Encyclopedia of Special Education

FOURTH EDITION

Encyclopedia *of* Special Education

A Reference for the Education of Children, Adolescents, and Adults with Disabilities and Other Exceptional Individuals

FOURTH EDITION

Volume 2: D–J

Edited by

Cecil R. Reynolds, Kimberly J. Vannest, and Elaine Fletcher-Janzen

WILEY

Cover design: Wiley

This book is printed on acid-free paper. ∞

Published by John Wiley & Sons, Inc., Hoboken, New Jersey.
Published simultaneously in Canada.

Library of Congress Cataloging-in-Publication Data:

Encyclopedia of special education: a reference for the education of children, adolescents, and adults with disabilities and other exceptional individuals / edited by Cecil R. Reynolds, Kimberly J. Vannest, and Elaine Fletcher-Janzen.—Fourth edition.

    pages cm

  Includes bibliographical references.

  ISBN 978-0-470-64216-0 (set); ISBN 978-0-470-94938-2 (v. 1); ISBN 978-0-470-94939-9 (v. 2); ISBN 978-0-470-94940-5 (v. 3); ISBN 978-0-470-94941-2 (v. 4); 978-1-118-62830-0 (ebk.); 978-1-118-62845-4 (ebk.); 978-1-118-66058-4 (ebk.).

  1. Children with disabilities—Education—United States—Encyclopedias. 2. Special education—United States—Encyclopedias. 3. People with disabilities—Education—United States—Encyclopedias. I. Reynolds, Cecil R., 1952– editor of compilation. II. Vannest, Kimberly J., 1967– ; editor of compilation. III. Fletcher-Janzen, Elaine, editor of compilation.

  LC4007.E53 2013

  371.903—dc23
                                                   2012048628

Printed in the United States of America

10 9 8 7 6 5 4 3 2 1

ENCYCLOPEDIA OF SPECIAL EDUCATION ENTRIES

EDITORIAL STAFF

Heather Davis
Texas A&M University
Letters A–M

Heather Hatton
Texas A&M University
Letters N–Z

Frank E. Vannest
San Pasqual High School,
Retired
Letters A–Z

Contributing Editors

Heather Peshak George
University of South Florida
Positive Behavior supports

Richard Parker
Texas A&M University
Single Case Research

John Davis
Texas A&M University
Single Case Research

Ben Mason
Juniper Gardens,
University of Kansas
Gifted and Talented

Mary Wagner
Principal Scientist in the
Center for Education and
Human Services
Longitudinal Studies

Stacey Smith
Texas A&M University
Reading

Ron Dumont
Fairleigh Dickinson University
Assessments

John O. Willis
Rivier College
Assessments

Kathleen Viezel
Fairleigh Dickinson University
Assessments

Jamie Zibulsky
Fairleigh Dickinson University
Assessments

Mary Capraro
Texas A&M University
Mathematics

Jennifer Ganz
Texas A&M University
Autism

Dalun Zhang
Texas A&M University
Transition

Mitchell Yell
University of South Carolina
Legal Issues in Special Education

Dave Edyburn
University of Wisconsin
Assistive Technology

Sandra Lewis
Florida State University
Visual Impairments

Pat Scherer
International Center on
Deafness and the Arts
Deaf Education

Amanda Chow
Texas A&M University
Biographies and
    Autobiographies

Lauren Williams
Texas A&M University
Organizations and
    Publications

Rose Mason
Juniper Gardens,
University of Kansas
Intelligence

Nancy Hutchins
Texas A&M University
Behavior

CONTRIBUTORS

Susanne Blough Abbott
Bedford Central School District
Mt. Kisco, New York

Marty Abramson
University of Wisconsin at Stout
Menomonie, Wisconsin

Patricia Ann Abramson
Hudson Public Schools
Hudson, Wisconsin

Salvador Hector Achoa
Texas A&M University
College Station, Texas

William M. Acree
University of Northern Colorado
Greeley, Colorado

Tufan Adiguzel
Bahcesehir Unviersity
Isantbul, Turkey

Theresa T. Aguire
Texas A&M University
College Station, Texas

Patricia A. Alexander
University of Maryland
College Park, Maryland

Vincent C. Alfonso
Fordham University
New York, New York

Nancy Algert
Texas A&M University
College Station, Texas

Bob Algozzine
University of North Carolina
at Charlotte
Charlotte, North Carolina

Kate Algozzine
University of North Carolina
at Charlotte
Charlotte, North Carolina

Thomas E. Allen
Gallaudet College
Washington, DC

Marie Almond
The University of Texas of the
Permian Basin
Odessa, Texas

Anna Pat L. Alpert
Texas A&M University
College Station, Texas

Geri R. Alvis
Memphis State University
Memphis, Tennessee

Daniel G. Amen
University of California
School of Medicine
Irvine, California

Megan Amidon
Texas State University–
San Marcos
San Marcos, Texas

C. H. Ammons
*Psychological Reports /
Perceptual and Motor Skills*
Missoula, Montana

Song An
Texas A&M University
College Station, Texas

Carol Anderson
Texas A&M University
College Station, Texas

Cynthia Anderson
University of Oregon
Eugene, Oregon

Kari Anderson
University of North Carolina
at Wilmington
Wilmington, North Carolina

Peggy L. Anderson
University of New Orleans,
Lakefront
New Orleans, Louisiana

Candace Andrews
California State University,
San Bernardino
San Bernardino, California

Karal Anhalt
Texas A&M University
College Station, Texas

Jean Annan
Massey University
New Zealand

Stephanie Anselene
University of North Carolina
at Wilmington
Wilmington, North Carolina

J. Appelboom-Fondu
UniversitéLibre de Bruxelles
Brussels, Belgium

James M. Applefield
University of North Carolina
at Wilmington
Wilmington, North Carolina

Pauline F. Applefield
University of North Carolina
at Wilmington
Wilmington, North Carolina

Kimberly F. Applequist
University of Colorado at Colorado
Springs
Colorado Springs, Colorado

Anna M. Arena
Academic Therapy Publications
Novato, California

John Arena
Academic Therapy Publications
Novato, California

Martin Argan
University of Wyoming
Laramie, Wyoming

Julie A. Armentrout
University of Colorado at Colorado
Springs
Colorado Springs, Colorado

Laura Arnstein
State University of New York
Binghamton, New York

Patricia Ann Arramson
Hudson Public Schools
Hudson, Wisconsin

Gustavo Abelardo Arrendondo
Monterrey, Mexico

Bernice Arricale
Hunter College, City University
of New York
New York, New York

H. Roberta Arrigo
Hunter College, City University
of New York
New York, New York

Alfredo J. Artiles
University of California,
Los Angeles
Los Angeles, California

Maria Arzola
University of Florida
Gainesville, Florida

Michael J. Ash
Texas A&M University
College Station, Texas

Adel E. Ashawal
Ain Shams University
Cairo, Egypt

Michelle S. Athanasiou
University of Northern Colorado
Greeley, Colorado

Shannon Atwater
Branson School Online
Branson, Colorado

William G. Austin
Cape Fear Psychological Services
Wilmington, North Carolina

Anna H. Avant
University of Alabama
Tuscaloosa, Alabama

Dan G. Bachor
University of Victoria
Victoria, British Columbia, Canada

John Baer
Rider University
Lawrenceville, New Jersey

Rebecca Bailey
Texas A&M University
College Station, Texas

Morgan Baker
Texas A&M University
College Station, Texas

Timothy A. Ballard
University of North Carolina
at Wilmington
Wilmington, North Carolina

Melanie Ballatore
University of Texas at Austin
Austin, Texas

Tanya Y. Banda
Texas A&M University Press
College Station, Texas

Monique Banters
Centre d'Etudeet de Reclassement
Brussels, Belgium

Deborah E. Barbour
University of North Carolina
at Wilmington
Wilmington, North Carolina

Russell A. Barkley
University of Massachusetts
Medical Center
Worchester, Massachusetts

Charles P. Barnard
University of Wisconsin at Stout
Menomonie, Wisconsin

David W. Barnett
University of Cincinnati
Cincinnati, Ohio

Ellis I. Barowsky
Hunter College, City University
of New York
New York, New York

Susan B. Barrett
Sheppard Pratt Health System
Towson, Maryland

Amanda L. Barth
The Chicago School of Professional
Psychology
Chicago, IL

Lyle E. Barton
Kent State University
Kent, Ohio

Vicki Bartosik
Stanford University
Stanford, California

Paul Bates
Southern Illinois University
Carbondale, Illinois

Stacey L. Bates
University of Texas at Austin
Austin, Texas

Anne M. Bauer
University of Cincinnati
Cincinnati, Ohio

Elizabeth R. Bauerschmidt
University of North Carolina
at Wilmington
Wilmington, North Carolina

Michael Bauerschmidt
Brunswick Hospital
Wilmington, North Carolina

Emily R. Baxter
University of Colorado
Colorado Springs, Colorado

John R. Beattie
University of North Carolina
at Charlotte
Charlotte, North Carolina

George R. Beauchamp
Cleveland Clinic Foundation
Cleveland, Ohio

Melissa Beckham
The Citadel
Charleston, South Carolina

Pena Bedesem
Kent State University
Kent, Ohio

Ronald A. Beghetto
University of Oregon
Eugene, Oregon

Julie Bell
University of Florida
Gainesville, Florida

Karen Bender
University of Northern Colorado
Greeley, Colorado

Ana Yeraldina Beneke
University of Oklahoma
Norman, Oklahoma

Randy Elliot Bennett
Educational Testing Service
Princeton, New Jersey

Richard A. Berg
West Virginia University
Medical Center
Charleston, West Virginia

John R. Bergan
University of Arizona
Tucson, Arizona

Dianne E. Berkell
C.W. Post Campus, Long Island
University
Greenvale, New York

Gary Berkowitz
Temple University
Philadelphia, Pennsylvania

Shari A. Bevins
Texas A&M University
College Station, Texas

John Bielinski
AGS Publishing
St. Paul, Minnesota

Kristan Biernath
The Hughes Spalding International
Adoption Evaluation Center
Atlanta, Georgia

Erin D. Bigler
Brigham Young University
Provo, Utah

Tia Billy
Texas A&M University
College Station, Texas

Roseann Bisighini
The Salk Institute
La Jolla, California

Kendra J. Bjoraker
University of Northern Colorado
Greeley, Colorado

Jan Blacher
University of California, Riverside
Riverside, California

Jose Blackorby
SRI International
Menlo Park, California

Jamie Bleiweiss
Hunter College, City University
   of New York
New York, New York

Gérard Bless
University of Fribourg
Fribourg, Switzerland

Richard Boada
University of Denver
Denver, Colorado

Margot Boles
Texas A&M University
College Station, Texas

L. Worth Bolton
Cape Fear Substance Abuse
   Center
Wilmington, North Carolina

Andy Bondy
Pyramid Educational Consultants
Newark, Delaware

Gwyneth M. Boodoo
Texas A&M University
College Station, Texas

Nancy Bordier
Hunter College, City University
   of New York
New York, New York

Jeannie Bormans
Center for Developmental Problems
Brussels, Belgium

Morton Botel
University of Pennsylvania
Philadelphia, Pennsylvania

Daniel J. Boudah
Texas A&M University
College Station, Texas

Michael Bourdot
Centre d'Etudeet de Reclassement
Brussels, Belgium

E. Amanda Boutot
Texas State University–San Marcos
San Marcos, Texas

Lisa Bowman-Perrott
Texas A&M University
College Station, Texas

Bruce A. Bracken
University of Memphis
Memphis, Tennessee

Mary Brady
Pennsylvania Special Education
   Assistive Device Center
Elizabethtown, Pennsylvania

Tammy Branan
University of Northern Colorado
Greeley, Colorado

Janet S. Brand
Hunter College, City University
   of New York
New York, New York

Don Braswell
Research Foundation, City
   University of New York
New York, New York

T. Berry Brazelton
Children's Hospital
Boston, Massachusetts

Adam S. Bristol
Yale University
New Haven, Connecticut

Courtney Britt
Texas State University–San Marcos
San Marcos, Texas

Warner H. Britton
Auburn University
Auburn, Alabama

Debra Y. Broadbooks
California School of Professional
   Psychology
San Diego, California

Melanie L. Bromley
California State University,
   San Bernardino
San Bernardino, California

Shannon R. Brooks
University of Minnesota
Minneapolis, Minnesota

Michael G. Brown
Central Wisconsin Center for the
   Developmentally Disabled
Madison, Wisconsin

Robert T. Brown
University of North Carolina
   at Wilmington
Wilmington, North Carolina

Ronald T. Brown
Emory University School of Medicine
Atlanta, Georgia

Tina L. Brown
Memphis State University
Memphis, Tennessee

Robert G. Brubaker
Eastern Kentucky University
Richmond, Kentucky

Catherine O. Bruce
Hunter College, City University
   of New York
New York, New York

Andrew R. Brulle
Wheaton College
Sycamore, Illinois

Virdette L. Brumm
Children's Hospital Los Angeles
Kreck/USC School of Medicine
Los Angeles, California

Laura Kinzie Brutting
University of Wisconsin at Madison
Madison, Wisconsin

Donna M. Bryant
University of North Carolina
   at Chapel Hill
Chapel Hill, North Carolina

Elizabeth A. Bubonic
Texas A&M University
College Station, Texas

Milton Budoff
Research Institute for Educational
   Problems
Cambridge, Massachusetts

Carolyn L. Bullard
Lewis & Clark College
Portland, Oregon

Melissa R. Bunner
Austin Neurological Clinic
Austin, Texas

Thomas R. Burke
Hunter College, City University
   of New York
New York, New York

Leslie Burkholder
Idea Infusion Consulting and
   Contracting
Denver, Colorado

Alois Bürli
Swiss Institute for Special Education
Lucerne, Switzerland

Matthew K. Burns
University of Minnesota
Minneapolis, Minnesota

Jason Burrow-Sanchez
University of Utah
Salt Lake City, Utah

Thomas A. Burton
University of Georgia
Athens, Georgia

Michelle T. Buss
Texas A&M University
College Station, Texas

James Button
United States Department of
   Education
Washington, DC

Glenda Byrns
Texas A&M University
College Station, Texas

Catherine M. Caldwell
University of Texas at Austin
Austin, Texas

Siglia Camargo
Texas A&M University
College Station, Texas

Claudia Camarillo-Dievendorf
Pitzer College, Claremont
Claremont, California

Anne Campbell
Purdue University
West Lafayette, Indiana

Frances A. Campbell
University of North Carolina
   at Chapel Hill
Chapel Hill, North Carolina

Mary Capraro
Texas A&M University
College Station, Texas

Robert M. Capraro
Texas A&M University
College Station, Texas

Elaine Carlson
Westat, Incorporated
Rockville, Maryland

Steven A. Carlson
Beaverton Schools
Beaverton, Oregon

Douglas Carnine
University of Oregon
Eugene, Oregon

Deborah Birke Caron
St. Lucie County School District
Ft. Pierce, Florida

Janet Carpenter
University of Oklahoma
Norman, Oklahoma

Edward G. Carr
State University of New York
   at Stony Brook
Stony Brook, New York

Nicole M. Cassidy
The Chicago School of Professional
   Psychology
Chicago, Illinois

Suzanne Carreker
Nehaus
Bellaire, Texas

Jodi M. Cholewicki-Carroll
University of South Carolina
Columbia, South Carolina

Eric Carter
Vanderbilt University
Nashville, Tennessee

Stephanie Caruthers
Texas State University–San Marcos
San Marcos, Texas

Catharina Carvalho
Texas A&M University
College Station, Texas

Tracy Calpin Castle
Eastern Kentucky University
Richmond, Kentucky

John F. Cawley
University of New Orleans
New Orleans, Louisiana

Carla C. de Baca
University of Northern Colorado
Colorado Springs, Colorado

Christine D. C. de Baca
University of Northern Colorado
Greeley, Colorado

Constance Y. Celaya
Irving, Texas

Sandra Chafouleas
University of Connecticut
Storrs, Connecticut

James C. Chalfant
University of Arizona
Tucson, Arizona

Mei-Lin Chang
Emory University
Atlanta, Georgia

Elaine A. Cheesman
University of Colorado at Colorado
   Springs
Colorado Springs, Colorado

Nina Cheng
University of Texas at Austin
Austin, Texas

Rebecca Wing-yi Cheng
The University of Hong Kong
Hong Kong, China

Robert A. Chernoff
Harbor—UCLA Medical Center
Los Angeles, California

Chris Cherrington
Lycoming College
Williamsport, Pennsylvania

Karen Elfner Childs
University of South Florida
Tampa, Florida

Robert Chimedza
University of Zimbabwe
Harare, Zimbabwe

Kathleen M. Chinn
New Mexico State University
Las Cruces, New Mexico

Mary M. Chittooran
Saint Louis University
Saint Louis, Missouri

Amanda C. Chow
Texas A&M University
College Station, Texas

Elizabeth Christiansen
University of Utah
Salt Lake City, Utah

Elaine Clark
University of Utah
Salt Lake City, Utah

Gary M. Clark
Kansas State University
Manhattan, Kansas

Deanna Clemens
College Station Independent School
   District
College Station, Texas

LeRoy Clinton
Boston University
Boston, Massachusetts

Renato Cocchi
Pesaro, Italy

Cynthia Price Cohen
Child Rights International Research
   Institute
New York, New York

Shirley Cohen
Hunter College, City University
   of New York
New York, New York

Ginga L. Colcough
University of North Carolina
at Wilmington
Wilmington, North Carolina

Christine L. Cole
University of Wisconsin at Madison
Madison, Wisconsin

Rhonda Collins
Florida State University
Tallahassee, Florida

Sarah Compton
University of Texas at Austin
Austin, Texas

Jennifer Condon
University of North Carolina
at Wilmington
Wilmington, North Carolina

Jane Close Conoley
University of Nebraska–Lincoln
Lincoln, Nebraska

Benjamin J. Cook
The Chicago School of Professional
Psychology
Chicago, Illinois

Bryan Cook
University of Hawaii
Honolulu, Hawaii

Clayton R. Cook
University of California, Riverside
Riverside, California

Krystal T. Cook
Texas A&M University
College Station, Texas

Carey E. Cooper
University of Texas at Austin
Austin, Texas

Mary Corlett
University of Texas at Austin
Austin, Texas

M. Sencer Corlu
Texas A&M University
College Station, Texas

Emily Cornforth
University of Colorado
Colorado Springs, Colorado

Vivian I. Correa
University of Florida
Gainesville, Florida

Barbara Corriveau
Laramie County School District # 1
Cheyenne, Wyoming

Lawrence S. Cote
Pennsylvania State University
University Park, Pennsylvania

Kathleen Cotton
Northwest Regional Educational
Laboratory
Portland, Oregon

Katherine D. Couturier
Pennsylvania State University
King of Prussia, Pennsylvania

Murray Cox
Southwest Adventist University
Keene, Texas

J. Michael Coxe
University of South Carolina
Columbia, South Carolina

Julia H. Coyne
The Chicago School of Professional
Psychology
Chicago, Illinois

Anne B. Crabbe
St. Andrews College
Laurinburg, North Carolina

Lindy Crawford
University of Colorado at Colorado
Springs
Colorado Springs, Colorado

M. Franci Crepeau-Hobson
University of Northern Colorado
Greeley, Colorado

Sergio R. Crisalle
Medical Horizons Unlimited
San Antonio, Texas

Chara Crivelli
Vito de Negrar
Verona, Italy

Jill E. Crowley
Saint Louis University
Saint Louis, Missouri

John Crumlin
University of Colorado at Colorado
Springs
Colorado Springs, Colorado

Jack A. Cummings
Indiana University
Bloomington, Indiana

Jacqueline Cunningham
University of Texas
Austin, Texas

Susan Curtiss
University of California,
Los Angeles
Los Angeles, California

Juliette Cutillo
Fountain–Fort Carson School
District 8
Colorado Springs, Colorado

Rik Carl D'Amato
University of Northern Colorado
Greeley, Colorado

Amy J. Dahlstrom
University of Northern Colorado
Greeley, Colorado

Elizabeth Dane
Hunter College, City University
of New York
New York, New York

Louis Danielson
American Institutes for Research
Washington, DC

Craig Darch
Auburn University
Auburn, Alabama

Barry Davidson
Ennis, Texas

Andrew S. Davis
University of Northern Colorado
Greeley, Colorado

Barbra L. Davis
University of Texas
Austin, Texas

Heather S. Davis
Texas A&M University
College Station, Texas

Jacqueline E. Davis
Boston University
Boston, Massachusetts

John L. Davis
Purdue University
West Lafayette, Indiana

Trina J. Davis
Texas A&M University
College Station, Texas

Raymond S. Dean
Ball State University
Indiana University School
of Medicine
Muncie, Indiana

Lori Dekeyzer
University of Utah
Salt Lake City, Utah

Elizabeth Delaune
Texas State University–San Marcos
San Marcos, Texas

Jozi De Leon
New Mexico State University
Las Cruces, New Mexico

Bernadette M. Delgado
University of Nebraska–Lincoln
Lincoln, Nebraska

Kendra De Loach
University of South Carolina
Columbia, South Carolina

Allison G. Dempsey
The University of Health Science
    Center at Houston
Houston, Texas

Jack R. Dempsey
University of Florida
Gainesville, Florida

Randall L. De Pry
Portland State University
Portland, Oregon

Lizanne DeStefano
University of Illinois,
    Urbana-Champaign
Champaign, Illinois

S. De Vriendt
Vrije Universiteit Brussel
Brussels, Belgium

Maria Rae Dewhirst
Illinois PBIS Network
La Grange Park, Illinois

Caroline D'Ippolito
Eastern Pennsylvania Special
    Education Resources
Center King of Prussia, Pennsylvania

Mary D'Ippolito
Montgomery County Intermediate
    Unit
Norristown, Pennsylvania

Roja Dilmore-Rios
California State University,
    San Bernadino
San Bernadino, California

Jeffrey Ditterline
University of Florida
Gainesville, Florida

Marilyn P. Dornbush
Atlanta, Georgia

Amanda Jensen Doss
Texas A&M University
College Station, Texas

Susann Dowling
University of Houston
Houston, Texas

Darrell L. Downs
Mount Sinai Medical Center and
    Miami Heart Institute
Miami, Florida

Jonathan T. Drummond
Princeton University
Princeton, New Jersey

Elizabeth McAdams Ducy
Texas A&M University
College Station, Texas

Sharon Duffy
University of California, Riverside
Riverside, California

Jengjyh Duh
National Taiwan Normal University
Taipei, Taiwan

Ron Dumont
Fairleigh Dickinson University
Teaneck, New Jersey

Glenn Dunlap
University of South Florida
Tampa, Florida

Jamie Duran
Texas A&M University
College Station, Texas

V. Mark Durand
University of South Florida
Saint Petersburg, Florida

Brooke Durbin
Texas A&M University
College Station, Texas

Abbey-Robin Durkin
University of Colorado
Colorado Springs, Colorado

Mary K. Dykes
University of Florida
Gainesville, Florida

Alan Dyson
University of Manchester
Manchester, England

Peg Eagney
School for the Deaf
New York, New York

Theresa Earles-Vollrath
University of Central Missouri
Warrensburg, Missouri

Ronald C. Eaves
Auburn University
Auburn, Alabama

Lucille Eber
Illinois PBIS Network
La Grange Park, Illinois

Lauren K. Eby
The Chicago School of Professional
    Psychology
Chicago, Illinois

Jana Echevarria
California State University,
    Long Beach
Long Beach, California

Danielle Edelston
University of California, Riverside
Riverside, California

Retha M. Edens
Saint Louis University
Saint Louis, Missouri

Heather Edgel
University of Utah
Salt Lake City, Utah

Amita Edran
California State University,
    Long Beach
Long Beach, California

Dave Edyburn
University of Wisconsin–Milwaukee
Milwaukee, Wisconsin

John M. Eells
Souderton Area School District
Souderton, Pennsylvania

Cassie Eiffert
University of Florida
Gainesville, Florida

Stephen N. Elliott
University of Wisconsin at Madison
Madison, Wisconsin

Julie Ellis
University of Florida
Gainesville, Florida

Fara El Zein
Texas State University–San Marcos
San Marcos, Texas

Ingemar Emanuelsson
Goteburg University
Goteburg, Sweden

Petra Engelbrecht
University of Stellenbosch
Stellenbosch, South Africa

Carol Sue Englert
Michigan State University
East Lansing, Michigan

Chaz Esparaza
California State University,
    San Bernardino
San Bernardino, California

Christine A. Espin
University of Minnesota
Minneapolis, Minnesota

Kimberly M. Estep
University of Houston–Clear Lake
Houston, Texas

Carol Anne Evans
University of Utah
Salt Lake City, Utah

Michelle Evans
California State University,
 San Bernardino
San Bernardino, California

Rand B. Evans
Texas A&M University
College Station, Texas

Rose Fairbanks
Temecula, California

Sarah Fairbanks
University of Connecticut
Storrs, Connecticut

Katherine Falwell
University of North Carolina
 at Wilmington
Wilmington, North Carolina

Jennie L. Farmer
University of South Florida
Tampa, Florida

Judith L. Farmer
New Mexico State University
Las Cruces, New Mexico

Stephen S. Farmer
New Mexico State University
Las Cruces, New Mexico

Peter Farrell
University of Manchester
Manchester, England

MaryAnn C. Farthing
University of North Carolina
 at Chapel Hill
Chapel Hill, North Carolina

Sharla Fasko
Rowan County Schools
Morehead, Kentucky

Lisa A. Fasnacht-Hill
Keck/USC School of Medicine
Children's Hospital of Los Angeles
Los Angeles, California

Elizabeth I. Fassig
University of Northern Colorado
Greeley, Colorado

Mary Grace Feely
School for the Deaf
New York, New York

John F. Feldhusen
Purdue University
West Lafayette, Indiana

Laurie L. Ferguson
Wright Institute
Berkeley, California
and The Children's Hospital
Denver, Colorado

John M. Ferron
University of South Florida
Tampa, Florida

Britt-Inger Fex
University of Lund
Lund, Sweden

MaryLynne D. Filaccio
University of Northern Colorado
Greeley, Colorado

Donna Filips
Steger, Illinois

Marni R. Finberg
University of Florida
Gainesville, Florida

Jeffrey Finlayson
The Chicago School of Professional
 Psychology
Chicago, Illinois

Krista Finstuen
Texas A&M University
College Station, Texas

Luke W. Fischer
The Chicago School of Professional
 Psychology
Chicago, Illinois

Sally L. Flagler
University of Oklahoma
Norman, Oklahoma

Dawn P. Flanagan
St. John's University
Jamaica, New York

Dennis M. Flanagan
Montgomery County Intermediate
 Unit
Norristown, Pennsylvania

K. Brigid Flannery
University of Oregon
Eugene, Oregon

Kelly Ann Fletcher
Ohio State University
Columbus, Ohio

David Fletcher-Janzen
Colorado Springs, Colorado

Elaine Fletcher-Janzen
Chicago School of Professional
 Psychology
Chicago, Illinois

Wendy L. Flynn
Staffordshire University
Staffordshire, United Kingdom

Cindi Flores
California State University,
 San Bernardino
San Bernardino, California

Peter T. Force
International Center for Deafness
 and the Arts
Northbrook, Illinois

Stephanie R. Forness
University of Northern Colorado
Greeley, Colorado

Constance J. Fournier
Texas A&M University
College Station, Texas

Rollen C. Fowler
Eugene 4J School District
Eugene, Oregon

Emily Fox
University of Michigan
Ann Arbor, Michigan

Jessica H. Franco
University of Texas at Austin
Austin, Texas

Thomas A. Frank
Pennsylvania State University
University Park, Pennsylvania

Leslie Coyle Franklin
University of Northern Colorado
Greeley, Colorado

Mary M. Frasier
University of Georgia
Athens, Georgia

Brigitte N. Fredrick
Texas A&M University
College Station, Texas

Rachel Freeman
University of Kansas
Lawrence, Kansas

Christine L. French
Texas A&M University
College Station, Texas

Joseph L. French
Pennsylvania State University
University Park, Pennsylvania

Alice G. Friedman
University of Oklahoma Health
 Services Center
Norman, Oklahoma

Douglas L. Friedman
Fordham University
Bronx, New York

Douglas Fuchs
Peabody College, Vanderbilt
 University
Nashville, Tennessee

Lynn S. Fuchs
Peabody College, Vanderbilt
 University
Nashville, Tennessee

Gerald B. Fuller
Central Michigan University
Mt. Pleasant, Michigan

Rosemary Gaffney
Hunter College, City University
of New York
New York, New York

Marie Galan
The Chicago School of Professional
Psychology
Chicago, Illinois

Sherri L. Gallagher
University of Northern Colorado
Greeley, Colorado

Jason Gallant
University of Florida
Gainesville, Florida

Diego Gallegos
Texas A&M University
College Station, Texas

Cynthia A. Gallo
University of Colorado
Colorado Springs, Colorado

Jennifer B. Ganz
Texas A&M University
College Station, Texas

Clarissa I. Garcia
Texas A&M University
College Station, Texas

Shernaz B. Garcia
University of Texas
Austin, Texas

Roman Garcia de Alba
Texas A&M University
College Station, Texas

Katherine Garnett
Hunter College, City University
of New York
New York, New York

Jeff Garrison-Tate
Texas A&M University
College Station, Texas

Carrie George
Texas A&M University
College Station, Texas

Heather Peshak George
University of South Florida
Tampa, Florida

Melissa M. George
Montgomery County Intermediate
Unit
Norristown, Pennsylvania

Phil Bless Gerard
University of Fribourg
Fribourg, Switzerland

Verena Getahun
AGS Publishing
St. Paul, Minnesota

Violeta Gevorgianiene
Vilnius University
Vilnius, Lithuania

Harvey R. Gilbert
Pennsylvania State University
University Park, Pennsylvania

Jennifer M. Gillis
University of California, Irvine
Irvine, California

Theresa M. Gisi
Colorado Neurological Associates, PC
Denver and Colorado Springs,
Colorado

Grazina Gintiliene
Vilnius University
Vilnius, Lithuania

Elizabeth Girshick
Montgomery County Intermediate
Unit
Norristown, Pennsylvania

Joni J. Gleason
University of West Florida
Pensacola, Florida

Sharon L. Glennen
Pennsylvania State University
University Park, Pennsylvania

Dianne Goldsby
Texas A&M University
College Station, Texas

Sam Goldstein
University of Utah
Salt Lake City, Utah

Maricela P. Gonzales
Texas A&M University
College Station, Texas

Rex Gonzales
University of Utah
Salt Lake City, Utah

Rick Gonzales
Texas A&M University
College Station, Texas

Jorge Gonzalez
Texas A&M University
College Station, Texas

Suzanne Gooderham
University of Ottawa
Ottawa, Ontario, Canada

Libby Goodman
Pennsylvania State University
King of Prussia, Pennsylvania

Steve Goodman
Michigan Integrated Behavior and
Learning Support Initiative
Holland, Michigan

Fara D. Goodwyn
Texas A&M University
College Station, Texas

Carole Reiter Gothelf
Hunter College, City University
of New York
New York, New York

Elizabeth Ann Graf
University of Northern Colorado
Greeley, Colorado

Steve Graham
University of Maryland
College Park, Maryland

Shannon A. Grant
Texas A&M University
College Station, Texas

Jeffrey W. Gray
Ball State University
Muncie, Indiana

P. Allen Gray, Jr.
University North Carolina at
Wilmington
Wilmington, North Carolina

Ashley T. Greenan
The Chicago School of Professional
Psychology
Chicago, Illinois

Darielle Greenberg
California School of Professional
Psychology
San Diego, California

Jacques Grégoire
Catholic University of Louvain
Louvain, Belgium

Laurence C. Grimm
University of Illinois
Chicago, Illinois

Lindsay S. Gross
University of Wisconsin
Milwaukee, Wisconsin

Suzanne M. Grundy
California State University,
San Bernardino
San Bernardino, California

Amy R. Guerette
Florida State University
Tallahassee, Florida

Nonna Guerra
Texas A&M University
College Station, Texas

John Guidubaldi
Kent State University
Kent, Ohio

Laura A. Guli
University of Texas at Austin
Austin, Texas

J. C. Guillemard
Dourdan, France

Deborah Guillen
The University of Texas of the
Permian Basin
Odessa, Texas

Steven Gumerman
Temple University
Philadelphia, Pennsylvania

Thomas Gumpel
The Hebrew University of Jerusalem
Jerusalem, Israel

Rumki Gupta
Indian Statistical Institute
Kolkata, India

Terry B. Gutkin
University of Nebraska–Lincoln
Lincoln, Nebraska

Kathryn L. Guy
University of Texas at Austin
Austin, Texas

Patricia A. Haensly
Texas A&M University
College Station, Texas

George James Hagerty
Stonehill College North
Easton, Massachusetts

Angelroba Hairrell
Texas A&M University
College Station, Texas

Danny B. Hajovsky
University of Kansas
Lawrence, Kansas

Robert Hall
Texas A&M University
College Station, Texas

Winnifred M. Hall
University of West Indies
Kingston, Jamaica

Lindsay Halliday
California State University,
San Bernardino
San Bernardino, California

Richard E. Halmstad
University of Wisconsin at Stout
Menomonie, Wisconsin

Glennelle Halpin
Auburn University
Auburn, Alabama

Donald D. Hammill
PRO-ED, Incorporated
Austin, Texas

Monika Hannon
University of Northern Colorado
Colorado Springs, Colorado

Harold Hanson
Southern Illinois University
Carbondale, Illinois

Elise Phelps Hanzel
California School of Professional
Psychology
San Diego, California

Jennifer Hargrave
University of Texas at Austin
Austin, Texas

Jennifer Harman
University of Florida
Gainesville, Florida

Janice Harper
North Carolina Central University
Durham, North Carolina

Gale A. Harr
Maple Heights City Schools
Maple Heights, Ohio

Karen L. Harrell
University of Georgia
Athens, Georgia

Frances T. Harrington
Radford University
Blacksburg, Virginia

Karen R. Harris
University of Maryland
College Park, Maryland

Kathleen Harris
Arizona State University
Tempe, Arizona

Patti L. Harrison
University of Alabama
Tuscaloosa, Alabama

Joshua Harrower
Cal State University
Seaside, California

Beth Harry
University of Miami
Miami, Florida

Stuart N. Hart
University of Victoria
Victoria, British Columbia, Canada

Lawrence C. Hartlage
Evans, Georgia

Patricia Hartlage
Medical College of Georgia
Evans, Georgia

Melissa M. Harvey
University of Colorado
Colorado Springs, Colorado

Dan Hatt
University of Oklahoma
Norman, Oklahoma

Anette Hausotter
Bis Beratungsstelle Fur Die
Intergration
Germany

Leanne S. Hawken
University of Utah
Salt Lake City, Utah

Krista D. Healy
University of California, Riverside
Riverside, California

Lora Tuesday Heathfield
University of Utah
Salt Lake City, Utah

Kathleen Hebbeler
SRI International
Menlo Park, California

Jeff Heinzen
Indianhead Enterprise
Menomonie, Wisconsin

Floyd Henderson
Texas A&M University
College Station, Texas

Rhonda Hennis
University of North Carolina
at Wilmington
Wilmington, North Carolina

Latanya Henry
Texas A&M University
College Station, Texas

Arthur Hernandez
Texas A&M University
College Station, Texas

Robyn S. Hess
University of Colorado
Denver, Colorado

E. Valerie Hewitt
Texas A&M University
College Station, Texas

Julia A. Hickman
Bastrop Mental Health Association
Bastrop, Texas

Meme Hieneman
Behavioral Services Program
All Children's Hospital
Tampa, Florida

Craig S. Higgins
Stonehill College
North Easton, Massachusetts

Kellie Higgins
University of Texas at Austin
Austin, Texas

Alan Hilton
Seattle University
Seattle, Washington

Delores J. Hittinger
The University of Texas of the
    Permian Basin
Odessa, Texas

Sarah L. Hoadley
Appalachian State University
Boone, North Carolina

Harold E. Hoff, Jr.
Eastern Pennsylvania Special
    Education Resources Center
King of Prussia, Pennsylvania

Elizabeth Holcomb
*American Journal of Occupational
Therapy*
Bethesda, Maryland

E. Wayne Holden
University of Oklahoma Health
    Sciences Center
Norman, Oklahoma

Andrea Holland
University of Texas at Austin
Austin, Texas

Ivan Z. Holowinsky
Rutgers University
New Brunswick, New Jersey

Kristin T. Holsker
The Chicago School of Professional
    Psychology
Chicago, Illinois

Thomas F. Hopkins
Center for Behavioral Psychotherapy
White Plains, New York

Robert H. Horner
University of Oregon
Eugene, Oregon

Najmeh Hourmanesh
University of Utah
Salt Lake City, Utah

Wayne P. Hresko
Journal of Learning Disabilities
Austin, Texas

Carolyn Hughes
Vanderbilt University
Nashville, Tennessee

Charles A. Hughes
Pennsylvania State University
University Park, Pennsylvania

Jan N. Hughes
Texas A&M University
College Station, Texas

Kay E. Hughes
The Riverside Publishing Company
Itasca, Illinois

Aimee R. Hunter
University of North Carolina
    at Wilmington
Wilmington, North Carolina

Nancy Hutchins
Texas A&M University
College Station, Texas

Nancy L. Hutchinson
Simon Fraser University
Buraby, British Columbia

Beverly J. Irby
Sam Houston State University
Huntsville, Texas

Paul Irvine
Katonah, New York

Cornelia L. Izen
George Mason University
Fairfax, Virginia

Lee Anderson Jackson, Jr.
University of North Carolina
    at Wilmington
Wilmington, North Carolina

Elisabeth Jacobsen
Copenhagen, Denmark

Markku Jahnukainen
University of Helsinki
Helsinki, Finland

Emma Janzen
University of Colorado
Colorado Springs, Colorado

Diane Jarvis
State University of New York
    at Buffalo
Buffalo, New York

Phillip Jenkins
University of Kentucky
Lexington, Kentucky

Helen G. Jenne
Alliant International University
California School of Professional
    Psychology
San Diego, California

Jenise Jensen
University of Utah
Salt Lake City, Utah

Jacqueline Jere
University of Zambia
Lusaka, Zambia

Olga Jerman
University of California, Riverside
Riverside, California

Brian D. Johnson
University of Northern Colorado
Greeley, Colorado

Judy A. Johnson
Goose Creek Consolidated
    Independent School District
Baytown, Texas

Kristine Jolivette
Georgia State University
Atlanta, Georgia

Elizabeth Jones
Texas A&M University
College Station, Texas

Gideon Jones
Florida State University
Tallahassee, Florida

Meredith Jones
Texas A&M University
College Station, Texas

Philip R. Jones
Virginia Polytechnic Institute
    and State University
Blacksburg, Virginia

Shirley A. Jones
Virginia Polytechnic Institute
    and State University
Blacksburg, Virginia

Tarcia Jones
Texas A&M University
College Station, Texas

R. Malatesha Joshi
Texas A&M University
College Station, Texas

Diana Joyce
University of Florida
Gainesville, Florida

Song Ju
Texas A&M University
College Station, Texas

David Kahn
Texas A&M University
College Station, Texas

Araksia Kaladjian
University of California, Riverside
Riverside, California

James W. Kalat
North Carolina State University
Raleigh, North Carolina

Maya Kalyanpur
Towson University
Towson, Maryland

Michele Wilson Kamens
Rider Universtiy
Lawrenceville, New Jersey

Randy W. Kamphaus
Dean, College of Education,
    Georgia State University
Atlanta, Georgia

Harrison Kane
University of Florida
Gainesville, Florida

Stan A. Karcz
University of Wisconsin at Stout
Menomonie, Wisconsin

Dilip Karnik
Children's Hospital of Austin
Austin, Texas

Austin J. Karpola
The Chicago School of Professional
    Psychology
Chicago, Illinois

Maribeth Montgomery Kasik
Governors State University
University Park, Illinois

Allison Katz
Rutgers University
New Brunswick, New Jersey

Jen Katz-Buonincontro
University of Oregon
Eugene, Oregon

Alan S. Kaufman
Yale University School of Medicine
New Haven, Connecticut

James C. Kaufman
California State University,
    San Bernardino
San Bernardino, California

Nancy J. Kaufman
University of Wisconsin at Stevens
    Point
Stevens Point, Wisconsin

Scott Barry Kaufman
Yale University
New Haven, Connecticut

Elizabeth Kaufmann
University of Texas at Austin
Austin, Texas

Kenneth A. Kavale
Regent University
Virginia Beach, Virginia

Hortencia Kayser
New Mexico State University
Las Cruces, New Mexico

Forrest E. Keesbury
Lycoming College
Williamsport, Pennsylvania

Jennifer Keith
University of Northern Colorado
Greeley, Colorado

Kristy K. Kelly
The Chicago School of Professional
    Psychology
Chicago, Illinois

Theresa Kelly
University of Northern Colorado
Greeley, Colorado

Courtney A. Kemp
The Chicago School of Professional
    Psychology
Chicago, Illinois

Barbara Keogh
University of California,
    Los Angeles
Los Angeles, California

Leanne Ketterlin-Gellar
University of Oregon
Eugene, Oregon

Kay E. Ketzenberger
The University of Texas of the
    Permian Basin
Odessa, Texas

Eve Kikas
University of Tartu
Tartu, Estonia

Paula Kilpatrick
University of North Carolina
    at Wilmington
Wilmington, North Carolina

Donald Kincaid
University of South Florida
Tampa, Florida

Peggy Kipping
PRO-ED, Incorporated
Austin, Texas

Gonul Kircaali-Iftar
Anadolu University
Eskişehir, Turkey

Bob Kirchner
University of Northern Colorado
Greeley, Colorado

Donald A. Kirson
Counseling Center, University
    of San Diego
San Diego, California

Margie K. Kitano
New Mexico State University
Las Cruces, New Mexico

Howard M. Knoff
University of South Florida
Tampa, Florida

Tim Knoster
Bloomsburg University
Bloomsburg, Pennsylvania

Brandi Kocian
Texas A&M University
College Station, Texas

Dana R. Konter
University of Wisconsin–Stout
Menomonie, Wisconsin

Peter Kopriva
Fresno Pacific University
Fresno, California

F. J. Koopmans-Van Beinum
Amsterdam, The Netherlands

Mark A. Koorland
Florida State University
Tallahassee, Florida

Peter Kopriva
Fresno Pacific University
Fresno, California

L. Koulischer
Institut de Morphologie
Pathologique Belgium

Martin Kozloff
University of North Carolina
    at Wilmington
Wilmington, North Carolina

Kathleen S. Krach
Texas A&M University
College Station, Texas

Thomas R. Kratochwill
University of Wisconsin at Madison
Madison, Wisconsin

Bob Krichner
Laramie City School District #1
Cheyenne, Wyoming

James P. Krouse
Clarion University of Pennsylvania
Clarion, Pennsylvania

Louis J. Kruger
Tufts University
Medford, Pennsylvania

Moana Kruschwitz
University of Texas at Austin
Austin, Texas

Miranda Kucera
University of Colorado at Colorado
    Springs
Colorado Springs, Colorado

Loni Kuhn
University of Utah
Salt Lake City, Utah

Alexandra S. Kutz
University of Texas at Austin
Austin, Texas

Paul G. Lacava
Rhode Island College
Providence, Rhode Island

Michael La Conte
District 11 Public Schools
Colorado Springs, Colorado

Timothy D. Lackaye
Hunter College, City University
of New York
New York, New York

Iman Teresa Lahroud
University of Texas at Austin
Austin, Texas

Shui-fong Lam
The University of Hong Kong
Hong Kong, China

C. Sue Lamb
University of North Carolina
at Wilmington
Wilmington, North Carolina

Gordon D. Lamb
Texas A&M University
College Station, Texas

Nadine M. Lambert
University of California, Berkeley
Berkeley, California

Russell Lang
Texas State University–San Marcos
San Marcos, Texas

Louis J. Lanunziata
University of North Carolina
at Wilmington
Wilmington, North Carolina

Rafael Lara-Alecio
Texas A&M University
College Station, Texas

Franco Larocca
The University of Verona
Verona, Italy

Kerry S. Lassiter
The Citadel
Charleston, South Carolina

Jeff Laurent
University of Texas
Austin, Texas

Mark M. Leach
University of Southern Mississippi
Hattiesburg, Mississippi

Samuel LeBaron
University of Texas Health Science
Center
San Antonio, Texas

Yvan Lebrun
School of Medicine
Brussels, Belgium

Jillian N. Lederhouse
Wheaton College
Sycamore, Illinois

Donghyung Lee
Texas A&M University
College Station, Texas

Linda Leeper
New Mexico State University
Las Cruces, New Mexico

Ronald S. Lenkowsky
Hunter College, City University
of New York
New York, New York

Mary Louise Lennon
Educational Testing Service
Princeton, New Jersey

Carmen Léon
Andrés Bello Catholic University
Caracas, Venezuela

Richard Levak
California School of Professional
Psychology
San Diego, California

J. Patrick Leverett
The Citadel
Charleston, South Carolina

Allison Lewis
University of North Carolina
at Wilmington
Wilmington, North Carolina

Lucy Lewis
University of North Carolina
at Wilmington
Wilmington, North Carolina

Sandra Lewis
Florida State University
Tallahassee, Florida

Tim Lewis
University of Missouri
Columbia, Missouri

Collette Leyva
Texas A&M University
College Station, Texas

Elizabeth O. Lichtenberger
The Salk Institute
La Jolla, California

Xiaobao Li
University of Houston
Houston, Texas

Ping Lin
Elmhurst College
Elmhurst, Illinois

Janet A. Lindow
University of Wisconsin at Madison
Madison, Wisconsin

Ken Linfoot
University of Western
Sydney
Sydney, Australia

Daniel D. Lipka
Lincoln Way Special Education
Regional Resources Center
Louisville, Ohio

Brittany Little
The Chigo School of Professional
Psychology
Chicago, IL

Cornelia Lively
University of Illinois,
Urbana-Champaign
Champaign, Illinois

Antolin M. Llorente
Baylor College of Medicine
Houston, Texas

Lisa A. Lockwood
Texas A&M University
College Station, Texas

Jeri Logemann
Northwestern University
Evanston, Illinois

David Lojkovic
George Mason University
Fairfax, Virginia

Charles J. Long
University of Memphis
Memphis, Tennessee

Linda R. Longley
University of North Carolina
at Wilmington
Wilmington, North Carolina

Emilia C. Lopez
Fordham University
New York, New York

Esmerelda Lopez
Texas A&M University
College Station, Texas

Araceli Lopez-Arenas
Texas A&M University
College Station, Texas

Patricia A. Lowe
University of Kansas
Lawrence, Kansas

Michael T. Lucas
California State University,
San Bernardino
San Bernardino, California

Emily L. Lund
Texas A&M University
College Station, Texas

Marsha H. Lupi
Hunter College, City University
of New York
New York, New York

Ann E. Lupkowski
Texas A&M University
College Station, Texas

Teresa M. Lyle
University of Texas at Austin
Austin, Texas

Patricia S. Lynch
Texas A&M University
College Station, Texas

Loleta Lynch-Gustafson
California State University,
San Bernardino
San Bernardino, California

Philip E. Lyon
College of St. Rose
Albany, New York

James Lyons
University of California, Riverside
Riverside, California

John W. Maag
University of Nebraska–Lincoln
Lincoln, Nebraska

Charles A. MacArthur
University of Maryland
College Park, Maryland

John MacDonald
Eastern Kentucky University
Richmond, Kentucky

Taddy Maddox
PRO-ED, Incorporated
Austin, Texas

Danielle Madera
University of Florida
Gainesville, Florida

Ghislain Magerotte
Mons State University
Mons, Belgium

Susan Mahanna-Boden
Eastern Kentucky University
Richmond, Kentucky

Charles A. Maher
Rutgers University
New Brunswick, New Jersey

Richard Mahoney
Texas State University–San Marcos
San Marcos, Texas

Kebangsaan Malaysia
Texas A&M University
College Station, Texas

Elba Maldonado-Colon
San Jose State University
San Jose, California

David C. Mann
St. Francis Hospital
Pittsburgh, Pennsylvania

Douglas L. Mann
V. A. Medical Center, Medical
University of South Carolina
Charleston, South Carolina

Lester Mann
Hunter College, City University
of New York
New York, New York

Denise E. Maricle
University of Wisconsin–Stout
Menomonie, Wisconsin

Donald S. Marozas
State University of New York
at Geneseo
Geneseo, New York

Ellen B. Marriott
University of North Carolina
at Wilmington
Wilmington, North Carolina

James E. Martin
University of Oklahoma
Norman, Oklahoma

Tamara J. Martin
The University of Texas of the
Permian Basin
Odessa, Texas

Stephanie Martinez
University of South Florida
Tampa, Florida

Benjamin A. Mason
Texas A&M University
College Station, Texas

Patrick Mason
The Hughes Spalding International
Adoption Evaluation Center
Atlanta, Georgia

Rose Mason
University of Kansas
Lawrence, Kansas

Margo A. Mastropieri
Purdue University
West Lafayette, Indiana

Heidi Mathie
University of Utah
Salt Lake City, Utah

Jill Mathis
Laramie School District #1
Cheyenne, Wyoming

Darin T. Matthews
The Citadel
Charleston, South Carolina

Jon Maxwell
Texas A&M University
College Station, Texas

Deborah C. May
State University of New York
at Albany
Albany, New York

Joan W. Mayfield
Baylor Pediatric Specialty Services
Dallas, Texas

Liliana Mayo
Centro Ann Sullivan
Lima, Peru

James K. McAfee
Pennsylvania State University
University Park, Pennsylvania

Heidi A. McCallister
University of Texas at Austin
Austin, Texas

Cristina McCarthy
University of Utah
Salt Lake City, Utah

Eileen F. McCarthy
University of Wisconsin at Madison
Madison, Wisconsin

Elizabeth McClellan
Council for Exceptional Children
Reston, Virginia

Dalene M. McCloskey
University of Northern Colorado
Greeley, Colorado

George McCloskey
Philadelphia College of Osteopathic
Medicine
Philadelphia, Pennsylvania

Laura S. McCorkle
Texas A&M University
College Station, Texas

Linda McCormick
University of Hawaii, Manoa
Honolulu, Hawaii

Ryan E. McDaniel
The Citadel
Charleston, South Carolina

Paul A. McDermott
University of Pennsylvania
Philadelphia, Pennsylvania

Breeda McGrath
The Chicago School of Professional
Psychology
Chicago, Illinois

Kelly McGraw
The Chicago School of Professional
  Psychology
Chicago, Illinois

Kevin S. McGrew
St. Joseph, Minnesota

Stacy E. McHugh
The Children's Hospital
Denver, Colorado

Kent McIntosh
University of British Columbia
Vancouver, British Columbia,
  Canada

Phillip J. McLaughlin
University of Georgia
Athens, Georgia

James A. McLoughlin
University of Louisville
Louisville, Kentucky

James K. McMee
Pennsylvania State University
King of Prussia, Pennsylvania

Paolo Meazzini
University of Rome
Rome, Italy

Frederic J. Medway
University of South Carolina
Columbia, South Carolina

Brenda Melvin
New Hanover Regional Medical
  Center
Wilmington, North Carolina

Marissa I. Mendoza
Texas A&M University
College Station, Texas

James F. Merritt
University of North Carolina
  at Wilmington
Wilmington, North Carolina

Judith Meyers
San Diego, California

Danielle Michaux
VrijeUniversiteit Brussel
Brussels, Belgium

Jennifer Might
University of North Carolina
  at Wilmington
Wilmington, North Carolina

Stephen E. Miles
Immune Deficiency Foundation
Towson, Maryland

Susie Miles
University of Manchester
Manchester, United Kingdom

James H. Miller
University of New Orleans
New Orleans, Louisiana

Kevin Miller
University of Central Florida
Orlando, Florida

Ted L. Miller
University of Tennessee at
  Chattanooga
Chattanooga, Tennessee

Norris Minick
Center for Psychosocial Studies, The
  Spencer Foundation
Chicago, Illinois

Anjali Misra
State University of New York
Potsdam, New York

Andrew A. Mogaji
University of Lagos
Lagos, Nigeria

Lisa Monda
Florida State University
Tallahassee, Florida

Marcia L. Montague
Texas A&M University
College Station, Texas

Lourdes Montenegro
Andrés Bello Catholic University
Caracas, Venezuela

Judy K. Montgomery
Chapman University
Irvine, California

Linda Montgomery
The University of Texas of the
  Permian Basin
Odessa, Texas

Hadley Moore
University of Massachusetts
Boston, Massachusetts

Melanie Moore
University of North Carolina
  at Wilmington
Wilmington, North Carolina

Luis Benites Morales
Universidad San Martin de Porres
Lima, Peru

Susannah More
University of Texas at Austin
Austin, Texas

Marianela Moreno
Andrés Bello Catholic University
Caracas, Venezuela

Mary E. Morningstar
University of Kansas
Lawrence, Kansas

Richard J. Morris
University of Arizona
Tucson, Arizona

Amy Morrow
University of North Carolina
  at Wilmington
Wilmington, North Carolina

Lonny W. Morrow
Northeast Missouri State University
Kirksville, Missouri

Sue Ann Morrow
EDGE, Incorporated
Bradshaw, Michigan

Elias Mpofu
Pennsylvania State University
Harrisburg, Pennsylvania

Tracy A. Muenz
Alliant International University
San Diego, California

Mary Murray
Journal of Special Education
Ben Salem, Pennsylvania

Gladiola Musabelliu
University of Tirana
Tirana, Albania

Magen M. Mutepfa
Zimbabwe Schools Special Services
  and Special Education
  Department
Zimbabwe

Jack Naglieri
The Ohio State University
Columbus, Ohio

Sigamoney Naicker
Western Cape Educational SI
  Department
South Africa

Michael Nall
Louisville, Kentucky

Nicole Nasewicz
University of Florida
Gainesville, Florida

Robert T. Nash
University of Wisconsin at Oshkosh
Oshkosh, Wisconsin

Bonnie K. Nastasi
Kent State University
Kent, Ohio

Diana L. Nebel
University of Northern Colorado
Greeley, Colorado

Cameron L. Neece
University of California,
  Los Angeles
Los Angeles, California

Leslie C. Neely
Texas A&M University
College Station, Texas

Thomas Neises
California State University,
    San Bernardino
San Bernardino, California

Brett R. Nelson
University of Northern Colorado
Greeley, Colorado

Michael Nelson
University of Kentucky Louisville
Louisville, Kentucky

Joyce E. Ness
Montgomery County Intermediate
    Unit
Norristown, Pennsylvania

Ulrika Nettelbladt
University of Lund
Lund, Sweden

Lori Newcomer
University of Missouri
Columbia, Missouri

Lynn Newman
SRI International
Menlo Park, California

Jennifer Nicholls
Dysart Unified School District
El Mirage, Arizona

Robert C. Nichols
State University of New York
    at Buffalo
Buffalo, New York

Sandra Nite
Texas A&M University
College Station, Texas

Matthew K. Nock
Yale University
New Haven, Connecticut

Nancy L. Nassbaum
Austin Neurological Clinic
Austin, Texas

Etta Lee Nurick
Montgomery County Intermediate
    Unit
Norristown, Pennsylvania

Christopher Oakland
New York, New York

Thomas Oakland
University of Florida
Gainesville, Florida

Festus E. Obiakor
Emporia State University
Nigeria

Hector Salvia Ochoa
Texas A&M University
College Station, Texas

Jessica Oddi
The Chicago School of Professional
    Psychology
Chicago, Illinois

Louise O'Donnell
University of Texas Health Science
    Center
San Antonio, Texas
and University of Texas at Austin
Austin, Texas

Joy O'Grady
University of Memphis
Memphis, Tennessee

Masataka Ohta
Tokyo Gakujei University
Tokyo, Japan

Ed O'Leary
Utah State University
Logan, Utah

Daniel Olympia
University of Utah
Salt Lake City, Utah

John O'Neill
Hunter College, City University
    of New York
New York, New York

Robert O'Neill
University of Utah
Salt Lake City, Utah

Ause Tugba Oner
Texas A&M University
College Station, Texas

Caitlin Onks
Bryan ISD
Bryan, Texas

Alba Ortiz
University of Texas
Austin, Texas

Samuel O. Ortiz
St. John's University
Jamaica, New York

Andrew Oseroff
Florida State University
Tallahassee, Florida

Lawrence J. O'Shea
University of Florida
Gainesville, Florida

Marika Padrik
University of Tartu
Tartu, Estonia

Doris Paez
New Mexico State University
Las Cruces, New Mexico

Ellis B. Page
Duke University
Durham, North Carolina

Kathleen D. Paget
University of South Carolina
Columbia, South Carolina

Douglas J. Palmer
Texas A&M University
College Station, Texas

Hagop S. Pambookian
Elizabeth City, North Carolina

Ernest L. Pancsofar
University of Connecticut
Storrs, Connecticut

Sara Pankaskie
Florida State University
Tallahassee, Florida

Maryann Toni Parrino
Montclair University
Upper Montclair, New Jersey

Linda H. Parrish
Texas A&M University
College Station, Texas

Daniel R. Paulson
University of Wisconsin at Stout
Menomonie, Wisconsin

Nils A. Pearson
PRO-ED, Incorporated
Austin, Texas

Mary Leon Peery
Texas A&M University
College Station, Texas

Kathleen Pelham-Odor
California State University,
    San Bernardino
San Bernardino, California

Shelley L. F. Pelletier
Dysart Unified School District
El Mirage, Arizona

Michelle Perfect
University of Texas at Austin
Austin, Texas

Olivier Périer
Université Libre de Bruxelles Centre
    Comprendreet Parler
Brussels, Belgium

Paula Perrill
University of Northern Colorado
Greeley, Colorado

Joseph D. Perry
Kent State University
Kent, Ohio

Richard G. Peters
Ball State University
Muncie, Indiana

Brooke Pfeiffer
Texas State University–San Marcos
San Marcos, Texas

Faith L. Phillips
University of Oklahoma Health
    Sciences Center
Norman, Oklahoma

Jeffry L. Phillips
University of North Carolina
    at Wilmington
Wilmington, North Carolina

Kathleen M. Phillips
University of California, Riverside
Riverside, California

Lindsey A. Phillips
University of Utah
Salt Lake City, Utah

Yongxin Piao
Beijing Normal University
Beijing, China

Diana Piccolo
Missouri State University
Springfield, Missouri

Sip Jan Pijl
Gion University of Groningen
Groningen, The Netherlands

John J. Pikulski
University of Delaware
Newark, Delaware

Casey Pilgrim
The Chicago School of Professional
    Psychology
Chicago, Illinois

Diana E. Pineda
The Chicago School of Professional
    Psychology
Chicago, Illinois

Sally E. Pisarchick
Cuyahoga Special Education Service
    Center
Maple Heights, Ohio

Anthony J. Plotner
University of South Carolina
Columbia, South Carolina

Cynthia A. Plotts
Southwest Texas State University
San Marcos, Texas

Janiece Pompa
University of Utah
Salt Lake City, Utah

Brenda M. Pope
New Hanover Memorial Hospital
Wilmington, North Carolina

John E. Porcella
Rhinebeck County School
Rhinebeck, New York

James A. Poteet
Ball State University
Muncie, Indiana

Michelle W. Potter
University of California, Riverside
Riverside, California

Shawn Powell
United States Air Force Academy
Colorado Springs, Colorado

Kristiana Powers
California State University,
    San Bernardino
San Bernardino, California

David P. Prasse
University of Wisconsin
Milwaukee, Wisconsin

Jennifer Dawn Pretorius
Vaal University of Technology
South Africa

Marianne Price
Montgomery County Intermediate
    Unit
Norristown, Pennsylvania

Elisabeth A. Prinz
Pennsylvania State University
University Park, Pennsylvania

Philip M. Prinz
Pennsylvania State University
University Park, Pennsylvania

Antonio E. Puente
University of North Carolina
    at Wilmington
Wilmington, North Carolina

Krista L. Puente
University of North Carolina
    at Wilmington
Wilmington, North Carolina

Nuri Puig
University of Oklahoma
Norman, Oklahoma

Adam C. Pullaro
California State University,
    San Bernardino
San Bernardino, CA

Elizabeth P. Pungello
University of North Carolina
    at Chapel Hill
Chapel Hill, North Carolina

Robert F. Putnam
May Institute
Randolph, Massachusetts

Shahid Waheed Qamar
Lahore, Pakistan

Cathy Huaqing Qi
University of New Mexico
Albuquerque, New Mexico

Jennifer M. Raad
University of Kansas
Lawrence, Kansas

Linda Radbill
University of Florida
Gainesville, Florida

Shannon Radcliff-Lee
University of North Carolina
    at Wilmington
Wilmington, North Carolina

William A. Rae
Texas A&M University
College Station, Texas

Paige B. Raetz
Western Michigan University
Kalamazoo, Michigan

Katrina Raia
University of Florida
Gainesville, Florida

Craig T. Ramey
University of North Carolina
    at Chapel Hill
Chapel Hill, North Carolina

Sylvia Z. Ramirez
University of Texas
Austin, Texas

Christine D. Ramos
University of Northern Colorado
Greeley, Colorado

Noe Ramos
Texas A&M University
College Station, Texas

Arlene I. Rattan
Ball State University
Muncie, Indiana

Gurmal Rattan
Indiana University of Pennsylvania
Indiana, Pennsylvania

Nancy Razo
Texas A&M University
College Station, Texas

Anne Reber
Texas A&M University
College Station, Texas

April Regester
University of Missouri
Saint Louis, Missouri

Robert R. Reilley
Texas A&M University
College Station, Texas

Fredricka K. Reisman
Drexel University
Philadelphia, Pennsylvania

Kimberly M. Rennie
Texas A&M University
College Station, Texas

Daniel J. Reschly
Peabody College, Vanderbilt
    University
Nashville, Tennessee

Cecil R. Reynolds
Texas A&M University
and Bastrop Mental Health
    Associates
College Station, Texas

Robert L. Rhodes
New Mexico State University
Las Cruces, New Mexico

William S. Rholes
Texas A&M University
College Station, Texas

Cynthia A. Riccio
Texas A&M University
College Station, Texas

James R. Ricciuti
United States Office of Management
    and Budget
Washington, DC

Teresa K. Rice
Texas A&M University
College Station, Texas

Laura Richards
University of Utah
Salt Lake City, Utah

Paul C. Richardson
Elwyn Institutes
Elwyn, Pennsylvania

Sylvia O. Richardson
University of South Florida
Tampa, Florida

Pamela M. Richman
University of North Carolina
    at Wilmington
Wilmington, North Carolina

Bert O. Richmond
University of Georgia
Athens, Georgia

Richard Rider
University of Utah
Salt Lake City, Utah

Michelle Ries
University of Memphis
Memphis, Tennessee

Catherine Hall Rikhye
Hunter College, City University
    of New York
New York, New York

T. Chris Riley-Tillman
University of Missouri
Columbia, Missouri

Judy Ripsch
The Chicago School of Professional
    Psychology
Chicago, Illinois

Mandi Rispoli
Texas A&M University
College Station, Texas

Selina Rivera-Longoria
Texas A&M University
College Station, Texas

Eric Roberts
Texas A&M University
College Station, Texas

Gary J. Robertson
American Guidance Service Circle
Pines, Minnesota

Kathleen Rodden-Nord
University of Oregon
Eugene, Oregon

Kimberly M. Rodriguez
Texas A&M University
College Station, Texas

Olga L. Rodriguez-Escobar
Texas A&M University
College Station, Texas

Anita M. Roginski
The Chicago School of Professional
    Psychology
Chicago, IL

Matthew Roith
University of Colorado
Colorado Springs, Colorado

Dahl A. Rollins
Texas A&M University
College Station, Texas

Cassandra Burns Romine
Texas A&M University
College Station, Texas

Jean A. Rondal
University of Liege
Liege, Belgium

Sheldon Rosenberg
University of Illinois
Chicago, Illinois

Leslie D. Rosenstein
Neuropsychology Clinic, PC
Austin, Texas

Bruce P. Rosenthal
State University of New York
New York, New York

Eve N. Rosenthal
Texas A&M University
College Station, Texas

Rosalinda Rosli
Texas A&M University
College Station, Texas

Michelle Ross
The Chicago School of Professional
    Psychology
Chicago, IL

Eric Rossen
University of Florida
Gainesville, Florida

Beth Rous
University of Kentucky Human
Development Institute Lexington,
    Kentucky

Amy Loomis Roux
University of Florida
Gainesville, Florida

Kathy L. Ruhl
Pennsylvania State University
University Park, Pennsylvania

Elsa Cantu Ruiz
University of Texas at San Antonio
San Antonio, Texas

Joseph M. Russo
Hunter College, City University
    of New York
New York, New York

Robert B. Rutherford, Jr.
Arizona State University
Tempe, Arizona

Kim Ryan-Arredondo
Texas A&M University
College Station, Texas

Daniel J. Rybicki
ForenPsych Services
Agoura Hills, California

Anne Sabatino
Hudson, Wisconsin

David A. Sabatino
West Virginia College of Graduate
    Studies
Morgantown, West Virginia

Susan Sage
Dysart Unified School District
El Mirage, Arizona

Monir Saleh
Beheshti University
Tehran, Iran

Lisa J. Sampson
Eastern Kentucky University
Richmond, Kentucky

Alfred Sander
Universitat des Saarlandes
Saarbruecken, Germany

Tiffany D. Sanders
University of Florida
Gainesville, Florida

Polly E. Sanderson
Research Triangle Institute
Research Triangle Park, North
    Carolina

Therese Sandomierski
University of Florida
Tampa, Florida

Derek D. Satre
University of California
San Francisco, California

Scott W. Sautter
Peabody College, Vanderbilt
    University
Nashville, Tennessee

Robert F. Sawicki
Lake Erie Institute of
    Rehabilitation
Lake Erie, Pennsylvania

Nancy K. Scammacca
University of Texas at Austin
Austin, Texas

Walter R. Schamber
University of Northern Colorado
Greeley, Colorado

Patrick J. Schloss
Pennsylvania State University
University Park, Pennsylvania

Ronald V. Schmelzer
Eastern Kentucky University
Richmond, Kentucky

Carol Schmitt
San Diego Unified School District
San Diego, California

Carol S. Schmitt
Eastern Kentucky University
Richmond, Kentucky

Sue A. Schmitt
University of Wisconsin at Stout
Menomonie, Wisconsin

Sarah Schnoebelan
University of Texas at Austin
Austin, Texas

Lyle F. Schoenfeldt
Texas A&M University
College Station, Texas

Jacqueline S. Schon
University of Kansas
Lawrence, Kansas

Eric Schopler
University of North Carolina
    at Chapel Hill
Chapel Hill, North Carolina

Fredrick A. Schrank
Olympia, Washington

Louis Schwartz
Florida State University
Tallahassee, Florida

Adam J. Schwebach
University of Utah
Salt Lake City, Utah

Krista Schwenk
University of Florida
Gainesville, Florida

June Scobee
University of Houston,
    Clear Lake
Houston, Texas

Terrance Scott
University of Louisville
Louisville, Kentucky

Thomas E. Scruggs
Purdue University
West Lafayette, Indiana

Denise M. Sedlak
United Way of Dunn County
Menomonie, Wisconsin

Robert A. Sedlak
University of Wisconsin at Stout
Menomome, Wisconsin

Katherine D. Seelman
University of Pittsburgh
Pittsburgh, Pennsylvania

John D. See
University of Wisconsin at Stout
Menomonie, Wisconsin

Margaret Semrud-Clikeman
University of Texas at Austin
Austin, Texas

Amy Sessoms
University of North Carolina
    at Wilmington
Wilmington, North Carolina

Sandra B. Sexson
Emory University School of Medicine
Atlanta, Georgia

Susan Shandelmier
Eastern Pennsylvania Special
    Education Regional Resources
    Center
King of Prussia, Pennsylvania

Alison Shaner
University of North Carolina
    at Wilmington
Wilmington, North Carolina

Deborah A. Shanley
Medgar Evers College, City
    University of New York
New York, New York

William J. Shaw
University of Oklahoma
Norman, Oklahoma

Patricia Scherer
International Center on Deafness
    and the Arts
Northbrook, Illinois

Kaci Deauquier Sheridan
Texas A&M University
College Station, Texas

Susan M. Sheridan
University of Wisconsin at Madison
Madison, Wisconsin

Vedia Sherman
Austin Neurological Clinic
Austin, Texas

Naoji Shimizu
Tokyo Gakujei University
Tokyo, Japan

Agnes E. Shine
Barry University
Miami Shores, Florida

Erin K. Shinners
The Chicago School of Professional
    Psychology
Chicago, Illinois

Ludmila Shipitsina
Institute of Special Education and
    Psychology
Saint Petersburg, Russia

Edward A. Shirkey
New Mexico State University
Las Cruces, New Mexico

Gerald L. Shook
Behavior Analyst Certification Board
Tallahassee, Florida

Dakum Shown
University of Jos
Jos, Nigeria

Almon Shumba
University of KwaZulu-Natal
South Africa

Lawrence J. Siegel
University of Texas Medical Branch
Galveston, Texas

Jeff Sigafoos
University of Wellington at Victoria
Wellington, New Zealand

Rosanne K. Silberman
Hunter College, City University
of New York
New York, New York

Brandi Simonsen
University of Connecticut
Storrs, Connecticut

Lissen Simonsen
University of North Carolina
at Wilmington
Wilmington, North Carolina

Richard L. Simpson
University of Kansas
Lawrence, Kansas

Paul T. Sindelar
Florida State University
Tallahassee, Florida

Jessica L. Singleton
University of Northern Colorado
Greeley, Colorado

Jaime Slappey
University of North Carolina
at Wilmington
Wilmington, North Carolina

Jerry L. Sloan
Wilmington Psychiatric Associates
Wilmington, North Carolina

Jamie Slowinski
The Chicago School of Professional
Psychology
Chicago, Illinois

Julie E. Smart
Utah State University
Logan, Utah

April M. Smith
Yale University
New Haven, Connecticut

Craig D. Smith
Georgia College
Milledgeville, Georgia

E. S. Smith
University of Dundee
Dundee, Scotland

Maureen A. Smith
Pennsylvania State University
University Park, Pennsylvania

Stacey L. Smith
Texas A&M University
College Station, Texas

Judy Smith-Davis
Counterpoint Communications
Company
Reno, Nevada

Mary Helen Snyder
Devereux Cleo Wallace
Colorado Springs, Colorado

Latha V. Soorya
Binghamton University
The Institute for Child Development
Binghamton, New York

Cesar Merino Soto
University Privada San Juan
Bautista
Lima, Peru

Jane Sparks
University of North Carolina
at Wilmington
Wilmington, North Carolina

Jessica Spata
The Chicago School of Professional
Psychology
Chicago, Illinois

Barbara S. Speer
Shaker Heights City School
District
Shaker Heights, Ohio

Donna Spiker
SRI International
Menlo Park, California

Vicky Y. Spradling
Austin State Hospital
Austin, Texas

Harrison C. Stanton
Las Vegas, Nevada

Shari A. Stanton
Las Vegas, Nevada

Tilly R. Steele
National Center for Leadership in
Visual Impairment
Elkins Park, Pennsylvania

J. Todd Stephens
University of Wisconsin at Madison
Madison, Wisconsin

Bernie Stein
Tel Aviv, Israel

David R. Steinman
Austin Neurological Clinic and
Department of Psychology
University of Texas at Austin
Austin, Texas

Cecelia Steppe-Jones
North Carolina Central University
Durham, North Carolina

Linda J. Stevens
University of Minnesota
Minneapolis, Minnesota

Rachael J. Stevenson
Bedford, Ohio

Mary E. Stinson
University of Alabama
Tuscaloosa, Alabama

Roberta C. Stokes
Texas A&M University
College Station, Texas

Doretha McKnight Stone
University of North Carolina
at Wilmington
Wilmington, North Carolina

Eric A. Storch
University of Florida
Gainesville, Florida

Laura M. Stough
Texas A&M University
College Station, Texas

Michael L. Stowe
Texas A&M University
College Station, Texas

Edythe A. Strand
University of Wisconsin at Madison
Madison, Wisconsin

Elaine Stringer
University of North Carolina
at Wilmington
Wilmington, North Carolina

Dorothy A. Strom
Ball State University Indiana
School of Medicine
Muncie, Indiana

Sheela Stuart
Georgia Washington University
Washington, DC

Sue Stubbs
Save the Children Fund
London, United Kingdom

George Sugai
University of Connecticut
Storrs, Connecticut

Jeremy R. Sullivan
Texas A&M University
College Station, Texas

Kathryn A. Sullivan
Branson School Online
Branson, Colorado

Shelley Suntup
California School of Professional
Psychology
San Diego, California

Emily G. Sutter
University of Houston, Clear Lake
Houston, Texas

Lana Svien-Senne
University of South Dakota
Vermillion, South Dakota

Tricia Swan
University of Colorado
Colorado Springs, Colorado

H. Lee Swanson
University of California, Riverside
Riverside, California

Beth Sweeden
University of Wisconsin
Madison, Wisconsin

David Sweeney
Texas A&M University
College Station, Texas

Mark E. Swerdlik
Illinois State University
Normal, Illinois

Thomas G. Szabo
Western Michigan University
Kalamazoo, Michigan

Henri B. Szliwowski
HôpitalErasme, UniversitéLibre de
    Bruxelles
Brussels, Belgium

Pearl E. Tait
Florida State University
Tallahassee, Florida

Paula Tallal
University of California, San Diego
San Diego, California

Mary K. Tallent
Texas Tech University
Lubbock, Texas

Melody Tankersly
Kent State University
Kent, Ohio

C. Mildred Tashman
College of St. Rose
Albany, New York

James W. Tawney
Pennsylvania State University
University Park, Pennsylvania

Joseph R. Taylor
Fresno Pacific University
Fresno, California

Leslie Taylor
University of South Carolina
Columbia, South Carolina

Therese Tchombe
University of Yaounde
Cameroon

Ellen A. Teelucksingh
University of Minnesota
Minneapolis, Minnesota

Tirussew Teferra
Addis Ababa University
Addis Ababa, Ethiopia

Cathy F. Telzrow
Kent State University
Kent, Ohio

Yolanda Tenorio
California State University,
    San Bernardino
San Bernardino, California

David W. Test
University of North Carolina
    at Charlotte
Charlotte, North Carolina

Coleen Thoma
Virginia Commonwealth University
Richmond, Virginia

Carol Chase Thomas
University of North Carolina
    at Wilmington
Wilmington, North Carolina

Jo Thomason
Council of Administrators of Special
    Education
Fort Valley, Georgia

Bruce Thompson
Texas A&M University
College Station, Texas

Spencer Thompson
The University of Texas of the
    Permian Basin
Odessa, Texas

Sage Thornton
University of California, Riverside
Riverside, California

Eva Tideman
Lund University
Lund, Sweden

Steven R. Timmermans
Mary Free Bed Hospital and
    Rehabilitation Center
Grand Rapids, Michigan

Gerald Tindal
University of Oregon
Eugene, Oregon

Renze M. Tobin
Texas A&M University
College Station, Texas

Anne W. Todd
University of Oregon
Eugene, Oregon

Francine Tomkins
University of Cincinnati
Cincinnati, Ohio

Carol Tomlinson-Keasey
University of California, Riverside
Riverside, California

Rachel M. Toplis
Falcon School District 49
Colorado Springs, Colorado

Keith. J. Topping
University of Dundee
Dundee, Scotland

Raymond Toraille
Public Education
Paris, France

Jose Luis Torres
Texas A&M University
College Station, Texas

Audrey A. Trainor
University of Wisconsin–Madison
Madison, Wisconsin

Stanley O. Trent
University of Virginia
Charlottesville, Virginia

David M. Tucker
Austin Neurological Clinic
and University of Texas at Austin
Austin, Texas

Timothy L. Turco
Louisiana State University
Baton Rouge, Louisiana

Mary Turri
University of British Columbia
Vancouver, British Columbia,
    Canada

Lori E. Unruh
Eastern Kentucky University
Richmond, Kentucky

Susan M. Unruh
University of Kansas
Wichita, Kansas

Marilyn Urquhart
University of South Dakota
Vermillion, South Dakota

Cynthia Vail
Florida State University
Tallahassee, Florida

Greg Valcante
University of Florida
Gainesville, Florida

Hubert B. Vance
East Tennessee State University
Johnson City, Tennessee

Aryan Van Der Leij
Free University
Amsterdam, The Netherlands

Heather S. Vandyke
Falcon School District 49
Colorado Springs, Colorado

Christina E. Van Kraayenoord
The University of Queensland
Brisbane, Australia

K. Sandra Vanta
Cleveland Public Schools
Cleveland, Ohio

Juana Vaquero
Texas A&M University
College Station, Texas

Rebecca Vaurio
Austin Neurological Clinic
and University of Texas
at Austin
Austin, Texas

Kathleen Veizel
Farliegh Dickinson University
Teaneck, New Jersey

Donna Verner
Texas A&M University
College Station, Texas

Don Viglione
California School of Professional
Psychology
San Diego, California

Judith K. Voress
PRO-ED, Incorporated
Austin, Texas

Mary Wagner
SRI International
Menlo Park, California

Emily Wahlen
Hunter College, City University
of New York
New York, New York

Christy M. Walcott
East Carolina University
Greenville, North Carolina

Deborah Klein Walker
Harvard University
Cambridge, Massachusetts

Donna Wallace
The University of Texas of the
Permian Basin
Odessa, Texas

Raoul Wallenberg
International University for Family
and Child
Saint Petersburg, Russia

James E. Walsh
The Chicago School of Professional
Psychology
Chicago, Illinois

Marjorie E. Ward
The Ohio State University
Columbus, Ohio

Nicole R. Warnygora
University of Northern
Colorado
Greeley, Colorado

Sue Allen Warren
Boston University
Boston, Massachusetts

John Wasserman
The Riverside Publishing
Company
Itasca, Illinois

Sharine Webber
Laramie County School
District #1
Cheyenne, Wyoming

Lauren M. Webster
Wake Forest University
Winston-Salem, North Carolina

Danny Wedding
Marshall University
Huntington, Virginia

Paul Wehman
Virginia Commonwealth
University
Richmond, Virginia

Michael Wehmeyer
University of Kansas
Lawrence, Kansas

Frederick F. Weiner
Pennsylvania State University
University Park, Pennsylvania

Marjorie Weintraub
Montgomery County Intermediate
Unit
Norristown, Pennsylvania

Bahr Weiss
University of North Carolina
at Chapel Hill
Chapel Hill, North Carolina

Mark Weist
University of South Carolina
Columbia, South Carolina

Shirley Parker Wells
University of North Carolina
at Wilmington
Wilmington, North Carolina

Louise H. Werth
Florida State University
Tallahassee, Florida

Catherine Wetzburger
Hôpital Erasme, Université Libre de
Bruxelles
Brussels, Belgium

Jessi K. Wheatley
Falcon School District 49
Colorado Springs, Colorado

Larry J. Wheeler
Southwest Texas State University
San Marcos, Texas

Annika White
University of California, Riverside
Riverside, California

Michelle White
University of Florida
Tampa, Florida

Jessica Whitely
University of Ottawa
Ottawa, Ontario, Canada

Susie Whitman
Immune Deficiency Foundation
Odessa, Texas

Thomas M. Whitten
Florida State University
Tallahassee, Florida

J. Lee Wiederholt
PRO-ED, Incorporated
Austin, Texas

Lisa Wildmo
Bryan, Texas

Saul B. Wilen
Medical Horizons Unlimited
San Antonio, Texas

Karen Wiley
Universtiy of Northern Colorado
Colorado Springs, Colorado

Greta N. Wilkening
University of Colorado Health
Sciences Center
Children's Hospital
Denver, Colorado

C. Williams
Falcon School District 49
Colorado Springs, Colorado

L. Williams
Falcon School District 49
Colorado Springs, Colorado

Lauren E. Williams
Texas A&M University
College Station, Texas

Mary Clare Williams
Ramey, Pennsylvania

Meredith Williamson
Texas A&M University
College Station, Texas

Diane J. Willis
University of Oklahoma Health
Sciences Center
Oklahoma City, Oklahoma

John O. Willis
Rivier College
Nashua, New Hampshire

Melissa T. Willison
The Chicago School of Professional
Psychology
Chicago, IL

Victor L. Willson
Texas A&M University
College Station, Texas

John D. Wilson
Elwyn Institutes
Elwyn, Pennsylvania

Kimberly D. Wilson
University of Texas
at Austin
Austin, Texas

Margo E. Wilson
Lexington, Kentucky

Carol Windmill
University of Ottawa
Ottawa, Ontario, Canada

Kelly Winkels
University of Florida
Gainesville, Florida

Anna Winneker
University of South Florida
Tampa, Forida

Britt L. Winter
Western Michigan
University
Kalamazoo, Michigan

Joseph C. Witt
Louisiana State University
Baton Rouge, Louisiana

Monica E. Wolfe
Texas A&M University
College Station, Texas

Bencie Woll
University of Bristol
Bristol, United Kingdom

Bernice Y. L. Wong
Simon Fraser University
Buraby, British Columbia

Mary M. Wood
University of Georgia
Athens, Georgia

Diane E. Woods
World Rehabilitation Fund
New York, New York

Lee L. Woods
University of Oklahoma
Norman, Oklahoma

Frances F. Worchel
Texas A&M University
College Station, Texas

Patricia Work
University of South Dakota
Vermillion, South Dakota

Eleanor Boyd Wright
University of North Carolina
at Wilmington
Wilmington, North Carolina

Logan Wright
University of Oklahoma
Norman, Oklahoma

Karen F. Wyche
Hunter College, City University
of New York
New York, New York

Martha Ellen Wynne
Loyola University, Chicago
Chicago, Illinois

Susan Yarbrough
Florida State University
Tallahassee, Florida

Mitchell Yell
University of South Carolina
Columbia, South Carolina

James E. Yeseldyke
University of Minnesota
Minneapolis, Minnesota

Pui-sze Yeung
The University of Hong Kong
Hong Kong, China

Roland K. Yoshida
Fordham University
New York, New York

Mantak Yuen
The University of Hong Kong
Hong Kong, China

Thomas Zane
Johns Hopkins University
Baltimore, Maryland

Ronald Zellner
Texas A&M University
College Station, Texas

Lonnie K. Zeltzer
University of Texas Health Sciences
Center
San Antonio, Texas

Paul M. Zeltzer
University of Texas Health Sciences
Center
San Antonio, Texas

Dulan Zhang
Texas A&M University
College Station, Texas

Xinhua Zheng
University of California, Riverside
Riverside, California

Jamie Zibulsky
Farliegh Dickinson University
Teaneck, New Jersey

Walter A. Zilz
Bloomsburg University
Bloomsburg, Pennsylvania

Elizabeth M. Zorn
The Chicago School of Professional
Psychology
Chicago, Illinois

Kenneth A. Zych
Walter Reed Army Medical Center
Washington, DC

PREFACE TO THE FOURTH EDITION

Work on the first Encyclopedia of Special Education originated in 1982 and the first edition was published in 1987. In this 4th edition we welcome Editor Dr. Kimberly Vannest to the project team. Since the first edition of nearly 2,000 pages, this current version includes nearly 3,000. This encyclopedia both historically captures the terms, individuals, laws, and societal movements of more than 4 decades of Special Education, it also chronicles the evolution of special education.

We remain well aware of how life, research, and standards have changed for those of us who practice in special education. It is an interesting process to look back and see how the *Encyclopedia* has changed over the years and how it has really provided a mirror of the zeitgeist of the times in which we live and practice.

The first edition was full of new ideas such as profile analysis, direct instruction, and terms such as "trainable" and "educable." The field had license to imagine and try ways to rewire the brain that was having trouble in school. This fourth edition clearly marks the federal and state demands for evidence-based practices in classrooms and methodologically rigorous research, perhaps reflecting the end of imagination and the beginning of an era of proof or accountability. Hence, we see behavioral terms and behavioral-oriented credentials enjoying resurgence because they allow for documentation of behaviors that are easy to observe. Accountability is a force to be noticed as it infiltrates and guides current practice even accountability has evolved from a focus on student activities or opportunities, to student outcomes and performance and now teacher evaluation. It will be fascinating to see where we are in another decade.

The first edition was full of new and somewhat untested laws: We were still trying to interpret Public Law 94-142! Since then, we are in the reauthorization of what has evolved into IDEIA (Individuals with disabilities education Act) as Special Education Law has involved eight presidents over time. And conceptualization of disability for accessing services is under new scrutiny for learning disabilities and expanded definitions for autism to reflect the meteoric rise in prevelance. The advocacy and self-advocacy network that surrounds and includes special education students today is vast, connected, and accessible. The Internet has exponentially changed the individual's abilities to learn about support organizations and to reach out to others who have similar concerns and

conditions. This movement is not just on a national level, the World Health Organization is rallying the international community to connect the daily living experiences of individuals with disabilities in the *International Classification of Functioning, Disability, and Health*. This classification system was designed to describe the *individual* with a disability, not just to classify the disability itself. Indeed, we remember that in the first edition of the *Encyclopedia*, it was acceptable to label individuals via the disability; therefore, individuals with Schizophrenia were schizophrenics and individuals with Mental Retardation were the mentally retarded. The disability came first and the individual came second. In the second edition of the *Encyclopedia*, we remember stressing heavily with all of our editors and authors that all language referring to clinical populations would have to reflect the individual first and his or her handicapping condition second. This was a major literary turn at the time! The third edition may best be characterized as disability and ability now living side by side as the 3rd edition marked a time beyond mainstreaming, beyond inclusion but of expectation for a respect of difference, and expectation for accommodation and natural adaptation of the environment or curriculum to meet the needs of people, not of the disabled. Humanness is central and our similarities outweigh our differences, even in special education.

The four editions of the *Encyclopedia* have also reflected the evolution of test construction and interpretation. The level of psychometric design is higher than ever before, providing many benefits to the population such as increased specificity in assessing executive functions, trauma, study skills, and so on. The major broadband assessment batteries that measure cognitive abilities and psychological constructs are excellent, theory-based measures that have imaginative and careful design. Therefore, our ability to include well-designed tools in the assessment process has never been better. The fourth edition of the *Encyclopedia* catalogues many new tests and revisions of old and true instruments.

The demand for "countable" accountability of special education outcomes is upon these days. For the past 20 years, the *Encyclopedia* reflected exploration, and now exploration is passé and counting and demanding results is the zeitgeist of the times. Renegades as we are, we have included more and more neuropsychological principles and terms into the various editions of the *Encyclopedia* as we have paid homage to the vast mystery of the human brain and personality that will most likely never be reduced down to accountable facts. Herein lies the rub for those with interests in brain-behavior relationships, the very thing that we seek is unattainable and therein provides continuous wonder, curiosity, and frustration! We are confident that the most important aspect of future research that seeks to improve the daily lives of children with disabilities lies in the study of the brain and its relationship to learning and daily living skills. This process will always be a study of one, and not given to group statistics. Therefore, regardless of the political zeitgeist, we have expressed our desire to support clinical excellence throughout the third edition of the *Encyclopedia* and minimize old ideas that have been parceled out as new and redesigned to fit ends that are not apolitical. The original *Encyclopedia* was bursting with curiosity and wonder about a new field. We wish to maintain this tribute in the current edition and support the continued innocence of true scientific exploration.

New to the ESE-IV were entries on Positive Behavior Supports. We would like to give many thanks to Heather Peshak George, University of South Florida, as a Contributing Editor and her amazing contribution and coverage of this topic. Areas such as autism were brought up-to-date to reflect the most recent knowledge by Jeni Ganz at Texas A&M University as a Contributing Editor and entries reflecting changes in transition services were updated by Dulan Zhang at Texas A&M University. Last but not least, the Drs. Ron Dumont and John Willis again provided a completely new thread of reviews of standardized assessments throughout the *Encyclopedia*. Joining their expertise in assessment reviews were Drs. Kathleen Viezel and Jamie Zibulsky. We once again are pleased to have them as part of our effort in updating over 100 assessment entries. Without the work of many contributing editors and authors, the Encyclopedia would not have been possible.

Please allow us to apologize to our authors if their affiliations or names have changed over the past 20 years and the most recent changes are not incorporated into the fourth edition. We have tried to keep up with the changes but are sure that we have missed a few and promise to remediate in future editions! We also had to make editorial decisions about giving credit where credit was due for updates of entries. Therefore, the reader will notice that we have taken painstaking efforts to list the authors and to which editions they contributed. Minor edits to update references, change archaic terminology, add web pages or update addresses were completed throughout the volumes. We kept a historical "chronicling of the field" approach in our edits so entries for some entities, journals, educational methods, assessments or instructional strategies were maintained in the Encyclopedia, albeit updated by "this term is no longer in use" or "this organization closed in . . ." these types of edits are not attributed to the editors In every instance but we take responsibility for any updates beyond the original contribution of the authors.

There are, as usual, many individuals to thank for assisting with the creating and preparation of this volume of work. First, let us thank the contributing editors to the previous and current editions. These individuals took on the responsibilities of looking at where the field has been and where it is going in their respective areas of expertise. They then shepherded many authors into taking on smaller parts to reflect important aspects of the basics and documenting growth. Without their commitment and dedication, we would be bereft of hope for a renovation of this size of work! We would also like to thank the individual authors for their cheerful attitude and dedication to their contributions: They are representatives of the best the field has to offer and we are very grateful for their efforts.

On a personal note - this edition comes at a time of unique personal challenges for each of us. The types of challenges where an individual may question their role in the greater societal fabric or reorder the time spent on things of value. As the newest member of the Editorial team, KV would like to express her belief that this work is not just work, it is a living contribution and documentation of the countless and untold hours of teachers, parents, students, legislators to improve the educational experiences and outcomes of students with disabilities. For every biography there are thousands who dedicate their lives in service. This encyclopedia represents so much more than the sum of the entries, it represents a commitment of people and our culture to improve the lives of others In a way that makes us unique as living organisms on this planet. This work was and is of great value and I'm privileged to be a part of the project.

Cecil would like to thank Julia, as he does so untiringly, for her support in so many ways, and his long-deceased Dad, who gave him the gift of a model of service. Elaine would like to thank Cecil for the opportunity that he gave her many years ago to be a part of this historical project: Words cannot reflect the depth of appreciation. Elaine would also like to thank Kimberly for taking up the baton and continuing the Encyclopedia of Special Education standard of excellence—it is in the best of hands! Kimberly would like to express deep appreciation for the work of her colleagues Cecil and Elaine, and express enduring thankfulness for her father Frank Vannest, who painstakingly checked references and web links for the 3,000-page manuscript. Thanks also to staff and students Heather Davis, Heather Hatton, Amanda Chow, and Erica Strickland for your excellent work. Finally, a personal thank you to Jack—your cheerful patience shooting baskets while I edited from the bleachers, your piano concerts in the background, and most compelling, learning the Aggie war hymn on the bass. Thank you all for the support.

Lastly, we would like to thank the editors at John Wiley & Sons, Inc., Marquita Flemming, Sherry Wasserman, and Kim Nir. What started as a description of the field of special education became a history of special education and a chronicle of its life and times. We have been honored to witness this process and, as always, look forward to future growth.

D

DAILY LIVING SKILLS

The purpose of a functional life skills curriculum for students with disabilities is to maximize their independent functioning in everyday settings where people without disabilities live, work, and spend time. Early instructional programs in Madison, Wisconsin schools that addressed naturally occurring, functional activities in everyday contexts, including general education and the community, resulted in improved postschool outcomes for students, including increased employment in integrated settings with coworkers without disabilities (Van Deventer et al., 1981). Similarly, Benz, Lindstrom, and Yovanoff (2000) demonstrated that a functional skills curriculum (Youth Transition Program) was associated with improved postschool outcomes for participating students, including higher rates of graduation, employment, and participation in postsecondary education.

More than 30 years after the first of these early demonstrations of the effectiveness of a functional curriculum for students with disabilities, the field of special education appears to be in a quandary about what comprises an appropriate curriculum for these students (Alper, Ryndak, Hughes, & McDonnell, 2011; Hughes, 2011). On the one hand, federal legislation (e.g., No Child Left Behind Act [NCLB] of 2001) calls for an increased access to general education curricula and focus on academic outcomes and standardized testing. On the other hand, special education is not producing the positive postschool outcomes nationwide demonstrated in the early studies. Having a disability is persistently associated with poor postschool outcomes, such as low graduation and postsecondary enrollment rates and increased unengagement, unemployment, and underemployment (Newman, Wagner, Cameto, & Knokey, 2009). For example, Newman et al. (2009) reported that, after leaving high school, only 33% of youth with intellectual disabilities are employed (primarily part time), only 7% attend postsecondary school as a sole postschool activity, only 14% live independently or semi-independently, only 26% have a checking account, and only 11% participate in a community group, such as a sports team or church club. One factor related to such poor postschool outcomes may be the inappropriateness of the prevailing special education curriculum, instructional strategies, and service delivery model, which have increasingly deemphasized a functional skills curriculum.

Balancing Academic and Functional Skills

Increasing numbers of special educators are beginning to question the relevance of a curriculum strictly focused on achieving grade-level general education standards versus functional skills (e.g., Bouck, 2009; Patton, Polloway, & Smith, 2000; Wehman, 2009). For example, Storey and Miner (2011) remind us that "although specific curriculum content decisions must be based on standards and benchmarks as well as more individualized preferences and interests, the general goal of all instruction must be to enhance a person's capacity to function successfully in the community" (p. 4). Therefore, the curriculum should comprise skills that teach a person to function in employment, residential, community living, and recreational/leisure domains and that are personally meaningful and valuable to the individual (Hughes, 2011). Similarly, the curriculum should consist of skills that are useful in an immediate (e.g., learning to operate a microwave in order to cook and eat breakfast) or future environment (e.g., learning to ride the bus to get to work). When we consider the poor adult outcomes generally experienced by individuals with disabilities (e.g., Newman et al., 2009), a renewed emphasis in the curriculum on the "criterion of ultimate functioning"—the skills a person must possess "to function as productively and independently as possible in socially, vocationally, and domestically integrated adult community environments" (Brown, Nietupski, & Hamre-Nietupski, 1976, p. 8)—is invaluable as we enter an era of "curriculum wars" in special education.

Critical Skills Areas

Test, Walker, and Richter (2008) referred to functional skills as "skills that help a person to live in, and get around in, the community" (p. 132). The breadth of such skills is extensive, given the range of community and home environments and sub-environments that individuals frequent. Test et al. suggest five general skills areas: travel and community safety (e.g., transportation, pedestrian safety), grocery and general shopping (e.g., preparing a shopping list, finding items, purchasing), eating out (e.g., ordering and paying for meals), community services (e.g., using medical and recreational services, post office), and money and budgeting (e.g., banking, using credit cards). The extent to which individuals achieve mastery in these skills areas will clearly enhance their independence and competence and both increase and broaden their participation in their respective communities.

Additional skills areas include those skills needed to function independently at home. Steere and Burcroff (2004) suggest competence in nine general activity areas is necessary. These areas include: planning and preparing meals; self-care, bathing, and hygiene; cleaning and care of the home; cleaning and care of clothing; telephone use; leisure activities; safety procedures; time management and scheduling; and negotiating with others (roommates) and self-advocacy.

Successful performance of these and the community functional skills mentioned earlier require that individuals know when to perform these skills, how their actions may impact others (e.g., waiting to use the shower), and what support they may need to complete tasks. Also, one issue that warrants serious attention is that participants need to be aware of the numerous risks that exist in home and community environments (e.g., crosswalks, appliances) (Agran, 2004). Learning how to recognize such risks (e.g., spilled water on kitchen floor) and appropriately responding to risk stimuli (e.g., extinguishing a fire) must be included in instruction.

Teaching in Community and Home Settings

As discussed in the entry *Community-Based Instruction*, there is considerable controversy regarding where the instruction of independent living skills should be conducted. Numerous researchers have suggested that instruction should be delivered in natural settings in which the tasks are typically performed (e.g., using a public Laundromat). That said, this focus precludes or limits student participation in inclusive, general education setting (Fisher & Sax, 1999) and may limit instruction in academics. Conversely, proponents of community-based instruction maintain that failure to teach independent living skills in community environments will only compromise generalization and skill transfer. When planning instructional programs, it is critical that the planning team consider the relative benefits of both approaches when determining the instructional site. As a reasonable compromise, several researchers suggest that both general education and community settings be used (e.g., teach skill in school but probe in community) (Agran et al., 1999; Test et al., 2008).

Systematic Instruction and Promoting Generalization

Direct instruction in the actual settings in which students are expected to perform valued behavior has been shown to be effective in teaching critical functional and independent living skills to students, especially those with severe disabilities (e.g., Downing, 2010; McDonnell & Hardman, 2010). The first step is to analyze the performance demands in a setting or across different settings and then observe the student performing these skills. Areas in which the student is not performing required skills should then be taught by direct instructional methods, such as modeling, prompting, reinforcing, and providing corrective feedback (Downing, 2010). As the student acquires targeted skills, the teacher, job coach, or other instructor should begin fading assistance to promote the student's independent performance. For example, if a teacher has been accompanying a student on a bus route from school to a job site, the teacher can begin fading assistance by sitting in a different section of the bus, checking to see that the student gets off at the correct bus stop. When the student is performing all steps of the bus riding routine independently (e.g., boarding the correct bus, paying for the ride, finding and sitting in an unoccupied seat, signaling for and disembarking at the correct bus stop), the teacher can replace accompanying the student on each ride with occasional spot checks.

To promote generalization of acquired skills across people, settings, tasks, and time, instructional personnel should introduce into training multiple exemplars of stimuli that occur across environmental settings (Horner, Sprague, & Wilcox, 1982; Stokes & Baer, 1977). For example, if a student is learning to use a bank card at an ATM machine, the teacher should expose the student to ATM machines that have different stimulus features, such as where to insert the bank card and information provided on the keypad. If students learn to perform a task across a variety of relevant stimuli, they are more likely to generalize tasks to new situations and environmental demands. For example, Hughes et al. (2000) taught four high school students with intellectual disabilities and autism to initiate conversation across a variety of peers and settings (multiple exemplars). All four students generalized their initiations to novel peers in both trained and untrained settings after instruction had been terminated.

Summary

Grigal, Test, Beattie, and Wood (1997) examined a sample of IEPs of students with disabilities to examine the transition components in their IEPs. Independent living skills were included in just over one-half of the IEPs; home making skills were in about 40%; and transportation, financial, and medical-related skills were in less than 25%. Additionally, IEP goals were evaluated to determine if they were: *detailed, adequate,* or *minimal*. The majority of goals in the area of living skills were determined to be at best minimal, with many goals being "vague and illegible." Last, in a study by Lynch and Beare (1990) on IEP objectives for students with intellectual disabilities or behavioral disorders, their education was exclusively on academic skills. From the available data, it appears that a large number of students with disabilities are not receiving satisfactory, if any, instruction in living skills. This is regrettable given the many challenges that individuals with disabilities will face as they transition into the myriad of employment, residential, commercial, public, and medical environments and services available to them as adults. Instruction in independent living skills is a curriculum domain that cannot be neglected for many students with disabilities.

REFERENCES

Agran, M., et al. (Spring, 1999). A survey of secondary level teachers' opinions on community-based instruction and inclusive education. *Journal of the Association for Persons with Severe Handicaps, 24*, 58–62.

Alper, S., Ryndak, D. L., Hughes, C., & McDonnell, J. (2011). *Documenting long-term outcomes of inclusive education for students with significant disabilities: Methodological issues.* Manuscript submitted for publication.

Benz, M. R., Lindstrom, L. E., & Yanvanoff, P. (2000). Improving graduation and employment outcomes of students with disabilities: Predictive factors and student perspectives. *Exceptional Children, 66*, 509–529.

Bouck, E. C. (2009). No Child Left Behind, the Individuals with Disabilities Education Act, and functional curricula: A conflict of interest? *Education and Training in Developmental Disabilities, 44*, 3–13.

Brown, L., Nietupski, J., & Hamre-Nietupski, S. (1976). Criterion of ultimate functioning. In M. A. Thomas (Ed.), *Hey, don't forget about me!* (pp. 2–15). Reston, VA: Council for Exceptional Children.

Downing, J. E. (2010). *Academic instruction for students with moderate and severe intellectual disabilities in inclusive classrooms.* Thousand Oaks, CA: Corwin.

Fisher, D., & Sax, C. (1999). Noticing differences between and postsecondary education: Extending Agran, Snow, and Swaner's discussion. *Journal of the Association for Persons with Severe Handicaps, 24*, 303–305.

Grigal, M., Test, D., Beattie, J., & Wood, W. M. (1997). An evaluation of transition components of Individualized Education Programs. *Exceptional Children, 63*(3), 357–372.

Horner, R. H., Sprague, J., & Wilcox, B. (1982). Constructing general case programs for community activities. In B. Wilcox & G. T. Bellamy (Eds.), *Design of high school programs for severely handicapped students* (pp. 61–98). Baltimore: Paul H. Brookes.

Hughes, C. (2011). Foreword. In K. Storey & C. Miner, *Systematic instruction of functional skills for students and adults with disabilities.* Springfield, IL: Charles Thomas.

Hughes, C., Rung, L. L., Wehmeyer, M. L., Agran, M., Copeland, S. R., & Hwang, B. (2000). Self-prompted communication book use to increase social interaction among high school students. *Journal of the Association for Persons with Severe Handicaps, 25*, 153–166.

Lynch, E. C., & Beare, P. L. (1990). The quality of IEP objectives and their relevance to instruction for students with mental retardation and behavior disorders. *Remedial and Special Instruction, 11*, 44–55.

McDonnell, J., & Hardman, M. L. (2010). *Successful transition programs: Pathways for students with intellectual disabilities and developmental disabilities.* Thousand Oaks, CA: Sage.

Newman, L., Wagner, M., Cameto, R., & Knokey, A. M. (2009). *The post-high school outcomes of youth with disabilities up to 4 years after high school. A report of findings from the National Longitudinal Transition Study-2 (NLTS2).* Menlo Park, CA: SRI International.

No Child Left Behind Act of 2001, Pub. L. No. 107-110, 115 Stat. 1425 (2002).

Patton, J. R., Polloway, E. A., & Smith, T. E. C. (2000). Educating students with mild mental retardation. *Focus on Autism and Other Developmental Disabilities, 15*, 80–89.

Steere, D. E., & Burcroff, T. L. (2004). Living at home. In P. Wehman & J. Kregel (Eds.), *Functional curriculum* (pp. 293–316). Austin, TX: PRO-ED.

Stokes, T., & Baer, D. (1977). An implicit technology of generalization. *Journal of Applied Behavior Analysis, 10*, 349–367.

Storey, K., & Miner, C. (2011). *Systematic instruction of functional skills for students and adults with disabilities.* Springfield, IL: Charles Thomas Publishers.

Test, D., Walker, A., & Richter, S. (2008). Community functioning skills. In K. Storey, P. Bates, & D. Hunter (Eds.), *The road ahead: Transition to adult life for persons with disabilities* (pp. 131–150). St. Augustine, FL: Training Resource Network.

Van Deventer, P., Yelinek, N., Brown, L., Schroeder, J., Loomis, R., & Gruenewald, L. (1981). A follow-up examination of severely handicapped graduates of the Madison Metropolitan School District from 1971–1978. In L. Brown, K. Baumgart, I. Pumpian, J. Nisbet, A. Ford, A. Donnellan, M. Sweet, R. Loomis & J. Schroeder (Eds.), *Educational programs for severely handicapped students, Vol, XI.* Madison, WI: Madison Metropolitan School District.

Wehman, P. (2009, October). *Transition from school to adulthood for youth with disabilities: Where are we in 2009?* Paper presented to the U.S. Department of Education, Office of Special Education and Rehabilitative Services, Washington, DC.

CAROLYN HUGHES
Vanderbilt University

MARTIN AGRAN
University of Wyoming
Fourth edition

DANCE THERAPY

Dance therapy is a method by which movement is incorporated into a therapeutic or educational program. As a therapy approach, dance has been used to enhance traditional methods of medical and verbal group therapies with numerous populations, including the aged, the mentally ill, and the mentally retarded. Dance is especially useful with the retarded because it does not require verbal abilities (Rogers, 1977). Benefits noted through informal observations of dance therapy programs have included improvements in general motility, speech patterns, locomotion, and social ability (Barteneiff & Lewis, 1980).

Dance therapy has also resulted in reduction of muscle tension and trait anxiety (Kline et al., 1978).

Dance has also been used in a broader context to promote physical and social development. Crain, Eisenhart, and McLaughlin (1984) implemented a dance program with mildly retarded adolescent students that included movement orientation, movement exploration, dance foundations, rhythms, and traditional dances. They noted improvements for 11 of 13 participants in areas of physical and social development.

Dance therapy is useful with special populations both as an adjunct to normal group verbal therapies and as a method to enhance physical, social, and educational development (Gladding, 1992).

REFERENCES

Barteneiff, I., & Lewis, D. (1980). *Body movement: Coping with the environment*. New York, NY: Gordon & Breach.

Crain, C., Eisenhart, M., & McLaughlin, J. (1984). The application of a multiple measurement approach to investigate the effects of a dance program on educable mentally retarded adolescents. *Research Quarterly for Exercise & Sport*, *55*, 231–236.

Gladding, S. T. (1992). *Counseling as an art: The creative arts in counseling*. Alexandria, VA: American Counseling Association.

Kline, F., Burgoyne, R. W., Staples, F., Moredock, P., Snyder, V., & Ioerger, M. (1978). A report on the use of movement therapy for chronic, severely disabled outpatients. *Art Psychotherapy*, *5*, 181–183.

Rogers, S. B. (1977). Contributions of dance therapy in a treatment program for retarded adolescents and adults. *Art Psychotherapy*, *4*, 195–197.

CHRISTINE A. ESPIN
University of Minnesota

See also Recreation for Individuals With Disabilities; Recreational Therapy

DANDY-WALKER SYNDROME

Dandy-Walker syndrome (DWS) is a congenital anomaly that involves the formation of a large cyst in the posterior region of the brain (known as a Dandy-Walker Formation) that results in hydrocephalus and agenesis of the central region or vermis of the cerebellum (Greenspan, 1998). It is similar to Joubert syndrome in the latter respect and has some overlapping symptoms. Etiology is unknown, but DWS is thought to be not genetic, but related to some invasive organism, possibly cytomegalovirus. It is sometimes diagnosable via ultrasound in utero but is more likely to be detected in infancy and early childhood.

There are significant impairments associated with most cases of DWS including mental retardation of varying degrees (in about 50% of cases), nonverbal learning disabilities in higher functioning DWS patients, sporadic cases including agenesis of the corpus callosum (Tucker & Vaurio, 2003), and many social and behavioral problems.

Specific psychoeducational recommendations cannot be made for all DWS patients due to the degree of variability in outcome. Most will require special education services, often as Other Health Impaired, but consistent assessment and modification of programming are typically necessary. The successfulness of the shunt for the hydrocephalus is crucial to a positive outcome, and the earlier the shunting takes place, the better the prognosis.

REFERENCES

Greenspan, S. (1998). Dandy-Walker syndrome. In L. Phelps (Ed.), *Health-related disorders in children and adolescents* (pp. 219–223). Washington, DC: American Psychological Association.

Tucker, D. M., & Vaurio, R. (2003). Agenesis of the corpus callosum. In E. Fletcher-Janzen & C. R. Reynolds (Eds.), *Childhood disorders diagnostic desk reference* (pp. 15–16). Hoboken, NJ: Wiley.

STAFF

DARIER DISEASE

Darier disease is a skin disorder in which a red rash appears on parts of the body, particularly the forehead, ears, neck, chest, groin, and back. This rash often has a foul odor and is accompanied by weakening of the fingernails causing V-shape indentations. The rash may also itch. Darier disease is not contagious. Darier disease has also been loosely correlated with certain neurological and psychological disorders (Cordeiro, Werebe, & Vallada, 2000).

Darier disease normally manifests itself in the teenage years, and symptoms are gradually progressive. It begins with small bumps and may lead to scaly or blistery skin. It is thought to be inherited genetically through an autosomal dominant gene.

Characteristics

1. Red rash on skin, particularly neck, forehead, ears, back, chest, and groin areas.
2. Foul odor from affected areas.
3. V-shape notches in the fingernails.

There is no cure for Darier disease. It can, however, be treated in several ways to help alleviate the symptoms. Doctors may prescribe Accutane, a topical gel or cream, a regimen of dry skin lotion, vitamins A and E (Randle, Diaz-Perez, & Winkelmann, 1980), and avoidance of sunlight. Additionally, a strong antiodor soap may be helpful.

In an educational setting, it is important to be sensitive to the psychological needs of a child with Darier disease. The child will most likely be subject to more teasing from his or her peers than would unaffected children. A visit from a doctor or nurse may help to sensitize other children. Lastly, there are many online support groups that are available to individuals with this disorder.

REFERENCES

Cordeiro, Q. Jr., Werebe, D. M., & Vallada, H. (2000). Darier's disease: A new paradigm for genetic studies in psychiatric disorders. *Sao Paulo Medical Journal, 118*, 201–203.

Randle, H. W., Diaz-Perez, J. L., & Winkelmann, R. K. (1980). Toxic doses of vitamin A for pityriasis rubra pilaris. *Archives of Dermatology, 116*, 888–892.

ALLISON KATZ
Rutgers University

See *also* **Response to Intervention**

DATA-BASED DECISION MAKING, POSITIVE BEHAVIOR SUPPORT

Data-based decision making has been a preferred practice in education for many years (Boudett, City, & Murnane, 2006b; Carroll & Johnson, 1990; Chalfant, Pysh, & Moultrie, 1979; Deno, 1985; Deno, Fuchs, Marston, & Shin, 2001; D'Zurilla, Nezu, & Maydeu-Olivares, 2002; Gilbert, 1978; Hamilton et al., 2009; Idol-Maestas, 1983; Pidgeon & Gregory, 2004; Pugach & Johnson, 1995; West & Idol, 1990; White & Haring, 1980; Zins, Curtis, Graden, & Ponti, 1988). The process is known in special education by different names (e.g., collaborative problem solving, collaborative teaming, instructional consultation, instructional support, mainstream assistance, prereferral intervention, psychoanalytic consultation, school assistance centers, and teacher assistance teams), but it typically involves groups meeting regularly to review and uses data to make decisions about administrative, academic, and social problems (Boudett, City, & Murnane, 2006a, 2006b; Burns & Symington, 2002; Chalfant et al., 1979; Deno, 1985; Deno et al., 2001; Fuchs, 1991; Fuchs, Fuchs, Bahr, Fernstrom, & Stecker, 1990; Graden, 1989; Graden, Casey, & Bonstrom, 1983; Graden, Casey, & Christenson, 1985; House & McInerney, 1996; Kerzner, 2009; Phillips & McCullough, 1990; S. Safran & Safran, 1996; Santangelo, 2009; Snell & Janney, 2000).

Landmark federal legislation (Public Law 94–142) and its reauthorizations direct that decision making in special education should be guided by teams of qualified professionals (Individuals with Disabilities Education Improvement Act, 2004). Architects of the principles and practices that became team decision making believed that working together in groups to review data would provide assurances against individual errors in judgment when solving the complex problems sometimes encountered in providing services for individuals with disabilities (Algozzine & Ysseldyke, 2006; Pfeiffer, 1982). In a broader sense, effective schools use data-based decision making to inform, monitor, and improve instruction, to document progress and outcomes, and to inform parents and other stakeholders on key performance indicators (Bernhardt, 2009; Blanc et al., 2010; Blankenstein, Houston, & Cole, 2010; Boudett et al., 2006a, 2006b; Burke, 2010; Deno, 2005; Hill, 2010; Houston, 2010; Newton, Horner, Algozzine, Todd, & Algozzine, 2009; Pidgeon & Gregory, 2004; Renfro & Grieshaber, 2009).

At the summative level, data-based decision making involves answering questions that illustrate comparisons of performance over time as well as across schools, districts, states, or other education agencies; and, at the formative level, it focuses more on what and how students are being taught, what levels of success are being achieved, and what additional supports are needed for teachers and students (Hill, 2010). In this context, formative use of data to monitor progress is the foundation for summative evaluations that document outcomes and performance (B. Algozzine & Algozzine, 2009; Hill, 2010; Stiggins & Duke, 2008; Sugai et al., 2005). Schools implementing response-to-intervention (RtI) and school-wide positive interventions and behavior support (SWPBIS) use data-based decision making teams to frequently monitor a broad range of systems and strategies for achieving important academic and social outcomes for all students (B. Algozzine & Algozzine, 2009; Anderson & Spaulding, 2007; Bradley, Danielson, & Doolittle, 2007; Brown-Chidsey & Steege, 2005; Fuchs & Deshler, 2007; L. Fuchs, 2004; Newton et al., 2009; Sailor, Doolittle, Bradley, & Danielson, 2009; Scott & Martinek, 2006; Sugai et al., 2005; Sugai & Horner, 2008, 2009; Ysseldyke & Algozzine, 1984, 2006; Ysseldyke, Algozzine, & Thurlow, 2000).

The commonalities in the early and growing array of data-based decision-making models for solving problems reflect the view that (a) most decisions of substance involve repeated cycles that involve ongoing evaluation and adaptation, and (b) decision making is most effective when individuals as members of teams engage in a series of systematic and iterative activities (Newton et al., 2009). The first step in most of these models is reviewing expectations and performance and identifying problems. A "problem" is generally defined as a discrepancy between an actual condition and an expected or desired condition and "problem solving" in many educational models begins by addressing "who, what, where, and when" questions about the problem. Developing and refining a hypothesis about "why" the problem exists is the next step before discussing and developing solutions and developing and implementing an action plan to address the problem. The final step typically involves evaluating and revising the implemented solution to identify the need and direction for additional actions.

Illustrations From Practice

Data-based decision making occurs at many levels in effective schools. The examples that follow illustrate how schools using data-based decision making (a) to address schoolwide instructional concerns (Data Wise Improvement Process), (b) to maximize student achievement and reduce behavior problems with a tiered prevention system (Response to Intervention Teams), and (c) to prevent the development and increase of problem behaviors that limit student success (Positive Behavior and Intervention Support Teams).

Data Wise Improvement Process

At Denver Middle School, Principal Josh McDaniel had established his school data team and created a schedule for them to meet twice a month. The team consisted of the principal, principal intern, assistant principal, academic facilitator, and a teacher from each subject area as well as EC and Bilingual/ESL. Every teacher in the school was a member of at least one instructionally oriented team (such as a grade-level or departmental team) and each team sent at least one representative to the school data team.

On Tuesday at 11 a.m., team members gathered in the testing room and the agenda for the meeting was distributed. The following items were printed on the front page of the agenda: meeting norms (i.e., phone on vibrate, start on time/end on time, suspend all hierarchy, stay on task, and adjust agenda as needed), team member names and their roles on the team (i.e., facilitator, data analyst, scribe, alternate scribe), and questions that guided the discussion at every meeting (i.e., What do we expect our students to learn? How will we know that the intervention was implemented with fidelity? How will we know when our students have learned it? How will we respond when our students don't?). The meeting began with the facilitator reading the team norms and saying how important it was to follow them as all members engaged in crucial conversations.

Prior to this meeting, the team had used formative assessment data to target a gap in student understanding. Only 60% of seventh graders earned 80% or higher when answering questions related to comprehension of text. A closer look at student work indicated that the learner-centered problem involved analyzing the effects of mood and style in the genres nonfiction and poetry. The academic facilitator collaborated with teachers at the weekly seventh grade language arts planning meeting to create a rubric of indicators of best practice when teaching mood and style. Using these common indicators, administrators and support staff conducted walkthroughs to determine the degree to which teachers were using best practice when providing instruction in analyzing the effect of mood and tone in nonfiction and poetry.

The purpose of this meeting was to share walkthrough data, identify a problem of practice related to the learner-centered problem, create an action plan documenting a solution to the problem of practice, and a plan for implementing and monitoring the effects of the solution. Data overviews were displayed for all to see using a laptop and projector (*reviewing expectations and performance and identifying problems*). They revealed that although indicators on the rubric were present in classrooms, the content teachers were using to teach mood and style was not nonfiction or poetry. The academic facilitator then e-mailed all seventh grade language arts teachers a request to bring five samples of each genre to the next planning meeting so that they could review them and decide on those most appropriate for their purpose (*developing and refining a hypothesis*). It was agreed that the academic facilitator would also guide teachers (*discussing and developing solutions*) as they created common assessments to determine the extent to which students were meeting the targeted goal "100% of our seventh grade students will be able to analyze the effect of mood and style on samples of writing from the genres nonfiction and poetry" (*developing and implementing an action plan*). Administrators and support staff agreed to continue walkthroughs for the purpose of monitoring the extent to which teachers were using the selected samples to teach the elements of mood and style (*evaluating and revising the solution*).

Throughout the meeting the scribe recorded minutes on a laptop. She created an action plan documenting the solution (i.e., providing nonfiction and poetry samples for teachers to use), and a plan for implementing and monitoring the effects of the solution (i.e., the creation of common assessment questions and walkthroughs). She listed additional instructional problems observed by administrators and support staff as they conducted their walkthroughs to assess the fidelity of implementation. These included: too much teacher-led instruction, minimal checks for understanding during a lesson or activity, need to link content to other subjects, and lack of scaffolding. The decision was made to conduct walkthroughs across grade and subject levels to define these problems with more precision. Before the meeting adjourned, the assistant principal asked team members to respond to the following evaluation questions. "Did we achieve our objectives? What could we have done better? How did we establish and maintain focus? Did we use effective meeting methods? How could we improve?"

Response to Intervention Team

At Hickory Hill Elementary School, a Response to Intervention (RtI) approach includes school-wide screenings, progress monitoring, and a 3-tiered service delivery. The school has adopted Tier 1 core curricula for reading, math, social studies, and science. School-wide screenings include common and authentic assessments that monitor student performance related to core curricula objectives, Dynamic Indicators of Basic Early Literacy Skills (DIBELS) assessments in the fall, winter, and spring for kindergartners and first graders, DIBELS fluency and accuracy assessments for students in the second and third grades, and Fuchs' fluency and accuracy assessments for students in the fourth and fifth grades. In addition to these measures, students in the second through fifth grades are given formative assessments linked to the state standards as well as other assessments to measure specific district benchmarks.

Administrators and support staff meet weekly with each grade level team to review assessment data (*reviewing expectations and performance and identifying problems*), to interpret and analyze data, to identify possible explanations of the data (*developing and refining a hypothesis*) and develop SMART goals (*discussing and developing solutions*), and develop interventions for target groups of students scoring below the benchmark performance (*developing and implementing an action plan*). These students receive Tier 2 level of support, remaining in the core curriculum with changes to instruction/practice or supplemental support. A 6-week rotation exists in which the teams spend 2 weeks discussing reading, 2 weeks discussing social studies/science, and 2 weeks discussing math. A 6-week action plan for each content area and target group is created and implementation of plans and progress of groups is monitored (*evaluating and revising the solution*).

If a student continues not to make progress with Tier 2 levels of support, he or she is referred to a Tier 3 Intervention Team. At these meetings, a problem-solving approach occurs in which the problem is identified, an individual intervention and action plan is developed, and a progress monitoring plan is established. Implementation of each plan and progress of each individual is monitored. Hickory Hill uses a web-based data management and reporting system to determine response to intervention. It is through the use of data-based decision making to inform instruction during grade level team meetings and a problem solving student intervention team process that Hickory Hill provides differentiated instruction to its students through a 3-tiered delivery approach.

School-Wide Positive Behavior Interventions and Support (SWPBIS) Team

At a monthly SWPBIS Team meeting, Brighton Elementary (565 K-5 students, Title I) SWPBIS Team members reviewed their office discipline patterns and trends (www.swis.org) and found that inappropriate language, disrespect, and physical aggression were the most frequent problem behaviors and those behaviors were occurring on the playground (*reviewing expectations and performance and identifying problems*). Before defining the problem with more precision, it was determined to teach all students how to play respectfully on the playground. Each classroom participated in a 45-minute instructional session on the playground, learning the rules and expectations of all equipment, games, and boundaries. Planning time for implementation of a teaching recess plan involved a total of 21 hours across staff, while implementation time required about 18 hours of direct teaching time. As the team reviewed their data to define the problem with more precision, they found that the problems were *not* occurring at all recess times; but were occurring during the second and third grade recesses due to the students trying to get access to the new equipment and games (*developing and refining a hypothesis*). With these additional elements of precision (who, when, and why) came problem solving (*discussing and developing solutions*) and action planning based on contextual fit and the perceived motivation of the problem (*developing and implementing an action plan*). After a 15-day intervention phase, which included periodic fidelity checks verifying that the plan was being properly implemented, the team met again to review progress and consider next steps (*evaluating and revising the solution*).

REFERENCES

Algozzine, B., & Algozzine, K. (2009). Facilitating academic achievement through schoolwide positive behavior support. In W. Sailor, G. Dunlap, R. Horner, & G. Sugai (Eds.), *Handbook of positive behavior support* (pp. 521–550). New York, NY: Springer.

Algozzine, B., & Ysseldyke, J. (2006). *The fundamentals of special education*. Thousand Oaks, CA: Corwin.

Anderson, C., & Spaulding, S. (2007). Using positive behavior support to design effective classrooms. *Beyond Behavior, 16*(2), 27–31. Retrieved from ERIC database.

Bernhardt, V. L. (2009). Data use: Data-driven decision making takes a big picture view of the needs of teachers and students. *Journal of Staff Development, 30*(1), 24–27.

Blanc, S., Christman, J., Liu, R., Mitchell, C., Travers, E., & Bulkley, K. (2010). Learning to learn from data: Benchmarks and instructional communities. *Peabody Journal of Education, 85*, 205–225. doi:10.1080/01619561003685379

Blankenstein, A. M., Houston, P. D., & Cole, R. W. (Eds.). (2010). *Data enhanced leadership*. Thousand Oaks, CA: Corwin Press.

Boudett, K. P., City, E. A., & Murnane, R. J. (2006a). Introduction. In K. P. Boudett, E. A. City, & R. J. Murname (Eds), *Data wise: A step-by-step guide to using assessment results to improve teaching and learning* (pp. 1–8). Cambridge, MA: Harvard University Press.

Boudett, K. P., City, E. A., & Murnane, R. J. (Eds.). (2006b). *Data wise: A step-by-step guide to using assessment results to improve teaching and learning*. Cambridge, MA: Harvard University Press.

Bradley, R., Danielson, L., & Doolittle, J. (2007). Responsiveness to intervention: 1997 to 2007. *Teaching Exceptional Children*, *39*(5), 8–12.

Brown-Chidsey, R., & Steege, M. W. (2005). *Response to intervention: Principles and strategies for effective practice*. New York, NY: Guilford Press.

Burke, K. (2010). Using data to drive instruction and assessment in the standards-based classroom. In A. M., Blankenstein, P. D. Houston, & R. W. Cole (Eds.), *Data enhanced leadership* (pp. 75–93). Thousand Oaks, CA: Corwin Press.

Burns, M. K., & Symington, T. (2002). A meta-analysis of pre-referral intervention teams: Student and systemic outcomes. *Journal of School Psychology*, *40*, 437–447.

Carroll, J. S., & Johnson, E. J. (1990). *Decision research: A field guide*. Newbury Park, CA: Sage.

Chalfant, J. C., Pysh, M. V., & Moultrie, R. (1979). Teacher assistance teams: A model for within-building problem solving. *Learning Disability Quarterly*, *2*, 85–96.

D'Zurilla, T. J., Nezu, A. M., & Maydeu-Olivares, A. (2002). *Social Problem-Solving Inventory—Revised (SPSI—R): Technical manual*. North Tonawanda, NY: Multi-Health Systems.

Deno, S. L. (1985). Curriculum-based measurement: The emerging alternative. *Exceptional Children*, *52*, 219–232.

Deno, S. L. (2005). Problem-solving assessment. In R. Brown-Chidsey (Ed.), *Assessment for intervention: A problem-solving approach* (pp. 10–40). New York, NY: Guilford Press.

Deno, S. L., Fuchs, L. S., Marston, D., & Shin, J. (2001). Using curriculum-based measurements to establish growth standards for students with learning disabilities. *School Psychology Review*, *30*, 507–524.

Fuchs, D. (1991). Mainstream assistance teams: A prereferral intervention system for difficult-to-teach students. In G. Stoner, M. Shinn, & H. Walkers (Eds.), *Interventions for achievement and behavior problems* (pp. 241–268). Silver Springs, MD: National Association of School Psychologists.

Fuchs, D., & Deshler, D. D. (2007). What we need to know about responsiveness to intervention (and shouldn't be afraid to ask). *Learning Disabilities Research & Practice*, *22*, 129–136.

Fuchs, D., Fuchs, L. S., Bahr, M. W., Fernstrom, P, & Stecker, P. M. (1990). Prereferral intervention: A prescriptive approach. *Exceptional Children*, *56*, 493–513.

Fuchs, L. S. (2004). The past, present, and future of curriculum-based measurement research. *School Psychology Review*, *33*(2), 188–192.

Gilbert, T. F. (1978). *Human competence: Engineering worthy performance*. New York, NY: McGraw-Hill.

Graden, J. L. (1989). Redefining prereferral intervention as intervention assistance: Collaboration between general and special education. *Exceptional Children*, *56*, 227–231.

Graden, J. L., Casey, A., & Bonstrom, O. (1983). Pre-referral interventions: Effects on referral rates and teacher attitudes. Minneapolis: Institute for Research on Learning Disabilities, University of Minnesota. (ERIC Document Reproduction Services No. ED 244438)

Graden, J. L., Casey, A., & Christenson, S. L. (1985). Implementing a prereferral intervention system: Part 1. The Model. *Exceptional Children*, *51*, 377–384.

Hamilton, L., Halverson, R., Jackson, S., Mandinach, E., Supovitz, J., & Wayman, J. (2009). *Using student achievement data to support instructional decision making* (NCEE 2009–4067). Washington, DC: National Center for Education Evaluation and Regional Assistance, Institute of Education Sciences, U.S. Department of Education. Retrieved from http://ies.ed.gov/ncee/wwc/publications/practiceguides/

Hill, P. W. (2010). Using assessment data to lead teaching and learning. In A. M. Blankenstein, P. D. Houston, & R. W. Cole (Eds.), *Data enhanced leadership* (pp. 31–50). Thousand Oaks, CA: Corwin Press.

House, J. E., & McInerney, W. F. (1996). The school assistance center: An alternative model for the delivery of school psychological services. *School Psychology International*, *17*, 115–124.

Idol-Maestas, L. (1983). *Special educator's consultation handbook*. Rockville, MD: Aspen.

Individuals with Disabilities Education Improvement Act of 2004. (2004, December 3). Public Law 108–446, 118 STAT. 2647. Retrieved from http://idea.ed.gov/download/statute.html

Individuals with Disabilities Education Improvement Act, H.R. 1350, 108th Congress (2004).

Kerzner, S. (2009). Psychoanalytic school consultation: A collaborative approach. *Schools: Studies in Education*, *6*, 117–128.

Newton, J. S., Horner, R., Algozzine, R., Todd, A., & Algozzine, K. (2009). Using a problem-solving model for data-based decision making in schools. In W. Sailor, G. Dunlap, G. Sugai, & R. Horner (Eds.), *Handbook of positive behavior support* (pp. 551–580). New York, NY: Springer.

Pfeiffer, S. (1982). The superiority of team decision making. *Exceptional Children*, *49*, 68–69.

Phillips, V., & McCullough, L. (1990). Consultation-based programming: Instituting the collaborative ethic in schools. *Exceptional Children*, *56*, 291–304.

Pidgeon, N. F., & Gregory, R. (2004). Judgment, decision making and public policy. In D. Koehler & N. Harvey (Eds.), *Blackwell handbook of judgment and decision making* (pp. 604–623). Oxford, England: Blackwell.

Pugach, M. C., & Johnson, L. J. (1995). *Collaborative practitioners—collaborative schools*. Denver, CO: Love.

Renfro, L., & Grieshaber, A. (2009). Focus, feedback, follow-through: Professional development basics guide district's plan. *Journal of Staff Development*, *30*(4), 26–31.

Safran, S. P., & Safran, J. S. (1996). Intervention assistance programs and prereferral teams: Directions for the twenty-first century. *Remedial Special Education*, *17*, 363–369.

Sailor, W., Doolittle, J., Bradley, R., & Danielson, L. (2009). Response to intervention and positive behavior support. In W. Sailor, G. Dunlap, G. Sugai, & R. Horner (Eds.), *Handbook of positive behavior support* (pp. 729–753). New York, NY: Springer.

Santangelo, T. (2009). Collaborative problem solving effectively implemented, but not sustained: A case for aligning the sun, the moon, and the stars. *Exceptional Children*, *75*, 185–209.

Scott, T. M., & Martinek, G. (2006). Coaching positive behavior support in school settings: Tactics and data-based decision making. *Journal of Positive Behavior Interventions, 8,* 165–173.

Snell, M., & Janney, R. (2000). Teachers' problem-solving about children with moderate and severe disabilities in elementary classrooms. *Exceptional Children, 66,* 472–490.

Stiggins, R., & Duke, D. (2008). Effective instructional leadership requires assessment leadership. *Phi Delta Kappan, 94,* 285–291.

Sugai, G., & Horner, R. H. (2006). A promising approach for expanding and sustaining school-wide positive behavior support. *School Psychology Review, 35,* 245–259.

Sugai, G., & Horner, R. H. (2009). Defining and describing school-wide positive behavior support. In W. Sailor, G. Dunlap, G. Sugai, & R. Horner (Eds). *Handbook of positive behavior supports* (pp. 307–329). New York, NY: Springer.

Sugai, G., Horner, R. H., Sailor, W., Dunlap, G., Eber, L., Lewis, T.,...Nelson, M. (2005). *School-wide positive behavior support: Implementers' blueprint and self-assessment.* Eugene: University of Oregon Press.

West, J. E., & Idol, L. (1990). Collaborative consultation in the education of mildly handicapped and at-risk students. *Remedial and Special Education, 11,* 22–31.

White, O. R., & Haring, N. G. (1980). *Exceptional teaching* (2nd ed.). Columbus, OH: Charles E. Merrill.

Ysseldyke, J. E., & Algozzine, B. (1984). *Introduction to special education.* Boston, MA: Houghton Mifflin.

Ysseldyke, J. E., Algozzine, B., & Thurlow, M. L. (2000). *Critical issues in special education* (3rd ed.). Boston, MA: Houghton Mifflin.

Ysseldyke, J., & Algozzine, B. (2006). *Effective assessment for students with special needs.* Thousand Oaks, CA: Corwin.

Zins, J. E., Curtis, M. J., Graden, J. L., & Ponti, C. R. (1988). *Helping students succeed in the regular classroom: A guide for developing intervention assistance programs.* San Francisco, CA: Jossey-Bass.

ANNE W. TODD
University of Oregon

BOB ALGOZZINE
University of North Carolina at Charlotte

ROBERT H. HORNER
University of Oregon

KATE ALGOZZINE
University of North Carolina at Charlotte
Fourth edition

DAY-CARE CENTERS

Formal day-care programs originated during the Industrial Revolution with custodial care in factory rooms for young children of working mothers. Early in this century, the Salvation Army in Baltimore and Hull House in Chicago began day-care programs for infants and children of working mothers. Beginning in 1933, the Federal Work Relief Project supported Emergency Nursery Schools (ENS) as a way of providing jobs for unemployed teachers. The ENS programs were similar to the later Head Start programs in that they were for preschool children, offered medical services, emphasized nutrition, and provided in-service staff training; however, ENS emphasized nurturing care while Head Start emphasizes more formal education. When the ENS program ended, day care for mothers working in war industries was funded under the Lanham Act until 1946. Other day-care programs were supported by industry during World War II. None of those early programs were intended for children with disabilities, but probably some with mild problems were admitted.

Programs exclusively for children with disabilities began in the 1950s. Sponsored and conducted by parent groups, most were for children with intellectual developmental delays. In the 1960s the Massachusetts Department of Mental Health added a day-care program to its preschool program because many severely retarded children were excluded from schools. Few private preschools, kindergartens, or public schools accepted children with severe disabilities until the late 1970s. Most children diagnosed with blindness, deafness, intellectual developmental delays, and severe physical disabilities were excluded from day-care services and parents looked to state-supported residential facilities for supports and services for their children. After implementation of PL 94-142 in 1977, school systems supported educational programs that replaced (and were often similar to) the private day-care facilities for school-age children. Day-care services were developed for preschool- and postschool-age children with disabilities. This is noted in the American Association on Mental Deficiency's definition of day care: "extended care services provided on an ongoing basis for individuals residing in the community and not eligible for school programs or workshops; involves social, physical, recreational, and personal-care training and activity" (Grossman, 1983).

Efforts to integrate students with disablties into preschool day-care programs with nondisabled peers has increased over the past decades (Barnett, 2008, 2010; Branca, 1988; Guralnick, 1978, 1994, 1995; Templeman, 1989). Providing early intervention programs to children at-risk or identified with a disability has increased the importance of receiving early childhood services (Barnett, 2010). Previously 70% of children ages 3 to 4 received services in private programs. Although 70% of children ages 3 to 4 continue to attend early childhood programs, only 50% attend private programs, which are often funded through public subsidies (Barnett, 2010). Funding to support early childhood programs has increased to promote parents to enroll students in early intervention programs. However, with the increase of funding, many children still do not attend early childhood programs or the program quality is often inadequate (Barnett, 2010). Effective preschool programs have been linked to increasing achievement, school success, and social behavior of children at-risk for future disabilities (Barnett, 2008; Camilli, Vargas, Ryan, & Barnett, 2010).

Creating preschool and day-care programs, which provide well-designed instruction provided by trained teachers increases the positive effects on children's learning and development. With an increase in public subsidies and the inclusion of all students from varying socioeconomic backgrounds greater outcomes could be achieved (Barnett, 2008).

REFERENCES

Barnett, S. (2010). Universal and targted approaches to preschool programs in the United States. *International Journal of Child Care and Education Policy, 4*, 1–12.

Barnett, W. S. (2008). Preschool education and its lasting effects: Research and policy implications. Boulder, CO and Tempe, AZ: Education and Public Interest Center & Education Policy Research Unit. Retrieved from http://nieer.org/resources/research/PreschoolLastingEffects.pdf

Branca, R. A. (1988). *Implementing a program of supportive services to severely handicapped preschool age children in community programs.* (ERIC Clearinghouse No. EC212115)

Camilli, G., Vargas, S., Ryan, S., & Barnett, W. S. (2010). Meta-analysis of the effects of early education interventions on cognitive and social development. *Teachers College Record,* (3), Article 15440. Retrieved from http://www.tcrecord.org/content.asp?contentid1415440

Grossman, H. J. (1983). *Classification in mental retardation.* Washington, DC: American Association on Mental Deficiency.

Guralnick, M. J. (1978). *Early intervention and the integration of handicapped and nonhandicapped children.* Baltimore, MD: University Park Press.

Guralnick, M. J. (1994). Mother's perceptions of the benefits and drawbacks of early childhood mainstreaming. *Journal of Early Intervention, 18*(2), 168–138.

Guralnick, M. J. (1995). Parent perspectives of peer relationships and friendships in integrated and specialized programs. *American Journal on Mental Retardation, 99*(5), 457–476.

Templeman, T. P. (1989). Integration of children with moderate and severe handicaps into a daycare center. *Journal of Early Intervention, 13*(4), 315–328.

Sue Allen Warren
Boston University
First edition

Heather Davis
Texas A&M University
Fourth editon

See also Head Start; Least Restrictive Environment; Mainstreaming; Respite Care

DEAF-BLIND

There exists a broad range of visual and auditory impairments among deaf-blind persons, indicating an enormous diversity in the severity of disabilities within this population. The term deaf-blind (also called *dual sensory impairment*) covers persons with severe visual and hearing disabilities who are unable to profit from special programs designed solely for deaf or blind children and youths (*Federal Register*, 1975).

It is estimated that there are more than 5,000 children and youth who are deaf-blind in the United States (Arizona Deaf-Blind Project, 1998). Maternal rubella, CHARGE Association, Usher's syndrome, and meningitis are among the top four causes of deaf-blindness in the United States. Additionally, deaf-blind persons often are afflicted with congenital heart disease, mental retardation (Vernon, Grieve, & Shaver, 1980), physical handicaps, social/emotional issues, and communication delays (Arizona Deaf-Blind Project, 1998).

Deaf-blindness has often been associated with Helen Keller and her teacher Anne Sullivan (Lash, 1980). Although some deaf-blind people function within or above normal intelligence, many require extraordinary educational training. The separate disabilities are not additive but multiplicative in nature (Warren, 1984), and often cause severe learning problems. Deaf-blind children have often been referred to as the most difficult group of children to educate (Sims-Tucker & Jensema, 1984). They frequently engage in stereotypic behaviors that interfere with learning and communication. In an attempt to meet the special needs of this population, Regional Centers for Services for Deaf-Blind Children was established in 1967 (Sims-Tucker & Jensema, 1984).

Educational programming for deaf-blind children, including assessment and evaluation, continues to be a difficult task. The trend in educating children with severe disabilities has emphasized a more functional curriculum (Brown et al., 1979). Similarly, educators of deaf-blind children are turning to these curricular approaches for developing intervention programs in such areas as self-help, prevocational and vocational skills, communication, and sensory development (VaDAS-IIy & Fewell, 1984). Programming developed by Van Dijk (1971) has provided teachers, parents, and therapists with an invaluable communication curriculum that incorporates movement theory, which is often associated with the coactive movement. In addition, the emphasis on visual as well as auditory training can be seen in educational programs developed by Goetz and Utley (undated) and Efron and DuBoff (1979).

The Arizona Deaf-Blind Program was established as a federally funded free resource for professionals and families working with deaf-blind individuals. It is housed at the Arizona School for the Deaf and Blind. The program provides consultation services for families of deaf-blind children, provides a lending library, and maintains an online interactive webpage. The project can be contacted at P.O. Box 88510, Tucson, AZ, 85754. Tel.: (520) 770-3680 or at http://www.asdb.state.az.us/ Other resources are: American Association of the Deaf-Blind, Inc., Silver Spring, MD 20901. Tel.: (301) 588-6545, TTY: (301) 523-1265, http://www.aadb.org/ Helen Keller National Center for Deaf-Blind, 111 Middle Neck Road, Sands Point, NY 11050. Tel.: (516) 944-8900, TTY: (516) 944-8637, http://www.hknc.org/

REFERENCES

Arizona Deaf-Blind Program. (1998). *Deaf-blindness fact sheet.* Retrieved from www.azdb.org

Brown, L., Branston, M., Hamre-Nietupski, S., Pumpian, I., Certo, N., & Gruenewald, L. (1979). A strategy for developing chronological age appropriate and functional curricular content for severely handicapped adolescents and young adults. *Journal of Special Education, 13*, 81–90.

Efron, M., & DuBoff, B. (1979). *A vision guide for teachers of deaf-blind children.* Raleigh, NC: South Atlantic Regional Center for Services to Deaf-Blind Children.

Federal Register. (1975). Education for All Handicapped Children Act. http://sitemaker.umich.edu/356.zipkin/the_education_for _all_handicapped_children_act

Goetz, L., & Utley, B. (undated). *Auditory assessment and program manual for severely handicapped deaf-blind students.* Parsons, KS: Words & Pictures.

Lash, J. P. (1980). *Helen and teacher: The story of Helen Keller and Anne Sullivan Macy.* New York, NY: Delacorte.

Sims-Tucker, B., & Jensema, C. (1984). Severely and profoundly auditorially/visually impaired students: The deaf-blind population. In P. Valletutti & B. Sims-Tucker (Eds.), *Severely and profoundly handicapped students: Their nature and needs* (pp. 269–317). Baltimore, MD: Paul H. Brookes.

VaDAS-IIy, P., & Fewell, R. (1984). Predicting the futures of deaf-blind adolescents: Their living and vocational options. *Education of the Visually Handicapped, 16*, 12–19.

Van Dijk, J. (1971). *Learning difficulties and deaf-blind children.* Proceedings of the Fourth International Conference on Deaf-Blind Children. Watertown, MA: Perkins School for the Blind.

Vernon, M., Grieve, B., & Shaver, K. (1980). Handicapping conditions associated with the congenital rubella syndrome. *American Annals of the Deaf, 125*(8), 993–997.

Warren, D. (1984). *Blindness and early childhood development.* New York, NY: American Foundation for the Blind.

VIVIAN I. CORREA
University of Florida
First edition

ELAINE FLETCHER-JANZEN
Chicago School of Professional Psychology
Second edition

See also **Deaf; Keller, Helen; Movement Therapy; Visual Impairment**

DEAF CULTURE

Culture is a term used to identify similar values, norms, beliefs, traditions, behaviors, and language that bind together a group of people usually residing in a specific geographic area sometimes as large as a nation. American Deaf Culture refers to those behaviors, beliefs, and traditions, which characterize the majority of individuals who have experienced severe hearing loss from birth or early childhood and who reside in the United States. Because severe hearing loss is a low-incidence disability there is a strong tendency on the part of the population all over the world who are deaf to feel a closer bond with other deaf individuals who live in other parts of the world than they do with hearing individuals in their own local area.

The major component of Deaf Culture is the use of sign language. In the United States this language is known as American Sign Language or ASL. Sign Language is a visual language based heavily on visual components of the idea being expressed. Therefore it is far easier for an American who is deaf to quickly identify with and understand a person from a different country who utilizes a different form of sign language used in their country than it is for a hearing person in the United States to make the same adjustment to a person from a different country speaking the language native to their own country. Because it is through spoken communication that most hearing individuals establish long-lasting and supportive relationships, it is not surprising that individuals who are deaf seek others like themselves who utilize a visually based communication system to experience the same satisfying and supportive relationships.

Hearing individuals who cannot use American Sign Language are often ignored and rejected by the deaf community. Those who can use sign language are allowed to participate but are not accepted as members of the culture. Those individuals who belong to the culture are referred to as Deaf with a capital "D" while those with hearing loss who do not associate or belong to the culture are referred to as deaf with a lower case "d." Other characteristics of Deaf Culture include the rejection of the term *hearing impaired*. Deaf Culture does not accept the concept that deafness is a disability that needs to be fixed but prefers to think of themselves as normal people who use a visual communication system that does not need to be changed or improved. For this reason the term *impaired* is not acceptable as it suggests that people who are deaf are broken or inferior and need to be fixed. People who are Deaf use the word *hearing* to refer to people who can hear. However, they do not use the ASL sign for hear but instead use the sign for talking. From the perspective of Deaf people it is clearly apparent that it is the visible act of *talking* that separates the two groups rather than the nonvisual act of hearing.

Individualization is a dominant characteristic of American Culture as is expressed in the popular song "I Did

It My Way." The journey through life is viewed as the ultimate experience of who the individual is and what attributes make him or her unique. In sharp contrast the Deaf population functions on the theory of collectivism. People who are Deaf view themselves as belonging to the group that truly represents Deafness. It is the membership in this group that defines them and gives them the sense of belonging that they seek.

Concepts of time are different in Deaf Culture much like they are in some other countries. Deaf Time is a concept openly referred to by hearing individuals who work with people who are Deaf and by Deaf people themselves. Comments such as "We will start the meeting on Deaf Time" are meant to infer that the meeting will start whenever the Deaf people arrive. At the conclusion of any social gathering of Deaf people, departure time is almost always extended until some act of turning off the lights as a signal or an announcement by someone in charge that the evening is concluded, must occur before everyone leaves.

Art Forms in Deaf Culture

Within Deaf Culture a variety of art forms have been developed. For example, in the area of the visual arts of drawing and painting a name has been given to the form of Deaf Culture Art and is known as DE'VIA (Deaf View Image Art). In this art form some aspect of Deafness is incorporated into the picture, which may take the form of a common sign that communicates a concept or an attribute. Eyes are often used frequently in the drawings as a way of expressing the need for visual information and the idea that the eyes are the ears of people who are Deaf.

Deaf Poetry, frequently called ASL Poetry, is another art form found in Deaf Culture. Rhyming, which is found in many poems enjoyed by hearing people, is an auditory experience, so it holds little pleasure for the person who is Deaf. For that reason Deaf people have used a visual technique and have created a new poetry form. They have selected a visual component found in American Sign Language as their means of creating beautiful poetry. The component that is used is the hand shapes on which signs are based. Poets select one hand shape used in ASL and their theme and then they must compose a poem of beauty utilizing that hand shape as the basis of all the words they select for their poem. This is a difficult task and requires an individual with a good grasp of the language and a high degree of linguistic ability.

Theater performance has also been influenced by Deaf Culture. Because few people who are Deaf have intelligible speech that can be used in a theater performance, their acting ability as well as their ability to communicate nonverbally is the way by which their talent is judged.

Therefore, time is given to learning how to use the body to the fullest degree possible to convey meaning. Facial expression is equally important and rehearsals often give time to discussions of how best to use the body, movement,

and facial expression to enhance the visual quality of the play. Hearing people who are seeing deaf theater for the first time often comment on how the visual content of the play also enhances the performance for them. The name given to this area in Deaf Theater is *Visual Vernacular*.

Many individuals who are Deaf have excelled in the field of the arts. Many of the professionals in the arts who are Deaf also claim membership in Deaf Culture and freely contribute their talents to broaden and enhance the understanding of the Deaf community and its culture.

This entry has been informed by the source listed below.

REFERENCE

Schein, J. D. (1989). *At home among strangers*. Washington, DC: Gallaudet Press.

PATRICIA SCHERER
International Center on Deafness and the Arts
through Education
Fourth edition

DEAF EDUCATION

The history of deaf education is relatively short because no records exist of organized teaching in prehistoric times or in the ancient civilizations of Egypt, Greece, and Rome. Although a few records exist of previous isolated examples of deaf individuals reaching some degree of education, Pedro Ponce de Leon (1520–1584) is generally considered to be the first teacher of the deaf. A Benedictine monk, he was entrusted with the education of several deaf children of Spanish nobility, and received wide publicity as a result of his successes. The records concerning the first teachers of the deaf are full of information showing that many of the techniques used today find their roots in the work of those pioneers. The reader is referred to the excellent survey by Moores (1978) for a review. However, it is necessary to mention the Abbott de l'Epée and Samuel Heinicke, because confrontation between their methods was at the heart of the oral versus manual controversy that has profoundly divided deaf educators for two centuries.

De l'Epée established the first public school for the deaf in the world in 1755 in his Paris home. He started it when he was asked to give religious instruction to deaf twin sisters who used signs to communicate between them. De l'Epée understood that gestures could express human thought as much as spoken language and believed sign language to be the natural language of the deaf. He, therefore, set out to learn it from his pupils, but felt compelled to supplement their natural signs by newly formed "methodical" signs in order to obtain a complete sign counterpart of French syntax and morphology. The teaching of articulation was regarded by him as of lesser importance than that of signs and written language.

Samuel Heinicke taught several deaf children as a private tutor in different parts of Germany and established a school in Leipzig in 1778. He prided himself on being able to teach his pupils to speak clearly, and was strongly opposed to the teaching of written before spoken language, which he considered the only appropriate vehicle of thought. Heinicke and his followers Graser and Hill bitterly criticized de l'Epée's method, considering speech to be the first priority of teaching and sign language detrimental to that cause.

Controversy between the advocates of oralism and manualism, which started with de l'Epée and Heinicke, was lively during most of the 19th century, not only in Europe, but also in the United States. The first school for the deaf in the United States was founded by Thomas Hopkins Gallaudet, in 1847, with Laurent Clerc, a deaf teacher trained in Paris by de l'Epée's successor, Sicard. Other manual schools were created along the same lines, most of them paying little or no attention to the teaching of speech and articulation. Other U.S. educators responded with the creation of strictly oral schools. The controversy between manual and oral methods was later embodied by two exceptional personalities: Edward Miner Gallaudet (Thomas's son) and Alexander Graham Bell. The former was convinced of the importance of spoken as well as sign language and was instrumental in establishing an oral-manual combined method in most American schools. Bell observed that education of the deaf in residential schools isolated them from the hearing society, and claimed that sign language was detrimental to the acquisition of English. He advocated the elimination of both sign language and the deaf teachers who used it.

In 1880 an international congress of educators of the deaf convened in Milan, Italy. It adopted two resolutions:

1. Considering the unquestionable superiority of speech over signs for the most perfect knowledge of language, the oral method must be preferred to the gestual method.

2. Considering that the simultaneous use of signs and speech has the disadvantage of being noxious to speech, to lip reading, and to the precision of ideas, the purely oral method must be preferred.

These resolutions were enforced in all European countries, but in the United States Edward Gallaudet opposed Bell and managed to restrict their application. Not only did he maintain a school system using the combined oral-manual method, but he was also able to educate teachers of the deaf in this method at the National Deaf Mute College in Washington, DC; that school was to become the present Gallaudet College. From that time on, the opposition between Bell and Gallaudet increased. It led to the formation of two rival groups of schools and teachers: the exclusively oral and the combined oral-manual.

In Europe, oral education continued to prevail, unchallenged, during more than half of the 20th century. After World War II, progress in electroacoustic technology gave new impetus to oralism. Hopes arose that auditory training with sophisticated apparatus and efficient individual hearing aids combined with lip reading would enable hearing-impaired children to develop their speech skills, both receptively and expressively, to a much larger extent then previously. Whetnall and Fry in London (1964) and the John Tracy Clinic in Los Angeles (Thielman, 1970), among many others, considered that early intervention would allow most deaf children to attend ordinary schools for the normally hearing or special units attached to those schools. The integration—or mainstreaming—movement that they initiated progressively gathered more and more strength in Great Britain than in the United States and continental Europe.

It is generally accepted today that many hearing-impaired children, with early education, proper hearing aid fitting, and continued support, can successfully be educated with the normally hearing (Nix, 1976; Webster & Ellwood, 1985). Although the degree of hearing loss is an important factor in determining which hearing-impaired children can be mainstreamed, it is generally recognized that this factor is by no means decisive in itself. Some profoundly deaf children can succeed in ordinary schools, while others with more residual hearing may not be able to do so (Périer et al., 1980). There is, therefore, no consensus concerning the proportion of deaf and hard-of-hearing children that should be integrated. The present situation varies greatly among nations. In some such as Italy, the official policy is that all handicapped children should be mainstreamed. Other countries, like West Germany, maintain separate special school systems for the profoundly deaf and the hard of hearing, so that even the majority of the latter are not educated with the normally hearing. Several developing countries where special education has yet to be organized view mainstreaming as a tempting alternative to the building and maintaining of special schools. Cautions against the excesses of such a trend are voiced by numerous educators of the deaf, who argue that most of the profoundly deaf will continue to need special education. The pros and cons of mainstreaming have been aptly described by Meadows (1980), who argues that the options should carefully be weighed for each child.

Sign language interpretation services for the deaf have been developed primarily in the United States to assist the deaf in all circumstances in which they may benefit from them. Legal provisions ensuring that a deaf child has the right to the best possible education has made it possible in some cases to provide support services in schools or universities, allowing more deaf children and students to be mainstreamed than was formerly possible. In addition to sign language interpretation, other forms of interpretation are beginning to be developed in some countries: oral interpretation and oral interpretation with cued speech.

Although the trend toward mainstream education has steadily increased over the years, the hope that early speech and hearing training would solve the language and education difficulties of most hearing-impaired children has proved overly optimistic. Several studies, among them Conrad's (1979), demonstrated that whatever method was used, whether oral or manual, the majority of deaf school graduates reached a mean reading age equivalent only to that of 9- to 10-year-old hearing children. Thus, the existing methods had not prevented relative failure to develop good command of the societal language (English in this case), even in its written form. Other studies reviewed by Quigley and Kretschmer (1982) showed that deaf children of deaf parents who had had signs as their first language were not disadvantaged in the oral skills and had slightly but significantly better gradings in overall language evaluation when compared with deaf children of hearing parents.

These results, together with the rehabilitation of sign language, were largely instrumental in the birth and development of the total communication (TC) philosophy. This, as defined by Denton (1970), is the right of a deaf child to learn to use all forms of communication available to develop language competence. This includes the full spectrum: child-devised gestures, speech, formal sign language, finger spelling, speech reading, reading, writing, as well as any other methods that may be developed in the future. Every deaf child should also be provided with the opportunity to learn to use any remnant of residual hearing he or she may have by employing the best possible electronic equipment for amplifying sound. Many schools in the United States, and a growing number throughout the world, have adhered to the principle of TC, although there are various interpretations of its meaning. More and more infant programs throughout the world are using it from the earliest age; many are urging parents to learn to communicate with their children through signs in addition to speech. Such combination of signs and speech has been termed bimodal communication by Schlesinger (1978).

Several types of manual aids other than signs are used to facilitate the reception or the production of spoken language. While many educators are using these or some form of bimodal communication for the profoundly deaf, others continue to use exclusively oral methods.

Table D.1 is an attempt at classification of the methods currently used. It must be borne in mind, however, that various combinations are possible; some techniques developed within the framework of a given method are applicable in other contexts. For instance, in some Belgian centers, cued speech (3.1) is used in combination with bimodal communication (4.1) and with the verbo-tonal method (1). Five groups can be distinguished: auditory, oral, oral plus manual aids, combined, and manual.

Table D.1. Classifications of Methods Used in Deaf Education

1. Auditory		Auditory unisensory or acoupedic
2. Oral		Oral-aural, multisensory
3. Oral + Manual Aids	3.1	Oral-aural + lip-reading complements
	3.2	Oral-aural + manual representation of phonemes
	3.3	Oral-aural + finger spelling
4. Combined	4.1	Unilingual bimodal communication or simultaneous method
	4.2	Bilingual bimodal communication
5. Manual		Visual unisensory communication by sign language alone

1. *Auditory unisensory or acoupedic* methods rely on auditory training to develop spoken language. Speech reading is either not encouraged or suppressed during training periods (Pollack, 1964). In the verbo-tonal method (Guberina, Skaric, & Zaga, 1972), perception of acoustic features through the tactile sense is used in addition to hearing. The auditory global approach of Calvert and Silverman (1975) stands at the margin between the acoupedic and the oral-aural, because "the primary, although not always the exclusive, channel for speech development is auditory."

2. *Oral also called oral-aural* (Simmons-Martin, 1972). Auditory perception and speech reading are used as well as other modalities, but signs are excluded. Ling (1976) describes systematic speech development procedure primarily based on audition though not neglecting tactile and visual support, as in Calvert and Silverman's multisensory approach, used when the auditory global is not sufficient. Van Uden's maternal reflective method (1970) insists on the necessity of active oral-aural dialogue and natural prosody.

3.1. *Oral-aural plus lip-reading complements.* In cued speech (Cornett, 1967) and related systems, the oral-aural approach is combined with a system of hand shapes executed near the mouth, synchronously with speech. The hand brings only that part of the information that is not supplied by lip reading. The combination of this information allows the deaf child to unequivocally identify by sight the speech sounds and syllables that the hearing identify through the ear (Nicholls & Ling, 1982; Périer et al., 1986).

3.2. *Oral-aural plus manual representation of phonemes.* In the French Borel-Maisonny method (1979), and in the German Phonembestimmte Manual System (PMS) of Schulte (1974), the oral-aural methodology is aided by contrived gestures that correspond to some of the characteristics of speech sounds and thus help in their identification and production. The gestures bring independent information that is not linked to lip reading.

3.3. *Oral-aural plus finger spelling*. These are the U.S. Rochester (Scouten, 1942) and U.S.S.R. neo-oralism (Morkovin, 1960) methods. Finger spelling is executed by the teacher simultaneously with speech; the child is asked to accompany his or her own speech by finger spelling. Since the latter is a representation of written language, reading and writing are strongly emphasized.

4.1. *Unilingual bimodal communication or simultaneous method*. One language, that of the hearing society and of most deaf children's parents, is simultaneously expressed in speech and signs. There are numerous varieties of signed representations of spoken language. Some are close to the regional sign language of the deaf, differing mostly in word order; others use additional signs to convey syntactical and morphological information; still others are wholly contrived (Crystal & Craig, 1978).

4.2. *Bilingual bimodal communication*. Spoken language in an oral-aural approach is used in certain situations by hearing persons, although sign language is used in other situations by deaf and hearing persons. In early education, it is often considered acceptable for hearing parents who have not yet mastered sign language to use those signs they have learned in combination with their spoken language (Bouvet, 1981; Erting, 1978).

5. *Visual unisensory communication by sign language alone*. Although no educators advocate that deaf children should not learn the major societal language, a few favor the exclusive use of sign language for early education. Only when sign language is firmly established as a first language is the majority's societal language taught as a second language (Ahlgren, 1980). In some programs, teaching is first done in the written form, spoken language being delayed (Malé & Rickli, 1983).

The status of deaf education in 1985 was characterized by a great vitality and a large diversity, although the antagonism between methods has somewhat abated. The oral-manual controversy is not as bitter as before, with most people on each side now recognizing the merits of the other (Tervoort, 1982a, 1982b). The question is not so much of a choice between exclusively oral and combined oral-manual methods as of deciding for whom, when, how, and how much each modality should be used. General agreement exists on the paramount importance of early detection, assessment, and intervention, including proper hearing aid fitting and maintenance. The role of parents as the first educators of their deaf children, already stressed

by Whetnall and Fry and the John Tracy Clinic, is widely recognized (UNESCO, 1985). Their full participation is essential for the success of any method. Parents should, therefore, be thoroughly informed about the different programs available so that they can make their own choices. The fact that more than 90% of deaf children's parents are normally hearing must be taken into account in any decision about education policy. Whichever method is adopted, and whether priority is given to speech or sign, educators of today all have common goals: to enable deaf children to acquire the mastery of language needed to assert their personalities and attain full accomplishment; to bring deaf children to complete literacy, through which they will be able to reach the degree of academic achievement corresponding to their intellectual capacities and personal motivation.

REFERENCES

Ahlgren, E. (1980). The sign language group in Stockholm. In E. Ahlgren & Bergman (Eds.), *Papers from the first international symposium on Sign Language research* (pp. 3–7). Leksand, Sweden: Swedish National Association for the Deaf.

Borel-Maisonny, S. (1979). *Absence d'expression verbale*. Paris, France: A.R.P.L.O.E.

Bouvet, D. (1981). *La Parole de l'enfant sourd*. Paris, France: Presses Universitaires de France, Collection Le Fil Rouge.

Calvert, D. R., & Silverman, S. R. (1975). *Speech and deafness: A text for learning and teaching*. Washington, DC: Bell.

Conrad, R. (1979). *The deaf school child*. London, England: Harper & Row.

Cornett, R. O. (1967). Cued speech. *American Annals of the Deaf*, *112*, 3–13.

Crystal, D., & Craig, E. (1978). Contrived sign language. In I. M. Schlesinger & L. Namir (Eds.), *Sign language of the deaf* (pp. 141–168). New York, NY: Academic Press.

Denton, D. (1970). *Remarks in support of a system of total communication for deaf children*. Communication Symposium. Frederick: Maryland School for the Deaf.

Erting, C. (1978). Language policy and deaf ethnicity in the United States. *Sign Language Studies*, *19*, 139–152.

Guberina, P., Skaric, I., & Zaga, B. (1972). *Case studies in the use of restricted bands of frequencies in auditory rehabilitation of the deaf*. Zagreb, Yugoslavia: Institute of Phonetics Faculty of Arts.

Ling, D. (1976). *Speech and the hearing-impaired child: Theory and practice*. Washington, DC: Bell.

Malé, A., & Rickli, F. (1983). *Introduction au bilinguisme: Langue des signes française—français oral, à l'école de Montbrillant*. Geneva, Switzerland: Départment de l'Instruction Publique.

Meadows, K. P. (1980). *Deafness and child development*. Berkeley: University of California Press.

Moores, D. F. (1978). *Educating the deaf: Psychology, principles, and practices*. Boston, MA: Houghton Mifflin.

Morkovin, B. (1960). Experiment in teaching deaf preschool children in the Soviet Union. *Volta Review, 62,* 260–268.

Nicholls, G. H., & Ling, D. (1982). Cued speech and the reception of spoken language. *Journal of Speech and Hearing Research, 25,* 262–269.

Nix, G. (1976). *Mainstream education for hearing impaired children and youth.* New York, NY: Grune & Stratton.

Périer, O., Capouillez, J. M., & Paulissen, D. (1980). The relationship between the degree of auditory deficiency and the possibility of successful mainstreaming in schools for hearing children. In H. Hartmann (Ed.), *1st International Congress of the Hard of Hearing* (pp. 348–353). Hamburg, Germany: Deutscher Schwerhorigenbund.

Périer, O., Charlier, B., Hage, C., & Alegria, J. (1986). Evaluation of the effects of prolonged cued speech practice upon the reception and internal processing of spoken language. *Proceedings of the 1985 International Congress of Educators of the Deaf.* Manchester, England.

Pollack, D. (1964). Acoupedics: An unisensory approach to auditory training. *Volta Review, 66,* 400–409.

Quigley, S. P., & Kretschmer, R. F. (1982). *The education of deaf children: Issues, theory and practice.* London, England: Arnold.

Schlesinger, H. S. (1978). The acquisition of bimodal language. In I. M. Schlesinger & L. Namir (Eds.), *Sign language of the deaf.* New York, NY: Academic Press.

Schulte, K. (1974). *The phonemetransmitting manual system* (PMS). Heidelberg, Germany: Verlag.

Scouten, E. (1942). *A reevaluation of the Rochester method.* Rochester, NY: Rochester School for the Deaf.

Simmons-Martin, A. (1972). The oral/aural procedure: Theoretical basis and rationale. *Volta Review, 74,* 541–551.

Tervoort, B. T. (1982a). Communication and the deaf. *Proceedings of the International Congress on Education of the Deaf* (pp. 219–229). Heidelberg, Germany: Verlag.

Tervoort, B. T. (1982b). The future: Oralism versus manualism? *Proceedings of the International Congress on Education of the Deaf* (pp. 544–547). Heidelberg, Germany: Verlag.

Thielman, V. (1970). John Tracy Clinic correspondence course for parents of preschool deaf children. *Proceedings of the International Congress on Education of the Deaf* (pp. 156–158). Stockholm, Sweden: Sveriges Lärarförbundet.

UNESCO. (1985). *Consultation on alternative approaches for the education of the deaf.* Paris, France: UNESCO.

Van Uden, A. (1970). New realizations in the light of the pure oral method. *Volta Review, 72,* 524–536.

Webster, A., & Ellwood, J. (1985). *The hearing-impaired child in the ordinary school.* London, England: Croom Helm.

Whetnall, E., & Fry, D. (1964). *The deaf child.* Springfield, IL: Thomas.

OLIVIER PÉRIER
Université Libre de Bruxelles
Centre Comprendre et Parler, Belgium

See also American Sign Language; Fingerspelling; Total Communication

DEAF EDUCATION, HISTORY OF

A review of the history of the development of deaf education is both interesting and complex. As each historical time period is reviewed it becomes readily apparent that the social attitude and beliefs that existed in the environment had significant impact on the opportunities, which were offered to deaf children in order that they might become educated and able to learn. These early beliefs and attitudes often came from the thinking of philosophers who were the intellects who lived in that period of time. The inaccuracy of their beliefs established laws and procedures that were discriminatory against which deaf individuals have struggled for centuries.

For example, during the period of time from 427 BC to 347 BC Socrates fostered the philosophy of Innate Intelligence. He stated that all intelligence was present at birth and included language and concepts, which then developed over time. Without speech as an indicator of language there was no observable sign of intelligence and it was therefore assumed that deaf people were incapable of thought. Plato furthered the ideas that had been originated by Socrates during the time period of 384 BC to 322 BC building on the thought that the deaf cannot reason. These beliefs were accepted and followed for hundreds of years and so permeated society that it was not until the 1500s AD that a few educational pioneers established educational classes and schools for deaf children.

These early beliefs appeared in the Hebrew law of 1000 BC, which state that deaf individuals are not allowed to participate fully in the rituals of the Temple. Special laws preventing marriage and the right of individuals who were deaf to own properties were established. The ability of an individual who was deaf to serve as a witness in court was also withheld. The early Christians led by Saint Augustine during the time period of 345 AD to 555 AD taught that deafness was an indication of God's anger toward the parents of the deaf person. During the Dark and through the Middle Ages, 476 AD to 1453 AD, it was believed that people born deaf could not have faith and could not be saved and were therefore barred from churches.

Two major events occurred that raised doubts concerning the prevailing thoughts about deaf people. The first of these events was initiated by wealthy citizens who had a son or daughter who was deaf. Refusing to believe that their children had no intelligence they hired monks to find a way to teach their children so they could be saved and could also inherit property which heretofore had been prevented. These private tutors were located mainly in Italy and Spain but gradually spread across Europe and America ideas to use in their teaching, none of which were proven but all of which were successful with certain individuals. Some tutors experimented with hand signals that were similar to gestures while others tried to form a more complete language with visual movements of the hand. Some attempted to teach speech by using drawings of the tongue positions to formulate words. These tutors had a sufficient degree of success that the word spread that some individuals who were deaf were capable of learning.

The second event that changed thinking was the Renaissance. Individuals who were deaf and who resided in different countries began to contribute works of art and poetry, which indicated their ability to think and create. This evidence was sufficient to prompt educators to become interested in establishing schools and methods for teaching children who were deaf and schools began to spring up across Europe. Il Abbe de L'Epp. of Paris known as the Father of Sign Language and Deaf Education established the first free public school for deaf children in 1771. He watched the gestures of the children under his care on the playground and tried to create a bridge between the deaf and hearing worlds by taking the children's gestures and using them to formulate a symbolic language of signs and in 1778 published a dictionary of French sign language.

Meanwhile in Germany in 1755 a German oral teacher of the deaf by the name of Samuel Heinicke established an Oral School for the Deaf in the world. He used techniques taught by a Dutch doctor and named his approach "the German method." He initiated a series of debates with Abbe de L'Epp. in which each one of these teachers tried to prove the superiority of their method of teaching, which led to an oral versus manual conflict that continues to exist even today due to the lack of scientific methodology to identify the most effective approach for each child based on his or her type and degree of hearing loss. In England in 1760 Thomas Braidwood established the first school for the deaf. The methodology that he utilized was also oral but his approach to teaching was secretive and not shared with the world. In the United States a man named Thomas Hopkins Gallaudet became interested in deafness and traveled to Europe to learn how to teach the deaf so that he could set up a school in the United States. His interest was motivated by a neighbor's child, Alice Cogswell, who was deaf but appeared to Gallaudet as a bright child capable of learning. He went first to England to study at the Braidwood School but because it did not share its techniques with others, he crossed the channel to France and visited the Abbe's school where he met one of the deaf teachers named Laurent Clerc. Gallaudet convinced Clerc to return to the United States with him. Together they founded the first permanent school for the deaf in the United States, originally named the Connecticut Asylum for the Education and Instruction of Deaf and Dumb Children. Schools in the United States began to spread and by 1912 more than 30 schools were established and the Connecticut school was renamed as it is known today, the American School for the Deaf.

From the time of Gallaudet's visit to the Abbe's school in the 1800s to the 1920s many important events occurred that helped shape the progress of deaf education in the United States. In the schools existing at that time 40% of the instruction was taught by deaf teachers and the instructional methodology was through American Sign Language. The original thought about deafness was that it left people without the ability to think, so the influence of this concept was still present and caused most teaching to be done through memory in a rote manner. Several curricula in the area of teaching language to deaf children were developed and used in the various schools. This approach resulted in a deficit in the acquisition of language and in the development of critical thinking skills causing some dissatisfaction with the use of American Sign Language for instructional purposes. Again wealthy parents took a lead role and hired tutors for their children and demanded that they be taught to speak using the oral method. In some instances this was successful and caused the dissatisfaction with the use of ASL to grow. In 1880 an international Congress of educators of the deaf was held in Milan, Italy and the educators present voted that the oral method of teaching was superior to manual communication systems. The only country in opposition to this vote was the United States, which had a well-developed national system utilizing manual communication. However, this vote caused a sharp reduction in the schools using manual communication and oral education became the primary mode of instruction until the 1970s. In an attempt to combat this change and the rejection of sign language, the National Association of the Deaf was established.

During this period of time the two major events impacting education of the deaf were the establishment of Gallaudet as a liberal arts college for the deaf located in Washington, DC, and the invention of the telephone by Alexander Graham Bell in 1876. Bell was a teacher of the deaf whose father had been interested in education of the deaf and had invented a system for teaching the deaf called "Visible Speech." He was married to a deaf woman and was responsible for many ideas of ways to enhance education of the deaf. In his attempt to develop an amplification system for the deaf he invented the telephone, which made him both rich and famous. As a result he formed the Volta Bureau to promote oral-based education for deaf children and a period of great upheaval began spurred on by ongoing debates between Gallaudet and Bell concerning the two systems of oral and manual communication.

Gradually oral education became primary throughout Europe and the United States and day schools and public school classes began to form. Most children still attended the state residential schools but there was a strong encouragement given to parents to keep their children at home. During the latter part of the 1890s work began on the development of hearing aids. The first aids were too heavy to be worn and used carbon-based microphones and were powered by 3- and 6-volt batteries. The system was usually placed on a desk making it awkward to use but it did give deaf people their first experience with amplified sound. World War II caused a renewed interest in deafness as many soldiers returning from war faced hearing loss resulting from bomb explosions and gunfire. The need for assessment of individuals with hearing loss began to develop along with the need for more thorough techniques of remediation. Hearing aids were designed that could be worn on the body comfortably. The term *audiology* was developed at that time to represent the science of measuring hearing loss and prescribing amplification appropriate to the degree of loss. Surgical procedures were also developed and the field in general became more sophisticated with services medically, surgically, technically, and educationally. The war also brought about a need for employment and deaf people were employed in factories where employers for the first time became aware of their skill and ability to be good employees.

During the 1960s there was a movement to study Sign Language linguistically to determine if it was in reality a true language as it had never been considered to fulfill the criteria of a language system in the past. The first book analyzing ASL and defending it as a language was written in 1960 by William Stoke.

In 1964 the first telephone system for the deaf was developed by Robert Weitbrecht. Weitbrecht, a deaf inventor, utilized phone lines to transmit calls with a teletypewriter. In this way deaf people using the phone placed in a specially designed cradle could type their message to a deaf person who also had a teletypewriter system. This advancement changed the lives of deaf individuals and allowed them a freedom of communication that they had never previously experienced. Also occurring in 1964 was the issuance of a congressional report known as the Babbidge Report on oral deaf education. The report concluded that oral education had been a failure and that not only did its graduates fail to read and write successfully but that the individual failed to acquire a communication system that was functional for either relating to a hearing person or a deaf person. As a result of these findings a new system appeared in the schools, called *Total Communication* and consisted of the simultaneous use of both sign language and spoken language-based instruction. ASL, a language in its own right, did not follow English word order and did not specify vocabulary in the same manner as spoken language. To use the two systems simultaneously it became necessary to change some of the sign language to match the English and two forms, Signed English, and Seeing Essential English, came into existence. Eventually most prefixes and suffixes in English were dropped and the signing became known as Pidgin English as it expressed main ideas but did not carry the visual component of total English syntax.

In 1981 a deaf cable channel was established and began broadcasting as the Silent Network reaching approximately 2 million homes during its first year. It operated 24 hours a day, 7 days a week. By the end of a 10-year period of broadcasting it was reaching 14 million homes.

In 1985 a program entitled Deaf Mosaic began a 10-year run broadcasting from Gallaudet University. This was an extremely popular program with deaf people and professionals in the field of deafness. It won Emmy awards for both the producers and the hosts who were themselves deaf.

Also in 1985 the cochlear implant was approved for clinical trials in individuals 18 years and older. The implant is a device providing sound to the cochlea, which is then transmitted to the auditory nerve and carried to the brain for interpretation. This was a startling new concept to bring sound to deaf individuals. At first it was viewed with great skepticism but as individuals began to report success attitudes gradually changed and now most deaf children receive an implant during the first 2 years of life. The implant is not successful with all children or adults but at this time there is no pretest, which will definitively indicate the success or failure the user will experience. The implant has had a major impact on the field as it required new teaching techniques, which are designed to change the processing of information in the child's brain to be predominately auditory rather than visual. There is controversy about the techniques that should be used to accomplish this goal. Some advocates indicate that the child needs auditory listening experience only without the use of visual cues to accomplish this change while others believe that both stimuli should be used much like the normal experience of learning spoken language by a normal hearing child. Because there was so much doubt as to the potential success of the implant in the beginning it was necessary to carefully supervise the procedures of using the implant in adults for several years before children were even attempted. During this time little was done by most schools to prepare their teachers for the change in teaching techniques. The lag in preparation continues to exist today and is partially a product of the difference of opinion in exactly what the teaching strategy should be.

From the 1960s until the current time there has been a gradual increase in the demands of deaf people for their civil rights. In 1988 there was the need to select a new president of Gallaudet University. Up until this point the person had always been a hearing individual and the board of directors continued that criteria in selecting the new president in 1988. The students rallied and voices were heard from all over the United States demanding a president who was deaf. The slogan used during that campaign was "Deaf President Now." After eight days of protest and headlines in newspapers as well as TV newscasts all over the United States, I. King Jordan became the first Deaf President of Gallaudet.

In 2007 the movement toward equality took a giant step with the passage of the Americans with Disabilities Act in Congress. This Act outlawed any act of discrimination or any obstacle to accessibility for individuals with a disability. It provided for more accessibility to communication for the deaf and included the provision of captions in TV through the use of a decoder chip. Currently these chips are required in all TV sets with screens larger than 13 inches. This Act also included an educational section known as IDEA (Individual with Disabilities Education Act). It stated that children should be educated in the least restrictive environment, which was intended to mean their home school. Eventually this statement was modified for deaf students to say that the least restrictive environment for deaf students may not be the school closest to their home. Nevertheless the intent of this Act to provide equal education for all was destructive to the existence of residential state schools for the deaf, which prior to this time had been the main source of education. Some residential schools closed due to declining enrollment and day classes began to develop wherever there were enough children to form one. The residential schools began to serve those children who came from small towns and rural areas where no classes or support services existed. Because the source of public education was a parent's right to choose, many deaf children from deaf families continued in the residential school feeling that the environment met more of their cultural needs. In the residential schools many of the faculty were also deaf so the school provided a job outlet for college educated deaf students who wanted to teach. As the day classes increased and it became evident how important a role model was for the deaf children, deaf teachers also began to find employment in the day school programs. Mainstreaming or placement in a regular classroom with hearing children also increased, particularly for the gifted deaf child and hard of hearing children. IDEA, the Education Act for Children with Disabilities, also provided the child with the modifications they needed to succeed in school as well as interpreters, note takers, and itinerant teachers.

If we pause to reflect on the 3,000 years of history known to man concerning the development of individuals who are deaf and hard of hearing we realize that the early concept that people who were deaf were helpless and could not be educated because they had no ability to think was very destructive to the deaf individual. The laws of society concerning deaf individuals differed depending on their cultural beliefs and background. Laws varied from thinking that it was society's responsibility to protect and care for these helpless deaf individuals and to severely punish anyone who attempted to harm them or take advantage of them to a practice of putting them out to die as little children once it was discovered that they were deaf and without thought. Even though time brought about an awareness that deaf people had the same brain as any human and could learn, the past thinking was reflected in the very rote style that early education used to present the curriculum. The educators perceived the need that everything they were taught had to be very rigidly organized and then memorized by the student. They felt that the deaf child did not have the capacity to learn naturally as hearing children do. Most importantly, we must remember that all throughout the 3,000 years of development the question of the appropriate communication system, sign language or spoken language, has never been resolved. Although some research has occurred particularly in the past 100 years but due to the low incidence nature of the disability and the variance of the intensity of the problem from person to person it has been most difficult to find an answer to this question of communication modalities. Because of the difficulty for the deaf person to easily and naturally acquire language and communication, the deficit they generally demonstrate separates them from the majority of speaking people and as a result they have formed a culture of their own where they are comfortable and feel accepted. The American Sign Language is the core of the culture and its use by a deaf individual is the signal to others that the individual belongs to and is accepted by the culture.

The current time is most difficult for the child with hearing loss, the parents of the child, the teacher of the child, the school system accepting the responsibility to provide a program for deaf children, and the universities that must decide on the appropriate training program for all children with hearing loss despite the variance of the impact on learning each child demonstrates. It is the sincere hope of most individuals interested in bettering the lives of children with hearing loss so they can fulfill their individual potential, that science will lead us to the answers we need to better understand the way in which deafness impacts the brain and to identify the appropriate interventions, which will finally answer the questions pertaining to learning and language acquisition.

This entry has been informed by the sources listed below.

REFERENCE

Lang, H. (1994). *Silence of the spheres: The deaf experience in the history of science*. Westport, CT: Praeger.

PATRICIA SCHERER
International Center on Deafness and the Arts
Fourth edition

DEAF, INTERPRETERS FOR (See Interpreters for the Deaf)

DEAFNESS, CAUSES AND TYPES OF

There are two major types of hearing loss that are classified.

The first type is classified as a conductive hearing loss, indicating that it is occurring in the conductive mechanism of the middle ear. Conductive hearing loss does not occur at the severe levels of loss that are associated with sensory neural hearing loss. In general the loss of discrimination ability is also far less than that associated with sensory neural loss.

The second type is known as a sensory neural hearing loss and is a disorder of the inner ear that disrupts the transmission of sound to the auditory nerve, which leads to the brain for recognition. This type of hearing loss occurs as a result of damage to the external or internal hair cells in the cochlea. When the damage is located on the internal hair cells the condition is known as *auditory neuropathy*.

Hearing loss can occur at levels that are usually referred to as *mild, moderate, severe*, or *profound*. Hearing loss often occurs at birth and is known as a congenital loss of hearing. However, hearing loss can occur at any time in life and it is common for most elderly adults to experience some level of hearing loss.

Causes of Deafness

Causes of deafness include:

- Genetic hearing loss.
- Diseases such as meningitis, scarlet fever, mumps, and measles.
- Ototoxic drugs used to save life when there is a dangerous life-threatening illness.
- Immunological and neurological diseases such as multiple sclerosis.
- Trauma such as skull fracture or explosions, fireworks or gunfire too close to the head.
- Tumors frequently on the eighth auditory nerve.
- Circulatory problems.
- Genetic hearing loss.
- Age-related hearing loss.
- Noise exposure over a period of time that exceeds safety limits of loudness and can injure hair cells in the cochlea.
- Syndromes including deafness.

Syndromes Including Deafness

A syndrome can be defined as a group of symptoms, features, and signs that occur together to the extent that they become recognized as an association of characteristics that is then given the name of a syndrome. The following syndromes are commonly associated with deafness.

Charge Syndrome

The title word *Charge* is an acronym with the letters representing the disabilities associated with deafness:

C—**C**oloboma of the eye, which is defined as a cleft occurring in one or more areas of the eye leading to visual problems and possible blindness.

H—**H**eart defects.

A—**A**tresia of the choanae, which impacts breathing properly through the nose.

R—**R**etardation of growth and development.

G—**G**enital hypoplasia (a lack of cells in the sex organs).

E—**E**ar malformations leading to hearing loss.

Charge children may often suffer from many other disorders, most of which are related to malformations or abnormalities of body parts and organs.

Ushers Syndrome

The major symptoms of Ushers syndrome are hearing and vision loss. The eye disorder is retinitis pigmentosa commonly called RP. Individuals with RP experience night blindness and a narrowed field of vision with little use of peripheral vision. This occurs due to the gradual deterioration of the retina. There are three types of Ushers although Type 3 is rarely found in the United States. The rate of incidence of Ushers is 4 out of every 100,000 births. The hearing loss associated with Ushers is often congenital with the visual loss occurring later in childhood or early adolescence. As the progression occurs, both vision and hearing deteriorate and in many instances the individual becomes both deaf and blind. Because this is a serious disability and individuals are aware of what is happening to them, the progression is often accompanied with an emotional disability that compounds the difficulties for adjustment.

Waardenberg Syndrome

This syndrome is associated with hearing loss and by changes in skin pigmentation and hair coloring. Individuals often display one blue or green eye and one brown eye. The syndrome is named after a Dutch eye doctor who noted that people with two eyes that differed in color often had a hearing loss. Hair coloring can also be a part of this syndrome with a strand of gray or white hair often appearing as young as age 12. It has been discovered that there are four different genes causing Waardenbergs. The two types with the greatest frequency of occurrence are Type 1 and 2. The physical characteristics of the individual determine which type of Waardenbergs Syndrome (WS) he or she has; for example, a wide space between the inner corners of the eyes indicates WS Type 1. About 20% of individuals with WS Type 1 have a hearing loss. Individuals without the wide space between the inner corners of the eye but who demonstrate other physical characteristics form WS Type 2. In this group 50% of the individuals have hearing loss. WS is a dominant genetic disorder and therefore a child can inherit the abnormal genes from one parent with a 50% chance of occurrence.

Stickler Syndrome

This syndrome is generally observed in the facial features of the individual. The face is often flattened, caused by underdeveloped bones in the mid-section of the face. Problems with both vision and hearing are frequently present in individuals with Stickler syndrome. The visual problem and the hearing loss can be progressive and in some cases can cause deafness and blindness. Stickler syndrome has an occurrence rate of 1 in 7,500 to 9,000 births. It is a dominant disorder that can be passed to a child by one parent who carries the altered gene.

Large Vestibular Aqueduct Syndrome (LVAS)

This syndrome is sometimes also known as the *Large Endolymphatic Duct and Sac Syndrome* (LEDS). This condition is caused by a very large endolymphatic duct and sac, which allows the endolymphatic fluid to flow back into the hearing and balance mechanisms. It is the enlarged duct that creates the hearing loss not the enlarged vestibular aqueduct. It is for this reason that some research labs changed the name from LVAS (Enlarged Vestibular Aqueduct Syndrome) to LEDS (Large Endolymphatic Duct and Sac Syndrome). This syndrome causes sudden hearing loss that fluctuates. Of those individuals in the population with hearing loss it is estimated that between 1% and 7% of the cases result from LVAS. The hearing disorder is generally sensorineural in type although some cases of conductive loss have also been observed. The hearing loss usually occurs either in a pattern of gradual loss or in episodes of sudden serious loss, which may have been caused by a blow to the head. When the sudden loss episode ends the individual usually does not return to the previous level of hearing. Many individuals with LVAS gradually become deaf in their adult years.

Kabuki Syndrome

The Kabuki syndrome is rare, occurring in 1 out of 32,000 births. The name of the syndrome, which was identified by Japanese scientists, is derived from the similarity of the facial appearance to the appearance of the Japanese Kabuki Theater character. The most common characteristics of the Kabuki syndrome are heart disorders (30%), hearing loss (50%), hypotonia and postnatal growth deficiencies (83%). In 92% of the cases there is mild to moderate intellectual delay. These children usually display a happy personality and often have learning disabilities.

Mondini Syndrome

The cause of the Mondini syndrome is related to malformations of the inner ear. A variance of malformations can occur, which usually results in a sensorineural hearing loss. In some instances the loss on the audiogram appears to be conductive, which probably results from better bone conduction resulting from the type and location of the malformation. In some cases dizziness may accompany the hearing loss. The associated malformation of the cochlea, which results in one and a half turns instead of the normal two and a half turns results in gradual hearing loss during the first 3 years of life, which may progress to a profound loss.

Goldenhar Syndrome

The associated characteristics of the Goldenhar syndrome include incomplete development of the ear, nose, soft palate, lip, and mandible. In some cases there are also problems with internal organs including the heart, kidneys, and lungs. This is a rare syndrome being observed in only 1 of 26,000 births. Hearing loss differs from individual to individual depending on the area of the hearing mechanism that has been impacted by the malformation. The use of hearing aids is frequently required for these children.

Pendred Syndrome

This syndrome is a genetic disorder, which causes hearing loss in children. Other characteristics include the thyroid gland and the balance mechanism. The hearing loss occurs at birth or during the first years of life and is progressive. It is almost always expressed bilaterally with one ear indicating a more severe loss than the other. Because of the associated problem with the thyroid, 60% of all cases develop a goiter by adulthood. Almost half of the individuals with Pendred syndrome will also have difficulties with balance. This may delay walking skills but most children are able to develop compensatory skills, which reduce the impact of the balance deficits.

Pendred syndrome is a genetic recessive disorder, which means that the child must inherit the altered gene from each of the parents. Hearing loss resulting from Pendred syndrome results in about 5% to 10% of all hereditary cases of deafness.

Treacher-Collins Syndrome

Treacher-Collins syndrome is characterized by problems in the structure of the face. The symptoms include malformation of the outer ear accompanied by hearing loss, a very small jaw, a very large mouth, a defect in the lower eyelid, scalp hair that reaches to the cheeks and a cleft palate. Children with Treacher-Collins syndrome usually demonstrate normal intelligence and grow to be normal functioning adults. Plastic surgery is needed by most of the children to correct the deformities that can be corrected. Treatment for the hearing loss and hearing aids are usually needed. The loss is generally conductive in type and therefore these children do not have severe and profound hearing loss.

PATRICIA SCHERER
International Center on Deafness and the Arts, Chicago, Illinois

DEAF PRESIDENT NOW

The history of Gallaudet begins with Thomas Hopkins Gallaudet, a hearing person, who became interested in deaf education in 1814 when he met a young deaf child that he felt was not receiving a proper education. Gallaudet was interested in manual communication for the deaf, that is, sign language, and ultimately secured the services of a French educator, Laurent Clerc. Together they cofounded the American School for the Deaf in Hartford, Connecticut in 1817, the nation's first school for deaf children.

One of Thomas Gallaudet's children, Edward Minor Gallaudet, established another school for deaf children in 1857. The school became so successful that in 1864 a collegiate division was added, becoming the world's only university for deaf and hard of hearing students—Gallaudet University.

Six different hearing individuals served as president of Gallaudet University from 1864 to 1988. During this time discrimination and prejudices against deaf and hard of hearing people continued to grow, ultimately splitting the community into two primary groups; the manualists, led by Edward Minor Gallaudet and the oralists, led by Alexander Graham Bell, the inventor of the telephone.

The seeds of discontent can be traced back to 1880 when an international meeting of educators of deaf children in Milan, Italy banned the use of sign language in the teaching of deaf children, which also led to the dismissal of deaf teachers from most classrooms. The exception was at Gallaudet University where sign language continued to be used. Another result of the Milan meeting was the formation of the National Association of the Deaf (NAD), the first self-help and advocacy group formed by deaf adults. However, the oral method of instruction from primarily hearing teachers continued well into the 20th century, thereby denying deaf children little if any exposure to deaf role models.

Over the years, more and more in the deaf community felt it was time for a Deaf person to become the President of Gallaudet University. This opportunity presented itself in the latter part of 1987 when then President Dr. Jerry Lee tendered his resignation. A committee was formed to find a successor and this process ultimately reduced the initial applicants down from 87 to 3 finalists, two of whom were deaf. The board of trustees was made aware by the deaf community that now was the time to select a deaf person as the next Gallaudet University president. This support also included politicians at the highest levels including Vice-President George Bush. Neither the mainstream media nor Gallaudet students had become involved at this point.

This all changed on March 6, 1988, when the board of trustees shocked everyone by selecting the lone hearing finalist, Dr. Elisabeth Zinser, to become the next president of Gallaudet University. Additionally, instead of announcing their decision in person on campus, they had the university's public relations office hand out a press release an hour and a half prior to the previously agreed on time.

The campus reaction was swift and in total disagreement with the decision of the board, especially Jane Spilman the board chair who was quoted as saying, "Deaf people are not able to function in a hearing world." Student unrest and various demonstrations ensued for 8 days thereafter. Protest leaders formalized their demands and presented them to the board but all of the demands were initially rejected:

- Zinser must resign and a deaf president elected.
- Spilman must resign from the board.
- The percentage of deaf members on the board of trustees must be increased to at least 51%.
- There must be no reprisals against any of the protesters.

Additional protests continued with more individuals and groups getting involved, as well as becoming better coordinated, so that by the end of the third protest day this story was being covered by the national media in print and on TV. As support continued to grow for the protestors, Elisabeth Zinser announced her resignation on Day 5.

On Day 8, it was announced at a special press conference that all of the protest demands would be met and that the eighth, and first deaf president of Gallaudet University would be Dr. I. King Jordan. Dr. Jordan was president from 1988 to 2006 and has since been succeeded by two more deaf presidents: Dr. Robert Davila from 2007 to 2009, and the current president, Dr. T. Allan Hurwitz.

Deaf President Now (DPN) week helped to improve relationships between the deaf and hearing communities as well as to increase the nation's understanding and awareness of the rights and abilities of deaf and hard of hearing people.

REFERENCE

Gallaudet University, 800 Florida Avenue, Northeast Washington, DC 20002, (202) 651–5000, www.Gallaudet.edu

Peter T. Force
*International Center on Deafness and the Arts
through Education*
Fourth edition

DEAN-WOODCOCK NEUROPSYCHOLOGICAL BATTERY

The Dean-Woodcock Neuropsychological Battery (DWNB, 2003b) is a comprehensive battery that assesses individuals' emotional, sensory and motor functioning. The DWNB consists of the Dean-Woodcock Sensory-Motor Battery, the Dean-Woodcock Structured Neuropsychological Interview, and the Dean-Woodcock Emotional Status Examination. The DWNB is designed to be administered to individual's ages 4 through 80 (and older). The entire DWNB takes approximately 1 hour and 45 minutes to administer. The Dean-Woodcock Sensory-Motor Battery takes 30- to 45 minutes to administer, and the Structured Neuropsychological Interview and Emotional Status Examination each take 30 minutes. The latter two may be given before or after the Sensory-Motor Battery.

During the Structured Neuropsychological Interview, the examinee is asked questions about their medical and family background. The Emotional Status Examination includes signs and symptoms of major disorders. The Sensory-Motor Battery is composed of 18 subtests divided into four major areas: Sensory Tests, Tactile Tests, Subcortical Motor Tests, and Cortical Motor Tests. The DWNB contains an examiners manual, stimulus book, and manipulatives kit. The DWNB is easily transported, including record forms in its carrying case.

Norms for the Dean-Woodcock Sensory Motor Battery are based on a sample of 1,011 individuals that ranged in age from 4 to 80 years. The sample was representative of the U.S. population with respect to sex, race, age, and handedness according to the 2000 census. Individuals with a history of psychiatric, neurological, orthopedic disorders were excluded, as were those with a history of sensory motor impairment and/or head injury. Studies indicated that the Sensory Motor Battery was both reliable and valid.

Many of the tests and procedures are not new; rather the battery is a compilation of neuropsychological measures that have been demonstrated as having high clinical utility. What sets this battery apart is the standard administration procedures and normative sample base (Dean & Woodcock, 2003a).

This entry has been informed by the sources listed below.

REVIEWED IN:

Geisinger, K. F., Spies, R. A., Carlson, J. F., & Plake, B. S. (Eds.). (2007). *The seventeenth mental measurements yearbook.* Lincoln, NE: Buros Institute of Mental Measurements.

Davis, A. S. (2008). Understanding and using the Dean-Woodcock Neuropsychological Battery with children, youth, adults, and in geriatrics. In R. C. D'Amato & L. C. Hartlage (Eds.), *Essentials of neuropsychological assessment: Treatment planning for rehabilitation* (2nd ed., pp. 172–206). New York, NY: Springer.

Davis, A. S., & D'Amato, R. C. (2005). Evaluating and using contemporary neuropsychological batteries: The NEPSY and the Dean-Woodcock assessment system. In R. C. D'Amato, E. Fletcher-Janzen, and C. R. Reynolds (Eds.), *Handbook of school neuropsychology* (pp. 265–286). Hoboken, NJ: Wiley.

Dean, R. S., & Woodcock, R. W. (2003a). *Examiner's manual: Dean-Woodcock neuropsychological battery.* Itasca, IL: Riverside.

Dean, R. S., & Woodcock, R. W. (2003b). *Dean-Woodcock neuropsychological battery.* Itasca, IL: Riverside.

RON DUMONT
Fairleigh Dickinson University

JOHN O. WILLIS
Rivier College

KATHLEEN VIEZEL
JAMIE ZIBULSKY
Fairleigh Dickinson University

DEBORAH P. VERSUS TURLINGTON

Deborah P. v. Turlington (1979) is the federal district court case that struck down the competency testing program requirements for high-school graduation in the state of Florida. Deborah P. represented the class of all students in the state who were in danger of failing the test, including students of all ethnic backgrounds. The federal district court found that the competency testing program was unconstitutional for two reasons. The program had failed to provide students with adequate notice of the changes in requirements for a diploma, and the program was held to be racially discriminatory under the 14th Amendment. According to the court, the competency testing program tended to perpetuate preexisting patterns of racial discrimination within the Florida school system. Children in special education programs were not specifically addressed in *Deborah P.*, however, similar issues may be raised if special education students are required to pass competency tests or denied diplomas on the basis of testing programs that discriminate on the basis of race or disability.

REFERENCE

Deborah P. v. Turlington. (1979). #78-892-CIV-T-C, U.S. District Court, Middle District, Tampa Division, July 12 (slip opinion).

CECIL R. REYNOLDS
Texas A&M University
First edition

KIMBERLEY APPLEQUIST
University of Colorado at Colorado Springs
Third edition

DECROLY, OVIDE (1871–1932)

Ovide Decroly, a Belgian physician whose hospital work brought him into contact with many handicapped children, reasoned that the best treatment for such children would be a sound educational program. He established a special school for "the retarded and abnormal" in 1901. A few years later, he founded a school for normal children, where he demonstrated that the methods he was using successfully with handicapped children were equally effective with the nonhandicapped.

Decroly's educational methods were unique. The cornerstone of his method was what he called the "center of interest." Centers of interest were developed around four basic needs: food, protection from the elements, defense against common dangers, and work. Emphasis was placed on learning through activities that grow out of the interests and needs of the students. As much as a year's study could grow out of one topic or theme.

Decroly's work profoundly influenced the European concept of education for both normal and handicapped children. Many of his ideas were similar to those of John Dewey, but Decroly was more a practitioner than a philosopher and his foremost contribution was the establishment of schools that served as models of education based on the needs of children.

This entry has been informed by the sources listed below.

REFERENCES

Hamaide, A. (1924). *The Decroly class.* New York, NY: Dutton.

Kajava, K. (1951). *The traditional European school and some recent experiments in the new education.* Doctoral dissertation. New York, NY: Columbia University.

PAUL IRVINE
Katonah, New York

DEINSTITUTIONALIZATION

Deinstitutionalization has been a movement based on the principles of normalization. Individuals with disabilities, mostly the retarded and emotionally disabled, have been moved out of institutions into alternative community living arrangements. Wolfensberger (1972), one of the most outspoken advocates of both deinstitutionalization and normalization, maintained that normalization referred not to treatment but to services, situations, and attitudes that would bring about humane care for the disabled. The practice called for small, community-based group homes that permitted residents to participate in local activities and be closer to their families as opposed to long-term, total life care in institutions. Community residential facilities were small in size, house an equally small number of persons, and were meant to be either a permanent residence or a transitional training residence for retarded adults. These facilities ranged in design from loosely supervised apartments to group homes with live-in house parents (Baker, Seltzer, & Seltzer, 1977).

The trend toward deinstitutionalization of retarded persons began approximately 45 years ago when President Kennedy remarked that the practice of institutionalized segregation from the rest of society was immoral. In 1974 President Nixon announced the goal of returning half of all institutionalized retarded individuals to community settings (Braddock, 1977). The basic construct for the deinstitutionalization movement included: (1) the creation and maintenance of environments that did not impose excessive restrictions on disabled persons; (2) the creation of arrangements that brought persons as close as possible to the social and cultural mainstream; and (3) guarantees that the human and legal rights of disabled citizens were protected (Neufeld, 1979, p. 115).

Numerous studies have been conducted over the past 45 years to assess outcomes for individuals who were a part of deinstitutionalization. The results of these studies are mixed. Many studies cite improvement in quality of life, adaptive behavior skills, and self-care skills (Fine, 2007; Larson & Lakin, 1989; Lord & Pedlar, 1991).

Other studies present a more negative outcome, with deinstitutionalized mentally retarded individuals being overrepresented in the homeless (Roleff, 1996). Indeed, Craig and Paterson (1988) cited lack of long-term support for mentally ill individuals, and estimated that there are 300,000 mentally ill homeless persons in the United States. Perhaps the most disturbing of studies regarding deinstitutionalization is by Strauss and Kastner. In 1996 they compared risk-adjusted odds of mortality of people with mental retardation living in institutions or the community from 1980 to 1992 in California. It was estimated that the mortality was 72% higher in the community. It was suggested that the reason for the difference was the availability and adherence to health care (Strauss & Kastner, 1996).

For children, deinstitutionalization has had mixed results. Many children return to their families and research suggests that one third will return to state schools. However, daily living skills training and vocational training are widely available, and many children who were originally placed in contained classrooms are included in the mainstream in less than a year (Laconia State School, 1987).

In summary, outcome studies for deinstitutionalization indicate that many individuals with mental retardation achieve much better self-help and daily living skills when living in the community. However, many do not receive the community support or health care that is necessary for day-to-day living. Indeed, many individuals who are psychiatrically disabled may live in homeless conditions.

For deinstitutionalization to produce effective results, several issues should be considered. Adequate alternatives that are properly designed, properly maintained, and properly supervised should be developed. In addition, comprehensive evaluations of the individual's ability to succeed in a community-based facility should be made.

REFERENCES

Baker, B. L., Seltzer, G. B., & Seltzer, M. M. (1977). *As close as possible. Community residences for retarded adults.* Boston, MA: Little, Brown.

Braddock, D. (1977). *Opening closed doors: The deinstitutionalization of disabled individuals.* Reston, VA: Council of Exceptional Children.

Craig, R. T., & Paterson, A. (1988). The homeless mentally ill: No longer out of sight and out of mind. *State Legislative Report, 13,* 30. National Conference of State Legislatures, Denver, CO.

Fine, M. (1990). Changes in adaptive behavior of older adults with mental retardation following deinstitutionalization. *American Journal on Mental Retardation, 94,* 6, 661–668.

Laconia State School. (1987). Deinstitutionalization of minors with mental retardation. *Abstract X: Research & resources on special education.* Reston, VA: ERIC Clearinghouse on Handicapped and Gifted Children.

Larson, S. A., & Lakin, C. (1989). Deinstitutionalization of persons with mental retardation: The impact on daily living skills. *Policy Research Brief, 1,* 1.

Lord, J., & Pedlar, A. (1991). Life in the community: Four years after closure of an institution. *Mental Retardation, 29*(4), 213–221.

Roleff, T. L. (1996). *The homeless: Opposing viewpoints.* San Diego, CA: Greenhaven Press.

Strauss, D., & Kastner, T. A. (1996). Comparative mortality of people with mental retardation in institutions and the community. *American Journal on Mental Retardation, 101*(1), 26–40.

Neufeld, G. R. (1979). Deinstitutionalization procedures. In R. Wiegerink & J. W. Pelosi (Eds.), *Developmental disabilities: The DD movement* (pp. 115–126). Baltimore, MD: Paul H. Brookes.

Wolfensberger, W. (1972). *The principle of normalization in human services.* Toronto, Ontario: National Institute on Mental Retardation.

CECELIA STEPPE-JONES
North Carolina Central University
First edition

ELAINE FLETCHER-JANZEN
Chicago School of Professional Psychology
Second edition

See also Community-Based Services; Normalization; Rehabilitation

DELACATO, CARL H. (1923–   )

Carl H. Delacato earned his BS in education from West Chester State College in 1945. He continued his education, obtaining the MS in 1948 and EdD in 1952 from the University of Pennsylvania. From 1945 to 1964, he was assistant headmaster at Chestnut Hill Academy in Philadelphia, and in 1948, he founded and directed the Chestnut Hill Reading Clinic. During his distinguished career, he has served as associate director and instructor at the Institutes for the Achievement of Human Potential, Philadelphia, Pennsylvania (1953–1973); professor and chairman of the Department of Developmental Education, University of Plano, Plano, Texas; and director of the Institute for Rehabilitation of the Brain Injured, Morton, Pennsylvania (1974–1989).

Delacato (1968) has focused his study on neurological organization and patterning. The Doman-Delacato Treatment Method for children with neurological disabilities, developed by Delacato and Glenn Doman, is a remedy based on the neurological organization of the individual. Neurological organization is defined by Delacato as a physiologically optimum condition existing uniquely and most completely in man, resulting from total, uninterrupted ontogenetic development. Delacato discovered that learning, behavioral, and motor disorders were disabilities that occurred along a continuum of severity as a result of brain injury or incomplete neural development. Delacato contends that assessment and modification of neurological organization can be utilized for the diagnosis, treatment, and prevention of language problems.

Delacato's numerous awards include the Distinguished Alumnus award of West Chester College (1978), the Gold Medal Honor of Brazil (1960), and the first Trailblazer award of the University of Plano (1966). His major publications include *The Diagnosis and Treatment of Speech* (1968), *Neurological Organization and Reading* (1966), *A New Start for the Child with Reading Problems* (Delacato, 1982), and *The Ultimate Stranger: The Autistic Child* (Delacato, 1984). In addition, Delacato has contributed numerous articles on rehabilitation and education to professional journals, and has served as editor of *American Lectures in Education and Learning*.

REFERENCES

Delacato, C. H. (1966). *Neurological organization and reading.* Springfield, IL: Thomas.

Delacato, C. H. (1968). *The diagnosis and treatment of speech and reading problems.* Springfield, IL: Thomas.

Delacato, C. H. (1982). *A new start for the child with reading problems: A manual for parents* (Rev. ed.). Morton, PA: Morton.

Delacato, C. H. (1984). *The ultimate stranger: The autistic child.* Novato, CA: Arena.

ELIZABETH JONES
Texas A&M University
First edition

TAMARA J. MARTIN
The University of Texas of the Permian Basin
Second edition

JESSI K. WHEATLEY
Falcon School District 49, Colorado Springs, Colorado
Third edition

DELAYED LANGUAGE (See Language Delays)

DE LEON, PEDRO (See Ponce De Leon, Pedro De)

DE L'EPÉE, ABBÉ CHARLES MICHEL (1712–1789)

Abbé Charles Michel de l'Epée founded in Paris in 1755 the first public school for the deaf, the *Institution Nationale des Sourds Muets*. The Abeé developed a systematic language of signs based on the earlier work of Jacob Rodrigues Pereire. His system of signs was the basis of the instructional system in the United States' first school for the deaf, the American School for the Deaf. It is still in use today in modified form (Lane, 1984).

REFERENCE

Lane, H. (1984). *When the mind hears.* New York, NY: Random House.

PAUL IRVINE
Katonah, New York

DELINQUENCY, DISABILITIES AND

It has been estimated that between 30% and 70% of juvenile offenders have disabilities which require special education services (National Center on Education, Disability, and Juvenile Justice [EDJJ], 2006; Office of Juvenile Justice and Delinquency Prevention [OJJDP], 1998). This number may be low because many youths are identified with a disability before their incarceration (Perryman, DiGangi, & Rutherford, 1989). In addition, it is estimated that 22% of incarcerated youth have significant mental health problems (OJJDP, 1998). Estimates of prevalence of disabilities among juvenile delinquents vary dramatically (Crawford, 1982; Murphy, 1986; Nelson & Rutherford, 1989; OJJDP, 1998). These disparities largely can be attributed to methodological inconsistencies in identification of the disabilities. Further methodological inconsistencies exist in the defining of juvenile delinquency. The criteria for identifying juvenile delinquents are not uniform across state departments of correction (Murphy, 1986). Indeed, differential diagnosis of a disability as well as juvenile delinquency appear, in part, to be a state phenomenon.

Though tenuous, the accumulated body of research indicates that the prevalence of disabilities among juvenile delinquents is disproportionate to that reported in non-delinquent populations (Crawford, 1982; Keiltz & Dunivant, 1986; Murphy, 1986; OJJDP, 1998). However, the actual prevalence of the major handicaps among juvenile delinquents is difficult to establish. This difficulty can be attributed to the lack of uniform procedures in identifying disabilities and juvenile delinquency. These findings have important implications concerning the identification and servicing of delinquents with disabilities under the provision of the Individuals with Disabilities Education Improvement Act (IDEIA, 2004) and its predecessor in 1975. Many states were slow to provide special education services to incarcerated youth, which resulted in more than 20 class action lawsuits involving special education over the years. Unfortunately, few of the cases went to court; therefore, very few published judicial opinions exist (OJJDP, 1998). The Office of Juvenile Justice and Delinquency Prevention (OJJDP) has advocated for stronger links between correctional facilities and school districts, fiscal autonomy for cost-per-pupil budgeting, adherence to the standards for correctional education programs put out by the Correctional Education Association, and avoidance of litigation.

Leone (1991) suggests that the social disadvantages and characteristics associated with juvenile delinquents may lead to increased likelihood of contact with the criminal justice system. Although there is a correlation between poor social and conflict resolution skills and delinquent behavior, no causality can be inferred. Several studies are available that address the effectiveness of special education programs in corrections. Bachara and Zaba (1978) found that the juvenile offenders who were offered remediation in the form of special education, tutoring, or perceptual-motor training exhibited a significantly lower recidivism rate than those who were not offered these programs (Karcz, 1987). Other researchers of the juvenile delinquent population have found that there exists an overall impoverishment of adaptive skill behaviors for this population (Berman & Siegal, 1976). Other studies

(Forbes, 1991; Grande & Koorland, 1988) suggest that the uniqueness of the correctional setting realizes special problems with staff training, special educator training for correctional settings, curriculum design, and interagency cooperation.

Several successful approaches to assisting special education students who are incarcerated utilize research-based reading instruction (Brunner, 1993), cite cooperative learning techniques as being successful with this population (Ragan, 1993), and have found support for Team-Assisted Individualization (TAI; Salend & Washin, 1988).

OJJDP (1998) has suggested the following recommendations to parents or guardians of incarcerated youth who have disabilities:

Discuss the need for appropriate services at the facility with:

> Teachers and tutors at the facility.
> A facility administrator.
> A special education attorney in the area or a law school clinical program.
> A professor of education.
> Parents.

Obtain the Correctional Education Association standards on correctional education programs.

Review the facility's educational standards.

Establish a committee of educators, advocates, and administrators to:

> Ensure that IEPs are conducted in a timely fashion by qualified personnel.
> Revise the educational standards of the facility.
> Simplify the eligibility determination for special education services.
> Ensure that the facility has qualified teachers.

Involve local advocacy groups that support children and persons with disabilities.

Contact an attorney who can assist you in bringing litigation against the facility if education services not improve.

The National Center on Education, Disability, and Juvenile Justice (EDJJ) is funded by the Office of Special Education Programs. EDJJ has produced a readily available CD-ROM, *Meeting the Educational Needs of Students with Disabilities in Short-Term Detention Facilities*, which provides an overview of the issues and strategies involved in the delivery of special education and related services in jails and detention centers. The CD will be most useful to educators, administrators, and policymakers who work with this population of students, and is designed as a guide for the implementation of basic components of special education programs and practices in short-term detention facilities. The procedures and practices described on the CD are based on available research, best practice, and the experiences of the authors. It can be obtained from the EDJJ website at www.edjj.org/.

REFERENCES

Bachara, G. H., & Zaba, J. N. (1978). Learning disabilities and juvenile delinquency. *Journal of Learning Disabilities, 11,* 58–62.

Berman, A., & Siegal, A. (1976). Adaptive and learning skills in juvenile delinquents: A neuropsychological analysis. *Journal of Learning Disabilities, 9,* 51–53.

Brunner, M. (1993). *Reduced recidivism and increased employment opportunity through research-based reading instruction.* Clearinghouse No. CS011379. Washington, DC: U.S. Department of Justice.

Crawford, D. (1982). *Prevalence of handicapped juveniles in the justice system: A study of the literature.* Phoenix, AZ: Research & Development Training Institutes.

Forbes, M. A. (1991). Special education in juvenile correctional facilities: A literature review. *Journal of Correctional Education, 42*(1), 31–35.

Grande, C. G., & Koorland, M. A. (1988). A complex issue: Special education in corrections. *Children and Youth Services Review, 10*(4), 345–350.

Individuals with Disabilities Education Improvement Act (IDEIA 2004). U.S. Department of Education. idea.ed.gov/

Karcz, S. A. (1987). Delinquency and special education. In C. R. Reynolds & L. Mann (Eds.), *Encyclopedia of special education* (1st ed.). New York, NY: Wiley.

Keiltz, I., & Duvinant, N. (1986). The relationship between learning disability and juvenile delinquency: Current state of knowledge. *Remedial & Special Education, 7*(3), 18–26.

Leone, P. E. (1991). *Juvenile corrections and the exceptional student.* (ERIC Digest No. E509)

Murphy, D. A. (1986). The prevalence of handicapping conditions among juvenile delinquents. *Remedial and Special Education, 7,* 7–17.

National Center on Education, Disability, and Juvenile Justice (EDJJ). (2006). Retrieved from http://edjj.org/

Nelson, C. M., & Rutherford, R. B. (1989). *Impact of the correctional special education training (C/SET) project on correctional special education.* Paper presented at the CEC/CCBD National Topical Conference on Behavior Disorders, Charlotte, NC.

Office of Juvenile Justice and Delinquency Prevention (OJJDP). (1998). *Educational advocacy for youth with disabilities. Beyond the walls: Improving conditions of confinement for youth in custody.* Rockville, MD: Juvenile Justice Clearing House.

Perryman, P., DiGangi, S. A., & Rutherford, R. B. (1989). *Recidivism of handicapped and nonhandicapped juvenile offenders: An exploratory analysis.* Paper presented at the Learning Handicapped Offender Conference, Pittsburgh, PA.

Ragan, P. E. (1993). Cooperative learning can work in residential care settings. *Teaching Exceptional Children*, 25(2), 48–51.

Salend, S. J., & Washin, B. (1988). Team-assisted individualization with handicapped adjudicated youth. *Exceptional Children*, 55(2), 174–180.

HARRISON C. STANTON
Las Vegas, Nevada
First edition

ELAINE FLETCHER-JANZEN
Chicago School of Professional Psychology
Second edition

See also Juvenile Delinquency; Learning Disabilities

DELIS-KAPLAN EXECUTIVE FUNCTION SYSTEM

The Delis-Kaplan Executive Function System (D-KEFS, 2001) is a comprehensive assessment of higher-level thinking and cognitive flexibility, key components of executive functions believed to be mediated primarily by the frontal lobe. It is the first nationally standardized set of tests to evaluate higher-level cognitive functions in both children and adults, ages 8 to 89 years. There are two forms available; the Standard Record Forms include nine D-KEFS tests:

1. *Sorting test* assesses problem-solving, verbal and spatial concept formation, and flexibility of thinking on a conceptual task.

2. *Trail making test* assesses flexibility of thinking on a visual-motor task.

3. *Verbal fluency test* assesses fluent productivity in the verbal domain.

4. *Design fluency test* assesses fluent productivity in the spatial domain.

5. *Color-word interference test* assesses verbal inhibition.

6. *Tower test* assesses planning and reasoning in the spatial modality as well as impulsivity.

7. *20 Questions test* assesses hypothesis testing, verbal and abstract thinking, and impulsivity.

8. *Word context test* assesses deductive reasoning and verbal abstract thinking.

9. *Proverb test* assesses metaphorical thinking and the ability to generate versus comprehend abstract thought.

The Alternate Record Forms include alternate versions of the Sorting, Verbal Fluency, and 20 Questions Tests, the three tests most susceptible to practice effects. An alternate set of Sorting Cards is also available.

The D-KEFS is individually administered, and its game-like format is designed to be interesting and engaging for examinees, encouraging optimal performance without providing "right/wrong" feedback that can create frustration for some examinees. It can be administered as a complete set in 90 minutes, or individual tests can be administered in varying time frames. The complete testing kit includes an examiner's manual that provides clear instructions for administration and interpretation, as well as guidance for choosing appropriate subtests if the entire battery is not being administered. The D-KEFS can either be hand scored or scored using the D-KEFS Scoring Assistant, which is convenient and dramatically reduces scoring time. The nine D-KEFS subtests can either be recorded and scored as a complete battery or as individual subtests. With this software, the score reports can be produced, viewed, and printed on a PC in either tabular or graphic format.

The national standardization of the D-KEFS (1998–2000) included more than 1,700 children and adults, from ages 8 to 89 years, demographically and regionally matched with the U.S. population. D-KEFS is correlated with the Wechsler Abbreviated Scale of Intelligence (WASI) and the California Verbal Learning Tests–Second Edition (CVL T-II), providing information concerning the role of intellectual ability and memory on D-KEFS performance. No factor analyses were done.

Reliability scores for the D-KEFS are generally below .80, the minimum value that has been suggested for both internal consistency and test-retest reliability. Only 53 of the 316 reliability values presented (17%) met this standard. The reliability may be lowered by constricted ranges of scores among normal participants. Alternatively, several of the tests are fairly short, which may adversely affect reliability and sensitivity. Evidence regarding validity is not strong. Data are presented for two small clinical groups that are of questionable usefulness in demonstrating specific deficits in executive functions.

This entry has been informed by the sources listed below.

REVIEWED IN:

Delis, D. C., Kaplan, E., & Kramer, J. H. (2001). *Delis-Kaplan executive function system: Examiner's manual*. San Antonio, TX: Psychological Corporation.

Delis, D. C., Kramer, J. H., & Kaplan, E. (2004). Reliability and validity of the Delis-Kaplan executive function system: An update. *Journal of the International Neuropsychological Society*, *10*, 301–303.

Floyd, R. G., Bergeron, R., Hamilton, G., & Parra, G. R. (2010). How do executive functions fit with the Cattell-Horn-Carroll model? Some evidence from a joint factor analysis of the Delis-Kaplan executive function system and the Woodcock-Johnson III Tests of Cognitive Abilities. *Psychology in the Schools, 47,* 721–738.

Latzman, R. D., & Markon, K. E. (2010). The factor structure and age-related factorial invariance of the Delis-Kaplan executive function system (D-KEFS). *Assessment, 17,* 172–184.

Plake, B. S., Impara, J. C., & Spies, R. A. (Eds.). (2003). *The fifteenth mental measurements yearbook.* Lincoln, NE: Buros Institute of Mental Measurements.

Schmidt, M. (2003). Hit or miss? Insight into executive functions: Review of Delis-Kaplan executive function system, by D. C. Delis, E. Kaplan, and J. H. Kramer (2001). *Journal of International Neuropsychological Society, 9,* 960–965.

Shunk, A. W., Davis, A. S., & Dean, R. S. (2006). Review of "Delis Kaplan Executive Function System (D-KEFS)." *Applied Neuropsychology, 13,* 275–279.

RON DUMONT
Fairleigh Dickinson University

JOHN O. WILLIS
Rivier College

KATHLEEN VIEZEL
JAMIE ZIBULSKY
Fairleigh Dickinson University

DE LORENZO, MARIA E.G.E. (1927–)

Maria E. De Lorenzo is a noted Uruguayan special educator. She obtained her BA in education at Teacher's College, Montevideo, Uruguay (1941), and her MA in clinical psychology at the University of Michigan, Ann Arbor (1948). She served as director of School No. 1 for mentally retarded children (1949–1967) and as a member of the National Board of Elementary Education in Uruguay from 1967 to 1972. From 1966 to the present, De Lorenzo has been chief of the Mental Retardation Unit of the Inter-American Children's Institute, a specialized agency of the Organization of American States.

She frequently acts as a consultant for numerous international organizations such as the United Nations, the Organization of American States, Partners of the Americas, the President's Committee on Mental Retardation (U.S.), and the International League of Societies for Persons with Mental Handicaps. Since 1967, De Lorenzo has been a member of various UN organizations, among them the World Health Organization, UN Educational, Scientific, and Cultural Organization, and UN International Children's Emergency Fund. She is a member of numerous professional associations and of the editorial boards of the *International Journal of Rehabilitation Research*, the *Journal of Learning, Disabilities*, and the *Infant Mental Health Journal*.

De Lorenzo received numerous honors and special appointments, such as the Joseph P. Kennedy Award (1966), the Leadership Award for Achievements in Mental Deficiency (1976), and the Award of Merit granted by the President's Committee on Mental Retardation (1977). She also received the associate researcher *honoris causa* at the Research Department of the Bureau of Child Research, University of Kansas (1972). In 1978, De Lorenzo was invited to be the main speaker at the opening session of the World Congress on Future Social Education, organized by the Council for Exceptional Children in Sterling, Scotland. Her work was featured in the 1994 publication, *Comparative Studies in Special Education*, an examination of special education provisions throughout the world.

This entry has been informed by the source listed below.

REFERENCE

Mazurek, K., & Winzer, M. A. (Eds.). (1994). *Comparative studies in special education.* Washington, DC: Gallaudet University.

IVAN Z. HOLOWINSKY
Rutgers University
First edition

TAMARA J. MARTIN
The University of Texas of the Permian Basin
Second edition

DELUSIONS

Delusions are false or erroneous ideas that people believe wholeheartedly but that have no basis in fact and may involve a misinterpretation of perceptions or experiences (American Psychiatric Association, 1994; Barlow & Durand, 2005). Making a professional distinction between a delusion and a strongly held belief is not easy, and may come down to the person's degree of conviction for holding on to the idea despite compelling, contradictory evidence; the tenacity of which Jaspers (1963) thought of as a basic characteristic of "madness."

Delusions are most often associated with the psychotic mental disorder of schizophrenia, but can occur in other disorders such as dementia of Alzheimer's type or major depressive disorder with psychotic features (American Psychiatric Association, 1994; Barlow & Durand, 2005). Mack, Franklin, and Frances (2003) describe, too, how delusions can also occur in substance use disorders. For example, amphetamine use stimulates the nervous system by enhancing activity of norepinephrine and dopamine, making them more available throughout the brain, which can lead to hallucinations and paranoid delusions.

Concerning Schizophrenia, delusions are regarded as one of four major "Characteristic" symptoms (i.e., criterion A) associated with the disorder; the other symptoms being hallucinations, disorganized speech, grossly disorganized or catatonic behavior, and negative symptoms (i.e., affective flattening, alogia, avolition). If delusions are considered so bizarre, that is, they are implausible and not understandable and do not seem to come from ordinary life experiences, then only this single symptom is needed to satisfy criterion A instead of the required two of the four listed (Criteria B, C, D, E, and F, still must be considered before making a formal diagnosis).

In addition to being considered one of the major characteristic symptoms, delusions are also referred to as one of the "positive symptoms," along with hallucinations, disorganized speech (i.e., frequent derailment or incoherence), and grossly disorganized or catatonic behavior, because of the observed excess or distortion of normal functions (Barlow & Durand, 2005). "Negative" symptoms are regarded as those in which a diminution or loss of normal functions has occurred, such as is the case with symptoms like flattening of affect or loss of personal volition (American Psychiatric Association, 1994). Moreover, delusions are included in the top 10 "first rank" symptoms list psychiatry uses for diagnosing schizophrenia—a diagnostic list that is meant to strike an optimal balance between efficient classification and comprehensive description of the disorder (Andreasen & Flaum, 1991).

A variety of delusional types exist but perhaps the more well known are delusions of grandeur, delusions of persecution, delusions of reference, and delusions of control. *Delusions of grandeur* are marked by the belief that one is a great inventor, religious savior, or other specially empowered person. *Delusions of persecution* are probably the most common form of delusion among individuals with schizophrenia (Barlow & Durand, 2005) and center on the belief that they are being plotted or discriminated against, spied on, slandered, threatened, attacked, or deliberately victimized. *Delusions of reference* occur when individuals with schizophrenia attach special and personal meaning to the actions of others or to various objects or events. When individuals with schizophrenia believe their feelings, thoughts, and actions are being controlled by other people, then *delusions of control* are in operation (American Psychiatric Association, 1994; Barlow & Durand, 2005; Ho, Black, & Andreasen, 2003).

Other unique forms of delusions known as *Capgras syndrome* and *Cotard's syndrome* are also described in the literature (cf. Black & Andreasen, 1999). Capgras syndrome is the belief that someone a person knows has been replaced by a double. Cotard's syndrome is the belief that a part of one's body has been changed in some impossible way. More recently in the literature, *erotomanic delusions*

have been the topic of discussion due to their association with criminal stalking behavior. This particular delusion describes the individual's belief that, without any basis whatsoever, he or she is loved by someone who may actually be a casual acquaintance or even a complete stranger. These individuals develop far-fetched fantasies that drive them to protect, harm, or even kill the person they desire (Silva, Derecho, Leong, & Ferrari, 2000).

Assessing and classifying delusions is no simple task; in fact, they are seen as a multidimensional and varied phenomenon. Individuals with schizophrenia, for example, are often full of conviction and convinced of the reality of their beliefs; their delusions often extend into various areas of their lives, such as only at work with the boss versus being convinced that everyone in the world is persecuting them. Delusions are often bizarre and depart from culturally determined consensual reality, such as believing they are the Creator of the universe or hear "strange buzzing" sounds in their head: proof positive of alien brain-washing activity. Delusions can be very logical, consistent, and systematic; or the converse. Delusions can exert low or extreme pressure on a person, keeping a person only occasionally distracted by fleeting thoughts of being a famous movie star versus being totally obsessed and energized by a delusion, devoting themselves day and night to figuring out how the CIA has recruited them into their organization without their consent and knowledge. Suffice it to say, delusions are not static experiences, but are extremely dynamic in nature and come in a full range of expression.

In an intriguing discussion by Roberts (1991), the idea is posited that delusions may give purpose for people with schizophrenia who are otherwise quite upset by the strange changes taking place within themselves. The emerging idea has little support, but in Roberts's (1991) study, "deluded" individuals expressed a much stronger sense of purpose and meaning in life, and less depression than compared to matched individuals who previously had delusions but were recovering. This suggests that delusions might serve as an adaptive function for individuals with schizophrenia.

For further investigation into the phenomenon of delusions, the reader is directed to the classic "three Christs" study of Rokeach (1964) where the author spent a great deal of time at a mental hospital interviewing three individuals with schizophrenia who all held the same delusion that they were Jesus Christ. Also, Fleschner (1995) presents a fascinating, first-person account of the insights of a patient with schizophrenia.

REFERENCES

American Psychiatric Association. (1994). *Diagnostic and statistical manual of mental disorders* (4th ed.). Washington, DC: Author.

Andreasen, N. C., & Flaum, M. (1991). Schizophrenia: The characteristic symptoms. *Schizophrenia Bulletin, 17*, 27–49.

Barlow, D. H., & Durand, V. M. (2005). *Abnormal psychology: An integrative approach* (4th ed.). Belmont, CA: Wadsworth.

Black, D. W., & Andreasen, N. C. (1999). Schizophrenia, schizophreniform disorder and delusional (paranoid) disorders. In R. E. Hales, S. C. Yudofsky, & J. A. Talbott (Eds.), *Textbook of clinical psychiatry* (3rd ed., pp. 425–477). Washington, DC: American Psychiatric Press.

Fleschner, C. L. (1995). First person account: Insight from a schizophrenia patient with depression. *Schizophrenia Bulletin, 21,* 703–707.

Ho, B-C., Black, D. W., & Andreasen, N. C. (2003). Schizophrenia and other psychotic disorders. In R. E. Hales & S. C. Yudofsky (Eds.), *Textbook of clinical psychiatry* (4th ed., pp. 379–438). Washington, DC: American Psychiatric Press.

Jaspers, K. (1963). *General psychopathology* (J. Hoeing & M. W. Hamilton, Trans.). Manchester, England: Manchester University Press.

Mack, A. H., Franklin, J. E., & Frances, R. J. (2003). Substance use disorders. In R. E. Hales & S. C. Yudofsky (Eds.), *Textbook of clinical psychiatry* (4th ed., pp. 309–377). Washington, DC: American Psychiatric Press.

Roberts, G. A. (1991). Delusional belief and meaning in life: A preferred reality? *British Journal of Psychiatry, 159,* 20–29.

Rokeach, M. (1964). *The three christs of Ypsilanti.* New York, NY: Random House.

Silva, J. A., Derecho, D. V., Leong, G. B., & Ferrari, M. M. (2000). Stalking behavior in delusional jealousy. *Journal of Forensic Science, 45,* 77–82.

ROLLEN C. FOWLER
Eugene 4J School District, Eugene Oregon

See also Childhood Psychosis; Childhood Schizophrenia

DEMENTIA

Dementia is a generic term applied to a pattern of observable abnormalities in mental abilities, with impairment in at least three of the following five functions: memory, visuospatial skills, emotion or personality, language, and cognition. Combinations of symptoms are caused by many different etiologies (Hegde, 1994). Some literature agrees that irreversible dementia can be subdivided into three major areas: primary degenerative dementia, multi-infarct dementia, and all other dementia diagnoses of terminal diseases collectively (Shekim, 1997). Dementia of the Alzheimer's type is the most common, and it is caused by structural and chemical changes in the brain. The second most common, multi-infarct dementia, is caused by repeated focal lesions from strokes. Dementia is associated with acquired immunodeficiency syndrome (AIDS), Pick's disease, Parkinson's disease, supranuclear palsy, Binswanger's disease, Creutzfeldt-Jakob disease, Huntington's disease, and Korsakoff's disease (Payne, 1997). In addition, reversible dementias arise from adverse drug interactions or toxicity, metabolic and endocrine disorders, infections, intracranial masses, normal-pressure hydrocephalus, alcohol abuse, vitamin deficiencies, neurosyphilis, arteriosclerotic complications, and epilepsy (Tonkovich, 1988).

Assessment and diagnosis of dementia is a team effort involving physicians, speech-language pathologists, psychologists, and other specialists. The final determination is made on the basis of case history, clinical examination, neurological tests, brain imaging, laboratory tests, communication assessment, and assessment of intellectual functions. Analysis of higher intellectual and language functions include verbal description of common objects, immediate and delayed story retelling, and verbal fluency ("Tell me all the words you can think of beginning with T"; Hegde, 1994).

Language problems frequently observed in early stages of dementia are mild naming problems, verbal paraphasia (saying words that are similar to the target word), subtle problems in comprehending abstract meanings, impaired picture description, difficulty in topic maintenance, and repetitious speech. As the disease progresses, symptoms include severe memory problems in all forms of memory; generalized intellectual deterioration; profound disorientation to place, person, and time; speech at a rapid rate with echolalia (repeating what was said to them); pallilalia (repeating one's own utterances); jargon; and inattention to social conventions (Hegde, 1994).

REFERENCES

Hegde, M. N. (1994). *A coursebook on aphasia and other neurogenic language disorders.* San Diego, CA: Singular.

Payne, J. C. (1997). *Adult neurogenic language disorders: Assessment and treatment.* San Diego, CA: Singular.

Shekim, L. (1997). Dementia. In L. L. LaPointe (Ed.), *Aphasia and related neurogenic language disorders* (2nd ed., pp. 238–249). New York, NY: Thieme.

Tonkovich, J. L. (1988). Communication disorders in the elderly. In B. B. Shadden (Ed.), *Communication behavior and aging: A sourcebook for clinicians* (pp. 197–218). Baltimore, MD: Williams & Wilkins.

SHEELA STUART
George Washington University

DEMENTIAS OF CHILDHOOD

Dementia refers to a global cognitive decline that impacts more than one component of cognitive functioning and involves a memory impairment. The term *decline* indicates deterioration in cognitive functioning from a previous higher level of functioning (American Psychiatric Association, 2000). The etiology of dementia may be traced to a general medical condition, persistent effects of a substance, or multiple causes. The acquired nature of dementia suggests that it results in decreased mental functioning over time, as compared to an acute or sudden onset. Dementia describes conditions that are usually "both progressive and irreversible" (Lezak, 1995, p. 204).

Characteristics

1. Clinically significant deterioration in cognitive functioning that gets progressively worse over time.
2. Memory deficits including difficulties with registration, retention, recall, or recognition of new information.
3. Slowed reaction time.
4. Deficits in cognitive processes possibly including aphasia (language disturbance), apraxia (impaired motor functioning), agnosia (inability to recognize or identify objects), or impaired executive abilities.
5. Typically dementia presents as a gradual onset of symptoms and continued cognitive decline.
6. No evidence of impaired consciousness or awareness (not the result of delirium or amnesia).

Although degenerative disorders affect less than 1% of people under 65 year of age, many conditions that occur during childhood can produce dementia (Gurland & Crass, 1986). Dementia in children can be classified similar to how they are identified in adults. They are the result of general medical conditions, persistent substance exposure, or a mixture of the two. Medical conditions that may cause dementia include brain tumors or neoplasms, which can lead to changes in cognitive functioning. The impact of a medical condition on declining mental abilities in dementia depends on the size, location, and rate of growth of the tumor or neoplasm (Lezak, 1995). Children treated with chemotherapy for acute lymphocytic leukemia or childhood leukemia have also been known to suffer from neuropsychological impairments (Teeter & Semrud-Clikeman, 1997). Dementia resulting from kidney dialysis affects less than 1% of individuals undergoing dialysis (Lezak, 1995).

Cerebrovascular disease, or strokes, can produce impairments in cognitive ability and are referred to as vascular dementia. Dementia may also be associated with traumatic brain injuries. The juvenile type of Huntington's disease can cause cognitive impairments, memory retrieval deficits, and difficulties with planning and attention (American Psychiatric Association,

2000). Lastly, medical conditions such as brain lesions (hydrocephalus), endocrine disorders (hypothyroidism), nutritional deficiencies (Vitamin B_{12} deficiency), immune conditions, and metabolic diseases can produce symptoms of dementia (American Psychiatric Association, 2000).

Children infected with HIV may develop symptoms of progressive neurodevelopment degeneration termed HIV encephalopathy, neuroaids, or AIDS dementia complex (Aylward, 1997). This condition initially consists of mild symptoms such as depression, forgetfulness, or difficulty sustaining attention but can develop into complete dementia (Lezak, 1995). There is no known treatment for AIDS dementia.

There is evidence that individuals with Trisomy 21, commonly referred to as Down syndrome, may experience aspects of dementia by the time they are adolescents. One possible explanation for this occurrence is an accelerated rate of aging and reduced temporal lobe functioning in this population (Miezejeski, Devenny, Krinsky-Mchale, Zigman, & Silverman, 2000). Research suggests that some individuals with Trisomy 21 experience brain atrophy and metabolic deficits similar to those associated with Alzheimer's disease (Nadel, 1999).

Acute or chronic exposure to substances can produce symptoms of dementia in children. Contact with neurotoxins, such as lead, mercury, certain insecticides, solvents, or carbon monoxide can lead to significant cognitive impairments. Ingestion of alcohol, inhalants, sedatives, hypnotics, anxiolytics, or medications such as anticonvulsants or intrathecal methotrexate can also produce indications of dementia (American Psychiatric Association, 2000).

Although it can be difficult to assess the degree of cognitive deterioration in young children, worsening school performance, significant developmental delays, or divergence from normal development can be early signs of dementia (American Psychiatric Association, 2000). Mental status examinations and neuropsychological assessment can be useful for identifying cognitive assets and deficits. Assessment of memory functioning including short-term memory, long-term retrieval, and recognition can also provide valuable information. Deficits in expressive and receptive language abilities and executive functioning are often present.

For special education purposes, children with dementias may be eligible to receive services under the classification Other Health Impairment. If they are eligible to receive special education services, academic support could be beneficial. Treatment typically consists of cognitive rehabilitation techniques to compensate for memory impairment (e.g., the use of visual imagery and verbal encoding strategies). External memory aids, such as tape recorders and notebooks, also can be helpful. Pharmacological interventions such as cholinergically active drugs that are known to impact memory and cognition positively may also be useful.

REFERENCES

American Psychiatric Association. (2000). *Diagnostic and statistical manual of mental disorders* (4th ed., text rev.). Washington, DC: Author.

Aylward, G. P. (1997). *Infant and early childhood neuropsychology*. New York, NY: Plenum Press.

Gurland, B. J., & Crass, P. S. (1986). Public health perspectives on clinical memory testing of Alzheimer's disease and related disorders. In L. W. Poon (Ed.), *Clinical memory assessment of older adults*. Washington, DC: American Psychological Association.

Lezak, M. D. (1995). *Neurological assessment* (3rd ed.). New York, NY: Oxford University Press.

Miezejeski, C. M., Devenny, D. A., Krinsky-Mchale, S., Zigman, W., & Silverman, W. (2000). Aging in persons with Down syndrome and mental retardation: Receptive language, visual motor integration, and fluency [Abstract]. *Archives of Clinical Neuropsychology, 15*.

Nadel, L. (1999). Down syndrome in cognitive neuroscience perspective. In H. Tager-Flusberg (Ed.), *Neurodevelopmental disorders*. Cambridge, MA: MIT Press.

Teeter, P. A., & Semrud-Clikeman, M. (1997). *Child neuropsychology: Assessment and interventions for neurodevelopmental disorders*. Boston, MA: Allyn & Bacon.

BOB KIRCHNER
University of Northern Colorado

SHAWN POWELL
United States Air Force Academy

DENDRITES

A typical neuron is depicted in Figure D.1. Two views at different magnifications are seen in Figure D.2. The nucleus of the cell, called the *soma* or *perikaryon*, has various protruding elements. The main protruding element is the axon.

Typically surrounding the soma, except where the axon exits, are a variety of smaller protruding elements that form the dendritic network of the neuron. The dendrites have an appearance somewhat akin to branches of a leafless tree and *dendron* is the Greek stem meaning tree. The dendrites serve as the neurotransmitter receptacle sites, as does the soma itself, from neurotransmitter release from the axon of a different neuron. The synaptic termination actually occurs on little spines that arise from the dendrite. These spines are numerous. For example, a single motor neuron may have as many as 4,000 spines on its dendrites. Although it was originally assumed that the dendrite served a rather passive role in neuronal transmission, it is now speculated that the dendritic processes play a much more dynamic and active role in neurotransmission (Cooper, Bloom, & Roth, 1978; Cotman & McGaugh, 1980) and neurobehavioral (i.e., learning) functions.

REFERENCES

Cooper, J. R., Bloom, F. E., & Roth, R. H. (1978). *The biochemical basis of neuropharmacology* (3rd ed.). New York, NY: Oxford University Press.

Cotman, C. W., & McGaugh, J. L. (1980). *Behavioral neuroscience*. New York, NY: Academic Press.

ERIN D. BIGLER[1]
Austin Neurological Clinic
University of Texas

See also **Central Nervous System; Glial Cells**

DENMARK, SPECIAL EDUCATION IN THE FOLKESKOLE IN

The term *Folkeskole* refers to the Danish municipal primary and lower secondary school system. All children of compulsory education age, despite the nature of their special needs, have a right to free education in the Folkeskole. Education, not schooling, is compulsory. Whether education is received in the publicly provided municipal school, in a private school, or at home, is a matter of parental choice provided certain standards are met.

In Denmark pupils with special needs that attend a private school are offered special education for free provided their special educational needs are assessed by a local pedagogical-psychological counseling center. Under Danish laws, its so-called welfare system offers persons full compensation for services that address needs persons have not personally caused. As noted in the following, achieving this status has taken years.

Since the founding of the Folkeskole in 1814, children were guaranteed the right to 7 years of education in religion, reading, writing, and arithmetic. Special education services initially were not provided.

During the early 20th century, teachers began to focus more on individual pupils. After 1924, children with severe sensory, motor, and mental handicaps received training in schools administrated by the Ministry of Social Affairs. This ministry provided free educational services independent of the Folkeskole. Around 1930, some more wealthy municipalities established special education services for children with minor special educational needs even though they had no legal duty to do so. The School Act of 1937 established the first national services for children who were unable to benefit from ordinary teaching, if conditions allowed.

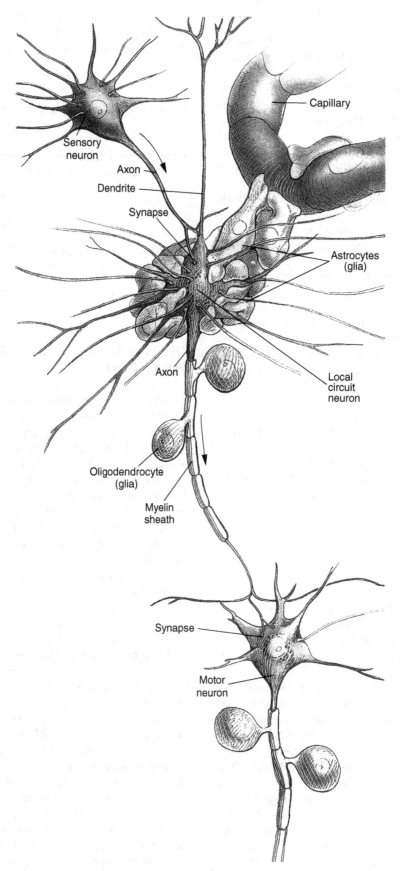

Figure D.1. Left, a neural circuit. A large neuron with multiple dendrites receives synaptic contact from another neuron at upper left. It sends its myelinated axon into a synaptic connection with a third neuron at bottom. These neural surfaces are shown without the extensive investment of glia that envelop the branch extending toward the capillary at upper right.

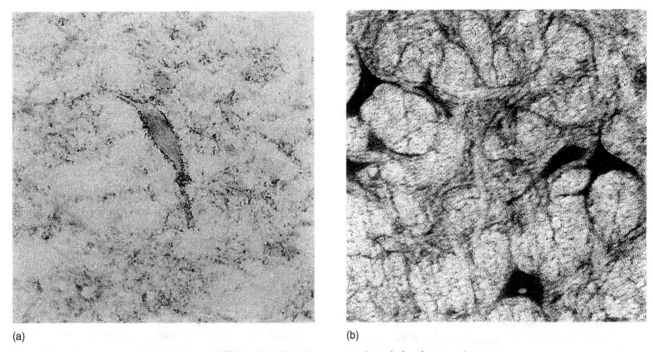

(a) (b)

Figure D.2. Two views (a and b) of synapses at different magnifications, as seen through the electron microscope.

World War II delayed the development of special education to some degree. However, following a report from the Commission for Special Education, special training services were introduced in the School Act of 1958. From that time, municipalities have provided special education services for the most chronic disabilities.

At first, care for the handicapped was guided by the desire to provide mutual protection to those with and without handicaps by separating them. This lead to the construction of residential institutions in rural areas in which the handicapped could receive various forms of care and live throughout one's life. Teaching cognitive skills was not emphasized in that cognitive abilities were not seen as important. Parents of children with handicaps began to protest the nature of these services. They wanted their child to remain in their home during childhood and to be prepared to lead an ordinary life as much as possible by receiving adequate training, including the acquisition of academic skills. These desires challenged local public school. With support from some politicians and school officials, some children with quite severe handicaps became integrated in some mainstream local schools.

Since the 1960s, children who are blind and visually impaired have been integrated in local school. Later, those with other disabilities increasingly were integrated in the local school, most often in special classes. Children with the most severe sensory, motor, and mental handicaps continued to receive their teaching and training in institutions run by the Ministry of Social Affairs.

The School Act of 1975 required all municipalities to provide special education services for every pupil who could not benefit from the ordinary education. The Act made education compulsory for ages 7 through 16, with 10th grade optional. Moreover, municipal Folkeskoles were required to provide a 1-year preschool program. Although voluntary, 98% of Danish children attend these classes. In 1980, the Ministry of Social Affairs' responsibilities for providing educational services to children from birth to 18 were transferred to the Ministry of Education. Special education assistance to infants is provided only to those with speech and/or language difficulties. However, municipalities often interpret this policy broadly by providing services to young children with various needs.

Consistent with Danish traditions, the development of integrated social and school services for special needs children has been initiated by a group of dedicated persons (e.g., parents, politicians, teachers) who eventually prevailed by convincing the Danish Parliament to enact laws favoring a more inclusive policy. Thus, since 1980, the Folkeskole has provided educational services to all children in a manner consistent with the Act.

In accord with this change favoring a more inclusive tone in education, municipalities modified social programs to provide support that enabled parents of special needs children to have them live at home.

Responsibility for educating pupils of the most severe handicaps (approximately 1.35% of all children) was placed in counties that developed a special school system and a consultant service. In addition, over time, municipal governments assumed more responsibility for providing special education services, resulting in significant developments in these services at the local municipal level.

New models of special education were introduced, including the provision of intensive training to a child the entire school day (e.g., intensive reading for 3 or more weeks) in a clinic setting. The term *clinic* in the Folkeskole refers to special rooms in a school well equipped for special training of children by well-trained teachers. These services generally provide part-time training in one or two subjects (e.g., reading, arithmetic). Children with attention problems or other behavior disorders also may receive training in a specific subject. If approved by parents, pupils may receive training in their free time in a clinic in addition to their fully integrated program in an ordinary class. A two-teacher model for use in mainstream classrooms also has been introduced.

Parents are centrally involved in decisions regarding their special needs children. Part 9 of the Folkeskole Act addresses parent complaints. Complaints about decisions taken by school officials may be brought before municipal authorities (Section 51 [1]). In addition, municipal council's decisions regarding referral or refusal to refer to special education can be brought before a Complaints Commission for Extensive Special Education (Section 51 a [1] and [3]).

In 2007, a new reform was implemented, resulting in reducing the former 275 municipalities to 98. These municipalities have assumed total responsibility for the education of all children, including special needs children. The change was triggered by knowledge that the former system that divided responsibilities between municipalities and counties was inefficient. It happened that neither of the two government bodies accepted responsibility for needed services, believing the other was responsible. This change has helped to ensure that needed services are delivered.

Each municipality must establish a pedagogical-psychological counseling service. The Danish Folkeskole is centrally regulated by the Act on the Folkeskole, which establishes the framework for a school's services and activities. Although all municipal schools have common aims, individual municipalities are responsible for deciding how its schools are to function within the framework of the Act on the Folkeskole (Part 1 of the Folkeskole Act).

The use of diagnostic categories has been discussed lively in Denmark. Diagnoses by medical personnel generally have become less common. Decisions as to whether a child requires special support are dependent on an individual assessment (the Act on the Danish Folkeskole).

Referral to special education in more than one subject or in cases where there is a disagreement between school and parents shall be made on pedagogical and psychological assessment and on consultation with the pupil and his or her parents (Part 2 of the Folkeskole Act, Section 12 [2]). These and other legal provisions underscore the need for school officials and the pedagogical-psychological

counseling service to closely cooperate when providing special education services to students.

Due to the decentralization of the educational system, the pedagogical-psychological counseling centers have developed unevenly. Staff normally consists of some psychologists trained in different areas (e.g., learning difficulties, social-emotional problems). Special education instructional assistance may include teaching pupils all subjects specified by the Folkeskole and providing training and preparation for later work, special educational assistance to parents and teachers, special educational materials and technical aids, and personal assistance through counseling and other sources. Moreover, a child with a severe motor handicap may have his or her own helper to assist as needed.

During the 2008 to 2009 school year, 716,209 pupils attended primary and lower secondary education, 87% of whom attended the Danish Folkeskole. The remaining 13% received their education in private schools, and a few were taught by their parents.

About 10% of Danish pupils receive special education services in various degrees according to their individual needs. During the 2008 to 2009 school year, 1.7% (12,476) received special education in special schools and 2.7% (19,812) in regular schools 4.0% (27,974) regular class students received special education as a part time supplement. About 1% (3,131) received special education in boarding schools. There are no valid statistics on diagnostic categories. http://www.dst.dk/pukora/epub/Nyt/2010/NR311.pdf

New initiatives on special education in the Folkeskole outline the importance of inclusiveness and differentiated teaching to all pupils. Those providing educational-psychological advisory services play an important role in promoting inclusiveness in mainstream schools, in that they are involved with all three types of education: ordinary education, education of pupils with ordinary special educational needs, and pupils with profound special educational needs. The counseling and guidance services provided to schools and parents greatly influence local attitudes and decisions regarding educational and organizational action programs (http://european-agency.org/ European Agency: National Overview in the Field of Special Needs Education).

Teacher training has since 2007 included special education in its syllabus, until then they received most of their training in special education after being certificated as a teacher. Teachers responsible for the total teaching of one or more pupils with special needs often will have completed a program of education that qualifies them for their responsibilities. However, this is not a legal responsibility. For all teachers there is a possibility to take a 1-year course for a Diploma in special education on University Colleges, and a 1-year master program has also been established on Aarhus University.

This entry has been informed by the sources listed below.

REFERENCES

Directions on the Folkeskole's efforts to students, whose development demands special considerations and support. http://www.uvm.dk/Uddannelse/Folkeskolen/Specialundervisning.aspx

The Folkeskole Act as per 2010. https://www.retsinformation.dk/Forms/R0710.aspx?id=133039 (in Danish)

European Agency. (n.d.) National overview in the field of special needs education. http://european-agency.org/

MIELS EGELUND
Copenhagen, Denmark

See also Belgium, Special Education in; France, Special Education in

DENO, EVELYN N. (1911–2005)

As a developmental psychologist, Evelyn Deno specialized in the design and delivery of helping services for handicapped children and their parents. As a preschool, elementary, and college teacher of 17 years, Deno earned her MA in 1950, and PhD in 1958, in child development and clinical psychology from the University of Minnesota, where she taught graduate-level classes in child development. She then went on to become director of special education and rehabilitation for the Minneapolis public schools. She returned to the University of Minnesota in 1967 as professor of educational psychology and director of the Psycho-Educational Center. She was also codirector of the Leadership Training Institute for the USOE Bureau of Professional Development.

Best known for her "cascade of special education services" concept and diagram, Deno always saw the need for "helping service systems and political agents to promote a more compatible match between individual aspirations and the constraining social and physical environmental realities" (personal communication, August 27, 1985). She applied developmental theory to see how people with special adjustment problems can be helped to survive in a culture and society inclined to regard deviance from the "norm" (or what is expected) as a problem of the deviant one, not a challenge to society's ability and obligation to respect individual differences" (personal communication, August 27, 1985).

Deno's interests were with the adjustment problems of older persons and the design and implementation of programs for them to serve as counselors to their peers, tutors, and as "special friends" to learning-disabled and emotionally disturbed children. She received a number of awards for outstanding contributions in her field. Service delivery models designed and tested under her direction have been designated as national service prototypes. Her ideas on merging special and general education, labeling, and blaming students' failure to learn solely on teachers were analyzed in an article in the *Journal of Special Education* (Hallahan & Kauffman, 1994).

Deno retired from the University of Minnesota in the mid-1970s, and lived in the Twin Cities area of Minnesota. She edited an anthology of personal experiences of those involved in the major paradigm shift in 1955 in special education, when Minnesota passed into law the requirement that individual school systems provide educational services to all handicapped children, rather than placing them in residential state institutions.

Deno received numerous local, state, and national awards for her many contributions to the education and habilitation of people with disabilities. She lived a well and full life, passing away June 4, 2005.

REFERENCE

Hallahan, D. P., & Kauffman, J. M. (1994). Toward a culture of disability in the aftermath of Deno and Dunn. *Journal of Special Education, 27,* 496–508.

ELAINE FLETCHER-JANZEN
Chicago School of Professional Psychology
First edition

KAY E. KETZENBERGER
The University of Texas of the Permian Basin
Second edition

JESSI K. WHEATLEY
Falcon School District 49, Colorado Springs Colorado
Third edition

DENTISTRY AND THE EXCEPTIONAL CHILD

The physical consequences and personal discomfort of dental disorders and untreated oral diseases for disabled individuals are obvious; they include pain, oral abscesses, and loss of teeth (DECOD, 2006). The educational and social implications are, perhaps, just as important. Bad teeth, gum disorders, and so on can cause bad breath and cosmetic disabilities and thus make the social acceptance of disabled children and adults more difficult. The cosmetic implications of good dental health for the disabled have been recognized by many states that provide dental care to vocational rehabilitation clients, though the need for services usually outstrips the resources available to meet them.

A number of diverse physiological social and economic factors have been identified as being responsible for the greater degree of dental and oral disorders in disabled populations. Malformations and abnormal development of certain teeth are thus coincidental with certain types of disabilities. Particular dental difficulties have been found to be associated with various types of disabilities. Individuals with Down syndrome have been found to experience a relatively low incidence of tooth decay but a high incidence of periodontal or gum disease (Pugliese, 1978), while the gums of many epileptic individuals have been found to overgrow as a consequence of dilantin use (Nowak, 1976). Neurological seizures or motor disabilities may result in head injuries that cause serious damage to oral structures. Motor impairments, limited cognitive understanding of the importance of good dental habits, and poor motivation often limit the carrying out of oral hygiene practices by children with disabilities and frustrate parents' training and monitoring efforts.

The strained economic conditions of many disabled children is another reason for the high incidence of oral disease in special education populations. Many disabled children come from socioeconomically disadvantaged families that are not likely to emphasize the precepts of oral hygiene in their daily living or to afford dental care. Furthermore, there has been a reduction of dental support for such families in Medicaid programs. Indeed, the federal government, under Title XIX, does not require that states provide any dental services to adult Medicaid recipients.

Additionally, until recently, barrier restrictions, difficulties in patient management, and negative attitudes have limited receptivity in dental professionals with regard to the provision of services to difficult patients. Difficulties in patient management and negative attitudes on the part of dental health professionals negatively affect the provision of dental care to difficult to treat patients with disabilities. Beyond such problems, even when willing and proficient service providers are available, parents of exceptional children and agencies serving them are often unaware of their availability.

Specific difficulties with respect to preventing or ameliorating dental problems and oral disease in students with disabilities are attributable to the attitudes of school personnel generally and special education personnel in particular. There is little attention paid to the dental/oral needs and problems of exceptional children in our schools currently. This is in part a consequence of changing conditions of service provision to disabled children. Increasingly, as that provision has moved from segregated circumstances such as institutions in which health care considerations are predominant over educational ones, to the less restrictive environments of day and public school programs, there has been a decided shift from concern with the physical (care) needs of disabled schoolchildren to their specific instructional needs. Although the health professionals and special education teachers serving special education populations undoubtedly recognize the needs of disabled children for good oral training and dental health care, they are not likely to emphasize these in their day to day individualized education plan practices. Present-day special education requires the provision of so many mandated educational services that the laborious training of children in instructionally peripheral areas of brushing, flossing, and so on is likely to be neglected.

The 1970s were a particularly active period with respect to comprehensive investments of time and effort in improving dental care for individuals with disabilities. One of the most important efforts in this respect was the funding by the Robert Wood Johnson Foundation during 1974 to 1978 of 11 dental schools across the country. This funding was to support the development of comprehensive dental school training programs relative to the provision of services to disabled individuals (i.e., to develop specialized skills and technology, to create positive attitude change in dental professionals, to develop referral and service delivery capabilities at dental schools, and to institutionalize aspects of these programs at dental schools following funding).

Evaluation of these projects revealed decreased anxiety in faculty, staff, and students in working with exceptional students, increased ability to communicate with individuals with disabilities regarding their dental problems, and improved dental care practices. Positive attitude changes were reported in persons affected by the program (e.g., decreased fear and anxiety), as well as a better understanding of handicapped dental patients. A comprehensive report on the Robert Wood Johnson Foundation's program, the most ambitious privately funded one to date, is available from the Educational Testing Service (Campbell, Esser, & Flaugher, 1982).

Apropos of the Robert Wood Johnson Foundation's work, Stiefel and Truelove (1985) reported on the 5-year postgraduate program at the University of Washington that resulted in significant cognitive changes and gains in confidence respecting the treatment of individuals with disabilities by dentists, dental hygienists, and assistants who participated in a postgraduate program. Curricula guidelines are also available (DECOD, 2006; Jolly, 2007).

Although there has been a steady if meager stream of publications concerning the dental management of children with disabilities, of interest is the work of such investigators as Price (1978) and Pugliese (1978). Much of this interest, as might be expected, has been in the direction of preventive dentistry, and in the participation of home, school, and community in the dental management of individuals with disabilities. The Association for Retarded Citizens' position is that dental treatment should "be of the same quality as received by other people, preserve or enhance the individual's health and be administered only with the *informed consent* of the person or his or her surrogate decision maker" (ARC, 1992, p. 1). Callahan (1983a, 1983b), among others, has emphasized that effective dental care for individuals with disabilities must go beyond the improvement of dental services per se and improved technology to improving the willingness of dental practitioners to engage school and other service providers in the dental care of exceptional students. Callahan emphasizes the value of preventive services that will improve the dental status of individuals with disabilities and reduce the costs of their dental care. For those individuals with disabilities who will remain school and community based (this means most disabled children and adults), programs of comprehensive preventive dental care should be emphasized over those of costly treatment.

What can be accomplished through preventive programs has been demonstrated through model outreach programs implemented by the National Foundation of Dentistry for the Handicapped (Callahan, 1983b; NFDH, 2006). These programs have incorporated daily oral hygiene programs into the practices at a variety of special education schools, sheltered workshops, and group homes at relatively modest costs. They rely on periodic screening to detect dental disorders while they are still easily manageable. They use referral networks to coordinate the delivery of dental treatment to those disabled individuals who require it. Most important, they use teachers, counselors, vocational rehabilitation personnel, houseparents, and other service personnel, in addition to those from the dental professions, on their service delivery teams. Similar concerted efforts might be valuable in bringing special education and special educators fully into the teaching and training of oral hygiene methods and precepts.

Interest in applying dental and oral hygiene principles in work with more severely disabled populations is evidenced by the work of Feldman and Elliot (1981). Finally, because the vast majority of special education students these days reside at home, it is encouraging to observe recent efforts directed toward parents as oral hygiene trainers and monitors. Thus an article by Stark, Markel, Black, and Greenbaum (1985) provides guidelines to parents respecting their children's dental needs with regard to nutrition, medication, visits to the dentist, and the inculcation of proper dental care habits. In addition the American Academy of Pediatric Dentistry (AAPD, 2006) has developed a video for parents of exceptional children.

REFERENCES

American Academy of Pediatric Dentistry (AAPD). (2006). *Dental care for a special child*. Retrieved from http://www.aapd.org/

Association for Retarded Citizens (ARC). (1992). *Position paper on medical and dental treatment*. Arlington, TX: Author.

Callahan, W. P. (1983a). Dental disease: A continuing education problem for the disabled individual. *Journal of Special Education, 17*, 355–359.

Callahan, W. P. (1983b). The effectiveness of instructional programming on the reduction of dental diseases in mentally retarded individuals. *Mental Retardation, 21*, 260–262.

Campbell, J. Y., Esser, B. F., & Flaugher, R. L. (1982). *Evaluation of a program for training dentists in the care of handicapped patients* (Report No. QAT24225). Princeton, NJ: Educational Testing Service.

DECOD. (2006). *Dental education in the care of persons with disabilities*. Retrieved from http://dental.washington.edu/

Feldman, D., & Elliot, T. A. (1981). A multidimensional oral hygiene curriculum for the severely and profoundly handicapped. *Journal of Special Education Technology, 4*, 33–45.

Jolly, D. E. (2007). Curriculum guidelines for training general practice residents to treat the person with a handicap. *Journal of Dental Education, 54*(5), 293–297.

NFDH. (2006). *National Foundation of Dentistry for the Handicapped*. Retrieved from http://nfdh.org/

Nowak, A. J. (1976). *Dentistry for the handicapped patient*. St. Louis, MO: Mosby.

Price, J. H. (1978). Dental health education for the mentally and physically handicapped. *Journal of School Health, 48*, 171–173.

Pugliese, R. (1978). Oral health status in a group of mentally retarded patients. *Rhode Island Dental Journal, 11*, 6–9.

Stark, J., Markel, G., Black, C. M., & Greenbaum, J. (1985). Day to day dental care: A parents' guide. *Exceptional Parent, 15*, 15–17.

Stiefel, D. J., & Truelove, E. L. (1985). A postgraduate dental training program for treatment of persons with disabilities. *Journal of Dental Education, 49*, 85–90.

David C. Mann
St. Francis Hospital

See also Bruxism and the Student With Disabilities; Individualized Educational Plan; Self-Help Training

DENYS-DRASH SYNDROME

Denys-Drash syndrome, also known as *Drash syndrome*, is the combination of Wilms tumor (a malignant cancerous tumor of the kidney), pseudohermaphroditism (unambiguous gonadal sex with ambiguous external genitalia), and nephrotic syndrome (the deterioration of the kidney's renal tubular epithelium). This syndrome is characterized as a rare genetic disorder caused by the mutation of the Wilms tumor suppressor gene (WT1; Thoene, 1995). The majority of the 150 identified cases of Denys-Drash have been male (Mueller, 1994). This syndrome is usually detected during early infancy and most commonly results in chronic renal failure (Busey, 1990).

Characteristics

Wilms Tumor

1. Abdominal pain
2. Nausea and vomiting
3. High blood pressure
4. Blood in urine (Olendorf, Jeryan, & Boyden, 1999)

Pseudohermaphroditism (Male)

1. XY karyotype
2. Male gonads
3. Female genitalia or ambiguous genitalia

Pseudohermaphroditism (Female) (Mueller, 1994)

1. XX karyotype
2. Female gonads
3. Male genitalia or ambiguous genitalia

Nephrotic Syndrome (Rx Med Health Resource Centre, 2001)

1. Lack of appetite
2. Irritability
3. Vomiting
4. Diarrhea
5. Swelling and possible significant weight increase
6. Protein malnutrition

Genetic counseling is useful in facilitating the understanding of the diagnosis, course of syndrome, and treatment (Thoene, 1995). Individuals suffering from Denys-Drash syndrome may need to undergo surgery, chemotherapy, and radiation in order to treat the Wilms tumor (Olendorf et al., 1999). Because of the potential development of gonadal malignancy associated with pseudohermaphroditism, removal of the ovaries or testes may be necessary (Thoene, 1995). Treatment of the nephrotic syndrome is likely to include any combination of dialysis, kidney transplant, or renal transplant (Jensen, Ehrlich, Hanna, Fine, & Grunberger, 1989). The dietary requirements while undergoing dialysis, a renal transplant, or a kidney transplant are different. Therefore, nutritional counseling with a registered dietitian is essential to facilitate ongoing extensive nutritional management specific to each procedure necessary to treat the nephrotic syndrome (National Kidney Foundation, 2001). Attending individual and family psychological counseling helps to promote acceptance and adjustment surrounding this serious illness and the psychosocial issues typically associated with gender ambiguity.

Individuals suffering from Denys-Drash disease may be eligible for special education services under the Other Health Impairment or Physical Disability handicapping condition. Excessive school absences due to medical treatment may warrant homebound instruction or specialized instruction within the school environment. Information gained by the family through genetic counseling should be provided to the multidisciplinary team evaluating the current level of functioning and educational needs of the student. Although it may be necessary for the student to bring lunch from home, the school's nutritional services staff should be made aware of the dietary requirements in the event that they need to provide the student with a meal. If excessive absences prove to make social integration difficult for the student, a social skills group may be helpful.

The prognosis for those suffering from Denys-Drash syndrome is variable. However, without treatment, death usually occurs during infancy (Busey, 1990). Therefore, early diagnosis and treatment are necessary for survival. Despite timely diagnosis and treatment, those cases resulting in death are most commonly due to renal failure (Mueller, 1994).

REFERENCES

Busey, M. L. (1990). *Birth defects encyclopedia*. Boston, MA: Blackwell.

Jensen, J. C., Ehrlich, R. M., Hanna, M. K., Fine, R. N., & Grunberger, I. (1989). A report of 4 patients with the Drash syndrome and a review of the literature. *Journal of Urology*, *141*, 1174–1176.

Mueller, R. F. (1994). The Denys-Drash syndrome. *Journal of Medical Genetics*, *31*, 471–477.

National Kidney Foundation. (2001). *Nutritional support for kidney disease patients*. Retrieved from http://kidney.org/

Olendorf, D., Jeryan, C., & Boyden, K. (1999). *The* Gale *encyclopedia of medicine* (Vol. 5). Ann Arbor, MI: Gale.

Rx Med Health Resource Centre. (2001). *Nephrotic syndrome*. Retrieved from http://www.rxmed.com/b.main/b1.illness/b1.illness.html

Thoene, J. (1995). *Physician's guide to rare diseases* (2nd ed.). Lawrenceville, NJ: Dowden.

JULIETTE CUTILLO
Fountain-Fort Carson School District 8 Colorado Springs

DEPAKENE

Depakene is an antiepileptic agent known generically as *valproic acid*. Depakene is the most recently introduced anticonvulsant medication. It differs both chemically and in clinical action from most other anticonvulsants (Goldensohn, Glaser, & Goldberg, 1984). Generally this medication is used either as the sole or adjunctive treatment for simple (petit mal) and complex absence seizures as well as generalized seizure disorders. The precise mechanism by which Depakene works is unknown; however, some research has suggested that its activity is related to increased brain levels of gamma-aminobutyric acid.

Although there is little research on the behavioral effects of Depakene, uncontrolled trials suggest that it may improve visual-motor coordination (Schlack, 1974), alertness, and school performance (Barnes & Bower, 1975). Nausea and gastrointestinal irritation are common side effects of Depakene, but these can be controlled through dosage or by giving the drug with food. If Depakene is given with other medications, particularly phenobarbital, there can be extreme, temporary sedation as well as awkward motor movements. Some of the more extreme side effects include a disruption of platelet functioning, liver damage, and pancreas failure, all of which have the potential to be fatal. For these reasons, Depakene typically is held in reserve as a medication of final resort for those individuals with seizures that cannot be controlled by other medication. For those who are using the ketogenic diet there may also be possible interactions (Ballaban-Gil, O'Dell, Pappo, Moshe, & Shinnar, 1998).

REFERENCES

Ballaban-Gil, K., Callahan, C., O'Dell, C., Pappo, M., Moshe, S., & Shinnar, S. (1998). Complications of the ketogenic diet. *Epilepsia, 39*(7), 744–748.

Barnes, S. E., & Bower, B. D. (1975). Sodium valproate in the treatment of intractible childhood epilepsy. *Developmental Medicine and Child Neurology, 17*, 175–181.

Goldensohn, E. S., Glaser, G. H., & Goldberg, M. A. (1984). Epilepsy. In L. P. Rowland (Ed.), *Merritt's textbook of neurology* (7th ed., pp. 629–650). Philadelphia, PA: Lea & Febiger.

Schlack, H. G. (1974). Ergenye in the treatment of epilepsy. *Therapiewoche, 24*, 39–42.

RICHARD A. BERG
*West Virginia University Medical Center,
Charleston Division*

See also Anticonvulsants; Seizure Disorders

DEPENDENT VARIABLE

Dependent variable operationally defines a behavior you wish to measure and change as part of an experimental study (Alberto & Troutman, 2006). Bailey and Burch (2002) write that the word "*dependent* refers to the fact that this variable *depends upon* some experimental manipulations that you will make in the course of the experiment" (p. 64). Examples of dependent variables include (a) number of times a student raises her hand following a teacher's question, (b) the percent of time a student is academically engaged during a defined instructional period, (c) the reading rates of a small group of students who are at risk for reading failure, (d) the amount of time a student participates in nonstructured activities during recess, and (e) the percent correct on weekly spelling tests for a student during baseline and intervention phases.

Each of the dependent variables listed previously can be measured and manipulated as part of an experimental design. For example, a teacher reported that her student rarely raises her hand and often blurts out answers to the teacher's question. After reviewing the baseline data, the teacher learns that this student only raises her hand on the average of 1 time per instructional period, but blurts out answers nearly 10 times per instructional period. The teacher implements an intervention in which prior to the beginning of class she verbally precorrects the student to remember to raise her hand and wait to be called on by the teacher. This antecedent-based instructional strategy (i.e., "precorrection"; see De Pry & Sugai, 2002) is implemented and the observer continues to collect data on hand raising in exactly the same manner as she did during the baseline phase. Following the procedures for the experimental design, the teacher manipulates the dependent variable by introducing and removing the intervention to measure the effect of the precorrection intervention on the frequency of hand raising. Data illustrated that the student increased hand raising to nearly eight times during intervention phases. Measurement of the dependent variable in baseline and intervention phases demonstrates the effect of precorrection on hand raising during instruction.

Operational definitions require that the teacher or researcher consider the relevant behavioral dimensions of the behavior of concern prior to writing the definition. Behavioral dimensions include consideration for how often a behavior occurs (frequency), how long the behavior occurs (duration), where the behavior occurs (locus), how hard or damaging the behavior is (magnitude), and the amount of time that it takes for the person to engage in the behavior following the antecedent stimulus (latency; Wolery, Bailey, & Sugai, 1988). An operational definition is a written statement that precisely defines the behavior you wish to measure in terms that are observable, measurable, and replicable (Fletcher-Janzen & De Pry, 2003).

Bailey and Burch (2002) suggest that the following factors be considered when defining the dependent variable. First, the teacher or researcher should consider the face validity of the definition, that is, how it agrees with the standard usage of the proposed dependent variable. Next, the teacher or researcher should determine if the dependent variable has been previously defined as part of his or her review of the extant research literature and to what degree the same definition can be used (replicated) as part of the proposed study. If an existing definition is not available or appropriate for the study, then creating and pilot testing a new definition is appropriate. This process includes carefully defining the dependent variable as previously described and testing for reliability prior to implementing data collection on the dependent variable.

Once defined, the dependent variable informs the teacher or researcher on the appropriate data-collection strategy. For example, if you want to count the frequency of a discrete behavior, then event recording is the most effective method. If you are interested in examining how long a person engages in a behavior, then duration recording is the best choice. And if you are interested in the amount of time it takes from the time a teacher gives a request until the student engages in behavior, then latency recording is the appropriate data-collection method. Data collected on the dependent variable is always plotted along the ordinate or Y-axis of a graph and interobserver reliability data is collected (approximately 20% of the total sample) to document consistency between the primary observer and an independent observer.

REFERENCES

Alberto, P. A., & Troutman, A. C. (2006). *Applied behavior analysis for teachers* (7th ed.). Upper Saddle River, NJ: Prentice Hall.

Bailey, J. S., & Burch, M. R. (2002). *Research methods in applied behavior analysis*. Thousand Oaks, CA: Sage.

De Pry, R. L., & Sugai, G. (2002). The effect of active supervision and precorrection on minor behavioral incidents in a sixth grade general education classroom. *Journal of Behavioral Education, 11*, 255–267.

Fletcher-Janzen, E., & De Pry, R. L. (2003). *Teaching social competence and character: An IEP planner with goals, objectives, and interventions*. Longmont, CO: Sopris West.

Wolery, M., Bailey, D. B. Jr., & Sugai, G. M. (1988). *Effective teaching: Principles and procedures of applied behavior analysis for exceptional students*. Boston, MA: Allyn & Bacon.

RANDALL L. DE PRY
Portland State University

See also Research in Special Education

DEPRESSION, CHILDHOOD AND ADOLESCENT

Depression is a mood (affective) disorder that affects approximately 2% of children and adolescents in the general population (Kashani et al., 1983). Once considered

exclusively the domain of psychiatry, depressive disorders can and should be considered by school personnel in identification, assessment, and treatment (Reynolds & Stark, 1987). Students with emotional or behavioral disorders (EBD) and learning disabilities (LD) may be particularly at risk for developing depression. For example, Maag and Behrens (1989a) found that about 21% of EBD and LD students experienced significant depressive symptomatology. However, an important distinction should be made between depressive symptomatology and the clinical disorder.

As a symptom, depression refers to sad affect and as such is a common experience of everyday life. As a syndrome or disorder, depression refers to a group of symptoms that go together. Sadness may be part of a larger set of problems that include the loss of interest in activities, feelings of worthlessness, sleep disturbances, changes in appetite, and others (Kazdin, 1987, p. 121).

These distinctions may explain part of the discrepancy and debate over the actual prevalence of depression among students with EBD and LD. For example, Maag and Reid (1994) found that 10% of students with LD experienced significant depressive symptomatology. However, only 2% of them obtained Beck Depression Inventory (BDI) scores that corresponded to levels of clinical depression. This prevalence estimate is the same that exists in the general population of youngsters. In their meta-analytic review, Maag and Reid (2006) concluded that, although students with LD have statistically greater depressive symptomatology than their nondisabled peers, the magnitude was most likely not great enough to place them in the clinical range for a depressive disorder.

Much less is known about depression in students with EBD than those with LD. This lack of data is anomalous because one of the five federal criteria for students being identified and served under the emotional disturbance category is "a general pervasive mood of unhappiness or depression" (U.S. Department of Education, 1999, p. 12422). On the other hand, it may be a fait accompli that students with EBD experience depression because it is one of the defining criteria.

One of the first studies examining depression among students with EBD was conducted by Cullinan, Schloss, and Epstein (1987). They found that students with EBD displayed greater depression scores than their nondisabled peers. However, depression was measured using a subscale of the Behavior Problem Checklist (BPC), which was not designed to specifically assess depression. Several years later, Maag and his colleagues examined depression among this population using instruments specific to depression in correctional settings and public schools using a variety of constructs and analyses including gender, age, and extreme scores (DiGangi, Behrens, & Maag, 1989; Maag & Behrens, 1989a, 1989b; Maag, Behrens, & DiGangi, 1992). They concluded that students with EBD obtained statistically higher depression and negative cognition scores than their nondisabled peers. Since that time, a smattering of studies have been conducted with results indicating students with EBD displayed mild but insignificant differences in depression as compared to their nondisabled peers (Allen-Meares, 1991; Stanley, Dai, & Nolan, 1997), the presence of depressive subtypes (Carmanico et al., 1998), and a greater number of externalizing versus internalizing comorbid disorders (Pellegrino, Singh, & Carmanico, 1999).

Characteristics of Childhood and Adolescent Depression

There are a variety of characteristics associated with childhood and adolescent depression including, but not limited to, low-self esteem, cognitive disturbances, deficient social skills, locus of control, substance abuse, familial stressors, and poor academic skills (e.g., Maag & Forness, 1991; Maag & Rutherford, 1987, 1988; Reynolds, 1985). Kazdin (1990; 2007) stated that three specific characteristics have received the most research: prevalence, gender, and age.

Prevalence

Most prevalence estimates address the severity of depressive symptoms as reported from rating scales. In the general population, estimates range from 1.3% to 7.3% with an acknowledged prevalence around 2% (Kazdin, 2007). In clinic samples (i.e., youngsters receiving inpatient or outpatient treatment for a psychiatric disorder), estimates of depressive disorders range between 10% to 20% (Kashani et al., 1983). Perhaps the greatest disparity in prevalence estimates involves samples of students with EBD and LD. Researchers have consistently found that students with EBD and LD obtained statistically significant higher depression scores than their nonhandicapped peers with prevalence estimates topping off at 21% (e.g., Maag & Behrens, 1989a; Maag et al., 1992; Maag & Reid, 2006). However, there is a difference between statistical and clinical significance. The prevalence of depression among students with EBD and LD when using cutoff scores reflecting clinical depression mirrors the general population at 2%. Some of the discrepancies in prevalence estimates result, in part, from the impact of gender and age.

Gender and Age Differences

Gender and age are related variables that are difficult to separate. Depression tends to be more prevalent among women than men (Kazdin, 2007). Gender differences typically do not surface until adolescence, when more females than males experience severe depressive symptomatology (Angold, Weissman, John, Wickramaratne, & Drusoff, 1991; Mezzich & Mezzich, 1979; Teri, 1982). Similar results were obtained by Maag and Behrens (1989a) with adolescent females 3 times more likely to report severe depressive symptomatology than their male counterparts. In general, except for very young children (aged 1 to 6), who have low rates of depression (Kashani, Cantwell, Shekim, & Reid, 1982; Kashani, Ray, & Carlson, 1984), age differences in both youngsters with and without disabilities tend to be mediated by gender (e.g., Fleming & Offord, 2007; Maag & Behrens, 1989a; Rutter, 1986).

Smucker, Craighead, Craighead, and Green (1986) found several age- and gender-related differences with respect to specific characteristics of depression. For adolescent males, acting-out behaviors were more highly correlated with overall depression scores than for adolescent females. These gender differences were not observed in children (grades 3 to 6). They also found that a generally dysphoric mood and a negative view of self correlated more highly with total depression scores for both preadolescent and adolescent females (grades 3 to 9) than for same-aged males.

Assessment of Depression

There are generally four ways to assess depression. The most robust method is for a licensed child psychologist or psychiatrist to render a diagnosis based on a clinical interview. Self-report rating scales such as the *Beck Depression Inventory* (BDI), *Children's Depression Inventory* (CDI), and *Reynolds Adolescent Depression Scale* (RADS) may be used in conjunction with a clinical interview but are also sometimes used in isolation to estimate prevalence (Maag & Forness, 1991; Maag & Reid, 2006). Rating scales completed by others (i.e., parents or teachers), such as the *Children's Depression Rating Scale* (CDRS) and *Depression and Anxiety in Youth Scale* (DAYS), are also commonly used. Less frequently used are peer report measures such as the *Peer Nomination Inventory for Depression* (PNID). These scales have been the subject of extensive reviews (e.g., Kazdin, 1987, 2007; Maag & Forness, 1991; Reynolds, 1985) and, therefore, are not reviewed again here. Rather, issues related to the use of ratings scales and the role of school personnel in early identification of depression are presented.

Issues in the Use of Rating Scales

Many prevalence estimates of depression (using general, clinical, and special education samples), including conclusions reached regarding gender and age differences, are based on scores obtained from rating scales either completed by the child or others that have flawed or inadequate psychometric properties. For example, high scores on the BDI may nevertheless only represent a normal scattering of depressive symptoms among nonclinical populations (Beck, Steer, & Garbin, 1988). CDI scores of children diagnosed as depressed by *DSM* criteria have not always differed from those of nonclinically diagnosed children (Saylor, Finch, Spirito, & Bennett, 1984). The DAYS has been touted as a good measure for depression among children because it is completed by children, teachers, and parents (Newcomer, Berenbaum, & Bryant, 1994). However, it is fairly new—compared to the BDI and CDI—and less is known about its psychometric properties and normative sample sizes have been small.

Another key methodological consideration is that empirically derived cutoff scores typically yield a high percentage of false positives and false negatives (Kazdin, 1987). False positives and negatives will be influenced by the sensitivity and specificity of an instrument (Reid & Maag, 1994). Sensitivity refers to the percentage of students who receive a statistically significant cutoff score on a depression measure and have also been diagnosed as depressed by a clinician (true positives). Specificity refers to the percentage of students that have not obtained a statistically significant cutoff score and also have not been diagnosed as depressed by a clinician (true negatives). Although youngsters who have been diagnosed as clinically depressed have scored higher on self-report measures than those without a diagnosis, results have not always been clinically or statistically significant (Kazdin, 1987; Maag & Reid, 1994). Furthermore, Saylor et al. (1984) found that the breadth of CDI scores for students diagnosed as clinically depressed was quite broad—ranging from 4 to 32.

Role of School Personnel in Early Identification

Educators should play a strategic role in the early identification of depression. Youngsters spend more time in school than in most other structured settings outside the home, and their most consistent and extensive contact is with educators. Furthermore, students' behaviors, interpersonal relationships, and academic performance— all important indicators of mood and the ability to cope—are subject to ongoing scrutiny in the classroom. Consequently, school personnel may be the first professionals to notice developing problems. Unfortunately, school personnel have not always possessed specific and accurate information about childhood and adolescent depression (Clarizio & Payette, 2007; Maag, Rutherford, & Parks, 1988; Peterson, Wonderlich, Reaven, & Mullins, 1987).

Reynolds (1996) developed a three-stage screening program to identify depression in students: (1) conducting large-group screening with self-report depression measures, (2) retesting children 3 to 6 weeks later who met cutoff score criteria for depression during Stage 1 screening, and (3) conducting individual clinical interviews with students who manifest clinical levels of depression at both Stage 1 and Stage 2 evaluations. The easy part of this process is conducting activities during Stages 1 and 2 that can be undertaken by classroom teachers. Retesting children during Stage 2 is important to weed out students who

experience a transient depressed mood during the initial screening or exaggerated their depressive symptomatology. Stage 3 is more problematic because it requires conducting individual clinical interviews by a licensed psychologist or psychiatrist. School psychologists who are state licensed may conduct these interviews. Otherwise, the school can only recommend to parents that they take their child to see a child psychologist or psychiatrist for further evaluation.

School-Based Interventions

More than 15 years ago, Reynolds and Stark (1987) began describing school-based intervention strategies to treat depression in children and adolescents and described difficulties in implementing them. First, treating depression should not be approached in a cavalier fashion. Depression is a serious mental disorder that may have life-threatening consequences. Second, clinically trained individuals, such as school psychologists, counselors, and social workers, should work collaboratively with teachers to provide consultation in the development and implementation of interventions. Third, prevention may be the best approach for treating depression in schools.

A variety of school-based interventions have been used to treat depression in children and adolescents. Behaviorally oriented social-skills training interventions emerged in the 1980s (e.g., Schloss, Schloss, & Harris, 1984). Activity scheduling—a process that involves the systematic planning of a child's daily activities—has been recommended to increase activity level and reduce time spent in negative ideation (Reynolds & Stark, 1987; Stark et al., 1996). Three components of self-control training have been used to successfully treat depression in youths: self-monitoring, self-evaluation, and self-reinforcement (e.g., Reynolds & Coats, 1986; Stark, Reynolds, & Kaslow, 1987). Finally, cognitive-behavioral interventions have received the most attention and offer the greatest nonpharmaceutical promise for treating childhood and adolescent depression (Maag & Swearer, 2006). In this section, the roles of school psychologists, school counselors, and special educators in treating depression is described.

Primary Role of School Psychologists and Counselors

School psychological and counseling services have evolved to the point of considerable compatibility (Murphy, DeEsch, & Strein, 1998). Training accreditation standards for both professions include skill development in the areas of assessment, consultation, and counseling and in facilitating the delivery of comprehensive services within a multidisciplinary team concept (Council for Accreditation of Counseling and Related Educational Programs, 1994; National Association of School Psychologists, 1994). In addition, school psychologists and counselors alike obtain licenses in their respective areas that permit them to conduct psychotherapy and receive third party reimbursement. They also have unique training and expertise that complement each other—especially when it comes to addressing the needs of students who display depressive symptomatology. School counselors have skills in small group counseling, large group developmental interventions, and vocational and career development. School psychologists possess expertise in applied behavior analysis, cognitive and personality assessment, individual therapy, and organizational consultation. Although there are some administrative, professional, and personal barriers, the partnership between both professionals greatly enhance outcomes for students with depression.

Nastasi, Varjas, Bernstein, and Pluymert (1997) described four levels of services across which school psychologists can be involved either directly or indirectly in developing mental health programs in schools:

1. *Prevention*: Helping a school choose a program for students to manage their feelings.
2. *Risk reduction*: Helping counselors target students whose parents suffer from depressive disorders and work with these students in a support group.
3. *Early intervention*: Helping preschool and elementary teachers recognize the signs and symptoms of depressive disorders.
4. *Treatment*: Delivering direct treatment to students experiencing a depressive disorder.

School counselors have been assuming an increased role as mental health therapists in schools (Lockhart & Keys, 1998). Nowhere is this role as important as it is in providing services for students who are depressed or experiencing depressive symptomatology. Evans, Van Velsor, and Schumacher (2002) described the role of school counselors in using cognitive behavioral interventions as that of active collaboration with the student. They described three classic levels of prevention using cognitive-behavioral interventions (CBI) that school counselors can undertake: primary, secondary, and tertiary.

Ancillary Role of Special Educators

Special educators are not trained, nor do they hold licenses to provide counseling services to students with disabilities. That is not to say, however, that they cannot play an important ancillary role because many have received training in various techniques associated with cognitive-behavioral interventions such as self-monitoring, cognitive strategy instruction, social skills training, and problem-solving training (Maag & Katsiyannis, 1996). It would be a relatively simple matter for school psychologists or counselors to modify these approaches and consult with special educators who would implement these techniques for treating students who are depressed (Maag & Swearer, 2006).

Conclusion

Clinical depression affects about 2% of children in the general population, including those identified by schools as EBD and LD. The prevalence of depression is similar for boys and girls, but increases for females when they reach adolescence. Boys typically display externalizing behaviors while girls manifest depression with internalizing symptoms. A variety of self and other report rating scales have been developed to assess depression. However, a diagnosis of depression should be made by a licensed child psychologist or psychiatrist using a clinical interview and perhaps including scores from depression rating scales. School-based treatments for depression have appeared in the literature for the past 15 years. The most common approaches are social skills training, self-management, and cognitive-behavioral interventions. School psychologists and counselors can coordinate and implement treatment with special educators providing ancillary support.

REFERENCES

Allen-Meares, P. (1991). A study of depressive characteristics in behaviorally disordered children and adolescents. *Children and Youth Services Review, 13*, 271–286.

Angold, A., Weissman, M. M., John, K., Wickramaratne, P., & Drusoff, B. (1991). The effects of age and sex on depression ratings in children and adolescents. *Journal of the American Academy of Child and Adolescent Psychiatry, 30*, 67–74.

Beck, A. T., Steer, R. A., & Garbin, M. G. (1988). Psychometric properties of the Beck Depression Inventory: Twenty-five years of evaluation. *Clinical Psychology Review, 8*, 77–100.

Carmanico, S. J., Erickson, M. T., Sing, N. N., Best, A. M., Sood, A. A., & Oswald, D. P. (1998). Diagnostic subgroups of depression in adolescents with emotional and behavioral disorders. *Journal of Emotional and Behavioral Disorders, 6*, 222–232.

Clarizio, H. F., & Payette, K. (2007). A survey of school psychologists' perspectives and practices with childhood depression. *Psychology in the Schools, 27*, 57–63.

Council for the Accreditation of Counseling and Related Educational Programs. (1994). *Accreditation procedures manual and application*. Alexandria, VA: Author.

Cullinan, D., Schloss, P. M., & Epstein, M. H. (1987). Relative prevalence and correlates of depressive characteristics among seriously emotionally disturbed and nonhandicapped students. *Behavioral Disorders, 12*, 90–98.

DiGangi, S. A., Behrens, J. T., & Maag, J. W. (1989). Dimensions of depression: Factors associated with hopelessness and suicidal intent among special populations. *Monograph in Behavioral Disorders, 12*, 47–53.

Evans, J. R., Van Velsor, P., & Schumacher, J. E. (2002). Addressing adolescent depression: A role for school counselors. *Professional School Counseling, 5*, 211–219.

Fleming, J. E., & Offord, D. R. (1990). Epidemiology of childhood depressive disorders: A critical review. *Journal of the American Academy of Child and Adolescent Psychiatry, 29*, 571–80.

Kashani, J. H., Cantwell, D. P., Shekim, W. O., & Reid, J. C. (1982). Major depressive disorder in children admitted to an inpatient community mental health center. *American Journal of Psychiatry, 139*, 671–672.

Kashani, J. H., McGee, R. O., Clarkson, S. E., Anderson, J. C., Walton, L. A., Williams, S.,...McKnew, D. H. (1983). Depression in a sample of 9-year old children. *Archives of General Psychiatry, 40*, 1217–1233.

Kashani, J. H., Ray, J. S., & Carlson, G. A. (1984). Depression and depression-like states in preschool-age children in a child development unit. *American Journal of Psychiatry, 141*, 1397–1402.

Kazdin, A. E. (1987). Assessment of childhood depression: Current issues and strategies. *Behavioral Assessment, 9*, 291–319.

Kazdin, A. E. (1990). Childhood depression. *Journal of Child Psychology and Psychiatry, 31*, 121–160.

Kazdin, A. E. (2007). Mediators and mechanisms of change in psychotherapy research. In S. Nolen-Hoeksema, T. D. Cannon, & T. Widiger, (Eds.). *Annual Review of Clinical Psychology, 3*, 1–27.

Lockhart, E. J., & Keys, S. G. (1998). The mental health counseling role of school counselors. *Professional School Counseling, 1*, 3–6.

Maag, J. W., & Behrens, J. T. (1989a). Depression and cognitive self-statements of learning disabled and seriously emotionally disturbed adolescents. *Journal of Special Education, 23*, 17–27.

Maag, J. W., & Behrens, J. T. (1989b). Epidemiologic data on SED and LD adolescents reporting extreme depressive symptomatology. *Behavioral Disorders, 15*, 21–27.

Maag, J. W., Behrens, J. T., & DiGangi, S. A. (1992). Dysfunctional cognitions associated with adolescent depression: Findings across special populations. *Exceptionality, 3*, 31–47.

Maag, J. W., & Forness, S. R. (1991). Depression in children and adolescents: Identification, assessment, and treatment. *Focus on Exceptional Children, 24*(1), 1–19.

Maag, J. W., & Katsiyannis, A. (1996). Counseling as a related service for students with emotional or behavioral disorders: Issues and recommendations. *Behavioral Disorders, 21*, 293–305.

Maag, J. W., & Reid, R. (1994). The phenomenology of depression among students with and without learning disabilities: More similar than different. *Learning Disabilities Research and Practice, 9*, 91–103.

Maag, J. W., & Reid, R. (2006). Depression among students with learning disabilities: Assessing the risk. *Journal of Learning Disabilities, 39*, 3–10.

Maag, J. W., & Rutherford, R. B. (1987). Behavioral and learning characteristics of childhood and adolescent depression: Implications for special educators. In S. Braaten, R. B. Rutherford Jr., & J. W. Maag (Eds.), *Programming for adolescents with behavioral disorders* (Vol. 3, pp. 55–70). Reston, VA: Council for Children with Behavioral Disorders.

Maag, J. W., & Rutherford, R. B. Jr. (1988). Review and synthesis of three components for identifying depressed students. In R. B. Rutherford Jr., C. M. Nelson, & S. R. Forness (Eds.), *Bases of severe behavioral disorders in children and youth* (pp. 205–230). San Diego, CA: College-Hill.

Maag, J. W., Rutherford, R. B. Jr., & Parks, B. T. (1988). Secondary school professionals' ability to identify depression in adolescents. *Adolescence, 23*, 73–82.

Maag, J. W., & Swearer, S. M. (2006). Cognitive-behavioral interventions for depression: Review and implications for school personnel. *Behavioral Disorders, 30*, 116–119.

Mezzich, A. C., & Mezzich, J. E. (1979). Symptomatology of depression in adolescence. *Journal of Personality Assessment, 43*, 267–275.

Murphy, J. P., DeEsch, J. B., & Strein, W. O. (1998). School counselors and school psychologists: Partners in student services. *Professional School Counseling, 2*, 85–87.

Nastasi, B. K., Varjas, K., Bernstein, R., & Pluymert, K. (1997). *Exemplary mental health programs: School psychologists as mental health service providers.* Bethesda, MD: National Association of School Psychologists.

National Association of School Psychologists. (1994). *Standards for training and credentialing in school psychology.* Washington, DC: Author.

Newcomer, P. L., Berenbaum, E. M., & Bryant, B. R. (1994). *Depression and anxiety in youth scale: Examiner's manual.* Austin, TX: PRO-ED.

Pellegrino, J. F., Singh, N. N., & Carmanico, S. J. (1999). Concordance among three diagnostic procedures for identifying depression in children and adolescence with EBD. *Journal of Emotional and Behavioral Disorders, 7*, 118–127.

Peterson, L., Wonderlich, S. A., Reaven, N. M., & Mullins, L. L. (1987). Adult educators' response to depression and stress in children. *Journal of Social and Clinical Psychology, 5*, 51–58.

Reid, R., & Maag, J. W. (1994). How many fidgets in a pretty much: A critique of behavior rating scales for identifying students with ADHD. *Journal of School Psychology, 32*, 339–354.

Reynolds, W. M. (1985). Depression in children and adolescence: Diagnosis, assessment, intervention strategies, and research. In T. R. Kratochwill (Ed.), *Advances in school psychology* (Vol. 4, pp. 133–189). Hillsdale, NJ: Erlbaum.

Reynolds, W. M. (1996). A model for screening and identification of depressed children and adolescents in school settings. *Professional School Psychology, 1*, 117–129.

Reynolds, W. M., & Coats, K. I. (1986). A comparison of cognitive-behavioral therapy and relaxation training for the treatment of depression in adolescents. *Journal of Consulting and Clinical Psychology, 54*, 653–660.

Reynolds, W. M., & Stark, K. D. (1987). School-based intervention strategies for the treatment of depression in children and adolescents. In S. G. Forman (Ed.), *School-based affective and social interventions* (pp. 69–88). New York, NY: Haworth.

Rutter, M. R. (1986). The developmental psychopathology of depression: Issues and perspectives. In M. R. Rutter, C. E. Izard, & P. B. Read (Eds.), *Depression in young people: Developmental and clinical perspectives* (pp. 3–30). New York, NY: Guilford Press.

Saylor, C. F., Finch, A. J., Jr., Spirito, A., & Bennett, B. (1984). The children's depression inventory: A systematic evaluation of psychometric properties. *Journal of Consulting and Clinical Psychology, 52*, 955–967.

Schloss, P. J., Schloss, C. N., & Harris, L. (1984). A multiple baseline analysis of an interpersonal skills training program for depressed youth. *Behavioral Disorders, 9,* 182–188.

Smucker, M. R., Craighead, W. E., Craighead, L. W., & Green, J. J. (1986). Normative and reliability data for the Children's Depression Inventory. *Journal of Abnormal Child Psychology, 14,* 25–39.

Stanley, P. D., Dia, Y., & Nolan, R. F. (1997). Differences in depression and self-esteem reported by learning disabled and behavior disordered middle school students. *Journal of Adolescence, 20,* 219–222.

Stark, K. D., Kendall, P. C., McCarthy, M., Staford, M., Barron, R., & Thomeer, M. (1996). *ACTION: A workbook for overcoming depression.* Ardmore, PA: Workbook.

Stark, K. D., Reynolds, W. M., & Kaslow, N. J. (1987). A comparison of the relative efficacy of self-control and behavior therapy for the reduction of depression in children. *Journal of Abnormal Child Psychology, 15,* 91–113.

Teri, L. (1982). The use of the Beck Depression Inventory with adolescents. *Journal of Abnormal Child Psychology, 10,* 277–282.

U.S. Department of Education. (1999). Assistance to states for the education of children with disabilities and the early intervention program for infants and toddlers. *Federal Register, 64*(48), CFR Parts 300 and 303.

JOHN W. MAAG
University of Nebraska–Lincoln

See also Emotional Disorders; Emotional Lability

DEPRIVATION (*See* Postinstitutionalized Child)

DEPRIVATION, BIONEURAL RESULTS OF

The term *deprivation* is usually used to mean the absence or reduction of normal sensory input to the nervous system. Its meaning is sometimes extended to include restriction or suppression of opportunities for normal motoric activities associated with exploration, play, and social intercourse. The bioneural results of deprivation have mostly been investigated through animal experiments.

The visual system has been studied extensively. Various changes reviewed by Vrensen and De Groot (1974) have been observed in the visual cortex of animals reared in the dark. Monocular deprivation has been shown to produce more salient changes than binocular; competition between the two sides seems to be a more important factor than deprivation per se. The changes are particularly marked, and largely irreversible, when deprivation occurs during a critical period of early life. The best-known examples are the protracted loss of vision through one eye in kittens (Wiesel & Hubel, 1965) and monkeys (Hubel,

Wiesel, & LeVay, 1976), resulting from a brief period of interference with that eye's function shortly after birth. Stimulation of the deprived eye no longer elicits normal activity in the visual area of the brain because this has become reorganized in favor of the other eye.

In the auditory system, complete suppression of input is impossible without destruction of both inner ears, since otherwise there is always some perception of the sounds produced in the animal's own body. Temporary restriction of auditory stimuli can be achieved by rearing in a sound-attenuated environment or by interfering with the external or middle ear structures that transmit sound to the inner ear. Both methods produce perturbations of the auditory function and neuronal alterations of brain stem auditory nuclei (Webster & Webster, 1979). Significant changes in the microscopic structure of the auditory cortex have been observed in mutant mice with hereditary deafness owed to inner ear degeneration (Périer et al., 1984). As in the visual system, there are critical or sensitive periods of development during which plasticity is greatest and the results of deprivation most evident (Eggermont, 1986).

Nonspecific reduction of sensory stimulation is achieved by rearing animals in standard or isolated laboratory conditions as opposed to environmental complexity. In these experiments, there is a reduction of the normal span of sensory experiences, motor activities, and social exchanges. Behavioral differences as well as differences in cerebral structures are observed. Both have been extensively reviewed by Walsch (1980, 1981a, 1981b).

In man, the counterpart of animal experiments on the visual system is functional amblyopia, a condition observed in some children who have suffered from unattended squinting or other conditions interfering with the vision of one eye. Even after correction of the pathological condition, the deprived eye may remain largely nonfunctional. Partial auditory deprivation is a frequent occurrence in small children as a result of serous otitis media. It seems to cause long-lasting learning difficulties, even after normal hearing has been restored. All degrees of hearing loss, from mild to profound, might affect the human auditory pathways and cortex, as shown in animals. These possible effects in man have been discussed by Ruben and Rapin (1980). Studies in language development indicate that infants possess a capacity for making phonetic distinctions that must, to persist, be confirmed by the corresponding sounds of language spoken in their environment. Some studies indicate that children with congenital or early-acquired hearing loss might lose this early competence (Serniclaes, D'Alimonte, & Alegria, 1984).

Examples of extreme multisensory and social deprivation in man are afforded by "wolf" children and exceptional cases such as that of Genie, a girl maintained in isolation for years by psychotic parents (Curtiss, 1977). The complexity of such cases as well as the lack of sufficient information about their early life make their interpretation difficult. Less severe but more frequent deprivation situations occur in hospitalism (Spitz, 1945) and in poorly stimulating familial background. It is probable, though yet unproven, that these have bioneural consequences in addition to the well-known psychological ones.

REFERENCES

Curtiss, S. (1977). *Genie, a psycholinguistic study of a modern day "wild child."* New York, NY: Academic Press.

Eggermont, J. (1986). Critical periods in auditory development. Proceedings of the Nijmegen Workshop. *Acta Otolaryngologica (Stockholm)* (Supplement *491*), 153–160.

Hubel, D. H., Wiesel, T. N., & LeVay, S. (1976). Functional architecture of area 17 in normal and monocularly deprived Macaque monkeys. *Cold Spring Harbor Symposium on Quantitative Biology, 40*, 581–589.

Périer, O., Alegria, J., Buyse, M., D'Alimonte, G., Gilson, D., & Serniclaes, W. (1984). Consequences of auditory deprivation in animals and humans. *Acta Otolaryngologica (Stockholm), 411*, 60–70.

Ruben, R. J., & Rapin, I. (1980). Plasticity of the developing auditory system. *Annals of Otology Rhinology and Laryngology, 89*, 303–311.

Serniclaes, W., D'Alimonte, G., & Alegria, J. (1984). Production and perception of French stops by moderately deaf subjects. *Speech Communication, 3*, 185–198.

Spitz, R. A. (1945). Hospitalism—An inquiry into the genesis of psychiatric conditions in early childhood. *Psychoanalytic Study of the Child, 1*, 53–74.

Vrensen, G., & De Groot, D. (1974). The effect of dark rearing and its recovery on synaptic terminals in the visual cortex of rabbits. A quantitative electron microscopic study. *Brain Research, 78*, 263–278.

Walsch, R. (1980). Effects of environmental complexity and deprivation on brain chemistry and physiology: A review. *International Journal of Neuroscience, 11*, 77–89.

Walsch, R. (1981a). Effects of environmental complexity and deprivation on brain anatomy and histology: A review. *International Journal of Neuroscience, 12*, 33–51.

Walsch, R. (1981b). Sensory environments, brain damage, and drugs: A review of interactions and mediating mechanisms. *International Journal of Neuroscience, 14*, 129–137.

Webster, D. B., & Webster, M. (1979). Effects of neonatal conductive hearing loss on brain stem auditory nuclei. *Annals of Otology Rhinology, & Laryngoly, 88*, 684–688.

Wiesel, T. N., & Hubel, D. H. (1965). Comparison of the effects of unilateral and bilateral eye closure on cortical unit responses in kittens. *Journal of Neurophysiology, 28*, 1029–1040.

OLIVIER PÉRIER
Université Libre de Bruxelles

Centre Comprendre et Parler, Belgium

See also Early Experience and Critical Periods; Genie; Language, Absence of; Language Delays

DEPRIVATION, EARLY AUDITORY

Early auditory deprivation occurs when auditory stimuli during early childhood are not sufficient for adequate development of the auditory system. Variations in quantity, quality, or timing of exposure can lead to atypical development (Ruben & Rapin, 1980). In general, the more severe or complete and early the deprivation, the more detrimental the effects (Ruben & Rapin, 1980). The implications of such deprivation are great in that early deprivation can have a long-term impact on an individual's ability to hear, produce, and understand speech sounds (Finitzo, Gunnarson, & Clark, 1990; Werner & VandenBos, 1993). In most cases, the auditory system is fully mature by age 10, so auditory deprivation that occurs before then is likely to have a greater detrimental effect (Werner & VandenBos, 1993). Premature infants are believed to be at exceptional risk for the detrimental effects of auditory deprivation because their auditory system is less developed at birth (Ruben & Rapin, 1980). A common source of early auditory deprivation is otitis media (Finitzo et al., 1990).

Characteristics

1. Poor differential hearing.
2. Decreased sensitivity to sound in the end of the range.
3. Difficulty localizing sound.

Early identification of hearing loss is imperative if the aim of treatment is the prevention of long-term impairment (Rubin, 1972). The early use of hearing aids may be especially important in aiding the development of the auditory system (Ruben & Rapin, 1980). Otitis media has been associated with subsequent hearing impairment, and prompt treatment is thus likely to be critical to facilitating the normal development of hearing (Ruben & Rapin, 1980; Sak & Ruben, 1981).

Rubin (1972) suggests the use of individualized treatment to maximize the utility of any hearing present, especially regarding the generation and understanding of verbal language. The participation of caretakers in such a program is a necessity. They often need to be taught how to communicate with their children in ways that facilitate the child's developing ability to communicate. Treatment should be sensitive to the difficulty that many parents may have in accepting their child's hearing deficit. Home visits by therapists are recommended (Rubin, 1972).

Children with a hearing loss that has a negative impact on their ability to learn should qualify for special education services. If hearing is not sufficient to allow for verbal communication, American Sign Language should be taught. Educators should remember that although a child may not be able to speak, it is important for others to communicate visually as well as auditorily to maximize the utility of whatever level of hearing they do have (Rubin, 1972).

Whenever possible, children with hearing difficulties should be seated near the teacher so that the child can hear and see the teacher clearly (Bess, Klee, & Culbertson, 1986). Because difficulty with sound discrimination is a characteristic of those with early auditory deprivation, efforts should be made to provide a quiet setting that is free of auditory distractions.

There is some evidence that early auditory deprivation leads to difficulties with language-related cognition (Neville & Lawson, 1987; Sak & Ruben, 1981). Thus, children with hearing difficulties may struggle with tasks such as spelling and auditory decoding. Although the evidence is inconsistent, some research suggests superiority in visual skills compared to non-hearing-impaired peers (Neville & Lawson, 1987; Sak & Ruben, 1981). It should be noted that there is some indication that these differences may be due, at least in part, to the early acquisition and use of visual language rather than to the effects of auditory deprivation (Neville & Lawson, 1987). Regardless of the cause for these differences, results suggest the importance of incorporating visual modalities into instruction when working with this population.

It is believed that early auditory deprivation leads to atypical neuronal development in areas pertaining to hearing (Ruben & Rapin, 1980). Currently, there is no treatment that can repair the irregularities in development. However, the interventions just mentioned can minimize the degree of functional impairment.

A goal for future research is to continue to test the generalizability of animal studies (Rubin, 1972). In addition, future research should attempt to clarify whether the cognitive differences in those with hearing impairment are due to the effects of deprivation or the result of visual language use.

REFERENCES

Bess, F. H., Klee, T., & Culbertson, J. L. (1986). Identification, assessment, and management of children with unilateral sensorineural hearing loss. *Ear and Hearing*, 7(1), 43–51.

Finitzo, T., Gunnarson, A. D., & Clark, J. L. (1990). Auditory deprivation and early conductive hearing loss from otitis media. *Topical Language Disorders*, 11(1), 29–42.

Neville, H. H., & Lawson, D. (1987). Attention to central and peripheral visual space in a movement detection task: III. Separate effects of auditory deprivation and acquisition of a visual language. *Brain Research*, 405, 284–294.

Ruben, R. J., & Rapin, I. (1980). Plasticity of the developing auditory system. *Annals of Otology, Rhinology, and Laryngology*, 89, 303–311.

Rubin, M. (1972). Auditory deprivation in infants. *Journal of Communication Disorders*, 5, 195–204.

Sak, R. J., & Ruben, R. J. (1981). Recurrent ear effusion in childhood: Implications of temporary auditory deprivation for language and learning. *Annals of Otology, Rhinology, and Laryngology*, 90, 546–551.

Werner, L. A., & VandenBos, G. R. (1993). Developmental psychoacoustics: What infants and children hear. *Hospital and Community Psychiatry*, 44(7), 624–626.

MELANIE E. BALLATORE
University of Texas at Austin

DEPRIVATION, EARLY VISUAL

Early visual stimulation is critical to the normal development of the visual system. Early visual deprivation occurs when exposure to visual stimuli is limited in amount or intensity during initial stages of development (Jackson & Ellis, 1971; Perier, 2000). The outcome of early visual deprivation varies according to a variety of factors. Deprivation that is monocular and more severe and that occurs early in development generally leads to greater impairment (Boothe, Dobson, & Teller, 1985; Hyvarinen & Hyvarinen, 1982). Length of deprivation also has an impact on the amount of impairment, and longer periods of deprivation lead to more detrimental outcomes (Boothe et al., 1985). Additionally, when the previous factors are present, the duration of deprivation needed to result in negative consequences is lessened (Boothe et al., 1985).

Research indicates that specific forms of deprivation lead to differential effects on the visual pathways (Boothe et al., 1985). In cases of long-term monocular deprivation, change in ocular dominance appears to be mirrored in brain structure (Boothe et al., 1985). When early visual deprivation is long term, it appears that other sensory modalities utilize multimodal neurons, limiting those available to the visual modality on recovery of visual input (Boothe et al., 1985; Perier, 2000). There is evidence that in cases of congenital blindness, there is some compensatory development of the auditory system (Roder, Rosler, & Neville, 1999).

Characteristics

1. Impaired spatial resolution.
2. Poor visual acquity.
3. In cases of monocular visual deprivation, poor binocular vision.

Long-term, correctable, binocular visual deprivation is fairly rare, most commonly occurring as a result of cataracts. Some form of congenital cataracts occurs in approximately 1 out of every 250 births (Potter, 1993). In cases of short-term monocular deprivation, it is necessary not only to reinstate vision but also to allow the previously impaired eye to gain strength by temporarily limiting the use of the unaffected eye by using an eye patch. Simple reinstatement of vision in the deprived eye has little or no effect on negative symptoms. When cataracts are present, treatment generally consists of surgical removal followed by optical correction devices such as glasses or contact lenses (Boothe et al., 1985).

Children experiencing the negative effects of early visual deprivation may qualify for special education services depending on the extent of visual impairment. Possible accommodations include instruction in braille and use of large type. To maximize the use of any vision present, the child should be seated near the instructor. Whenever possible, instruction should incorporate multiple sensory modalities, especially auditory.

The most common outcome of monocular deprivation is amblyopia, or lazy eye, which occurs when one eye is deprived of visual input relative to the other eye (Boothe et al., 1985). In such cases both spatial resolution and binocular function are negatively affected (Boothe et al., 1985). When deprivation is not long term and treatment follows, prognosis is good (Boothe et al., 1985). In cases of long-term binocular deprivation, prognosis is poor, resulting in a general lack of visual responsiveness (Boothe et al., 1985).

Prognosis following treatment for cataracts is dependent on several factors (Boothe et al., 1985). For cataracts that are thick, present at birth, and cover the entire eye, prognosis is relatively poor (Boothe et al., 1985). In cases where cataracts are present at birth, immediacy of treatment is critical to maximizing vision (Boothe et al., 1985; Potter, 1993). Even when treatment is fairly successful, visual acquity is generally impaired (Boothe et al., 1985; Potter, 1993).

For ethical reasons, early visual deprivation cannot be induced in human subjects. Therefore, the bulk of research into early visual deprivation is done with animals. A goal for research is work that seeks to confirm the generalizability of such research to humans.

REFERENCES

Boothe, R. G., Dobson, V., & Teller, D. Y. (1985). Postnatal development of vision in human and nonhuman primates. *Annual Review of Neuroscience, 8,* 495–545.

Hyvarinen, J., & Hyvarinen, L. (1982). Higher functions and plasticity in visual pathways. *Acta Opthalmologica, 157*(Suppl.), 9–17.

Jackson, C. W. Jr., & Ellis, R. (1971). Sensory deprivation as a field of study. *Nursing Research, 20*(1), 46–54.

Perier, O. (2000). Deprivation, bioneural results of. In C. R. Reynolds & E. Fletcher-Janzen (Eds.), *Encyclopedia of special education: A reference for the education of the handicapped and other exceptional children and adults* (2nd ed., Vol. 1, pp. 558–559). New York, NY: Wiley.

Potter, W. S. (1993). Pediatric cataracts. *Pediatric Opthamology, 40*(4), 841–853.

Roder, B., Rosler, F., & Neville, H. J. (1999). Effects of inter-stimulus interval on auditory event-related potentials in congenitally blind and normally sighted humans. *Neuroscience Letters, 264,* 53–56.

MELANIE E. BALLATORE
University of Texas at Austin

DERMATITIS, ATOPIC

Atopic dermatitis is a skin disorder that occurs in adults and children. The skin is hypersensitive and reacts with inflammation. The skin can become extremely itchy, and if the condition becomes chronic, the skin may become scaly and thick.

Atopic dermatitis has a 12% prevalence rate in the United States, and 60% of the patients will show signs of this condition by the end of their first year; 90% of all the patients will show signs by the end of their fifth year (Ghidorzi, 2001). The condition occurs equally in males and females, but females do have more severe symptoms (Ghidorzi, 2001). A genetic predisposition in combination with other environmental influences seems to cause the condition. By adulthood, 70% of all patients report less severe symptoms or even disappearance of the symptoms (DermIS, 2001).

Characteristics

1. An infant is brought to the physician with a rash that seems to be resistant to over-the-counter medications.

2. The child's rash causes extreme itching but is not accompanied by fever or other symptoms.

3. The skin where the rash is present is dry and forms blisters that may ooze—leading to crusting when the ooze dries.

4. Commonly affected areas in infants and children are cheeks, trunk (diaper rash), elbows, and knees. Commonly affected areas in adults are face, neck, elbows, knees, and genital areas.

5. Skin condition is judged according to appearance:
   • Acute. Eczema is blistered and shows inflammation.

- Subacute. Skin appears to be scaling and leathery (lichenification).
- Chronic. Skin may appear lighter or darker due to pigmentation change (Ghidorzi, 2001).

6. Complications include secondary skin infections and scaring (Atopic dermatitis, 2002).

Treatment should be supervised by a physician to provide the necessary differential diagnosis as well as a treatment plan to reduce the associated symptoms of this often-chronic condition. Treatment varies according to the different stages (acute, subacute, and chronic) as well as the causes of the disorder, which can include food allergies and environmental factors such as wool and lanolin (Atopic dermatitis, 2002). To prevent irritation to the skin, bathing and the use of cosmetics and soaps should be avoided. Common treatments include anti-itch lotions as well as topical steroids under more severe circumstances. Flare-ups can be caused by change in climate, sweating, tight and irritating clothing (especially wool), exposure to tobacco smoke, and emotional stress (Ghidorzi, 2001).

To address the issues related to emotional stress and depression that often accompany a chronic condition, psychological guidance and support groups are recommended. These issues should be considered by all professionals involved in the child's daily life in school and at home. By reducing emotional stress, understanding of the condition by the patient and all involved will decrease the possibility of flare-ups and therefore enable the child to live life with the least amount of disturbances. Although atopic dermatitis cannot be cured, with appropriate treatment the causes of flare-ups can be avoided and symptoms can be managed (Greene, 2001). The majority of patients will experience a fading of their symptoms by the time they reach adulthood.

REFERENCES

Atopic dermatitis. (2002). *Mosby's medical, nursing, and allied health dictionary* (6th ed., p. 154). St. Louis, MO: Harcourt Health Sciences.

DermIS. (2001). *Einleitende Informationen zur Neurodermitis.* Retrieved from http://dermis.net/dermisroot/en/home/index.htm

Ghidorzi, A. J. (2001, June 28). Atopic dermatitis. *eMedicine Journal, 2*(6). Retrieved from http://www.emedecine.com/emerg/topic130.html

Greene, A. R. (2001). *Disease—Atopic dermatitis.* Retrieved from www.medseek.com

MONIKA HANNAN
University of Northern Colorado

DERMATITIS, CONTACT

Contact dermatitis is an inflammation of the skin that follows contact with various irritants and allergic substances (Contact dermatitis, 2002). Contact dermatitis is differentiated according to the causes of the skin condition. The skin reacts with itching, tenderness, blistering, and swelling.

Ninety percent of all workers' compensation claims in the United States are caused by contact dermatitis (Michael, 2001). Twenty percent of all women have contact dermatitis at least once during their lifetime with the highest occurrence after childbirth. Women are twice as likely to get contact dermatitis, and 2% of the population has dermatitis affecting their hands at any given time. Children of affected individuals are 60% more likely to react positively when patch tests are administered (Michael, 2001). Overall, Caucasians tend to have a greater likelihood of developing contact dermatitis, but it might be harder to detect in other ethnic groups.

Characteristics

1. Itching of affected areas.
2. Redness or inflammation and swelling of skin.
3. Skin reacting to exposure with rash or blisters, which in turn might ooze or form a crust.
4. Skin reaction occurring after exposure to allergic substances.

Source: Greene, 2001.

Contact dermatitis is divided into four types:

1. Allergic contact dermatitis is a reaction to specific allergens. Such reactions can change depending on genetic predisposition, intensity, and duration of contact. There is a wide range of possible allergens that can include plants (e.g., poison ivy), metals found in jewelry (e.g., nickel sulfate), household cleaners, medications, and other chemicals (Michael, 2001).

2. Irritant contact dermatitis is a reaction to mild or strong irritants. Among the irritants are acids, alkalis, solvents, and plants. The exposed area, depending on the irritant, should be thoroughly flushed with water.

3. Photodermatitis is a reaction to exposure to the sun. Certain medications and foods seem to predispose some individuals to these reactions. Among the medications implicated are tetracycline and sulfa drugs, and among the foods are citrus fruits, parsnip, and celery (Michael, 2001).

4. Contact urticaria is an extreme reaction to different allergens. Such allergens can be found in food or in

latex. Anaphylactic shock has been reported in some cases (Michael, 2001).

Treatment is dependent on the cause of the contact dermatitis. Treatment could include flushing with water, applying soothing and wet dressings, or using medication and lotions (Greene, 2001). Symptoms related to acute discomfort (anxiety, sleeplessness, lack of concentration, irritability, and mood swings) should be considered by all professionals involved in the child's daily life. The impact of the symptoms on the child's mental health depends on the severity of the dermatitis and can influence a child's ability to focus and concentrate on curricular activities. It might be necessary to examine whether the child is exposed to irritants in her or his school environment. For example, schedule changes might be necessary following a diagnosis of photo dermatitis so that the child's exposure to sun during recess is reduced.

The proper diagnosis by a physician can help the individual by identifying environmental allergens. The primary concern then must be avoidance of the allergen (Dermatitis and eczema, 1999). Following the removal of the allergen from the child's environment, the healing process may take up to 3 weeks.

Proper education by the physician of the child, and his or her parents, about the treatment of dermatitis is essential. This education can help the patient to avoid specific substances that have been shown to cause symptoms. Equipped with the appropriate knowledge, the child should be able to enjoy life to the fullest extent possible.

REFERENCES

Contact dermatitis. (2002). *Mosby's medical, nursing, and allied health dictionary* (6th ed., pp. 421–422). St. Louis, MO: Harcourt Health Sciences.

Dermatitis and eczema. (1999). *Harvard Medical School family health guide* (pp. 549–550). New York, NY: Simon & Schuster.

Greene, A. R. (2001). *Disease—Contact dermatitis*. Retrieved from www.medseek.com

Michael, J. A. (2001, November 15). Contact dermatitis. *eMedicine Journal, 2*(11). Retrieved from www.medseek.com

MONIKA HANNAN
University of Northern Colorado

DERMATOMYOSITIS

Dermatomyositis is a rheumatological disorder that involves multiple systems including skeletal muscle, skin, the gastrointestinal tract, and the central nervous system. Irregular skin lesions and muscle inflammation are among the most common clinical signs; however, patients may have arthralgias, arthritis, or cardiopulmonary dysfunction. Onset of dermatomyositis usually occurs in school-age children between ages 8 and 9 and rarely occurs before the age of 2 years. Dermatomyositis malignancies occur in 20% of patients and more often in adults. However, other complications such as calcinosis occurs in approximately 20% to 50% of childhood cases.

Incidence of juvenile dermatomyositis has been previously estimated as 4 in 1,000,000 annually (Cawkwell, 2000). Although the etiology of dermatomyositis is unknown, involvement of cellular immune mechanisms is suspected.

Characteristics

1. Muscle weakness and tenderness, surface skin rash, and constitutional symptoms are common. Arthritis can occur, and gastrointestinal vasculitis is a potentially fatal complication.
2. Muscle atrophy and calcinosis may be severe long-term sequelae of muscle inflammation.
3. Onset usually occurs between ages 8 and 9.
4. Occlusive vasculities are the most prominent lesions found in children.
5. Twenty to 50% of childhood cases have calcinosis.
6. The disorder often involves severe muscle weakness, atrophy, contracture. Involvement of palatorespiratory muscles may lead to serious respiratory difficulties and death.
7. Cardiac complications have also been reported.

The prevalence of dermatomyositis is unknown; however, it is less common than other rheumatological diseases, such as rheumatoid arthritis, systemic lupus erythematosus, or Henoch-Schonlein purpura.

Treatment has changed dramatically in recent years with more aggressive management becoming more prevalent. However, little substantive research has been published on therapeutics (Cawkwell, 2000). Available treatments usually include systemic corticosteroids to suppress clinical symptoms with or without an immunosuppressive agent (Callen, 2000). Intravenous immunoglobulin therapy may be used to boost the immune system. Physical therapy is imperative to preserve and increase muscle strength and to prevent crippling contractures or deformities. Hygienic skin maintenance also is imperative. In cases where palatorespiratory muscles are involved, management of respiratory function is maintained with constant care and use of respiratory equipment.

Special education services may be required in the form of accommodation due to the long-term effect of chronic illness on school achievement. Many of these children will qualify for services under the classification of Other Health Impairment as a result of their medical condition.

Early treatment intervention can help modify the progression of dermatomyositis. If treated early, symptoms may subside for a number of years. The prognosis for treated children is good; however, the prognosis for untreated patients is poor, and complications may lead to death. It is estimated that approximately 40% will die from complications of dermatomyositis. Research continues to focus on outcome and disease activity markers, as well as on further delineation of the role of genetics, environment, and immunity in the pathogenesis and course of the juvenile idiopathic inflammatory myopathies (Cawkwell, 2000). New understanding of the pathobiology of the disease should lead to improved, less toxic treatments (Laxer & Feldman, 1997).

REFERENCES

Callen, J. P. (2000). Dermatomyositis. *Lancet, 355*(9197), 53–57.

Cawkwell, G. M. (2000). Inflammatory myositis in children, including differential diagnosis. *Current Opinion in Rheumatology, 12*, 430–434.

Laxer, R. M., & Feldman, B. M. (1997). General and local scleroderma in children and dermatomyositis and associated syndromes. *Current Opinion in Rheumatology, 9*, 458–464.

VIRDETTE L. BRUMM
Children's Hospital Los Angeles
Keck/USC School of Medicine

DE SANCTIS-CACCHIONE SYNDROME

De Sanctis-Cacchione (DSC) syndrome is a very rare, more severe variant of xeroderma pigmentosum (XP) that also includes mental retardation, numerous neurological abnormalities, dwarfism, and hypogonadism.

Xeroderma pigmentosum (XP) is itself uncommon, with an incidence of only 1 in 250,000 in the United States, and a somewhat higher rate in Japan (1 in 40,000). However, cases have been found worldwide (e.g., Lincheta, Balea, Simón, & Otano, 1998; Niederauer, Bohnert, Altmeyer, & Jung, 1992). Impaired intelligence with one or a few neurological features is seen in about 20% of the number of total XP cases (Buyse, 1990). These cases often display hyporeflexia, impaired intelligence, and progressive hearing loss. DSC patients, however, make up an even more severely affected subgroup of these, displaying intellectual impairment, numerous neurological abnormalities, and stunted physical growth and sexual development (Jones, 1997).

Characteristics

1. XP syndrome, including ultraviolet photosensitivity of exposed skin and eye tissue, leading to increased cancer risk.
2. Mental retardation, including progressive cognitive deterioration.
3. Progressive sensorineural hearing loss.
4. Dwarfism, including microcephaly.
5. Hypogonadism, leading to delayed sexual development.
6. Neurological abnormalities including hyporeflexia, areflexia, ataxia, spasticity, choreoathetosis, brain atrophy, abnormal electroencephalograms (EEGs), and electromyograms (EMGs).

DSC patients belong to either Group A or D of about 10 complementation groups of XP that vary in severity (Buyse, 1990). The XP-related skin and ocular features reflect the cellular vulnerability to ultraviolet radiation due to defective DNS repair mechanisms. Photosensitivity of exposed skin leads to increased freckling, blistering, poikiloderma, and other skin anomalies, as well as a predisposition to develop neoplasia of both the skin and conjunctivas. Heightened photosensitivity as well as increased freckling can be seen in the first year of life, with most cases showing these signs by age 5. Photophobia can be seen in the neonate. As progressive damage of the eyes occurs, corneal opacities, conjunctivitis, keratitis, ectropion, and entropion may occur. In DSC the onset of these skin and ocular features may be earlier and more severe than in XP without neurological abnormalities (Buyse, 1990).

In addition to the features of XP, in DSC there are many neurological abnormalities that are typically noted in childhood, although some may have onset as late as the second decade of life. Defects include mental retardation and further progressive dementia, progressive sensorineural deafness, stunted growth (e.g., microcephaly, dwarfism), delayed sexual development (gonadal hypoplasia likely due to hypothalamic dysfunction), hyporeflexia and areflexia, spasticity, and later the onset of ataxia and choreoathetoid movements. EEGs and EMGs are often abnormal, and there may be radiological evidence of neuronal loss leading to olivopontocerebellar and cerebral atrophy, as well as signs of demyelination and neuropathy (Kanda et al., 1990).

There is no known prevention, except genetic counseling. Heterozygote carriers are thought to be clinically normal, but there may be a heightened risk of skin cancer. Prenatal screening can be done via DNA repair studies of cultured amniotic fluid cells. Life span in XP is shortened, with a 70% probability of survival attained at age 40. The survival rate of DSC patients is similar to that for XP patients without neurological compromise and depends on the degree of exposure to UV light as well as on the level of cell repair deficiency (which varies by complementation subgroup). Death is typically due to complications of associated CNS dysfunction or more commonly lethal cancers.

Treatment of the XP-related features consists primarily of avoidance of ultraviolet radiation, which in some cases may lead to a total avoidance of exposure to sunlight and indoor ultraviolet sources (e.g., fluorescent or halogen lights). For some cases, an adaptive reversal in diurnal schedule is made. These patients have sometimes been called "children of the moon" because they live their normal waking hours during the night to maximize avoidance of exposure to sunlight (Xeroderma Pigmentosum Society, Inc., 2001). Home schooling may be the only option in these cases. However, in less severe cases, accommodations (e.g., protective sunscreen and clothing, staying indoors) may allow children to attend regular school. In more serious cases, dermatome shaving or dermabrasion and corneal transplants may be indicated. Oral retinoids to prevent new neoplasms have been studied. Avoidance of additional carcinogens, including cigarette smoke and other environmental sources, is also recommended.

Treatment of the neurological abnormalities will depend on the degree and kind. Special education services are available for associated mental retardation, developmental delays, or further deterioration of cognitive function. Hearing aids and occupational and physical therapies may be warranted, and children may qualify for special services under Other Health Impairment or Physical Disability.

REFERENCES

Buyse, M. L. (1990). *Birth defects encyclopedia*. Cambridge, MA: Blackwell Scientific.

Jones, K. L. (1997). *Smith's recognizable patterns of human malformation* (5th ed.). Philadelphia, PA: Saunders.

Kanda, T., Oda, M., Yonezawa, M., Tamagawa, K., Isa, F., Hanakago, R., & Tsukagoshi, H. (1990). Peripheral neuropathy in xeroderma pigmentosum. *Brain, 113*(Pt. 4), 1025–1044.

Lincheta, L., Balea, A., Simón, R., & Otano, E. (1998). Xeroderma pigmentosum syndrome of De Sanctis-Cacchione: Presentation of one case. *Cuban Review of Pediatrics, 70*(2), 113–116.

Niederauer, H., Bohnert, E., Altmeyer, P., & Jung, E. (1992). De Sanctis-Cacchione syndrome: Xeroderma pigmentosum with oligophrenia, short stature and neurologic disorders. *Hautarzt, 43*(1), 25–27.

Xeroderma Pigmentosum Society, Inc. (2001, May 1). Retrieved from http://www.xps.org

VICKY Y. SPRADLING
Austin State Hospital

DESENSITIZATION

Desensitization is a behavioral-based procedure developed by psychiatrist Joseph Wolpe, in 1958 (Gerald, 2001). Wolpe based his desensitization procedure on the classical conditioning methods developed in the 1920s by John Watson and Mary Cover Jones. The use of desensitization peaked in the 1960s and 1970s; nevertheless, it is still widely used. The decline has been attributed to more rapidly moving techniques, such as flooding and implosive therapy. Also, the shift toward cognitive-behavioral therapy is seen as a factor, however, less direct (McGlynn, Smitherman, & Gothard, 2004).

With desensitization, the therapist begins by asking the client questions regarding his or her anxieties or phobias. The client is then asked to monitor himself or herself to see how and when his or her anxieties or phobias are provoked. The therapist begins with relaxation techniques to allow the client to feel safe and calm. Once the client is relaxed the therapist asks the client to imagine neutral scenes that do not provoke anxiety and eventually to imagine scenes related to his or her anxiety or phobia. The client is relaxed again, and this process evolves in a hierarchy of anxiety-eliciting scenes. Throughout sessions, the therapist may model for the client and respond to the client with prompts or reinforcements to eventually fade out the anxiety-producing response. When the client can imagine the anxiety- or phobia-eliciting scene and remain calm, treatment ends. This form of treatment is efficient because it only requires the use of imagery of the anxiety-producing situation. The client in pure desensitization therapy is never brought face to face with the stimulus. However, the therapist may introduce the stimulus by way of in vivo desensitization or flooding (Gerald, 2001).

Desensitization is currently used for test anxiety (Powell, 2004), performance anxiety (Lazarus & Abramovitz, 2004), and has proven to be effective. Although these are its primary uses it has also been used effectively in treating anorexia nervosa, obsessions, compulsions, stuttering, body image disturbances, nightmares, and depression (Gerald, 2001).

REFERENCES

Gerald, C. (2001). Behavior therapy. In J. Martinez & A. Berterretche (Eds.), *Theory and practice of counseling and psychotherapy* (pp. 266–269). Belmont, CA: Wadsworth/Thomson.

Lazarus, A. A., & Abramovitz, A. (2004). A multimodal behavioral approach to performance anxiety. *Journal of Clinical Psychology, 60*, 831–840.

McGlynn, F. D., Smitherman, T. A., & Gothard, K. D. (2004). Comment on the status of systematic desensitization. *Behavior Modification, 28*, 194–205.

Powell, D. H. (2004). Behavioral treatment of debilitating test anxiety among medical students. *Journal of Clinical Psychology, 60*, 853–865.

SELINA RIVERA-LONGORIA
Texas A&M University

See also Behavior Therapy; Cognitive Behavior Therapy; Intervention

DES LAURIERS, AUSTIN M. (1917–1983)

Austin Des Lauriers earned his PhD in 1942 from the University of Montreal. From 1967 to 1970, he was professor and director of research and training at the University of Missouri Medical Center in Kansas City. He also served as professor and director of the Child Study Center at Ottawa, where he maintained a private practice.

Des Lauriers' work primarily centered on school psychology, autism, and schizophrenia. However, his views on functional literacy in business were featured in the quarterly publication *Learning in the Workplace* (Des Lauriers, 2007); and at the Working Conference on Vermont's Heritage for Teachers, his work contributed to the proceeding devoted to the development of teaching materials to be used in Vermont's classrooms (True, 1984).

Des Lauriers' research interests have focused on topics of childhood schizophrenia (Des Lauriers, 1962) and autism. He held that the autistic child's condition and behavior (in an arrested form) involve the same conflicts that a normal child experiences. His book, *Your Child Is Asleep* (Des Lauriers & Carlson, 1969), is considered a classic in the field.

REFERENCES

Des Lauriers, A. M. (1962). *The experience of reality in childhood schizophrenia.* New York, NY: I.V.P.

Des Lauriers, A. M. (2007). *Learning in the workplace.* Toronto, Canada: Toronto Frontier College.

Des Lauriers, A. M., & Carlson, C. F. (1969). *Your child is asleep: Early infantile autism.* Homewood, IL: Dorsey.

True, M. (1984). *Teaching Vermont's heritage.* Proceedings of the Working Conference on Vermont's Heritage for Teachers. Burlington: Vermont University.

RICK GONZALES
Texas A&M University
First edition

TAMARA J. MARTIN
University of Texas of the Permian Basin
Second edition

DES LAURIERS–CARLSON HYPOTHESIS

The Des Lauriers-Carlson hypothesis suggests that underarousal in individuals with autism spectrum disorders (ASD) leads to both echolalia and maladaptive behaviors (Rogers & Ozonoff, 2005). In 1969, Austin Des Lauriers and Carole Carlson suggested that the reticular activating system, the area of the brain stem that regulates arousal, was involved in the cause of early infantile autism. They proposed an imbalance in the relationship between the reticular activating system and the limbic system. The limbic system, which is involved in emotion, motivation, and reinforcement, is thought to be inhibited by the reticular activating system, causing an individual with ASD to be unable to make associations between behavior and positive or negative consequences, thus leading to echolalia and challenging behaviors (Des Lauriers & Carlson, 1969).

The etiology of ASD was once thought to be based on abnormal family relationships and early parenting experiences (Kanner, 1943). There have since been many theories that attempt to understand the complicated disorder (Zimmerman, 2008), including abnormal parenting and family relationships (a theory that has been discounted; Schopler, 2007), the social environment, and biochemical and genetic deficits as contributing factors (James, 2008; Pessah & Lein, 2008; Rossman & DiCicco-Bloom, 2008). Although it does appear that ASD is correlated to atypical sensory responses, what is apparent is that further empirical research is necessary to understand that link (O'Neill & Jones, 1997; Rogers & Ozonoff, 2005).

REFERENCES

Des Lauriers, A. M., & Carlson, C. F. (1969). *Your child is asleep: Early infantile autism.* Homewood, IL: Dorsey.

James, S. J. (2008). Oxidative stress and the metabolic pathology of autism. In A. Zimmerman (Ed.), *Autism: Current theories and evidence* (pp. 245–268). New York, NY: Humana Press.

Kanner, L. (1943). Autistic disturbances of affective contact. *Nervous Child, 2*, 217–250.

O'Neill, M., & Jones, R. S. P. (1997). Sensory perceptual abnormalities in autism: A case for more research. *Journal of Autism and Developmental Disorders, 27*(3), 283–293.

Pessah, I. N., & Lein, P. J. (2008). Evidence for environmental susceptibility in autism: What we need to know about gene x environmental interactions. In A. Zimmerman (Ed.), *Autism: Current theories and evidence* (pp. 409–428). New York, NY: Humana Press.

Rogers, S. J., & Ozonoff, S. (2005). Annotation: What do we know about sensory dysfunction in autism? A critical review of the empirical evidence. *Journal of Child Psychology and Psychiatry, 46*, 1255–1268.

Rossman, I. T., & DiCicco-Bloom, E. (2008). ENGRAILED2 and cerebellar development in the pathogenesis of autism spectrum disorders. In A. Zimmerman (Ed.), *Autism: Current theories and evidence* (pp. 3–40). New York, NY: Humana Press.

Schopler, E. (2007). *Neurobiological correlates of autism*. Reston, VA: ERIC Publications. (ERIC Clearinghouse No. EC300540)

Zimmerman, A. W. Preface. In A. Zimmerman (Ed.), *Autism: Current theories and evidence* (pp. v–ix). New York, NY: Humana Press, 2008.

STEVEN GUMERMAN
Temple University

LESLIE C. NEELY
Texas A&M University
Fourth edition

See also Autism

DESPERT, JULIETTE L. (1892–1982)

Juliette L. Despert, MD, child psychiatrist and researcher, received her education in her native France and in the United States. During her many years as a practicing psychiatrist, she contributed numerous articles to professional journals and published over half a dozen books, including *The Emotionally Disturbed Child: An Inquiry into Family Patterns* (Despert, 1970), *Schizophrenia in Childhood, Children of Divorce* (Despert, 1953), and *Schizophrenia in Childhood* (Despert, 1968) and developed the Despert Fables.

REFERENCES

Despert, J. L. (1953). *Children of divorce*. New York, NY: Doubleday.

Despert, J. L. (1968). *Schizophrenia in childhood*. New York, NY: Brunner.

Despert, J. L. (1970). *The emotionally disturbed child: An inquiry into family patterns*. New York, NY: Doubleday.

PAUL IRVINE
Katonah, New York

DESTRUCTIVE BEHAVIORS

To specify all acts in which persons engage that could be considered destructive is impossible; the topography of various destructive behaviors is at least as diverse as the people who exhibit them. A number of factors mitigate against a universally acceptable definition of destructive behaviors and are generally accounted for in operational definitions of such acts. There are at least three elements that should be implicitly or explicitly incorporated into operational definitions of destructive behaviors. One element is that of intentionality. For example, a child who accidentally breaks a dish is not generally considered destructive, but one who deliberately breaks a dish is considered destructive. Second, characteristics of the behavior itself (e.g., intensity, frequency) play a definitional role. For instance, children who occasionally bite their fingernails are not considered to be self-destructive, while those who often bite their hands until they bleed generally are considered self-destructive. Third, situational factors influence definitions. Persons who intentionally break a glass in a restaurant are considered destructive; in contrast, in some wedding ceremonies the intentional breaking of a glass is a socially sanctioned event. Much has been asserted in recent years that society has redefined destructive behavior in a more innocuous fashion: a statement about society's increasing tolerance for deviant behaviors (Moynihan, 1994).

A multitude of treatment programs that have successfully reduced various types of destructive behaviors have been reported. These programs have ranged in scope from large district-wide programs to reduce vandalism to interventions that have reduced the destructive behavior of a single individual. Likewise, the programs have varied a great deal according to the procedures used. As in the case with selecting any procedure to reduce behavior, a host of ethical, moral, legal, empirical, and practical issues must be attended to (see Foxx, 1982; Polsgrove, 1983; Repp. 1983). In the following paragraphs, effective programs for reducing various destructive behaviors are briefly discussed in approximate order of increasing intrusiveness. It should be stressed, however, that ineffective programs, regardless of their level of intrusiveness, should never be perpetuated.

There have been many examples of positively based programs to reduce destructive behaviors. An interesting large-scale program to reduce acts of vandalism was reported by Mayer, Butterworth, Nefpaktitis, and Sulzer-Azaroff (1983). Selected teachers in 18 schools participated in workshops and consultation sessions. Over the three-year study, the teachers significantly increased their rates of praise. Acts of vandalism were significantly reduced and decreases in other disruptive and destructive student behaviors were also observed. Russo, Cataldo, and Cushing (1981) reported that positively reinforcing compliance resulted in decreased acts of self-destruction among three children, although no contingencies were in effect for the self-destructive behaviors. Using a DRO procedure (reinforcement delivered for nonoccurrence of behavior), Frankel, Moss, Schofield, and Simmons (1976) eliminated aggressive and self-destructive acts.

Extinction combined with positive reinforcement was used by Martin and Treffry (1970) to eliminate poor posture and self-destructive behaviors in a 16-year-old partially paralyzed mentally retarded girl with cerebral palsy. She was positioned in such a manner that if she slouched she was not visible to the persons administering the reinforcers. If she was engaging in self-destructive behaviors, she was also not reinforced.

A variety of destructive behaviors exhibited by five mentally retarded boys were reduced by a nonexclusionary timeout procedure (Foxx & Shapiro, 1978). A number of advantages are associated with this technique compared with other forms of timeout procedures.

An overcorrection procedure (a punishment technique involving the correction of the undesirable behavior followed by practicing the desirable behavior) was used by Foxx and Azrin (1972) to eliminate the destructive behavior of a profoundly retarded adult female. Other punishment procedures (e.g., contingent electric shock, aromatic ammonia, citric acid) have also been used to decrease destructive behaviors.

Irrespective of the particular type of destructive behavior, these responses merit our best professional interventions. A variety of treatments (in addition to the ones mentioned here) have proven successful, but careful attention to aspects of individual cases is essential.

REFERENCES

Foxx, R. M. (1982). *Decreasing behaviors of severely retarded and autistic persons*. Champaign, IL: Research Press.

Foxx, R. M., & Azrin, N. H. (1972). Restitution: A method of eliminating aggressive-disruptive behavior of retarded and brain damaged patients. *Behavior Research and Therapy, 10,* 15–27.

Foxx, R. M., & Shapiro, S. T. (1978). The timeout ribbon: A nonexclusionary timeout procedure. *Journal of Applied Behavior Analysis, 11,* 125–136.

Frankel, F., Moss, D., Schofield, S., & Simmons, J. Q. (1976). Use of differential reinforcement to suppress self-injurious and aggressive behavior. *Psychological Reports, 39,* 843–849.

Martin, G. L., & Treffry, D. (1970). Treating self-destruction and developing self-care skills with a severely retarded girl: A case study. *Psychological Aspects of Disability, 17,* 125–131.

Mayer, G. R., Butterworth, T., Nafpaktitis, M., & Sulzer-Azaroff, B. (1983). Preventing school vandalism and improving discipline: A three-year study. *Journal of Applied Behavior Analysis, 16,* 355–369.

Moynihan, P. (1994). Defining deviancy down: How we've become accustomed to alarming levels of crime and destructive behavior. *American Educator, 17,* 10–18.

Polsgrove, L. (Ed.). (1983). Aversive control in the classroom. *Exceptional Education Quarterly, 3*(4).

Repp, A. C. (1983). *Teaching the mentally retarded*. Englewood Cliffs, NJ: Prentice Hall.

Russo, D. C., Cataldo, M. F., & Cushing, P. J. (1981). Compliance training and behavioral covariation in the treatment of multiple behavior problems. *Journal of Applied Behavior Analysis, 14,* 209–222.

JAMES P. KROUSE
Clarion University of Pennsylvania

See also Acting Out; Applied Behavior Analysis; Emotional Disorders; Reality Therapy

DETROIT TESTS OF LEARNING APTITUDE, FOURTH EDITION

The Detroit Tests of Learning Aptitude, Fourth Edition (DTLA-4; Hammill, 1998) is intended for use with children and adolescents ages 6 to 0 to 17 to 0. There is also an adult version for ages 16 to 0 through 79 to 0 and a primary version for children age 3 to 0 to 9 to 11. It was designed to (a) measure both general intelligence and discrete ability areas; (b) show the effects of language, attention, and motor abilities on test performance; (c) allow interpretation in light of current theories of intellect.

The DTLA-4 consists of 10 subtests, which take between 40 minutes and 2 hours to administer. Administration time varies by individual as none of the subtests are timed. To administer the test, an examiner's manual, two color picture books for the subtests, profile/summary forms, examiner's record booklets, response forms, story sequence chips, and design sequence cubes are needed. Percentiles, standard scores, and age equivalents can be derived from this test. A computerized scoring program is available to convert raw scores to the three types of scores, as well as to calculate intra-ability differences.

The 10 subtests of the DTLA-4 include Word Opposites, Design Sequences, Sentence Imitation, Reversed Letters, Story Construction, Design Reproduction, Basic Information, Symbolic Relations, Word Sequences, and Story Sequences. The Picture Fragments subtest found in previous editions has been removed to shorten the length of administration. These subtests measure a variety of specific cognitive abilities, including vocabulary, auditory and visual memory, and visual problem solving. Scoring of the subtests results in scaled scores ($M = 10$; $SD = 3$), which are then compiled into 16 composite scores ($M = 100$; $SD = 15$), including the Overall Composite, Optimal Level Composite, Domain Composites, and Theoretical Composites. The Overall Composite is formed from the scaled scores of all of the subtests in the battery. The Optimal Level Composite is comprised from the four highest subtest scores, giving an estimate of the individual's potential, or highest level of performance possible when any inhibiting influences are disregarded. Domain Composites are given for language, attention, and manual dexterity, while Theoretical Composites allow for interpretation in terms of major theories proposed by Horn and Cattell, Jensen, DAS-II, and Wechsler.

The DTLA-4 was standardized on 1,350 students in 37 states, stratified by age. This sample was representative of the 1996 U.S. Census with respect to gender, race, ethnicity, urban/rural residence, family income, educational attainment of parents, and geographic distribution. With respect to reliability, test-retest studies range from .71 to .96 for the subtests while coefficients for the composites exceed .90. Internal consistency was shown to exceed .80 for the subtests and .90 for the composites. Scorer reliability coefficients were in the .90s for all tests. Several factor analyses have been completed regarding the validity of the DTLA-4 showing intercorrelation between the subtests, chronological age, and tests of academic achievement. Criterion-prediction validity has been examined through the comparison of the DTLA-4 with various aptitude tests, including the TONI3, WISC, KABC, PPVT, and WJPEB.

Test bias was considered throughout test construction. The effects of bias in terms of culture, race, and gender were controlled and minimized by the inclusion of minority and disabled groups within the normative sample. Internal consistency was seen throughout these subgroups. Differential item functioning analysis was used to reduce item bias and delta score values were used to identify potential bias.

This entry has been informed by the sources listed below.

REVIEWED IN:

Hammill, D. (1998). *Detroit Tests of Learning Aptitude-4*. Austin, TX: PRO-ED.

Plake, B. S., & Impara, J. C. (Eds.). (2001). *The fourteenth mental measurements yearbook*. Lincoln, NE: Buros Institute of Mental Measurements.

JOHN DUMONT
Fairleigh Dickinson Unviersity

JOHN O. WILLIS
Rivier College

KATHLEEN VIEZEL
JAMIE ZIBULSKY
Fairleigh Dickinson University

DEVELOPMENTAL APHASIA (See Childhood Aphasia; Language Disorders)

DEVELOPMENTAL APRAXIA

Developmental apraxia is a childhood disorder of sensory integration interfering with ability to plan and execute skilled or nonhabitual motor tasks in the absence of muscle weakness or paralysis (Davis, Jakielski, & Marquardt, 1998; Hall, Jordan, & Robin, 1993). Voluntary or purposeful motor acts are inconsistently produced while involuntary movements remain intact. The condition is characterized by difficulty in articulation of speech (oral, speech, or verbal apraxia); formation of letters in writing; difficulty with visual-spatial tasks such as drawing, block arrangements, assembling stick designs or shapes in drawing; or problems in sequential movements of gesture, pantomime, dressing, grooming, or eating (Hall et al., 1993; Shriberg, Aram, & Kwiatkowski, 1997). In less severe forms, apraxia may be referred to as dyspraxia (Dewey, 1995; Missiuna & Polatajko, 1995).

Developmental apraxia of speech (DAS-II) is a nonlinguistic sensorimotor disorder of articulation characterized by impaired capacity to program and position the speech musculature and the sequencing of muscle movements (respiratory, laryngeal, and oral) for the volitional production and sequencing of phonemes. Children with developmental apraxia of speech have more addition errors (producing extra phonemes), prolongation errors, repetitions of sounds and syllables, and nonphonemic productions such as glottal plosives, bilabial fricatives, nasal assimilation and distortions such as subtle voicing and devoicing errors that are not overt substitution errors (Davis et al., 1998; Hall et al., 1993; Shriberg et al., 1997).

Whereas speech-language pathologists may be more familiar with the term developmental apraxia of speech, occupational and physical therapists may use the term developmental coordination disorders (DCD; David, 1995; Willoughby & Polatajko, 1995). This condition is also referred to as *clumsy child syndrome, mild motor problems, incoordination, developmental apraxia or dyspraxia, perceptual motor dysfunction, visual-motor problems*, and *sensory-integrative dysfunction*. The *Diagnostic and Statistical Manual of Mental Disorders* (*DSM-IV*; American Psychiatric Association, 1994) description of DCD implicitly excludes the coordination disturbances affecting speech motor skill development, even though phonological awareness deficits are frequently found in children diagnosed with DCD. A consensus does not exist for etiology of the condition (Davis et al., 1998; Dewey, 1995; Hall et al., 1993; Shriberg et al., 1997). Developmental apraxia of speech and developmental coordination disorders can impact on the social and academic dimensions of the communication-learning process across the life course, but particularly do so in childhood.

REFERENCES

American Psychiatric Association. (1994). *Diagnostic and statistical manual of mental disorders* (4th ed.). Washington, DC: Author.

David, K. S. (1995). Developmental coordination disorders. In S. Campbell (Ed.), *Physical therapy for children* (pp. 425–456). Philadelphia, PA: Saunders.

Davis, B. L., Jakielski, K. J., & Marquardt, T. P. (1998). Developmental apraxia of speech: Determiners of differential diagnosis. *Clinical Linguistics and Phonetics, 12,* 25–45.

Dewey, D. (1995). What is developmental dyspraxia? *Brain and Cognition, 29,* 254–274.

Hall, P. K., Jordan, L. S., & Robin, D. A. (1993). *Developmental apraxia of speech: Theory and clinical practice.* Austin, TX: PRO-ED.

Missiuna, C., & Polatajko, H. (1995). Developmental dyspraxia by any other name: Are they all just clumsy children? *The American Journal of Occupational Therapy, 49,* 619–627.

Shriberg, L., Aram, D., & Kwiatkowski, J. (1997). Developmental apraxia of speech: I. Descriptive and theoretical perspectives. *Journal of Speech, Language and Hearing Research, 40,* 273–285.

Willoughby, C., & Polatajko, H. (1995). Motor problems in children with developmental coordination disorder: Review of the literature. *The American Journal of Occupational Therapy, 49,* 787–793.

STEPHEN S. FARMER
New Mexico State University

DEVELOPMENTAL ASSESSMENT OF YOUNG CHILDREN

The Developmental Assessment of Young Children (DAYC, 1998) is designed for children between birth and 5 years 11 months. It is an individually administered test of developmental abilities in the adaptive, cognitive, communication, physical, and social-emotional domains. Each of the 5 domains reflects areas that are required for assessment and intervention for young children according to the Individuals with Disabilities Education Act (IDEA). This particular measure can be tailored to the specific assessment needs of each child or all domains may be administered. The DAYC has four uses: the identification of children with developmental delays, recognition of strengths and weaknesses, documentation of child's progress, and measurement of children's developmental abilities for research purposes (Plake & Impara, 2001).

The Cognitive subtest consists of 78 items that assess concept development. The Communication subtest consists of 78 items measuring receptive/expressive language and verbal/nonverbal abilities. The Social-Emotional subtest is comprised of 58 items that assess social awareness in relationships and social competence. The Physical Development subtest consists of 87 items measuring motor development. The last subtest, Adaptive Behavior, is comprised of 62 items that assess independent functioning in self-help.

Administration time is approximately 1 hour and 40 minutes for the comprehensive battery. Each subtest requires about 20 minutes to complete. Testing may occur over more than one session; however, it should be completed as soon as possible. Administration is fairly straightforward. Items passed receive 1 point and those failed receive 0 points. Basal and ceilings are utilized for each subtest. Data are recorded on the subtest scoring forms. The DAYC provides standard scores, percentile scores, and age equivalents as well as a General Development Quotient (GDQ) if all five subtests are completed.

Normative data was collected on a national sample of 1,269 individuals consistent with the 1996 United States Census. The sample also includes an "at-risk" category of children with no present disability but an identified risk factor. Internal consistency reliability coefficients range from .90 to .99 and test-retest reliability was good ($r = .90$). Three types of validity were reported in the manual. Content-description validity correlations range from .94 to .99. Criterion-related validity was examined through comparison with the Battelle Developmental Inventory Screening Test and the Revised Gesell and Amatruda Developmental and Neurologic Examination. Coefficients were significant at the .01 level with the Batelle (range from .47 to .61) and at the .05 level with the Gesell (range from .41 to .53). Construct validity was assessed but statistical data was not reported in the available reviews.

Reviews state that the DAYC is well organized, easy to understand, and simple to use. One limitation of the DAYC is the lack of research regarding treatment effects. It is suggested that the DAYC is not appropriate for evaluating change after a program intervention.

This entry has been informed by the sources listed below.

REVIEWED IN:

Plake, B. S., & Impara, J. C. (Eds.). (2001). *The fourteenth mental measurements yearbook.* Lincoln, NE: Buros Institute of Mental Measurements.

RON DUMONT
Fairleigh Dickinson University

JOHN O. WILLIS
Rivier College

KATHLEEN VIEZEL
JAMIE ZIBULSKY
Fairleigh Dickinson University

DEVELOPMENTAL DELAY

Arnold Gessell (1925, 1946), in his pioneering research at the Yale Institute for Child Development, established a sequence of developmental norms, or milestones, through which individuals progress on their way toward normal development. Under his maturational conceptualization, individuals achieve certain developmental milestones that represent indicators of both current and future development and adjustment. Most infants and children reach these critical milestones within expected time frames. Such milestones include the abilities to make eye contact, exhibit fine and gross motor skills, develop language, achieve continence, reciprocate during play, and read independently. In some cases, however, developmental delays can occur, which portend possible developmental disabilities. The early pioneering work on developmental milestones has made it possible for the early identification of delays to occur (Baron-Cohen, 1989; Passey & Feldman, 2004).

Developmental delay is a term used to denote when babies or children *fail* to reach certain developmental milestones, or do so at a *markedly slow* rate (First & Palfrey, 1994). It is well understood that infants and children develop at varying rates. Some sit at 6 months, others at 4 months, and still others at 8 months. Given the fact that slight variations in normal development unequivocally exist, the term *developmental delay* is generally reserved for instances when infants or children have more than one delay or exhibit significant maturational lag in a critical, functional skill (Squires, Nickel, & Eisert, 1996). For example, the inability to develop adequate verbal skills by the age of 5 would represent a developmental delay of notable concern. The defining feature of developmental delays is the relationship with untoward outcomes. For example, recent research has suggested that 3-year-old children with developmental delays present significantly greater behavior problems than typically developing same-age peers (Baker, Blacher, & Olsson, 2005; Baker, Blacher, Crnic, & Edelbrock, 2002). The phenomena of developmental delays have also been referred to as a young child's "failure to thrive," and is typically characterized by slow weight gain (Corbett & Drewett, 2004). However, while some studies suggest a specific linkage between failure to thrive in infancy and its adverse effects on cognitive development (e.g., cognitive delay), to date there is no clear consensus in the literature as to the relation between an infant's failure to thrive and developmental delay (Batchelor, 1999; Boddy, Skuse, & Andrews, 2000; Wright, 2000).

Developmental delays are capable of being measured on both quantitative (i.e., by degree or extent of delay) and qualitative (i.e., by kind or type of delay) dimensions. A delay, for example, in developing ambulation until age 4 is quantitatively more severe than a delay in walking until age 3. Moreover, a noticeable maturational lag in developing language skills has qualitatively different implications than a delay in responding adequately to visual stimuli. A diagnosis of developmental delays is best performed using a multimethod, multi-informant, and multisetting approach to determine whether target pupils can or cannot perform certain behavioral markers or do so at a rate that

is significantly below that observed in normal children the same age (Salvia & Ysseldyke, 2003).

Developmental delays can have many different causes, such as genetics (i.e., Down syndrome) or complications during pregnancy and birth (i.e., prematurity, infection). Recent studies have focused on the most common known cause of developmental delay, Fragile X syndrome. Specifically, investigators have found that the silencing of the FMR-1 gene is singly involved in the pathogenesis of Fragile X syndrome at the molecular level, leading to a lack of production of the FMR-1 protein (FMRP) synthesis. There is increasing evidence that suggests a correlation between higher FMRP levels and greater phenotypic expression (e.g., developmental delays). Often, however, the specific cause is unknown, although some causes can be reversed if caught early enough, such as hearing loss from chronic ear infections, or lead poisoning. In any case, whether the causes can be reversed or whether the delay suggests an unalterable, lifelong condition, it is important to identify developmental delays so that families can seek appropriate treatment for their child or begin to cope and adjust to the difficulties that lie ahead.

Early diagnosis in infants and children depends on early identification of features associated with particular developmental disabilities. As a result, early screening for developmental delays has become the gold standard of clinical practice when assessing for the early warning signs of developmental disabilities (Gray & Tonge, 2005). The use of developmental screening questionnaires by primary care physicians and early childhood professionals is the best and most frequently employed method to identify developmental disorders (Fenton et al., 2003; Filipek et al., 1999). The theoretical importance of identifying infants and young children with developmental problems through the use of developmental screening measures and linking the data to services has been recognized by a number of professional organizations including the American Academy of Pediatrics, the Child Welfare League of America, and the American Academy of Child and Adolescent Psychiatry.

Contemporaneously, the notion of developmental delay is used in a variety of contexts to guide important professional practices: education, clinical, and legal/political. Indeed, developmental delays play a vital role in the clinical diagnosis of several *DSM-IV* disorders including, but not limited to, pervasive developmental disorder, autistic disorder, mental retardation, specific learning disability, and Asperger syndrome. To receive a diagnosis of autistic disorder, for instance, individuals must have pronounced delays in acquiring language skills and in responding appropriately to social cues, both of which should occur regularly by the age of 3—a point at which most children are identified with autistic disorder (American Psychiatric Association, 2000; Howlin & Moore, 1997).

Children with developmental delay are eligible to receive services as mandated under federal law. They are also the subject of early "child find" and intervention efforts. The category "developmental delay" was first incorporated into the 1986 revision of the Individuals with Disabilities Education Act (IDEA), and more recently has been retained in the 2004 Individuals with Disabilities Education Improvement Act (IDEIA). The description of developmental delay in IDEIA (2004) is as follows:

> (i) experiencing developmental delays, as defined by the State and as measured by appropriate diagnostic instruments and procedures, in 1 or more of the following areas: physical development; cognitive development; communication development; social or emotional development; or adaptive development;

> (1) A rigorous definition of the term "developmental delay" that will be used by the State in carrying out programs under this part in order to appropriately identify infants and toddlers with disabilities that are in need of services under this part. (p. 2739)

In sum, the development of norms pertaining to child development helped in the identification of children who were delayed in meeting developmental milestones. Early screening efforts aimed at identifying children at risk of, or having, developmental delays are now part of state mandated child find efforts. Many developmental delays can lead to developmental, educational, or social problems for the child. Fortunately, early intervention efforts can ameliorate or even prevent subsequent delays.

REFERENCES

American Psychiatric Association. (2000). *Diagnostic and statistical manual of mental disorders* (4th ed., text rev.). Washington, DC: Author.

Baker, B. L., Blacher, J., Crnic, K. A., & Edelbrock, C. (2002). Behavior problems and parenting stress in families of three-year-old children with and without developmental delays. *American Journal on Mental Retardation, 107*, 433–444.

Baker, B. L., Blacher, J., & Olsson, M. B. (2005). Preschool children with and without developmental delay: Behavior problems, parents' optimism and well-being. *Journal of Intellectual Disability Research, 49*, 575–590.

Batchelor, J. (1999). *Failure to thrive in young children: Research and practice evaluated*. London, England: Children's Society.

Baron-Cohen, S. (1989). The autistic child's theory of mind: A case of specific developmental delay. *Journal of Child Psychology and Psychiatry, 30*(2), 285–297.

Boddy, J., Skuse, D., & Andrews, B. (2000). The developmental sequelae of non-organic failure to thrive. *Journal of Child Psychology and Psychiatry, 41*, 1003–1014.

Corbett, S. S., & Drewett, R. F. (2004). To what extent is failure to thrive in infancy associated with poorer cognitive development? A review and meta-analysis. *Journal of Child Psychology and Psychiatry, 45*, 641–654.

Fenton, G., D'Ardia, C., Valente, D., Del Vecchio, I., Fabrizi, A., & Bernabei, P. (2003). Vineland adaptive behavior profiles in children with autism and moderate to severe developmental delay. *Autism, 7*, 269–287.

Filipek, P. A., Accardo, P. J., Baranek, G. T., Cook, E. H., Dawson, G., Gordon, B.,...Volkmar, F. R. (1999). The screening and diagnosis of autism spectrum disorders. *Journal of Autism and Developmental Disorders, 29*, 439–484.

First, L. R., & Palfrey, J. S. (1994). The infant or young child with developmental delay. *New England Journal of Medicine, 330*, 478–483.

Gessel, A. (1925). *The mental growth of the pre-school child*. New York, NY: MacMillan.

Gessel, A., & Ilg, F. L. (1946). *The child from five to ten*. New York, NY: Harper & Brothers.

Gray, K. M., & Tonge, B. J. (2005). Screening for autism in infants and preschool children with developmental delay. *Australian & New Zealand Journal of Psychiatry, 39*(5), 378–386.

Howlin, P., & Moore, A. (1997). Diagnosis in autism: A survey of over 1,200 patients in the UK. *Autism: The International Journal of Research and Practice, 1*, 135–162.

Individuals with Disabilities Education Act Amendments of 1986, 20. U.S.C. § 1400 *et seq.*

Passey, J., & Feldman, M. (2004). Descriptive analysis of parent-child interactions in young children with or at risk for developmental delay. *Behavioral Interventions, 19*(4), 233–246.

Salvia, J., & Ysseldyke, J. (2003). *Assessment in special and inclusive education* (9th ed.). New York, NY: Houghton Mifflin.

Squires, J., Nickel, R. E., & Eisert, D. (1996). Early detection of developmental problems: Strategies for monitoring young children in the practice setting. *Journal of Developmental and Behavioral Pediatrics, 17*, 420–427.

Wright, C. M. (2000). Identification and management of failure to thrive: A community perspective. *Archives of Disease in Childhood, 82*, 5–9.

CLAYTON R. COOK
JAMES LYONS
JAN BLACHER
University of California, Riverside

See *also* Individuals with Disabilities Improvement Education Act of 2004 (IDEIA); Early Experiences

DEVELOPMENTAL DISABILITIES

Developmental disabilities is a term representing an umbrella category referring to a diverse group of physical, cognitive, psychological, sensory, and speech impairments that begin anytime during an individual's development up to 22 years of age. According to the Developmental Disabilities Assistance and Bill of Rights Act of 2000

(Public Law 106-402), a developmental disability results in substantial functional limitations in three or more of the following seven areas of major life activity: (1) self-care, (2) receptive and expressive language, (3) learning, (4) mobility, (5) self-direction, (6) capacity for independent living, and (7) economic self-sufficiency. Individuals from birth to age 9, who have a substantial developmental delay or a specific congenital or acquired condition, may be considered to have a developmental disability without meeting three or more of the criteria described *if* there is a high probability of the individual meeting those criteria later in life. Additionally, the term *developmental disabilities* reflects the individual's need for support services or other forms of assistance requiring individual planning or coordination, and that are lifelong or of extended duration.

In the past four decades, the field of developmental disabilities has undergone a series of social, political, and scientific changes. These changes have resulted in many modifications to the definition of developmental disabilities and societal responses to individuals with these disabilities. The Developmental Disabilities Services and Facilities and Construction Act of 1970 (Public Law 91-517) defined the term developmental disabilities as follows:

> Disabilities attributable to mental retardation, cerebral palsy, epilepsy or another neurological condition of an individual found by the Secretary [Health, Education, and Welfare] to be closely related to mental retardation or to require treatment similar to that required for a mentally retarded individual, which disability originates before such an individual attains age 18, which has continued or can be expected to continue indefinitely, and constitutes a substantial handicap to the individual. (sec. 6001)

Public Law 91-517 came from the efforts of a national coalition to minimize categories of exceptionality and to make services more available to people who did not meet the criteria for mental retardation but still showed evidence of multiple handicaps and adaptive delays. The Act brought under a single federal legislative umbrella three major disorders: mental retardation, cerebral palsy, and epilepsy. It also included all other neurological conditions occurring before age 18 that produce consequences similar to those of the main three. The intent of the legislation was to bring together under one law disability groups that have comparable service needs. The goal was to improve services and increase coordination among the many public and private agencies that provide such services.

Following the 1970 legislation, the term *developmental disabilities* was altered to include autism and a few specific learning disabilities (e.g., dyslexia) in the Developmentally Disabled Assistance and Bill of Rights Act of 1975 (Public Law 94-103). However, these pieces of federal legislation still reflected a categorical definition of developmental disabilities, where the needs and services of people were classified under disparate descriptions that focused on etiological and medical origins. The original intent of coining the term *developmental disabilities* was to reflect a functional definition that focused on common adaptive problems. This was finally accomplished with the enactment of the Rehabilitation Comprehensive Services and Developmental Disabilities Amendments of 1978 (Public Law 95-602). All other legislation following the 1978 Act have used a functional definition of developmental disabilities, replacing the terminology of specific conditions (e.g., mental retardation, cerebral palsy) and focusing solely on the effects of the disabilities, especially when they are severe and chronic in nature.

These modifications to the definition of developmental disabilities were significant in that they were ultimately translated into guidelines for the delivery of special education services and related support services in community-based rehabilitation and treatment settings. Currently, there are approximately 4.5 million individuals with developmental disabilities in the United States. Without appropriate services and supports, options (e.g., education, employment, housing) for these individuals are minimal. The most recent piece of legislation pertaining to developmental disabilities is the Developmental Disabilities Assistance and Bill of Rights Act of 2000 (Public Law 106-402). This Act ensures that people with developmental disabilities and their families receive the services and supports they need to participate in the planning and designing of those services. The Administration on Developmental Disabilities (ADD), the federal agency responsible for implementation and administration of Public Law 106-402, focuses on eight areas for services and programs: Employment, Education, Child Care, Health, Housing, Transportation, Recreation, and Quality Assurance.

Currently, the field of developmental disabilities has become more progressive. There has been an expansion of inclusive community options and the number of people in large congregate facilities continues to decline. Furthermore, research, policy, and practice now emphasize quality-of-life issues, self-determination, and services required by individuals with dual-diagnoses or other psychopathologies. A robust self-advocacy movement has also emerged and person-centered planning is an aspiration in virtually every state. It is also likely that with the burgeoning emphasis on the genetic origins of behavior and disability, the developmental disabilities concept may broaden. Roles for family members of persons with developmental disabilities continue to expand.

In summary, the term *developmental disability* means a severe, chronic disability of an individual that is attributable to a mental or physical impairment or combination of mental and physical impairments. The impairment must manifest before the individual attains age 22 and must be likely to continue indefinitely. Former definitions involved the removal of explicit references to the specific categories of developmental disabilities. The current definition emphasizes considerable functional limitations and identifies individuals whose disabilities will create needs in particular activities.

This entry has been informed by the sources listed below.

REFERENCES

Blacher, J., & Baker, B. L. (2002). *The best of AAMR. Families and mental retardation: A collection of notable AAMR journal articles across the 20th century*. Washington, DC: American Association on Mental Retardation.

Kazdin, A. E. (2000). *Encyclopedia of psychology* (Vol. 3). Washington, DC: Oxford University Press.

Luckasson, R., Borthwick-Duffy, S., Buntinx, W. H. E., Coulter, D. L., Craig, E. M., Reeve, A., … Tasse, M. J. (2002). *Mental retardation: Definition, classification, and systems of supports* (10th ed.). Washington, DC: American Association on Mental Retardation.

McLaughlin, P. J., & Wehman, P. (1996). *Mental retardation and developmental disabilities* (2nd ed.). Austin, TX: PRO-ED.

Schalock, R. L. (2004). The emerging disability paradigm and its implications for policy and practice. *Journal of Disability Policy Studies, 14*(4), 204–215.

Thompson, R. J., & O'Quinn, A. N. (1979). *Developmental disabilities*. New York, NY: Oxford University Press.

ARAKSIA KALADJIAN
University of California, Riverside

CAMERON L. NEECE
University of California, Los Angeles

See also **Cerebral Palsy; Mental Retardation**

DEVELOPMENTAL DISABILITIES ASSISTANCE ACT AND BILL OF RIGHTS

The Developmental Disabilities Assistance and Bill of Rights Act Amendments of 1994 was originally enacted as Title 1 of the Mental Retardation Facilities and Construction Act of 1963, Public Law, 88-164 and was amended in 1981, 1987, 2007, and 1994. The purpose of the Act is to:

> [A]ssure that individuals with developmental disabilities and their families participate in the design of and have access to needed community services, individualized supports, and other forms of assistance that promote self-determination, independence, productivity, and integration and inclusion in all facets of community life, through culturally competent programs authorized under this title. (42 U.S.C. §15001[b])

This is carried out through the participation of State Councils on Developmental Disabilities, the development of state protection and advocacy systems, the support of university-affiliated programs, and the support of national initiatives to collect data and provide technical assistance to state Councils.

The Act also states Congress's findings with respect to the rights of individuals with developmental disabilities:

1. Individuals with developmental disabilities have a right to appropriate treatment, services, and habilitation for such disabilities.

2. The treatment, services, and habitation [sic] for an individual with developmental disabilities should be designed to maximize the potential of the individual and should be provided the setting that is least restrictive of the individual's personal liberty.

3. The Federal Government and the States both have an obligation to ensure that public funds are provided only to institutional programs, programs, and other community programs, including educational programs in which individuals with developmental disabilities participate, that

   a. provide treatment, services, and habilitation that are appropriate to the needs of such individuals, and

   b. meet minimum standards relating to:

      i. provision of care that is free of abuse, neglect, sexual and financial exploitation, and violations of legal and human rights and that subjects individuals with developmental disabilities to no greater risk of harm than others in the general population;

      ii. provision to such individuals of appropriate and sufficient medical and dental services;

      iii. prohibition of the use of physical restraint and seclusion for such an individual unless absolutely necessary to ensure the immediate physical safety of the individual or others, and prohibition of the use of such restraint and seclusion as a punishment or as a substitute for a habilitation program;

      iv. prohibition on the excessive use of chemical restraints on such individuals and the use of such restraints as punishments or as a substitute for a habilitation program or in quantities that interfere with services, treatment, or habilitation for such individuals; and

      v. provision for close relatives or guardians of such individuals to visit the individuals without prior notice.

4. All programs for individuals with developmental disabilities should meet standards:

   a. that are designed to assure the most favorable possible outcome for those served; and

b.   i. in the case of residential programs serving individuals in need of comprehensive health-related, habilitative, assistive technology or rehabilitative services, that are at least the equivalent to those standards applicable to intermediate care facilities for the mentally retarded, promulgated in regulations of the Secretary on June 3, 1988, as appropriate, taking into account the size of the institutions and the service delivery arrangements of the facilities of the programs;

ii. in the case of other residential programs for individuals with developmental disabilities, that assure that

    I. care is appropriate to the needs of the individuals being served by such programs;

    II. the individuals admitted to facilities of such programs are individuals whose needs can be met through services provided by such facilities; and

    III. the facilities of such programs provide for the humane care of the residents of the facilities, are sanitary, and protect their rights; and

iii. in the case of nonresidential programs, that assure that the care provided by such programs is appropriate to the individuals served by the programs. (42 U.S.C. §15009[a]).

Congress specifically indicated within the statute that these rights are "in addition to any constitutional or other rights otherwise afforded to all individuals" (42 U.S.C. §15009[b]).

Under Part B of the Act, the State Developmental Disabilities Council program provides financial assistance to each state to support the activities of State Councils on Developmental Disabilities. The councils are made up of individuals who have developmental disabilities, family members, and representatives of state agencies that provide services to individuals with developmental disabilities. The council develops and implements a statewide plan to address employment (which is a federally mandated priority) and case management, child development, and community living. Fiscal year 2004 funding for the Act was $149,861,569, according to the Administration on Developmental Disabilities website.

The Administration on Developmental Disabilities receives annual reports from states and provides its own annual report on the implementation of the Act. The Administration is located at Administration on Developmental Disabilities Administration for Children and Families, U.S. Department of Health and Human Services, Mail Stop: HHH 405-D, 370 L'Enfant Promenade, S.W., Washington, DC 20447. Tel.: (202) 690-6590 (voice) and (202) 245-2890 (TDD). The Administration on Developmental Disabilities also maintains an extensive webpage: http://www.acf.hhs.gov/.

ELAINE FLETCHER-JANZEN
Chicago School of Professional Psychology
Second edition

KIMBERLY F. APPLEQUIST
University of Colorado at Colorado Springs
Third edition

See also Individuals with Disabilities Education Improvement Act of 2004 (IDEIA)

DEVELOPMENTAL DISABILITIES LEGAL RESOURCE CENTER (*See* Protection and Advocacy System—Developmentally Disabled)

DEVELOPMENTAL DYSLEXIA, HISTORY OF

Developmental dyslexia is typically perceived as a complex heterogeneous reading disorder. It appears to stem from a selective disturbance of the maturation of neurological functions thought to be responsible for the acquisition of reading and writing skills. It is genetically determined and thus distinct from acquired alexia from traumatic brain injury (Gaddes, 1976). Critical components of the disorder that are relative to the individual's unique patterns of intrinsic abilities and extrinsic assets dictate that the dyslexic must have at least average intelligence; sufficient cultural and linguistic opportunity; emotional stability; access to appropriate instruction; and approximately normal sensory acuity (Rourke & Gates, 1981). Prognosis of relative success in compensating for the disorder's consequences is based on early identification, delineation of the individual's unique pattern of strengths and weaknesses, capitalization on unique educational strategies, and concomitant appropriate sociocultural/familial support systems.

More than 90 years worth of published material (Benton, 1980) has been generated by the disorder; its history has been rich with conflicting information. To state that developmental dyslexia has been a confusing disorder would be diplomatic at best; however, continued research in the differentiation of subtypes, longitudinal studies on developmental changes, technological advances related to etiology, and empirical results from promising intervention programs continue to refine conceptualizations of dyslexia.

The origin of the term *dyslexia* has been attributed to Kausmaul, who in 1877 defined the word *alexia* as word blindness. In 1891 Dejerine provided autopsy data on individuals who had suffered cerebrovascular injury and were left with reading disabilities. In 1896 Morgan described a famous dyslexic case study concerning an intelligent 14-year-old male who could not read or write but could perform algebra. These studies indicated specific deficits or abnormal development of the angular gyrus region in the dominant hemisphere (Dalby, 1979).

In 1900 Hinshelwood reported that the disorder caused partial or complete loss of visual memory for letters and words. In 1901 Nettleship observed that a disproportionate number of males had dyslexia, the disorder tended to run in families, and there was the presence of a linguistic factor. Four years later, Fisher recommended implementation of a "look and say" method of instruction for individuals who had a phonemic analysis deficit. This remediation used global word recognition. Interestingly, he also advocated teaching children to write with their left hands, based on the assumption that the right hemisphere subserved the learning process in children with faulty left hemispheres. Marie, in 1906, disagreed with the localizationalist theories of brain functioning, then the prevalent school of thought, which assumed specific behaviors were attributed to specific brain areas. He argued that there could not be specific centers for reading because reading was a new development in humans (Pirozzolo, 1981).

Educational and clinical psychologists' interest in dyslexia gained momentum during the first two decades of the 20th century. Research focused on the basic underlying factors that presumably caused failure in learning to read, and two schools of thought emerged. The first emphasized the relation of perceptual and cognitive disabilities and the second concentrated on environmental factors (Benton, 1980). A new perspective on dyslexia was formulated by Orton toward the end of the second decade.

Orton related reading disability to a defective interhemispheric organization of cerebral function. It was assumed to be the result of a faulty maturational process of establishing specialization of function in a single hemisphere. The consequences of incomplete hemispheric dominance were said to lead to confusion and failure to read effectively (Johnson & Myklebust, 1967).

Behavioral and personality disorders in dyslexics were investigated in the 1930s. It was assumed that psychotherapy should be the primary mode of intervention before and during educational remediation. In the early 1940s, Werner and Strauss (Dalby, 1979) stated that brain damage was present, whether detectable by neurological means, as long as similar behavior patterns were exhibited. They initiated the term minimal brain damage (MBD), which, unfortunately, was embraced by zealous individuals who then attributed MBD to the entire population of persons with learning disorders. Without substantial evidence to support the conclusion that brain

damage existed minimally, dissimilar disorders were erroneously lumped together (e.g., attention deficit disorders, developmental dyslexia). The devastating impact of these erroneous labels was unfortunately incurred by the child (Hobbs, 1975).

To complicate this picture further, incidence rates for dyslexics in the general population ranged from 10% to 30%, as reported in the voluminous post–World War II research on dyslexia. It became clear, however, that many researchers had failed to differentiate specific reading disability from failure to read owing to other factors (e.g., lack of normal intelligence, primary sensory impairments, lack of adequate educational and cultural opportunities, and emotional instability). The field of developmental dyslexia became clouded, and, as Benton and Pearl (1978) note, this large volume of research did little to differentiate distinct subtypes of dyslexia. The concept of dyslexia appeared to mean different things to different people. Adams (1967) found 23 definitions of dyslexia in the literature and he argued for abandonment of the term. It has been observed that the particular way in which research in developmental dyslexia is conducted stems directly from its definition, and if that definition is not one that is commonly accepted, researchers' results will differ accordingly (Rourke, 1976; Sawyer, 1992). It is currently estimated that 15% of the school population is dyslexic, as are over 85% of adult illiterates (Griesbach, 1993; Orton-Gillingham Practitioners and Educators, 1998).

From the 1960s to the present, research proceeded by varied means. Renewed interest in Orton's work followed advances in asymmetrical hemispheric specialization research (e.g., dichotic listening, dichaptic discrimination, and tachistoscopic methods). Medical technology has furthered investigations in the neurological basis of dyslexia by means of electroencephalography, computerized tomography scanning, cerebral blood flow studies, positron emission tomography, and autopsies on dyslexic and normal brains. Current research in the educational/neuropsychological literature (Hynd & Obrzut, 1981; Knights & Bakker, 1976; Lyon, Fletcher, & Barnes, 2003) has supported the involvement of higher cortical impairment in developmental dyslexia.

Evidence from research on pre- and perinatal events in relation to dyslexia has demonstrated the importance of this period on the child's development. However, there is no strong evidence to substantiate that abnormalities in this period lead directly to specific reading disability. Extensive data from twin research (Herschel, 1978) showed a genetic basis to developmental dyslexia, although there is little evidence to support particular biochemical, physiological, or behavioral attributes linked specifically to dyslexia.

Sex differences are apparent in that males are disproportionately represented in reading-disabled populations. Data exist that indicate even normal girls are more adept at the learning-to-read process than normal boys.

Anatomical data further substantiate those claims, since myelination occurred more rapidly in the left hemisphere for girls and the right hemisphere for boys (Dalby, 1979). Other sex differences have been hypothesized to be maturational lags in hemispheric specialization shifts in the learning-to-read process (Rourke, 1982), where girls pass through the stages faster than boys (Gaddes, 1976). These hypotheses suggest that the right hemisphere-mediated functions may have a critical role in the initial stages of the acquisition of the reading process, whereas the left hemisphere-mediated functions may be more efficient in using a routinized mode that stems from that acquisition. This right-to-left shift in hemispheric specialization may be a function of increased competence with the learning-to-read process.

The current perspective on developmental dyslexia has focused on more stringent methods of research in the identification of distinct subtypes (Rourke & Gates, 1981). Converging data from this body of research suggested a need for a multidimensional definition; it was clear that appropriate identification of dyslexics could not be made solely on the basis of poor reading achievement with approximately average intelligence (Yule & Rutter, 1976). The presence of differences in the types of dyslexia necessitates different strategies of educational interventions. Recognition of these differences became more pronounced following multivariate analyses of clinical neuropsychological methods (Lyon et al., 2003; Petrauskas & Rourke, 1979) and important developmental changes, described in longitudinal research (Satz, Taylor, Friel, & Fletcher, 1978).

The neuropsychological evidence has suggested the presence of several subtypes of dyslexic readers, two of which are fairly distinct in older children and adults: auditory-linguistic deficient (dysphonetic) readers and visual-spatial deficient (dyseidetic) readers, as described by Pirozzolo (1981). Others have described a mixed dyslexic group (both dysphonetic and dyseidetic); an unspecified group (of which subcortical impairment cannot be completely ruled out), and a normal group; or linguistic, perceptual, and mixed groups (Masutto, 1994); and phonological and surface types (Lyon et al., 2003; Murphy & Pollatsek, 1994).

REFERENCES

Adams, R. B. (1967). *Dyslexia: A discussion of its definition.* Paper prepared for the second meeting of the Federal Government's Attack on Dyslexia. Washington, DC: Bureau of Research, U.S. Office of Education.

Benton, A. L. (1980). Dyslexia: Evolution of a concept. *Bulletin of the Orton Society, 30,* 10–26.

Benton, A. L., & Pearl, D. (1978). *Dyslexia: An appraisal of current knowledge.* New York, NY: Oxford University Press.

Dalby, J. T. (1979). Deficit or delay: Neuropsychological models of developmental dyslexia. *Journal of Special Education, 3,* 239–264.

Gaddes, W. H. (1976). Prevalence estimates and the need for definition of learning disabilities. In R. Knights & D. Bakker (Eds.), *The neuropsychology of learning disorders: Theoretical approaches* (pp. 3–24). Baltimore, MD: University Park Press.

Griesbach, G. (1993). *Dyslexia: Its history, etiology, and treatment.* (ERIC Clearinghouse No. CS011300)

Herschel, M. (1978). Dyslexia revisted: A review. *Human Genetics, 40,* 115–134.

Hobbs, N. (1975). *The futures of children: Categories, labels, and their consequences.* San Francisco, CA: Jossey-Bass.

Hynd, G. W., & Obrzut, J. E. (1981). *Neuropsychological assessment and the school-age child: Issues and procedures.* New York, NY: Grune & Stratton.

Johnson, D. J., & Myklebust, H. R. (1967). *Learning disabilities: Educational principles and practices.* New York, NY: Grune & Stratton.

Knights, R., & Bakker, D. (1976). *The neuropsychology of learning disorders: Theoretical approaches.* Baltimore, MD: University Park Press.

Lyon, G. R., Fletcher, J. M., & Barnes, M. C. (2003). Learning disabilities. In E. J. Mash & R. A. Barkley (Eds.), *Child Psychopathology* (2nd ed., pp. 520–586). New York, NY: Guilford Press.

Masutto, C. (1994). Neurolinguistic differentiation of children with subtypes of dyslexia. *Journal of Learning Disabilities, 27*(8), 520–526.

Murphy, L., & Pollatsek, A. (1994). Developmental dyslexia: Heterogeneity without discrete subgroups. *Annals of Dyslexia, 44,* 120–146.

Orton-Gillingham Practitioners and Educators. (1998). *Dyslexia.* Retrieved from http://www.ortonacademy.org/approach.php

Petrauskas, R. J., & Rourke, B. P. (1979). Identification of subtypes of retarded readers: A neuropsychological multivariate approach. *Journal of Clinical Neuropsychology, 1,* 17–37.

Pirozzolo, F. J. (1981). Language and brain: Neuropsychological aspects of developmental reading disability. *School Psychology Review, 3,* 350–355.

Rourke, B. P. (1976). Reading retardation in children: Developmental lag or deficit? In R. Knights & D. Bakker (Eds.), *The neuropsychology of learning disorders: Theoretical approaches* (pp. 125–137). Baltimore, MD: University Park Press.

Rourke, B. P. (1982). Central processing deficiencies in children: Toward a developmental neuropsychological model. *Journal of Clinical Neuropsychology, 4,* 1–18.

Rourke, B. P., & Gates, R. D. (1981). Neuropsychological research and school psychology. In G. W. Hynd & J. E. Obrzut (Eds.), *Neuropsychological assessment and the school-age child: Issue and procedures* (pp. 3–25). New York, NY: Grune & Stratton.

Satz, P., Taylor, H. G., Friel, J., & Fletcher, J. M. (1978). Some developmental and predictive precursors of reading disabilities: A six year follow-up. In A. L. Benton & D. Pearl (Eds.), *Dyslexia: An appraisal of current knowledge* (pp. 313–347). New York, NY: Oxford University Press.

Sawyer, D. J. (1992). Dyslexia: Introduction to special series. *Journal of Learning Disabilities, 25,* 1, 38.

Yule, W., & Rutter, M. (1976). Epidemiological and social implications of specific reading retardation. In R. Knights & D. Bakker (Eds.), *The neuropsychology of learning disorders: Theoretical approaches* (pp. 25–39). Baltimore, MD: University Park Press.

Scott W. Sautter
Peabody College, Vanderbilt University

DEVELOPMENTAL MATHEMATICS AT THE COLLEGE LEVEL

College level developmental mathematics is part of the developmental education program, an all-encompassing approach to providing students with an improved ability to learn. The concept of developmental education involves putting into action strategies, which help underprepared students to succeed academically. These strategies include instruction in study skills, providing tutoring sessions, and availability of prerequisite courses (Illich, Hagan, & McCallister, 2004).

The U.S. Department of Education (1996) defined developmental education as courses for college students who lack the skills needed to perform the required work of the attended institution. The classification of *remedial* depends on who is using the term. Each college maintains its own standards, and, therefore, developmental education is defined by individual institutions (Kozeracki & Brooks, 2006). In other words, a remedial student is deemed as such only by the institutional standards of the college the student attends. A student is designated remedial by the particular test that he/she takes, and there is no consensus on a single metric. Finding the appropriate policies for the optimal placement of students continues to elude those who have tried (Rodgers & Wilding, 1998).

Mathematics courses such as introduction to algebra and intermediate algebra are typically part of the developmental mathematics program. Remedial courses, a subset of developmental education, are non-credit bearing courses and made up of content considered to be pre-college. Students who enroll in remedial courses are by definition, remedial students (Boylan & Bonham, 2007). The purpose of these mathematics classes is to facilitate students' transition into college-level courses. Prerequisite courses are put into place in order to improve students' chances at overall collegiate success (Kozeracki & Brooks, 2006).

Standardized achievement tests are not typically sufficient for diagnostic decision making as they do not indicate the source of poor achievement, and, unfortunately, little is truly known about the sources of mathematical disabilities (Geary, 1999). Students with disorders in mathematics by definition have a learning disability. Discrimination against individuals with disabilities is prohibited by two federal laws: the Rehabilitation Act (Section 504) and the Americans with Disabilities Act (ADA). Both of these laws require the applicant to provide documentation of the disability (Arizona Center for Disability Law, 2001). Though special education services are typically provided on the basis of reading disability, difficulties in mathematics are just as pervasive as those found in reading. Students experience differing types and intensities of math dilemmas (Garnett, 1998).

Beyond using the words to label students is the question of their definition. In practice, the terms *remedial* and *developmental* are used synonymously. In actuality, there are a number of terms that refer to the same category of student. Young (2002) stated that students considered remedial are also given the term *under-prepared*. These students may be part of an educational program also termed *developmental, remedial*, or even *preparatory*, terms often used synonymously (Kozeracki & Brooks, 2006). Another term that is sometimes heard in similar discussions is that of the *at-risk* student. Though these students are often found in the same classes as remedial students, their classification is a bit different. Students referred to as at-risk are students guaranteed to fail if no intervention takes place (Young, 2002). Therefore, while neither remedial students nor at-risk students are performing at the college-level, remedial students may go on to find success while at-risk students will not succeed without intervention.

REFERENCES

Arizona Center for Disability Law. (2001). *Legal rights of students with disabilities in post-secondary schools: A self-advocacy guide*. U.S. Department of Health and Human Services. Retrieved from http://www.acdl.com/selfguides.html

Boylan, H. R., & Bonham, B. S. (2007). 30 years of developmental education: A retrospective. *Journal of Developmental Education, 30*, 2–4.

Garnett, K. (1998). Math learning disabilities. *LD Online*. Retrieved from http://www.ldonline.org/article/5896

Geary, D. C. (1999). Mathematical disabilities: What we know and don't know. *LD Online*. Retrieved from http://www.ldonline.org/article/5881

Illich, P. A., Hagan, C., & McCallister, L. (2004). Performance in college-level courses among students concurrently enrolled in remedial courses: Policy implications. *Community College Journal of Research & Practice, 28*, 435–453.

Kozeracki, C. A., & Brooks, J. B. (2006). Emerging institutional support for developmental education. *New Directions for Community College, 136*, 63–73.

Rodgers, K. V., & Wilding, W. G. (1998). Studying the placement of students in the entry-level college mathematics courses. *Primus, 8*, 203–208.

U.S. Department of Education, National Center for Education Statistics (1996). *Remedial Education at Higher Education*

Institutions in Fall 1995 (NCES 97–584). Washington, DC: U.S. Department of Education.

Young, K. M. (2002). *Retaining underprepared students enrolled in remedial courses at the community college.* Informative Analysis. (ERIC Document Reproduction Service No. ED46 7850)

MURRAY COX
Southwest Adventist University
Fourth edition

DEVELOPMENTAL MILESTONES

Childhood development is marked by a number of developmental milestones. While brain maturation and physical development are continuous throughout childhood, the resulting acquisitions of and improvements in abilities can cause the sudden emergence of behaviors or ways of thinking that were not possible previously. For example, the infant's first smile, first unaided steps, and first words that bring joy to parents represent milestones resulting from continuous and interrelated developmental processes and interaction with the environment. Relatively obvious physiological developments together with less obvious brain maturation, cognitive development, and stimulation from the environment result in the apparently sudden emergence of new skills and abilities. While the first responsive smile, those first wobbly steps, and the first recognizable words are three of the most obvious milestones of early childhood, there are a host of physical, biological, cognitive, emotional, and social milestones that, taken together, allow us to form a normative picture of childhood development.

Physical Milestones

In infancy, milestones in motor development tend to be the most noticeable. Most parents will eagerly announce their child's first success at standing unaided or his or her first steps. Developmentalists distinguish between gross and fine motor skills, gross motor skills being those that involve large muscle groups (crawling, walking, running, etc.) and fine motor skills being those involving smaller muscles such as the fingers and including grasping objects and manipulating tools. Both gross and fine motor skills develop out of innate reflexes present at birth and follow a predictable series of developmental milestones with each skill built on the previous one. As infants' brains develop and they gain muscle strength and coordination, their reflexes begin to come under conscious control. As gross motor skills develop, they become able to coordinate arm and leg movements and by about 7 months many are

able to coordinate their limbs sufficiently well to move by crawling on their stomach. Crawling then develops into creeping, or moving on hands and knees with the stomach raised off the ground. As balance, strength, and coordination continue to develop infants become able to pull themselves to a sitting position and to support themselves in a sitting position. As balance continues to improve, they are able to take tentative steps with support, to stand unaided, and ultimately to walk unaided (Bayley, 1969).

The development of fine motor skills follows a parallel sequence. Newborns have a reflexive grasp and will close their palms around any object their hand contacts. In the first few months of life, infants bat at objects in their environment. As fluid eye-hand coordination develops, infants become able to direct their hands effectively to objects in their environment (White, 1971). They can open their fist en route and, once contact is made, grasp the object with their palms. This *palmar grasp* works well for handling wooden blocks and rattles, but is not effective for picking up smaller objects. As muscle development and eye-hand coordination improves, the palmar grasp is replaced by the *pincer grasp*, in which the thumb and fingers and then the thumb and forefinger are opposed (Bayley, 1969).

Typical ages for the emergence of various motor skills among healthy children have been determined and some examples are given in Table D.2 (Bayley, 1969; Frankenberg, Dodds, Archer, Shapiro, & Bresnick, 2001).

It is important to note that, although the developmental sequence is the same for all normal children, there is a great deal of individual variation in the age at which specific abilities emerge. Most of the range data in Table D.2 are for the 25th to 75th percentiles, and they give a misleadingly small picture of the amount of variation among the majority of children. For example, as the table indicates, the average age for children to pull themselves to a standing position was 8.3 months and the range for the 25th and 75th percentiles was 7.8 to 9.0 months (Frankenberg et al., 2001). However, the range for the 5th and 95th percentiles for the same skill was 5 to 12 months (Bayley, 1969). Thus, there was a full 7-month spread between the ages at which most children first demonstrated the ability to pull themselves to a standing position.

Although physical milestones occur in rapid succession during the infant and toddler years, as the child enters the play years, physical milestones become less apparent as growth slows and the child masters and integrates existing physical abilities. Things remain relatively calm until the hypothalamus in the brain triggers the period of rapid physical growth and sexual maturation known as puberty (Berger, 2005). As with other developmental domains, the *sequence* of events experienced in puberty is more or less constant, although there is some variation to the sequence among normal adolescents (Rogol, Roemmich, & Clark, 2002). However, as in other domains, there is great variation in the ages at which individuals experience specific milestones. For example, for the majority of

Table D.2. Gross and Fine Motor Skill Development (approximate ages in months)

Gross Motor Skills	Age for Mastery		Fine Motor Skills	Age for Mastery	
	Median	Range[a]		Median	Range[a]
Able to lift head to 45°	0.9	0–1.8	Holds onto ring	.8	.3–3[b]
Able to lift head to 90°	2.1	1.4–2.9	Able to grasp rattle	3.2	2.7–3.6
Bear weight on legs	2.6	1.8–3.5	Partially opposes thumb	4.9	4–8[b]
Able to roll over	3.2	2.0–4.2	Reaches for pellet	5.6	4–8[b]
Pull self to sitting position	3.4	2.9–4.0	Thumb opposed to fingers	6.9	5–9[b]
Pull self to standing position	8.3	7.8–9.0	Bang two cubes held in hands	7.7	6.7–10.6
Stand unaided	11.5	10.2–12.5	Thumb-finger grasp	8.0	7.4–9.0
Walk well	12.2	10.9–13.6	Able to place block in cup	9.9	11.0–12.3
Kick ball forward	18	16–21	Scribbling	13.1	12.0–14.3
Hopping	42	39–45	Able to build a tower of four cubes	19.2	16.1–22.4

[a]Lower limit of range = 25th percentile and upper limit = 75th percentile unless otherwise noted.
[b]Lower limit of range = 25th percentile and upper limit = 95th percentile.

Table D.3. Typical Developmental Sequence of Puberty

Girls	Approximate Average Age (years)	Boys
Ovaries increase production of estrogen and progesterone	9	
Uterus and vagina enlarge	9.5	Testes increase production of testosterone
Breast bud stage	10	Testes and scrotum enlarge
Appearance of public hair	11	
Weight spurt begins		
Peak height spurt	11.5	Appearance of pubic hair
Peak muscle and organ growth	12	Penis growth begins
Hips noticeably widen		
First menstrual period	12.5	First ejaculation
		Weight spurt begins
First ovulation	13	Peak height spurt
Voice lowers	14	Peak muscle and organ growth
		Shoulders noticeably broaden
Final public hair pattern	15	Voice lowers
		Facial hair appears
Full breast growth	16	
	18	Final public hair pattern

girls, the appearance of breast buds can occur anywhere between the ages of 8 and 13 years. The typical developmental sequence is also different for girls and boys, and girls generally experience earlier onset of puberty than do boys. Table D.3 shows the typical sequence of pubertal development for girls and boys (Berger, 2005).

Among boys, the most noticeable signs of puberty are the growth spurt, the deepening of the voice, and the appearance of secondary sex characteristics, such as facial hair. In females, menstruation is the primary indication of the change from girlhood to womanhood, although girls also go through a growth spurt at the beginning of puberty.

Cognitive Milestones

Physical and motor developmental milestones are relatively easy to identify because they are characterized by discrete changes. Cognitive development also results in various developmental milestones, but these are more difficult to identify because they are subtle and they appear gradually. To developmentalists, however, these milestones are just as significant as a child's first step or the growth spurt of puberty. In the 1950s, Piaget described a stage theory of cognitive development in children and adolescents that has been supported, with some modifications, by a large body of research data. Piaget proposed four major stages in cognitive development: the sensorimotor, preoperational, concrete-operational, and formal-operational stages.

According to Piaget, during the first 2 years of life, infants are in the sensorimotor stage. During this stage the child changes dramatically, from a wordless newborn, whose behaviors are primarily reflexive, to a talking 2-year-old who has developed an impressive mastery of his or her immediate environment. Two major accomplishments during the sensorimotor stage are the development of the concept of object permanence and the beginnings of symbolic thought (Piaget, 1954).

In the first few months of life, the infant's world is largely restricted to the immediate environment. "Out of sight, out of mind" is an appropriate description for the infant's understanding of objects. Until about 6 months of age, infants typically lose interest in objects or people when they are removed from the sensory field. Beginning at about 6 months, infants will stare at the doorway and may cry when their caregivers "disappear." This change in behavior seems to indicate an awareness, on the infant's part, that the caregiver is a separate entity that has somehow exited from the world.

Piaget investigated the development of object permanence in his own children, using an infant version of hide-and-seek, in which he hid a toy, in full view of the child, under a cloth or pillow and this technique has been used innumerable times since then to investigate children's understanding of object permanence. Children under about 8 months of age will often reach for the cloth, but then soon abandon the search. However, children more than 10 months old will pull the cloth away to reveal the toy. Piaget interpreted this difference as indicating that the older children had developed the ability to hold an image of an object in memory long enough to search for it. That is, they understood that an object still existed even when it had disappeared from view. The development of object permanence represents a milestone in memory development. Once infants can represent objects in their minds they are no longer limited to reacting to the immediate environment and they become more effective at acting on their environment. This development combined with infants' developing gross and fine motor skills sets the stage for active exploration of the environment.

The second major accomplishment of the sensorimotor stage is the development of symbolic thought, or the ability to think using symbols, which is the foundation of language. However, the roots of language development actually begin much earlier than this. Bloom (1998) noted that the turn-taking behavior seen in conversation is evident in the behavior of 3-month-old infants and their caregivers. Physical and cognitive development allows infants to vocalize certain syllables by age 6 to 9 months. Deaf infants born to signing parents begin to babble with their hands and fingers at the same age (Bloom, 1998). As with the development of motor skills, children's language development follows an invariant sequence of stages, although the ages at which individual children reach specific milestones vary significantly. An infant's random vocalizations evolve into babbling, which, in turn, evolves into the first recognizable words, typically soon after the infant's first birthday. There follows a period of relatively slow acquisition of additional words until, by about 18 months old, the typical infant knows about 50 words. Around the 19th

month, the pace of word acquisition increases dramatically, beginning a period known as the *vocabulary spurt*. During this period children learn new words at rates of between 5 and 13 words per day, such that by the time the child reaches first grade he or she has an impressive vocabulary of about 10,000 words (Bloom, 1998). However, language acquisition is not just about vocabulary. Children have to learn how to put words together to make meaningful sentences. The first words are followed by holophrases, in which a single word is used to express a complete thought, additional information being supplied through the tone, loudness, and cadence with which the word is spoken (Berger, 2005). Then come two-word phrases and eventually simple sentences at about 24 months. As with all areas of development, it is important to note that there is significant interindividual variation in achievement of these milestones, as Table D.4 indicates (Bloom, 1998).

The development of effective symbolic thought marks the transition to the preoperational stage of cognitive development, usually at about age 2 years. In this stage, children are able to represent objects in their environment, but cannot yet use logical operations in their thinking, which is egocentric and illogical, and is often referred to as *magical thinking*. The primary obstacles to logical thought in this stage are *centration*, or the tendency to focus on only one aspect of the situation; *irreversibility*, or the inability to understand that some operations can be reversed to produce the initial state; and focusing too much on appearances. Egocentrism prevents a child from viewing a situation from another person's perspective. For example, when asked if his brother has a brother, the preoperational child is likely to answer "no," unable to comprehend that he is his brother's brother. (Obviously this does not work if there is a third brother in the picture!) Centration, irreversibility, and a focus on appearances lead to an ability to understand the principle of conservation. This is usually demonstrated by pouring an equal amount of liquid into a tall and a short glass. The preoperational child will believe that the tall glass now contains more liquid than the short glass, because he or she is influenced by the appearances and focuses on only one aspect of the situation—the height of the liquid in the glass (Lefrancois, 1995).

Around the age of 5 or 7, children become less focused on appearances and are more able to think about more than one aspect of a situation simultaneously. As they begin to understand the concepts of conservation and reversibility, they move into Piaget's third stage, concrete operations.

Table D.4. Language Milestones

	Age of Emergence (months)	
	Mean	Range
First words	13	10–17
Vocabulary spurt	19	13–25
First complete sentences	24	18–32

Children are now able to think logically and to use logical operations. However, they are able to apply these to concrete, or real-world, situations only. They are not yet able to think in the abstract or to contemplate things that do not exist. However, they are now able to understand that actions and relationships follow logical rules (Lefrancois, 1995). A major hallmark of the concrete operational stage is the understanding of classification, the ability to organize items into groups based on some attribute, and children in this stage become avid collectors of all sorts of things such as baseball cards and coins. Related to classification is seriation, another skill that becomes apparent in the concrete operational stage. Children in this stage are able to rank order numbers of items accurately, based on some variable (e.g., height, length), a task that generally stumps children in the preoperational stage. The ability of children in the concrete operational stage to consider more than one aspect of a situation allows them to view situations from more than one perspective. Now the child who is asked if his brother has a brother can answer that he is his brother's brother.

Other observable abilities include the concept of *identity*, or the awareness that certain characteristics of an object can remain the same even when others change (such as the volume of liquid remaining the same even though the height increases when it is poured into a tall thin glass) and *reciprocity*, or the concept that a change in one attribute can compensate for a change in another (e.g., the increased height of liquid in a tall thin glass is compensated by the reduced width).

The transition to Piaget's fourth stage, formal operational thought, occurs when brain maturation has progressed to the point where abstract thought is possible, usually in mid to late adolescence (Berger, 2005; Inhelder & Piaget, 1958). Piaget viewed this stage as the culmination of cognitive development, but more recent researchers have provided evidence for additional development and the emergence of postformal thinking in early adulthood. With the attainment of formal operational thought, thinking becomes independent of the constraints of the real world. Adolescents become able to think about how things could be. They develop *counterfactual thinking*, or the ability to reason logically about situations that do not or could not exist in reality. Often this results in their becoming highly critical of the way things are. They become much more adept at solving logical problems as the trial-and-error approach of concrete operations is replaced by hypothetico-deductive thought in which hypotheses are developed and tested in a logical and systematic fashion (Lefrancois, 1995).

Although Piaget's descriptions of the stages of cognitive development have generally held up well, his predictions of the ages of transition have not. Research has shown that evidence of specific abilities is dependent on the technique used to assess children's thinking and that specific abilities can often be detected at significantly earlier ages

than Piaget originally proposed. Also, children's development does not occur in a vacuum and social, cultural, and environmental factors have been shown to exert significant influences on the emergence of specific abilities. In addition, it appears that achievement of formal operations is not as universal as Piaget believed. In one study, only about 50% of adults were estimated to have achieved formal operational thought (REF). Nevertheless, Piaget's stage theory of cognitive development remains a useful description of the development of cognition among children and it has served as the foundation for a number of other developmental theories including Kohlberg's stages of moral development (Reimer, Paolito, & Hersh, 1983) and Selman's stages of social-perspective taking (Selman & Schulz, 2007).

Social Milestones

Human infants rely on parental care and protection to survive. It has been proposed that this need may have resulted in the development of the specific signs and signals that infants use to keep their caregivers nearby (Bowlby, 1980). The first social smile, noticed by all parents, is part of a larger system known as the *attachment behavioral system*. This system appears to operate to ensure the infant is kept safe and protected. By using different attachment behaviors, infants signal their need for attention, express preferences for particular people, object angrily if they are separated from an attachment figure, and seek comfort from their attachment object when the environment is threatening (Main, 1981). Smiling is one example of an attachment behavior. Infants' smiles strengthen when their caregiver is nearby, encouraging social interaction between caregiver and infant. Bowlby proposed four developmental phases in the attachment behavioral system. In Phase I, which under ideal conditions lasts for 8 to 12 weeks after birth, the infant responds reflexively to human contact in ways that tend to prolong contact, but is unable to discriminate self from other or between other people. During Phase II, which lasts until age 6 to 9 months, the reflexive behaviors of Phase I come under conscious control and the infant is able to integrate attachment behaviors into more complex chains of behavior. Also, the infant becomes able to discriminate between significant caregivers and other people and is likely to direct attachment behaviors at one or two principal caregivers. In addition, infants begin to initiate attachment behaviors instead of simply responding to contact with the caregiver (Marvin & Britner, 1999).

With the development of locomotion and the consequent ability to control the proximity to the caregiver, the infant transitions to Phase III. According to Bowlby, the infant now has an internal image of the goal state (contact with the caregiver) and is able to select behaviors that will realize the goal. At the same time, the infant begins to use communicative signals as means to achieve the goal state. During Phase III wariness of unfamiliar people increases markedly, and, in the presence of unfamiliar others, the infant will retreat to the caregiver for safety. In Phase IV, which develops sometime between the ages of 3 and 4 years, the child becomes less dependent on physical proximity with the caregiver, and attachment is perceived more as an ongoing relationship with the caregiver. Beyond the preschool years, Bowlby believed that the attachment behavioral system continues to develop, but that this development does not represent any qualitative change to a new stage (Marvin & Britner, 1999).

It should be clear from this very brief description of Bowlby's ideas that each developmental phase in attachment behaviors depends on the successful resolution of the previous stage. The formation of adequate caregiver-infant attachments during the first year of life appears to be a requirement for healthy development during the toddler, preschool, and later years. Once formed, the benefits of secure attachment appear to continue into the toddler, preschool, and school years (Bretherton & Waters, 1985). Securely attached toddlers seem competent and self-assured as they explore their environments and are likely to become preschoolers who are regarded as leaders and sought by other children as playmates (Bronson, 1981). In addition, a positive relationship with a caregiver seems to set the stage for the development of successful friendships, which provide social and cognitive support, ease the normative transitions of childhood, and are crucial to successful social development (Berndt, 2004; Hartup, 1996; Rubin, Bukowski, & Parker, 1998).

Closing Thoughts

While it is convenient to divide human development into specific domains, it is important to remember that all developmental domains are interlinked and that none occurs in isolation. Brain maturation affords improvements in cognition that allow the emergence of language, but the emergence of language, in turn, influences cognition. Developing motor skills eventually lead to independent locomotion that opens up multiple opportunities for exploration of the environment and for cognitive stimulation. Each domain of development affects and is affected by all others. In addition, social, biological, cultural, and environmental factors exert significant influences on development and should never be ignored. Skills and abilities tend to emerge earlier among cultures that value and encourage them, while genetic and racial differences result in differences in the ages at which milestones are reached among different groups. As an example, in the United States, African-American girls tend to mature earlier than Caucasian girls, with mean ages for menstruation of 12.0 years for African Americans and 12.7 years for Caucasians (Biro et al., 2001). The impact of environmental factors is

evidenced by the fact that in contemporary western cultures the average age of the onset of menstruation is now 3 years lower than it was in European countries during the late 1800s (Tanner & Eveleth, 1975). This shift is believed to be due to better nutrition, more favorable socioeconomic conditions, and improvements in general health.

Developmental milestones take many forms. The rapid physical changes that occur during infancy and the physical milestones that herald a new period of life are readily identified because they represent an abrupt break with the past. Similar milestones characterize cognitive and social development, but they tend to emerge gradually and to be subtler. Object permanence, the first words, and the attainment of concrete-operational thinking are each noticeable milestones in a continuously unfolding developmental process. Each milestone represents both the culmination of previous processes and the foundation for further development. Social and emotional milestones include attachment behaviors and the establishment of supportive friendships. In assessing the achievement of any milestone, but a social milestone in particular, it is essential that it be investigated and assessed in a culturally competent fashion, because family and social relationships are contextually and culturally loaded concepts (Nissani, 1993; Rocco, 1993; Winborne & Randolf, 1991). Examined together, the succession of physical, mental, and social milestones chart an individual's progress on the journey of life, but it must be remembered that, for each of us, that journey is unique, and that difference does not necessarily imply deficit.

REFERENCES

Bayley, N. (1969). *Manual for the Bayley scales of infant development*. New York, NY: Psychological Corporation.

Berger, K. (2005). *The developing person through the life span*. New York, NY: Worth.

Berndt, T. J. (2004, July). Children's friendships: Shifts over a half-century in perspectives on their development and their effects. *Merrill-Palmer Quarterly, 50*(3), 206–223.

Biro, F. M., MacMahon, R. P., Striegel-Moore, R., Crawford, P. B., Obarzanek, E., & Morrison, J. A. (2001). Impact of timing of pubertal maturation on growth in black and white female adolescents: The National Heart, Lung, and Blood Institute Growth and Health Study. *Journal of Pediatrics, 138*(5), 636–643.

Bloom, L. (1998). Language acquisition in its developmental context. In W. Damon & N. Eisenberg (Eds.), *Handbook of child psychology: Vol 2. Cognition, perception, and language* (5th ed., pp. 309–370). New York, NY: Wiley.

Bowlby, J. (1980). *Attachment and loss: Loss, sadness, and depression* (Vol. 3). New York, NY: Basic Books.

Bretherton, I., & Waters, E. (1985). Growing points of attachment theory and research. *Monographs for the Society for Research in Child Development, 50*, 209.

Bronson, W. C. (1981). *Toddlers' behavior with agemates: Issues of interaction, cognition, and affect.* Norwood, NJ: Ablex.

Frankenberg, W. K., Dodds, J., Archer, P., Shapiro, H., & Bresnick, B. (2001). The Denver II: A major revision and restandardization of the Denver Developmental Screening Test. *Pediatrics, 89*(1), 91–97.

Hartup, W. W. (1996). The company they keep: Friendships and their developmental significance. *Child Development, 67,* 1–13.

Inhelder, B., & Piaget, J. (1958). *The growth of logical thinking from childhood to adolescence.* New York, NY: Basic Books.

Lefrancois, G. R. (1995). *Theories of human learning.* Pacific Grove, CA: Brooks/Cole.

Main, M. (1981). Avoidance in the service of attachment. In K. Immelmann, G. W. Barlow, L. Petrinovich, & M. Main (Eds.), *Behavioral development: The Bielefeld Interdisciplinary Project.* London, England: Cambridge University Press.

Marvin, R. S., & Britner, P. A. (1999). Normative development. In J. Cassidy & P. R. Shaver (Eds.), *Handbook of attachment* (pp. 44–67). New York, NY: Guilford Press.

Nissani, H, (1993). *Early childhood programs for language minority students.* (ERIC Digest No. ED355836)

Piaget, J. (1954). *The construction of reality in the child.* New York, NY: Ballantine.

Reimer, J., Paolitto, D. P., & Hersh, R. (1983). *Promoting moral growth: From Piaget to Kohlberg* (2nd ed.). New York, NY: Longman.

Rocco, S. (1993). New visions for the developmental assessment of infants and young children. (ERIC Clearinghouse No. EC302834)

Rogol, A. D., Roemmich, J. N., & Clark, P. A. (2002). Growth at puberty. *Journal of Adolescent Health, 31,* 192–200.

Rubin, K. H., Bukowski, W., & Parker, J. G. (1998). Peer interactions, relationships, and groups. In W. Damon & N. Eisenberg (Eds.), *Handbook of child psychology: Vol 3. Social, emotional, and personality development* (5th ed., pp. 619–700). New York, NY: Wiley.

Selman, R. L. & Schulz, L. H. (2007). *Making a friend in youth.* Chicago, IL: University of Chicago Press.

Tanner, J. M., & Eveleth, P. B. (1975). Variability between populations in growth and development at puberty. In S. R. Berenberg (Ed.), *Puberty: Biologic and psychosocial components.* Leiden, Netherlands: Stenfert Kroese.

White, B. L. (1971). *Human infants: Experience and psychological development.* Englewood Cliffs, NJ: Prentice Hall.

Winborne, D. G., & Randolf, S. M. (1991). *Developmental expectations and outcomes for African-American infants.* (ERIC Clearinghouse No. PS019880)

JOHN CRUMLIN
University of Colorado at Colorado Springs

See also Developmental Delay; Developmental Norms

DEVELOPMENTAL NORMS

Developmental norms describe the position of an individual along a continuum of development. Two fundamental types of developmental norms are age equivalents and grade equivalents. They are obtained by administering a test to several successive age or grade groups; the average, or typical, performance of each age or grade group is subsequently determined and becomes the norm for a particular age or grade group (Anastasi, 1982).

A number of human traits demonstrate growth with increasing age, including abstract intelligence, vocabulary or language acquisition, and motor skill development. Age equivalents have frequently been used to interpret performance for age-related traits. The average test score obtained by successive age or grade groups is determined based on the performance of a carefully selected sample of individuals. The age (in years and months) for which a particular test score was the average becomes the age equivalent for that particular test score (e.g., a child who answered 35 questions correctly on a receptive language test received an age equivalent of 4 to 6, meaning that 35 was the average, or typical, score for children aged 4 years, 6 months tested in the norming program). The term *mental age* refers to an age equivalent obtained from an intelligence test. A child with a mental age of 6 years, 3 months, for example, performed as well as the average child aged 6 years, 3 months.

Skills that develop as a direct result of school instruction such as reading or mathematics have frequently been assessed with tests that yield grade equivalents. The typical, or average, performance of successive grade groups is determined for a carefully selected sample of pupils. The grade for which a certain test score was the average becomes the grade equivalent for that particular test score (e.g., a pupil who answered 40 questions correctly on a mathematics concepts test received a grade equivalent of 6.2, meaning that 40 was the average score for pupils in the second month of grade 6; Thorndike & Hagen, 1977).

Age and grade equivalents have come into disfavor for three reasons:

1. They represent scales having unequal units because human traits typically develop faster in the earlier years and slow down in adolescence and adulthood. Thus, the difference in performance between ages 3 and 4 (e.g., may be much greater than the difference in performance between ages 14 and 15 for a particular trait). Similarly, the difference in performance between grade equivalents 1.0 and 2.0 may be much greater than that between 8.0 and 9.0. This characteristic makes interpretation difficult.

2. They are not as rich in meaning as within-group norms (standard scores and percentile ranks) because they "match" the individual's performance

to the age or grade group for which that performance was just average.

3. They can imply a level of functioning or skill development that is misleading. A fifth-grade pupil who receives a reading comprehension grade equivalent of 10.8 is not necessarily reading at the same level as a student in the eighth month of the tenth grade. The grade equivalent of 10.8 is to some extent a contrivance of the grade equivalent score scale and simply means the pupil is reading very well for a fifth grader (Cronbach, 1984). Grade equivalents are especially difficult to interpret when obtained from group achievement tests. Mental ages for adolescence and adulthood likewise do not describe actual performance at those ages and often represent an arbitrary and artificial extension of the mental age scale.

In summary, age and grade equivalents are developmental norms that, when interpreted cautiously, can sometimes provide useful information; however, within group norms such as standard scores and percentile ranks they are the preferred method of test interpretation.

REFERENCES

Anastasi, A. (1982). *Psychological testing* (5th ed.). New York, NY: Macmillan.

Cronbach, L. J. (1984). *Essentials of psychological testing* (4th ed.). New York, NY: Harper & Row.

Thorndike, R. L., & Hagen, E. P. (1977). *Measurement and evaluation in psychology and education*. New York, NY: Wiley.

GARY J. ROBERTSON
American Guidance Service

See also Grade Equivalents; Norm-Referenced Testing

DEVELOPMENTAL OPTOMETRY

The relationship between vision, sight, and learning took on a new meaning in 1922 when A. M. Skeffington, an optometrist who help found the Postgraduate Optometric Extension Program, lectured on the concept that Snellen visual acuity (sight) and visual effectiveness (vision) were not one and the same. In the 1930s George Crow and Margaret Eberl expanded this concept by instituting the use of preventive lenses and visual training to enhance visual abilities, promote visual efficiency, and reduce or eliminate visual anomalies such as amblyopia, strabismus, and binocular dysfunction. At the same time, the American Optometric Association published a pamphlet, "It is a

Cruel Test," stating that "Optometry is not interested in merely whether the child sees well—it is interested in whether he sees efficiently."

Clinical studies in the visual development of the school-age child took a dramatic step forward in the 1940s at the Clinic of Child Development at Yale University. Gesell, Ilg, and Bullis (1949) established that the eye and the other sensory modalities take turns in the development of the mind. They stated that vision is so fundamental in the growth of the mind that the body takes hold of the physical world with his eyes long before he takes hold with his hands. The eyes lead in the patterning of behavior.

The team at the Clinic of Child Development Center observed visual behavior from the earliest stages. It was noted, for example, that the newborn eyes wander without a stimulus. However, after a few hours, the child can often fixate briefly. By 16 weeks the eyes are leading the other senses, but they also begin to team with the hands. Through these observations, it was established that visual development began at birth despite the fact that vision appeared to be a "fleeting, discontinuous performance."

At the Child Development Center, Getman also developed, applied, and modified optometric techniques to test the visual development of the child from 21 to 48 months. These new tests and modifications were necessitated by the fact that adult testing procedures were of little value in the testing of children.

Getman found that monocular and binocular fixation, near and far point shifting of attention, and depth perception and spatial awareness develop and increase throughout childhood at varying rates. The studies revealed the importance of how the visual mechanism is involved in the total performance of the child. The concept of developmental vision that Getman and Kephart elaborated on also established a causal relationship between early motor patterns and the development of binocularity. Therefore, any delay or omission in development could result not only in binocular defects but in amblyopias and anisometropias. According to Solan (1979) any deviation from the normal ontogeny of motor and sensory maturation is considered to be significant.

Renshaw, Getman, and Skeffington studied the retinoscopic reflex during reading in conjunction with the lie detector test. They noted that when reading, stress could be revealed by the blood pressure, respiration, galvanic skin response, and retinoscopic reflex. These studies, along with the work of Huebal, Wiesel, and others, established that vision is not just genetically endowed; it develops. The concept of function altering structure rather than structure altering function became embodied in developmental vision theory. Solan (1979) states that by integrating the concepts of Myklebust, Strauss, Werner, Birch, Kephart, Piaget, Jensen, and others, the developmental optometrist is able to construct a diagnostic and therapeutic regimen. Developmental and perceptual therapy provides a child experiencing a learning disability with those characteristics normally associated with good students who are efficient learners.

The optometrist specializing in the field of developmental vision includes in the basic vision examination a careful case history that covers any significant information on the prenatal, perinatal, and postnatal disorders and any delays in the developmental milestones. The visual examination includes the standard testing procedures such as visual acuity, ocular health status of the eyes, binocular status, refractive status, and accommodative facility. Additional tests may probe the child's concept of laterality, directionality, dominance, eye-hand coordination, and visual perception.

Training of the child with developmental vision problems encompasses the standard visual training procedures. These include enhancement of ocular motility, stereopsis, eye-hand coordination, and accommodation. Additional techniques may emphasize bilateral and binocular integration. It is also important for the optometrist to collaborate with special services personnel to assist in the psychological conditions that sometimes exist with vision difficulties (Biaggo & Bittner, 2007).

The optometrist, as Solan (1979) states, blends professional and intellectual skills to develop in the learning-disabled child a suitable level of visual functional readiness for learning, the sensory-motor skills necessary for a child to respond to classroom instruction, and cognitive skills and conceptual tempo required for assimilation and generalization in learning reasoning and problem solving.

This entry has been informed by the sources listed below.

REFERENCES

Barsch, R. H. (1964, January). The role of cognition in movement. *Optometric Child Vision Care & Guidance, 8*(4), 17–23.

Biaggio, M. K., & Bittner, E. (2007). Psychology and optometry: Interaction and collaboration. *American Psychologist, 45*(12), 1313–1315.

Gesell, A., Halverson, A. Z., & Amstruda, C. (1940). *The first five years of life.* New York, NY: Harper & Brothers.

Gesell, A., Ilg, F. L., & Bullis, G. E. (1949). *Vision: Its development in infant and child.* New York, NY: Harper & Brothers.

Getman, G. (1960). *Techniques and diagnostic criteria for the optometric care of children's vision,* Duncan, OK: Occupational Education Programs.

Getman, G. (1962). *How to develop your child's intelligence.* Luverne, MI: Author.

Getman, G., & Bullis, G. (1950). *Developmental vision* (Vol. 1). Duncan, OK: Occupational Education Programs.

Getman, G., & Kephart, N. (1957). *Developmental vision* (Vol. 2). Duncan, OK: Occupational Education Programs.

Kephart, N. C. (1960). *The slow learner in the classroom.* Columbus, OH: Charles E. Merrill.

Lavatelli, C. (1973). *Piaget's theory applied to an early childhood curriculum.* Boston, MA: Center for Media Development.

Piaget, J., & Inhelder, B. (1956). *The child's conception of space.* London, England: Routledge & Kegan Paul.

Skeffington, A. (1957). *Developmental vision* (Vol. 1). Duncan, OK: Occupational Education Programs.

Solan, H. (1979). *Learning disabilities: The role of the developmental optometrist, 50*(11), 1265. St. Louis, MO: American Optometric Association.

Bruce P. Rosenthal
State University of New York

DEVELOPMENTAL PSYCHOLOGY

Developmental Psychology is a publication of the American Psychological Association (APA). Founded in 1969, *Developmental Psychology's* first editor was Boyd R. McCandless of Emory University.

The journal's primary purpose is to publish articles that advance knowledge and theory about development across the life span. The journal includes significant empirical contributions as well as scholarly reviews and theoretical or methodological articles. Developmental psychology is defined as the scientific study of systematic psychological changes, emotional changes, and perception changes that occur in human beings over the course of their life span. Studies cover multiple topics, including biological, social, and cultural factors that affect development. The journal's website highlights special issues that cover the topics of violent children, social and emotional development, transitions and adjustment in adolescence, and sexual orientation and human development.

Developmental Psychology is published bimonthly. A yearly print subscription to the journal can be ordered online through www.apa.org. Discounts are provided to APA members and to students. Individual articles can also be purchased through the website and viewed electronically. The American Psychological Association is located at 750 First Street NE, Washington, DC 20002.

Manuscripts to be considered for publication should be submitted electronically to the "Manuscript Submission Portal," found on the website. All other correspondence regarding the journal can be sent to the current editor, Jacque Eccles, at the University of Michigan, P.O. Box 1248, 426 Thompson St., Ann Arbor, MI, 48106.

REFERENCE

Developmental Psychology. (2011). Retrieved from www.apa.org/pubs/journals/dev/index.aspx

Elizabeth Jones
Texas A&M University
Third edition

Lauren K. Eby
Chicago School of Professional Psychology
Fourth edition

DEVELOPMENTAL TEST OF VISUAL PERCEPTION, SECOND EDITION

The Developmental Test of Visual Perception, Second Edition (DTVP-2; 1993) 1993 is a revision of The Marianne Frostig Developmental Test of Visual Perception originally authored by Frostig, Maslow, Lefever, & Whittlesey (1963). The new edition includes numerous improvements, is suitable for children ages 4 to 10, measures both visual perception and visual-motor integration skills, has eight subtests, is based on updated theories of visual perception development, and can be administered to individuals in 35 minutes. The DTVP-2 subtests are Eye-Hand Coordination, Copying, Spatial Relations, Position in Space, Figure-Ground, Visual Closure, Visual-Motor Speed, and Form Constancy.

The DTVP-2 is unique among other tests of visual perception and visual-motor integration because (1) its subtests are reliable at the .8 or .9 levels for all age groups; (2) its scores are validated by many studies; (3) its norms are based on a large representative sample keyed to the 2007 census data; (4) it yields scores for both pure visual perception (no motor response) and visual-motor integration ability; and (5) it has been proven to be unbiased relative to race, gender, and handedness.

The DTVP-2 was standardized on 1,972 children from 12 states. Characteristics of the normative sample approximate those provided in the 2007 *Statistical Abstract of the United States* with regard to gender, geographical region, ethnicity, race, and urban/rural residence. Standard scores, normal curve equivalents (NCEs), percentiles, and age equivalents are provided in the Examiner's Manual.

This test was reviewed in *The Twelfth Mental Measurements Yearbook* by Bologna (1995) and Tindal (1995). Bologna stated that the revised test was an impressive revision of a previously weak instrument; Tindal described the test as useful in determining General Visual Perception, Motor Reduced Visual Perception, and Visual-Motor Integration.

This entry has been informed by the sources listed below.

REFERENCES

Bologna, N. B. (1985). Review of the developmental test of visual perception: Second edition. In J. C. Conoley & J. C. Impara (Eds.), *The twelfth mental measurements yearbook* (pp. 289–292). Lincoln: Buros Institute of Mental Measurements, University of Nebraska Press.

Frostig, M., Maslow, P., Lefever, D. W., & Whittlesey, J. R. B. (1963). *The Marianne Frostig developmental test of visual perception*. Palo Alto, CA: Consulting Psychologists Press.

Hammill, D. D., Pearson, N. A., & Voress, J. K. (1993). *Developmental test of visual perception–Second edition*. Austin, TX: PRO-ED.

Tindal, G. (1985). Review of the developmental test of visual perception: Second edition. In J. C. Conoley & J. C. Impara (Eds.), *The twelfth mental measurements yearbook* (pp. 289–292). Lincoln: Buros Institute of Mental Measurements, University of Nebraska Press.

NILS A. PEARSON
PRO-ED, Inc

DEVELOPMENTAL THERAPY

Developmental therapy is a method of educating severely socially, emotionally, and behaviorally disabled children. It has normal social-emotional development as its goal. Developmental sequences in behavior, social communication, socialization, and cognition provide the framework for the curriculum. Devised by Mary M. Wood (1979, 1986), developmental therapy links theory and research about normal social-emotional development to classroom practices. It was first demonstrated in 1970 at the Rutland Psychoeducational Center in Athens, Georgia, in a collaborative effort between the public school system, the mental health system, the University of Georgia, and the U.S. Department of Education.

Developmental therapy has been used successfully with severely emotionally disturbed and autistic children from age 2 to 16 years in preschool, elementary, middle school, and high-school classes. It also has been used effectively in day-treatment settings and residential facilities. Educators have adapted aspects of developmental therapy to resource rooms, self-contained classrooms, and regular education classes. It has extensive applications in the therapeutic arts, including art, music, and recreation therapies. It has also been adapted for use in camp settings and leisure programs, and for parents in home programs with autistic children. It was approved by the U.S. Office of Education, National Institute of Education Joint Dissemination Review Panel in 1975 as an exemplary educational program with documented effectiveness. It received validation again in 1981 from the same panel as an exemplary training model for teachers.

The foundation for developmental therapy is based on theory and research about social, emotional, cognitive, communication, and behavioral development. There is agreement that social knowledge, language, and judgment play important roles in governing behavior and that these are acquired through social experience. There also is agreement that the quality of interactions with others influences the form behavior will take. In addition, developmental theorists provide the concept of ordered, sequential processes in thinking, feeling, behaving, and relating from infancy through adolescence. Their work provides a reference for understanding the extent to which social and affective skills can be taught and the limitations that can be expected at any particular stage (Erikson, 1977;

Flavell, 1977; Kohlberg, 1983; Piaget, 1977). Social learning and behavioral theorists provide knowledge about the impact of others on the development of self-control and self-regulated behavior. Studies of modeling, imitation, punishment, discipline, aggression by adults toward children, and the role of reasoning in behavioral management provide understanding about how social behavior emerges (Bandura, 1977; Selman, 1980; Turiel, 1983). Psychoanalytic theorists focus on feelings, anxieties, defense mechanisms, ego functions, and relationships with adults (Freud, 1965; Loevinger, 1976; Maccoby, 1980). These major constructs from different theoretical orientations have been integrated into the practices of developmental therapy.

Students are grouped for developmental therapy according to their stage of social-emotional development. Groups range in size from 4 to 12 students, with the smaller groups used for students at lower developmental stages and those with severe psychopathology. Each group is conducted by a lead teacher-therapist and a support teacher aide. The goals and specific program (treatment) objectives and procedures for each stage are based on individual assessment of each student's social-emotional development. Characteristic roles for adults and the activities, materials, schedules, and behavior management strategies are specified by the stage.

The instrument used to assess each student's social-emotional development is the Developmental Therapy Objectives Rating Form (DTORF). This instrument provides specific individual education plan (IEP) short-term objectives and long-range program goals. Since the first field testing, the DTORF has been used with several thousand students ages 2 to 16 with a range of disabilities, including children who are autistic, intellectually and developmentally delayed, multiple disabilities, deaf, schizophrenic, typically developing, and gifted. Several studies provide adequate support for the effectiveness of developmental therapy (Kaufman, Paget, & Wood, 1981; Wood, 1997; Wood & Swan, 1978).

Developmental therapy has received contextual endorsement because of the directives for Part H of the Individuals with Disabilities Education Act (IDEA) and its amendments. Professionals working with young children with behavioral disorders and their families have adopted developmental therapy because it is based on the child's current level of performance rather than chronological age. This concept is conducive to the practicalities of working within the family system as mandated by IDEA (Hanft & Striffler, 1995; Zabel, 1991).

REFERENCES

Bandura, A. (1977). *Social learning theory*. Englewood Cliffs, NJ: Prentice Hall.

Erikson, E. H. (1977). *Toys and reasons*. New York, NY: Norton.

Flavell, J. H. (1977). *Cognitive development*. Englewood Cliffs, NJ: Prentice Hall.

Freud, A. (1965). *Normality and pathology in childhood: Assessment of development*. New York, NY: International Universities Press.

Hanft, B., & Striffler, N. (1995). Incorporating developmental therapy in early childhood programs: Challenges and promising practices. *Infants and Young Children, 8*(2), 37–47.

Kaufman, A., Paget, C., & Wood, M. M. (1981). Effectiveness of developmental therapy for severely emotionally disturbed children. In F. H. Wood (Ed.), *Perspectives for a new decade: Education's responsibility for seriously emotionally disturbed and behaviorally disordered children and youth*. Reston, VA: Council for Exceptional Children.

Kohlberg, L. (1983). *Essays on moral development* (Vol. 2). San Francisco, CA: Harper & Row.

Loevinger, J. (1976). *Ego development*. San Francisco, CA: Jossey-Bass.

Maccoby, E. E. (1980). *Social development*. New York, NY: Harcourt, Brace & Jovanovich.

Piaget, J. (1977). *The development of thought*. New York, NY: Viking.

Selman, R. (1980). *The growth of interpersonal understanding*. New York, NY: Holt, Rinehart & Winston.

Turiel, E. (1983). *The development of social knowledge*. Cambridge, MA: Cambridge University Press.

Wood, M. M. (1979). *The developmental therapy objectives: A self-instructional workbook*. Austin, TX: PRO-ED.

Wood, M. M. (1986). *Developmental therapy in the classroom*. Austin, TX: PRO-ED.

Wood, M. M. (1997). *Social competence for young children: An outreach project for inservice training*. (ERIC Clearinghouse No. EC305787)

Wood, M. M., & Swan, W. W. (1978). A developmental approach to educating the disturbed young child. *Behavioral Disorders 3*, 197–209.

Zabel, M. K. (1991). Teaching young children with behavior disorders: Working with behavior disorders. *ERIC Clearinghouse on Handicapped and Gifted Children*. Reston, VA: Council for Exceptional Children. (ERIC Document No. EC300413)

MARY M. WOOD
University of Georgia
First edition

See also Emotional Disorders; Social Learning Theory

DEVEREUX BEHAVIOR RATING SCALE-SCHOOL FORM

The Devereux Behavior Rating Scale-School Form (DSF) is based on federal criteria and is designed to evaluate behaviors of children and adolescents that may be indicative of moderate to severe emotional disturbances. This instrument is also useful for providing normative comparisons of behavior and for comparative results from different informants (e.g., parents, teachers). It is used for assessing a child or adolescent in a variety of settings. The information derived from the DSF can be used for treatment planning and for the evaluation of pre-/postmeasures of treatment. It is effective in evaluating progress during educational interventions and can be helpful in determining whether a child or adolescent should be placed in a special education program due to a serious emotional disturbance. The DSF has two forms that include separate sets of items appropriate for children ages 5 to 12 and for adolescents ages 13 to 18. The scale includes 40 items consisting of four subscales that address areas identified in the federal definition of Serious Emotional Disturbance. The areas are Interpersonal Problems, Inappropriate Behaviors/Feelings, Depression, and Physical Symptoms/Fears. It takes approximately 5 minutes to administer.

The Devereux Behavior Rating Scale-School Form results are compared to a nationally standardized sample of more than 3,000 cases that are approximated closely to the 2007 Census data on all demographic variables. There are separate norms for age and sex for both parent and teacher raters. The form is easy to administer and score with items and directions written at the sixth grade reading level. There is multilevel analysis and interpretation with the Total Scale Score and subscale scores assisting the evaluator in eligibility determination. The subscale scores help facilitate IEP planning and the design of preferred intervention. The Problem Item Scores help to identify specific behavioral problems for treatment.

The DSF internal consistency estimates are calculated according to age and gender, age and rater, and age, rater, and gender. The DFS Total Scale internal reliability coefficients range from .92 (parent ratings for females age 13 to 18) to .97 (teacher ratings for males and females age 5 to 12). The median Total Scale reliability coefficients by age are .96 (ages 5 to 12) and .94 (ages 13 to 18), by gender, .95 (males) and .94 (females), and by rater, .93 (parents) and .96 (teachers). The median internal reliability coefficients for the four subscales across rater, gender, and age are .85 (Interpersonal Problems), .84 (Inappropriate Behaviors/Feelings), .84 (Depression), and .82 (Physical Symptoms/Fears). The median reliability coefficient across all subscales, age, rater, and gender is .84. The DFS has very good test-retest reliability (24-hours, 2-weeks, and 4-weeks) and inter-rater reliability.

The construct-related validity of the DSF indicate that all item total correlations are significant (p < .01) and clearly indicate that the items are highly correlated to the total score. A considerable amount of data was collected and evaluated by the authors to determine the criterion-related validity of the DSF. The examination included ratings of regular education children and adolescents comparing them to seriously emotionally disturbed children and adolescents from a number of different settings. In addition, another study examined whether the criterion-related validity of the Devereux Behavior Rating Scale-School Form could be generalized to racial/ethnic subpopulations. Results based on this study support the DSF's usefulness in screening for serious emotional disturbances and suggest that the criterion-related validity is generalizable to Caucasian, African-American, and Hispanic children (Goh, 1997).

This entry has been informed by the sources listed below.

REVIEWED IN:

Impara, J. C., & Plake, B. S. (Eds.). (1998). *The thirteenth mental measurements yearbook*. Lincoln, NE: Buros Institute of Mental Measurements.

Floyd, R. G., & Bose, J. E. (2003). Behavior rating scales for assessment of emotional disturbance: A critical review of measurement characteristics. *Journal of Psychoeducational Assessment, 21*, 43–78.

Gimpel, G. A., & Nagle, R. J. (1996). Factorial validity of the Devereux behavior rating scale-School form. *Journal of Psychoeducational Assessment, 14*, 334–348.

Goh, D. S. (1997). Clinical utility of the Devereux behavior rating scale: School form among culturally diverse children. *Psychology in the Schools, 34*, 301–308.

Naglieri, J. A., LeBuffe, P. A., & Pfeiffer, S. I. (1993). *Devereux behavior rating scale-School form test manual*. San Antonio, TX: Psychological Corporation.

Naglieri, J. A., & Gottling, S. H. (1995). Use of the teacher report form and the Devereux behavior rating scale-School form with learning disordered/emotionally disordered students. *Journal of Clinical Child Psychology, 24*, 71–76.

Nickerson, A. B., & Nagle, R. J. (2001). Interrater reliability of the Devereux behavior rating scale-School form: The influence of teacher frame of reference. *Journal of Psychoeducational Assessment, 19*, 299–316.

DEVEREUX SCALES OF MENTAL DISORDERS

The Devereux Scales of Mental Disorders (DSMD; Naglieri, LeBuffe, & Pfeiffer, 1994) is designed to assess whether a child or adolescent is experiencing, or is at risk for, psychopathology, including externalizing disorders (attention/delinquency and conduct scales), internalizing disorders (anxiety and depression scales), and critical pathology disorders (acute problems and autism scales). It is useful for evaluating treatment effectiveness and in analyzing information for treatment planning. The DSMD has two levels: a 111-item child form for ages 5 to 12 and a 110-item adolescent form for ages 13 to 18. The content of the items are based on the diagnostic criteria of the *Diagnostic and Statistical Manual of Mental Disorders, Fourth Edition (DSM-IV)*. The DSMD takes 15 minutes to complete and the rater can be any adult who has known the child for at least 4 weeks. Parent and teacher raters use the same form, with separate norms provided for each. The scales are easily completed, scored, and interpreted and are written at the sixth grade reading level. Items are rated on a 5-point Likert-type scale ranging from 0 (never) to 4 (very frequently).

The DSMD can be hand-scored or computerized scored, and helps professionals assess behavior in a variety of settings. The results are compared to a national standardized sample of more than 3,000 cases approximated closely to the 2007 Census. There are separate norms for females and males. The DSMD scoring method allows professionals to compare DSMD scores of the same child or adolescent at different points in time during treatment.

The DSMD Total Score internal consistency coefficients were .98 by age, .98 by gender, and .97 (parents) and .98 (teachers) by rater. The median reliability coefficients for the composite scales on the child form are .97 (Externalizing), .94 (Internalizing), and .90 (Critical Pathology). For the six scale scores on the child form, the median reliability coefficients are .96 (Conduct), .84 (Attention), .88 (Anxiety), .89 (Depression), .90 (Autism), and .78 (Acute Problems). The median reliability coefficients for the composite scales on the adolescent form are .94 (Externalizing), .96 (Internalizing), and .92 (Critical Pathology). For the six scale scores on the adolescent form, the median reliability coefficients are .96 (Conduct), .75 (Delinquency), .84 (Anxiety), .93 (Depression), .88 (Autism), and .90 (Acute Problems). The DSMD has good test-retest (24-hour and 1-week intervals) and interrater reliability.

The DSMD authors have cited in the test manual numerous studies conducted that provide support for the DSMD's differential validity including adolescents diagnosed with anxiety disorders, conduct disorders, and depressive disorders. In addition, the DSMD T-scores are distinguished between children and adolescents with psychiatric diagnoses and nonclinical children and adolescents. Other studies conducted have found the DSMD to be able to differentiate between inpatient children and adolescents diagnosed with ADHD and those with a conduct disorder diagnosis and the DSMD Composite and Subscales Scales accurately differentiate between inpatient children and adolescents diagnosed with depressive disorders, disruptive disorders, and psychotic disorders. The DSMD has been reported to produce greater classification accuracy that the REIS Scales and the Teacher Report Form (TRF) in finding behavioral and emotional disturbances in children and adolescents with mental retardation. The DSMD also has been found to have higher specificity and positive predictive power that the TRF when evaluating serious emotional problems in children

and adolescents (Smith & Reddy, 2000). The DSMD was also compared to the Child Behavior Checklist (CBCL) for diagnostic classification accuracy in adolescents. The DSMD and CBCL were comparable in classifying oppositional or conduct disorder; the CBCL was superior for classifying major depression; and the DSMD was superior for classification of substance abuse (Curry & Ilardi, 2000).

This entry has been informed by the sources listed below.

REVIEWED IN:

Curry, J. F., & Ilardi, S. S. (2000). Validity of the Devereux scales of mental disorders with adolescent psychiatric inpatients. *Journal of Clinical Child Psychology, 29,* 578–588.

Gimpel, G. A., & Nagle, R. J. (1999). Psychometric properties of the Devereux scales of mental disorders. *Journal of Psychoeducational Assessment, 17,* 127–144.

Hussey, D., & Guo, S. (2005). Forecasting length of stay in child residential treatment. *Child Psychiatry and Human Development, 36*(1), 95–111.

McTaggart, S. (2005). Toward inclusion: Predictors and outcomes for SED students in an alternative program. *Dissertation Abstracts International Section A, 66.* Retrieved from PsycINFO database.

Naglieri, J. A., LeBuffe, P. A., & Pfieffer, S. I. (1994). *The Devereux scales of mental disorders test manual.* San Antonio, TX: Psychological Corporation.

Naglieri, J., & Pfeiffer, S. (2004). Use of the Devereux scales of mental disorders for diagnosis, treatment planning, and outcome assessment. *The use of psychological testing for treatment planning and outcomes assessment: Volume 2: Instruments for children and adolescents* (3rd ed., pp. 305–330). Mahwah, NJ: Erlbaum. Retrieved from PsycINFO database.

Plake, B. S., & Impara, J. C. (Eds.). (2001). *The fourteenth mental measurements yearbook.* Lincoln, NE: Buros Institute of Mental Measurements.

Reddy, L., Pfeiffer, S., & Files-Hall, T. (2007). Use of the Devereux scales of mental disorders for children and adolescents with emotional disturbance. *Journal of Psychoeducational Assessment, 25*(4), 356–372.

Reddy, L., & Pfeiffer, S. (2007). Behavioral and emotional symptoms of children and adolescents with Prader-Willi syndrome. *Journal of Autism and Developmental Disorders, 37*(5), 830–839.

Smith, S. A., & Reddy, L. A. (2000). A test review of the Devereux scales of mental disorders. *Canadian Journal of School Psychology, 15,* 85–91.

Smith, S. R., Reddy, L. A., & Wingenfeld, S. A. (2002). Assessment of psychotic disorders in inpatient children and adolescents: Use of the Devereux scales of mental disorders. *Journal of Psychopathology & Behavioral Assessment, 24,* 269–273.

Smith, S. R., & Reddy, L. A. (2002). The concurrent validity of the Devereux scales of mental disorders. *Journal of Psychoeducational Assessment, 20,* 112–127.

Smith, S. R., Wingenfeld, S. A., & Hilsenroth, M. J. (2002). The use of the Devereux scales of mental disorders in the assessment of attention-deficit/hyperactivity disorder and conduct disorder. *Journal of Psychopathology & Behavioral Assessment, 22,* 237–255.

DEVIATION IQ

A deviation IQ is a commonly used standard score of cognitive ability that refers to an individual's score relative to his or her age group. The deviation IQ was introduced to overcome the technical problems inherent in the ratio IQ, such as issues of comparability across age. A standard score is obtained by converting raw test scores from a standardization sample into a normalized score distribution with a fixed mean and standard deviation. This normalized score distribution takes the form of a Gaussian bell-curve where a universe of infinite random samples can be drawn from the population to form a probability distribution that contains a fixed mean and standard deviation (Jaccard & Jacoby, 2010). Thus, the deviation IQ provides a meaningful comparison of an individual's score in reference to their age group.

Deviation IQ scores typically have a mean of a 100 with a standard deviation of 15 and they can be produced from a normalized z-score distribution that has a mean of 0 and a standard deviation of 1. Standard (normalized) scores provide equal variability at each age level and standard scores from one test can be directly compared with standard scores from another. In individual assessment, David Wechsler introduced the deviation IQ with his Wechsler-Bellevue scale in 1939. (The deviation IQ had been used with some group tests earlier.) Wechsler chose to use a standard score with a standard deviation of 15 (instead of 16, the median standard deviation of the Binet at the time) because most people are more familiar with units of 5 (i.e., 5, 10, 15) than of 4 (i.e., 4, 8, 12, 16).

The construct of intelligence—and moreover the term intellectual quotient, has been the subject of heated academic and political debate (Elliott, 1987), thus researchers and clinical practitioners alike often refer to intelligence with more accepted euphemisms such as General Cognitive Ability, General Intelligence or *g*. IQ is also often broken down into specific composites that refer to different broad abilities. The Cattell-Horn-Carroll (CHC) theory serves as the hierarchical factor analytic structure that most modern test developers follow (McGrew, 2009). Test scores are based on an individual's performance on a test, but that performance is not determined in absolute, but relative to one's peers. That is, their derivation from a mental ability test are interpreted as deviation IQs, where the individual stands in relation to others of his or her age on the content of the test.

With adults, as with children, a deviation IQ is a useful index for indicating the current level of intellectual development and functioning relative to others. Because intelligence scores have been found to generally rise three points every decade, a phenomenon known as the Flynn Effect, intelligence test batteries must be renormed frequently (Flynn, 2007). This allows the normalized score distribution to retain a mean of 100 and a standard deviation of 15. Moreover, the deviation IQ does not inflate over time because the process of norming occurs roughly every 10 years.

REFERENCES

Elliott, Rogers (1987). *Litigating intelligence: IQ tests, special education, and social science in the courtroom.* Dover, MA: Auburn.

Flynn, J. R. (2007). *What is intelligence? Beyond the Flynn effect.* New York, NY: Cambridge University Press.

Jaccard, J., & Jacoby, J. (2010). *Theory construction and model building skills: A practical guide for social scientists.* New York, NY: Guilford Press.

McGrew, K. (2009). Editorial: CHC theory and the human cognitive abilities project: Standing on the shoulders of the giants of psychometric intelligence research. *Intelligence, 37,* 1–10.

DANNY B. HAJOVSKY
University of Kansas
Fourth edition

DEXEDRINE

Dexedrine (dextroamphetamine sulfate), an amphetamine, is used in the treatment of attention deficit disorder with hyperactivity (RxList, 1997), narcolepsy, and as short-term therapy for exogenous obesity. Although amphetamines are known to work as central nervous stimulants, the mechanism whereby they produce mental and behavioral effects in children is not known. Adverse reactions can include palpitations and rapid heartbeat; euphoria, restlessness, and insomnia; and exacerbation of motor and vocal tics and Tourette's syndrome. Overdose may result in assaultiveness, confusion, hallucinations, and panic states usually followed by fatigue and depression.

A brand name of Smith, Kline, and French, Dexedrine is available in 5 mg tablets; 5, 10, and 15 mg sustained released capsules, and elixir. Recommended dosage for attention deficit disorder with hyperactivity in children 6 years of age and older is to start with 5 mg once or twice daily, with daily dosage to be raised, if needed, in increments of 5 mg at weekly intervals, typically not to exceed a total of 40 mg per day.

This entry has been informed by the sources listed below.

REFERENCE

Physicians' desk reference. (1984). (pp. 1878–1880). Oradell, NJ: Medical Economics.

RxList. (1997). Internet drug index. Retrieved from http://www.rxlist.com/script/main/hp.asp

LAWRENCE C. HARTLAGE
Evans, Georgia

See also Attention Deficit/Hyperactivity Disorder; Ritalin

DHAT

Dhat is a culture-bound syndrome that is considered a "hypochondriacal concern associated with the discharge of semen, whitish discoloration of the urine, and feelings of weakness and exhaustion" (American Psychiatric Association, 1994, p. 849). This disorder is found primarily among males in India, Sri Lanka, Nepal, Bangladesh, and Pakistan. Other terms for this disorder are jiryan (India), sukra prameba (Sri Lanka), and shen-k'uei (China).

There are no known prevalence or incidence studies, such that Bhatia and Malik (1991, p. 692) observed in their study of the disorder that the "syndrome has not been studied in detail." However, according to their study, presented in the British Journal of Psychiatry, this disease seems to affect men exclusively, with adolescence as the earliest reported onset. The age range of dhat onset is reportedly 16 to 24 years of age, with the mean age of onset 21.8 years (Bhatia & Malik, 1991). This syndrome is a commonly recognized clinical entity in Indian culture. The afflicted is typically more likely to be married or recently married and of average or low socioeconomic status (perhaps a student, laborer, or farmer by occupation) and to come from a rural area and belong to a family with conservative attitudes toward sex (Bhatia & Malik, 1991).

Characteristics

1. Weakness
2. Fatigue
3. Heart palpitations
4. Sleeplessness
5. Protein in urine

Dhat syndrome is a true culture-bound sex neurosis quite common in the natives of the Indian subcontinent.

The word dhat is derived from the Sanskrit word dhatu, which means "the elixir that constitutes the body" (Bhatia & Malik, 1991, p. 691). It is a commonly held belief both culturally and within the Indian system of medicine that "disturbances in the 'Dhatus' result in an increased susceptibility to physical and mental disease" (Bhatia & Malik, 1991, p. 691).

The belief that semen is precious and life preserving is deeply ingrained in Indian culture. Practitioners of traditional systems of medicine reinforce this belief and have specific clinics to treat dhat (Bhatia & Malik, 1991). When a patient afflicted with dhat syndrome is referred to medical personnel, typical treatment is to administer antianxiety or antidepressant drugs. Some patients are also treated with a 4-week course of psychotherapy.

The likelihood of this disorder occurring in the United States is rare, and studies of affliction among emigrant Indian populations have not been formulated at this time. However, this disorder is deeply ingrained within Indian cultures, and family history as well as assimilation studies could be useful in determining dhat syndrome in afflicted students presenting dhat-like characteristics.

REFERENCES

American Psychiatric Association. (1994). Diagnostic and statistical manual of mental disorders (4th ed.). Washington, DC: Author.

Bhatia, M. S., & Malik, S. C. (1991). Dhat syndrome: A useful diagnostic entity in Indian culture. British Journal of Psychiatry, 159, 691–695.

KIELY ANN FLETCHER
Ohio State University

DIABETES

Diabetes is a chronic metabolic disease affecting approximately 18 million Americans. Common symptoms of diabetes include extreme hunger and thirst, frequent urination, irritability, weakness, fatigue, nausea, and high blood and urine sugar levels. Two major types of diabetes have been identified. Type I, or insulin dependent diabetes, was formerly called juvenile-onset because it usually occurred in children and adolescents. Type II, or noninsulin dependent, was formerly called maturity-onset. In Type I diabetes, the pancreas does not function properly, resulting in little to no insulin production and a build-up of sugar in the bloodstream. Treatment involves insulin injections, diet, and regular exercise. Approximately 1.5 million Americans are Type I diabetics. It is thought that there is a genetic predisposition for diabetes. At present there is no known cure. Obesity and stress can contribute to the onset of diabetes.

Hypoglycemia (low blood sugar) and hyperglycemia (high blood sugar) are the two most common emergencies encountered by diabetics. Hypoglycemia occurs when the blood sugar drops too low because of too much insulin, not enough food, or too much exercise. Symptoms include anger or bad temper, sudden staggering and poor coordination, pale color, disorientation, confusion, and sweating, eventually leading to stupor or unconsciousness, also called *insulin shock*. This condition is treated by administering some form of sugar such as fruit juice or candy. If unconsciousness occurs, a child should receive emergency medical care.

Hyperglycemia occurs when there is too little insulin, when infection or illness is present, or when too much food or drink is consumed. Symptoms of hyperglycemia include drowsiness, extreme thirst and frequent urination, fruity or wine-smelling breath, heavy breathing, flushed skin, vomiting, and eventually stupor or unconsciousness, called a *diabetic coma*. Treatment of this condition is usually the administration of insulin with the supervision of a health-care professional.

Some diabetics develop complications such as retinopathy, that sometimes result in blindness, diabetic neuropathy or nerve disease, diabetic nephropathy or kidney disease, cardiovascular disease, or respiratory failure. Diabetes and its complications is the number three cause of nonaccidental death among children in the United States (Wright, Schafer, & Solomons, 1979).

It has been suggested by researchers that by the time a child reaches the developmental age of 12, he or she should be able to take the lead by doing his or her own urine or blood sugar tests and administration of insulin. Keep in mind that children in special education classes may reach these developmental ages at slower rates and thus may be more reliant on teachers and parents for assistance in complying with their diabetic regimen. In such cases teachers must be aware of the regimen. Parents should inform teachers about their child's needs, which may include a special diet, especially at lunch and snack time, time to run tests and take insulin injections, exercise, and signs of emergency, especially hyperglycemia and hypoglycemia. However, teachers should make every effort not to separate the child from the peer group. The diabetic child has the same needs for support, encouragement, and understanding as other children and should be encouraged to participate in all activities.

Compliance with the diabetic treatment regimen is usually difficult for a child and it may be more difficult for a child in special education who does not understand all of the rules of diabetes. It is important in this case that the teacher and school staff work with the child's parents to understand the special needs and restrictions diabetes places on the child. Teachers need to be aware of the diabetic child's developmental age and work with the child to develop responsibility, independence, and self-reliance compatible with his or her age of development. Should parents prove either unsophisticated or unresponsive, direct teacher-physician contact becomes essential. Indeed, school districts have been found in violation of the Americans with Disabilities Act (2007) with respect to their treatment of students with diabetes (Vennum, 1995). In addition, most parents surveyed by the American Diabetes Association (1996) indicate dissatisfaction with their child's diabetes management in school. Certainly, higher expectations for school involvement are the current trend.

This entry has been informed by the sources listed below.

REFERENCES

American Diabetes Association. (1984). *A word to . . . teachers and school staff*. Alexandria, VA: Author.

American Diabetes Association. (1984). *Your child has diabetes: What you should know*. Alexandria, VA: Author.

American Diabetes Association. (1984). *An Introduction: What you need to know about diabetes*. Alexandria, VA: Author.

American Diabetes Association. (1996). This can't be happening in our schools! *Diabetes Forecast, 49*(2), 61–66.

Carpenter, J. (1976). *Diabetes: A handicap*. Unpublished manuscript.

Vennum, M. K. (1995). Students with diabetes: Is there legal protection? *Journal of Law and Education, 24*(1), 33–69.

Wright, L., Schafer, A., & Solomons, G. (1979). *Encyclopedia of pediatric psychology*. Baltimore, MD: University Park Press.

JANET CARPENTER
LOGAN WRIGHT
University of Oklahoma

See also Family Response to a Child With Disabilities; Health Impairments

DIAGNOSIS IN SPECIAL EDUCATION

Diagnosis or evaluation is an essential step in the process of identifying those children in need of special education services. Matarazzo and Pankratz (1984) define psychological diagnosis as: "(1) the process of classifying information relevant to an individual's emotional and behavioral state, and (2) the name assigned the state, taken generally from a commonly accepted classification system" (p. 369). Based on this definition, diagnosis in special education involves taking the information obtained through the assessment of a student's emotional, behavioral, academic, and intellectual functioning and classifying that information based on some accepted diagnostic system. The specific diagnostic system used determines the specific classification or name given to that student's level of functioning or condition.

The diagnostic procedure traditionally employed in special education has been one based on a medical model (Reynolds, 1984; Ysseldyke & Algozzine, 1982). This model is one borrowed from psychological diagnostic systems. It consists of preparing catalogs of systems of various special and remedial conditions and determining the extent to which an individual has characteristics similar to those of the known condition (Ysseldyke & Algozzine, 1982). According to Reynolds (1984), the focus has been on "intrapsychic causes of psychological dysfunction to the exclusion of extrapersonal factors, and on the deficiencies and weaknesses of individuals rather than on their strengths" (p. 453).

There have been many problems associated with the use of this type of a diagnostic model in special education. One problem centers on the fact that a wide variety of diagnostic systems have been developed. This has resulted in a situation in which the assessment of one student can produce very different diagnoses depending on the diagnostic system being referred to. There also tends to be considerable variations among the diagnoses of individuals classified under the same diagnostic system (Edgar & Hayden, 1985; Reynolds, 1984). These inconsistencies have made the process of special education diagnosis complicated and controversial.

The passage of PL 94-142, the Education for All Handicapped Children Act of 1975, began the formal process of diagnosis in special education. Subsequent amendments defined and redefined the different disabilities; and as the Act changed its name in 2007 to the Individuals with Disabilities Education Act (IDEA), so did the idea of "handicaps" change to "disabilities."

The emphasis on cultural competency in diagnosis is not new, but it is much more emphasized in the scientific literature and in current law. Cultural competence also refers to the individual who is conducting the evaluation. The individual must have professional training in multicultural issues and demonstrate competence in assessment and diagnosis of children and adolescents of different socioeconomic status, gender, ethnicity, disabilities, and acculturation.

School psychologists traditionally have been the gatekeepers in the diagnosis/eligibility process. School psychology emphasized classification. Rosenfield and Nelson (1995) state:

But as the current ethical, political, legal and educational context has evolved, there has been a re-examination of the purposes and applications of data gathered during assessment process (Taylor et al., 1993). In a position paper on the Role of the School Psychologist in Assessment (1994), the National Association of School Psychologists endorsed the proposition that assessment practices must be linked to prevention and intervention to provide positive outcomes for students. Thus, there is an increasing emphasis on information that is "useful in designing, implementing, monitoring, and evaluating interventions."

(Reschly, Kicklighter, & McKee, 1988, pp. 9–50)

Diagnosis in special education, therefore, has taken on a broader definition and is linked much more to intervention than ever before. Rosenfield and Nelson (1995) suggest that there are three purposes of school psychological assessment: (1) informing/entitlement/classification decisions, (2) planning interventions, and (3) evaluating outcomes. Diagnosis and outcome are on the same continuum as opposed to being discrete entities. This shift in paradigm has also changed assessment instrument usage. The use of more natural and dynamic forms of assessment that directly impact instructional delivery and behavior management are common (Rosenfield & Nelson, 1995).

It is obvious that there is much diversity in the diagnosis of the mildly mentally retarded, learning disabled, and emotionally disturbed. According to Edgar and Hayden (1985), these disabilities belong to a large percent of the total handicapped population and are the ones that are most difficult to quantify. These categories are basically indistinguishable from one another, and the population of children within these categories is indistinguishable from the larger group of children with general learning problems (e.g., disadvantaged, slow learner).

Each of these nonquantifiable categories has a history of problems in terms of the criteria used in their identification. For example, mild retardation is defined based on an IQ; there has been continual criticism of the use of IQ tests with minority population (Edgar & Hayden, 1985). The high percentage of minority students diagnosed as mentally retarded has brought charges from some that the traditional IQ tests cannot be reliably used to diagnose mental retardation. It has also been virtually impossible to define the distinction between seriously emotionally disturbed and socially maladjusted. There are no quantitative measures available for determining who is seriously emotionally disturbed. Emotional disturbance tends to be a socially defined condition, as do mild mental retardation and learning disabilities. Many of the problems associated with the diagnosis of learning disabilities have already been discussed. Edgar and Hayden (1985) feel that the only quantifiable aspect of the learning disabled definition is low achievement, which could classify 20% to 30% of all school-age children. Reynolds (1984) concludes that a large segment of children being served as learning disabled may not, in fact, be learning disabled. These are usually the intellectually borderline and low average children. According to Reynolds (1984), this is due, in part, to the diversity of models of severe discrepancy as well as to biases in the referral process favoring low-IQ, low-achieving children. It will be interesting to see if the demise of the discrepancy model will alter the amount of children identified as needing special education.

Diagnosis in special education has attempted and failed to follow the traditional model of psychological diagnosis. This model has not been proven to be an effective one for special education. One of the main criticisms of this diagnostic system has been its inability to provide reliable and valid classifications of the conditions involved in special education diagnosis. Conditions such as mental retardation, emotional disturbance, and learning disabilities have not been quantifiably defined and are therefore difficult to classify. Despite these serious flaws, the concept of formal diagnosis is still considered to be of vital importance, and has changed to fit the current demands of the Individuals with Disabilities Education Improvement Act (IDEIA) and intervention and outcome-focused needs of special education.

This entry has been informed by the sources listed below.

REFERENCES

Edgar, E., & Hayden, A. H. (1985). Who are the children special education should serve? And how many children are there? *Journal of Special Education, 18,* 523–539.

Grossman, H. J. (Ed.). (1983). *Classification in mental retardation.* Washington, DC: American Association on Mental Deficiencies.

Hammill, D. D., Larsen, S. C., Leigh, J., & McNult, G. (1981). A new definition of learning disabilities. *Learning Disabilities Quarterly, 4,* 336–342.

Matarazzo, J. D., & Pankratz, L. D. (1984). Diagnosis. In R. J. Corsini (Ed.), *Encyclopedia of psychology* (pp. 369–372). New York, NY: Wiley.

Mercer, C. D., Hughes, C., & Mercer, A. R. (1985). Learning disabilities definitions used by state education departments. *Learning Disabilities Quarterly, 8,* 45–55.

National Information Center for Children and Youth with Disabilities. (1998). *Evaluation and testing guidelines.* Washington, DC: Author.

Reynolds, C. R. (1984). Critical measurement issues in learning disabilities. *Journal of Special Education, 18,* 451–475.

Reschly, D. J., Kicklighter, R., & McKee, W. (1988). *School Psychology Review, 17*(1), 9–50.

Reynolds, C. R., Gutkin, T. B., Elliot, S. N., & Witt, J. C. (1984). *School psychology: Essentials of theory and practice.* New York, NY: Wiley.

Rosenfield, S., & Nelson, D. (1995). *The school psychologist's role in school assessment.* (ERIC Digest No. ED391985)

Ysseldyke, J. E., & Algozzine, B. (1982). *Critical issues in special and remedial education.* Boston, MA: Houghton Mifflin.

LORI E. UNRUH
Eastern Kentucky University

DIAGNOSTIC ACHIEVEMENT BATTERY, SECOND EDITION

The Diagnostic Achievement Battery, Second Edition (DAB-2; Newcomer, 1990) uses 12 subtests divided into five areas: listening (Story Comprehension, Characteristics), speaking (Synonyms, Grammatic Completion), reading (Alphabet/Word Knowledge, Reading Comprehension), writing (Capitalization, Punctuation, Spelling, Writing Composition), and mathematics (Mathematics Calculation, Mathematics Reasoning) for children between the ages of 6 and 14. Subtest raw scores convert to standard scores ($M = 10$, $SD = 3$) and percentile ranks. By combining subtests, composite scores ($M = 100$, $SD = 15$) are generated that reliably assess global strengths and weaknesses. The composites are Listening, Speaking, Reading, Writing, Mathematics, Spoken Language, Written Language, and Total Achievement.

The test was normed on 2,623 students residing in 40 states. The sample is representative of the nation as a whole with regard to gender, race, ethnicity, geographic region, and urban/rural residence. Reliability coefficients are high. Evidence of content, concurrent, and construct validity also is provided.

Compton (1996) reports that the DAB-2 measures a wide variety of skills that are directly related to classroom performance. Bernier and Hebert (1995) find that the DAB-2 is a well-designed individual diagnostic test. Brown (1995) reports that the subtests seem to measure common constructs.

REFERENCES

Bernier, J., & Hebert, M. (1995). Review of the diagnostic achievement battery, second edition. In J. C. Conoley & J. C. Impara (Eds.), *The twelfth mental measurements yearbook* (pp. 294–295). Lincoln: Buros Institute of Mental Measurements, University of Nebraska Press.

Brown, R. (1995). Review of the diagnostic achievement battery, second edition. In J. C. Conoley & J. C. Impara (Eds.), *The twelfth mental measurements yearbook* (pp. 295–296). Lincoln: Buros Institute of Mental Measurements, University of Nebraska Press.

Compton, C. (1996). *A guide to 100 tests for special education.* Upper Saddle River, NJ: Globe Fearon.

Newcomer, P. L. (1990). *Diagnostic achievement battery*: Second edition. Austin, TX: PRO-ED.

Taddy Maddox
PRO-ED, Inc

DIAGNOSTIC AND STATISTICAL MANUAL OF MENTAL DISORDERS

The most widely used system for psychiatric diagnosis and classification in the United States is the fourth edition of the *Diagnostic and Statistical Manual of Mental Disorders* (*DSM-IV;* American Psychiatric Association, 1994). The current version of the *DSM*, called the *DSM-IV-TR*, was published in July 2000. It is considered to be a minor revision confined to the descriptive text that accompanies each disorder (American Psychiatric Association, 2000). The first edition of the *DSM* was published in 1952, with the first revision appearing in 1968. All revisions of the *DSM* were developed for use with children, adolescents, and adults. The revision process included literature reviews, data reanalyses, and field trials. The American Psychiatric Association also publishes the *DSM-IV* Sourcebook, which provides a comprehensive and convenient reference record of the clinical and research support for the various revision decisions.

The purpose of the *DSM* "is to provide clear descriptions of diagnostic categories in order to enable clinicians and investigators to diagnose, communicate about, study, and treat people with various mental disorders" (American Psychiatric Association, 1994). The *DSM* uses a multiaxial classification system. Each axis refers to a different domain of information that may help the professional plan treatment plans and advice, and predict outcomes for the patient or student.

Axis I: Clinical Disorders
    Other Conditions That May Be a Focus of Clinical Attention
Axis II: Personality Disorders
    Mental Retardation
Axis III: General Medical Conditions
Axis IV: Psychosocial and Environmental Problems
Axis V: Global Assessment of Functioning

The multiaxial system assists the clinician in making a diagnosis that is biopsychosocial in nature. In other words, the information given is holistic and takes the mental, physical, and social aspects of the individual's life

into consideration. This is particularly appropriate for the 1990s, where the field of psychology has recognized the need for cultural competence in diagnosis.

The *DSM-IV* includes a section on "Disorders Usually First Diagnosed in Infancy, Childhood, or Adolescence." The diagnoses included in this section are: mental retardation, learning disorders, motor skills disorder, communication disorders, pervasive developmental disorders, attention-deficit and disruptive behavior disorders, feeding and eating disorders of infancy or early childhood, tic disorders, elimination disorders, and a category of other disorders of infancy childhood or adolescence. The latter diagnoses include separation anxiety disorder, selective mutism, reactive attachment disorder of infancy or early childhood, stereotypic movement disorder and disorder of infancy, childhood, or adolescence NOS.

The *DSM-IV* defines "mental disorder" in much the same way as its predecessors:

> [A] clinically significant behavioral or psychological syndrome or pattern that occurs in an individual and that is associated with present distress (e.g., a painful symptom) or disability (i.e., impairment in one or more important areas of functioning) or with a significantly increased risk of suffering death, pain, disability, or an important loss of freedom. In addition, this syndrome or pattern must not be merely an expectable and culturally sanctioned response to a particular event, for example, the death of a loved one. Whatever its cause, it must currently be considered a manifestation of a behavioral, psychological, or biological dysfunction in the individual. (American Psychiatric Association, 1994, p. xxi)

A criticism of this definition of mental disorder that is particularly relevant to children is that it includes areas not typically regarded as mental disorders such as developmental disorders and learning disabilities. Concerns have been expressed that children diagnosed with specific developmental or learning problems will be diagnosed and stigmatized as having a mental disorder (Rutter & Schaffer, 1980). The issue of labeling children for special education placement decisions has been controversial over the years, and it continues to be a source of frustration for many students, professionals, and parents. Therefore, the *DSM-IV* is probably best used in clinical settings where specific psychiatric treatment plans follow the specific psychiatric diagnoses. The *DSM-IV* provides at best only a basis for diagnosis and treatment for learning problems. In educational settings, special education professionals have the expertise to specify learning strengths and weaknesses and develop individual academic treatment plans that are carried out in the most appropriate learning environment.

A *DSM-IV* for primary care physicians has been developed, *DSM-IV* Primary Care Version (American Psychiatric Association, 1995), which is a volume devised to assist the primary care physician during routine patient visits. This version focuses on common conditions such as anxiety, depression, and substance abuse, diagnoses that the primary care physician is likely to encounter and to need specialized knowledge. The volume also assists in communication between primary care physicians and psychiatrists. Children and adolescents presenting with the more common mental disorders may be identified by their primary physicians, and this may help in prevention and the availability of treatment.

This entry has been informed by the sources listed below.

REFERENCES

American Psychiatric Association. (1994). *Diagnostic and statistical manual of mental disorders* (4th ed.). Washington, DC: Author.

American Psychiatric Association. (1995). *Diagnostic and statistical manual of mental disorders, fourth edition, primary care version*. Washington, DC: Author.

American Psychiatric Association. (2006). *Frequently asked questions: Diagnostic and statistical manual of mental disorders*. Retrieved from http://www.psychiatry.org/about-apa-psychiatry

Rutter, M., & Shaffer, D. (1980). DSM-III: a step forward or backward in terms of the classification of child psychiatric disorders? *Journal of the American Academy of Child Psychiatry, 19*, 37, 1–394.

LAWRENCE J. SIEGEL
University of Texas Medical Branch, Galveston
First edition

ELAINE FLETCHER-JANZEN
Chicago School of Professional Psychology
Second edition

See also Clinical Psychology; Mental Illness; Mental Status Exams

DIAGNOSTIC ASSESSMENTS OF READING WITH TRIAL TEACHING STRATEGIES

The DARTTS program is a two-component program (Diagnostic Assessment of Reading [DAR] and Trial Teaching Strategies [TTS]) designed for reading teachers, classroom teachers, special education and Title I teachers, and other professionals.

The *DAR* component is an individually administered criterion-referenced assessment of reading. The six subtests that make up the scale are Word Recognition (reading words from graded word lists), Word Analysis (letter-knowledge, matching letters and words, and letter-sound correspondence knowledge), Oral Reading (graded reading passages), Silent Reading Comprehension (graded reading passages with comprehension assessed with multiple choice questions), Spelling (writing dictated words), and Word Meaning (words from graded word lists are presented orally, and the student provides a definition for each word). For the *DAR*, the examiner simultaneously administers and scores the tests, marking students' responses as correct, incorrect, or omitted. A mastery criterion has been established for each test, and the student continues with each test until a highest mastery level has been established.

The Trial Teaching Strategies (TTS) component identifies how each student learns best through microteaching sessions. The TTS procedures are suitable for all teaching approaches and are used flexibly to aid any student reading at any level.

Raw scores can be converted to national percentile ranks. This assessment was standardized nationally on 1,664 students, and validity measures were determined using the Gates-MacGinitie Vocabulary Test. During the 1990–1991 school year, a validation study was conducted with about 4000 students on the DARTTS program. Participating students were tested with a nationally standardized reading test immediately before and then again after the use of the DARTTS materials to measure short-term gains. Then they were retested at the end of the school year to assess long-term stability of gains. Data from the validation study are included in the *DARTTS Technical Manual*.

This entry has been informed by the sources listed below.

REVIEWED IN:

Conoley, J. C., & Impara, J. C. (Eds.). (1995). *The twelfth mental measurements yearbook*. Lincoln, NE: Buros Institute of Mental Measurements.

FLORENCE G. ROSWELL
City College, City University of New York

JEANNE S. CHALL
Harvard Graduate School of Education

DIAGNOSTIC PRESCRIPTIVE TEACHING

Diagnostic prescriptive teaching "refers to the practice of formulating instructional prescriptions on the basis of differential diagnostic results" (Arter & Jenkins, 1979, p. 518). Although any educational plan for an individual learner should spring from assessment, diagnostic prescriptive teaching has had a more specific meaning. The key idea underlying diagnostic prescriptive teaching is that a given diagnostic pattern is linked differentially to a specific instructional strategy (methods, materials, techniques, etc.). That a given set of assessment findings implies an accompanying set of instructional strategies is assumed.

In the early 1970s, when ability training began to receive criticism from within the field of learning disabilities (Hammill, 1972; Hammill, Goodman, & Wiederholt, 1974), Ysseldyke and Salvia (1974) suggested that diagnostic prescriptive teaching should be based on one of two theoretical models. The first model is the ability training model. From this perspective, the diagnosed strengths and weaknesses are conceptualized primarily as perceptual or psycholinguistic in nature and understood to be the basis for academic skills. Training programs are then differentially prescribed to improve the underlying abilities demonstrating weaknesses. For example, if a student is diagnosed as expressing figure-ground errors, the prescribed educational plan would include remedial figure-ground activities, without any "advice" from the diagnostic pattern to suggest how teaching the ability will or should relate to the level of academic skill. The second model is the task analysis model. From this perspective, the diagnosis or assessment targets are the specific academic skills for the purpose of identifying the skills within the learner's repertoire. The goal of instruction is then the attainment of those new or missing skills. For example, if assessment identifies a student knows only 75% of the addition facts through 10, the prescription is that the student should be taught the remaining 25% without any "advice" from the assessment results of how those skills should be taught.

Since the early 1970s, diagnostic prescriptive teaching has taken on a meaning broader than the two theoretical models. Smead and Schwartz (1982) developed a model that is integrative in nature. Moving beyond the ability training model with its focus nearly completely on perceptual or psycholinguistic processes, they identified three learner-focused areas from which diagnostic information has relevance for instruction: motivational-emotional, cognitive-perceptual, and neurological-physical. In a similar manner, they focused on a greater variety of dimensions than did those previously concerned solely with the application of task analysis to special education. In addition, they suggested that a third set of factors must be considered: the environmental characteristics of the learning situation, which include sociological, emotional, pedagological, contingency, standing patterns of behavior, and physical factors. Finally, they suggested that the interactions among these three sets of factors—learner focused, task focused, and environmental focused—must also be diagnosed and related to the instructional prescription.

Thus, diagnostic prescriptive teaching has become better understood with the realization that a series of diagnostic patterns with related prescribed activities is simplistic given the complexity and variety of learners, tasks, and environments—and how they interact. Prescribed instructional goals must flow from assessment, addressing the learner and his/her style of learning, the skills or abilities that must be learned, and the situation and contingencies under which learning will be best facilitated. More recent studies (Covey, 1991; Fox & Thompson, 1994) suggest that diagnostic-prescriptive teaching techniques such as multisensory approaches, mapping strategies, peer learning, and process writing have achieved good outcomes with learning disabled students.

REFERENCES

Arter, J. A., & Jenkins, J. R. (1979). Differential diagnosis-prescriptive teaching: A critical appraisal. *Review of Educational Research, 49*, 517–555.

Covey, D. G. (1991). *The influence of teaching the main idea, drawing conclusions, and making inferences on the improvement of writing skills.* (ERIC Clearinghouse No. CS213114)

Fox, L. H., & Thompson, D. L. (1994). *Bringing the lab school method to an inner-city school.* (ERIC Clearinghouse No. EC304266)

Hammill, D. (1972). Training visual perceptual processes. *Journal of Learning Disabilities, 5*, 39–44.

Hammill, D., Goodman, L., & Wiederholt, J. L. (1974). Visual-motor processes: Can we train them? *Exceptional Children, 41*, 5–14.

Smead, V. S., & Schwartz, N. H. (1982, August). *An integrative model for instructional planning.* Paper presented at the 19th Annual Meeting of the American Psychological Association, Washington, DC.

Ysseldyke, J. E., & Salvia, J. (1974). Diagnostic-prescriptive teaching: Two models. *Exceptional Children, 41*, 17–32.

STEVEN R. TIMMERMANS
Mary Free Bed Hospital and Rehabilitation Center

See also Diagnostic Teaching; Direct Instruction

DIAGNOSTIC TEACHING

Diagnostic teaching is the name given an instructional process used to discover the instructional and environmental conditions under which student learning is most productive. Diagnostic teaching is also referred to as *clinical teaching* and *data-based instructional decision making*.

Diagnostic teaching differs from a diagnostic-prescriptive model of instruction. In a diagnostic-prescriptive approach, a student's achievement and learning characteristics are assessed. Subsequently, recommendations for instructional delivery are drawn from this information. This model relies on inference from a static data base (e.g., test information) for prediction of optimal instructional arrangements. In common use, such a model often fails to make use of information gained during the instructional process.

Diagnostic teaching, although sometimes included as a step in a diagnostic-prescriptive model of instruction (Reynolds & Birch, 1977), is more commonly viewed as an alternative assessment system. Like a diagnostic-prescriptive approach, diagnostic teaching makes use of test information about a student's achievement and learning characteristics, but it differs from a diagnostic-prescriptive model in a number of significant ways.

Diagnostic teaching is a process of systematic discovery rather than prediction. Reisman (1982), in discussing application of diagnostic teaching to mathematics, describes a process with five steps: (1) identify strengths and weaknesses in mathematics; (2) hypothesize reasons for achievement and nonachievement; (3) formulate instructional objectives; (4) teach to the objectives; and (5) evaluate student learning.

Zigmond, Vallecorsa, and Silverman (1983) propose a model of diagnostic teaching that is similar to that of Reisman but that is more detailed; it contains 12 discrete steps. Other and different models of diagnostic teaching are available (Walker, 1988). Differences tend to be in the thoroughness of description. Most have a set of common characteristics.

Diagnostic teaching is a cyclical process that is continued throughout the duration of student instruction. It involves planning, executing, and evaluating teaching hypotheses (Wixson, 1991). It is used to find the most effective match of learner characteristics and instructionally relevant variables. However, there is a recognition that because the difficulty of material and the demands of schooling change over time, the most appropriate combinations of instructional variables will change over time as well.

Since diagnostic teaching is an ongoing process, the diagnostician is most properly a skilled teacher rather than a diagnostic specialist who does not have continual contact with the student. The child's teacher is also in the best position to judge whether student performance or a particular instructional interchange is typical and of significance or merely an exception to the norm. The teacher's ability to note student habits and learning strategies, likes and dislikes, reactions to grouping arrangements, and so on, provides the basis on which trial modifications in instruction can be made.

Diagnostic teaching requires the diagnostician to be familiar with a variety of different curricular approaches. For any given approach, the diagnostician must be able to determine where the student might encounter difficulty. This allows the teacher to provide instruction at an appropriate level of difficulty using curricula that require different student behaviors, capacities, and experiences.

Howell and Kaplan (1980) demonstrate how basic skills can be analyzed for use in diagnostic teaching.

Diagnostic teaching also requires the diagnostician to be culturally competent (Baca & Valenzuela, 1994) and familiar with instructional variables that can be used differently in conjunction with various curricular approaches. Among these are engaged time, the immediacy and nature of performance feedback, grouping practices, and presentation and questioning techniques. For example, one exploratory combination within the diagnostic teaching process might be an increase in the engaged time a student spends being directly taught (instructional variables) phonics (curricular approach). If student learning did not meet expectations, one or more of the critical variables would be systematically altered.

Historically, the effects of different instructional combinations have been judged subjectively by the diagnostic teacher. The decision whether to continue instruction or to test another combination of variables was equally subjective. During the past two decades, there has been a growing sophistication in the use of student performance data to judge instructional effect more effectively. There has also been an increase in the sophistication of decision rules that can be used to guide the course of diagnostic teaching.

Procedures for the collection of student performance data are integral to most models of diagnostic teaching. These range from the use of special recording paper and elaborate techniques for performance analysis (White & Haring, 1980) to the use of checklists and behavioral tallies (Zigmond, Vallecorsa, & Silverman, 1983). Decision rules are usually presented within the context of a particular model but generally indicate what to do if student performance is deficient and how long instruction should continue before some systematic modification in instruction is made.

REFERENCES

Baca, L., & de Valenzuela, J. S. (1994). *Reconstructing the bilingual special education interface*. Washington, DC: National Clearinghouse for Bilingual Education.

Howell, K. W., & Kaplan, J. S. (1980). *Diagnosing basic skills*. Columbus, OH: Merrill.

Reisman, F. K. (1982). *A guide to the diagnostic teaching of arithmetic*. Columbus, OH: Merrill.

Reynolds, M. C., & Birch, J. W. (1977). *Teaching exceptional children in all America's schools*. Reston, VA: Council for Exceptional Children.

Walker, B. J. (1988). *Diagnostic teaching of reading: Techniques for instruction and assessment*. (ERIC Clearinghouse No. CS0103329)

White, O. R., & Haring, N. G. (1980). *Exceptional teaching*. Columbus, OH: Merrill.

Wixson, K. K. (1991). Diagnostic teaching. *Reading Teacher, 44*(6), 420–422.

Zigmond, N., Vallecorsa, A., & Silverman, R. (1983). *Assessment for instructional planning in special education.* Englewood Cliffs, NJ: Prentice Hall.

STEVEN A. CARLSON
Beaverton Schools, Beaverton, Oregon

See also Diagnostic Prescriptive Teaching; Direct Instruction; Teacher Effectiveness

DIALYSIS AND SPECIAL EDUCATION

Dialysis, the process of flushing kidney wastes by artificial means in cases of acute or chronic renal failure, has been increasingly used with children during the past 35 years. Dialysis methodology is viewed as a drastic mode of treatment for children, necessitated in advanced cases of kidney disease prior to, or as the result of, failed transplantation (Czaczkes & De-Nour, 1979).

While individual differences make generalization difficult, Whitt (1984) indicates that the complex and time-consuming dialysis schedule places most children at educational and emotional risk, as the time spent in hemodialysis treatment interrupts the normal pace and progress of the child's schooling. Hobbs and Perrin (1985) found the result of this loss of school time and educational opportunity to be academic underachievement and missed and splintered basic skills. In addition, the disruption of normal school progress and success weakens children's emotional stability and their feelings of competence and control (Stapleton, 1983).

During periods of school attendance, the primary role of special education is to maintain the independence of the child in dialysis. This is best accomplished by providing resource assistance to allow that child to function effectively within the regular classroom whenever possible while remediating educational weaknesses and gaps (Kleinberg, 1982). As the school experience for the dialysis child represents one of the few opportunities for that child to be in control of the environment, to gain competence and skill, and to prepare for the future in a normalized setting, special education must be used to modify programs, instruction, and the learning environment to ensure optimal educational progress (Sirvis, 1989; Van Osdol, 1982).

Special education services are also required for those periods of time (each week) during which a child is undergoing hemodialysis. Children in such treatment report concerns with the boredom imposed by the length of the sessions and the anxiety associated with the process and its discomforts (Amonette, 1984). Special education must provide instructional materials and programs for children to be used during treatment to relieve anxiety and boredom and effective home and hospital instructors to apply them.

Technological advances in computer and telecommunication strategies hold promise for upgrading the educational experience for the dialysis student during nonattendance periods.

REFERENCES

Amonette, L. (1984). *Kidney dialysis patients discover new hope through ABE Program.* Paper presented at the National Adult Education Conference, Louisville, KY.

Czaczkes, J. W., & De-Nour, A. K. (1979). *Chronic hemodialysis as a way of life.* New York, NY: Brunner/Mazel.

Hobbs, N., & Perrin, J. M. (Eds.). (1985). *Issues in the care of children with chronic illness.* San Francisco, CA: Jossey-Bass.

Kleinberg, S. (1982). *Educating the chronically ill child.* Baltimore, MD: Aspen Systems.

Sirvis, B. (1989). *Students with specialized health care needs.* ERIC Clearinghouse on Handicapped and Gifted Children. Reston, VA: Council for Exceptional Children. (ERIC Digest No. 458)

Stapleton, S. (1983). Recognizing powerlessness: Causes and indicators in patients with chronic renal failure. In J. F. Miller (Ed.), *Coping with chronic illness: Overcoming powerlessness.* Philadelphia, PA: Davis.

Van Osdol, W. R. (1982). *Introduction to exceptional children* (3rd ed.). Dubuque, IA: Brown.

Whitt, J. K. (1984). End stage renal disease. In M. G. Eisenberg, L. C. Sutkin, & M. A. Jansen (Eds.), *Chronic illness and disability through the life span: Effects on self and family.* New York, NY: Springer.

RONALD S. LENKOWSKY
Hunter College, City University of New York

See also Physical Disabilities

DIANA VERSUS STATE BOARD OF EDUCATION

Diana v. *State Board of Education* (1970) and *Guadalupe* v. *Tempe Elementary School District* (1972) were highly similar cases that were never actually brought to trial but that have nevertheless had a significant impact on special education assessment and placement procedures. In each case, civil rights organizations filed suit in federal courts on behalf of all bilingual students attending classes for the mildly mentally retarded (or the respective state's cognate designation). Both cases noted disproportionate representation of bilingual, Spanish-surnamed children in programs for the mentally retarded. Additionally, the plaintiffs in each case argued that intelligence tests administered in English to Spanish-speaking children were the principal reason for the overrepresentation. Other charges were made raising concerns about the quality of programs for the mentally retarded in both cases and violations of the equal protection clause of the Fourteenth Amendment to the U.S. Constitution, including lack of due process considerations. As Reschly (1979) has noted, in both cases the school districts involved were engaged in unsound, unprofessional assessment procedures and had developed much of their special education processes around what most in the field would consider bad professional practice.

Each case was resolved on the basis of similar consent decrees, agreements entered into by each party and then certified by the court to avoid further litigation. Issues regarding the quality of direct service were virtually ignored in the decrees, which centered on assessment and placement procedures. In *Diana*, for example, the consent decree certified by the court required assessment of each child's primary language competence; if the primary language was found to be other than English, tests used in the assessment had to be nonverbal, translated, or administered using an interpreter. The decree also required that unfair portions of English-language tests were to be deleted and more influence accorded to the results of nonverbal intelligence tests when placement decisions were being made.

Guadalupe, in the consent decree, mandated the same changes in testing practices as *Diana*. *Guadalupe* went on to add four additional statements:

1. IQ tests were not to be the exclusive or the primary basis for the diagnosis of mild mental retardation.

2. Adaptive behavior in other than school settings would be assessed.

3. Due process procedures were to be developed and instituted before individual assessment or any movement toward diagnosis and placement could occur.

4. Special education would be provided to each child in the most normal setting or environment possible.

Since *Diana* and *Guadalupe* were settled by consent decrees, no judicial opinion is available and there are no findings to be reviewed and discussed. Neither case set legal precedent. Both were strongly influential, however, in subsequent legislation passed at the state and federal levels. Wording from the two decrees is now commonplace in many state and federal regulations governing the education of the handicapped.

REFERENCE

Reschly, D. J. (1979). Nonbiased assessment. In G. Phye & D. Reschly (Eds.), *School psychology: Perspectives and issues*. New York, NY: Academic Press.

CECIL R. REYNOLDS
Texas A&M University

See also Consent Decree; Equal Protection; Individuals with Disabilities Education Improvement Act of 2004 (IDEIA); Larry P.; Marshall v. Georgia

DIAZEPAM

Diazepam (Valium) is a minor tranquilizer with relatively few side effects compared with other psychotropic medications. It is prescribed primarily with adult populations for symptoms of anxiety. Clinically, diazepam seems to be prescribed infrequently as a psychotropic, particularly as an antianxiety drug in children.

Although diazepam is used only infrequently as a psychotropic agent in pediatric populations, it is often used as an adjunct in the treatment of seizure disorders. When administered intravenously in repeated dosages as deemed necessary, diazepam has been found to be effective in the initial management of uncontrolled, continuous seizures, or status epilepticus (Behrman, Vaughn, Victor, & Nelson, 1983). In general, diazepam is not used in the long-term management of seizure disorders because of the likelihood of the development of tolerance to the drug. Tolerance often develops very rapidly, sometimes as quickly as 3 to 14 days after initiation of therapy (Behrman et al., 1983). Increasing the dosage when the tolerance develops may help control the seizures, but, frequently, side effects such as drowsiness, ataxia, and slurred speech make the increased dosage intolerable. Occasionally, diazepam may be indicated therapeutically in the treatment of petit mal seizures, refractory to Zarontin and other agents, and in combination with phenobarbital and phenytoin in the treatment of seizures associated with central nervous system disease (Behrman et al., 1983).

Diazepam has been used to some extent in the treatment of sleep disturbances in children. It should be noted that insomnia and night waking, although common in childhood, are typically transitory. The practitioner must carefully rule out other dysfunctions such as phobic and separation disorders, as well as psychosocial stressors that may result in sleep disturbances. Further, psychostimulant medications used during the day for the treatment of hyperactivity may also cause sleep disturbances (Brown & Borden, 1989). However, if the etiology of the sleep disturbance is an identifiable stressor that cannot be alleviated, the short-term use of diazepam at low dosages, administered in a single dose at bedtime, may be a temporary treatment for both the child and the parent (Shaffer & Ambrosini, 1985). Diazepam may also be particularly effective for those sleep disturbances termed parasomnias; they include nightmares, sleep terrors, and sleepwalking. Because these disorders typically dissipate with age, the need for continued medication must be reassessed frequently.

The side effects attributed to diazepam are often further elaborations of the desired therapeutic effects. Those of primary concern include confusion, disinhibition, incoordination, drowsiness, and depression (Jaffe & Magnuson, 1985; Konopasek, 2004; Rapoport, Mikkelsen, & Werry, 1978). Both physiological and psychological dependence may also develop as a function of prolonged usage (Rapoport et al.,

1978). Following prolonged usage, diazepam should be discontinued slowly with decreasing dosages because seizures may occur in response to abrupt withdrawal.

REFERENCES

Behrman, R. E., Vaughn, V. C., Victor, B., & Nelson, W. E. (1983). Convulsive disorders. In R. Behrman & V. Vaughn (Eds.), *Nelson textbook of pediatrics* (pp. 1531–1545). Philadelphia, PA: Saunders.

Brown, R. T., & Borden, K. A. (1989). Neuropsychological effects of stimulant medication on children's learning and behavior. In C. R. Reynolds (Ed.), *Child neuropsychology: Techniques of diagnosis and treatment*. New York, NY: Plenum Press.

Jaffe, S., & Magnuson, J. V. (1985). Anxiety disorders. In J. Wiener (Ed.), *Diagnosis and psychopharmacology of childhood and adolescent disorders* (pp. 199–214). New York, NY: Wiley.

Konopasek, D. E. (2004). *Medication factsheets*. Longmont, CO: Sopris West.

Rapoport, J. L., Mikkelsen, E. J., & Werry, J. S. (1978). Antimanic, antianxiety, hallucinogenic, and miscellaneous drugs. In J. Werry (Ed.), *Pediatric psychopharmacology* (pp. 316–355). New York, NY: Brunner/Mazel.

Shaffer, D., & Ambrosini, P. J. (1985). Enuresis and sleep disorders. In J. Wiener (Ed.), *Diagnosis and psychopharmacology of childhood and adolescent disorders* (pp. 305–331). New York, NY: Wiley.

RONALD T. BROWN
SANDRA B. SEXSON
Emory University School of Medicine

See also Anticonvulsants; Phenobarbital; Tranquilizers

DICHOTIC LISTENING

Dichotic listening is an auditory task used in clinical practice and research. The paradigms use simultaneous presentation of differing auditory stimuli to both ears. It has been used in the assessment of selective attention as well as for determination of cerebral hemisphere specialization of language. In the free-recall consonant-vowel (CV) syllable paradigm, for example, presentation to the right ear might be /ba/ simultaneous with presentation to the left ear of /ta/. The child is asked to repeat what he or she hears (e.g., Cohen, Riccio, & Hynd, 1999). Based on the accuracy of free recall for right and left ear presentations, a dominant ear or "ear advantage" is determined. To control for potential differences in absolute hearing between left and right ears, some dichotic listening tasks, such as the Staggered Spondaic Word test (SSW; Katz, 1962), require pure tone testing first, and then presentation of the auditory stimulus at a set decibel level above hearing level for each ear. In contrast to the CV paradigm, the SSW presents a single word to one ear, then different words simultaneously to each ear, and then a single word to the second ear. Thus, the SSW yields right only, competing, and left only conditions for evaluation of ear advantage.

Regardless of the specific task, results of dichotic listening tasks are presumed to provide information on hemispheric lateralization of language (Hugdahl, Carlsson, Uvebrant, & Lundervold, 1997; Kimura, 1961). In the normal population, the typical person demonstrates a right ear advantage on dichotic listening tasks, consistent with left hemisphere specialization for language. In clinical populations, particularly those with involvement of the central auditory system, the laterality ratio or extent of ear advantage is not as great, or the population may evidence a left ear advantage. For example, Cohen et al. (1999) found that children with speech-language impairments demonstrated one of three patterns: (1) weak right ear advantage; (2) left ear advantage or right ear deficiency; or (3) bilateral deficits. Similarly, in comparing children with expected reading levels to those with dyslexia, Asbjornsen, Helland, Obrzut, and Boliek (2003) found that children with dyslexia demonstrated lower laterality indexes (i.e., less pronounced right ear advantage) than would be expected.

At the same time, it is important to remember that dichotic listening tasks also involve attentional processes and memory; performance is not solely determined by language. For this reason, attentional priming has been investigated to determine effects of attention on CV tasks (e.g., Asbjornsen & Bryden, 1998; Obrzut, Horgesheimer, & Boliek, 1999; Riccio, Hynd, Cohen, & Molt, 1996; Riccio, Cohen, Garrison, & Smith, 2005). Additional research is needed before it is possible to dissociate attention, memory, and language components of the various dichotic listening tasks. Until then, caution should be used when making inferences related to cerebral lateralization or localization of function using dichotic listening tasks. Further, if there is no control for potential pure tone differences between right and left ear, additional caution is needed in determining ear advantage for language (or attention or memory).

REFERENCES

Asbjornsen, A. E., & Bryden, M. P. (1998). Auditory attentional shifts in reading-disabled students: Quantification of attentional effectiveness by the Attentional Shift Index. *Neuropsychologia, 36*, 143–148.

Asbjornsen, A. E., Helland, T., Obrzut, J. E., & Boliek, C. A. (2003). The role of dichotic listening performance and tasks of executive functions in reading impairment: A discriminant function analysis. *Child Neuropsychology, 9*, 277–288.

Cohen, M. J., Riccio, C. A., & Hynd, G. W. (1999). Children with specific language impairment: Quantitative and qualitative analysis of dichotic listening performance. *Developmental Neuropsychology, 16*, 243–252.

Hugdahl, K., Carlsson, G., Uvebrant, P., & Lundervold, A. J. (1997). Dichotic listening performance and intracarotid injections of amobarbital in children and adolescents: Preoperative and postoperative comparisons. *Archives of Neurology, 54,* 1494–1500.

Katz, J. (1962). The use of staggered spondaic words for assessing the integrity of the central auditory nervous system. *Journal of Auditory Research, 2,* 237–337.

Kimura, D. (1961). Cerebral dominance and the perception of verbal stimuli. *Canadian Journal of Psychology, 15,* 166–171.

Obrzut, J. E., Horgesheimer, J., & Boliek, C. A. (1999). A "threshold effect" of selective attention on the dichotic REA with children. *Developmental Neuropsychology, 16,* 127–137.

Riccio, C. A., Cohen, M. J., Garrison, T., & Smith, B. (2005). Auditory processing measures: correlation with neuropsychological measures of attention, memory, and behavior. *Child Neuropsychology, 11,* 363–372.

Riccio, C. A., Cohen, M. J., Hynd, G. W., & Molt, L. (1996). The staggered spondaic word test: Performance of children with attention deficit hyperactivity disorder. *American Journal of Audiology, 5,* 55–62.

CYNTHIA A. RICCIO
Texas A&M University

See also Auditory Processing; Language Disorders; Reading Disorders

DICTIONARY OF OCCUPATIONAL TITLES

The *Dictionary of Occupational Titles* (DOT) is prepared and published by the U.S. Department of Labor, Employment and Training Administration. It provides comprehensive occupational information to serve the labor market in job placement, employment counseling, and guidance. Concise standardized definitions (12,741) are alphabetized by title with coding arrangements for occupational classifications. Blocks of jobs are assigned to one of 550 occupational groups using a 5- or 6-digit code. Skilled, semiskilled, or unskilled categories are specified. The format for each definition is occupational code number; occupational title; industry designation; alternate title (if any); body of the definitional lead statement; task element statement; undefined related title (if any).

Consumers may reproduce any part of this public document without special permission from the federal government. Source credit is requested but not required. The DOT has 1,404 pages. A computerized version of the DOT is available and provides the benefit of a searchable database.

This entry has been informed by the source listed below.

REFERENCE

U.S. Department of Labor, Employment, and Training Administration. (1996). *Dictionary of occupational titles* (4th ed.). Washington, DC: Author.

C. MILDRED TASHMAN
College of St. Rose

DIFFERENTIAL ABILITY SCALES–SECOND EDITION

The Differential Ability Scales–Second Edition (DAS-II-II; 2007a) is an individually administered measure of cognitive ability and achievement designed to measure specific abilities and assist in determining strengths and weaknesses for children and adolescents age 2 years, 6 months through 17 years, 11 months. The DAS-II-II is composed of 20 cognitive subtests that include 10 "core" subtests and 10 "diagnostic" subtests. The core subtests are used to calculate a high-level composite score called the General Conceptual Ability (GCA) score (i.e., "the general ability of an individual to perform complex mental processing that involves conceptualization and transformation of information"; Elliott, 2007, p. 17) and three lower-level composite scores: Verbal Ability, Nonverbal Reasoning Ability, and Spatial Ability cluster scores. With lower g-loadings, the diagnostic subtests are used predominantly to assess strengths and weaknesses and do not contribute to the composite scores. Administration time is estimated to be 45 to 70 minutes for the full cognitive battery.

Three batteries comprise the DAS-II-II: a lower early years level battery for ages 2:6 to 3:5, an upper early years level battery for ages 3:6 to 6:11, and a school-age level battery for ages 7:0 to 17:11. These batteries differ with regard to subtests included and the number of abilities measured. The lower early years level is made up of 4 core cognitive subtests, which yield the GCA score as well as verbal ability and nonverbal ability cluster scores. Three diagnostic cognitive subtests are also available. In comparison, the upper early years level is comprised of 6 core cognitive subtests, which yield a GCA score and verbal ability, nonverbal reasoning ability, and spatial ability cluster scores. Additionally this level provides 3 to 10 diagnostic cognitive subtests that yield working memory, processing speed, and school readiness cluster scores. The school-age level battery consists of 6 core cognitive subtests, and 7 to 10 diagnostic cognitive subtests that yield a GCA score and 5 cluster scores: verbal ability, nonverbal reasoning ability, spatial ability, working memory, and processing speed. At each level, subtests can be combined to provide a "Special Nonverbal Composite" score. The DAS-II-II, like many other standardized cognitive ability tests, uses the Deviation IQ ($M = 100$, $SD = 15$) for the composite scores and T scores ($M = 50$, $SD = 10$) for the 20 individual subtests.

The DAS-II-II was standardized on a stratified sample of 3,480 American children and adolescents. Data from the 2005 U.S. Census Bureau was used to stratify the sample. Strata included age, sex, ethnicity, parental education, educational preschool enrollment, and geographic location. Between the ages of 2:6 and 4:11, age groups consisted of 176 children; between the ages of 5:0 and 17:11, age groups consisted of 200 children.

Reliability and validity data are very good. Average internal consistency reliability coefficients for the GCA are .94 for the lower early years level, .96 for the upper early years level, and .96 for the school-age level (Elliott, 2007). Internal consistency of the clusters is also very good; reliability coefficients range from .87 for the nonverbal ability cluster in the lower early years level to .95 for the spatial ability cluster in the upper early years and school-age level. Median test-retest reliability coefficients ranged from .92 for the GCA; .89 for the verbal and spatial clusters; .88 for the school readiness cluster; .87 for working memory cluster .83 for processing speed; and .81 for the nonverbal reasoning cluster. Finally, with regard to concurrent validity, the GCA correlates well with other measures of intelligence ($r = .80$).

Overall, the DAS-II-II is a well-standardized instrument with strong psychometric properties. Additional strengths are that the GCA is highly g-saturated, that the time of administration is relatively short, that the test is adaptive in nature and that children as young as 2 and 3 years of age can be assessed. The DAS-II-II is not effortless to administer, but it is not unduly or unnecessarily difficult. As with most individual tests covering a wide range of ages, there is more hardware to cope with when testing younger children, but it is not too challenging to learn to keep track of and manipulate the cards and objects needed for picture similarities and verbal comprehension. Examiners need to use both the administration manual and the record form along with the stimulus books for some subtests, especially word definitions, copying, and recall of designs, but this divided-attention task is not difficult to master. Despite these assets, the DAS-II-II has some limitations. As noted above, the DAS-II-II is not unduly difficult to administer and score. Although easier to administer than many comparable tests, it is a complex instrument that does require training, practice, and careful attention, especially with verbal comprehension, recall of designs, and recall of objects. New examiners will need to be thoughtful and thorough in their preparation. In particular, caution must be exercised when scoring word definitions, verbal similarities, recall of designs, and

copying, as these subtests require considerable judgment by the examiner. In addition, the range of possible GCA scores varies from age group to age group, and GCA scores are derived from different combinations of subtests in each of the three batteries.

REVIEWED IN:

Beran, T. N. (2007). Review of "Differential Ability Scales" (2nd ed.). *Canadian Journal of School Psychology*, 22(1), 128–132.

Dumont, R., Willis, J., & Elliott, C. D. (2008). *Essentials of DAS-II-II Assessment*. Hoboken, NJ: Wiley.

Dumont, R., Willis, J., Salerno, J. D., & Sattler, J. M. (2008). Differential Ability Scales–Second Edition. (Chapter 17). In J. Sattler, *Assessment of children: Cognitive applications* (5th ed.). San Diego, CA: Sattler.

Elliott, C. D. (2007). *Differential ability scales, 2nd edition: Introductory and technical handbook*. San Antonio, TX: Psychological Corporation.

Elliott, C. D., Hale, J. B., Fiorello, C. A., Dorvil, C., & Moldovan, J. (2010). Differential Ability Scales-II prediction of reading performance: Global scores are not enough. *Psychology in the Schools*, 47(7).

Hale, J. B., Fiorello, C. A., Dumont, R., Willis, J. O., Rackley, C., & Elliott, C. E. (2008). Differential ability scales–Second edition (neuro)psychological predictors of math performance for typical children and children with math disabilities. *Psychology in the Schools*, 45(9), 1–21.

Marshall, S., McGoey, K. E., & Moschos, S. (2011). Test review: Differential ability scales—Second edition. *Journal of Psychoeducational Assessment*, 29, 1, 89–93.

Reddy, L. A., Braunstein, D. J., & Dumont, R. (2008). Use of the differential ability scales for children with attention-deficit hyperactivity disorder. *School Psychology Quarterly*, 23, 1, 139–148.

Spies, R. A., Carlson, J. F., & Geisinger, K. F. (Eds.). (in press). *The eighteenth mental measurements yearbook*. Lincoln, NE: Buros Institute of Mental Measurements.

RON DUMONT
Fairleigh Dickinson University

JOHN O. WILLIS
Rivier College

KATHLEEN VIEZEL
Fairleigh Dickinson University

JAMIE ZIBULSKY
Fairleigh Dickinson University
Fourth edition

DIFFUSION TENSOR IMAGING

There have been a number of advances in magnetic resonance imaging facilitating access to new opportunities for gathering functional information about the brain. The development of Diffusion Tensor Imaging (DTI) has enabled researchers to go beyond anatomical imaging and study tissue structure at a microscopic level in vivo. DTI was first introduced in the mid-1980s by Le Bihan et al. (1986). DTI is a method of magnetic resonance imaging that measures water diffusion across several tissue axes. With DTI, diffusion anisotropy effects can be fully characterized and exploited providing better details on tissue microstructure (Basser, Mattiello, & Le Bihan, 1994). This is useful in studying the brain because water displacements are not the same throughout the brain. White-matter displacements are smaller or often more restricted than and perpendicular to myelinated fibers as they create physical boundaries that slow the diffusion of water molecules. DTI measures the movement of water in the brain, detecting areas where the normal flow of water is disrupted. A disrupted flow of water indicates the possibility of an underlying abnormality.

One of the most useful applications of DTI has included an understanding of brain ischemia (Warach, 1992). Currently, DTI is useful in the study and diagnosis of white-matter diseases including traumatic brain injuries or neurological insults such as strokes and even epilepsy. DTI may not only be useful in studying white-matter diseases and other neural abnormalities, but it could be used to assess brain maturation in children, newborns, or premature infants (Le Bihan et al., 2001). Increasing research has placed a focus on studying neuronal connectivity (Le Bihan et al., 2001). An important application of DTI is fiber tracking, which allows elucidation of white-matter tracts. DTI is the only noninvasive approach to track brain white-matter fibers. This allows for visualization of various anatomic connections between different parts of the brain on an individual basis. When used in collaboration with fMRI, information about white-matter tracts reveals important information about neurocognitive networks, and provides a quick way to improve our understanding of brain function. Future research will concentrate on improving the accuracy and robustness of the technique, as well as enhanced visualization of the white fiber tracts in three dimensions. Advances in this imaging technique will continue to provide useful information to scientists in better understanding brain function and improving the accuracy and ability to improve the lives of patients.

REFERENCES

Basser, P. J., Mattiello J., & Le Bihan D. (1994). Estimation of the effective self-diffusion tensor from the NMR spin echo. *Journal of Magnetic Resonance Imaging, 103*, 247–254.

Le Bihan, D., Breton, E., Lallemand, D., Grenier, P., Cabanis, E., & Laval-Jeantet, M. (1986). MR Imaging of intravoxel incoherent motions: Applications to diffusion and perfusion in neurological disorders. *Radiology, 161*, 401–407.

Le Bihan, D., Mangin, J. F., Poupon, C., Clark, C. A., Pappata, S., Molko, N., & Chabriat, H. (2001). Diffusion tensor imaging: Concepts and applications. *Journal of Magnetic Resonance Imaging, 13*, 534–546.

Warach, S., Chien, D., Li, W., Ronthal, M., & Edelman, R. R. (1992). Fast magnetic resonance diffusion-weighted imaging of acute human stroke. *Neurology, 42*, 1717–1723.

ADAM J. SCHWEBACH
University of Utah

See also Biofeedback; Magnetic Resonance Imaging; Spect

DIGEORGE SYNDROME

DiGeorge syndrome (DGS) is a set of phenotypic abnormalities including T-cell–mediated immune deficits, thymic aplasia, congenital hypoparathyroidism, mild facial anomalies, developmental delay, and congenital heart defects (Thomas & Graham, 1997). The syndrome was initially described in 1965. Simultaneously, other overlapping syndromes were identified, including velocardiofacial syndrome (VCFS). Ultimately, secondary to an overlap of clinical symptoms, as well as chromosomal investigations of affected families, it was recognized that most individuals with the characteristic features of these and other syndromes have a deletion of 22q11 and that these disorders represent a set of related developmental abnormalities (Thomas & Graham, 1997) categorized under the heading of Chromosome 22q11 deletion syndrome.

The 22q11 deletion syndrome may be inherited in an autosomal dominant fashion or arise secondary to de novo deletions or translocations (Thomas & Graham, 1997). Individuals with similar deletions may have variable clinical presentation. Not all affected individuals have a 22q11 deletion, although 85% to 90% of those diagnosed with DGS do. Teratogenic exposure, maternal diabetes, or other in utero perturbation can also cause the same series of abnormalities. The syndrome is thought to be a developmental field defect occurring in about the third or fourth week of gestation (Thomas & Graham, 1997).

There are varying estimates of the incidence of a 22q11 deletion. They have ranged from 1:4,727 to 1:10,000 births (Devriendt et al., 1999). Five percent of children with congenital heart disease are found to have this deletion.

Characteristics

1. Structural heart abnormalities (85%), with multiple anomalies, occur in a great number of identified patients.

2. A cleft palate is present in 80% to 85% of the patients, although this may represent an overestimation based on ascertainment bias (Graham & Thomas, 1997).

3. Infants appear normal at birth but often experience failure to thrive.

4. The typical facies become more identifiable with age. The key features include a long face with a prominent bulbar nose accompanied by a squared nasal root, minor ear abnormalities, narrow palpebral fissures, retrognathia, and abundant hair. Slender, tapered, and hyperextensible fingers are associated (58% to 63%).

5. Patients with DGS often have compromised immunologic function. One group with "complete" DGS has deficiency of T-cell function and has increased susceptibility to infection. A second group with "incomplete" DGS has decreased immune function early in life but eventually develops adequate T-cell numbers and function.

6. Learning disabilities, complicated by hearing loss associated with otitis media, are evident in 100% of those with 22q11 deletions. Mild to moderate mental retardation is evident in 40% to 50% of the population. Some authors identify the pattern of performance as typical of those with nonverbal learning disorders (Swillen et al., 1999).

7. Children with this syndrome are described as demonstrating impulsivity and disinhibition but also can be shy and withdrawn (Swillen et al., 1999). There is an unusual predilection for development of overt psychosis during late adolescence or early adulthood, with the prevalence of psychosis in the DGS population estimated at 10% to 22% (Thomas & Graham, 1997).

8. Hypocalcemia is an early problem with 10% to 20% of the children experiencing seizures or rigidity. The hypocalcemia most often remits with time.

Educational intervention is a necessary aspect of treatment. Audiologic function must be monitored. Speech therapy has been found to be more useful after surgical correction, if the patient has velopharyngeal insufficiency (> 85% of these patients). Computer-assisted instruction has been found helpful. Treatment of the nonverbal learning disorder, including the social learning deficit, is required (Derynck et al., 1999).

Future research will include attempts at greater understanding of the relationship between the specific genetic abnormality and clinical presentation. An understanding of how DGS and VCFS are related to schizophrenia and other psychiatric illnesses may shed light on the neurologic abnormalities in these disorders as well.

REFERENCES

Derynck, F., Sokolowsky, M., Pech, C., Henin-Brun, F., Rufo, M., & Philip, N. (1999). Psychiatric and mother-child relational disorders in children with chromosomal deletion 22q11. *Genetic Counseling, 10*(1), 110–111.

Devriendt, K., Mathijs, G., Van Dael, R., Gewillig, M., Eyskens, B., Hjalgrim, H., ... & Vermeesch, J. R. (1999). Delineation of the critical deletion region for congenital heart defects, on chromosome, *American Journal of Human Genetics, 64* (4), 119–126.

McDonald-McGinn, D. M., La Rossa, D., Godmuntz, E., Sullivan, K., Eicher, P., Gerdes, M., ... Zackai, E. H. (1999). The variable expression of the chromosome 22q11.2 deletion: Findings in 216 patients. *Genetic Counseling, 10*(1), 96–98.

Swillen, A., Devriendt, K., Legius, E., Prinzie, P., Vogels, A., Ghesquiere, P., & Fryns, J. P. (1999). The behavioural phenotype in velocardio-facial syndrome (VCFS): From infancy to adolescence. *Genetic Counseling, 10*(1), 79–88.

Thomas, J. A., & Graham, J. M. (1997). Chromosome 22q11 deletion syndrome: An update and review for the primary pediatrician. *Clinical Pediatrics, 36*(5), 253–266.

GRETA N. WILKENING
University of Colorado Health Sciences Center
The Children's Hospital

Individuals with DGS require careful medical surveillance. The cardiac defect is the most pressing issue initially. If the lesion is not lethal, the abnormality is often correctable. Hypocalcemia must be managed aggressively to limit neurologic compromise. Feeding difficulties are frequent, sometimes requiring gastrostomy or nasogastric feeding (McDonald-McGinn et al., 1999). Aggressive immunotherapy is necessary. Immune function often improves after the preschool years (Thomas & Graham, 1997). There has been successful use of bone marrow transplantation in patients who have complete DGS or VCFS and lack immunologic function (Thomas & Graham, 1997).

DILANTIN

Dilantin is an antiepileptic drug that can be useful in the treatment of seizure disorders. Generically, it is known as phenytoin. It was introduced in 1938 by Merritt and Putnam, who discovered its anticonvulsant activity in animals. It has proven remarkably effective in treating both partial seizures and generalized tonic-clonic seizure activity. Dilantin appears to work primarily in the motor cortex of the brain; it acts to inhibit the spread of seizure activity by preventing the extension of seizure activity from abnormally discharging neurons to surrounding cells

(Mosby, 1997). It is thought that Dilantin tends to stabilize the threshold of neurons against the hyperexcitability caused by excessive stimulation or environmental changes that can lead to seizures. Additionally, Dilantin appears to reduce brain stem center activity responsible for the tonic phase of tonic clonic (grand mal) seizures.

Some minor toxic symptoms such as gastric discomfort and nausea are frequent at the onset of Dilantin therapy. These tend to disappear rapidly. In children, a common effect of chronic use is gingival hyperplasia, which may cause bleeding gums. This condition generally can be prevented by good oral hygiene. Hirsutism occurs frequently, and may be aesthetically distressing, especially in girls. Toxic reactions to Dilantin include blurring of vision or ataxia. The onset of pruritus (severe itching), rash, or fever is an indication for immediate drug withdrawal, as liver damage or bone marrow suppression may occur, as may a syndrome resembling systemic lupus. However, drug withdrawal should always be done on physician's orders. Abrupt withdrawal of Dilantin may precipitate status epilepticus (Mosby's GenRX, 1997).

This entry has been informed by the sources listed below.

REFERENCES

Goldensohn, E. S., Glaser, G. H., & Goldberg, M. A. (1984). Epilepsy. In L. P. Rowland (Ed.), *Merritt's textbook of neurology* (7th ed., pp. 629–650). Philadelphia, PA: Lea & Febiger.

Mosby's GenRx. (1997). *Phenytoin sodium*. Rx List Monographs. Linn, MO: Mosby.

RICHARD A. BERG
*West Virginia University Medical Center,
Charleston Division*

See also Anticonvulsants; Epilepsy

DIPLEGIA

Diplegia is a topographic term used to describe a movement disorder predominantly affecting the lower extremities, with only mild involvement of the upper extremities. The term diplegia frequently is used as a description of a kind of cerebral palsy in which the arms are less involved than in a quadriplegia and more involved than in a paraplegia (McCloskey, 2003). The term quadriplegia indicates both arms and both legs are involved to a similar degree, and the term paraplegia denotes involvement of both legs only.

Clinical practice suggests the term diplegia is somewhat misleading, as the primary emphasis truly is on the movement disorder of the lower extremities; however, the upper extremities show so little involvement that a casual observer may not detect deficits that could impair function seriously. Often these deficits are sensory-motor-vestibular in nature and interfere with acquisition of fine motor skills such as dressing and handwriting.

The etiology of diplegia may be developmental delay, anoxia, trauma, jaundice, neonatal seizures, reflex suppression, or other factors that suggest the possibility of certain progressive biochemical disorders or spinocerebellar degenerative diseases. Differential diagnosis by a skilled pediatric neurologist, with ongoing follow-up by appropriate therapists, is essential to provide appropriate medical and educational intervention for children with diplegia.

This entry has been informed by the sources listed below.

REFERENCES

Berkow, R. (Ed.). (1982). *The Merck manual of diagnosis and therapy* (14th ed.). Rahway, NJ: Merck.

McCloskey, D. (2003). Diplegia. In E. Fletcher-Janzen & C. R. Reynolds (Eds.), *Childhood disorders diagnostic desk reference* (pp. 183–184). Hoboken, NJ: Wiley.

RACHAEL J. STEVENSON
Bedford, Ohio

See also Chorea; Dyskinesia; Neuropsychology

DIPLOPIA

The basis for understanding diplopia (double vision) requires an appreciation of the physiologic mechanisms of binocularity within the visual cortex (Records, 1979). Evidence suggests there are four classes of cortical neuronal receptive fields for common visual direction—monocular left eye, monocular right eye, binocular corresponding, and binocular disparate. Presumably, each neuron derives stimulation from a specific visual direction; the visual direction is unambiguous for all classes except binocular disparate, where it falls between the visual directions of the two monocular receptive fields for that neuron. Consider stimuli to two eyes, presented on corresponding retinal points and moved gradually away in disparity; in time, fusion breaks and diplopia is perceived. When stimuli are presented to corresponding points only, as with a point of light, binocular corresponding neurons and monocular right and left neurons are stimulated. All three types have the same visual direction label and there is no conflict, resulting in single vision. When a small disparity is introduced, some binocular disparate neurons are stimulated and binocular corresponding neurons should cease responding. However, the monocular right and left neurons each are stimulated for a visual direction slightly to either side of the mean visual direction for binocular disparate neurons. These are integrated with a third set of responses from the binocular disparate neuron; therefore, there should be a range of small disparities for which binocular response gives a unitary perception of a fused stimulus. In essence, it is this disparity that permits stereopsis, a specialized form of depth perception.

Diplopia may be physiologic or pathologic (McCloskey, 2003; Von Noorden, 1985). Physiologic diplopia is normal and results from stimulation and appreciation of objects simultaneously with the area of disparities that may be fused within the cortex and those outside. Object points in visual space stimulating corresponding retinal elements may be constructed to form a plane known as horopter. Both in front of and behind this plane is Panum's fusional space, an area in space that can be integrated cortically without perceiving objects as double. Physiologic diplopia occurs outside this space, and may be appreciated by observing an object in the distance and holding a pencil near. While attending to the distant object, the pencil will be seen as double. Most of the time, physiologic diplopia is cortically suppressed and not appreciated. Its clinical significance is twofold. Occasionally, schoolchildren become aware of and concerned about physiologic diplopia; reassurance is warranted. Second, diplopia may be useful from a diagnostic and therapeutic perspective in the presence of strabismus.

Pathological diplopia may be characterized as either monocular or binocular. Monocular diplopia results from defects in the refractive media or retinal pathology. Examples are high astigmatic refractive error, cataract, ectopic lens position, or macular edema. If diplopia is binocular, image positions may be separated horizontally, vertically, or obliquely; may vary with different directions of gaze and head position; and may be constant or variable.

Extraocular muscle paresis in adults almost always yields diplopia. However, patients with strabismus from early life rarely perceive diplopia. A series of adaptive mechanisms in infancy and childhood avoid this symptom: abnormal head position, binocular rivalry, suppression, and abnormal retinal correspondence. In the presence of a weak extraocular muscle, moving the head to a position that avoids the field of action of the paretic muscle often will prevent diplopia; therefore, an abnormal head position may be an indicator of extraocular muscle paresis. Binocular rivalry is a function that can be present normally or abnormally. When viewing with one eye through a monocular telescope or microscope, it often is unnecessary to close the other eye to avoid confusion of images. This cortical phenomenon, known as *retinal rivalry*, is a normal adaptation to avoid diplopia. In the presence of strabismus, particularly in a strabismic circumstance where there is alternation of fixation from one eye to the other, retinal rivalry is apparently the operant mechanism. In a constant strabismic circumstance, one eye assumes fixation to the exclusion of the other, and the image from the deviating eye is suppressed (McCloskey, 2003). Suppression

is a mechanism, largely limited to infancy and youth, one consequence of which is decreased vision (amblyopia). Thus, amblyopia develops and is treatable in infancy and early childhood; however, once maturation of the system is complete (about age 9 years), amblyopia is neither a threat nor effectively treated.

Where strabismus is of early onset and long-standing duration, the cortical adaptation of abnormal retinal correspondence may ensue. In this instance, noncorresponding retinal points are cortically integrated, presumably to avoid diplopia. Thus diplopia may be monocular or binocular, physiologic or pathologic (McCloskey, 2003). The presence of diplopia may be detrimental to school performance.

REFERENCES

McCloskey, D. (2003). Diplopia. In E. Fletcher-Janzen & C. R. Reynolds (Eds.), *Childhood disorders diagnostic desk reference* (pp. 184–185). Hoboken, NJ: Wiley.

Records, R. E. (1979). *Physiology of the human eye and visual system*. Hagerstown, MD: Harper & Row.

Von Noorden, G. K. (1985). *Binocular vision and ocular motility*. St. Louis, MO: Mosby.

GEORGE R. BEAUCHAMP
Cleveland Clinic Foundation

DIRECT INSTRUCTION

The term direct instruction arose from two complementary lines of research and development. Rosenshine (1976) introduced the term into the mainstream of educational research. His synthesis of many classroom observation studies indicated that students consistently demonstrate higher reading achievement scores when their teachers:

- Devote substantial time to active instruction.
- Break complex skills and concepts into small, easy-to-understand steps and systematically teach in a step-by-step fashion.
- Ensure that all students operate at a high rate of success.
- Provide immediate feedback to students about the accuracy of their work.
- Conduct much of the instruction in small groups to allow for frequent student-teacher interactions.

The other source of direct instruction derives from the work of curriculum developers rather than researchers. In the early 1960s in Israel, Smilarsky taught preschoolers from peasant immigrant families from surrounding Arab nations. The method, called *direct promotion*, taught in a direct manner toward specific goals. In the mid-1960s

Bereiter and Engelmann (1966) formed an academically oriented preschool based on direct-instruction principles. In the late 1960s, Engelmann articulated the concept of direct instruction in the form of specific curricular materials and in a comprehensive model for teaching low-performing students. Direct instruction was incorporated as part of the acronym for DISTAR (Direct Instruction System for Teaching and Remediation) and as part of the title of the direct instruction model that took part in the U.S. Office of Education Follow Through Project. The key to direct instruction, as envisioned by Engelmann and his colleagues, is a comprehensive intervention, addressing teacher expectations for student learning, the curriculum, teaching skills, time spent engaged in academic activities, administrative support, and parental involvement.

At the heart of the direct instruction intervention was the conviction that student failure could be prevented or at least remedied, regardless of the label placed on the child. The empirical basis for this conviction is found in a number of sources, ranging from an annotated bibliography of 188 articles and books on direct instruction in special education (Fabre, 1983) to an article reviewing 20 direct instruction studies in special education in Australia (Maggs & Maggs, 1979). Other sources include a review of special education studies in the United States (Gersten, 1985) and an overview of articles on direct instruction (Carnine, 1983). These various reports frequently emphasize the academic gains of students in direct instruction (ABT Associates, 1977).

The national evaluation of the Follow Through (FT) Project yielded another finding that surprised many educators:

> The performance of FT children in direct instruction sites on the affective measures is an unexpected result. The direct instruction model does not explicitly emphasize affective outcomes of instruction, but the sponsor has asserted that they will be the consequence of effective teaching. Critics of the model have predicted that the emphasis on tightly controlled instruction might discourage children from freely expressing themselves, and thus inhibit the development of self-esteem and other affective skills. In fact, this is not the case.
> (ABT Associates, 1977, p. 73)

These outcomes reflect the basic philosophy of direct instruction: Student failures are school failures. School failures are not remedied by showing teachers research findings in an attempt to increase teacher expectations; however, teachers need well-designed curricular materials, substantial instructional time to teach students, and teaching techniques for motivating and helping students who are making numerous mistakes.

Curricular materials guide teachers in explaining, reviewing, and giving practice on academic content. Direct instruction materials are designed in part to minimize student confusions. In a simple example, subtracting 3,942 from 6,000 often confuses students as they try to rename in one column at a time. In direct instruction, students rewrite 600 tens as 599 tens and 1 ten in a single step:

$$599 + 1$$
$$6/,0/0/0$$
$$-3,942.$$

Recognizing that $600 = 599 + 1$ is much less confusing than crossing out successive zeroes and rewriting the value represented by each renamed zero.

Direct instruction materials also teach students strategies that allow them to handle a wide range of tasks. In intermediate spelling, students learn a few rules and 655 word roots; they then can spell over 10,000 words. The instructional design principles are articulated in several books: *Theory of Instruction* (Engelmann & Carnine, 1982); *Direct Instruction Reading* (Carnine & Silbert, 1979); *Direct Instruction Mathematics* (Silbert, Carnine, & Stein, 1981); and *Applied Psychology for Teachers: A Behavioral Cognitive Approach* (Becker, 1986).

Direct instruction teaching techniques are designed to maximize the quality and amount of academic engaged time. The amount of time is increased by showing teachers how to schedule instructional time more effectively and how to keep students attending by using reinforcement, rapid pacing, challenges, and so on. The quality of learning is particularly influenced by how teachers react to student errors. For memorization errors, teachers give the answers and periodically review the missed questions. For errors reflecting inappropriate strategy selection or application, the teacher asks questions based on prior instruction to guide the student in using the strategy to arrive at an appropriate answer.

Familiarity with direct instruction curriculas and teaching techniques requires intensive staff development. Staff development occurs primarily in individual teachers' classrooms. A supervisor observes and sets priorities for training on teaching techniques. A supervisor might model a correction procedure with a teacher's students one day, observe the teacher applying the procedure immediately, and then return a few days later to see whether the teacher is comfortable with the procedure. If the teacher has mastered the correction procedure, the supervisor will commence training in the next teaching technique on the priority list.

Supervision of direct instruction can be difficult. Supervisors must have tact as well as skill in diagnosing teaching deficiencies, identifying and prioritizing remedies, modeling and prompting remedies, and managing their time efficiently in order to spend sufficient time making classroom observations.

Although some sources point to the success (broad-ranged) of direct instruction (Adams & Siegfried, 1996; White, 2005), others have suggested that there are no significant differences between direct instruction and regular classroom reading outcomes (Mosley, 1997). Findings suggest that students have to be taught by direct instruction for 2 years or more before effects are noted (Mosley, 1997).

On the other hand, one recent study about Direct Instruction conducted in Milwaukee Public Schools (MPS; White, 2005) examined third- through fifth-grade students' progress and found:

- Despite students being exposed to DI being even lower income, on average, than other MPS low-income students, those individuals with long-term exposure to DI (defined as 5 years) do better, on average, than all low-income MPS students. In fourth grade, students with 5 years of DI had higher average scores, 4 points in reading and 3 points in math, than non-DI students and 8 points in reading and 7 points in math among relatively comparable students with 1 or 2 years of DI. These differences reflect several months of learning.

- Among low-income students tracked between third and fourth grades 2002 to 2003 to 2003 to 2004, those with 5 years of DI increased their math scores by 6.6% whereas nonlow-income students increased their scores by 4.7%. This difference is statistically significant and is evidence of substantial progress.

- Among students moving from fourth to fifth grade on reading those same years, low-income students with 5 years of DI gained 4.2% on their test scores versus 3.9% for nonlow-income. The differences are not statistically significant. But it is significant in the sense that these are very different sets of students making about the same academic progress.

- Those low-income, fourth-grade, regular education (no special education) students with 5 years of DI averaged 633 in reading versus 625 for all low-income students, again a substantial difference, especially when one knows the DI students are lower income and more likely to have limited English proficiency.

- Among fifth graders, those with 5 years of DI averaged 660 on reading (and 630 on math) compared to all low-income fifth graders who averaged 646 on reading (626 on math). The difference in reading is about equivalent to one-half year of progress, and the 660 is again earned by a lower-income population, suggesting an even greater achievement.

- These and other higher scores and gains by those with long-term DI experience developed despite these students having more challenges to success and attending schools that usually did not have the resources to fully implement DI.

- In the few schools that did completely implement DI, defined as DI in every grade and continuous professional development for the staff, students did even better, on average. Among low-income students, with a mix of regular and special education, students scored an average of 654 on reading and 647 on math versus other low-income students who averaged 648 in

reading and 622 on math. These differences suggest that full implementation leads to even greater academic gains. (pp. 1–2)

These data are impressive when considering the special needs of low-income children and the pressures of accountability induced by current legislation.

REFERENCES

ABT Associates. (1977). *Education as experimentation: A planned variation model* (Vol. 4). Cambridge, MA: Authors.

Adams, G. L., & Siegfried, L. (1996). *Research on direct instruction: 25 years beyond DISTAR*. Seattle, WA: Educational Achievement Systems.

Becker, W. C. (1986). *Applied psychology for families*. Chicago, IL: Science Research Associates.

Bereiter, C., & Engelmann, S. (1966). *Teaching disadvantaged children in the preschool*. Englewood Cliffs, NJ: Prentice Hall.

Carnine, D. W., & Silbert, J. (1979). *Direct instruction reading*. Columbus, OH: Merrill.

Carnine, D. (1983). Direct instruction: In search of instructional solutions for educational problems. In D. Carnine, D. Elkind, D. Melchenbaum, R. Lisieben, & F. Smith (Eds.), *Interdisciplinary voices in learning disabilities and remedial education* (pp. 1–66). Austin, TX: PRO-ED.

Engelmann, S., & Carnine, D. W. (1982). *Theory of instruction*. New York, NY: Irvington.

Fabre, T. (1983). *The application of direct instruction in special education: An annotated bibliography*. Unpublished manuscript, University of Oregon.

Gersten, R. (1985). Direct instruction with special education students: A review of evaluation research. *Journal of Special Education, 19*, 42–58.

Maggs, A., & Maggs, R. K. (1979). Direct instruction research in Australia. *Journal of Special Education Technology, 81*(3), 26–34.

Mosley, A. M. (1997). *The effectiveness of direct instruction on reading achievement*. (ERIC Clearinghouse No. CS012664)

Rosenshine, B. (1976). Classroom instruction. In N. L. Gage (Ed.), *Psychology of teaching. The 77th yearbook of the National Society for the Study of Education*. Chicago, IL: National Society for the Study of Education.

Silbert, J., Carnine, D. W., & Stein, M. (1981). *Direct instruction mathematics*. Columbus, OH: Merrill.

White, S. (2005). *The benefits from phonics and direct instruction. Wisconsin Policy Research Institute, Inc.* Retrieved from http://wpri.org/

DOUGLAS CARNINE
University of Oregon
First edition

ELAINE FLETCHER-JANZEN
Chicago School of Professional Psychology
Second edition

See also Distar; Reading Disorders; Reading Remediation; Response to Intervention

DISABILITY

The term disability is derived from the Latin prefix *dis-*, meaning negation, separation, lack of, or opposite of; and the Latin *habilitas*, meaning fitness, and *habere*, indicating to have or to be easily handled. Disability today indicates the lack of power or ability to do something. It is usually regarded as a negative attribute. The prefix contributes to our English word some of the connotations of its association with Dis, the god of the underworld in Roman mythology with whom the Greeks identified Pluto, and with Hades and the realm of the dead.

Some writers distinguished disability from impairment and handicap. Wright (1960) viewed a disability as mainly a medical condition; however, she saw a handicap reflecting the demands placed on an individual in a particular situation. An individual may indeed have a disability but may not have a handicap except in certain situations. Wright's elaboration on the significance of physical disability is essential reading for persons interested in a psychological perspective of body physique.

Stevens (1962) formulated a taxonomy for special education in which he distinguished among disability, impairment, and handicap. Stevens regarded disability as a loss of function, impairment as tissue damage or disease, and handicap as "the burden which is imposed on the learner when confronted with educational situations which cannot be resolved by reason of body dysfunction or impairment" (p. 65). While the progression may be from tissue damage to loss of function to certain situational difficulties, Stevens argued that the extent or severity of any disability cannot be directly predicted from evaluation of the impairment only. Nor can the behavior one exhibits, or the burden that one elects to carry or that is assigned by society to a person with a certain disability or impairment, be accurately determined from knowledge about the disability only. Disabilities in motion, sensation, intelligence, emotion, and physiological processes do not necessarily translate into specific handicaps in situations requiring mobility, communication, healthy self-concept, or social interaction skills.

The World Health Organization (WHO) has made many efforts over the past 30 years to clarify terms and extend the medical model of disease per se to account for the consequences of disease (1980). In 1980, the International Classification of Impairments, Disabilities, and Handicaps (ICIDH) was formed. The ICIDH bridged the former medical model with a social model and facilitated the recognition of the contributions of medical services, rehabilitation agencies, and social welfare personnel to the care of people with conditions that interfere with everyday life, especially those people who have chronic, progressive, and irreversible conditions. The medical model of disease (WHO, 1980, p. 10) was illustrated as:

etiology → pathology → manifestation

The extended model, a biopsychosocial model (WHO, 1980, p. 11), was presented as:

disease → impairment → disability → handicap

Disability in the WHO classification system denoted the "consequences of impairment in terms of functional performance and activity by the individual" (p. 14). An impairment was defined as "any loss or abnormality of psychological, physiological, or anatomical structure or function" (p. 47). Handicap was defined as "a disadvantage for a given individual, resulting from an impairment or a disability, that limits or prevents the fulfillment of a role that is normal (depending on age, sex, and social and cultural factors) for that individual" (p. 183). Thus impairment represents "exteriorization of a pathological state" (p. 47) and occurs at the tissue level; disability refers to "excesses or deficiencies of customarily expected activity, performance, and behavior" (p. 142) and was located at the level of the person; and handicap "reflects the consequences for the individual—cultural, social, economic, and environmental—that stem from the presence of impairment and disability" (p. 183).

After 9 years of international revision efforts coordinated by the WHO, the World Health Assembly on May 22, 2001, approved the International Classification of Functioning, Disability and Health and its abbreviation of "ICF." This classification was first created in 1980 (and then called the International Classification of Impairments, Disabilities, and Handicaps, or ICIDH) by WHO to provide a unifying framework for classifying the consequences of disease.

Revision activities for ICIDH in the United States and Canada have been under the auspices of the WHO Collaborating Center for the Classification of Diseases for North America since 1993. The North American Collaborating Center (NACC), which recently has been renamed the WHO Collaborating Center for the Family of International Classifications for North America, is housed at the National Center for Health Statistics (NCHS). The Collaborating Center for the Family of International Classifications for North America (NACC):

- Represents the United States and Canada in international activities related to study and revision of the ICIDH/IC.
- Works with U.S. researchers conducting ICIDH/ICF studies and evaluations.
- Collaborates with Canadian researchers through the Canadian Institute for Health Information (CIHI).

The ICF classification complements WHO's International Classification of Diseases, 10th Revision (ICD), which contains information on diagnosis and health condition, but not on functional status. The ICD and ICF constitute the core classifications in the WHO Family of International Classifications (WHO-FIC). The NACC has responsibilities to WHO in its "Terms of Reference" to promote the development and use of ICF in the light of practical experience.

The ICF is structured around the following broad components: Body functions and structure, Activities (related to tasks and actions by an individual), and Participation (involvement in a life situation), and Additional information on severity and environmental factors.

Functioning and disability are viewed as a complex interaction between the health condition of the individual and the contextual factors of the environment, as well as personal factors. The picture produced by this combination of factors and dimensions is of "the person in his or her world." The classification treats these dimensions as interactive and dynamic rather than linear or static. It allows for an assessment of the degree of disability, although it is not a measurement instrument. It is applicable to all people, whatever their health condition. The language of the ICF is neutral as to etiology, placing the emphasis on function rather than condition or disease. It also is carefully designed to be relevant across cultures as well as age groups and genders, making it highly appropriate for heterogeneous populations.

The NACC has sponsored 10 annual ICF revision meetings in the United States and Canada from 1993 to 2004, hosted the annual WHO ICD meeting in 1993, and did so again in October 2001. The North American Collaborating Center also has sponsored several other ICF activities, such as the development of web-based training for ICF (called "CODE ICF"), the production of ICF videos, and the production of internationally comparable disability tabulations from six national disability surveys (called "DISTAB") back coded to ICF. In this effort, the DISTAB group worked closely with the United Nations (U.N.) in New York, which in June 2001 sponsored a Seminar on the Measurement of Disability. The background papers, and many of the papers presented, are on the U.N. website. A searchable version of the ICF is available at the WHO website at http://www.who.int/en/.

In the present context of special education and rehabilitation, the term disability is frequently changed to the adjectival form and used to describe individuals. Thus we hear talk about disabled persons. Note, however, the affect of this change; instead of considering a disability or the lack of power to act, attention is directed to people who are characterized as not having power to act, with no distinction as to what actions might be limited. Wright (1960), in her discussion of physical disabilities, has pointed out the distinction between calling someone a physically disabled person as opposed to a person with a physical disability: "it is precisely the perception of a person with a physical disability as a *physically disabled person* that has reduced all his life to the disability aspects of his physique. The short cut distorts and undermines" (p. 8). Consider the impact of further streamlining our language when we talk about the disabled and characterize as disabled an entire group of people who may share nothing other than their membership in the amorphous group labeled disabled. A common example is the group called the learning disabled (LD); the extreme heterogeneity among the individual group members is obscured by the blanket term or its abbreviation to LD.

Attempts to define the term disability and differentiate it from related terms is more than an exercise in semantics. Precise definitions are needed for determining who is eligible for services; what the incidence and prevalence of conditions are; what projected health care, educational, rehabilitation, and welfare assistance may be required from a local, state, national, or international perspective; and what efforts might facilitate the development of appropriate housing and employment opportunities. It seems likely that as long as the term disability carries a strong pejorative connotation, attempts will be made to limit its denotation and increase the objectivity of its meaning.

REFERENCES

Stevens, G. D. (1962). *Taxonomy in special education for children with body disorders*. Pittsburgh, PA: Department of Special Education and Rehabilitation, University of Pittsburgh.

World Health Organization (WHO). (1980). *International classification of impairments, disabilities, and handicaps: A manual of classification relating to the consequences of disease*. Geneva, Switzerland: Author.

World Health Organization (WHO). (1998). *ICIDH-2 Beta 1 Field Trials*. Retrieved from http://www.who.int/en/

World Health Organization (WHO). (2006). *International classification of functionality*. Retrieved from http://www.who.org

Wright, B. (1960). *Physical disability—A psychological approach*. New York, NY: Harper & Row.

MARJORIE E. WARD
Ohio State University
First edition

ELAINE FLETCHER-JANZEN
Chicago School of Professional Psychology
Second edition

See *also* Child With a Disability, Definition of; Individuals with Disabilities Improvement Education Act of 2004 (IDEIA); Labeling

DISABILITY ETIQUETTE

The following text consists of excerpts from the City of San Antonio's (Texas) Planning Department *Disability Etiquette Handbook*. The *Handbook* is featured on the city's website (http://www.sanantonio.gov/publicworks/dao/) and has won a great deal of positive comments and is being used by other city governments, such as the city of Sacramento, California. It is a positive example of institutional respect and support of individuals with disabilities.

People With Disabilities

People with disabilities are not conditions or diseases. They are individual human beings. For example, a person is not an epileptic, but rather a person who has epilepsy. First and foremost they are people. Only secondarily do they have one or more disabling conditions. Hence, they prefer to be referred to in print or broadcast media as People with Disabilities.

In any story, article, announcement, or advertisement, *people with disabilities* should be used either exclusively or, at a minimum, as the initial reference. Subsequent references can use the terms *person with a disability* or *individuals with disabilities* for grammatical or narrative reasons. In conclusion, the appropriate and preferred initial reference is *people with disabilities*.

Distinction Between Disability and Handicap

A *disability* is a condition caused by an accident, trauma, genetics, or disease that may limit a person's mobility, hearing, vision, speech, or mental function. Some people with disabilities have one or more disabilities.

A *handicap* is a physical or attitudinal constraint that is imposed upon a person, regardless of whether that person has a disability. Webster's Ninth New Collegiate Dictionary defines handicap as "to put at a disadvantage."

For example, some people with disabilities use wheelchairs. Stairs, narrow doorways, and curbs are handicaps imposed upon people with disabilities who use wheelchairs. People with disabilities have all manners of disabling conditions:

- Mobility impairments.
- Blindness and vision impairments.
- Deafness and hearing impairments.
- Speech and language impairments.
- Mental and learning disabilities.

Conversation Etiquette

- When talking to a person with a disability, look at and speak directly to that person, rather than through a companion who may be along.
- Relax. Don't be embarrassed if you happen to use accepted common expressions, such as "See you later" or "Got to be running along," that seem to relate to the person's disability.

- To get the attention of a person with a hearing impairment, tap the person on the shoulder or wave your hand. Look directly at the person and speak clearly, naturally, and slowly to establish if the person can read lips. Not all persons with hearing impairments can lip read. Those who cannot will rely on facial expression and other body language to help in understanding. Show consideration by placing yourself facing the light source and keeping your hands, cigarettes, and food away from your mouth when speaking. Keep mustaches well-trimmed. Shouting won't help. Written notes may.
- When talking with a person in a wheelchair for more than a few minutes, use a chair, whenever possible, in order to place yourself at the person's eye level to facilitate conversation.
- When greeting a person with a severe loss of vision, always identify yourself and others who may be with you. For example: "On my right is Penelope Potts."
- When conversing in a group, give a vocal cue by announcing the name of the person to whom you are speaking. Speak in a normal tone of voice, indicate in advance when you will be moving from one place to another, and let it be known when the conversation is at an end.
- Listen attentively when you're talking to a person who has a speech impairment. Keep your manner encouraging rather than correcting. Exercise patience rather than attempting to speak for a person with speech difficulty. When necessary, ask short questions that require short answers or a nod or a shake of the head. Never pretend to understand if you are having difficulty doing so. Repeat what you understand, or incorporate the interviewee's statements into each of the following questions. The person's reactions will clue you in and guide you to understanding.
- If you have difficulty communicating, be willing to repeat or rephrase a question. Open-ended questions are more appropriate than closed-ended questions. For example:
  - *Closed-ended question.* You were a tax accountant in XYZ Company in the corporate planning department for 7 years. What did you do there?
  - *Open-ended question.* Tell me about your recent position as a tax accountant.
- Do not shout at a hearing impaired person. Shouting distorts sounds accepted through hearing aids and inhibits lip reading. Do not shout at a person who is blind or visually impaired—he or she can hear you!
- To facilitate conversation, be prepared to offer a visual cue to a hearing impaired person or an audible cue to a vision impaired person, especially when more than one person is speaking. See Table D.5.

Table D.5. Glossary of Acceptable Terms

Acceptable Terms	Unacceptable Terms
Person with a disability.	Cripple, cripples—the image conveyed is of a twisted, deformed, useless body.
Disability, a general term used for functional limitation that interferes with a person's ability, for example, to walk, hear, or lift. It may refer to a physical, mental, or sensory condition.	Handicap, handicapped person, or handicapped.
People with cerebral palsy, people with spinal cord injuries.	Cerebral palsied, spinal cord injured, and so on. Never identify people solely by their disability.
Person who had a spinal cord injury, polio, a stroke, and so on, or a person who has multiple sclerosis, muscular dystrophy, arthritis, and so on.	Victim. People with disabilities do not like to be perceived as victims for the rest of their lives, long after any victimization has occurred.
Has a disability, has a condition of (spina bifida, etc.), or born without legs, and so on.	Defective, defect, deformed, vegetable. These words are offensive, dehumanizing, degrading, and stigmatizing.
Deafness/hearing impairment. Deafness refers to a person who has a total loss of hearing. Hearing impairment refers to a person who has a partial loss of hearing within a range from slight to severe.	
Hard of hearing describes a hearing-impaired person who communicates through speaking and speech-reading, and who usually has listening and hearing abilities adequate for ordinary telephone communication. Many hard of hearing individuals use a hearing aid.	Deaf and Dumb is as bad as it sounds. The inability to hear or speak does not indicate intelligence.
Person who has a mental or developmental disability.	Retarded, moron, imbecile, idiot. These are offensive to people who bear the label.
Uses a wheelchair or crutches; a wheelchair user; walks with crutches.	Confined/restricted to a wheelchair; wheelchair bound. Most people who use a wheelchair or mobility devices do not regard them as confining. They are viewed as liberating; a means of getting around.
Able-bodied; able to walk, see, hear, and so on; people who are not disabled.	Healthy, when used to contrast with "disabled." Healthy implies that the person with a disability is unhealthy. Many people with disabilities have excellent health.
People who do not have a disability.	Normal. When used as the opposite of disabled, this implies that the person is abnormal. No one wants to be labeled as abnormal.
A person who has (name of disability.) Example: A person who has multiple sclerosis.	Afflicted with, suffers from. Most people with disabilities do not regard themselves as afflicted or suffering continually. Afflicted: A disability is not an affliction.

Reasonable Accommodations in the Workplace

Reasonable accommodations enhance the opportunity for qualified persons with disabilities who may not otherwise be considered for reasons unrelated to actual job requirements to be or remain employed. The purpose of providing reasonable accommodations is to enable employers to hire or retain qualified job candidates regardless of their disability by eliminating barriers in the workplace.

Types of accommodations include:

- Assistive devices.
- Reassignment.
- Modified work schedules.
- Job modifications.
- Relocation.
- Change in the physical plant.

Examples of assistive devices often used in the workplace include:

- Teletypewriter (TTY) or telephone amplifier, often used by persons with hearing impairments.
- Wooden blocks to elevate desks and tables for wheelchair users.
- Large-type computer terminals and braille printers to assist persons with vision impairments.

Decisions to implement an accommodation should include making a choice that will best meet the needs of the individual by minimizing limitation and enhancing his or her ability to perform job tasks, while serving the interests of your majority work force.

Reception Etiquette

Know where accessible restrooms, drinking fountains, and telephones are located. If such facilities are not available, be ready to offer alternatives, such as the private or employee restroom, a glass of water, or your desk phone.

Use a normal tone of voice when extending a verbal welcome. Do not raise your voice unless requested.

When introduced to a person with a disability, it is appropriate to offer to shake hands. People with limited hand use or who wear an artificial limb can usually shake hands.

- Shaking hands with the left hand is acceptable.
- For those who cannot shake hands, touch the person on the shoulder or arm to welcome and acknowledge their presence.
- Treat adults in a manner befitting adults.
- Call a person by his or her first name only when extending that familiarity to all others present.
- Never patronize people using wheelchairs by patting them on the head or shoulder.
- When addressing a person who uses a wheelchair, never lean on the person's wheelchair. The chair is part of the space that belongs to the person who uses it.
- When talking with a person with a disability, look at and speak directly to that person rather than through a companion who may be along.
- If an interpreter is present, speak to the person who has scheduled the appointment, not to the interpreter. Always maintain eye contact with the applicant, not the interpreter.
- Offer assistance in a dignified manner with sensitivity and respect. Be prepared to have the offer declined. Do not proceed to assist if your offer to assist is declined. If the offer is accepted, listen to and accept instructions.
- Allow a person with a visual impairment to take your arm (at or about the elbow). This will enable you to guide rather than propel or lead the person.
- Offer to hold or carry packages in a welcoming manner. For example: "May I help you with your packages?"
- When offering to hand a coat or umbrella, do not offer to hand a cane or crutches unless the individual requests otherwise.

Service Animals

Background

More than 12,000 people with disabilities use the aid of service animals. Although the most familiar types of service animals are guide dogs used by people who are blind, service animals are assisting persons who have other disabilities as well. Many disabling conditions are invisible. Therefore, every person who is accompanied by a service animal may or may not "look" disabled. A service animal is *not* required to have any special certification.

What Is a Service Animal?

A service animal is *not* a pet! According to the Americans with Disabilities Act of 2007 (ADA) a service animal is any animal that has been individually trained to provide assistance or perform tasks for the benefit of a person with a physical or mental disability that substantially limits one or more major life functions.

Service Dog Etiquette

- Do not touch the service animal, or the person it assists, without permission.
- Do not make noises at the service animal—it may distract the animal from doing its job.
- Do not feed the service animal—it may disrupt his or her schedule.
- Do not be offended if the person does not feel like discussing his or her disability or the assistance the service animal provides. Not everyone wants to be a walking-talking "show and tell" exhibit.

Sign Language Interpreters

The professional interpreter is always considered to be an extension of and part of the event. Interpreters are part of the team meant to deliver accurate and intended messages given by the presenters or performers. The further in advance notice is provided to the interpreter, the more prepared they will be. This process will allow the interpreter to have the proper time needed for an event and prevent "cold" interpreting. Time for preparation is essential to allow accurate dissemination of the intended messages to the audience.

For instance, an interpreter needs to spend an average of 15 to 20 hours of practice for a 2-hour musical concert. With this in mind, the following information given to the interpreter will enhance the quality of the interpreted performance/event:

- Name and type of event.
- Name of event contact person with a phone number.
- Correct billing address.
- Clear address and directions to the event and the location where the interpreter is to check in.
- Parking passes or information on any kind of special arrangements for parking.
- Correct spellings of all names of those speaking or performing.
- A summary of subjects that will be presented by each speaker.
- A list of any musical lyrics in advance, ideally at the time of request.
- Communication and shared information to all persons directly involved with the event regarding the arrangements for the interpreter.

If any information to be presented is other than English, a written interpretation in English will be needed in advance, or an advance notice of at least 3 weeks will be needed to allow adequate time to secure an appropriate interpreter.

STAFF

DISADVANTAGED CHILD

Most writings about disadvantaged children first gained attention during the 1940s and 1950s; lower-class youths and racial minorities were identified as the populace of this educationally disenfranchised group of learners. Historically we can identify the roots of this population in terms of their educational needs, but it was not until the mid-1960s that writers such as Riessman and Havighurst had their turns at defining the characteristics that constitute this deprived population. As indicated by Riessman (1962), the terms culturally deprived, educationally deprived, deprived, underprivileged, disadvantaged, lower class, and lower socioeconomic group, could all be used interchangeably.

Ornstein (1976) has presented an interesting and basic critique of the attempts made by Havighurst and Riessman to provide us with the characteristics of the disadvantaged. Havighurst began by attempting to provide the traditional conceptualization of the disadvantaged that grew out of the earliest of writings. The disadvantaged youth is seen as coming primarily from a low-income family and most likely from a racial minority. Havighurst emphasizes the social, economic, and personal handicaps of the disadvantaged and sees this youth at the lowest end of several strata. Ornstein interprets this as providing the unwary reader with a convenient label that is essentially laden with negativism.

On the other hand, we have Ornstein's interpretation of what he refers to as a positive trend exemplified in Riessman's (1962) classic book *The Culturally Deprived Child*, in which he views the disadvantaged youth as having many positive characteristics. With the emphasis now on a more positive outlook, readers are encouraged to note and develop qualities within this population such as physical orientation, hidden verbal ability, creative potential, group cohesiveness informality, and sense of humor.

Although Riessman has made great efforts to identify some characteristics that might be construed as potentially positive qualities, he also is cognizant of the negative criteria used by Havighurst and others. An examination of *The Culturally Deprived Child* (1962) results in the reader's awareness that Reissman understood the enormity of the problems encountered by the deprived children of our nation.

Karnes, Reid, and Jones (1971), in the Guidance Monograph Series, provide us with an approach to the identification process in that they refer to a difference between middle class and lower class in only the six areas of: (1) self-concept, (2) motivation, (3) social behavior, (4) language, (5) intellectual functioning, and (6) physical fitness. With such broad categories, each educator can conceivably provide us with information applicable to either the Havighurst or Riessman model. In addition, the term *disadvantaged youth* is also seen as being too nebulous and having a degree of relativism that in turn reduces the selection process for innovative educational programs to confront this issue. Loss of objectivity in the identification and ultimate selection of students for educational enrichment often results in failure to meet the program's goals.

Without many of the precise criteria needed to identify the disadvantaged population, the educational community moved ahead with special programs with a financial base from congressional legislation. In 1965, Congress passed the Elementary and Secondary Education Act (ESEA) and for the first time in U.S. history, federal financial support was provided to both public and nonpublic schools. From this legislation came Title I—Education of Children of Low-Income Families. Title I was designed to support and provide financial incentives for special programs to meet the special needs of socially and educationally deprived children of low-income families. Congress amended and expanded the ESEA many times over the next 30 years. The major criticism of the Act was that funds were spread thinly instead of being focused in areas of most need (Department of Education, 1993). In 2001, the ESEA was again amended and heavily revised by the No Child Left Behind Act, which shifted the focus of funding from schools with a high concentration of low-income families to underperforming schools without regard to the socioeconomic status of children attending such schools. The impact of this change remains unclear, and the ultimate effect in terms of educational outcomes will likely not be known for several more years.

In addition, a crisis developed in urban schools, where an exodus of White middle-class families from the city to private and/or suburban schools created a buildup of educationally disadvantaged minority students (Ornstein, 1989). Issues of cultural competence have also been included recently to the evaluation of services to disadvantaged children. There have been requests (Lake, 2007) to distinguish between the terms "culturally disadvantaged" and "culturally different."

Specific learning characteristics of the deprived or disadvantaged student might include many of the following: (1) oriented to the physical and visual rather than to the oral; (2) content-centered rather than form-centered; (3) externally oriented rather than introspective; (4) problem-centered rather than abstract-centered; (5) inductive rather than deductive; (6) spatial rather than temporal; (7) slow, careful, patient, and persevering (in areas of importance) rather than quick, clever, facile, and flexible; (8) inclined to communicate through actions rather than words; (9) deficient in auditory attention and interpretation skills; (10) oriented toward concrete application of what is learned; (11) short attention span; (12) characteristic gaps in knowledge and learning; (13) lacking experiences of receiving approval for success in tasks (Conte & Grimes, 1969).

Meeting the needs of the disadvantaged child is a relatively new educational approach when viewed within the context of America's education history. Efforts to define this population have not been without conflict, and massive expenditures of monies by the federal government have also stirred controversy. However, studies indicate that enrichment programs (Kaniel & Richtenberg, 1992), mentoring (Shaughnessy, 1992), and appropriate curricula design (Gemma, 1989) have very positive outcomes with children who are disadvantaged.

REFERENCES

Conte, J. M., & Grimes, G. H. (1969). *Media and the culturally different*. Washington, DC: National Education Association.

Gemma, A. (1989). *A comparison of the child-centered curriculum model, the direct instruction curriculum model, and the open-framework curriculum model: Three curriculum models for disadvantaged preschool children*. (ERIC Clearinghouse No. PS018905)

Kaniel, S., & Richtenberg, R. (1992). Instrumental enrichment: Effects of generalization and durability with talented adolescents. *Gifted Education International, 8*(3), 128–35.

Karnes, M. B., Reid, J., & Jones, G. R. (1971). *The culturally disadvantaged student and guidance*. Boston, MA: Houghton Mifflin.

Lake, R. (1990). An Indian father's plea. *Teacher Magazine, 2*(1), 48–53.

Ornstein, A. C. (1976). Who are the disadvantaged? In J. H. Cull & R. E. Hardy (Eds.), *Problems of disadvantaged and deprived youth* (pp. 5–15). Springfield, IL: Thomas.

Ornstein, A. C. (1989). Enrollment trends in big city schools. *Peabody Journal of Education, 66*(4), 64–71.

Riessman, F. (1962). *The culturally deprived child*. New York, NY: Harper & Row.

Shaughnessy, M. F. (1992). *Mentoring disadvantaged gifted children and youth*. (ERIC Clearinghouse No. UD028765)

U.S. Department of Education. (1993). *Improving America's Schools Act of 1993: The Reauthorization of the Elementary and Secondary Education Act*. Washington, DC: Author.

RICHARD E. HALMSTAD
University of Wisconsin at Stout
Second edition

KIMBERLY F. APPLEQUIST
University of Colorado at Colorado Springs
Third edition

See also No Child Left Behind Act

DISASTERS AND DISABILITIES

Disasters affect millions of people worldwide each year. Disasters involve the occurrence of a natural catastrophe, technological accident, or human-caused hazard that results in severe property damage, deaths, and/or multiple injuries (Federal Emergency Management Agency, 2009). Disaster events occur when the resources needed due to an unexpected impact exceed the capacity of a community or society to respond to that impact (World Health Organization, 2008). Among those who are affected by disasters are individuals with disabilities. People with physical disabilities are placed at risk in disaster when they have difficulties evacuating from the direct impact of a disaster or must rely on physical assistance from others when evacuating. Individuals with cognitive impairments may have difficulty understanding or following emergency instructions during disasters. People with sensory disabilities, such as blindness or hearing impairments can experience difficulties in receiving timely communication about emergency events. In addition, people with disabilities are more likely to live in housing that places them at risk in disaster, such as in flood plains or in substandard structures (Hemingway & Priestly, 2006; Peek & Stough, 2010). Together these factors can place individuals with disabilities at disproportionate risk in disaster situations.

Research and governmental reports document discrepancies in disaster services provided to individuals with disabilities during the response and recovery phases of disaster (Rowland, White, Fox, & Rooney, 2007; Stough, 2009). Accounts report difficulties in physically evacuating buildings, finding accessible transportation, and obtaining sheltering postdisaster. For example, the National Council on Disability (2006) reported that many people with physical disabilities were unable to evacuate during Hurricane Katrina due to inaccessible transportation. Three weeks later, during Hurricane Rita, deaf evacuees encountered numerous communicational barriers when staying in large public shelters (White, 2006). During the Southern California wildfires of 2008 individuals with disabilities had difficulties in getting transportation between shelters and disaster assistance centers (Kailes, 2008). Studies have also found difficulties in accessing services, such as case management or unemployment benefits, following disaster (Stough, Sharp, Decker & Wilker, 2010). Children with disabilities can be particularly affected by disaster as they are physically more vulnerable and rely on adults for psychological and custodial support (Peek & Stough, 2010). Educational programs for children may also be affected, for example, special education services were disrupted for several months following Hurricane Ike when schools were closed and programs were reorganized (McAdams Ducy & Stough, 2011).

Individuals with disabilities in the United States are entitled to equal access to emergency services, such as evacuation procedures and sheltering. The Stafford Act, which gives the Federal Emergency Management Agency (FEMA) the responsibility for coordinating government-wide disaster efforts, specifies that the needs of individuals with disabilities be included in the components of the national preparedness system (FEMA, 2007). Title II of the Americans with Disabilities Act requires modifications to policies, practices, and procedures to avoid discrimination against people with disabilities. State and local governments must comply with Title II of the ADA in the emergency and disaster programs, services, and activities they provide. This requirement also applies to programs, services, activities provided through third parties, such as the American Red Cross, private nonprofit organizations, or religious entities. Specifically, entities must make reasonable modifications and accommodations, cannot use eligibility criteria to screen out people with disabilities, and must provide effective communication to individuals with disabilities (American with Disabilities Act, 2007).

Most individuals with disabilities live and work in the community, as do those without disabilities. However, approximately 600,000 people with disabilities spend significant parts of their day in some type of congregate care (Braddock et al., 2011). For individuals with disabilities who live in group homes, nursing facilities, or hospitals, most state preparedness plans include point-to-point evacuation plans to ensure that these groups are moved in advance of predictable natural events such as hurricanes or floods. Plans also are made for relocation of these groups postdisaster in events such as earthquakes or tornados. An important factor in both cases is that caretaker and medical supports are ensured to provide continuity of care during the disaster event (National Council on Disability, 2009). Consideration for caretaker supports is also essential in the case of young children and school-age children with disabilities who may need supervision from day care providers or teachers to take preparedness measures or to follow evacuation orders. Children with disabilities also may need provisions for medical and special nutritional needs if separated from their parents during disaster. In addition, some researchers (e.g., Christ & Christ, 2006; McAdams Ducy, & Stough, 2011) have documented that teachers can provide effective emotional, as well as instrumental, support to students with disabilities during disasters. Similarly, employers who provide supported work environments need to consider medical and other special needs of their employees with disabilities should a disaster occur during the work day. In both congregate housing and work environments, an accessible built environment (Christensen, Collins, Holt, & Phillips, 2006) is an important element to consider when determining evacuation routes or areas in which to shelter-in-place.

Historically, emergency management tended to segregate people with disabilities in separate shelters and provided differentiated services for those labeled as having "special needs" (U.S. Department of Justice, 2006). A focus on the functional needs of individuals with disabilities, rather than on their diagnostic label or limitations, is the current and most appropriate, practice in emergency situations (FEMA, 2010). The functional needs approach to emergency management identifies disaster supports that individuals require in the five areas of communication, health, maintaining independence, transportation, or supervision (Kailes & Enders, 2006). For example, individuals with auditory limitations may need modifications in how they receive emergency communications, while individuals with remembering or decision making may require some supervision while in a shelter. The functional needs approach to disaster services also may benefit individuals who are not labeled as having a disability; for example, providing text announcements about emergency procedures in a noisy environment may not only assist individuals who are deaf, but also be helpful to seniors who use hearing aids.

Recent attention on national policies concerning the needs of individuals with disabilities has resulted in changes to the Stafford Act and led to the inclusion of the functional needs approach in the U.S. National Incident Management System, which guides governmental and nongovernmental agencies in providing a coordinated response to disasters. In addition, disability experts and individuals with disabilities themselves are increasingly included by emergency managers and disaster personnel in designing and carrying out emergency plans that incorporate provisions for individuals with functional needs.

REFERENCES

Americans with Disabilities Act. (2007, July). *The ADA and emergency shelters: Access for all in emergencies and disasters.* Retrieved from http://www.ada.gov/pcatoolkit/chap7shelter prog.htm

Braddock, D., Hemp, R., Rizzolo, M., Haffer, L., Shea, E., & Wu, J. (2011). *State of the states in developmental disabilities.* Retrieved from University of Colorado Department of Psychiatry website, http://sos.arielmis.net/documents/United States.pdf

Christ, G. H., & Christ, T. W. (2006). Academic and behavioral reactions of children with disabilities to the loss of a firefighter father. *Review of Disability Studies, 2*(3), 68–77.

Christensen, K. M., Collins, S. D., Holt, J. M., & Phillips, C. N. (2006). The relationship between the design of the built environment and the ability to egress of individuals with disabilities. *Review of Disability Studies, 2*(3), 24–34.

Federal Emergency Management Association (FEMA). (2010). *Guidance on planning for integration of functional needs support services in general population shelters.* Retrieved from http://www.fema.gov/pdf/about/odic/fnss_guidance.pdf

Federal Emergency Management Association (FEMA). (2009, July). *Acronyms, abbreviations, and terms* (FEMA P-524). Retrieved from http://training.fema.gov/EMIWeb/emischool/ EL361Toolkit/assets/FAATBook.pdf

Federal Emergency Management Association (FEMA). (2007). *Robert T. Stafford Disaster Relief and Emergency Assistance*

Act, as amended, and Related Authorities. Retrieved from https://www.fema.gov/library/viewRecord.do?fromSearch= fromsearch&id=3564

Hemingway, L., & Priestley, M. (2006). Natural hazard, human vulnerability and disabling societies: A disaster for disabled people? *Review of Disability Studies, 2*(3), 57–59.

Kailes, J. I. (2008, September). *Southern California wildfires report.* Prepared in partnership with the Access to Readiness Coalition, the California Foundation for Independent Living Centers, and the Center for Disability Issues and the Health Professions at Western University of Health Sciences. Retrieved from www.jik.com/CaliforniaWildfires.pdf

Kailes, J. I., & Enders, A. (2006). Moving beyond "special needs." A function based framework for emergency management and planning. *Journal of Disability Policy Studies, 17*(4), 230–237.

McAdams Ducy, E., & Stough, L. M. (2011). Exploring the support role of special education teachers after Hurricane Ike: Children with significant disabilities. *Journal of Family Issues, 32*(10), 1325–1345.

National Council on Disability. (2009). *Effective emergency management: Making improvements for communities and people with disabilities.* Retrieved from http://www.ncd.gov/policy/ emergency_management

National Council on Disability. (2006). *The impact of Hurricanes Katrina and Rita on people with disabilities: A look back and remaining challenges.* Retrieved from http://www.ncd.gov/ policy/emergency_management

Peek, L., & Stough, L. M. (2010). Children with disabilities in disaster. *Child Development, 81*(4), 1260–1270.

Rowland, J. L., White, G. W., Fox, M. H., & Rooney, C. (2007). Emergency response training practices for people with disabilities. *Journal of Disability Policy Studies, 17*(4), 216–222.

Stough, L. M. (2009). The effects of disaster on the mental health of individuals with disabilities. In Y. Neria, S. Galea, & F. H. Norris (Eds.), *Mental health and disasters* (pp. 264–276). New York, NY: Cambridge University Press.

Stough, L. M., Sharp, A. N., Decker, C., & Wilker, N. (2010). Disaster case management and individuals with disabilities. *Rehabilitation Psychology, 55*(3), 211–220.

U.S. Department of Justice. (2006, August). An ADA guide for local governments—Making community emergency preparedness and response programs accessible to people with disabilities. Retrieved from http://www.ada.gov/emergencyprep .htm

White, B. (2006). Disaster relief for Deaf persons: Lessons from Hurricanes Katrina and Rita. *Review of Disability Studies, 2*(3), 49–56.

World Health Organization (2008, July). *ReliefWeb glossary of humanitarian terms.* Retrieved from http://www.who.int/hac/ about/reliefweb-aug2008.pdf

Laura M. Stough
Texas A&M University

Elizabeth McAdams Ducy
Texas A&M University

DISCIPLINE

The noun *discipline* comes from the Latin word *disciplina*, meaning teaching, learning. However, a more common use of the word connotes either training that corrects or molds or punishment for transgressions against societal or parental rules.

Discipline begins with the efforts of parents to teach the mores of their culture. Almost all of this early discipline begins when the infant becomes mobile and can therefore behave in ways that parents believe need to be changed. Early parental discipline usually focuses on behavioral control (e.g., not touching the untouchable or not running in the street). Difficulties can arise if parents think that the child can control a behavior that the child in fact cannot—at least not at that age. A good example of this is toilet training of toddlers. Parents continue to carry the responsibility for disciplining children until they enter school. From the time children enter school until they leave, a partnership begins with others, such as teachers to discipline children as well (Foster & Robin, 1998).

Parents seem to discipline their children either through power-assertion techniques or through love-oriented techniques (Hoffman, 1970). In the former style of parental discipline, power-assertion, the parent uses physical punishment, deprives the child of material objects or privileges, directly applies force, or threatens. Control is exercised by taking advantage of greater physical strength and/or control of home environment.

Love withdrawal, a form of love-oriented discipline, uses direct but nonphysical expressions of anger or disappointment when the child misbehaves. For example, the parent may discipline by explicitly stating negative feelings, ignoring, isolating, or turning away from the child.

The use of power-assertive discipline such as spanking or love-oriented techniques such as withdrawal of affection may produce resentment or anxiety and cause the child to focus attention on his or her own negative consequences. These procedures are punitive rather than altruistic, that is, they decrease the child's appreciation of another person's distress.

Through induction, another form of love-oriented parental discipline, the parent appeals to the child's affection or respect for another. In essence, the child may be reminded that someone else will be hurt, disappointed, or suffer from his or her actions.

In comparison, inductive discipline is a nonpunitive technique that communicates the harm caused by a child's actions and encourages the child to place himself or herself in the victim's place. Hoffman (1975) believes that children are likely to develop a strong altruistic orientation if their parents often use inductive disciplinary techniques.

A popular perspective on discipline in the educational setting was espoused by William Glasser (1969). Glasser suggested that children be allowed to determine their own discipline and to set consequences for their behavior.

Adults (parents, teachers, etc.) who use Glasser's style of discipline often play a low-key role that reduces immediate application of reward and punishment and supplants both with discussion in which the adult serves as mediator for decision making.

Although Glasser's approach may be effective with bright, middle-class, high-school students, it may not be effective with young children or with older adolescents who have grown up in a lower-class setting. If children have not developed the requisite skills for deciding on a socially competent course of action when disciplinary decisions are required, this approach is not suggested. The effectiveness of each technique varies, perhaps influenced most by such factors as the age, verbal reasoning abilities, and cultural background of the child.

On entering the school setting, previously learned behavior patterns emerge when children are faced with adapting to participating in a room where waiting, sharing, instruction, and learning must take place. The term control is often viewed as a convenient catchall for what should be termed classroom management. One is never sure whether the meaning is intended in the broad sense (to cover all of classroom management), or the literal sense, that of keeping pupil behavior so curbed that the classroom is totally teacher-dominated.

Discipline, like control, is often incorrectly used to mean various aspects of classroom management. Good discipline may be considered maintaining an orderly classroom. A classroom and/or school environment that supports good student behavior must also expect the student to make good choices. Students that only respond to external structures such as rewards or punishments learn very little self-discipline and the gains are usually only short term (Short, 1994).

A more acceptable use of the term in the educational setting would describe discipline as an imposition of self-control in order to promote efficient habits of learning, proper conduct, consideration for others, and a positive learning environment. From the educator's point of view, preventing misbehavior is much more important than imposing control after the fact (Baron, 1992). Teachers working in teams to create positive classroom climates have much better support and success than individual efforts (Bell-Ruppert, 1994). In addition, democratic rather than authoritarian values have emerged in recent classroom discipline models. However, democratic values require flexible problem-solving skills that both the teacher and the students must value (Lewis, 1997).

To maintain discipline in the classroom, the student must be given as much independence as the teacher and child can tolerate. Classroom management should yield neither highly structured teacher-dominated environments nor completely permissive ones. To facilitate the development of self-control and discipline, a teacher's managerial style should attempt to promote active participation and a positive learning environment.

REFERENCES

Baron, E. B. (1992). *Discipline strategies for teachers*. (ERIC Clearinghouse No. SP034413)

Bell-Ruppert, N. (1994, November). *Discipline plans in middle schools*. Paper presented at the Annual Conference and Exhibit of the National Middle School Association.

Foster, S. L., & Robin, A. L. (1998). Parent-adolescent conflict and relationship discord. In E. J. Mash & R. A. Barkley (Eds.), *Treatment of childhood disorders* (2nd ed., pp. 601–646). New York, NY: Guilford Press.

Glasser, W. (1969). *Schools without failure*. New York, NY: Harper & Row.

Hoffman, M. L. (1970). Moral development. In P. H. Mussen (Ed.), *Carmicheal's manual of child psychology* (Vol. 2, 3rd ed.). New York, NY: Wiley.

Hoffman, M. L. (1975). Altruistic behavior and the parent-child relationships: *Journal of Personality & Social Psychology, 40*, 121–137.

Lewis, R. (1997). *The discipline dilemma: Control Management, Influence* (2nd ed.). Melbourne, Australia: Australian Council for Educational Research.

Short, P. (1994). *Rethinking student discipline: Alternatives that work*. (ERIC Clearinghouse No. EA026417)

MICHAEL J. ASH
JOSE LUIS TORRES
Texas A&M University
First edition

ELAINE FLETCHER-JANZEN
Chicago School of Professional Psychology
Second edition

See *also* Classroom Management; Self-Control Curriculum; Self-Monitoring

DISCOURSE

Discourse are oral and literate units of language that are usually larger than a sentence and show a common theme as well as local and global cohesion and coherence patterns (Schiffrin, 1994). It creates representation of events, objects, beliefs, personalities, and experiences. Discourse includes a variety of cues that include not only words and sentences, but also the tone, the overall purpose, and the relative formality of a communication event. In addition, oral discourse involves gestures, body positions, facial expressions of the speaker, and context (Brownell & Joanette, 1993). Two major types of discourse exist: Basic Interpersonal Communication Skills (BICS) or "everyday language," and Cognitive-Academic Language Proficiency (CALP) or "instructional language" (Chamot & O'Malley,

1994; Cummins, 1983). Both BICS and CALP contribute to education success. Characteristics of discourse associated with BICS and CALP are divided into three categories that occur across a developmental continuum: (1) conversation, (2) narration, and (3) exposition (Larson & McKinley, 1995; Merritt & Culatta, 1998; Naremore, Densmore, & Harman, 1995; Nelson, 1998; Wallach & Butler, 1994).

Conversation is used to request and report concrete items and actions (informal or personal oral or written interactions; Halliday, 1975; Hoskins, 1996; Naremore et al., 1995; Nelson, 1998; Tough, 1979). Conversation is a type of BICS that can be oral (e.g., social group, family conferences, telephone calls, "rap" sessions, gossip) or literate (e.g., personal notes, a diary, e-mail). Conversational discourse is context-embedded and has a structure of topics, initiations, responses, turns, exchanges, topic maintenance, reaction time latency, breakdowns, repairs, pacing/leading, and closure. Conversation competence is measured by quantity, quality, relationship, and manner, as well as nonverbal dimensions of communication. Individuals who do not develop conversational skills may experience difficulty with the second level of discourse, narration.

Narration is used to report what happened, to talk or write about, or to read about the there and then (recounts, eventcasts, accounts, fictional stories; Esterreicher, 1995; Hedberg & Westby, 1993; Hughes, McGillivray, & Schmidek, 1997; Naremore et al., 1995; Nelson, 1998). Narrative competence includes the understanding and use of *story grammars* (characters, place, time, initiating event, problem, internal response, resolution, and ending). Story grammars develop through the process of centering and chaining involved in learning *story types* (heaps, sequences, primitive narratives, unfocused chains, focused chains, and eventually true narratives represented by complex, multiple, embedded, or interactive episodes). Narration, a combination of BICS and CALP discourse, is a bridge between conversation and exposition because narration develops the cognitive, linguistic, and contextual structures introduced in conversation and required by exposition. For some individuals, reading problems may be related to poorly developed productive narrative abilities.

Exposition, an oral and literate CALP communication form, is a context-reduced and abstract form of language used to generalize about and infer what happens in the there and then (Chamot & O'Malley, 1994; Cummins, 1983; Larson & McKinley, 1995; Merritt & Culatta, 1998; Naremore et al., 1995; Nelson, 1998; Ripich & Creaghead, 1994; Wallach & Butler, 1994). Expository language includes understanding and producing speeches, lectures, discussions, classroom discourse, textbooks, reaction papers, essays, and technical, research, or term papers. Expository forms are structured through genres such as description, collection, sequence/procedure, compare-contrast, cause-effect, problem-solution, and argue-persuade. Exposition competence requires the understanding and use of precise vocabulary (often associated with academic content or career areas), pronunciation, grammar, organization, sequencing, transitions, cohesion, coherence, spelling, proofreading, and editing. Individuals who have not developed the oral and literate communication skills associated with narration may experience difficulties with expository language.

Critical elements that serve as building blocks for successful discourse abilities include *communication-learning functions* (instrumental, regulatory, interactional, personal, heuristic, imaginative, informational/representational, performatives, responsives, expressive; Halliday, 1975), *language-thinking functions* (maintaining, reporting, applying, analyzing, logical reasoning, evaluating, synthesizing, imagining, projecting, predicting, inferencing; Tough, 1979), and *executive functions* (awareness, goal setting, planning, self-initiating, self-inhibiting, self-monitoring, self-evaluating, ability to change set, strategic behavior; Ylvisaker & Szekeres, 1989). These various communication-learning functions are used in the process of *heuristics*, the reciprocal system of requesting information (asking questions) and responding (answering questions).

Discourse problems may be caused by developmental or acquired conditions. Oral and literate discourse rules and use vary from culture to culture (Hedberg & Westby, 1993). However, the consensus is that for social and academic success throughout life, individuals must be able to understand and use the communication-learning conventions associated with conversation, narration, and exposition (Nelson, 1998; Wallach & Butler, 1994).

REFERENCES

Brownell, H. H., & Joanette, Y. (Eds). (1993). *Narrative discourse in neurologically impaired and normal aging adults*. San Diego, CA: Singular.

Chamot, A. U., & O'Malley, J. M. (1994). *The CALLA handbook: Implementing the cognitive academic language learning approach*. Reading, MA: Addison-Wesley.

Cummins, J. (1983). Language proficiency and academic achievement. In J. W. Oller, Jr. (Ed.), *Issues in language testing research* (pp. 108–130). Boston, MA: Newbury House.

Esterreicher, C. A. (1995). *Scamper Strategies: FUNdamental activities for narrative development*. Eau Claire, WI: Thinking.

Halliday, M. A. K. (1975). *Learning how to mean: Exploration in the development of language*. London, England: Edward Arnold.

Hedberg, N. L., & Westby, C. E. (1993). *Analyzing storytelling skills: Theory to practice*. Tucson, AZ: Communication Skill Builders.

Hoskins, B. (1996). *Conversations: A framework for language intervention*. Eau Claire, WI: Thinking.

Hughes, D., McGillivray, L., & Schmidek, M. (1997). *Guide to narrative language*. Eau Claire, WI: Thinking.

Larson, V. L., & McKinley, N. (1995). *Language disorders in older students: Preadolescents and adolescents.* Eau Claire, WI: Thinking.

Merritt, D. D., & Culatta, B. (1998). *Language intervention in the classroom.* San Diego, CA: Singular.

Naremore, R. C., Densmore, A. E., & Harman, D. R. (1995). *Language intervention with school-aged children: Conversation, narrative, and text.* San Diego, CA: Singular.

Nelson, N. W. (1998). *Childhood language disorders in context: Infancy through adolescence* (2nd ed.). Boston, MA: Allyn & Bacon.

Ripich, D. N., & Creaghead, N. A. (Eds.). (1994). *School discourse problems* (2nd ed.). San Diego, CA: Singular.

Schiffrin, D. (1994). *Approaches to discourse.* Cambridge, MA: Blackwell.

Tough, J. (1979). *Talk for teaching and learning.* Portsmouth, NJ: Heinemann.

Wallach, G. P., & Butler, K. G. (1994). *Language learning disabilities in school-age children and adolescents: Some principles and applications.* New York, NY: Merrill/Macmillan College.

Ylvisaker, M., & Szekeres, S. (1989). Metacognitive and executive impairments in head injured children and adults. *Topics in Language Disorders, 9,* 34–49.

STEPHEN S. FARMER
New Mexico State University

DISCREPANCY ANALYSIS (See Learning Disabilities, Severe Discrepancy Analysis in)

DISCREPANCY FROM GRADE

Discrepancy model analysis is used in the assessment of learning disabilities to determine if a difference exists between the level of achievement and ability. Levels of achievement and intelligence are measured reliably by using standardized tests. Results, however, may not always be accurate owing to error in measurement (Connell, 1991). Attempts to measure discrepancy may also be complicated by age or grade level. A discrepancy of 1 year at the third grade for a 9-year-old is more severe than a similar discrepancy for a 16-year-old. In addition, cognitive language relationships change over time, which may make eligibility decision-making inappropriate using these models (Cole, 1992).

Several techniques using expectancy analysis are used in quantifying learning disabilities (Mercer, 1983). They are the mental grade method, the learning quotient method, and the Harris method. Harris (1961) provided a

method to determine an individual's reading expectancy grade (RE). The examiner subtracts 5 years from the individual's mental age:

$$RE = MA - 5$$

To determine if a discrepancy exists, a comparison is made between the individual's reading expectancy and the present reading level. The learning quotient method was developed by Myklebust (1968); it includes mental age, chronological age, and grade age (GA). The learning quotient is the ratio between the present achievement age and expectancy age with a score of 89 or below resulting in classification as learning disabled.

A third technique once commonly used to determine discrepancy in learning disabilities was proposed by Harris (1970). This method includes both mental age and chronological age but gives priority to mental age:

$$EA = \frac{2MA + CA}{3}$$

These methods for determining discrepancy have been criticized in that difference scores between two tests were less reliable than each score separately (Salvia & Clark, 1973). It has also been noted that a large number of children might exhibit discrepancy by pure chance. These techniques were also criticized because of their failure with nonreaders.

REFERENCES

Cole, K. (1992). Stability of the intelligence quotient-language quotient relation. *American Journal of Mental Retardation, 97*(2), 131–143.

Connell, P. H. (1991). *An analysis of aptitude-achievement discrepancy formulas in learning disability assessment.* (ERIC Clearinghouse No. TM017793)

Harris, I. (1961). *Emotional blocks to learning.* New York, NY: Free Press.

Harris, A. J. (1970). *How to increase reading ability* (5th ed.). New York, NY: McKay.

Mercer, C. D. (1983). *Students with learning disabilities* (2nd ed.). Columbus, OH: Merrill.

Myklebust, H. (1968). Learning disabilities: Definition and overview. In H. Myklebust (Ed.), *Progress in learning disabilities.* New York, NY: Grune & Stratton.

Salvia, J., & Clark, J. (1973). Use of deficits to identify the learning disabled. *Exceptional Children, 39,* 305–308.

CRAIG D. SMITH
Georgia College

See also Grade Equivalents; Learning Disabilities; Learning Disabilities, Problems in Definition of; Learning Disabilities, Severe Discrepancy Analysis in

DISCRIMINANT ANALYSIS

Discriminant analysis is a statistical technique used to predict group membership from two or more interval dependent variables. It is similar to multiple regression in conception. For example, a researcher might be interested in determining if dyslexic students are distinguishable from other learning-disabled students using the subtests of the Wechsler Intelligence Scale for Children–Revised (WISC-R). Discriminant analysis can be used to determine the optimal set of weights for the WISC-R subtests that maximally separate the two groups on a new variable composed of the weighted sum of the WISC-R subtests.

Discriminant analysis may also be viewed as a data reduction technique. Instead of needing a large number of variables to categorize subjects, the researcher applies discriminant analysis so that a new variable or set of variables is created that uses the information of the original variables. The new variables are linear combinations, or weighted sums, of the original variables. It is anticipated that fewer new variables are needed than in the original set, hence the idea of data reduction. Mathematically, more than one unique solution to the problem is possible. The number of solutions will be equal to the smaller of two numbers: the number of predictors or the degrees of freedom for groups (number of groups minus one). Each solution corresponds to a new variable independent statistically of all the other new solution variables. For two groups there is only one solution since the smaller of the two numbers is equal to one (two groups minus one). This solution is also equal to the multiple regression of the group variable (mathematically defined as, for example, one or two on the predictor variables). The regression weights and the discriminant analysis weights in this case are identical.

For three or more groups, there will be two or more solutions to the problem of maximally distinguishing between the groups. Each solution corresponds to constructing a straight line on which the groups differ most in the sense of squared distance from the mean of the groups on the line. Each solution line is perpendicular in a Euclidean geometric sense from each other solution line. Computer programs are used to solve these problems, and the programs are designed to find the best solution first. The best solution is one in which the variance between the groups is greatest in relation to average variance within the groups for all possible lines. Once this solution is found, the next one is found from the residuals of fit to the first solution. A statistical test, Wilks lambda, is a multivariate analog to the ratio of the sum of squares within groups to the sum of the squares' total. An F-test may be used to test significance. For each new solution, test the additional error reduced in a manner similar to that employed in multiple regression to test a new predictor's additional contribution to prediction. Also, stepwise procedures can be employed in discriminant analysis to select the subset of predictors

that maximally separate the groups. Predictors that do not contribute to separation in a given solution are dropped.

Discriminant analysis is widely used in both social and physical sciences. Its mathematical solutions are straightforward for a computer; discriminant analysis programs for computers are widely used (Huberty & Lowman, 1997).

This entry has been informed by the sources listed below.

REFERENCES

Cohen, J., & Cohen, P. (1983). *Applied multiple regression / correlation analysis for the social sciences* (3rd ed.). Hillsdale, NJ: Erlbaum.

Huberty, C., & Lowman, L. L. (1997). Discriminant analysis via statistical packages. *Educational and Psychological Management, 57*, 759–784.

Pedhazur, E. (1982). *Multiple regression in behavioral research* (2nd ed.). New York, NY: Holt, Rinehart & Winston.

VICTOR L. WILLSON
Texas A&M University

See also Factor Analysis; Multiple Regression

DISCRIMINATION LEARNING

Discrimination learning refers to the process of learning to respond differentially to relevant dimensions of a stimulus event. As a fundamental construct of behaviorally oriented learning explanations, this type of learning emphasizes events that occur before a behavior(s); the relationship of these events to the strength and contextual appropriateness of the behavior(s); and the resulting consequences that serve to maintain, strengthen, or punish the behavior(s).

During the teaching of discriminations, a stimulus event is presented to the student. Following this presentation, the student independently or, if necessary, with prompts, exhibits a behavioral response. If the behavior that the individual engages in is appropriate relative to the stimulus event, the learner is rewarded with a potentially reinforcing outcome. If the behavior is not appropriate with regard to the stimulus event, the consequent alternatives might include not attending to the response (ignoring), or systematic presentation of consequences aimed at reducing the future probability of the behavior occurring (punishment).

As a function of the consequences that occur in this S > R > C relationship, the stimulus events that have historically led to reinforcement become cues for the learner to engage in particular behaviors that will result in rewarding consequences. These stimulus events are referred to as discriminative stimuli (S^D). Conversely, those stimulus events that have not resulted in reinforcement (S^Δ) do not cue the individual to respond. Discrimination learning, then, teaches an individual when to engage in a particular behavior to obtain desirable outcomes, and by contrast clarifies when behavior will not lead to desirable consequences.

The teaching of discriminations constitutes one of the major tasks for individuals who are involved in educating the exceptional needs learner. Although this type of learning is often assumed to take place in an almost incidental fashion, with most exceptional learners this outcome is not as likely. A host of variables, including diverse cognitive skills, inconsistent learning opportunities, and nefarious reinforcement contingencies, may interact to limit such individual's development of accurate discriminations. Effective educational service delivery for the exceptional child or youth often necessitates the use of more systematic methods of teaching discriminations.

Planned teaching of discriminations has involved simple to complex presentations of the attributes of the stimulus events (e.g., size, shape, volume, color, or combinations of these) and varied reinforcement schedules (e.g., movement from fixed to variable schedules of reinforcement) aimed at strengthening the discriminative potential of the stimulus event. Following accurate individualized assessment, discriminations are taught beginning at a level that increases the opportunity for success. Based on continuing assessment, teaching complexity is systematically moved in the direction of more normative skill development.

Teaching of discriminated responses has been used in vocationally oriented curricula, social skills programs, and many other curriculum areas targeted for the exceptional needs learner. By teaching individuals to exhibit specified behaviors under certain stimulus conditions, many of the inconsistent and inappropriate behaviors exhibited by this diverse group have been strengthened or replaced with more environmentally appropriate responses. For a comprehensive explanation of discrimination learning, the reader is referred to texts by Alberto and Troutman (1977) and Sulzer-Azaroff and Mayer (1977). Both texts provide clear examples of the application of this learning principle to educational programming. McDonald and Martin (1993) recommend the use of the Assessment of Basic Learning Abilities Test to assess discrimination acquisition with individuals who have profound disabilities.

REFERENCES

Alberto, P. A., & Troutman, A. C. (1977). *Applied behavior analysis for teachers: Influencing student performance*. Columbus, OH: Merrill.

McDonald, L., & Martin, G. L. (1993). Facilitating discrimination learning for persons with developmental disabilities. *International Journal of Rehabilitation Research*, 16(2), 160–164.

Sulzer-Azaroff, B., & Mayer, G. R. (1977). *Applying behavior-analysis procedures with children and youth*. New York, NY: Holt, Rinehart & Winston.

J. TODD STEPHENS
University of Wisconsin–Madison

See also Applied Behavior Analysis; Behavior Modification; Data-Based Instruction; Precision Teaching

DISPROPORTIONALITY

Disproportionality in special education denotes unequal percentages of students with various demographic characteristics in special education classifications and programs. Disproportionality most often occurs in disability classifications of intellectual and developmental disabilities, emotional behavior disorders, and specific learning disability (SLD), or in programs for the talented and gifted (TAG). The demographic variables in which disproportionality is most often observed, and sometimes seen as a problem, are ethnic/racial status, sex, and socioeconomic status. Disproportionality related to these student characteristics is well known, but highly controversial (Reschly, 1986, 1991, 1997).

The most widely studied disproportionality phenomenon is the overrepresentation of minorities, males, and economically disadvantaged students in the exceptional child classification of MMR. The same groups are also overrepresented, according to some studies, in programs for the SLD and ED. However, the overrepresentation in SLD and ED is rarely of the same magnitude as in MMR.

In Table D.6, data compiled from a Federal Office of Civil Rights (OCR) survey of school districts in the United States, reported in a National Academy of Sciences monograph (Heller, Holtzman, & Messick, 1982), are presented. In 1978, these national results indicated that the only significant area of disproportionality was MMR, where the percentage of Black students classified as MMR was 3 times the percentage of White students so classified. Relatively equal percentages of Black, White, and Hispanic students were found in all other classifications except for ED, where Black students were again overrepresented, but the numbers of students were small. The national results also indicated that Hispanic students were not overrepresented in special education programs for the mildly handicapped, an apparent reversal of a phenomenon that led earlier to placement bias litigation in Arizona and California.

Other studies have indicated minority disproportionality in SLD and ED. For example, data for the state of

Table D.6. National Projections From 1978 OCR Survey (%)

Classification	Minority	Anglo American	Hispanic	African American
Mildly mentally retarded	2.54	1.07	0.98	3.46
Seriously emotionally disturbed	0.42	0.29	0.29	0.50
Learning disabled	2.29	2.04	1.78	2.23
Speech impaired	1.82	2.04	1.78	1.87
Totally (mildly handicapped)	7.07	5.72	5.63	8.06

Source: Based on Finn (1982), Table 1, p. 324, and Table 3, p. 330.

Florida presented in the *S1* v. *Turlington* trial (1986) indicated that Black students were overrepresented in SLD, ED, and MMR.

Males and economically disadvantaged students generally are overrepresented in special education programs for the MMR. This overrepresentation sometimes approaches a ratio of two males for every female in SLD, ED, and MMR programs. Although studied far less frequently, overrepresentation of economically disadvantaged students is at least as ubiquitous as minority overrepresentation. Indeed, minority overrepresentation is probably best understood as reflecting the effects of poverty circumstances (Reschly, 1986).

The disproportionate representation of students in TAG programs is a virtual mirror image of representation in programs for the mildly handicapped. Economically disadvantaged minority students are underrepresented in programs for the gifted. The degree of underrepresentation is highly variable, but for Black students, it is approximately the same as the degree of overrepresentation in programs for the mildly handicapped. The representation of males and females is approximately equal in TAG programs except in very specialized programs that attempt to select the markedly gifted (IQ greater than 150) or in programs for markedly advanced students in the areas of science and mathematics. In the latter kinds of programs, there is considerable underrepresentation of females, a phenomenon that also evokes considerable controversy.

Disproportionality statistics are easily confused and often distorted. In the *Larry P.* case, undisputed facts established that Black students constituted 10% of the total enrollment in California, but 25% of the MMR enrollment. However, only 1% of all California Black students were in MMR programs. These seeming disparities arise from the low base rate of MMR (and other exceptional conditions) and the failure to clearly distinguish between percent of group in the general population (10%), percent of group in the program (1%), and percent of the program by group (25%; Reschly, 1986). Interpretation of disproportionality statistics must carefully distinguish among these different percentages.

The two general causes of disproportionality suggested in the literature are bias or discrimination and genuine individual differences. In short, the disproportionality is seen by some as a reflection of genuine differences among students and by others as a reflection of pernicious bias and discrimination from a variety of sources.

Allegations of bias or discrimination generally implicate the processes and procedures in which students are selected to be considered for placement in various kinds of programs. Thus bias or discrimination has been alleged in referral procedures, in the assessment process and assessment instruments (especially in intelligence tests), and in decision making by persons responsible for classification and placement decisions. Results of research on referral, assessment process and procedures, and decision making are far from definitive or unequivocal. Thus far, there is little evidence that intentional bias or discrimination is a primary cause of disproportionality (Bickel, 1982; Reschly, 1986).

There is ample evidence establishing an association between extreme poverty and the incidence of mild mental retardation (MMR). This evidence has been gathered over the past 80 years with different racial or ethnic groups throughout western Europe and the United States. The MMR is to a large degree a phenomenon of poverty, but the vast majority of poor persons are not mildly mentally retarded (Reschly, 1986, 1991). The mechanisms whereby poverty increases risk for MMR are not clearly understood, but a variety of conditions are implicated (Robinson & Robinson, 1976).

Explanations for the sex disproportionality within the mildly handicapped and in certain types of programs for the gifted are far less clear, but no less controversial. These explanations range from constitutional factors (e.g., suggesting that the greater susceptibility of males to various constitutional disorders explains the overrepresentation of males in the mildly handicapped classifications) to the hypothesis that lower amounts of testosterone in females might account for the underrepresentation of women in programs for extremely advanced students in science and mathematics. Experiential or environmental influences are also suggested for sex disproportionality (e.g., suggestions that sex-typed behavior accounts for greater male referral for learning problems as well as fewer females excelling in math and science). Again, definitive, unequivocal results have not been established, and probably cannot be established in the foreseeable future.

Disproportionality, whether it involves overrepresentation of Black students in programs for the mildly retarded or underrepresentation of women in programs for mathematically precocious youths, should be seen as a symptom, but only a symptom. Factors that might lead to disproportionality should be investigated, including possible bias or discrimination in procedures and processes whereby students are selected or placed in various programs.

Disproportionality, particularly overrepresentation of minority students in programs for the mildly mentally retarded, has provoked extensive and enormously expensive litigation beginning in about 1968 and continuing through present day (Bersoff, 1982; Prasse & Reschly, 1986; Reschly, 1986, 1991). The common features of the placement bias cases are: (a) overrepresentation of minority students, usually Blacks, in self-contained MMR special classes; (b) class-action suits filed in federal district courts; and (c) allegations of bias in various aspects of the referral, preplacement evaluation, and classification/placement decision making. The outcomes of these cases have been extremely diverse, ranging from judicial decrees banning overrepresentation and forbidding the use of individually administered intelligence tests in certain circumstances to judicial decrees indicating that overrepresentation as such is not discriminatory and upholding the use of IQ tests along with other measures as an important protection for all children in the referral and classification/placement process. Federal circuit courts have upheld trial decisions in two cases, *Larry P.* v. *Riles* (1984) and *Marshall* v. *Georgia* (1985). However, the *Larry P.* and *Marshall* opinions reached opposite conclusions on a similar set of issues. Further litigation is likely.

Research methods designed to develop valid ways to screen, refer, and classify/place students that also eliminate disproportionality have been unsuccessful to date, although significant strides have been made toward reducing the cultural bias of some screening tools, such as the Kaufman Assessment Battery for Children. However, inclusive programming (Kovach & Gordon, 1997; Markowitz, 1997) has reduced many instances of placement from service provision to special education outcomes. Processes and procedures that maintain the integrity of programs in meeting the needs of students; apply reliable and valid screening, referral, and classification/placement procedures; and are being consistently implemented and assessed. Centers such as COMRISE (Center of Minority Research in Special Education) are attempting to increase the number and research capacity of minority scholars in institutions of higher education with high minority enrollments. They are building a community of minority scholars within the larger special education research community and are trying to improve the quality and effectiveness of culturally competent special education services for minority students (COMRISE, 1998). The U.S. Department of Education reports disproportionality statistics on an annual basis, and is currently focusing much attention to the less than adequate special education services delivered to inner-city students (U.S. Dept. of Education,

1996). The Office of Civil Rights (OCR) conducts compliance reviews on such issues as ensuring nondiscriminatory practices are followed in the placement of minority students in special education and low-track courses, ensuring that access to English language instruction as well as content courses and other educational benefits are afforded to limited-English proficient students, ensuring student assessment practices are nondiscriminatory, and providing nondiscriminatory access to gifted and talented and other high-ability programs (OCR, 1998). There also has been a national shift toward prereferral intervention, better interventions in regular education, orienting assessment procedures toward intervention rather than classification, the use of court orders, and the use of alternative criteria and assessment procedures (Reschly, 1991, 1997).

Recent years have seen a legislative effort to address the phenomenon of disproportionality in special education. Indeed, the major federal statute in this area, the Individuals with Disabilities Education Act, includes requirements that states develop policies and procedures to prevent overidentification as children with disabilities or disproportionality by student race or ethnicity in this regard, that they collect and report data regarding any such disproportionality, and that they review and revise any relevant policies upon detecting any such disproportionality.

REFERENCES

Bersoff, D. N. (1982). The legal regulation of school psychology. In C. R. Reynolds & T. B. Gutkin (Eds.), *The handbook of school psychology* (pp. 1043–1074). New York, NY: Wiley.

Bickel, W. E. (1982). Classifying mentally retarded students: A review of placement practice in special education. In K. A. Heller, W. H. Holtzman, & S. Messick (Eds.), *Placing children in special education: A strategy for equity* (pp. 182–229). Washington, DC: National Academy.

COMRISE. (1998). *Center of Minority Research in Special Education*. Charlottesville: University of Virginia, Curry School of Education.

Finn, J. D. (1982). Patterns in special education placement as revealed by OCR surveys. In R. A. Heller, W. H. Holtzman, & S. Messick (Eds.), *Placing children in special education: A strategy for equity* (pp. 322–381). Washington, DC: National Academy.

Heller, K., Holtzman, W., & Messick, S. (Eds.). (1982). *Placing children in special education: A strategy for equity*. Washington, DC: National Academy.

Kovach, J. A., & Gordon, D. E. (1997). Inclusive education: A modern-day civil-rights struggle. *Educational Forum, 6*(3), 247–57.

Markowitz, J. (1997). *Addressing the disproportionale representation of students from racial and ethnic minority groups in special education: A resource document*. Alexandria, VA: National Association of State Directors of Special Education.

Office of Civil Rights. (1998). *Annual report to Congress, fiscal year 1996*. Washington, DC: U.S. Department of Education.

Prasse, D. P., & Reschly, D. J. (1986). *Larry P*: A case of segregation, testing, or program efficacy? *Exceptional Children, 52,* 333–346.

Reschly, D. J. (1986). Economic and cultural factors in childhood exceptionality. In R. T. Brown & C. R. Reynolds (Eds.), *Psychological perspectives on childhood exceptionality: A handbook* (pp. 423–466). New York, NY: Wiley.

Reschly, D. J. (1991). Bias in cognitive assessment: Implications for future litigation and professional practices. *Diagnostique,* *17*(1), 86–90.

Reschly, D. J. (1997). *Disproportionate minority representation in general and special education: Patterns, issues, and alternatives.* Des Moines: Iowa State Department of Education.

Robinson, N., & Robinson, H. (1976). *The mentally retarded child* (2nd ed.). New York, NY: McGraw-Hill.

U.S. Department of Education. (1996). *Eighteenth annual report to Congress: To assure the free appropriate public education of all children with disabilities: Implementation of the Individuals with Disabilities Education Act (IDEA).* Washington, DC: Author.

DANIEL J. RESCHLY
Iowa State University
Second edition

KIMBERLY F. APPLEQUIST
University of Colorado at Colorado Springs
Third edition

See also Cultural Bias in Testing; Culturally/Linguistically Diverse Students in Special Education, Representation of; Individuals with Disabilities Education Improvement Act of 2004 (IDEIA); Larry P.; Marshall v. Georgia; Nondiscriminatory Assessments

DISSOCIATIVE IDENTITY DISORDER

Dissociative identity disorder (DID), formerly known as multiple personality disorder (MPD), occurs when a child experiences more than one identity or personality state controlling the child's behavior at different times. The child may or may not be aware that he or she possesses different identities (or "alters"), and switching between alters may occur within seconds. As a result, the child often suffers lapses of memory, which represent failure to recall information that was presented, or events that occurred, when the child was in a different identity or personality state. Children with DID may experience periods of time for which they cannot account for, find items in their possession without knowing how or when they acquired them, meet people who know them but whom they do not recognize, and fail to remember material that they have learned in class. Although many individuals with DID can function well for a time, most will experience periods of decompensation marked by severe anxiety, depression, hallucinations, flashbacks, or other psychiatric symptoms.

DID is thought to be precipitated by severe abuse or trauma in childhood. Although dissociation may occur as a symptom of other disorders, genuine cases of dissociative identity disorder are thought to be very rare. The incidence is thought to be far higher in females than in males. Kluft (1991) has noted that only about 10% of individuals with MPD or DID were diagnosed prior to age 20, and only 3% were diagnosed at age 11 or younger.

Characteristics

1. Two or more identities with distinct personalities.
2. Personalities take control of an identified persons behavior.
3. Unable to recall important facts that may occur when other personalities are present.
4. Subtance abuse (e.g., blackouts or chaotic behavior during alcohol intoxication) or a general medical condition (e.g., complex partial seizures) is not to blame for erratic behavior.

Source: Adapted from American Psychiatric Association, 1994.

Treatment of dissociative identity disorder may include medication, psychotherapy, or a combination of both. Medications are used to reduce the intensity of the child's reaction to external triggers and stressors and to treat psychological symptoms such as depression, anxiety, panic symptoms, attention and concentration problems, flashbacks, nightmares, sleep problems, and poor impulse control. Medications such as clonidine and propranol may be used to reduce hyperarousal, anxiety, poor impulse control, disorganized thinking, and rapid switching. Anxiety may be treated with benzodiazepines, sedative antihistamines, buspirone, beta-blockers, and small doses of neuroleptics. Depression may be treated with tricyclic antidepressants, monoamine oxidase inhibitors (MAOIs), or selective serotonin reuptake inhibitors (SSRIs; Torem, 1996).

Children suffering from severe DID resulting in behavior that is harmful to themselves or others may be psychiatrically hospitalized. Inpatient and outpatient individual psychotherapy may focus on establishing safety, teaching the child relaxation techniques to help calm anxiety, and modifying environmental stressors or desensitizing the child to them. Cognitive-behavioral techniques may focus on correcting thinking errors and erroneous beliefs, whereas experiential techniques such as play therapy with younger children, art, and movement therapy encourage expression of feeling and abreaction. Hypnosis, often used in the past to "discover" and "integrate" alter personalities, has fallen into disfavor because of the risk of creating new alters and personalities, and lawsuits have resulted. Family therapy can provide psychoeducational guidance in helping families learn to deal with the stresses of parenting a DID child and in addressing pathological family dynamics. Group therapy may be used to promote age-appropriate socialization.

Children suffering from DID may be eligible for special education services under the classification of Emotional Disturbance. Support by the school psychologist may be necessary to help the child cope with and reduce anxiety, memory, and cognitive problems caused by anxiety secondary to stimulation of traumatic memories. In extreme cases, homebound and hospitalized services may be necessary.

REFERENCES

American Psychiatric Association. (1994). *Diagnostic and statistical manual of mental disorders* (4th ed.). Washington, DC: Author.

Kluft, R. P. (1991). Clinical presentations of multiple personality disorder. *Psychiatric Clinics of North America, 3*, 605–630.

Torem, M. (1996). Medications in the treatment of dissociative identity disorder. In J. Spira & I. Yalom (Eds.), *Treating dissociative identity disorder*. San Francisco, CA: Jossey-Bass.

JANIECE POMPA
University of Utah

DISTAL ARTHROGRYPOSIS SYNDROME

Distal arthrogryposis syndrome (DAS) is a hereditary, congenital neuromuscular disorder. It is distinguished by multiple contractures of the fingers, hands, and feet. Less frequently there may be hip, knee, or shoulder involvement. Two distinct clinical forms exist.

DAS is very rare. There are fewer than 50 reported cases in the literature. DAS is transmitted in an autosomal dominant manner. There is considerable variability in the severity of the physical abnormalities in children with DAS, even among sibling groups and their affected parents. This interesting phenomenon is caused by wide swings in the abnormal gene's expressivity.

Characteristics

Type I (typical)

1. In the newborn the hand is tightly fisted. The thumb is laid flat across the palm. The index and middle fingers overlap the thumb. They are, in turn, overlapped by the ring and little fingers. This unusual finger positioning is the most distinguishing physical finding of the syndrome.
2. Positional deformities of the feet, including outward deviation and clubfoot.
3. Congenital hip dislocation and decreased hip mobility.
4. Mild flexion contractures of the knee.
5. Stiff shoulders (at birth).

Type II (atypical)

All or some of the above, in conjunction with all or some of the following:

1. Cleft lip and/or cleft palate.
2. Small tongue.
3. Droopy eyelids (ptosis).
4. Short stature.
5. Scoliosis.
6. "Borderline" intellectual functioning.

Treatment of this disorder involves rectifying the orthopedic problems, which, fortunately, are remarkably responsive to therapy. Feeding difficulties may occur with the atypical forms and require medical intervention.

Because of the rarity of the diagnosis, there is no research to indicate an educational prognosis. It is expected that children diagnosed with Type I DAS would not require special education because of the reported normal intelligence. In contrast, children with Type II DAS may require educational modifications because of borderline intellectual functioning. The amount of modification needed would be based on the intellectual functioning and academic need of the individual child. In both cases, however, children with Type I or Type II DAS may require modifications in their educational environment because of their orthopedic problems. Evaluation and treatment by an occupational and physical therapist may be warranted, as well as assistive devices or technology in the classroom to facilitate learning.

The prognosis for Type I DAS is favorable. These children have normal intelligence and orthopedic abnormalities that either improve with age or are readily correctable. However, as adults these patients may continue to have mild contractures of the fingers and outward deviation of the hands.

Patients with Type II DAS have more dysmorphic features and lower intelligence than do their Type I counterparts. Therefore, they do not fare as well.

REFERENCE

Jones, K. (1997). *Smith's recognizable patterns of human malformations* (5th ed.). Philadelphia, PA: Saunders.

BARRY H. DAVISON
Ennis, Texas

JOAN W. MAYFIELD
Baylor Pediatric Specialty Services
Dallas, Texas

DISTAR

DISTAR (Direct Instructional System for Teaching and Remediation) was a product name for an instructional system published by Science Research Associates Inc. (SRA). From 1964 to 1966, Siegfried Engelmann and Carl Bereiter developed the teaching methods used in the DISTAR program, which is based on a task analysis of basic skills and presentation of materials in a direct teaching model. In 1967 SRA contracted with Engelmann to develop, write, and test DISTAR reading, language, and arithmetic materials. His co-authors were Elaine Bruner, reading; Douglas Carnine, arithmetic; and Jean Osborn and Therese Engelmann, language. In 1968 Wesley Becker joined Engelmann's Follow-Through Project and in 1969 they formed the Engelmann-Becker Corporation, a private nonprofit organization providing teacher training in the Engelmann-Becker instructional model and the production of materials for Follow-Through sites. Although developmental work took place at the Engelmann-Becker Corporation, product development for DISTAR per se was performed under contract between SRA and the individual authors involved (Brinckerhoff, 1983).

The DISTAR system was originally designed to teach basic skills and concepts in reading, arithmetic, and language to disadvantaged preschoolers (Guinet, 1971). However, the scope broadened to include average, above average, learning-disabled, and educable and trainable mentally retarded children (Kim, Berger, & Kratochvil, 1972). Reviews of research (Cotton & Savard, 1982; Gersten, 1981) revealed that the direct instruction method was proven successful with socioeconomically disadvantaged primary age children and special education students through age 13.

Research results comparing the DISTAR program with other direct instruction curricula indicated that DISTAR was comparable in outcomes (Kuder, 1990; Traweek & Berniger, 1997).

REFERENCES

Brinckerhoff, L. (1983, Spring). Siegfried Engleman—Prophet or Profiteer. *ADI NEWS*, p. 1.

Cotton, K., & Savard, W. G. (1982). *Direct instruction: Research on school effectiveness project*. Portland, OR: Northwest Regional Educational Lab. (ERIC Document Reproduction Service No. ED 214 909)

Gersten, R. M. (1981, April). *Direct instruction programs in special education settings: A review of evaluation research findings*. Paper presented at the annual international convention of the Council for Exceptional Children, New York. (ERIC Document Reproduction Service No. ED 204 957)

Guinet, L. (1971). *Evaluation of DISTAR materials in three junior learning assistance classes* (Report No. 71-16). Vancouver, BC: Board of School Trustees, Department of Planning and Evaluation. (ERIC Document Reproduction Service No. ED 057 105)

Kim, Y., Berger, B. J., & Kratochvil, D. W. (1972). *DISTAR instructional system* (Report No. OEC-0-70-4892). Washington, DC: Office of Education, Office of Program Planning and Evaluation. (ERIC Document Reproduction Service No. ED 061 632)

Kuder, S. J. (1990). Effectiveness of the DISTAR reading program for children with learning disabilities. *Journal of Learning Disabilities, 23*(1), 69–71.

Traweek, D., & Berniger, V. (1997). Comparison of beginning literacy programs. *Learning Disability Quarterly, 20*(2), 160–168.

MARY D'IPPOLITO
Montgomery County Intermediate Unit, Norristown,
Pennsylvania

See also Direct Instruction; Follow Through

DISTRACTIBILITY

Distractibility refers to difficulties in sustaining attention to tasks, concentrating, tracking, and screening out interfering distractions (Lezak, 1995). A child who is distractible may appear to be daydreaming, doodling, or paying unnecessary attention to what others are doing (Children and Adults with Attention Deficit Disorders [CHADD], 2000). Children described as distractible typically display shorter attention spans than do their same-age peers, and they usually have difficulty completing assignments when multitasking is involved. Their inability to focus attention may result in uncompleted assignments and forgotten items. Distractibility negatively impacts a child's ability successfully to complete school and household tasks.

Characteristics

1. Difficulty maintaining attention to expected tasks or activities.

2. Limited follow-through of required tasks.

3. Slow response to directions.

4. Failure to devote sufficient attention to tasks so that crucial components of the task are left out and finished products are often messy and unorganized.

5. Difficulty listening and apparent inability to follow directions.

6. High susceptibility to environmental distractions.

7. Limitations in organizing tasks and activities; frequently loss of items needed for task completion or day-to-day items (e.g., homework or lunch money).

8. Avoidance or inability to complete assignments involving continued concentration.

9. Appearance of forgetfulness with daily activities.

10. Sluggish reaction time.

Much of the information and research related to the topic of distractibility is derived from the inattentive subtype of attention-deficit/hyperactivity disorder (ADHD). The term ADHD is a relatively common neurobiological disorder that affects between 3% and 7% of school-age children, with males being between 2 and 9 times more likely to exhibit these concerns than females (American Psychiatric Association, 2000). Between 40% and 60% of children with ADHD also exhibit characteristics of other disorders including learning disabilities, emotional-behavioral disorders, mood disorders, tics or Tourette syndrome, and anxiety disorders (CHADD, 2000). Additionally, frontal lobe injuries or deficits have been associated with limitations in focusing and shifting attention (Mirsky, 1989).

A multimodal treatment approach incorporating medical, psychological, educational, and behavior management interventions has been found to produce the best results in treating children who are distractible (Gaddes & Edgell, 1994). Psychostimulant medication is effective with 70% to 80% of children diagnosed with ADHD (CHADD, 2000); methylphenidate (Ritalin), dextroamphetamine (Dexedrine), and pemoline (Cylert) are usually prescribed. These medications are used to improve a child's ability to attend to tasks and to decrease off-task behavior. Frequently reported side effects of stimulant medication include insomnia, headaches, appetite suppression, and irritability when the dose wears off. Growth suppression can be an issue with long-term medication usage. Overall, research indicates that medication helps students with distractibility obtain maximum benefit from educational and behavioral interventions (Bohlmeyer, 1998).

Psychological interventions often include group or individual counseling. The focus of counseling interventions may include social skills development, behavioral self-monitoring, and classroom management regarding the nature of this condition. Parents are also targeted for intervention by providing them with information about distractibility and connecting them with available support groups. Parents, teachers, and others involved with the child on a daily basis can also receive training on using behavioral signals that redirect a child back to the task at hand. Behavioral contracts that outline expectations and rewards for meeting expectations are also effective in many cases (Bohlmeyer, 1998). The use of a coach who offers reminders, feedback, and encouragement may improve a child's work-completion rate and time on task (Hallowell & Ratey, 1994).

Educational techniques designed to reduce a student's level of distractibility generally involve interventions in which the child's teacher implements classroom accommodations to address the child's needs. Efficacious techniques include: (a) providing brief, clear, and specific directions; (b) establishing eye contact prior to giving directions; (c) asking the child to repeat verbal directions for clarification; (d) providing the child with frequent feedback regarding performance; (e) breaking down lengthy assignments into small steps; (f) allowing students a choice of academic assignments; and (g) maintaining a consistent structure so that the child understands the expectations. Peer tutoring and self-monitoring are also school interventions that have been helpful in reducing distractibility by providing children who are distractible with exposure to a model of appropriate behavior and a source of frequent feedback (Brock, 1998).

Other alternative approaches to treating distractibility have been developed to help children stay on task. However, there is no credible scientific evidence to support the use of alternative treatments, such as dietary intervention (e.g., the Feingold diet), electroencephalogram biofeedback, applied kinesiology, optometric vision training, mineral supplements, candida yeast, or anti–motion sickness medications (CHADD, 2000).

Children who have difficulty sustaining attention are at risk for academic difficulties and emotional concerns such as lowered self-esteem. Although it once was thought that children outgrew ADHD in adolescence, it is now understood that the effects of the disability may continue into adulthood. The long-term prognosis is hopeful for those children who receive individual interventions early in life designed to meet their needs and help them succeed at home and school. Longitudinal research indicates that children who obtain appropriate interventions for ADHD exhibit fewer school, substance abuse, and interpersonal problems while demonstrating greater overall functioning than do those who do not receive individualized treatment. Although some children may continue to display distractible behaviors as adults, most can learn compensation strategies and access sources of support that help them remain on task and attain their goals.

REFERENCES

American Psychiatric Association. (2000). *Diagnostic and statistical manual of mental disorders* (4th ed., text rev.). Washington, DC: Author.

Bohlmeyer, E. M. (1998). Attention deficit disorder: A primer for parents. In A. S. Canter & S. A. Carroll (Eds.), *Helping children at home and school: Handouts from your school psychologist* (pp. 539–541). Bethesda, MD: National Association of School Psychologists.

Brock, S. E. (1998, February). Classroom-based interventions for students with ADHD. *Communiqué, 8–10.*

Children and Adults with Attention Deficit Disorders (CHADD). (2000, November 18). Retrieved from http://www.chadd.org/

Gaddes, W. H., & Edgell, D. (1994). *Learning disabilities and brain function: A neuropsychological approach.* New York, NY: Springer.

Hallowell, E. M., & Ratey, J. J. (1994). *Driven to distraction.* New York, NY: Pantheon Books.

Lezak, M. D. (1995). *Neuropsychological assessment* (3rd ed.). New York, NY: Oxford University Press.

Mirsky, A. S. (1989). The neuropsychology of attention: Elements of a complex behavior. In E. Perecman (Ed.), *Integrating theory and practice in clinical neuropsychology.* Hillsdale, NJ: Erlbaum.

BOB KIRCHNER
University of Northern Colorado

SHAWN POWELL
United States Air Force Academy

See also Attention Deficit/Hyperactivity Disorder; Attention Span; Conners' Rating Scales; Freedom from Distractibility; Hyperkinesis; Impulse Control

DIVISION WITH MODELS, BEST PRACTICES FOR TEACHING

Mathematic disabilities are common in students with learning disabilities (LD) and mild levels of mental retardation (MMR) (Van Luit & Naglieri, 1999). Most students who have mathematics learning difficulties are not able to successfully become proficient in the four basic math operations before leaving elementary education (Van Luit & Kroesbergen, 2003). According to Van Luit and Naglieri (1999), instruction for students with learning disabilities should be appropriate for children with special needs, and utilize special strategies and processes such as working with concrete materials or working with mental representations. When solving word problems in mathematics and advanced problem solving, these students tend to use strategies that include drawing, modeling, and the use of idiosyncratic representations in order to understand the problem situations (Carpenter, Fennema, Franke, Levi, & Empson, 1999; Fuson, 2003).

One of the most important parts of problem solving is understanding the correct operation to use. The division operation is considered the most difficult operation to understand. However, it is also one of the most familiar operations that children use in their daily life. They understand the idea of "sharing" before they start to use "sharing" as a mathematical operation. According to Thompson and Saldanha (2003), there are two types of division: measuring (segmenting) and partitioning (sharing). In the measurement model, students need to put an amount into groups of a certain size. Partitioning is the action of distributing an amount of something to a number of recipients (Thompson & Saldanha, 2003).

Students with learning disabilities need special attention to obtain the skills necessary for solving division problems. To provide this special attention, teachers should use different kinds of teaching strategies. Using visual materials might be more helpful than teaching in a traditional manner. When humans learn sensory stimuli it may expedite learning. Using models, seeing materials, and touching them is the sensory part of learning; also letting students solve problems with these materials is the cognitive part of the learning. Using direct modeling strategies is useful in teaching division to students with special needs. Using base 10 blocks and units of these blocks (one cube) can be especially helpful because by using these materials students are able to understand the meaning or division by sharing materials, to see the division operation in a sensory way, allowing them to use the division model in two different ways. As a physical model is used and demonstrated, students can remember a certain arithmetic operation and recognize the relationship between a physical situation and the operation (Thornton, Tucker, Dossey, & Bazik, 1983). To make the usage of direct modeling strategy more concrete, this example can be given: the problem situation is to divide 27 by 3. There are two ways to solve this division problem using two models of division, partition and measurement. According to the partition model, student should choose three subgroups; each group has nine counters. To help understanding students can choose three counters (i.e., block units or cubes) at a time. After that the student puts one counter side by side the first chosen three counters and continues until they are all used up. At the end they will have three groups, which have nine counters in each group. Another way to solve the problem is to use the measurement division model. Students should make nine sets with three counters in each set. To understand that, the student can choose three counters and put them in one spot, then choose three counters and put them in another spot, and continue in this way until they get nine sets and use up all counters. It is possible to use base 10 blocks to solve multidigit division problems by using the same kind of division models. To sum up, whatever material or model is used, the important idea is the necessity of teaching the division operation with concrete models and leading students to learn by activities and guiding them to understand the basic idea of the division operation.

REFERENCES

Carpenter, T. P., Fennema, E., Franke, M. L., Levi, L., & Empson, S. B. (1999). *Children's mathematics: Cognitively guided instruction*. Portsmouth, NH: Heinemann.

Fuson, K. C. (2003). Developing mathematical power in whole number operations. In J. Kilpatrick (Ed.), *A research companion to principle and standards for school mathematics* (1st ed., pp. 68–94). Reston, VA: National Council of Teachers of Mathematics.

Thompson, P. W., & Saldanha, L. A. (2003). Fractions and multiplicative reasoning. In J. Kilpatrick, W. G. Martin, & D. Schifter (Eds.), *A research companion to principles and standards for school mathematics* (pp. 95–113). Reston, VA: NCTM.

Thornton, C. A., Tucker, B. F., Dossey, J. A., & Bazik, E. F. (1983). *Teaching mathematics to children with special needs*. Menlo Park, CA: Addison Wesley.

Van Luit, J. E. H., & Kroesbergen, E. H. (2003). Mathematics interventions for children with special educational needs: A meta-analysis. *Remedial and Special Education, 24*, 97–114.

Van Luit, J. E. H., & Naglieri, J. A. (1999). Effectiveness of the MASTER program for teaching special children multiplication and division. *Journal of Learning Disabilities, 32*, 98–107.

AYSE TUGBA ONER
Texas A&M University
Fourth edition

DIVORCE AND SPECIAL EDUCATION

Since the mid-1970s, the impact of parental divorce on children has been an area of concern for professionals in psychology and education. This interdisciplinary consensus has been generated in part by alarming Census descriptions of rapidly changing adult lifestyles. For example, Census reports indicate that the divorce rate more than quadrupled from 1970 to 1994. These figures did not account for those who were divorced and remarried at the time of the survey, so they actually underestimate the total incidence of divorce in our society. Similarly, the incidence of single-parent child rearing also increased markedly from 11.9% in 1970 to 29% in 1994. These figures did not include those who have previously experienced a single-parent situation but were living in reconstituted two-parent families.

A central issue is whether adjustment to divorce represents a transitory stressor or is associated with long-term disorders. Longitudinal studies provide a consensus that divorce should be conceptualized as a multistage process (Hetherington, Cox, & Cox, 1978, 1985; Wallerstein, 1985; Wallerstein & Kelly, 1974). These studies, conducted over periods of 6 and 10 years, respectively, reveal complex interactions and altered family relationships that result in long-term maladjustment for children. They also illustrate substantial age and sex differences in adjustment.

Wallerstein and Kelly (Kelly & Wallerstein, 1976; Wallerstein, 1984, 1985; Wallerstein & Kelly, 1974, 1975, 1976, 1980a, 1980b) conducted a 10-year longitudinal study of 131 children residing in Marin County, California, whose parents were divorced. This was a nonclinical sample of children, ages 2½ to 18 years, from White, middle-class families. Clinical interviews were conducted just after separation, and at 1-, 5-, and 10-year intervals following divorce. Initial results revealed that children responded differently by age. At the 1-year follow-up, adjustment problems persisted, although most adolescents had made adequate adjustments (attributed to distancing from parents and successful mastery experiences during the past year). At the 5-year follow-up, variables that mediate children's adjustment to divorce were identified—resolution of parental conflict, child's relationship with noncustodial parent, quality of parenting by custodial parent, personality and coping skills of the child, child's support system, diminished anger and depression in the child, and age and sex of the child. A positive relationship with the father was more important for boys than girls. Results of the 10-year follow-up (of 113 original subjects) confirmed the long-term impact of divorce. Difficulties at 10 years were characterized by poor parenting (diminished capacity to parent) and an overburdened child (taking on of adult responsibility).

Hetherington, Cox, and Cox (Hetherington, 1979; Hetherington et al., 1978, 1979a, 1979b, 1982, 1985) used a sample of 96 divorced- and intact-family preschool-age children from White, middle-class families in Virginia. Children were assessed at 2 months, and 1, 2, and 6 years after divorce. A comprehensive, multifactored, multisource approach to assessment was used to assess sex-role typing and cognitive and social development of the child.

Results indicated severe disorganization and stress during the first year. Difficulties were evident in parenting behavior and child adjustment. Divorced parents were less able than nondivorced parents to cope with parenting. They made fewer maturity demands, were less consistent in discipline, used less reasoning, communicated less with the child, and displayed less interaction with and affection toward the child. Children were more dependent, disobedient, aggressive, demanding, unaffectionate, and whining. Mother-son relationships were particularly affected, characterized by a cycle of poor parenting, child aggression, coercive parenting, increased negative child behavior, and parental feelings of helplessness and incompetence. By 2 years, most of the negative effects had abated. Factors that facilitated adjustment included low parental conflict and parental agreement on child rearing. Results at 6 years (which included a remarried sample) indicated that divorce had a more negative impact on boys and remarriage had a more negative impact on girls. Externalizing problems were more stable across time for boys and internalizing problems more stable for girls. Divorced-family children experienced more negative life changes, which were, in turn, related to more behavior problems at follow-up.

Kurdek et al. (Kurdek, 1981, 1983, 1985, 1987; Kurdek & Berg, 1983; Kurdek, Blisk, & Siesky, 1981; Kurdek & Siesky, 1980a, 1980b; Kurdek & Sinclair, 1985) examined the role of cognitive mediators in children's adjustment to divorce. Their initial study included a sample of 70 divorced-family children, mean age of 9.92 years, from White middle-class families in Dayton, Ohio, whose parents were members of Parents Without Partners. Results revealed that children's adjustment to divorce was facilitated by an internal locus of control, accurate perceptions of social situations (i.e., understanding of interpersonal relations), low interpersonal stress, and good father-child relationships. They found that children's reasoning about divorce was linked to the development of logical and social reasoning. Further, the level of cognitive understanding determined whether the child's thinking about divorce was nonegocentric; focused on parents' thoughts, feelings, and intentions; and was grounded in an appreciation of the complex dynamics of interpersonal relations.

Using a national sample of 18,000 elementary and secondary students from 14 states, Brown (1980) compared one-parent (divorced, separated, widowed, unmarried) and two-parent families. Global measures of adjustment such as grade point average, attendance, suspensions, truancy, and referral for discipline problems were obtained from school records. Findings indicated that the impact for elementary-aged children was evident on behavioral (e.g., suspensions and truancy) and academic indexes. For high-school children, differences were evident on behavioral indexes (e.g., expulsions, tardiness, suspensions); however, there appeared to be little impact on academic achievement.

The research of Stolberg et al. (Stolberg, 1987; Stolberg & Anker, 1983; Stolberg & Bush, 1985; Stolberg & Cullen, 1983; Stolberg, Kiluk, & Garrison, 1986) has focused on environmental factors that mediate children's adjustment to divorce, including such factors as parenting skills, visitation, and family changes associated with divorce. Local samples obtained through Parents Without Partners, newspaper ads, and schools were used. They found parenting skills, frequency of life changes, and marital hostility to be successful predictors of prosocial skills and psychopathology of divorced-family children. Parenting skills (of the mother/custodial parent) were found to be the single most significant influence on child adjustment, particularly affecting prosocial skills. There was no direct relationship between parent and child adjustment when effects of parenting skills were removed.

Furstenberg et al. (Furstenberg, Nord, Peterson, & Zill, 1983; Furstenberg & Spanier, 1984) used data from a national sociological study of children's well being. The representative sample included 1,300 U.S. children (ages 11 to 16) and their families, and subsequent subsamples of divorced and remarried families. Findings from this study revealed a racial difference in divorce and remarriage rates, with Blacks one and a half times as likely to divorce but less likely to remarry than Whites (remarriage rate: one out of eight for Blacks, four out of seven for Whites). Frequent contact (at least once per week) of the child with the noncustodial parent was evident in only 17% of the divorced sample. Those variables that best predicted amount of contact with the noncustodial parent, irrespective of the child's sex, included provision of child support and residential propinquity, which were positively related to amount of contact, and length of time since separation, which was negatively related.

Findings from other studies relevant to determinants of children's postdivorce adjustment indicate that adjustment is facilitated by availability of the noncustodial parent and a positive relationship with the custodial parent (Hess & Camara, 1979); parent-child discussion of divorce-related topics (Jacobson, 1978a, 1978b); low interpersonal hostility prior to separation (Berg & Kelly, 1979; Jacobson, 1978a, 1978b, 1978c); and more time spent with the father (Jacobson, 1978a, 1978c).

In reviewing the literature on remarriage, Kurdek and Sinclair (1985) conclude that similarities exist between children's adjustment to divorce and to remarriage in that children from both situations (compared with those in intact families) exhibit higher deviance rates, more difficulty in management, and lower self-esteem, as do their parents. Although findings are conflicting, past research generally indicates that (a) remarriage does not necessarily stabilize the family; (b) children reexperience the disruption associated with divorce when parents remarry; and (c) the parent's situation in reference to role strain does not necessarily improve with remarriage.

Critical reviews of past research have consistently indicated severe methodological limitations (Atkeson, Forehand, & Rickard, 1982; Clingempeel & Reppucci, 1982; Kurdek, 1981, 1983). Major limitations include (a) small and biased samples that limit generalizability of the findings; (b) inadequate or nonexistent control groups, which precludes the study of divorce-specific effects; (c) failure to control for socioeconomic status in comparisons between divorced and intact families; and (d) failure to include multimethod, multifactored criteria to control for measurement bias.

The NASP-KSU (National Association of School Psychologists—Kent State University) Impact of Divorce

Project was directed at minimizing the limitations of the cited research in order to provide more definitive conclusions about the long-term impact of divorce on children (Guidubaldi, 1983, 1985; Guidubaldi & Cleminshaw, 1985; Guidubaldi, Cleminshaw, & Perry, 1985; Guidubaldi, Cleminshaw, Perry, & Mcloughlin, 1983; Guidubaldi, Cleminshaw, Perry, & Nastasi, 1984; Guidubaldi, Cleminshaw, Perry, Nastasi, & Lightel, 1986; Guidubaldi & Nastasi, 1984; Guidubaldi & Perry, 1985, 1987; Guidubaldi, Perry, & Cleminshaw, 1984; Guidubaldi, Perry, & Nastasi, 1986). Results on 699 children from 38 states at the initial data-gathering period (Time-1) demonstrated more conclusively than previous studies that, during middle childhood (ages 6 to 11), youths are adversely affected by divorce. Because the average length of time in a single-parent home at Time-1 was 3.98 years ($SD = 2.54$), these effects were interpreted as long term. Specific criteria on which children from divorced homes performed more poorly than those from intact homes are as follows: (a) social-behavioral measures from parent and teacher ratings of peer popularity status, anxiety, dependency, aggression, withdrawal, inattention, and locus of control; (b) Wechsler IQ scores; (c) Wide Range Achievement Test scores in reading, spelling, and math; (d) school performance indexes, including grades in reading and math and repeating of a school grade; (e) adaptive behaviors (measured by the Vineland Teacher Rating Scale) in the areas of daily living, social skills, and communication; and (f) physical health ratings of the children in the study as well as of parents and siblings. Intact-family children showed superior performance on 21 of 27 social competence criteria and 8 of 9 academic competence criteria. Additionally, analyses revealed that divorced-family children were far more likely to have been previously referred to a school psychologist, to have been retained in grade, and to be in special class placements, including programs for reading difficulties.

Definition of the sequelae of divorce is a complex process, and assessment must therefore include not only multidimensional aspects of child and parent adjustment but also a longitudinal-ecological approach. The NASP-KSU study thus included follow-up samples of 229 children at 2- and 3-year intervals, and examined environmental factors as mediators of children's postdivorce adjustment. Eleven major findings from this nationwide study are:

1. The negative, differential effects of divorce on children and young adolescents are long term where the average length of time since divorce was 6.41 years ($SD = 2.35$) at Time-2 of this study.

2. Children's reactions to divorce are especially influenced by sex and age, with boys during late childhood and early adolescence being more adversely affected on multiple criteria than 6- and 7-year-old boys. Late childhood and young adolescent girls were much better adjusted than those at the 6- and 7-year age levels.

3. Single-parent, divorced-family households have significantly less income than intact families. This difference accounts for significant academic achievement variance between divorced- and intact-family children.

4. The socioeconomic measures of parents' educational and occupational levels moderate some of children's divorce adjustment. This is especially apparent in regard to the educational level of the same sex parent.

5. A positive relationship with both the custodial and noncustodial parent predicted positive adjustment for both girls and boys of divorce concurrently and across time. The noncustodial parent-child relationship was noticeably more important for boys.

6. More frequent and reliable visitation with the noncustodial parent (typically, the father) was associated with better adjustment for both girls and boys.

7. Diminished degree of conflict between parents predicted improved children's adjustment, especially for boys across time to early adolescence.

8. Authoritarian (i.e., punitive) child-rearing styles in comparison with authoritative (i.e., more democratic) and permissive styles predicted more adverse child adjustment, especially for boys.

9. The home routines of less television viewing, regular bedtimes, maternal employment, and helpfulness of maternal grandfather predict positive adjustment for both boys and girls.

10. Family support factors that promote positive postdivorce adjustment are availability of helpful relatives, including in-laws, availability of friends, paid child care assistance such as nursery schools and babysitters, and participation in occupational and educational endeavors by the custodial parent.

11. When the total sample of male and female divorced-family children are considered, school environment variables of smaller school population, safe and orderly atmosphere, fewer miles bused to school, and traditional rather than open classroom structure are associated with better adjustment. However, several school and classroom climate factors relate to better adjustment for girls only. These include safe and orderly environment, frequent monitoring of student progress, high expectations for academic achievement, and time on task.

The impact of divorce on children has appropriately become a central concern of mainstream education. Special educators perhaps need to focus even more on this rapidly increasing disruption of children's lives. As evidenced in the NASP-KSU nationwide study and in Beattie and Maniscalo (1985), children in special education programs disproportionately come from divorced, single-parent homes. Income levels, home routines, and parental supports are adversely affected by this condition and children from these homes, particularly boys, show overwhelming evidence of maladjustment in both academic and social-emotional areas of performance. Understanding conditions that can ameliorate the negative impact of divorce on children may be one of the most critical bases for development of preventive mental health interventions as well as remedial techniques for children already identified as special.

REFERENCES

Atkeson, B. M., Forehand, R. L., & Rickard, K. M. (1982). The effects of divorce on children. In B. B. Lahey & A. E. Kazdin (Eds.), *Advances in clinical child psychology* (Vol. 5). New York, NY: Plenum Press.

Beattie, J. R., & Maniscalo, G. O. (1985). Special education and divorce. Is there a line? *Techniques, 1*(5), 342–345.

Berg, B., & Kelly, R. (1979). The measured self-esteem of children from broken, rejected, and accepted families. *Journal of Divorce, 2*, 263–369.

Brown, B. F. (1980). A study of the school needs of children from one-parent families. *Phi Delta Kappa, 62*, 537–540.

Clingempeel, W. G., & Reppucci, N. D. (1982). Joint custody after divorce: Major issues and goals for research. *Psychological Bulletin, 91*, 102–127.

Furstenberg, F. F., Nord, C. W., Peterson, J. L., & Zill, N. (1983) The life course of children of divorce: Marital disruption and parental contact. *American Sociological Review, 48*, 656–668.

Furstenberg, F. F., & Spanier, G. B. (1984). *Recycling the family*. Beverly Hills, CA: Sage.

Guidubaldi, J. (1983, July). Divorce research clarifies issues: A report on NASP's nationwide study. *Communiqué, 10*, 1–3.

Guidubaldi, J. (1985). Differences in children's divorce adjustment across grade level and gender: A report from the NASP-Kent State University Nationwide Project. In S. Wolchik & P. Karoly (Eds.), *Children of divorce: Perspectives on adjustment*. Lexington, MA: Lexington.

Guidubaldi, J., & Cleminshaw, H. (1985). Divorce, family health and child adjustment. *Family Relations, 34*, 35–41.

Guidubaldi, J., Cleminshaw, H., & Perry, J. (1985). The relationship of parental divorce to health status of parents and children. *Special Services in the Schools, 1*, 73–81.

Guidubaldi, J., Cleminshaw, H. K., Perry, J. D., & Mcloughlin, C. S. (1983). The impact of parental divorce on children: Report of the nationwide NASP study. *School Psychology Review, 12*, 300–323.

Guidubaldi, J., Cleminshaw, H. K., Perry, J., & Nastasi, B. (1984). Impact of family support systems on children's academic and social functioning after divorce. In G. Rowe, J. DeFrain, H. Lingrin, R. MacDonald, N. Stinnet, S. Van Zandt, & R.

Williams (Eds.), *Family strengths 5: Continuity and diversity* (pp. 191–207). Newton, MA: Education Development Center.

Guidubaldi, J., Cleminshaw, H. K., Perry, J. D., Nastasi, B. K., & Lightel, J. (1986). The role of selected family environment factors in children's post-divorce adjustment. *Family Relations, 35*, 141–151.

Guidubaldi, J., & Nastasi, B. (1984, April). Classroom climate and post-divorce child adjustment. In J. Guidubaldi (Chair), *Factors related to academic and social adjustment of elementary grade divorced-family children*. Symposium conducted at the annual convention of the American Educational Research Association, New Orleans.

Guidubaldi, J., & Perry, J. D. (1985). Divorce and mental health sequelae for children: A two-year follow-up of a nationwide sample. *Journal of the American Academy of Child Psychiatry, 24*, 531–537.

Guidubaldi, J., Perry, J. D., & Cleminshaw, H. K. (1984). The legacy of parental divorce: A nationwide study of family status and selected mediating variables on children's academic and social competencies. In B. B. Lahey & A. E. Kazdin (Eds.), *Advances in clinical child psychology* (Vol. 7, pp. 109–151). New York, NY: Plenum Press.

Guidubaldi, J., Perry, J. D., & Nastasi, B. K. (1986). Growing up in a divorced family: Initial and long-term perspectives on children's adjustment. In S. Oskamp (Ed.), *Annual review of social psychology*. Beverly Hills, CA: Sage.

Hess, R. D., & Camara, K. A. (1979). Post-divorce family relationships as mediating factors in the consequences of divorce for children. *Journal of Social Issues, 35*(4), 79–96.

Hetherington, E. M. (1979). Divorce: A child's perspective. *American Psychologist, 34*, 851–858.

Hetherington, E. M., Cox, M., & Cox, R. (1978). The aftermath of divorce. In J. H. Stevens, Jr., & M. Mathews (Eds.), *Mother-child, father-child relationships* (pp. 149–176). Washington, DC: National Association for Education of Young Children.

Hetherington, E. M., Cox, M., & Cox, R. (1979a). Family interaction and the social-emotional and cognitive development of children following divorce. In V. Vaughn & T. Brazelton (Eds.), *The family setting priorities*. New York, NY: Science and Medicine.

Hetherington, E. M., Cox, M., & Cox, R. (1979b). Play and social interaction in children following divorce. *Journal of Social Issues, 35*, 26–49.

Hetherington, E. M., Cox, M., & Cox, R. (1982). Effects of divorce on parents and children. In M. E. Lamb (Ed.), *Nontraditional families: Parenting and child development* (pp. 233–288). Hillsdale, NJ: Erlbaum.

Hetherington, E. M., Cox, M., & Cox, R. (1985). Long-term effects of divorce and remarriage on the adjustment of children. *Journal of the American Academy of Child Psychiatry, 24*, 518–530.

Jacobson, D. S. (1978a). The impact of marital separation/divorce on children. I. Parent-child separation and child adjustment. *Journal of Divorce, 1*(4), 341–360.

Jacobson, D. S. (1978b). The impact of marital separation/divorce on children: II. Interparent hostility and child adjustment. *Journal of Divorce, 2*, 3–19.

Jacobson, D. S. (1978c). The impact of marital separation/divorce on children: III. Parent-child communication and child adjustment, and regression analysis of findings from overall study. *Journal of Divorce, 2,* 175–194.

Kelly, J. B., & Wallerstein, J. S. (1976). The effects of parental divorce: Experiences of the child in early latency. *American Journal of Orthopsychiatry, 46,* 20–23.

Kurdek, L. A. (1981). An integrative perspective on children's divorce adjustment. *American Psychologist, 36,* 856–866.

Kurdek, L. A. (Ed.). (1983). *Children and divorce.* San Francisco, CA: Jossey-Bass.

Kurdek, L. A. (1985). Children's reasoning about parental divorce. In R. D. Ashmore & D. M. Brodzinsky (Eds.), *Perspectives on the family* (pp. 1–48). Hillsdale, NJ: Erlbaum.

Kurdek, L. A. (1987). Cognitive mediators of children's adjustment to divorce. In S. Wolchick & D. Karoly (Eds.), *Children of divorce: Perspectives on adjustment.* New York, NY: Gardner.

Kurdek, L. A., & Berg, B. (1983). Correlates of children's adjustment to their parents' divorces. In L. A. Kurdek (Ed.), *Children and divorce* (pp. 47–60). San Francisco, CA: Jossey-Bass.

Kurdek, L. A., Blisk, D., & Siesky, A. E. (1981). Correlates of children's long-term adjustment to their parents' divorce. *Developmental Psychology, 17,* 565–579.

Kurdek, L. A., & Siesky, A. E. (1980a). Sex role self-concepts of single divorced parents and their children. *Journal of Divorce, 3,* 249–261.

Kurdek, L. A., & Siesky, A. E. (1980b). Children's perceptions of their parents' divorce. *Journal of Divorce, 3,* 339–378.

Kurdek, L. A., & Sinclair, R. (1985). *The relation between adolescent adjustment and family structure, grade, and gender.* Unpublished manuscript, Wright State University, Department of Psychology, Dayton, OH.

Stolberg, A. L. (1987). Prevention programs for divorcing families. In L. Bond (Ed.), *Vermont Conference on the Primary Prevention of Psychopathology.* Burlington, VT: Author.

Stolberg, A., & Anker, J. (1983). Cognitive and behavioral changes in children resulting from parental divorce and consequent environmental changes. *Journal of Divorce, 7,* 23–41.

Stolberg, A. L., & Bush, J. P. (1985). A path analysis of factors predicting children's divorce adjustment. *Journal of Clinical Child Psychology, 14,* 49–54.

Stolberg, A. L., & Cullen, P. M. (1983). Preventive interventions for families of divorce: Divorce Adjustment Project. In L. A. Kurdek (Ed.), *Children and divorce* (pp. 71–82). San Francisco, CA: Jossey-Bass.

Stolberg, A. L., Kiluk, D., & Garrison, K. M. (1986). A temporal model of divorce adjustment with implications for primary prevention. In S. M. Auerbach & A. L. Stolberg (Eds.), *Issues in clinical and community psychology: Crisis intervention with children and families.* Washington, DC: Hemisphere.

Wallerstein, J. S. (1984). Children of divorce: Preliminary report of a ten-year follow-up of young children. *American Journal of Orthopsychiatry, 54,* 444–453.

Wallerstein, J. S. (1985). Children of divorce: Preliminary report of a ten-year follow-up of older children and adolescents. *Journal of the American Academy of Child Psychiatry, 24,* 545–553.

Wallerstein, J. S., & Kelly, J. B. (1974). The effects of parental divorce: The adolescent experience. In E. Anthony & C. Koupanik (Eds.), *The child and his family* (Vol. 3, pp. 479–505). New York, NY: Wiley.

Wallerstein, J. S., & Kelly, J. B. (1975). The effects of parental divorce: Experiences of the preschool child. *Journal of the American Academy of Child Psychiatry, 14,* 600–616.

Wallerstein, J. S., & Kelly, J. B. (1976). The effects of parental divorce experiences of the child in later latency. *American Journal of Orthopsychiatry, 46,* 256–267.

Wallerstein, J. S., & Kelly, J. B. (1980a). California's children of divorce. *Psychology Today, 13,* 66–67.

Wallerstein, J. S., & Kelly, J. B. (1980b). *Surviving the break-up: How children and parents cope with divorce.* New York, NY: Basic Books.

JOHN GUIDUBALDI
BONNIE K. NASTASI
Kent State University

DIX, DOROTHEA L. (1802–1887)

Dorothea Dix, a humanitarian and social reformer, was responsible for major reforms in the care of the mentally ill in the United States and abroad. Shocked by the common practice of incarcerating mentally ill people in jails with criminals, she spent a year and a half investigating conditions in her home state of Massachusetts and, in 1843, reported her findings to the state legislature. Her description of the abhorrent conditions that existed (including the use of chains for restraint) and her argument that mentally ill persons could be properly treated and cared for only in hospitals, resulted in substantial enlargement of the state hospital at Worcester, which was one of only eight mental hospitals in the United States at that time. Capitalizing on her success in Massachusetts, Dix turned her attention to other states and countries. She was responsible for the construction of 32 hospitals in the United States and others in Canada, Europe, and Japan.

During the Civil War, Dix served as superintendent of women nurses, the highest office held by a woman during the war. After the war she returned, at age 65, to her work with hospitals. In 1881 she retired to the New Jersey State Hospital at Trenton, the first hospital established through her efforts, where she remained until her death.

REFERENCE

Marshall, H. E. (1937). *Dorothea Dix, forgotten samaritan.* Chapel Hill: University of North Carolina Press.

PAUL IRVINE
Katonah, New York

DOCTORAL TRAINING IN SPECIAL EDUCATION

The common purpose of doctoral-level education training programs is to prepare leaders for the field, but the programs themselves are as diverse as the roles their graduates assume. Many local, state, and federal administrators, college and university teacher trainers, scholars, and researchers hold the doctorate in special education. Both the doctor of philosophy (PhD) and the doctor of education (DEd or EdD) are awarded. Although the PhD is considered an academic degree and the DEd a professional degree, this distinction does not hold up in practice because many prominent scholars hold the DEd and many practitioners the PhD.

Students are typically selected for doctoral training on the basis of their potential for success in advanced graduate training and the potential they exhibit as special education leaders. Programs frequently use the previous academic achievement of their applicants and Graduate Record Examination scores (or both) to predict success in advanced graduate work. Leadership potential is evaluated through previous professional experience, professional references, and, occasionally, statements of professional goals (by which the seriousness of an applicant's intent may be judged). Typically, admission is competitive.

A program of study is planned under the direction of an advisor (or major professor) and a supervisory committee. The program typically derives from the aspirations of the student and the strengths of the program offerings. In addition to special education course work, doctoral programs may include concentrations in a related field of study or cognate area and work in research methodology and statistics. The successful completion of course work, however, represents only a fraction of the formal requirements that a doctoral candidate must meet. Many programs require a qualifying examination before formal admission to candidacy and, later in the program, a comprehensive examination to determine mastery of the program of studies. Doctoral programs culminate with the completion of an independent research project and the preparation and defense of the dissertation. The supervisory committee evaluates the student's performance at each of these checkpoints.

These formal requirements represent only part of what students learn during their doctoral studies. Many have the opportunity (often as graduate assistants) to develop skills in teaching, supervision, administration, and research. Initially, their participation in these activities is guided by the faculty. With experience, candidates may take on more responsibility and operate with greater independence. Many programs provide financial support for graduate assistants with funds from leadership preparation grants awarded by the U.S. Department of Education's Office of Special Education and Rehabilitative Services.

The importance of these informal experiences in the full preparation of doctoral students was established in an analysis of the credentials of recent graduates. Rose, Cullinan, and Heller (1984) reported that recent graduates who were considered competitive applicants for college and university positions had published at least three articles, presented more than four papers at national conferences, written or assisted in the writing of two grant applications, taught at least one course independently, and conducted numerous workshops and consultancies. Clearly, there is much to be accomplished beyond the formal requirements of a doctoral program for its graduates to compete successfully in the academic job market.

Finally, it must be emphasized that leadership preparation programs have undertaken a critical self-evaluation in response to the common and difficult problems they face: the quantity and quality of students, the poor focus of their offerings, faculty dissatisfaction, and low faculty productivity (Prehm, 1984). With regard to this final concern, research (Schloss & Sindelar, 1985) has shown that productive researchers are the exception and not the rule, even for faculties of doctoral-granting programs. The recent efforts of the Higher Education Consortium for Special Education, an organization representing institutions with comprehensive programs in special education, in developing indicators of quality in leadership training represent a positive first step in addressing these issues. There has been a call for a national data collection system to address a critical shortage of doctoral-level specialists (Smith, 1990).

REFERENCES

Prehm, H. J. (1984). Preparation for leadership in personnel preparation. *Teacher Education & Special Education, 7,* 59–65.

Rose, T. L., Cullinan, D., & Heller, H. W. (1984). A consumer's report of special education doctoral programs. *Teacher Education & Special Education, 7,* 88–91.

Schloss, P. J., & Sindelar, P. T. (1985). Publication frequencies of departments conferring the PhD in special education. *Teacher Education and Special Education, 8,* 67–76.

Smith, D. D. (1990). *History and future needs of doctoral training in special education.* (ERIC Clearinghouse No. EC301042)

PAUL T. SINDELAR
Florida State University

See *also* Specialnet; Supervision in Special Education; Teacher Centers

DOG GUIDES

The use of dogs to guide people who are blind has a long history. However, it was not until after World War I that the dog was systematically trained to guide German veterans blinded during the war. The veterans were taught to follow the trained dog's movements through the use of a specially designed harness.

An American living in Switzerland, Dorothy Harrison Eustis, described the use of German shepherds as dog guides for people who were blind in a 1927 article published in the *Saturday Evening Post*. One of the Americans who got in touch with Eustis after the publication of the article was Morris Frank, a young man from Tennessee who had been recently blinded. He persuaded Eustis to have a dog trained for him and he traveled to Switzerland to be trained with the dog.

After Frank's success with the first American dog guide, the legendary Buddy, Eustis returned to the United States in 1929 and established the Seeing Eye Inc., the first school to train dog guides for people who have visual impairments in America. There are now dozens of programs in the United States that prepare dog guides and there are similar training programs throughout the world. The introduction of dog guides led to a greater acceptance of travelers who are blind and has helped a shift in perception of people with visual impairments (Blasch & Stuckey, 1995).

Dog guides are first socialized and then trained to detect obstacles on the ground, as well as overhanging or projecting objects that have the potential to come into contact with the user. Unlike the long cane, the use of which depends on the user coming into contact with objects, dogs lead their users around environmental obstacles. As such, it is possible for the user to be unaware of the reasons for slight changes in direction when traveling. Most dog guide schools carefully match the user and dog on specific characteristics and then provide a course of training for several weeks to develop the skills of the human-dog team.

Dog guides, due to a variety of limitations, provide mobility assistance to a small percentage of people who are visually impaired. Personal preferences, remaining vision, activity level, age, physical and mental health, the presence of hearing impairment, vocation, and life circumstances often dictate the advisability of the use of a dog guide. Very few school-age students with visual impairments use dog guides, although the practice is not prohibited.

Individuals using dog guides must be mature enough to handle the dog in a variety of complex public environments, as well as to care for the dog appropriately. Dogs need to be fed and groomed daily, and their elimination needs to be addressed in a timely way. They must be vigorously exercised and their skills at detecting obstacles and guiding maintained through frequent practice and correction (Frank, Haneline, & Brooks, 2010). In addition, individuals who use dog guides must have well-developed orientation skills, for it is they who direct the dog from one destination to another. For this reason, school age students who see themselves as potential dog users should be provided with a strong foundation in skills related to both orientation and mobility.

REFERENCES

Blasch, B. B., & Stuckey, R. A. (1995). Accessibility and mobility of persons who are visually impaired: A historical analysis. *Journal of Visual Impairment and Blindness, 89*(5), 417–422.

Frank, L., Haneline, R., & Brooks, A. (2010). Dog guides and the orientation and mobility specialist. In W. R. Wiener, R. L. Welsh, & B. B. Blasch (Eds.), *Foundations of orientation and mobility (3rd ed.): Vol. II: Instructional strategies and practical applications* (pp. 519–534). New York, NY: AFB Press.

SANDARA LEWIS
Florida State Unviersity
Fourth edition

DOLCH WORD LIST

The Dolch Word List of 220 common words constitutes more than 65% of the words found in elementary reading materials and 50% of all reading materials (Dolch, 1960). These high-frequency words form the framework for all reading materials. The list, developed by Edward W. Dolch, includes prepositions, conjunctions, pronouns, adjectives, adverbs, and the most common verbs. There are no nouns included in this list since each noun, according to Dolch, is tied to subject matter (Johns, 1971). The list is comprised of *structure words*, words that hold language together, as opposed to content words.

The average third-grade reader should be able to identify these 220 service words at sight. Many of the words have irregular spellings and cannot be learned by picture cues. Dolch (1939) reports that if the reader is able to recognize more than half the words at the sight reading rate of 120 words per minute, he or she will have confidence and will be able focus on the meaning of the material.

The Dolch Word List is frequently used as a diagnostic tool to identify poor readers (Elmquist, 1987). Many struggling readers are deficient in recognizing and understanding the proper use of these words. The list also serves as the basis of remedial instruction. Garrard Publishers produces several materials, Popper Words, Basic Sight Vocabulary Cards, and Basic Sight Word Test, based on the list. The actual list can be found at http://kidzone.ws/ or on many other websites.

REFERENCES

Dolch, E. W. (1939). *A manual of remedial reading.* Champaign, IL: Garrard.

Dolch, E. W. (1960). *Teaching primary reading.* Champaign, IL: Garrard.

Elmquist, E. (1987). *Improving reading skills and attitudes through the reading and writing connection.* (ERIC Clearinghouse No. CS010210)

Johns, J. L. (1971). The Dolch Basic Word List—Then and now. *Journal of Reading Behavior, 3,* 35–40.

JOYCE E. NESS
Montgomery County Intermediate

DOLL, EDGAR A. (1889–1968)

Edgar A. Doll joined the staff of the Training School at Vineland, New Jersey, as a research and clinical psychologist in 1913. There he worked with E. R. Johnstone and H. H. Goddard in the Vineland Laboratory: the first laboratory devoted solely to the study of mental retardation.

Following service in World War I, 3 years with New Jersey's State Department of Classification and Education, completion of the doctorate in psychology at Princeton University, and 2 years of teaching at Ohio State University, Doll returned to Vineland as director of research. His studies of social competence led to the publication, in 1935, of the *Vineland Social Maturity Scale,* a revolutionary instrument that provided an objective basis for measuring social functioning that was more useful than mental age for classifying people for purposes of training and care.

Doll left Vineland in 1949 to serve as coordinator of research for the Devereux Schools. He was later consulting psychologist for the Bellingham, Washington public schools. He served as president of the American Association of Applied Psychology, the American Association on Mental Deficiency, and the American Orthopsychiatric Association.

This entry has been informed by the sources listed below.

REFERENCES

Doll, E. A. (1953). *The measurement of social competence: A manual for the Vineland Social Maturity Scale.* Minneapolis, MN: Educational Test Bureau.

Doll, E. E. (1969). Edgar Arnold Doll, 1889–1968. *American Journal of Mental Deficiency, 73,* 680–682.

PAUL IRVINE
Katonah, New York

DOMAN, GLENN (1919–)

Glenn Doman is internationally known for his interest and pioneering work in child brain development and function. He attended Drexel Institute in 1938, graduated from the University of Pennsylvania in 1940 and in 1965 went on to graduate from the University of Pennsylvania School of Physical Therapy. He was certified at the perceptor level in human brain development in 1969.

Doman has studied children for more than 40 years. He founded the Institutes for the Achievement of Human Potential in 1955 and served as its director until 1981; subsequently, he has served as the chairman of its board. He is known for the formulation of the Doman-Delacato treatment method for children with neurological disabilities, a treatment that was popular during the 1960s. The theory stresses that an individual's development in mobility, vision, audition, and language follows specific neurological stages that are correlated with anatomical progress. The Institutes have worked with thousands of brain-injured children.

Doman's publications include *How to Teach Your Baby to Read* (1964/1994), *What to Do About Your Brain-Injured Child* (1974/1994), *How to Teach Your Baby Math* (1979/1994), *How to Multiply Your Baby's Intelligence* (1984/1994), and *How to Teach Your Baby to Be Physically Superb* (1988/1994). These books are available in 20 languages.

Among his numerous honors, Doman was knighted by the Brazilian government for his work on behalf of the children of the world. In 1994, he was presented with the European prize "Lorenzo, the Magnificent" by the Accademia Internazionale Medicea for his work in the field of science. In 1996, the Institutes for Functional Medicine awarded Doman the first annual Linus Pauling Functional Medicine Award.

REFERENCES

Doman, G. (1994). *How to teach your baby to read* (2nd ed.). New York, NY: Avery.

Doman, G. (1994). *What to do about your brain-injured child* (2nd ed.). New York, NY: Avery.

Doman, G. (1994). *How to teach your baby math* (2nd ed.). New York, NY: Avery.

Doman, G. (1994). *How to multiply your baby's intelligence* (2nd ed.). New York, NY: Avery.

Doman, G. (1994). *How to teach your baby to be physically superb* (2nd ed.). New York, NY: Avery.

ROBERTA C. STOKES
Texas A&M University
First edition

TAMARA J. MARTIN
The University of Texas of the Permian Basin
Second edition

DOPAMINE

Dopamine (DA) is a catecholamine class neurotransmitter. Dopamine has been one of the most studied neurotransmitters because of observed roles for DA in schizophrenia, obsessive-compulsive behavior (Lewis, 1996), conduct disorder (Galvin, 1995) tardive dyskinesia, and Parkinson's disease. Dopaminergic pathways are located throughout the limbic system (area of the brain often associated with emotional reactivity and memory), the basal ganglia (area of the brain associated with motor timing and complex integration), and frontal brain areas. Animal studies of DA depletion and studies of neurological disorders with motor manifestations (i.e., Parkinson's disease) produce results supportive of DA's contributory role in brain systems involved in normal locomotion (Seiden & Dykstra, 1977). Similarly, researchers working with drugs that stimulate DA in animal brains have noted increases in spontaneous aggression during chemical stimulation of DA receptor sites (Senault, 1970). Introduction of haloperidol (Haldol), a DA-blocking agent, reduces the frequency of such fighting (Leavitt, 1982). The role of DA in sexual activity appears similar, that is, increased availability of DA increases sexual behavior in rats. In humans, however, the latter effect appears more indirect. When L-Dopa, a precursor of DA, was administered to male Parkinson's patients, its observed effect on sexual potency appeared more the result of removing other disabling motor symptoms than a result of direct stimulation of libido (Leavitt, 1982). In addition, DA appears to play a role in the regulation of food intake. Investigators (Seiden & Dykstra, 1977) also have noted a role for DA in the maintenance of avoidance behavior and in the facilitation of behavior on positive reinforcement schedules.

REFERENCES

Galvin, M. (1995). Serum dopamine beta Hydroxylase and maltreatment in psychiatrically hospitalized boys. *Child Abuse & Neglect: The International Journal, 19*(7), 821–832.

Leavitt, F. (1982). *Drugs and behavior.* New York, NY: Wiley.

Lewis, M. H. (1996). Plasma HVA in adults with mental retardation and stereotyped behaviors: Biochemical evidence for a dopamine deficiency model. *American Journal on Mental Retardation, 100*(4), 413–418.

Seiden, L. S., & Dykstra, L. A. (1977). *Psychopharmacology: A biochemical and behavioral approach.* New York, NY: Van Nostrand Reinhold.

Senault, B. (1970). Comportement d'aggressivité intraspécifique induit par l'apomorphine chez le rat. *Psychopharmacologia, 18,* 271–287.

ROBERT F. SAWICKI
Lake Erie Institute of Rehabilitation

See also **Haldol; Tranquilizers**

DOUBLE-BLIND DESIGN

One frequently encountered problem in research involving the administration of medication, particularly psychotropic drugs, is that some children or adults may be improved solely as a function of their knowledge that a drug has been administered. The degree to which this effect, frequently referred to as a *placebo effect,* is present and affecting the outcome of research is unknown and uncontrolled in any specific situation. Experimenters may also be influenced by administration of medication, particularly if the researcher developed the pharmaceutical agent or has other subjective reasons to be biased toward a particular outcome. In such cases, investigators may observe differential rates of behavioral or physiological change in those subjects receiving medication in comparison with those individuals receiving no drug therapy (Babbie, 1979). In either of these cases, the subject's or experimenter's expectation of a certain outcome represents a threat to the validity of the research design. Validity is compromised when the effect of the drug administered is confounded with the expectation of what, if any, the effects of the drug might be.

To control for the effect of patients merely taking medication, as would be the case if those taking medication were compared with a nonmedicated control group, subjects who are not receiving an active drug substance are administered a placebo that appears identical to the active medication in every regard, with the exception that its active ingredients are inert. Thus, the drug under study is not present in the placebo dose and the patients are unaware of whether their medication is in fact active or a placebo. In research terminology, then, the patients are blind to their own drug condition. In order to control for the effect of experimenter bias, it is also necessary for the investigators who administer medication and those who evaluate the outcome (the presence or absence of the drug effect) to be blind to the drug condition of the patients. When these precautions are followed, the research design is said to employ a double-blind procedure, since neither the patients nor the researchers are cognizant of the drug condition to which patients may be assigned (Sprague, 1979).

Obviously, there must be records of which patients have received active medication and which have received placebos in order for the results of the study to be interpretable. However, it is critical that this information not be available to researchers who may have contact with the patients or to the patients themselves until after the study has been completed. Thus, by following a strict double-blind research design, drug effects may be distinguished from actual patient and experimenter expectations regarding the drug under investigation (Sprague, 1979). Unless these two types of effects can be separated, the validity of such a study would be compromised seriously (Sprague, 1979; Sprague & Werry, 1971).

In summary, the double-blind condition exists when neither the subject involved nor the investigator evaluating the drug trial is cognizant of the control condition (placebo) or the active pharmacological intervention. Such a procedure precludes the investigator's expectations and hopes from influencing any physiological or behavioral changes that may occur as a function of active pharmacotherapy (Sprague, 1979).

In reviews of the massive literature pertaining to the psychopharmacology of hyperactive and mentally retarded populations, Sprague (Sprague, 1979; Sprague & Werry, 1971) has underscored that the use of double-blind procedures is a minimum requisite in evaluating psychotropic drugs for these groups. Nonetheless, ethical considerations may preclude withholding an effective medication for a child despite the requirements of rigorous empirical research. Thus, investigators must carefully weigh the mandates of controlled clinical trials research with the special needs of some children. Moreover, some research (Whalen & Henker, 1980) in the field of pediatric psychopharmacology has provided rather convincing evidence to suggest that the notion of being administered any pill, whether placebo or active medication, exerts a specific effect on children's views of personal causality (Margraf, 1991). This is particularly true for hyperactive or conduct-disordered children (Ross & Ross, 1982). Should these findings be upheld in future research, the use of active medication as well as both a placebo and a no-pill condition will in fact be necessary in clinical trials, particularly those that involve stimulant medications or other psychotropic drugs prescribed for behavior disorders in children.

REFERENCES

Babbie, E. R. (1979). *The practice of social research*. Belmont, CA: Wadsworth.

Margraf, J. (1991). How "blind" are doubled blind studies? *Journal of Consulting and Clinical Psychology, 59*(1), 184–187.

Ross, D. M., & Ross, S. A. (1982). *Hyperactivity*. New York, NY: Wiley.

Sprague, R. L. (1979). Assessment of intervention. In R. L. Trites (Ed.), *Hyperactivity in children: Etiology, measurement and treatment implications* (pp. 217–229). Baltimore, MD: University Park Press.

Sprague, R. L., & Werry, J. S. (1971). Methodology of psychopharmacological studies with the retarded. In N. R. Ellis (Ed.), *International review of research in mental retardation* (Vol. 5). New York, NY: Academic Press.

Whalen, C. K., & Henker, B. (1980). *Hyperactive children: The social ecology of identification and treatment*. New York, NY: Academic Press.

MARTHA ELLEN WYNNE
Loyola University of Chicago

RONALD T. BROWN
Emory University School of Medicine

See also **Hawthorne Effect; Research in Special Education; Single Case Research**

DOWN, J. (JOHN) LANGDON (1828–1896)

J. (John) Langdon Down, an English physician, in 1866 described the condition that he called mongolism and that is now known as Down syndrome. Although there had been earlier descriptions in the medical literature of individuals who appeared to belong to the same category, Down is credited with the discovery and description of this clinical entity (Penrose, 1966).

Down was concerned with the prevention of mental retardation. He recommended attention to good parental health and sound prenatal care and child-rearing practices. He advocated education for mentally retarded individuals and recognized the efficacy of early training.

REFERENCES

Down, J. L. (1866). Observations on an ethnic classification of idiots. *London Hospital Clinical Lecture Reports, 3*, 259–262.

Down, J. L. (1887). *Mental affectations of childhood and youth*. London, England: Churchill.

Penrose, L. S., & Smith, G. F. (1966). *Down's anomaly*. Boston, MA: Little, Brown.

PAUL IRVINE
Katonah, New York

DOWN SYNDROME

Down syndrome, occurring in approximately 1 out of 800 to 1,000 live births (National Dissemination Center for Children with Disabilities, 2004), is the most frequent genetic cause for Mild to Moderate Mental Retardation and associated medical problems (National Institute of Child Health and Human Development, 2005). Down syndrome is a genetic disorder caused by a chromosomal abnormality. An English physician, John Langdon Down, first identified the condition in 1866. Dr. Down did not understand the cause of the disorder and attributed its physical manifestations as regression to a Mongolian and primitive racial type (Selikowitz, 1997). Thus, he coined the term *mongolism*. Down syndrome is unrelated to race, nationality, religion, or socioeconomic status (National Association for Down Syndrome, 2005). Advanced maternal age is the only substantiated risk factor for babies with Down syndrome (Centers for Disease Control and Prevention, 2005). The probability that a woman under 30 will have a baby with Down syndrome is less than 1 in 1,000, but for a woman who is 35, the chance increases to 1 in 400 (National Institutes of Health, 2005).

In 1959, Lejeune, a French geneticist, discovered that Down syndrome is caused by an extra copy of chromosome 21 (Down Syndrome Association United Kingdom, 2005). People with the disorder have an extra, crucial portion of the number 21 chromosome in some or all of their cells. Thus, Down syndrome is commonly known as Trisomy 21. The additional genetic material modifies the course of prenatal development and results in the characteristics associated with the syndrome. Methods for identifying Down syndrome in the prenatal period are screening tests (e.g., triple screen, alphafetoprotein plus, the quad test) that measure the amounts of certain hormones and proteins in the blood, and diagnostic tests (including amniocentesis, chorionic villus sampling, and percutaneous umbilical blood sampling; National Down Syndrome Congress, 2005).

Down syndrome typically is identified at birth or shortly thereafter due to the physical features that frequently are associated with the disorder. The most common physical characteristics include muscle hypotonia (i.e., low muscle tone), flat facial profile (i.e., somewhat depressed nasal bridge and small nose), oblique palperbral fissures (i.e., upward slant to the eyes), an abnormal shape of the ear, a single crease across the center of the palm as opposed to the average double crease, hyperflexibility (i.e., excessive ability to extend the joints), dysplastic middle phalanx of the fifth finger (i.e., little finger curved inward), epicanthal folds (i.e., small skin folds on the inner corner of the eyes), excessive space between the large and the second toe, and enlargement of the tongue in relationship to the size of the mouth (National Down Syndrome Society, 2005). A test of one's chromosomal karyotype analyzes the child's chromosomes to determine whether an extra chromosome 21 is present in some or all of the cells, confirming a diagnosis that has been made at birth (National Institutes of Health, 2005).

Nondisjunction, the most common chromosomal abnormality, refers to faulty cell division resulting in three rather than two number 21 chromosomes. This extra chromosome originates in the development of either the egg or the sperm, and is replicated in every cell of the body as the embryo develops. Therefore, three copies of chromosome 21 exist in all cells of the individual. Nondisjunction is responsible for roughly 95% of all cases of Down syndrome (National Down Syndrome Society, 2005).

Mosaicism takes place when nondisjunction of the 21st chromosome occurs in one of the initial cell divisions after fertilization. Mosaicism involves a mixture of two types of cells, some with 46 chromosomes, and some with 47. Mosaicism is responsible for about 1% to 2% of Down syndrome cases (National Down Syndrome Society, 2005).

The third type of abnormality, translocation, occurs when part of the 21st chromosome breaks off during cell division and attaches to another chromosome, typically the 14th chromosome. About 3% to 4% of Down syndrome cases are accounted for by translocation (National Down Syndrome Society, 2005). Translocation may occur spontaneously and may be passed from parent to child. One or both parents may be a balanced carrier of translocation (e.g., they exhibit no symptoms yet can pass the condition to their offspring). The mother transmits 88% of the cases of translocation, fathers transmit 8% of the cases,

and mitotic errors comprise the remaining 2% (National Institute of Child Health and Human Development, 2005).

Individuals with Down syndrome usually are smaller, develop more slowly intellectually than their peers, and have health-related problems, including respiratory difficulties due to a lowered resistance to infection, rates of mild to moderate hearing loss, speech difficulty, and visual problems including crossed eyes and far- or nearsightedness. Babies with Down syndrome frequently have heart defects, the majority of which are surgically correctable. Some with Down syndrome may have atlantoaxial instability, a misalignment of the top two vertebrae of the neck that can result in neck injuries (National Dissemination Center for Children with Disabilities, 2004). Those with Down syndrome have a greater likelihood to develop leukemia in childhood, dementia later in life, gastrointestinal blockage, and thyroid problems (Mayo Clinic, 2005). There is a tenfold greater incidence of seizure disorders in individuals with Down syndrome than in the regular population (National Institute of Child Health and Human Development, 2005).

The National Association for Down Syndrome stresses the crucial need for early intervention services for children with the condition and recommends physical, speech, and developmental therapies should be started shortly after birth. Academic placement should consider the strengths, limitations, and needs of the individual child. Partial or full inclusion is somewhat common (National Down Syndrome Society, 2005). Families and schools are encouraged not to place limitations on potential abilities of children with Down syndrome in light of their large range of abilities (National Dissemination Center for Children with Disabilities, 2005). Life expectancy for individuals with Down syndrome is age 50 or older (National Institute of Child Health and Human Development, 2005).

REFERENCES

Centers for Disease Control and Prevention. (2005, June 17). *Risk factors for Down syndrome (Trisomy 21): Maternal cigarette smoking and oral contraceptive use in a population-based case-control study.* Retrieved from http://www.cdc.gov/

Down Syndrome Association United Kingdom. (2005). *New parents.* Retrieved from http://downsyndrome.org/

Mayo Clinic. (2005, April 7). *Down syndrome.* Retrieved from http://www.mayoclinic.com/

National Association for Down Syndrome. (2005). *Down syndrome facts.* Retrieved from http://nads.org/

National Dissemination Center for Children with Disabilities. (2004, January). *Fact sheet four.* Retrieved from http://nichey.com/

National Down Syndrome Congress. (2001). *Facts about Down syndrome.* Retrieved from http://ndsccenter.org/

National Down Syndrome Society. (2005). *General information.* Retrieved from http://www.ndss.org/

National Institute of Child Health and Human Development: National Institutes of Health. (2005, March 29). *Facts about Down syndrome*. Retrieved from http://nichd.nih.gov/Pages/index.aspx

Selikowitz, Mark. (1997). *Down syndrome: The facts*. Oxford, England: Oxford University Press.

MARNI R. FINBERG
University of Florida

See also Developmental Delay; Genetic Counseling; Mental Retardation; Mosaicism; Trisomy 21

THE DRAW-A-PERSON INTELLECTUAL ABILITY TEST FOR CHILDREN, ADOLESCENTS, AND ADULTS

The DAP:IQ (Reynolds & Hickman, 2003) provides an objective scoring system that is applied to a standardized method for obtaining a drawing of a human figure from which an IQ estimate is then derived. The test is normed for ages 4 years 0 months 0 days through 89 years 11 months 30 days on a population proportionate representative sample of 2,295 individuals from across the United States. All that is necessary for administration and scoring of the DAP:IQ is the test manual, the Administration/Scoring Form, and a sharpened pencil. The examinee is asked to draw a picture of him- or herself using the standard instructions provided in the manual. The drawing is not timed but most examinees (children and adults) complete the drawing in 5 minutes or less. Once the examiner has learned the scoring system and is comfortable with the examples in the manual, scoring is completed typically in only 2 to 3 minutes. In most cases, the total time required to collect the drawing, score it, and interpret it will be less than 10 to 12 minutes. The DAP:IQ may be administered individually or in groups, the latter being primarily for screening purposes.

The DAP:IQ provides a common set of scoring criteria across its full age range of 4 years through 89 years and is the first draw-a-person test to do so. This not only eases the burden on the examiner but allows for more direct, continuous measurement of a common construct across the age range.

The value of using human figure drawings (HFDs) as a component of the psychoeducational and psychological evaluation has been recognized across 3 centuries. Goodenough (1926), in her groundbreaking, comprehensive study also reviews prior research on using human figure drawings in psychological assessment, going back to at least 1885. Exposure to human figures and the commonality of our fundamental features are universal phenomena among humans. Humans drawing pictures of humans is a common, universal activity as well. Cave drawings and petroglyphs that predate recorded history commonly contain pictures of humans of the era as well as abstract depictions.

Standardized instructions for the task are easy to derive. The drawings are collected in a rapid, efficient manner, and standardized scoring systems emphasize conceptual aspects of the drawings, not their artistic qualities. Drawing itself is a universal activity and few people are resistant to providing a drawing of the human figure once reassured the artistic qualities of their efforts are not being evaluated. Human figure drawings typically can be obtained in even the most challenging of clinical situations, such as the assessment of individuals with pervasive developmental disorder or severely hyperactive children, or when a large number of nonreading or non-English speaking persons must be examined.

As a measure of cognitive ability, scoring criteria for the DAP:IQ should not include motor coordination as a salient component, and subsequently the DAP:IQ does not include or emphasize motor coordination in deriving the scores. Instead it emphasizes the conceptual aspects of the drawing.

REFERENCES

Goodenough, F. (1926). *Measurement of intelligence by drawings*. Chicago, IL: World Book.

Reynolds, C. R., & Hickman, J. A. (2003). DAP:IQ, *The Draw-A-Person intellectual ability test for children, adolescents, and adults*. Austin, TX: PRO-ED.

CECIL R. REYNOLDS
Texas A&M University

See also Intelligence; Intelligent Testing

DRAW-A-PERSON TEST

The draw-a-person (DAP) is an assessment technique used with both children and adults for a variety of purposes. Harris (1963) provided a set of instructions, a scoring system, and norms for using the technique as a measure of children's intelligence. The test has also been widely used as a projective personality assessment technique following a suggestion by Machover (1949). Although specific instructions vary, the examinee is typically asked to draw a picture of a person. The examiner provides as little structure as possible; however, if necessary, the subject is encouraged to draw an entire person and not to use stick figures. The subject is then asked to draw a person of the opposite sex. These basic instructions are often embellished to include a drawing of oneself and an inquiry phase during which the subject may be asked to make up a story about the person in the drawing or to explain various details included in the picture. Several scoring systems are available (Naglieri, 1988; Shaffer, Duszynski, & Thomas, 1984), and they have moderate to high test-retest reliability based on global quantitative ratings (Naglieri, 1988; Swenson, 1968).

However, the DAP, along with other projective tests, has serious validity problems as a tool for diagnosing emotional disorders. The problems have two sources. First, subjects are drawing the person at only one point in time, and their drawings may vary from one test to another owing to a variety of circumstances. Second, clinical interpreters or researchers may be biased owing to their own theoretical perspective (e.g., psychoanalysis) or desired outcome.

Even with its drawbacks, the DAP is still popular and may provide a reasonable estimate of the cognitive abilities of people across a wide age range. Unfortunately, its effectiveness in diagnosing emotional disorders is limited at best (Groth-Marnat, 1997). Commonly used with standardized tests such as the MMPI, the DAP can be used alone as a means of initiating a conversation with a child or adult in a counseling situation (Groth-Marnat, 1997). A standardized version of the draw-a-person test has been developed to assist with estimations of an individual's cognitive ability. The Draw-a-Person Intellectual Ability Test (DAP:IQ) was published in 2005 (Reynolds & Hickman, 2005).

REFERENCES

Groth-Marnat, G. (1997). *Handbook of psychological assessment* (3rd ed.). New York, NY: Wiley.

Harris, D. B. (1963). *Children's drawings as measures of intellectual maturity*. New York, NY: Harcourt, Brace, & World.

Machover, K. (1949). *Personality projection in the drawing of the human figure*. Springfield, IL: Thomas.

Naglieri, J. A. (1988). *Draw a person: A quantitative scoring system*. San Antonio, TX: Psychological Corporation.

Reynolds, C. R., & Hickman, J. A. (2005). *The draw-a-person intellectual ability test for children, adolescents, and adults*. Lutz, FL: PAR.

Shaffer, J., Duszynski, K., & Thomas, C. (1984). A comparison of three methods for scoring figure drawings. *Journal of Personality Assessment, 48*, 245–254.

Swenson, C. H. (1968). Empirical evaluation of human figure drawings. 1957–1966. *Psychological Bulletin, 70*, 20–44.

ROBERT G. BRUBAKER
Eastern Kentucky University
First edition

WENDY L. FLYNN
Staffordshire University
Second edition

See also **Bender Visual-Motor Gestalt Test; House-Tree-Person; Kinetic-Family-Drawing**

DROPOUT

A dropout is generally considered to be an individual who leaves school before graduation. Yet, Block, Covill-Servo, and Rosen (1978) found a serious problem with this definition and the reporting of dropouts. They found many inconsistencies in the way school districts define and report dropouts. New York defines a dropout as "any pupil who leaves school prior to graduation for any reason except death and does not enter another school" (p. 15). Under this definition, an average of 25% of the students entering high school drop out.

In recent years the dropout rate has been declining. For example, the event dropout rate for ages 15 through 24 in grades 10 through 12 has fallen from 6.1% in 1972 to 4.5% in 1993. However, these figures still constitute a large number of individuals. In 1993, approximately 381,000 students in grades 10 through 12 dropped out of school (National Center for Education Statistics, 1993).

For special education students and children with disabilities, the dropout rate is twice that of their nondisabled peers (Office of Special Education [OSERS], 1997). In addition, dropouts with disabilities do not return to school, and females became unwed mothers at a much higher rate than nondisabled peers (OSERS, 1997).

One of the six national education goals for the United States was to achieve a 90% graduation rate by the year 2000 (Dorn, 1996). Reasons for leaving school include a dislike of school, involuntary exclusion, academic problems, problems with teachers, marriage, and pregnancy. These reasons are determined ex post facto and do not have a high predictive value in identifying potential dropouts. Most dropouts are 16 years old and from families with lower socioeconomic status where parental attitudes toward education and parental supervision are low. Dropouts generally are of lower intellectual ability, have poor personal-social skills, and have academic problems.

The consequences of dropping out of school are seen when compared with the results of graduating. Dropouts generally earn significantly less money and are more likely to be unemployed. Contributing to these effects is the finding that dropouts have no postsecondary training because, as an entrance requirement, most postsecondary training programs require a high-school diploma or equivalent.

Dorn (1996) argues that "instead of seeing different educational outcomes as evidence of remaining equities in schooling, Americans have focused instead on the social costs of dropping out." Schools are expected to ameliorate problems that are essentially socioeconomic in nature and many times beyond their scope and jurisdiction.

The National Dropout Prevention Center for Students with Disabilities (NDPC-SD) was created to assist in dropout prevention and reentry programs for students with disabilities. The center is a convenient resource for information about effective dropout-prevention strategies, technical assistance, and program replication. Assistance is available for state and local education agencies, policymakers, administrators, researchers, parents, teachers, and other practitioners. NDPC-SD is housed at the National Dropout Prevention Center/Network (NDPC/N) at Clemson University and is part of OSEP's Technical Assistance and Dissemination (TA&D) Center Network.

NDPC-SD identifies evidence-based programs through research synthesis and assists state agencies to support local education agencies that implement model programs and effective practices. NDPC-SD partners with the Education Development Corporation (EDC) Inc. of Newton, Massachussetts, and the Intercultural Development Research Association (IDRA) of San Antonio, Texas, to carry out its activities.

A major goal of NDPC-SD is to provide effective technical assistance activities to "scale up" the use of research-validated programs and interventions in dropout prevention. NDPC-SD employs various strategies to transfer knowledge and to support systems change. One strategy used by NDPC-SD is to assist states in building infrastructures by using local districts as implementation sites. This is a part of OSEP's concept of continuous improvement through focused monitoring and technical assistance processes. This strategy reflects research's best-known evidence about sustaining systemic reform efforts and is on point with the 2004 Individuals with Disabilities Education Improvement Act (IDEIA 2004), which calls for aligning all monitoring and technical assistance efforts. These include direct consultation in conducting root/cause analysis, designing state-level initiatives based on state-identified needs, and offering professional development institutes and web-based resources.

NDPC-SD has access to a broad range of expertise and experience through its national partners and other collaborators, including the What Works Clearinghouse, the What Works Synthesis Center, the National Center for Secondary Education and Transition, the Exiting Community of Practice, and other OSEP-supported TA&D projects. Many NDPC-SD programs and services receive guidance from a national advisory committee that includes members of special and regular education practices, administrators at the state and local levels, parents, and researchers.

NDPC-SD is funded by the U.S. Department of Education's Office of Special Education Programs Cooperative Agreement No. H326Q030002. It can be reached at National Dropout Prevention Center for Students with Disabilities, Clemson University, 209 Martin Street, Clemson, SC 29631-1555. Tel.: (800) 443-6392, TDD/TDY (866) 212-2775, fax (864) 656-0136, e-mail: NDPCSD-L@clemson.edu, website www.dropoutprevention.org

REFERENCES

Block, E. E., Covill-Servo, J., & Rosen, M. F. (1978). *Failing students—Failing schools: A study of dropouts and discipline in New York State*. Rochester, NY: Statewide Youth Advocacy Project.

Dorn, S. (1996). *Creating the dropout: An institutional and social history of school failure*. Westport, CT: Praeger.

Office of Special Education. (1997). *An overview of the bill to provide a broad understanding of some of the changes in IDEA '97*. Retrieved from http://www.ed.gov/offices/OSERS/IDEA/overview.html

U.S. Department of Education National Center for Education Statistics. (1993). *High school dropout rates*. Washington, DC: National Institute on the Education of At-Risk Students.

DANIEL R. PAULSON
University of Wisconsin at Stout
First edition

ELAINE FLETCHER-JANZEN
Chicago School of Professional Psychology
Second edition

DRUG ABUSE

Drug abuse, or more currently *substance abuse*, is defined by the *Diagnostic and Statistical Manual of Mental Disorders*, fourth edition, text revision (*DSM-IV-TR;* American Psychiatric Association, 2000) as a "a maladaptive pattern of substance use manifested by recurrent and significant adverse consequences related to the repeated use of substances" (p. 182). The criteria for a substance abuse diagnosis are:

A. A maladaptive pattern of substance use leading to clinically significant impairment or distress, as manifested by one (or more) of the following, occurring within a 12-month period:

1. Recurrent substance use resulting in a failure to fulfill major role obligations at work, school, or home (e.g., repeated absences or poor work performance related to substance use; substance-related absences, suspensions, or expulsions from school; neglect of children or household).

2. Recurrent substance use in situations in which it is physically hazardous (e.g., driving an automobile or operating a machine when impaired by substance use).

3. Recurrent substance-related legal problems (e.g., arrests for substance-related disorderly conduct).

4. Continued substance use despite having persistent or recurrent social or interpersonal problems caused or exacerbated by the effects of the substance (e.g., arguments with spouse about consequences of intoxication, physical fights).

B. The symptoms have never met the criteria for Substance Dependence for this class of substance. (pp. 182–183)

Drug abuse is one of the six categories of behaviors that contribute to the leading causes of morbidity and mortality in the United States (National Clearinghouse for Alcohol and Drug Information [NCADI], 1998). It has only been in the 1980s and 2007s that the neuropsychological effects of drug abuse have started to be understood. This new understanding has been due to technological advances in the study of the brain, and the rise and development of pediatric neurology and neuropsychology. It is during adolescence that the more abstract and sophisticated cognitive skills develop in the human brain. Planning, evaluation, flexibility, internalized behavioral controls, higher-level abstracting skills, and higher levels of moral awareness are some of these sophisticated skills. The use of drugs during this period many have long-lasting effects on frontal and prefrontal regions of the brain (Elliott, 1998). For each insult to the brain there is a concomitant negative consequence for cognitive functions and behavior; therefore, the prevention of drug abuse in youth is extremely important if individual and social consequences are to be avoided.

The Centers for Disease Control (CDC) has developed a Youth Risk Behavior Surveillance System (YRBSS) to monitor the health-risk behaviors among youth and young adults (CDC, 1996). The system includes national, state, and local school-based surveys of high school students and gives a shocking picture of how students in the United States are involved in drug abuse.

According to the 1995 YRBSS, more than 80% of high school students have used alcohol; more than 40% have used marijuana; 16% have used cocaine, crack, or freebase; and more than 20% have sniffed or inhaled intoxicating substances. Of the students who had experienced drug abuse, 40% initiated drug-related behaviors before the age of 13. More than 30% of the students reported using alcohol or drugs at the last episode of sexual intercourse.

In addition, more than 40% of the students had ridden with a driver who had been drinking alcohol.

For the past 30 years, significant efforts have been made with private and public monies to prevent drug abuse. Schools have been a primary vehicle for prevention monies because education has been shown to assist in prevention, and education is a compatible goal with school missions (Bosworth, 1997). Education programs begin as early as the elementary years, and try to eliminate myths that support student use (such as "everybody is doing it") with normative information that gives students statistics. There is no conclusive evidence on what types of programs or strategies are effective or ineffective; however, there is some evidence that scare tactics, providing only information on drugs and their effects, self-esteem building, values clarification, large assemblies, and didactic presentation of material have not been shown to be particularly effective (Tobler & Stratton, 1997, cited in Bosworth, 1997). Skill building and experiential teaching techniques (roleplaying, simulations, and so on) have been successful in helping students utilize positive approaches to avoiding drug use (Bosworth, 1997).

The following resources are cited in Bosworth (1997):

For educators exploring possible drug prevention approaches and curricula, several excellent guides to curriculum selection are available from the National Clearinghouse for Alcohol and Drug Information (NCADI), P.O. Box 2345, Rockville, MD 20852. Tel.: (800) 729-6686. NCADI is the public information arm of the U.S. Department of Health and Human Services. Free titles include:

Drug Prevention Curricula: A Guide to Selection and Implementation

Community Creating Change: Exemplary Alcohol and Other Drug Prevention Programs

Prevention Plus II: Tools for Creating and Sustaining Drug-Free Communities

Learning to Live Drug Free: A Curriculum Model for Prevention

Prevention Resource Guides for Elementary Youth and Secondary School Students

Also serving as a programming resource are the Drug-Free Schools and Communities Regional Centers established in 1986 as part of the Drug-Free Schools and Communities Act to help schools and communities eliminate drug and alcohol use among youth. The three regional centers are: Northeast Regional Center, Sayville, NY. Tel.: (516) 589-7022; Southeast Regional Center, Louisville, KY. Tel.: (502) 588-0052; Midwest Regional Center, Oak Brook, IL. Tel.: (708) 571-4710.

An organization dedicated to the promotion and improvement of peer leader programs may also be of help: The National Peer Helpers Association, P.O. Box 2684, Greenville, NC. Tel.: (919) 328-6923.

882 DUE PROCESS

REFERENCES

American Psychiatric Association. (2000). *Diagnostic and statistical manual of mental disorders* (4th ed., text rev.). Washington, DC: Author.

Bosworth, K. (1997). Drug abuse prevention: School-based strategies that work. *ERIC Clearinghouse on Teaching and Teacher Education.* Washington, DC. (ERIC Digest No. ED409316)

Centers for Disease Control (CDC). (1996). *Youth risk behavior surveillance United States*, 1995, *45*, SS-4.

Elliot, R. (1998). Neuropsychological sequelae of substance abuse by youths. In C. R. Reynolds & E. Fletcher-Janzen (Eds.), *Handbook of clinical child neuropsychology* (pp. 311–331). New York, NY: Plenum Press.

National Clearinghouse for Alcohol and Drug Information (NCADI). (1998). *Youth risk behavior surveillance United States*, 1995. http://healthliteracy.worlded.org/docs/culture/materials/orgs_015.html

Elaine Fletcher-Janzen
Chicago School of Professional Psychology

See also Al-Anon; Alcohol and Drug Abuse Patterns; Chemically Dependent Youths; Substance Abuse

DRUGS (*See specific drugs*)

DUE PROCESS

"Due process" in the field of special education has its roots in the U.S. Constitution. The Fifth and Fourteenth Amendments prohibit the deprivation of any person's life, liberty, or property without due process of law by, respectively, the federal and state governments. More commonly in the field of special education, due process is the shorthand term applied to the procedural safeguards and due process procedures stated in the Individuals with Disabilities Education Act (IDEA) reauthorizations and regulations. These procedures offer parents the right to share with schools in decision making that could result in their child's being found eligible for and placed in special education classes. Because these placements may segregate children from the typical school environment, courts and laws have mandated that schools follow particular procedures to ensure that parents and other guardians have the opportunity to review and give their consent to changes in their child's educational program. Bersoff (1978) and Kotin (1978) provide a discussion of the legal theory underlying the due process requirements.

The due process requirements in special education can be classified under six headings addressed by the IDEA: prior notice requirements, opportunity to examine records, independent educational evaluation, informed consent, impartial due process hearing and appeal (including opportunity for mediation), and requirements for when parents cannot be located. First, the educational agency must provide written notice within a reasonable time frame before any action is initiated to propose or reject (e.g., when parents request special education for their child) a change in the identification, evaluation, or educational placement of a child. The notice must be written in the parents' native language or other mode of communication, such as braille, and in a way that results in parents understanding the notice. The notice must contain a description of the action proposed or refused by the agency, an explanation of why such action was considered, a description of any options to be considered in making a decision, and a full explanation of all procedural safeguards available to the parents. These procedural safeguards allow the parents, at no cost, the opportunity to inspect and review all education records of their child and to obtain an independent educational evaluation conducted by a qualified examiner who is not employed by the agency. The intent of these provisions is to fully inform parents.

With this information, the parents are presumed able to give voluntary informed consent to the actions proposed. Consent must be obtained before the agency conducts a preplacement evaluation and before initial special education placement.

When parents and schools disagree about any issue concerning the evaluation, placement, or educational program for a special education student, either party may request an impartial due process hearing. A hearing officer is presented evidence under conditions that are similar to those in a court. Either party can call witnesses and cross-examine the other party's witnesses. A verbatim record is taken of the proceedings. The hearing officer writes a decision that may be appealed to the state education agency and, if desired, to a civil court. Given the emotional and financial costs of this procedure, several states have initiated a mediation process as an alternative for settling disputes before a due process hearing is conducted; however, mediation is not a substitute for a due process hearing. As noted previously, the IDEA now permits mediation, as well.

Finally, public agencies are required to identify surrogate parents to represent a disabled child when no parent or guardian can be located. Several issues have been raised about this requirement, such as qualifications to be a surrogate parent, training for this role, and liability protection, among others (U.S. Department of Education, 1977).

REFERENCES

Bersoff, D. N. (1978). Procedural safeguards. In L. G. Morra (Ed.), *Developing criteria for the evaluation of due process procedural safeguards provision of Public Law 94-142* (pp. 63–142). Washington, DC: U.S. Office of Education.

Kotin, L. (1978). Recommended criteria and assessment techniques for the evaluation by LEAs of their compliance with the notice and consent requirements of PL 94-142. In L. G. Morra (Ed.), *Developing criteria for the evaluation of due process procedural safeguards provision of Public Law 94-142* (pp. 143–178). Washington, DC: U.S. Office of Education.

U.S. Department of Health, Education, and Welfare. (1977). Education of handicapped children: Implementation of Part B of the Education of the Handicapped Act. *Federal Register, 42*(163), 42474–42518.

ROLAND K. YOSHIDA
Fordham University
First edition

KIMBERLY F. APPLEQUIST
University of Colorado at Colorado Springs
Third edition

See also Consent, Informed; Individuals with Disabilities Education Improvement Act of 2004 (IDEIA); Surrogate Parents

DUHRING DISEASE

Duhring disease, also known as *dermatitis herpetiformis*, is a rare and chronic skin disorder that is characterized by the presence of skin lesions that cause severe itching, burning, and stinging. The etiology of the disease, which is not fully understood, is believed to be genetic predisposition. Approximately 90% of people with Duhring disease are positive for HLA B8-DR3, a genetic marker that may predispose them to the disease (National Organization for Rare Disorders [NORD], 1998)

Although Duhring disease can occur at any age, it is more common in middle adulthood and is very rare in childhood. In the United States about 1 in 10,000 are diagnosed with the disease, and the male/female ratio is 2:1. The disease is more common in Caucasian Americans and rare in African Americans and Asian Americans (Celiac Sprue Association [CSA], 1998)

Characteristics

1. Small blisters, fluid-filled sores, red bumps that resemble hives, and/or raised papules.
2. Severe itching, burning, and stinging of affected areas.
3. Lesions on both sides of body, especially the head, elbows, knees, lower back, and buttocks.
4. Loss of the ability properly to digest gluten (approximately 75% of cases).

A clinical evaluation and blood tests that show the presence of certain antibodies such as reticulin and endomysium confirm a diagnosis of Duhring disease. Immunofluorescence can also be used to show the presence of IgA, a protein antibody (immunoglobulin) that usually protects the body from viral and bacterial infections (NORD, 1998).

Typically, people with Duhring disease are treated with the medication Dapsone in a dose of 25 to 50 mg daily. The symptoms are often relieved and the condition of the skin lesions improved 1 to 2 days after drug therapy is started. The dosage of Dapsone may be adjusted to maintain relief of the symptoms, and some patients take up to 100 mg daily. Dapsone can cause the destruction of red blood cells (hemolysis), so patients taking the drug must have periodic blood tests to monitor blood counts. Sulfapyridine may be used an alternative to Dapsone, especially in patients with coronary disease. A topical cortisone cream can also be used to help relieve the itching and burning associated with the disease. It is important to note that in most cases the skin lesions reappear 24 to 48 hours after the Dapsone therapy is discontinued (NORD, 1998).

For the percentage of the diagnosed population who also have gluten-sensitive enteropathy, following a strict gluten-free diet may relieve their symptoms. Gluten is found in all grains except rice and corn. Special gluten-free foods can be purchased commercially. It has also been shown that the gluten-free diet may benefit most patients with Duhring disease. The diet reduces the dosage of Dapsone needed, improves gastrointestinal symptoms, and focuses on the cause of the disease rather than the symptoms (CSA, 1998).

Special education for patients with Duhring disease does not seem necessary, but supportive counseling may help the child cope with the chronic and sometimes painful condition. Also, because of the social and emotional issues of the potential chronicity, it is important that the child have some form of support to use as an outlet for any problems or concerns. It might also be helpful to teach children how to dress in a manner that would minimize exposure of the rashes to help eliminate any social torment that they may experience at school or in other social settings.

The prognosis for Duhring disease is very positive if patients take their medications and follow up with their doctor. In addition, by following the gluten-free diet, they might be able to prevent future outbreaks or minimize the severity. There is ongoing research to determine the relationship between Duhring disease and the function of the digestive system. For more information the NORD website recommends contacting Russell P. Hall, III, M.D., Box 3135, Duke University Medical Center, Durham, NC 27710. Tel.: (919) 684–3110.

REFERENCES

Celiac Sprue Association. (1998). *Dermatitis herpetiformis defined*. Retrieved from http://www.csaceliacs.info/

National Organization for Rare Disorders. (1998). *Duhring disease*. Retrieved from http://www.rarediseases.org

CYNTHIA A. GALLO
University of Colorado

DUNLAP, GLEN

Glen Dunlap is a prominent and respected researcher and scholar who has dedicated his career to advancing the field of applied behavior analysis to improve the lives of individuals with disabilities and their families. Along with a few close colleagues, Dr. Dunlap is responsible for the establishment of positive behavior support as a comprehensive and widely accepted approach for supporting people with difficult behavior in the community (Carr, Dunlap, Horner, et al., 2002; Horner et al., 1990). His areas of specialization have included, but are not limited to instructional strategies for children with autism (Dunlap, 1984; Koegel, Dunlap, & Dyer, 1980; Winterling, Dunlap, & O'Neill, 1987); curricular modifications to improve student behavior (Dunlap, Kern-Dunlap, Clarke, & Robbins, 1991; Foster-Johnson, Ferro, & Dunlap, 1994), engaging families as partners in assessment and intervention (Vaughn, Clarke, & Dunlap, 1997; Vaughn, Dunlap, Fox, Clarke, & Bucy, 1997), working with young children (Duda, Dunlap, Fox, Lentini, & Clarke, 2004; Dunlap & Fox, 1999; Fox, Dunlap, & Philbrick, 1997), and extending behavioral assessment practices to students with emotional and behavioral disorders (Dunlap et al., 1994; Dunlap et al., 1993; Dunlap, White, Vera, Wilson, & Panacek, 1996). Dr. Dunlap's contributions to the field have been honored by his receipt of the DEC Mary McEvoy Award for Service to the Field and Thomas G. Haring Award for Research.

Dr. Dunlap earned his bachelor's degree in psychology in 1973, and then his PhD in 1981 in speech and hearing, education, and psychology in a joint doctoral program at the University of California at Santa Barbara and the University of California at San Francisco. Between his undergraduate and graduate work, he directed a program at Princeton Child Development Institute and worked for Father Flanagan's Boys' Home. During his doctoral program, Dr. Dunlap conducted research with Dr. Bob Koegel focused on educational interventions for children with autism. He continued as an assistant research psychologist at the UCSB for three years following graduation. In 1984, Dr. Dunlap moved to Marshall University in West Virginia. There he served as the site coordinator for the Research and Training Center on Community-Referenced Behavior Management (which preceded the RRTC on Positive Behavior Support), directed a model preschool training project, and oversaw training and research activities at the West Virginia Autism Training Center.

In 1989, Dr. Dunlap was enticed to leave Marshall University to develop programs at the University of South Florida in Tampa. Working with parent advocates, he established Florida's Center for Autism and Related Disabilities—a program that has served as a model for agencies throughout the country. In his role as director of DARES (Division of Applied Research and Educational Support) at USF, Glen served as the executive director for CARD and Headstart. He was the principal investigator and project director for the NIDRR RRTC on PBS and OSEP Center for Evidence-Based Practices for Young Children with Challenging Behavior and the Prevent-Teach-Reinforce program. He was Co-PI and provided leadership for numerous large projects including the Technical Assistance Center on Social-Emotional Interventions, Behavior Analysis Services Program, Florida's Team Training and Technical Assistance Project and Tampa Bay Partnership on Parent Involvement. Collectively, Dr. Dunlap is responsible for acquiring and managing grant funds related to PBS well in excess of $50 million.

Dr. Dunlap in now residing in Reno, Nevada and continues his work on research grants, while traveling and lecturing extensively. He is a member of several professional associations, including the Association for Behavior Analysis, Autism Society of America, Division of Early Childhood, Council for Exceptional Children, Council for Children with Behavior Disorders, and Association for Positive Behavior Support—an organization for which he was president (2006–2007). He has served as founding editor for the *Journal of Positive Behavior Interventions* (1998–2004) and *Topics in Early Childhood Special Education* (2006-present) and as associate editor for *Journal of the Association for Severe Handicaps, Journal of Early Intervention*, and *Education and Treatment of Children*. He has served on 18 additional journal editorial boards.

Dr. Dunlap is a prolific author, producing an extensive array of scholarly contributions. Thus far in his impressive career, he has written more than 110 articles for peer-reviewed journals and 50 book chapters, as well as a lengthy list of training manuals, reports, and other publications. He is the author of six books (Bambara, Dunlap, & Schwartz, 2004; Dunlap et al., 2010; Horner, Dunlap, & Koegel, 1988; Koegel, Koegel, & Dunlap, 1996; Lucyshyn, Dunlap, & Albin, 2002; Sailor, Dunlap, Sugai, & Horner, 2009). Glen has conducted hundreds of presentations at behavior analytic, educational, disability, and psychological conferences, with keynote presentations at APBS and other international conferences.

As one looks back over Dr. Dunlap's contributions to positive behavior support as a discipline and practice, three key themes seem evident. The first is Dr. Dunlap's commitment to collaboration. Essentially all of his publications have multiple authors—students and respected colleagues with whom he has worked extensively. The second is his willingness to reach beyond a single field of study to create important advancements in behavioral intervention. Dr. Dunlap has published in a tremendous array of journals, representing various professions charged with serving individuals with disabilities and behavioral challenges and the people who care for them. By reaching out to these disciplines, he has bolstered PBS's theoretical foundation and solidified current practice. And finally, this inclusive, creative thinking has led Dr. Dunlap to employ an increasingly diverse range of research methods to investigate and evaluate phenomena, thereby strengthening the empirical support for this field.

REFERENCES

Bambara, L., Dunlap, G., & Schwartz, I. (Eds.). (2004). *Positive behavior support: Critical articles on improving practice for individuals with severe disabilities.* Austin, TX: PRO-ED.

Carr, E. G., Dunlap, G., Horner, R. H., Koegel, R. L., Turnbull, A. P., Sailor, W., . . . Fox, L. (2002). Positive behavior support. Evolution of an applied science. *Journal of Positive Behavior Interventions, 4,* 4–16.

Duda, M. A., Dunlap, G., Fox, L., Lentini, R., & Clarke, S. (2004). An experimental evaluation of positive behavior support in a community preschool program. *Topics in Early Childhood Special Education, 24,* 143–155.

Dunlap, G. (1984). The influence of task variation and maintenance tasks on the learning and affect of autistic children. *Journal of Experimental Child Psychology, 37,* 41–64.

Dunlap, G., dePerczel, M., Clarke, S., Wilson, D., Wright, S., White, R., & Gomez, A. (1994). Choice making to promote adaptive behavior for students with emotional and behavioral challenges. *Journal of Applied Behavior Analysis, 27,* 505–518.

Dunlap, G., & Fox, L. (1999). A demonstration of behavioral support for young children with autism. *Journal of Positive Behavior Interventions, 1,* 77–87.

Dunlap, G., Iovannone, R., Wilson, K., Kincaid, D., Christiansen, K., Strain, P, & English, C. (2010). *Prevent-Teach-Reinforce: A school-based model of positive behavior.* Baltimore, MD: Paul H. Brookes.

Dunlap, G., Kern-Dunlap, L., Clarke, S., & Robbins, F. R. (1991). Functional assessment, curriculum revision, and severe behavior problems. *Journal of Applied Behavior Analysis, 24,* 387–397.

Dunlap, G., Kern, L., dePerczel, M., Clarke, S., Wilson, D., Childs, K. E., . . . Falk, G. D. (1993). Functional analysis of classroom variables for students with emotional and behavioral challenges. *Behavioral Disorders, 18,* 275–291.

Dunlap, G., White, R., Vera, A., Wilson, D., & Panacek, L. (1996). The effects of multi-component, assessment-based curricular modifications on the classroom behavior of children with emotional and behavioral disorders. *Journal of Behavioral Education, 6,* 481–500.

Foster-Johnson, L., Ferro, J., & Dunlap, G. (1994). Preferred curricular activities and reduced problem behaviors in students with intellectual disabilities. *Journal of Applied Behavior Analysis, 27,* 493–504.

Fox. L., Dunlap, G., & Philbrick, L. A. (1997). Providing individual supports to young children with autism and their families. *Journal of Early Intervention, 21,* 1–14.

Horner, R. H., Dunlap, G., & Koegel, R. L. (1988). *Generalization and maintenance: Lifestyle changes in applied settings.* Baltimore, MD: Paul H. Brookes.

Horner, R. H., Dunlap, G., Koegel, R. L., Carr. E. G., Sailor, W., Anderson, J., . . . O'Neill, R. E. (1990). Toward a technology of "nonaversive" behavioral support. *Journal of the Association for Persons with Severe Handicaps, 15,* 125–132.

Koegel, L. K., Koegel, R. L., & Dunlap, G. (Eds.). (1996). *Positive behavioral support: Including people with difficult behavior in the community.* Baltimore, MD: Paul H. Brookes.

Koegel, R. L., Dunlap, G., & Dyer, K. (1980). Intertrial interval duration and learning in autistic children. *Journal of Applied Behavior Analysis, 13,* 91–99.

Lucyshyn, J., Dunlap, G., & Albin, R. W. (Eds.) (2002). *Families and positive behavior support: Addressing problem behaviors in family contexts.* Baltimore, MD: Paul H. Brookes.

Sailor, W., Dunlap, G., Sugai, G., & Horner, R. (2009). (Eds). *Handbook of positive behavior support.* New York, NY: Springer.

Vaughn B. J., Dunlap, G., Fox, L., Clarke, S., & Bucy, M. (1997a). Parent-professional partnership in behavioral support: A case study of community-based intervention. *Journal of the Association for Persons with Severe Handicaps, 22,* 185–197.

Vaughn, B. J., Clarke, S., & Dunlap, G. (1997b). Assessment-based intervention for severe behavior problems in a natural family context. *Journal of Applied Behavior Analysis, 30,* 713–716.

Winterling, V., Dunlap, G., & O'Neill, R. E. (1987). The influence of task variation on the aberrant behavior of autistic students. *Education and Treatment of Children, 10,* 105–119.

MEME HIENEMAN
Behavioral Services Program Coordinator,
*   All Children's Hospital*
Fourth edition

DUNN, LLOYD M. (1917–   )

Lloyd Dunn was born in Saskatchewan, Canada, and received his U.S. citizenship in 1963. He obtained his

BEd (1949) and MEd (1950) from the University of Saskatchewan, later earning his PhD in special education at the University of Illinois. From 1953 to 1969, he was a faculty member of Peabody College, now part of Vanderbilt University. Dunn has served as affiliate professor of education at the University of Hawaii, and was past president and recipient of the Wallin Award of the Council for Exceptional Children.

His major works are in the areas of psychometrics, language development, and education of the mentally retarded. Dunn (1968) has taken the position that much of the past and present practices of special education for minority children who are labeled mildly retarded are morally and educationally wrong. He believes that regular class placement without special education services is needed for most such children (Dunn, 1968). He was an early advocate of small, special-purpose residential facilities for the more severely retarded, rather than large, impersonal state residential institutions (Dunn, 1963).

Dunn is best known for the textbook, *Exceptional Children in the Schools;* the article "Special Education for the Mildly Retarded—Is Much of It Justifiable!"; and various assessment tools and instructional programs, including the Peabody Picture Vocabulary Test, the Peabody Individual Achievement Test, and the Peabody Early Languages Kit. His work, outlining a progressive plan to improve special education by merging it with general education, has been extensively analyzed and very influential on policy change and legislation in Canada and the United States (Dahl & Sanche, 1997; Hallahan & Kauffman, 1994; Snell & Drake, 1994).

Dunn was one of the founders of the Kennedy Center in 1965. He was director of Peabody's Mental Retardation Research Training Program, the first doctoral program in the nation for training researchers in this field. He conceived of the Institute on Mental Retardation and Intellectual Development, which came to be known IMRID, and was its first director. The Kennedy Center continues to bring expertise in the biomedical and behavioral sciences to bear in understanding and preventing problems of development and learning.

REFERENCES

Dahl, H., & Sanche, R. (1997). *Special education policy: A retrospective and future prospective—A view from Saskatchewan.* Salt Lake City, UT: Council for Exceptional Children.

Dunn, L. M. (1963). *Exceptional children in the schools.* New York, NY: Holt, Rinehart, & Winston.

Dunn, L. M. (1968). Special education for the mildly retarded—Is much of it justifiable? *Exceptional Children, 35,* 5–22.

Hallahan, D. P., & Kaufmann, J. M. (1994). Toward a culture of disability in the aftermath of Deno and Dunn. *Journal of Special Education, 27*(4), 496–508.

Snell, M. E., & Drake, George, P. (1994). Replacing cascades with supported education. *Journal of Special Education, 27*(4), 393–409.

ELIZABETH JONES
Texas A&M University
First edition

TAMARA J. MARTIN
The University of Texas of the Permian Basin
Second edition

JESSI K. WHEATLEY
Falcon School District 49,
   Colorado Springs, Colorado

DUODENAL ATRESIA AND DUODENAL STENOSIS

Duodenal atresia (DA) is a rare congenital anomaly of the duodenum, the first section of the small intestine, which lies adjacent to and just downstream from the outlet of the stomach. In DA there is disruption and occlusion of the tubular continuity (lumen) of the gut. Duodenal stenosis refers to a narrowing of the intestinal lumen.

DA is felt to occur around the fourth or fifth week of gestation. At this time the intestine develops from a solid structure, which is normally canalized from the upper esophagus to the rectum. Intestinal atresia is caused by a failure of this process to evolve completely.

DA has many different anatomic variations, which can be classified by intrinsic and extrinsic etiologies. The intrinsic form is the most common. The usual appearance is a thin membrane across the bowel lumen.

DA occurs in about 1 in 10,000 births. It has no clear pattern of genetic transmission. It accounts for about 30% to 35% of all intestinal atresias. There is an equal male-to-female ratio for this disorder. About a third of infants with DA have other severe, life-threatening congenital malformations. These defects can affect other sites in the gut, as well as the heart, kidney, and anorectal area. DA is a common finding in Down syndrome, occurring in 20% to 30% of these babies. It is also far more frequent in premature infants than in those born at term.

Characteristics

1. Vomiting bile, usually on the first day of life, without abdominal distention. This symptom is a classic sign of upper intestinal blockage.

2. Polyhydramnios (excessive amount of amniotic fluid) is present in about 50% of pregnancies. This finding is secondary to the failure of swallowed amniotic fluid to reach the lower intestine, where it is normally absorbed.

3. X rays of the abdomen show a "double bubble sign," the result of a distended, air-filled stomach and upper segment of the duodenum.

4. Prenatal diagnosis is becoming more frequent because of the widespread use of ultrasound evaluations during pregnancy.

Treatment of DA requires surgical correction of the defect. However, that procedure is often postponed until a search for other, possibly even more serious, anomalies is concluded. Initial therapy consists of decompression of the distended stomach by nasogastric tube, intravenous fluid administration, and diagnostic studies that attempt to define other malformations.

Following operative repair of their problem, babies with DA may be unable to take oral feedings for several days, until their gut resumes normal activity. During this time they are given intravenous nutritional support composed of amino acids, glucose, fatty acids, vitamins, and minerals. This regimen promotes healing of surgical sites and, incredibly, weight gain. After gut function and continuity recover, oral feedings start, and intravenous alimentation is slowly withdrawn.

There is no research to indicate that children with DA have cognitive deficits. Problems with learning ability or developmental delay would be related to the associated anomalies present.

Prognosis for DA is largely dependent on what associated anomalies are present. Clearly, infants with Down syndrome, complex congenital heart disease, serious kidney defects, or extreme prematurity will have a much less favorable outlook than will newborns in whom DA is an isolated finding.

This entry has been informed by the sources listed below.

REFERENCE

Wylie, R. (2000). Intestinal atresia, stenosis, and malrotation. In R. E. Behrman, R. M. Kleigman, & H. B. Jenson (Eds.), *Nelson's textbook of pediatrics* (16th ed., pp. 1132–1136). Philadelphia, PA: Saunders.

BARRY H. DAVISON
Ennis, Texas

JOAN W. MAYFIELD
Baylor Pediatric Specialty Services, Dallas, Texas

DURATION RECORDING

Duration recording is a direct observation method that is used in a systematic fashion to determine how long a person engages in a behavior. Duration recording is used for behaviors that have a distinguishable beginning and end, that is, discrete behaviors (Alberto & Troutman, 2006). Examples of behaviors that are suitable for measurement using duration recording include academic engagement, remaining in seat, time participating as a member of a group, engaging in an activity, and tantruming.

To record behavior using duration recording, you first need to operationally define the target behavior. An operational definition is a written statement that precisely defines the behavior you wish to measure in terms that are observable, measurable, and replicable (Fletcher-Janzen & De Pry, 2003). Next, the observer should define the observation period, including recording the start and stop times. A device for measuring time, such as a stopwatch, is used to measure the amount of time the person engages in the targeted behavior. The stopwatch should be allowed to run when the person is meeting the operational definition and stopped when the person does not meet the operational definition. This method continues throughout the observation session.

For example, a sixth-grade teacher has expressed concern about a student who has low levels of academic engagement. In collaboration with her paraprofessional, they operationally define academic engagement as "eyes on the teacher, eyes on the assigned instructional task, or being engaged in a task-related activity." The paraprofessional positions herself so that she can fully observe the student of concern. During several instructional periods, observations are made. The stopwatch is allowed to run as long as the student meets the operational definition of academic engagement, however, the paraprofessional stops the stopwatch each time the student is not meeting the definition, that is, when he is not academically engaged. This method continues until the observation period has concluded. When the observation session is finished, the paraprofessional records the amount of minutes and seconds that she has on the stopwatch. This number is converted to seconds and divided by the total number of seconds for the observation period. In our example, the paraprofessional observed the student for 30 minutes, or 1,800 seconds. Data from her stopwatch indicated that the student was academically engaged for 22 minutes and 30 seconds (1,350 seconds) during one of her observation sessions. She takes the observation total and divides by the observation period (1,350/1,800 = .75 × 100 = 75%) and learns that the student was academically engaged for 75% of the observation period. The data for this observation period is then recorded and graphed for future reference. In some cases, the teacher or researcher might collect data at several times throughout the day. At the end of the day, the totals would be averaged and recorded as the average duration of the targeted behavior for that day (Alberto & Troutman, 2006). As with all direct observation systems, collecting interobserver reliability data is critical. The formula for calculating interobserver reliability for duration recording is taking the shorter number of minutes (or total seconds) and dividing by the larger number of minutes (or total seconds) then multiplying by 100. This formula will give you the percentage of agreement between the primary observer and an independent observer.

REFERENCES

Alberto, P. A., & Troutman, A. C. (2006). *Applied behavior analysis for teachers* (7th ed.). Upper Saddle River, NJ: Prentice Hall.

Fletcher-Janzen, E., & De Pry, R. L. (2003). *Teaching social competence and character: An IEP planner with goals, objectives, and interventions.* Longmont, CO: Sopris West Educational Services.

RANDALL L. DE PRY
University of Colorado at Colorado Springs

See also **Behavioral Assessment; Research in Special Education**

DWARFISM

Dwarfism is a genetic condition that results in an extremely short stature. There are several hundred different diagnosed types of dwarfism. The most common form of short limb dwarfism is achondroplasia. Achondroplasia occurs in approximately 1 in 26,000 to 40,000 births, results in disproportionately short arms and legs ("Little people in America," n.d.), and affects about 80% of all Little People with equal frequency in males and females in all races ("Reaching new heights," n.d.). The average height of adults with this condition is about 4 feet. Other less-frequent types of dwarfism include spondyloepiphyseal dysplasia congenital (SED) and diastrophic dysplasia ("Little people in America," n.d.). Advances in genetics have led to the identification of the genes that result in the characteristics of the different types of dwarfism; however, mass genetic testing for this genetic condition is not practiced. Proportionate dwarfism, another commonly recognized type of dwarfism, is often the result of hormonal deficiency and can be treated medically ("Little people in America," n.d.), yet neonatal testing for growth hormone deficiency is controversial (Gandrud & Wilson, 2004).

There is variability in the extent to which a person is affected by the condition; however, for the most part those with dwarfism have normal intelligence, normal life spans, and are in good health ("Little people in America," n.d.). A small number of those with dwarfism may be affected by compression of the brain stem, hydrocephalus, and obstructive apnea. Motor development may be delayed in infants and young children, often resulting in delays in sitting, standing, and walking ("Achondroplasia," n.d). Often, those with dwarfism have a prominent forehead, short fingers, and a flat nose due to abnormalities in cartilage development ("Achondroplasia," n.d.). The small stature that characterizes dwarfism is generally untreatable; however, some people opt to undergo limb-lengthening surgery that is often painful and is still extremely controversial in Little People circles ("Little people in America," n.d.). Currently, dwarfism is recognized as a disability under the Americans with Disabilities Act ("Little people in America," n.d.).

When working with those affected by dwarfism one should keep in mind that with the exception of height-related challenges, they are equally productive citizens who engage in similar activities and careers as other average-height individuals. The biggest challenge is to encourage acceptance and understanding, while working to dismiss stereotypes that have historically been intertwined with this condition. Furthermore, a person with dwarfism may experience self-esteem issues that could be addressed with therapy or support groups (Theunissen et al., 2002).

REFERENCES

Achondroplasia. (n.d.). *March of Dimes quick reference and fact sheets.* Retrieved from http://www.marchofdimes.com/

Gandrud, L. M., & Wilson, D. M. (2004). Is growth hormone stimulation testing in children still appropriate? *Growth Hormone & IGF Research, 14,* 185–194.

Little people in America. (n.d.). *LPA online.* Retrieved from http://www.lpaonline.org/

Reaching new heights. (n.d.). Retrieved from http://www.lpaonline.org/

Theunissen, N. C. M., Kamp, G. A., Koopman, H. M., Zwinderman, K. A. H., Vogels, T., & Wit, J. M. (2002). Quality of life and self-esteem in children treated for idiopathic short stature. *Journal of Pediatrics, 140,* 507–515.

MICHELLE T. BUSS
Texas A&M University

See also **Physical Anomalies**

DYSCALCULIA

Dyscalculia is a mathematical learning disability, specific to understanding and retaining knowledge of mathematical concepts. Frequency rates for school age children diagnosed with dyscalculia are between 3% and 8% (Geary, 2000). Specific features of dyscalculia include: (1) having difficulty in performing calculations in math problems, especially solving word problems and multistep problems (Geary, 1993); (2) retaining mathematical knowledge learned through instruction, such as remembering multiplication and division facts; (3) having spatial and symbolic disparity of mental images for mathematical concepts or processes (Vaidya, 2004); and (4) having difficulty in developing "number sense" of mathematical relationships.

Dyscalculia occurs in both males and females and many times those diagnosed with dyscalculia also display other disabilities, such as attention-deficit/hyperactivity disorder (ADHD) or dyslexia (Landerl, Bevan, & Butterworth, 2004). There is also evidence to suggest that dyscalculia is based on neurological or genetic factors (Geary, 2000; Rourke, 1989). However, dyscalculia is not necessarily associated with below-average or low intelligence.

Not as much research has been devoted to diagnosing and testing this disability, as others, such as dyslexia. Standard achievement tests, such as the Woodcock-Johnson III Test of Achievement, may include assessments that measure math achievement and knowledge, but few tests have been designed to specifically assess and measure dyscalculic tendencies and behaviors. Diagnosing dyscalculia is a multifaceted process, and should include a variety of assessments and data collection techniques, such as assessments, tests, anecdotal records and classroom observations. Just because an individual has poor math skills does not necessarily mean they have dyscalcuia.

Early detection of dyscalculic tendencies is still being researched in preschool children. A milestone for early mathematical development in young children is developing principles of counting before being introduced to place value. For example, children should understand the cardinality principle, which states that the last word in a number series, such as "seven" stands for the number of objects being counted (Geary, 2006). Children that have difficulty learning these counting principles may need further testing into possible dyscaculia tendencies that may inhibit their success and understanding of formal place value concepts during their school-age years. However, more research and testing needs to be developed in this area.

Even though there is no cure for dyscalculia, there are several interventions and techniques to help those with dyscalculia improve their understanding and retention of mathematical concepts and methods. Using *tactile* learning approaches, such as math manipulatives, counting on fingers, writing out the problem in shaving cream, or physically acting out or modeling the problem can aid in unpacking the mathematical information within concepts and problems. Using an *oral* or *written* learning approach, such as drawing what the math problem or answer means, to them, and orally explaining the drawing can also be beneficial in understanding misconceptions and error patterns within their mathematical reasoning of the problem. Using a variety of *cooperative learning techniques*, such as think, pair, share, or four corners, can also give opportunities for both oral discussion of the problem and ability to verify and explain their mathematical reasoning and better learn math terminology. Since individuals with dyscalculia also tend to display other disabilities, such as ADHD, these interventions and techniques can also be useful for individuals diagnosed with this disability, as well.

REFERENCES

Geary, D. (1993). Mathematical disabilities: Cognition, neuropsychological and genetic components. *Psychological Bulletin*, *114*, 345–362.

Geary, D. (2000). Mathematical disorders: An overview for educators. *Perspectives*, *26*, 6–9.

Geary, D. (2006). Dyscalculia at an early age: Characteristics and potential influence on socio-emotional development. *Encyclopedia on Early Childhood Development*. Retrieved from http://web.missouri.edu/~gearyd/files/GearyANGxp.pdf

Landerl, K., Bevan, A., & Butterworth, B. (2004). Developmental dyscalculia and basic numerical capacities: A study of 8–9 year old students. *Cognition*, *93*, 99–125.

Rourke, B. P. (1989). *Nonverbal learning disabilities: The syndrome and the model*. New York, NY: Guilford Press.

Vaidya, S. R. (2004, Summer). Understanding dyscalculia for teaching. *Education*, *124*, 717.

D. DIANA PICCOLO
Missouri State Unviersity
Fourth edition

DYSCOPIA (*See Developmental Apraxia*)

DYSFLUENCY (*See Stuttering*)

DYSGRAPHESTHESIA

Dysgraphesthesia is the inability to recognize symbols drawn on parts of the body (Spreen, Risser, & Edgell, 1995). Often referred to as a neurological *soft sign*, dysgraphesthesia is more common in children with learning disabilities or behavior disorders, although a direct causal relationship has not been found (Bigler & Clement, 1997; Spreen et al., 1995). Dysgraphesthesia has also been associated with cortical motor deficit (Spreen et al., 1995), parietal lobe dysfunction, peripheral neuropathy, vascular lesions, temporal lobe dysfunction, and inattention or confusion (Broshek & Barth, 2000; Reitan & Wolfson, 1985). There is no information available regarding prevalence or incidence.

Characteristics

1. Indicated by a significant number of errors on tactile-perception tests.
2. Correlated with learning disabilities and behavior disorders.

Dysgraphesthesia is assessed through the use of tests of sensory perception, specifically skin writing procedures, most often with symbols or numbers traced on the palm of the hand or on the fingertips. Fewer errors on these kinds of assessment measures are expected as children become older, and reliability of soft neurological signs such as dysgraphesthesia is greater in 8- to 11-year-olds than it is in 5- to 6-year-olds (Stevenson, 2000). Tests of dysgraphesthesia are useful for determining the lateralization of brain lesions, especially when there are no other obvious neurological signs such as aphasia (Lezak, 1995). It has been suggested that contralateral parietal lobe damage or dysfunction can be inferred when one hand is significantly more impaired than the other (Reitan & Wolfson, 1985). More pronounced deficits have been found as the lesion approaches postcentral gyrus (Spreen et al., 1995).

Clusters of low scores on sensory perception tests may be associated with apraxia, or difficulty planning nonhabitual movement (Stevenson, 2000). This may lead to problems with fine motor skills such as writing or getting dressed, necessitating the use of developmentally appropriate interventions such as occupational therapy (Broshek & Barth, 2000; Stevenson, 2000). Longitudinal studies have shown the persistence over time of soft neurological signs such as dysgraphesthesia in children who are diagnosed with learning or emotional disorders and who continue to exhibit these disorders as adults (Spreen et al., 1995).

Future research may be aimed at better defining relationships between neurological status and soft signs such as dysgraphesthesia (Spreen et al. 1995).

REFERENCES

Bigler, E. D., & Clement, P. F. (1997). *Diagnostic clinical neuropsychology* (3rd ed.). Austin: University of Texas Press.

Broshek, D. K., & Barth, J. T. (2000). The Halstead-Reitan neuropsychological test battery. In G. Groth-Marnat (Ed.), *Neuropsychological assessment in clinical practice* (pp. 223–262). New York, NY: Wiley.

Lezak, M. D. (1995). *Neuropsychological assessment* (3rd ed.). New York, NY: Oxford University Press.

Reitan, R. M., & Wolfson, D. (1985). *The Halstead-Reitan neuropsychological test battery: Theory and clinical interpretation.* Tucson, AZ: Neuropsychology Press.

Spreen, O., Risser, A. H., & Edgell, D. (1995). *Developmental neuropsychology.* New York, NY: Oxford University Press.

Stevenson, R. J. (2000). Graphesthesia. In C. R. Reynolds & E. Fletcher-Janzen (Eds.), *Encyclopedia of special education* (p. 837). New York, NY: Wiley.

KATHRYN L. GUY
MARGARET SEMRUD-CLIKEMAN
University of Texas

DYSGRAPHIA

Dysgraphia is a disorder characterized by writing difficulties. More specifically, it is defined as difficulty in automatically remembering and mastering the sequence of muscle motor movements needed in writing letters or numbers. The difficulty writing is incongruent with the person's ability and is not due to poor instruction. The disorder varies in terms of severity, ranging from mild to severe.

Problems in writing and difficulty with other motor skills related to instruction are not uncommon among school-age children. Although the prevalence of dysgraphia is unknown, it is estimated that 5% to 20% of children demonstrate some form of deficient writing behavior (Smits-Engelman & Van Galen, 1997). Although a neurologic basis is suspected, the exact cause is unknown. What is known is that it is a problem that results from an integration failure, that is, a deficit in visual-motor integration rather than a deficit in either visual skill or motor skill alone (Bain, Bailet, & Moats, 1991). Dysgraphia is also considered to be caused by difficulty sequencing information as well as a more general auditory or language-processing problem.

Dysgraphia seldom exists in isolation but more commonly occurs with other coordination and learning problems (e.g., dyslexia, dyscalculia, and developmental coordination disorder). The problem has also been found among children who have attention problems and hyperactivity. Because fine motor coordination improves with maturation and instruction, dysgraphia is seldom recognized before the end of the first grade. In fact, the *Diagnostic and Statistical Manual of Mental Disorders,* fourth edition's (*DSM-IV*) diagnosis of Disorders of Written Expression, which dysgraphia may be a part of, stipulates that to be diagnosed with a disorder, the individual's writing problem must interfere with learning. In other words, children whose only problem is poor handwriting (i.e., they have no other problem with written expression) are not given a *DSM-IV* diagnosis.

Characteristics

1. Generally illegible writing despite appropriate attention and time given to the task.
2. Mix of print and cursive and upper and lower case and changes in shapes, size, and slant.
3. Failure to attend to writing details, unfinished words and letters, and omitted words.
4. Irregular spacing between words and letters.
5. Standard lines and margins not adhered to.
6. Unusual grip on writing tool and unusual wrist/body/paper position.
7. Excessive erasures.
8. Self-talking while writing or close observation of the writing hand.
9. Slow or labored writing and copying even if neat and legible.

Although writing samples and behavioral observations of the child are often used to diagnose the problem, a number of standardized assessment instruments may also be helpful. This includes the Developmental Test of Visual-Motor Integration, Coding/Digit Symbol and Symbol Search subtests of the Wechsler intelligence scales (WISC-III/WAIS-III), Bender-Gestalt, and Jordan Left-Right Reversal Test. A variety of written language achievement measures may also be useful, including tests such as the Woodcock Johnson Achievement Test (WJ-3) and Test of Written Language (TOWL). In addition to assessing student characteristics, it is also important to assess the type of instruction that has been provided to the child and his or her response to the writing task. Classroom observations may be helpful in ruling out contextual variables as a significant factor in the writing problem.

Treatment of dysgraphia may include interventions to assist the child in better controlling fine motor skill. Although the classroom teacher and parent may be helpful in this regard, in some cases the child may need to be evaluated and seen by the occupational therapist to work on controlling the writing movements. Few children with dysgraphia actually qualify for special education services under the Individuals with Disabilities in Education Act (IDEA) of 1997; however, some may if the problem in writing is associated with other learning problems (e.g., written language). In the cases where dysgraphia is comorbid with other learning disabilities, children may be served under the category Specific Learning Disabilities. In most cases, children can be accommodated in the regular classroom.

Educators can employ a number of accommodations, modifications, and remediation strategies to help students with dysgraphia. Some of these include allowing the student to use a computer or typewriter to do written work, having them use special writing implements (e.g., grippers or extra-large pencils and pens), or allowing the child to write in whatever form of manuscript is easiest and most legible (e.g., print or cursive). Giving children extra time for writing assignments and allowing them to audiotape assignments, take oral tests, and do more self-correction of their written work may be beneficial. Some children, however, may need further instruction and practice in handwriting. For an excellent resource refer to the Resource Room website (Jones, 1998).

If untreated, the prognosis for dysgraphia is generally thought to be poor. Although some writing problems persist regardless of intervention, many children can be helped by attention paid to the problem. Not only do children need to be made aware of the problem, but also specific strategies need to be put in place to assist the child. Knowing what strategies are most effective, however, is unclear. Perhaps further studies of other associated conditions will shed light on this otherwise neglected disorder.

REFERENCES

Bain, A. M., Bailet, L. L., & Moats, L. C. (1991). *Written language disorders: Theory into practice.* Austin, TX: PRO-ED.

Jones, S. (1998). *Accommodations and modifications for students with handwriting problems and/or dysgraphia.* Retrieved from www.resourceroom.us

Smits-Engelman, B. C. M., & Van Galen, G. P. (1997). Dysgraphia in children: Lasting psychomotor deficiency or transient developmental delay? *Journal of Experimental Child Psychology, 67*(2), 164–184.

LINDSEY A. PHILLIPS
ELAINE CLARK
University of Utah

See also **Visual-Motor and Visual-Perceptual Problems; Writing Disorders; Writing Remediation**

DYSKINESIA

Dyskinesia is a collection of movement disorders involving impairment of central nervous system motor control. It is thought to be due to damage or abnormal development of the basal ganglia, the deep subcortical nuclei in the cerebral cortex. Involuntary movement, irregular motions, or lack of coordinated voluntary movement characterizes dyskinesia (Fredericks & Saladin, 1996). Dyskinetic movement disorders include dystonia, tremor, chorea, tics, and myoclonus. Each movement disorder is uniquely characterized. For example, dystonia is characterized by involuntary, sustained posturing. Small oscillating movements at rest or with effort characterize tremor. Random, excessive, irregularly timed movements characterize chorea. Tics are brief, repetitive, involuntary movements. Involuntary movements that are rapid, shock-like, and arrhythmic (unpatterned) characterize myoclonus (Weiner & Goetz, 1999).

Each movement disorder is unique in regard to the somatic distribution and quality of movement, the age of onset, and etiology. Dyskinesia may be the primary sign or symptom or may be included with the other signs or symptoms of a syndrome. Childhood dyskinetic movement disorders include Tourette syndrome, choreoathetoid cerebral palsy, Wilson's disease, Lesch-Nyhan syndrome, and dystonia. The etiology of a dyskinetic movement disorder is variable and may be due to genetic transmission, brain anoxia, infection, or neoplasm (Weiner & Goetz, 1999).

Prevalence and incidence of dyskinesia in childhood is not documented due to the varied nature of the etiology.

Characteristics

1. Involuntary sustained muscle contractions producing unusual postures.
2. Involuntary oscillating movement at rest or during effort.
3. Excessive, irregularly timed involuntary movement.
4. Repetitive, brief, purposeless involuntary movement.
5. Rapid, often repetitive involuntary movement.

Medical intervention includes pharmacologic treatment or intramuscular injections to control the involuntary movement (Kurlan, 1995). Supportive counseling services may be helpful in educating families, peers, and school personnel regarding the nature of the dyskinesia. The school and home environment may need to be restructured or adapted to improve function depending on the severity of the dyskinesia.

In older children and adults tic disorders are a fairly common type of dyskinesia. They may include rapid repetitive facial movements such as blinking, coughing, sniffing, or lip smacking. These, too, are typically treated symptomatically. They may be treated through the use of relaxation techniques or antianxiety medications in an effort to reduce the stress associated with increased demonstration of this type of dyskinesia (Fredericks & Saladin, 1996). In patients treated with neuroleptic drugs, tardive dyskinesia may develop as a result of this family of drugs. This is more common in adults but may also occur in

older adolescents. Unfortunately, this condition may be irreversible (NIH Health Information Index, 2000).

The impact this group of movement disorders may have on the development of children depends in part on the age at onset, the range and severity of symptoms exhibited, and the developmental level of the child. One of the key components of movement and exploration is stability and predictability of postural tone. Without this stability in the trunk, a child may be unwilling or unable to maintain a sitting position necessary to reach, grasp, and explore objects. Cognitive and perceptual motor skills exhibited in refined searching also require stability of movement. Success in this skill depends on the infant's ability to watch an item being hidden, remember where it went, and retrieve it (Piaget, 1952). Without adequate support and predictable movement patterns, this behavior may be difficult or impossible.

Moving independently in the environment, using independent self-help behaviors such as eating and fine motor skills such as stacking blocks and puzzles also requires stable and predictable movements. A very young infant just learning to crawl may be hesitant to proceed if he or she is unable to maintain stability necessary for movement. Moving out into the environment provides opportunities to explore and increase social and language development. Without this ability, the secondary disabilities that may result include delayed cognitive, language, and social skills necessary for smooth transition to the next levels of development.

Thus, delays in development resulting from dyskinesia may not only potentially affect motor development but also impact development in social and cognitive areas as well as other areas depending on the severity of the dyskinesia. Special education placement will depend on the nature of the disability and the level of involvement for each child. A variety of special education service categories (e.g., Mental Disability, Preschool Services, Traumatic Brain Injury, and Physical Disability) may be considered, and services provided should stem from the special needs of each child. Therefore, it is critical that intervention programs address all areas potentially impacted, such as speech, occupational, and physical therapy in addition to academic areas. The ideal program would include a transdisciplinary model in which counseling, physical, occupational, and speech therapy are incorporated into the child's daily activities.

REFERENCES

Fredericks, C. M., & Saladin, L. K. (1996). *Pathophysiology of the motor systems*. Philadelphia, PA: Davis.

Kurlan, R. (1995). *Treatment of movement disorders*. Philadelphia, PA: Lippincott.

NIH Health Information Index: National Institute of Neurological Disorders and Stroke. (2000). *Dyskinesias*. Retrieved from http://www.ninds.nih.gov/

Piaget, J. (1952). *The origin of intelligence in children*. New York, NY: International Universities Press.

Weiner, W. W., & Goetz, C. G. (1999). *Neurology for the non-neurologist* (4th ed.). Philadelphia, PA: Lippincott Williams & Wilkins.

PATRICIA WORK
MARILYN URQUHART
LANA SVIEN-SENNE
University of South Dakota

DYSLEXIA (*See Developmental Dyslexia, History of; Reading Disorders*

DYSLOGIC SYNDROME

Dyslogic syndrome, sometimes referred to as *developmental* or *congenital aphasia*, consists of the inability to express oneself through language due to a central nervous system dysfunction. Symptoms may not be the result of a sensory or cognitive deficit, nor may they occur due to loss of prior linguistic abilities (Eisenson, 1972; Nicolosi, Harryman, & Kresheck, 1983; Telzrow, 2000). The primary characteristic of dyslogia is difficulty with communication, which is likely to make learning more difficult and to cause frustration to the child. At times children with dyslogia may be misdiagnosed with mental retardation, deafness, auditory deficit, or psychological disorder due to similarities in behavioral patterns (Telzrow, 2000). True dyslogia is believed to be quite rare, although epidemiological information is not available (Eisenson, 1972).

Eisenson (1972) cited several diagnostic criteria for dyslogia that differentiate it from other language disorders. Children with dyslogia often have difficulty with integrating sensory information. This can occur across sensory modalities but in all cases includes the auditory modality. It appears that those with dyslogia have a particularly difficult time making sense of auditory information. More specifically, he suggested that they struggle to find meaningful patterns in auditory input (Chappell, 1970; Eisenson, 1972).

Characteristics

1. Perceptual dysfunction within or across sensory modalities. In nearly all cases auditory perception is impaired.

2. Auditory perceptual difficulties despite intact hearing.

3. Sequencing difficulties for auditory and sometimes visual events.

4. Child's performance on intellectual tasks below that of children of a similar age. Eisenson (1972) described this as intellectual inefficiency rather than impairment.

5. Delayed language development. Children may be effectively nonverbal until the age of 4 or 5 years. Subsequent language is lacking in vocabulary and syntax.

In addition to their struggles with language, Eisenson (1972) believes that those with dyslogia have difficulty with sequencing in general. Children with dyslogia may also exhibit symptoms of inattention and distractibility that can prevent them from working up to their cognitive ability. As these children approach ages where higher cognitive functioning is more frequently required, their difficulties with sequencing become more apparent.

It appears that with patient training, children with dyslogia may learn to recognize and understand simple words, especially nouns that can be represented by physical objects. There is less evidence for the acquisition of understanding of words that represent less concrete concepts such as feelings or actions. With some training, these children may learn to respond to specific, short directive sentences (e.g., "Come, Mary"). However, it appears that these children have a hard time generalizing their understanding, and responses may be situationally specific. Thus, a child who learns to come to the teacher may not respond to the same command when spoken at home (Chappell, 1970).

Prognosis in cases of dyslogia is varied. In some cases, the ability to communicate effectively by language may never develop. In others, the development of language will be permanently impaired, but improvement does occur (Chappell, 1970; Eisenson, 1972). It should be noted that development or recovery of language among those with dyslogia is generally less successful than is that of children with acquired aphasia (Eisenson, 1972).

The language impairment in these children may be so great that when language does begin to develop, it is likely to be impaired in its syntax and complexity. The pattern of language development is likely to be somewhat idiosyncratic and is unlikely to present as merely delayed. These children may be able to speak, but their ability to communicate verbally is likely to remain impaired (Chappell, 1970; Eisenson, 1972).

In an educational environment, care should be taken to provide these children with nonauditory cues for learning. Attempts to teach language should include simple (two to three word) sentences, extensive and patient repetition, and the pairing of vocabulary with concrete objects. It appears that these children require an optimal environment in order to reach their intellectual potentials. Eisenson (1972) suggested that factors such as irrelevant stimuli, fatigue, and frustration may be especially detrimental to children struggling with dyslogia. In such cases, common accommodations for children with attentional difficulties would likely be helpful.

REFERENCES

Chappell, G. E. (1970). Developmental aphasia revisited. *Journal of Communication Disorders, 3*, 181–197.

Eisenson, J. (1972). *Aphasia in children*. New York, NY: Harper & Row.

Nicolosi, L., Harryman, E., & Kresheck, J. (1983). *Terminology of communication disorders*. Baltimore, MD: Williams & Wilkins.

Telzrow, C. T. (2000). Dyslogic syndrome. In C. Reynolds & E. Fletcher-Janzen (Eds.), *Encyclopedia of special education: A reference for the education of the handicapped and other exceptional children and adults* (2nd ed., Vol. 1, pp. 636–637). New York, NY: Wiley.

MELANIE E. BALLATORE
University of Texas at Austin

See *also* Childhood Aphasia; Language Disorders

DYSMETRIA

Dysmetria is defined as an aspect of ataxia in which the ability to control the distance, power, and speed of an act is impaired (Stedman, 2000). The term originates from the Greek *dys*, meaning difficult or disordered, and *metron*, meaning measure. Individuals with dysmetria have problems judging the extent to which they must move their body to reach a desired goal and often have difficulty stopping their movement in a precise manner to reach the goal. Movements, therefore, undershoot (hypometria) or overshoot (hypermetria) the distance (Telzrow, 2000). Individuals with dysmetria may have difficulty raising their arms parallel to the floor (i.e., arms extended at the shoulder level). Some may also have problems moving their arms above their heads from their shoulders and back down while keeping their eyes closed.

The prevalence of dysmetria is unknown, but it has been shown to co-occur with other conditions. Some of these associated conditions include neurologic disorders (e.g., cerebellar dysfunction), learning problems (e.g., dyslexia),

and psychiatric conditions (e.g., schizophrenia). Unless dysmetria is detected while evaluating for problems associated with related conditions, it is likely to remain undiagnosed. There have been cases of children with traumatic brain injury (TBI) who after being hit by a vehicle are found to have a cerebellar tumor thought to be responsible for the initial misjudgment of distance, and thus the accident. Had imaging not been done to evaluate the TBI, it is likely that the tumor would not have been detected and that the dysmetria would not have been diagnosed.

Characteristics

1. Disturbance in the ability to judge distance and control the range of movement in muscle action to reach precisely a desired goal.
2. Rapid, brusque movements with more force than is typical.
3. Often associated with other conditions (e.g., neurologic and psychiatric).
4. Difficult to diagnose.

There is no prescribed treatment for dysmetria, and the literature is almost nonexistent. Frank and Levinson (1976) studied the effectiveness of seasick medications to treat "dysmetric dyslexia." The researchers hypothesize that dysmetric dyslexia may be due to vestibular dysfunction and respond to a specific intervention of the eyes being prevented from moving beyond printed letters and words. In the end, it may be that interventions used to correct dysmetria will be those that are designed to address related problems, including reading disabilities and other learning difficulties. Research is clearly needed to understand this condition better and to find ways to determine when dysmetria signals a more serious problem (e.g., brain tumors).

REFERENCES

Frank, J., & Levinson, H. N. (1976). Seasickness mechanisms and medications in dysmetric dyslexia and dyspraxia. *Academic Therapy, 12*(2), 133–153.

Stedman, T. L. (2000). *Stedman's medical dictionary* (27th ed., p. 553). Baltimore, MD: Lippincott Williams & Wilkins.

Telzrow, C. F. (2000). In C. R. Reynolds & E. Fletcher-Janzen (Eds.), *Encyclopedia of special education* (2nd ed., p. 637). New York, NY: Wiley.

LINDSEY A. PHILLIPS
ELAINE CLARK
University of Utah

See *also* Mobility Instruction

DYSMORPHIC FEATURES

Dysmorphic features are those physical anomalies that identify the presence of congenital syndromes or acquired disabilities. Dysmorphic features may be present in a variety of body parts, including the head, face, hands, and feet. Most congenital syndromes are associated with dysmorphic features that are specific to and, in fact, represent signs of the condition. Dysmorphic features associated with Down syndrome, for example, include a single palmar crease (Simian crease) on one or both hands, epicanthus, and microcephaly (Kelly, 1975). Apert's syndrome, another condition frequently associated with mental retardation, is characterized by syndactyly (webbing) of the hands and feet and a flat, narrow head owing to closure of the bony sutures (Batshaw & Perret, 1981). Some dysmorphic features (e.g., anencephaly or absence of the cortical brain tissues) are severe and typically result in death (Batshaw & Perret, 1981).

Although dysmorphic features may occur in the absence of any known syndrome and without apparent mental or physical impairment, in most cases such anomalies are suggestive of moderate to severe impairment. Dysmorphic features may represent malformations that occur during the first trimester (Batshaw & Perret, 1981). Malformations may result from genetic abnormalities (e.g., Down syndrome, phenylketonuria); cell migration defects (e.g., cleft palate, spina bifida); maternal infection (e.g., rubella, cytomegalovirus); drugs (e.g., fetal alcohol syndrome, fetal dilantin syndrome); and other teratogens (Batshaw & Perret, 1981; Casey & Collie, 1984). The presence of dysmorphic features often is used to infer level and type of associated impairment. A study of the relationship between physical appearance and mental retardation syndromes reported that atypical appearance increases with the severity of mental retardation; greater atypical appearance is associated with more severe organic impairment in populations of severely and profoundly retarded persons; and mildly retarded persons with positive neurologic findings demonstrated greater degrees of atypical appearance (Richardson, Koller, & Katz, 1985).

Dysmorphic features of a less severe nature also have been identified in populations of mildly handicapped children. Waldrop and Halverson (1971) described findings from five separate studies in which congenital anomalies such as epicanthus, curved fifth digits, and a wide gap between the first and second toes were associated with hyperactive behavior in children. The authors suggest that "the same factors operating in the first weeks of pregnancy influenced the occurrence of *both* the morphological aberrations and the predisposition for impulsive, fast-moving behavior" (Waldrop & Halverson, 1971, p. 343). Subsequent studies demonstrated such minor physical anomalies could be identified in infants, were stable overtime, and were associated with infant irritability (Quinn, Renfield, Burg, & Rapaport, 1977). Although these and other authors (e.g., Rosenberg & Weller, 1973) suggest minor congenital anomalies may be useful in predicting at-risk status for mild learning problems, other findings suggest the quality of the child's environment may represent an important intervening variable (LaVeck, Hammond, Telzrow, & LaVeck, 1983).

REFERENCES

Batshaw, M. L., & Perret, Y. M. (1981). *Children with handicaps: A medical primer*. Baltimore, MD: Paul H. Brookes.

Casey, P. H., & Collie, W. R. (1984). Severe mental retardation and multiple congenital anomalies of uncertain cause after extreme parental exposure to 2, 4-D. *Journal of Pediatrics, 104*, 313–315.

Kelly, T. E. (1975). The role of genetic mechanisms in childhood handicaps. In R. H. A. Haslam & P. J. Valletutti (Eds.), *Medical problems in the classroom* (pp. 193–215). Baltimore, MD: University Park Press.

LaVeck, F., Hammond, M. A., Telzrow, R., & LaVeck, G. D. (1983). Further observations on minor anomalies and behavior in different home environments. *Journal of Pediatric Psychology, 8*, 171–179.

Quinn, P. O., Renfield, M., Burg, C., & Rapaport, J. L. (1977). Minor physical anomalies: A newborn screening and 1-year follow-up. *Journal of Child Psychiatry, 16*, 662–669.

Richardson, S. A., Koller, H., & Katz, M. (1985). Appearance and mental retardation: Some first steps in the development and application of a measure. *American Journal of Mental Deficiency, 89*, 475–484.

Rosenberg, J. B., & Weller, G. M. (1973). Minor physical anomalies and academic performance in young school-children. *Developmental Medicine & Child Neurology, 15*, 131–135.

Waldrop, M. F., & Halverson, C. F. (1971). Minor physical anomalies and hyperactive behavior in young children. In J. Hellmuth (Ed.), *The exceptional infant* (Vol. 2, pp. 343–380). New York, NY: Brunner/Mazel.

CATHY F. TELZROW
Kent State University

See also Congenital Disorders; Minor Physical Anomalies; Physical Anomalies

DYSNOMIA

Dysnomia and anomia are used interchangeably to denote problems in finding and using an intended word. Eisenson (1973) defines dysnomia as "difficulty in invoking an appropriate term regardless of its part of speech" (p. 19). It is frequently evidenced in dysphasic patients as a residual of central nervous system dysfunction. The dysphasic individual may substitute a word related by class or function to the intended word (e.g., knife for ford; Eisenson, 1973). Fewer problems were noted on common words than those used less frequently in the language (Jenkins, Jiménez-Pabón, Shaw, & Sefer, 1975).

A dysphasic individual tends to talk around the elusive word and sometimes may remark that he or she knows it but cannot say it. He or she may attempt a gesture to illustrate the word's meaning or may give several functional cues, sometimes achieving successful recall through associations. Some dysphasics recognize the word when it is said to them. Word-finding difficulties also have been found among learning-disabled children with language disorders (Wiig & Semel, 1984) and among children diagnosed as being developmentally dysphasic (Myklebust, 1971). In such cases, the child cannot name an object or picture, but is aware of the error and can recognize the intended word when it is supplied because auditory monitoring processes are intact (Myklebust, 1971).

Dysnomic difficulties are evident in picture-naming tasks, characterized by use of an associated word (e.g., door for key). Use of an opposite such as "brother" for "sister" also is a common error in both children and adults. Verbal association tasks that require a child to name items within categories (e.g., animals) may produce rapid naming of several items and then either silence or incorrect responses. Errors may occur on words that a child has evidenced knowing on previous occasions (Wiig & Semel, 1984). German (1982) studied 8- to 11-year-old learning-disabled children to identify types of substitutions unique to this group when the children were unable to retrieve words. The strongest pattern noted was the substitution of a word of lesser complexity and with wider application (e.g., "string" for "rein"); the weakest pattern was the repetition of initial sound(s) of a related word before the target word was uttered (e.g., "br, br, comb").

Word-finding problems in spontaneous speech may be signaled by inappropriate pauses, use of filler ("um" and "er") and nonmeaningful phrases ("whatchama call it"), substitution of a functional description (circumlocution), or overuse of nonspecific words ("stuff," "place," "something," "thing"; Wiig & Semel, 1984). Classroom tasks involving rhyming words, silent picture naming, matching initial-, medical-, and final-consonant sounds, and look-say methods of reading may prove troublesome for dysnomic children (Wiig, Semel, & Nystrom, 1982). German (1982) suggests that a thorough evaluation of a child's pattern of word substitutions may prove helpful in intervention techniques.

REFERENCES

Eisenson, J. (1973). *Adult aphasia: Assessment and treatment.* New York, NY: Appleton-Century-Crofts.

German, D. (1982). Word-finding substitutions in children with learning disabilities. *Language, Speech & Hearing Services in Schools, 13,* 223–230.

Jenkins, J. J., Jiménez-Pabón, E., Shaw, R. E., & Sefer, J. W. (1975). *Schuell's aphasia in adults: Diagnosis, prognosis, and treatment.* Hagerstown, MD: Harper & Row.

Myklebust, H. (1971). Childhood aphasia: An evolving concept. In L. E. Travis (Ed.), *The handbook of speech pathology and audiology* (pp. 1181–1201). New York, NY: Appleton-Century-Crofts.

Wiig, E., & Semel, E. (1984). *Language assessment and intervention for the learning disabled* (2nd ed.). Columbus, OH: Merrill.

Wiig, E., Semel, E., & Nystrom, L. A. (1982). Comparison of rapid naming abilities in language learning disabled and academically achieving eight-year olds. *Language, Speech & Hearing Services in Schools, 13,* 11–25.

K. SANDRA VANTA
Cleveland Public Schools,
Cleveland, Ohio

See also Aphasia; Communication Disorders; Language Disorders

DYSPEDAGOGIA

Dyspedagogia refers to poor teaching. It has been cited as a major cause of reading retardation and other learning disorders. Though the term is used as one of the etiological agents for a wide array of problems, dyspedagogia is commonly associated with the field of learning disabilities (Epstein, Cullinan, Hessen, & Lloyd, 1980), mathematics (Maree, 1992), and currently in general areas that require cross-cultural competency for learners outcomes (Truscott & Truscott, 2005). Indeed, general and special education has been placed under great scrutiny by the No Child Left Behind law and the reauthorization of IDEA in 2004.

Early research in reading disorders and learning disabilities looked for psychophysiological dysfunctions or psychological information-processing deficits as the cause of a child's inefficient learning. Once various forms of testing established a supposed etiology, specific treatment regimens were to flow directly from the diagnosis. Although this approach to special and remedial education, often referred to as ability training, has been questioned (Ysseldyke, 1973), it remains a dominant force in practice. Learning problems were seen as based in the individual child, whether because of psychoneurological dysfunction or sociocultural disadvantage. Improper choice of teaching materials or methodology, or an inappropriate match between learning style and pedagogy, were rarely viewed as contributing factors in a student's academic retardation.

Cohen (1971) cites Harris's research (1968) on teaching beginning reading as an early example of dyspedagogia as an etiological agent in poor reading achievement. When comparisons were made between different beginning reading programs, matching classrooms across and within each program, the achievement discrepancies were greater between classrooms using the same program than across the different types of beginning reading programs. This was generally interpreted to indicate that the teacher variable is a more powerful determinant of student achievement than the actual programs or materials employed.

Cohen (1971) believed that dyspedagogia is the norm for most children, both in regular and special education. Many children, however, learn well enough despite poor or inappropriate teaching. The problem lies in the fact that those children who come to the educational setting with negatively predisposing social, psychological, neurological, or linguistic differences need effective, intensive teaching, and will suffer inordinately from dyspedagogia (Wertsch, 1985). The presenting background problems are not ignored, but the burden falls on educators to minimize their deleterious effects on learning by providing sound, skill-oriented instruction.

As a result of research in regular education on effective teaching (e.g., Brophy, 1979; Lyon, 2003; Rosenshine, 1978), a good deal of attention is being given to issues such as direct instruction, time on task, academically engaged time, instructional management, performance monitoring, success-oriented learning, feedback, reflective teaching, and related practices. This research has offered promise for special and general education (Englert, 1984; Goodman, 1985; Rieth, Edsgrove, & Semmel, 1979).

REFERENCES

Brophy, J. E. (1979). Teacher behavior and its effects. *Journal of Educational Psychology, 71*, 733–750.

Cohen, S. A. (1971). Dyspedagogia as a cause of reading retardation: Definition and treatment. In B. Bateman (Ed.), *Learning disorders* (Vol. 4). Seattle, WA: Special Child.

Englert, C. S. (1984). Effective direct instruction practices in special education settings. *Remedial & Special Education, 5*(2), 38–47.

Epstein, M. H., Cullinan, D., Hessen, E. L., & Lloyd, J. (1980). Understanding children with learning disabilities. *Child Welfare, 59*(1), 3–14.

Goodman, L. (1985). The effective schools movement and special education. *Teaching Exceptional Children, 17*, 102–105.

Harris, A., Morrison, C., Serwa, B., & Gold, L. (1968). *A continuation of the craft project: Comparing approaches with disadvantaged urban Negro children in primary grades* (U.S.O.E. #6-10-063). New York, NY: City University of New York.

Lyon, R. (2003). Reading disabilities: Why do some children have difficulty learning to read? *International Dyslexia Association Perspectives, 29*(2), 111–114.

Maree, J. G. (1992). Problems in mathematics: Moving towards a holistic approach. *Journal of Special Education, 16*(2), 174–182.

Rieth, H. J., Edsgrove, L., & Semmel, M. I. (1979). Relationship between instructional time and academic achievement: Implications for research and practice. *Education Unlimited, 1*(6), 53–56.

Rosenshine, B. (1978). *Academic engaged time, content covered and direct instruction* (ERIC Document No. 152 776). Champaign: University of Illinois.

Truscott, S. D., & Truscott, D. M. (2005). Challenges in urban and rural education. In C. L. Frisby & C. R. Reynolds (Eds.), *Multicultural school psychology* (pp. 357–393). Hoboken, NJ: Wiley.

Wertsch, J. (1985). *Vygotsky and the social formation of mind.* London, England: Harvard University Press.

Ysseldyke, J. E. (1973). Diagnostic-prescriptive teaching: The search for aptitude-treatment interactions. In L. Mann & D. Sabatino (Eds.), *First review of special education.* New York, NY: Grune & Stratton.

JOHN D. WILSON
Elwyn Institutes

DYSPHAGIA

Dysphagia has been defined in several different ways. For example, Buchholz (1996) offered a broad definition in which dysphagia is considered a condition resulting from some interference in eating or the maintenance of nutrition and hydration; Groher (1997) stated that dysphagia is an "abnormality in the transfer of a bolus from the mouth to the stomach" (p. 1). However, a general definition of dysphagia is having difficulty swallowing. This difficulty could be caused by a number of different conditions. The more common causes of swallowing difficulty are neurologic damage such as stroke or progressive neurologic disease such as Parkinson's disease, head and neck tumors and their treatment, medical problems such as rheumatoid arthritis, scleroderma, diabetes, and induced trauma to the esophagus, larynx, tongue, or pharynx (New York Eye and Ear Infirmary [NYEEI], 2000).

Dysphagia typically falls into one of two categories. Oropharyngeal dysphagia is the result of a stroke or neuromuscular disorder that leaves the throat muscles weakened, making it difficult to get food from the mouth into the throat. This condition is often accompanied by choking or coughing when attempting to swallow and the sensation of food going down the windpipe. The most common type of dysphagia, however, is esophageal dysphagia, which refers to the sensation of food sticking or getting caught in the base of one's throat or chest and may be accompanied by pressure or pain in the chest (Mayo Foundation for Medical Education and Research [MFMER], 1998).

A narrowing of the lower esophagus, known as *peptic stricture*, is a common cause of esophageal dysphagia. The resulting condition, known as gastroesophageal reflux, is a result of stomach acid bubbling up into the esophagus, causing inflammation and scarring in the esophagus. Another cause of esophageal dysphagia is a formation of a pouch in the back of the throat or esophagus, known as diverticulum.

Despite the many medically identifiable causes of dysphagia, many people experience swallowing problems that seem to have no medical basis (e.g., difficulty swallowing pills or the feeling of a lump in the throat). These problems persist in some people even though they have no other difficulty swallowing.

The incidence of dysphagia is approximately 13% to 14% in inpatient hospital settings, 40% to 50% in nursing homes, and approximately 33% in rehabilitation centers (NYEEI, 2000).

Acute forms of dysphagia are typically diagnosed by tests such as drinking a barium solution that coats the esophagus and enables an X-ray to show abnormalities in the esophagus; an endoscopy, in which a tube with a special camera at the tip allows the esophagus to be viewed from the inside; or a procedure known as a manometry test, in which an instrument is inserted into the esophagus and pressure readings of esophageal muscle contractions are taken.

Characteristics

1. Pain while swallowing.
2. Coughing while eating or drinking or very soon after eating or drinking.
3. Wet-sounding voice during or after eating.
4. Increased congestion in the chest after eating or drinking.
5. Slow eating.
6. Multiple swallows on a single mouthful of food.
7. Obvious extra effort or difficulty while chewing or swallowing.
8. Fatigue or shortness of breath while eating.
9. Temperature rise 30 minutes to 1 hour after eating.
10. Weight loss associated with increased slowness in eating.
11. Frequent heartburn.
12. Repetitive pneumonias.

The causes of dysphagia determine the course of treatment. Pharyngeal dysphagia may be treated by a throat specialist, neurologist, or a speech pathologist for therapy. Typically, special throat exercises, liquid diets, and

in severe cases a feeding tube may be recommended. Esophageal stricture may be treated by a procedure known as dilatation, in which an endoscope is inserted into the esophagus and a special balloon attached to the endoscope is inflated to expand the constricted areas of the esophagus. Acid reflux or esophageal spasms that result in dysphagia may be treated with prescription medication. In some cases, such as diverticulum or the presence of a tumor, surgery may be necessary (MFMER, 1998).

Children with dysphagia may require extra care at lunch and snack times, such as additional time to eat, adult supervision, and education of peers about the disorder.

REFERENCES

Buchholz, D. (1996). Editorial: What is dysphagia? *Dysphagia, 11*, 23.

Groher, M. E. (1997). *Dysphagia: Diagnosis and management* (3rd ed.). Boston, MA: Butterworth-Heinemann.

Mayo Foundation for Medical Education and Research (MFMER). (1998). Dysphagia: When swallowing becomes difficult. *Condition Centers*. Retrieved from http://www.mayoclinic.com/

New York Eye and Ear Infirmary (NYEEI). (2000). Dysphagia: What is a normal swallow? *Health matters*. Retrieved from http://nyee.edu/

TRACY A. MUENZ
Alliant International University

DYSPHASIA (See Language Disorders)

DYSPHONIA

Dysphonia is a general term referring to any voice disorder of phonation. Dysphonia is a deviation in pitch, intensity, and quality resulting primarily from the action of the vocal folds. Included in this definition are characteristics of the voice that consistently interfere with communication, draw unfavorable attention, adversely affect the speaker or listener, or are inappropriate to the age, sex, or perhaps the culture or class of the individual. Dysphonia is inclusive of more than 30 specific types and can be organic, psychogenic, or functional in nature (Nicolosi, Harryman, & Kresheck, 1996).

The incidence of voice disorders has proved difficult to establish: figures range from 6% (Senturia & Wilson, 1998) to 23.4% (Silverman & Zimmer, 1975) in the school age population, with the generally accepted number being closer to the 6% figure. In a study describing laryngeal disorders in children evaluated by otolaryngologists, Dobres Lee, Stempler, Kummer, and Kretchmer (1990) found the top five pathologies presented by children to be (1) subglottic stenosis, (2) vocal nodules, (3) laryngomalacia, (4) dysphonia with normal folds, and (5) vocal fold paralysis. Subglottic stenosis and laryngomalacia are considered to be congenital laryngeal pathologies. Subglottic stenosis is the maldevelopment of the cricoid cartilage causing a subglottal narrowing of the larynx. The narrowing produces an obstruction of the airway that causes the voice to be stridulous. In most cases, the cricoid cartilage continues to develop, and the problem self-corrects in infancy or early childhood (Aronson, 1990). Surgery is required in more severe cases. Laryngomalacia occurs when the epiglottis fails to develop normally, remaining very soft and pliable and causing stridor. No treatment is required for this condition, as the epiglottis will continue to grow and the condition will spontaneously clear by the third year with normal maturation (Aronson, 1990). Vocal nodules and dysphonia with normal folds are highly correlated with disorders of abuse and misuse. Vocal fold nodules are benign, callous-like growths resulting from frictional rubbing of the vocal fold edges (Nicolosi et al., 1996). Nodules can disappear following vocal rest or voice therapy, but surgical removal may be required. When the etiology of the nodules is vocal abuse or misuse, voice therapy is highly indicated to modify the behavior in order to prevent a recurrence of the condition. Disorders of phonation with normal folds result in vocal characteristics of a number of symptoms of dysphonia, which are not specific to a single etiology or dysphonia type. Vocal fold paralysis is the most common type of neurogenic voice disorder. It is typically caused by peripheral involvement of the recurrent laryngeal and the superior laryngeal nerves (Willatt & Stell, 1991). Location of the lesion along the nerve pathway will determine the type of paralysis and the resultant voice quality.

Characteristics

1. Aphonia: Complete loss of voice, involuntary whispering.
2. Breathiness: Excessive air loss accompanying vocal tone.
3. Dipolophonia: Two tones produced simultaneously, one from the ventricular folds and one from the vocal folds.
4. Glottal attack: Extreme glottal closure prior to exhalation for speech.
5. Glottal fry: Crackling type of low-pitched phonation.
6. Harshness: Milieu of hard glottal attacks, pitch and intensity problems, and overadduction of the vocal folds.
7. Hoarseness: Low pitch with restricted pitch range, pitch breaks, and aphonic episodes.
8. Pitch break: Sudden shift of pitch during speech, usually related to an individual's speaking at an inappropriate pitch level.
9. Stridor: Tense laryngeal noise associated with respiration.

Treatment for dysphonia varies with type and etiology. For disorders associated with vocal abuse and misuse, voice therapy by a speech-language pathologist is warranted. Treatment approaches are numerous and varied, but inclusion of vocal hygiene counseling is typical.

Students may receive voice therapy under the category of Speech-Language Impairment, but it is often difficult to meet the requirement of educational necessity. It should be noted that although it is not required, it is considered unethical among the speech pathology community to treat a student for a voice disorder without an examination from a physician, preferably an otolaryngologist. The responsibility for funding such an examination is often an issue.

Prognosis for recovery from dysphonia varies according to type, etiology, and student motivation and participation in a therapy program. When the dysphonia stems from vocal abuse or misuse, the lifestyles of the student and his or her family will often dictate the ease or difficulty they will have in attempting to make vocal modifications. Some students and families are not willing to modify their lifestyles for the health of their voice. A reasonable period of time and a concerted trial of therapy should always be administered.

Current research is focused on many adult dysphonias, primarily spasmodic dysphonia, and on medical management of such conditions. Research regarding children and adolescents is focused on issues of vocal hygiene, abuse, and misuse.

REFERENCES

Aronson, A. (1990). *Clinical voice disorders: An interdisciplinary approach* (3rd ed.). New York, NY: Marcel Decker.

Dobres, R., Lee, L., Stemple, J., Kummer, A., & Kretchmer, L. (1990). Description of laryngeal pathologies in children evaluated by otolaryngologists. *Journal of Speech and Hearing Disorders, 55,* 526–533.

Nicolosi, L., Harryman, E., & Kresheck, J. (1996). *Terminology of communication disorders: Speech-language-hearing* (4th ed.). Baltimore, MD: Williams & Wilkins.

Senturia, B., & Wilson, F. (1998). Otorhinolaryngologic findings in children with voice deviations: Preliminary report. *Annals of Otology, Rhinology, and Laryngology, 77,* 1027–1042.

Silverman, E., & Zimmer, C. (1975). Incidence of chronic hoarseness among school-age children. *Journal of Speech and Hearing Disorders, 40,* 211–215.

Willatt, D., & Stell, P. (1991). Vocal cord paralysis. In S. Paparella & D. Shumrick (Eds.), *Otolaryngology* (3rd ed., pp. 2289–2307). Philadelphia, PA: Saunders.

SHELLEY F. PELLETIER
JENNIFER L. NICHOLLS
Dysart United School District El Mirage, Arizona

DYSPRAXIA (*See Developmental Apraxia*)

DYSTHYMIA

Dysthymia is one of the predominant types of depressive disorders in children and adolescents. It is an affective disorder characterized by chronically depressed mood (or irritable mood) that occurs most of the time for at least one year (American Psychiatric Association [APA], 1994). In differentiating dysthymia from major depressive disorder, the mood disturbance in dysthymia is typically less severe, lasts longer, and may not remit (Stark, Bronik, Wong, Wells, & Ostrander, 2000). Additionally, dysthymia is thought to have an earlier onset than major depressive disorder (Kovacs, Akiskal, Gatsonis, & Parrone, 1994).

The prevalence of dysthymia in the general population of the United States is approximately 3%, and it occurs equally in males and females in childhood (APA, 1994). Average age of onset ranges from 6 to 13 years. It is reported to be more common among first-degree biological relatives with major depression.

Characteristics

1. Minimum 1-year history of chronic depressed (or irritable) mood for much of the day, more days than not. Mood disturbances are difficult to distinguish from the child's typical functioning. The child's depressed mood is considered less severe than that characterizing major depressive disorder.

2. At least two of the following symptoms must be present: (a) poor appetite or overeating, (b) sleep disturbances (insomnia or hypersomnia), (c) low energy or fatigue, (d) low self-esteem and self-deprecation, (e) poor concentration or difficulty making decisions, (f) feelings of hopelessness or pessimism.

3. Associated characteristics include poor social skills, irritability, and anger.

4. Relief from depressive symptoms does not last longer than 2 months at a time.

5. Exclusionary criteria include major depressive episode, manic episode, hypomanic episode, or symptoms due primarily to substance abuse, medication, or medical condition.

6. Accompanied by impairment in social or academic functioning.

Source: Adapted from APA, 1994.

A variety of psychosocial treatment approaches have been documented in the literature, including psychoeducational, psychodynamic, cognitive-behavioral, and family systems interventions. Outcome data suggest that cognitive-behavioral approaches are the most thoroughly evaluated and most promising interventions in the treatment of childhood depression (Harrington, Whittaker, & Shoebridge, 1998). Clinical practice typically combines psychosocial treatment with pharmacological interventions. Although antidepressants are commonly used in the treatment of childhood depression, to date there is a lack of well-controlled studies documenting their efficacy (Stark et al., 2000).

Children with dysthymia may qualify for special education services under the category Serious Emotional Disturbance. Because dysthymia is associated with higher than average rates of academic failure (Keller, 1994), these children may also qualify for special education services under the category Specific Learning Disability. Impaired social interaction skills are a prominent characteristic of dysthymia, so social skills training may be one component of the special education services that these children require. Additionally, the presence of depression is one of the risk factors in suicide attempts among youth, so these children should be appropriately monitored in school settings.

The majority of children diagnosed with dysthymia (onset occurs before age 21) are likely to develop major depressive episodes, with a median duration of 5 years before onset (Kovacs et al., 1994). Children with dysthymia also are at greater risk for recurrent major depression, bipolar disorder, and other affective illnesses (Keller, 1994; Kovacs et al., 1994). Comorbidity rates are high for a variety of disorders, the predominant ones being anxiety disorders and disruptive behavior disorders. There is considerable need for further empirical research on the effective treatment of dysthymia and other depressive disorders specific to children and adolescents as well as research highlighting the comparative efficacy of specific therapeutic and pharmacological interventions.

REFERENCES

American Psychiatric Association. (1994). *Diagnostic and statistical manual of mental disorders* (4th ed.). Washington, DC: Author.

Harrington, R., Whittaker, J., & Shoebridge, P. (1998). Psychological treatment of depression in children and adolescents: A review of treatment research. *British Journal of Psychiatry*, *173*, 291–298.

Keller, M. B. (1994). Dysthymia in clinical practice: Course, outcome and impact on the community. *Acta Psychiatrica Scandinavica*, *89*(Suppl. 383), 24–34.

Kovacs, M., Akiskal, H. S., Gatsonis, C., & Parrone, P. L. (1994). Childhood-onset dysthymic disorder: Clinical features and prospective naturalistic outcome. *Archives of General Psychiatry*, *51*, 365–374.

Stark, K. D., Bronik, M. D., Wong, S., Wells, G., & Ostrander, R. (2000). Depressive disorders. In M. Hersen & R. T. Ammerman (Eds.), *Advanced abnormal child psychology* (2nd ed., pp. 291–326). Mahwah, NJ: Erlbaum.

LORA TUESDAY HEATHFIELD
University of Utah

DYSTONIA

Dystonia is a neurologic movement disorder characterized by sustained muscle contractions that frequently cause twisting or repetitive movements and abnormal, sometimes painful, postures or positions. This disorder may involve any voluntary muscle in the body. Defined as a syndrome of sustained muscle contractions, dystonia encompasses motor syndromes that vary as a function of age of onset, cause, and body distribution (King, Tsui, & Calne, 1995). The symptoms of dystonia may begin during early childhood, in adolescence, or during adulthood. Dystonia may frequently be misdiagnosed or confused with other disorders. The diagnosis may be missed as the movements and resulting postures are often unusual and the condition is rare. The exact prevalence of dystonia in the general population is not known; however, an estimate of 330 cases per million has been made (King et al., 1995).

Characteristics

1. Movement is characterized by an excess of involuntary muscle activity (Rothwell, 1995).
2. Childhood dystonia often presents as abnormal foot inversions, awkward gait, and contractions of many different muscle groups and may involve one or more limbs of the proximal or distal muscle groups.
3. Dystonic movements tend to increase with fatigue, stress, and emotional states; they tend to be suppressed with relaxation, hypnosis, and sleep.
4. Dystonia is usually present continually throughout the day whenever the affected body part is in use and disappears with deep sleep.
5. Common misdiagnoses are clubfoot, scoliosis, stress, and psychogenic disorder.
6. Pain is common in some individuals.

Although dystonia has no cure, there are successful treatments that greatly reduce the symptoms and restore individuals to many daily living activities. The first step in treatment is attempting to determine the cause of the dystonia. Dystonia is classified as being primary or idiopathic, in which there is no known organic lesion, but is believed to be hereditary and to occur as the result of a faulty genes (King et al., 1995). It is also classified as being secondary, which generally arises from some insult to the basal ganglia of the central nervous system such as trauma, toxins, drugs, neoplasm, or infarction; another underlying disease process such as Wilson disease, multiple sclerosis, or stroke; or as a result of the use of certain neuroleptic or antipsychotic drugs. For secondary dystonias, treating the underlying cause may improve the dystonia. For instance, treatments for neurological conditions such as multiple sclerosis may reduce dystonic symptoms. Withdrawing or reducing neuroleptic drugs leads to slow improvement in some cases.

There are three main approaches to the treatment of primary dystonia: drug therapy, injections of therapeutic agents (botulinum toxin) directly into dystonic muscle, and surgery (Greene & Fahn, 1992). Drug therapy may include benzodiazepines, which are a class of drugs that interfere with chemical activities in the nervous system and brain, serving to reduce communication between nerve cells; baclofen, which is a drug that is used to treat individuals with spasticity; and anticholinergics, which block the action of the neurotransmitter acetylcholine, thereby deactivating muscle contractions (King et al., 1995). Surgical intervention may be considered in those individuals with severe dystonia who have not responded or have become nonresponders to drug therapy. The goal of surgery for individuals with dystonia is to attempt to rebalance movement and posture control by destroying specific regions in the brain (King et al., 1995).

Special education services may be available to children diagnosed with dystonia by providing services under IDEA categorical areas of other health impairment or physical impairment. Movement problems usually start on the lower limbs and can progress to other parts of the body. At times they may then reach a plateau. Therefore, input from a physical therapist may be required to provide advice, monitoring, and exercises. An occupational therapist may be necessary to identify areas of concern in regard to work, play, and self-care. Speech therapy is often warranted and varies depending on the type of dystonia. A therapy program is then designed to meet individual needs, and information can be provided to the child and family about ways to promote optimal communication. Due to extensive medical intervention, school absences may require home schooling or tutoring by a special educator. Counseling services may be appropriate due to the psychosocial aspects of the physical distortions caused by muscular contractions. Finally, for the dystonic child, most all life activities take longer; this and the effect of the medication may cause fatigue. Consequently, it is important to have realistic expectations of the child's physical performance. The overall goal should be to foster a feeling of successful achievement, emphasizing the activities that children can accomplish rather than focusing on their limitations.

Research evaluating the ideology and a potential cure for dystonia has begun. Some professionals research the effects of dystonia such as the short- and long-term outcomes for afflicted children. Will the child's abilities decline over time? Will there be some psychosocial problems? What is the appropriate educational placement for children with dystonia? Reflecting on the implications of this disorder, these simple questions need further empirical study before clear answers can be provided.

REFERENCES

Greene, P. E., & Fahn, S. (1992). Baclofen in the treatment of idiopathic dystonia in children. *Movement Disorders, 7*, 48–52.

King, J., Tsui, C., & Calne, D. B. (1995). *Handbook of dystonia.* New York, NY: Marcel Dekker.

Rothwell, J. C. (1995). *The physiology of dystonia.* New York, NY: Marcel Dekker.

KENDRA J. BJORAKER
University of Northern Colorado

See also Mobility Instruction

E

EAR AND HEARING

The ear is the sensory organ of hearing, and hearing is the sense by which sound waves are recognized and interpreted. The ear can be divided into four parts: the outer, middle, and inner ear, and central pathways. Sound waves enter the outer ear via the auricle (or pinna) on the side of the head and then go through the ear canal (external auditory meatus) to the middle ear. The middle ear consists of the eardrum (tympanic membrane) and three articulated bones (malleus, incus, and stapes), collectively called the ossicles, which extend from the eardrum to the inner ear. The middle ear transforms the acoustic energy of the sound waves impinging on the eardrum to mechanical energy.

The inner ear is divided into a vestibular (balance) and cochlear (hearing) section. The cochlea consists of three fluid-filled ducts. The middle duct contains the Organ of Corti, which houses the sensory nerve endings for hearing. The cochlea transforms the mechanical sound wave energy from the middle ear to electrical energy to initiate a neural response. The neural response of the cochlea is carried by the central auditory pathways to the brain. The central pathways consist of the auditory nerve (eighth cranial nerve), which starts in the inner ear, interacts with neural complexes in the brain stem, and terminates in Heschel's gyri, which is the primary auditory reception center in the temporal cortex on each side of the brain.

This entry has been informed by the sources listed below.

REFERENCES

Moore, B. C. J. (1982). *An introduction to the psychology of hearing* (2nd ed.). New York, NY: Academic Press.

Pickles, J. O. (1982). *An introduction to the physiology of hearing.* New York, NY: Academic Press.

THOMAS A. FRANK
Pennsylvania State University

See also Deaf; Deaf Education

EARLY CHILDHOOD, CULTURALLY AND LINGUISTICALLY DIVERSE ISSUES IN

Young children enter formal schooling differentially prepared to benefit from their educational experiences (Farver, Xu, Eppe, & Lonigan, 2006). Among these children are those from culturally and linguistically diverse backgrounds. As early as preschool and kindergarten, linguistically and culturally diverse young children demonstrate varying levels of readiness skills including language development (Miccio, Tabors, Páez, Hammer, & Wagstaff, 2005), with first language and second language oral skills both often falling below national norms for monolingual English speakers (Cobo-Lewis, Pearson, Eilers, & Umbel, 2002; Tabors, Páez, & López, 2003).

Young children whose first language is not English represent a growing share of the population in the United States (O'Bryon & Rogers, 2010). Although Spanish is the most spoken language among the CLD students, Chinese, French, German, and Tagalog are also popular among the more than 400 languages spoken in the schools and early childhood centers nationwide (Halle, Hair, Wandner, McNamara, & Chien, 2011).

In schools, linguistically and culturally diverse children are often categorized under different names; including English language learners (ELLs), linguistic minority students, culturally and linguistically diverse (CLD) students, and more recently dual language learners (DLLs). In recent years, the designation of Limited English Proficiency has been discouraged owing to a deficit focus (Castro, Espinosa, & Paez, 2011). In the field of special education, the provision of services to CLD infants, toddlers, and preschoolers with a disability started with the passage in 1986 of the Amendments to the Education of the Handicapped Act and is now ensured by Part C of the 2004 reauthorization of the Individuals with Disabilities Education Improvement Act (IDEIA). This legislation makes the early provision of special services a mandated requirement for infants and toddlers with disabilities from birth through age 3, with a free and appropriate public education for children 3 to 5 years of age. The provision of these services often takes the form of wraparound services that focus on recommendations found in an Individualized Family Service Plan (IFSP) (IDEA, 2004). In accordance with Part C of the IDEA, an IFSP is as a guide that helps families navigate the process of early intervention for children with disabilities. The IFSP subsumes collaboration between family members and professionals who provide services to the children in the process of planning, implementation, and delivery of the early interventions. As such, an IFSP places the child's disability in the context of the family and their culture.

CLD students in early childhood face a variety of barriers and mitigating circumstances that place them at high risk for less optimal outcomes. Many children growing up in linguistically and culturally diverse homes often experience substantially fewer opportunity for language development, including limited opportunity to engage in literacy activities with parents impoverished home learning environments; infrequent access to books; less exposure to print media (Neuman & Roskos, 1993) and teachers unprepared to work with second languages. This lack of opportunity and access often translates into poorly developed oral language skills, placing them at high risk for early delays. The most salient among them are their low academic achievement that stems from low expectations from teachers, inadequate instruction, and the inappropriate assessment procedures and instruments that can result in the over-representation of CLD children among students receiving special education services (Xu & Drame, 2008). In order to improve the outcomes of early childhood services for CLD children, the National Association of School Psychologists (2006) published a position statement in which best practice early childhood assessment are described as being nondiscriminatory, technically and developmentally appropriate, and conducted by a multidisciplinary team who strives to link intervention strategies based on comprehensive, educational, and behavioral concerns expressed by families and school personnel.

These factors notwithstanding, difficulties experienced by CLD young children are confounded by the dual task of learning a second language as well as the content being taught. Not only are the younger CLD children prone to lag behind their English speaking peers academically, they also face an added risk for poor academic achievement when they lose the fluency they already have in their primary language. CLD children also tend to come from families who live in poverty and from parents who have low educational attainment. Latino children, in particular, face added challenges because they are more likely than their peers to come from parents with little education and who live in poverty (Halle et al., 2011). The combination of these factors places the culturally diverse early childhood population with disabilities as prime candidates for early intervention measures that are aimed at improving their future outcomes (Aud, Fox, & KewalRamani, 2010; Dinan, 2006).

In the process of early identification for special education services of CLD infants, toddlers, and preschoolers,

school personnel face the dual task of identifying a disability and ensuring that testing results cannot be better accounted for by linguistic or cultural differences between a CLD child and the test's norming sample. For example, it is not uncommon for the testing results of inappropriately conducted evaluations to fail to differentiate between a disability and a cultural/linguistic difference and thus misdiagnose students (Artiles & Ortiz, 2002). Examples of inappropriate evaluations include the use of assessment tools that have not been psychometrically validated to be used with linguistically diverse populations, the devalue of home languages other than English, and the use of teaching techniques that do not optimize the strengths of the CLD students' primary languages (Nieto, 2004). Comprehensive culturally competent assessment among the CLD population has, therefore, been advocated as a way to ensure that ethical standards proposed by professional associations such as the National Association of School Psychologists (NASP) and the National Association for the Education of Young Children (NAEYC) are followed in the process of determining if developmental trends or behaviors are due to a disability or to the student's diverse background. One way that professionals can ensure that multicultural attitudes, knowledge, and skills are incorporated into their practice include decisions pertaining to: (a) the language to use during assessment (dominant versus not), (b) what instruments and tests to administer, (c) the involvement of the culturally diverse families in the assessment process and (d) the best practices when dealing with interpreters (NAEYC, 2009; NASP, 2006). Furthermore, these professionals need to understand the evidence-based instructional strategies that are effective with CLD children. Some of these strategies include presenting CLD students with a challenging curricular content, setting high expectations for them, using technology effectively, recognizing sociocultural factors that affect the learning process, and utilizing their native languages and home environments as valuable resources for their learning (Artiles & Ortiz, 2002).

Another important aspect to attend to when dealing with CLD young students relates to how they are tested and the adaptation procedures applied during the process of conducting assessments that are comprehensive and culturally competent. Specifically, important adjustments in multicultural evaluations include allowing more time during the sessions, alternative assessment strategies (e.g., nonverbal measures and classroom observations), and allowing for additional interpretation questions (e.g., the roles played by the child's language, family, and culture in the findings) (Paéz, 2004).

REFERENCES

Artiles, A. J., & Ortiz, A. A. (2002). *English language learners with special education needs.* McHenry, IL: Center for Applied Linguistics and Delta Systems.

Aud, S., Fox, M., & KewalRamani, A. (2010). *Status and trends in the education of racial and ethnic groups (NCES 2010-015).*

U.S. Department of Education, National Center for Education Statistics. Washington, DC: U.S. Government Printing Office. Retrieved from http://nces.ed.gov/pubs2010/2010015.pdf

Castro, D., Espinosa, L. M., & Paez, M. (2011). Defining and measuring quality early childhood practices that promote dual language learners' development and learning. In M. Zaslow, I. Martinez-Beck, K. Tout, & T. Halle (Eds.), *Next steps in the measurement of quality in early childhood settings* (pp. 257–280). Baltimore, MD: Paul H. Brookes.

Cobo-Lewis, A. B., Pearson, B. Z., Eilers, R. E., & Umbel, V. C. (2002). Effects of bilingualism and bilingual education on oral and written Spanish skills: A multifactor study of standardized test outcomes. In D. K. Oller & R. E. Eilers (Eds.), *Language and literacy in bilingual children* (pp. 98–117). Clevedon, UK: Multilingual Matters.

Dinan, K. A. (2006). *Young children in immigrant families: The role of philanthropy. Sharing knowledge, creating services and building supportive policies.* New York, NY: National Center for Children in Poverty.

Farver, J. M., Xu, Y., Eppe, S., & Lonigan, C. J. (2006). Home environments and young Latino children's school readiness. *Early Childhood Research Quarterly, 21,* 196–212.

Halle, T., Hair, E., Wandner, L., McNamara, M., & Chien, N. (2011). Predictors and outcomes of early versus later English language proficiency among English language learners. *Early Childhood Research Quarterly,* doi:10.1016/j.ecresq.2011.07 .004. Retrieved from http://www.sciencedirect.com.lib-ezproxy .tamu.edu:2048/science?_ob=MiamiImageURL&_cid=272055 &_user=952835&_pii=S0885200611000603&_check=y&_ori gin=browse&_coverDate=19-Aug-2011&view=c&wchp=dGL bVBA-zSkzk&md5=e675e3411f8a0e04ed4b762ebb2855e1/1- s2.0-S0885200611000603-main.pdf

Individuals with Disabilities Education Improvement Act of 2004. P.L. 108-446 Sta. 2647 (2004). Retrieved from http:// www.copyright.gov/legislation/pl108-446.pdf

Miccio, A., Tabors, P., Páez, M., Hammer, C., & Wagstaff, D. (2005). Vocabulary development in Spanish-speaking Head Start children of Puerto Rican descent. In J. Cohen, K. McAlister, K. Rolstad, & J. MacSwan (Eds.), *ISB4: Proceedings of the 4th International Symposium on Bilingualism.* Somerville, MA: Cascadilla Press.

National Association for the Education of Young Children (2009). *Where we stand on assessing young English language learners.* Retrieved from http://www.naeyc.org/files/naeyc/file/ positions/WWSEnglishLanguageLearnersWeb.pdf

National Association of School Psychologists (2006). *NASP Position Statement on Early Childhood Assessment.* Retrieved from http://caspsurveys.org/NEW/pdfs/nasppp1.pdf

Neuman, S. & Roskos, K. (1993). Access to print for children of poverty: Differential effects of parent mediation and literacy-enriched play settings on environmental and functional print tasks. *American Educational Research Journal, 30,* 95–122.

Nieto, S. (2004). *Affirming diversity: The sociopolitical context of multicultural education* (4th ed.). Boston, MA/New York, NY: Pearson/Allyn & Bacon.

O'Bryon. E. C., & Rogers, M. R. (2010) Bilingual school psychologists' assessment practices with English language learners. *Psychology in the Schools, 47*(10), 1018–1034. doi: 10.1002/pits.20521

Páez, D. (2004). *Culturally competent assessment of English language learners: Strategies for school personnel.* Helping Children at Home and School II: Handouts for Families and Educators. National Association of School Psychologists. Retrieved from http://www.nasponline.org/resources/ culturalcompetence/cca_personnel.pdf

Tabors, P. O., Páez, M. M., & López, L. M. (2003). Dual language abilities of Spanish-English bilingual four-year-olds: Initial finding from the Early Childhood Study of Language and Literacy Development of Spanish-speaking children. *NABE Journal of Research and Practice, 1,* 70–91.

Xu, Y., & Drame, E. (2008). Culturally appropriate context: Unlocking the potential of response to intervention for English language learners. *Early Childhood Education Journal 35,* 305–311. doi: 10.1007/s10643-007-0213-4

CATHARINA CARVALHO
JORGE E. GONZALEZ
Texas A&M University

EARLY CHILDHOOD INTERVENTION, POSITIVE BEHAVIOR SUPPORT

Positive behavior support (PBS) is an approach that emerged in the late 1980s as a framework for developing and implementing effective supports and interventions in order to promote adaptive social behavior and to prevent and remediate maladaptive patterns of undesirable behavior. Positive behavior support is comprised of (a) an overall process of data-based problem solving and decision making, (b) a commitment to strength-based goals that are guided by person-centered values and the perspectives of direct and indirect consumers, (c) implementation of evidence-based prevention and intervention strategies, and (d) utilization of systems variables to help enhance implementation and sustainability. Positive behavior support has been used with individuals and groups across the life span, including young children and their families.

PBS in the context of early childhood intervention, like PBS in other contexts, is conceptualized best in the larger framework of prevention. The general framework of prevention that has been adopted by many authors in PBS is the tiered model derived from the fields of public and behavioral health (Simeonsson, 1991; Sugai et al., 2000; Walker, Colvin, & Ramsey, 1995). This framework is constructed usually of three tiers or levels, with the levels consisting of a hierarchy of interventions that increase in degrees of intensity, required effort and resources, and individualization. A widely adopted tiered model that addresses social-emotional development and challenging behaviors of young children is the "Pyramid Model" (Fox, Dunlap, Hemmeter, Joseph, & Strain, 2003). The Pyramid Model (Figure E.1) is based on two primary assumptions.

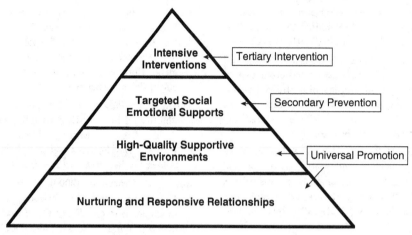

Figure E.1. The pyramid model.

The first assumption is that a child's problem behavior is related to the child's social-emotional and communication skill development. Children with normative social emotional skills, the ability to solve problems, well-developed communication skills, and the ability to regulate their emotions are less likely to have problem behavior. The second assumption is that early childhood practitioners and programs need a comprehensive range of strategies to address the social-emotional and behavioral needs of all children.

In the pyramid model framework, the *universal* level, relevant for all young children, consists of primary prevention practices intended to promote healthy social-emotional development and reduce the chances that a child will develop patterns of challenging behaviors. The universal level includes practices related to the development of nurturing and responsive relationships with children and the provision of environments that are characterized as safe, responsive, stimulating, instructive and comprehensible. Important universal practices include: actively supporting children's play and communication with others; providing specific praise and contingent positive attention; developing relationships with children and their families; collaborative teaming with colleagues; offering developmentally appropriate instructional activities; structuring transitions; supporting children's active engagement in activities; providing clear directions, and teaching rules and expectations explicitly (Hemmeter, Ostrosky, & Fox, 2006).

When children present with identified risk factors (e.g., poverty, maternal depression, learning or perceptual disabilities) and when children show signs of behavioral or social difficulties, secondary prevention strategies are implemented. This second tier of interventions is focused on the child's development of critical social emotional skills and may include the use of specialized social-emotional curricula (Joseph & Strain, 2003), individualized systematic teaching of social skills, and focused parent education programs. Secondary prevention efforts might focus on helping the child develop skills in self-regulation, social problem solving, friendship, identifying and expressing emotions appropriately, and cooperative responding. Data collection regarding these children's social-emotional development becomes more frequent and more individualized.

The third and top level of the pyramid calls for relatively intensive and individualized strategies that have been referred to as individualized PBS. These strategies are for young children with persistent challenging behaviors that have not been resolved satisfactorily with Tier 1 and 2 procedures. The PBS approach that has been commonly adopted for children with serious challenging behavior is comprised of five steps: (1) establishing a team and setting short- and long-term goals, (2) conducting a functional assessment of the child's challenging behaviors and deriving hypotheses that summarize the team's understanding of the relation between environmental factors and the occurrence and nonoccurrence of the targeted behaviors, (3) creating a multicomponent behavior support plan involving antecedent manipulations, instructional strategies and arrangements of positive reinforcement, redirection, and other consequences, (4) implementing the plan with high fidelity in all relevant environments, and (5) evaluating progress and making adjustments to the plan as necessary. This general approach has been described and evaluated many times over the past two decades and has been shown to be effective in home, preschool, and child care settings (Dunlap & Fox, 1996; 2009).

Positive behavior support (PBS) for young children has emerged in the past two decades as an approach that has been empirically validated on many levels. For individual children with serious challenging behaviors, a large number of investigations have demonstrated the efficacy of the PBS strategy with a variety of challenging behaviors (e.g., Conroy, Dunlap, Clarke, & Alter, 2005). Furthermore, researchers and practitioners have adopted PBS principles and procedures for application at classroom and program levels. Assessment and intervention strategies have been implemented across entire programs (e.g., preschool, Head Start) in order to promote healthy social-emotional development and prevent or resolve challenging behaviors for diverse populations of young children (Fox & Hemmeter, 2009). Although considerable research remains to be conducted, the promise of PBS in early intervention and for early childhood programs in general, has been clearly established.

REFERENCES

Conroy, M. A., Dunlap, G., Clarke, S., & Alter, P. J. (2005). A descriptive analysis of positive behavioral intervention research with young children with challenging behavior. *Topics in Early Childhood Special Education, 25,* 157–166.

Dunlap, G., & Fox, L. (1996). Early intervention and serious problem behaviors: A comprehensive approach. In L. K. Koegel, R. L. Koegel, & G. Dunlap (Eds.), *Positive behavioral support: Including people with difficult behavior in the community* (pp. 31–50). Baltimore, MD: Paul H. Brookes.

Dunlap, G., & Fox, L. (2009). Positive behavior support and early intervention. In W. Sailor, G. Dunlap, G. Sugai, & R. H. Horner (Eds.), *Handbook of positive behavior support* (pp. 49–71). New York, NY: Springer.

Fox, L., Dunlap, G., Hemmeter, M. L., Joseph, G. E., & Strain, P. S. (2003). The teaching pyramid: A model for supporting social competence and preventing challenging behavior in young children. *Young Children, 58*(4), 48–52.

Fox, L., & Hemmeter, M. L. (2009). A programwide model for supporting social emotional development and addressing challenging behavior in early childhood settings. In W. Sailor, G. Dunlap, G. Sugai, & R. H. Horner (Eds). *Handbook of positive behavior support* (pp. 177–202). New York, NY: Springer.

Hemmeter, M. L., Ostrosky, M., & Fox, L. (2006). Social and emotional foundations for early learning: A conceptual model for intervention. *School Psychology Review, 35*(4), 583–601.

Joseph, G. E., & Strain, P. S. (2003). Comprehensive evidence-based social-emotional curricula for young children: An analysis of efficacious adoption potential. *Topics in Early Childhood Special Education, 23,* 65–76.

Simeonsson, R. J. (1991). Primary, secondary, and tertiary prevention in early intervention. *Journal of Early Intervention, 15,* 124–134.

Sugai, G., Horner, R. H., Dunlap, G., Hieneman, M., Lewis, T. J., Nelson, C. M., . . . Wilcox, B. (2000). Applying positive behavior support and functional behavioral assessment in schools. *Journal of Positive Behavior Interventions, 2,* 131–143.

Walker, H., Colvin, J. & Ramsey., E. (1995). *Antisocial behavior in schools: Strategies and best practices.* Pacific Grove, CA: Brooks/Cole.

GLEN DUNLAP
University of South Florida

LISE FOX
University of South Florida
Fourth edition

EARLY EXPERIENCE AND CRITICAL PERIODS

Early experience has long been presumed to have great impact on later development. Even into the beginning of the 20th century, many lay people and professionals believed that experiences, particularly traumatic ones, suffered by a pregnant woman could be transmitted to the embryo or fetus through a form of prenatal imprinting. In his autobiography, Joseph Merrick, the "Elephant Man," for example, attributed his gross deformities to his mother's being pushed under an elephant during a parade (Howell & Ford, 1980). In what may be the first book devoted to mental retardation and related conditions in children, Ireland (1898, p. 24) suggested that:

> In all ages women have believed that fright or extreme distress is dangerous to their offspring, causing weakness, deformities, or deafness. . . . Mr. Paget gave a case where a young girl bore a great resemblance to a monkey, and had a crop of brown, harsh, lank hair on the back and arms. The mother had in an early period of pregnancy been terrified by a monkey jumping on her back from a street organ.

Both Merrick and Ireland were wrong (see Elephant Man entry in this volume) about the transmission of prenatal experiences to offspring; they were only among the first of many misclaims about the effects of early experience.

Early experience and critical periods have traditionally been given important roles in intellective, personality, social, and emotional development. Briefly, early experience is viewed as having greater and more lasting impact on development than merely prior experience. Events that occur during certain discrete early critical periods, during which development is rapidly occurring, may have irreversible effects on later behavior. A partial list of proposed critical periods is in Table E.1. Summaries of supporting research are in Denenberg (1972) and Scott (1978).

Persisting influence of early experience is implicit in the continuity position on development, which dominated both psychology and education for much of the 20th century. It holds that later development is continuous with, and thus grows out of, earlier behavior, which in turn is molded by early experience. As an example, Pasamanick and Knoblock (1966) proposed a continuum of reproductive casualty: The degree of perinatal insult suffered by a newborn directly relates to the degree of later impairment it will show. Thus, early plasticity and response to stimulation is replaced by later rigidity and resistance to change. The proposed generality of the continuity view was well expressed by Kelly (1955): "Whether one is an extreme hereditarian, an environmentalist, a constitutionalist, or an orthodox psychoanalyst, he is not likely to anticipate major changes in personality after the first years of life" (p. 659).

Beginning in the 1950s and 1960s, however, and burgeoning in the 1970s and 1980s, a number of researchers

Table E.1. Some Suggested Behavioral Critical Periods

Species	Early Manipulation	Later Effect
Precocial birds	Exposure to parent surrogate	Filial imprinting
Birds	Exposure to potential mate	Sexual imprinting
Mammals	Hormone presentation or removal	Sexual and agonistic behavior
Songbirds	Exposure to adult song; surgery	Acquisition of adult song
Mice	Exposure to noise	Susceptibility to audiogenic seizures
Cats and monkeys	Visual environment	Pattern vision; brain structure and function
Rats and mice	Mild stress	Resistance to stress
Rats	Rearing environment	Learning; brain structure and function
Dogs and monkeys	Social environment	Sexual and social behavior
Sheep and goats	Social environment	Mother-infant bond
Human infants and children	Exposure to toxins	Intellective and sensory functioning
Human children	Exposure to language; brain damage	Language acquisition
Humans	Social environment	Caretaker-infant bond
Human children	Rearing environment	Social, emotional, intellective functioning

and theorists began to produce data and reviews of previous research that supported the noncontinuity view that early experience and behavior did not necessarily predispose humans—or nonhumans for that matter—to particular later behavior (Brim & Kagan, 1980; Emde & Harmon, 1984; Erikson, 1950; Kagan, 1984; Kagan, Kearsley, & Zelazo, 1978; Kagan & Moss, 1962). As one example, Sameroff and Chandler (1975) found little evidence to suggest that degree of perinatal insult directly caused degree of later impairment. Most children who had suffered low or even moderate degrees of perinatal insult could not be differentiated from those who had suffered none. Problems were shown by children whose perinatal insult was combined with inadequate caretaking behavior. Sameroff and Chandler proposed a dynamic and interactive "continuum of caretaking casuality" to replace Pasamanick and Knoblock's linear "continuum of reproductive casuality." Lerner (1986) has provided a thoughtful discussion of the continuity-noncontinuity dispute.

Emphasis on early experience and critical periods initially came independently from two distinct disciplines: psychoanalysis and biology. In virtually all his writings on psychoanalysis and the psychodynamic theory of personality development, Sigmund Freud proposed that traumatic emotional experiences in infancy and early childhood had lasting, usually permanent, effects on personality. Such experiences, often of a sexual nature and involving the parents, were repressed into the unconscious where they later manifested themselves as neurotic behaviors. Freud viewed personality development as essentially complete and set by 6 years of age (Freud, 1938). Freud's views persist in many contemporary psychodynamically oriented theorists and practitioners. Some in the Freudian tradition

extended psychodynamic theory to account for psychoses. Bettelheim (1967), for example, proposed that autistic children withdraw into themselves and shut out others as a defense against their cold, hostile parents. Generations of parents were blamed for their children's schizophrenia and autism as well as other less disturbed behaviors. Others (Bowlby, 1951) proposed that early maternal deprivation would lead to later maladjusted behavior.

The biological concept of critical periods refers to times, generally in prenatal development, when organ systems are undergoing rapid differentiation. Early in embryonic development, tissue transplanted from a donor site to a host site develops as appropriate to the host site. If transplanted later, however, the tissue continues to develop as appropriate to the original donor site, demonstrating an irreversible loss of plasticity. Teratogens introduced during these critical periods activate irreversible changes in development, frequently producing gross abnormalities. Organ systems have individual, but largely overlapping, critical periods. Most end shortly after the embryonic period (8 weeks of gestation), but those for the central nervous system, eyes, and external genitalia extend well after birth (see Figure E.3 in Etiology entry, this volume). The classic, if tragic, example of a brief critical period for teratogenic action is that of thalidomide, a mild tranquilizer. Depending on when it was taken by the pregnant woman, between days 34 and 50 past her last menstrual period, thalidomide produced various finger, limb, external ear, and other anomalies in the fetus. Ingestion before day 34 or after day 50 had essentially no effect.

Thus, outside these critical periods, the developing embryo generally is well-buffered against adverse prenatal environmental influences through what Waddington

(1962) called canalization. In the absence of any adverse influence, the embryo is predicted to develop along its normal pathway. Gottlieb (1983) has cogently criticized the canalization concept as being little more than a new term for innate, and it indeed minimizes the role that a variety of experiences may play in pre- and postnatal development. However, canalization remains a useful descriptive term for biological influences, such as the thalidomide situation described earlier.

The importance of these biological influences cannot be exaggerated. The devastating and irreversible effects of numerous prenatal and postnatal experiences are well documented (e.g., Gandelman, 1992). Known prenatal teratogens include alcohol, antiseizure and anticancer medications, x-irradiation, maternal infections (toxoplasmosis, rubella, cytomegalovirus, herpes, syphilis, and HIV), and cocaine (Behnke & Eyler, 1993; Shriver & Piersel, 1994). Teratogens that can have major impact early in postnatal development include lead (e.g., Needleman, 1993). Also of concern are effects that may be seen as genetic in women but as prenatal environmental for embryos and fetuses. Consider women with phenylketonuria (PKU) who have received dietary treatment during their development. The diet largely prevents brain damage, and their IQs will approach normal. However, those with PKU have traditionally been taken off the diet no later than adolescence. Thus, when pregnant, women with PKU on normal diets transmit unmetabolized phenylalanine through the placenta, producing brain damage in their embryos and fetuses.

The ethologist Konrad Lorenz (1937) observed that newly hatched precocial birds such as ducklings and goslings appeared to form filial attachments that could not be reversed by later experiences only during short periods of time early in life. He thus provided evidence for a behavioral critical period. Later research (Hess, 1959) corroborated Lorenz's work. Further, particular experience seems to affect a variety of behaviors only if presented at particular times, and deprivation of experience beyond a certain point appears permanently to alter certain behaviors (see Table E.1). Researchers proposed, for example, that (a) early, but not later, rearing in complex environments improves rats' problem-solving performance and increases their brain weight; (b) rearing monkeys in social isolation for 1 year hinders permanently their acquisition of appropriate social behavior; (c) exposure to particular auditory stimuli during certain early periods only primes mice to have audiogenic seizures in later life; (d) human infants become imprinted or attached to their mothers only in the first 6 months of life; and (e) mothers can become adequately attached to their infants only in the first few days of life.

In an important theoretical paper, Scott (1962) proposed a "general principle of organization" that integrated biological and psychological critical periods:

Once a system becomes organized, whether it is the cells of the embryo that are multiplying and differentiating or the behavior patterns of a young animal that are becoming organized through learning, it becomes progressively more difficult to reorganize the system. That is, organization inhibits reorganization. Further, organization can be strongly modified only when active processes are still going on, and this accounts for critical periods of development (p. 11).

Regardless of the wealth of evidence for the importance of early experience and critical periods in development and functioning of biological systems, research suggests that many purported permanent effects of early behavioral experiences are either transitory, reversible, not as time-limited as originally thought, or not due to experience at all.

Some areas in which research questions a critical role of early experience are:

1. Early feeding, toilet training, and other experiences are not correlated with later behavior. In addition, although a few behaviors are stable over age, little consistency in personality is seen from infancy or even early childhood to adulthood (Kagan & Moss, 1962).

2. No overall continuum of reproductive casualty exists. In addition to Sameroff and Chandler's emphasis on interaction between infant characteristics and caretakers' behavior, perinatal insult appears to affect development according to threshold, rather than continuous model. Most children appear to recover from mild perinatal insult; recovery from severe insult is much less likely.

3. Some types of early experiences thought to be permanent are reversible under certain conditions and do not operate in the restricted time frame once proposed. For example, ducklings will show strong imprinting long after the normal end of the critical period if allowed sufficient time to follow the object (Brown, 1975). Of particular interest, monkeys raised in isolation for a year will develop a considerable amount of normal social behavior if put in the unusual therapeutic context of living with a young monkey (Suomi & Harlow, 1972).

4. A number of severely deprived children have shown surprising degrees of intellective and social development after initiation of intensive therapy (Clarke & Clarke, 1976; Skuse, 1984). Genie, a severely deprived child, is of particular interest because of her acquisition of language long after the purported critical period had ended.

5. Proposed critical periods for attachment of infants to their caretakers, and vice versa, have not been found by a variety of researchers.

6. Virtually no evidence supports the claim that certain disorders result from aberrant parental behavior. Parents were inappropriately blamed for their children's autism and schizophrenia for decades, regardless of evidence that the disorders have genetic or other organic origins (Torrey, 1977). However, children of schizophrenic mothers are themselves more likely to manifest schizophrenia if their adoptive parents are maladjusted than if their adoptive parents are normal.

7. As early deprivation may not necessarily produce irreversible deficits, so early enrichment does not necessarily produce lasting gains. Brief early intervention does not inoculate children against adverse environmental factors. On the other hand, programs such as Head Start do produce meaningful changes in children's behavior, and highly intrusive compensatory programs, such as the Abecedarian Project, have produced dramatic results.

8. Maternal deprivation, in and of itself, does not provide lasting deleterious effects on children (Rutter, 1981).

9. Children's personality characteristics once attributed to parental behavior (Baumrind, 1989; Kagan & Moss, 1962) are being reinterpreted. Directionality of relationships is questionable, since the data are largely correlational and could reflect children's influences on parents instead of parents' influences on children (Bell, 1968; Maccoby & Martin, 1983) or genetic influences (Plomin & McClearn, 1993). In a very controversial review of the literature, Harris (1995) has suggested that parents influence their children's behavior largely only within the home context and that socialization in other situations is largely through peer interactions.

10. The oft-proposed theory that work-related separations between a mother and young child have negative effects on the child's personality or development does not have consistent support. In one follow-up study of 6- to 7-year-old children whose mothers had worked during their first year of life, Barglow, Contreras, Kavesh, and Vaughn (1998) reported that maternal employment during their children's infancy had few adverse long-term consequences on the children's social behavior and none on IQ in children.

On the other hand, some early learning and other experiences may be necessary for appropriate later development or may predispose individuals to later inappropriate development. Indeed, Brown (1986) and Gottlieb (1991) proposed that behavioral canalization or experiential canalization, respectively, may, to an extent, parallel Waddington's biological canalization. Early learning experiences may predispose an infant or child to certain later behaviors that, in the absence of intense relearning, become highly prepotent in his or her repertoire. Further, the first 3 years of life are very important for brain development and differentiation. For decades, we have known that varied early environmental experiences increase brain development in animals (Bennett, Diamond, Krech, & Rosenzweig, 1964). More recently, evidence has accumulated supporting similar phenomena in humans (Schroeder, 1996; Shore 1997). Thus, we might expect early experiences to persist in the absence of some countering force. For example, parents of different socioeconomic status (SES) speak in very different amounts and ways to their children (Hart & Risley, 1995). Upper SES professional parents not only speak much more, but are more responsive, use more varied words and sentences, and use many more approvals and fewer prohibitions than do working-class or welfare parents. Of particular interest, overall family SES rating correlated positively with the children's IQs at 3 and 9 years of age. Unfortunately, interpretation is complicated by the fact that the authors did not statistically control for parents' IQs, leading to a confounding of environmental and possible genetic factors.

Early experience indeed plays an important role in development, but the degree of that role varies greatly with the type and timing of the experience. Evidence for critical periods in some areas of development is strong (Colombo, 1982; Gandelman, 1992). Further, evidence that change in normal development occurs throughout life and that effects of extreme deprivation can be partially countered with intensive therapy should not be misread as implying that plasticity is equivalent across life. Humans are more responsive to many types of experience at a relatively early age. Indeed, MacDonald (1985) suggests that plasticity declines with age and that more intense therapy may be necessary with older individuals. Similarly, Brown (1986) proposes a continuum of therapeutic environments, suggesting that the greater the degree of early impairment, the greater—and more unusual—may be the needed intervention. Recovery from some early experiences will occur only in response to therapies that are not part of the normal environment. Recovery from others that involve manifest brain damage may not be possible under any condition. A question of considerable current interest is whether recovery from early brain damage is more complete than recovery after later damage. Further, we need to distinguish between different types of early experiences and critical periods (Brown, 1981). Areas in which adverse early experiences have disrupted a developing organic system will be more resistant to therapy than areas where the experiences have resulted in the learning of particular behaviors. Early interference with organization of an organ system is likely to be permanent, whereas interference with the organization of behavior through learning can be overcome through relearning.

Parents should not be blamed for their children's autistic or schizophrenic behavior, nor should complete recovery of most such children, particularly autistic ones, be expected. Much recovery from early psychological deprivation or adverse conditions can be effected with sensitive and intensive therapy. Psychodynamic explanations of childhood and adult behavior in terms of infant experiences have little scientific support. Early intervention programs can be effective in increasing the intellective, emotional, and social development of high-risk infants and children, but they need to be intensive and long term (Bricker, Bailey, & Bruder, 1984; Ramey & Ramey, 1998). Finally, therapy or rehabilitation of children with manifest brain damage should be undertaken as soon as realistically possible in order to effect maximum recovery.

Those in special education should be aware of the varied ways in which prenatal and early postnatal experiences can affect children. Different educational approaches likely will be different owing not only to the types of experience children have had, but the way in which those experiences may have interacted with the children's own characteristics. Finally, and obviously, we should all be sensitive to the extent to which inappropriate behaviors that children show in school are likely to persist.

REFERENCES

Barglow, P., Contreras, J., Kavesh, L., & Vaughn, B. E. (1998). Developmental follow-up of 6–7 year old children of mothers employed during their infancies. *Child Psychiatry and Human Development, 29,* 3–19.

Baumrind, D. (1989). Rearing competent children. In W. Damon (Ed.), *Child development today and tomorrow* (pp. 349–378). San Francisco, CA: Jossey-Bass.

Behnke, M., & Eyler, F. D. (1993). The consequences of prenatal substance use for the developing fetus, newborn, and young child. *International Journal of the Addictions, 28,* 1341–1391.

Bell, R. Q. (1968). A reinterpretation of the direction of effects in studies of socialization. *Psychological Review, 75,* 81–95.

Bennett, E. L., Diamond, M. C., Krech, D., & Rosenzweig, M. R. (1964). Chemical and anatomical plasticity of the brain. *Science, 146,* 610–619.

Bettelheim, B. (1967). *The empty fortress: Infantile autism and the birth of the self.* New York, NY: Free Press.

Bowlby, J. (1951). Maternal care and child health. *Bulletin of the World Health Organization, 3,* 355–534.

Bricker, D., Bailey, E., & Bruder, M. B. (1984). The efficacy of early intervention and the handicapped infant: A wise or wasted resource. In M. Wolraich & D. K. Routh (Eds.), *Advances in developmental and behavioral pediatrics* (Vol. 5, pp. 331–371). Greenwich, CT: JAI.

Brim, O. G., Jr., & Kagan, J. (Eds.). (1980). *Constancy and change in human development.* Cambridge, MA: Harvard University Press.

Brown, R. T. (1975). Following and visual imprinting in ducklings across a wide age range. *Developmental Psychobiology, 8,* 187–191.

Brown, R. T. (1981). *Should we be sensitive about critical periods?* Annual meeting of the Psychonomic Society, Philadelphia, PA.

Brown, R. T. (1986). Etiology and development of exceptionality. In R. T. Brown & C. R. Reynolds (Eds.), *Psychological perspectives on childhood exceptionality: A handbook.* New York, NY: Wiley.

Clarke, A. M., & Clarke, A. D. B. (Eds.). (1976). Early experience: Myth and evidence. New York, NY: Free Press.

Colombo, J. (1982). The critical period concept: Research, methodology, and theoretical issues. *Psychological Bulletin, 91,* 260–275.

Denenberg, V. H. (Ed.). (1972). *The development of behavior.* Sunderland, MA: Sinauer.

Emde, R. N., & Harmon, R. J. (Eds.). (1984). *Continuities and discontinuities in development.* New York, NY: Plenum Press.

Erikson, E. (1950). *Childhood and society.* New York, NY: Norton.

Freud, S. (1938). *A general introduction to psychoanalysis.* New York, NY: Garden City.

Gandelman, R. (1992). *Psychobiology of behavioral development.* New York, NY: Oxford University Press.

Gottlieb, G. (1983). The psychobiological approach to developmental issues. In P. H. Mussen, M. M. Haith, & J. J. Campos (Eds.), *Handbook of child psychology* (4th ed., Vol. 2, pp. 1–26). New York, NY: Wiley.

Gottlieb, G. (1991). Experiential canalization of behavioral development: Theory. *Developmental Psychology, 27,* 4–13.

Harris, J. R. (1995). Where is the child's environment? A group socialization theory of development. *Psychological Review, 102,* 458–489.

Hart, B., & Risley, T. R. (1995). *Meaningful differences in the everyday experience of young American children.* Baltimore, MD: Paul H. Brookes.

Hess, E. H. 1959. Imprinting. *Science, 130,* 133–141.

Howell, M., & Ford, P. (1980). *The true history of the Elephant Man.* London, England: Allison & Busby.

Ireland, W. W. (1898). *Mental affections of children, idiocy, imbecility, and insanity.* London, England: J. & A. Churchill.

Kagan, J. (1984). *The nature of the child.* New York, NY: Basic Books.

Kagan, J., Kearsley, R., & Zelazo, P. (1978). *Infancy: Its place in human development.* Cambridge, MA: Harvard University Press.

Kagan, J., & Moss, H. A. (1962). *From birth to maturity.* New York, NY: Wiley.

Kelly, E. L. (1955). Consistency of the adult personality. *American Psychologist, 10,* 659–681.

Lerner, R. M. (1986). *Concepts and theories of human development* (2nd ed.). New York, NY: Random House.

Lorenz, K. (1937). The companion in the bird's world. *Auk, 54,* 245–273.

Maccoby, E. E., & Martin, J. A. (1983). Socialization in the context of the family: Parent-child relationships. In P. H. Mussen & E. M. Hetherington (Eds.), *Handbook of child development* (4th ed., Vol. 4, pp. 1–101). New York, NY: Wiley.

MacDonald, K. (1985). Early experience, relative plasticity, and social development. *Developmental Review, 5*, 99–121.

Needleman, H. L. (Ed.). (1993). *Human lead exposure.* Boca Raton, FL: CRC.

Pasamanick, B., & Knoblock, H. (1966). Retrospective studies on the epidemiology of reproductive casualty: Old and new. *Merrill-Palmer Quarterly, 12*, 7–26.

Plomin, R., & McClearn, G. E. (Eds.). (1993). *Nature, nurture, & psychology.* Washington, DC: American Psychological Association.

Ramey, C. T., & Ramey, S. L. (1998). Early intervention and early experience. *American Psychologist, 53*, 109–120.

Rutter, M. (1981). *Maternal deprivation reassessed* (2nd ed.). New York, NY: Penguin.

Sameroff, A. J., & Chandler, M. J. (1975). Reproductive risk and the continuum of caretaking casualty. In F. D. Horowitz, M. Hetherington, S. Scarr-Salapotek, & G. Siegel (Eds.), *Review of child development research* (Vol. 4). Chicago, IL: University of Chicago Press.

Schroeder, S. R. (1996). *Cognitive and neurological importance of first and early experience.* Paper presented at annual convention of the American Psychological Association, Toronto, Canada.

Scott, J. P. (1962). Critical periods in behavioral development. *Science, 138*, 949–958.

Scott, J. P. (Ed.). (1978). *Critical periods.* Stroudsburg, PA: Dowden, Hutchinson, & Ross.

Shore, R. (1997). *Rethinking the brain: New insights into early development.* New York, NY: Families and Work Institute.

Shriver, M. D., & Piersel, W. (1994). The long-term effects of intrauterine drug exposure: Review of recent research and implications for early childhood special education. *Topics in Early Childhood Special Education, 14*, 161–183.

Skuse, D. (1984). Extreme deprivation in early childhood-II. Theoretical issues and a comparative review. *Journal of Child Psychology & Psychiatry, 25*, 543–572.

Suomi, S., & Harlow, H. (1972). Social rehabilitation of isolate-reared monkeys. *Developmental Psychology, 6*, 487–496.

Torrey, E. F. (1977). A fantasy trial about a real issue. *Psychology Today, 10*(10), 24.

Waddington, C. H. (1962). *New patterns in genetics and development.* New York, NY: Columbia University Press.

ROBERT T. BROWN
University of North Carolina at Wilmington
First edition

WENDY L. FLYNN
Staffordshire University
Second edition

See also Abecedarian Project, The; Autism; Brain Damage; Etiology; Genie; Head Start; Thalidomide

EARLY INFANTILE AUTISM (*See* Autism)

EARLY SCREENING PROFILES

The Early Screening Profiles (ESP; Harrison et al., 1990) is a developmental screening test of young children ages 2 years 0 months through 6 years 11 months of age. It is designed to identify children who require further testing or early intervention services. The ESP is comprised of seven components: (1) the Cognitive/Language Profile, Motor Profile, (2) Self-Help/Social Profile, (3) Articulation Survey, (4) Home Survey, (5) Health History Survey, and (6) Behavior Survey. The parts may be used independently or in combination with other parts. Only three components (Cognitive/Language Profile, Motor Profile, and Articulation Survey) are administered directly to the child. Test administration time for these three components ranges from 15 to 30 minutes. The Cognitive/Language Profile consists of two cognitive subtests that measure nonverbal reasoning (Visual Discrimination and Logical Relations) and two language subtests that measure receptive and expressive language (Verbal Concepts and Basic School Skills). The Motor Profile consists of two subtests, assessing gross motor and fine motor skills. The Articulation Survey measures the child's speech production. The examiner completes the Behavior Survey, with regard to the child's behaviors during the test administration. The Home Survey (assessing aspects of home environment and parent-child interactions) and Health History Survey (a list of past and present health problems) are both brief questionnaires completed by the parent. The Self-Help/Social Profile is also a questionnaire completed by the parent and/or the child's teacher. It measures the child's performance of everyday activities required to take care of oneself and interact with others. The parent and teacher questionnaires take 10 to 15 minutes to complete.

Scoring the ESP occurs in two levels: Level I and Level II. Level I scoring yields numerical values of 1 to 6, indicating from below average to above average performance, for three Profiles (Cognitive/Language, Motor, and Self-Help/Social) and for a composite or Total Screening. Scores can be obtained quickly and directly from the tables packaged with the components. Level II scoring yields more detailed normative scores for the three Profiles and Total Screening, providing standard scores (M = 100, SD = 15), national percentile ranks, normal curve equivalents, stanines, and age equivalents. The Articulation, Home, and Behavior Surveys are scored only with descriptive categories (below average, average, or above average) and the Health History Survey is not scored.

The ESP was standardized on a sample of 1,149 children from 2 years 0 months through 6 years 11 months of age. The number of subjects in each of the five 1-year intervals ranged from 163 to 303. There were approximately equal distributions of males and females per group. Data from the 1985 and 1990 U.S. Census Bureau was used to stratify the sample on variables including age, sex, parent education, geographic region, and race/ethnicity. The sample matches the U.S. population well on all variables, although there are slight differences in parental education. The manual contains specific characteristics of the sample. A high degree of reliability was found of the profiles and Total Screening, with the exception of the Motor Profile and Behavior Survey, which were less reliable, and the Home Survey, which was quite low, which the author notes may be due to the diverse items on the scale.

Critiques of the ESP have been mixed. Telzrow (1995) reveals a favorable impression. She notes that the manual is comprehensive and detailed in its discussion of its development, technical adequacy, and scoring, including limitations to using age equivalents, which makes the ESP a "comprehensive addition to a total program in early childhood identification and service delivery." However, Barnett (1995) criticizes that the ESP lacks ecological validity and does not improve on the limitations of most screening instruments. Additional information may found about ESP at: http://www.nectac.org/~pdfs/pubs/screening.pdf or http://www.pearsonassessments.com/HAIWEB/Cultures/en-us/Productdetail.htm?Pid=PAa3500&Mode=summary.

REFERENCES

Barnett, D. W. (1995). AGS Early Screening Profiles. In J. C. Conoley & J. C. Impara (Eds.), *The twelfth mental measurements yearbook*. Lincoln, NE: Buros Institute of Mental Measurements.

Harrison, P. L., Kaufman, A. S., Kaufman, N. L., Bruininks, R. H., Rynders, J., Ilmer, S., . . . Cicchetti, D. V. (1990). *Early Screening Profiles manual*. Circle Pines, MN: American Guidance Service.

Telzrow, C. (1995). AGS Early Screening Profiles. In J. C. Conoley & J. C. Impara (Eds.), *The twelfth mental measurements yearbook*. Lincoln, NE: Buros Institute of Mental Measurements.

DEBRA Y. BROADBOOKS
California School of Professional Psychology

EATING DISORDERS

Eating disorders involve some form of disturbance in regular eating behaviors that is characterized as severe. Such disturbances can involve either eating too much or too little food. In addition, individuals with eating disorders usually experience feelings of emotional distress concerning body weight and shape.

The *Diagnostic and Statistical Manual of Mental Disorders*, fourth edition, text revision (*DSM-IV-TR*) recognizes three specific categories of eating disorders, anorexia nervosa, bulimia nervosa, and eating disorder not otherwise specified (American Psychiatric Association, 2000). Women who meet criteria for any of the three categories of eating disorder have higher rates of other psychopathologies than do women without eating disorders (Ekeroth, Broberg, & Nevonen, 2004).

Anorexia nervosa, a disease in which a person willfully resists maintaining a body weight that is at or above the health limit, affects an estimated 0.5% to 3.7% of females some time in their lifetime (American Psychiatric Association Work Group on Eating Disorders, 2000). People with anorexia nervosa may attempt to control weight through caloric restriction, excessive exercise, and purging (e.g., vomiting, using laxatives or other diuretics). Despite being underweight, many persons who suffer from anorexia develop obsessive fears of weight gain. Although many people recover from anorexia after receiving appropriate intervention services, mortality can result for those who do not seek or respond to treatment. Caucasian females constitute the most likely demographic group to report symptoms of anorexia nervosa.

Bulimia nervosa is another eating disorder in which individuals experience an obsessive fear of weight gain. However, unlike individuals who suffer from anorexia nervosa, people with bulimia nervosa usually maintain or exceed a healthy body weight. Bulimia nervosa is characterized by episodes of binge eating at least two times per week, in which a large amount of food is consumed in a small amount of time. During binge eating episodes, individuals frequently experience a lack of control and feelings of shame and guilt. In addition, people with bulimia nervosa attempt to compensate for their binge eating disorder through inappropriate behaviors, such as excessive exercise and/or purging.

Individuals whose eating disturbances that fall into the category of eating disorder not otherwise specified may exhibit symptoms consistent with anorexia nervosa or bulimia nervosa but do not meet full criteria for either diagnosis.

All three categories of eating disorders are considered culture-bound disorders. Eating disorders are more common in women than in men. Three culture-related conditions seemingly influence prevalence rates of eating disorders: eating behaviors, body image ideals, and perceptions of health (Markey, 2004). Twin studies have revealed the existence of an underlying genetic component (Bulik, Sullivan, Wade, & Kendler, 2000).

REFERENCES

American Psychiatric Association. (2000). *Diagnostic and statistical manual of mental disorders* (4th ed., text rev.). Washington, DC: Author.

American Psychiatric Association Work Group on Eating Disorders. (2000). Practice guideline for the treatment of patients with eating disorders (revision). *American Journal of Psychiatry, 157*, 1–39.

Bulik, C. M., Sullivan, P. F., Wade, T. D., & Kendler, K. S. (2000). Twin studies of eating disorders: A review. *International Journal of Eating Disorders, 27*, 2–20.

Ekeroth, K., Broberg, A. G., & Nevonen, L. (2004). Eating disorders and general psychopathology: A comparison between young adult patients and normal controls with and without self-reported eating problems. *European Eating Disorders Review, 12*, 208–216.

Markey, C. N. (2004). Culture and the development of eating disorders: A tripartite model. *Eating Disorders, 12*, 139–156.

ALLISON G. DEMPSEY
University of Florida

See also Anorexia; Bulimia Nervosa

ECHOLALIA

Echolalia is a strong tendency to repeat what has been said by another person (Benson & Ardila, 1996; Stribling, 2007). Echolalia has been noted in those with degenerative brain disease, psychosis (both children and adults), Tourette syndrome, childhood dysphasia, severe intellectual disabilities, autism spectrum disorders (ASD), and some forms of aphasia, as well as in some congenitally blind children (Cummings & Benson, 1989; Fay, 1980a; Stribling, 2007). Many typically developing children who acquire normal speech and language practice some echolalia during the developmental speech and language period of infancy and early childhood, although these echolatic behaviors generally disappear by 2.5 to 3 years of age (Fay, 1980a; Gerber, 2003; Loveland, McEvoy, & Tunali, 1990). A message may be repeated in its entirety or partially, with repetition usually following immediately after the initial presentation.

There are two types of echolalia: immediate and delayed echolalia. Immediate echolalia is the tendency to repeat what was just said, and is frequently associated with ineffective communication skills (Carr, Schreibman, & Lovass, 1975). Delayed echolalia is a form of echolalia in which the repetition of utterances made by oneself or others are stored and repeated at a later time, ranging from minutes to weeks. Repetition of television commercials, songs, and lines from movies by children with autism are examples of delayed echolalia. Unlike immediate repetitions, delayed echolalia may serve a communicative purpose (Rydell & Prizant, 1995). Children have been reported to use stored utterances to express an intention or to verbalize a behavioral self-reminder (Fay, 1980b; Stribling, 2007). An echoed utterance preceded or followed by an appropriate self-formulated comment evidences comprehension. The repetition seems to facilitate understanding in much the same manner as in typically developing adults and children when confronted with difficult messages.

REFERENCES

Benson, D. F., & Ardila, A. (1996). *Aphasia: A clinical perspective*. New York, NY: Oxford University Press.

Carr, E. G., Schreibman, L., & Lovass, O. I. (1975). Control of echolalic speech in psychotic children. *Journal of Abnormal Child Psychology, 3*, 331–351.

Cummings, J. L., & Benson, D. F. (1989). Speech and language alterations in dementia syndromes. In A. Ardila & F. Ostrosky (Eds.), *Brain organization of language and cognitive processes* (pp. 107–120). New York, NY: Plenum Press.

Fay, W. H. (1980a). Aspects of speech. In R. L. Schiefelbush (Ed.), *Language intervention series* (Vol. 5, pp. 21–50). Baltimore, MD: University Park Press.

Fay, W. H. (1980b). Aspects of language. In R. L. Schiefelbush (Ed.), *Language intervention series* (Vol. 5, pp. 53–85). Baltimore, MD: University Park Press.

Gerber, S. (2003). A developmental perspective on language assessment and intervention for children on the autistic spectrum. *Topics in Language Disorders, 23*, 74–94.

Loveland, K. A., McEvoy, R. E., & Tunali, B. (1990). Narrative story telling in autism and Down's syndrome. *British Journal of Developmental Psychology, 8*, 9–23.

Rydell, P. J., & Prizant, B. M. (1995). Assessment and intervention strategies for children who use echolalia. In K. A. Quill (Ed.) *Teaching children with Autism* (pp. 114–117). New York, NY: Delmar.

Stribling, P. (2007). Two forms of spoken repetition in a girl with autism. *International Journal of Language and Communication Disorders, 42*, 427–444.

K. SANDRA VANTA
Cleveland Public Schools, Cleveland, Ohio
First edition

ROBERT L. RHODES
New Mexico State University
Second edition

LESLIE C. NEELY
Texas A&M University
Fourth edition

See also Autism

ECHOPRAXIA

Echopraxia is defined as the involuntary and spasmodic imitation of movements made by another person (Goodwin, 1989). The imitation or repetition of body movements characteristic of echopraxia may be concomitant with a variety of disorders. Echopraxia serves as a diagnostic marker for specific developmental, psychiatric, and neurological disorders because of the frequent incidence of involuntary movement or gesture imitation associated with certain disorders. Echopraxic behavior is often a symptom of the low-incidence disorders of autism (Malvy et al., 1999), childhood schizophrenia (Schopler & Sloan, 2000), and Tourette syndrome (National Institute of Neurological Disorders and Stroke, 2000).

The imitative motor movements of a child with Tourette syndrome may represent one of the most common manifestations of echopraxia. The atypical gesture imitation of a child with autism or childhood schizophrenia with catatonic symptoms is also considered to be a type of echopraxia. Although no specific prevalence estimate is currently available for echopraxia as an isolated characteristic, the concomitant occurrence of echopraxia with childhood onset disorders underscores the importance of a clear understanding of this trait.

Characteristics

1. The child displays automatic imitation of another person's movements or gestures (e.g., scratching head or raising hand in air).
2. The imitation appears to be involuntary and occurs across a variety of settings and situations.
3. The child does not appear able to alter echopraxic behavior successfully despite frequent redirection and intervention attempts.
4. Periods of heightened anxiety and stress may result in more frequent occurrence.
5. Child may display additional behaviors and mannerisms that interfere with daily functioning (e.g., vocal tics or echolalic speech).

The neural mechanisms involved with echopraxia seem to differ from true voluntary imitation. In contrast to the involuntary and spasmodic nature of echopraxia, voluntary imitation usually represents a developmental milestone that is associated with typical growth and development (Rhodes, 2000; Stevenson, 1987). Echopraxia is also different from mirrored movements. The phenomenon of mirrored movements is observed when the simultaneous identical movement of one hand accompanies the voluntary movement of the other hand. Mirrored movements may be the result of a developmental delay in inhibition rather than a deficit in inhibition resulting in echopraxia (Rhodes, 2000; Stevenson, 1987).

A deficit in inhibition resulting in echopraxia may also be seen in individuals with frontal lobe lesions (Neurology and Neurosurgery Forum, 1997). Lesions in the frontal lobe may damage the regulatory system that assists individuals in deciding whether their bodies should move in response to stimuli or whether body movements should be inhibited. As a result, individuals with frontal lobe lesions and corresponding deficits in inhibition may move involuntarily in response to external movements or gestures.

The treatment of echopraxia is typically focused on the alleviation of symptoms through a regimen of behavioral interventions and medication. Depending on the severity of symptoms, children with Tourette syndrome, for example, may benefit from neuroleptic and antihypertensive medication in addition to biofeedback and behavioral interventions.

Special education services are typically available to children with echopraxia under the disability categories of autism, other health impairment, physical disability, or emotional/behavioral disability. Through the child's Individualized Education Plan (IEP), a prescriptive intervention plan is established that consistently implements behavioral interventions and modifications for motor-based tasks or assignments. The unusual behaviors associated with echopraxia and resulting social considerations may also be addressed through emotional-behavioral support for the child as well as peer education and sensitivity training.

There is currently no known cure for many of the disorders with which echopraxia is associated. Increased use of biofeedback and behavioral interventions in combination with advances in medicine may further assist individuals with echopraxia to control the involuntary symptoms that they experience.

REFERENCES

Goodwin, D. M. (1989). *A dictionary of neuropsychology*. New York, NY: Springer.

Malvy, J., Roux, S., Zakian, A., Debuly, S., Sauvage, D., & Barthelemy, C. (1999). A brief clinical scale for the early evaluation of imitation disorders in autism. *Autism, 3*(4), 357–369.

National Institute of Neurological Disorders and Stroke. (2000, August 1). *Tourette syndrome*. Retrieved from http://www.ninds.nih.gov/health_and_medical/disorders/tourette.htm

Neurology and Neurosurgery Forum (June 9, 1997). *Instantaneous dexterous reflex*. Retrieved from http://www.medhelp.org/

Rhodes, R. L. (2000). Echopraxia. In C. R. Reynolds & E. Fletcher-Janzen (Eds.), *Encyclopedia of special education* (2nd ed.). New York, NY: Wiley.

Schopler, E., & Sloan, J. L. (2000). Childhood schizophrenia. In C. R. Reynolds & E. Fletcher-Janzen (Eds.), *Encyclopedia of special education* (2nd ed.). New York, NY: Wiley.

Stevenson, R. J. (1987). Echopraxia. In C. R. Reynolds & L. Mann (Eds.), *Encyclopedia of special education*. New York, NY: Wiley.

ROBERT L. RHODES
New Mexico State University

ECOLOGICAL ASSESSMENT

The purpose of ecological assessment is to understand the complex interactions that occur between an individual who is the focus of assessment and his or her environment. Representing what is essentially an expansion of traditional behavior assessment techniques, ecological behavior assessment is similar to behavioral assessment with two important distinctions. First, in ecological behavior assessment, emphasis is placed on the quantification of behavior and its controlling environmental factors from a systems level perspective. That is, rather than focusing exclusively on molecular units of targeted behaviors and consequences directly responsible for their maintenance, the goal of ecological behavior assessment is to generate an understanding of the total behavior-environment system. This "system mapping" is typically accomplished through the measurement of behaviors and persons other than those to which an intervention is to be applied. For example, research conducted by Wahler (1975), in which observational data were taken on a variety of child behaviors, suggested that behavioral interventions targeted at a single response are likely to result in complex patterns of collateral and inverse changes in behavior within a child's repertoire. Second, in ecological behavior assessment, emphasis is placed on the measurement of existing patterns of teacher and student behavior with the goal of using this information in the development of intervention alternatives.

Given the complexity of the classroom ecology, how then is it possible to adequately assess the myriad interactions among behaviors of students, behaviors of students and teachers, and behaviors of students and teachers and the physical environment? With the finite nature of the assessment process and the functionally infinite possibilities for behavior-setting interactions, such a task would indeed be formidable. Fortunately, by drawing on concepts employed in the area of statistical analysis, the task need not be that of documenting all interactions but merely of observing those that contribute to a significant proportion of variance in possible classroom behavior.

The following steps, then, are presented as suggestions in the ecological assessment of behavior in any classroom setting. First, it is important to assess teacher expectations for what constitutes "good" and "bad" regularities in classroom behavior. Because teachers are typically the rule makers for such behavior, and because they are the individuals most responsible for making decisions regarding behavior appropriateness, assessment of their expectations is likely to provide an important criterion by which to evaluate intervention success.

Second, once teacher expectations for student behavior have been identified, the next step is to assess regularities in student behavior that actually exist in the classroom setting. Here it is necessary to identify and observe multiple categories of student behavior at both the individual and group level. Because of the emphasis of ecological behavior assessment on molar units of student behavior (i.e., patterns of behavior that occur across students), techniques such as momentary time sampling, sequential interval time sampling of several students chosen at random, self-monitoring, and review of permanent products may be useful in obtaining frequency measures at the group level. Whatever the technique employed, one goal of ecological behavioral assessment is to identify relative frequencies of both appropriate and inappropriate classroom behaviors that are descriptive for the class as a whole.

The third and perhaps most important task in the ecological assessment of classroom behavior is the identification of regularities in teacher behaviors. Whether they are aware of it or not, teachers play critical roles in the establishment of classroom ecology especially in the awareness of cross-cultural variables in the environment (Truscott & Truscott, 2005). They generate rules for behavior that are specific to the classroom setting and deliver consequences to children in accordance with these rules.

The fourth and final step in the ecological assessment of classroom behavior involves the assessment of behavioral processes. Specifically, once regularities in both teacher and student behavior have been identified, the issue becomes one of determining just how the behaviors in which the teacher engages are used to consequence the behaviors in which students engage. Through an ecological mapping of contingencies common to classroom settings, it becomes possible to draw comparisons between behaviors that teachers would like to encourage in students and behaviors that they actually do encourage through their interactions.

Ecological assessment can be time-consuming and complex, but it is often a rewarding process for truly understanding the behavior of children. The present summary draws heavily on the work of Kounin (1970), Gump (1975), Martens et al. (1999), and Reynolds, Gutkin, Elliott, and Witt (1984). Readers interested in cross-cultural aspects of ecological assessment are referred to Truscott and Truscott (2005).

REFERENCES

Gump, P. V. (1975). Ecological psychology and children. In M. Hetherington (Ed.), *Review of child development research* (Vol. 5). Chicago, IL: University of Chicago Press.

Kounin, J. S. (1970). *Discipline and group management in classrooms*. New York, NY: Holt, Rinehart & Winston.

Martens, B., Witt, J., Daly, E., & Vollmer, T. (1999). Behavior analysis: Theory and practice in educational settings. In C. R. Reynolds & T. B. Gutkin (Eds.), *The handbook of school psychology* (3rd ed., pp. 638–663). New York, NY: Wiley.

Reynolds, C. R., Gutkin, T. B., Elliott, S. N., & Witt, J. C. (1984). *School psychology: Essentials of theory and practice*. New York, NY: Wiley.

Truscott, S. D., & Truscott, D. M. (2005). Challenges in urban and rural education. In C. L. Frisby & C. R. Reynolds (Eds.), *Handbook of multicultural school psychology* (pp. 357–391). Hoboken, NJ: Wiley.

Wahler, R. G. (1975). Some structural aspects of deviant child behavior. *Journal of Applied Behavior Analysis, 8*, 27–42.

JOSEPH C. WITT
Louisiana State University

See also **Applied Behavior Analysis; Clinical Interview**

ECOLOGICAL EDUCATION FOR CHILDREN WITH DISABILITIES

Ecology refers, generally, to the study of the relationship between an organism and its environment. Although the roots of ecology as a field of study are found in early anthropology, the application of ecological theories, models, and principles in special education is relatively new. The first attempt to examine the interaction of environmental effects and certain persons with disabilities, and to specify related treatment approaches, is found in the works of Heinz Werner, Alfred A. Strauss, Lora Lehtinen, and William M. Cruickshank. These researchers of the 1940s, 1950s, and 1960s studied children with brain injuries and adults and the effects that various environmental stimuli had on their learning and overall behavior. An important concept derived from their research was the idea of the "stimulus-reduced" environment, first prescribed for classically brain-injured adults and children, then extended to certain "exogenous" mentally retarded children, and finally to children with learning disabilities. Although this work began in the 1940s, these researchers, and those who built on their pioneering efforts, did not refer formally to their efforts as ecological in nature. The term *ecology* itself, derived primarily from the biological sciences, surfaced as an educational variable with studies of emotionally disturbed children in the late 1960s and early 1970s.

The most notable contributions to the field include the work of Hobbs (1966) with Project Re-Ed and the University of Michigan studies in child variance (Feagans, 1972). Project Re-Ed recognized that many of the socialization problems experienced by so-called emotionally disturbed children did not have a locus within the child. Rather, problems existed in the interaction between the labeled child and the important social institutions in which he or she acted. Because there was a bad fit between child and environment (i.e., home, family, school, community), it was necessary to remove the child temporarily from this failure situation, not just to work with the child, but also to change contributing factors in the environment. Although specially trained teachers aided the student, social services personnel and mental health consultants worked with the significant others in the child's world before re-merging the two again. Segregation was to be as brief as possible; normalization was always the goal.

The Michigan work, accomplished within the university's Institute for Mental Retardation and Related Disorders, reviewed, integrated, and synthesized the research, theories, and conceptual models bearing on childhood emotional disturbance. The group then developed and implemented various dissemination and training activities based on their synthesis of differing approaches to emotional disturbance. Though ecological theory was only one of six major approaches studied, the Michigan efforts helped in large part to enhance the role of ecological theory in special education.

Broadly, the ecological approach to the study and treatment of emotionally disturbed and other children with disabilities attempts to break down traditional views of disabilities as something found exclusively in the involved child. The disturbance is not intrinsic per se, but a description of the interaction of a particular child with a particular environment. The search is for the source of the mismatch in the ecosystem. The study of the child occurs not in the sterility of the psychological laboratory, but in the naturalistic, real-world, holistic settings in which the child's problems occur. This is not to deny that emotional disturbance, or mental retardation, or learning disabilities are not real, or that problems in learning or adjustment that certain children experience may not have contributing neurological or biochemical substrata. The ecological focus in special education tries to show that looking only at internal factors cannot give the whole picture, and that treatment approaches based on simplified, historical, etiological views can limit the success parents and professionals might have with handicapped learners.

Because a purely medical, psychological, or multicultural explanation alone is not sought when students with disabilities are viewed through ecological theory, a multidisciplinary team approach to diagnosis, classification, education, and treatment emerges. Special education ecologists look not only at how the child acts on his or her environment, but how the environment in its broadest sense acts on the child. Rather than overemphasize causal factors, proponents of the ecological approach seek to find or establish a state of equilibrium between child and surroundings. Specific coping skills may be taught to bring about a greater match between the child's behavior and the expectations placed on him or her by the physical and social environment. Rather than just attempting to change, or cure, what is purportedly going on within the child, the ecological special educator seeks to study the cultural relativity of the child's behavior, and adaptation (or synomorphy) between child and environment. The focus is on the reciprocity of behavior and reaction. Algozzine, Schmid, and Mercer (1981) ask: Is the disturbance merely in the eye of the beholder? Is the child really disturbed, or just disturbing?

The ecological approach to special education goes by many names. It has been termed environmental psychology, architectural psychology, ecological psychology, sociophysical technology, person-environment relations, man-environment studies, and environmental design cybernetics (Preiser & Taylor, 1983). Ecological principles have been used to examine not only brain-injured and socially/emotionally maladjusted students, but also children and youths with other conditions. Some of these studies found, for example, that the mere proximity of toys led to greater interaction and gradual expansion of the recreation setting for individuals with severe/profound disablities (Wehman, 1978). Other writers (Marsh & Price, 1980) looked into the interaction of environmental variables such as flexibility of school settings and information reception or reading disabilities and academic achievement, in secondary-age learning-disabled youth. Sarason and Doris (1979) coined the phrase "iatrogenic educable mental retardation" in describing the school-related disabilities found in learners from lower socioeconomic status backgrounds. Autistic, brain-injured, and normal children have been shown to demonstrate differential social responses to the density of the class or group setting in which they are placed (Hutt & Viazey, 1966). Even classroom lighting amounts and types have been examined to determine any possible effects they may have on student learning and behavior (Fletcher, 1983). As Zentall (1983) notes, professionals place regular and special education students in learning environments for about 1,100 hours per year, without any empirical basis for the design of that environment—a design that, to a large extent, can be modified or controlled.

Though special and regular educators have shown cognizance of the environmental needs of certain physically and sensorily disabled children (e.g., preferential seating for the hard of hearing, plant modifications for children with physical disabilities, magnifiers and enlarged

materials for partially sighted students), they still have not totally embraced the prosthetic environments described by behavioral engineers such as Ogden Lindsley (1964). Ecologists in the field would claim that special educators should continue to move away from the former child-focus approach, and more toward a pedagogy in which they test, observe, and teach in the real-world settings where skills must ultimately be generalized and successfully demonstrated if they are to say that learning truly has occurred (Hutchins & Renzaglia, 1983). Ecologically valid assessment has moved forward in recent years due to the increase of cultural competency expectations for teachers and researchers in special education (Frisby & Reynolds, 2005).

REFERENCES

Algozzine, B., Schmid, R., & Mercer, C. D. (1981). *Childhood behavior disorders: Applied research and educational practice.* Rockville, MD: Aspen.

Feagans, L. (1972). Ecological theory as a model for constructing a theory of emotional disturbance. In W. C. Rhodes & M. L. Tracy (Eds.), *A study in child variance* (Vol. 1). Ann Arbor: University of Michigan Press.

Fletcher, D. (1983). Effects of classroom lighting on the behavior of exceptional children. *Exceptional Education Quarterly, 4*(2), 75–89.

Frisby, C. L., & Reynolds, C. R. (2005). *The handbook of multicultural school psychology.* Hoboken, NJ: Wiley.

Hobbs, N. L. (1966). Helping disturbed children: Psychological and ecological strategies. *American Psychologist, 21,* 1105–1115.

Hutchins, M. P., & Renzaglia, A. (1983). Environmental considerations for severely handicapped individuals: The needs and the questions. *Exceptional Education Quarterly, 4*(2), 67–71.

Hutt, C., & Viazey, J. M. (1966). Differential effects of group density on social behavior. *Nature, 209,* 1371–1372.

Lindsley, O. R. (1964). Direct measurement and prosthesis of retarded behavior. *Journal of Education, 147,* 62–81.

Marsh, G. E., & Price, B. J. (1980). *Methods for teaching the mildly handicapped.* St. Louis, MO: Mosby.

Preiser, W. F. E., & Taylor, A. (1983). The habitability framework: Linking human behavior and physical environment in special education. *Exceptional Education Quarterly, 4*(2), 1–15.

Sarason, S. B., & Doris, J. (1979). *Educational handicaps, public policy and social history.* New York. NY: Free Press.

Wehman, P. (1978). Effects of different environmental conditions on leisure time activity of the severely and profoundly handicapped. *Journal of Special Education, 12*(2), 183–193.

Zentall, S. S. (1983). Learning environments: A review of physical and temporal factors. *Exceptional Education Quarterly, 4*(2), 90–115.

JOHN D. WILSON
Elwyn Institutes

See also Ecological Assessment

ECSTASY ABUSE

Ecstasy (3,4-methylenedioxymethamphetamine, or MD-MA) is a popular party drug that has a chemical structure similar to amphetamine and mescaline, a hallucinogen (McCann, Mertl, & Ricaurte, 1998). Ecstasy belongs to a group of drugs known collectively as "club drugs" because they are frequently used at dance clubs and all-night dance parties called raves (Stocker, 2000). Ecstasy is typically sold on the street in pill form and is ingested orally. It is also sold as a powder that can be snorted, smoked, or injected. Street names besides ecstasy include "XTC," "clarity," "essence," "Adam," and "X" (National Institute on Drug Abuse [NIDA], 1999).

Ecstasy results in a high by stimulating the release of the neurotransmitter serotonin in the neurons (NIDA, 1999). Serotonin plays a direct role in regulating mood, aggression, sleep, sexual activity, and sensitivity to pain (NIDA, 2001). Ecstasy use can result in both psychedelic and stimulant effects that can last from several minutes to an hour. Users report feelings of peacefulness, empathy, and acceptance, as well as an enhanced sense of pleasure, self-confidence, and increased energy. In addition, ecstasy can result in feelings of closeness with others and a desire to touch them. The effects related to intimacy and trust have led some clinicians to suggest that ecstasy has some potential value as a psychotherapeutic agent. However, the federal government has classified ecstasy as a drug with no accepted medical use (NIDA, 1999).

Research examining general drug use trends among America's youth indicates that use remained relatively stable over the past 2 years, except for ecstasy and steroids. For these drugs, increases were observed across grade levels. For 8th graders, past-year use of ecstasy increased from 1.7% in 1999 to 3.1% in 2000. For 10th graders, the increase was from 4.4% to 5.4%; and for 12th graders, past-year use rose from 5.6% in 1999 to 8.2% in 2000. Reported use is significantly higher among White and Hispanic students than among African Americans. Data for adolescents indicate that 7.6% of Whites and 10.6% of Hispanics reported using ecstasy in 2000, whereas only 1.3% of African Americans reported using the drug during the same year (NIDA, 2001).

Short-Term Effects

1. Euphoria
2. Elevated self-confidence
3. Heightened sensory awareness
4. Increased feelings of empathy and closeness with others
5. Decreased appetite
6. Elevated anxiety and paranoia
7. Increased heart rate and blood pressure
8. Dizziness and confusion
9. Chills, sweating, faintness, and vomiting
10. Malignant hyperthermia
11. An acne-like rash

Ecstasy's rewarding and negative effects vary with the dose and purity of the drug, the environment in which it is taken, and the individual user (NIDA, 1999). Both short- and long-term use of ecstasy can result in a variety of adverse, long-lasting effects (NIDA, 2001).

Long-Term Effects

1. Panic disorder
2. Psychosis
3. Flashbacks
4. Major depressive disorder
5. Addiction
6. Brain damage

Chronic use of ecstasy has been found to harm brain neurons that release serotonin, which can result in persistent cognitive disturbances and memory problems (Mathias, 1999). Ecstasy may also cause degeneration of neurons containing the neurotransmitter dopamine. Damage to these neurons can cause motor disturbances (NIDA, 2001). A number of ecstasy-related deaths have also been reported. The stimulant effects of ecstasy can enable the user to dance for long periods, and often the end result is dehydration, hyperthermia, and heart or kidney failure (NIDA, 1999).

Most students who use ecstasy will not qualify for special education services, although psychological services may be warranted.

With the increase in the use of ecstasy and other club drugs, NIDA recently announced an increase of 40% in its funding for research on club drugs. NIDA has also joined a multimedia campaign with other national organizations to educate the public about the dangers of these drugs (NIDA, 1999). Future research is also focusing on determining more specifically the extent of long-term negative effects that result from ecstasy use, as well as evaluating the eficacy of various prevention programs and therapeutic interventions.

REFERENCES

Mathias, R. (1999). *"Ecstasy" damages the brain and impairs memory humans*. Retrieved from http://www.drugabuse.gov/

McCann, U. D., Mertl, M., & Ricaurte, G. A. (1998). Ecstasy. In R. E. Tarter, R. T. Ammerman, & P. J. Ott (Eds.), *Handbook of substance abuse: Neurobehavioral pharmacology* (pp. 567–577). New York, NY: Plenum Press.

National Institute on Drug Abuse. (1999). *Facts about MDMA (ecstasy)*. Retrieved from http://www.drugabuse.gov/

National Institute on Drug Abuse. (2001). *MDMA (ecstasy)*. Retrieved from http://www.drugabuse.gov/

Stocker, S. (2000). Overall teen drug use stays level, use of MDMA and steroids increases. Retrieved from http://www.drugabuse.gov/NIDA_Notes/NNVol15N1/Overall.html

M. Franci Crepeau-Hobson
University of Northern Colorado

ECTODERMAL DYSPLASIA

Ectodermal dysplasia refers to a group of genetic disorders that involve abnormalities in the layer of cells known as the ectoderm. During prenatal development, the ectoderm is the outer layer of cells in the fetus that grow into the skin, hair, nails, teeth, nerve cells, sweat glands, and parts of the ear, eye, and other organs (National Foundation for Ectodermal Dysplasias [NFED] Scientific Advisory Board, 2000). The prevalence of ectodermal dysplasias of all types is estimated to be as high as 7 of every 10,000 births (NFED Scientific Advisory Board, 2000).

Different forms of ectodermal dysplasia are evidenced by different constellations of the characteristics. Most forms of ectodermal dysplasia involve at least two of the characteristics listed here.

Characteristics

1. Fair skin, skin rashes (especially severe diaper rash in infants), extremely dry skin
2. Frequent high fevers, inability or diminished ability to sweat, very low heat tolerance
3. Absent or very sparse and fine scalp hair; absence of eyebrows, eyelashes, and other body hair
4. Thin, ridged, cracked, brittle, small, or poorly developed nails
5. Eruption of some or all teeth delayed or absent, malformed teeth, widely spaced teeth, excessive tooth decay
6. Underproduction of bodily fluids such as tears and saliva
7. Hearing or vision loss
8. Cleft lip or cleft palette

Ectodermal dysplasia is caused by a gene mutation that is inherited or a new mutation that occurs during fetal development. Some types of ectodermal dysplasias are sex-linked and occur more often in males, whereas others are transmitted on autosomal chromosomes and occur equally frequently in both genders (NFED Scientific Advisory Board, 1999).

Treatment for ectodermal dysplasia is palliative and aimed at the constellation of characteristics evident in the individual affected. Moisturizing ointments and sunscreens are used to prevent damage to the skin. Missing teeth are replaced by bridges, dentures, or implants. Avoiding excessive heat, taking cool baths, and intaking fluids is recommended for those with a decreased ability to sweat. Lubricating eyedrops and saliva substitutes should be used by those with decreased tear and saliva production. In cases of ectodermal dysplasia that result in cleft lip or palette, corrective surgery is available (NFED Scientific Advisory Board, 2000).

Ectodermal dysplasia is not associated with deficits in intelligence or developmental delays (NFED Scientific Advisory Board, 1999). Some classroom modifications may be needed for those individuals with inadequate sweat production (such as an air-conditioned classrooms or removal of physical education requirements). Children with ectodermal dysplasia are eligible for needed modifications under the Other Health Impairment handicapping condition. In those cases where cleft lip or cleft palette is involved or where hearing loss develops, children may qualify for special education services, in particular speech therapy. Children with ectodermal dysplasia differ in appearance from most other children and may suffer adjustment problems in school if they are ridiculed or ostracized by others as a result of their appearance. Teachers and school administrators should take whatever steps are necessary to prevent this behavior toward affected children.

Ectodermal dysplasia is not a progressive disorder. The life spans of affected individuals tend to be normal (NFED Scientific Advisory Board, 2000). Genetic counseling may be helpful to those with ectodermal dysplasia or with a family history of it in order to determine their risks of transmitting the disorder to their progeny. Recent research has isolated the gene for one common type of ectodermal dysplasia (NFED Scientific Advisory Board, 2000). Researchers are also working to determine what protein or enzyme deficiency is responsible for ectodermal dysplasia in order to develop treatments that address the root cause of the disorder (NFED Scientific Advisory Board, 2000).

REFERENCES

National Foundation for Ectodermal Dysplasias Scientific Advisory Board. (2000). *A family guide to the ectodermal dysplasias*. Mascoutah, IL: National Foundation for Ectodermal Dysplasias.

National Foundation for Ectodermal Dysplasias Scientific Advisory Board. (1999). *The multi-syndrome guide to the ectodermal dysplasias*. Mascoutah, IL: National Foundation for Ectodermal Dysplasias.

NANCY K. SCAMMACCA
University of Texas at Austin

See also APECED Syndrome; Hypohidrotic Ectodermal Dysplasia; Rapp-Hodgkin Syndrome

ECTRODACTALY ECTODERMAL DYSPLASIA (EEC SYNDROME)

Ectrodactyly ectodermal dysplasia is a rare form of ectodermal dysplasia involving missing or webbed fingers and/or toes, cleft lip and/or palate, and abnormalities of the eyes and urinary tract in addition to the aberrations normally present with ectodermal dysplasia, such as usually dry hair, light colored and sparse eyebrows, dry skin, and missing teeth or teeth lacking enamel. Ectodermal dysplasias are a group of inherited syndromes derived from the ectodermal germ layer.

EEC syndrome is a rare autosomal dominant genetic trait in which symptoms vary greatly. Prevalence is unknown, and treatment is symptomatic. Surgery can be performed to correct abnormalities of the fingers and toes as well as cleft palate and lip. Families dealing with children with EEC syndrome could benefit from genetic counseling. Overall, a team of specialists is required to manage the treatment and amelioration of complications associated with this disorder. With the aid of this multidisciplinary team, children affected with ectrodactyly ectodermal dysplasia can lead long lives.

Characteristics

1. The individual has missing or irregular fingers and/or toes, commonly seen in the third digit.
2. There are abnormalities of the eyes in which the glands needed to allow tears to escape and to secrete fluid onto the back of the eyelid are absent, triggering frequent eye infections as well as vision problems.
3. Cleft palate and cleft lip are common; however, if these conditions are not present, an underdeveloped jaw, broad nose, slanted or widely spaced eyes, and a short groove in the center of the upper lip may still be present.
4. In some cases, an obstructed tube carrying urine from the kidney into the bladder causes kidney and pelvis inflammation. A deleted or duplicate kidney has been documented in some cases.

Special education issues also vary greatly among these children. Although some children present with mental retardation, many cases of normal mental functioning have been documented. However, even if mental deficits are not present, remediation may become necessary in children who present with hearing loss, speech difficulties, and visual impairment or loss, all of which are commonly found in children with EEC syndrome.

Prognosis is generally good, but symptomology varies greatly between cases. Individualized assessment on a case-by-case basis is necessary. The most serious complication of EEC syndrome is kidney difficulties, but even these can be treated effectively. Future research includes genetic mapping in an attempt to find a cure and more effective treatment.

This entry has been informed by the sources listed below.

REFERENCES

Buss, P. W., Hughes, H. E., & Clarke, A. (1995). Twenty-four cases of the EEC syndrome: Clinical presentation and management. *Journal of Medical Genetics, 32*(9), 716–723.

Jones, K. L. (Ed.). (1997). Smith's recognizable patterns of human malformation (5th ed.). Philadelphia, PA: W. B. Saunders.

Miller, C. I., Hashimoto, K., Shwayder, T., el-Hoshy, K., & Horton, S. (1997). What syndrome is this? Ectrodactyly, ectodermal dysplasia, and cleft palate (EEC) syndrome. *Pediatric Dermatology, 14*(3), 239–240.

KIMBERLY M. ESTEP
University of Houston–Clear Lake

EDGERTON, ROBERT B. (1931–   )

Robert Edgerton was introduced to the study of mental retardation at the Pacific State Hospital, California, after completing his PhD in anthropology (1960) from the University of California, Los Angeles (UCLA). He has taught at UCLA since that time in the departments of psychiatry and anthropology, becoming professor in 1972 and an administrator of socio-behavioral studies in the Mental Retardation Research Center in 1970.

Edgerton provided major contributions to the study of mental retardation primarily through his intensive and atypical methods of research. As a strong advocate of participant/observation and the qualitative approach to gathering scientific data, he conducted research using anthropological perspectives and methodologies.

At a time when deinstitutionalization is in practice, the qualitative results of Edgerton's research have been useful for social policy evaluation. He has provided insights into the everyday lives of persons with intellectual delay and developmental disabilities that directly affected the design of community residential policies and criteria for reinstitutionalization. Author of over 75 books, articles, and monographs, Edgerton's principal publications include *The Cloak of Competence, Mental Retardation,* and *Environments and Behavior: The Adaptation of Mentally Retarded Persons.* His work has been featured in Schalock and Siperstein's (1996) publication, *Quality of Life,* dealing with the conceptualization and measurement of quality of life for persons with intellectual delay and developmental disabilities.

This entry has been informed by the sources listed below.

REFERENCES

Edgerton, R. B. (1967). *The cloak of competence.* Berkeley and Los Angeles: University of California Press.

Edgerton, R. B. (1979). *Mental retardation.* Cambridge, MA: Harvard University Press.

Kernan, K., Begab, M., & Edgerton, R. B. (Eds.). (1983). *Environments and behavior: The adaptation of mentally retarded persons.* Baltimore, MD: University Park Press.

Schalock, R. L., & Siperstein, G. N. (Eds.). (1996). *Quality of life: Vol. 1. Conceptualization and measurement.* Washington, DC: American Association on Mental Retardation.

ELAINE FLETCHER-JANZEN
Chicago School of Professional Psychology
First edition

TAMARA J. MARTIN
The University of Texas of the Permian Basin
Second edition

EDUCABILITY

Is a term no longer used in education science, but the term is relevant to our history. In its broadest sense, educability

refers to the likelihood of a child diagnosed with intellectual developmental disabilteis benefiting from and progressing in a course of education. The term has become part of the nomenclature because historically children were classified by their "educability." In fact, the concept of educability can be viewed as the driving force behind the development and growth of psychometrics.

In 1904 Alfred Binet was charged with developing a process by which children unlikely to pass a standard curriculum could be identified and placed in alternative settings or excluded altogether. Working from a viewpoint that normal children achieved certain developmental stages at predictable rates, Binet and his associate Theodore Simon developed an instrument for evaluating a child's mental age. This allowed for projections of the child's functioning in school and for more heterogeneous groupings.

Although the concept of intellectual developmental disabilities had long been accepted as a separate entity, Binet's scale had the unexpected side effect of demonstrating that the differences were on a quantitative continuum rather than being qualitatively distinct. A new group of individuals emerged. MacMillan (1977) points out that such individuals were identified prior to intelligence testing, because they were generally able-bodied, socially competent, and typical looking. Only when placed in academic situations were their learning difficulties recognized.

In 1969, this led to what the President's Committee on Mental Retardation termed the "six-hour retardate." This is the child who is considered challenged only during that period of the day that he or she is in school, and who is indistinguishable from others for the remaining time. By extension, many of these individuals are fine leaving school and entering the workforce.

In addition, these individuals often have marked language difficulties and decreased personal/social skills. Lambert, Wilcox, and Gleason (1974), Sedlak and Sedlak (1985), and the American Association on Mental Retardation (2006) provide more in-depth analyses of the issues related to assessment, programming, and expectations for these children.

REFERENCES

American Association on Mental Retardation. (2005). *AAMR home page.* Retrieved from http://www.aamr.org

Grossman, H. J. (1973). *Manual on terminology and classification in mental retardation.* Washington, DC: American Association on Mental Deficiency.

Lambert, N. M., Wilcox, M. R., & Gleason, W. P. (1974). *The educationally retarded child: Comprehensive assessment and planning for slow learners and the educable mentally retarded.* New York, NY: Grune & Stratton.

MacMillan, D. C. (1977). *Mental retardation in school and society*. Boston, MA: Little, Brown.

Sedlak, R. A., & Sedlak, D. M. (1985). *Teaching the educable mentally retarded*. Albany: State University of New York Press.

DENNIS M. FLANAGAN
Montgomery County Intermediate Unit, Norristown, Pennsylvania

See also AAIDD, American Association on Intellectual Developmental Disabilities; Intellectual Disability; Six-Hour Retarded Child

EDUCABLE INTELLECTUALLY DEVELOPMENTALLY DELAYED (See Intellectually Developmentally Delayed)

EDUCATEUR

The educateur, sometimes referred to as the psychoeducateur, is a trained generalist whose primary concern goes beyond that of the traditional teacher's interest in student learning to include a focus on the personality and emotional development of the child (Morse & Smith, 1980). The role of the educateur dates to the years immediately following World War II, when the presence of large numbers of displaced emotionally disturbed children (victims of the psychological traumas of war) were identified in France and Scotland (Daly, 1985). Inadequate numbers of qualified mental health workers to meet the many needs of these children led to the development of a new profession, that of the educateur, a professional trained in the skills of teaching, social work, psychology, and recreation.

In the mid-1950s in Canada, Guindon (1973) adapted the European educateur model for use with delinquent and emotionally disabled children and youths. Guindon's psychoeducateur intervention had an ecological orientation, emphasizing the significance of change in the child's environment and using interventions associated with other perspectives.

Drawing from a combination of psychodynamic and developmental approaches, educateur treatment seeks to restructure completely all activities and relationships in the child's environment. To accomplish this, the child is placed in a residential setting for an average period of 18 months. Here, the educateur initially works to provide a highly structured environment with maximum external control. Then external controls are gradually reduced with concomitant increase in flexibility and individual expression for the child.

Linton (1971) described the educateur working in these specialized facilities as being trained to effect positive changes by focusing specifically on the interaction between child and environment and on the natural support systems such as family and community. Thus the educateur functions as a child advocate and environmental change agent to reduce discord and restore harmony in a manner that ultimately permits complete withdrawal of external intervention. The educateur's goal is to help the child acquire problem-solving skills and behavioral repertoires for successfully meeting both known and unfamiliar situations (Goocher, 1975).

Project Re-ED (Hobbs, 1982) is considered by some individuals to represent an Americanized version of the educateur model with the term teacher-counselor replacing educateur. For those individuals interested in acquiring educateur skills, Daly (1985) reports that at least four American colleges or universities (Ohio State University, Southern Connecticut State College, Western Michigan University, and the University of Virginia) provide training programs using the term educateur. The training in these programs includes recreation, special education, and behavioral sciences as well as an internship in a child service agency.

REFERENCES

Daly, P. M. (1985). The educateur: An atypical childcare worker. *Behavioral Disorders*, *11*, 35–41.

Goocher, B. E. (1975). Behavioral applications of an educateur model in child care. *Child Care Quarterly*, *4*, 84–92.

Guindon, J. (1973). The reeducation process. *International Journal of Mental Health*, *2*(1), 15–26, 27–32.

Hobbs, N. (1982). *The troubled and troubling child*. San Francisco, CA: Jossey-Bass.

Linton, T. E. (1971). The education model: A theoretical model: A theoretical monograph. *Journal of Special Education*, *5*, 155–190.

Morse, W., & Smith, J. (1980). *Understanding child variance*. Reston, VA: Council for Exceptional Children.

KATHY L. RUHL
Pennsylvania State University

See also Project RE-ED

EDUCATIONAL AND PSYCHOLOGICAL MEASUREMENT

Educational and Psychological Measurement is a bimonthly journal devoted to the development and application of measures of individual differences. The Journal was founded in 1941 by Frederick Kuder and continues to publish the most current theoretical papers in the field. As the field of educational and psychological measurement evolves at an exponential rate, *Educational and Psychological Measurement* publishes scholarly work from all academic disciplines Interested in measurement theory, problems, and Issues. George A. Marcoulides at the University of California, Riverside is the current Editor. For more information regarding this journal, please visit: http://epm.sagepub.com/

Gwyneth M. Boodoo
Texas A&M University
First edition

Bruce Thompson
Texas A&M University
Second edition

Heather Davis
Texas A&M University
Fourth edition

EDUCATIONAL DIAGNOSTICIAN

An educational diagnostician reviews and determines the need for psychoeducational assessments for students suspected of having a disability. The educational diagnostician differs from the school psychologist both in preparation and function. Generally, the educational diagnostician is a certified or licensed regular or special education teacher with 3 or more years of experience in the classroom. Graduate training, typically a two-semester master of education program, is focused on content and techniques concerned with diagnosis and remediation of learning problems. Educational diagnosticians' roles differ significantly between states and possibly even school districts. Federal laws require diagnosticians to work as part of a multidisciplinary team to assess students in all suspected areas of concern. Educational diagnosticians often are responsible for the initial and ongoing psychoeducational assessments and timelines. Collaborating with parents and other professionals in the field of special education to develop appropriate individual educational plans for students identified with a disability is often the responsibility of a diagnostician. Also, the interpretation of data from psychoeducational assessments and the contribution of input on student strengths and weaknesses to admission, review, and dismissal

teams is typically a responsibility of the educational diagnostician. Although roles and responsibilities of an educational diagnostician may vary from state to state, collaboration and assessment of students suspected with a disability is the primary role and contribution of an educational diagnositican. For more information on educational diagnosticians, see http://www.cec.sped.org/

Philip R. Jones
Virginia Polytechnic Institute and State University

Heather Davis
Texas A&M University
Fourth edition

See also **Multidisciplinary Teams; School Psychology**

EDUCATIONAL HIGH SCHOOL REFORM

"Good enough for yesterday will not serve as good enough for tomorrow." (Sizer, 2004)

Preparing all students for life after high school has changed drastically from a generation or more ago. High schools are charged with preparing students for college and careers. More importantly, high schools are preparing students with the skills, knowledge, habits, and confidences for a global workforce and society.

Early high school reform efforts have been influenced by Ernest Boyer's work *High School: A Report on Secondary Education in America (1983);* Ted Sizer's writing on the study of high schools, *Horace's Compromise, (1984)*; and *A Nation at Risk* (National Commission on Excellence in Education (1983). More recently, one of the more comprehensive and practical reports was *Breaking Ranks II: Strategies for Leading High School Reform (2004)* that exemplifies how high schools might look differently to better meet the needs of all students. Each of these landmark works have common elements that include greater personalization, increased rigor, learning driven by student inquiry, reflection and interests, and developing student's mind and character.

Personalization is enhanced by organizing high schools into smaller units. Smaller units may have different structures and names: houses or schools within schools, magnet programs and academies, charter schools and minischools and small learning communities. Regardless of the structure or name, a team of teachers shares several hundred students in common for instruction and assumes responsibility for their educational progress across school years. Creative and flexible structures (e.g., student schedules, school day, school year, advisories, and organizational units) provide opportunities for students to build meaningful relationships with adults and peers. Based on research, the strategies of smaller learning communities or units that have had positive effects on student achievement include interdisciplinary teams of teachers, school and district level policies and supports, rigorous and relevant curriculum, inclusive program practices and continuous program improvement.

Rigor in the high school curriculum requires that all students are provided the appropriate challenge and supports to ensure that they meet high standards. From the standards-based education movement of the late 1990s to the Common Core Standards (2010), rigor defines the knowledge and skills students should have within their K–12 education so that they will graduate high school fully prepared for college and/or be successful in a career. A quality high school curriculum must also provide high quality instruction. Staff must use a variety of instructional strategies and assessments to accommodate individual learning styles.

Successful high schools not only provide rigorous academic coursework, but relevant and meaningful learning experiences that include multiple pathways to graduation and linking core content to personal experiences, student interests and connections to the world of work. Inquiry-based learning acknowledges the different perspectives and experiences that learners bring to the lesson or activity. It teaches students to seek knowledge and information through questioning.

Schools must not only develop students' intellectual and academic minds but prepare them for productive citizenry. Character formation helps to shape students' attitudes and behaviors that are reflected in the values of integrity, respect, responsibility, self-discipline, honesty, and care.

High School Reform Initiatives Affect Transition Services

Paralleling reforms in secondary education for all students are new policy and practices aimed at improving access and progress for students with disabilities. Because high schools are the final level of compulsory schooling, they must prepare students for different postsecondary destinations—both into postsecondary education and the workforce. Three generations of reform efforts illustrate these endeavors to assist youth with high school transition.

First Generation of Reform: Practical Skill Development. The *first generation* of transition services (1960s to 1980s) was characterized by early definition of career development and transition services, establishment of a delivery system for services and supports, and emerging evidence of the relationships between transition planning and successful student transition to postsecondary education and employment.

The federal government assumed an important role in the expansion of the career-vocational education movement, including vocational rehabilitation, with the creation of the Commission on National Aid to Vocational Education (1914) and passage of the Smith-Hughes Act (P.L. 64-347, 1917). The career education movement in the United States gained additional momentum in the 1960s when it became a high priority of the then U.S. Office of Education's Bureau of Adult, Vocational and Technical Education (Halpern, 1999). During the 1960s and 1970s, policy makers recognized that high dropout rates in the United States were due in part to the failure of the educational system to provide students with a relevant education that was aligned with their future goals and potentials. As a result, vocational programs began to target the needs of special populations, including those with disabilities, limited English proficient, economically disadvantaged, teen parents, and those in correctional settings. The work of Dr. Gary Clark greatly influenced practice and policy related to the career development of children and youth with disabilities, cautioning policy makers that students with disabilities continued to experience limited access to educational and employment programs. His lifespan approach to career development contributed greatly to the early development of the concept of career development.

Second Generation of Reform: Accountability for Student Achievement. In the 1990s, partly in reaction to public concerns about the eroding quality of education in the United States and weakening economic competitiveness, policy makers turned their attention to improving the academic achievement of all students. Policy initiatives reflected the belief that improving education depended upon the creation of national standards that defined what every student should know and be able to do (Jennings, 2000). The *standards-based reform movement* led to a shift in the attention of educators from work and career-preparation to academic performance outcomes.

The *second generation* of transition services that began in the 1990s was characterized by federal policy initiatives that further defined transition services and provided resources to build capacity in the states and local communities. In 1990, the amendments to IDEA (PL 101-476) defined transition services and activities, including formal agreements with school-linked agencies to share the responsibility for long-range transition planning. Adding to the development of transition services were the passage of the Americans with Disabilities Act in 1990 (ADA;

P.L. 101-336) which prohibited workplace discrimination against persons with disabilities; (2) amendments to the Rehabilitation Act to promote coordination with secondary schools to improve transition services, and (3) the School to Work Opportunities Act (STWOA) of 1994 (PL 103-239) to advance job training programs. These initiatives were based on accumulating research evidence that transition planning and supports lead to improved postsecondary outcomes, and that states need assistance to build their capacity.

Third Generation of Reform: Equity and Accountability. Since the 1980s, educational improvement legislation, including IDEA 2004 and the No Child Left Behind Act of 2001 (NCLB, 107-110), have sought to improve public school programs for all students (National Center on Secondary Education and Transition, (2004). These laws promoted state assessments, curriculum standards and comprehensive planning to enable all students to achieve high academic standards, while holding educators responsible for the progress of student (Kochhar & Bassett, 2002). NCLB and IDEA 2004 requires that children with disabilities be considered general education students first, and, therefore, be included, to the extent possible, in the general education curriculum and in standardized assessments. To support these goals, educational laws reflect stronger mandates for collaboration between general and special education teachers; teachers and related services professionals; teachers, families and students; preschool and elementary schools; elementary and middle schools; middle and high schools; high schools and postsecondary institutions (colleges and universities); and school and community agencies. States are responsible for implementing a single accountability system for all students based on strong academic standards for what every child should know and learn, including children with disabilities.

The *third generation* of transition services (in the 2000s) has been characterized by more explicit definition and guidance in IDEA 2004 for developing a comprehensive and systematic transition planning process that is individualized for each student and validated by research. In secondary education, in order for students with disabilities to have meaningful access to the general curriculum, transition planning and services must be tailored to individual needs and preferences, relevant to postsecondary goals, and use flexible curricula and environments. Such a transition program recognizes different pathways to graduation for students, incorporates the concept of integrated transition planning and participation in a general education course of study, and employs flexible combinations of academic, career-technical education classes and community-based work experiences to achieve different pathways to graduation.

Implications for Transition

Secondary educational reform by right includes a strong foundation of transition competencies. A variety of approaches to such reform fall into four basic categories: targeted, comprehensive, collaborative, and systemic (Müller & Burdette, 2007). The first category, *targeted* approaches, includes *instructional interventions* (designed to improve classroom teaching and student achievement), *student support programs* (designed for students who may need extra support), *and school restructuring* (designed to alter the organization structure of the school). Targeted approaches generally attempt to alter one particular facet of the school, rather than all facets of the school. The second category, *comprehensive* approaches, involves altering all aspects of the school, under the assumption that the school itself is not performing adequately for most students. Two strategies within this category are *reforming existing high schools* by developing a comprehensive set of practices and programs locally or by adopting an externally developed comprehensive school reform model or *creating new* schools, by either developing a new school locally or by adopting an externally developed whole school model. Both of these strategies can be used to create comprehensive high schools to serve all students or to create specialized high schools to serve specific populations of students, such as students who are at risk or have already dropped out of school. The third category, *collaborative* approaches, involves attempts to create partnerships between schools and local government and community agencies, under the assumption that schools alone cannot successfully address the needs of students and improve their performance in school. Instead, schools are more likely to be successful if they work with outside agencies to provide more support to students, and to all the institutions—families, schools, communities—that serve them. The fourth category, *systemic* approaches, emphasize making changes to the entire state educational system, under the assumption that such changes can transform how all schools function in the system, a sort of "systemic school reform."

Given the philosophical alignment between general education and transition initiatives, there are a number of initiatives that provide a transition-focused foundation. These include such initiatives as vocational education, school dropout prevention programs, and smaller learning communities programs. Private efforts, too, have sought to provide guidance to secondary reform. The National High School Center provides current research and resources regarding high school improvement issues. The Center includes students with disabilities in high school settings, including those students with mental health issues, access to general education, significantly struggling learners, and strategies for dropout prevention, and access to academic and career readiness. The National Community of Practice in Support of Transition, sponsored by the IDEA Partnership at the National Association of State Directors of Special Education, works collaboratively with state and local education agencies to improve interagency transition-focused initiatives and to promote the role of youth and high school reform issues.

According to the National Longitudinal Transition Study 2, youth with disabilities more engaged in school and community, dropout rates are decreasing, employment and wages are increasing, and postsecondary enrollment and community engagement are also increasing (Newman, Wagner, Cameto, & Knokey, 2009). The field of transition has been using many "best practices" for over 20 years that general education reform could embrace for all students: planning for transition to employment or further schooling, active student participation and advocacy; job development and career planning; contextual teaching practices in academic environments; early warning systems for dropout prevention; collaboration with teachers, families, and students; and personalized postsecondary planning within the secondary setting. Secondary educational reform is now beginning to embrace many of these transition-based tenets for students with and without disabilities.

REFERENCES

Boyer, E. L. (1983). *High school: A report on secondary education in America*. The Carnegie Foundation for the Advancement of Teaching. New York, NY: Harper & Row.

Breaking Ranks II: Strategies for leading high school reform (2004). Reston, VA: National Association of Secondary High School Principals.

Halpern, A. (1999). *Transition: Is it time for another rebottling?* Paper presented at the 1999 Annual OSEP Project Directors' Meeting, Washington, DC.

Jennings, J. (2000). *The future of the federal role in elementary and secondary education*. Washington, DC: Center on Education Policy.

Kochhar-Bryant, C. A., & Bassett, D. (2002). Challenge and promise in aligning transition and standards-based education. In C. A. Kochhar-Bryant & D. Bassett (Eds.), *Aligning transition and standards-based education: Issues and strategies*. Arlington, VA: Council for Exceptional Children.

Müller, E., & Burdette, P. (2007, December). *High school reform: Integration of special education*. In *Forum* (pp. 1–9). Washington, DC: National Association of State Directors of Special Education.

National Center on Secondary Education and Transition. (2004). U.S. Department of Education.

National Commission on Excellence in Education. (1983). *A nation at risk: The imperative for educational reform*. Washington, DC: U.S. Government Printing Office.

Newman, L., Wagner, M., Cameto, R., & Knokey, A-M. (2009). *The post-high school outcomes of youth with disabilities up to 4 years after high school: A report from the National Longitudinal Transition Study-2 (NLTS2)* (NCSER 2009-3017). Menlo Park, CA: SRI International.

Sizer, T. (1984) *Horace's compromise: The dilemma of the American high school*. Boston, MA: Houghton Mifflin.

DIANE S. BASSETT
University of Northern Colorado

CAROL A. KOCHHAR-BRYANT
George Washington University

TERESA GROSSI
Indiana University
Fourth edition

EDUCATIONALLY DISADVANTAGED

According to the Office of Elementary and Secondary Education, educationally deprived children are children whose educational attainment is below the level that is appropriate for children their age. These children are often referred to as educationally disadvantaged. A cause for this scholastic retardation in depressed areas is attributed to the attitudes and behavior of school personnel (Passow, 1967). These children often come from culturally deprived homes that fail to equip the children to fit into and adapt well to the school environment (Passow, 1967). Daniels (1967) adds that the disadvantaged have become disabled because of social or environmental conditions in their ability to learn and to acquire skills and abilities for coping with the problems of earning a living and enjoying a satisfying life. He accepts the estimate that the disadvantaged constitute 25% of the school population, and in larger cities 30% to 40%.

Title I of the Elementary and Secondary Education Act was designed to overcome the debilitating burdens placed on educationally disadvantaged students by certain school personnel and culturally deprived families. Title I was one in a series of legislative efforts aimed at addressing the needs of the culturally disadvantaged. Some of the others were the Civil Rights Act of 1964, the Economic Opportunity Act of 1964, the Vocational Act of 1963, and the National Defense Act (revised in 1965). Additional related legislation aimed at reducing discrimination policies toward the educationally disadvantaged and other specific targeted populations were Title IX of the Education Amendments of 1972 (PL 92-318), the Education for All Handicapped Children Act (PL 94-142), the Rehabilitation Act of 1973 (PL 93-112), and the Individuals with Disabilities Education Act (IDEA).

Chapter 1 of PL 97-35 addresses the issue of financial assistance to meet the educational needs of disadvantaged children. This legislation replaced Title I of the Elementary and Secondary Act of 1965. Chapter 1 continues to be the main legislation addressing the educational needs of deprived children. The act will fund local education agency school programs to meet the needs of educationally deprived children. According to PL 97-35:

Such programs and projects may include the acquisition of equipment and instructional materials, employment of special instructional and counseling and guidance personnel, employment and training of teacher aides, payments to teachers in amounts in excess of regular salary schedules (as a bonus for service in schools serving project areas), the training of teachers, the construction, where necessary, of school facilities, other expenditures authorized under Title I. (p. 1701)

The law in this area has undergone a major change with the passage, in 2001, of the No Child Left Behind Act, which shifted focus of federal assistance from educationally disadvantaged and low-income students to "underperforming" schools without regard to the socioeconomic status of the students who attend them. For a more complete discussion of the new law, see the entry on No Child Left Behind, elsewhere in this encyclopedia.

Passow's (1967) assessment of the underlying causes for educational deprivation and cultural deprivation still appear to be valid, even though much federal legislation has been written to address this American educational need. Passow has stated that educationally disadvantaged children's problems stem from poverty, unemployment, segregation, discrimination, and lack of equal opportunity in housing and employment. In addition, he suggests that discontinuities with the majority culture, rising out of difference in lifestyle, child rearing practices, and skills for urban living; and inadequate educational attainment of those skills essential in a technical society are also problematic. Promising practices, he states, fall into nine categories: in-service education and recruitment, reading, summer programs, community-school aspects, guidance activities, early admissions programs, team teaching programs, special placement classes, and job-retraining programs. The challenge for schools in developing promising practices is to keep in mind the question, How can the school educate inner-city children out of their subcultures into society's mainstream while preserving and developing their individuality and diversity, as well as the positive elements of their cultures?

The current literature suggests that schools can increase their effectiveness by changing their focus from considering the culturally disadvantaged as disadvantaged to considering them as culturally different. This shift in focus permits one to accept the fact that the culturally different may continue having disadvantages, but they also have benefits for society. Programs that include emphasis on the benefits to society by the culturally different are basically encompassed in the concept of multicultural education.

Rodriguez (1983) defines multicultural education as education that values cultural pluralism. Multicultural education recognizes that cultural diversity is a valuable resource and should be extended into American society. Schools should not melt away cultural differences or merely tolerate cultural pluralism. Each cultural unit lives as part of an interrelated whole. According to Bennett (1986), the goal of multicultural education is to change the total educational environment so that it will develop competencies in multiple cultures and provide members of all cultural groups with equal educational opportunity. Equity is at the heart of multicultural education.

It appears, therefore, that effective programming for the educationally disadvantaged can be enhanced if the needs of the disadvantaged are perceived in an educational milieu that also recognizes the benefits to society of the students' culture.

REFERENCES

Bennett, C. I. (1986). *Comprehensive multicultural education: Theory and practice* (p. 53). Boston, MA: Allyn & Bacon.

Daniels, W. G. (1967). Some essential ingredients in educational programs for the socially disadvantaged. In J. Hellmuth (Ed.), *Disadvantaged child. Vol. 1: Special child* (pp. 202–221). Seattle, WA: Seguin School.

Passow, H. A. (1967). Education of the culturally deprived child. In J. Hellmuth (Ed.), *Disadvantaged child. Vol. 1: Special child* (pp. 171–180). Seattle, WA: Seguin School.

Rodriguez, F. (1983). Education in a multicultural society. Lanham, MD: University Press of America.

STAN A. KARCZ
University of Wisconsin at Stout

See also Cultural Bias in Testing; No Child Left Behind; Pluralism, Cultural

EDUCATIONAL RESOURCES INFORMATION CENTER

The Educational Resources Information Center (ERIC) is a national system that has provided access to an online library of educational research and information. The collection, begun in 1966, includes journal articles, books, research, conference and policy papers, technical reports, and other education-related materials. The mission of ERIC is to provide a comprehensive easy-to-use, searchable, Internet-based bibliographic and full-text database of education research and information to improve practice in learning; teaching; educational decision making; and research for educators, researchers and the general public. ERIC provides access to more than 1.4 million bibliographic records of journal articles and other educational related materials with hundreds of new records added weekly. More than 100,000 articles on ERIC are available in full text free of charge, in Adobe PDF or other formats; materials published after 2004 are available through links to others sources (e.g., publishers' websites).

ERIC is sponsored and funded by the Institute of Education Sciences (IES) of the United States Department of Education. Computer Sciences Corporation (CSC) operates ERIC and provides support, development, and management of the digital collection, ERIC thesaurus, website, associated technologies, and outreach to ERIC users. The ERIC system has been authorized by the U.S. Department of Education to utilize three expert advisory panels made up of members with expertise in information management, research methodology, academic librarians and K–12 librarians, and many others. These three committees assist in ERIC's ongoing development: steering committee, content experts, and library committee. The ERIC Steering Committee is an expert technical group that provides guidance and recommendations on usability of the website, database search engine, and various other technologies related to the digital library. Content experts provide advice on setting standards and acquiring subject-specific, education related resources for the library. The Library Committee provides input regarding collection development, service delivery, and outreach. The ERIC network consisted of 16 subject-specific clearinghouses that prepared abstracts for relevant documents prior to January 2004. The U.S. Department of Education consolidated the program into a single body, upgraded systems, streamlined operations, and sped up delivery of content. ERIC Digests, created by the former clearinghouses, are available in full text on the ERIC website, as are many articles previously available only through microfiche collections or through a paper copy. ERIC is available at www.eric.ed.gov.

This entry has been informed by the sources listed below.

REFERENCES

About the ERIC Program. Educational Resources Information Center. (n.d.). Retrieved October 27, 2011, from http://eric.ed.gov/about

Education Resources Information Center. Institute of Education Sciences. (n.d.). Retrieved October 27, 2011, from http://ies.ed.gov/ncee/projects/eric.asp

KACI DEAUQUIER SHERIDAN
Texas A&M University
Fourth edition

EDUCATIONAL TESTING SERVICE

Educational Testing Service (ETS) is a nonprofit corporation established in 1947. It was originally intended to carry out the College Entrance Examination Board (CEEB) testing program. The ETS also was involved in assisting the testing functions of the Carnegie Corporation and the American Council on Education. In addition to providing contract services to these, and now many other agencies (ETS develops and is responsible for carrying out the Law School Admissions Test, Graduate Record Examination, and numerous other programs), ETS has a world-renowned research and development staff.

The largest percentage of ETS's activity is devoted to developing, administering, scoring, and reporting services for the Scholastic Aptitude Test (SAT). The SAT is administered regularly at more than 5,000 testing centers to more than 1 million college applicants each year. The use of ETS-administered admissions testing programs periodically stirs great controversy, mostly centering around charges of unfairness to certain classes of individuals.

In all of its testing programs, ETS regularly makes accommodations for individuals with disabilities. Not only are readers or recorded tests provided for the blind and for the dyslexic, but prostheses and special administrative procedures for orthopedically disabled individuals are provided as well; such special arrangements must be requested far in advance of the intended testing date.

ETS has become heavily involved in competency testing and examinations for licensure and certification of professions.

ETS has pioneered educational measurement research and analysis, innovative product development, and original policy studies to advance learning worldwide. ETS has a PATHWISE® series which includes professional development workshops, mentor training, support materials, advanced courses for experienced teachers, online instruction, and professional development programs for school leaders. These include a School Leadership Series for principals, superintendents, and other school leaders.

ETS also provides licensure programs in most states. These programs include the Praxis Series: Professional Assessments for Beginning Teachers, and the National Board for Professional Teaching Standards® assessments for accomplished teaching practice.

In addition, ETS offers products and services in support of nonnative speakers of English. The Test of English as a Foreign Language Program provides a complement of assessments and other information to assist in the evaluation, admission, placement, and education of nonnative speakers of English. Additional information can be found at www.ets.org.

CECIL R. REYNOLDS
Texas A&M University

JESSI K. WHEATLEY
Falcon School District 49, Colorado Springs, Colorado,
Third edition

EDUCATION AND TREATMENT OF CHILDREN

Education and Treatment of Children (*ETC*) is a refereed, scholarly journal published quarterly by West Virginia University Press. The journal's goal is to disseminate reliable information related to educational and treatment services for children and youth. Manuscripts accepted for publication are judged on their relevance to a variety of childcare professionals for improving the effectiveness of teaching and training techniques for those currently in the field.

ETC utilizes a broad base of educators, researchers, clinical practitioners, and graduate students in the editorial review process, representing most geographic areas of the United States and portions of Canada.

Since its initial publication in 1976, *ETC* has published manuscripts describing a wide variety of experimental studies as well as nonexperimental procedures and/or services and programs for exceptional and normal children and youths. A considerable portion of each issue is devoted to reviews of books and other published materials in the areas of education and treatment of children and youths. The content of the journal is informative and practical for practitioners and researchers alike and should prove useful in improving treatment practices.

JULIA A. HICKMAN
Bastrop Mental Health Association

JESSI K. WHEATLEY
Falcon School District 49, Colorado Springs, Colorado
Third edition

KACI DEAUQUIER SHERIDAN
Texas A&M University
Fourth edition

EDUCATION FOR ALL HANDICAPPED CHILDREN ACT OF 1975 (PL 94-142) (*See* Individuals with Disabilities Education Improvement Act of 2004 (IDEIA); Categorical Education; Cerebral Palsy; Education for the Terminally Ill; Other Health Impaired; Spina Bifida)

EDUCATION FOR THE TERMINALLY ILL

There are several stages of instruction to be observed in the education of terminally ill children. The initial phase should begin with the instruction and counseling of those who will teach them. It is necessary for educators to face, express, and deal with their own feelings toward death and dying before they can effectively identify and meet the emotional needs and presenting problems of such children. Denial, avoidance, fear, and helplessness are attitudes commonly encountered in unprepared teachers that directly affect the quality of the terminally ill child's experiences in school (Cairns, 1980). Instructional modules devoted to teacher self-awareness and the reality of facing and coping with death and dying are recommended for inclusion in teacher preparation programs (Sirvis, 1981).

As terminally ill children often choose a caring adult other than a parent with whom to communicate and express their feelings, the second stage in teacher preparation must be familiarization and understanding of the psychological stages encountered by the terminally ill and the "language of feelings" employed by such children. Professionals must be aware of the different ways children may select to communicate those feelings in order to be helpful and supportive (Kübler-Ross, 1983).

The second phase in a comprehensive education program for the terminally ill must address the needs and fears of the peers and classmates of the dying child. Wass and Corr (1982) stress the need for curriculum units on death and terminal illness to prepare teachers to instruct on such topics, and Jeffrey and Lansdown (1982) also recommend the inclusion of curriculum units on death and dying for both regular and special education class pupils.

The final phase in educating the terminally ill child offers directed strategies for the teacher. These include: (a) the maintenance of regular classroom routines for such children and the continued application of rules, limits, and reasonable goal-setting (Noore, 1981); (b) the use by teachers of such methods as life space interviews, adjunctive therapy, expressive writing, bibliotherapy (literature), role playing, magic circle discussions, art therapy, and play therapy to cope with the child's presenting problems (Ainsa, 1981); (c) the preparation by teachers to deal effectively with behaviors that may range from withdrawal to defiance while helping friends and classmates grieve and recover on the death of the child; (d) the maintenance by teachers of a primary role and the fulfillment of teaching responsibilities while emphasizing views in the classroom that stress maintaining meaning in the life of the terminally ill child (Stuecher, 1980). Most terminally ill children continue to receive educational services until they are too ill to benefit from them and may receive in-home teaching services as Other Health Impaired through special education.

There are many online resources for teachers, parents, and caregivers on terminal illness. In addition, online resources for children with terminal illnesses are plentiful and can be accessed at http://www.musckids.com, http://www.patient.co.uk/, http://www.webmd.com/hw/raising_a_family

REFERENCES

Ainsa, T. (1981). Teaching the terminally ill child. *Education*, *101*, 397–401.

Cairns, N. (1980). The dying child in the classroom. *Essence: Issues in the Study of Aging, Dying, and Death, 4*, 25–32.

Eklof, M. (1984). The terminally ill child: How peers, parents and teachers can help. *PTA Today, 10*, 8–9.

Jeffrey, P., & Lansdown, R. (1982). The role of the special school in the care of the dying child. *Developmental Medicine & Child Neurology, 24*, 693–696.

Kubler-Ross, E. (1983). *On children and death*. New York, NY: Macmillan.

Noore, N. (1981). The damaged child. *Journal for Special Educators, 17*, 376–380.

Sirvis, B. (1981). Death and dying: An instructional module for special educators. *Dissertation Abstracts International*, Order no. 76-21039, *39*, 164 pp.

Stuecher, U. (1980). Supporting chronically and terminally ill children in hospitals: A challenge for educators. *Education Unlimited, 2*, 5, 22–27.

Wass, H., & Corr, C. A. (1982). *Helping children cope with death: Guidelines and resources*. New York, NY: Hemisphere.

RONALD S. LENKOWSKY
Hunter College, City University of New York

See also Family Counseling; Family Response to a Child With Disabilities; Physical Disabilities

EDUCATION OF CHILDREN WITH BLINDNESS/VISUAL DISABILITIES

Educationally significant, noncorrectable vision impairments are prevalent in approximately 1 in 1,000 students (Council for Exceptional Children, 2011), About 10% of visually impaired children are blind (Council for Exceptional Children, 2011). Identification categories for children who have visual impairment fall into two classification categories: blind and visually impaired/low vision. Those who are blind may have no light perception or may have some light perception without projection. The low-vision learner is considered severely impaired (even with corrective assistance such as glasses), but is able to read print (often in modified form). Children who are born with siginficant visual impairments or who are blind, may begin to receive services through federal monies from birth to age 3. Early intervention is critical to provide parents and caregivers early interventions to address each individual chid's needs.

According to Kirk and Gallagher (1986), research on the impact of visual impairments indicates that, for the vast majority of students, (a) intellectual abilities are not markedly affected; (b) the perception of other senses is not substantially different from that of persons who can see; (c) language development is affected only in those areas where the meanings of words are dependent on visual concepts; and (d) self-esteem and self-confidence are not distorted except when a peer group has negatively influenced the individual's attitude.

The influence of recent social and educational movements to serve disabled citizens in less restrictive settings has realized a particular impact on the education of visually impaired students. Prior to 1960, approximately 80% of learners who were visually impaired were prepared in residential schools; currently over 70% of learners who are visually impaired are served in local educational programs. The integration of students who are visually impaired into regular school environments such as the innovative local programming promoted by Barraga (1983) focuses on adaptations in the presentation of learning experiences, modifications in instructional materials, and refinements in the learning environment.

Depending on the nature and severity of the visual impairment, Reynolds and Birch (1982) have identified the continuum of services that should be available to appropriately serve the students with low-vision or blindness placed in local school programs. The range of services and other resources includes specialized instruction directed to the unique learning needs and style of the visually impaired. This instruction may be offered by consultants, itinerant teachers, resource teachers, or specially assisted regular classroom teachers or teacher aides. Particularly important in the development of effective programming for this population is the substitution of auditory or tactual learning programs to compensate for the loss of visual capabilities (NICCYD, 2006).

The range of services also includes instruction in orientation and mobility and the availability of readily accessible programs and facilities. To ensure the maximum possible classroom integration, modifications in facility structure, classroom arrangement, and lighting may be necessary. In addition, specialized materials and technologies such as braille, advanced reading machines (e.g., Kurzweil Reader, Optacon), recorded information, and large print documents and magnifiers are offered, along with comprehensive early intervention programming for infants and young children and a strong, ongoing program of career preparation and placement.

REFERENCES

Barraga, N. (1983). *Visual handicaps and learning* (Rev. ed.). Austin, TX: Exceptional Resources.

Council for Exceptional Children. (n.d.). *Blindness and visual impairments*. Prepared by the Institute of Education Sciences (IES), U.S. Department of Education, under Contract No. ED-99-CO-0026. Retrieved January 12, 2012, from http://www.cec.sped.org/

Kirk, S. A., & Gallagher, J. J. (1986). *Educating exceptional children* (5th ed.). Boston, MA: Houghton Mifflin.

National Information Center for Children and Youth with Disabilities (NICCYD). (2006). *Visual impairments fact sheet*. Retrieved from http://nichcy.org/

Reynolds, M. C., & Birch, J. W. (1982). *Teaching exceptional children in all America's schools* (rev. ed.). Reston, VA: Council for Exceptional Children.

GEORGE JAMES HAGERTY
Stonehill College

KACI DEAUQUIER SHERIDAN
Texas A&M University
Fourth edition

See also **Visual Impairment**

EDUCATION WEEK

Education Week is a weekly newspaper published 42 times during the typical academic year by Editorial Projects in Education Inc., a Washington, DC based corporation. *Education Week* carries news, comment, and editorials of interest and concern to professional educators and researchers in the field, and it monitors budgetary concerns and federal policy. Special-education news is regularly included, as are position papers on topics of special interest such as learning disabilities, diagnosis, and mainstreaming.

Each year in January, *Education Week* issues a new edition of *Quality Counts*. *Quality Counts* examines a central issue in education and each edition also includes state report cards and extensive data on state education policy. Available both in print and on the web, *Quality Counts*

has become an essential resource for educators, policy makers, and researchers at all levels. Letters to the editor and commentary on current events in education and previously published news items, features, or commentaries are accepted. Classified ads and listings of job openings are also included.

Education Week can also be accessed online at http://www.edweek.org/ew/index.html. The website offers access to present and past editions of both *Education Week* and *Quality Counts*, information on specific topic areas, a section for teachers, and discussion boards and blogs. The address for *Education Week* is 6935 Arlington Road, Bethesda MD 20814.

CECIL R. REYNOLDS
Texas A&M University
Second edition

JESSI K. WHEATLY
Falcon School District, 49, Colorado Springs, Colorado
Third edition

JESSICA ODDI
JEFFRY FINLAYSON
The Chicago School of Professional Psychology
Fourth edition

EEG ABNORMALITIES

The electroencephalogram (EEG) is a graphic representation of the electrical activity of the brain that is generated in the cortex by the flow of synaptic currents through the extracellular space. Electrical changes in the brain that manifest in EEG abnormalities represent the heart of the epileptic attack (Bennett & Ho, 1997; Camfield & Camfield, 1999; Kandel, Schwartz, & Jessell, 1991). When an epileptic seizure occurs, large populations of neurons are activitated synchronously in regions of the cortex. During the evaluation of a patient, it is not uncommon to find an abnormal EEG when there is no overt evidence of a seizure disorder. The criteria for determining the presence of a seizure disorder in an individual with an abnormal EEG are rarely stated explicitly. Hill (1957) has reported that a high percentage of schizophrenic patients show paroxysmal abnormalities in their EEGs (e.g., synchronous spikes, spike and wave complexes, and slow wave bursts). The relationship between an abnormal EEG and behavioral disturbances in nonepileptic individuals is more difficult to define. It also has been demonstrated that commonly used drugs can often cause EEG changes that can mimic seizure activity (Fink, 1963; Ulett, Heusler,

Table E.2. Effect of commonly used drugs on the EEG[a]

Drug Type	Effect on Basic Frequencies	EEG Change Synchronization	New Waves	Persistence After Drug Discontinued
Phenothiazine	Beta slowing (occasional)	Increased	High voltage sharp	6–10 weeks
Tricyclics	Increased beta	Increased	Sharp	Unknown
Barbiturates	Increased beta; slowing	Increased in low doses; decreased in high doses	Spindles	3–6 weeks
Meprobamate	Increased beta	Increased	Spindles	3–6 weeks
Benzodiazepines	Increased beta	Increased	Fast, sharp	3–6 weeks

[a]All of these drugs except barbiturates tend to increase preexisting dysrhythmias. Withdrawal from high levels of barbiturates and meprobamate can induce increased slowing, synchronization, and paroxysmal activity, and may result in seizures.

& Word, 1965). Some of these changes are described in Table E.2.

Defining the limits of normality in an EEG presents a major problem with which clinicians and investigators have struggled for years. There is no doubt that spikes, spike-wave discharges, focal slowing with phase reversal, and paroxysmal activity during wakefulness are always abnormal; however, there are many instances and EEG patterns that do not contain any of the aforementioned but still may be considered abnormal. In patients who drink alcohol heavily or who have received tranquilizers or other medications, EEG abnormalities may be seen and represent the effect of these drugs or withdrawal from them. EEG abnormalities seen in some psychopathic individuals with a history of aggressive behavior may be due to brain damage. Positive electroencephalographic abnormalities and brain damage thus may be a result and not the cause of emotional disturbance. Even with these possibilities there remains impressive literature correlating EEG abnormalities with certain psychiatric symptomatology (e.g., Dodrill, 1981; Hartlage & Hartlage, 1997).

In a large study of unselected, nonepileptic individuals, it was possible to differentiate those with abnormal EEGs from those with normal EEGs on the basis of their symptoms (Tucker, Detre, Harrow, & Glaser, 1965). Symptoms classically associated with schizophrenia were significantly more common in psychiatric patients with abnormal EEGs; they included impaired associations, flattened affect, religiosity, persecutory and somatic delusions, auditory hallucinations, impaired personal habits, and destructive-assaultive behavior. The group with abnormal EEGs also exhibited symptoms normally associated with neurological diseases such as time disorientation, perseveration, recent memory difficulties, and headaches. Neurotic and depressed individuals had approximately the same incidence of abnormal EEGs as the general population (18%). (Also see reviews by Bennett & Ho, 1997; Hartlage & Hartlage, 1997; and Murphy & Heller, 1994.)

Research by Wilkus and Dodrill (1976) demonstrated that increasing involvement of the brain with epileptiform discharges (epilepticlike EEG abnormalities) is related to decreased cognitive performance. Furthermore, the decreased performances associated with this condition are conspicuously widespread and involve many different kinds of functions. The EEGs of epileptics have been studied with respect to abnormalities in rhythm frequency. Generally, decreased abilities were associated with slower rhythm frequencies. For example, Dodrill and Wilkins (1976) studied the performance of a large group of epileptic individuals on a broad range of tests and found that performance was not substantially decreased until the dominant posterior rhythm frequency dropped below 8 Hz, when performance decreased precipitously. Although decreased abilities were seen across a wide range of skills, those requiring simultaneous attention and complex mental manipulations showed the greatest losses. However, the social and emotional consequences of epilepsy are the most serious consequences of this disorder (Camfield & Camfield, 1999; Murphy & Heller, 1994).

REFERENCES

Bennett, T., & Ho, M. (1997). The neuropsychology of pediatric epilepsy and antiepileptic drugs. In C. R. Reynolds & E. Fletcher-Janzen (Eds.), *Handbook of clinical child neuropsychology* (2nd ed., pp. 517–538). New York, NY: Plenum Press.

Camfield, P. R., & Camfield, C. S. (1999). Pediatric epilepsy: An overview. In K. F. Swaiman & S. Ashwal (Eds.), *Pediatric neurology* (pp. 629–633). St. Louis, MO: Mosby.

Dodrill, C. B. (1981). Neuropsychology of epilepsy. In S. B. Filskov & T. J. Boll (Eds.), *Handbook of clinical neuropsychology* (pp. 366–395). New York, NY: Wiley.

Dodrill, C. B., & Wilkus, R. J. (1976). Neuropsychological correlates of the electroencephalogram in epileptics: II. The waking posterior rhythm and its interaction with epileptiform activity. *Epilepsia, 17*, 101–109.

Fink, M. (1963). Quantitative EEG in human psychopharmacology: Drug patterns. In G. H. Glaser (Ed.), *EEG and behavior* (pp. 143–169). New York, NY: Basic Books.

Hartlage, P. L., & Hartlage, L. C. (1997). The neuropsychology of epilepsy: Overview and psychosocial aspects. In C. R. Reynolds

& E. Fletcher-Janzen (Eds.), *Handbook of clinical child neuropsychology* (2nd ed., pp. 506–516). New York, NY: Plenum Press.

Hill, D. (1957). Electroencephalogram in schizophrenia. In R. Richter (Ed.), *Schizophrenia: Somatic aspects* (pp. 30–72). London, England: Pergamon Press.

Kandel, E., Schwartz, J., & Jessell, T. (1991). *Principles of neural science* (3rd ed.). New York, NY: Elsevier.

Murphy, S., & Heller, W. (1994). Seizure disorder: Psychological issues. In R. Olson, L. Mullins, J. Gillman, & J. Chaney (Eds.), *The sourcebook of pediatric psychology* (pp. 185–198). Boston, MA: Longwood.

Tucker, G. J., Detre, T., Harrow, M., & Glaser, G. H. (1965). Behavior and symptoms of psychiatric patients and the electroencephalogram. *Archives of General Psychiatry, 12,* 278–292.

Ulett, G. A., Heusler, A. F., & Word, T. J. (1965). The effect of psychotropic drugs on the EEG of the chronic psychotic patient. In W. P. Wilson (Ed.), *Applications of electroencephalography in psychiatry: A symposium* (pp. 23–36). Durham, NC: Duke University Press.

Wilkus, R. J., & Dodrill, C. B. (1976). Neuropsychological correlates of the electroencephalogram in epileptics. I. Topographic distribution and average rate of epileptiform activity. *Epilepsia, 17,* 89–100.

Richard A. Berg
West Virginia University Medical Center, Charleston Division

See also Epilepsy; Neuropsychology

EEOC (*See* Equal Employment Opportunity Commission)

EFFECTIVENESS OF SPECIAL EDUCATION

The work of Jean-Marc-Gaspard Itard with Victor, the "wild boy of Aveyron," usually marks the beginning of modern special education (Itard, 1806/1962). Although innovative and comprehensive, the education program developed by Itard produced only modest improvement in Victor's performance. The enduring perception was that the Itard experiment "failed" (e.g., Kirk & Johnson, 1951) but, in reality, the modest gains were substantial and become more meaningful when emphasis shifts from results to methods (Gaynor, 1973).

Questions about the efficacy of special education remain: Is special education special? Unequivocal answers are difficult to attain and this has resulted in a cyclical nature for special education that oscillates between optimism and pessimism (Sarason & Doris, 1979). Answers to questions about efficacy are typically sought in the research literature, but difficulties arise when individual study findings do not agree. The disagreement makes it necessary to combine findings to produce "usable knowledge" (Lindblom & Cohen, 1979) that can provide a basis for decision making about efficacy.

Special education has historically assumed a goal of correcting or reversing the altered learning functions of students. Beginning with Itard, special education has focused on enhancing cognitive *processes* so special education students may then be able to learn in the same way as general education students. Consequently, process training has long been a primary form of special education (see Mann, 1979). Although intuitively appealing, does research support the theoretical assumption that training processes enhance learning ability?

A large body of empirical research has investigated the efficacy of process training, but difficulties arise in deciding what the research says, as illustrated in the case of psycholinguistic training, a prominent form of process training during the 1960s and 1970s. Psycholinguistic training was developed by Samuel A. Kirk and embodied in the *Illinois Test of Psycholinguistic Abilities* (ITPA). The model was based on the assumption that psycholinguistic ability is comprised of discrete components and that these components can be improved with training. By the mid-1970s, empirical research summaries revealed very different interpretations.

A review of 39 studies offered by Hammill and Larsen (1974) concluded that, "the idea that psycholinguistic constructs, as measured by the ITPA, can, in fact, be trained by existing techniques remains nonvalidated" (p. 11). In response, Minskoff (1975) offered a more positive evaluation and concluded that psycholinguistic deficits can be remediated. The Minskoff review was immediately challenged by Newcomer, Larsen, and Hammill (1975) who concluded that, "the reported literature raises doubts regarding the efficacy of presently available Kirk-Osgood psycholinguistic training programs" (p. 147). The divergent interpretations made it increasingly difficult to determine "what the research says" about the efficacy of psycholinguistic training.

Several years later, Lund, Foster, and McCall-Perez (1978) reevaluated the original 39 studies and concluded that, "It is, therefore, not logical to conclude either that all studies in psycholinguistic training are effective or that all studies in psycholinguistic training are not effective" (p. 319). Hammill and Larsen (1978) contested the Lund et al. analysis and concluded that, "the cumulative results...failed to demonstrate that psycholinguistic training has value" (p. 413). Although polemics abounded, a primary question remained unanswered: What is really known about the efficacy of psycholinguistic training?

The difficulty is that traditional means for combining research findings does not eliminate potential bias in evaluating outcomes. To exclude the subjectivity associated with traditional methods of reviewing research findings (see Cooper & Rosenthal, 1980), quantitative methods, usually termed "meta-analysis" (Glass, 1976), have become an accepted means of combining empirical findings. Meta-analysis is the application of statistical procedures to collections of empirical findings from individual studies for the purpose of integrating, synthesizing, and making sense of them (Glass, McGaw, & Smith, 1981).

As a research methodology, meta-analysis uses rigorous and systematic procedures that permit quantification and standardization of individual study findings with the "effect size" (ES) statistic (Kavale, 2001a). An ES is most often interpreted as a z-score indicating level of improvement on an outcome assessment for students initially at the 50th percentile. To gain greater insight, an ES may also be interpreted with the "binomial effect size display" (BESD; Rosenthal & Rubin, 1982), which addresses the question: What is the percentage increase in the number of successful responses when using a new instructional practice? Based on converting an ES to r, the BESD for the use of intervention (ES = 1.6, for example) would show an increase in success rate from 25 to 75%. The 50-percentage-point spread between treatment (75%) and comparison (25%) success rate shows that the use of intervention Z possesses not only statistical significance, but also *practical* significance. Another ES interpretation is based on notions of statistical power where Cohen (1988) offered "rules of thumb" for classifying ES as small (0.20), medium (0.50), or large (0.80).

To accumulate findings about the effectiveness of psycholinguistic training in a more objective manner, Kavale (1981) conducted a meta-analysis on 34 studies that yielded an average ES of 0.39. In a statistical sense, an ES shows outcomes in standard deviation (SD) units that can be interpreted in terms overlapping distributions (treatment versus control). The ES of 0.39 indicates that the average treated subject would gain 15 percentile ranks on the ITPA and would be better off than 65% of control (no treatment) subjects. The BESD ($r = .19$) for psycholinguistic training shows a success rate increase from 40% to 60%. Using Cohen's (1988) rules of thumb, the ES approaches a "medium" level. The 15 percentile rank gain, 20% increase in success rater, and almost medium statistical power level suggest modest efficacy for psycholinguistic training.

The modest efficacy does not represent an unequivocal endorsement of psycholinguistic training, however, and suggests the need for further analysis to determine where psycholinguistic training may be more or less effective. When ES data were aggregated by ITPA subtest, five of nine ITPA subtests revealed "small," albeit positive, effects. Such a modest level of response suggests that training would not be warranted in these five cases. For four subtests (auditory and visual association, verbal and manual expression), however, training improves performance from 15 to 24 percentile ranks and makes the average trained subject better off than approximately 63–74% of untrained subjects.

The findings regarding the associative and expressive constructs appear to belie the conclusion of Hammill and Larsen (1974) that, "neither the ITPA subtests nor their theoretical constructs are particularly ameliorative" (p. 12). The meta-analytic findings should *not*, however, be interpreted as approval for psycholinguistic training. In the case of auditory association, for example, there are difficulties in defining the skill: What is auditory association? Additionally, it is important to determine whether improvement in auditory association provides enhanced functioning in other than that discrete ability. In contrast, the case for expressive constructs, particularly verbal expression, presents a different scenario because it represents the tangible process of productive language behavior whose improvement is critical for school success. In fact, the verbal expression ES (0.63) exceeds what would be expected from 6 months of general education language instruction (ES = 0.50). Thus, the Kavale (1981) meta-analysis showed where psycholinguistic training might be effective and might be initiated when deemed an appropriate part of an intervention program.

Mann (1979) suggested that, "process training is, in fact, one of the oldest forms of education and that, despite periodic discontinuities in its practice, it has continued unabated into our own day" (p. 537). Table E.3 reveals that popular forms of process training demonstrate limited efficacy. (The reported ES were obtained from the meta-analyses listed in Appendix A and represent either the ES reported in a single meta-analysis investigating a particular intervention or a weighted mean ES from meta-analyses investigating the same intervention.) For example, perceptual-motor training, the embodiment of 1960s special education, had practically no effect on improving educational performance. In fact, perceptual-motor training has a small effect on improving perceptual-motor functioning (ES = 0.17). The popular programs developed during the 1960s revealed very modest effectiveness (see Table E.4). For example, the BESD reveals

Table E.3. Effectiveness of Process Training

Method	Mean Effect Size	Percentile Rank Equivalent	Power Rating
Irlen Lenses	−.02	49	Negative
Perceptual-Motor Training	.08	53	Negligible
Diet Modification (Feingold)	.12	55	Small
Modality-Matched Instruction	.14	56	Small
Social Skills Training	.36	64	Small
Psycholinguistic Training	.39	65	Small–Medium

Table E.4. Average Effect Size for Perceptual-Motor Training Programs

Training Program	Mean Effect Size	Percentile Equivalent	Power Rating
Kephart	.06	52	Small
Frostig	.10	54	Small
Cratty	.11	54	Small
Getman	.12	55	Small
Barsch	.16	56	Small
Delacato	.16	56	Small

that the Kephart program produces only a slight increase in success rate (6%).

The limited efficacy of process training may be related to difficulties in attempting to ameliorate unobservable (hypothetical) constructs. The outcomes of training (products) are the only observable component, whereas the means by which those products were achieved (process) are not observable. Although these difficulties are evident for constructs like perception, the same problems can be identified for, as an example, social skills training where the actual skills represent products that are presumed related to the hypothetical construct of social competence. The limited efficacy of social skills training is found across special education populations. Forness and Kavale (1996) found an ES of 0.21 for students with LD, whereas Quinn, Kavale, Mather, Rutherford, and Forness (1999) found an ES of 0.20 for students with EBD. Thus, regardless of special education designation, social skill deficits appear difficult to remediate.

Although attacks on process training have been vigorous and long-standing (e.g., Mann, 1971), its historical, clinical, and philosophical foundation creates a resistance to accepting negative evidence (e.g., Hallahan & Cruickshank, 1973) because "the tension between belief and reality provides a continuing sense of justification for process training" (Kavale & Forness, 1999, p. 35). The failure to change beliefs about efficacy is also found for modality-matched instruction (ES = 0.14), which has received a number of negative evaluations (e.g., Arter & Jenkins, 1979; Larrivee, 1981; Tarver & Dawson, 1978). Nevertheless, teachers maintain a strong belief that students learn best when instruction is modified to match individual modality patterns (Kavale & Reese, 1991). In addition to low effects for modality matching, only two out of three correct decisions are made for preference (ES = 0.51) Considered with the modest 6-percentile-rank gain, modality-matched instruction does not appear warranted. Thus the empirical evidence demonstrating the limited efficacy of process training suggests that it should not be a major focus in program planning.

The long dominant tradition of process training in special education reflected a pathology model; academic problems were regarded as a "disease" and interventions were aimed at "curing" the disease (i.e., removing the pathology; Kauffman & Hallahan, 1974). By about 1975, the realization that process training was not producing desired outcomes shifted attention to an "instructional-imbalance" model in which school failure was viewed as the result of a mismatch between instructional methods and student developmental level. The "effective schools" research (see Bickel & Bickel, 1986) was a major influence stressing the importance of teachers believing that all students can achieve, that basic skill instruction should be emphasized, and that clear instructional objectives should be used to monitor student performance.

At the same time, a "learning process" model emerged that viewed teaching within a "process-product" paradigm in which variables that depict what occurs during teaching are correlated with products (i.e., student outcomes; Needels & Gage, 1991). Research revealed the importance of a number of principles, for example, encouraging student's active engagement in learning, exploring innovative approaches to grouping and organizing classroom instruction, and making learning meaningful by keeping it enjoyable, interesting, student centered, and goal oriented (see Brophy & Good, 1986). These principles became "best practice" and were interpreted for special education (e.g., Christenson, Ysseldyke, & Thurlow, 1989; Reith & Evertson, 1988; Reynolds, Wang, & Walberg, 1992).

Research investigating the teaching-learning process has identified a number of effective instructional practices. Table E.5 shows a sample of effective instructional practices and reveals that substantial positive influence on learning are possible by modifying the way instruction is delivered.

The use of effective instructional practices moves special education toward the general education teaching-learning model and away from a reliance on "special" interventions (e.g., process training). For example, mnemonic instruction (MI) is a strategy that transforms difficult-to-remember facts into a more memorable form through recoding, relating, and retrieving information (Mastropieri & Scruggs, 1991). The BESD for a student receiving MI shows a 64% increase in success rate, which indicates substantial practical significance. Compare the success rate of MI to, for example, perceptual-motor training (ES = 0.08) where the modest 4% increase in success rate indicates a negligible statistical effect and almost no practical significance.

The ultimate purpose of implementing effective instruction is to enhance academic performance. Achievement outcomes are shown in Table E.6 and indicate the potential for substantial gains across subject areas. All achievement domains show large ES, with gains ranging from 29 to 41 percentile ranks on academic achievement measures. The BESD reveals a success rate increase from 27% to 73% indicating an average 46% improvement in the number of students showing a positive response to instruction.

Table E.5. Effective Instructional Practices

Practice	Mean Effect Size	Power Rating	Binomial Effect Size Display (success rate increase) From (%)	To (%)
Mnemonic Instruction	1.62	Very large	18	82
Self-Monitoring	1.36	Very large	22	78
Reinforcement	1.17	Very large	25	75
Self-Questioning	1.16	Very large	25	75
Drill and Practice	.99	Large	28	72
Strategy Instruction	.98	Large	28	72
Feedback	.97	Large	28	72
Direct Instruction	.93	Large	29	71
Applied Behavior Analysis	.93	Large	29	71
Visual Displays	.90	Large	29	71
Computer-Assisted Instruction	.87	Large	30	70
Repeated Reading	.76	Large	32	68
Error Correction	.72	Medium large	33	67
Formative Evaluation	.70	Medium large	33	67
Peer Mediation	.64	Medium	35	65
Diagnostic-Prescriptive Teaching	.64	Medium	35	65
Peer Tutoring	.62	Medium	35	65
Positive Class Morale	.60	Medium	36	64
Grouping	.43	Small medium	40	60
Increased Time	.38	Small medium	41	59

The example of reading comprehension demonstrates how meta-analysis can be useful for judging the magnitude of "real" effects. Two meta-analyses contributed almost all ES measurements and produced ESs of 1.13 and 0.98, a modest three percentile rank difference in outcomes (87% versus 84%). When specific methods for improving reading comprehension are compared, the two meta-analyses revealed similar findings. The largest effects (ES = 1.60 and 1.33) were found for metacognitive techniques (e.g., self-questioning, self-monitoring). Text-enhancement procedures (e.g., advanced organizers, mnemonics) produced ES of 1.09 and 0.92. The least powerful (but nevertheless effective) techniques involved skill-training procedures (e.g., vocabulary, repeated reading) with ES of 0.79 and 0.62. The meta-analytic evidence suggests that, on average, the "real" effect of reading comprehension instruction is 1.04, a level comparable to 1 year's worth of reading comprehension instruction in general education (ES = 1.00). Thus, methods adapted for the purposes of special education produced the same effect as 1 year of general education instruction, but did so in approximately 20 hours. Clearly, special education students can significantly improve their ability to better understand what they read.

Table E.6. Effective Special Education Instruction

Subject Area	Mean Effect Size	Percentile Rank Equivalent	Binomial Effect Size Display (success rate increase) From (%)	To (%)
Handwriting	1.32	91	22	78
Oral Reading	1.31	90	22	78
Language	1.27	90	23	77
Reading Comprehension	1.04	85	27	73
Word Recognition	.98	84	28	72
Narrative Writing	.97	83	28	72
Math	.96	83	28	72
Spelling	.87	81	30	70
Vocabulary	.85	80	30	70
Problem-Solving	.82	79	31	69

Table E.7. Effective Special Education–Related Services and Activities

Service	Mean Effect Size	Power Rating	Binomial Effect Size Display (success rate increase) From (%)	To (%)
Memory Training	1.12	Very large	25	75
Prereferral	1.10	Very large	26	74
Cognitive Behavior Modification	.74	Large	32	68
Psychotherapy	.71	Medium large	33	67
Stimulant Medication	.62	Medium	35	65
Counseling	.60	Medium	35	65
Consultation	.55	Medium	36	64
Rational-Emotive Therapy	.50	Medium	38	62
Attribution Training	.43	Small medium	39	61
Placement	.12	Small	47	53

A hallmark of special education is the provision for related services to be provided when deemed appropriate in augmenting the instruction program. Table E.7 shows a sample of adjunct activities and most demonstrate, at least, "medium" ES. On average (ES = 0.65), related services produce a 24 percentile rank gain on an outcome assessment with the BESD (r = .30), showing a 20% increase in success rate (45–65%). Thus, related services appear to be useful supplements to the instructional program.

Placement has often been viewed as having a positive influence on student performance (see Kavale & Forness,

2000). The ES magnitude (0.12) negates such a view and indicates that the success rate associated with placement increases only 6%, from 47% to 53% (BESD). Although the ES (0.12) favors placement in general education, the actual advantage is small and is found only for students with MR (IQ < 75) and "slow learners" (IQ 75–90). In contrast, for students with LD or EBD, placement in special classes appears more advantageous (ES = 0.29). The average students with LD or EBD placed in a special class would be better off than 61% of those who remained in a general education class. Nevertheless, ES associated with placement are "small" suggesting that "what" (i.e., nature of the instruction) is a more important influence on student outcomes than "where" (i.e., placement). This data led to the expression "special education is a service not a place." Efforts aimed at preventing the need for special education appear to be effective. Prereferral activities produce significant positive efforts (ES = 1.12) and appear successful in about 78 out of 100 cases. Prereferral "works" because it is predicated on modification of *instructional* activities, and its 48% success rate means that almost half of students given preferential activities will *not* need to enter special education. Responses to intervention models are built in part on the assumptions of prevention science and the improvement seen with early intervention.

Pharmacological treatment is often an integral part of the treatment regimen for special education students. Stimulant medication is the most popular and produces significant positive changes in behavior, averaging 23 percentile ranks on behavior ratings and checklists. The ES (0.62) was obtained primarily from a meta-analysis done in 1982 (ES = 0.58) and a replication completed in 1997 (ES =0.64). The consistency of the ES found (i.e., 0.58 and 0.64) provides confirmation for the positive influence of stimulant medication. The use of stimulant medication has long been criticized and more natural and unobtrusive treatments have been sought. One such alternative, popularized during the 1970s, was the Feingold diet designed to eliminate all foods containing artificial substances from the diet. The ES (0.12) obtained for the Feingold diet (see Table E.3) clearly indicates that it has limited influence on modifying behavior. A comparison of the two treatments shows stimulant medication to be greater than 5 times more effective than the Feingold diet.

Special education demonstrates efficacy that may be attributable to a change in instructional emphasis. Until about 25 years ago, special education emphasized its "special" nature by developing singular and different methods not found in general education. The goal was to enhance hypothetical constructs (e.g., "processes") that were presumed to be the cause of learning deficits. Basic skill instruction was a secondary consideration until processes were remediated and learning became more efficient. When intervention activities emphasize, for example, process training and basic skill instruction is subordinate, the nature of special education can be conceptualized as

SPECIAL education, use of unique and exclusive "special" interventions. The limited efficacy of *SPECIAL education* (see Table E.3) suggests that process deficits are difficult to "fix" and such a focus in intervention activities produces little benefit.

The recognition that "special" interventions did not produce desired outcomes moved special education to emphasize "education" in an effort to enhance academic outcomes. When intervention activities emphasize alternative instructional "education" techniques, the nature of special education can be conceptualized as *special EDUCATION*. Such instructional techniques would also be beneficial to monitor all students (i.e. general education) and are adapted to assist students with disabilities in acquiring and assimilating new knowledge; *special EDUCATION* demonstrates significant success (see Table E.6) and produces improved *achievement* outcomes (see Table E.5).

The difference between the two forms of special education are seen in the mega ES (mean of means) for "special" (0.15) versus "education" (0.89) techniques. The comparison reveals *special EDUCATION* to be 6 times more effective than *SPECIAL education*, as defined here; it produces achievement outcomes (mega ES = 1.04) that exceed 1 year's worth of general education instruction (ES = 1.00). On average, SPECIAL education provides only a 6% advantage, meaning that the group receiving "special" interventions exceeds only about 56% of the group not receiving such interventions; a modest level of improvement slightly above chance (50%). Additionally, across meta-analyses investigating *SPECIAL education*, about 25% of the calculated ES were negative, indicating that in one out of four cases the student *not* receiving the "special" intervention performed better. Clearly, there is little reason to include *SPECIAL education* in most intervention programs.

In contrast, the methods associated with *special EDUCATION* provide an efficacious foundation for designing an instructional program. The use of effective techniques is likely to move the average student in special education from the 50th to the 81st percentile. The 31-percentile-rank gain is better than 5 times the gain found with the use of "special" interventions, and indicates students are better off than 81% of those not receiving *special EDUCATION*. For example, Direct Instruction (DI), a teaching procedure based on an explicit step-by-step strategy (ES = 0.93) is 6.5 times more effective than the intuitively appealing modality-matched instruction that attempts to enhance learning by capitalizing on learning style differences (ES = 0.14). Students in special education taught with DI would be better off than 87% of students not receiving DI and would gain over 11 months' credit on an achievement measure compared to about 1 month for modality-matched instruction. With its grounding in effective instructional methodology, *special EDUCATION* can sometimes be up to 20 times more effective than *SPECIAL education*. The critical point in determining the effectiveness of special education is to first define the procedures.

The meta-analyses summarized provide insight into the indications and contraindications of special education interventions (Lipsey & Wilson, 2001). The interventions associated with *special EDUCATION* may be considered a form of "evidenced-based practice" (EBP; Odom et al., 2005) where intervention decisions are based on empirical findings demonstrating that the actions produce efficacious and beneficial outcomes. The use of EBP promotes *instructional validity* where changes can be attributed to the specific activities and can be used to produce similar results with other students (generalization).

Because students in special education, by definition, possess unique learning needs, instructional decisions are critical in the design of *individualized* programs. The complexities surrounding the instructional decision making introduces a degree of "uncertainty" (i.e., the program may not work; Glass, 1979). Besides uncertainty, there is also the possibility of "risk" (i.e., negative outcomes) that can be described in meta-analysis by the standard deviation (SD), a measure of dispersion around the mean ES, representing an index of variability. Taken together, the ES and SD provide a theoretical expectation about intervention efficacy (i.e., ES ± SD). For example, psycholinguistic training (0.39 ± 0.54) spans a theoretical range (−0.15 to 0.93) from negative ES to "large" ES; the difficulty is the inability to predict the outcome (i.e., ES) for a particular student. The mega ES for *SPECIAL education* (0.15) is associated with a larger mega SD (.48) making "special" interventions actually more variable than effective (0.15 ± 0.48). The theoretical range for *SPECIAL education* (−0.33 to 0.63), although possibly producing "medium" effects, also includes significant risk (i.e., the possibility of a negative ES indicating that those *not* receiving the intervention perform better). In contrast, *special EDUCATION* (0.89 ± 0.87) reveals itself to be more effective than variable and, although the theoretical range shows that it may not "work" in some cases (ES = 0.02), there also exists the possibility of being almost twice as effective (ES = 1.76).

Although the use of *special EDUCATION* can reduce risk (i.e., no negative ES), the special education teaching-learning process remains a capricious enterprise (i.e., variable, unpredictable, and indeterminate). To create more certainty, instructional decisions should not be prescriptive (i.e., do A in circumstance X or Y, and do B in circumstance Z) but rather based on an assortment of effective options (i.e., practices with large ES) and data about the characteristics of the student in need of support. This means that teachers are central characters in the special education decision-making process who must replace dogmatic beliefs with rational choices about "what works." Instructional decisions thus include elements of science (theoretical and empirical knowledge) and art (interpretation necessary to initiate action; see Gage, 1978). The teacher's goal is to narrow the gap between the state of the art (what has been demonstrated to be possible) and the state of practice (current ways of providing instruction).

REFERENCES

Arter, J. A., & Jenkins, J. R. (1977). Examining the benefits and prevalence of modality considerations in special education. *Journal of Special Education, 11*, 281–298.

Bickel, W. E., & Bickel, D. D. (1986). Effective schools, classrooms, and instruction: Implications for special education. *Exceptional Children, 52*, 489–500.

Brophy, J., & Good, T. (1986). Teacher behavior and student achievement. In M. C. Wittrock (Ed.), *Handbook of research on teaching* (Vol. 3, pp. 328–375). New York, NY: Macmillan.

Christenson, S. L., Ysseldyke, J. E., & Thurlow, M. L. (1989). Critical instructional factors for students with mild handicaps: An integrative review. *Remedial and Special Education, 10*, 21–31.

Cohen, J. (1988). *Statistical power analysis for the behavioral sciences* (2nd ed.). Hillsdale, NJ: Erlbaum.

Cooper, H., & Hedges, L. V. (Eds.). (1994). *Handbook of research synthesis.* New York, NY: Sage.

Cooper, H. M., & Rosenthal, R. (1980). Statistical versus traditional procedures for summarizing research findings. *Psychological Bulletin, 87*, 442–449.

Forness, S. R., & Kavale, K. A. (1996). Treating social skill deficits in children with learning disabilities: A meta-analysis of the research. *Learning Disability Quarterly, 19*, 2–13.

Gage, N. L. (1978). *The scientific basis of the art of teaching.* New York, NY: Teachers College Press.

Gaynor, J. F. (1973). The "failure" of J. M. G. Itard. *Journal of Special Education, 7*, 439–445.

Glass, G. V. (1976). Primary, secondary, and meta-analysis of research. *Educational Researcher, 5*, 3–8.

Glass, G. V. (1979). Policy for the unpredictable (uncertainty research and policy). *Educational Researcher, 8*, 12–14.

Glass, G. V., McGaw, B., & Smith, M. L. (1981). *Meta-analysis in social research.* Beverly Hills, CA: Sage.

Hallahan, D. P., & Cruickshank, W. (1973). *Psychological foundations of learning disabilities.* Englewood Cliffs, NJ: Prentice-Hall. (Translated 1979). Lernstorungen bzw. lernbehinderung: Padagogisch—psychologische grundlagen. Munchen, Germany: E. Reinhardt.

Hammill, D. D., & Larsen, S. C. (1974). The effectiveness of psycholinguistic training. *Exceptional Children, 41*, 5–14.

Hammill, D. D., & Larsen, S. C. (1978). The effectiveness of psycholinguistic training: A reaffirmation of position. *Exceptional Children, 44*, 402–414.

Hedges, L. V., & Olkin, I. (1985). *Statistical methods for meta-analysis.* San Diego, CA: Academic Press.

Itard, J. M. G. (1962). *The wild boy of Areyron.* (G. Humphrey & M. Humphrey, trans.). New York, NY: Appleton-Century-Crafts. (Original work published 1806)

Kauffman, J. M., & Hallahan, D. P. (1974). The medical model and the science of special education. *Exceptional Children, 41*, 97–102.

Kavale, K. A. (1981). Functions of the Illinois Test of Psycholinguistic Abilities (ITPA): Are they trainable? *Exceptional Children, 47*, 496–510.

Kavale, K. A. (1984). Potential advantages of the meta-analysis technique for research in special education. *Journal of Special Education, 18,* 61–72.

Kavale, K. A. (2001a). Meta-analysis: A primer. *Exceptionality, 9,* 177–183.

Kavale, K. A. (2001b). Decision making in special education: The function of meta-analysis. *Exceptionality, 9,* 245–268.

Kavale, K. A., & Forness, S. R. (1999). *Efficacy of special education and related services.* Washington, DC: American Association on Mental Retardation.

Kavale, K. A., & Forness, S. R. (2000). History, rhetoric, and reality: Analysis of the inclusion debate. *Remedial and Special Education, 21,* 279–296.

Kavale, K. A., & Reese, J. H. (1991). Teacher beliefs and perceptions about learning disabilities: A survey of Iowa practitioners. *Learning Disability Quarterly, 14,* 141–160.

Kirk, S. A., & Johnson, G. O. (1951). *Educating the retarded child.* New York, NY: Houghton-Mifflin Company.

Larrivee, B. (1981). Modality preference as a model for differentiating beginning reading instruction: A review of the issues. *Learning Disability Quarterly, 4,* 180–188.

Lindblom, C. E., & Cohen, D. K. (1979). *Usable knowledge: Social science and social problem solving.* New Haven, CT: Yale University Press.

Lipsey, M. W., & Wilson, D. B. (2001). *Practical meta-analysis* (Vol. 49). Thousand Oaks, CA: Sage.

Lund, K. A., Foster, G. E., & McCall-Perez, G. C. (1978). The effectiveness of psycholinguistic training: A reevaluation. *Exceptional Children, 44,* 310–319.

Mann, L. (1971). Psychometric phrenology and the new faculty psychology: The case against ability assessment and training. *Journal of Special Education, 5,* 3–14.

Mann, L. (1979). *On the trail of process: A historical perspective on cognitive processes and their training.* New York, NY: Grune & Stratton.

Mastropieri, M. A., & Scruggs, T. E. (1991). *Teaching students ways to remember: Strategies for learning mnemonically.* Cambridge, MA: Brookline Books.

McGraw, K. O., & Wong, S. P. (1992). A common language effect size. *Psychological Bulletin, 111,* 361–365.

Minskoff, E. (1975). Research on psycholinguistic training: Critique and guidelines. *Exceptional Children, 42,* 136–144.

Needels, M. C., & Gage, N. L. (1991). Essence and accident in process-product research on teaching. In H. C. Waxman & H. J. Walberg (Eds.), *Effective teaching: Current research* (pp. 3–31). Berkeley, CA: McCuthan.

Newcomer, P., Larsen, S., & Hammill, D. (1975). A response. *Exceptional Children, 42,* 144–148.

Odom, S. L., Brantlinger, E., Gersten, R., Horner, R. H., Thompson, B., & Harris, K. R. (2005). Research in special education: Scientific methods and evidence-based practices. *Exceptional Children, 71,* 137–148.

Quinn, M. M., Kavale, K. A., Mathur, S., Rutherford, R. B., & Forness, S. R. (1999). A meta-analysis of social skill interventions for students with emotional or behavioral disorders. *Journal of Emotional and Behavioral Disorders, 1,* 54–64.

Reith, H. J., & Evertson, C. (1988). Variables related to the effective instruction of difficult-to-teach children. *Focus on Exceptional Children, 20,* 1–8.

Reynolds, M. C., Wang, M. C., & Walberg, H. J. (1992). The knowledge bases for special and general education. *Remedial and Special Education, 13,* 6–10, 33.

Rosenthal, R., & Rubin, D. B. (1982). A simple, general purpose display of magnitude of experimental effect. *Journal of Educational Psychology, 74,* 166–169.

Sarason, S. B., & Doris, J. (1979). *Educational handicap, public policy, and social history.* New York, NY: Cambridge University Press.

Tarver, S. G., & Dawson, M. M. (1978). Modality preference and the teaching of reading: A review. *Journal of Learning Disabilities, 11,* 5–17.

U.S. Department of Education. (1999). Assistance to states for the education of children with disabilities program and the early intervention program for infants and toddlers with disabilities: Final regulations. *Federal Register, 64*(48), CFR Parts 300 and 303.

APPENDIX A

Reported Effect Sizes were obtained from the following sources:

Adams, G. L., & Englemann, S. (1996). *Research on Direct Instruction: 25 years beyond DISTAR.* Seattle, WA: Educational Achievement Systems.

Ang, R. P., & Hughes, J. N. (2002). Differential benefits of skills training with antisocial youth based on group composition: A meta-analytic investigation. *School Psychology Review, 31,* 164–186.

Arnold, K. S., Myette, B. M., & Casto, G. (1986). Relationships of language intervention efficacy to certain subject characteristics in mentally retarded preschool children: A meta-analysis. *Education and Training of the Mentally Retarded, 21,* 108–116.

Beelman, A., Pfingsten, U., & Losel, F. (1994). Effects of training social competence in children: A metaanalysis of recent evaluation studies. *Journal of Clinical Psychology, 23,* 260–271.

Borman, G. D., Hewes, G. M., Overman, L. T., & Brown, S. (2002). *Comprehensive school reform and student achievement: A meta-analysis* (Report No. 59). Baltimore, MD: Center for Research on Education of Students Paced At-Risk, Johns Hopkins University.

Browder, D. M., & Xin, Y. P. (1998). A meta-analysis and review of sight word research and its implications for teaching functional reading to individuals with moderate and severe disabilities. *Journal of Special Education, 32,* 130–153.

Burns, M. K. (2004). Empirical analysis of drill ratio research: Refining the instructional level for drill tasks. *Remedial and Special Education, 25,* 167–173.

Burns, M. K., & Symington, T. (2002). A meta-analysis of prereferral intervention teams: Student and systemic outcomes. *Journal of School Psychology, 40,* 437–447.

Carlberg, C., & Kavale, K. (1980). The efficacy of special versus regular class placement for exceptional children: A meta-analysis. *Journal of Special Education, 14,* 296–309.

Casto, G., & Mastropieri, M. A. (1986). The efficacy of early intervention programs: A meta-analysis. *Exceptional Children, 52,* 417–424.

Conners, F. A. (1992). Reading instruction for students with moderate mental retardation: Review and analysis of research. *American Journal on Mental Retardation, 96,* 577–597.

Cook, S. B., Scruggs, T. E., Mastropieri, M. A., & Casto, G. C. (1985–86). Handicapped students as tutors. *Journal of Special Education, 19,* 483–492.

Crenshaw, T. M., Kavale, K. A., Forness, S. R., & Reeve, R. E. (1999). Attention deficit hyperactivity disorder and the efficacy of stimulant medication: A meta-analysis. In T. E. Scruggs & M. A. Mastropieri (Eds.), *Advances in learning and behavioral disabilities* (Vol. 13, pp. 135–165). Stamford, CT: JAI Press.

de Castro, B., Veerman, J. W., Koops, W., Bosch, J. D., & Monshouwer, H. J. (2002). Hostile attribution of intent and aggressive behavior: A meta-analysis. *Child Development, 73,* 916–934.

Didden, R., Duker, P. C., & Karzilius, H. (1997). Meta-analytic study on treatment effectiveness for problem behaviors with individuals who have mental retardation. *American Journal on Mental Retardation, 101,* 387–399.

Dunn, R., Griggs, S. A., Olson, J., Beasley, A., & Gorman, B. S. (1995). A meta-analytic validation of the Dunn and Dunn model of learning style preferences. *Journal of Educational Research, 88,* 353–362.

Durlak, J. A., Fuhrman, J., & Lampman, C. (1991). Effectiveness of cognitive-behavior therapy for maladapting children: A meta-analysis. *Psychological Bulletin, 110,* 204–214.

Elbaum, B., Vaughn, S., Hughes, M., Moody, S. W., & Schumm, J. S. (2000). How reading outcomes of students with disabilities are related to instructional grouping formats: A meta-analytic review. In R. Gersten, E. Schiller, & S. Vaughn (Eds.), *Contemporary special education research* (pp. 105–135). Mahwah, NJ: Erlbaum.

Engles, G. I., Garnefski, N., & Diekstra, R. F. W. (1993). Efficacy of rational emotive therapy: A quantitative analysis. *Journal of Consulting and Clinical Psychology, 61,* 1083–1090.

Forness, S. R. (2001). Special education and related services: What have we learned from meta-analysis? *Exceptionality, 9,* 185–198.

Forness, S. R., & Kavale, K. A. (1993). Strategies to improve basic learning and memory deficits in mental retardation: A meta-analysis of experimental studies. *Education and Training in Mental Retardation, 28,* 99–110.

Forness, S. R., & Kavale, K. A. (1996). Treating social skill deficits in children with learning disabilities: A meta-analysis of the research. *Learning Disability Quarterly, 19,* 1–13.

Forness, S. R., Kavale, K. A., Blum, I. M., & Lloyd, J. W. (1997). Mega-analysis of meta-analysis: What works in special education and related services. *Teaching Exceptional Children, 29*(6), 4–9.

Fuchs, L. S., & Fuchs, D. (1986). Effects of systematic evaluation. A meta-analysis. *Exceptional Children, 53,* 199–208.

Gersten, R., & Baker, S. (2001). Teaching expressive writing to students with learning disabilities: A meta-analysis. *Elementary School Journal, 101,* 251–272.

Glass, G. V., & Smith, M. L. (1979). Meta-analysis of research on class size and achievement. *Educational Evaluation and Policy Analysis, 1,* 2–16.

Gonzalez, J. E., Nelson, J. R., Gutkin, T. B., Saunders, A., Galloway, A., & Shwery, G. S. (2004). Rational emotive therapy with children and adolescents: A meta-analysis. *Journal of Emotional and Behavioral Disorders, 12,* 222–235.

Gresham, F. M. (1998). Social skills training: Should we raze, remodel, or rebuild? *Behavioral Disorders, 24,* 19–25.

Gresham, F. M., Sugai, G., & Horner, R. H. (2001). Interpreting outcomes of social skills training for students with high-incidence disabilities. *Exceptional Children, 67,* 331–344.

Hedges, L. V., & Stock, W. A. (1983). The effects of class size: An examination of rival hypotheses. *American Educational Research Journal, 20,* 63–85.

Hillocks, G. (1984). What works in teaching composition: A meta-analysis of experimental treatment studies. *American Journal of Education, 93,* 133–170.

Horn, W. F., & Packard, T. (1985). Early identification of learning problems: A meta-analysis. *Journal of Educational Psychology, 77,* 597–607.

Innocenti, M. S., & White, K. R. (1993). Are more intensive early intervention programs more effective? A review of the literature. *Exceptionality, 4,* 31–50.

Joseph, L. M., & Scery, M. E. (2004). Where is the phonics? A review of the literature on the use of phonetic analysis with students with mental retardation. *Remedial and Special Education, 25,* 88–94.

Kavale, K. (1981a). Function of the Illinois Test of Psycholinguistic Abilities (ITPA). Are they trainable? *Exceptional Children, 47,* 496–510.

Kavale, K. (1982a). The efficacy of stimulant drug treatment for hyperactivity: A meta-analysis. *Journal of Learning Disabilities, 15,* 280–289.

Kavale, K. (1982c). Psycholinguistic training programs: Are there differential treatment effects? *The Exceptional Child, 29,* 21–30.

Kavale, K. A. (1984). A meta-analytic evaluation of the Frostig test and training program. *The Exceptional Child, 31,* 134–141.

Kavale, K. A. (1990). Variances and verities in learning disability interventions. In T. E. Scruggs & B. Y. L. Wong (Eds.), *Intervention research in learning disabilities* (pp. 3–33). New York, NY: Springer-Verlag.

Kavale, K. A., & Dobbins, D. A. (1993). The equivocal nature of special education interventions. *Early Child Development and Care, 86,* 23–37.

Kavale, K. A., & Forness, S. R. (1983). Hyperactivity and diet treatment: A meta-analysis of the Feingold hypothesis. *Journal of Learning Disabilities, 16,* 324–330.

Kavale, K. A., & Forness, S. R. (1987). Substance over style: Assessing the efficacy of modality testing and teaching. *Exceptional Children, 54,* 228–239.

Kavale, K. A., & Forness, S. R. (2000). Policy decisions in special education: The role of analysis. In R. Gersten, E. Schiller,

& S. Vaughn (Eds.), *Contemporary special education research* (pp. 281–326). Mahwah, NJ: Erlbaum.

Kavale, K. A., & Glass, G. V. (1982). The efficacy of special education interventions and practices: A compendium of meta-analysis findings. *Focus on Exceptional Children, 15*(4), 1–14.

Kavale, K. A., & Glass, G. V. (1984). Meta-analysis and policy decisions in special education. In B. K. Keogh (Ed.), *Advances in special education* (Vol. IV, pp. 195–247), Greenwich, CT: JAI.

Kavale, K. A., Mathur, S. R., Forness, R., Rutherford, R. B., & Quinn, M. M. (1997). Effectiveness of social skills training for students with behavior disorders: A meta-analysis. In T. E. Scruggs & M. A. Mastropieri (Eds.), *Advances in learning and behavioral disabilities* (pp. 1–28). New York, NY: Elsevier.

Kavale, K. A., & Mattson, P. D. (1983). "One jumped off the balance beam": Meta-analysis of perceptual-motor training. *Journal of Learning Disabilities, 16*, 165–173.

Kroesbergen, E. H., & VanLuit, J. E. H. (2003). Mathematics interventions for children with special educational needs: A meta-analysis. *Remedial and Special Education, 24*, 97–114.

Lapadat, J. C. (1991). Pragmatic language skills of students with language and/or learning disabilities: A quantitative synthesis. *Journal of Learning Disabilities, 24*, 147–158.

Lipsey, M. W., & Wilson, D. B. (1993). The efficacy of psychological, educational, and behavioral treatment. *American Psychologist, 48*, 1181–1209.

Mastropieri, M. A., Bakken, J. P., & Scruggs, T. E. (1991). Mathematics instruction for individuals with mental retardation: A perspective and research synthesis. *Education and Training in Mental Retardation, 26*, 115–129.

Mastropieri, M. A., & Scruggs, T. E. (1985–86). Early intervention for socially withdrawn children. *Journal of Special Education, 19*, 429–441.

Mastropieri, M. A., Scruggs, T. E., & Casto, G. (1985). Early intervention for behaviorally disordered children: An integrative review. *Behavior Disorders Monograph, 11*, 27–35.

Mastropieri, M. A., Scruggs, T. E., & Casto, G. (1985–86). Early intervention for behaviorally disordered children: An integrative review [Monograph]. In R. B. Rutherford, Jr. (Ed.), *Monographs in behavior disorders* (pp. 27–35). Tempe, AZ: Council for Children with Behavior Disorders.

Mathur, S. R., Kavale, K. A., Quinn, M. M., Forness, S. R., & Rutherford, R. B. (1998). Social skills interventions with students with emotional and behavioral problems: A quantitative synthesis of single-subject research. *Behavioral Disorders, 23*, 193–201.

Niemiec, R., & Walberg, H. J. (1987). Comparative effects of computer-assisted instruction: A synthesis of reviews. *Journal of Educational Computing Research, 3*, 19–37.

Nye, C., Foster, S. H., & Seaman, D. (1987). Effectiveness of language intervention with the language/learning disabled. *Journal of Speech and Hearing Disorders, 52*, 348–357.

Quinn, M. M., Kavale, K. A., Mathur, S., Rutherford, R. B., & Forness, S. R. (1999). A meta-analysis of social skill interventions for students with emotional or behavioral disorders. *Journal of Emotional and Behavioral Disorders, 7*, 54–64.

Robinson, T. R., Smith, S. W., Miller, M. D., & Brownell, M. T. (1999). Cognitive behavior modification of hyperactivity-impulsivity and aggression: A meta-analysis of school-based studies. *Journal of Educational Psychology, 91*, 195–203.

Schmidt, M., Weinstein, T., Niemic, R., & Walberg, H. J. (1985–86). Computer-assisted instruction with exceptional children. *Journal of Special Education, 19*, 494–501.

Schumm, J. S., Moody, S. W., & Vaughn, S. (2000). Grouping for reading instruction: Does one size fit all? *Journal of Learning Disabilities, 33*, 477–488.

Scotti, J. R., Evans, I. M., Meyer, L. H., & Walker, P. (1991). A meta-analysis of intervention research with problem behavior: Treatment validity and standards of practice. *American Journal on Mental Retardation, 96*, 233–256.

Scruggs, T. E., Mastropieri, M. A., Cook, S., & Escobar, C. (1986). Early intervention for children with conduct disorders: A quantitative synthesis of single-subject research. *Behavioral Disorders, 11*, 260–271.

Scruggs, T. E., Mastropieri, M. A., Forness, S. R., & Kavale, K. A. (1988). Early language intervention: A quantitative synthesis of single-subject research. *Journal of Special Education, 22*, 259–283.

Shonkoff, J. P., & Hauser-Cram, P. (1987). Early intervention for disabled infants and their families: A quantitative analysis. *Pediatrics, 80*, 650–658.

Skiba, R. J., & Casey, A. (1985). Interventions for behaviorally disordered students: A quantitative review and methodological critique. *Behavioral Disorders, 10*, 239–252.

Smith, M. L., & Glass, G. V. (1980). Meta-analysis of research on class size and related estimators. *American Educational Research Journal, 17*, 419–433.

Smith, M. S., Glass, G. V., & Miller, T. I. (1980). *The benefits of psychotherapy*. Baltimore, MD: Johns Hopkins University Press.

Soto, G., Toro-Zambrana, W., & Belfiore, P. J. (1994). Comparison of two instructional strategies on social skills acquisition and generalization among individuals with moderate and severe mental retardation working in a vocational setting: A meta-analytical review. *Education and Training in Mental Retardation and Developmental Disabilities, 29*, 307–320.

Swanson, H. L. (1999a). *Interventions for students with learning disabilities: A meta-analysis of treatment outcomes*. New York, NY: Guilford Press.

Swanson, H. L. (1999b). Reading research for students with LD: A meta-analysis of intervention outcomes. *Journal of Learning Disabilities, 32*, 504–532.

Swanson, H. L. (2001). Research on interventions for adolescents with learning disabilities: A meta-analysis of outcomes related to higher-order processing. *Elementary School Journal, 101*, 331–348.

Swanson, H. L., Carson, C., & Sachsee-Lee, C. M. (1996). A selective synthesis of intervention research for students with learning disabilities. *School Psychology Review, 25*, 370–391.

Swanson, H. L., & Hoskyn, M. (1998). Experimental intervention research on students with learning disabilities: A meta-analysis of treatment outcomes. *Review of Educational Research, 68,* 277–321.

Swanson, H. L., & Hoskyn, M. (2000). Intervention research for students with learning disabilities: A comprehensive meta-analysis of group design studies. In T. E. Scruggs & M. A. Mastropieri (Eds.), *Advances in learning and behavioral disabilities* (Vol. 14, pp. 1–153). Stamford, CT: JAI Press.

Swanson, H. L., O'Shaughnessy, T. E., McMahon, C. M., Hoskyn, M., & Sachsee-Lee, C. M. (1998). A selective synthesis of single subject design intervention research on students with learning disabilities. In T. E. Scruggs & M. A. Mastropieri (Eds.), *Advances in learning and behavioral disabilities* (Vol. 12, pp. 79–126). Greenwich, CT: JAI Press.

Therrien, W. J. (2004). Fluency and comprehension gains as a result of repeated readings: A meta-analysis. *Remedial and Special Education, 25,* 252–261.

Thurber, S., & Walker, C. E. (1983). Medication and hyperactivity: A meta-analysis. *Journal of General Psychology, 108,* 79–86.

VanIjzendoorn, M. H., & Bus, A. G. (1994). Meta-analytic confirmation of the nonword reading deficit in developmental dyslexia. *Reading Research Quarterly, 29,* 267–275.

Vaughn, S., Gersten, R., & Chard, D. J. (2000). The underlying message in LD intervention research: Findings from research syntheses. *Exceptional Children, 67,* 99–114.

Walberg, H. J. (1984). Improving the productivity of America's schools. *Educational Leadership, 41,* 19–30.

Wang, M. C., & Baker, E. T. (1985–86). Mainstreaming programs: Design features and effects. *Journal of Special Education, 19,* 503–521.

Waxman, H. C., Wang, M. C., Anderson, K. A., & Walberg, H. J. (1985). Adaptive education and student outcomes: A quantitative synthesis. *Journal of Educational Research, 78,* 228–236.

Weisz, J. R., Weiss, B., Han, S. S., Granger, D. A., & Morton, T. (1995). Effects of psychotherapy with children and adolescents revisited: A meta-analysis of treatment outcome studies. *Psychological Bulletin, 117,* 450–468.

White, K. R. (1985–86). Efficacy of early interventions. *Journal of Special Education, 19,* 401–16.

White, W. A. T. (1988). A meta-analysis of the effects of direct instruction in special education. *Education and Treatment of Children, 11,* 364–374.

Whiteley, B. E., & Frieze, I. H. (1985). Children's causal attributions for success and failure in achievement settings: A meta-analysis. *Journal of Educational Psychology, 77,* 608–616.

Wilson, S. J., Lipsey, M. W., & Derzon, J. (2003). The effects on aggressive behavior: A meta-analysis. *Journal of Consulting and Clinical Psychology, 71,* 136–149.

Xin, Y. P., & Jitendra, A. K. (1999). The effects of instruction in solving mathematical word problems for students with learning problems: A meta-analysis. *Journal of Special Education, 32,* 207–225.

KENNETH A. KAVALE
Regent University

See also Individuals with Disabilities Education Improvement Act of 2004 (IDEIA); Response to Intervention

EGBERT, ROBERT L. (1923–2001)

Robert L. Egbert obtained his BS and MS degrees from Utah State University, later earning his doctorate at Cornell University, Ithaca, New York. He was a full professor at the Center for Curriculum and Instruction of the University of Nebraska, Lincoln for 28 years and the college's dean from 1971 to 1982. He was a member of the boards of directors of the High/Scope Educational Research Foundation and American Association of Colleges for Teacher Education, and a director of the National Commission for Excellence in Teacher Education.

Used both regionally and nationally, his articles and reports have focused on improvement and change in teacher education (Egbert, 1971, 1974, 1985). In 1985, he directed the preparation of the report, "A Call for Change in Teacher Education," and in February 1991, his paper presenting a history of project Head Start and the four phases of the Follow Through Program between 1967 and 1991 was featured in a conference sponsored by the U.S. Office of Educational Research and Improvement. As a leading expert in the field of education, he addressed the 1985 annual meeting of the American Association of Colleges for Teacher Education, delivering the Charles W. Hunt Lecture, "A Time for Beginnings."

A lifelong educator and a specialist in early childhood education, Egbert officially retired in 1999, but remained active in the college until shortly before his death, never ceasing to be a strong advocate for the teaching profession.

REFERENCES

Egbert, R. L. (1971). Follow through. *National Elementary Principal, 51,* 104–109.

Egbert, R. L. (1974). Improving teacher education through the use of research information. *Journal of Teacher Education, 35*(4), 9–11.

Egbert, R. L. (1985). *A call for change in teacher education.* Washington, DC: National Commission for Excellence in Teacher Education.

ROBERTA C. STOKES
Texas A&M University
First edition

TAMARA J. MARTIN
*The University of Texas
of the Permian Basin*
Second edition

JESSI K. WHEATLEY
*Falcon School District
49 Colorado Springs,
Colorado*
Third edition

EHLERS-DANLOS SYNDROME

Ehlers-Danlos syndrome (EDS) is not a single, homogeneous disorder, but a group of nine different types of genetically inherited disorders characterized by hyperelastic skin that is fragile and bruises easily, excessive laxity (looseness) of the joints, easily damaged blood vessels, and excessive bleeding (Ainsworth & Aulicino, 2001). The syndrome is caused by abnormal formation of connective tissue due to mutations in collagen genes. Symptoms range from mild to severe within the six most prevalent types of the disorder.

There are three ways in which the various types of EDS can be inherited: The majority are autosomal dominant, but some are autosomal recessive and X-linked recessive inheritance. Carriers of one type of EDS can transmit only that specific type of gene for EDS and thus will not have a child with a type different from their own (Matsen, 2001).

EDS occurs in approximately 1 in 5,000 individuals (Ainsworth & Aulicino, 2001). EDS is most commonly found in Caucasians with European ancestry and in males, although both males and females of all races and ethnic backgrounds can be affected. There are some specific complications that can occur depending on the gender of the individual with EDS. Adolescent males are at particular risk for arterial ruptures, presumably due to defective collagen that is taxed during prepubertal growth spurts (Barabas, 2000). Pregnant females are at risk for miscarriage and premature delivery due to rupture of the uterus or fetal membrane fragility (Beers & Berkow, 1999).

Although nine different types of EDS have been identified, each with a distinctive set of features, the most common forms of EDS (Types I, II, and III) are characterized by phenotypic overlap:

Characteristics

1. Hyperelastic skin
2. Cutaneous fragility (easy to bruise, tear, and excessively scar the skin)
3. Articular hypermobility of joints (the ability to flex joints beyond the "normal" range)
4. Joint dislocation (usually occurring in the shoulders, knees, hips, collar bone, or jaw)
5. Molluscoid pseudotumors (firm, fibrous lumps that develop over elbows and knees or other pressure points)
6. Varicose veins
7. Visual difficulties (usually severe nearsightedness)

The following characteristics are usually found in the rarer forms of EDS:

1. Gum disease (Type VII)
2. Curvature of the spine (Type VI)
3. Blood clotting problems (Type IV)
4. Severe eye complications (Type VI)
5. Pulmonary difficulties (Type IV)
6. Rupture of the intestines, mitral heart valve, or uterus (from pregnancy; Type IV)

Due to the rarity of EDS and the often apparent health of individuals with this syndrome, many physicians are unaware of the symptoms of this disorder and can easily misdiagnose patients (Wilson, 2000). Doctors or other professionals who come into contact with children with EDS may also mistake bruises and torn skin for child abuse. The actual diagnosis of EDS is made based on the patient's family history and skin biopsy to determine the chemical makeup of the individual's connective tissue.

There is no specific treatment for EDS because individual problems must be evaluated and treated accordingly. Due to the extremely fragile skin and tissue of children with EDS, precautions should be taken to prevent injury. Toddlers and young children should be protected from slipping, falling, or overextending their joints by keeping hallways and doorways clear of toys and other objects and avoiding the use of stairs (Matsen, 2001).

Additional precautionary measures such as padding the legs and elbows of children will greatly lessen the chance of accidental trauma, such as scarring and bruising. Physical and occupational therapy may be beneficial in strengthening muscles and in providing information to improve daily living. Unstable joints can be treated with braces. Fragile skin should also be protected with sunscreen to prevent damage. Surgery and sutures of wounds need to be undertaken with great care, as fragile tissues may tear and excessive bleeding can occur due to ruptured blood vessels and arteries (Barabas, 2000; Beers & Berkow, 1999; Pepin, Schwarze, Superti-Furga, & Byers, 2000).

Although EDS does not affect intelligence, children may experience difficulties both emotionally and academically because of absences from school for medical problems. Due to the variety of physical disabilities that are associated with EDS, children with this syndrome can qualify for special education services. Teachers should be made aware of the nature of the illness, with its associated bruising and injuries, as well as the need for any medications that are required for the child. Children with EDS may benefit from psychological services and support groups for children with illnesses to cope with feelings of sadness and alienation. Despite the special considerations and limitations that children with EDS have, it is important that they be allowed to play with friends and be involved in activities in which they can safely participate (Matsen, 2001).

Prognosis depends on the type of EDS from which an individual suffers. People with EDS generally have normal life spans, although life expectancy can be shortened from life-threatening complications that can occur in various types of the syndrome. Examples of potentially fatal complications include failure of surgical wounds to close and rupture of major vessels and organs (Barabas, 2000; Beers & Berkow, 1999; Pepin et al., 2000; Wilson, 2000).

Genetic counseling is recommended for prospective parents with a family history for EDS. Affected parents should be made aware of the type of EDS they have and its mode of inheritance. Information about genetic counseling available in a specific area can be obtained by contacting the March of Dimes or may be determined through a knowledgeable health-care provider.

REFERENCES

Ainsworth, S. R., & Aulicino, P. L. (2000, December). *A survey of Ehlers-Danlos syndrome: Ehlers-Danlos National Foundation.* Retrieved from http://ednf.org/

Barabas, A. (2000). Correspondence: Letter to the editor. *New England Journal of Medicine, 343,* 366–368.

Beers, M. H., & Berkow, R. (Eds.), (1999). *The* Merck *manual of diagnosis and therapy* (17th ed.). Lawrenceville, NJ: Merck.

Matsen, F. (Ed.). (2001). *Ehlers-Danlos syndrome.* University of Washington: Orthopaedics & Sports Medicine. Retrieved from http://www.orthop.washington.edu/

Pepin, M., Schwarze, U., Superti-Furga, A., & Byers, P. H. (2000). Clinical and genetic features of Ehlers-Danlos syndrome, type IV, the vascular type. *New England Journal of Medicine, 342,* 673–680.

Wilson, F. (2000). Rare Ehlers-Danlos syndrome type IV presents in common patient symptoms. *Dermatology Times.*

ANDREA HOLLAND
University of Texas at Austin

EISENSON, JON (1907–2001)

Jon Eisenson received his BSS from the College of the City of New York in 1928. He earned both his MA in 1930 and his PhD in clinical psychology in 1935 from Columbia University. In his early years as a psychologist, he believed that understanding the nature of language, its relationship to thinking and learning, and how it is used and abused by humans was important to understanding the behavior of persons with or without disabilities.

His major fields of interest included language and the brain, aphasia, stuttering, dyslexia, and communication. Eisenson served as the assistant chief clinical psychologist in the United States War Department in 1944 and 1945 during World War II. For many years, his primary interests were the effects of brain damage on language behavior

and developing techniques for recovery and reading problems, both congenital and acquired.

Eisenson's principal publications included *Aphasia in Children,* which addressed the problems of severely linguistically impaired children with aphasia, and *Communicative Disorders in Children,* written for professionals who wish to improve the communicative abilities of children with impairments severe enough to interfere with normal communication. Additional writings include *Adult Aphasia,* dealing with aphasia acquired as a result of disease or accident, *Reading for Meaning,* a psycholinguistic approach to the teaching of reading, *Is My Child's Speech Normal?,* and *How to Speak American English.*

Eisenson was a fellow and past president of the American Speech and Hearing Association and the American Speech and Hearing Foundation.

Eisenson authored numerous articles and books, and was an experienced teacher and guest lecturer. In addition to his many professional pursuits, he wrote poetry for children and adults.

This entry has been informed by the sources listed below.

REFERENCES

Eisenson, J. (1984a). *Adult aphasia* (2nd ed.). Englewood Cliffs, NJ: Prentice Hall.

Eisenson, J. (1984b). *Language and speech disorders in children.* Elmsford, NY: Pergamon Press.

Eisenson, J. (1985). *My special zoo.* Tulsa, OK: Modern Education.

Eisenson, J. (1998). *Reading for meaning* (rev. ed.). Austin, TX: PRO-ED.

Eisenson, J., & Ogilvie, M. (1983). *Communication disorders* (5th ed.). New York, NY: Macmillan.

TAMARA J. MARTIN
The University of Texas of the Permian Basin

JESSI K. WHEATLEY
Falcon School District 49 Colorado Springs, Colorado
Third edition

ELABORATED VERSUS RESTRICTED VERBAL CODES

The expressions "elaborated" and "restricted" code were introduced by the British sociologist Basil Bernstein in 1974 and were defined:

on a linguistic level, in terms of the probability predicting for any one speaker which syntactic elements will be used to organize meaning. In the case of an elaborated code, the speaker will select from a relatively extensive range of alternatives and therefore the probability of predicting the pattern of organizing elements is considerably reduced. In the case of a restricted code, the number of these alternatives is often severely limited and the probability of predicting the pattern is greatly increased. (pp. 76–77)

Bernstein hypothesized that these different codes were functions of different social structures. Comparisons of groups of middle-class and working-class children showed significant differences for grammatical and lexical features. Middle-class children used a significantly higher proportion of subordinations, complex verbal stems, the passive voice, uncommon adjectives, adverbs, and conjunctions, and the pronoun I.

In later publications, Bernstein refined and extended his theory. A code was then said to be "a regulative principle controlling speech realizations in diverse social contexts" (Bernstein, 1974, p. 12). "Elaborated codes give access to universalistic orders of meaning, which are less context bound, whereas restricted codes give access to particularistic orders of meaning, which are far more context bound, that is, tied to a particular context" (p. 197).

The four contexts Bernstein cites are the regulative, instructional, imaginative, and interpersonal. In each of these contexts, speech variants can be observed that are characteristically elaborated or restricted (codes cannot be observed because they belong to the deep structure of communication). The variants are elaborated if they appear to be selected from a wide range of syntactic alternatives that can be used in various contexts (universality); they are restricted if they are chosen from a much more limited, and, therefore, more predictable, number of possibilities. The distinction between speech variants and codes is important because elaborated speech variants can appear in elaborated and restricted codes, as can restricted variants. What distinguishes the codes is the relative frequency of the two types of variants in both codes.

As social roles are first learned in the family, the way socialization occurs is of crucial importance for the development of one or the other coding activity. Bernstein distinguished two kinds of families. Person-oriented families, in which the child learns to play his or her part among the other members of the family, are more likely to endow a child with an elaborated code. The child growing up in a positional family, in which roles are preestablished, is less likely to learn to adapt his or her language to that of interlocutors and, as a consequence, is more likely to build up a restricted code.

Bernstein insists that a restricted code is not in itself inferior to an elaborated code. The main problem for working-class children belonging to families that seem to be predominantly of the positional type is that their restricted code will constitute a severe hinderance when they go to school. "For the schools are predicated on elaborated code and its system of social relationships. Although

an elaborated code does not entail any specific value system, the value system of the middle class penetrates the texture of the very learning context itself" (Bernstein, 1974, p. 186).

Bernstein was criticized, on the one hand, for the vagueness of his definitions and the crudeness of the linguistic distinctions he operated with, and on the other hand, for having given scientific support to the theory of linguistic deprivation (Labov, 1970) and eventually to compensatory education programs (Bereiter & Engelmann, 1966). The latter criticism does not seem to be justified, as it ignores the evolution in Bernstein's ideas after 1962.

REFERENCES

Bereiter, G., & Engelmann, S. (1966). *Teaching disadvantaged children in the pre-school.* Englewood Cliffs, NJ: Prentice Hall.

Bernstein, B. (1974). *Class, codes and control* (Vol. 1). London, England: Routledge & Kegan Paul.

Labov, W. (1970). The logic of non-standard English. In J. Alatis (Ed.), *Report of the 20th Annual Round Table Meeting on Linguistics and Language Studies.* Washington, DC: Georgetown University Press.

S. De Vriendt
*Vrije Universiteit Brussels
Brussels, Belgium*

See also Expressive Language Disorders; Language Delays; Language Disorders

ELAVIL

Elavil is the trade name for the generic tricyclic antidepressant amitriptyline. Elavil and other tricyclic antidepressants (TCA) usually are prescribed for endogenous depressions. These are affective disorders that present with vegetative disturbance (i.e., psychomotor slowing, poor appetite/weight loss, loss of sexual interest) and usually cannot be ascribed to a situational cause. Persons with endogenous depression often have positive familial histories for an affective disorder.

Therapeutically, TCAs are intended to reduce symptom intensity, increase mood elevation and physical activity, reestablish appetite and sleep patterns, and, in general, facilitate activity levels that will promote social adjustment (Blum, 1984). Such effects are assumed to be a result of TCA's blocking brain amine reuptake, thus making more of the various catecholamines available at their specific receptor sites (Seiden & Dykstra, 1977).

Elavil differs from other TCAs in that it tends to produce greater sedation and a greater degree of anticholinergic side effects: visual blurring, urinary retention, constipation, concentration difficulties (Katzung, 1982). The TCAs are not often used in the treatment of children, because children appear to be more at risk for cardiovascular side effects and seizure-facilitating side effects of high doses (Blum, 1984). However, in titrated doses, TCAs have been used to treat enuresis and severe obsessive-compulsive disorders in children (Detre & Jarecki, 1971). In the 1990s, widespread use of TCAs was curtailed in favor of the SSRIs, selective serotonin reuptake inhibitors, such as Prozac. It is not recommended for children under 12 years (Fletcher-Janzen & Williams, 2005).

REFERENCES

Blum, K. (1984). *Handbook of abusable drugs.* New York, NY: Gardner Press.

Detre, T. P., & Jarecki, G. H. (1971). *Modern psychiatric treatment.* Philadelphia, PA: Lippincott.

Fletcher-Janzen, E., & Williams, J. (2005). Medications and the special education student. In E. Fletcher-Janzen & C. R. Reynolds (Eds.), *Special education almanac* (pp. 405–480). Hoboken, NJ: Wiley.

Katzung, B. G. (1982). *Basic and clinical pharmacology.* Los Altos, CA: Lange Medical.

Seiden, L. S., & Dykstra, L. A. (1977). *Psychopharmacology: A biochemical and behavioral approach.* New York, NY: Van Nostrand Reinhold.

ROBERT F. SAWICKI
Lake Erie Institute of Rehabilitation

See also Dopamine; Haldol; Tranquilizers

ELECTIVE MUTISM

Elective mutism (now commonly referred to as selective mutism) is a disorder of infancy, childhood, and adolescence that consists of a child's consistent failure to speak in certain social situations, in which there is an expectation for speaking, despite speaking in other situations (American Psychiatric Association, 2000). The Classification of Mental and Behaviour Disorder: Clinical Description and Diagnostic Guidelines (ICD-10; World Health Organization, 1992) defines elective mutism as a condition characterized by a marked, emotionally determined selectivity in speaking, such that the child demonstrates a language competence in some situations but fails to speak in other (definable) situations.

The disorder usually is associated with marked personality features involving social anxiety, withdrawal, sensitivity, or resistance (Sharkey & McNicholas, 2008). Onset usually occurs during the preschool years, before age 5. Characteristics associated with elective mutism include shyness, anxiety, fear of social embarrassment, social isolation, withdrawal, dependency upon parents, negative controlling personality, oppositional behavior, enuresis, encopresis, depression, separation anxiety, and language dysfunction (Black & Uhde, 1995; Dummit, Klein, Tancer, Asche, & Martin, 1996; Schum, 2002; Tatem & DelCampo, 1995).

Elective mutism occurs in less than 1 percent of the population (Ford et al., 1998; Powell & Dalley, 1995; Tatem & DelCampo, 1995). This prevalence rate is the same for the school age as well as the general population. Elective mutism occurs more often in females than males, with sex ratio estimates ranging from 1.6:1 to 2:1 (Anstendig, 1998; Tatem & DelCampo, 1995).

Etiology of elective mutism is largely unknown. Theories about what causes elective mutism have focused on individual or family dynamics, anxiety, overprotection, developmental language and speech disorders, mild mental retardation, immigration, hospitalization or trauma before age 3, and extreme shyness or anxiety disorders (Ford, Sladeczek, Carlson, & Kratochwill, 1998; Joseph, 1999; Tatem & DelCampo, 1995).

A diagnosis of selective mutism (elective mutism) must include the absence of speech that interferes with educational or occupational achievement or with social communication, that lasts at least 1 month (not limited to the first month of school), is not due to a lack of knowledge of or comfort with the spoken language required in the social situation, is not better accounted for by a communication disorder, and does not occur exclusively during the course of a pervasive developmental disorder, schizophrenia, or other psychotic disorders (American Psychiatric Association, 2000).

Guidelines exist for a two-part assessment of elective mutism (Dow, Sonies, Scheib, Moss, & Leonard, 1995). A parental interview should occur first. It should provide a description of the child's symptom history, whether the child is verbally and nonverbally inhibited, the child's academic and medical history, family history, and an informal evaluation of speech and language ability. A child interview should be made, using nonverbal means (e.g., observation, play therapy) to allow for direct observation of the severity and nature of the child's mutism. During this interview the child can respond to questions by using puppets, pantomime, or writing, if he or she is old enough. In addition, physical examination is necessary to rule out any medical problems. Auditory testing as well as a speech and language evaluation should be completed to ensure that the elective mutism is not due to hearing or receptive and/or expressive language difficulties. Finally, standardized psychological nonverbal tests should be used to acquire an understanding of the child's cognitive abilities.

Elective mutism often is highly resistant to treatment (Kehle, Madaus, Baratta, & Bray, 1998). Effective treatments of elective mutism may occur through several modalities, including family systems therapy, behavioral interventions, psychopharmacological interventions, and individual psychotherapy (Anstendig, 1998).

The family treatment approach views elective mutism as a result of inadequate familial relationships characterized by heightened dependence and ambivalence coupled with an excessive need to control. Families with electively mute children are characterized by intense attachments, interdependency, fear and distrust of the outside world, fear and distrust of strangers, language and cultural assimilation difficulties, marital disharmony, and withholding of speech by one or more of the parents in the home. The child's mutism is a way to keep family secrets and withhold involvement with his/her outside environment (Anstendig, 1998). Interventions are designed to help the problematic dynamics of the family by modifying the communication and interaction patterns within the family unit.

Behavioral treatment approaches views elective mutism as a learned response in which the refusal to speak is a method for manipulating the environment. The behavioral approach also views the child's silence as functional in an environment that helps to create and maintain this way of interacting. Behavioral approaches include contingency management, positive reinforcement, shaping, stimulus fading, escape-avoidance, self-modeling techniques, labeling and functional language, and social-psychological functions of reward. Interventions begin with an in-depth analysis of the nonverbal behavior, including an ecological analysis to examine cues in the environment that help him/her unlearn this way of operating (Anstendig, 1998). Multimethod interventions, where a combination of techniques serves to address different aspects of the child's mutism, work best (Anstendig, 1998; Watson & Kramer, 1992). The main goal of behavioral interventions is to extinguish all reinforcement for the child's mutism (Dow et al., 1995).

Psychopharmacological treatments view elective mutism as a variant of an anxiety disorder (i.e., a social phobia; Anstendig, 1998). The main intervention is the use of medication (fluoxetine [Prozac], phenelzine, fluvoxamine) alone or in combination with other interventions. Psychopharmacological treatments are effective in eliminating the disorder. However, whether psychopharmacological treatments can be generalized to all children with elective mutism or only those who are electively mute and anxiety disordered is unclear (Anstendig, 1998).

Psychodynamic methods view elective mutism as a symptom of a severe underlying intrapsychic conflict related to psychotic spectrum disorders or part of another specific disorder of childhood (e.g., stranger anxiety, selective attention, Dissociative Identity Disorder; Anstendig, 1998). Consistent with psychodynamic approaches to therapy, verbal interactions, art, or play typically are used.

Various school interventions may be helpful, including involving the child with peers in various activities, promoting more spontaneity in behavior, and watching for opportunities to reinforce small improvements (Schum, 2002).

The longer elective mutism persists, the more resistant it becomes to intervention (Kehle et al., 1998). Also, some individuals with a history of elective mutism continue to experience social anxiety later in life (Bergman et al., 2002). After elective mutism is treated, expressive language delays may become obvious because a child did not speak during critical periods of language development. Thus, language intervention may be needed.

REFERENCES

American Psychiatric Association. (2000). *Diagnostic and statistical manual of mental health disorders* (4th ed., text rev.). Washington, DC: Author.

Anstendig, K. (1998). Selective mutism: A review of the treatment literature by modality from 1980–1996. *Psychotherapy, 35*(3), 381–391.

Bergman, L. R., Piacentini, J., & McCracken, J. T. (2002). Prevalence and description of selective mutism in a school-based sample. *Journal of the American Academy of Child and Adolescent Psychiatry, 41*(8), 938–946.

Black, B., & Uhde, T. W. (1995). Psychiatric characteristics of children with selective mutism: A pilot study. *Journal of the American Academy of Child and Adolescent Psychiatry, 34*(7), 847–857.

Dow, S. P., Sonies, B. C., Scheib, D., Moss, S. E., & Leonard, H. L. (1995). Practical guidelines for the assessment and treatment of selective mutism. *Journal of the American Academy of Child and Adolescent Psychiatry, 34*(7), 836–846.

Dummit, E. S., III., Klein, R. G., Tancer, N. K., Asche, B., & Martin, J. (1996). Fluoxetine treatment of children with selective mutism: An open trial. *Journal of the American Academy of Child and Adolescent Psychiatry, 35*(5), 15–21.

Ford, M. A., Sladeczek, I. E., Carlson, J., & Kratochwill, T. R. (1998). Selective mutism: Phenomenological characteristics. *School Psychology Quarterly, 13*(3), 192–227.

Joseph, P. R. (1999). Selective mutism: The child who doesn't speak. *Pediatrics, 104*, 308.

Kehle, T. J., Madaus, M. R., Baratta, V. S., & Bray, M. A. (1998). Augmented self-modeling as a treatment for children with selective mutism. *Journal of School Psychology, 36*(3), 247–260.

Powell, S., & Dalley, M. (1995). When to intervene in selective mutism: The multimodal treatment case of persistent selective mutism. *Psychology in the Schools, 32*, 114–123.

Schum, R. L. (2002). Selective mutism: An integrated treatment approach. *ASHA Leader, 7*, 4–6.

Sharkey, L., & McNicholas, F. (August 01, 2008). "More than 100 years of silence," elective mutism: A review of the literature. *European Child and Adolescent Psychiatry, 17*(5), 255–263.

Sheridan, S. M., Kratochwill, T. R., & Ramirez, S. Z. (1995). Assessment and treatment of selective mutism:

Recommendations and a case study. *Special Services in the Schools, 10*(1), 55–78.

Tatem, D. W., & DelCampo, R. L. (1995). Selective mutism in children: A structure family therapy approach to treatment. *Contemporary Family Therapy, 17*(2), 177–194.

Watson, S. T., & Kramer, J. J. (1992). Multimethod behavioral treatment of long-term selective mutism. *Psychology in the Schools, 29*, 359–366.

World Health Organization (WHO). (1992). *Classification of mental and behaviour disorder: Clinical description and diagnostic guidelines (ICD-10)*. Geneva, Switzerland: Author.

KATRINA RAIA
University of Florida

See also **Language Disorders**

ELECTROENCEPHALOGRAPH

An electroencephalograph is a machine that is used to measure the electrical activity of the brain. Fluctuations in brain electrical activity are recorded by electrodes attached to the scalp. The placement of the electrodes has been standardized for clinical use and is accepted internationally (Jasper, 1958). The potentials of the brain are shown on paper in a record called an electroencephalogram (EEG). The amplitude of the brain's electrical activity is small; it is measured in microvolts (millionths of a volt) and must be amplified by the electroencephalograph. The fluctuations in voltage that appear on the EEG have a fairly rhythmic character. The wavelike patterns that are produced will vary with the brain region being recorded as well as with the age and state of alertness of the patient.

The primary information in the EEG is its frequency, which varies from 0.5 to 60 Hz (cycles per second). Attempts have been made to provide rough categories for the classification of frequency. The characteristic pattern for adults in the waking state is dominated by the so-called alpha frequencies, a roughly sinusoidal shape pattern ranging from 8 to 12.5 Hz. Current usage usually identifies five frequency bands that are used in both clinical practice and research, particularly sleep research: delta, 0.5–4 Hz; theta, 4–8 Hz; alpha, 8–13 Hz; beta 1, 13–20 Hz; and beta 2, 20–40 Hz (Greenfield & Sternbach, 1972).

As a general rule, it is possible to predict what sort of brain wave pattern an individual will produce in the absence of brain damage. Variations from expected patterns can constitute a basis for postulating impaired brain functioning. Lewinsohn (1973) notes that the major pathologic changes include waves that are too fast, too slow, or too flat, with all of these conditions being either focal or diffuse.

A major limitation of the EEG is that normal-appearing records may be obtained in the presence of clear-cut evidence of severe organic brain disease (Chusid, 1976). Additionally, about 15% to 20% of the normal population produce abnormal EEG recordings (Mayo Clinic, 1976). Diagnostically, EEGs have been found to be about 60% accurate (Filskov & Goldstein, 1974). EEGs have proven most useful in the diagnosis of seizure disorders (Camfield & Camfield, 1999).

REFERENCES

Camfield, P. R., & Camfield, C. S. (1999). Pediatric epilepsy: An overview. In K. F. Swaiman & S. Ashwal (Eds.), *Pediatric neurology* (pp. 629–633). St. Louis, MO: Mosby.

Chusid, J. G. (1976). *Correlative neuroanatomy and functional neurology*. Los Altos, CA: Lange Medical Publications.

Filskov, S. B., & Goldstein, S. G. (1974). Diagnostic validity of the Halstead-Reitan Neuropsychological Battery. *Journal of Consulting & Clinical Psychology, 42*, 382–388.

Greenfield, N. S., & Sternbach, R. A. (1972). *Handbook of psychophysiology*. New York, NY: Holt, Rinehart & Winston.

Jasper, H. H. (1958). The ten-twenty electrode system of the International Federation. *Electroencephalography & Clinical Neurophysiology, 10*, 371–375.

Lewinsohn, P. M. (1973). *Psychological assessment of patients with brain injury*. Washington, DC: Division of Research, Department of Health, Education and Welfare.

Mayo Clinic. (1976). *Clinical examinations in neurology*. Philadelphia, PA: Saunders.

RICHARD A. BERG
West Virginia University Medical Center
Charleston Division

See also **Absence Seizures; EEG Abnormalities; Epilepsy; Grand Mal Seizures**

ELECTROENCEPHALOGRAPHY (EEG) BIOFEEDBACK

Electroencephalography (EEG) biofeedback is a learning strategy that enables individuals to alter brain wave activity and theoretically then alter behavior or emotions (*see* Biofeedback). EEG biofeedback is a painless, noninvasive procedure typically measuring six electrical signals in the brain: alpha, beta, theta, delta, SMR, and high beta. Researchers have demonstrated that individuals with certain conditions, including those related to psychiatric illness, typically exhibit atypical patterns of electrical activity in the brain often measured as ratio differences between certain brain waves at certain parts of the brain (e.g., theta/beta ratio in the right prefrontal cortex). EEG biofeedback has become particularly popular for the evaluation and treatment of Attention-Deficit/Hyperactivity Disorder (ADHD) despite absence of strong scientific support. Electrophysiological measures were among the first to be used to study brain processes among children with ADHD. These measures have been used both in research to describe and quantify the neurophysiology of ADHD and also in the clinical assessment, diagnosis, and treatment. Early EEG studies found that children with ADHD exhibited abnormalities such as excess slow-wave activity and eleptiform spike and wave activity. These findings were interpreted as indicating abnormal brain processes among children with ADHD, specifically a maturational delay marked by underarousal. Proponents of EEG biofeedback promise success rates of 90% in treating ADHD and other conditions absent well-accepted, supportive scientific literature. Proponents of this treatment suggest that the treatment represents a learning process and results are seen gradually over time. Twenty to 40 sessions are recommended for most conditions at a rate of 2 or more sessions per week.

SAM GOLDSTEIN
University of Utah

ELECTRONIC TRAVEL AIDS

Individuals with visual impairments who travel independently rely on essentially three kinds of travel aids: long canes, dog guides, and electronic travel aids. Electronic travel aids serve as guidance devices that extend the range of perception of the environment beyond the fingertip, tip of the long cane, or handle of the dog guide's harness. These sensory aids enable individuals with visual impairments to determine the approximate elevation, dimensions, azimuth, and possibly surface texture of objects detected within the range that the ultrasonic or electromagnetic waves penetrate. Information put out as auditory sounds or tactile vibrations permits the user to decide whether to avoid direct contact with the source of the signal, make contact with it, or simply use it as a reference point for orientation and navigation purposes (Harper, 1998; Yang et al., 2011).

Of the four most commonly used electronic travel aids, three are considered secondary aids that complement and enrich information received from the long cane or dog guide. The Russell Pathsounder is a small battery-operated unit that can be mounted on the user's chest. The unit emits ultrasonic waves that penetrate the area in front of the unit to a distance of 6 feet. If the invisible waves hit an object and produce an echo picked up by the receiver in the unit, then an auditory and/or vibrating

signal is triggered. The chest unit vibrates until the object appears in the inner protection zone less than inches from the traveler's chest. Once within that zone, the vibrator in the back of the neck strap is activated to signal the closer proximity. The auditory warning signal is a buzzing sound that switches to a high-pitched beep when objects enter the inner protection zone. The Pathsounder can supplement the long cane by protecting the upper body. Wheelchair users also find the device helpful (Farmer, 1980).

The Sonicguide developed in New Zealand is another secondary aid that provides protection for the vulnerable area between the knees and the head. The unit emits pulses of ultrasonic waves from a source mounted in eyeglass frames. The pitch of the sound represents distance from an object within a 20-foot range; the stereophonic effect reveals location to the left or right of the head direction; and the sound quality or timbre suggests characteristics of the surface texture (Mellor, 1981).

The LASER (light amplification by stimulated emission of radiation) cane is considered both a primary and secondary aid. It is an adaptation of the long cane with three built-in laser sources that send out beams of infrared light in three directions. The beams are only 1 inch wide at 10 feet from the source to permit rather precise location of objects. The upward beam detects objects in line with the head, the forward beam locates objects in the direct line of travel, and the downward beam picks up drop-offs such as curbs or stairs (Farmer, 1980). For a more detailed discussion of mobility aids in general and electronic travel aids in particular, see Farmer's chapter on mobility devices in Welsh and Blasch (1980) and Yen (2006).

REFERENCES

Farmer, L. (1980). Mobility devices. In R. Welsh & B. Blasch (Eds.), *Foundations of orientation and mobility*. New York, NY: American Foundation for the Blind.

Harper, S., Green, P. N., & UMIST. (1998). *Standardising electronic travel aid interaction for visually impaired people*. Manchester, England: UMIST.

Mellor, C. M. (1981). *Aids for the 80's: What they are and what they do*. New York, NY: American Foundation for the Blind.

Welsh, R., & Blasch, B. (1980). *Foundations of orientation and mobility*. New York, NY: American Foundation for the Blind.

Yang, R., Park, S., Mishra, S., Hong, Z. H., Newsom, C., Joo, H., Hofer, E., & Newman, M. W. (2011). Supporting spatial awareness and independent wayfinding for pedestrians with visual impairments. *Proceedings of the 13th international ACM SIGACCESS conference* on *computers and accessibility (ASSETS '11)*, Dundee, Scotland.

Yen, D. H. (2006). *Electronic travel aids for the blind*. Retrieved from http://www.noogenesis.com/eta/current.htm

MARJORIE E. WARD
Ohio State University

See *also* Mobility Instruction; Vision Training

ELEMENTARY AND SECONDARY EDUCATION ACT (ESEA)

The Elementary and Secondary Education Act (ESEA) became law in 1965. The ESEA was an important part of President Lyndon Johnson's war on poverty. When he signed the ESEA into law, President Johnson said, "I believe deeply no law I have ever signed or will ever sign means more to the future of America" (Remarks, 1965). Because he had been a teacher, President Johnson saw the effects that poverty had on his students. Thus, he believed that equal access to a quality education for disadvantaged children was absolutely essential to improving their quality of life.

The purpose of the ESEA, which was the first major federal educational law and also the most expansive, was to provide funding to states to improve educational opportunities for disadvantaged children. The law dramatically changed the role of the federal government in education.

The ESEA originally consisted of the following six titles or sections:

1. Title I—Financial Assistance to Local Educational Agencies for the Education of Children of Low-Income Families
2. Title II—School Library Resources, Textbooks, and other Instructional Materials
3. Title III—Supplementary Educational Centers and Services
4. Title IV—Educational Research And Training
5. Title V—Grants to Strengthen State Departments of Education
6. Title VI—General Provisions

The largest, and perhaps important, section was Title I. In this title the federal government developed funding formulas to determine which schools would be Title I schools. The formulas involved collected data such as the number of student's in a school who are eligible to receive free or reduced lunch or the percentage of students within a school's attendance zone who received public assistance. If either of the two types of data exceeded a poverty cutoff rate, the school is eligible to receive Title I funds. Title I provides funding and the guiding principles for educating disadvantaged children.

Title II provides funding for purchasing materials for media centers and audio/visual equipment. Title III provides funding for programs that meet the educational needs of students who are at risk of school failure. Title IV provides funding for college and universities. Title V provides funding to state departments of education.

When Congress passes statutes that appropriate money they authorize the statute. The ESEA was authorized through 1970. This meant that every 4 or 5 years Congress had to reauthorize funding for the law. When Congress revisited the law it also amended and changed the law. For example, the ESEA was reauthorized in 1994 in a law called the Improving America's Schools Act of 1994 and again in the No Child Left Behind Act of 2001.

In the 1994 Improving American's School Act, which reauthorized and amended the ESEA, states were required to develop or adopt challenging content, demanding proficiency standards, and rigorous assessments. Moreover, Title I schools had to meet adequate yearly progress (AYP). Schools that did not meet AYP had to develop corrective action plans. In the 2001 No Child Left Behind Act, which also amended the ESEA, public schools were required to bring all students to proficiency in reading and math by the 2013–2014 school year. The law included sanctions for schools that failed to make AYP. The law also required that schools use reading and math curricula based on scientifically based research. Another provision of the law required that all teachers had to be "highly qualified," which was defined as (a) having an undergraduate degree, (b) be certified or licensed in the areas in which they taught, and (c) demonstrate knowledge in the area in which they taught.

Since the original passage of the ESEA in 1965, the federal role in education has evolved from primarily providing federal funding assistance to the states to holding states and school districts accountable for improving learning outcomes and achievement of America's students.

This entry has been informed by the sources listed below.

REFERENCES

Remarks of President Lyndon Johnson upon signing the Elementary and Secondary Education Bill. (1965). Lyndon Baines Johnson Library and Museum. Retrieved from http://www.lbjlib.utexas.edu/johnson/archives.hom/speeches.hom/650411.asp

Yell, M. L. (2012). *The law and special education* (3rd ed.). Upper Saddle River, NJ: Pearson/Merrill Education.

Yell, M. L., & Drasgow, E. (2005). *No Child Left Behind: A guide for practitioners*. Upper Saddle River, NJ: Pearson/Merrill Education.

MITCHELL YELL
South Carolina University
Fourth edition

ELEMENTARY MATHEMATICS CONTENT SPECIALISTS

Elementary mathematics specialists are elementary classroom teachers who want to improve instructional skills as well as develop their understanding and abilities in mathematics. Well-prepared teacher leaders in a specialist's role can have a significant influence on strengthening assessment and pedagogical content knowledge of those classroom teachers who are inadequately prepared to deliver effective math instruction. These specialists provide professional development that is critical for improving instruction and student learning in math (Campbell & Malkus, 2011).

There are nearly 1 million teachers at the elementary level most who teach mathematics. There are variables that can improve the quality of math instruction at the elementary level but the teacher is key (Reys & Fennel, 2000). Research has shown that students learn more from teachers who are skilled, experienced, and know what and how to teach (Darling-Hammond & Youngs, 2002; Rice, 2003). Dossey (1984) felt it was important that elementary teachers understand the vital role they play in teaching mathematics and called for specialists in math at the elementary level. Again Fennel in 2006 called for math specialists at the elementary level reminding us about Dossey's call.

In recent years there has been an increasing call for content specialists at the elementary school level, particularly in the areas of math and science (National Mathematics Advisory Council, 2008; Reys & Fennell, 2003; Schwartz, Lederman, & Abd-El-Khalick, 2000). The content specialist approach contrasts with the traditional approach employed by most schools, in which teacher generalists provide instruction to students in all core subject areas, including mathematics, science, social studies, and literacy. Content specialist have been conceived as professionals who will improve student learning outcomes by providing teachers with professional development and building their content specific knowledge and understanding of instructional and pedagogical techniques (Gerretson, Bosnick, & Schofield, 2008). The use of content specialists in math is supported by research indicating that teachers' mathematical knowledge for teaching is significantly related to student learning outcomes (Hill, Rowan, & Ball, 2005). Although research evaluating the effectiveness of mathematics specialists in promoting student-learning outcomes is limited and insufficient to draw conclusions, existing findings suggest positive outcomes for students when content specialists are employed (Schwartz et al., 2000). Gerretson et al. (2008) surveyed school principals in employing math specialists and comparison schools without math specialists. In schools with these specialists, principals reported that teachers had more planning time and professional development focused on effectively and efficiently delivering content to students showing that they were highly valued by principals and staff.

Additionally, Rowan and Campbell (1995) reported that math specialists were especially beneficial in schools experiencing severe economic or social stresses and schools with large populations of special education students. Specialists have conducted workshops for parents of special education and Title I students on math skills, assisting them in supporting their children at home, and they have distributed information with parents via school newsletters on how to help their children with math. These specialists can be used for assistance with a range of diverse learners. When certain students with disabilities require alternative testing, specialists can ensure that the individual assessment used for each student is aligned with the grade-level objectives and in keeping the individual student's education folders up to date (Blount & Singleton, 2007).

Specialists can also assist with an inclusion model by helping general education teachers within the confines of their classrooms rather than in a pull-out situation on strategies to reinforce skills of students who lack a strong math background. There has been considerable evidence that math specialists collaborate with and serve as resources for special education teachers. Sometimes math specialists serve on district teams for special education and help identify gaps in special education math instruction (Blount & Singleton, 2007).

REFERENCES

Blount, D. & J. Singleton, J. (2007). The role and impact of the mathematics specialist from the principal's perspectives. *The Journal of Mathematics and Science: Collaborative Explorations, 9*, 69–77.

Campbell, P. F., & Malkus, N. N. (2011). The impact of elementary mathematics specialists. *The Journal of Mathematics and Science: Collaborative Explorations, 12*, 1–28.

Darling-Hammond, L., & Youngs, P. (2002). Defining "highly qualified teachers": What does "scientifically-based research" actually tell us? *American Educational Research Association, 31*, 13–25.

Dossey, J. A. (1984). Pre-service elementary mathematics education: A complete program. *Arithmetic Teacher, 31*, 6–8.

Fennel, F. (2006). We need elementary school mathematics specialists now. *NCTM New Bulletin, 43*.

Gerretson, H., Bosnick, J., & Schofield, K. (2008). A case for content specialists as the elementary classroom teacher. *The Teacher Educator, 43*, 302–314.

Hill, H., Rowan, B., & Ball, D. L. (2005). Effects of teachers' mathematical knowledge for teaching on student achievement. *American Educational Research Journal, 42*, 371–406.

National Mathematics Advisory Council. (2008). *Foundations for success: The final report of the national mathematics advisory council*. Washington, DC: U.S. Department of Education.

Reys, B. J., & Fennell, F. (2003). Who should lead mathematics instruction at the elementary school level? A case for mathematics specialists. *Teaching Children Mathematics, 9*, 277–282.

Rice, J. K. (2003). *Teacher quality: Understanding the effectiveness of teacher attributes*. Washington, DC: Economic Policy Institute.

Rowan, T. E., & Campbell, P. F. (1995, April). *School-based mathematics specialists: Providing on-site support for instructional reform in urban mathematics classrooms. The Project IMPACT model.* Paper presented at the annual meeting of the American Educational Research Association, San Francisco.

Schwartz, R. S., Lederman, N. G., & Abd-El-Khalick, F. (2000). Achieving the reforms vision: The effectiveness of a specialists-led elementary science program. *School Science and Mathematics, 100,* 181–193.

MARY MARGARET CAPRARO
Texas A&M University
Fourth edition

THE ELEPHANT MAN

Renowned in both late Victorian England during his life-time and contemporarily more by his professional name, the "Elephant Man," than his real one, Joseph Carey Merrick has been fascinating to both professionals and the public for over 100 years. First brought to recent attention by Ashley Montagu (1972) in his biography, *The Elephant Man: A Study in Human Dignity,* Merrick has been the subject of at least one other biography (Howell & Ford, 1980), a successful play and subsequent movie, and numerous professional and popular articles. Howell and Ford's book not only contains a detailed biography, but many photographs and drawings, contemporary accounts, and Merrick's autobiography, which serve as the sources for this entry.

Merrick may well as an adult have been the "ugliest man in the world," as he was frequently called. Born normal to lower-class parents in Leicester, England in 1860, Merrick began to develop deformities in the head, limbs, and back such that regular employment became impossible, although he held several jobs for a short time in early adulthood. His mother died when he was young, and his father virtually abandoned him when he remarried. Unable otherwise to make a living, Merrick allowed himself for many years to be exhibited as a sideshow freak as the "Elephant Man." When a London physician, Frederick Treves, saw him in Whitechapel, he left Merrick one of his cards. When the show was closed in England as an affront to human decency, Merrick and a manager went to Belgium, where the manager abandoned him when the show was again pursued by police. With money gained by pawning some possessions, Merrick made his way back to London. This time, he was pursued and jeered by curious crowds. Finally, he ended up at London Hospital where Treves worked. After some difficulty. Treves arranged for a room to be furnished in the hospital, where Merrick spent most of the rest of his life.

Treves at first thought Merrick was retarded, but found that he was intelligent, and, perhaps surprising given his years of mistreatment, sensitive, friendly, and sociable.

Indeed, he became a society celebrity, and was visited by many notables, including the Prince and Princess of Wales and the Duke of Cambridge in 1887. Visitors frequently brought small gifts, which Merrick treasured. His head was so large that he could only sleep with his head between his knees. Unfortunately, his condition became progressively more serious and debilitating. He was found dead in his room, lying flat on his bed, on April 11, 1890. Treves suggested that he had tried to rest more like normal people and had lain down. Pressure from the weight of his head suffocated him. The *London Times* published an announcement of his death.

How ugly was he? Perhaps his own words serve best:

> The measurement around my head is 36 inches, there is a large substance of flesh at the back as large as a breakfast cup, the other part in a manner of speaking is like hills and valleys, all lumped together, while the face is such a sight that no one could describe it. The right hand is almost the size and shape of an Elephant's fore-leg, measuring 12 inches round the wrist and 5 inches round one of the fingers; the other hand and arm is no larger than that of a girl 10 years of age, although it is well proportioned. My feet and legs are covered with thick lumpy skin, also my body, like that of an Elephant, and almost the same colour, in fact, no one would believe until they saw it, that such a thing could exist. (Howell & Ford, 1980, p. 168)

What caused his deformities? He thought that he knew. Again in his words:

> The deformity which I am now exhibiting was caused by my mother being frightened by an Elephant; my mother was going along the street when a procession of animals were passing by, there was a terrible crush of people to see them, and unfortunately she was pushed under which frightened her very much; this occurring during a time of pregnancy was the cause of my deformity. (Howell & Ford, 1980, p. 168)

But, however popular such explanations were at the time, he was, of course, wrong. Treves had viewed the disorder as being congenital, but neither he nor anyone else at the time could suggest a specific disorder. However, as early as 1909, a diagnosis of neurofibromatosis was suggested. Now known to be a single-gene dominant disorder, it is a likely candidate since many of the symptoms fit with Merrick's condition and it frequently arises through spontaneous mutation. The most characteristic manifestation is neurofibromas, masses of tumors comprised of densely packed nerve and fibrous tissue. Common also are patches of darkened skin, termed café au lait spots. Recently, however, alternatives have been suggested, most notably Proteus syndrome. Proteus is characterized by "macrocephaly, hyperostosis of the skull; hypertrophy of long bones; and thickened skin and subcutaneous tissues, particularly of the hands and feet, including plantar hyperplasia, lipomas, and other unspecified subcutaneous masses" (Tibbles & Cohen, 1986, p. 683). Over 100 years after his death, Joseph Merrick indeed remains a subject of fascination.

REFERENCES

Howell, M., & Ford, P. (1980). *The true history of the elephant man.* London, England: Allison & Busby.

Montagu, A. (1972). *The elephant man: A study in human dignity.* New York, NY: Outerbridge & Dienstfrey.

Tibbles, J. A., & Cohen, M. M., Jr. (1986). The Proteus syndrome: The Elephant Man diagnosed. *British Medical Journal (Clinical Research Edition), 293,* 683–685.

ROBERT T. BROWN
University of North Carolina at Wilmington

ELLIS, NORMAN R. (1924–   )

Norman R. Ellis, born in Springville, Alabama, September 14, 1924, is known for his theoretical work on mental retardation, for research on memory and learning by persons with mental retardation, and for editing major works on mental retardation. He is a major proponent of the difference or deficit theory, which proposes that people with mental retardation have mental processes that are in some ways qualitatively different from those of persons with normal intelligence. From this model, it follows that the goal of research should be to discover and study those processes that predict differences in intellectual ability. In the area of research, Ellis is credited with formulating the stimulus trace deficit theory, which states that short-term memory deficits of subjects who are mentally retarded are due to rapid deterioration of stimulus traces in the brain. He also proposed a three-stage model of memory: primary memory, secondary memory, and tertiary memory (Borkowski, Peck, & Damberg, 1983; Determan, 1983). Ellis is editor of major works on mental retardation, including two editions of the *Handbook in Mental Deficiency* (1963, 1979) and 13 volumes of the *International Review of Research in Mental Retardation* (1966–1986). He is the author of nearly 100 scholarly articles, including "Further Evidence for Cognitive Inertia of Persons with Mental Retardation," a study examining postpractice interference effects in naming colors of Stroop words (Ellis & Dulaney, 1991), and "Automatized Responding and Cognitive Inertia in Individuals with Mental Retardation," research providing some support for age-related inherent structural differences leading to greater rigidity in older adults (Dulaney & Ellis, 1994).

Ellis received his BA degree in 1951 from Howard College, an MA in general experimental psychology from the University of Alabama in 1952, and a PhD from Louisiana State University in 1956 in general experimental psychology. He is professor of psychology and director of the doctoral training program in mental retardation and developmental disabilities, University of Alabama. He previously held positions at George Peabody College, Louisiana State University, and State Colony and Training School, Pineville, Louisiana.

Ellis is a fellow of the American Association on Mental Retardation and American Psychological Association. He received the American Association on Mental Retardation Award for Outstanding Research in 1972 and the Edgar A. Doll Award for Outstanding Research from the American Psychological Association in 1986. He has received numerous awards from the University of Alabama. He is listed in the 12th edition of *American Men and Women in Science* and is Professor Emeritus of the University of Alabama.

REFERENCES

Borkowski, J. G., Peck, V. A., & Damberg, P. R. (1983). Attention, memory, and cognition. In J. L. Matson & J. A. Mulick (Eds.), *Handbook of mental retardation* (pp. 479–497). New York, NY: Pergamon Press.

Determan, K. D. (1983). Some trends in research design. In J. L. Matson & J. A. Mulick (Eds.), *Handbook of mental retardation* (pp. 527–539). New York, NY: Pergamon Press.

Dulaney, C. L., & Ellis, N. R. (1994). Automatized responding and cognitive inertia in individuals with mental retardation. *American Journal on Mental Retardation, 99*(1), 8–18.

Ellis, N. R., & Dulaney, C. L. (1991). Further evidence for cognitive inertia of persons with mental retardation. *American Journal on Mental Retardation, 95*(6), 13–21.

ELEANOR BOYD WRIGHT
University of North Carolina at Wilmington

ELWYN INSTITUTES

Elwyn Institutes was founded in 1852. It is located on a 400-acre campus near Media, Pennsylvania. It is a comprehensive service facility, and it provides day and residential programs for children and adults with learning disabilities, intellectual developmental disabilities, deaf/blind, neurologically disabled, brain damaged, visually impaired, physically disabled, deaf, hard of hearing, or multidisabled and deaf.

Elwyn Institutes' continuum of services features rehabilitation programs that coordinate residential and community living arrangements with special education, vocational training, and sequential programs that lead to independence in the community. Students in residence live in modern living accommodations on campus and in apartments within the local communities.

Elwyn Institutes maintains programs in Philadelphia; Wilmington, Delaware; Fountain Valley, California; and

Israel. Management and administrative supervision is provided at the American Institute for Mental Studies, also known as the Vineland Training School, in Vineland, New Jersey.

Elwyn Institutes' educational programs are offered to students with day and residential accommodations from preschool years through to 21 years. These programs provide a wide range of educational services, including comprehensive evaluations, preschool programs, daycare facilities, and elementary and secondary levels of education and training. Ancillary services include audiological evaluations, speech and language therapy, mobility training, occupational therapy, psychiatric and psychological services, and medical and dental care.

Elwyn Institutes is located at 111 Elwyn Road, Elwyn, PA 19063. More information can be found at http://www.elwyn.org/

REFERENCE

Sargent, J. K. (1982). *The directory for exceptional children* (9th ed.). Boston, MA: Porter Sargent.

PAUL C. RICHARDSON
Elwyn Institutes

EMBEDDED FIGURES TEST

The Embedded Figures Test (EFT; Witkin, 1950) is an individually administered test designed to measure field dependence-independence. Field-independent individuals are able to locate the previously viewed geometric figure within the larger figure more quickly than field-dependent individuals. It consists of 16 simple straight-line figures to be traced within a larger, more complex figure. This test is designed for individuals 12:0 and older, whereas the Children's EFT is for ages 5:0 through 11:0, and the Preschool EFT is for ages 3:0 through 5:0. A group test is also available. A shorter form was developed during a factor analysis study that eliminates the two most difficult items and reduces the administration time (Mumma, 1993). The EFT was designed to measure field dependence-independence.

The EFT consists of 24 complex figure cards, 8 sample figure cards, and a stylus used to trace the embedded figures. Twelve cards are administered during the test. Standard scores are developed after an average disembedding time is determined by dividing the total search time by 12. During administration, the item to be disembedded is presented beside the larger figure. The simple figure is presented to the right of the complex figure for right-handed individuals and to the left of the complex figure for left-handed subjects.

Reliability studies show both internal consistency and test-retest stability. The EFT correlates well with other measures of field dependence-independence.

REFERENCES

Mumma, G. H. (1993). The Embedded Figures Test: Internal structure and development of a short form. *Personality & Individual Differences, 15,* 221–224.

Witkin, H. A. (1950). Individual differences in ease of perception of embedded figures. *Journal of Personality, 19,* 1–15.

RON DUMONT
Fairleigh Dickinson University

JOHN O. WILLIS
Rivier College
Third edition

EMOTIONAL DISORDERS

The greatest amount of progress on behalf of individuals who were emotionally disturbed (ED) occurred in the 20th century. Assessment instruments, residential schools for the emotionally disturbed, special classes in public schools, child guidance clinics, juvenile courts and legal statutes specifically written for delinquent and abused children, and hundreds of texts dealing with the etiology, diagnosis, and treatment of children were all products of the 20th century.

By the 1960s and 1970s, dramatic progress had been made on behalf of children and youth. Behavior modification techniques became a popular treatment method and ecological approaches to treatment of the disturbed child were developed. Public Law 94-142 mandated an appropriate education for all children. Efforts were made to deinstitutionalize children and to mainstream them in the public schools. By the late 1970s and early 1980s, a family systems approach to treatment of the disturbed child came into vogue. Today efforts are being made to educate the emotionally disturbed child in the classroom and to supplement education with a therapeutic treatment program.

The problems in defining normal functioning in children make it difficult to classify abnormalities. This is particularly the case in emotional disturbance, where behavioral rather than academic criteria are primarily employed. Stemming from the realities of providing educational remediation, however, Bower (1969) spearheaded efforts to conceptualize emotional disturbances in children. He provided a practical definition consisting of the following five characteristics: (1) learning problems are not explained by intellectual, sensory, or health factors;

(2) there are difficulties in initiating and maintaining interpersonal relationships; (3) behavioral or emotional reactions are not appropriate to circumstances; (4) there is pervasive unhappiness or depression; and (5) there is the development of physical symptoms or fears related to school or personal problems. Any one or more of these five characteristics occurring to a marked extent over a long period of time are sufficient for diagnosis. Bower's criteria were adopted verbatim in PL 94-142. Public Law 94-142 additionally labeled schizophrenic and autistic children as seriously emotionally disturbed and differentiated socially maladjusted from emotionally disturbed children. Autistic children were dropped from the emotionally disturbed category and placed in the health-impaired category in 1981, and later received their own category.

Despite its official sanction as a category of childhood exceptionality, the label *emotional disturbance* has evoked considerable debate in the literature. It has been reported that the differentiation of emotional and behavioral disorders in children is difficult to make (Boyle & Jones, 1985), and that the distinction between primary and secondary emotional disturbance in learning disabilities is similarly confused (Chandler & Jones, 1983). Inadequacies in definition may have resulted in the underdetection and underserving of emotionally disturbed children (Long & McQueen, 1984). Although Bower (1981) has openly discussed the nebulous nature of basing a classification category on disturbances in emotion, he has continued to advocate the application of the revised term *emotionally handicapped* and his original diagnostic criteria.

Incidence rates of emotional disturbances, or the number of newly diagnosed cases at any point in time, are practically nonexistent because of the difficulties in accurately defining the onset and duration of childhood psychiatric disorders. Estimates of prevalence, or the number of existing cases at any point in time, however, are available and are based on data collected from educational and psychiatric perspectives.

A number of individual difference variables have been identified as significant correlates of childhood emotional disturbance. Sex is a particularly important factor. Males are more likely than females to be identified throughout the school years, with more males receiving the psychiatric diagnosis of conduct disorder and more females receiving the psychiatric diagnoses of specific emotional disorders, especially during adolescence (Offord, 1983). Racial and family characteristics have also been implicated. Blacks are more likely than Whites to be identified, and identification varies inversely with parent education level as well as family socioeconomic status (Zill, 1985). The importance of family variables is supported by the strong association between childhood psychiatric diagnoses in general and broken homes, marital discord, and parental deviance (Offord, 1983).

The etiology of mild to moderate emotional disturbances may not always be precise, but two major causative factors seem to predominate. These include socioenvironmental factors and biological factors. Genetic factors are important, but from the information to date, only the more severe forms of psychopathology seem to result from a genetic predisposition. This will be discussed in the section on seriously emotionally disturbed children.

Etiology

In the last quarter of the 20th century, marked changes occurred in the family as we knew it. Single-parent families, blended families ("his and her children" in second marriages), parents working outside the home, "latchkey" children, apartment living, and family mobility all contributed to socioenvironmental factors as one of the major etiologies of emotional disturbances in children. Parental deprivation or distortions in parent-child relationships as a result of parental psychopathology are all too common. Many children are seriously neglected, and/or emotionally, physically, and even sexually abused by a parent or surrogate parent. Chronic neglect of a pervasive nature can and does affect the child's emotional and personal development. Physically and sexually abused children often exhibit depression or emotional agitation, poor self-image, cognitive deficits, and difficulties interrelating with peers (Willis, 1985).

Children and youth reared in extreme poverty are at higher risk for developing personality disorders and delinquent behavior. These disadvantaged children often exhibit cognitive delays. Thus, early school performance may be deficient, which may further accentuate a negative self-image.

In the biological realm, children with chronic health or other physical disorders may create added stress within the family. The exceptional child may be overprotected or rejected. In addition, the parent(s) may feel ambivalent toward the child. Any or all of these reactions can lead to maladaptive parental behaviors that can then create problems for the child and family.

A child's temperament may also determine, to an extent, a predilection toward emotional problems, especially if the child's temperament does not match parental and other environmental expectations. Ten temperament characteristics are described by Thomas, Chess, and Birch (1968): activity level, approach-withdrawal, rhythmicity, adaptability, mood, threshold, intensity, distractibility, persistence, and attention span. A difficult child is characterized by being slow to adapt to change, withdrawing from new stimuli, exhibiting a negative mood, manifesting biological irregularity, and demonstrating a high level of expressiveness. The difficult child is more likely to develop behavior disorders because his or her ability to interact with the environment and others is not always easy and nonstressful. This child may be at greater risk for abuse merely because he or she is, by nature, difficult. Children who present with neurological dysfunction or brain damage as the result of prematurity, pre- or postnatal infections, complications during pregnancy, and head trauma owed to accidents or injuries, may present with a diagnosis of emotional disturbance.

Classification of ED

Bower's (1969) definition of emotional disturbance provides a set of criteria for labeling and differentiating a group of children who may respond to educational remediation. From a psychiatric perspective, however, the label *emotional disturbance* encompasses a wide range of childhood psychopathology. A number of different psychiatric disorders are included; they are the product of disparate etiologies and respond differentially to the treatment strategies that are available. Once a child receives the categorical label of emotionally disturbed, it is important to provide a more specific psychiatric diagnosis to facilitate effective treatment.

A brief discussion of some of the major childhood psychiatric syndromes included under the emotional disturbance label follows. The reader is referred to texts on childhood psychopathology or exceptionality by Achenbach (1982), Brown and Reynolds (1986), and Steinhauer and Rae-Grant (1983), and to the fourth edition of the *Diagnostic and Statistical Manual of Mental Disorders* of the American Psychiatric Association (*DSM-IV;* 1994) for more specific and comprehensive information.

Childhood depression has been recognized as a viable diagnosis in recent years. Estimates of prevalence vary according to diagnostic criteria, but one study placed the prevalence rate of depression at just over 5% for elementary school-aged children (Leftowitz & Tesiny, 1985). The rising incidence of suicide in children and adolescents is undoubtedly linked to increasing rates of childhood depression. With pervasive unhappiness or depression included as one of the diagnostic criteria for emotional disturbance, it is clear that childhood depression or depressive affect related to other psychological problems will appear frequently in groups of emotionally disturbed children.

Childhood depression differs from adult depression along a number of lines. The major presenting complaints in children are extreme sadness and accompanying withdrawal. Masked versions, in which the presenting complaints involve acting out behaviors, are not uncommon. Vegetative symptoms do not occur as frequently in children as they do in adults. However, both acute and chronic depression in children have been reported. The withdrawn, uncommunicative child is definitely a candidate for this diagnosis. Rapid, unexplained increases in acting out behaviors also necessitate consideration of an underlying depressive reaction.

A number of childhood psychiatric problems are linked directly to anxiety disorders. Anxiety may be the primary symptom or reactions to anxiety may produce somatic complaints and/or behavioral changes.

Phobias occur when anxiety and its somatic or behavioral concomitants are displayed in the presence of a feared object or situation. School phobia is a specific phobic reaction resulting from fears about school experiences, about separation from parents, or a combination of both. Panic disorder and generalized anxiety reactions refer to more global anxiety responses that are not linked to specific aspects of the environment yet may reflect underlying emotional conflict. In posttraumatic stress disorder, symptoms based on both anxiety and depression occur following a traumatic event that a child reexperiences repeatedly on a psychological level. With the incidence of child abuse increasing, the latter diagnosis is appearing more frequently in populations of emotionally disturbed children.

Other childhood disorders such as psychosomatic disorders may be seen in the special education child. Psychosomatic disorders are any physical conditions that can be initiated, exacerbated, or prolonged by psychosocial factors (Schaefer, Millman, & Levine, 1979).

The notion that health-related problems are caused by the interaction of biological, social, and psychological factors constitutes the cornerstone of psychosomatic disorders. Indeed, psychosomatic dysfunction is one of the major causes of school absence. For example, the child who presents with asthma, gastrointestinal disorders such as ulcers, diarrhea, vomiting, or abdominal pain, migraine headaches or hypertension, skin disorders such as dermatitis, and even hysterical symptoms may manifest an exaggeration of symptoms secondary to emotional stress. The stress may result from environmental demands, learning problems, or parent-child problems. Basically, physical symptoms that are rooted in or exacerbated by emotional conflict are the primary presenting complaints in psychosomatic disorders. Preexisting physiological vulnerability, such as ulcers or asthma, can be worsened by emotional stresses within the individual or family.

Children who have a history of multiple or prolonged hospitalization, or a history of chronic illness, may also present with emotional disturbance secondary to the trauma of medical surgeries or procedures. The effects of hospitalization and physical illness on the developing child can be understood best by reading Willis, Elliot, and Jay (1982) and Olson, Mullins, Gillman, & Chaney (1994).

Personality disorders are characterized by maladaptive and inflexible patterns of behaviors, thoughts, and emotions that affect an individual's functioning across situations and time. The symptoms of personality disorders are ego syntonic, meaning that they are not viewed by the individual as problematic. They are diagnosed more frequently in adults than in children because rapid developmental changes in children complicate predictions regarding stability of functioning. Childhood precursors of personality disorders have been applied as specific diagnoses in childhood populations.

Based on symptom clusters, personality disorders and their childhood precursors have been grouped into three categories (Steinhauer & Berman, 1983). The first group is defined by emotional constriction, rigidity, aloofness, and the inability to maintain interpersonal relationships. Schizoid disorders of childhood and adolescence are included in this category, as well as schizoid, paranoid, and schizotypal personality disorders. The second group is defined by dramatic, emotional, self-centered, and unstable behaviors. Identity disorders of childhood and adolescence and conduct disorders are the childhood precursors within this category. Histrionic, narcissistic, and antisocial personality disorders are also included. Intrapsychic struggles between anxiety and defenses against anxiety characterize the third group. Avoidant disorder and oppositional disorder are diagnoses applied to children manifesting these characteristics. Avoidant, dependent, compulsive, and passive-aggressive are labels used to describe fully developed personality disorders based on these intrapsychic struggles.

Children who present with a behavior disorder are often seen in the school setting. This population differs from children who present with social maladjustment when the following criteria are present: the presence of guilt or anxiety; a specific etiology; and responsiveness to treatment. Often these children experience enormous frustration, intrapsychic conflicts, poor self-esteem, feelings of failure, and high anxiety levels. They may act out their frustrations in an aggressive way (Group for the Advancement of Psychiatry, 1966); as opposed to socially maladjusted children, they frequently feel remorse for their aggressive acts.

Immature behaviors displayed in the school setting (thumb sucking, crying, whining, negativism, baby talk) are often seen in children under stress and are indicative of some underlying, perhaps transient problem occurring at home or elsewhere in the child's environment. Some children who have been overprotected by their parents may be bright, but immature in their social and environmental behavior. The withdrawn child does not interact with peers, is often viewed as a loner, is overly shy, and may be deficient in social skills. The immature or withdrawn child requires intervention but does not necessarily require individual treatment.

Treatment

Since there is no cookbook method of treating all disorders with which a child might present, the mental health professional treating an emotionally disturbed child must consider a number of factors when planning treatment strategies. It is not within the scope of this section to advocate one therapeutic orientation over another. Rather, an overview of psychodynamic therapy, behavior therapy, family and group therapy, and parent consultation will be presented.

Psychodynamic therapy deals with the underlying psychological causes creating a child's disturbance rather than overt symptoms. Feelings, fantasies, and fears are played out by the child in play therapy. The therapist may make dynamic interpretations of the child's verbal or non-verbal communication. It is hoped that the interpretations will make the child aware of unconscious thoughts and feelings that perpetuate his or her overt symptoms and that change in behavior may result from this therapeutic and educational style of interaction. In behavior therapy, the notion is that all behavior is learned and that some children learn maladaptive ways of interacting or relating or do not learn appropriate behaviors and social skills. The behavior therapist focuses on symptoms rather than causes, and seeks to actively manipulate the unacceptable behavior. This is an excellent technique to use when children present with discrete symptoms or present with a paucity of verbal insight skills. Relaxation training, a specific behavioral technique, might be used to aid children who are experiencing stress and other tension-related disorders.

Group psychotherapy is especially helpful for children experiencing peer or social interaction problems, since in group therapy usually two or more children are seen by a therapist. The orientation of the group can be behavioral, psychodynamic, or supportive, but the goal of the therapist is usually to increase the child's awareness and control of his or her emotions.

The decision to treat a child in the context of family therapy is made when the therapist perceives the family as maintaining and perpetuating the child's problem. The therapists attempts to identify and modify maladaptive family patterns that perpetuate the child's problems (Jay, Waters, & Willis, 1986). Parent consultation is also used to teach parents means of modifying behavior at home, to offer advice on child rearing, to explain a child's behavior, and to give support. A more detailed account of treatment methods used with children can be found in Jay et al. (1986), Olson et al. (1994), and Ollendick (1998).

REFERENCES

Achenbach, T. M. (1982). *Developmental psychopathology*. New York, NY: Wiley.

American Psychiatric Association. (1994). *Diagnostic and statistical manual of mental disorders* (4th ed.). Washington, DC: Author.

Bower, E. M. (1969). *Early identification of emotionally handicapped children in school* (2nd ed.). Springfield, IL: Thomas.

Bower, E. M. (1981). *Early identification of emotionally handicapped children in school* (3rd ed.). Springfield, IL: Thomas.

Boyle, M. H., & Jones, S. C. (1985). Selecting measures of emotional and behavioral disorders of childhood for use in general populations. *Journal of Child Psychology & Psychiatry, 26,* 137–159.

Brown, R. T., & Reynolds, C. R. (1986). *Psychological perspectives on childhood exceptionality*. New York, NY: Wiley.

Chandler, H. N., & Jones, K. (1983). Learning disabled or emotionally disturbed: Does it make any difference? *Journal of Learning Disabilities, 16*, 432–434.

Group for the Advancement of Psychiatry. (1966). *Psychopathological disorders in childhood: Theoretical considerations and a proposed classification* (Vol. 6, Report No. 2). New York, NY: Author.

Jay, S., Waters, D. B., & Willis, D. J. (1986). The emotionally exceptional. In R. T. Brown & C. R. Reynolds (Eds.), *Psychological perspectives on childhood exceptionality*. New York, NY: Wiley.

Leftowitz, M. M., & Tesiny, E. P. (1985). Depression in children: Prevalence and correlates. *Journal of Consulting & Clinical Psychology, 53*, 647–656.

Long, K. A., & McQueen, D. V. (1984). Detection and treatment of emotionally disturbed children in schools: Problems and theoretical perspectives. *Journal of Clinical Psychology, 40*, 378–390.

Offord, D. R. (1983). Classification and epidemiology in child psychiatry: Status and unresolved problems. In P. D. Steinhauer & Q. Rae-Grant (Eds.), *Psychological problems of the child in the family* (2nd ed.). New York, NY: Basic Books.

Ollendick, T. (1998). Children and adolescents: Clinical formulation and treatment. In A. Bellack & M. Hersen (Eds.), *Comprehensive clinical psychology* (Vol. 5). New York, NY: Elsevier.

Olson, R., Mullins, L., Gillman, J., & Chaney, S. (1994). *The sourcebook of pediatric psychology*. Boston, MA: Longwood.

Schaefer, C. E., Millman, H. L., & Levine, G. (1979). *Therapies for psychosomatic disorders in children*. San Francisco, CA: Jossey-Bass.

Steinhauer, P. D., & Berman, G. (1983). Anxiety, neurotic, and personality disorders in children. In P. D. Steinhauer & Q. Rae-Grant (Eds.), *Psychological problems of the child in the family* (2nd ed., pp. 230–257). New York, NY: Basic Books.

Steinhauer, P. D., & Rae-Grant, Q. (Eds.). (1983). *Psychological problems of the child in the family* (2nd ed.). New York, NY: Basic Books.

Thomas, A., Chess, S., & Birch, H. G. (1968). *Temperament and behavior disorders in children*. New York, NY: New York University Press.

Willis, D. J. (1985). *Psychological investigation of physical and sexual abuse of children*. Presidential address. Los Angeles, CA: American Psychological Association.

Willis, D. J., Elliot, C., & Jay, S. (1982). Psychological effects of physical illness and its concomitants. In P. Magrab (Ed.), *Handbook for the practice of pediatric psychology*. New York, NY: Wiley.

Wright, L., Schaefer, A. B., & Solomons, G. (1979). *Encyclopedia of pediatric psychology*. Baltimore, MD: University Park Press.

Zill, N. (1985). *The school-age handicapped*. Prepared by Child Trends, incorporated under Department of Education contract number 300-83-0198. Washington, DC: U.S. Department of Education.

DIANE J. WILLIS
E. WAYNE HOLDEN
University of Oklahoma Health Sciences Center
Previous edition

BRYAN COOK
University of Hawaii

MELODY TANKERSLY
Kent State University

PENA BEDESEM
Kent State University
Fourth edition

See also Childhood Psychosis; Childhood Schizophrenia; Conduct Disorder; Psychoneurotic Disorders; Seriously Emotionally Disturbed

EMOTIONAL LABILITY

Emotional lability refers to rapidly shifting or unstable emotions (American Psychiatric Association, 2000). It is a psychiatric term that developed from attempts to classify the qualitative aspects of inappropriate emotional functioning in clinical cases. Lability has been most frequently applied in descriptions of serious emotional disturbance where rapid changes in emotional status are readily apparent. Unstable emotions are also characteristic of less severe psychopathologies and can be used to describe normal children's functioning during periods of stress or crisis. Sustained emotional lability, however, is considered to be pathological and results from a number of different causative factors. The primary etiological agents in children are fragile central nervous system functioning and frustration in meeting environmental demands (Swanson & Willis, 1979).

Some familiarity with the psychiatric terminology used to describe emotion (Kaplan, Freedman, & Saddock, 1980) is needed to clearly understand the role of lability in the description of a child's functioning. Mood refers to sustained internal sensations that are stable and influence all aspects of an individual's functioning. Affect, on the other hand, is the immediate expression of emotion that is attached to specific environmental events. Affect can vary from situation to situation, while mood is pervasive emotional tone occurring across situations. The outward manifestations of affect are the basis for describing emotional responding. Lability refers to changes in affect that are repetitious and abrupt; both negative and positive affect may be displayed. Emotional responding is intense and typically does not fit environmental demands. Lability can be contrasted with other terms used to describe affective expression. Restricted affect is characterized by a reduction in the range and intensity of responding; blunted affect refers to a severe reduction in the intensity of responding; and flat affect is the complete absence of emotional responding.

Children receiving special education services who are classified emotionally disturbed are at greatest risk for displaying emotional lability. Unstable emotions are a primary diagnostic feature in a number of childhood psychiatric conditions included under the emotional disturbance label. Other categories of childhood exceptionality, however, are not exempt from rapidly shifting or unstable emotions. Labile affect is frequently displayed secondary to cognitive disturbance in learning-disabled and mentally retarded children. Emotional lability may also be present in children with sensory or physical disabilities owed to frustrations with meeting environmental demands. Even gifted children can display emotional lability when they are not appropriately challenged in the classroom setting. It is clear that emotional lability can be applied to all categories of childhood exceptionality and not restricted to children who have been diagnosed with a psychiatric condition.

REFERENCES

American Psychiatric Association. (2000). *Diagnostic and statistical manual of mental disorders* (4th ed., text rev.). Washington, DC: Author.

Kaplan, H. I., & Freedman, A. M., & Saddock, B. J. (1980). *Comprehensive textbook of psychiatry / III*. Baltimore, MD: Williams & Wilkins.

Swanson, B. M., & Willis, D. J. (1979). *Understanding exceptional children and youth*. Chicago, IL: Rand McNally.

E. Wayne Holden
Diane J. Willis
University of Oklahoma Health Sciences Center

See also Acting Out; Emotional Disorders; Seriously Emotionally Disturbed

EMPHYSEMA, CONGENITAL LOBAR

Congenital lobar emphysema is a chronic disease involving progressive hyperinflation of one or more pulmonary lobes, resulting in the trapping of air in the affected lobes. There are two distinct types of congenital lobar emphysema:

(1) an overexpansion of the normal lung lobe and (2) a polyalveolar lobe, in which there are an increased number of normally expanded alveoli. Although half of all cases have an etiology that is idiopathic, this disease can also be caused by lung obstructions or failure of the lungs to develop properly (Bhutani, 1996).

This disease has a peak incidence between birth and 6 months and is 1.5 to 3 times more prevalent in males than in females. Congenital lobar emphysema affects the left upper lobe in 41% of cases, the right middle lobe in 34% of cases, and the right upper lobe in 21% of cases (De Milto, 1999). No research could be found about whether ethnicity or socioeconomic plays any role in the prevalence of congenital lobar emphysema.

Characteristics

1. Infant presents with wheezing, chronic coughing, shortness of breath, and difficulty in exhaling and may have a blue tinge to both skin and fingernail beds.
2. X ray reveals hyperinflation of the affected lobe with mediastinal shift away from the affected side.

Congenital lobar emphysema ranges in severity from severe to virtually undetectable, with many cases being mild with no need for supplemental oxygen. For those with mild or no symptoms, no treatment may be required. For those with acute or severe symptoms, surgery—either segmentectomy or lobectomy—is a common treatment (Hansen, Corbet, & Avery, 1991; Ordonez, 1997).

In most cases, whether treated medically or surgically, respiratory symptoms typically disappear by age 1. Almost all children with congenital lobar emphysema, however, show evidence of mild pulmonary obstruction by age 10, indicative of a more generalized abnormality (Hansen et al., 1991).

Congenital lobar emphysema does not often result in severe physical or cognitive disability. Like children with asthma, children with congenital lobar emphysema may require modified activities and classes. Typically, this includes allowing the child more frequent rests during strenuous physical exercise and providing alternatives for activities in which the child is unable to participate. During recess or other play periods, and in physical education classes, nonstrenuous games or tasks should be made available to the child, and the child should be allowed to choose not to participate in an activity that he or she finds difficult. Additionally, the child may have a heightened sensitivity to chemical irritants such as cleansers or other substances and should be given the same consideration when these irritants are present as he or she would be given in the case of strenuous activity. Due to the chronic nature of this illness, counseling may be required for the child and his or her family.

Congenital lobar emphysema is a chronic condition and will therefore be present throughout the child's life. In acute or severe cases, treatment results in an excellent outcome, with respiratory symptoms disappearing in most children by the end of their first year.

REFERENCES

Bhutani, V. K. (1996). *Intensive care of the fetus and neonate.* St. Louis, MO: Mosby.

De Milto, L. (1999). *Gale encyclopedia of medicine* (1st ed.). Farmington Hills, MI: Gale Research.

Hansen, T., Corbet, A., & Avery, M. E. (1991). *Diseases of the newborn* (6th ed.). Philadelphia, PA: Harcourt Brace Jovanovich.

Ordonez, P. (1997). *Congenital lobar emphysema.* Retrieved from http://www.neonatology.org/index.html

MELISSA M. HARVEY
University of Colorado at Colorado Springs

EMPIRICALLY SUPPORTED TREATMENT

Empirically supported treatments (ESTs) are psychological interventions that have been tested in research studies and have exceeded certain levels of research support. The term "empirically supported treatments" (also sometimes referred to as "empirically validated treatments") is most closely associated with efforts initiated by the American Psychological Association (APA) during the 1990s to identify effective psychological treatments. These efforts were in part a response to the evidence-based medicine movement (see entry for Evidence-Based Practice) and were based on the premises that (a) client care can be enhanced by empirical knowledge, (b) it is difficult for clinicians to keep up with new research relevant to their practice, (c) if clinicians do not keep up with new research their knowledge will deteriorate after their training, and (d) clinicians will benefit from summaries of evidence provided by expert reviews and guidelines on how to apply this evidence to clinical practice (Chambless & Ollendick, 2001). The purpose of the APA's Task Force on the Promotion and Dissemination of Psychological Procedures (referred to here as the Task Force) was to maintain a current list of effective practices for distribution to practitioners and training programs in clinical psychology.

The criteria for ESTs developed by the Task Force consist of three levels of empirical support (Chambless et al., 1998): Well-established treatments, probably efficacious treatments, and experimental treatments.

Well-established treatments are supported by at least two randomized clinical trials demonstrating superiority to a pill or placebo condition or another treatment or equivalence to another well-established treatment. Alternatively, these treatments could have been supported by a large series of single-case design studies comparing the intervention to another treatment. Additional requirements for well-established treatments include that the treatments must be clearly described in treatment manuals, the characteristics of the treated samples must be clearly defined, and the efficacy of the treatments have to have been established by at least two different teams of investigators. Probably efficacious treatments are treatments that have been supported by at least one randomized clinical trial or by single-case design studies, but do not meet all criteria for well-established treatments (e.g., the treatment has only been studied by one group of investigators). Finally, the Task Force defined treatments not meeting either level of support as experimental treatments.

The original APA Task Force published two lists of ESTs (Chambless et al., 1998; Task Force, 1995) and led to the establishment of a second APA task force focused on child clinical psychology and to other efforts to define ESTs. In 2001, Chambless and Ollendick published a summary of these efforts, combining them into a single list of ESTs, spanning the adult and child literatures, including interventions for geriatric populations and children being seen in medical settings. Efforts to identify new ESTs are ongoing, including a special issue of the *Journal of Clinical Child and Adolescent Psychology* (Silverman & Hinshaw, 1995) published in 1995 with a list of treatments for children. Other similar ongoing efforts include the Evidence-Based Intervention Workgroup in school psychology (see Kratochwill & Shernoff, 2003) and the U.S. Department of Education's What Works Clearinghouse, listing effective practices in all areas of education (2005).

These efforts to identify ESTs have not been without controversy. One of the concerns most commonly raised by opponents of this movement is that ESTs will not work in clinical care settings because the samples they were tested on are not representative of typical clients (e.g., Westen, Novotny, & Thompson-Brenner, 2004). Although some evidence exists to counter this argument (see Chambless & Ollendick, 2001, for a summary of this evidence), these concerns have led to a call for increased research to test these treatments outside research settings with typical clinical settings, practitioners, and clients (e.g., the National Advisory Mental Health Council Workgroup on Child and Adolescent Mental Health Intervention Development and Deployment, 2001).

REFERENCES

Chambless, D. L., Baker, M. J., Baucom, D. H., Beutler, L. E., Calhoun, K. S., Crits-Christoph, P., . . . Woody, S. R. (1998).

Update on empirically validated therapies II. *The Clinical Psychologist, 51*, 3–16.

Chambless, D. L., & Ollendick, T. H. (2001). Empirically supported psychological interventions: Controversies and evidence. *Annual Reviews of Psychology, 52*, 685–716.

Kratochwill, T. R., & Shernoff, E. S. (2003). Evidence-based practice: Promoting evidence-based interventions in school psychology. *School Psychology Quarterly, 18*, 389–408.

The National Advisory Mental Health Council Workgroup on Child and Adolescent Mental Health Intervention Development and Deployment. (2001). *Blueprint for Change: Research on Child and Adolescent Mental Health*. Washington, DC.

Silverman, W. K., & Hinshaw, S. P. (1995). Empirically supported psychosocial interventions for children: An overview. *Journal of Clinical Child and Adolescent Psychology, 34*, 11–24.

Task Force on Promotion and Dissemination of Psychological Procedures. (1995). Training in and dissemination of empirically validated psychological treatments: Report and recommendations. *The Clinical Psychologist, 48*, 3–23.

Westen, D., Novotny, C. M., & Thompson-Brenner, H. (2004). The empirical status of empirically supported therapies: Assumptions, findings, and reporting in controlled trials. *Psychological Bulletin, 130*, 631–663.

U.S. Department of Education's Institute of Education Sciences. (2005). *What works clearinghouse*. Retrieved from http://ies.ed.gov/ncee/wwc/

AMANDA JENSEN DOSS
TIA BILLY
Texas A&M University

See also Effectiveness of Special Education; Evidence-Based Practice; Intervention; Intervention in School and Clinic

EMPLOYMENT OPTIONS

Employment options are different choices that an individual with a disability can make in pursuing job opportunities when transitioning to adulthood. Individuals with disabilities have the power to make choices and take actions in making a decision about employment. However, a few decades ago, there were very few work options other than competitive employment due to the lack of support and accommodation for individuals with disabilities. As a result, individuals with disabilities encountered serious problems of unemployment or underemployment. Thanks to advocacy and the civil rights movement since the 1960s, federal laws and policies, such as the Rehabilitation Act and the Americans with Disabilities Act (ADA), have been established to ensure equal employment opportunities and improve employment outcomes for individuals with disabilities. A variety of employment options have been evolved when implementing federal laws and policies. As more employment options are available, individuals with

disabilities are more likely to gain employment. The most popular employment options include sheltered employment, supported employment, customized employment, competitive employment, and self-employment.

Competitive employment is when people with disabilities work, like those without disabilities, in the community and are paid equally as those who do the same job. They may or may not receive supports from vocational rehabilitation (VR) agencies. Supported employment, customized employment and self-employment are different types of competitive employment designed for individuals with disabilities. Self-employment is to own and operate a small business and receive financial benefits. Individuals with disabilities who start self-employment may receive technical assistance and supports from VR and other programs.

Sheltered employment refers to vocational or nonvocational programs for individuals who need more support and are placed in segregated settings, such as day-treatment centers, activity centers, and sheltered workshops, which are offered to individuals who were perceived as incapable of working in competitive and integrated settings (Kregel & Dean, 2002). Day-treatment programs provide multidimensional treatment and rehabilitative services to individuals who have mental disorders outside the hospital. The program was popular and grew fast during 1970s and 1980s. However, research examining employment outcomes indicated that rehabilitative day-treatment programs were not as effective as supported-employment programs. In response to this research finding, many mental health centers have changed from day-treatment programs to supported-employment programs (Drake, Becker, Biesanz, Torrey, McHugo, & Wyzik, 1994). Work activity center is also a type of sheltered employment that provides a variety of trainings and services to people with disabilities who need rehabilitative services. Individuals receive training on independent living skills and prevocational skills. They also perform some relatively simple tasks, such as sorting, assembling, wrapping, and so forth. Sheltered workshops are facility-based programs that provide employment to individuals with disabilities. The program offers benefits including paychecks, job training, employment experience, socialization with peers, leisure activities, and so on. Kregel and Dean (2002) divided these sheltered employment into two categories: one is transitional-employment programs, which focus on preparing individuals for future successful competitive employment; the other is extended-employment programs, which are designed to provide long-term work placements for individuals as a source of income. Although they vary in objectives, services, and functions; a common feature of these sheltered employment programs is segregated placement.

Supported employment is competitive employment with ongoing support, especially for individuals with significant disabilities. It emerged as an alternative to sheltered employment when the effectiveness of segregated employment was questioned during 1980s. As defined in Act Amendments of 1986, key features of supported employment include paid employment, integrated work sites for people with severe disabilities, and ongoing support and services. In supported employment, individuals are provided person-centered planning, job coaches, on-site work training, supervision, assistive technology, and natural support (e.g., support from co-workers and supervisors; Wehman, Brooke, & West, 2006). There are four models of supported employment including individual placement, enclave, mobile work crew, and small business (ODEP, 1993). Individual placement model means to place an individual in a community business and provide onsite job training and a job coach. The job coach is always available to provide follow-up or new training as needed. Enclave model is implemented for a small group of individuals, who work as a team in a single work site and receive training and support from one onsite supervisor. Another type of enclave model is called the "dispersed enclave," which is used when members of the enclave work on different jobs in the same company. In the mobile work crew model, people work together as a unit and sell service (e.g., groundskeeping). Under the supervision of a job coach, they work with people who do not have disabilities at different locations within the community. The small business model includes more employees with disabilities than without disabilities. It operates like any other business that generates revenues and pays employees from the revenues they made. Overall, supported employment is an evidence-based practice found to be effective on promoting long-term employment, independence, and community integration (Bond, 2004; Wehman, 1986). Since the passage of the Rehabilitation Act Amendments of 1992, increasing number of consumers of VR services receive supported employment services instead of sheltered employment services (Wehman, Revell, & Kregel, 1998). Supported employment is a preferred employment option for individuals with significant cognitive disabilities.

Customized employment is a relatively new and growing employment option for individuals with disabilities. The term was introduced by the U.S. Department of Labor, Office of Disability Employment Policy (ODEP) in 2001 as a new approach to increase employment opportunities for individuals with disabilities and facilitate their integration to global workforce (Inge, 2006). Customized employment is a process for an employee and an employer to negotiate and build employment relationships based on the needs of both. It is to match a work candidate's strengths, needs, and interests to an employer's or a business' demands and needs. Activities in customized employment generally include individual assessment, negotiation with employers, modification of job responsibilities, and providing ongoing supports. Customized employment may be developed through job-carving, self-employment, and business ownership. Supports and funding may come from various sources based on an individual's needs (Griffin, Hammis, Geary, & Sullivan, 2008).

The availability of employment options greatly increases employment opportunities for individuals with disabilities who have difficulties in traditional competitive employment. It is important for individuals with disabilities to understand these options, so that they can make informed decisions about employment based on their own strengths, needs and interests with the assistance from VR counselors, special educators, family members, other service providers.

REFERENCES

Bond, G. R. (2004). Supported employment: Evidence for an evidence-based practice. *Psychiatric Rehabilitation Journal, 27*, 345–359.

Drake, R. E., Becker, D. R., Biesanz, J. C., Torrey, W. C., McHugo, G. J., & Wyzik, P. F. (1994). Rehabilitative day treatment vs. supported employment: I. Vocational outcomes. *Community Mental Health Journal, 30*, 519–532.

Griffin, C., Hammis, D., Geary, T., & Sullivan, M. (2008). Customized employment: Where we are; where we're headed. *Journal of Vocational Rehabilitation, 28*, 1–5.

Inge, K. J. (2006). Customized employment: A growing strategy for facilitating inclusive employment. *Journal of Vocational Rehabilitation, 24*, 191–193.

Kregel, J., & Dean, D. H. (2002). Sheltered vs. supported employment: A direct comparison of long-term earnings outcomes for individuals with cognitive disabilities. In J. Kregel, D. Dean, & P. Wehman (Eds)., *Achievements and challenges in employment services for people with disabilities* (pp. 63–83). Retrieved from http://www.worksupport.com/main/downloads/dean/shelteredchap3.pdf

Office of Disability Employment Policy (ODEP). (1993, October). *Supported employment.* Retrieved from http://www.dol.gov/

Wehman, P. (1986). Supported competitive employment for persons with severe disabilities. *Journal of Applied Rehabilitation Counseling, 17*, 24–29.

Wehman, P., Brooke, V., & West, M. (2006) Vocational placements and careers: Toward inclusive employment. In P. Wehman (Eds)., *Life beyond the classroom.* Baltimore, MD: Paul H. Brookes.

Wehman, P., Revell, G., & Kregel, J. (1998). Supported employment: A decade of rapid growth and impact. *American Rehabilitation, 24*(1), 31–43.

SONG JU
Texas A&M University
4th edition

ENCEPHALITIS, MYCOPLASMA PNEUMONIAE

Mycoplasma pneumoniae encephalitis is a bacterial infection that mimics a virus; that is, the bacterias lack a cell wall and receptor sites for common antibiotics. Mycoplasmas are transmitted via the respiratory route and are the smallest free-living parasites known to exist (Clyde, 1997). This type of pneumonia occurs more often in the winter months and is often accompanied by bulbous myringitis (eardrum inflammation) and otitis media (ear infections). The infection is more commonly found in school-age children and adolescents. Neurologic complications are rare: 1% to 7% of pneumoniae cases (Johnson, 1998), but the condition has been associated with a variety of serious problems, including lethargy, altered consciousness, agitation, psychotic behavior, seizures, aphasia, paresthesis, cranial nerve palsies, and cerebellar ataxia (Thomas, Collins, Robb, & Robinson, 1993). It has also been found in patients diagnosed with meningitis and Guillain-Barré syndrome.

The pathogenesis of mycoplasma infection is not known; however, researchers have hypothesized that the condition is due to one of three causes. The most likely explanation is that the infection results from an autoimmune response in which free-floating antibodies in the brain react with complementary mycoplasma antibodies. Other explanations include a direct insult of the central nervous system (CNS) by bacteria crossing the blood-brain barrier and bacteria releasing a neurotoxin that damages the CNS (Thomas et al., 1993); however, few cases have been found in which bacteria has been isolated in the CNS, and the release of neurotoxins has only been shown in animals.

Characteristics

1. The bacterial infection mimics a virus and occurs more commonly in school-age children and adolescents than adults.
2. Eardrum inflammation and ear infections are common.
3. Neurologic symptoms include lethargy, agitation, seizures, and altered consciousness.
4. Prognosis is generally good, but in some cases sequelae persist such as optic atrophy, intellectual deterioration, and spastic quadriplegia.

Although respiratory infection typically precedes neurological symptoms, in some cases there is no known antecedent respiratory illness or infection. Mycoplasma pneumoniae infection, however, should be considered a possibility in all cases of acute encephalitis. The diagnosis is typically made through serologic tests that detect the antibodies (i.e., IgG and IgM). Lumbar puncture, magnetic resonance imaging, and computerized tomography scanning have all been used, but these tests are often inconclusive. Although increased levels of protein concentrations and lymphocytes are often found, bacteria in the CSF is not typically found.

The most effective treatment is that of an antibiotic, such as erythromycin and tetracycline. Penicillin and cephalosporin are not effective despite their frequent use. These antibiotics are helpful in treating bacterial infections, but there is no evidence that there is any impact on the neurologic sequelae. Further, there is no evidence that corticosteroids are effective with this infection and its aftermath (Thomas et al., 1993). Fortunately, prognosis is generally good. There are very few cases of death caused by mycoplasma pneumoniae infections; however, the seriousness of certain sequelae means that these children need to be evaluated carefully for problems such as intellectual deterioration, short-term memory impairment, seizures, optic atrophy, and movement disorders (e.g., spastic quadriplegia).

Treatment depends on the severity and the nature of the impact. For example, in cases of physical impairment, services from physical and occupational therapists are often warranted. These children may qualify for special education services under Other Health Impairment or even Section 504. In most cases, certain classroom accommodations will be needed. When cognitive impact is severe, school-age children may even warrant services for students with Intellectual Disabilities and Specific Learning Disabilities. When emotional and behavioral needs become so great as to interfere with learning and social progress, special education services for students with Emotional Disturbance may be needed. Given the impact that eardrum inflammation and ear infection can have on hearing, audiologists and speech and language pathologists should be consulted so that the child can be properly evaluated for services. Furthermore, school psychological services should be obtained to ensure that the student's educational and emotional needs are properly assessed (e.g., pre- and postencephalitis functioning and educational needs) and that interventions are appropriately designed and implemented. Children with mycoplasma pneumoniae encephalitis should also be offered counseling services to help them cope with the sudden onset of this illness (and its sequelae) and the fears and uncertainty about the future. It is critical that parents be involved in the assessment and intervention process to insure that the child with mycoplasma pneumoniae encephalitis has the benefit of state-of-the-art services.

REFERENCES

Clyde, W. A. (1997). Mycoplasmal diseases. In W. M. Scheld, R. J. Whitley, & D. T. Durack (Eds.), *Infections of the central nervous system* (2nd ed., pp. 283–293). New York, NY: Lippincott Raven.

Johnson, R. T. (1998). *Viral infections of the nervous system*. New York, NY: Lippincott Raven.

Thomas, N., Collins, J., Robb, S., & Robinson, R. (1993). Mycoplasma pneumoniae infection and neurological disease. *Archives of Disease in Childhood, 69*, 573–576.

Loni Kuhn
Elaine Clark
University of Utah

ENCEPHALITIS, POSTHERPETIC

Postherpetic encephalitis, or herpes simplex encephalitis (HSVE), is caused by the herpes simplex virus–1 (HSV-1) and is characterized by inflammation of the parenchyma and the surrounding meninges. The herpes simplex virus has a predilection for certain areas of the brain, specifically, the frontotemporal region. HSVE accounts for 10% of all cases of encephalitis and is one of the most common types of fatal sporadic encephalitis (Clifton, 1991). This type of encephalitis is uncommon: It occurs annually in an estimated 1 in 250,000 individuals but is more prevalent in children than in adults. It is not entirely clear how the virus gains access to the brain, but some researchers question olfactory and orbital routes.

Symptoms of HSVE include alterations in mental status (e.g., loss of consciousness, confusion, and memory loss), headache, fever, lethargy, nausea and vomiting, generalized and focal seizures, and hemiparesis. Neurologic impairment can be permanent, including impairment in sensorimotor, language (e.g., dysnomia), intellectual skills, and behavioral functions.

Characteristics

1. HSVE is caused by the herpes simplex virus–1 and affects more children than adults.

2. Herpes simplex viruses have a predilection to the frontotemporal region of the brain and are characterized by inflammation of the parenchyma and the surrounding meninges.

3. Rapid onset of symptoms is common and can include alterations in mental status, headache, vomiting, fever, lethargy, seizures, and hemiparesis.

4. Mortality rates are as high as 70% if untreated, but drug therapies such as Acyclovir help.

5. Sensorimotor, intellectual, language, and behavioral changes are common.

HSVE is diagnosed by a number of methods, including electroencephalograms (EEGs), computed tomography (CT), tissue biopsies, and cerebral spinal fluid (CSF) evaluation. Brain biopsies have been shown to be the most reliable diagnostic tools, but examining CSF for lymphocytes, antibodies, and red blood cells has also been shown to be the most practical (Ratho, Sethi, & Singh, 1999). EEG and neuroimaging have been useful in identifying areas of the brain impacted by the virus, and they predict sequelae from the infection.

If untreated, HSVE can result in death—in some cases in 70% of all individuals infected (Clifton, 1991). The antiviral drug Acyclovir has been successful in reducing mortality rates (in some studies to 28%) and morbidity. In addition to Acyclovir, cortcosteroids are occasionally given to reduce intracranial pressure. Concern has been expressed about a potential negative interaction among steroid use, the antiviral agent, and the virus itself; however, recent research in rats has failed to show an increase in herpes simplex replication using the two treatments (Blessing, Blessing, & Wesselingh, 2000).

The prognosis is improved with early diagnosis and treatment, but problems can persist long after the acute phase of illness. Educators need to be aware of potential long-term neurologic impairments caused by HSVE. This includes problems with memory and cognition, motor and language problems, and aggression, to name a few. Special education is likely to be needed, so children who have had HSVE need to be evaluated for special education—as well as regular education—needs. Speech and language therapists, as well as occupational and physical therapists, may play an important role in the child's ability to achieve.

Future research is needed to better explain the pathogenesis of the infection, in particular, where the virus is more likely to gain access. This may provide critical information for finding ways to prevent the encephalitis and facilitate early diagnosis and treatment.

REFERENCES

Blessing, K. A., Blessing, W. W., & Wesselingh, S. L. (2000). Herpes simplex replication and dissemination is not increased by corticosteroid treatment in a rat model of focal herpes encephalitis. *Journal of Neurovirology, 6*(1), 25–32.

Clifton, E. R. (1991). Herpes simplex encephalitis: An overview. *Journal of Mississippi State Medical Association, 32*(12), 437–440.

Ratho, R. K., Sethi, S., & Singh, S. (1999). Role of serology in the diagnosis of herpes simplex encephalitis. *Indian Journal of Pathological Microbiology, 42*(3), 333–337.

Loni Kuhn
Elaine Clark
University of Utah

ENCEPHALITIS, POSTINFECTIOUS MEASLES

Postinfectious measles encephalitis is an autoimmune response characterized by inflammation and demyelination that is triggered by the measles virus. The measles virus is transmitted through respiratory droplets and is thought to have impacted civilizations as early as 4000 B.C. A young Danish physician, Peter L. Panum, however, is credited with much of the information that is now known about measles, including the highly contagious nature of the disease. Panum was sent to the Faroe Islands in the mid-1800s to assist with a large-scale measles outbreak and discovered that measles have an incubation period of about 14 days (Griffin, Ward, & Esolen, 1994). In most cases, individuals begin to show signs of improvement about five days after the measles rash appears. It is not clear how the measles virus triggers the autoimmune reaction that causes encephalomyelitis. However, when this occurs, there is considerable neurologic involvement, and prior to the introduction of the measles vaccine, it was the most common cause of neurological disability. Encephalitis-associated symptoms include fever, headache, seizures, and coma. It has been estimated that 50 percent of individuals who contract postinfectious measles encephalitis develop seizures and nearly 100 percent show impaired consciousness during the episode (Scheld, Whitley, & Durack, 1997). Other neurologic-related sequelae include intellectual deterioration, hemiparesis, paraplegia, and ataxia (Scheld et al., 1997).

Characteristics

1. An autoimmune response characterized by demyelinization and inflammation
2. Triggered by the measles virus, and affecting 1 per 1,000 measles cases
3. Commonly diagnosed following neurological complications from rashes
4. Mortality rate of approximately 25%
5. Neurologic sequelae including intellectual decline, hemiparesis/plegia, and ataxia

---

Because the measles vaccine is commonly administered in North America and Europe, measles infections are fairly infrequent. In other areas of the world, measles epidemics occur often, as does the corresponding encephalitis. Encephalitis occurs in 1 of every 1,000 cases of measles and is more commonly found among young people and the elderly (Griffin et al., 1994). There does not appear to be a sex difference, as males and females are equally affected.

Most often, the diagnosis of postinfectious encephalitis is made based on clinical signs and symptoms of neurological complication (i.e., following the measles rash). In some cases, the disease is found in the urine, blood, and cerebral spinal fluid (CSF), and especially in increased levels of mononuclear cells and protein (Johnson, 1998), but these are not consistent findings. Therefore, follow-up is needed even in cases in which there is no evidence of the disease in the blood or urine and the lumbar puncture is clean. Other methods to follow up on the disease include use of electroencephalograms (EEGs) and magnetic resonance imaging (MRI). In cases of postinfectious measles encephalitis, the EEG commonly displays diffuse, symmetric slowing, and the MRI often shows demyelination in the cerebellum and brain stem.

The prognosis for individuals who contract postinfectious measles encephalitis is often poor: Approximately 25% die from the disease. There are no antiviral drug treatments to treat postinfectious measles encephalitis. Although the administration of immunoglobulins following exposure has been shown to alter the course some, conflicting evidence has been found, and the overall consensus seems to be that corticosteroid treatments are not very helpful in alleviating the disease. Clearly, the most effective treatment is prevention through vaccines. In countries in which the vaccine is widely used, the disease is essentially nonexistent.

For those who survive, special education services may be necessary. This includes services under the category of other health impairment, intellectual disabilities, and specific learning disabilities. Given the complexity and severity of symptoms following the contraction of the disease, regardless of special education eligibility, children will likely need some accommodations in the classroom and ancillary services such as occupational and physical therapies. Psychological services are likely to be critical to evaluate the neuropsychological consequence of the disease and determine necessary services. Home-school collaborations are likely to be necessary to ensure that the child is receiving appropriate services and making the expected progress educationally and socially. Depending on the severity of the disability caused from the disease, vocational testing and services may also be called for; therefore, children need to be evaluated early to reduce frustration and provide them with the best education possible.

REFERENCES

Griffin, D., Ward, B., & Esolen, L. (1994). Pathogenesis of measles virus infection: An hypothesis for altered immune responses. *Journal of Infectious Diseases, 170*(Suppl. 1), 24–31.

Johnson, R. T. (1998). *Viral infections of the nervous system.* New York, NY: Lippincott Raven.

Scheld, M., Whitley, R., & Durack, D. (1997). *Infections of the central nervous system.* New York, NY: Lippincott Raven.

LONI KUHN
ELAINE Clark
University of Utah

ENCOPRESIS

Encopresis involves the repeated passage of feces into inappropriate places (e.g., clothing or the floor), whether involuntarily or intentional. It is differentiated into either primary or secondary subtypes: The primary subtype indicates that the individual has never established fecal continence, whereas the secondary subtype indicates the disturbance developed after a period of established continence. Encopresis may stem from psychological reasons such as anxiety about defecating in a public place, a more generalized anxiety, or oppositional behavior or may be caused by physiologically induced dehydration related to hypothyroidism, a febrile illness, or a side effect of medications. Secondary encopresis may begin following a stressful event, such as the birth of a sibling, the beginning of school, or separation from a parent due to divorce or death.

Encopresis cannot be diagnosed prior to the age of 4, and there must be at least one event per month for at least 3 months. It is estimated that 1 percent of 5-year-olds have encopresis, and the disorder is 5 to 6 times more prevalent in males. Referrals for encopresis account for approximately 3% of pediatric outpatient referrals (Abrahamin & Lloyd-Still, 1984) and 5% of referrals to psychiatric clinics. A history of constipation, developmental delays in other areas, attention-deficit/hyperactivity disorder, or coercive or premature bowel training increases the risk for developing encopresis (Maxmen & Ward, 1995). Frequency of encopresis decreases with age, with a spontaneous remission rate of about 28% per year (Schaefer, 1979). Encopresis can persist intermittently for years but rarely becomes a chronic condition.

In addition to the primary and secondary distinctions of encopresis, three major categories of encopresis exist (Howe & Walker, 1992). The most common is retentive encopresis, which accounts for 80–95 percent of all encopretic cases (Christopherson & Rapoff, 1983). Retentive encopresis occurs when a child becomes constipated and liquid fecal mater leaks around the fecal obstruction and soils undergarments. The second type of encopresis includes chronic diarrhea and irritable bowel syndrome, most commonly associated with stress and anxiety. The third and least common form of encopresis is manipulative, intentional soiling, most commonly associated with oppositional defiance or conduct disorders.

Characteristics

1. Repeated passage of feces into inappropriate places whether involuntarily or intentionally.

2. Primary encopresis: At least one such event per month for at least 3 months.

3. Secondary encopresis: One full year of being continent prior to current episode of encopresis.

4. Chronological age is at least 4 years (or equivalent developmental level).

5. The behavior is not exclusively due to direct physiological effects of a substance (e.g., laxatives) or a general medical condition except constipation.

6. Code as either with constipation and overflow incontinence or without constipation and overflow incontinence.

7. Treatment usually includes both medical and behavioral interventions.

Treatment of encopresis usually includes both medical and behavioral interventions (Mash & Barkley, 1996). It is believed that a multifaceted approach that treats a wide range of systems (organic, behavioral, cognitive, and environmental) will achieve the most efficacious results. To avoid the retention-leakage cycle, a combination of enemas, laxatives, stool softeners, or increased dietary fiber are used to evacuate the colon. In rare cases surgical extraction of the fecal material may be required. Children are then scheduled to have regular sessions on the toilet for the purpose of muscle retraining. They are given the responsibility of cleaning both themselves and any soiled clothing or surrounding areas after bowel movements. Rewards for appropriate toileting behavior and establishing a regular time for bowel movements (usually immediately after a meal) are also helpful for treating encopresis. Shaping and fading, behavioral modification techniques, are often used to increase stimulus control as a child transitions from a diaper to the toilet (Smith, Smith, & Lee, 2000). Parents are encouraged to keep a matter-of-fact approach in helping their children in order to avoid inadvertently reinforcing attention-seeking behaviors.

The child with encopresis often feels ashamed and embarrassed, which can lead to avoidance of school and other social situations. The amount of impairment is a direct function of the effect on the child's self-esteem, social ostracism by peers at school and in the community, and rejection by the caregiver. Special education accommodations may be made if the encopresis falls under the handicapping condition of Other Health Impairment. Support and planning by the school personnel may assist the child and parent in creating a plan to decrease school absenteeism and peer isolation. Due to the nature of the disorder, children with involuntary encopresis often experience psychological problems stemming from the encopresis, rather than causing encopresis. Children with deliberate soiling behaviors may receive rewards (i.e., parental attention, school absence, etc.) that inadvertently reinforce the soiling and smearing behaviors. When incontinence is deliberate, features of oppositional defiant disorder or conduct disorder may also be present.

The frequency of encopresis decreases with age, with a spontaneous remission rate of 28% per year (Schaefer, 1979). Therefore, the initial prognosis for encopresis is good. However, the psychological impact may reach farther because the child faces the social isolation and stigmatism already created within his or her peer group. School-based interventions may decrease peer isolation and increase the child's feelings of mastery of bowel control while in social situations. School personnel may provide discrete scheduled toileting times during the school day, enhance effective toileting strategies by providing rewards for reduction of soiling, and providing a place for cleaning of clothes and self if a soiling incident occurs. The school psychologist or counselor can facilitate increased communication between school, medical personnel, and the school, encouraging consistent intervention strategies. Encopresis can persist intermittently for years, but it rarely is a chronic condition. Intervention at the school level is critical for continued social and academic success for the child experiencing encopresis.

The need for future research is evident, primarily because available studies addressing encopresis are based on case studies. Valid experimental designs to evaluate treatment effectiveness, such as random assignment of cases to experimental and control groups or to alternate treatment groups, reversal designs (ABAB), and multiple baseline design studies are needed (Schaefer, 1979) in order to rule out spontaneous remission or extraneous effects on bowel control. There is also a need for further study in identifying differential treatment for continuous versus discontinuous encopresis and for longitudinal investigations of the natural history of encopresis (Schaefer, 1979).

REFERENCES

Abrahamin, R., & Lloyd-Still, J. D. (1984). Chronic constipation in childhood: A longitudinal study of 186 patients. *Journal of Pediatric Gastroenterology and Nutrition, 3*, 460–467.

Christopherson, E. R., & Rapoff, M. A. (1983). Toileting problems in children. In C. E. Walker & M. C. Roberts (Eds.), *Handbook of clinical child psychology* (pp. 593–615). New York, NY: Wiley.

Howe, A. C., & Walker, C. E. (1992). Behavioral management of toilet training, enuresis, and encopresis. *Pediatric Clinics of North America, 39*, 413–432.

Mash, E. J., & Barkley, R. A. (1996). *Child psychopathology*. New York, NY: Guilford Press.

Maxmen, J., & Ward, N. (1995). *Essential psychopathology and its treatment* (2nd ed.). New York, NY: W. W. Norton.

Schaefer, C. E. (1979). *Childhood encopresis and enuresis*. New York, NY: Van Nostrand Reinhold.

Smith, L., Smith, P., & Lee, K. (2000). Behavioral treatment of urinary incontinence and encopresis in children with learning disabilities: Transfer of stimulus control. *Developmental Medicine and Child Neurology, 42*, 276–279.

LESLIE COYLE FRANKLIN
BRIAN JOHNSON
University of Northern Colorado

ENDOCARDIAL FIBROELASTOSIS

Characterized by an increased amount of connective tissue and elastic fibers causing a thickening in the muscular lining of the heart, endocardial fibroelastosis (EFE) is a rare condition eventually leading to congestive heart failure if it is not diagnosed early. Whereas some studies advocate that EFE may be the result of an X-linked, autosomal recessive trait, others support that EFE is caused by intrauterine viral infections, impaired lymphatic drainage of the heart, or carnitine deficiency.

Prevalence rates were once estimated at 1 in 5,000 live births; however, that number has decreased over the years, and EFE has become virtually nonexistent with the advent of vaccinations and improved neonatal health care. As expected, undiagnosed problems such as congestive hearth failure lead to problems in brain perfusion, with significant cognitive sequelae in some cases.

Treatments vary by seriousness of the condition. Drug therapies that have been found effective include diuretics used to eliminate fluid retention and cardiac glycosides that can be administered to ameliorate symptoms such as increased heart rate, myocardial contractility, and other symptoms of chronic heart failure. Anticoagulants aid in the reduction of blood clots. Heart transplants also are a viable option for some children with EFE.

Characteristics

1. Thickening of the linings of heart chambers
2. Difficulty breathing, coughing, irritability, fatigue, failure to thrive, and sometimes a bluish skin discoloration of the feet and hands
3. Unusual chest sounds, such as bubbling, rales, and murmurs, often heard with a stethoscope during routine physicians' examinations
4. Life-threatening complications, including rapid heartbeat, irregular heart rhythms, and congestive cardiomyopathy

Although the prognosis is generally poor, especially in children who present with EFE at birth, children who respond to drug therapies have been known to live healthy lives. Some children may also be caught in the middle of the spectrum and experience persistent symptoms requiring medical intervention above and beyond drug therapies. Because roughly only one third of the children survive to school age, little is known with regard to psychosocial and educational determinants. Children who respond well to drug treatments go on to live seemingly unaffected lives as long as medication is continued and the condition is monitored. Educational placement may require labeling of the child under other health impairment. Future research is focusing on prevention and etiology of this lethal disorder.

This entry has been informed by the sources listed below.

REFERENCES

Keith, J. D., Rose, V., & Manning, J. A. (1978). Endocardial fibroelastosis. In J. D. Keith, R. D. Rowe, & P. Vlad (Eds.), *Heart disease in infancy and childhood* (3rd ed., pp. 941–957). New York, NY: Macmillan.

Nelson, W. E., Behrman, R. E., Kliegmen, R. M., & Arvin, A. M. (1996). *Nelson textbook of pediatrics* (15th ed.). Bangalore, India: Prism Books.

Venugopalan, P. (2001). Endocardial fibroelastosis. *eMedicine*, 2. Retrieved from http://emedicine.medscape.com/

KIMBERLY M. ESTEP
University of Houston–Clear Lake

ENDOCRINE DISORDERS

The endocrine system consists of the pituitary, thyroid, parathyroid, adrenal, pancreas, gonads, and placenta. The general function of the endocrine system is to control growth and reproduction and to maintain chemical homeostasis in the body.

Disorders associated with the endocrine system may result from partial or total insensitivity of tissue to endogenous hormones, hypersecretion of hormones, or hyposecretion of hormones. Endocrine disorders may have a variety of etiologies including chromosomal abnormalities, prenatal deficiencies, maternal hormonal deficiencies during gestation, and a variety of environmental variables (e.g., toxins, traumatic brain injury, brain tumors, and viruses).

Endocrine disorders also vary in prevalence and in the age at which symptoms appear. Commonly, endocrine disorders in children are detected because a child's development is premature or delayed (Sandberg & Barrik, 1995). Relatively common endocrine disorders of childhood include Turner syndrome, Klinefelter syndrome, congenital adrenal hyperplasia, hyperthyroidism, diabetes mellitus, and obesity. Rarer forms of the disorders may include hypothyroidism, which rarely appears as a birth defect, and multiple endocrine neoplasia Type 2 (MEN 2), which involves an overactivity and enlargement of the endocrine glands.

Characteristics

1. Effects of the disorders can be direct (i.e., alteration of physical state), indirect (i.e., secondary effects based on social consequences of atypical physical or hormonal development), or a combination of both direct and indirect effects

2. Endocrine dysfunction can have direct and indirect effects on physical, sexual, behavioral, and emotional development depending on the glands involved

3. Cognitive, motor, and speech delays are common in hypothyroidism and Klinefelter syndrome but may appear in other disorders if appropriate treatment is not provided.

4. Behavioral, emotional, and social problems are common with many endocrine disorders and may result from the following:

   a. Hormonal imbalances

   b. Early or delayed development of secondary sexual characteristics leading to age-inappropriate sexual behavior

   c. Feelings of isolation or rejection because of physical abnormalities

5. The severity of symptoms varies widely across disorders. Some endocrine disorders such as congenital adrenal hyperplasia can be fatal. Other disorders such as diabetes are chronic conditions in which symptoms can be maintained with few functional impairments. There are also disorders such as benign tumors of the parathyroid gland in which individuals may not have noticeable symptoms. These patients may initially report feeling normal and then report improved sleep and concentration following surgical removal of the benign tumor.

Medical treatment for the hormonal imbalance is the standard defense against endocrine disorders. Hormone replacement therapy is widely used for disorders of hyposecretion or tissue insensitivity such as Turner's syndrome or hypopituitary syndromes. Estrogen replacement therapy is used to supplement the underproductive gonads of females with Turner syndrome. In hypopituitary syndromes, growth-hormone replacement therapy is used to stimulate growth. For disorders involving hypersecretion of endocrine glands, medical treatment seeks to reduce hormone levels through the use of natural or synthetic hormones (e.g., gonadatropin-releasing hormone for overactive pituitary glands).

The psychoeducational sequelae of endocrine disorders vary as widely as do the etiology and symptoms. Disorders associated with under- or overactive pituitary glands are typically not associated with cognitive deficits. At the other extreme, global deficits in cognitive functioning can result from endocrine disorders such as hypothyroid disorders. Furthermore, domain-specific deficits may also be associated with endocrine problems. For example, chromosomal disorders such as Klinefelter syndrome and Turner syndrome are associated with average intelligence but with specific deficits in reading and visual-spatial processing, respectively.

The psychological sequelae of endocrine disorders are also important to consider in managing these conditions. Behavioral and emotional problems may result from hormonal imbalances, reactions to treatments, or reactions to looking and feeling different from peers. Future research should focus on the direct and indirect effects of the various disorders on academic and social development. The effects on school performance and behavior of the intrusive or chronic medical procedures associated with these disorders should also be evaluated.

REFERENCE

Sandberg, D. E., & Barrick, C. (1995). Endocrine disorders in childhood: A selective survey of intellectual and educational sequelae. *School Psychology Review*, *24*(2), 146–170.

LATHA V. SOORYA
Binghamton University and The Institute for Child Development

ENDORPHINS

Endorphins are neurochemicals that modify they way nerve cells respond to transmitters. Defined as endogenous opioid peptides, endorphins exhibit pharmacological properties like morphine substances within the body (Boecker et al., 2008). Since the first report by Hughes in 1975 of the isolation of a morphinelike substance in brain tissue, there has been much research and speculation as to the biological function of these peptides. Many of the first studies concentrated on locating and identifying the compounds. In addition to brain tissue, endorphins have also been found in the pituitary gland and gastrointestinal tract (Cooper, Bloom, & Roth, 1982). Within the brain, endorphins have been located in a number of areas. In particular, high concentrations have been found in areas

involved in pain perception, memory, and arousal of emotions (Synder, 1977). Endorphins work as natural pain relievers by blocking the transmission of pain signals after injury.

Considerable effort has also been made to understand the physiological and behavioral effects of the endorphins. Injection of endorphins produces many of the same physiological effects of morphine such as analgesia, hypothermia, nausea, vomiting, muscular rigidity, and severe akinesia (Cooper et al., 1982). Endorphins have been found to relieve pain, enhance immune systems, reduce stress levels, modulate appetites, lower blood pressures, and induce calm sensations over the body (Boecker et al., 2008). The number of whole-animal effects that have been attributed to the endorphinergic system has grown considerably in the past few decades, but still remains open to much more comprehensive analysis.

Akil (1977) has hypothesized that the endorphins evolved from primitive systems involved with pain and stress modulation and later become important in drives, emotions, and mood states, and in interfacing sensory and hormonal mechanisms. Studies do suggest that the role of the endorphins is multiple and involves much more than dulling the sensation of pain.

REFERENCES

Akil, H. (1977). Opiates: Biological mechanisms. In J. D. Barchas, P. A. Berger, R. D. Ciaranello, & G. R. Elliot (Eds.), *Psychopharmacology: From theory to practice*. New York, NY: Oxford University Press.

Boecker, H., Sprenger, T., Spilker, M. E., Henriksen, G., Koppenhoefer, M., Wagner, K. J., . . . Tolle, T. R. (2008). The runner's high: Opioidergic mechanisms in the human brain. *Cerebral Cortex* doi: 10.1093/cercor/bhn013

Cooper, J. R., Bloom, F. E., & Roth, R. H. (1982). *The biochemical basis of neuropharmacology*. New York, NY: Oxford University Press.

Synder, S. H. (1977, March). Opiate receptors and internal opiates. *Scientific American*, pp. 44–56.

POLLY E. SANDERSON
Research Triangle Institute

***See also* Metabolic Disorders; Stress and Individuals With Disabilities**

ENGELMANN DISEASE

Engelmann disease is a rare genetic disorder characterized by progressive widening and malformation of the shafts of the long bones (diaphyseal dysplasia). This disease is also referred to as Camurati-Engelmann disease, osteoathia hyperostotica scleroticans multiplex infantalis, progressive diaphyseal dysplasia, or ribbing disease.

This disease presents in midchildhood, often before age 10, and symptoms usually resolve by age 30 (*Merck Manual of Diagnosis and Therapy*, 2001). All races and both sexes are affected (*Online Mendelian Inheritance in Man*, 2000). Engelmann disease is inherited as an autosomal dominant genetic trait.

Characteristics

1. Symptoms include muscular pain, weakness, and wasting, typically in the legs.

2. Skeletal abnormalities or weakness and underdevelopment (hyopoplasia) of various muscles are present.

3. Pain and weakness of the leg muscles may result in an unusual "waddling" walk or gait (National Organization for Rare Disorders, 1997).

4. Skeletal malformations may include abnormal side-to-side or inward curvature of the spine (scoliosis or lumbar lordosis) or hardening (sclerosis) of the bones near the base of the skull and, in rare cases, the jaw.

5. The predominant X-ray feature is marked thickening of the periosteal and medullary surfaces of the long bones' diaphyseal cortices.

6. Often, the patient has a loss of appetite (anorexia), leading to a malnourished appearance.

Treatment usually involves corticosteroids, such as cortisone or prednisone, for relief of symptoms. Eye surgery to decompress the optic nerves is most often ineffective and usually not recommended. Other treatment is symptomatic and supportive.

Children with Engelmann disease would benefit from particular special-education services, such as physical and occupational therapy. Due to the various degrees of pain that may be present with the disease; pain management intervention may also be necessary.

Although the bone malformations and muscle atrophy are somewhat progressive over time, the symptoms do seem to resolve by the age of 30. Thus, although the prognosis is not optimistic for most individuals, there is some hope for at least stability of the symptoms of the disease.

REFERENCES

Merck Manual of Diagnosis and Therapy. (2001). *Diaphyseal dysplasia*. Retrieved from http://www.merck.com/pubs.mmanual/section19/chapter270/2701.htm

National Organization for Rare Disorders. (1997). *Engelmann disease*. Retrieved from http://www.rarediseases.org

Online Mendelian Inheritance in Man. (2000). *Camurti-Engelmann disease*. Retrieved from http://www.omim.org/

SARAH COMPTON
University of Texas at Austin

ENGLAND, SPECIAL EDUCATION IN

Special education in England and Wales is heavily influenced by the Warnock Report (Department of Education and Science, 1978). The Report formulated a framework for the special educational needs system that largely was established in a 1981 Act and that continues to underpin special needs education in England. This framework has five significant elements: (1) children's special educational needs were defined in very general terms as difficulty in learning; (2) a large minority of children (one in six at any one time) was deemed to have these needs, and many of these would be maintained in mainstream schools; (3) special educational needs were to be assessed on an individual basis by teachers, educational psychologists, doctors, and other professionals; (4) the assessment would lead to the local education authorities making provisions to meet the needs; and (5) provision could be made equally well in mainstream as in special settings.

Children are identified as having special educational needs on the basis of difficulties they experience in school rather than simply on the basis of any impairments or medical conditions that they experience (Department for Education and Skills, 2001a). In 1994, the Code of Practice on the Identification and Assessment of Special Educational Needs was developed (Department for Education, 1994) and revised in 2001. This Code provides guidance for schools and local education authorities on the stage-approach to conceptualizing special needs in mainstream schools. Schools are legally bound to provide services for children who have been placed on their special needs register. During the early stages of implementing the Code of Practice, this service is provided from within the school. However, if the child's needs require external support, the local education authority is legally obliged to provide them. Finally, if the needs are severe, then a Statement of Special Educational Need is prepared. This legal process is designed to help ensure that a child has a full and comprehensive assessment of his or her needs. Parents have the right to see all copies of reports and the right to appeal decisions. All children being educated in special schools have this Statement.

Approximately 18% of children in primary schools and 15% in secondary schools (National Statistics, 2003a) are identified as having special educational needs. In 2004 the average percentage of pupils ages 0–19 who are placed in special schools and other segregated settings is 0.82% (101,612 pupils; Rustemier & Vaughan, 2005). Since the nature of services is determined at the local level, this figure varies enormously between local education authorities, from 0.06% in a local education authority in London to 1.46% in a local education authority in the north of England (Rustemier & Vaughan, 2005). Local education authorities determine how many special school places to fund and which students to place in them. Private providers are being used increasingly for a small minority of children. However, figures relating to special school placement are misleading as many students are placed in specialist units or resource rooms within mainstream schools. In addition, approximately 32,000 students (0.34%) excluded from school for disciplinary reasons are in pupil referral units (National Statistics, 2003a, 2003b).

In October 1997, the government announced its support for inclusive education (Department for Education and Employment, 1997) by endorsing the Salamanca Statement on Special Needs Education (United Nations Educational, Scientific and Cultural Organization, 1994). This move was unusual because the language of inclusion was relatively new in England in that English governments usually do not align themselves with international declarations in education or look elsewhere for models on which to develop policy (Dyson, 2005). In 1998, a Programme of Action was produced with the goal to identify practical ways to make inclusive education a reality (Department for Education and Employment, 1998). In the following year, as part of a major revision of the curriculum in 1999, statutory guidance on inclusion was issued by the agency responsible for overseeing the national curriculum (Department for Education and Employment and Qualifications and Assessment Authority, 1999).

In 2001, legislation was passed to protect pupils against discrimination on the grounds of their disability. The Special Educational Needs and Disability Act also gave parents of children with special educational needs stronger rights to choose a mainstream placement. At about the same time, the national schools inspectorate, the Office for Standards in Education, issued guidance on how to inspect the inclusiveness of schools (Office for Standards in Education, 2000) and the government issued guidelines to local education authorities on how best to fund inclusive provision (Department for Education and Skills, 2001b) and to schools on how to interpret the new legislation (Department for Education and Skills, 2001c). In 2004, a second Programme of Action was produced that promised to give new impetus to the inclusion agenda (Department for Education and Skills, 2004).

The emergence of parental choice has had a considerable impact on special needs provision. The education reforms of the 1980s and 1990s, focusing on the 1988 Education Reform Act, removed the power of local education authorities to place children in local schools and gave parents the right (with certain restrictions) to choose a school for their child. There often is a contest between parents, who want to secure additional resources by having children's needs recognized and others (e.g., local education authorities) that must manage the budgets out of which resources to meet those needs must be found. The sometimes-bitter disputes that arise around the formal statements of the needs of individual children pose a major challenge to the English special education system (Audit Commission, 2002a). The new Programme of Action (Department for Education and Skills, 2004) has strengthened and formalized procedures, such as independent tribunals where parents can appeal against local education authority decisions (Department for Education, 1994) and determine the placement of their children (Department for Education and Skills, 2001b).

Special-needs education has been aligned more closely with the mainstream standards agenda, as the title of the new Programme of Action reveals: Removing Barriers to Achievement (Department for Education and Skills, 2004). This new strategy attempts to promote personalized learning for all children and innovative education that responds to the diverse needs of individual children, thus reducing reliance on separate special-educational-needs structures and processes. Removing Barriers to Achievement builds on the current reform of children's services outlined in *Every Child Matters* (Department for Education and Skills, 2004). The development of integrated services involving education, health, social care, and juvenile justice is part of the government's commitment to reducing child poverty, investing in early-years education, and delivering lasting benefits to children with special educational needs and their families.

REFERENCES

Audit Commission. (2002). *Policy focus paper: Statutory assessment and statements of special educational needs.* London, England: Author.

Department for Education. (1994). *Code of practice on the identification and assessment of special educational needs.* London, England: Author.

Department for Education and Employment. (1997). *Excellence for all children: Meeting special educational needs.* London, England: The Stationery Office.

Department for Education and Employment. (1998). *Meeting special educational needs: A programme of action.* London: Department for Education and Employment. Retrieved from http://www.teachernet.gov.uk/_doc/5915/Action_Programme_Full.doc

Department for Education and Employment and Qualifications and Assessment Authority (Qualifications and Assessment Authority). (1999). *The National Curriculum: Handbook for primary/secondary teachers in England.* London, England: Author.

Department for Education and Science. (1978). *Special educational needs: Report of the Committee of Enquiry into the Education of Handicapped Children and Young People (The Warnock Report)*. London, England: Her Majesty's Stationery Office.

Department for Education and Skills. (2001a). *Special educational needs code of practice*. London, England: Author.

Department for Education and Skills. (2001b). *The distribution of resources to support inclusion*. London, England: Author.

Department for Education and Skills. (2001c). *Inclusive schooling: Children with special educational needs*. London, England: Author.

Department for Education and Skills. (2004). *Removing barriers to achievement: The government's strategy for special educational needs*. London, England: Author. Retrieved from http://www.teachernet.gov.uk/wholeschool/sen/senstrategy/

Dyson, A. (2005). Philosophy, politics and economics? The story of inclusive education in England. In D. Mitchell (Ed.), *Contextualising inclusive education*. London, England: Routledge.

National Statistics. (2003a). *Statistics of education: Special educational needs in England: January 2003*. London, England: The Stationery Office. Retrieved from http://www.dfes.gov.uk/rsgateway/DB/SBU/b000429/specialneeds.pdf

National Statistics. (2003b). *Statistics of education: Schools in England*. London, England: The Stationery Office. Retrieved from http://www.dfes.gov.uk/rsgateway/DB/VOL/v000417/schools_volume_2003.pdf

Office for Standards in Education. (2000). *Evaluating educational inclusion*. London, England: Author.

Rustemier, S., & Vaughan, M. (2005). *Segregation trends—Local education authorities in England 2002–2004. Placement of pupils with statements in special schools and other segregated settings*. Bristol, England: Centre for Studies on Inclusive Education.

United Nations Educational, Scientific and Cultural Organization. (1994). *Salamanca statement and framework for action on special needs education*. Paris, France: Author.

SUSIE MILES
ALAN DYSON
PETER FARRELL
University of Manchester

See *also* Belgium, Special Education; Denmark, Special Education; France, Special Education

ENGLEMANN, SIEGFRIED E. (1931–   )

Siegfried E. Englemann obtained his BA in education at the University of Illinois in 1955. He was a research associate at the University of Illinois from 1964 to 1966; from 1966 to 1977 he was a senior educational specialist at the University of Illinois. From 1970 to 1974 he was associate professor at the University of Oregon. Since 1974 he has been a professor of special education at the University of Oregon.

Englemann's major area of study is working with disadvantaged children in the classroom setting. Englemann and Bereiter (1966) believe that the "how" of educating disadvantaged children is as important as the "what," and that to fail in developing more effective teaching methods is perhaps to fail completely in equalizing the educational attainment of children from differing cultural backgrounds. Englemann and Bereiter (1966) also feel that direct instruction is a thoroughly feasible and highly effective way of teaching needed academic skills to the young. The most important side effect of the direct teaching is the development of self-conscious pride and confidence in one's own ability to learn and think. The American Psychological Association presented Englemann with the Fred Keller Award of Excellence in 1994.

Some of Englemann's major works include *Teaching: A Basic Course in Applied Psychology, Teaching I: Classroom Management,* and *Teaching II: Cognitive Learning and Instruction.* He also contributed chapters to many books and has written over 80 articles, including "Observations on the Use of Direct Instruction with Young, Disadvantaged Children," "Teaching Formal Operations to Preschool Children," and many others. Englemann also served as senior author on over 100 instructional programs.

This entry has been informed by the sources listed below.

REFERENCES

Becker, W. C., Englemann, S. E., & Thomas, D. R. (1969). *Teaching: A basic course in applied psychology*. Chicago, IL: Science Research Associates.

Englemann, S. E. (1969). *Preventing failure in the primary grades*. Chicago, IL: Science Research Associates.

Englemann, S. E., & Bereiter, C. (1966). Observations on the use of direct instructions with young, disadvantaged children. *Journal of School Psychology, 4*(3), 55–62.

ELIZABETH JONES
Texas A&M University

ENGLISH AS A SECOND LANGUAGE (ESL) AND SPECIAL EDUCATION (See Second Language Learners in Special Education)

ENGRAMS

Psychologists have long questioned how information is stored and subsequently retrieved from the brain. As early as 1900, Müller and Pilzecker argued that memory involves an unobservable physical change in the central nervous system that becomes relatively permanent as a result of repeated presentation of information. In keeping with this notion, most neurobiological theories of memory have hypothesized the existence of a memory trace or engram. Generally, engram is used to denote the relatively permanent structural or biochemical change in the brain consistent with the long-term storage of information (Hillgard & Bower, 1975). Information in short-term memory, on the other hand, appears to be less stable and is inaccessible unless converted into the enduring long-term store.

Retrieval of the memory trace is seen to be based on a reactivation of the same physical structure or biochemical conditions that were responsible for the initial storage or encoding process (Bloch & Laroche, 1984). This reactivation process seems to be triggered by stimuli that are the same or similar to the original stimulus event. From this point of view, both storage and retrieval are based on similar "neuronal circuits."

REFERENCES

Bloch, V., & Laroche, S. (1984). Facts and hypotheses related to the search for the engram. In G. Lynch, J. L. McGaugh, & N. M. Weinberger (Eds.), *Neurobiology of learning and memory* (pp. 249–260). New York, NY: Guilford Press.

Hillgard, E. R., & Bower, G. H. (1975). *Theories of learning.* Englewood Cliffs, NJ: Prentice Hall.

Müller, G. E., & Pilzecker, A. (1900). Experimentelle beitrage zur lehre von gedachtniss. *Zeitschrift fur Psychologie, 1*, 1–300.

JEFFREY W. GRAY
Ball State University

RAYMOND S. DEAN
Ball State University
Indiana University School of Medicine

See also Memory Disorders

ENRICHMENT

Enrichment is a term that is frequently used to denote one form or approach to differentiating instruction for gifted youth. It is also often used to denote supplementary curriculum for youth at any level of ability. When the term refers to a form of instruction for gifted youth, it may be defined, by contrast, with terms such as acceleration, individualization, or grouping. These terms may, however, relate chiefly to administrative arrangements,

just as enrichment may relate to an approach that administratively refers to provision for the gifted by the regular teacher in a typical heterogeneous classroom. Administrative acceleration may simply refer to a gifted child's early admission to school, grade skipping in the elementary school, or early admission to college. Individualization may refer to the administrative arrangement of continuous progress in an ungraded school. Finally, grouping may refer to the gathering of all mathematically talented youth into a single "honors" mathematics class in seventh grade. Although these administrative approaches may stem in part from concern with the nature or needs of gifted youth, they tend to acquire a functional autonomy that makes them independent alternatives or options, regardless of gifted youths' specific needs.

Masse and Gagne (1983) argued that proper definitions of the term *enrichment* and the associated terms, *acceleration, individualization*, and *grouping*, must grow out of consideration of the special and unique characteristics of the gifted and their correlated special needs. They noted, however, that lists of characteristics of gifted (and talented) youths can be extensive and even contradictory. From their own review of research on characteristics of the gifted they concluded that there are four basic and pervasive characteristics: (1) rapid learning; (2) ease in learning complex material; (3) diversity of interests; and (4) depth of specific interests. Renzulli's (1979) three-ring conception of giftedness would probably be similar in stressing the components of ability (rapid learning, complex learning, and task commitment) and depth of interest, but Renzulli's third component, creative ability, is probably not reflected in Masse and Gagne's concept. However, in his enrichment triad instructional model, Renzulli (1977) proposed a Type I enrichment that provides gifted youths with an opportunity for exploratory learning in areas of varied interests. Such activity might meet the need generated by the characteristic of "varied interests" noted by Masse and Gagne. Type II enrichment in the triad model refers to group instructional activities to teach thinking and feeling processes, whereas Type III refers to enrichment through opportunities to investigate real problems. Type III activities tie in with depth of specific interest, which Masse and Gagne identified as a primary characteristic of gifted students.

Stanley (1979) proposed four types of enrichment. The first is busywork, or simply more of the same type of work done by all students. A second type is irrelevant academic enrichment, which is supplementary instruction that pays no attention to the special talents or characteristics of gifted youth. The third type is cultural enrichment, which ignores the student's talents or abilities but offers curriculum in the arts and foreign languages. The fourth type, relevant enrichment, provides special instruction directly related to gifted youths' special talents or characteristics (e.g., an enriched mathematics course for mathematically talented youths). In contrast to these four types of enrichment, Stanley proposed that acceleration is always vertical, moving a gifted youth to higher levels. In contrast to his use of the term *vertical* to refer to acceleration, the term *horizontal* is often used to refer to enrichment. Stanley characterized it as a process of teaching more content but at the same level of difficulty or complexity.

Tannenbaum (1983) argued that enrichment for the gifted always requires a curriculum that is differentiated from the regular curriculum in that it is designed to meet the special needs of gifted youths. Tannenbaum (1983) went on to propose a five-point enrichment matrix that can be used to design a curriculum for the gifted. The matrix calls for five types of content adjustment: (1) expansion of basic skills; (2) teaching core content in less time; (3) broadening the knowledge base; (4) teaching content related to the teacher's special expertise; and (5) out-of-school mentoring experiences. The matrix also attends to teaching higher-level thinking skills (Baer, 1988) and social-affective modification. These modifications can be applied to all curricular areas.

The term *enrichment* is best used to refer to curriculum experiences that are supplements to or replacements for the regular curriculum. Enrichment for the gifted should be designed to meet their specific needs and their capacity to learn more complex material. The term acceleration refers to instruction or learning at an earlier age than normal and at a faster pace. Administrative acceleration should be used to meet the needs of gifted youths for instruction at a level that matches their readiness or achievement levels and their need to learn rapidly or at a faster pace.

The ideal educational program for gifted youths offers a combination of enriched curriculum and accelerated instruction. That is, these students are allowed to move into higher and appropriate levels of the regular school curriculum, to be taught at a pace that matches their capacity to learn, and to experience an enriched or augmented curriculum that meets their need for extended and more complex learning.

REFERENCES

Baer, J. (1988). Let's not handicap gifted thinkers. *Educational Leadership, 45*(7), 66–72.

Masse, P., & Gagne, F. (1983). Observations on enrichment and acceleration. In B. M. Shore, F. Gagne, S. Larivee, R. H. Tali, & R. E. Tremblay (Eds.), *Face to face with giftedness* (pp. 395–413). New York, NY: Trillium.

Renzulli, J. S. (1977). *The enrichment triad model: A guide for developing defensible programs for the gifted and talented.* Mansfield Center, CT: Creative Learning Press.

Renzulli, J. S. (1979). *What makes giftedness?* Los Angeles: National State Leadership Training Institute for the Gifted/Talented.

Stanley, J. C. (1979). Identifying and nurturing the intellectually gifted. In W. C. George, S. J. Cohn, & J. C. Stanley (Eds.), *Educating the gifted, acceleration and enrichment* (pp. 172–180). Baltimore, MD: Johns Hopkins University Press.

Tannenbaum, A. J. (1983). *Gifted children, psychological and educational perspectives.* New York, NY: Macmillan.

JOHN FELDHUSEN
Purdue University
First edition

JOHN BAER
Rider University
Third edition

See also Creativity; Creativity Tests

ENRICHMENT TRIAD MODEL

The Enrichment Triad Model is a teaching-learning model developed by J. S. Renzulli (1977) specifically for teaching gifted children. Renzulli's model is designed to be used with students who have three interacting clusters of traits—creativity, high ability, and task commitment. Identified students with these traits take part in a program based on three interrelated categories of enrichment that are depicted in Figure E.2. These categories include (1) Type I, general exploratory activities; (2) Type II, group training activities; and (3) Type III, individual and small group investigations of real problems. The first two categories (Types I and II) are considered appropriate for all

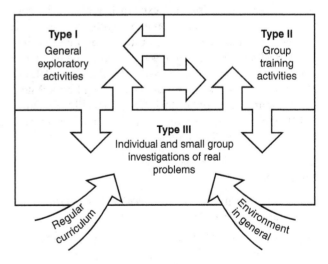

Figure E.2. The enrichment triad module.

learners, whereas the third category (Type III) consists of advanced-level experiences that gifted students pursue on a self-selected basis.

Type I enrichment consists of general exploratory experiences that are designed to expose students to a variety of topics or areas of study that are not ordinarily covered in the regular curriculum. This type of enrichment is provided through a variety of activities such as interest or learning centers, audio-visual materials, field trips, guest speakers, or teacher demonstrations.

In Type II enrichment, the teacher uses special methods, materials, and instructional techniques that are specifically designed to develop higher-level thinking processes, research skills, and processes related to personal and social development. These are exercises that will help students deal more effectively with content and solve problems in a variety of areas and new situations.

Type III enrichment activities are individual and small-group investigations, and these are the major focus of this model. These activities are considered especially appropriate for gifted students. Students are encouraged to gather new data, use the authentic methods of researchers in particular fields of knowledge, and share the results of their work with appropriate audiences. According to Renzulli (1977), when students have superior potential for performance in particular areas of sincere interest, they "must be allowed the opportunity to pursue topics therein to unlimited levels of inquiry" (p. 17). To develop his model, Renzulli investigated the characteristics of eminent adults (Roe, 1952), studied Ward's (1961) ideas for inquiry, and adopted Bruner's (1960) and Torrance's (1965) conclusions that young children are able to engage in critical and creative investigations.

The Enrichment Triad Model has been popular in many schools because it is very inclusive. All students may participate in Type I and Type II activities, and students who have the ability and interest can design their own Type III investigations for in-depth explorations of topics of special interest. These individual and small-group research projects are often carried out during school time that has been freed up through compacting requirements of the regular curriculum. In recent years the Enrichment Triad Model has been subsumed into Renzulli and Reis's School Enrichment Model (1985, 1994, 1997; Renzulli & Renzulli, 2010), which is a system for school-wide implementation of the Enrichment Triad Model.

REFERENCES

Bruner, J. S. (1960). *The process of education*. Cambridge, MA: Harvard University Press.

Renzulli, J. S. (1977). *The Enrichment Triad Model*. Wethersfield, CT: Creative Learning Press.

Renzulli, J. S., & Reis, S. M. (1985). *The schoolwide enrichment model: A comprehensive plan for educational excellence*. Mansfield Center, CT: Creative Learning Press.

Renzulli, J. S., & Reis, S. M. (1994). Research related to the Schoolwide Enrichment Model. *Gifted Child Quarterly*, *38*, 2–14.

Renzulli, J. S., & Reis, S. M. (1997). *The schoolwide enrichment model: A how-to guide for educational excellence*. Mansfield Center, CT: Creative Learning Press.

Renzulli, J. S., & Renzulli, S. R. (2010). The schoolwide enrichment model: A focus on student strengths and interests. *Gifted Education International*, *26*(2–3), 140–157.

Roe, A. (1952). *The making of a scientist*. New York, NY: Dodd & Mead.

Torrance, E. P. (1965). *Gifted children in the classroom*. New York, NY: Macmillan.

Ward, V. S. (1961). *Educating the gifted: An axiomatic approach*. Columbus, OH: Merrill.

JUNE SCOBEE
University of Houston, Clear Lake

JOHN BAER
Rider University
Fourth edition

See also Creativity; Creativity, Theories of

ENURESIS

Enuresis may be broadly defined as the repeated involuntary voiding of urine that occurs beyond the age at which bladder control is expected and for which there is no organic or urologic explanation. According to the American Psychiatric Association (1994), diagnostic criteria include at least two events per month for children between the ages of 5 and 6, or at least one monthly episode for older children. However, many (e.g., Campbell, 1970; Doleys, 1977; Eufemia, Wesolowski, Trice, & Tseng, 1984) note that children as young as 3 years old may be considered enuretic.

Childhood enuresis is classified as either nocturnal (occurring during sleep) or diurnal (occurring during waking hours). Distinctions have also been made between primary enuresis (child has always been enuretic) and secondary enuresis (child loses previously acquired control). According to Sorotzkin (1984), the view that secondary enuresis is related to higher levels of psychological stress or organic etiology is not based on empirical evidence. Furthermore, the lack of prognostic value of distinguishing primary and secondary enuresis also attests to not making such a distinction.

Reported prevalence estimates vary greatly. In a review of literature, Siegel (1983) reports that there are more than 3 million enuretic children in America. He also states that approximately 20 percent of all children are nocturnal enuretics at age 5, with half of these children remaining enuretic at age 10. The American Academy of Family Physicians (AAFP; 2006) reports that between 5 and 7 million children experience enuresis. Most researchers report that enuresis is about twice as prevalent among males than females.

Enuresis has been studied from a variety of theoretical perspectives. Although there are many variants of the psychoanalytic orientation, all share the assumption that enuresis is merely the symptomatic expression of intrapsychic problems. For example, enuresis has been variously viewed as an expression of repressed sexual drives, an act of displaced aggression against parents, a masochistic expulsion of destructive energy, a functional equivalent of a fetish, and a desire for regression that frequently occurs with the birth of a sibling or separation (Mountjoy, Ruben, & Bradford, 1984; Sorotzkin, 1984). Siegel (1983) concludes that empirical evidence does not support the view of enuresis as a symptom of underlying psychological disturbance.

A number of biological factors have been studied in relation to enuresis. The maturational lag hypothesis, for example, posits that neurological immaturity is responsible for primary enuresis; this perspective has been seriously questioned, however, since nearly all 5-year-old nocturnal enuretics have occasional dry nights, indicating maturation has occurred (Sorotzkin, 1984). Other biological variables that have been implicated include genetic factors, infections, atypical sleep patterns, and small functional bladder capacities (Sorotzkin, 1984). Of these factors, diminished functional bladder capacity is most supported by research although even that support is equivocal.

From a behavioral perspective, enuresis is essentially viewed as the failure to appropriately respond to both physiological and environmental cues for urination. Current behavioral theories consider both classical and operant factors.

Although a diverse array of treatments for enuresis have been reported (e.g., drug therapy, psychotherapy, hypnotherapy, fluid restrictive diets, elimination diets, and surgery), behavioral approaches have unquestionably received the most empirical attention. Among the many behavioral treatments, the most frequently employed are urine alarm procedures, retention control training, and treatment packages that incorporate multiple components.

The urine alarm procedure involves the use of an apparatus by which an alarm is activated at the onset of urination. Although the device was originally developed for (and most often used for) treating nocturnal enuresis, it has been adapted and used to treat diurnal enuresis as well. There is some disagreement regarding whether the procedure represents classical conditioning (i.e., after repeated pairings of the bell, which causes the child to awaken and inhibit urination and heed full-bladder cues, distention of the bladder eventually acquires discriminative stimulus properties) or operant conditioning (i.e., the bell is an aversive stimulus that is avoided by inhibiting urination and awakening). Empirical evidence attests to the efficacy of the procedure. Doleys (1985) reports that typical data indicate a 75% success rate, with relapse rates of 40%; reapplication of the procedure is typically successful with 60% to 70% of those who initially relapse. Procedural variations such as gradually requiring the child to drink large quantities prior to bedtime and using an intermittent schedule of alarm presentation have yielded higher success rates and/or lower relapse rates (Doleys, 1977).

Retention-control training is a procedure in which the child is required to refrain from urinating for progressively longer periods of time. It is based on the premise that such training increases functional bladder capacity (i.e., the volume at which evacuating contractions occur). Although some evidence exists to support the procedure, it has not proven universally successful (Doleys, 1977; Siegel, 1983).

A multicomponent treatment for nocturnal enuresis is the dry-bed training procedure of Azrin, Sneed, and Foxx (1974). Among the features of this intensive program are the use of a urine alarm, increased intake of liquids, retention control training, practice in toileting, positive reinforcement for appropriate urination, hourly awakenings, and verbal reprimands and positive practice overcorrection for accidents. The dry-pants training program (Azrin & Foxx, 1974) is directed at diurnal enuresis and is procedurally similar to the dry-bed program. The total program is regarded as highly successful; however, program modifications such as eliminating the alarm should be made with caution (Eufemia et al., 1984; Siegel, 1983; Sorotzkin, 1984).

REFERENCES

American Academy of Family Physicians (AAFP). (2006). *Enuresis (bed wetting)*. Retrieved from http://familydoctor .org/familydoctor/en.html

American Psychiatric Association. (1994). *Diagnostic and statistical manual of mental disorders* (4th ed.). Washington, DC: Author.

Azrin, N. H., & Foxx, R. M. (1974). *Toilet training in less than a day*. New York, NY: Simon & Schuster.

Azrin, N. H., Sneed, T. J., & Foxx, R. M. (1974). Dry-bed training: Rapid elimination of childhood enuresis. *Behavior Research and Therapy, 12*, 147–156.

Campbell, M. F. (1970). Neuromuscular neuropathy. In M. F. Campbell & T. H. Harrison (Eds.), *Urology* (Vol. 2, pp. 1935–1948). Philadelphia, PA: Saunders.

Doleys, D. M. (1977). Behavioral treatment of nocturnal enuresis in children: A review of the recent literature. *Psychological Bulletin, 84*, 30–54.

Doleys, D. M. (1985). Bell and pad conditioning. In A. S. Bellack & M. Hersen (Eds.), *Dictionary of behavior therapy techniques* (pp. 46–48). New York, NY: Pergamon Press.

Eufemia, R. L., Wesolowski, M. D., Trice, A. D., & Tseng, M. S. (1984). The long and short term effects of dry bed training. *Education and Treatment of Children, 7*, 61–66.

Mountjoy, P. T., Ruben, D. H., & Bradford, T. S. (1984). Recent technological advances in the treatment of enuresis: Theory and research. *Behavior Modification, 8*, 291–315.

Siegel, L. J. (1983). Psychosomatic and psychophysiological disorders. In R. J. Morris & T. R. Kratochwill (Eds.), *The practice of child therapy* (pp. 253–286). New York, NY: Pergamon Press.

Sorotzkin, B. (1984). Nocturnal enuresis: Current perspectives. *Clinical Psychology Review, 4*, 293–315.

JAMES P. KROUSE
Clarion University of Pennsylvania

See also **Applied Behavior Analysis; Encopresis**

EOSINOPHILIC FASCIITIS

Eosinophilic fasciitis (Shulman's syndrome) involves inflamed fascia (layer of fibrous tissue below the skin) and muscles of the extremities due to eosinophil (a certain type of white blood cells) infiltration, which causes tenderness and swelling. It is classified as a diffuse connective tissue disease (Beers, Mark, & Berkow, 1999). The arms and forearms are affected more often than are the thighs and legs. Presence on the trunk of the body occurs in approximately 50% of the cases, but the face is usually spared (Thoene & Jess, 1995). The etiology of this disease has been linked to aberrant immune responses as well as toxic, environmental, or drug exposures (Graham & Brad, 2000). Another cause is thought to be due to sudden, strenuous physical exertion in an otherwise sedentary person (Beers et al., 1999).

This condition is very rare, and primarily affects Anglo-Americans. There is no difference in the occurrence in males versus females. Most patients are between the ages of 30 and 60 at first report, but childhood cases have been reported (Graham & Brad, 2000).

Characteristics

1. Skin appears thickened and develops a symmetric, puckered, orange-peel-like appearance, mainly over the extremities.
2. Child complains of pain in muscles and joints and may experience joint contractures (permanent tightening of the muscles, skin, and ligaments surrounding the joint) with gradual restriction of arm and leg movement.
3. The child complains that his or her hands feel weak and occasionally numb or tingly.
4. Extremities become tender and swollen.
5. Child has unusual fatigue and weight loss.

A child with eosinophilic fasciitis will endure many tests, including muscle and skin biopsies and tests of erythrocyte (a type of red blood cell) sedimentation rates (a type of blood test; Beers et al., 1999). Eosinophilic fasciitis can induce many physical limitations, such as "claw hand," and carpal tunnel-like symptoms, so the child might find himself or herself unable to engage in many of his previous activities. Fatigue and weight loss may also limit the child to low-stress activities. Arthritis and neuropathy (loss of feeling from nerve damage) are commonly present in patients with eosinophilic fasciitis.

The treatment of a patient with eosinophilic fasciitis is long and arduous. It is directed at reducing tissue inflammation. Medications such as prednisone, to which many patients respond rapidly, help alleviate the symptoms (Beers et al., 1999). Patients may need to continue low doses of these medications for 2–5 years. Glucocorticoids (which raise blood sugar and reduce inflammation), as well as oral steroids (Guttman, 1999, April), are common medications to prescribe to a child with eosinophilic fasciitis (Meszaros, 1995, April). Treatment is directed at eliminating inflammation. Although the duration of medical treatment is undetermined, most patients have a resolution of the disease within 3–5 years, with some recurrences being reported. Many patients have spontaneous remission, whereas others will see a gradual decrease in symptoms.

Eosinophilic fasciitis alters a child's physical image, and some children will find this hard to deal with. Support from family and friends will help this child with emotional difficulties associated with his or her changing physical appearance. Eosinophilic fasciitis is somewhat debilitating at its most active stages, so it is sometimes hard for a child with the disorder to function well enough to attend school daily and function better in the daily environment. At-home schooling should be considered as an option for this child. Special education services may be available under the other health impairment category due to the chronic-illness nature of this disorder. The student may also need supportive counseling for pain management and hospitalization issues. Pain management will help children be able to attend school more often. Family members of a child with eosinophilic fasciitis should be encouraged to attend pain management and counseling sessions when appropriate.

REFERENCES

Beers, M. D., Mark, H., & Berkow, M. D. (Eds.). (1999). *The Merck manual of diagnosis and therapy* (17th ed.). Lawrenceville, NJ: Merck Research Laboratories.

Graham, M. D., & Brad, S. (2000, October 15). *Eosinophilic fasciitis from dermatology*. Retrieved from http://emedicine .medscape.com/

Guttman, C. (1999, April). Unusual aspects of connective tissue diseases demand different approaches. *Dermatology Times, 20*, 34.

Meszaros, L. (1995, April). Monitor patients on glutocorticoid therapy carefully. *Dermatology Times, 16*, 65–66.

Thoene, M. D., & Jess, G. (Ed.). (1995). *Physicians' guide to rare diseases* (2nd ed.). Lawrenceville, NJ: Dowden.

EMILY R. BAXTER
University of Colorado–Colorado Springs

EPICANTHIC FOLD

The epicanthic fold, also known as epicanthus, refers to the vertical fold of skin from the upper eyelid covering the lacrimal caruncle at the inner canthus of the eye (the point where the upper and lower eyelids meet) (Rosenburg & Weller, 1973). The expression of epicanthus may be extreme, covering the entire canthus, or mild. Although the epicanthal fold is typical in people of Asiatic decent, epicanthal folds seen in other young children of other races can be an indicator of a medical condition. Epicanthic folds can be seen in medical conditions such as: Down syndrome, fetal alcohol syndrome, Turner syndrome, and phenylketonuria (PKU) (Roizen & Patterson, 2003).

REFERENCES

Rosenberg, J. B., & Weller, G. M. (1973). Minor physical anomalies and academic performance in young school children. *Developmental Medicine & Child Neurology, 15*, 131–135.

Roizen, N. J., Patterson, D. (2003). Down's syndrome. *Lancet, 361*, 1281–1289.

CATHY F. TELZROW
Kent State University

See also Dysmorphic Features; Epidemiology; Minor Physical Anomalies

EPIDEMIOLOGY

Epidemiology is reviewed within two models: medical and psychological. Epidemiology is the study of specific medical disorders within communities to measure risk of attack and to uncover etiological clues and modes of spread. Reid (1960) defines epidemiological inquiry as "the study of the distribution of diseases in time and space, and of the factors that influence this distribution."

Although elucidating etiology is a prime concern, collected data are used in planning services and devising treatment modes (Graham, 1979). Basic data include (a) identification of a particular disorder in a defined population, (b) incidence rates, (c) prevalence rates, and (d) dynamic patterns of occurrence over time. In addition to identifying disease syndromes and origins, epidemiology serves to test the reliability of concepts derived solely from clinical studies, thus avoiding assumptions based on relationships that may be merely correlational rather than causative. Correlational data do not permit inferences of causality.

Epidemiology employed to study psychological disorders uncovers common underlying factors in nonmedical problems. The premise of both models remains unchanged: to complete the clinical picture (Morris, 1964). Neither model is used solely to collect information but to use data to further effective treatment and services for disordered populations.

One basic difference between medical and psychological epidemiology is that the former has definitive criteria for judging physical normalcy while the latter, focusing primarily on behavior, is left with a range of altering, social criteria that are difficult to quantify. Another difference between the models concerns the search for etiology that may or may not be relevant to nonmedical surveys, depending on the conceptual perspective of the researcher (e.g., psychoanalytic, behavioral systems theory). Nevertheless, a profitable psychological inquiry employs quantitative cut-off points, if defined arbitrarily, to identify deviations from the norm (Rutter et al., 1970). Epidemiologists who take behavior as the starting point define disorders according to social criteria, itemize behaviors, count behaviors empirically, and factor analyze data to examine the amount of variance explained by particular behavior dimensions for different populations (Rutter, 1977).

Methodological problems in the psychological approach include (a) whether the population is represented in sampling; (b) questionnaire reliability; (c) whether nonresponders represent an atypical group; and (d) whether observed behavior is related to events and people in a subject's life. Psychological epidemiology is the vehicle for a number of comprehensive studies along a wide range of topics: child abuse (Baldwin & Oliver, 1975; Light, 1973); specific reading retardation in relation to deviant behavior (Rutter & Yule, 1973); disorders of middle childhood (Pringle et al., 1966; Rutter et al., 1970); adolescent turmoil (Rutter, Graham, Chadwick, & Yule, 1976); autism (Folstein & Rutter, 1977); and a host of others (see especially Ollendick, 1998).

REFERENCES

Baldwin, J. A., & Oliver, J. E. (1975). Epidemiology and family characteristics of severely abused children. *British Journal of Preventive & Social Medicine, 29*, 205–221.

Folstein, S., & Rutter, M. (1977). Generic influences and infantile autism. *Nature, 265*, 726–728.

Graham, P. (1979). Epidemiological studies. In H. C. Quay & J. S. Werry (Eds.), *Psychopathological disorders of childhood.* New York, NY: Wiley.

Light, R. J. (1973). Abused and neglected children in America: A study of alternative policies. *Harvard Educational Review, 43*, 556.

Morris, J. N. (1964). *Uses of epidemiology.* Baltimore, MD: Williams & Wilkins.

Ollendick, T. (Ed.). (1998). *Children and adolescents: Clinical formulation and treatment.* In A. Bellack & M. Hersen (Eds.), *Comprehensive clinical psychology* (Vol. 5). New York, NY: Elsevier.

Pringle, M. L. K., Butler, N. R., & Davie, R. (1966). *11,000 seven-year-olds.* London, England: Longmans.

Reid, D. D. (1960). *Epidemiological methods in the study of mental disorders.* Geneva, Switzerland: World Health Organization.

Rutter, M. (1977). Surveys to answer questions. In P. J. Graham (Ed.), *Epidemiological approaches in child psychiatry.* New York, NY: Academic Press.

Rutter, M., Graham, P., Chadwick, O., & Yule, W. (1976). Adolescent turmoil: Fact or fiction. *Journal of Child Psychology & Psychiatry, 17*, 35–56.

Rutter, M., Tizard, J., & Whitmore, K. (Eds.). (1970). *Education, health and behavior.* London, England: Longmans.

Rutter, M., & Yule, W. (1973). Specific reading retardation. In L. Mann & D. Sabatino (Eds.), *The first review of special education* (pp. 49–62). Philadelphia, PA: JSE.

C. MILDRED TASHMAN
College of St. Rose

See also Diagnosis in Special Education; Etiology; Research in Special Education

EPILEPSY (*See* Seizure Disorders)

EPILEPSY FOUNDATION OF AMERICA

The Epilepsy Foundation of America (EFA) is a nonprofit, voluntary agency established in 1967. The agency is devoted to epilepsy care, treatment, research, and education for the almost 3 million people with epilepsy in the United States and their families. The national foundation, together with its numerous local chapters, provides information on a wide variety of issues related to epilepsy, including low-cost anticonvulsant medication, legal rights, and employment. The foundation provides a discount drug pharmacy service for its members.

Numerous excellent publications relevant to the school-age child with epilepsy are available from the foundation. These include pamphlets such as "What Everybody Should Know About Epilepsy," "Epilepsy: The Teacher's Role," and "Epilepsy School Alert (1974)." School Alert is one of two major annual educational programs sponsored by the foundation. In operation since 1972, the School Alert program was developed in conjunction with the Department of School Nurses and the National Education Association; it is designed for EFA chapter use with schools in the local chapter vicinity. Some state departments of education have officially endorsed the School Alert program.

The address for the Epilepsy Foundation of America is 8301 Professional Place, Landover, MD 20785-7223. Additional information is available online at http://www .epilepsyfoundation.org/. All information retrieved from: http://www.epilepsyfoundation.org/aboutus/ on December 14, 2011.

REFERENCE

Epilepsy School Alert. (1974). Washington, DC: Epilepsy Foundation of America.

CATHY F. TELZROW
Kent State University

EPINEPHRINE

Epinephrine is one of the naturally occurring catecholamines (together with norepinephrine and dopamine). Its action sites are mainly in the sympathetic nervous system (Katzung, 1982). Leavitt (1982) suggests wider involvement of epinephrine in automatic processes owing to its presence in the hypothalamus. The gross actions of epinephrine are to relax bronchial muscles, constrict bronchial vasculature, and increase cardiac output, thus increasing overall oxygenation. Secondary central nervous system effects may occur through the overall increase in blood pressure and oxygen availability (McEvoy, 1984). Thus, the overall action of epinephrine is that of a mild stimulant. Because of its action as a bronchodilator, one of the chief uses of epinephrine is in providing symptomatic relief for sufferers of asthma and chronic obstructive pulmonary diseases and allergic reactions (MedlinePlus, 2006).

Side effects of epinephrine overdosage or sensitivity are similar to those of other stimulants (i.e., fear, anxiety, tenseness, restlessness, sleeplessness, or excitability;

Blum, 1984). More serious reactions appear similar to amphetamine toxicity and include psychomotor agitation, assaultiveness, disorientation, impaired memory, panic, hallucinations, and homicidal or suicidal ideation/tendencies (McEvoy, 1984). Toxicity is more likely to occur among persons who are hypertensive or hyperthyroid (McEvoy, 1984).

REFERENCES

Blum, K. (1984). *Handbook of abusable drugs*. New York, NY: Gardner Press.

Katzung, B. G. (1982). *Basic and clinical pharmacology*. Los Altos, CA: Lange Medical.

Leavitt, F. (1982). *Drugs and behavior*. New York, NY: Wiley.

McEvoy, G. K. (1984). *American hospital formulary service: Drug information 84*. Bethesda, MD: American Society of Hospital Pharmacists.

MedlinePlus. (2006). Epinephrine injection. Retrieved from http://www.nlm.nih.gov/medlineplus/druginfo/

ROBERT F. SAWICKI
Lake Erie Institute of Rehabilitation

See also Catecholamines; Dopamine

EQUAL EDUCATIONAL OPPORTUNITY

In its earliest form, equal educational opportunity referred to a belief that education would "close no entrance to the poorest, the weakest, the humblest. Say to ambition everywhere, the field is clear, the contest fair; come, and win your share if you can!" (Woodard & Watson, 1963). A number of judicial decisions have affirmed this basic premise that underlies equal educational opportunity (e.g., *Brown v. Board of Education*, 1954, 1955; *Lau v. Nichols*, 1974; *Regents of California v. Bakke*, 1978).

Although there is general agreement on what constitutes equal educational opportunity, there is some uncertainty about whether this implies equal access to education, the process of education, or the outcomes of education (Hyman & Schaaf, 1981). In the case of disabled learners, the concept of equal opportunity has focused on equal access and equity in the process of education.

The first equal opportunity decision involving disabled students (*PARC v. Commonwealth of Pennsylvania*, 1971) resulted in an order providing that the state of Pennsylvania could not postpone or deny disabled children access to a publicly supported education. In addition, those school districts that provided education to preschool children were required to provide such education for disabled children. A similar case in the District of Columbia (*Mills v. Board of Education*, 1972) resulted in a similar judicial order,

with the court indicating that if sufficient funds are not available to finance all of the services and programs that are needed and desirable in the system, then the available funds must be expended equitably in such a manner *that* no child is entirely excluded from a publicly supported education consistent with his or her needs and ability to benefit therefrom.

Apart from protections afforded by the judiciary, attorney generals in a number of states interpreted state laws, regulations, and administrative guidelines to include the public education of disabled children and youths (e.g., Arkansas, 1973; Wisconsin, 1973).

With the passage of PL 94-142, the Education of All Handicapped Children Act, the federal government extended the concept of equal educational opportunity to include the process by which education is delivered. These rights are reaffirmed in the Individuals with Disabilities Education Act and in the Americans with Disabilities Act. Not only was access to education required, but it was to he provided, to the extent possible, with nondisabled students in regular education classrooms. Moreover, disabled students were to receive specially designed instruction to meet their unique needs, as well as the related services (e.g., audiology, psychological services) required for disabled students to benefit from special education.

REFERENCES

Hyman, J. B., & Schaaf, J. M. (1981). *Educational equity: Conceptual problems and prospects for theory*. Washington, DC: National Institute of Education.

Woodard, C. V., & Watson, T. (1963). *Agrarian rebel*. New York, NY: Oxford University Press.

PATRICIA ANN ARRAMSON
Hudson Public Schools, Hudson, Wisconsin
Second edition

KIMBERLEY APPLEQUIST
University of Colorado at Colorado Springs
Third edition

See also Americans with Disabilities Act; *Brown v. Board of Education*; Individuals with Disabilities Education Improvement Act of 2004 (IDEIA); Mainstreaming; *Mills v. Board of Education*; Pennsylvania Association for Retarded Citizens v. Pennsylvania

EQUAL EMPLOYMENT OPPORTUNITY COMMISSION

The purpose of the Equal Employment Opportunity Commission (EEOC) is to eliminate discrimination based on race, ethnicity, religion, national origin, sex (including pregnancy), genetic information, disability, previous complaint of discrimination and age (over 40) in hiring, promoting, firing, wages, testing, training, apprenticeship, and all other conditions of employment. The commission also promotes voluntary action programs by employers, unions, and community organizations to make equal employment opportunity an actuality, for those businesses with 15 employees or more (20 employees in age-discrimination cases). The EEOC also is responsible for all compliance and enforcement activities relating to equal employment among federal employees and applicants, including discrimination on the basis of disability.

The EEOC was created under Title VII of the Civil Rights Act of 1964. Title VII was amended by the Equal Employment Opportunity Act of 1972 and the Pregnancy Discrimination Act of 1978. In 1990, the EEOC's authority was expanded to include enforcement of claims of discrimination on the basis of disability status under Title I of the Americans with Disabilities Act, which prohibits private employers, state and local governments, employment agencies, and labor unions from discriminating against individuals with disabilities in employment matters. In 2008, EEOC began to include the Genetic Information Nondiscrimination Act of 2008 (GINA), which makes it illegal to discriminate based on genetic information (i.e., family medical history, diseases, genetic tests of applicant/employee or family member). GINA also made it illegal to retaliate based on a complaint, charge, or lawsuit based on discrimination. The commission consists of five commissioners appointed by the president with advice and consent of the Senate to 5-year terms. The president designates a commissioner as chairperson and appoints a counsel general. The work of the commission has been credited with widespread banning of various forms of discrimination against a variety of groups. Reorganization Plan One of 1978 transferred to the EEOC Section 501 of the Rehabilitation Act of 1973, which pertains to employment discrimination against individuals with disabilities in the federal government.

The EEOC has field offices that receive written complaints against public or private employers, labor organizations, joint labor management, and apprenticeship programs for charges of job discrimination or age discrimination. Charges of Title VII violations in private industry or state or local government must be filed with the commission within 180 days of the alleged violation. The commission has the authority to bring suit in federal district court if a negotiated settlement cannot be found. The commission encourages settlements prior to determination by the agency through fact-finding conferences and informal methods of conciliation, conference, and persuasion.

The EEOC has issued several guidelines on employment policies and practices, the most comprehensive of which are the Guidelines on Discrimination Because of Sex (May 23, 2007), Race and Color (April 19, 2006), Religious Discrimination (July 22, 2008), Disabilities (October 17, 2002), and the Guidelines on Employee Selection Procedures through the Compliance Manual (Office of Federal Contract Compliance Programs, 2008). The commission is also a major publisher of employment data on minorities and women. For further information, contact the EEOC's National Contact Center at U.S. Equal Employment Opportunity Commission, 131 M Street, NE, Washington, DC 20507.

REFERENCES

Equal Employment Opportunity Commission (EEOC). (1983). 17th annual report. *American statistics index* (Suppl. 10). Washington, DC: U.S. Government Printing Office.

U.S. Equal Employment Opportunity Commission (EEOC). (2009). Retrieved from http://www.eeoc.gov/eeoc/jobs/index.cfm

Office of Federal Contract Compliance Programs (OFCCP). (2008). *EEO is the law poster supplement: private employers, state and local governments, educational institutions, employment agencies and labor organizations revisions.* Washington, DC: U.S Department of Labor.

DANIEL R. PAULSON
University of Wisconsin at Stout
Second edition

KIMBERLY F. APPLEQUIST
University of Colorado at Colorado Springs
Third edition

KACI DEAUQUIER SHERIDAN
Texas A&M University
Fourth edition

See also **Americans with Disabilities Act; Civil Rights of Individuals with Disabilities; Equal Education Opportunity**

EQUAL PROTECTION

Equal protection is a term often applied to the need for due process in the differential treatment of any persons in society. In special education, equal protection applies to placement proceedings or any other action that might result in differential treatment of a child. The term is derived from the Fourteenth Amendment to the U.S. Constitution.

The Fourteenth Amendment equal protection clause provides, in a simple, straightforward statement, the far-reaching assertion that "no state shall.... deny to any person within its jurisdiction the equal protection of the laws." The court system has interpreted this statement in numerous cases and generally holds that it does not require that all persons be treated equally under all laws at all times. According to Overcast and Sales (1982), the essence of the constitutional guarantee provided by the equal protection clause of the Fourteenth Amendment is that any classifications made in a rule or a law must be reasonable and not of an arbitrary nature. In determining the reasonableness of a classification, the courts normally look to see whether (1) the classification itself is a reasonable one, (2) the classification furthers an appropriate or legitimate government purpose, and (3) the classification's subgroups, or classes, are treated equally (Overcast & Sales, 1982; Sales et al., 1999).

Whenever the classification affects a fundamental right or is related to suspect criteria (e.g., is statistically related to membership in a protected class such as race or handicap), the judiciary also will examine two additional criteria. The court wishes to determine in these circumstances, which circumstances are always extant in special education, whether the classification is necessary to promote some compelling state interest, and whether the classification represents the least burdensome alternative available or that can be designed. Suspect criteria that have been identified by the courts include race, religion, national origin, alien status, legitimacy, poverty, and sex. Discrimination related to these categories takes place almost daily in the schools, however, it must be based on a valid distinction among the groups.

The courts have held that they have the right to intervene in the actions of schools and others when any basic constitutional safeguard is violated, including the equal protection clause (e.g., *Epperson v. Arkansas*, 1968; *Ingraham v. Wright*, 1977). The equal protection clause has been used to protect students' right to an education on a number of occasions; this clause may be (and certainly has been) interpreted as granting the right to equal educational opportunity. School systems cannot discriminate among groups of people when providing an education unless there is a substantial and legitimate purpose for the discrimination (Bersoff, 1982). Prior to the passage of PL 94-142, the Education for All Handicapped Children Act of 1975, advocates fighting for the right of individuals with disabilities to attend public schools, from which they were frequently excluded, relied heavily on the equal protection clause of the Fourteenth Amendment in winning their cases. The equal protection clause also has been invoked in favor of children classified as disabled who have argued they are not disabled and claimed that by placing them in special education programs, they have been denied equal protection through exclusion from access to regular education with normal children (Bersoff, 1982; Reschly & Bersoff, 1999).

REFERENCES

Bersoff, D. N. (1982). The legal regulation of school psychology. In C. R. Reynolds & T. B. Gutkin (Eds.), *The handbook of school psychology* (pp. 1043–1074). New York, NY: Wiley.

Overcast, T. D., & Sales, B. D. (1982). The legal rights of students in the elementary and secondary public schools. In C. R. Reynolds & T. B. Gutkin (Eds.), *The handbook of school psychology* (pp. 1075–1100). New York, NY: Wiley.

Reschly, D., & Bersoff, D. (1999). Law and school psychology. In C. R. Reynolds & T. B. Gutkin (Eds.), *The handbook of school psychology* (3rd ed., pp. 1077–1112). New York, NY: Wiley.

Sales, B. D., Krauss, D., Sacken, D., & Overcast, T. (1999). The legal rights of students. In C. R. Reynolds & T. B. Gutkin (Eds.), *The handbook of school psychology* (3rd ed., pp. 1113–1145). New York, NY: Wiley.

CECIL R. REYNOLDS
Texas A&M University

See also Larry P.; *Marshall v. Georgia*; *Matty T. v. Holladay*

EQUINE THERAPY

Equine therapy refers to a prescribed medical treatment that uses horsemanship to alleviate an extensive array of physical, psychological, cognitive, and social disabilities. Brought to the United States from Europe during the 1970s, its popularity has steadily grown since. Equine therapy relies upon the integration of services provided by a physician who prescribes medical treatment, a physical therapist who designs the therapeutic regimen, and an instructor who implements the program. Equine therapy activities include feeding, tacking, grooming, riding, and vaulting (Ewing, MacDonald, Taylor, & Bowers, 2007).

Kuprian (1981) distinguishes between hippotherapy, in which the horse's symmetrical rhythms are transferred to a rider's body passively, and riding therapy, in which a rider engages in active exercise (relaxation, stretching, strengthening). Still more advanced is vaulting, in which gymnastics are introduced (Kroger, 1981), and riding as sport, in which an individual competes against others, having accomplished a sufficient degree of fitness and skill (Heipertz, 1981). All equine therapy is strength-based and ability focused (Yorke, Adams, & Coady, 2008).

It is theorized that equine therapy is particularly effective at treating psychological, cognitive, and social disabilities because of unique circumstances using horses as cotherapists presents. Because of the intimate and broad body contact involved in hippotherapy, riding, and vaulting, a kind of "physical sign language" develops between client and horse, making clients more aware of body language and communication (Edgette, 1996). Unlike conventional therapy, horses as cotherapists are available to clients at all times; moreover, horses provide unconditional responsiveness to clients through body language (York, Adams, & Coady, 2008). Ewing, MacDonald, Taylor,

& Bowers (2007) argue that the sheer size and stature of a horse solicits respect from clients. This size differential may make the therapist seem less threatening in contrast to the horse, allowing for more participative therapy sessions and greater client progress (Beck, Seraydarian, & Hunter, 1986).

Despite numerous qualitative accounts of the effectiveness of equine therapy, quantitative research is still sparse (Ewing, MacDonald, Taylor, & Bowers, 2007; Klontz, Bivens, Leinart, & Klontz, 2007; Vidrine, Owen-Smith, & Faulkner, 2002; York, Adams, & Coady, 2008). However, existing quantitative research suggests that equine therapy supports improved physical mobility, stability, muscle tone, coordination, and balance; sensory integration; cognitive training and retraining; academic performance; emotional stability (self-esteem, accountability, diminished aggression); communication facility; and the ability to relate to others and function within a group.

Equine therapy is not recommended for all disabilities. Individuals who have seizures or bone and joint anomalies are considered poor candidates for equine therapy because of the physical risk involved.

Additional information may be obtained from the North American Riding for the Handicapped Association (NARHA) P.O. Box 33150, Denver, Colorado 80233. 1-800-369-RIDE, or online at NARHA@NARHA.org.

REFERENCES

Beck, M., Seraydarian, L., & Hunter, G. (1986). The use of animals in the rehabilitation of psychiatric inpatients. *Psychological Reports, 58,* 63–66.

Chardonnens, E. (2009). The use of animals as co-therapists on a farm: The child-horse bond in person-centered equine assisted psychotherapy. *Person-Centered and Experiential Psychotherapies 8*(4), 319–32.

Edgette, J. (1996). *Heads up!: Practical sports psychology for riders, their trainers, and their families.* New York, NY: Doubleday.

Ewing, C., MacDonald, P., Taylor, M., & Bowers, M. (2007). Equine-facilitated learning for youths with severe emotional disorders: A quantitative and qualitative study. *Child and Youth Care Forum, 36*(1), 59–72.

Heipertz, W. (1981). Riding therapy for orthopaedic cases. In W. Heipertz (Ed.), *Therapeutic riding: Medicine, education, sports* (translated by M. Takeuchi; pp. 55–66). Ottawa, Canada: National Printers.

Klontz, B., Bivens, A., Leinart, D., & Klontz, T. (2007). The effectiveness of equine-assisted experiential therapy: Results of an open clinical trial. *Society and Animals, 15*(3), 257–267.

Kroger, A. (1981). Vaulting as an education aid in schools for behaviorally disturbed children. In W. Heipertz (Ed.), *Therapeutic riding: Medicine, education, sports* (translated by M. Takeuchi; pp. 40–54). Ottawa, Canada: National Printers.

Kuprian, W. (1981). Hippotherapy and riding therapy as physiotherapeutic treatment methods. In W. Heipertz (Ed.),

Therapeutic riding: Medicine, education, sports (translated by M. Takeuchi; pp. 14–39). Ottawa, Canada: National Printers.

Vidrine, M., Owen-Smith P., & Faulkner, P. (2002). Equine-facilitated group psychotherapy: Applications for therapeutic vaulting. *Issues in Mental Health Nursing, 23,* 587–603.

Yorke, J., Adams, C., & Coady, N. (2008). Therapeutic value of equine–human bonding in recovery from trauma. *Anthrozoos: A Multidisciplinary Journal of The Interactions of People & Animals, 21*(1), 17–30.

Casey Pilgrim
The Chicago School of Professional Psychology
Fourth edition

ERRORLESS LEARNING

Errorless and near-errorless learning describes a method of instruction designed specifically to prevent the production of errors and to develop appropriate stimulus control (i.e., correct responding in the presence of the discriminative stimulus). Specifically, systematic antecedent (i.e., instructional prompts), response, and consequence manipulations (i.e., differential reinforcement) are arranged to increase the likelihood that correct or desired responding will occur in the presence of the desired antecedent conditions and not occur when those antecedent conditions are not present.

Errorless learning is based on three premises. First, environmental stimuli occasion or establish the opportunity for specific responses. Second, to achieve errorless learning, differential reinforcement, or delivering reinforcement for target behaviors in the presence of target (discriminative) stimuli versus in their absence and withholding reinforcement in the presence of target stimuli when undesired behavior occurs, is necessary. Differential reinforcement ensures control over target responding will be governed by discriminative stimuli rather than irrelevant stimuli. Last, error production limits the possibility to present positive reinforcement for the target behavior and the establishment of desired stimulus control (i.e., correct responding in the presence of the discriminative stimulus). Further, practicing errors may expose the learner to repeated failure and frustration. Instead, providing carefully sequenced stimulus examples and scaffolded antecedent instruction increases the learner's access to positive reinforcement and learning success.

Errorless learning methods are dependent on the use of either stimulus prompts or response prompts. The use of prompts increases the likelihood that a target behavior will occur and reinforcement be delivered, in the presence of the desired antecedent stimulus. Prompts can take many forms, including (a) verbal cues, (b) physical prompts, or

(c) visual cues, and can be of full or partial intensity and intrusiveness.

Errorless learning approaches can be categorized as stimulus shaping and fading procedures and response-prompting procedures. Stimulus shaping and fading are the processes of providing sequentially fewer prompts that emphasize the relevant features of discriminative stimuli and nondiscriminative stimuli, until accurate responding occurs in the presence of discriminative stimuli themselves. For example, emphasizing the long tail of the letter /h/ with a different color, length, or width initially may help a student correctly identify the letter. Prompts may be removed gradually as the student continues to identify the letter /h/ correctly. Additionally, minimally different nonexamples from the letter /h/, such as /n/, may be presented. The short tail length of letter /n/ may initially be emphasized and gradually minimized, as the learner continues to accurately discriminate the letter /h/ from /n/.

Response prompting is a process of providing prompts that increases the probability that the target behavior will occur. Four types of response prompting procedures exist (1) increasing assistance (least-to-most prompts), (2) graduated guidance, (3) time delay (constant and progressive), and (4) decreasing assistance (most-to-least prompts). Increasing-assistance procedures involve presenting a discriminative stimulus and providing the least intrusive prompt possible to ensure correct responding. If the target behavior does not occur, a more intrusive prompt is provided in the next instructional trial. This process of providing successively more intrusive prompts will continue, until the target behavior is performed.

Graduated guidance is most useful for teaching chained behaviors or complex skills (e.g., hand-washing, physical education skill), and refers to a procedure in which a discriminative stimulus is presented and full assistive prompts are immediately provided. As the learner independently engages in the target behavior, the pressure and intrusiveness of assistance is reduced (e.g., holding an arm versus touching it). However, if the learner begins to engage in an incorrect behavior, assistance is immediately reinstated. A teacher may eventually "shadow" the learner or follow the learner's movements closely without touching him or her, as they gain independence.

Time delay is a procedure in which a delay is imposed between the presentation of the discriminative stimulus and a prompt. A progressive time delay occurs when the time delay between the presentation of a discriminative stimulus and a prompt is initially brief. On successive trials, the time delay will increase until the target behavior is performed before the prompt is presented. A constant time delay is similar to a progressive time delay, except the delay is always the same length of time.

Decreasing assistance involves providing the most intrusive prompt after a discriminative stimulus is presented. As the learner engages in the target behavior, the intrusiveness of the prompt is systematically and gradually reduced, until the learner engages in the target behavior without a prompt.

Research

Studies demonstrating the effectiveness of errorless learning strategies span multiple areas of behavioral research and practice. Haupt, Van Kirk, and Terraciano (1975) used two prompting methods to teach math facts. Both methods involved presenting the learner with math facts with the answers clearly visible. Gradually, the answers were covered up and eventually the learner correctly answered the math facts without the answers being visible.

MacDuff, Krantz, and McClannahan (1993) found that graduated guidance procedures were effective in teaching participants with autism to engage in picture activity schedules. The participants were also able to correctly perform novel activity schedules. In another example, Lamm and Greer (1988) implemented a least-to-most prompting procedure to encourage swallowing behavior in three infants with gastronomy tubes. The procedure was successful in evoking swallowing behavior for all three infants and the feeding tubes were removed for two of the infants (the other tube remained due to unrelated health problems).

Errorless learning has been effectively used to teach a variety of behaviors such as dressing skills (Engelman, Altus, Mosier, & Mathews, 2003), grocery shopping skills (Morse & Schuster, 2000), and teaching an individual to identify his or her name (Malott, Whaley, & Malott, 1997). Stimulus shaping and fading and response prompting procedures continue to be popular instructional methods, assisting individuals to acquire new behaviors.

Guidelines for Practice

A multitude of errorless learning prompting procedures have been used to teach new skills. Some experts suggest that time-delay procedures may be the most efficient response-prompting strategies. Others state that both progressive time delay and decreasing assistance strategies are superior to increasing assistance strategies (Billingsley & Romer, 1983). Le Grice and Blampied (1997) suggest that increasing assistance strategies are not only effective but are less intrusive and require less teacher effort. In general, a substantial body of research evidence supports the use of a variety of errorless learning strategies to improve teaching outcomes in different contexts and with different populations.

When selecting prompts, a few guidelines will be helpful. Prompts should be selected that emphasize the relevant features that are desired to control responding. For example, when teaching "zebra," stripes would be one stimulus feature to emphasize. Consideration should be given to how prompts are presented, which prompts will be easiest to fade, and which stimulus conditions promote generalization. For example, verbal prompts may be difficult to fade or minimize and a prompt always presented by the same person may promote stipulated responding. Last, to avoid overstipulated responding, instructional prompts should be faded and removed as quickly as possible when correct responding is observed.

Complex or chained behaviors are more difficult to teach than discrete behaviors (requiring one response). When teaching complex behaviors, the chain of behaviors should be broken down (task analyzed) into discrete components so that each discrete behavior is shaped and gradually linked to other behaviors in the chain. The goal is to provide positive reinforcement contingent upon occurrences of larger "chunks" of linked behaviors.

Case Examples

Example 1

"Monica" is a 4-year-old who knows her colors but is learning to identify the word *red*. Her teacher has an index card with the word red printed on it with a piece of red fabric attached. Her teacher uses decreasing assistance by first presenting the index card and says "What word is this?" Immediately her teacher says, "Say red," and positively reinforces Monica's response. Next, her teacher presents the index card and question without the verbal prompt until Monica reliably and accurately responds. Monica's teacher then removes the red fabric and presents the index card and question by itself. After correct responding without the red fabric, Monica's teacher presents the word in different fonts and on different paper, to ensure Monica can identify the word red when it is presented in other ways.

Example 2

"Joseph" is learning to use a spoon. Joseph's father, Dan, uses the graduated-guidance technique to teach him this skill. First, Dan holds and guides Joseph's hand and wrist while he spoons preferred food to his lips. Next, Dan decreases the pressure used to hold Joseph's hand and wrist while using his spoon. Dan then stops holding Joseph's hand and wrist and moves to touching Joseph's arm lightly while using the spoon, later his shoulder, and then does not touch Joseph at all, unless he misses or performs a step incorrectly.

Example 3

"Miguel" is learning addition facts. His teacher uses a progressive time-delay procedure and asks Miguel to answer math-fact questions. Miguel's teacher provides the answer to the math-fact questions after waiting a second, when Miguel does not respond. After Miguel responds correctly within a second, his teacher begins to wait 3 seconds until providing the answer, then waits 9 seconds, 30 seconds, and finally does not provide the answer for any of the math facts, as Miguel reliably answers them all correctly.

REFERENCES

Billingsley, F. F., & Romer, L. T. (1983). Response prompting and the transfer of stimulus control: Methods, research, and a conceptual framework. *Journal of the Association for Persons with Severe Handicaps, 8*, 3–12.

Engelman, K. K., Altus, D. E., Mosier, M. C., & Mathews, R. M. (2003). Brief training to promote the use of less intrusive prompts by nursing assistants in a dementia care unit. *Journal of Applied Behavior Analysis, 36*, 129–132.

Haupt, E. J., Van Kirk, M. J., & Terraciano, T. (1975). An inexpensive fading procedure to decrease errors and increase retention of number facts. In E. Ramp & G. Semb (Eds.), *Behavior analysis: Areas for research and application*. Upper Saddle River, NJ: Prentice Hall.

Lamm, N., & Greer, R. D. (1988). Induction and maintenance of swallowing responses in infants with dysphagia. *Journal of Applied Behavior Analysis, 21*, 143–156.

Le Grice, B. & Blampied, N. M. (1997). Learning to use video recorders and personal computers with increasing assistance prompting. *Journal of Developmental and Physical Disabilities, 9*, 17–29.

MacDuff, G. S., Krantz, P. J., & McClannahan, L. E. (1993). Teaching children with autism to use photographic activity schedules: Maintenance and generalization of complex response chains. *Journal of Applied Behavior Analysis, 26*, 89–97.

Malott, R. W., Whaley, D. C., & Malott, M. E. (1997). *Elementary principles of behavior*. Upper Saddle River, NJ: Prentice Hall.

Morse, T. E. & Schuster, J W. (2000). Teaching elementary students with moderate disabilities how to shop for groceries. *Exceptional Children, 66*, 273–288.

SARAH FAIRBANKS
GEORGE SUGAI
University of Connecticut
Fourth edition

See also Direct Instruction; Teaching Strategies

ERTL INDEX

The problem of cultural bias in traditional measures of intelligence led to the development of alternative assessment strategies. One rather exotic strategy is the use of the Neural Efficiency Analyzer (NEA). Introduced by Ertl (1968), this instrument was purported to measure the reaction time of brain waves to 100 randomly presented flashes of light. Ertl argued that in contrast to traditional methods of intellectual assessment, the score obtained from the Neural Efficiency Analyzer (Ertl Index) was free of cultural influences and thus was appropriate for use with any ethnic group regardless of age.

The Ertl Index consists of the average time from the onset of the stimulus light to the appropriate brain wave change. Based on this average evoked potential, an estimate of the subject's performance on a more traditional measure of cognitive functioning (e.g., Wechsler Intelligence Scale for Children) is also calculated. In support of this proposed relationship between the Ertl Index and intellectual functioning, Ertl (1968) presented data suggesting a concomitant decrease in the neural efficiency score upon ingestion of chemicals known to impede cognitive functioning (e.g., alcohol). Moreover, Ertl found that when these chemicals were removed, the neural efficiency scores returned to normal limits.

Clinically, Ertl proposed that the Ertl Index would serve as a screening measure for cognitive difficulties. He argued that special educational placement based on culturally free measures such as the Ertl Index would eliminate the educational misclassification of culturally deprived children. Moreover, Ertl proposed that the Ertl Index "should permanently dispel the myth of racial inequality in the United States" (Tracy, 1972, p. 90). In support of this argument, Ertl (Tracy, 1972) presented data suggesting that there were no significant differences between the brain wave activities (Ertl Index) of Blacks and Whites.

Although the Neural Efficiency Analyzer appeared to be an innovative attempt to minimize the cultural bias in intelligence testing, empirical evidence does not support the use of this measure on a clinical basis. Indeed, Evans, Martin, and Hatchette (1976) showed that the Ertl Index did not discriminate between children with learning problems and normal controls. Similarly, it was found that the Ertl Index did not significantly predict college grade-point averages (Sturgis, Lemke, & Johnson, 1977). A review of more than a dozen major texts in assessment, psychophysiology, and learning disabilities published in the 1990s failed to produce a reference to this method, and it appears to have faded from any serious consideration at this point.

REFERENCES

Ertl, J. (1968). *Evoked potential and human intelligence*. Final Report, USOE, Project No. 6-1454.

Evans, J. R., Martin, D., & Hatchette, R. (1976). Neural Efficiency Analyzer scores of reading disabled, normally reading and academically superior children. *Perceptual & Motor Skills, 43*, 1248–1250.

Sturgis, R., Lemke, E. A., & Johnson, J. J. (1977). A validity study of the Neural Efficiency Analyzer in relation to selected measures of intelligence. *Perceptual & Motor Skills, 45*, 475–478.

Tracy, W. (1972). Goodbye IQ, hello EI (Ertl Index). *Phi Delta Kappan, 54*, 89–94.

JEFFREY W. GRAY
Ball State University

RAYMOND S. DEAN
Ball State University
Indiana University School of Medicine

See also Intelligence; Intelligence Testing; Neural Efficiency Analyzer

ERYTHROKERATODERMIA WITH ATAXIA

Erythrokeratodermia with Ataxia, also known as Giroux-Barbeau syndrome, was first reported in 1972. In infancy and childhood, erythrokeratodermia with ataxia presents with groups of red, hardened, scaly skin plaques developing into a neurological syndrome in early adulthood consisting of impaired muscle coordination (ataxia), dysarthria (poorly articulated speech), decreased tendon reflexes, and involuntary, rhythmic movements of the eyes (nystagmus). In childhood the plaques usually disappear in the summer months. The plaques may completely disappear in young adulthood, only to reappear later in life. Normally, the neurological deficits become apparent when these plaques reappear; in rare cases, however, neurological abnormalities may be present early in life.

Characteristics

1. In infancy and childhood, red, hardened plaques appear on the skin, and these plaques may disappear during the summer months.
2. As the child reaches adulthood, a progressive neurological syndrome consisting of impaired muscle coordination, dysarthria, nystagmus, and decreased tendon reflexes replaces or accompanies the reappearance of the plaques.

Erythrokeratodermia with ataxia is a rare hereditary autosomal dominant skin disorder that equally affects males and females. Treatment is symptomatic and supportive with dermatological attention being given to the plaques early in life. When the neurological deficits appear, other support services may become needed. Special education needs may not arise because the deficits involving impaired muscle coordination, problems articulating speech, and decreased tendon reflexes occur mainly during adulthood. However, in the rare case that the neurological deficits begin during the school years, remediation requirements should be commensurate with degree and type of impairment including occupational and physical therapy, as well as speech therapy. Not much is known about erythrokeratodermia with ataxia, and research efforts are focused on learning more about the disorder and effective means of treatment.

REFERENCES

Giroux, J. M., & Barbaeu, A. (1972). Erythrokeratodermia with ataxia. *Archives of Dermatology, 106*(2), 183–188.

Magalini, S. I., & Magalini, S. C. (Eds.). (1997). *Dictionary of medical syndromes*. Philadelphia, PA: Lippincott-Raven.

KIMBERLY M. ESTEP
University of Houston–Clear Lake

ESQUIROL, JEAN E. (1722–1840)

Jean E. Esquirol, a French psychiatrist, studied under Philippe Pinel in Paris, and succeeded him as resident physician at the Salpetriere. His exposure of inhumane practices in French institutions for the mentally ill contributed greatly to the development of properly run hospitals in France. Esquirol identified and described the main forms of mental illness, and in 1838 published *Des Maladies Mentales*, the first scientific treatment of the subject.

REFERENCE

Esquirol, J. E. (1838). *Des maladies mentales*. Paris, France: Bailliere.

PAUL IRVINE
Katonah, New York

ESTONIA, SPECIAL EDUCATION IN

In Estonia, teaching children with special educational needs started in the 19th century. Due to the initiative of doctors and churchmen, charitable institutions for children with behavior problems, Mental Retardation, deafness, and blindness were established in 1845. The first special school for children with hearing impairments was founded in 1866. The ideas of special education were well received and encouraged, given the country's high literacy rates (at that time, 91% could read and 78% could write). A parliamentary republic was formed following Estonia's independence in 1918. Between 1920 and 1939, a restricted system of special educational services developed. State schools for children who were deaf, blind, and mildly to moderately mentally retarded were founded. Hugo Valma greatly influenced the ideology and development of special education. He published books and articles on educating children with Mental Retardation. In 1928, speech therapy developed as a specialization. In 1939, the Baltic countries were assigned to the Soviet sphere of influence and remained in isolation until 1991. During this period of Soviet influence, a system of special educational service was founded for children starting from age 3. A national curriculum for special schools was developed. However, education was available only for children with slight mental disabilities; children with moderate, severe, and profound mental disabilities were sent to nursing homes and were regarded as nonteachable. During the 1970s, special nursery schools were established. During the 1980s, speech therapists began serving children with reading and writing problems and with slight speech problems in mainstream schools.

From 1991, when the Republic of Estonia was restored, all discriminatory restrictions have been removed and all children have a right to education suitable for their abilities. In 1995, the Disability Policy of the Republic of Estonia was adopted on the basis of the United Nations rules of equal opportunities. Terminology has been changed; labeling has been removed.

Children with special needs, ages 3 to 7, may study in special nursery schools (*erilasteaed*), mainstream nursery schools in integration groups (*sobitusrühm*), or groups for children with special needs (*erirühm*). Although the number of special nursery schools has decreased (e.g., in 1995, there were seven special nursery schools and now there are three), the number of special groups has increased. Special groups are available for children with physical disabilities, sensory disabilities (deafness and hearing impairment; blindness and visual impairment), multiple disabilities, speech impairment and specific developmental disorders, and Mental Retardation (moderate, severe, and profound learning disabilities). In integration groups, children with special education needs (physical, speech, sensory, mental disabilities, psychiatric disorders, and specific developmental disorders) study together with their nondisabled peers. Groups are established by county or city administrations.

At ages 7 through 20, children with special needs may study in mainstream schools, in special classes of mainstream schools, receive various forms of support, or study in special schools, depending on a student's needs. The number of special needs students is increasing due, in part, to teachers becoming more skilled at identifying special needs children and new ways to think about special needs children. At the same time, the number of students in general education is decreasing.

Special needs children are recommended to a suitable school, group, class, or curriculum following a decision by a counseling committee composed of five members: special education teacher, speech therapist, psychologist, social worker, and a representative of the county administration or of the city administration. The parents decide whether the child attends a special school or a mainstream school. The number of special schools, about 46, has been consistent during the past 2 decades. Special needs children increasingly are being place in mainstream schools of which there are 603. Some special nursery and basic schools recently have been reorganized into regional counseling centers.

Special schools and classes are available for students with physical disabilities, speech impairments, sensory or learning disabilities, mental disorders, and behavior problems. Sanatorium schools are available for students with health disorders. Special needs children may study in vocational schools that offer a small group instruction for a special group together with individual instruction for special needs children who are studying in a mainstream or special group. Opportunity classes (*tasandusklass*) exist for children with learning difficulties, supplementary learning classes (*abiklass*) for children with slight learning disabilities, coping classes (*toimetulekuklass*) for children with moderate learning disabilities, and nursing classes (*hooldusklass*) for children with severe and profound learning disabilities. The following support systems are available in mainstreams schools: individual curricula; remedial groups that provide learning support for students with learning difficulties, speech therapy, long day groups, and home study (with the possibility to attend lessons of music, arts, handicraft, and physical education); and boarding school facilities for children who have social problems.

Education requirements are determined by a national curriculum for nursery schools, basic schools, and secondary schools. The simplified national curricula for basic schools (supplementary learning curriculum; students with a slight learning disability) and the national curriculum for students with moderate and severe learning disabilities determine the requirements of basic education of special needs children. A special national curriculum is being developed for students with profound learning disabilities. For special needs children, an individual curriculum may be specified based on the child's abilities. When evaluating special needs children, a differentiated evaluation allows knowledge and skills to be evaluated according to the student's individual characteristics. In conducting final examinations for graduation from basic school, the characteristics of the special needs child and the aims specified in the curriculum are considered. A final examination may not be conducted when the curriculum was simplified as a result of a student's moderate or severe learning difficulties.

Regular class teachers, special education teachers, and speech therapists teach special needs children. As a rule, teachers working in special or nursery schools or in special groups or classes must have advanced education, including special education or an education program that required 320 hours of in-service training in special education. Since 1968, the University of Tartu has prepared special education teachers. Earlier, special education teachers and speech therapists studied the same curriculum. However, after a curriculum reform in 1991, students specialize either in special education or speech therapy. Starting in 1997, special-education teacher-counselors (who work mainly in mainstream nursery and basic schools) are educated in the University of Tallinn. Both universities provide in-service courses in special education.

School psychologists, social workers, and social pedagogues also provide services for special needs children. School psychologists are involved in the assessment and counseling of children. During the last few years, their responsibilities for implementing individual instruction have grown. Specialists working with special-needs children in nursery and basic schools are employed by county and city governments. In towns, there are speech therapists in most nursery schools and mainstream schools and school psychologists in the majority of mainstream schools. In special schools and institutions for special groups, additional speech therapists and/or special teachers may be employed. A few schools have hired social workers. They serve several schools in towns and in rural areas. The number of special education teachers, speech therapists, and school psychologists who work in rural areas is insufficient.

Although some services for special needs children have been provided for decades, contemporary theoretical approaches together with policies promulgated by the European Union are profoundly impacting special education in Estonia. The state is obliged to have a clear education policy; to permit amendments, supplements, and adaptations of curricula depending on a student's needs; and to ensure the quality of study materials, in-service teacher training, and the existence of support teachers. Not all of these obligations are met. Obstacles arise due to the country's small size, limited financial and professional resources, and lack of regulations pertaining to the implementation of legislation in some areas. Considerable work is occurring in implementing laws and regulations and educating teachers, parents, politicians, and others who work with special needs children.

This entry has been informed by the sources listed below.

REFERENCES

LAWS AND ACTS

Alushariduse raamõppekava kinnitamine [National Curriculum for Nursery Schools], Riigi Teataja I 1999, 80, 737. Retrieved September 30, 2005, from https://www.riigiteataja.ee/ert/act.jsp?id=77809

Eesti Vabariigi Haridusseadus [Republic of Estonia Law on Education], Riigi Teataja I 2004, 75, 524. Retrieved July 30, 2005, from https://www.riigiteataja.ee/ert/act.jsp?id=816786

Individuaalse õppekava järgi õppimise kord [Regulation of Learning According to Individual Learning Curriculum], Riigi Teataja L 2004, 155, 2329. Retrieved July 30, 2005, from https://www.riigiteataja.ee/ert/act.jsp?id=824971

Koolieelse lasteasutuse seadus [Law On Pre-School Child Institutions], Riigi Teataja I, 2004, 41, 276. Retrieved July 30, 2005, from https://www.riigiteataja.ee/ert/act.jsp?id=754369

Kutseõppeasutuse seadus [Vocational Educational Institutions Act], Riigi Teataja I 2005, 31, 229. Retrieved July 30, 2005, from https://www.riigiteataja.ee/ert/act.jsp?id=908863

Kutseseadus [Professions Act], Riigi Teataja I 2003, 83, 559. Retrieved July 30, 2005, from https://www.riigiteataja.ee/ert/act.jsp?id=690522

Lasteaed-algkooli, algkooli, põhikooli ning gümnaasiumi eripedagoogide ja koolipsühholoogide miinimumkoosseis [Staff Minimum for special education teachers and school psychologists in Nursery-primary school, primary school, basic school, and upper secondary school], Riigi Teataja L 2003, 4, 39. Retrieved July 30, 2005, from https://www.riigiteataja.ee/

Pedagoogide kvalifikatsiooninõuded [Standards of Qualification for Teachers], Riigi Teataja I 2005, 6, 42. Retrieved July 30, 2005, from https://www.riigiteataja.ee/ert/act.jsp?id=839432

Põhikooli ja gümnaasiumi riiklik õppekava [National Curriculum for Basic Schools and Upper Secondary Schools], Riigi Teataja I 2004, 67, 468. Retrieved July 30, 2005, from https://www.riigiteataja.ee/ert/act.jsp?id=802290

Põhikooli- ja gümnaasiumiseadus [Basic School and Upper Secondary School Act], Riigi Teataja I 2004, 56, 404. Retrieved July 30, 2005, from https://www.riigiteataja.ee/ert/act.jsp?id=784125

Põhikooli lihtsustatud riikliku õppekava (abiõppe õppekava) kinnitamine [Simplified National Curriculum for basic schools (supplementary learning curriculum)], Riigi Teataja L 2004, 106, 1705. Retrieved July 30, 2005, from https://www.riigiteataja.ee/ert/act.jsp?id=792367

Toimetuleku riikliku õppekava kinnitamine [National Curriculum for Students with Moderate and Severe Learning Disabilities], Riigi Teataja L 2004, 106, 1705. Retrieved July 30, 2005, from https://www.riigiteataja.ee/ert/act.jsp?id=790670

LITERATURE

The Information Database on Education Systems in Europe. The Education System in Estonia. (2003/2004). Retrieved from http://www.eurydice.org/Eurybase/Application/frameset.asp?country=EE&language=EN

Kõrgesaar, J. (2002). "Sissejuhatus hariduslike erivajaduste k"sitlusse (Introduction into the field of special needs). Tartu, Estonia: Tartu Šlikooli Kirjastus.

Kõrgesaar, J., & Veskiväli, E. (1987). Eripedagoogika Eestis (Special Education in Etsonia). Tartu, Estonia: Tartu Ülikooli Kirjastus.

Padrik, M. (2002). Veränderungen der Behindertenpädagogik in einer veränderten Gesellschaft: das Beispiel Estland. In Reader Internationale Woche (pp. 73–83). Berlin, Germany: Universität Bremen.

Statistical Office of Estonia (2005). Statistical database. Retrieved from http://www.stat.ee/statistics

MARIKA PADRIK
EVE KIKAS
University of Tartu, Estonia

See also International Ethics and Special Education

ETHICS

In its broadest sense, *ethics* generally refers to a system of principles that guide how an individual or group of individuals should behave. The ethical principles that guide an individual may derive from a variety of sources, including family, religion, or culture. The ethical principles of members of a profession often derive from professional codes of ethics, which provide standards and guidelines by which professionals can guide their practice. These types of applied professional ethics will be the focus of this chapter.

Special-education professionals include special education teachers, counselors, social workers, psychologists, and researchers, and they work in a variety of settings that range from working with special needs children in mainstream classrooms, self-contained classrooms, residential settings, rehabilitation hospitals, homes of chronically ill children, and juvenile justice educational settings. As a result, these individuals may be guided by a variety of ethical codes, including those of the American Counseling Association (2005), the American School Counselors Association (2004), the American Psychological Association (2010), the National Association of School Psychologists (2010), the National Association of Social Workers (2008), the National Education Association (1985), and others. While the principles vary somewhat by organization and have changed over the years, there are several ethical principles that are consistent across time and organizations. The principles of *autonomy, justice, fidelity, nonmaleficence,* and *beneficence* are seen across ethical codes and will be described in more detail here.

Autonomy is one important ethical principle to consider when working with a special-education population. This refers to the importance of allowing an individual to make decisions about themselves free from undue pressure from the professional. Professionals should "respect student's values, beliefs, and cultural background and [should] not impose the school counselor's personal values on students and their families" (American School Counselors Association, 2004, ES A-1-C). In the special-education setting, this means that the professional needs to be respectful and welcoming of input from the child and family, and should refrain from interfering with their decisions.

Professional codes of ethics are also frequently concerned with the ethical principle of *justice*. This principle suggests the need to ensure that equal opportunities are available for all people. "Psychologists recognize that fairness and justice entitles all persons to access to and benefit from the contributions of psychology and equal quality in the processes, procedures, and services conducted by psychologists" (American Psychological Association EP Principle D). This suggests that professionals must not only refrain from discrimination but must actively pursue skills necessary to promote mental health and education of diverse students (National Association of School Psychologists, 2010, PPE II.1.2).

The principle of *fidelity* refers to the need to be truthful and open in interactions with others, and faithfulness to duties. Some codes prefer the term *integrity* to describe this concept. In the professional setting, this means that the professional must be honest and responsible, and must also promote honest and responsible behavior on the part of the organizations with which they are affiliated. For example, a school social worker must be honest when communicating with students or families, but he/she must also act to correct or prevent any misleading information from being disseminated by others in the school (National Association of Social Workers, 2008, Principle 5).

Non-Maleficence is the principle that reminds professionals to work to avoid harming others. For mental health professionals, this principle is often relevant when conducting research—it is vital for researchers to, "evaluate the potential risks...of their research and only conduct studies in which the risks to participants are minimized and acceptable" (National Association of School Psychologists, 2008, PPE IV.5.2). This means that even if a proposal provides benefits for some individuals, the professional must always consider possible harm caused by an activity.

A related principle is *beneficence*, which means responsible caring that is likely to benefit as many people as possible. In special education settings, this means that the professional should work to help as many children as possible receive as great a benefit as possible from their service. In many cases, this can lead to outreach efforts on the part of the professional to identify children and families who could benefit from services that do not currently receive them.

In many cases, it is fairly easy to determine whether a certain behavior is ethical. In certain situations, however, determining ethical behavior is quite challenging. This is often true when the ethical principles described earlier conflict with one another. Consider, for example, the decision of how to handle the case of a child whose behavior is disruptive to other children in the classroom. In this case,

a teacher who is concerned with beneficence may wish to remove the child from class because this would benefit the other children. On the other hand, the principle of nonmaleficence may be used to keep the child in class, especially if the teacher thought the child with the behavioral concern would be harmed by being removed from his/her peers. The principle of autonomy would encourage the teacher to emphasize the preferences of the child and guardians (who may not agree with each other), while the principle of justice would emphasize the need for the school and its teachers to improve their skills in working with children who have behavior problems. This is just one example of a difficult ethical dilemma commonly faced when working with children and adolescents.

Many of the codes of conduct describe recommended procedures for handling difficult ethical concerns. These procedures call for the professional to evaluate the ethical standards, the law, the rights of the parents and children, consulting with other professionals, making a decision that takes into account the likely consequences, implementing the action, and evaluating the impact of the decision (American Counseling Association, 2005, CE-Section H; American School Counselors Association, 2004, ES-G.3; American Psychological Association, 2010, EP Standard 1). Professionals who follow such procedures are not guaranteed to always make the best decisions, but these codes are in place to help reduce the likelihood of harm to children and families and increase the chances of helping as many people as possible.

REFERENCES

American Counseling Association (ACA). (2005). *Code of ethics and standards of practice.* Alexandria, VA: Author.

American Psychological Association (APA). (2010). *Ethical principles of psychologists and code of conduct with the 2010 amendments.* Retrieved from http://www.apa.org/ethics/code/index.aspx

American School Counselors Association (ASCA). (2004). Ethical standards for school counselors. Retrieved from http://www.schoolcounselor.org/files/EthicalStandards2010.pdf

National Association of School Psychologists (NASP). (2010). *Principles for Professional Ethics.* Bethesda, MD: Author.

National Association of Social Workers (NASW). (2008). *Code of ethics (Guide to the everyday professional conduct of social workers).* Washington, DC: Author.

National Education Association. (1985). *NEA Handbook: 1985–86.* Washington, DC: Author.

KAY KETZENBERGER
The University of Texas of the Permian Basin

JAMES E. WALSH
The Chicago School of Professional Psychology
Fourth edition

ETHICS, INTERNATIONAL, AND SPECIAL EDUCATION

Codes of ethics are found in numerous professional fields and are designed to protect the public by prescribing and proscribing behaviors professionals are expected to exhibit. Issues such as what constitutes professional practice, training, and licensure are intertwined with ethics. Ethics codes typically contain principles and standards that reflect both unenforceable general virtues (e.g., beneficence, fidelity) and specific, enforceable behaviors (e.g., research participant protection; Nagy, 1999). In most countries mature professional associations develop their own codes. Nevertheless, virtues and standards addressed in these codes often overlap across nations.

The need for codes of ethics is increasing due, in part, to growing skepticism of professionals, the growth of professionalism, and growing practice of professionals to transcend country and cultural boundaries because of business and technological changes.

International ethics codes allow for uniformity of appropriate professional behavior and highlight common threads that bridge multiple professions and countries. They can offer a shared meaning across cultures. For example, standards of care differ depending on one's country, yet an international code could solidify accepted standards. International codes also would facilitate international research by defining human participant protections that transcend cultures. Finally, they can help standardize acceptable training requirements that can be incorporated internationally.

The following provides information about the status of ethics codes regionally and internationally that may impact special education. Various professions are committed to work in special education, including educators, social workers, counselors, and those from medicine. Psychology has had an abiding interest in special education. Codes that emanate from psychology are discussed in the following paragraphs. They generally are well developed and often are on the cutting edge of ethics code development.

In 1995 the European Federation of Professional Psychologists Associations endorsed a Meta-Code of Ethics in the first attempt to present global unifying principles for psychological organizations and psychologists. This brief document addresses four main principles: respect for a person's rights and dignity, competence, responsibility, and integrity. Gauthier (2002) extended this work for individual psychologists by proposing the Universal Declaration of Ethical Principles for Psychologists. Its purpose is to promote professional unity within the profession internationally by including ethical practices regardless of country or culture. It is not intended to replace existing codes but it is predicted that a number of its elements will be included when countries revise their codes.

Ethics guidelines that extend across countries yet retain some cultural influences are needed. The International School Psychology Association devised an ethics code that covers professional responsibilities, confidentiality, professional growth and limitations, relationships, assessment, and research. It was developed following a review of ethics codes from psychological associations that are members of the International Union of Psychological Sciences.

Leach and Harbin (1997) compared psychological codes from 23 countries and found significant overlap among some codes (e.g., Australia, South Africa), and differences among others. As expected, there was considerable overlap with principles. However, the standards addressed in the codes tended to differ. Differences were noted based on topic area (e.g., testing and assessment) and unique features of countries' codes were also noted (e.g., prohibiting torture, policy statements; Leach, Glosoff, & Overmier, 2001).

Informed consent and confidentiality comprise legal and professional standards that often transcend countries. Both are important to special education. Parents and guardians have rights to receive and understand information generated by professionals who work with their children. Additionally, maintaining confidentiality of information pertinent to their family reflects a basic right to privacy and may be important to effective treatment (Ketzenberger, 2001). Informed consent and confidentiality are considered cornerstones of ethical behavior and are found in practically all ethics codes.

Psychologists and others working in special education often use testing and other assessment procedures. Test use is universal. However, some countries use them broadly and wisely, whereas others focus on specific areas (e.g., assessing Mental Retardation; Hu & Oakland, 1991; Leach & Oakland, 2007) and use them with little professional regard.

A number of organizations have developed test-related standards (e.g., International Test Commission, 2000; Joint Commission on Testing Practices, 2005; National Council on Measurement in Education, 1995), whereas others address theoretical and specialized areas of test development and use (e.g., American Educational Research Association, American Psychological Association, and National Council on Measurement in Education, 1999). The International Test Commission (ITC; www.intestcom.org) developed guidelines for adapting tests, including those that impact ethics (Oakland, 2005). The ITC recently developed guidelines for computer-based and Internet-delivered testing (Coyne & Bartram, 2004). It too has an ethics component.

Thus, as international professional boundaries continue to diminish, the need for ethics codes that transcend national boundaries becomes paramount. Although ethics codes always will reflect cultural differences and individual professional nuances, principles and standards exist with which all professions committed to working with special-needs children probably can agree. As codes continue to develop they are likely to include principles and standards advanced by international organizations. Thus, over time, codes are likely to increasingly reflect universal issues.

REFERENCES

American Educational Research Association, American Psychological Association, and National Council on Measurement in Education. (1999). *Standards for educational and psychological testing*. Washington, DC: American Educational Research Association.

Coyne, I., & Bartram, D. (2004). *International test commission computer-based and Internet delivered testing guidelines*. Draft March 5, 2002. Paper presented to the Council of the International Test Commission, Beijing, and The People's Republic of China.

Gauthier, J. (2002). *Toward a universal declaration of ethical principles for psychologists: A progress report*. Paper presented at the International Congress of Applied Psychology, Singapore.

Hu, S., & Oakland, T. (1991). Global and regional perspectives on testing children and youth: An international survey. *International Journal of Psychology 26*(3), 329–344.

International Test Commission. (2000). *International guidelines for test use*. Liverpool, England: Author.

Joint Commission on Testing Practices. (2005). *Code of fair testing practices in education*. Washington, DC: American Psychological Association.

Ketzenberger, K. (2001). Ethics. In C. R. Reynolds & E. Fletcher-Janzen (Eds.), *Encyclopedia of special education* (2nd ed., pp. 703–704). New York, NY: Wiley.

Leach, M. M., Glosoff, H., & Overmier, J. B. (2001). *International ethics codes: A follow-up study of previously unmatched standards and principles*. In J. B. Overmier & J. A. Overmier (Eds.), Psychology: CD-Rom; IUPsyS Global Resource.

Leach, M. M., & Harbin, J. J. (1997). Psychological ethics codes: A comparison of twenty-four countries. *International Journal of Psychology, 32*, 181–192.

Leach, M. M., & Oakland, T. (2007). Ethics standards impacting test development and use: A review of 31 ethics codes impacting practices in 35 countries. *International Journal of Testing, 7*, 1, 71–88.

Nagy, T. M. (1999). *Ethics in plain English: An illustrative casebook for psychologists*. Washington, DC: American Psychological Association.

National Council on Measurement in Education. (1995). *Code of professional responsibilities in educational measurement*. Washington, DC: Author.

Oakland, T. (2005). Selected ethical issues relevant to test adaptations. In R. Hambleton, C. Spielberger, & P. Meranda, (Eds.), *Adapting educational and psychological tests for cross-cultural assessment*. Mahwah, NJ: Erlbaum.

Mark M. Leach
University of Southern Mississippi

See also International School Psychology Association; International Test Use in Special Education

ETIOLOGY

Etiology is the study of causes of diseases and impairments. When considering those with disabilities, however, one must consider not only the specific cause, if known, but the affected individual's developmental history and exposure to intervention. Increasingly, technology is not only leading to increasing knowledge about the origins of various disorders but, also, to increasing ability to ameliorate some of the conditions. Only in the most severe cases is the relationship between cause and outcome one-to-one. Research is also leading to reconsideration of some presumed origins of disorders and the extent to which various factors may underlie these origins. In particular, findings from behavior genetics research is leading to changed views of both normal and abnormal development.

This research is having impact not only in the professional literature, but in the popular press as well. Consider the query on the April 1998 *Life* magazine cover, "Were you BORN that way? Personality, temperament, even life choices. New studies show that it's mostly in your genes." Well, perhaps, but the new studies actually suggest that genetic factors play varying roles in influencing human traits. The first page of the article itself hardly qualifies the cover: "It's not just brown eyes. Your inheritance could also include insomnia, obesity, and optimism. Yet scientists are saying that genes are not—quite—destiny" (Colt, 1998, p. 39). Not many years ago, such statements would have been almost inconceivable. After all, prevailing thought was that adult personality was largely determined by early experience, particularly before 5 to 6 years of age and particularly with the parents (see Early Experience and Critical Periods, this volume). Increasingly, research is indeed questioning the role of postnatal social experience in general, and that of parents in particular, in development of personality. However, research also is increasingly documenting the importance of both prenatal factors as causes of handicapping conditions and interactions between risk factors for handicapping conditions with other developmental factors.

Regardless of advances, however, the specific cause of most handicapping conditions still cannot be conclusively identified. This entry overviews various sources of handicapping conditions and developmental considerations, many of which are described in other individual entries. It also overlaps with a variety of others, particularly Early Experience and Critical Periods. A summary of the sources is in Table E.8.

Genetically Based Disorders

A variety of specific disorders have a specific chromosomal or single-gene basis. In the case of some disorders, family history and other methods support an OGOD (one gene, one disorder) basis, in which a single gene is both necessary and sufficient for the development of a disorder. Even in

Table E.8. Source of Handicapping Conditions

Source	Example or Effect
Genetic	
Chromosomal	
Autosomal trisomies	Down syndrome
Autosomal deletions and additions	Cri du chat
Sex-chromosome aneuploidies	Klinefelter, Turner, XXY syndromes
Constriction or weakness	Fragile X syndrome
Single-gene	
Dominant	Neurofibromatosis, tuberous sclerosis
Recessive	Inborn errors of metabolism (e.g., PKU, galactosemia, Tay Sachs)
Sex-linked	Lesch-Nyham syndrome
QTL	Mild mental retardation, predisposition toward variety of impairments
HIV	Mental retardation, variety of other impairments, progressive deterioration
Prenatal teratogens	
Radiation	Growth failure, major malformations
Maternal infections	
TORCH complex (toxoplasmosis, rubella, cytomegalovirus, herpes)	Growth retardation, visual and auditory impairments, mental retardation
Syphilis	Mental retardation, meningitis
Drugs and hormones	
Thalidomide	Limb, digit, external ear malformations
Alcohol	Fetal alcohol syndrome
Androgens	Masculinization of females
Antitumor agents	Major growth and central nervous system defects
Anticoagulants	Growth retardation, visual and auditory impairments
Anticonvulsants	Fetal hydantoin syndrome
Perinatal factors	
Maternal infection	
Herpes	Same as TORCH complex
Prematurity	Cerebral palsy, mental retardation
Low birth weight	Growth retardation, mental retardation, cerebral palsy
Asphyxia	Cerebral palsy, variety of other impairments
Postnatal chemical or traumatic factors	
Infection	
Encephalitis	Mental retardation
Toxins	
Lead	Mental retardation, epilepsy, sensory impairments
Accidents and child abuse, including shaken baby syndrome	Brain damage (specific) leading to variety of impairments
Learning	
Conditioning (Pavlovian)	Phobias
Operant conditioning	Negative self-concept, avoidant disorders, conduct disorders
Observational learning	Phobias, articulation disorders

such disorders, however, intervention may significantly reduce their adverse impact, PKU being perhaps the best-known example. Thus, owing to interaction among genes, and among genes and the pre- and postnatal environment, individuals' phenotypes (their actual appearances) often do not reflect their genotypes or genetic makeup (e.g., Kopp, 1983; Plomin & McClearn, 1993; Vogel & Motulsky, 1979). Many other disorders, as well as normal traits on which humans vary continuously (e.g., height, weight), have genetic predispositions that owe to the interaction among multiple genes, no one of which is either necessary or sufficient. These traits and disorders were formerly called polygenic, but that term, which implied a large number of genes each of unmeasurably small effect size, has been replaced. The new term, quantitative trait loci (QTL), implies that some potentially identifiable number of genes of varying effect size operate additively and interchangeably (Plomin, Owen, & McGuffin, 1994).

Chromosomal Abnormalities

Normal humans have 23 pairs of chromosomes in their body cells—22 pairs of similar autosomes and one pair of sex chromosomes. Females have two relatively long X, whereas males have one X and one shorter Y, sex chromosomes. In the development of germ cells (meiosis), each pair normally splits such that each germ cell has 23 chromosomes. However, occasionally one chromosome does not split (nondisjunction), resulting in a double dose or absence of that chromosome, or a chromosome breaks and becomes partly attached to another (translocation). These, and other processes, can lead to chromosomal abnormalities.

Most such abnormalities lead to spontaneous abortion, but the incidence in live births is about 1 in 200. Involving large numbers of genes, these abnormalities have broad and typical physical and behavioral effects. They tend to produce general intellective deficiency, minor in some syndromes but severe in others.

Autosomal trisomies involve an extra autosomal chromosome; affected individuals have 47 chromosomes. Down syndrome (trisomy 21) is the most common, but at least five others have been described. Virtually all increase in incidence with maternal age and result in growth failure and mental retardation.

Autosomal partial deletions and additions are low-incidence disorders that, except for 18 p-, which shows highly variable effects, generally result in severe mental retardation. The best known is 5 p-, cri du chat, so named because affected infants' cries sound like a cat's meows.

Sex chromosome aneuplodies involve an added or missing sex chromosome. Klinefelter (XXY) and XYY syndromes affect only males; Turner syndrome (XO) affects only females. Intelligence of affected individuals averages about 90, but this is highly variable.

Single-Gene Effects

Except for sex-linked recessive traits, individuals inherit a gene for each single-gene trait from each parent. Different forms (alleles) of a given gene can lead to different manifestations of a trait. Individuals are said to be homozygotic or heterozygotic for a given trait if they have inherited two similar or two different alleles, respectively. Single-gene traits follow Mendelian principles of inheritance: a dominant trait will be expressed if the individual has inherited at least one dominant gene for the trait, whereas a recessive trait will be expressed only if the individual inherits the recessive gene from both parents. An exception is sex-linked recessive traits, the genes for which are carried on the sex chromosomes. Such traits may be expressed if the recessive gene is inherited from one parent and no counterpart gene is inherited from the other parent to suppress its effects. In part because the Y-chromosome is shorter than the X and, therefore, carries fewer genes, such sex-linked traits appear much more commonly in males; these traits are transmitted by their mothers, who are carriers. Both X-linked dominant and X-linked recessive traits may

appear. Other patterns of inheritance such as codominance and partial dominance complicate the notion of simple dominance-recessiveness relations, as do the phenomena of penetrance, pleiotropy, and variable expressivity (e.g., Plomin & McClearn, 1993; Thompson & Thompson, 1980).

Dominant, recessive, and sex-linked single-gene disorders now number in the thousands (e.g., McKusick & Francomano, 1994), and new ones are discovered regularly. They lead to a variety of essentially OGOD conditions—over 100 are linked to mental retardation, 100 to hearing impairment, and 15 to spinocerebellar ataxia. A number are also invariably fatal in infancy. With the exception of sex-linked disorders, they occur in equal frequency in males and females. Because of their number and variety, only a few can be described.

Approximately 4,500 dominant single-gene disorders have been identified (McKusick & Francomano, 1994). If one parent is heterozygotic for the gene and manifests the disorder, offspring have a 50% chance of developing it. But about 50 percent of all cases arise from spontaneous mutation and thus have no family history. Obviously, individuals with the mutated gene can transmit the disorder to their children. Dominant disorders mainly involve structural abnormalities. Achondroplasia, for example, is a form of short-limb dwarfism. Many dominant disorders have highly variable expressivity, in which the manifestation is great in some individuals but hardly noticeable in others. Some disorders may appear to skip a generation when the effects are so minimal as to be essentially unseen (Thompson & Thompson, 1980). Further, dominant disorders, as well as many recessive ones, manifest pleiotropy, multiple effects of a single gene. An example is neurofibromatosis, a relatively high-incidence condition (approximate incidence: 1/3,000), which involves a variety of structural abnormalities. Its effects range from hardly noticeable to obvious deformities, with some risk of mental retardation and other developmental disabilities (e.g., Batshaw, 1997). Until recently, the most famous example of neurofibromatosis appeared to be Joseph Merrick, the Elephant Man (e.g., Howell & Ford, 1980), but he now appears likely to have had Proteus syndrome (see Elephant Man entry, this volume).

A child has a 25% chance of inheriting a recessive single-gene defect if both parents are heterozygotic (carriers) for the defect. Recessive single-gene defects may result in a variety of conditions, including sensory impairment, ataxia, and mental retardation.

In a large number of cases a defective gene results in impaired metabolism that, in turn, leads to the accumulation of some unmetabolized substance, which may be toxic. Among the more common and better understood of such inborn errors of metabolism or metabolic disorders are phenylketonuria, galactosemia, and Tay-Sachs disease. Some disorders can be detected through amniocentesis, and a few can be treated through dietary intervention.

A variety of single-gene-based defects that appear more commonly in males than females are sex-linked, frequently called X-linked. Among these are several forms of sensory impairments, the best known of which is red-green colorblindness. Lesch-Nyhan syndrome, which appears virtually solely in males, is an X-linked inborn error of metabolism that results in deterioration of motor coordination, mental retardation, and self-destructive behavior.

Beginning around 1980, improved test procedures enabled reliable identification of fragile chromosomal sites, where constriction or weakness occurs. Shortly thereafter, Fragile X was described, which now appears to be second only to Down syndrome as a genetically based cause of mental retardation. Although originally termed a chromosomally based disorder, Fragile X has recently been linked to a single gene on the X chromosome, and thus is more accurately described as sex-linked. It is unusual in that it affects females as well as males, although with a lower incidence and less severity, and has highly variable expressivity.

Higher incidence in males than females and familial patterns of incidence suggest that some types of attention deficit disorders and learning disabilities may have X-linked predisposition.

Quantitative Trait Loci (QTL)

As stated earlier, QTL traits are those influenced by a number of genes. Virtually all quantitatively varying human traits that have been studied have identifiable QTL bases (e.g., Plomin et al., 1994). Phenotypically, these traits are the outcome of the interaction among the genes themselves and among the genes and the developmental environment. Coming largely from adoption studies and concordance studies with monozygotic and dizygotic twins, identified traits include: general intelligence as well as verbal and spatial abilities (Plomin & DeFries, 1998); the "Big 5" personality traits (extraversion, neuroticism, conscientiousness, agreeableness, and openness) and temperament (Bouchard, 1994); and disorders such as mild mental retardation, alcoholism, criminality, schizophrenia, autism, major depression, reading disability, neural tube defects, and idiopathic seizure disorders. Particularly strong predisposition is indicated for autism. Interestingly, QTL predisposition toward diagnosed alcoholism, once thought to be fairly large, appears to be relatively small and occurs only in males; greater genetic influence is shown on amount of alcohol consumed (e.g., Plomin et al., 1994).

Other Presumed Genetic Disorders

Many low-incidence disorders have presumed genetic bases, owing to their patterns of inheritance, predominance in one gender, or concordance, although the exact basis has not been established. Autism and schizophrenia

have already been mentioned. An interesting and tragic example is Rett syndrome, a neurodevelopmental disorder that occurs only in females and is associated with apparently initial normal development followed by developmental arrest and deterioration (e.g., Brown & Hoadley, 1999).

Prenatal Influences

Prenatal development is generally divided into three periods: germinal or ovum (weeks 0–2), embryonic (weeks 3–8), and fetal (weeks 9–birth). Major developments in each period are germinal—the ovum (fertilized egg) becomes implanted on the uterine wall and differentiates into placental and embryonic tissue; embryonic—characterized by differentiation of all major organs and systems and external body features; and fetal—characterized by rapid growth and further differentiation of internal and external systems and features.

Although the embryo/fetus is generally well protected from environmental insult, a variety of chemicals, called teratogens, can cross the placenta and cause malformations (see Table 5.8). Teratogens have their major adverse impact during critical periods, times of most rapid tissue differentiations. There are less severe effects during sensitive periods. As shown in Figure E.3, systems have individual but overlapping critical periods, mainly around the time of the embryonic periods, and sensitive periods that extend into the fetal period. Sensitive periods for central nervous system, eyes, and external genitalia extend well after birth, so these systems are unusually sensitive to later teratogenic influence. During the early germinal period, teratogens generally either have no effects or are lethal, although they may cause certain major malformations (Moore, 1982).

Radiation, maternal infections, and a number of drugs have serious teratogenic impact (see Table 5.8). Maternal infections in general are a concern because the symptoms may be mild or absent in the pregnant woman, but have severe adverse effects on the embryo/fetus. Of major concern now is the growing number of cases, perhaps over 20,000, of pediatric HIV, transmitted through the mother. Affected children show a variety of CNS damage, including progressive encephalopathy, atrophy of the cortex, and an assortment of other conditions (Belfer, Krener, & Miller, 1987). Resulting neuropsychological, psychological, and social impairments include mental retardation, seizures, learning disabilities, motor coordination, language delays, and emotional and attentional disturbances (e.g., Armstrong, Seidel, & Swales, 1993). Recently, folic acid deficiency during pregnancy has been recognized as such a common cause of neural tube defects (e.g., spina bifida) that supplements are now being routinely supplied (Liptak, 1997).

Of the many teratogenic drugs (see Carta et al., 1994, for a review), the one of major concern is alcohol. Fetal

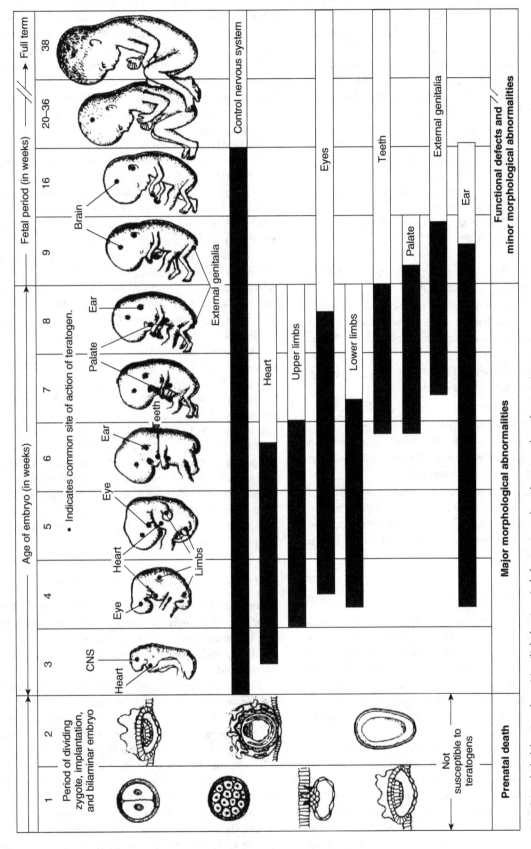

Figure E.3. Critical (dark bars) and sensitive (light bars) periods for teratogenic action on various tissue systems

Source: From Moore (1982).

alcohol syndrome is now, with Down and Fragile X syndromes, one of the three most common specific causes of mental retardation in the Western world, having an incidence of perhaps 1 in 1,000 births. Complicating outcomes for affected children is the likelihood that their mothers may be abusing multiple substances and live in poverty conditions. Interestingly, the predicted onslaught of "crack babies," essentially unteachable, aggressive children, into our schools has fortunately not materialized. Prenatal cocaine has adverse effects, but to a lesser extent than originally thought—and publicized in the popular media (see Day & Richardson, 1993, for a summary of the controversy).

Effects shown are of severe manifestations and are highly variable; in many cases exposed infants will be asymptomatic. The action of teratogens can be summarized as follows (Brown, 1986).

1. No agent is 100% teratogenic; influence is affected by both maternal and embryonic factors.

2. Teratogens act in specific ways and have specific effects, but some have multiple effects and different teratogens may have similar effects (e.g., TORCH complex).

3. Organ systems have individual but largely overlapping critical and sensitive periods.

4. Major effects of teratogens are death, malformations, growth retardation, and functional deficits.

5. Adverse effects are dose dependent, increasing in frequency and severity with increased degree and duration of exposure to a teratogen.

6. Some agents that have major teratogenic influence on the embryo may have little adverse effect or even positive effect on the mother. TORCH complex is an example of the former, and thalidomide and dilantin are examples of the latter.

Perinatal Influences

No single definition of the perinatal period has been universally accepted; Freeman (1985a) defines the period as a few hours or days before birth, whenever in gestation that occurs, to a few hours or days after delivery. Since herpes is almost always transmitted to the newborn as it passes through the birth canal, it is, strictly speaking, a perinatal influence, although it is classified as a member of the TORCH complex.

Major perinatal events are prematurity and low birth weight (LBW): "Premature birth, whether defined as either low birth weight (LBW) or as birth prior to term gestation [prematurity], remains the major contributing factor to neonatal morbidity and mortality" (Barden, 1983, p. 139). In the United States alone, each year some 350,000 LBW (<2,500 gm) infants are born, comprising about 8.5% of all births (Bernbaum & Batshaw, 1997).

Known correlates include amniotic fluid/membrane infection, substance abuse, young or old mother, poor prenatal care, African American mother, and maternal illness, but the specific cause in most cases is unknown. Physical characteristics of affected infants are presence of body hair, reddish skin color, and absence of skin folds. Behavioral characteristics include breathing difficulties, low motor tonus, absence of normal newborn reflexes, inability to maintain body temperature, high-pitched and irritating cries, and hyperreactivity to stimulation. Importantly, the behavioral characteristics may interfere with normal parent-child interactions and set the stage for future problems. Major complications of both conditions owe largely to asphyxia, which may result in hypoxic ischemic encephalopathy (HIE), intraventricular hemorrhage (IVH), and other conditions, which, themselves, result in brain damage. Retinopathy of prematurity is another problem. Although most premature/LBW infants with birthweights above 1,500 gm show normal development, incidence of mental retardation, cerebral palsy, visual and hearing impairments, and seizure disorders are increasingly likely outcomes with lower birth weights (Bernbaum & Batshaw, 1997).

Increases in knowledge about the effects of prematurity and LBW along with advances in treatment options have dramatically improved prognosis for premature/LBW infants and decreased mortality and morbidity. For example, survival rate for 1,500–2,500 gm and 1,000–1,500 gm infants has increased from 50% and 30% in 1960 to over 90% in the 1990s. Of surviving infants in 1950, over 90% of those with birthweights less than 1,500 showed serious later neurodevelopmental problems; in 1980, that figure had dropped to less than 20%. With extremely low birth weight infants, however, severe disability is still a likely outcome (Bernbaum & Batshaw, 1997).

Postnatal Chemical and Physical Effects

Birth is clearly a landmark, associated with adaptation to an external environment and self-breathing and feeding, but many developmental processes, begun prenatally continue, including development of the central nervous system and vulnerability to insult.

Brain damage can, of course, lead to virtually all impairments, with type and degree a function of the area damaged, the extent of damage, and the age at which the damage occurred. Infections, high fever, malnutrition, and certain toxins can cause diffuse damage to major areas of the brain, whereas physical insult can result in focal lesions, damage to more limited areas. A major issue is the effect of age at time of injury on recovery from brain damage. The Kennard principle that recovery is easier the earlier the brain damage is no longer accepted. Relations appear to be complicated, involving, in addition to age and type of damage, the individual's prior experience.

Infants are at particular risk for infection, and diseases such as meningitis may result in seizures and brain damage that can lead to later mental retardation, cerebral palsy, epilepsy, or specific learning disabilities (Thompson & O'Quinn, 1979).

Because of their effects on developing central nervous system tissue, certain toxins pose considerable risk for children. Of particular concern is lead poisoning, which in severe doses can produce devastating brain damage in children, resulting in severe mental retardation, sensory impairment, and seizures. In lesser doses, it may produce lowered intelligence, behavioral problems, and specific learning difficulties. The effects are dose dependent, and apparently no level of blood lead is safe (e.g., Needleman, 1993).

Malnutrition in infancy, particularly when severe enough to lead to marasmus or kwaskiorkhor, is a potential cause of diffuse brain damage and resulting mental retardation. Of particular concern is severe malnutrition occurring early in infancy or lasting more than 4 months; this may result in later retardation regardless of the adequacy of subsequent diet (Cravioto & Delicardie, 1970). Early effective treatment of malnutrition leads to "catch-up growth," lessening long-term consequences (Brann & Schwartz, 1983). However, even later sufficient dietary treatment may in some cases largely overcome the effects of early malnutrition, whereas later malnutrition can also lead to brain injury (Brown & Pollitt, 1996). Effects of less severe but chronic malnutrition manifest themselves less in terms of gross brain damage than in behavioral deficits, such as low energy, inattentiveness, and poor motor control, that interfere with normal education. Of importance is the extent to which other environmental factors can ameliorate or exacerbate the effects of malnutrition. As Brown and Pollitt (1996) emphasize, the traditional "main effects," or one-to-one, model developmental influences is oversimplified in the face of evidence for interactional processes.

Failure to thrive resulting from either parental neglect or infant-based impairments may have long-term consequences.

Accidents, particularly automobile accidents, are a common cause of specific brain damage in children. Child abuse is increasingly seen as another important factor.

Role of Learning

Learning plays such a ubiquitous role in the development of normal human behavior that its role in causing or exacerbating impaired behavior is sometimes overlooked in discussing etiology. Learning processes can result in direct impairments or the indirect exacerbation of other impairments. For example, phobias can be acquired through Pavlovian (classical or respondent) conditioning, in which an initially neutral stimulus such as a dentist is paired with pain, or through observational learning (imitation), in which a child observes a parent's severe fear of dentists.

Operant conditioning, or learning by consequences such as reinforcement and punishment, has an important influence on the way in which children with impairments react to those impairments and to themselves. If, for example, a retarded child's attempt to solve problems meets with failure (and perhaps ridicule as well), then the child may develop fear of failure and a poor self-concept. Through respondent conditioning, the child may become highly anxious in subsequent problem-solving settings. Anxiety, in turn, can lead to avoiding problem settings and increasing dependency on others, further reducing the child's own competence. Zigler (1967) has described the negative role that a number of such learned motivational-emotional factors can have on children with mental retardation. Research indicates that these factors adversely affect children with other impairments as well (Brown & Reynolds, 1986).

If a child's responses have no contingent impact on the environment and the child has no control over what happens, then learned helplessness may result, leading to an expectation of failure and apathy.

Reinforcement, particularly negative reinforcement of inappropriate emotional behaviors in boys by their parents, has been shown to be an important initial step in Patterson's (e.g., Patterson, Reid, & Dishion, 1992) coercion model of antisocial behavior. When a parent objects to a boy's behavior and the boy argues or throws a tantrum, the parent may back off, positively reinforcing the boy's inappropriate behavior. When the parent backs off, the boy stops his inappropriate behavior, which negatively reinforces the parent's backing off. In this way, a maladaptive behavioral cycle may result.

Developmental Considerations

Temperament

Children's own characteristics influence their development and the way in which others behave toward them. In reports from the landmark New York Longitudinal Study, Thomas, Chess, Birch, and their colleagues (e.g., Chess & Thomas, 1984) have documented the importance of temperament as a factor in children's development. Temperament is a relatively stable personality variable that affects such responses as adaptation to new situations and persistence. Children whose temperamental style is described as difficult are more likely to manifest behavior disorders than are other children.

Summaries of various approaches to temperament (Kagan, 1994; Strelau, 1998) further support the role of temperament as an important developmental factor. Temperament interacts with other developmental factors and may predispose children either to be abused or to develop conduct disorders.

Poverty

Poverty contributes to impairments both directly and indirectly and may be self-perpetuating. A number of factors that may lead to or exacerbate impairments are higher in low SES groups. These include poor prenatal care; obstetric and perinatal complications, especially prematurity and low birth weight; malnutrition; abusive parents; restricted verbal codes; and inadequate caretaking.

Birch and Gussow (1970) propose that a cycle of poverty acts to transmit poverty across generations. Risk factors associated with low-SES-based factors lead children to be more likely to suffer school failure. School failure leads to unemployment and underemployment which, in turn, maintain poverty conditions and thus perpetuate the cycle into another generation.

Inadequate caretaking behavior occurs in poorly trained parents, particularly under the stress of large families and low SES conditions. Such parents may be able to cope with a normal infant but be stretched beyond their limits in dealing with infants with pre- or perinatal complications. Such infants may, because of their behavioral characteristics, evoke inadequate and even abusive parenting behavior, exacerbating already present impairments and inducing them in infants who under more appropriate conditions would develop normally.

Interactions

The inadequacy of simple main-effects models has been apparent in several places in this entry. Development in general is characterized as being multicausal and interactional.

1. Interactions between infants and caretakers are crucial in the development of some impairments. Indeed, in a now-classic review, Sameroff and Chandler (1975) found little evidence for a "continuum of reproductive casualty." Instead, the way in which caretakers could or could not adequately cope with their infants determined later impairments, resulting in what they termed a "continuum of caretaking casualty." Interactions between characteristics of infants and characteristics of caretakers are important factors in development.

2. Depression is now seen to occur much more frequently in children than had been thought only a few years ago. Although a genetic predisposition for depression exists, its actual manifestation depends on interactions among a number of internal (biological, cognitive, and socioemotional) factors and external parental and broader contextual factors. The complexity of the developmental process is described admirably by Cicchetti and Toth (1998).

3. Evidence exists for both genetic and prenatal bases of schizophrenia. However, whether an individual actually develops schizophrenia or some other serious behavior disorder depends on factors in the developmental environment. If parents provide a disturbed family environment, children predisposed to develop schizophrenia are more likely actually to manifest the disorder. The Finnish Adoption Study (e.g., Tienari et al., 1994) has compared adopted children of biological mothers who had schizophrenia with adopted children of biological parents without schizophrenia. Of adopted children whose biological mothers had schizophrenia, only those raised in psychologically disturbed family settings were more likely to develop a serious disorder than those with no family history of schizophrenia. When raised by well-functioning parents, adopted children from both groups showed equivalent and low rates of serious disorders.

4. Environmental factors associated with poverty interact with biological risk factors to exacerbate developmental problems in children (as described in the entry for Social Class and Biological Factors). On the other hand, whether at-risk children, through prematurity or poverty, develop serious problems or school failure depends partly on their developmental environment. If raised under inadequate conditions, they are likely to show adverse consequences, but if provided with appropriate interventions, they may develop normally or at least more normally.

Prevention of Impairments

Applications of present knowledge and techniques could significantly reduce incidence and severity of impairments (Brown, 1986). Some methods are (a) wider use of genetic screening and counseling; (b) more adequate prenatal care for at-risk pregnant women; (c) training in parenting skills for prospective parents; (d) wider dissemination of information materials, and training on birth control to reduce family size in at-risk groups and early pregnancy in adolescents (school-based clinics should be considered); and (e) provision of adequate postnatal nutrition, medical care, and psychological stimulation for at-risk infants. Prevention, although expensive, is both less costly and more humane than remediation.

Additionally, adequacy of therapy has obvious impact on the development of children with conditions that may lead to impairments. The more serious the condition, the more extreme and unusual will be the necessary treatment, resulting in a "continuum of therapeutic environment" (Brown, 1986). In some cases, treatment will be required that simply does not exist in the natural environment. Thus PKU is treated with a synthetic diet, and newborns with perinatal complications or birth injuries are placed in increasingly sophisticated neonatal intensive care units.

Intervention through the broad-based Infant Health and Development Program significantly increased the number of premature, low-birthweight infants scoring in the normal range in cognitive, social, health, and growth measures at 3 years of age relative to nontreated controls (e.g., Bradley et al., 1994).

Although its effectiveness has frequently been questioned (e.g., Herrnstein & Murray, 1994), early intervention with children from poverty environments may, under appropriate conditions, have significant and long-term effects. The Abecedarian Project (e.g., Campbell & Ramey, 1995) began an intensive intervention program with poverty-level infants and carried it through early childhood. In adolescence, the subjects have maintained significantly higher levels of cognitive and social skills and particularly school performance over matched controls. Of particular importance, both school retention and assignment to special education are lower in the experimental children. To be effective, however, such programs must (a) begin early, preferably in infancy, and be maintained over a long period of time; (b) be intensive; (c) provide structured experiences directly rather than be mediated through the parents; (d) provide broad interdisciplinary assistance, including health and social services, individual therapy where needed, parent services and training, and optimal educational programs; (e) adjust to the varying needs of individual children; and (f) provide social and other support after the formal program has ended (e.g., Ramey & Ramey, 1998).

REFERENCES

Armstrong, F. D., Seidel, J. F., & Swales, T. P. (1993). Pediatric HIV infection: A neuropsychological and educational challenge. *Journal of Learning Disabilities, 26*, 92–103.

Barden, T. P. (1983). Obstetric management of prematurity. Part 2. Premature labor. In A. A. Fanaroff & R. J. Martin (Eds.), *Behrman's neonatal-perinatal medicine* (3rd ed., pp. 139–149). St. Louis, MO: Mosby.

Batshaw, M. L. (Ed.). (1997). *Children with disabilities* (4th ed.). Baltimore, MD: Paul H. Brookes.

Behrman, R. E. (1983). The field of neonatal-perinatal medicine. In A. A. Fanaroff & R. J. Martin (Eds.), *Behrman's neonatal-perinatal medicine* (3rd ed., pp. 1–3). St. Louis, MO: Mosby.

Belfer, M. L., Krener, P. K., & Miller, F. B. (1987). AIDS in children and adolescents. *Journal of the American Academy of Child and Adolescent Psychiatry, 27*, 147–151.

Bernbaum, J. C., & Batshaw, M. L. (1997). Born too soon, born too small. In M. L. Batshaw (Ed.), *Children with disabilities* (4th ed., pp. 115–139). Baltimore, MD: Paul H. Brookes.

Birch, H. G., & Gussow, J. D. (1970). *Disadvantaged children: Health, nutrition, and school failure.* New York, NY: Grune & Stratton.

Bouchard, T. J. (1994). Genes, environment, and personality. *Science, 264*, 1700–1701.

Bradley, R. H., Whiteside, L., Mundfrom, D. J., Casey, P. H., Kelleher, K. J., & Pope, S. K. (1994). Contributions of early intervention and early caregiving experiences to resilience in low birthweight, premature children living in poverty. *Journal of Clinical Child Psychology, 21*, 425–434.

Brann, A. W., Jr., & Schwartz, J. F. (1983). Central nervous system disturbances. In A. A. Fanaroff & R. J. Martin (Eds.), *Behrman's neonatal-perinatal medicine* (3rd ed., pp. 347–403). St. Louis, MO: Mosby.

Brown, J. L., & Pollitt, E. (1996). Malnutrition, poverty, and intellectual development. *Scientific American, 274*(2), 38–43.

Brown, R. T. (1986). Etiology and development of exceptionality. In R. T. Brown & C. R. Reynolds (Eds.), *Psychological perspectives on childhood exceptionality: A handbook* (pp. 181–229). New York, NY: Wiley.

Brown, R. T., & Hoadley, S. L. (1999). Rett syndrome. In S. Goldstein & C. R. Reynolds (Eds.), *Handbook of neurodevelopmental and genetic disorders in children.* New York, NY: Guilford Press.

Brown, R. T., & Reynolds, C. R. (Eds.). (1986). *Psychological perspectives on childhood exceptionality: A handbook.* New York, NY: Wiley.

Campbell, F. A., & Ramey, C. T. (1995). The effectiveness of early intervention on intellectual and academic achievement: A follow-up study of children from low-income families. *Child Development, 65*, 684–698.

Carta, J. J., Sideridis, G., Rinkel, P., Guimaraes, S., Greenwood, C., Baggett, K.,...McConnell, S. (1994). Behavioral outcomes of young children prenatally exposed to illicit drugs: Review and analysis of experimental literature. *Topics in Early Childhood Special Education, 14*, 184–216.

Chess, S., & Thomas, A. (1984). *Origins and evolution of behavior disorders.* New York, NY: Brunner/Mazel.

Cicchetti, D., & Toth, S. L. (1998). The development of depression in children and adolescents. *American Psychologist, 53*, 221–241.

Colt, G. H. (1998, April). Were you BORN that way? *Life, 39–50.*

Cravioto, J., & Delicardie, E. (1970). Mental performance in school-age children. *American Journal of Diseases in Children, 120*, 404–410.

Day, L., & Richardson, G. A. (1993). Cocaine use and crack babies: Science, the media, and miscommunication. *Neurotoxicology and Teratology, 15*, 293–294.

Freeman, J. M. (1985). Introduction. In J. M. Freeman (Ed.), *Prenatal and perinatal factors associated with brain disorders* (Publication No. 85-1149, pp. 1–11). Bethesda, MD: National Institutes of Health.

Herrnstein, R. J. & Murray, C. (1994). *The bell curve.* New York, NY: Free Press.

Howell, M., & Ford, P. (1980). *The true history of the Elephant Man.* New York, NY: Penguin.

Kagan, J. (1994). *Galen's prophecy: Temperament in human nature.* New York, NY: Basic Books.

Kopp, C. B. (1983). Risk factors in development. In P. H. Bertenthal, M. M. Haith, & J. J. Campos (Eds.), *Handbook of developmental psychology* (4th ed., Vol. 2, pp. 1081–1188). New York, NY: Wiley.

Liptak, G. S. (1997). Neural tube defects. In M. L. Batshaw (Ed.), *Children with disabilities* (4th ed., pp. 529–552). Baltimore, MD: Paul H. Brookes.

McKusick, V. A., & Francomano, C. A. (1994). *Mendelian inheritance in man: A catalog of human genes and genetic disorders* (11th ed.). Baltimore, MD: Johns Hopkins University.

Moore, K. L. (1982). *The developing human* (3rd ed.). Philadelphia, PA: Saunders.

Needleman, H. (1993). The lead controversy—Reply. *Pediatrics, 92*, 3, 509–509.

Patterson, G. R., Reid, J. B., & Dishion, T. J. (1992). *Antisocial boys*. Eugene, OR: Castalia.

Plomin, R., & DeFries, J. C. (1998, May). The genetics of cognitive abilities and disabilities. *Scientific American, 278*, 62–69.

Plomin, R., & McClearn, G. E. (Eds.). (1993). *Nature, nurture, & psychology*. Washington, DC: American Psychological Association.

Plomin, R., Owen, M. J., & McGuffin, P. (1994). The genetic basis of complex human behaviors. *Science, 264*, 1733–1739.

Ramey, C. T., & Ramey, S. L. (1998). Early intervention and early experience. *American Psychologist, 53*, 109–120.

Sameroff, A. J., & Chandler, M. J. (1975). Reproductive risk and the continuum of caretaking casualty. In F. D. Horowitz, M. Hetherington, S. Scarr-Salapatek, & G. Siegel (Eds.), *Review of child development research* (Vol. 4, pp. 187–244). Chicago, IL: University of Chicago Press.

Strelau, J. (1998). *Temperament: A psychological perspective*. New York, NY: Plenum Press.

Thompson, J. S., & Thompson, M. W. (1980). *Genetics in medicine* (3rd ed.). Philadelphia, PA: Saunders.

Thompson, R. J., & O'Quinn, A. N. (1979). *Developmental disabilities*. New York, NY: Oxford University Press.

Tienari, P., Wynne, L. C., Moring, J., Lahti, I., Naarala, M., Sorri, A., ... Lasky, K. (1994). The Finnish adoptive family study of schizophrenia: Implications for family research. *British Journal of Psychiatry, 164*(Suppl. 23), 20–26.

Vogel, F., & Motulsky, A. G. (1979). *Human genetics*. Berlin, Germany: Springer-Verlag.

Zigler, E. (1967). Familial mental retardation: A continuing dilemma. *Science, 155*, 292–298.

ROBERT T. BROWN
University of North Carolina at Wilmington

See also Autism; Brain Damage; Cafe au Lait Spots; Child Abuse; Conditioning; Inborn Errors of Metabolism; Lead Poisoning; Learned Helplessness; Low Birth Weight Infants; Malnutrition; Prematurity; Seizure Disorders; Spina Bifida; Temperament; Torch Complex

EUGENICS

The term *eugenics* refers to attempts to improve the hereditary characteristics of man through selective breeding. The idea of improving the human stock arose from the observation of the great diversity of human characteristics and abilities and the tendency for these characteristics to run in families. Thus, the theory arose that the human population might be improved by breeding from the best stock, as is commonly done with considerable success in plants and animals. This idea was expressed by the Greek poet Theognis as early as the sixth century BC, and various eugenics plans for the ideal state were included in the writings of Plato.

Although eugenics is an ancient idea, it gained intellectual credibility with the general acceptance of the Darwinian theory of evolution and the idea that man is a product of an evolutionary process that continues in the present and will extend into the future. Francis Galton, who was greatly influenced by the work of his cousin, Charles Darwin, coined the term *eugenics* in 1883. Galton's eugenics proposals centered around providing scholarships and other inducements for superior young people to marry and raise large families, as well as assistance to those of low ability in limiting family size.

The modern history of eugenics can be divided into two contrasting periods (Haller, 1984). In the first part of the 20th century, prior to World War II, there was widespread acceptance of the hereditary basis for human differences among scientists and the general public alike. The eugenics movement flourished, and in the United States was influential in the establishment of restrictive immigration and the passage of sterilization laws in a number of states. The second period, following the war, was characterized by the opposite trend. There was virtual consensus among behavioral scientists that the earlier conceptions were mistaken and research and publication concerning the hereditary basis of human behavior was inhibited and taboo. Eugenics became a bad word, and the term fell into disuse.

This massive swing of the pendulum appears to be purely ideological; it was not based on surprising new findings of any kind. No doubt the events of World War II, including the Holocaust and other excesses of the Nazis, created widespread revulsion toward attempts to change human populations. The civil rights movement and attempts to improve the lot of the disadvantaged probably also contributed to a new respect for human rights that seemed incompatible with many of the eugenics proposals of the earlier period.

Some eugenics proposals have been modest in scope and entirely voluntary. Muller (1965) proposed that sperm from outstanding males be stored and made available to women who voluntarily choose to conceive a child with it. Although such sperm banks are in existence, they have not yet gained the popularity that Muller invisioned. Shockley (1972) proposed that a bonus amounting to $1,000 for each IQ point below 100 be offered for voluntary sterilization to nonpayers of income tax. It is interesting to note that both Muller and Shockley are winners of the Nobel Prize and that both used their prestige to urge public acceptance of the eugenics idea, but the climate was turning in the opposite direction.

It seems clear that a properly administered eugenics program could achieve considerable success over a period of time, but it is instructive to note that no such program has been administered for a long enough time to demonstrate success on even a small scale. To have any effect on the course of human evolution, a eugenics program would have to alter the relative fertility of substantial segments of the world population over a long period of time. The human population is now so large and so disorganized politically that it is difficult to imagine how any of the past eugenics proposals could have a significant impact.

Sciene supports that Homo sapiens evolved over a period of about a million years. Although little is known about the details of this process, early people probably lived dangerously as hunters and gatherers in small isolated groups dispersed over a wide area. There must have been extremely strong selection for intelligence, language usage, and cooperativeness, since evolution of these traits was rapid. It seems likely that favorable cultural adaptations were selected along with favorable genetic traits, so that human culture evolved along with human biology.

For the past 10,000 years, humans have lived as farmers in fixed abodes. Osborn (1968) has reviewed studies of the fertility of agrarian primitive peoples performed before they were subjected to modern influences. These studies show that the more successful farmers tended to have larger families than the less successful, and that their offspring tended to have a better chance for survival. Statistics from the past century also tend to show that those more successful in terms of education and income tended to have more surviving children than did the less successful. Thus, during most of its history, humankind appears to have had a eugenic reproductive pattern. This is undoubtedly the basic cause of the current level of human achievement.

A dysgenic reproductive pattern has emerged worldwide. In the United States, for example, education and family income are now negatively related to births. Van Court and Bean (1985) have shown a significant negative correlation between vocabulary test score and number of children in a large and representative sample of American adults. In the past, differences in survival contributed significantly to differential fertility, but infant mortality has declined to the point that it is no longer a significant factor. Differential birth rates are now the only source of reproductive advantage.

On a larger scale, the most successful national populations are growing at less than half the rate of the less successful. The industrial democracies (such as Canada, Denmark, France, Germany, Japan, the United Kingdom, and the United States) had between 60 and 72 births per 1,000 women aged 15 to 49 in 1973, while virtually all less-developed nations had in excess of 100 births per 1,000 women. A number of those countries (such as Algeria,

Kenya, Mexico, and Nicaragua) had more than 200 births per 1,000 women. In aggregate, the less developed regions are increasing in population at 2.3% per year, whereas the developed regions are increasing at 0.9% per year.

These trends appear to be beyond rational control. Osborn (1968) attributed them to advances in birth-control technology, which provides effective methods that require information, foresight, planning, and money. Thus, the most successful have been the first to take advantage of the enhanced ability to control reproduction. Osborn optimistically predicted that this effect is likely to be temporary, and that favorable birth differentials will return when the new technology has been completely assimilated and everyone has the number of children they desire and can support.

In fact, the future of human heredity is exceptionally difficult to forecast at this time because of the rapid advances that are being made in genetics and biology that will likely result in new technologies of reproduction. Already we have in vitro fertilization, which could be used to separate genetic selection from childbearing and child rearing. Perhaps the future will bring the ability to clone humans and to alter the human genetic code. With these possibilities on the horizon, and others that cannot be foreseen, the present may not be the opportune time to undertake the politically awesome task of reversing the current dysgenic reproductive trends.

REFERENCES

Haller, M. H. (1984). *Eugenics*. New Brunswick, NJ: Rutgers University Press.

Muller, H. J. (1965). Means and aims in human genetic betterment. In T. M. Sonneborn (Ed.), *The control of human heredity and evolution*. New York, NY: Macmillan.

Osborn, F. (1968). *The future of human heredity*. New York, NY: Weybright & Talley.

Shockley, W. (1972). Dysgenics, geneticity, raceology: A challenge to the intellectual responsibility of educators. *Phi Delta Kappan, 53*, 297–312.

Van Court, M., & Bean, F. D. (1985). Intelligence and fertility in the United States: 1912–1982. *Intelligence, 9*, 23–32.

ROBERT C. NICHOLS
DIANE JARVIS
State University of New York at Buffalo

See also **Genetic Counseling; Genetic Factors in Behavior**

EUSTIS, DOROTHY HARRISON (1886–1946)

Dorothy Harrison Eustis introduced the use of guide dogs for the blind in the United States. Born in Philadelphia, Eustis established an experimental breeding kennel for dogs at her estate in Switzerland. With her husband, George Morris Eustis, and Elliott S. (Jack) Humphrey, an American horse breeder and trainer, she began a program of experimental breeding of dogs for police and army duty. She was also aware that the blind in Germany had used trained guide dogs successfully.

Convinced that guide dogs could make the difference between independent and dependent living for the blind, Eustis wrote an article, "The Seeing Eye," for *The Saturday Evening Post* (1927), urging the use of dogs as guides for the blind. The resulting deluge of mail from blind Americans led to the establishment, in 1929, of the United States' first guide-dog training school, in Nashville, Tennessee. Seventeen men and women and their dogs were trained the first year, after which the school was moved to Morristown, New Jersey, where it continues to the present day.

This entry has been informed by the sources listed below.

REFERENCES

Eustis, D. H. (1927, November 5). The seeing eye. *The Saturday Evening Post, 43–46.*

Putnam, P. B. (1979). *Love in the lead.* New York, NY: Dutton.

PAUL IRVINE
Katonah, New York

EVALUATING THE CORE CURRICULUM IN A RESPONSE TO INTERVENTION APPROACH

The reauthorization of the Individuals with Disabilities Education Improvement Act (IDEIA, 2004) has impacted researchers, policymakers, and education practitioners, particularly regarding the identification of specific learning disabilities (SLDs). The reauthorization has fueled debates in the field surrounding the use of the IQ-achievement discrepancy model and the implementation of Response to Intervention (RTI) (Machek & Nelson, 2010). These are important issues that require more research and discussion before consensus is reached. However, the use of RTI for LD classification truly misses the intent of the model: to use a preventive approach to assist *all* students. RTI is not the new method for LD eligibility and classification; RTI is a school-wide approach that supports the evaluation of curriculum, instruction, and assessment.

To that end, a primary component of the RTI framework is an evaluation of the core curriculum. By design, a core curriculum is the program that is used at each grade level delivered by general education teachers. When designed systematically using evidence-based practices, the core can meet the needs of most students at the school. This is important for several reasons. First, it allows schools to be efficient in meeting the needs of an entire school population. Adopted from the public health model (Simeonnson, 1994), this approach assumes that the core program will meet the needs of 80% of students. When this is achieved, around 15% of students may need some additional support and 5% of students will need intensive additional support. If school-wide data indicate that more than 20% of students require additional intervention, this becomes difficult, if not impossible to provide. Schools operate with finite resources, and without additional support, there is no funding for interventionists, supplemental and intensive programs, and assessment tools to monitor those students in need.

Second, evaluating the core curriculum allows schools to adopt and sustain preventative practices that support students earlier. In 2001, Reid Lyon and colleagues submitted a report to Congress titled *Rethinking Learning Disabilities*. The purpose of this report was to highlight the problems in the education of students with learning disabilities (LD) in schools and offer alternatives to the traditional identification and assessment for this category of disability (Yell & Walker, 2010). They argue that implementing school-wide programs that proactively assist students are beneficial because they target student needs and issues before they become so severe that they cannot be remediated. The authors noted that without early and effective intervention, "the poor first-grade reader almost invariably becomes a poor middle school reader, high school reader, and adult reader. In short children who get off to a poor start in reading rarely catch up. We wait—they fail" (p. 270).

More importantly, although there are many variations of RTI implementation, all primary models contain reference to the importance of the core curriculum. Proponents of the primary models are: Batsche, Curtis, Dorman, Castillo, and Porter, (2008); Fuchs and Fuchs (2005); Johnson, Mellard, Fuchs, and McKnight (2006); Vaughn (2005); Shinn (2008), and Sugai and Horner (2007a). Each model has a three-tier intervention structure. Consensus exists around the definition of the first tier, as Tier 1, as effective classroom instruction with a viable general education curriculum (Mellard, Stern, & Woods, 2011).

Screening Assessments

The success of RTI hinges on an accurate determination of which children are at risk for future difficulty (Compton, Fuchs, Fuchs, & Bryant, 2006; Fuchs & Fuchs, 2007; Good, Simmons, & Kame'enui, 2001; VanDerHeyden, Witt, & Gilbertson, 2007). Screening measures are administered to *all* children to identify who is at risk for future difficulty in relationship to the core curriculum. They are brief and provide a mechanism for identifying those children who are (a) at risk for academic failure, (b) in need of a more thorough assessment, and (c) in need of targeted intervention so they do not fall behind peers (Rathvon, 2004).

When coupled with a framework for decision-making, universal screening assists educators in early determination of who is in need. To provide valid information, the screening instrument must be both sensitive and specific. *Sensitivity* refers to the degree a measure correctly identifies children as at high risk (i.e., true positives). Conversely, *specificity* refers to how well a measure correctly identifies children at low risk (i.e., true negatives) (Compton et al., 2010). This is one reason that a decision-making framework is important in conjunction with screening. First, the framework details clear guidelines of how to interpret the data. Using cut points, students can be organized into three tiers based on need. Second, a framework provides guiding questions that assist the decision making process. Finally, it prompts educators to continuously review the data and determine what worked, what didn't, and how further educational needs should be addressed.

Decision-Making Framework

The three-tiered framework is based on the public health model (Walker, Horner, Sugai, Bullis, Sprague, Bricker, et al., 1996). This framework emphasizes prevention, rather than intervention, and systems, rather than individual students. It provides a way for schools to review data, determine if their core curriculum is effective, and assess how many students require additional support. The tiered approach to providing intervention to students in RTI mirrors that of a prevention science framework, as increasingly intense academic intervention is provided as part of the universal, strategic, and intensive tiers (Lembke, McMaster, & Stecker, 2010). These tiers parallel the universal, selective, and indicated prevention cycles that are described in a recent report by the National Research Council and the Institute of Medicine (2009). The framework consists of a triangle in which students are divided by how their needs are met. The target goals for each part of the triangle are 80-15-5, where 80% of students' needs should be met by the core curriculum, 15% met by a supplemental curriculum, and 5% met by an intensive curriculum.

The base of the triangle, representing 80% of students, is an approximation of the percentage of students who would respond well to the core curriculum and instructional practices. In academics, this refers to the core curriculum in the target area and includes reading, math, or written language. In behavior, this refers to the core curriculum or core expectations that students are taught regarding how to behave in school and may include social skills instruction or locally developed curriculum on school-wide expectations (school rules). Although features vary across RTI models, at least several tiers of

instructional support typically are used, and some type of data-based decision making occurs to direct student movement (Lembke, McMaster, & Stecker, 2010).

The middle part of the triangle represents those students who need additional support. These are students who require more instruction than the core curriculum to be successful. Vaughn and Denton (2008) identify several key features of appropriate secondary interventions: (a) identifying students at risk for reading difficulties through universal screening, (b) determining students' instructional needs and forming small groups, (c) providing daily, targeted instruction that is explicit and systematic, and (d) aligning reading instruction and text levels to student needs. The percentage of students that require support at this level should be around 15%. In the area of academics, this may consist of small-group instruction that is provided in addition to the core curriculum. In the area of behavior, this may consist of social skills instruction in addition to the school-wide behavioral expectations.

The top part of the triangle represents those students that have the most intense needs. These are individual students who require instruction that is of higher intensity and greater duration and assessment that is more frequent. These students require significant instruction that is above and beyond what is provided in the core curriculum. The percentage of students who require support at this level should be around 5%. Ideally, it is a small percentage of the total student population.

If data indicate that the number of students requiring core, supplemental, and intensive instruction are similar to the guidelines set above, the core curriculum can be said to be working. It is meeting the needs of most of the students, and fewer students are requiring supplemental and intensive support. If data indicate larger percentages of students who require supplemental and intensive instruction, this may be an indication that the core curriculum is ineffective.

The following steps are provided by NASDSE (2008) in the *Response to Intervention Blueprints for Implementation: School Building Level* to assist schools in evaluating their core curricula.

1. Identify screening tools. A list of technically adequate tools can be found on the National Center for Progress Monitoring website (http://www .studentprogress.org). These tools should be valid, reliable, brief, standardized, and linked to outcomes on state assessments.

2. Identify proficiency cut points. Cut points will identify those in need, and they should not be arbitrary but, rather, supported by research.

3. Collect universal screening data. Data should be collected three times per year using the approach that works best for the school (small teams approach, classroom approach, etc.).

4. Enter, organize, summarize, and display the data. The percent of students deemed proficient and non-proficient should be especially noted here.

5. Determine the acceptable percentage for proficiency. Although 80-15-5 is the educational norm, there may be instances where other definitions of proficiency are delineated.

6. Identify students who are proficient and not proficient. This is determined to allow a comparison of the current state to expectations.

7. Make a comparison. Ask the question, "Is our core program sufficient?"

8. Create a plan of action. What is working? What needs to be changed?

Using the 80-15-5 guidelines, one of three situations can result when data is reviewed. The possible outcomes are:

1. Data indicate that all grade levels have at least 80% of their students meeting grade level benchmarks. The entire school is successful with the core curriculum.

2. The data indicate that all grade levels do not have at least 80% of their students meeting grade level benchmarks. The entire school is *not* successful with the core curriculum.

3. The data indicate that some grade levels have 80% of their students meeting grade level criteria and some grade levels do not have 80% of their students meeting grade level criteria. Some of the school is successful with the core curriculum while some of the school is not successful with the core curriculum.

In the first outcome, it is clear that most students are successful with the core, across grade levels. Although supplemental and intensive groups are still needed, most students perform well in the core curriculum. In the second outcome, it is clear that many students are not successful with the core across grade levels. A school in this situation would benefit most by changing their entire core curriculum, so students can be supported most efficiently. In the third outcome, some grade levels are meeting expectations, but some grade levels clearly require more support.

Finally, if data indicate that more than 20% of students require additional support across all grade levels, then this represents a significant issue. There are a number of questions that need to be answered. First, if the core is not effective, why is it not effective? What components may be missing? Second, can we supplement the core curriculum with all students to provide what they need? Is this a feasible and manageable option? Finally, if there seem to be many issues, should the core curriculum be changed? If so, what components in a new core program are necessary? These questions should be part of a schoolwide action plan that guides the school team for short and long term planning.

In summary, a primary component of the RTI model is evaluating the core curriculum using schoolwide data. It is not the new method for LD evaluation, but rather a systemic approach designed to turn the spotlight on the system. For far too long, schools would look to within-student factors when they struggled, rather than considering the instruction and curriculum. By using schoolwide data, school teams can identify the impact of the core curriculum and its level of success. If data indicate that the core curriculum is not successful, it is clear that the most effective and efficient step to take is to change the core curriculum. By doing so, students are supported earlier, which is the greatest method for ensuring a trajectory of success.

[References omitted by the author.]

KELLY MCGRAW
The Chicago School of Professional Psychology
Fourth edition

EVALUATION (*See Curriculum-Based Assessment; Evidence-Based Practice; Response to Intervention*)

EVENT RECORDING

Event recording is a direct observation method that is used in a systematic fashion to determine the frequency of a targeted behavior. Event recording is most suitable for the measurement of discrete behaviors (Wolery, Bailey, & Sugai, 1988). A discrete behavior is a behavior that has a distinguishable beginning and end and that is typically equivalent in duration (Sulzer-Azaroff & Mayer, 1991). Examples of discrete behaviors include correct verbal responding, hand raising, hitting, and the number of questions a student asked during an instructional period.

As with any systematic direct observation system, the first step is to operationally define the target behavior. An operational definition is a written statement that precisely defines the behavior you wish to measure in terms that are observable, measurable, and replicable (Fletcher-Janzen & De Pry, 2003). Next, the observer should define the observation period, including recording the start and stop times. Finally, the data collector will carefully observe the person of concern. When he or she observes a behavior that matches the operational definition, a tally mark will be recorded on the data collection sheet. At the end of the observation period, the total number of tally marks will be added and graphed as the frequency of the behavior for that observation session. In some cases, the teacher or researcher might be interested in the rate of the targeted behavior. The rate of behavior can be calculated by dividing the frequency of the behavior over the total time of the observation period. For example, 60 behaviors over a 30-minute observation period would yield a rate of 2 behaviors per minute.

One of the many benefits of event recording is ease of use. Teachers and researchers typically tally the number of behaviors on a data-collection sheet. However, other methods, such as mechanical counters, moving paper clips from one pile to another, using computer software that is loaded on a laptop or a handheld device, and using a pocket calculator to count the occurrences of a behavior, are equally as effective and can increase the efficiency of this data collection method (Alberto & Troutman, 2006).

As with all direct observation systems, collecting interobserver reliability (IOR) data is critical. The formula for calculating simple interobserver reliability for event recording is taking the number of agreements divided by the number of agreements plus disagreements and then multiplying by 100. This formula will give you the percent of agreement between the primary observer and an independent observer. However, this simple calculation does not account for chance occurrence of agreement. To calculate the IOR and account for chance reporting Kappa is more appropriate. See Interrater Reliability for complete information

REFERENCES

Alberto, P. A., & Troutman, A. C. (2006). *Applied behavior analysis for teachers* (7th ed.). Upper Saddle River, NJ: Prentice Hall.

Fletcher-Janzen, E., & De Pry, R. L. (2003). *Teaching social competence and character: An IEP planner with goals, objectives, and interventions.* Longmont, CO: Sopris West Educational Services.

Sulzer-Azaroff, B., & Mayer, G. R. (1991). *Behavior analysis for lasting change.* Fort Worth, TX: Harcourt Brace.

Wolery, M., Bailey, D., Jr., & Sugai, G. (1988). *Effective teaching: Principles and procedures of applied behavior analysis with exceptional students.* Boston: Allyn & Bacon.

RANDALL L. DE PRY
University of Colorado at Colorado Springs

KIMBERLY VANNEST
Texas A&M University
Fourth edition

See also Behavioral Assessment; Interrater Reliability

EVIDENCE-BASED PRACTICE

Evidence-based practice (EBP) is a term broadly used in many health care and education fields to refer to practice that is informed by the findings and conclusions of research. The origins of the term are most often attributed to the evidence-based medicine movement, which formally begin in 1981 when a group of clinical epidemiologists published a series of articles in the *Canadian Medical Association Journal* to guide clinicians on how to read journal articles (Guyatt, 2002). This series spawned a similar series in the *Journal of the American Medical Association* between 1993 and 2000, resulting in the *Users' Guides to the Medical Literature: A Manual for Evidence-Based Clinical Practice* (Guyatt & Rennie, 2002), a definitive text on the principles and processes of EBP. Although this text was developed to specifically apply to evidence-based medicine, its guidelines can be applied to EPB in other fields.

According to Guyatt et al. (2002), EBP "acknowledges that intuition [and] unsystematic clinical experience... are insufficient grounds for clinical decision making; and it stresses the examination of evidence from clinical research" (p. 4). At the same time, one fundamental principle of EBP is that research evidence alone, without consideration of the individual situation, is never enough to make a clinical decision. Guyatt et al. assert that decisions must also include consideration of risks and benefits, inconvenience, costs, and patient values. Other factors to be considered when integrating research into practice include the similarity between the practice population and the participants of the research (e.g., the most well-tested intervention in the research literature for a particular problem might have only been tested with 12-year-olds, whereas a practitioner might be working with a 6-year-old) and the fit between the setting characteristics and the research recommendations (e.g., research might suggest that an intervention should be administered in the home, but the practice setting does not have the resources to do so). EBP requires practitioners to use their clinical training and decision-making skills to determine how best to apply research results to individual cases.

The second fundamental principle of EBP is that there is a hierarchy of evidence to guide decision making (Guyatt et al., 2002). For example, results from a study that tests a behavioral intervention in several different schools should be given more weight than the results of a study testing that intervention in a single classroom, which in turn would be given more weight than a case study testing that intervention with a single child. Factors to be considered when determining the relative utility of different forms of evidence include the type of study design (e.g., a randomized study comparing an intervention group with a control group provides stronger evidence than a single case study), the quality of the study design (e.g., a study involving random assignment of participants to groups likely provides stronger evidence than a study comparing self-selected groups), the quality of the study measurement (e.g., a study that demonstrates effects of an intervention on child mental health, family functioning, and academic outcomes provides stronger evidence than a study only demonstrating effects on child mental health alone), and the size of the evidence base (e.g., an intervention that has been tested in several studies has more evidence supporting its use than an intervention only tested in a single study).

Cournoyer and Powers (2002) have posited that EBP also dictates that "every client system, over time, should be individually evaluated to determine the extent to which the predicted results have been attained as a direct consequence of the practitioners' actions" (p. 15). In other words, EBP involves a scientific approach not only to making clinical decisions, but also to monitoring the consequences of those decisions.

The Empirically Supported Treatments (ESTs; e.g., Chambliss & Ollendick, 2001; see entry for Empirically Supported Treatment) movement in clinical psychology and other efforts to list specific EBPs (e.g., The Evidence-Based Intervention Workgroup in school psychology; e.g., Kratochwill & Shernoff, 2003) represent a form of EBP. However, EBPs are not necessarily limited to interventions on these types of lists, as these lists often only include treatments that have particular kinds and levels of evidence supporting their use and typically do not list treatments that fall below these evidence thresholds or that have different types of evidence for their support. By contrast, EBP, while placing preferential weight to more rigorously tested research conclusions, involves consideration of the full range of available evidence.

REFERENCES

Chambliss, D. L., & Ollendick, T. H. (2001). Empirically supported psychological interventions: Controversies and evidence. *Annual Review of Psychology, 52*, 685–716.

Cournoyer, B. R., & Powers, G. T. (2002). Evidence-based social work: The quiet revolution continues. In A. R. Roberts & G. Green (Eds.), *The social work desk references* (pp. 798–806). New York, NY: Oxford University Press.

Guyatt, C. (2002). Preface. In G. Guyatt & D. Rennie (Eds.), *Users' guide to the medical literature: A manual for evidence-based clinical practice* (pp. 3–12). Chicago, IL: American Medical Association.

Guyatt, G., & Rennie, D. (Eds.). (2002). *Users' guide to the medical literature: A manual for evidence-based clinical practice.* Chicago, IL: American Medical Association.

Guyatt, C., Haynes, B., Jaeschke, R., Cook, D., Greenhalgh, T., Meade, M., ... Richardson, W. S. (2002). Introduction: The philosophy of evidence-based medicine. In G. Guyatt & D. Rennie (Eds.), *Users' guide to the medical literature: A manual for evidence-based clinical practice* (pp. 3–12). Chicago, IL: American Medical Association.

Kratochwill, T. R. & Shernoff, E. S. (2003). Evidence-based practice: Promoting evidence-based interventions in school psychology. *School Psychology Quarterly, 18*, 389–408.

AMANDA JENSEN DOSS
Texas A&M University

See also Empirically Supported Treatment; Intervention in School and Clinic; Response to Intervention

EVIDENCE-BASED PROGRAMS

Evidence-based programs (EBP) in the field of special education are instructional practices that have been proven effective through the rigors of controlled scientific examination. The standards used in defining EBP may vary across disciplines, however prominent criteria include research design, quantity of research, methodological quality and magnitude of effect to evaluate research standards (Cook, Tankersley, & Landrum, 2009). The purpose for identifying and selecting EBP is to ensure that students receive the highest quality of instruction (Wang & Spillane, 2009) that enhances educational outcomes and improves students' quality of life.

Within the field of special education, research methods to determine effectiveness of an EBP may include sets of experimental, quasi-experimental group, single-subject design, or some combination (Reichow, Volkmar, & Cicchetti, 2008). Experimental designs must include a pretest and a posttest, a treatment group, a control group, and random assignment of study participants to either the treatment or control group. Quasi-experimental research incorporates many characteristics of the experimental design, but it does not include random assignment. Single-subject research designs focus on an individual or select group of individuals, who serve as their own control (Horner et al., 2005).

Multiple peer-reviewed studies must produce similar intervention results to verify effectiveness of treatment outcomes. Peer-review research refers to research that has been assessed by qualified independent evaluators who have determined that the procedures meet the standards of scientific rigor before the research is published (Federal Register, Aug. 14, 2006). This process ensures that educators can select instructional procedures that are empirically validated (Etscheidt & Curran, 2010) and, thus, are effective for teaching students with disabilities (Yell, Shriner, & Katsiyannis, 2006). The number of studies required to substantiate an intervention may vary depending on the organization determining EBP.

Methodological quality refers to the degree to which a study is free of bias or systematic errors. It should be determined through detailed reporting of participants, settings, independent and dependent variables, and include evidence of implementation fidelity (Cook et al., 2009). Additional methodological requirements include verification that the change in treatment is due to the intervention, demonstration that outcomes are deemed worthwhile to the subject and their environment and evidence of relevance for other participants, materials and behaviors (Horner et al., 2005). An evidence-based program employs empirical methods and relies on rigorous data analysis (No Child Left Behind, 2001, pp. 126–127) to demonstrate a meaningful degree of change.

Effect size refers to a statistical analysis that calculates the magnitude of change (Gersten et al., 2005) within a group design study. The degree of treatment effect in single-subject designs is determined through visual analysis of data for each condition of a study. A specific data pattern is required to verify change in the dependent variable as a function of the independent variable (Horner et al., 2005).

The selection of appropriate EBP for a student is determined through the analysis of the student characteristics, student assessment information, examination of current and future environmental needs, and individual and family preferences. Several EBP will typically be integrated throughout a single teaching session to provide competent instruction (Natinal Autism Center, 2008). For example, a teacher may employ the use of time-delay prompting and differential reinforcement while instructing a child to put materials away. When determining which teaching procedure to apply, consideration should be given to the educator's qualifications and their ability to identify and proficiently apply EBP. Program staff should have access to training that ensures comprehension and application of the selected practices supported by the latest research (Yell et al., 2006). To ensure efficacy, it is essential to adhere to the original research parameters; therefore, implementation fidelity should be regularly monitored. Assessment of intervention integrity may include direct measurements, indirect measures, and permanent products (Gresham, 2000) as methods to ensure program fidelity.

Although a large body of well-established programs supported by research exists, there remain issues surrounding EBP implementation. For example, although many programs have been identified as scientifically proven practices in general education, minimal evidence-based interventions have been supported for students with Autism Spectrum Disorders (Odom et al., 2010) and other severe disabilities. When research is available, educators may have misconceptions regarding the findings and the feasibility of implementing the practice. Studies conclude that a significant number of teachers lacked confidence in research results (Boardman, Arguelles, Vaughn, Hughes, & Klingner, 2005) and a low percentage of educational

Table E.9. Resources and Websites for Identifying Evidence-Based Practices in Special Education

Organization	Website
National Professional Development Center on Autism Spectrum Disorders	http://autismpdc.fpg.unc.edu/content/evidence-based-practices
Promising Practices Network	http://www.promisingpractices.net/programs.asp
What Works Clearinghouse	http://ies.ed.gov/

decision makers demonstrate familiarity with evidence-based interventions (Shernoff, Kratochwill, & Stoiber, 2003). In response to these concerns, government and professional organizations have been established to provide educators with resources to make informed programming decisions. The resources shown in Table E.9 may be useful in finding educational practices that have been identified as effective and supported by evidence.

REFERENCES

Boardman, A. G., Arguelles, M. E., Vaughn, S., Hughes, M. T., & Klingner, J. (2005). Special education teachers' views of research-based practices. *Journal of Special Education*, 39(3), 168–180. doi: 10.1177/00224669050390030401

Cook, B. G., Tankersley, M., & Landrum, T. J. (2009). Determining evidence-based practices in special education. *Exceptional Children*, 75(3), 365–383.

Etscheidt, S., & Curran, C. M. (2010). Peer-reviewed research and individualized education programs (IEPs): An examination of intent and impact. *Exceptionality*, 18(3), 138–150. doi: 10.1080/09362835.2010.491988

Federal Register. (2006, August 14). *Rules and Regulations, 71*, 466–464.

Gersten, R., Fuchs, L. S., Compton, D., Coyne, M., Greenwood, C., & Innocenti, M. S. (2005). Quality indicators for group experimental and quasi-experimental research in special education. *Exceptional Children*, 71(2), 149–164.

Gresham, F. (2000). Treatment integrity in learning disabilities intervention research: Do we really know how treatments are implemented? *Learning Disabilities Research & Practice*, 15(4), 198–205.

Horner, R. H., Carr, E. G., Halle, J., McGee, G., Odom, S., & Wolery, M. (2005). The use of single-subject research to identify evidence-based practice in special education. *Exceptional Children*, 71(4), 165–180.

Natonal Autism Center. (2008). *National Standards Project*. Retrieved from http://www.nationalautismcenter.org/affiliates/

National Professional Development Center on Autism Spectrum Disorders. *Evidence-based practice briefs*. (n.d.). Retrieved November 16, 2011, from http://autismpdc.fpg.unc.edu/content/briefs

Odom, S. L., Collet-Klingenberg, L., R., Rogers, S. J., & Hatton, D. D. (2010). Evidence-based practices in pnterventions for children and youth with autism spectrum disorders. *Preventing School Failure, 54*(4), 275–282. doi: 10.1080/10459881003785506.

Promising Practices Network. (n.d.). *Programs that Work.* Retrieved November 16, 2011, from http://www.promisingpractices.net/programs.asp

Reichow, B., Volkmar, F. R., & Cicchetti, D. V. (2008). Development of the evaluative method for evaluating and determining evidence-based practices in autism. *Journal of Autism and Developmental Disorders, 38*(7), 1311–1319. doi: 10.1007/s10803-007-0517-7

Shernoff, E. S., Kratochwill, T. R., & Stoiber, K. C. (2003). Training in evidence-based interventions (EBIs): What are school psychology programs teaching? *Journal of School Psychology, 41*(6), 467–483. doi: 10.1016/j.jsp.2003.07.002

Wang, P. S., & Spillane, A. (2009). Evidence-based social skills interventions for children with autism: A meta-analysis. *Education and Training in Developmental Disabilities, 44*(3), 318–342.

What Works Clearinghouse. (n.d.). Retrieved November 1, 2011, from http://ies.ed.gov/ncee/wwc/

Yell, M. L., Shriner, J. G., & Katsiyannis, A. (2006). Individuals with Disabilities Education Improvement Act of 2004 and IDEA regulations of 2006: Implications for educators, administrators, and teacher trainers. *Focus on Exceptional Children, 39*(1), 1–24.

JODI M. CHOLEWICKI-CARROLL
University of South Carolina
Fourth edition

EVIDENCE-BASED SECONDARY TRANSITION PRACTICES

Evidence-based practices (EBP) are an outgrowth of the call for teachers to use scientifically based instructional strategies in the early 2000s. First, the No Child Left Behind Act (NCLB, 2001) required schools to ensure that all students had access to effective, scientifically based instructional strategies derived from scientifically based research. Scientifically based research was defined as research that involved the use of "rigorous, systematic, and objective procedures to obtain reliable and valid knowledge relevant to education activities and programs" [20 U.S.C § 7901(37)]. Next, the Individuals with Disabilities Education Improvement Act (IDEA, 2004) reinforced this by calling for the use of scientifically-based instruction with students with disabilities.

In response to calls for teachers to use instructional strategies based on scientifically based research, the Division of Research of the Council for Exceptional Children published a special issue of *Exceptional Children* in December, 2005. In this special issue, Odom, Brantlinger, Gersten, Horner, Thompson, and Harris (2005) used the term "evidence-based practice" to refer to educational practices that have been demonstrated effective based on quality research. The remaining articles in the special issue suggested quality indicators for group and quasi-experimental research (Gersten et al., 2005), single-subject research (Horner et al., 2005), correlational research (Thompson, Diamond, McWilliam, Snyder, & Snyder, 2005), and qualitative research (Brantlinger, Jimenez, Klingner, Pugash, & Richardson (2005). However, to meet the requirements of NCLB and IDEA, instructional practices must be based on research that demonstrated a practice was the "cause" of improved student learning (Cook, Tankersley, Cook, & Landrum, 2008). As a result, the only research designs that can demonstrate experimental control of an independent variable (or practice) on a dependent variable (or student behavior) are group and quasi-experiment and single subject designs. Finally, Horner et al. (2005) defined a practice as "a curriculum, behavioral intervention, systems, change, or educational approach designed for use by…with the express expectation that implementation will result in measurable educational, social, behavioral, or physical benefit" (p. 175).

Recently, the National Secondary Transition Technical Assistance Center (NSTTAC) conducted a comprehensive literature review to identify evidence-based secondary transition practices (see Test et al., 2009 for a detailed description of inclusion criteria, procedures used to identify quality of research, and criteria used to identify a practice as "evidence-based"). Using criteria for high-quality research and evidence-based practice suggested by Gersten et al. (2005) and Horner et al. (2005) NSTTAC originally identified 32 secondary transition practices. These practices were labeled by the dependent variable (or skill learned) rather than the independent variable. This was done because NSTTAC assumed teachers would want information on teaching a specific skill (e.g., teaching grocery shopping), rather than the method used to teach the skill (e.g., using constant time delay). However, recently, NSTTAC updated the list of evidence-based secondary transition practices to include both the independent and dependent variables (see Table E.10).

Since the term *evidence-based practice* is relatively new, in order to avoid confusion, it must be differentiated from other terms such as *best practice* and research-based practice. First, over time, the term *best practice* has come to mean a practice supported by a wide range of evidence including personal experience and opinion, as well as possible research (Peters & Heron, 1993). As a result, it is difficult to be clear about whether a best practice is suppressed by research evidence. As a solution, the term *research-based practice* has been suggested. Research-based practices are based on research using rigorous designs and have a demonstrated record of success (i.e., more than one study) improving student outcomes. Although research-based practices are more clearly supported by multiple studies using rigorous research designs than are best-practices they are still not evidence-based

Table E.10. Current List of Evidence-Based Practices in Secondary Transition

Using **Backward Chaining** to teach
- Functional Life Skills

Using *Check and Connect* to promote:
- Student Participation in the IEP Meeting

Using **Computer Assisted Instruction** to teach:
- Food Preparation and Cooking Skills
- Grocery Shopping Skills
- Job Specific Skills
- Student Participation in the IEP Meeting

Using **Technology** to teach:
- Academic Skills

Using **Community Based Instruction** to teach:
- Banking Skills
- Grocery Shopping Skills
- Community Integration Skills
- Purchasing Skills
- Safety Skills
- Communication Skills
- Employment Skills

Using **Constant Time Delay** to teach:
- Banking Skills
- Food Preparation and Cooking Skills
- Functional Life Skills
- Leisure Skills
- Job Specific Skills

Using an **Extension of Career Planning Services after Graduation** to promote:
- Increased Finance Skills

Using **Forward Chaining** to teach:
- Home Maintenance Skills

Using the **One More Than Strategy** to teach:
- Counting Money
- Purchasing Skills

Using **Peer Assisted Instruction** to teach:
- Academic Skills

Using **Progressive Time Delay** to teach:
- Purchasing Skills
- Safety Skills
- Functional Life Skills

Using **Response Prompting** to teach:
- Food Preparation and Cooking Skills
- Grocery Shopping Skills
- Home Maintenance Skills
- Laundry Tasks
- Leisure Skills
- Purchasing Skills
- Sight Word Reading
- Social Skills
- Employment Skills

Table E.10. (Continued)

Using **Mnemonics** to teach:
- Completing a Job Application
- Academic Skills

Using **Static Picture Prompts** to teach:
- Purchasing Skills

Using **Video Modeling** to teach:
- Food Preparation and Cooking
- Home Maintenance Skills

Using **Visual Displays** to teach:
- Academic Skills

Using **Published Curricula** to teach:
- Student Involvement in the IEP

Using the *Self-Advocacy Strategy* to teach:
- Student Participation in the IEP Meeting

Using the *Self-Directed IEP* to teach:
- Student Participation in the IEP Meeting

Using The *Self Determined Learning Model of Instruction* to teach:
- Goal Attainment

Using *Whose Future Is It Anyway?* to teach:
- Self-Determination Skills
- Student Knowledge to Transition Planning

Using **Self-Management Instruction** to teach:
- Academic Skills
- Social Skills
- Job Specific Skills

Using **Self-Monitoring Instruction** to teach:
- Functional Life Skills

Using **Simulations** to teach:
- Banking Skills
- Purchasing Skills
- Social Skills

Using a **System of Least to Most Prompts** to teach:
- Food Preparation and Cooking Skills
- Grocery Shopping Skills
- Purchasing Skills
- Safety Skills
- Functional Life Skills
- Communication Skills
- Specific Job Skills

Using a **System of Most to Least Prompts** to teach:
- Functional Life Skills

Using **Total Task Chaining** to teach:
- Functional Life Skills

Using **Training Modules** to promote:
- Parent Involvement in the Transition Process

practices. Evidence-based practices are those based on research that have (a) used rigorous research designs, (b) demonstrated a record of success for improving student outcomes, and (c) undergone a systematic review process using quality indicators to evaluate level of evidence. As a result of Test et al. (2009) and NSTTAC, it is possible to state that Table E.10 is a list of evidence-based secondary transition practices.

REFERENCES

Cook, B. G., Tankersley, M., Cook, L., & Landrum, T. J., (2008). Evidence-based practices in special education: Some practical considerations. *Intervention in School and Clinic, 44*(2), 69–75.

Brantlinger, E., Jimenez, R., Klingner, J., Pugach, M., & Richardson, V. (2005). Qualitative studies in special education. *Exceptional Children, 71*, 195–207.

Gersten, R., Fuchs, L. S., Compton, D., Coyne, M., Greenwood, C., & Innocenti, M. S. (2005). Quality indicators for group experimental and quasi-experimental research in special education. *Exceptional Children, 71*, 149–164.

Horner, R. H., Carr, E. G., Halle, J., McGee, G., Odom, S., & Wolery, M. (2005). The use of single-subject research to identify evidence-based practice in special education. *Exceptional Children, 71*, 165–179.

Individuals with Disabilities Education Improvement Act of 2004, P. L. No. 108-446, 20 U.S.C.

No Child Left Behind Act of 2001, Pub. L. No. 107-110, 115 Stat.1425 (2002).

Odom, S. L., Brantlinger, E., Gersten, R., Horner, R. H., Thompson, B., & Harris, K. R. (2005). Research in special education: Scientific methods and evidence-based practices. *Exceptional Children, 71*, 137–148.

Peters, M. T., & Heron, T. E. (1993). When the best is not good enough: An examination of best practice. *Journal of Special Education, 26*, 371–385.

Test, D. W., Fowler, C. H., Richter, S. M., White, J., Mazzotti, V., Walker, A. R.,…Kortering, L. (2009). Evidence-based practices in secondary transition. *Career Development for Exceptional Individuals, 32*, 160–181.

Thompson, B., Diamond, K. E., McWilliam, R., Snyder, P., & Snyder, S. W. (2005). Evaluating the quality of evidence from correlational research for evidence-based practice. *Exceptional Children, 71*, 181–194.

DAVID W. TEST
University of North Carolina at Charlotte
Fourth edition

EXCEPTIONAL CHILDREN

Exceptional Children (EC) is the official scholarly journal of the Council for Exceptional Children (CEC), and has been published continuously since 1934. This peer-review journal publishes research, research reviews, methodological reviews of literature, data-based position papers, and policy analyses on the education and development of children and youth with exceptionalities. *EC* is published quarterly.

REFERENCE

Exceptional Children. Retrieved November 5, 2011, from http://www.cec.sped.org/

THOMAS E. ALLEN
Gallaudet College
First edition

TAMARA J. MARTIN
The University of Texas of the Permian Basin
Second edition

SHANNON A. GRANT
Texas A&M University
Third edition

EXHIBITIONISM

Exhibitionism is defined as the deliberate exposure of one's genitals in order to elicit shock and emotional distress from an unsuspecting person for the purpose of sexual gratification. The perpetrator is usually male, and the victim is usually a woman or a child. It is considered a paraphilia—a condition in which an individual is dependent on an unusual and personally or socially unacceptable stimulus for sexual arousal—and has been termed peiodeiktophilia when the penis is exposed (Money, 1984). Although the condition is considered common, there are no exact figures with regard to incidence or prevalence (Rhoads, 1989).

Characteristics

1. Sexual gratification is achieved by arousing shock or fear in victims. This arousal satisfies the exposer's sexual drive and replaces the desire for genital intercourse.

2. Exhibitionism can occur in children as young as 10, but the average age of diagnosis is 21 years old. Most diagnosed with the disorder display exhibitionistic behavior by the age of 17 (Abel, Osborn, Twigg, 1993; Smith & Monastersky, 1986).

3. The urge to expose one's genitals is compulsive and addictive in nature.
4. The frequency, intensity, and character of the behavior vary greatly from individual to individual.
5. Individuals are often socially isolated and socially immature.
6. "Mooning," or exposing the buttocks, which is considered a prank or an act of defiance, is not considered exhibitionism if it is not sexually arousing for the exposer (Arndt, 1995).

Children often engage in exhibitionistic and voyeuristic behaviors with other children and adults at an early age. By the age of 4 years, children typically initiate or become involved in games in which there is undressing or sexual exploration (Gil & Johnson, 1993). By school age, children develop feelings of privacy, and latency-aged children (approximately 7 to 12) may engage in a range of sexual interests that may or may not involve exhibitionistic behavior.

Because there is no physical contact involved, exhibitionism has been called a hands-off sexual offense and is one of the most often-reported hands-off offenses. Sixty-five percent of people who expose themselves have committed a prior sexual offense (Fehrenbach, Smith, Monastersky, & Deisher, 1986). The recidivism rate for exhibitionism is greater than for all other sex offenses (Kelley & Byrne, 1992). Some adolescent exhibitionists will go on to commit hands-on sexual offenses such as sexual assault. Exhibitionists often have habitual patterns of victim selection, styles of exposing, and preferred sites. Masturbatory behavior may occur before, during, or subsequent to the incident. Offenders often report antecedent fantasies as well (Ross & Loss, 1991). Hands-off adolescent offenders are typically better adjusted in school, less likely to be delinquent, less disturbed, and less likely to have a history of sexual abuse than are hands-on offenders (Saunders, Awad, & White, 1986). Exhibitionists are also more developmentally immature, have more issues of trust and shame, focus on short-term gratification, and exhibit more feelings of isolation and despair (Miner & Dwyer, 1997).

Treatment for children who expose their genitals usually includes individual and family therapy. For adolescent and adult offenders, a wide range of treatment modalities is available, including psychotherapy, cognitive therapy, and behavioral therapy. Some authors suggest that a multimodal therapeutic approach is warranted, usually initiated and backed by a court order. This approach involves behavioral-management techniques for quick control of the symptoms, combined with group therapy or individual therapy that addresses personality deficits and immaturities of the patient (Rhoads, 1989). Another approach is

hormone therapy with an antiandrogen concurrent with psychotherapy (Money, 1988). Moralizing, punishment, and legal threats are largely ineffective as treatments for adolescent and adult exhibitionists. Almost all interventions appear to produce only temporary reduction of the aberrant behavior (Rhoads, 1989).

Children and adolescents who expose themselves may have other behavioral or emotional problems that would come to the attention of the education system and qualify for services under a severely emotionally disturbed category. If the child's behavior is disruptive in the school or day-care setting, this may warrant contact with a mental health professional. Adolescents who expose themselves compulsively and for sexual gratification may not demonstrate the behavior within the school system, and any intervention would most likely be through the legal system.

Because exhibitionists are generally poorly motivated in therapy, prognosis for recovery is difficult to predict. Research is continuing with regard to prevention, assessment, and treatment of exhibitionists, especially in the area of pharmacological treatments.

REFERENCES

Abel, G. G., Osborn, C. A., & Twigg, D. A. (1993). Sexual assault through the life span: Adult offenders with juvenile histories. In H. E. Barbaree, W. L. Marshall, & S. M. Hudson (Eds.), *The juvenile sex offender* (pp. 104–117). New York, NY: Guilford Press.

Arndt, W. B. (1995). Deviant sexual behavior in children and adolescents. In G. A. Rekers (Ed.), *Handbook of child and adolescent sexual problems* (pp. 424–445). Lexington, MA: Lexington Books.

Fehrenbach, P. A., Smith, W., Monastersky, C., & Deisher, R. W. (1986). Adolescent sexual offenders: Offender and offense characteristics. *American Journal of Orhopsychiatry, 56*(2), 225–233.

Gil, E., & Johnson, T. E. (1993). *Sexualized children*. Rockville, MD: Launch Press.

Kelley, K., & Byrne, D. (1992). *Exploring human sexuality*. Englewood Cliffs, NJ: Prentice-Hall.

Miner, M. H., & Dwyer, S. M. (1997). The psychosocial development of sex offenders: Differences between exhibitionists, child molesters, and incest offenders. *International Journal of Offender Therapy and Comparative Criminology, 41*(1), 36–44.

Money, J. (1984). Paraphilias: Phenomenology and classification. *American Journal of Psychotherapy, 38*(2), 164–179.

Money, J. (1988). *Lovemaps: Clinical concepts of sexual/erotic health and pathology, paraphilia, and gender transposition in childhood, adolescence, and maturity*. Buffalo, NY: Prometheus Books.

Rhoads, J. M. (1989). Exhibitionism and voyeurism. In American Psychiatric Association Task Force on Treatments of Psychiatric Disorders (Ed.), *Treatments of psychiatric disorders: A task force report of the American Psychiatric Association*

(Vol. 1, pp. 670–673). Washington, DC: American Psychiatric Press.

Ross, J., & Loss, P. (1991). Assessment of the juvenile sex offender. In G. D. Ryan & S. L. Lane (Eds.), *Juvenile sexual offending: Causes, consequences, and correction* (pp. 199–251). Lexington, MA: Lexington Books.

Saunders, E., Awad, G. A., & White, G. (1986). Male adolescent sexual offenders: The offender and the offense. *Canadian Journal of Psychiatry, 3,* 542–549.

Smith, W. R., & Monastersky, C. (1986). Assessing juvenile sexual offenders' risk for reoffending. *Criminal Justice and Behavior, 13,* 115–140.

STEPHANIE R. FORNESS
BRIAN D. JOHNSON
University of Northern Colorado

EXPECTANCY AGE

Expectancy age refers to a method used to compare performance on an intelligence or scholastic aptitude measure with performance on an achievement measure. The practice most likely had its origins in the accomplishment ratio proposed by Raymond Franzen in 1920. Franzen advocated dividing a pupil's subject age, obtained from an achievement test, by his or her mental age, obtained from an intelligence test (Equation E.1):

$$100 = \frac{Subject\ age}{Mental\ age} = Subject\ ratio \qquad (E.1)$$

Equation E.1 was applied to each subject matter domain measured by a particular achievement test. Separate ratios were computed for reading, mathematics, and other subjects for which achievement test results were available. Subject ratios above 100 denoted performance greater than expected for the pupil's mental age, and subject ratios below 100 signified performance lower than expected for the pupil's mental age. The average of a pupil's subject ratios was termed the accomplishment quotient, an overall index of achievement in relation to mental age. A number of serious technical flaws resulted in the abandonment of the use of ratios in relating achievement to intellectual ability or capacity.

Present-day test developers and users, like their 1920 counterparts, continue to search for meaningful ways to relate intelligence and achievement test results. Government intervention in establishing procedures for identifying children with severe learning disabilities in connection with PL 94-142 has undoubtedly served to intensify pressures placed on test users. The proliferation of several discrepancy formulas that use age equivalents or grade equivalents has resulted in further confusion and inappropriate practices (Reynolds, 1981). For example, the use of a mental age, obtained either directly from an intelligence test or indirectly when only an IQ is available, to establish an expectancy age has sometimes occurred from solving for MA in Equation E.2:

$$MA = \frac{(CA)(IQ)}{100} \qquad (E.2)$$

Age equivalents in various achievement domains (e.g., reading, mathematics, spelling) are then compared one by one with the expectancy age to identify discrepancies between intelligence and achievement. Such practices are technically indefensible for the following reasons:

1. Age equivalents constitute a scale of unequal units. The difference in performance between an age equivalent of 6-0 and 7-0 is, for example, much greater than the difference in performance between an age equivalent of 14-0 and 15-0 for both the intelligence and the various achievement domains. In fact, an age equivalent must be extrapolated after about age 16 for most traits because there is little real growth beyond this age. Both the unequal units of the age equivalent scale and their artificial extension, or extrapolation, render them unsuitable for any sort of statistical manipulation. Thus the simple arithmetic operation of subtraction needed to search for discrepancies between ability and achievement is untenable.

2. Further difficulties with age equivalents result from their unequal variability, both at successive age levels within one subject matter domain as well as among different subject matter domains. The variability of age equivalents in arithmetic computation, for example, will be considerably smaller at a particular age level than that for reading comprehension. For this reason, there is no technically sound method to interpret discrepancies at different age levels within a single subject matter domain or across subject matter domains.

3. An added difficulty occurs when an attempt is made to compare age equivalents from tests having dissimilar norm groups. If the norming sample for an intelligence test differs from that for an achievement test, then observed discrepancies between age equivalents on the two measures may merely represent systematic differences between the two norm groups.

4. One other difficulty that must be mentioned in connection with such comparisons is the correlation between intelligence and achievement in various subject matter domains. Because the relationship between intelligence and reading comprehension, for example, differs from that for intelligence and arithmetic computation, the magnitude of observed discrepancies cannot be accepted at face

value without taking into account the phenomenon known as regression to the mean. Interpretation of differences is, thus, difficult because the correlation between each intelligence-achievement pairing differs both within a single age level as well as across age levels.

For these reasons, the practice of using an expectancy age as a benchmark for undertaking achievement test comparisons to identify pupils with suspected learning disabilities or atypical ability-achievement relationships cannot be recommended on technical or logical grounds.

This entry has been informed by the sources listed below.

REFERENCES

Franzen, R. (1920, November). The accomplishment quotient. *Teachers College Record*, 114–120.

Otis, A. S. (1925). *Statistical method in educational measurement.* New York, NY: Harcourt Brace Jovanovich.

Reynolds, C. (1981). The fallacy of "two years below grade level for age" as a diagnostic criterion for reading disorders. *Journal of School Psychology, 19*(4), 350–358.

GARY J. ROBERTSON
American Guidance Service

See also Grade Equivalents; Learning Disabilities, Severe Discrepancy Analysis In

EXPECTATIONS, POSITIVE BEHAVIOR SUPPORT

School-wide positive behavior support (SWPBS; Sugai & Horner, this volume) involves the establishment of processes and procedures intended for *all* students, staff, and settings across campus within a three-tiered continuum of support. The main components of primary-tier implementation include: (a) a committed team leading all PBS efforts, (b) establishing a data-based decision-making system, (c) positively stated behavior expectations and rules, (d) lesson plans to teach the expectations and rules, (e) procedures for encouraging expected behaviors, (f) procedures for discouraging violations of school-wide expectations and rules, and (g) a plan for monitoring effectiveness (Lewis & Sugai, 1999; George, Kincaid & Pollard-Sage, 2009). One overriding theme across components is the need to establish the expected (i.e., desired) behaviors across campus which would drive the data-based decision making (e.g., How many students are violating the expected behaviors? How many students are being rewarded for displaying the expected behaviors? What behaviors need to be retaught and encouraged?). Many students lose instructional time when the expectations for their performance (i.e., what is

expected of them behaviorally) are not defined, modeled, or practiced. By lacking a behavioral repertoire, students are more likely to create errors within their environment (i.e., break the rules), whether intentional or accidental.

Identifying Expected Behaviors

The identification and dissemination of behavioral expectations and rules are a critical component of establishing SWPBS with fidelity. Specifically, expectations are a list of broad, positively stated behaviors aligned with the school's mission statement that are desired of all students, faculty, and parents in all settings (Mayer, 1995; Mayer, 1999). Expectations are specific to a school, derived from the school's discipline data (i.e., what students are being referred for and need to do instead), and the values of the faculty and community. For example, if many students have been referred to the office for disrespect, tardies, fighting, and experience low achievement scores, a school may want their students to strive to be respectful, prepared, self-controlled, and active learners as indicated in Figure E.4.

Posters of the expectations throughout the school serve as visual reminders to students, staff, faculty, parents, and visitors of the campus and assist in building visibility, increasing buy-in, and maintaining support (George et al., 2009).

Defining Expected Behaviors

Once expectations are defined, rules for how these expectations look in particular settings are developed. A student displaying respect in the classroom may differ from how they are respectful in the cafeteria, restroom, or hallway. Therefore, rules are the specific, observable behaviors that assist in teaching the expectations across different settings. Table E.11 displays an example of an abbreviated "expectations by setting matrix" that

Figure E.4. School marquee displaying the school-wide behavioral expectations.

Table E.11. Expectations by Setting Matrix

Setting Rules → Expectations ↓	Hallways	Cafeteria	Recess
Be safe	Walk facing forward. Stay to the right except when directed otherwise.	Hold tray with two hands. Keep all food to self.	Use equipment safely. Follow game rules.
Be prepared	Have planner signed.	Have lunch money ready.	Be dressed out and in place on time.
Be respectful	Keep hands, feet, and objects to self. Use voices appropriately.	Keep hands, feet, and objects to self. Face forward and keep the line moving.	Keep hands, feet, and objects to self. Use polite language and respectful tone of voice.

identifies the school-wide expectations yet operationally defines the specific behavioral skills required across settings (only a few settings are displayed in the table). Establishing behavioral procedures for specific settings allows for uniform instruction across multiple programs; builds communication across faculty, staff, and parents; promotes curriculum design; and assists in professional accountability (George et al., 2009). By stating the rules positively, students can be easily taught what they are supposed to do rather than what they are not to do (Colvin, Kameenui, & Sugai, 1993; Mayer, 1995; Mayer, 1999).

Teaching Expected Behaviors

Once expectations and the operational definitions across settings (i.e., rules) have been developed, not only must they be posted on the walls throughout the school but these behavioral skills also must be taught. Appropriate behaviors are prerequisites for academics, procedures and routines create structure, and repetition is a factor in learning new skills. The school-based team may teach appropriate behavior through a variety of activities such as introductory kickoff events, ongoing direct instruction, embedding across curriculum and refresher trainings while the format may vary from rotating classes through stations, faculty coleading a school-wide assembly, and/or students performing skits on the morning news. The more that the expected (i.e., desired) behaviors are modeled by adults/staff on campus, students are provided with written and graphic cues in the setting where the behaviors are expected, efforts are acknowledged, plans to reteach and restructure teaching are developed, students participate in the development process, and "teachable" moments are used in core subject areas and during nonacademic times, the more likely the new skills will be acquired and successfully maintained (George et al., 2009).

Encouraging Expected Behaviors

Once the behavioral expectations and rules are developed and taught, the students, faculty and staff must be encouraged and acknowledged for displaying them

through rewards or incentives. Encouraging the expected behaviors increases the likelihood that desired behaviors will be repeated, focuses staff and student attention on the desired behaviors, fosters a positive school climate, reduces the need for engaging in time-consuming disciplinary measures, and continues to serve as an ongoing teaching tool (Florida's PBS Project, 2011). It is critical that rewards remain contingent on desired behavior despite the fact that the actual reward system is only one component of the primary-tier plan. Rewards should not drive the SWPBS process but rather assist in efforts by increasing awareness of positive behaviors and provide a reason for motivating students to use new skills such as the expected behaviors taught to them (George et al., 2009).

Conclusion

Establishing, teaching, and rewarding students, staff, and faculty the expected behaviors on campus not only increase the likelihood of behavior change but fosters a positive school environment focused on "what to do" as opposed to "what not to do," which is conducive to learning. Although expectations are established at the primary level of prevention and serve as the overall foundation of behavioral systems change, they are just as essential at the secondary and tertiary tiers of intervention. At the secondary level, students' behavior is compared across their peers and the expected behavioral goal is aligned with the school-wide expectations established at the school. For the tertiary tier, an individual student's behavior is compared with their peers, and interventions are identified to support the student in exhibiting the expected or desired behaviors, similar to their peers. The result is the establishment of expected behaviors of students, staff, and faculty, which is essential for overall systems change to occur across the continuum of supports.

REFERENCES

Colvin, G., Kameenui, E. J., & Sugai, G. (1993). Reconceptualizing behavior management and school-wide discipline in general education. *Education and Treatment of Children, 16,* 361–381.

Florida's Positive Behavior Support Project. Retrieved January 31, 2011, from http://flpbs.fmhi.usf.edu/

George, H. P., Kincaid, D. & Pollard-Sage, J. (2009). Primary tier interventions and supports. In W. Sailor, G. Dunlap, G. Sugai & R. Horner (Eds.), *Handbook of positive behavior support* (pp. 375–394). Lawrence, KS: Issues in Clinical Child Psychology.

Lewis, T. J., & Sugai, G. (1999). Effective behavior support: A systems approach to proactive school-wide management. *Focus on Exceptional Children, 31*, 1–24.

Mayer, G. R. (1995). Preventing antisocial behavior in schools. *Journal of Applied Behavior Analysis, 28*, 467–478.

Mayer, G. R. (1999). Constructive discipline for school personnel. *Education and Treatment of Children, 22*, 36–54.

HEATHER PESHAK GEORGE
University of South Florida–Tampa Bay
Fourth edition

EXPRESSIVE LANGUAGE DISORDERS (See Language Disorders)

EXPRESSIVE VOCABULARY TEST, SECOND EDITION

The Expressive Vocabulary Test, Second Edition (EVT-2, 2007) is an individually administered measure of expressive vocabulary and word retrieval. The battery is designed to be administered to individuals ages 2 years, 6 months through 90+ years and takes approximately 10 to 20 minutes to administer. Expressive vocabulary is tested through *labeling* items (designed for younger examinees) and *synonym* items (designed for older examinees). Word retrieval is determined through examination of the standard score differences between the EVT-2 and the Peabody Picture Vocabulary Test, Fourth Edition (PPVT-4; Dunn & Dunn, 2007), with which EVT-2 is co-normed. A computer scoring and report generation program is available for this instrument. A variety of scores are reported, including standard scores, percentile ranks, age equivalents, and growth scale values (a tool for monitoring progress over time).

Labeling items require children to name pictures or body parts presented, whereas synonym items require older examinees to provide a synonym for the target word and picture provided. Both labeling and synonym items are presented with pictures. The examinee responds to each item with a one-word answer. The presentation easel includes colorful pictures that are balanced for gender and ethnic representation, and these pictures were updated in this new edition of the test. The record form was updated to include all correct responses to each item, as well as the stimulus question itself. Additionally, the new edition

includes two forms of the test (Form A and Form B), each with 190 distinct items.

The EVT was co-normed with the PPVT-4, on a population of 3,540 examinees ages 2 years, 6 months to 90+ years (although fewer individuals were sampled who fell into the 70+ year age intervals). The sample was representative of the U.S. population in 2004 with respect to sex, gender, race/ethnicity, region, socioeconomic status, and special education status. Because the EVT and the PPVT-III were co-normed, scores from these measures are directly comparable.

The EVT-2 reliability analyses indicate a high degree of internal consistency. Spilt-half reliability coefficients ranged from 0.88 to 0.97, and the average internal alpha reliability was 0.96. Test-retest reliability coefficients derived from five studies of different aged samples ranged from 0.94 to 0.97, and alternate-forms reliability ranged from 0.83 to 0.91 with consistent reliability across age groups. Concurrent validation studies found EVT-2 scores to be moderately to highly correlated with other measures of vocabulary development, including the PPVT-4 (Dunn & Dunn, 2007), Comprehensive Assessment of Spoken Language (CASL; Carrow-Woolfolk, 1999), Clinical Evaluation of Language Fundamentals, Fourth Edition (CELF-4; Semel, Wiig, & Secord, 2003), and Group Reading Assessment and Diagnostic Evaluation (GRADE; Williams, 2001). Studies were also conducted to assess the different profiles of students with a variety of diagnoses associated with receiving special education services as compared to the profiles of students from the general population, and it was found that scores received by students in these populations did different from those scores received by other students.

Overall, the EVT-2 is a simple and well-constructed test that assesses one component of language development, and can be used in conjunction with the PPVT-4 to assess word retrieval problems. It should not be used as a solitary indicator of language disorders, but may be a useful tool when included in a broader battery.

REFERENCES

Carrow-Woolfolk, E. (1999). *Comprehensive assessment of spoken language*. Circle Pines, MN: American Guidance Service.

Dunn, L. M., & Dunn, D. M. (2007). *Peabody Picture Vocabulary Test, fourth edition*. Bloomington, MN: NCS Pearson.

Semel, E., Wiig, E. H., & Secord, W. A. (2003). *Clinical evaluation of language fundamentals, Fourth Edition*. San Antonio, TX: Psychological Corporation.

Williams, K. T. (2001). *Group reading assessment and diagnostic evaluation*. Circle Pines, MN: American Guidance Service.

ADDITIONAL READING

Graham, T. (2010). Review of the Expressive Vocabulary Test, second edition. In R. A. Spies, J. F. Spies, and K. F. Gesinger

(Eds.), *The eighteenth mental measurements yearbook*. Lincoln, NE: Buros Institute of Mental Measurements.

Rathvon, N. (2010). Review of the Expressive Vocabulary Test, second edition. In R. A. Spies, J. F. Spies, and K. F. Gesinger (Eds.), *The eighteenth mental measurements yearbook*. Lincoln, NE: Buros Institute of Mental Measurements.

Williams, K. T. (2007). *Expressive Vocabulary Test manual*. Circle Pines, MN: American Guidance Service, Inc.

JAMIE ZIBULSKY
Fairleigh Dickinson University

KATHLEEN VIEZEL
Fairleigh Dickinson University

RON DUMONT
Fairleigh Dickinson University

JOHN O. WILLIS
Rivier College
Fourth edition

EXTENDED SCHOOL YEAR FOR CHILDREN WITH DISABILITIES

Following the passage of the Education for All Handicapped Children Act of 1975, and between 1977 and 1981, 46 cases were filed in state and federal courts to contest the unwillingness of local educational agencies to provide special education for a period beyond the traditional school year (Marvell, Galfo, & Rockwell, 1981). The issue in those cases was whether a state or local policy of refusing to consider or provide education beyond the regular school year (usually 180 days) for children with disabilities violated mandates under Part B of the Education of the Handicapped Act (EHA).

In the leading case, *Battle* v. *Pennsylvania* (1980), the federal Third Circuit Court of Appeals held that Pennsylvania's inflexible application of a 180-day maximum school year prevented the proper formulation of appropriate educational goals and was, therefore, incompatible with the EHA's emphasis on the individual. Most of the courts that have considered limitations on the length of the school year, as applied to children with disabilities, have invalidated them for essentially the same reasons stated in the *Battle* decision.

The court decisions have provided some general guidelines, but controversial areas remain relative to the provision of extended-year services to children with disabilities. One major issue relates to determining which children with disabilities are eligible for extended-year services. Generally, the individual plaintiffs or class of plaintiffs involved in those lawsuits consisted of children with severe disabilities, a term that generally is not confined to a separate and specific category but indicates a degree of disability that necessitates intensified services. Courts have made it clear that determination of whether a child will receive a program in excess of the traditional school year must be made on an individual basis. To prevail, an individual must demonstrate that such a program is required for a particular child to benefit from the education provided during the preceding school year, in accordance with the interpretation of "free appropriate public education" set forth by the U.S. Supreme Court in *Board of Education* v. *Rowley* (1982).

Courts generally have accepted the argument advanced in the *Battle* case that children with severe disabilities, as compared with children without disabilities, have greater difficulty in acquiring and transferring skills, are more likely to lose a greater number of skills over time (or regress), and take a longer time to recoup those skills. There is disagreement, however, about whether a continuous program of education, without extended breaks, would lessen the likelihood of regression in certain children with severe disabilities. In accordance with the *Rowley* decision, courts have stressed the importance of the individualized education program (IEP) process mandated by the Individuals with Disabilities Education Act (IDEA) in educational decision making regarding extended-year services (e.g., *Crawford* v. *Pittman*, 1983).

Another major area of controversy concerns the cost of extended-year services. Courts have rejected arguments by school officials that limited fiscal resources justify limitations on the services that may be provided for children with disabilities. Since *Mills* v. *Board of Education* (1972), courts have almost uniformly held that lack of funds may not limit the availability of appropriate educational services for children with disabilities more severely than for children without disabilities (Sales et al., 1999).

More recently, IDEA, 2004 regulations require states to provide services to students receiving special education when the "likelihood of regression, slow recoupment, and predictive data based on the opinion of professionals" require schools to continue to provide Extended School Year (ESY) services (Individuals with Disabilities Education Act, Regulations, 2004). *Reusch* v. *Fountain* recommend six factors an IEP team should consider when determining ESY services:

1. Regression and recoupment
2. Degree of progress toward IEP goals
3. Emerging skills and breakthrough opportunities
4. Interfering behavior
5. Natures and/or severity of disability
6. Special circumstances

REFERENCES

IDEA. (2004). *Regulations: Subpart B—Extended School Year Services*. Retrieved from http://www.wrightslaw.com/idea/law/idea.regs.subpartb.pdf

Marvell, T., Galfo, A., & Rockwell, J. (1981). *Student litigation: A compilation and analysis of civil cases involving students, 1977–1981.* Williamsburg, VA: National Center for State Courts.

Reusch v Fountain, 1994. MJG-91-3124. United States District Court of Maryland, 872 F.Supp. 1421.

Sales, B., Krauss, D., Sacken, D., & Overcast, T. (1999). The legal rights of students. In C. R. Reynolds & T. B. Gutkin (Eds.), *The handbook of school psychology* (3rd ed., pp. 1113–1145). New York, NY: Wiley.

SHIRLEY A. JONES
Virginia Polytechnic Institute and State University
First edition

KIMBERLY F. APPLEQUIST
University of Colorado at Colorado Springs
Third edition

generalize to other conditions. Although extinction is an effective behavior-reduction technique, because of its limitations (considerations), it should not be used for the immediate reduction of dangerous or self-injurious behaviors.

REFERENCES

Spiegler, M. D. (1983). *Contemporary behavioral therapy.* Palo Alto, CA: Mayfield.

Sulzer-Azaroff, B., & Mayer, G. R. (1986). *Achieving educational excellence using behavioral strategies.* New York, NY: Holt, Rinehart, & Winston.

RHONDA HENNIS
LOUIS J. LANUNZIATA
University of North Carolina at Wilmington

See also Aversive Control; Aversive Stimulus; Behavior Modification; Punishment

EXTINCTION

Extinction, also termed planned ignoring, is a behavior-reductive procedure that occurs when a behavior that has been previously reinforced is no longer reinforced in order to reduce or eliminate the occurrence of that behavior (Sulzer-Azaroff & Mayer, 1986). Extinction has been used to effectively reduce a wide variety of inappropriate behaviors, usually those that are maintained by social attention (Spiegler, 1983).

The reductive effect on behavior is best demonstrated when extinction is effectively implemented as follows:

1. All sources of reinforcement to the behavior are identified and withheld.
2. Reinforcement of an alternative desirable behavior occurs along with extinction of the undesirable behavior.
3. Extinction is applied consistently following the emission of the response in question.
4. Extinction conditions are maintained for a sufficient period of trials until reduction in behavior is complete.

There are further considerations in the use of extinction. Extinction is a gradual behavior-reduction technique and does not work immediately. In addition, an immediate increase in the rate and intensity of the response under extinction conditions may occur temporarily before reduction in response. This is called a "response burst." Extinction conditions of one behavior may initially induce aggression in other behaviors. Finally, behaviors reduced under extinction may be situation-specific and may not

EYE-HAND COORDINATION

Eye-hand coordination (infrequently hand-eye coordination) refers to the ability of an individual to direct fine motor activities of the hand in response to directive input and feedback provided by the visual system. Proprioceptive input also plays a part in these finely coordinated movements. Eye-hand coordination is an important component of the larger concept of visual motor coordination, the latter concept referring to the role of vision in directing and controlling voluntary movements of the body.

As a result of its importance in so many common activities and its association with many disabling conditions, eye-hand coordination has been widely studied. Increasingly the research literature focuses on neurological correlates of eye-hand coordination and the gazing behavior typical of human vision in which the eyes appear to identify and monitor the target as a means of feedback to the hands. Gazing behavior varies under experimental conditions with eyes sometimes remaining on the targeted object and at other times seemingly scouting ahead. Study of eye-hand coordination in this area is entwined with the phenomenon of saccades, the rapid eye movement that characterizes human vision.

Eye-hand coordination is an extremely complex phenomenon and deficiency in eye-hand coordination can arise from many sources, including deficiency in visual perception, acuity, figure-ground distortion, and discrimination. Similarly, underdeveloped or damaged muscles of the hand or damage in the lower sensory neural pathways can affect the outcome of eye-hand coordination efforts. However, excluding obvious visual defects and/or disturbance in the lower neural or musculature systems, eye-hand coordination difficulty is most likely traceable to disruption within the cerebellum. Additionally, the frontal and parietal cortex of the brain are heavily involved with saccades and the use of the hands and have received considerable study.

A significant number of disabling conditions and other factors have been identified in eye-hand coordination deficits. Saavedra, Joshi, Woollacoot, and van Donkelarr (2009) studied individuals with cerebral palsy and found eye movement similar to normal expectations, but hand movements were slower, and children with cerebral palsy were unable to isolate eye, head, and hand movements. Sailer, Eggert, Strassnig, Riedel and Straube (2007) found schizophrenia patients required a longer period of time to initiate a hand movement than controls, whereas Wilmut, Wann, and Brown (2006) found slower and less accurate hand movement with children with Developmental Coordination Disorders. Deconinck, van Polanen, Savelsbergh, and Bennett (2011) found eye-hand movement to be affected by time pressure to task completion. This is only a partial list, and many other conditions have been investigated. For examples, Carmeli, Bar-Yossef, Ariav, Levy, and Liebermann (2008) found lagging perceptual motor (eye-hand) coordination in persons with mild intellectual disability, and the natural aging process seems to affect eye-hand coordination, usually in speed if not accuracy (Boisseau, Scherzer, & Cohen, 2002; Guan & Wade, 2000).

There is some evidence that training and experience can affect the quality of eye-hand coordination. Commercial programs for training eye-hand coordination are widely available although convincing documentation of program efficacy is probably less available. Despite this, research evidence does tentatively support the role of development and experience in the development of eye-hand coordination. As examples, Haines (1984) found TV viewing (and associated inactivity and physical passivity) negatively related to eye-hand coordination in young children. Sailer, Flanagan, and Johansson (2005) found evidence of learning and, importantly, stages of skill acquisition in subjects learning a visuomotor task. Finally, Shimizu, Yoon, and McDonough (2010) were able to teach preschoolers to use a computer mouse.

For educators, the importance of eye-hand coordination is intuitively apparent. However, central issues pertaining to advisability of assessment and training remain a source of empirical concern. Informal assessment often proceeds from the observation of daily skills thought to be dependent on eye-hand coordination ability. Formal procedures would now seem to be more in the realm of medical assessment than the "paper and pencil" tests of earlier work in special education (e.g., the Developmental Test of Visual-Motor Integration [Beery, 1982]). At least in some instances, training seems potentially plausible to improve eye-hand coordination. In general, educators can expect to observe deficits to appear in at least some typical school based activities, and persons with disabilities are probably more likely to demonstrate a greater incidence of difficulties in eye-hand coordination. Accommodations in testing and program activities seem fully justified and training may be explored based on the unique features of the particular case.

REFERENCES

Beery, K. E. (1982). *Revised administration, scoring and teaching manual for the Developmental Test of Visual-Motor Integration*. Cleveland, OH: Modern Curriculum Press.

Boisseau, E., Scherzer, P., & Cohen, H. (2002). Eye-hand coordination in aging in Parkinson's disease. *Aging, Neuropsychology, and Cognition, 9*(4), 266–275. doi: 10.1076/anec.9.4.266.8769

Carmeli, E., Bar-Yossef, T., Ariav, C., Levy, R. & Liebermann, D. G. (2008). Perceptual-motor coordination in persons with mild diasability. *Disability and Rehabilitation: An International, Multidisciplinary Journal, 30*(5) 323–329. doi: 10.1080/09638280701265398

Deconinck, F. J. A., van Polanen, V., Savelsbergh, G. H. P., & Bennett, S. J. ((2011). The relative timing between eye and hand in rapid sequential pointing is affected by time pressure, but not by advance knowledge. *Experimental Brain Research, 203*(1) 99–109. doi: 10.1007/s00221-011-2782-0

Guan, J. (2000). The effect of aging on adaptive eye-hand coordination. *The Journals of Gerontology: Series B: Psychological Sciences and Social Sciences, 55B*(3), 151–162.

Haines, K. C. (198). Eye-hand coordination as related to television watching among preschool children. *Early Child Development and Care, 13*(3–4), 391–397. doi:10.1080/0300443840130310

Saavedr, S., Joshi, A., Woollacott, M., & van Donkelaar, P. (2009). Eye hand coordination in children with cerebral palsy. *Experimental Brain Research, 192*(2), 155–165. doi: 10.1007/s00221-008-1549-8

Sailer, U., Flannagan, J. R., & Johansson, R. S. (2005). Eye-hand coordination during learning of a novel visuomotor task. *Journal of Neuroscience, 25*(39), 8833–8842. doi: 10.1523/JNEUROSCI.2658-05.2005

Sailer, U., Eggert, T., Strassnig, M., Riedel, M., & Straube, A. (2007). Predictive eye and hand movements are differentially affected by schizophrenia. *European Archives of Psychiatry and Clinical Neuroscience, 257*(7), 413–422. doi: 10.1007/s00406-007-0749-8

Shimuzu, H., Yoon, S., & McDonough, C. S. (2010). Teaching skills to use a computer mouse in preschoolers with developmental disabilities: Shaping moving a mouse and eye-hand coordination. *Research in Developmental Disabilities, 31*(6), 1448–1461. doi: 10.1016/j.ridd.2010.06.013

Wilmut, K., Wann, J. P., & Brown, J. H. (2006). Problem in coupling of eye and hand in the sequential movements of children with developmental coordination disorders. *Child: Care, Health and Development, 32*(6) 665–678. doi: 10.1111/j.1365-2214.2006.00678.x

TED L. MILLER
University of Tennessee at Chattanooga
Fourth edition

EYSENCK, HANS J. (1916–1997)

Eysenck was born and educated in Berlin, Germany, openly opposing Hitler and his requirement of Nazi Party membership for university admission, and moving to England in the late 1930s in protest. He received his BA in 1938 and PhD in psychology in 1949 from the University of London. In 1946 Eysenck became senior research psychologist at Maudsley Hospital, a year later becoming head of the psychology department, founded by him within the Institute of Psychiatry at that hospital. For over 30 years he was professor of psychology at the University of London and director of the psychology unit at Maudsley Hospital. Hans J. Eysenck died on September 4, 1997 at the age of 81.

Eysenck has been described as one of the most influential, provocative, and controversial psychologists of his generation. He was a persistent critic of psychoanalysis, psychotherapy, and projective assessment, and a moving force in the establishment of clinical psychology and behavior therapy. As a behaviorist, he advocated scientific methods of personality assessment and denied the theory of the subconscious, denouncing Freud as a charlatan in the process. Eysenck applied research methods traditionally used in the study of intelligence to the study of personality, utilizing factor analysis and discriminant function analysis to identify major factors. He attempted to develop hypotheses linking those factors to widely accepted psychological and physiological concepts. This approach to the treatment of scientific data was a general theme throughout his research.

Eysenck was a pioneer in defining the structure of personality, attracting students and collaborators from around the world with his analysis of the layers of personality. *Dimensions of Personality* (1947) and *The Structure of Human Personality* (1970) provide explanations of his theory of personality, identifying the measurable areas as intelligence, neurosis, psychosis, extroversion, and introversion, all later components of psychological tests. In the behaviorist tradition, Eysenck was unconcerned about aspects of personality that could not be measured, claiming that what was not measurable did not exist. His belief in interventions based on unlearning maladaptive behaviors that had been learned, drew criticism that he was merely treating symptoms of mental disorders, not the diseases themselves. He argued, however, that the symptoms were the disorders.

The most heated controversy of his career was prompted by Eysenck's publication of an article in *The Harvard Education Review* (1969), arguing that the difference between scores of Blacks and Whites on intelligence tests was due to genetic as well as environmental factors. At the height of this controversy, he was attacked by students calling him a racist and fascist while attempting to deliver a lecture, and he was accompanied by a bodyguard to ensure his safety.

Generating further criticism, Eysenck's book, *Smoking, Health and Personality*, was published in 1965. In it he described the "cancer-prone"-type personality, one characterized by feelings of hopelessness, helplessness, and depression, unable to express emotions and reacting inappropriately to stress. He argued that smoking itself does not cause cancer, and that both smoking and cancer are merely symptoms of the same personality disorder, one most likely of genetic origin.

During his career, Eysenck published some 80 books and 1,600 journal articles dealing with a vast array of subjects. In *Decline and Fall of the Freudian Empire* (Eysenck, 1985), he proposed that Freud was "a genius, not of science, but of propaganda," and despite his rationalism, in his later work he concluded that powerful evidence exists to support extra-sensory perception and found a significant correlation between personality and the position of the planets. His self-help books such as *Check Your Own IQ* sold in the millions, and he founded two journals, *Behavior Research and Therapy* and *Personality and Individual Differences*. In 1990 he published his autobiography, *Rebel With a Cause*.

REFERENCES

Eysenck, H. J. (1947). *Dimensions of personality*. London, England: Routledge & Kegan Paul.

Eysenck, H. J. (1965). *Smoking, health and personality*. London, England: Weidenfeld & Nicolson.

Eysenck, H. J. (1966). *Check your own IQ*. Harmondsworth, England: Penguin.

Eysenck, H. J. (1970). *The structure of human personality* (rev. ed.). London, England: Methuen.

Eysenck, H. J. (1985). *Decline and fall of the Freudian empire*. Harmondsworth, England: Penguin.

Eysenck, H. J. (1990). *Rebel with a cause: The autobiography of H. J. Eysenck*. London, England: Allen.

ELAINE FLETCHER-JANZEN
Chicago School of Professional Psychology
First edition

TAMARA J. MARTIN
The University of Texas of the Permian Basin
Second edition

F

FABRY DISEASE

Fabry disease, also known as angiokeratoma corpris diffusum, is a disorder of lipid metabolism caused by an alpha-galactosidase-A deficiency, which leads to an accumulation of glycolipid products in various muscle tissues and cells in the nervous system. Individuals inherit Fabry disease as an X-linked recessive trait (Rowland, 1995). It is caused by the gene located on the long arm of the X chromosome (Xq21.33-Xq22).

Prevalence of Fabry disease in the United States is estimated to be 2,500 individuals (Thoene & Coker, 1995). Fabry disease is most likely to affect males and individuals of Western European descent, but it can affect heterozygous females. Female carriers show signs of Fabry disease such as angiokeratomas, burning pains, and cloudiness of the cornea (Wynbrandt & Ludman, 1999).

Characteristics

1. Angiokeratomas or dark red, raised, dot-like lesions on the skin that appear during childhood and increase in size and number with age
2. Burning pain in the hands and feet triggered by exercise, fatigue, fever, emotional stress, or change in temperature; diminished ability to sweat
3. Nausea, vomiting, diarrhea, and abdominal or side pain
4. Retarded growth and delayed puberty
5. Swelling and distortion of the blood vessels in the conjunctiva and retina
6. Kidney failure or cardiovascular complications

Chronic pain in the hands and feet may be alleviated by daily doses of phenytoin (Dilantin) or low doses of diphenylhydantoin or carbamazepin (Tegretol). Other acute symptoms may be treated with Dexamethasone. Angiokeratomas may be removed with laser therapy (Thoene & Coker, 1995).

Special education services may be available for children with Fabry disease under the category of Other Health Impairment if the symptoms progress significantly.

Education providers should be alerted to possible side effects of medication used to alleviate pain symptoms.

Individuals affected by Fabry disease are at risk for kidney failure or cardiovascular complications, but kidney dialysis and transplantation have improved the prognoses for these individuals. Several companies and researchers are in the process of developing drugs for enzyme replacement therapy (Schiffmann et al., 2000; Takenaka et al., 2000).

REFERENCES

Rowland, L. P. (Ed.). (1995). *Merritt's textbook of neurology* (9th ed.). Baltimore, MD: Williams & Wilkins.

Schiffmann, R., Murray, G. J., Treco, D., Daniel, P., Sellos-Moura, M., Myers, M.,...Brady, R. O. (2000). Infusion of alpha-galactosidase A reduces tissue globotriaosylceramide storage in patients with Fabry disease. *National Institute of Health, 97*, 365–370.

Takenaka, T., Murray, G. J., Qin, G., Quirk, J. M., Ohshima, T., Qasba, P.,...Medin, J. A. (2000). Long-term enzyme correction and lipid reduction in multiple organs of primary and secondary transplanted Fabry mice receiving bone marrow cells. *Proceedings of the National Academy of Sciences, USA, 97*, 7515–7520.

Thoene, J. G., & Coker, N. P. (Eds.). (1995). *Physicians' guide to rare diseases* (2nd ed.). Montvale, NJ: Dowden.

Wynbrandt, J., & Ludman, M. D. (Eds.). (1999). *The encyclopedia of genetic disorders and birth defects*. New York, NY: Facts on File.

JENNIFER HARGRAVE
University of Texas at Austin

FACILITATED COMMUNICATION

Facilitated communication (FC) is among the most controversial techniques in special education in particular, and in education and psychology in general. Facilitated communication should not be confused with functional communication. In FC, a trained person, called a "facilitator," supports the hand, wrist, or arm of a communication-impaired individual, most commonly one with autism or another developmental disability. The individual is thus allegedly enabled to use a finger to point to or press the keys of a typewriter, computer keyboard, or alphabet facsimile. Supporters (e.g., Biklen & Cardinal, 1997) allege that this method allows the impaired individual to communicate by typing letters, words, sentences, and numbers (Jacobson, Mulick, & Schwartz, 1995).

FC first emerged in the 1970s in Australia. Rosemary Crossley initiated use of the technique while working with physically disabled persons (Prior & Cummins, 1992). Douglas Biklen, who observed Crossley's methods during a trip to Australia, introduced FC to the United States in 1989. Biklen extended use of the therapy to include those afflicted with cerebral palsy, autism, and Down syndrome (Kerrin et al., 1998).

Biklen's results using FC were purportedly successful. As Jacobson et al. (1995, p. 753) state, "... previously nonverbal students were typing, with facilitation, words, sentences, and paragraphs of remarkable clarity and intellect." Reports of FC's successes and Biklen (e.g., 1993) and his Syracuse University group's workshops, publications, and conferences led to widespread adoption of, and support for, the new technique. The media, combined with hopeful parents and teachers, aroused further excitement about FC's possibilities (Rimland, 1991).

With all of the support for FC, attention began to turn to exactly what the students were typing. Biklen (1993) stated that autistic individuals reported through their facilitators that they are of normal intelligence and social competence. However, not all facilitated messages reported such happy news. Some children and adolescents using FC apparently claimed that they had been physically and sexually abused for many years, although unable to report it (Zirkel, 1995). Outrage began to spread as criminal charges were filed against parents who were forcibly separated from their children. In one case, "Michael" supposedly alleged through FC that his father was sexually abusing him (Zirkel, 1995). Michael's father was criminally charged and Michael sent to live in a foster home. In an attempt to confirm Michael's alleged claim of abuse, two different facilitators working with Michael reported that he claimed to have been abused. However, prior to working with Michael, both facilitators had been informed of his previous claims. Importantly, the details of the reported abuse varied drastically between the facilitators (Zirkel, 1995). Michael's father was later cleared of all criminal charges, and he pressed charges against the facilitation agency.

The outrage caused by the claims of abuse and the skepticism of many scientists led to scientific investigations of FC. Questions were raised concerning the sophistication of the untaught skills that many disabled persons displayed. Those who had never been taught to read, write, spell, or add were seemingly able to produce complex and correctly spelled sentences, solve difficult math problems, and compose sensitive poetry. Describing use of FC with two boys diagnosed as autistic and severely mentally retarded, Donnellan, Sabin, and Majure (1992, p. 70) stated, "Neither young man had been given any formal training in reading, writing, or spelling, nor had either one shown any obvious interest in these skills. Yet, in the first ... sessions of facilitated communication ... both were able to produce meaningful complex sentences." Professionals began to question whether the students or the facilitators were really the ones communicating (Prior & Cummins, 1992; Silliman, 1992; Thompson, 1993). Skepticism of FC developed as quickly as had initial support. The results of numerous experiments suggested that FC was, in terms of actually enabling those with disabilities to communicate, a hoax. Well-controlled double-blind studies of FC demonstrated consistently that messages were coming not from the students, but from their facilitators. On trials where both the student and the facilitator had correct information, the facilitated message was correct, but on those trials on which only the student had correct information, the message was incorrect (Thompson, 1993). In other studies, researchers used screens to separate the student's and the facilitator's visual fields, showed them both a series of pictures, and asked the student to type what she or he saw. When student and facilitator saw the same picture, the facilitated answer was correct, but when the pictures were different, the answer corresponded to what the facilitator, not the student, had seen. Further, observations of students and facilitators consistently indicated that although the facilitators consistently looked at the keyboard, the students generally did not and had no home base, as do skilled typists. Without either looking at the board or having such a base, accurate typing is virtually impossible. Individuals with impairments using various methods of adapted communication always look at the instrument through which they are communicating. Much of this evidence may be seen in the videotape, *Prisoners of Silence* (Palfreman, 1993).

Virtually all well-controlled research indicated that the facilitators were themselves, although wholly without awareness, producing the messages (Jacobson, Mulick, & Schwartz, 1995). As several authors have suggested, this unconscious motor movement is similar to what occurs in dowsing, automatic writing, and Ouija. As an example of one study that supports this hypothesis, Burgess et al. (1998) showed a Biklen FC training videotape to 40 undergraduate students. They then asked the students to facilitate the communication of "Jackie," a confederate, who was described as disabled and unable to speak, but who was really a normal individual. Students were given different information about "Jackie" before the facilitation session. Eighty-nine percent of the answers that "Jackie" gave to questions about herself during the FC session corresponded to information provided to the particular student.

With all of the evidence against FC, however, Biklen and the Syracuse University group still support the technique, as reflected in a recent book (Biklen & Cardinal, 1997) and website (http://suedweb.syr.edu/thefci/). In addition, Vermont, Washington, and Indiana have facilitated communication coalitions where FC is still taught and implemented (http://www.bloomington.in.us). Perhaps Biklen and others are correct in claiming that FC is effective in some cases, but they need to provide stronger and more consistent evidence than they have to date. Unfortunately, the best conclusion at this time appears to be that, in spite of its hopes and bandwagon support, FC, as have so many other methods, appears to be wholly ineffective in enabling those with severe disabilities to communicate at all, let alone normally.

REFERENCES

Biklen, D. P. (1993). *Communication unbound: How FC is challenging traditional views of autism and ability/disability.* New York, NY: Teachers College Press.

Biklen, D., & Cardinal, D. N. (Eds.). (1997). *Contested words, contested science: Unraveling the facilitated communication controversy.* New York, NY: Teachers College Press.

Burgess, C. A., Kirsch, I., Shane, H., Niederauer, K. L., Graham, S. M., & Bacon, A. (1998). Facilitated communication as an ideomotor response. *Psychological Science, 9,* 71–74.

Donnellan, A. M., Sabin, L. A., & Majure, L. A. (1992). Facilitated communication: Beyond the quandary to the questions. *Topics in Language Disorders, 12,* 69–82.

Jacobson, J. W., Mulick, J. A., & Schwartz, A. A. (1995). A history of facilitated communication: Science, pseudoscience, and antiscience. *American Psychologist, 50,* 750–765.

Kerrin, R. G., Murdock, J. Y., Sharpton, W. R., & Jones, N. (1998). Who's doing the pointing? Investigating facilitated communication in a classroom setting with students with autism. *Focus on Autism and Other Developmental Disabilities, 13,* 73–75.

Palfreman, J. (1993, October 19). *Prisoners of silence.* Frontline, Public Broadcasting Service.

Prior, M., & Cummins, R. (1992). Questions about facilitated communication and autism. *Journal of Autism and Developmental Disorders, 22,* 331–336.

Rimland, B. (1991). Facilitated communication: Problems, puzzles and paradoxes: Six challenges for researchers. *Autism Research Review International, 5*(2), 3.

Silliman, E. R. (1992). Three perspectives of facilitated communication: Unexpected literacy, clever Hans, or enigma? *Topics in Language Disorders, 12*(4), 60–68.

Thompson, T. (1994). Reign of error: Facilitated communication. *American Journal on Mental Retardation, 98,* 670–673.

Zirkel, P. A. (1995). Facilitated communication of child abuse. *Phi Delta Kappan, 76,* 815–818.

LAUREN WEBSTER
ROBERT T. BROWN
University of North Carolina at Wilmington

See also **Asperger Syndrome; Autism**

FACTOR ANALYSIS

Factor analysis is a term encompassing several distinct statistical techniques, all intended to investigate the relationships among a set of variables. The primary purposes include (a) reducing a large set of variables to a smaller set that reproduces most of the properties of the initial set; and (b) verifying (or not) theoretically proposed relationships among a set of variables. A key concept in factor analysis is termed latent structure or latent factor. A latent factor is not directly observable, but inferred from the interrelationships among observed (also termed manifest) variables. One or more latent factors may be inferred from observed variables' relationships to each other, and any single observed variable may be related to one, some, or all latent factors.

Factor analysis has a long history in psychology, beginning with Charles Spearman's investigations in the early 1900s (Spearman, 1904) concerned with the measurement of intelligence. Indeed, most efforts to construct a theory of intelligence included concomitant developments in factor analysis over the next century. Parallel developments in biology and the physical sciences focused on data reduction under a method later termed *principal components*. This method was also termed dimensional reduction, and it created observed variables that were linear combinations of the original set. Again, the goal was fewer of the new principal component variables than the number of variables in the original set.

A major distinction between principal components analysis and the evolving factor analysis procedures due to Spearman, Cyril Burt, Karl Pearson, Karl Holzinger, and others (Harman, 1967) was the concept of measurement error. Principal components, followed from physical sciences in which measurement error was generally assumed to be near zero, while psychometric models of measurement developed with the concept of measurement error central to its theory. Measurement error remains the single most important aspect of factor analysis that differentiates it from physical science models of data.

Factor analysis initially focused on the Pearson correlation matrix for a set of variables. By necessity, various ad hoc procedures were developed to permit computations within the capabilities of paper and pencil or adding machines of the time. As solutions were generated, the issues of a best solution and of the most interpretable solution arose. The concept of simple structure, coined by Thurstone, was formulated by attempting to find a solution in which variables related mainly (or entirely) to one factor. This led to an interactive process in which observed variables, usually test scores, were changed in the test development so as to create near-simple structure or variables deleted to create it. The method of principal axes was developed by Hotelling by the 1930s and, with refinements, remains the primary method of analysis under the term *exploratory factor analysis* (EFA).

By the 1960s, the availability of computers permitted analysis of factor analysis models that previously had been too tedious for handwritten or adding-machine computations. New developments in interpretation of factor analysis solutions were created to "rotate" the solutions toward simple(r) structure. Two general approaches evolved: orthogonal rotation and oblique rotation. Orthogonal rotation effectively reoriented the factor solution within its space, assuming all factors were uncorrelated with all others. Conceptually, this was equivalent to starting with a spatial orientation such as a room of a house with one corner of walls and floor the origin and rotating the walls and floor while leaving alone the variables relationship to each other and to each factor. The intent was to align as closely as possible each factor to a subset of variables most closely associated with it while keeping each factor uncorrelated with any others. Oblique rotation permitted the factors to become correlated along with aligning each factor most closely with a subset of variables. Varimax rotation is the method most commonly used for orthogonal rotation, and methods such as oblimin and promax are commonly used for oblique rotations.

In the 1960s and 1970s, Swedish statistician Karl Jöreskog (1969, 1973) developed procedures for analyzing predetermined models for data. A major part of that development, termed *linear structural relations*, or LISREL, and later revised as structural equation modeling (SEM), was the specification of a factor structure for a set of observed variables. This procedure allowed testing of the adequacy of fit of the data to the theorized factor structure, and this has been termed *confirmatory factor analysis* or CFA. CFA permits an overall model test using a chi square statistic and various derivative standardized measures somewhat similar to squared multiple correlation-type indices. The most commonly used include the comparative fit index (CFI), normed fit index (NFI), adjusted goodness-of-fit index (AGFI), and root mean square error of approximation (RMSEA). General heuristic rules for acceptably good fit tend to require the fit indices to be above .90 or .95 and the RMSEA to be below .08. CFA can be conducted using various computer programs commercially available and many now include graphical drawing programs that do not require writing mathematical equations. Their proper use, however, should include consultation with an expert on CFA as there are many potential pitfalls in the estimation process.

EFA and CFA were intended to be complementary processes in that EFA explores the potential structure of a set of variables or test items, while CFA was intended to test a hypothesis concerning a specific factor model for the variables. There has been much blurring of the procedures in recent years, however, and unsatisfactory fit of CFA models now generally leads to a mixed use of EFA and CFA procedures. How adequate these are has yet to be determined.

REFERENCES

Harman, H. H. (1967). *Modern factor analysis*. Chicago, IL: University of Chicago Press.

Jöreskog, K. G. (1969). A general approach to confirmatory maximum likelihood factor analysis. *Psychometrika, 34*, 183–202.

Jöreskog, K. G. (1973). A general method for estimating a linear structural equation system. In A. S. Goldberger & O. D. Duncan (Eds.), *Structural equation models in the social sciences* (pp. 85–112). New York, NY: Academic Press.

Spearman, C. (1904). General intelligence, objectively determined and measured. *Applied Journal of Psychology, 14*, 201–293.

Victor L. Willson
Texas A&M University

See also Discriminant Analysis; Multiple Regression; Research in Special Education

FAILURE TO THRIVE

Failure to thrive (FTT) is defined as the failure of an infant or child to acquire height and weight normal for their ages as a result of inadequate calorie intake (Iwaniec, 2004). Failure to thrive has a long-standing history, with its origins dating specifically to Kasper Hauser syndrome and marasmus (Racicot, 2000). Failure to thrive originally was classified as having organic and nonorganic origins. However, these classifications have been replaced by broader classifications that incorporate medical and psychosocial factors. Although prevalence rates for FTT vary because of different criteria used for diagnosis, it accounts for 1% to 5% of all pediatric hospitalization and usually is seen in children ages 3 and under (Iwaniec, 2004; Racicot, 2000).

Although well-accepted indices or universal diagnostic criteria to diagnose FTT in children have not been established, the presence of height and weight growth trajectories below the 3rd to 5th percentiles in children, based on the National Center for Health Statistics norms (Marino, Weinman, & Soudelier, 2001; Phelps, 1991), often are used as the criterion for FTT. Consequences of FTT include growth deficits, decreased immunologic resistance, diminished physical activity, cognitive deficits, emotional and behavioral problems, and learning difficulties (Black, 1995; Iwaniec, 2004; Phelps, 1991).

Etiology of FTT focuses on medical and nonmedical issues and may be due to a combination of conditions. Medical factors include gastrointestinal, endocrine or genetic disorders, as well as illness (Black, 1995; Iwaniec, 2004). Nonmedical factors include family issues, psychological variables, and degree of social support. The home environments of infants with FTT often differ from those of normal growing infants (Casey, Bradley, & Wortham, 1984). Large family size, poor marital relationships, and lack of economic security may lead to severe stress levels in adults and inadequate attention to the nutritional needs of children (Alderette & DeGraffenried, 1986; Phelps, 1991). Substance abuse, maternal depression, infant temperament, and lack of social support also may contribute to FTT (Racicot, 2000). Mothers of children with FTT often have had negative childhoods characterized by inadequate nurturing, stress, and abuse and therefore develop poor parenting skills (Steward & Garvin, 1997). Children with FTT often display difficult temperaments including lethargy, hypervigilance, irritability, apathy, and poor feeding ability, which often results in deficient interactions with caregivers (Black, 1995; Steward & Garvin, 1997). Unsuitable relationships between the mother and child may be conditions that contribute to FTT.

Various treatments are available for children who display FTT. Food supplementation programs (e.g., Special Supplemental Food Program for Women, Infants, and Children) are an attempt at preventing nutritional problems (Black, 1995). Other interventions include parenting classes, home visits, and individual and family counseling. These are family-focused and concentrate on the relationship between the child and the caregiver (Black, 1995; Phelps, 1991; Racicot, 2000). Failure to thrive may have long-lasting effects for children even after their condition improves. They may show delays academically and socially and need intervention to combat their delays.

REFERENCES

Alderette, P., & DeGraffenried, D. F. (1986). Nonorganic failure-to-thrive syndrome and the family system. *Social Work, 31*(3), 207–211.

Black, M. M. (1995). Failure to thrive: Strategies for evaluation and intervention. *School Psychology Review, 24*(2), 171–185.

Casey, P. H., Bradley, R., & Wortham, B. (1984). Social and nonsocial home environments of infants with nonorganic failure-to-thrive. *Pediatrics, 73*, 348–353.

Iwaniec, D. (2004). *Children who fail to thrive: A practice guide.* London, England: Wiley.

Marino, R., Weinman, M. L., & Soudelier, K. (2001). Social work intervention and failure to thrive in infants and children. *Health & Social Work, 26*(2), 90–97.

Phelps, L. (1991). Nonorganic failure to thrive: Origins. *School Psychology Review, 20*(3), 417–427.

Racicot, L. C. (2000). *Lexis, my little fairy princess: Literature review and case report on non-organic failure to thrive (NOFTT).* (ERIC Document Reproduction Service No. ED481101)

Steward, D. K., & Garvin, B. J. (1997). Nonorganic failure to thrive: A theoretical approach. *Journal of Pediatric Nursing, 12*(6), 342–347.

KATRINA RAIA
University of Florida

See also Deprivation, Bioneural Results of; Developmental Delay; Malnutrition

FAIRBANK DISEASE

Fairbank disease is the name for one of two traditional categories of multiple epiphyseal dysplasia, or MED. Although other variations of MED are recognized, diagnoses are still often labeled by the former names. The Fairbank variant is the more severe of the two, and the milder version is referred to as the Ribbing variant. The affected epiphyses are small, irregular, or fragmented in the Fairbank variant, whereas in the Ribbing variant the involved epiphyses are often fat (Connors, 2000).

MED is genetically caused (Curcione, 1995), and three genes responsible for the condition have been identified (Connors, 2000). MED must be differentiated from Legg-Calve-Perthes disease, hypothyroidism, psuedoacoachondroplasia (PSACH), and from other dysplasias (Burns et al., 2000). Age of onset typically ranges from 2 to 6 years, although problems may not occur until much later in life (Gandy, 1997). The prevalence of MED is unknown.

Characteristics

1. Commonly begins with painful or stiff legs, especially knee and hip joints.
2. May have bowing of the knees, "knock-knees," or similar hip problems.
3. Joints are affected symmetrically.
4. May have short limbs or short and stubby hands and feet.
5. May exhibit a limp or a waddling walk.
6. Young children may have delayed walking ability.

Treatment for MED varies according to the symptoms expressed and the severity of those symptoms. Frequent X-rays can be expected in order to monitor the progression of the disease. Severe cases may require long spells of bed rest that will require a child to miss school and other daily activities. In milder cases, stretching exercises will be recommended as well as weight control to ensure that no additional stress is placed on the joints. High-impact sports should be avoided, and minor surgical procedures can be done to correct knee alignment when necessary (Li & Stanton, 1996).

Due to the extended absences from school that may be necessary during the initial stages of diagnosis and treatment, special education services may be available for children with MED. Home visits from educators are preferable because it is important that children remain actively involved in learning while away from the classroom (Kauffman & Hallahan, 1981).

Effects of MED persist throughout adulthood. Osteoarthritis tends to develop with advancing age (Gandy, 1997). Short stature is present but not severe. Joint replacements are usually necessary; typically hip replacements are required, but knee replacements may also be necessary (Li & Stanton, 1996).

REFERENCES

Burns, C., et al. (2000.) *Pediatric primary care: A handbook for nurse practitioners* (2nd ed.). Philadelphia, PA: W. B. Saunders.

Connors, M. (2001, April 5). *Multiple epiphyseal dysplasia.* Retrieved from http://www.mun.ca/biology/scarr/MED.htm

Curcione, P., & Stanton, R. (1995). *Multiple epiphyseal dysplasia.* Retrieved from http://gait.aidi.udel.edu/res695/homepage/pd_ortho/educate/clincase/epipdysp.htm

Gandy, A. (1997). *Multiple epiphyseal dysplasia.* Retrieved from http://www.pedianet.com/prof/disease/.les/multiple.htm

Kauffman, J., & Hallahan, D. (Eds.). (1981). *Handbook of special education.* Englewood Cliffs, NJ: Prentice Hall.

Li, C., & Stanton, R. (1996). *Multiple epiphyseal dysplasia: Clinical case presentation.* Retrieved from http://gait.aidi.udel.edu/res695/homepage/pd_ortho/educate/clincase/medyp.htm

Emily Cornforth
University of Colorado at Colorado Springs

FALSE POSITIVE AND FALSE NEGATIVE

The term *false positive*, developed in the vocabulary of medicine, is often confusing when used in other circles. In medicine, a condition is reported as positive when the condition is present. When the condition is reported as negative it is in the normal or average range. Therefore, a false positive refers to a judgment about the presence of an exceptional attribute that is actually in the average range or a score or judgment that incorrectly indicates a diagnosis (or a classification) of an individual who has been diagnosed as brain injured when in fact he or she is only exhibiting reasonably normal developmental delays. A false negative, the opposite of a false positive, results when an individual is determined to be average when in fact the individual is exceptional. For example, occasionally a child with cerebral palsy (who by medical diagnosis and by definition is brain injured) will reproduce, almost perfectly, drawings of geometric figures from a test for brain injury. By the results of the drawing test, the individual is a false negative. Whereas a negative interpretation of a clinical test indicates that nothing unusual has been found, a positive interpretation indicates exceptionality or pathology.

Further confusion may result when terms used in personnel selection are mixed with clinical terminology. In personnel selection, false rejections corresponds to false positives in clinical terminology. In the language of personnel specialists, a false rejection is an individual who has a score on a selection instrument that is below the cutoff (e.g., too exceptional to be successful on the job) but who is eventually successful on the job. False acceptances are those individuals who have scores on the selection tests above the cutoff but who are failures on the job. Even though nonnumerical conditions may influence the cutoff score, or various conditions may determine success on the job, such individuals are known as false negatives.

One of the most crucial factors in determining the number of false negative and false positive decisions is the cutoff score (which may be multiple scores on many parts of an assessment) used to indicate the presence (positive) or absence (negative) of pathology or whatever exceptional attribute is being evaluated. Personnel using a suicide prediction scale would be inclined to use a cutoff score that would deliberately decrease the number of persons who would be considered to be in the normal range (i.e., false negative) so that adequate protection could be put in place. Where incorrectly diagnosing pathology has dire implications but the condition itself is mild, a cutoff score would be set to underdiagnose, that is, to increase the number of false negatives and reduce the number of false positives.

Figure F.1 gives an illustration of the concept of false negative and false positive as it has been used in the diagnosis of learning disabilities (Reynolds, 1984). Four cells are illustrated: students who are learning disabled and are so diagnosed are true positives; students who are learning disabled but are diagnosed as normal are false negatives; students who are not in fact learning disabled are false positives; students who are not learning disabled and are not diagnosed as learning disabled are true negatives. Frequently, in deciding on a diagnosis, assessment

Natural
State of the
Organism

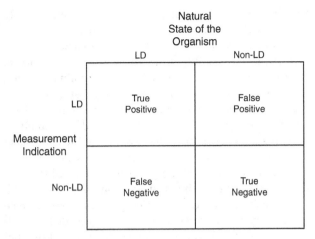

Figure F.1. Concept of false negative and false positive.

results are interpreted in a way to minimize either false negatives or false positives. In special education, learning disability diagnosis is best structured to minimize false negatives (Reynolds, 1984) while the diagnosis of mental retardation is best designed to minimize false positives.

Authors and publishers of tests and other predictive devices should provide an indication of the predictive confidence associated with each score. For many predictions, locally developed tables will be better than national data. Such tables should be developed, if they are not provided, to indicate the efficiency of various cutoff scores. Data should be provided about the percentage of correct classifications, especially for scores close to the cutoff, and about the expected percentage of false positive and false negative classifications for each group being considered. Prediction is often improved when more than one score is used, as in a formula derived from multiple regression. Data of various kinds and types usually produce better predictive information than scores from similar instruments.

REFERENCE

Reynolds, C. R. (1984). Critical measurements issues in learning disabilities. *Journal of Special Education, 18*, 451–476.

Joseph L. French
Pennsylvania State University

See also **Learning Disabilities, Severe Discrepancy Analysis in; Research in Special Education**

FAMILIAL MEDITERRANEAN FEVER

Familial Mediterranean fever (FMF) is a relatively common (in certain ethnic groups) inherited disorder of the immune system. It is classified as one of several rheumatic diseases that are characterized by an altered immune response that causes inflammation in specific organs.

The gene responsible for FMF is located on Chromosome 16. This site controls the synthesis of a protein, pyrin, which is present in neutrophils, a type of white blood cell. Although the role of pyrin in the immune response is not completely clear, it appears to function as an inhibiting agent. The underlying problem in FMF is a lack of inhibitor enzymes that can turn off the immune response and the ensuing inflammation it creates. Pleural (within the chest), peritoneal (within the abdomen), synovial (in joints), and pericardial (surrounding the heart) fluids are the most common substances affected by the inhibitor deficiency.

Several mutations of the abnormal gene in FMF cause variable severity in its symptoms. The forms with the poorest outlook and the best outlook are the most prevalent clinical types of FMF.

FMF is transmitted in an autosomal recessive manner. In certain populations, the estimation of the carrier state of the abnormal gene approaches 20%. The disorder is most common in Sephardic Jews (from Spain and Portugal), Armenians, Turks, and Arabs. Greeks, Hispanics, and Italians are less affected by FMF. It is interesting to note that FMF is rare in Ashkenazi Jews (from central and eastern Europe), Germans, and Anglo-Saxons.

Characteristics

1. Brief, acute episodes of fever and inflammation of serosal surfaces (previously mentioned) that end spontaneously and occur at irregular intervals.

2. Sixty-five percent of affected individuals will experience symptoms by 5 years of age. Ninety percent will have had at least one episode by age 20.

3. Acute attacks typically consist of fever (100%), abdominal pain (90%), arthritis and joint discomfort (85%), and chest pain (20%). Less frequent findings include pericarditis (inflammation of the membrane that encloses the heart), rash, muscle aches, splenic enlargement, and scrotal swelling.

4. Neurological complications are rare.

5. About 35–50% of untreated patients will develop amyloidosis, a condition in which an abnormal protein (amyloid) is deposited throughout the body. Unchecked amyloidosis will eventually cause kidney failure and death. This complication is most frequent among Sephardic Jews and Turks.

Treatment for FMF is prophylactic. The drug colchicine is taken daily. It not only prevents or significantly reduces the frequency of acute attacks, but also makes the development of amyloidosis much less likely. In some patients, colchicine has even caused partial reversal of amyloid deposition.

There is no research to indicate cognitive dysfunction or the need for special education services as a result of FMF.

The prognosis for FMF appears favorable, but is somewhat dependent on the clinical form (and genetic mutation) present in the individual patient. Evidence of amyloidosis is an ominous sign, but even this manifestation of FMF is responsive to therapy. For individuals with this disorder, colchicine is as close to a miracle drug as one could imagine.

This entry has been informed by the source listed below.

REFERENCE

Gedalia, A. (2000). Familial Mediterranean fever. In R. E. Behrman, R. M. Kleigman, & H. B. Jenson (Eds.), *Nelson textbook of pediatrics* (16th ed., p. 724). Philadelphia, PA: W. B. Saunders.

BARRY H. DAVISON
Ennis, Texas

JOAN W. MAYFIELD
Baylor Pediatric Specialty Services, Dallas, Texas

FAMILIAL RETARDATION

This term is rarely seen in the current nomenclature about intellectual disability but the concept remains intact. There was a time when the term *familial* was used in the field of intellectual disability as a synonym for familial influences on the individual and known heredity disorders. Discussions about whether intellectual disability is inherited or owed to inappropriate environmental stimulation are a part of the debate on the basis of intelligence—the nature-nurture or heredity-environment controversy—that dates back to the 1930s. That debate is unresolved, but it is now abundantly clear that some medical disorders associated with intellectual disability are transmitted genetically, whereas the etiology of others is uncertain (Westling, 1986).

Numerous studies have found evidence suggesting hereditability in the cultural-familial group associated with some degrees of disability. Reed and Reed (1965) provided extensive data on the issue. Of their 289 probands (initial cases), there were 55 who had the diagnosis of "cultural-familial, probably genetic" with no other medical diagnosis associated with retardation.

All of the 55 probands had at least one primary family member with ID and this was found across two or three generations. The Reeds estimated that when both parents have ID, the probability of occurrence in a child born to them is about 40%, in contrast to a probability of about 1% if neither parent is ID. The Reeds estimated that retardation incidence could be reduced by one third to one half if these couples chose not to have children. Analysis of the results of over 40 studies (excluding the challenged British studies) of identical and fraternal twins and other family relationships strongly suggests that hereditary factors are associated with intelligence, so the existence of a polygenic factor in is credible. Consensus now seems to be that a polygenic pattern in combination with adverse environmental factors best explains ID in the cultural-familial group.

Diagnosis of genetically based medical syndromes is more probable in cases where the degree of mental impairment is severe. Among the genetically determined disorders with which ID is associated are metabolic disorders such as phenylketonuria (PKU) and chromosomal anomalies such as cri du chat (5p monosomy). Genetic defect may be inherited from the parents, or it may be due to a mutation caused by viruses, certain chemicals, or radiation. Mutant genes may be dominant or recessive, and inheritance thereafter follows normal Mendelian laws.

Since about 1950, a large number of chromosomal anomalies, many associated with ID, have been described in the literature. The most common of these is Down syndrome, which has an incidence of about 1 in 700 births. It occurs most often in births to mothers over 35 years old. About 95% of the cases are due to gene mutations; most of the others are inherited from a parent who is a carrier of the gene. Males with Down syndrome do not reproduce, but the rare females who have children will pass on the affected gene to all offspring. Most people with Down syndrome have trisomy 21, meaning that they have three rather than two chromosomes at location 21. Translocations involve location of part or all of a chromosome in the wrong place and include D/G translocations involving chromosomes 13–15 with 21 and G/G translocations involving 21/22. The rare mosaic Down cases result from trisomy that begins after cells have begun to multiply; incidence of mosaicism is about 1 in 3,000 births overall, but about 1 in 10 if the mother shows a mosaic karyotype (a diagrammatic representation of form, size, and attachments of chromosomes). The retardation may be at any level, but IQ averages reported from surveys are around 35 to 50 for persons of school age or above. However, early reports on small numbers of children participating in two intensive early educational programs indicated that many of those children with Down syndrome scored at or above the mild retardation level on language or intelligence tests when tested after the preschool program or in primary grades (Hayden & Haring, 1976; Rynders & Horrobin, 1975). In cases of moderate or worse levels of mental retardation, about 82% have known causes but only 55% of mild cases have a known etiology. Familial retardation continues to be considered of unknown causes (Gillberg, 1995).

Nearly all abnormalities of amino acid metabolism are potential causes for mental retardation, but the likelihood of the ID varies greatly (Lee, 1980). The best-known cause is phenylketonuria (PKU), which has an incidence of between 1 in 5,000 and 1 in 20,000 in different countries. Fortunately, a simple blood screening test in the first week of life alerts physicians to the possibility of PKU and further diagnostic tests are easily made. Modification of diet beginning in infancy can prevent the extremely deleterious effects of PKU. However, women with hyperphenylalaniemia (silent PKU) are more likely than others to produce children with ID. Since inheritance follows the usual Mendelian laws for recessive genes, babies born to treated adults with PKU are at high risk for PKU or carrier status (Guthrie, 1972).

Other rare genetic metabolic disorders associated with ID include histidinemia, hereditary fructose intolerance, Wilson disease (hepatolenticular degeneration), galactosemia, maple syrup urine disease, Hartnup syndrome, Hurler disease (lipochondrodystrophy or gargoylism), and several of the amaurotic group, including infantile Tay-Sachs disease. Adults who are carriers of some of these disorders (e.g., Tay-Sachs) can be identified and may choose not to have children. Early death is associated with some metabolic disorders, but for some others medical treatments may prevent the severe disability associated with the disorder (Grossman, 1983; Lee, 1980).

Approximately one third of the cases of hypothyroidism (cretinism) are of the nonendemic familial type, which is hereditary. Untreated cretins have ID, short stature, and other physical signs. Hypothyroidism is readily diagnosed in infancy and most cases respond readily to medical treatment. Among other rare inherited conditions associated with retardation are cri du chat, Patou, Edwards, Lesch-Nyhan, Hunter, Duchenne, Williams, and Lawrence-Moon-Biedl syndromes, and tuberous sclerosis, congenital ectodermoses, neurofibromatosis, and trigeminal cerebral angiomatosis. Retardation is also found with greater than expected frequency in the genetic disorders of Turner and Klinefelter syndromes, but the majority of those victims are not retarded (Feingold, 1980; Grossman, 1983; Sciorra, 1980).

In summary, heredity is clearly a factor in some disorders with ID as a concomitant condition. However, those are the minority of ID cases, usually associated with severe ID, and found primarily in cases of chromosomal defects and endocrine dysfunction. In other disorders, genes are indicated, but the mechanism is unclear. It is probable that there is a hereditary component in cultural-familial retardation, but the mechanism and amount of genetic contribution is uncertain.

REFERENCES

Feingold, M. (1980). Delineation of human genetic syndromes with mental retardation. In M. M. McCormack (Ed.), *Prevention of mental retardation and other developmental disabilities.* New York, NY: Marcel Dekker.

Gillberg, C. (1995). *Clinical child neuropsychiatry.* Cambridge, England: Cambridge University Press.

Grossman, H. J. (Ed.). (1983). *Classification in mental retardation.* Washington, DC: American Association on Mental Deficiency.

Guthrie, R. (1972). Mass screening for genetic disease. *Hospital Practice, 7,* 93–100.

Hayden, A. H., & Haring, N. G. (1976). Programs for Down's syndrome children at the University of Washington. In T. D. Tjossem (Ed.), *Intervention strategies for high-risk infants and young children.* Baltimore, MD: University Park Press.

Lee, M-L. (1980). Aminoacidopathy and mental retardation. In M. M. McCormack (Ed.), *Prevention of mental retardation and other developmental disabilities.* New York, NY: Marcel Dekker.

Reed, E. W., & Reed, S. C. (1965). *Mental retardation: A family study.* Philadelphia, PA: Saunders.

Rynders, J. E., & Horrobin, J. M. (1975). Project EDGE: The University of Minnesota's communication simulation program for Down's syndrome infants. In B. Friedlander, G. Sterritt, & G. Kirk (Eds.), *Exceptional infant: Assessment and intervention* (Vol. 3). New York, NY: Brunner/Mazel.

Sciorra, L. J. (1980). Chromosomal basis for developmental disability and mental retardation. In M. M. McCormack (Ed.), *Prevention of mental retardation and other developmental disabilities.* New York, NY: Marcel Dekker.

Westling, D. L. (1986). *Introduction to mental retardation.* Englewood Cliffs, NJ: Prentice Hall.

SUE ALLEN WARREN
Boston University

See also Congenital Disorders; Cretinism; Cri du Chat Syndrome; Down Syndrome; Phenylketonuria; Tay-Sachs Disease

FAMILIAR DYSAUTONOMIA

Familial dysautonomia (FD) was first identified as a syndrome by Riley and his associates in 1949; it was named Riley-Day syndrome (Riley, Day, Greeley, & Langford, 1949). The symptomatology, which is extensive, results from involvement of the central (CNS) and peripheral nervous systems (PNS) and impacts on other developing systems of the body. Dysautonomia is transmitted genetically, with the mode of inheritance believed to be autosomal recessive. The disorder is prominently marked by the individual's insensitivity to pain, absence of lacrimation, and absence of taste buds, in addition to many functional incapacities from birth (Brown, 2003). Dysautonomia is rarely diagnosed during the neonatal period (Perlman, Benady, & Sassi, 1979), although early identification is important to its management and to provision of appropriate treatment and educational services. The disorder is progressive, with those involved rarely living beyond the fourth decade of life. Exceptions have been noted, however, and because improvement can occur, an optimistic attitude may enhance the emotional relationship between family members (Meijer & Hovne, 1981).

Neonatal functioning, when identified, may be marked by unusual posture and limb movements as well as difficulties in swallowing (Perlman et al., 1979). The latter may be associated with other oropharyngeal deficits, may interfere with subsequent normative speech development, and may require the assistance of speech therapy. With regard to problems of swallowing, early identification and the provision of a feeding program would greatly assist the young child, as feeding problems have also been found in a large percentage of this population (Ganz, Levine, Axelrod, & Kahanovitz, 1983). As an adult, the dysautonomic may be dysarthric, resulting from involvement of the CNS. The presence of altered posture and limb movements may further interfere with the integration of more complex motor patterns, and delayed developmental milestones may also be noted (Ganz et al., 1983).

Orthopedic problems, including scoliosis and kyphosis, may also develop, thus requiring the use of adaptive aids for positioning and, in severe cases, to aid in locomotion. Physical therapy input would probably be indicated by this time, as might occupational therapy to assist the individual in maintaining range of motion. If the disorder progresses to the point where hospitalization becomes necessary, as much contact as possible should be maintained with the child or adolescent's educational placement and home setting by the hospital. "Hospitalization is indeed a disrupting and threatening experience even for the older, more experienced adult patient... and the younger child with more limited coping skills... is at particular psychological risk" (Barowsky, 1978, p. 48). Decreased vitality, resulting from compromised vital functions that may occur with severe scoliosis and kyphosis, as well as with cardiovascular and pulmonary problems associated with dysautonomia, may dictate adjustment of the individual's activity levels and routines. Additionally, the presence of ataxia (difficulties with balance and maintaining position in space) presents problems of both coordination and safety to the dysautonomic individual.

Dysautonomia is generally not marked by a decrease in IQ, therefore individuals can benefit from full inclusion. They may also take an active role in the treatment and educational process and thus feel more in control of the disorder that has altered their lives. The maintenance of maximal functional ability can best be attained by the active involvement of dysautonomics on their own behalf, rather than through their passive compliance, often ascribed to the old medical model of treatment. Thus, individuals with familial dysautonomia require specialized educational, medical, and psychological treatment through their lifespans: the absence of any of these components represents a marked deficit in the management process.

Characteristics

1. Reduced or absent ability to produce tears
2. Lack of fungiform papillae on tongue
3. Excessive sweating
4. Vasomotor instability
5. Swallowing difficulties and episodic vomiting
6. Speech and motor dysfunction
7. Reduced heat, pain, and taste perception
8. Poor growth and scoliosis

REFERENCES

Barowsky, E. I. (1978). Young children's perceptions and reactions to hospitalization. In E. Gellert (Ed.), *Psychosocial aspects of pediatric care*. New York, NY: Grune & Stratton.

Brown, R. T. (2003). Familial dysautonomia. In E. Fletcher-Janzen & C. R. Reynolds (Eds.), *Childhood disorders diagnostic desk reference* (pp. 222–223). Hoboken, NJ: Wiley.

Ganz, S. B., Levine, D. D., Axelrod, F. B., & Kahanovitz, N. (1983). Physical therapy management of familial dysautonomia. *Physical Therapy, 63*(7), 1121–1124.

Meijer, A., & Hovne, R. (1981). Child psychiatric problems in "autonomous dysfunction." *Child Psychiatry & Human Development, 12*(2), 96–105.

Perlman, M., Benady, S., & Sassi, E. (1979). Neonatal diagnosis of familial dysautonomia. *Pediatrics, 63*(2), 238–241.

Riley, C. M., Day, R. L., Greeley, D. M., & Langford, W. S. (1949). Central autonomic dysfunction with defective lacrimation. I. Report of five cases. *Pediatrics, 3*, 468–478.

Ellis I. Barowsky
Hunter College, City University of New York

See also **Central Nervous System; Orthopedic Impairments**

FAMILIES FOR EARLY AUTISM TREATMENT

Families for Early Autism Treatment (FEAT) is "a nonprofit organization of parents, family members, and treatment professionals, designed to help families with children of all ages who have an Autism Spectrum Disorder (ASD), which includes Autistic Disorder, Pervasive Developmental Disorder, Not Otherwise Specified (PDD-NOS), and Asperger's Disorder (AS)" (n.d., para. 3). FEAT was started by a group of parents and professionals in Sacramento, California, in 1993. There are 27 independently run FEAT organizations across the United States and Canada. Web links to all 27 FEAT organizations can be found at http://www.feat.org. FEAT websites typically include information about autism diagnosis, applied behavior analysis (ABA) therapy, recommended readings and websites, local service providers, donations, and upcoming events.

Although each FEAT organization is run autonomously, the goals and structure of each organization are similar. FEAT organizations provide education on treatment options, federal and state education code, civil rights awareness, and early intervention. Many of the organizations hold trainings on research-based practices at monthly meetings or provide stipends for seminars or conferences. Advocacy resources (e.g., advocacy workshops, legal resources) are available for families and service providers of children with autism. In addition to gaining valuable information, members gain support from others through recreational events and support groups. FEAT membership is open to anyone interested in improving the life and education of individuals with ASD (Families for Early Autism Treatment, n.d.).

REFERENCES

Families for Early Autism Treatment. (n.d.). *Other FEAT websites*. Retrieved from http://www.feat.org

Families for Early Autism Treatment. (n.d.). *What is FEAT?* Retrieved from http://www.feat.org/AboutFEAT/tabid/145/Default.aspx

FAMILIES OF CULTURALLY/LINGUISTICALLY DIVERSE STUDENTS IN SPECIAL EDUCATION
(*See* Culturally/Linguistically Diverse Students in Special Education, Families of)

FAMILIES, POSITIVE BEHAVIOR SUPPORT

An essential goal of Positive Behavior Support has been and continues to be the improvement in the quality of the lives of people who receive behavioral supports (Dunlap, Sailor, Horner, & Sugai, 2009). Generating a positive and sustained impact on quality of life necessarily requires consideration of those closest to the individual. In the family is typically the most elemental and constant aspect in the lives of the individuals for whom PBS is being provided.

As the field of Positive Behavior Support has evolved from individually focused applications into a multitiered system of behavior support, the role of families has likewise developed in scope. However, the extent to which family involvement is evident in multitiered systems of School-wide PBS (SW-PBS) varies considerably across schools, districts, and states, as well as across the levels of behavioral support within schools. Unacceptably, parent involvement in PBS at any level has typically been limited (Gatti, Brusnahan, Ryan, & Nelson, 2008).

Federal education policy specifies the necessity of family involvement. Parents have fundamental rights as parents (IDEA, 2004) and are considered to be equal members of the Individual Education Plan teams along with the school staff. Federal legislation on early intervention dictates the creation of plans that address family needs (P.L. 99-457, the Infants and Toddlers With Disabilities Act, 1986). In legislation identifying requirements for receipt of Title I funding, school districts must involve parent in the planning, implementation, and evaluation of Title I programming [Title I, Part A, Section 1118(c)(4)(B) and Section 1118(e)(1)]. In spite of the general agreement that family involvement is essential to successful education for students, little agreement exists regarding the definition of family involvement and therefore the identification of what constitutes family involvement and the assessment of the impact of involved families on student behavior.

To demonstrate an optimal representation of engaging families in SW-PBS, three levels of "engagement" can be considered:

1. Awareness—families are familiar with features of PBS (knowledge)
2. Involvement—families attend meetings and assist in the school's implementation (participation)
3. Application—families use PBS related strategies at home and in the community (use)

Each of those three levels of engagement can be illustrated within the three most common levels (or tiers) of support:

1. Universal/Core supports (Tier 1)—those provided to all students across campus
2. Supplemental/Targeted supports (Tier 2)—those additional supports provided to some students with common needs
3. Individual/Intensive supports (Tier 3)—those intensive or individualized supports developed based on unique needs

Table F.1. Engaging Families Across the Levels of Support for Students in a Multitiered System

	Parental Awareness	Parental Involvement	Parental Application
Tier 1 (Core) Support	Include a review of the PBS expectations, rules and reinforcement system as part of orientation for parents of new students.	Identify at least one parent to be a team member on the schoolwide PBS team.	Provide a workshop for parents to demonstrate how they can extend the use of expectations, rules, and reinforcement into the home.
Tier 2 (Supplemental) Support	When a student is identified as needing additional behavioral support, meet with the parent to explain how the student was identified, what supports will be provided, and how the student's progress will be monitored.	Share with parents the social skills strategies covered in the skill building small group (i.e., steps on how to express "disagreement" appropriately).	Help parents learn how to identify situations at home in which the student may be lacking the social skill necessary to behave appropriately. Teach parents to review and reinforce the social skill strategies at home.
Tier 3 (Individual/ Intensive) Support	Provide parents with a graphic and narrative description of the Tier 3 process (assessment, intervention, and monitoring).	Include parents on the team that will be conducting the functional assessment and developing the intervention plan.	Teach parents how to identify the function of misbehavior and set up interventions to prevent, instruct, and reinforce to make it more likely their child will use appropriate behaviors.

Table F.1 provides examples of how schools engage families at increasing levels across the typical levels of support provided for students in a multitiered system.

The effectiveness of SW-PBS has been demonstrated at various levels of intervention, as has the value of parent involvement in their children's education (Henderson & Mapp, 2002). A blending of these two into cohesive systems that engage parents at multiple levels is likely to enhance the effectiveness and efficiency of SW-PBS and further enhance outcomes for students. Although the field has yet to develop valid instruments for assessing parent engagement and the impact that has on the success of students' academic and behavioral success, recently state educational agencies, districts, and schools have begun developing strategies to improve parent involvement in SW-PBS. Key exemplars include Colorado's PBS Project (http://www.cde.state.co.us/) and Iowa's Behavioral Alliance (www.educ.drake.edu/rc/alliance.html) and others are following suit.

REFERENCES

Dunlap, G., Sailor, W., Horner, R., & Sugai, G. (2009). Overview and history of positive behavior support. In *Handbook of positive behavior support* (pp. 3–16). Springer: New York, NY: Springer.

Gatti, S. N., Brusnahan, L. S., Ryan, C., & Nelson, R. (2008). Strategies for increasing parental involvement in schoolwide positive behavior support initiatives. Presentation delivered at the Association for Positive Behavior Support (March, 2008).

Henderson, N., & Mapp, K. (2002). A new wave of evidence: The impact of school, family, and community connections on student achievement: Annual synthesis. Retrieved from http://www.sedl.org

Individuals with Disabilities Education Act (IDEA). (2004). P.L. 99-457, the Infants and Toddlers with Disabilities Act, 1986 Title I, Part A, Section 1118(c)(4)(B) and Section 1118(e)(1).

KAREN ELFNER CHILDS
University of South Florida

FAMILY COUNSELING

Family counseling is an interactive process that aims to assist families in regaining a balance comfortable to all members (Mash, 2005; Perez, 1979). Family counseling is a therapeutic technique for exploring and alleviating the current interlocking emotional problems within a family system by helping family members to change dysfunctional transaction patterns together (Goldenberg & Goldenberg, 1985).

Family counseling is usually indicated when the family's ability to perform becomes inadequate. Unlike individual counseling, which focuses on the person's intrapsychic difficulties, family counseling emphasizes the relationships that transpire during therapeutic settings (Goldenberg & Goldenberg, 1983). Family counseling evolved from an extension of psychoanalytic treatment to coverage of a full range of emotional problems. The field includes work with families, the introduction of general systems theory, the evolution of child guidance and marital counseling, and an increased interest in new clinical techniques such as group therapy. It grew out of a need to expand traditional therapy from a linear approach to a multi-factor systematic view of individuals and their families (Frank, 1984).

Goals of family counseling include (a) increasing each member's tolerance for each member's uniqueness; (b) increasing each member's tolerance for frustration when loss, conflict, and disappointment are encountered; (c) increasing the motivation of each member to support, encourage, and enhance each other member; and (d) increasing congruent perceptions of family members (Perez, 1979).

Families of children in special education require family counseling frequently simply because of the multiplicity of crises with which they are faced. Black (1982) indicates that the treatment of children with disabilities and their families is as complex and diverse as are the disorders from which they suffer. The communication problems indigenous to handicapping conditions (sensory, affective, or cognitive) cause enormous problems of communication within the family. These problems can be mitigated through the use of family therapy. A frame of reference must be retained, however, in that the presence of a child with disabilities does not presume family problems.

Through the use of family counseling, parents and other family members may alter their behavior patterns to produce positive changes in the behaviors of their children (Kozloff, 1979).

REFERENCES

Black, D. (1982). Handicap and family therapy. In A. Bentovin, G. Barnes, & A. Cooklin (Eds.), *Family therapy* (Vol. 2). New York, NY: Grune & Stratton.

Frank, C. (1984). Contextual family therapy. *American Journal of Family Therapy, 12*(1), 3–12.

Goldenberg, I., & Goldenberg, H. (1983). Historical roots of contemporary family therapy. In B. B. Solman & G. Stricker (Eds.), *Handbook of family and marital therapy*. New York, NY: Plenum Press.

Goldenberg, I., & Goldenberg, H. (1985). *Family therapy: An overview*. Monterey, CA: Brooks/Cole.

Kozloff, M. A. (1979). *A program for families of children with learning and behavior problems*. New York, NY: Wiley.

Mash, E. J. (1998). Treatment of child and family disturbance. In E. J. Mash & R. A. Barkley (Eds.), *Treatment of childhood disorders* (pp. 3–50). New York, NY: Guilford Press.

Perez, J. (1979). *Family counseling: Theory and practice*. New York, NY: Van Nostrand.

ANNE M. BAUER
University of Cincinnati

See also Counseling Individuals With Disabilities; Family
Response to a Child With Disabilities; Family Therapy

FAMILY EDUCATIONAL RIGHTS AND PRIVACY ACT

The Family Educational Rights and Privacy Act (FERPA) (20 U.S.C. § 1232g; 34 CFR Part 99), also known as the Buckley Amendment, is a 1974 amendment to the Elementary and Secondary Education Act of 1965 (ESEA; Jacob-Timm & Hartshorne, 1995). FERPA is a federal law that protects the privacy of student records by allowing parents rights to their child's education records. Rights transfer to the student at the age of 18 or if the student attends a postsecondary institution.

Prior to the enactment of FERPA, numerous anomalies existed in the schools' record-keeping policies and procedures. First, many schools had exercised the authority of denying parents access to their child's educational records, while allowing many third parties, such as government agents and prospective employers, unlimited access to the education records. Second, certain types of information tended to accrete in the student's education records, and the information was not always based on fact or used for educational purposes. Third, the right of access to a student's education records varied from state to state and was often based on common case law and/or local policy. Fourth, parents were often denied the opportunity to challenge the accuracy of the content of their child's education records, and the parents' requests and the schools' denials went unrecorded (Rosenfield, 1989).

To address the preceding irregularities or anomalies in schools' record-keeping policies and procedures, the U.S. Congress passed FERPA, sponsored by U.S. Senator James Buckley, in 1974. However, it would take an additional 12 years before the final version of the FERPA regulations were promulgated, due to restructuring in the U.S. President's cabinet (specifically, establishment of the Department of Education, transferring of the FERPA regulations from what was once known as the Department of Health, Education, and Welfare and is now known as the Department of Health and Human Services to the Department of Education; and codifying the regulations in the Code of Federal Regulations). The final version of the FERPA regulations were published in 1988, although they have been revised several times since then, with the most recent revision effective in 2011.

The 1988 final version of the FERPA regulations were more simplified and clearer than the initial regulations issued in 1976. The 1988 final version of FERPA also reduced some of the regulatory burden placed on colleges and universities (American Association of Collegiate Registrars and Admissions Officers [AACRAO], 1995).

Since 1988, various acts and other amendments have modified FERPA. The Crime Awareness and Campus Security Act amended FERPA in 1990. This act led to modifications in the FERPA disclosure rules. In 1992, the Higher Education amendments also led to modifications in the FERPA provisions. The amendments excluded certain law enforcement records of institutes of higher education from being categorized as student education records. In 1995, modifications were made in the exclusion of certain law enforcement records as well (AACRAO, 1995). The Improving America's Schools Act in 1994 also had a major impact on the FERPA regulations. The Improving America's Schools Act essentially tightened privacy assurances for students and their families.

FERPA provides parents or eligible students the right to inspect and review the student's education records maintained by the school, request changes to school records in which the protected parties feel incorrect information may have been documented, obtain written permission to release information from a student's education record, and destroy records within specified timelines. While parent or student permission is required to release records, the following records are disclosed without consent: school officials with educational interest, schools to which a student is transferring, appropriate parties related to financial aid, organizations conducting research on behalf of the school, accrediting organizations, judicial orders or legally issued subpoena, officials dealing with health/safety emergencies, and state/local authorities of the juvenile justice system. Information related to the student's name, address, telephone number, date and place of birth, honors and awards, and dates of attendance may be released without consent, but parents and students must be provided a reasonable amount of time to request records of this nature not be disclosed. Schools are responsible for notifying students and parents annually about their specific rights under FERPA.

Recent amendments to FERPA allow education records to be protected, but allows states to effectively used the data needed to increase accountability. Schools are required to ensure limited resources are invested effectively, determine what is working and discontinue what is not, and further contribute to a culture of innovation and continuous improvement in education. Data-based decisions help educators to plan and provide the best education possible, but they must be aware of the balance between the use of student data and the protection of student privacy.

The Family Policy Compliance Office may be contacted at Family Policy Compliance Office, U.S. Department of Education, 400 Maryland Avenue, SW, Washington, DC 20202-8520.

REFERENCES

American Association of Collegiate Registrars and Admissions Officers (AACRAO). (1995). *Implementation of the Family Educational Rights and Privacy Act of 1974 as amended—revised edition* (Report No. ISBN-0-929851-26-9). Annapolis Junction, MD: AACRAO Distribution Center. (ERIC Document Reproduction Service No. ED 384 333)

Family Educational Rights and Privacy Act of 1974, 34 C.F.R. § Part 99 (2011). Retrieved from http://www2.ed.gov/policy/gen/guid/fpco/ferpa/index.html

Family Educational Rights and Privacy Act of 1974, 34 C.F.R. § Part 99 (2011). Retrieved from Federal Register https://www.federalregister.gov/articles/2011/12/02/2011-30683/family-educational-rights-and-privacy

Jacob-Timm, S., & Hartshorne, T. (1995). *Ethics and law for school psychologists*. Brandon, VT: Clinical Psychology Publishing.

Rosenfield, S. (1989). *EHA and FERPA confidentiality*. Washington, DC: EDLAW.

Patricia A. Lowe
University of Kansas

Cecil R. Reynolds
Texas A&M University
Second edition

Kimberly F. Applequist
University of Colorado
at Colorado Springs
Third edition

See also Buckley Amendment; Individuals With Disabilities Education Improvement Act of 2004 (IDEIA)

FAMILY INVOLVEMENT, TRANSITION

Family involvement is recognized in general education as among the strongest predictors of student achievement. The No Child Left Behind Act (NCLB) from 2001 underscored the critical role of families. Traditional types of parent involvement cited as beneficial include overseeing educational progress, helping with homework, volunteering at school events and in the classroom, and advocacy (Epstein, 2005).

The importance of family involvement for youth with disabilities in transition is perhaps even more critical in not just leading to academic success in school, but to positive postschool outcomes around employment, independent living, postsecondary educational pursuit, and more. The Individuals with Disabilities Education Improvement Act (IDEA) of 2004 requires parental involvement as part of the educational planning process. Because the support needs of students with disabilities can be significantly greater than their peers, the roles families play in the educational process may, by necessity, be broader.

In addition to typical school involvement efforts, families often support students with disabilities outside the school walls and beyond academic pursuits during the transition years. Families are students' first teachers, and can be instrumental in establishing a vision for the future and a culture of high expectations for students that starts at very young ages (Morningstar, Turnbull, & Turnbull, 1995). As students enter the transition years, families may act as coaches, moral supports, and sounding boards (Trainor, Carter, Swedeen, Cole, & Smith, in press) as students explore their strengths, interests, and future ambitions.

Because families are a permanent part of students' lives, they also have the ability to follow through on efforts long after the school day or calendar ends, helping students develop and practice critical skills, providing community experiences in which students learn and grow, and supporting development of increased self-determination and independence from very young ages and continuing into adulthood.

Families also may have connections to people and resources in their communities that can lead to expanded opportunities and relationships for students with disabilities, and they may partner with schools in providing important supports like transportation to activities or work.

Yet, many barriers exist that impact the ability of families to effectively partner with schools. These include a lack of family time and resources, cultural and language differences, a lack of understanding about the transition process, a history of bad experiences with the education system, a perception of not being heard or having no impact on the decision-making process, and more. Enlisting family and student participation has been cited as among the top five challenges facing secondary education transition (Johnson, Stodden, Emanuel, Luecking, & Mack, 2002).

Lack of perceived family involvement by schools does not mean families are not committed to seeing their children succeed as adults or to working on the skills and experiences necessary for that to happen. For instance, one study found that families of culturally and linguistically diverse students were actually much more engaged in supporting transition activities and goals than educators realized. The difference was one of approach: Families put high value in community and family contexts, rather than a school-based context for gaining the experiences and skills needed for successful transition to adulthood.

Some strategies that schools can use to more fully engage and partner with families in the transition process include:

- Helping families understand all aspects of the transition process, including other partner agencies in transition.
- Avoiding jargon and acronyms and explaining all terminology.

- Discussing future options with families, including employment, postsecondary, and other career opportunities.
- Connecting families to other families in transition so parents can learn from others in similar situations.
- Connecting families to parent leadership programs and other resources specifically designed for families. Every state has a Parent Training Initiative: Visit http://www.familyvillage.wisc.edu/index.html to locate the effort in your state.
- Encouraging multiple ways to connect and share updates, including by e-mail, ichat, in person at the family's home or a neighborhood location, and so forth.
- Respecting and seeking to understand the family's priorities and concerns, as well as their knowledge and understanding of their own child.
- Encouraging participation by and input from all family members, including siblings and extended family.

REFERENCES

Epstein, J. L. (2005) Attainable goals? The spirit and the letter of the No Child Left Behind Act on parents. *Sociology of Education*, 78(2), 179–182.

Johnson, D. R., Stodden, R., Emanuel, E., Luecking, R. & Mack, M. (2002). Current challenges facing secondary education and transition services: What research tells us. *Exceptional Children*, 68(4), 519–531.

Morningstar, M. E., Turnbull, A. P., & Turnbull, H. R. (1995). What do students with disabilities tell us about the importance of family involvement in the transition from school to adult life? *Exceptional Children*, 62, 249–260.

Trainor, A. A., Carter, E. W., Swedeen, B., Cole, O., & Smith, S. A. (in press). Perspectives of adolescents with disabilities on employment and community experiences. *Journal of Special Education*, 45(3), 157–170.

BETH SWEDEEN
University of Wisconsin
Fourth edition

FAMILY POLICY COMPLIANCE OFFICE

The Family Policy Compliance Office (FPCO) is an office of the U.S. Department of Education whose mission is to meet the needs of learners of all ages by effectively implementing legislation that seeks to ensure student and parental rights in education: the Family Educational Rights and Privacy Act (FERPA) and the Protection of Pupil Rights Amendment (PPRA).

Parents and eligible students who need assistance and/or wish to file a complaint under FERPA or PPRA should do so in writing to the FPCO at Family Policy Compliance Office, U.S. Department of Education, 400 Maryland Avenue, SW, Washington, DC 20202-5920.

STAFF

FAMILY RESPONSE TO A CHILD WITH DISABILITIES

Having a child with a disability can positively affect the family system and help the family become more resilient and healthy (Havens, 2008). Though learning that a child has a disability may cause a family to feel distressed and drift apart, this does not have to be the case. Initially, there can be a sense of family or sibling strain, but families can overcome these feelings and move forward. Maintaining perspective and keeping open communication are key in adjusting to having a child with a disability.

Acknowledging and accepting that a child has a disability is often a long journey for a family (Pfaff, 2002). Parents may struggle with the notions that their expectations for their child are shattered and that life will forever be different. After hearing the diagnosis, these feelings of being overwhelmed and uncertain can last anywhere from a few days to a few months. It is during this time that families begin to go through stages of adjustment.

A state of shock is typically the first reaction of parents to learning that their child has a disability (Healey, 1997). This period is characterized by a calm detachment from the actual problem. Parents eventually become aware that a real problem exists, but this takes time. Emotions during this phase are often heightened. Typical emotional reactions include inadequacy, uncertainty, disbelief, and confusion. Physical outbursts may also occur during this phase. As a way to combat these strong emotions, parents begin to deny the problem exists. This denial may take the form of seeking multiple professional opinions that are overly optimistic or becoming angry with professionals who present a modest prognosis for the child's development. Parents may search for cures or remedies in attempts to alter the reality that their child has a disability.

During the second phase of adjustment, feelings of anger arise. This anger could be expressed in two forms: outward anger, which could result in rage or an act of physical aggression, or inward anger, which emphasizes blame on oneself and internal guilt. Parents often find themselves displacing their anger on professionals and diagnosticians who confirm that their child has a disability. Feeling overwhelmed by the anger can leave parents feeling helpless, with low self-esteem. Throughout this phase, outsiders need to be aware that this is a crucial stage for the family and nothing they say or do should be taken personally (Healey, 1997).

In the third phase of adjustment, parents often begin bargaining in an attempt to make their child's disability disappear (Wilde, 2004). Bargaining also has many forms. Some parents might search for multiple medical opinions in hopes of one nullifying all of the others, while other parents may look to a "higher power" to solve their problems. Extreme examples of bargaining include seeking out a faith healer, visiting with a guru, or finding alternative medical treatment.

Stage four is often categorized by feelings of guilt and, sometimes, the onset of depression. This phase is often the time when parents express that they feel like they could have prevented the child from having a disability. Feelings of extreme anxiety and hopelessness, stemming from a newfound overwhelming sense of responsibility, are common during this time (Healey, 1997). Family isolation, an attempt to hide the child from society, and retreating frequently occur. Self-destructive behaviors, including the use of addictive substances, can also be an issue for the family (Wilde, 2004).

When parents begin to accept that the child does have a disability of some form, they may begin to discuss their child's problem with medical professionals, school staff, and friends. Parents in this phase become realistic when discussing the prognosis for their child's coping with the disability and begin helping their child strengthen their skills and abilities (Wilde, 2004). At this point, parents actually acknowledge their child's disability and understand that it is time to face reality. Acknowledgment clears the way for the final stage of hope, in which the parents actually adapt to the demands of having a child with a disability and begin to see that life can get better.

The final phase of hope places emphasis on bringing the members of the family back together and moving forward as one solid unit. Parents can commit to providing the experiences and opportunities necessary to maximize the child's potential because they have finally let go of the undue emotions. Each time a new stage is reached, like adolescence or adulthood for example, the parents will again have to acknowledge the problems that arise and take the steps necessary to solve them.

In some cases, however, parents may find themselves "stuck" in one of the stages of adjustment (Wilde, 2004). One reason for staying in a particular stage is because the family has a lack of professional or personal support. Outside support is of the utmost importance when moving through the stages of adjustment, so a lack of support can cause the family to get stuck in a stage. A second reason for families feeling "stuck" is that the parents might experience reinforcement for remaining in a stage, such as extra attention from family or professionals. Reinforcement could potentially keep the parents from wanting to move forward in the adjustment process. The third reason for being "stuck" pertains to the families living or working conditions. If the conditions are hostile or unsettling, adjustment might not possible for the parents. This issue, too, can cause a family to get stuck in a particular stage.

Siblings of the child with disabilities are equally as affected by the reactions of parents (Osman, n.d.). As parents progress through the stages of adjustment, their relationship with other children in the family can change. For the most part, the more time parents spend in the phases of acceptance and hope, the better the relationship with their other children turns out to be. Essentially, a positive attitude and outlook on life can drastically affect the functioning of the family unit (Pfaff, 2002).

Parents need to be honest and open when discussing their child's disability with siblings (Osman, n.d.). This allows the other children to fully understand their sibling's special needs. Also, parents should be accepting when their other children express their emotions. For example, the siblings may display jealousy due to lack of parental attention and guilt due to the fact that they are "normal" and their sibling has a disability.

The care and attention required by the child with a disability may substantially diminish the time available for other family members. When a parent spends an excessive amount of time with a child with a disability, it may deprive the other children of pertinent opportunities and experiences vital for their own growth and development. If parents set aside exclusive time for each of their children, it can ensure that all individual needs are being met (Pfaff, 2002).

In contrast, it is also important to note that not all families react to having a child with a disability by navigating through the stages of adjustment (Hanline, 1991). Some may experience certain stages and not others, the stages out of order, or no stages at all. In fact, some families report that having a child with a disability positively affected their family unit by bringing them closer together. The way a family adjusts to having a child with a disability is unique to their personal situation.

In conclusion, while some parents may adjust easily, other experience feelings of grief when learning that one of their children has a disability of some form. Though this reaction may begin with shock or denial, overtime the family can learn how function as a healthy, resilient unit. Successfully moving through each of the stages of grief can positively affect the family's ability to adjust overall.

REFERENCES

Hanline, M. F. (1991). Transitions and critical events in the family life cycle: Implications for providing support to families of children with disabilities. *Psychology in the Schools, 28,* 53–59.

Havens, A. (2008). *Becoming a resilient family: child disability and the family system.* National Center on Accessibility. Retrieved from http://www.ncaonline.org/.

Healey, B. (1997). *Helping parents deal with the fact that their child has a disability.* LD OnLine: The world. Retrieved from http://www.ldonline.org/article/5937/

Osman, B. (n.d.). *How learning disabilities affect a child.* Great Schools. Retrieved from http://www.greatschools.org/special-education/support/732-learning-disabilities-and-siblings.gs

Pfaff, L. (2002). *Raising a child with disabilities.* SMA Support Inc., Home of Spinal Muscular Atrophy. Retrieved from http://www.smasupport.com/NewsArticles/raisingachild.htm; http://www.ldonline.org/article/5937/

Wilde, J. (2004). *The disability journey: A bridge from awareness to action.* Lincoln, NE: iUniverse Inc. Retrieved from http://books.google.com/books?id=N5treWMW-wIC&pg=PA50&lpg=PA50&dq=bargaining stage of adjustment&source=bl&ots=CgajJEe3nA&sig=_R5GP6X33T3hsN5lNnUM4nOm-bU&hl=en&ei=hYG8Tv7YJufU2AXqzImTBQ&sa=X&oi=book_result&ct=result&resnum=4&ved=0CDMQ6AEwAw

MORGAN BAKER
Texas A&M University
Fourth edition

See *also* Parental Counseling; Parent Education

FAMILY SERVICE AMERICA

Founded in 1911 as the Family Welfare Association of America, and then the Family Service Association of America, the current name is Family Service America. The association is a federation of 280 local agencies located in over 1,000 communities. The local agencies provide a variety of services designed to resolve problems of family living, including family counseling, family life education, and family advocacy services dealing with parent-child, marital, and mental health problems. The association assists member agencies in developing and providing effective family services. In 1998, FSA was renamed the Alliance for Children and Families Inc. (ACF) and formed Ways to Work Inc. The Alliance, formed by the 1998 merger of Family Service America and the National Association of Homes and Services for Children, helps member agency leaders successfully meet today's and tomorrow's challenges by drawing upon its more than 90 years of leadership in the human services community. The ACF provides services to nonprofit child and family services and economic empowerment organizations. Motivated by a vision of a healthy society and strong communities, they work to strengthen America's nonprofit sector and through advocacy assure the sector's continued independence.

Strong family life is promoted through contact with the media, government, business, and industry. The ACF compiles statistics, conducts research, sponsors competitions, and bestows awards. Publications include books, the journal *Families in Society: The Journal of Contemporary Human Services*, and a directory of member agencies. Public information activities include the production and dissemination of manuals, pamphlets, brochures, and public service releases. Biennial meetings are held in odd-numbered years. The ACF maintains a library with primary holdings in social work, family life, psychology, and nonprofit agency management. A placement service is also available. ACF offices are located at 11700 W. Lake Park Drive, Milwaukee, WI 53224. Tel.: (414) 359-1040, website: http://www.alliance1.org/

PHILIP R. JONES
Virginia Polytechnic Institute and State University
First edition

MARIE ALMOND
The University of Texas of the Permian Basin
Second edition

JESSI K. WHEATLEY
Falcon School District 49, Colorado Springs, Colorado
Third edition

FAMILY THERAPY

Family therapy offers a distinctive theoretical approach for working with human problems, with the focus on the individual and their relationships with others, especially within the family structure. This interpersonal and systemic perspective challenged and revolutionized the etiology and treatment of psychological difficulties, and created advances in the way we view human functioning.

Prior to family therapy, methods of helping individuals focused on the individual, and sought to help the person resolve personal or intrapsychic conflicts. Thus, most therapists would treat the individual, and refuse to see the client's spouse or family members. Family therapy, however, believes that problems and solutions lie in the patterns and connections among people, that people exist in a context of mutual influence and interaction, and thus the individual must be considered part of a larger system, such as the family.

The theoretical foundations for family therapy began in the 1920s and came from diverse areas. First, research exploring the dynamics of small groups found similarities with family functioning, in that the individual exists as part of a social structure, and group membership defines various roles and interactions. Second, the child guidance movement discovered that families often played a part in the successful treatment of childhood difficulties. Third, social work, with their tradition of community service, provided additional support that the family is an important focus of intervention. Finally, research investigating family functioning and schizophrenia observed dramatic differences in the patient's behavior when family members were present, and concluded that families were a major influencing factor in mental disorders. All of these different sources suggested families play an important part in life and development, and an interpersonal approach to solving problems is the most appropriate model from which to provide treatment.

It was not until the 1950s that family therapy as a practice was initiated by a number of individuals from a wide range of professions including social work, psychiatry, and psychology. They included John Bell at Clark University, Murray Bowen at the Menninger Clinic and later at NIMH, Nathan Ackerman in New York, and Don Jackson and Jay Haley in Palo Alto. Others making significant contributions to the development of family therapy were Lyman Wynne, Theodore Lidz, Virginia Satir, Carl Whitaker, Ivan Boszormenyi-Nagy, Christian Midelfort, Robert MacGregor, and Salvador Minuchin.

Presently, family therapy practitioners are represented by several national organizations, with The American Association for Marriage and Family Therapy being the most prominent at over 24,500 members. The association is located in Washington, DC, and has primary responsibility for the certification and endorsement of training programs and individual practitioners.

Family therapy and the systemic principles on which it is founded continue to be utilized today in mental health centers, community agencies, and educational settings. Family therapy represents a challenging and beneficial method of intervention for many personal difficulties.

This entry has been informed by the sources listed below.

REFERENCES

Becvar, D. S., & Becvar, R. J. (1996). *Family therapy: A systemic integration* (3rd ed.). Boston, MA: Allyn & Bacon.

Gladding, S. T. (1998). *Family therapy: History, theory, and practice* (2nd ed.). Upper Saddle River, NJ: Prentice Hall.

Goldenberg, I., & Goldenberg, H. (1991). *Family therapy: An overview* (3rd ed.). Belmont, CA: Brooks/Cole.

Nichols, M. P., & Schwartz, R. C. (1998). *Family therapy: Concepts and methods* (4th ed.). Boston, MA: Allyn & Bacon.

LINDA M. MONTGOMERY
The University of Texas of the Permian Basin

See also Parental Counseling

FARRELL, ELIZABETH E. (1870–1932)

Elizabeth E. Farrell, who began her teaching career in an ungraded rural school in upstate New York, accepted a position as an elementary teacher in New York City in 1900. Observing that some children were unable to make satisfactory progress in the elementary classes, Farrell, using her experience in the rural school in which she had taught all grades, formed an ungraded class for these children, the first special class in the public schools of New York City. In 1906 a Department of Ungraded Classes was formed with Farrell as director, a position she held until her death.

Farrell designed the nation's first training program for special class teachers in 1911 at the Maxwell Training School in New York City, and she taught the first university courses for special class teachers at the University of Pennsylvania in 1912. Largely through her efforts, a program to prepare special class teachers was established at the Oswego (New York) Normal School in 1916.

Farrell originated and edited *Ungraded*, the journal of the Ungraded Class Teachers' Association. She was a founder of the Association of Consulting Psychologists. In 1922 she was one of 12 special educators who founded the International Council for Exceptional Children, and she served as its first president.

This entry has been informed by the source listed below.

REFERENCE

Warner, M. L. (1944). Founders of the International Council for Exceptional Children. *Journal of Exceptional Children, 10,* 217–223.

PAUL IRVINE
Katonah, New York

KIMBERLY VANNEST
Texas A&M University
Fourth edition

FEARS (*See Phobias and Fears*)

FEBRILE CONVULSIONS

Febrile convulsions are seizures associated with fevers or high body temperature in childhood and are a form of acute symptomatic seizures (Sinnar, 1999). Single or multiple generalized seizures in infancy or early childhood may be associated only with fever in about 4% of the population. Typically, febrile convulsions occur soon after the onset of a fever-producing illness not directly affecting the central nervous system. Usually the seizure occurs 3 to 6 hours after the onset of the fever (Livingston, 1972), although such seizures can be seen during the second or third day of an illness (Lennox-Buchtal, 1973). When the seizure begins, body temperature is usually at its peak at 39 to 40 degrees C (102 to 104 degrees F). Acute upper respiratory infection, tonsillitis, otitis media, and bronchial pneumonia are some common causes of febrile convulsions. The seizure is usually generalized and of short duration, although some may last as long as 20 minutes or more (Spreen, Tupper, Risser, Tuokko, & Edgell, 1984). The movements seen with these convulsions are bilateral but may show unilateral elements. Males have been found to be more susceptible to febrile seizures than females. Most investigators feel that there is an inherited susceptibility to seizure above a certain threshold of body temperature with autosomal dominant transmission (Brazier & Coceani, 1978; Sinnar, 1999).

Typically, this form of seizure activity is benign. Initially, it is difficult to separate these benign febrile convulsions from seizures caused by brain damage owed to unrecognized meningitis or congenital brain defects. The signs of a benign prognosis include (1) onset of the convulsions between the ages of 6 months and 4 years; (2) a normal EEG within a week after the seizure; (3) the absence of clinical signs of brain damage; and (4) the lack of atypical features or excessive duration of the attack. The chances of additional febrile seizures are about one in two if the first episode occurs before the age of 14 months, and much lower if the first attack occurs after 33 months of age. Few children have attacks later in life; however, it is not always possible to predict whether subsequent febrile or nonfebrile seizures will follow (Goldensohn, Glaser, & Goldberg, 1984).

Children who have a single febrile seizure have an excellent prognosis, as there appears to be little, if any, lasting neurological or mental deficit (National Institutes of Health, 1980; Sinnar, 1999). For those children who have a febrile convulsion in conjunction with a febrile seizure, preexisting central nervous system abnormalities, or a fever-inducing illness involving the central nervous system resulting in a convulsive episode, the prognosis is much less positive (Spreen et al., 1984).

REFERENCES

Brazier, M. A. B., & Coceani, F. (Eds.). (1978). *Brain dysfunction in infantile febrile convulsions.* International Brain Research Organization Monograph Series. New York, NY: Raven.

Goldensohn, E. S., Glaser, G. H., & Goldberg, M. A. (1984). Epilepsy. In L. P. Rowland (Ed.), *Merritt's textbook of neurology* (7th ed.) (pp. 629–650). Philadelphia, PA: Lea & Febiger.

Lennox-Buchtal, M. (1973). Febrile convulsions: A reappraisal. *Electroencephalography & Clinical Neurophysiology, 32* (Suppl. 1).

Livingston, S. (1972). Epilepsy in infancy, childhood, and adolescence. In B. Wolman (Ed.), *Manual of child psychopathology* (pp. 45–69). New York, NY: McGraw-Hill.

National Institutes of Health. (1980). Febrile seizures. A consensus of their significance, evaluation, and treatment. *Pediatrics, 66*, 1009–1030.

Sinnar, S. (1999). Febrile seizures. In K. F. Swaiman & S. Ashwal (Eds.), *Pediatric Neurology* (pp. 676–691). St. Louis, MO: Mosby.

Spreen, O., Tupper, D., Risser, A., Tuokko, H., & Edgell, D. (1984). *Human developmental neuropsychology.* New York, NY: Oxford University Press.

RICHARD A. BERG
West Virginia University Medical Center

See also Seizure Disorders

FEDERAL REGISTER

The *Federal Register (FR)* is a uniform system for publishing all executive orders and proclamations, proposed and final rules, regulations, and notices of agencies authorized by Congress or the president, certain documents required to be published by an act of Congress, and other documents deemed by the director of the *FR* to be of sufficient interest. It does not contain rules of Congress or of the courts. As such, it serves as formal notice to the public of legally significant actions and is typically the first place of public appearance of these documents (Cohen & Berring, 1984).

Since the *FR* publishes notices promulgated by federal agencies such as the U.S. Department of Education, it is an important source for regulations pertaining to special education. Regulations promulgated under the Education for All Handicapped Children Act (PL 94-142), for example, were first published here. Also, the *FR* is the primary source for the announcement of grant and contract competitions administered by special education programs. Guidelines and priorities for the spending of federal special education monies are contained therein as well.

The *FR* was established by the Federal Register Act of 1935 and is considered prima facie evidence of the filing and text of the original documents. It is issued each federal working day.

REFERENCE

Cohen, M. L., & Berring, R. C. (1984). *Finding the law.* St. Paul, MN: West.

DOUGLAS L. FRIEDMAN
Fordham University
Second edition

KIMBERLY F. APPLEQUIST
University of Colorado at Colorado Springs
Third edition

FEEBLE-MINDED

Feeble-minded is an historical term seen first in the early 16th century. The term was used to describe individuals with intellectual disabilities. The Swiss physician Aurealus Theophastus Bombastus von Hahenheim, better known as Paracelsus (1493–1541), used the term feeble-minded to describe individuals who act as "healthy animals."

J. Langdon Down (1826–1896) categorized distinct types of feeble-mindedness. Accidental feeble-mindedness resulted from trauma, inadequate prenatal care, prolonged delivery, inflammatory disease, or the unwise use of medication. Developmental feeble-mindedness resulted from disturbed mothers, parents inebriated at the time of conception, overexcitement during infancy through early childhood, or pressure from school at the time of second dentification or puberty. Although his patients were from poverty-stricken, urban neighborhoods, Down did not conceive of environmental factors as influencing development.

Edouard Seguin (1812–1880) offered yet another classification scheme: idiocy, or moderately to profoundly retarded; imbecility, or mildly retarded with defects in social development; backward or feeble-minded (enfant arriere); and simpleness or superficial retardation evidenced by the slowing down of development. The feeble-minded child was described by Seguin as a child who is retarded in development, and who has low muscle tone, uncoordinated use of the hands, and limited comprehension but no sensory deficits. Unlike Down, Seguin was sensitive to the fact that environmental factors and neglect could have a negative impact on development. Owing to the work of Samuel Gridley Howe (1801–1876) in the mid-1800s, it became more widely recognized that a percentage of feeble-minded children were the result of impoverished environments.

In the late 1800s, three broad categories of intellectual functioning appeared: idiot (severely and profoundly retarded), imbecile (moderately retarded), and feebleminded (mildly retarded). With the introduction of standardized tests of intelligence in the United States, the Committee on Classification of Feeble-Minded of the American Association for the Study of the Feeble-Minded (now the American Association on Mental Retardation) in 1910 issued a definition that set reasonable parameters on who could be classified as feeble-minded:

> The term feeble-minded is used generically to include all degrees of mental defect due to arrested or imperfect development as a result of which the person so affected is incapable of competing on equal terms with his normal fellows or managing himself or his affairs with ordinary prudence. The tripartite classification of mental retardation included: idiots (those so deeply defective that their mental development does not exceed that of a normal child of about 2 years); imbeciles (those whose mental development is higher than that of an idiot but does not exceed that of a normal child of about 7 years); and moron (those whose mental development is above that of an imbecile but does not exceed that of a child of about 12 years). (p. 61)

In the 1930s feeble-mindedness was defined as retarded intelligence with social incompetence. During the 1940s the term mentally deficient replaced feeble-minded as a generic label. The term is no longer applied in clinical or educational practice.

This entry has been informed by the sources listed below.

REFERENCES

Committee on Classification of Feeble-Minded. (1910). *Journal of Psycho-Asthenics, 15,* 61–67.

Kanner, L. (1967). Historical review of mental retardation (1800–1965). *American Journal of Mental Deficiency, 72,* 165–189.

Scheerenberger, R. C. (1983). *A history of mental retardation.* Baltimore, MD: Paul H. Brookes.

Seguin, E. (1971). *Idiocy and its treatment by the physiological method.* New York, NY: Kelly.

Sloan, W., & Stevens, H. (1976). *A century of concern: A history of the American Association on Mental Deficiency 1876–1976.* Washington, DC: American Association on Mental Deficiency.

CAROLE REITER GOTHELF
Hunter College, City University of New York

See also Idiot; Intellectual Developmental Delay

FEEDING DISORDER OF EARLY CHILDHOOD

Feeding disorder of early childhood is characterized by an enduring failure to eat adequately that is not due to a general medical condition of lack of available food and causes the infant or child (< 6 years) to fail to gain weight or to experience significant weight loss over a period of at least 1 month.

It has been estimated that 1–5% of all pediatric hospital admissions are due to failure to gain weight (i.e., failure to thrive), and as many as one half of these admissions may be associated with feeding disorders that are not due to any predisposing medical condition (Wolraich, Felice, & Drotar, 1996; Woolston, 1991). The prevalence of feeding disorder is equal in boys and girls.

Characteristics

1. Persistent failure to eat sufficiently, causing failure to gain weight or significant weight loss over at least 1 month that is present before age 6.
2. The feeding disturbance is not due to a gastrointestinal, endocrinological, neurological, or other medical condition, or to lack of available food.
3. Infants and children with feeding disorder may be irritable, inconsolable, withdrawn, or apathetic during feeding.
4. Associated problems include malnutrition, developmental delays, and growth retardation; parent-child interaction problems may also occur.

Given that the failure to gain weight or a significant loss of weight in infants and children can be due to a range of medical, psychological, and environmental conditions, a comprehensive multidimensional evaluation (integrating information from medical, nutritional, psychological, environmental, and parent-child interaction domains) is recommended in order to make a well-informed differential diagnosis and to focus treatment accordingly. After a diagnosis of feeding disorder has been made, treatment options are relatively straightforward and effective. Treatment typically involves parental education about the physiological development of eating behaviors, nutrition, child temperament, and the principles of learning and behavior change (Ramasamy & Perman, 2000; Ramsay, 1995). Effective treatments typically incorporate a behavior therapy component and include the use of a functional analysis to identify antecedents and consequences that can be manipulated in order to influence the child's eating behavior (e.g., prompting, reinforcement, and mild punishment).

Feeding disorder is more common in children with special needs due to developmental delays, chronic health conditions, communication difficulties, and physical limitations (Ramasamy & Perman, 2000). In such cases, feeding problems are most often due to an inability to manipulate or swallow certain foods, inappropriate or disruptive behavior during meals, or food selectivity. Assessment and treatment of children with special needs should employ a similar multidimensional approach and focus to that described previously (American Psychiatric Association, 1994).

If untreated, feeding disorder can lead to a range of negative outcomes such as malnutrition, growth retardation, developmental delays, susceptibility to infection and chronic illness, and possibly death; however, many children experience improved growth after some period of time. In addition, feeding disorder in infants and children is a risk factor for bulimia and anorexia nervosa later in life (Marchi & Cohen, 1990). The prognosis for feeding disorder is much more favorable if accurate diagnosis and empirically supported treatments are used early on in the course of this condition.

In an educational setting, children with feeding disorder may stand out for their lack of eating. It is necessary for a teacher to be aware of and well informed about this disorder, and special attention may be required for these children.

Although existing assessment and treatment techniques have proven effective in returning infants and children to normal eating and growth patterns, most studies have used single-case designs or small sample sizes without the use of randomization or control samples. Therefore, future research in this area should continue to explore the effectiveness of interdisciplinary assessment and treatment techniques using more complex research designs and larger and more diverse samples.

REFERENCES

American Psychiatric Association. (1994). *Diagnostic and statistical manual of mental disorders* (4th ed.). Washington, DC: Author.

Marchi, M., & Cohen, P. (1990). Early childhood eating behaviors and adolescent eating disorder. *Journal of the American Academy of Child and Adolescent Psychiatry, 29,* 112–117.

Ramasamy, M., & Perman, J. A. (2000). Pediatric feeding disorders. *Journal of Clinical Gastroenterology, 30,* 34–46.

Ramsay, M. (1995). Feeding disorder and failure to thrive. *Child and Adolescent Psychiatric Clinics of North America, 4,* 605–616.

Wolraich, M., Felice, M., & Drotar, D. (1996). The classification of child and adolescent mental diagnoses in primary care. In *Diagnostic and statistical manual for primary care (DSM-PC), child and adolescent version.* Elk Grove, IL: American Academy of Pediatrics.

Woolston, J. L. (1991). *Eating and growth disorders in infants and children.* Newbury Park, CA: Sage.

MATTHEW K. NOCK
Yale University

See also Feeding Disorders of Infancy

FEEDING DISORDERS OF INFANCY

Feeding disorders are characterized by any interference in the process of deglutition. Deglutition is the semiautomatic motor function of the muscles of the respiratory and gastrointestinal tracts that are responsible for moving food from the oral cavity (mouth) to the stomach (Miller, 1986). Normal oral motor function and swallowing are integral processes in oral feeding (Arvedson & Rogers, 1993).

Feeding and swallowing disorders in children (also known as dysphagia) are often part of a larger range of medical and health problems. Current advances in the medical field have led to increased survival rates of premature, low birth weight infants, as well as children who have undergone extensive medical or surgical procedures. As a result, a number of these infants and children experience complications. In particular, damage to the central nervous system, the airway, or both can occur, which results in a disruption of the oral feeding process (Arvedson & Rogers, 1993). The prevalence of feeding and swallowing disorders is not known. Additionally, there are no known variations among these children with regard to gender or ethnicity.

Characteristics

1. Extreme prematurity and very low birth weight.
2. Uncoordinated sucking, swallowing, and breathing that continues beyond 34–37 weeks gestation.
3. A history of long-term, nonoral feedings for a variety of reasons.
4. Cerebral palsy, mental retardation, or central nervous system dysgenesis (developmental anomalies of the brain) may be present in some children.
5. Some infants have experienced brain injury.
6. Disordered parent-child interactions, behavioral problems, or both are sometimes present (Arvedson & Rogers, 1993).

There are several known etiologies of feeding disorders. Arvedson and Rogers (1993) divide these etiologies into acute and chronic. Chronic disorders can be further classified as either static or progressive. Cerebral palsy is an example of a common static cause of dysphagia. Examples of progressive causes are destructive central nervous system tumors or neurodegenerative diseases.

Feeding disorders are often complicated by other factors. Respiratory distress interferes with oral feedings, as do abnormalities of the aerodigestive tract. These children frequently cough, have tachypnea, or gasp during oral feedings. Other less common complications are severe choking, apnea, and cyanosis. Aspiration pneumonia and various forms of lung disease have also been known to occur. Gastroesophageal reflux is frequently present in these children. Because feeding disorders typically result in prolonged oral feedings and a reduction of oral intake, malnutrition and growth failure may occur (Arvedson & Rogers, 1993).

A thorough clinical evaluation of feeding and swallowing commonly includes a review of the child's medical, developmental, and feeding history. A physical examination, prefeeding evaluation, and a feeding evaluation must also be conducted. Arvedson and Lefton-Grief (1998) stated that the clinical evaluation should provide the following information: the identification of possible causes of the dysphagia, a hypothesis about the nature and severity of the condition, a baseline of oral-motor skills and respiratory function, possible therapeutic techniques and feeding options, and a determination of the need for an instrumental assessment (e.g., video fluoroscopic swallow study). This process requires the collaboration of various professionals.

Infants and children who are candidates for oral-motor and feeding therapy require individualized treatment plans. These plans should be integrated into broad-based intervention plans with functional goals. A total sensory, oral-motor, and behavioral management program is recommended, as is an interdisciplinary, team-focused approach (Arvedson, 1993; Morris & Klein, 1987). It is important to note that total oral feeding may not be the final goal for all children.

Treatment involves compensatory procedures and direct therapy services. Compensatory strategies include changes in the child's posture, sensory enhancement (taste, thermal-tactile stimulation, temperature, size of the bolus) and changes in the child's feeding pattern. Examples of direct therapy are range of motion exercises for the lips, tongue, jaw, or all three; laryngeal elevation, tongue base retraction, and swallowing maneuvers. Swallowing maneuvers are voluntary strategies the child learns in order to change the timing or strength of certain movements during swallowing. In order to be effective, treatment should be delivered several times during the day. Therefore, it is crucial that family members or other caregivers be taught the specific techniques and strategies (Logemann, 2000). Prognosis depends upon the individual child, his or her level of functioning, and any comorbid

conditions (e.g., cerebral palsy) that may interfere with the normal feeding-swallowing process.

Medically based feeding and swallowing problems have increased dramatically in the public schools during the past 5 years (Logemann & O'Toole, 2000). Children with dysphagia usually meet the definition of a child with a disability because they lack the ability to successfully take in nutrition, and the risk of malnutrition can affect the child's ability to concentrate and learn (O'Toole, 2000). In addition, these children frequently have another disability, such as cerebral palsy, that further qualifies them for special education services in the public school.

Further research is needed with infants and young children, especially those with normal oral motor skills. Data-based research is needed in the area of treatment in order to prove the credibility of specific treatment approaches.

REFERENCES

Arvedson, J. C. (1993). Management of swallowing problems. In J. C. Arvedson & L. Brodsky (Eds.), *Pediatric swallowing and feeding: Assessment and management* (pp. 327–387). San Diego, CA: Singular Publishing Group.

Arvedson, J. C., & Lefton-Greif, M. A. (1998). *Pediatric video-fluroscopic swallow studies: A professional manual with caregiver guidelines.* San Antonio, TX: Communication Skill Builders.

Arvedson, J. C., & Rogers, B. T. (1993). Pediatric swallowing and feeding disorders. *Journal of Medical Speech-Language Pathology, 1*(4), 203–221.

Logemann, J. A. (2000). Therapy for children with swallowing disorders in the educational setting. *Language, Speech, and Hearing Services in Schools, 31,* 50–55.

Logemann, J. A., & O'Toole, T. J. (2000). Identification and management of dysphagia in the public schools. *Language, Speech, and Hearing Services in Schools, 31,* 26–27.

Miller, A. J. (1982). Deglutition. *Physiological Reviews, 62,* 129–184.

Morris, S. E., & Klein, M. D. (1987). *Prefeeding skills: A comprehensive resource for feeding development.* Tucson, AZ: Therapy Skill Builders.

O'Toole, T. J. (2000) Legal, ethical, and financial aspects of providing services to children with swallowing disorders in the public schools. *Language, Speech, and Hearing Services in Schools, 31,* 56–60.

THERESA T. AGUIRE
Texas A&M University

FEINGOLD DIET

One of the most widely acclaimed (particularly in the popular press) yet least empirically supported treatment modes for hyperactive children is the Feingold diet (Feingold, 1975, 1976). Specifically, Feingold (1975, 1976) has insisted that children with learning and behavioral disturbances have a natural toxic reaction to artificial food colors, flavorings, preservatives, and other substances that are added to foods to enhance their shelf life. The Feingold diet purports to be an additive-free dietary regimen that attempts to eliminate artificial flavorings, colorings, and even several nutritional fruits and vegetables containing salicylates. While the use of the Feingold diet has been frequently advocated in the therapeutic treatment of hyperactivity, learning disabilities, and other behavioral disorders, Feingold (1975) has claimed his additive-free diet to be effective in treating other handicapping conditions, including cognitive impairment, autism, and conduct disorders.

Feingold's claims that nearly 50% of hyperactive children in his clinical population have displayed marked improvements, and that in the majority of cases, the children have had a complete remission of symptoms as a result of the additive-free dietary regimen (Feingold, 1975, 1976). According to the Feingold group, these improvements have been demonstrated in both the social and cognitive domains. Feingold has even claimed striking academic improvements as a function of the additive-free diet, despite the fact that academic achievement has been an area little influenced by therapeutic efforts with this population (Barkley & Cunningham, 1978). Further, Feingold has insisted that the younger the child, the more expedient and pervasive the improvement that may be observed. For example, according to Feingold (1975), the efficacy of the additive-free diet in infants and toddlers may be documented in as little as 24 hours to one week. Feingold has noted that in adolescents, where improvement is predicted to be least successful, notable effects often take as long as several months to be seen.

The intense debate resulting from Feingold's claims has spawned a number of empirical studies supported by the federal government. A consensus of these studies (Conners, 1980; Spring & Sandoval, 1976) did not support Feingold's claims, and criticized Feingold's earlier work on the basis of its marginal research methodology, including poor placebo controls. Although Conners (1980) has accused Feingold of making "gross overstatements" (p. 109) regarding his diet, Conners does concede that a small number of hyperactive children (less than 5%) do respond favorably to the diet. Nonetheless, it is still unclear whether it is the Feingold diet that is responsible for the observed improvements in this small percentage of children or the regimen associated with the laborious preparations surrounding this special diet. For example, one research group (Harley & Matthews, 1980) has attributed any success of the Feingold diet to a placebo effect. They claim altered aspects of family dynamics often result from special procedures and efforts in implementing the Feingold diet. Others have attributed its effects to the familiar Hawthorne effect. A careful review and meta-analysis of the Feingold diet research by Kavale and Forness (1999) conclude there is little support for the Feingold hypothesis. Further, it must be cautioned that many practitioners have recognized that several of the foods Feingold has recommended for elimination from children's diets contain important nutrients necessary for their growth and development. Consequently, there has been concern in the pediatric community that the Feingold diet may not fulfill the nutritional needs of children treated with this approach.

Despite the frequent failures to corroborate Feingold's (1975, 1976) original claims (Conners, 1980; Kavale & Forness, 1999) the Feingold diet continues to have loyal followers. Many parents have even formed a national association, frequently contacting food manufacturers to provide additive-free food products. Perhaps contributing to its widespread acceptance is the fact that the Feingold diet is commensurate with society's penchant for dieting, health food fads, and natural foods. Further, the Feingold diet offers an alternative to psychotropic medication, which many parents perceive as risky and having side effects, although this has not been verified in the research literature (Ross & Ross, 1982). Citing the etiology and treatment of hyperactivity as an allergic reaction to food may be more palatable to parents than neurological or psychogenic hypotheses, but it is almost certainly less valid.

REFERENCES

Barkley, R. A., & Cunningham, C. E. (1978). Do stimulant drugs improve the academic performance of hyperactive children? A review of outcome studies. *Clinical Pediatrics, 17*, 85–92.

Conners, C. K. (1980). *Food additives and hyperactive children.* New York, NY: Plenum Press.

Feingold, B. F. (1975). *Why your child is hyperactive.* New York, NY: Random House.

Feingold, B. F. (1976). Hyperkinesis and learning disabilities linked to the ingestion of artificial food colors and flavors. *Journal of Learning Disabilities, 9*, 551–559.

Harley, J. P., & Matthews, C. G. (1980). Food additives and hyperactivity in children. In R. M. Knights & D. J. Bakker (Eds.), *Treatment of hyperactive and learning disordered children.* Baltimore, MD: University Park Press.

Kavale, K., & Forness, S. A. (1999). Effectiveness of special education. In C. R. Reynolds & T. B. Gutkin (Eds.), *Handbook of school psychology* (3rd ed.). New York, NY: Wiley.

Ross, D. M., & Ross, S. A. (1982). *Hyperactivity: Current issues, research and theory* (2nd ed.). New York, NY: Wiley-Interscience.

Spring, C., & Sandoval, J. (1976). Food additives and hyperkinesis: A critical evaluation of the evidence. *Journal of Learning Disabilities, 9,* 560–569.

EMILY G. SUTTER
University of Houston, Clear Lake

RONALD T. BROWN
Emory University School of Medicine

See also **Attention-Deficit/Hyperactivity Disorder; Hyperkinesis; Impulse Control**

FELDHUSEN, JOHN F. (1926–2009)

Excellence in Educating Gifted and Talented Learners, the title of a 1998 book with six chapters written by John Feldhusen and edited by Joyce Van Tassel-Baska, is also the definitive theme of the work that has evolved from Feldhusen's first publications on comparisons of mental performance among children of low, average, and high intelligence to his present studies on giftedness. Feldhusen, born in Waukesha, Wisconsin, received his BA in 1949, his MS in 1955, and his PhD in 1958 from the University of Wisconsin, Madison. An interim period as counselor and teacher provided practical background for his early studies on such diverse topics as programmed instruction, testing and measurement, delinquency, and classroom behavior. His contributions to the field of educational psychology culminated in his presidency of Division 15 of the American Psychological Association in 1975.

Feldhusen exhibited a continuing concern for instruction in creative thinking and problem solving. He was primarily interested in using research theory and evaluation to guide program and curriculum development in gifted education. His research interest became the impetus for advocacy of professional training for teachers of the gifted, numerous cooperative efforts with public school personnel, and in-service training throughout Indiana. It also resulted in a steady stream of publications and teacher-targeted presentations and workshops throughout the United States. Feldhusen was chairman of the Educational Psychology and Research Section of Purdue University in 1977 and Director of the Purdue Gifted Education Resource Institute in 1978. He was also an active promoter of graduate programs in gifted education.

Feldhusen was committed to the concept that gifted and talented youths are individuals who need special services not only to achieve as highly as possible, but also to experience self-fulfillment as human beings. Thus he believed that identification of the gifted must focus on finding those who need services, rather than on labeling youths, and on guiding development of individualized programs. Feldhusen's contributions to gifted education were recognized by his 1981 election to the presidency of the National Association for Gifted Children. He was awarded the status of distinguished scholar in that organization in 1983, and was appointed editor of the association's journal, *Gifted Child Quarterly,* in 1984. In 1991, he was named a Distinguished Professor at Purdue University, and in 2002 he was awarded the Mensa Lifetime Achievement Award.

This entry has been informed by the source listed below.

REFERENCE

Van Tassel-Baska, J. (Ed.). (1998). *Excellence in educating gifted and talented learners.* Denver, CO: Love.

PATRICIA A. HAENSLY
Texas A&M University
First edition

TAMARA J. MARTIN
*The University of Texas
   of the Permian Basin*
Second edition

FEMORAL HYPOPLASIA–UNUSUAL FACIES SYNDROME

Femoral hypoplasia–unusual facies syndrome (FH-UFS) is an exceedingly rare disorder. Its main features include short stature, mildly dysmorphic facial features, and absent or underdeveloped bones of the lower extremity. Short stature is the result of severely shortened legs.

The etiology of FH-UFS is unknown. Its incidence in the general population is unclear. Thus far only six cases have been reported. Most occurrences of FH-UFS appear to be sporadic. However, there is one instance in which an affected male had a similarly affected daughter. This example suggests the possibility of an autosomal dominant mode of inheritance. Maternal diabetes is also a common finding in infants with FH-UFS.

Characteristics

1. Short stature secondary to severely shortened legs.
2. Facial features include short nose with underdeveloped sides of the lower nose, thin upper lip, small jaw, cleft palate, upward slanting of the

outer corner of the eye, and malformed, low-set ears.

3. Limb deformities are bilateral (on both sides), but each extremity is not equally affected. Findings include underdeveloped (hypoplastic) or absent femur (thigh bone) and, occasionally, hypoplastic or absent tibia and fibula (bones of the lower leg, below the knee). There is usually some degree of hypoplasia of the humerus (bone of the upper arm). Fusion of the elbow joint and the adjacent radioulnar articulation is occasionally seen.

4. Other skeletal anomalies occasionally observed are underdevelopment of the pelvis, missing or deformed vertebrae, and scoliosis.

5. Associated genitourinary abnormalities have been described: undescended testicle; inguinal hernia; small penis and testes; and a variety of kidney anomalies, including complete absence of the kidney.

No treatment is available at this time for the majority of the skeletal pathology of FH-UFS. Some children are born with congenital heart defects that require surgical repair. Operative intervention may also be necessary to treat hernias, cleft palate, and esotropia (cross-eye). Although all of these patients have had normal intelligence, speech delays have been observed. These difficulties are best handled by referral to appropriate therapists.

A child with FH-UFS may require modifications in the physical environment due to physical limitations. Although referral to a speech pathologist may be needed to help with language delays, other modifications should not be required because no cognitive deficits have been reported. Because of the physical deformities, providing a positive environment that builds good self-image and education for his or her classmates will facilitate peer relationships.

Because there is such a small population of individuals with FH-UFS, prognostic discussion for the disorder is rather conjectural. However, in the absence of life-threatening cardiac or renal anomalies, there appears to be a reasonable hope for survival into adulthood.

This entry has been informed by the source listed below.

REFERENCE

Jones, K. (1997). *Smith's recognizable patterns of human malformations* (5th ed.). Philadelphia, PA: W. B. Saunders.

BERRY H. DAVISON, MD
Ennis, Texas

JOAN W. MAYFIELD
Baylor Pediatric Speciaalty Services, Dallas, Texas

FENICHEL, CARL (1905–1975)

Carl Fenichel was founder and director of the League School for Seriously Disturbed Children in Brooklyn, New York. At the school, Fenichel provided one of the early demonstrations that it is feasible to educate severely emotionally disturbed children in a day program when the parents are given intensive training in appropriate home management and care.

Educated at the City College of New York, the New School for Social Research, and Yeshiva University, where he earned the doctorate in education, Fenichel began his professional career as a teacher and psychologist. During his years at the League School, he served as professor of education at Teachers College, Columbia University, and as a lecturer at the Downstate Medical College in Brooklyn. Fenichel's pioneering League School, which he founded in 1953, served as a model for many of the first day programs for severely emotionally disabled children in the United States.

PAUL IRVINE
Katonah, New York

FERAL CHILDREN

Feral children is a term used to describe children who have spent various, usually unknown, amounts of their childhood living in wild or at least uncivilized conditions. From Peter in 1724 to Victor in 1799, Kasper Hauser in 1828, and Amala and Kamala—the "Wolf Children"—in 1920, feral children have fascinated philosophers, physicians, anthropologists, educators, and psychologists. Many have looked to them for answers to questions about the nature of man, the permanence of early experience, the efficacy of education in overcoming early deprivation, and, perhaps most basically, what each of us owes to heredity and what we owe to environment.

For convenience, feral children may be divided into two basic groups: (1) those who have grown up in open "wild" settings such as jungles or forests, and (2) those who have grown up under extreme environmental and social deprivation. In addition, a subgroup of "wild" children has supposedly been raised by animals. The mythology, romanticism, and/or fascination with the topic continues.

The antiquity of interest in using conditions of early rearing to learn of man's nature is indicated by King Psammitichus's experiment, as reported by Herodotus. To determine what language was the most ancient, the king ordered that two infants be nursed by goats and separated from all contact with humans. Supposedly the first word they said was Phrygian for bread, and the Egyptians yielded to the primacy of the Phrygians. Ireland (1898) indicated that similar experiments were conducted by Emperor Frederick II and James IV of Scotland. Interest in feral children peaked in the 18th century with scientific uncertainty about who are and are not humans (the word orangutan comes from Malaysian for wild man). There were attempts to discriminate between Descartes' endowment of humans with innate ideas and Locke's empiricist concept of the human mind as a blank slate. Feral children were studied as models of Rousseau's noble savage (Lane, 1986; Shattuck, 1980).

Craft's (1979) claim of "some 50 documented cases of animal-reared children..." (p. 139) notwithstanding, no fully documented examples of children reared by wolves, bears, gazelles, baboons, or any nonhumans, exist. Singh's claim that Amala and Kamala were reared by wolves was accepted by Zingg and the famous pediatrician-psychologist Arnold Gesell (1942), but the claim was convincingly disputed by Ogburn and Bose. Ogburn later detailed how a particular feral child falsely became converted into the "Wolf Boy of Agra," even though the child had not been with wild animals at all. Although Maclean (1977) claims evidence to support Amala and Kamala's wolf rearing, this is dubious and not subject to verification. We have no more hard evidence on the general subject than did Ireland (1898), who concluded that the notion of wolf children belonged with nursery myths.

Similar controversy exists over other questions asked about feral children related to cognitive abilities and the effects of deprivation (Bettelheim, 1959; Dennis, 1951; Lane, 1976, 1986).

Unfortunately, we probably will never have clear answers to any of the questions asked of feral children. Their stories have the shortcomings of all retrospective case histories—lack of complete information, potentially biased observers, the lack of repeatability and control, the impossibility of knowing how the children would have behaved if raised under normal conditions, and the virtual impossibility of empirical verification of events in the children's lives before their discovery. As one example, Dennis (1951) has pointed out that many of the children apparently did not disappear from their families until they were several years of age. How, then, can the supposed permanence of their primitive characteristics be attributed to their normal early experience? As another example, we do not know whether Genie, a contemporary deprived child, would have developed normal language under normal conditions. Given the limits of the data, the problem of direction of causality seems unsolvable. Attributing all behavioral deficits to these children's unnatural rearing environment is a clear case of illogical *post hoc ergo propter hoc* (after this, because of this) reasoning. Thus cases of feral children are almost inevitably open to alternative interpretations.

We do know from reports of numerous modern cases that considerable intellective, motor, social-emotional, and even language development can occur in formerly severely deprived, abused or neglected, and institutionalized children (Clarke & Clarke, 1976). Early deprivation, if not extremely prolonged, can be overcome, particularly with special and intensive intervention. Early adverse learning experiences are not irreversible, a message of considerable optimism to those in special education. Candland (1993) has sensitively portrayed the lives of many feral children and their relationships not only to the questions listed at the beginning of this entry but also to other interesting cases of humans and nonhumans.

REFERENCES

Bettelheim, B. (1959). Feral children and autistic children. *American Journal of Sociology, 64,* 455–467.

Candland, D. K. (1993). *Feral children and clever animals.* New York, NY: Oxford University Press.

Clarke, A. M., & Clarke, A. D. B. (Eds.). (1976). *Early experience: Myth and evidence.* New York, NY: Free Press.

Craft, M. (1979). The neurocytology of damaging environmental factors. In M. Craft (Ed.), *Tredgold's mental retardation* (12th ed., pp. 137–143). (Bailliere-Tindall.) Philadelphia, PA: W. B. Saunders.

Dennis, W. (1951). A further analysis of reports of wild children. *Child Development, 22,* 153–159.

Gesell, A. L. (1942). *Wolf child and human child.* New York, NY: Harper.

Ireland, W. W. (1898). *Mental affections of children, idiocy, imbecility, and insanity.* London, England: J. & A. Churchill.

Lane, H. (1976). *The wild boy of Aveyron.* Cambridge, MA: Harvard University Press.

Lane, H. (1986). The wild boy of Aveyron and Itard. *History of Psychology, 18,* 3–16.

Maclean, C. (1977). *The wolf children.* New York, NY: Hill & Wang.

Shattuck, R. (1980). *The forbidden experiment.* New York, NY: Farrar, Straus and Giroux.

ROBERT T. BROWN
University of North Carolina at Wilmington

See also Early Experience and Critical Periods; Genie; Itard, Jean M. G.; Kaspar Hauser Syndrome; Wild Boy of Aveyron

FERNALD, GRACE MAXWELL (1879–1950)

Grace Maxwell Fernald received her PhD in psychology from the University of Chicago in 1907. In 1911 she became head of the psychology department and laboratory at the State Normal School at Los Angeles. The remainder of her career was spent at the Normal School and the University of California at Los Angeles.

Fernald's lasting contribution to the field of education is her method for teaching disabled readers, a method that uses not only visual and auditory approaches, but kinesthetic and tactile cues as well. In 1921, UCLA's Clinic School, later renamed the Fernald School, was founded by Grace Fernald.

This entry has been informed by the sources listed below.

REFERENCES

Fernald, G. (1943). *Remedial techniques in basic school subjects*. New York, NY: McGraw-Hill.

Sullivan, E. B., Dorcus, R. V., Allen, R. M., Bennet, M., & Koontz, L. K. (1950). Grace Maxwell Fernald. *Psychological Review, 57*, 319–321.

PAUL IRVINE
Katonah, New York

FERNALD METHOD

A systematic, multisensory instructional approach, the Fernald Method, typically incorporates kinesthetic, visual, auditory, and tactile stimulation are used along with visual and auditory modalities. The multisensory programs that feature tracing, hearing, writing, and seeing are often referred to as VAKT (visual-auditory-kinesthetic-tactile; Hallahan, Kauffman, & Lloyd, 1985).

One of the most widely known and used multisensory approaches to teaching children struggling to read is the Fernald Method (Gearheart, 1985). The rationale for the Fernald Word Learning Approach, which is usually known as the VAKT approach, was described by Fernald in 1943; it works to improve sight word acquisition and word identification skills in students who have struggled to learn through other instructional methods. In practice, the VAKT approach is not confined to reading, but includes spelling and writing instruction

Fernald believed that overcoming the emotional problems failing students have with reading would be easier if their reading material were of interest to them. Therefore, stories are written down as suggested by the students, with as much help from the teacher as needed, and then read. Also, a student selects words that he or she wishes to learn and works on them, repeatedly feeling, spacing, seeing, saying, and hearing a word until it can be written from memory. Words that have been mastered are kept in a file so that a student may refer back to them as needed. Fernald was opposed to having the student sound out

words; she emphasized the reading and writing of words as a whole. Although the Fernald approach has strong advocates who can provide case studies documenting its successful use, research evidence does not reveal that it has been particularly successful (Myers, 1978).

REFERENCES

Fernald, G. (1943). *Remedial techniques in basic school subjects*. New York, NY: McGraw-Hill.

Gearheart, B. R. (1985). *Learning disabilities*. St. Louis, MO: Times Mirror/Mosby.

Hallahan, D. P., Kauffman, J. M., & Lloyd, J. W. (1985). *Introduction to learning disabilities*. Englewood Cliffs, NJ: Prentice Hall.

Kirk, S., & Chalfant, J. C. (1984). *Academic and developmental learning disabilities*. Denver, CO: Love.

Myers, C. A. (1978). Reviewing the literature on Fernald's technique of remedial reading. *Reading Teacher, 31*, 614–619.

JOSEPH M. RUSSO
Hunter College, City University of New York

See also Hegge, Kirk & Kirk Approach; Orton-Gillingham Method

FERNALD, WALTER E. (1859–1924)

Walter E. Fernald received his medical degree from the Medical School of Maine, served as assistant physician at the State Hospital in Minnesota, and then became the first resident superintendent of the Massachusetts School for the Feeble-Minded (later renamed the Walter E. Fernald State School). A leader in the movement for humane treatment of "mentally retarded persons," he developed an educational plan that provided a 24-hour-a-day program for each child. He devised a system for diagnosing and classifying individuals with cognitive impairment on the basis of total development rather than test results alone. Under his leadership, the Massachusetts school became an international center for the training of workers in the field of mental retardation. Fernald was also influential in the development of federal and state legislation relating to mental retardation (Wallace, 1924).

REFERENCE

Wallace, G. L. (1924). In memoriam Walter E. Fernald. *American Journal of Mental Deficiency, 30*, 16–23.

PAUL IRVINE
Katonah, New York

FETAL ALCOHOL SYNDROME

Fetal alcohol syndrome (FAS) is a complex of physical anomalies and neurobehavioral deficits that may severely affect the children of heavy-drinking mothers. More widespread than Down syndrome and Fragile X syndrome, FAS is the leading type of cognitive impairment in the Western world (Abel & Sokol, 1987; Cde Baca, 2003). FAS is certainly the most prevalent environmental and preventable type of cognitive impairment. In 2006, the National Organization on Fetal Alcohol Syndrome estimated that that the annual cost of treatment of all FAS-related effects was $5.4 billion (NOFAS, 2006). Prenatal exposure to alcohol has a range of effects, with less serious sequelae termed fetal alcohol effects (FAE) or alcohol-related neurodevelopmental disorder (ARND; Batshaw & Conlon, 1997). FAS is associated with three major effects, known as "the triad of the FAS" (Rosett & Weiner, 1984, p. 43): (1) growth retardation of prenatal origin, (2) characteristic facial anomalies, and (3) central nervous system dysfunction. First described in 1973 (Jones, Smith, Ulleland, & Streissguth; Jones & Smith), FAS has since been the subject of over 2,000 scientific reports (Streissguth et al., 1991). Follow-up studies, described below, confirm that alcohol is a teratogen that produces lifelong impairments.

Diagnostic Criteria and Common Characteristics

The Fetal Alcohol Study Group of the Research Society on Alcoholism (Rosett, 1980) established minimal criteria for diagnosis of FAS, based largely on Clarren and Smith's (1978) summary of 245 cases. FAS should be diagnosed only when all three criteria are met:

1. Prenatal and/or postnatal growth retardation (below 10th percentile for body weight, length, and/or head circumference, when corrected for gestational age). However, although growth retardation has been viewed as the most common characteristic of FAS, some suggest that it may not be a primary feature and perhaps not a defining characteristic (Carmichael Olson & Burgess, 1997).

2. Central nervous system dysfunction (neurological abnormality, developmental delay, or mental impairment < 10th percentile).

3. Characteristic facies (at least two of the following three facial dysmorphologies: (1) Microcephaly [head circumference < 3rd percentile]; (2) Microphthalmia and/or short palpebral fissures; (3) Poorly developed philtrum, thin upper lip, and flattening of the maxillary area). See Figure F.2.

In addition to these three diagnostic criteria, a history of drinking during pregnancy should be present for confident diagnosis, since no individual feature is specific to prenatal exposure to alcohol (Sokol et al., 1986). However, Streissguth, Sampson, Barr, Clarren, & Martin (1986, p. 64) have suggested that "... FAS and alcohol teratogenicity are reciprocal terms.... [I]dentifying a child with all the features of FAS strongly suggests that the child was affected by alcohol *in utero*." Of importance, they also stated (p. 64) that although alcohol teratogenicity may cause a "milder" FAS or FAE phenotype, such milder phenotypes should not be inferred to result necessarily from alcohol: "[O]ther environmental or genetic problems could produce similar manifestations.... When examining the individual patient, the examiner cannot be sure that alcohol produced a 'possible' fetal alcohol effect, even when a maternal history is positive for alcohol." An important attributional implication is that women who have occasionally consumed small amounts of alcohol during pregnancy and have slightly deformed infants should not be made to feel guilt or that alcohol caused the deformities. Women should certainly take precautions during their pregnancy, but do not have control over everything that may affect their babies (Rosett & Weiner, 1984).

Although low birth weight is associated with other maternal factors (several of which, including smoking, malnutrition, and drug abuse, are also associated with alcohol abuse), two lines of evidence suggest that alcohol induces prenatal growth retardation: (1) the other maternal factors are rarely associated with other defining features of FAS (Rosett & Weiner, 1984), and (2) offspring of pregnant animals given alcohol show both growth retardation and virtually all other physical and neurobehavioral features of FAS (e.g., Abel, 1984; Riley & Barron, 1989).

As West (1986b, p. vi) has observed, "Central nervous system dysfunction is the most devastating and one of the more consistently observed clinical abnormalities in surviving offspring of mothers known to have consumed large amounts of alcohol during pregnancy." Mental retardation or subnormality is the most common CNS indicator associated with FAS (see Streissguth, 1986, for a detailed review). Average IQ of affected children is about 65–75, but variability is high (Mattson & Riley, 1998). Children with the most severe morphology and growth indicators have the most severe intellectual and other CNS deficits. Affected infants and children may also show failure to thrive, poor sucking, retarded speech and motor development, fine-motor dysfunction, repetitive self-stimulating behaviors such as head rolling or head banging, auditory deficits, and seizures. Symptoms of attention-deficit/hyperactivity disorder (ADHD) are common and associated with school problems. Seizures occur in about 20% of cases, but are not considered characteristic of FAS. Prenatal alcohol has a variety of adverse effects on the developing CNS (see Abel, 1984 and West, 1986a for reviews). Underdiagnosis, even recently thought to be a problem (Little, Snell, Rosenfeld, Gilstrap, & Gant,

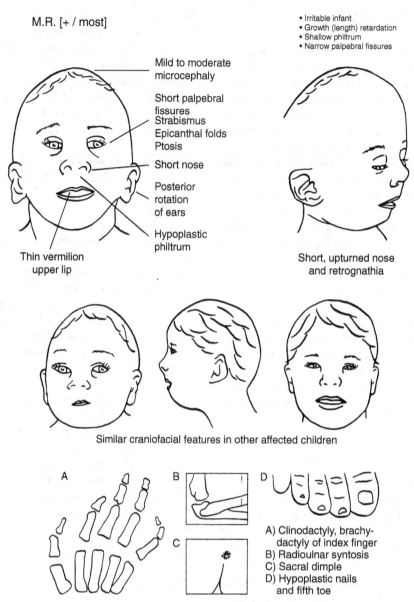

Figure F.2. Fetal alcohol syndrome.

1990), is now unlikely, owing to increased knowledge of FAS (Abel & Hannigan, 1995).

Historical Background

Although a number of authors have claimed to find ancient reference to damaging effects of maternal alcohol consumption, Abel (1984) suggested that those claims rest on erroneous secondary sources or mistranslations. Abel (1984) does report suggestions of adverse effects of maternal drinking in 17th century England and that several writers observed, during the "gin epidemic" in the early 18th century, that children of mothers who drank heavily were small, sickly, and mentally slow. Further, a number of 19th century reports linked stillbirth, infant mortality, and mental retardation to maternal drinking during pregnancy.

But studies in the 20th century failed to find a link between maternal drinking and adverse effects on offspring. Elderton and Pearson (1910) reported no relationship between parental drinking and intelligence or appearance of children, and suggested that children of alcoholics might have problems because parents and children shared "defective germ plasm" or because the parents provided a poor home environment. Although their claim was much criticized, it was later supported by Haggard and Jellinek (1942), who denied that prenatal alcohol produced malformations. Thus, however inaccurate from our perspective, Montagu's (1965, p. 114) conclusion was apparently well-founded at the time: "Unexpectedly, alcohol in the form of beverages, even in immoderate amounts, has no apparent effect on a child before birth.... (I)t now can be stated categorically...that no matter how great the amount of alcohol taken by the mother—or the father, for that matter—neither the germ cells nor the development of the child will be affected." The timing of Montagu's publication has a certain irony, appearing at about the time Lemoine, Harousseau, Borteryu, and Menuet began their study of the offspring of 127 alcoholic parents. In 1968, they reported that several of the children had such characteristic anomalies that maternal alcoholism could be inferred from them. The abnormalities were in the three areas now associated with FAS: growth retardation, low intelligence, and facial anomalies. Their paper, published in French with an English abstract, had little impact (Abel, 1984; Rosett & Weiner, 1984), and was unknown to Jones and Smith and their colleagues at the time of their initial reports in 1973 (Abel, 1984). Those reports brought the effects of maternal alcohol to international attention, in part by providing a name, fetal alcohol syndrome, that "dramatically refocused interest on an important perinatal risk" (Sokol et al., 1986, p. 88).

Incidence and Risk Factors

Although estimates vary widely across study and country, worldwide incidence of FAS is estimated as approximately 1.02 per 1,000 live births. However, most cases are in the United States, where incidence is estimated to be 1.9 per 1,000 births (Abel & Hannigan, 1995). The varying estimates may reflect sampling error and use of different diagnostic criteria as well as actual national/regional differences. As would be expected, incidence varies most with degree of prenatal maternal drinking. Full-blown FAS appears to be associated only with heavy maternal drinking; no cases have been reported among moderate drinkers (Abel & Sokol, 1987). FAS may occur in 30–50%, and FAE in 50–70%, of offspring of truly alcoholic women who consume eight or more drinks daily (Little et al., 1990). Some studies report incidence as high as 80% in low SES samples (Bingol et al., 1987).

Incidence of human newborns with some features of FAS also increases with amount of prenatal maternal alcohol consumption (Streissguth, Landesman-Dwyer, Martin, & Smith, 1980). Degree of physical growth retardation is also dose-related (Abel, 1984). A dose-response curve is found in virtually all animal studies: Number and severity of offspring anomalies increases with amount of prenatal exposure to alcohol (see Abel, 1984, for a summary). Well-controlled animal studies have confirmed that the damage is from prenatal alcohol and not secondary to some other effect (Abel, 1984; Streissguth et al., 1980).

Some effects of prenatal alcohol appear to occur only above a certain threshold level of exposure (Ernhart, Sokol, Ager, Morrow-Tlucak, & Martier, 1989; Streissguth, 1986). For example, Ernhart et al. (1989) reported that women who drank small amounts of alcohol early in pregnancy had children with no incidence of FAS-related neonatal physical anomalies above that of a control group. However,

teratogens typically have neurobehavioral effects at levels below those at which physical defects are shown (Abel, 1989). Indeed, Mattson and Riley (1998) report that groups of FAS children and alcohol-exposed children who had no characteristic physical features of FAS showed significant and largely similar deficits in IQs relative to normal children.

Importantly, FAS is seen much more commonly in offspring from lower socioeconomic status (SES) mothers (Abel, 1984; Abel & Hannigan, 1995; Bingol et al., 1987). A variety of possible reasons exist for this relationship, including the fact that alcoholism is inversely related to SES status. Even when alcohol intake was equated, however, Bingol et al. (1987) found that incidence of FAS and FAE was 71% in offspring of heavy-drinking low SES mothers and only 4.6% in offspring of heavy-drinking middle to upper SES mothers. SES was confounded with ethnicity, complicating interpretation, but Abel and Hannigan argue persuasively that SES is the major factor. Binge drinking, certain ethnic factors, smoking, and undernutrition also contribute to the manifestation of FAS in offspring of drinking mothers (Abel & Hannigan, 1995).

Both human and nonhuman research suggests that some of the variability in incidence of FAS/FAE stems from genetic factors. Clinical reports indicate that dizygotic (fraternal) twins of alcoholic mothers show differential development and performance (Streissguth, 1986). Maternal factors are implicated in research by Chernoff (1977, 1980): Pregnant mice from two different strains given comparable doses of alcohol had different blood-alcohol levels, and the strain with higher levels had offspring with higher incidence of anomalies.

FAS Effects From Childhood to Adulthood

FAS has effects, although in somewhat modified form, that last into adulthood. According to longitudinal studies (e.g., Streissguth, 1986; Streissguth, Clarren, & Jones, 1985; Streissguth et al., 1991), FAS/FAE adolescents and adults were about two standard deviations below the mean in height and head circumference, although variability was high; little overall catch-up growth had occurred. The characteristic low weight of FAS/FAE children had largely disappeared, although weight/height ratios were even more variable than other measures.

The facial dysmorphologies characteristic of FAS children became less distinctive with age. Although some features, such as short palpebral fissure length, remained, growth in a number of facial areas reduced the extent of the overall abnormal appearance.

The average IQ of the 61 FAS/FAE adolescents and adults reported by Streissguth et al. (1991) was 68, just into the mild retardation level. The FAS mean was 66 and the FAE was 73. Variability was again high, with IQ ranging from 20 to 105; no FAS individual's IQ was above the low 90s. Those with the most severe growth retardation and facial dysmorphologies in childhood continued to have the lowest later IQ scores. Only 6% of the 61 were in regular classes and not receiving special help; 28% were in self-contained special education classes, 15% were neither in school nor working, and 9% were in sheltered workshops. Although academic deficits were broad, arithmetic deficits were particularly large. Academic performance had not improved since childhood.

Children and adolescents with FAS/FAE show a number of additional behavioral deficits and excesses that present serious educational and other challenges (Carmichael Olson, & Burgess, 1997; Mattson & Riley, 1998; Steinhausen & Spohr, 1998). Among the more common features are hyperactivity, inattention, impaired learning (but not impaired memory of verbal material), a wide variety of receptive and expressive language problems, and fine motor coordination. Of particular concern are reports of temper tantrums in younger affected children and serious conduct disorders in older ones. Not surprisingly, FAS children have difficulty conforming to social norms.

In Streissguth et al. (1991), even FAS/FAE adolescents and adults who were not mentally retarded showed poor socialization scores and an unusually high level of maladaptive behaviors, including poor concentration and attention, sullenness, impulsivity, lying, and cheating. However, their family environments were highly unstable, making difficult the determination as to whether these effects owed to prenatal alcohol exposure, postnatal environment, or an interaction between difficult infants and inadequate parenting. Only 9% were still living with both parents; the mothers of 66% had died, many from alcohol-related causes.

Of particular concern for those in special education are the wide variety of behavioral sequelae, their varying degree, and the extent to which some may not be related to physical characteristics of FAS individuals. The suggestion that early stimulation may reduce the extent of some effects indicates the need for early and continued intervention (Phelps, 1995).

Prevention

Although 100% preventable theoretically, FAS may prove resistant to reduction efforts in practice (Cde Baca, 2003). Alcohol abuse is notably resistant to treatment, and relapse rates 12 months after treatment are as high as 75% (Tucker, Vuchinich, & Harris, 1985). Thus, education programs on the adverse effects of prenatal alcohol may lower alcohol consumption of moderately drinking women during pregnancy, but are unlikely to affect alcohol-abusing or alcoholic women, whose infants are most at risk. Although a variety of general approaches are available (Cox, 1987; Milkman & Sederer, 1990), treatment/prevention programs targeted specifically at

women (Kilbey & Asghar, 1992; National Institute on Alcohol Abuse and Alcoholism, 1987; Streissguth & LaDue, 1987) may be necessary if we wish to decrease the incidence of this tragic condition.

For more information, contact the National Organization on Fetal Alcohol Syndrome at http://www.nofas.org/

REFERENCES

Abel, E. L. (1984). *Fetal alcohol syndrome and fetal alcohol effects*. New York, NY: Plenum Press.

Abel, E. L. (1989). *Behavioral teratogenesis and behavioral mutagenesis*. New York, NY: Plenum Press.

Abel, E. L., & Hannigan, J. H. (1995). Maternal risk factors in fetal alcohol syndrome: Provocative and permissive influences. *Neurotoxicology and Teratology, 17,* 445–462.

Abel, E. L., & Sokol, R. J. (1987). Incidence of fetal alcohol syndrome and economic impact of FAS-related anomalies. *Drug and Alcohol Dependence, 19,* 51–70.

Batshaw, M. L., & Conlon, C. J. (1997). Substance abuse: A preventable threat to development. In M. L. Batshaw (Ed.), *Children with disabilities* (4th ed., pp. 143–162). Baltimore, MD: Paul H. Brookes.

Bingol, N., Schuster, C., Fuchs, M., Iosub, S., Turner, G., Stone, R. K., & Gromisch, D. S. (1987). The influence of socioeconomic factors on the occurrence of fetal alcohol syndrome. *Advances in Alcohol and Substance Abuse, 6*(4), 105–118.

Carmichael Olson, H., & Burgess, D. M. (1997). Early intervention for children prenatally exposed to alcohol and other drugs. In M. J. Guralnick (Ed.), *The effectiveness of early intervention* (pp. 109–145). Baltimore, MD: Paul H. Brookes.

Cde Baca, C. (2003). Fetal alcohol syndrome. In E. Fletcher-Janzen & C. R. Reynolds (Eds.), *Childhood disorders diagnostic desk reference* (pp. 233–238). Hoboken, NJ: Wiley.

Chernoff, G. F. (1977). The fetal alcohol syndrome in mice: An animal model. *Teratology, 15,* 223–230.

Chernoff, G. F. (1980). The fetal alcohol syndrome in mice: Maternal variables. *Teratology, 22,* 71–75.

Clarren, S. K., & Smith, D. W. (1978). The fetal alcohol syndrome. *New England Journal of Medicine, 298,* 1063–1067.

Cox, W. M. (Ed.). (1987). *Treatment and prevention of alcohol problems*. New York, NY: Academic Press.

Elderton, E. M., & Pearson, K. (1910). A first study of the effect influence of parental alcoholism on the physique and ability of the offspring. *Eugenics Laboratory Memoir, 10,* 1–46. (As described in Abel, 1984).

Ernhart, C. B., Sokol, R. J., Ager, J. W., Morrow-Tlucak, M., & Martier, S. (1989). Alcohol-related birth defects: Assessing the risk. In D. E. Hutchings (Ed.), *Prenatal abuse of licit and illicit drugs* (pp. 159–172). *Annals of the New York Academy of Sciences, 592.*

Haggard, H. W., & Jellinek, E. M. (1942). *Alcohol explored*. Garden City, NJ: Doubleday.

Jones, K. L., & Smith, D. W. (1973). Recognition of fetal alcohol syndrome in early infancy. *Lancet, 2,* 999–1001.

Jones, K. L., Smith, D. W., Ulleland, C. N., & Streissguth, A. P. (1973). Pattern of malformation in offspring of chronic alcoholic mothers. *Lancet, 1*, 1267–1271.

Kilbey, M. M., & Asghar, K. (Eds.). (1992). *Methodological issues in epidemiological, prevention, and treatment research on drug-exposed women and their children.* Research monograph 117. Rockville, MD: National Institute on Drug Abuse.

Lemoine, P., Harousseau, H., Borteryu, J. P., & Menuet, J. C. (1968). Les enfants de parents alcooliques: Anomalies observees a propos de 127 cas. *Ouest Medical 21*, 476–482. (As described in Abel, 1984).

Little, B. B., Snell, L. M., Rosenfeld, C. R., Gilstrap, L. C. III, & Gant, N. F. (1990). Failure to recognize fetal alcohol syndrome in newborn infants. *American Journal of Diseases in Children, 144*, 1142–1146.

Mattson, S. N., & Riley, E. P. (1998). A review of the neurobehavioral deficits in children with fetal alcohol syndrome or prenatal exposure to alcohol. *Alcoholism: Clinical and Experimental Research, 22*, 279–294.

Milkman, H. B., & Sederer, H. B. (Eds.). (1990). *Treatment choices for alcoholism and substance abuse.* New York, NY: Lexington.

Montagu, A. (1965). *Life before birth.* New York, NY: Signet.

National Institute on Alcohol Abuse and Alcoholism. (1987). *Program strategies for preventing fetal alcohol syndrome and alcohol-related birth defects.* Rockville, MD: Author.

Phelps, L. (1995). Psychoeducational outcomes of fetal alcohol syndrome. *School Psychology Review, 24*, 200–212.

Riley, E. P., & Barron, S. (1989). The behavioral and neuroanatomical effects of prenatal alcohol exposure in animals. In D. E. Hutchings (Ed.), *Prenatal abuse of licit and illicit drugs* (pp. 173–177). *Annals of the New York Academy of Sciences, 592.*

Rosett, H. L. (1980). A clinical perspective of the fetal alcohol syndrome. *Alcoholism: Clinical and Experimental Research, 4*, 119–122.

Rosett, H. L., & Weiner, L. (1984). *Alcohol and the fetus.* New York, NY: Oxford University Press.

Sokol, R. J., Ager, J., Martier, S., Debanne, S., Ernhart, C., Kuzma, J., & Miller, S. I. (1986). Significant determinants of susceptibility to alcohol teratogenicity. In H. M. Wisniewski & D. A. Snider (Eds.), *Mental retardation: Research, education, and technology transfer* (pp. 87–100). *Annals of the New York Academy of Sciences, 477.*

Steinhausen, H. C., & Spohr, H. L. (1998). Long-term outcome of children with fetal alcohol syndrome: Psychopathology, behavior, and intelligence. *Alcoholism: Clinical and Experimental Research, 22*(2), 334–338.

Streissguth, A. P. (1986). The behavioral teratology of alcohol: Performance, behavioral, and intellectual deficits in prenatally exposed children. In J. R. West (Ed.), *Alcohol and brain development* (pp. 3–44). New York, NY: Oxford University Press.

Streissguth, A. P., Aase, J. M., Clarren, S. K., Randels, S. P., LaDue, R. A., & Smith, D. F. (1991). Fetal alcohol syndrome in adolescents and adults. *Journal of the American Medical Association, 265*, 1961–1967.

Streissguth, A. P., Clarren, S. K., & Jones, K. L. (1985). Natural history of fetal alcohol syndrome: A 10-year follow-up of eleven children. *Lancet, 2*, 85–91.

Streissguth, A. P., & LaDue, R. A. (1987). *Fetal alcohol: Teratogenic causes of developmental disabilities in toxic substances and mental retardation: Neurobehavioral toxicology and teratology.* Monographs of the American Association on Mental Deficiency, no. 8. Washington, DC: American Association on Mental Retardation.

Streissguth, A. P., Landesman-Dwyer, S., Martin, J. C., & Smith, D. W. (1980). Teratogenic effects of alcohol in humans and laboratory animals. *Science, 209*, 353–361.

Streissguth, A. P., Sampson, P. D., Barr, H. M., Clarren, S. K., & Martin, D. C. (1986). Studying alcohol teratogenesis from the perspective of the fetal alcohol syndrome: Methodological and statistical issues. In H. M. Wisniewski & D. A. Snider (Eds.), *Mental retardation: Research, education, and technology transfer* (pp. 63–86). *Annals of the New York Academy of Sciences, 477.*

Tucker, J. A., Vuchinich, R. E., & Harris, C. V. (1985). Determinants of substance abuse relapse. In M. Galizio & S. A. Maisto (Eds.), *Determinants of substance abuse* (pp. 383–421). New York, NY: Plenum Press.

West, J. R. (Ed.). (1986a). *Alcohol and brain development.* New York, NY: Oxford University Press.

West, J. R. (1986b). Preface. In J. R. West (Ed.), *Alcohol and brain development.* New York, NY: Oxford University Press.

ROBERT T. BROWN

JENNIFER L. CONDON
University of North Carolina at Wilmington

See also Attention-Deficit/Hyperactivity Disorder; Fetal Hydantoin Syndrome; Teratogen

FETAL AMINOPTERIN/METHOTREXATE SYNDROME

Aminopterin is a folic acid antagonist occasionally used as an abortifacient (a drug to induce an abortion) in early pregnancy; methotrexate, the methyl derivative of aminopterin and also an abortifacient, is used to treat rheumatoid arthritis and psoriasis. Offspring of mothers treated with either drug early in pregnancy may show a complex of craniofacial, growth, and limb abnormalities. An apparent critical period for adverse effects occurs at 6 to 8 weeks postconception. Fetal or early postnatal death may occur. In survivors, the most apparent feature are facial dysmorphologies, which result in a characteristic appearance. Surprisingly, given frequent microcephaly, intelligence and motor behavior are largely unaffected

(Jones, 1997). The disorder is rare (Office of Rare Diseases, 2001), and accurate incidence figures are not available.

> ## Characteristics
>
> 1. Craniofacial dysmorphologies (microcephaly; severe hypoplasia of frontal, parietal, temporal, and occipital bones; broad nasal ridge; wide fontanels; low-set ears; prominent eyes; epicanthal folds; and micrognathia)
> 2. Postnatal growth retardation
> 3. Limb abnormalities (shortness of arms and legs, hypo- and syndactyly)
> 4. Apparently normal intelligence

As with many drug-induced abnormalities, knowledge that the pregnant woman actually ingested the drug is important for accurate diagnosis. Although the morphological effects are irreversible, surgery may help to alleviate some effects. The facial dysmorphologies may lead to speech impairments that will call for therapy, but normal classroom placement would be expected. However, affected individuals may benefit from counseling to help them deal with psychological consequences of their abnormal appearance.

REFERENCES

Jones, K. L. (1997). *Smith's recognizable patterns of human malformation* (5th ed.). Philadelphia, PA: W. B. Saunders.

Office of Rare Diseases. (2001). Rare diseases list. Retrieved from http://rarediseases.info.nih.gov/

ROBERT T. BROWN
University of North Carolina,
Wilmington

FETAL HYDANTOIN SYNDROME

Children of epileptic mothers who took phenytoin during pregnancy may show a complex of anomalies, known as fetal hydantoin syndrome (FHS) or fetal Dilantin syndrome, that include (a) mild to moderate growth deficiency, microcephaly (with associated mental deficiency); (b) cleft lip and palate, wide anterior fontanel, depressed nasal bridge, and other facies; (c) limb abnormalities, including hypoplasia of nails and terminal digits, a digitalized thumb, and dislocation of the hip; and (d) a variety of other abnormalities (Jones, 1997; Moore & Brown, 2003). The anticonvulsant agent phenytoin (Dilantin) has teratogenic effects. Uncertainty over whether negative effects in infants and children were caused by medication or seizures themselves has been eliminated, owing in part to successful animal models (e.g., Adams, Vorhees, & Middaugh, 1990). Risk of damage to infants exposed prenatally to hydantoin is relatively low; exposed infants are estimated to have about a 10% chance of developing the syndrome and approximately a 33% chance of showing some effects (Jones, 1997). The fetal genotype is an important influence on susceptibility to prenatal hydantoin (Jones, 1997), and rodent models additionally indicate a dose-response relationship (Adams et al., 1990).

The biggest concern for infants diagnosed with the syndrome is the degree of intellectual disability. Although effects are generally mild relative to some other teratogens, IQs of children with the full syndrome is 71 (Jones, 1997). The infants also show a failure to thrive in the early months of life for unknown reasons.

Many other anticonvulsant medications, including carbamazepine (Tegretol), valproic acid (Depakene), primidone (Mysoline), and phenobarbital also appear to have similar teratogenic effects, and prenatal exposure to multiple medications appear to increase risk to the fetus (Jones, 1997). Women with seizure disorders who are at risk for pregnancy should be tested to determine if medication can be suspended if they have been seizure-free for 2 years or at least maintained on as low a dose as possible. The conflict between potentially adverse effects of seizures on mother and fetus and of medication on the fetus may be difficult to resolve. For more information, contact the National Organization for Rare Disorders, Inc., website: http://www.rarediseases.org

REFERENCES

Adams, J., Vorhees, C. V., & Middaugh, L. D. (1990). Developmental neurotoxicity of anticonvulsants: Human and animal evidence on phenytoin. *Neurotoxicology and Teratology, 12,* 203–214.

Jones, K. L. (1997). *Smith's recognizable patterns of human malformation* (5th ed.). Philadelphia, PA: W. B. Saunders.

Moore, M., & Brown, R. T. (2003). Fetal hydantoin syndrome. In E. Fletcher-Janzen & C. R. Reynolds (Eds.), *Childhood disorders diagnostic desk reference* (pp. 238–239). Hoboken, NJ: Wiley.

ROBERT T. BROWN
JENNIFER L. CONDON
University of North Carolina at Wilmington

See also Dilantin; Fetal Alcohol Syndrome

FETAL RUBELLA SYNDROME

Rubella, or German measles, is a communicable RNA virus whose effects, including rash and fever, are generally mild when contracted in later childhood or adulthood. However, if contracted by a pregnant woman, rubella may cross the placental barrier and cause fetal death or serious deformities in her offspring. A congenital maternal infection, it is a member of the STORCH complex (syphilis, toxoplasmosis, varicella and other infections, rubella, cytomegalovirus, and herpes), a group of maternal infections that have similar effects on offspring (e.g., Graham & Morgan, 1997). A complex of effects, fetal rubella syndrome (FRS) or congenital rubella syndrome affects about 85% of offspring whose mothers contracted rubella during the first 20 weeks of pregnancy. Effects are greatest in offspring exposed to rubella during the embryonic period, although visual and auditory defects may occur with exposure up to 20 weeks gestation (Centers for Disease Control and Prevention, 2001; March of Dimes, 1999).

Characteristics

1. Intrauterine growth retardation
2. Sensory defects leading to profound hearing loss or deafness, defective vision or blindness, or both
3. Mental retardation and cerebral palsy
4. Congenital heart disease and widespread damage to other internal organs
5. Delayed motor development
6. Diabetes, first appearing in childhood or adulthood

Owing to widespread vaccination of children in developed countries, both postnatal and fetal rubella have declined in recent decades—in the United States, only 12 cases of confirmed FRS occurred during 1995–1996 (Dyne, 2001). However, risk remains high in countries where childhood vaccination is not routine. FRS can cause miscarriage or stillbirth, and survivors may show serious defects. The most common problems, in order, are severe hearing impairment, congenital heart disease, and visual impairments (Roizen & Johnson, 1996; Webster, 1998).

Apparently unaffected infants whose mothers had rubella early in pregnancy should be carefully monitored because sensory, learning, autistic signs, and behavior problems may not appear until childhood (Roizen & Johnson, 1996). Transient signs, including red-purple spots on skin, low birth weight, feeding problems, diarrhea, pneumonia, meningitis, anemia, and enlarged liver and spleen apparent at birth may identify potential cases (March of Dimes, 1999).

Prognosis depends on the number and severity of organic defects: "Of those children with congenital rubella who live to adulthood, one third will be unaffected, one third will have mild to moderate defects, and one third will have severe to profound impairment" (Roizen & Johnson, 1996, p. 183). Except for transient characteristics at birth, effects of FRS are permanent, and only supportive treatment is available. As with prognosis, type and extent of assistance required depend on the variety and severity of problems. Surgery may be required for cardiac and other organic defects. Special education treatment may include adaptive technology for sensory impairments (hearing aids, computer-based reading devices), speech and language therapy, special classroom placement, or—in severe cases—institutionalization. A team approach will be needed in many cases. Parents may need long-term help with in-home care, and many affected individuals will require some degree of lifelong assistance. Clearly, the best long-term approach for FRS is prevention through childhood immunization.

REFERENCES

Centers for Disease Control and Prevention. (2001). Rubella. In *Epidemiology and prevention of vaccine-preventable diseases: The pink book*. Retrieved from http://www.cdc.gov/nip/publications/pink/rubella.pdf

Dyne, P. (2001). Pediatrics, rubella. *eMedicine Journal, 2*(6). Retrieved from http://emedicine.com/emerg/topic388.htm

Graham, E. M., & Morgan, M. A. (1997). Growth before birth. In M. L. Batshaw (Ed.), *Children with disabilities* (4th ed., pp. 53–69). Baltimore, MD: Paul H. Brookes.

Roizen, N. J., & Johnson, D. (1996). Congenital infections. In A. J. Capute & P. J. Accardo (Eds.), *Developmental disabilities in infancy and childhood: Vol. 1. Neurodevelopmental diagnosis and treatment* (2nd ed., pp. 175–193). Baltimore, MD: Paul H. Brookes.

Webster, W. S. (1998). Teratology update: Congenital rubella. *Teratology, 58,* 13–23.

ROBERT T. BROWN

STEPHANIE ANSELENE
University of North Carolina, Wilmington

FETAL TRIMETHADIONE SYNDROME

Trimethadione and its congener paratrimethadione are highly teratogenic. Offspring of mothers treated with either drug during pregnancy are likely to show one or more of a variety of abnormalities. According to Jones

(1997), the effects are severe and predictable enough as to call for possible elective abortion if the mother is known to have used these drugs. In one review cited by Jones (1997), of pregnancies in women taking these drugs, about 25% spontaneously aborted and 83% of live births had one or more malformations, several of which were lethal. The disorder is rare (Office of Rare Diseases, 2001), and accurate incidence figures are not available.

Characteristics

1. Mental retardation
2. Intrauterine growth retardation
3. Craniofacial dysmorphologies (mild brachycephaly and midfacial hypoplasia, prominent forehead, and short upturned nose)
4. Cardiovascular defects

As with many drug-induced abnormalities, knowledge that the pregnant woman actually ingested the drug is important for accurate diagnosis. Prognosis is poor for those with severe mental retardation and cardiovascular defects. Surgery may help to alleviate the effects of some defects, but otherwise, only supportive treatment is available. Surviving children will need a variety of special education services, including special classroom placement and speech and physical therapy.

REFERENCES

Jones, K. L. (1997). *Smith's recognizable patterns of human malformation* (5th ed.). Philadelphia, PA: W B. Saunders.

Office of Rare Diseases. (2001). Rare diseases list. Retrieved from http://rarediseases.info.nih.gov/

ROBERT T. BROWN
University of North Carolina, Wilmington

FETAL VALPROATE SYNDROME

Fetal valproate syndrome (FVS) is caused by exposure to the anticonvulsant drug (AED) valproic acid (trade name Depakene, Depakote, among others). Valproic acid is a prenatal teratogen, and a small percentage of women who take the drug in the first trimester of pregnancy will have offspring with one or more signs of the syndrome. The effects, particularly craniofacial, of prenatal exposure to valproate are so similar to those of several other AEDs, including carbamazepine, hydantoin, mysoline, and phenobarbital, as to have led to the general descriptive term fetal antiepileptic drug syndrome (Jones, 1997; Zahn, Morrell, Collins, Labiner, & Yerby, 1998).

Incidence estimates are based on small sample studies and thus are subject to considerable error. About 35% of infants exposed prenatally to valproic acid will manifest characteristics of FVS (Jones, 1997), and approximately 2% will have spina bifida (Epilepsy Foundation, 2001). Dose-response curve or safe levels of exposure are unknown. Risk appears to be greater than with some other AEDs (Epilepsy Foundation, 2001), and the risk tends to increase if the pregnant woman takes multiple anticonvulsants (Jones, 1997; Zahn et al., 1998). No clear gender differences are apparent (Zahn et al., 1998). The following are only a few of numerous characteristics described in Jones (1997) and Jablonski's Multiple Congenital Anomaly/Mental Retardation (MCA/MR) Syndromes Database (1999), and they may appear in various combinations.

Characteristics

1. Numerous craniofacial dysmorphologies, including narrow bifrontal diameter, high forehead, epicanthal folds connecting to an infraorbital crease, low nasal bridge, short nose, anteverted nostrils, long philtrum, a thin upper and thick lower lip, cleft lip and palate, and low-set posteriorly rotated ears
2. Numerous deformities of cardiovascular, respiratory, and urogenital systems
3. Skeletal deformities, including spina bifida, hand and foot polydactyly, fingerlike thumbs, and rudimentary digits
4. Mild to moderate growth deficiency in some cases
5. Mental and motor retardation in some cases

Optimal treatment for FHS—and fetal antiepileptic drug syndromes in general—is preventive. Women who are taking anticonvulsants need to be aware of the risks involved before they become pregnant. Complicating the situation is the fact that uncontrolled seizures as well as exposure to AEDs put the embryo or fetus at risk. The Epilepsy Foundation (2001) has information of value to those with epilepsy who may become pregnant. Their physician should reduce the number of anticonvulsants to one at 6 months prior to conception. Folic acid supplements during pregnancy may also be recommended (Zahn et al., 1998).

Treatment and education of children with FVD or other AED syndrome need to be individualized owing to wide variations in the degree and type of resulting problems. A variety of special education services, including special classroom placement, may be necessary. Affected individuals with spina bifida will benefit from physical therapy and adaptive technology.

REFERENCES

Epilepsy Foundation. (2001). *Women and epilepsy*. Retrieved from http://www.efa.org

Jablonski's Multiple Congenital Anomaly/Mental Retardation (MCA/MR) Syndromes Database. (1999). *Fetal valproate syndrome (FVS)*. United States National Library of Medicine. Retrieved from http://www.nlm.nih.gov

Jones, K. L. (1997). *Smith's recognizable patterns of human malformation* (5th ed.). Philadelphia, PA: W. B. Sanders.

Zahn, C., Morrell, M., Collins, S., Labiner, D., & Yerby, M. (1998). Management issues for women with epilepsy: A review of the literature. *Neurology, 51*, 949–956.

ROBERT T. BROWN
University of North Carolina, Wilmington

FETAL VARICELLA SYNDROME

Varicella, or chicken pox, is an infection that if contracted by a pregnant woman may cross the placental barrier and cause serious deformities in her offspring. A congenital maternal infection, it is a member of the STORCH complex (syphilis, toxoplasmosis, varicella and other infections, rubella, cytomegalovirus, and herpes), a group of maternal infections that have similar effects on offspring (e.g., Graham & Morgan, 1997). An estimated 1–2% of offspring of mothers who contract varicella 8–20 weeks postconception show some aspects of the syndrome, and about 50% of those die in early infancy. The number and variety of defects that may be shown is large, and the range of effects is highly variable. Even basic characteristics will not appear in all cases (Jones, 1997; National Organization for Rare Disorders, 1997).

Characteristics

1. Intrauterine growth retardation
2. Mental retardation, learning disabilities, microcephaly, and cortical atrophy
3. Seizures
4. Eye deformities (including chorioretinitis, cataracts, microphthalmia)
5. Limb hypoplasia, possibly with rudimentary digits, paralysis, and limb atrophy
6. Cutaneous scars

Prevention is the best approach now that an effective vaccine is available. Approximately 50–70% of women in the Western world test immune, even if they have no memory of having had chicken pox in childhood. Women of childbearing age who test negative for immunity should receive the vaccine, but only if they are not pregnant because teratogenic effects of the vaccine are now not known (Koren, 2000).

Diagnosis is through blood and other fluid tests. Prognosis is highly variable, depending on number and severity of symptoms. Surgery may be necessary to alleviate the effects of some defects; adaptive technology may be required to help deal with the visual and limb problems, and a variety of special education services, ranging from special classroom placement to extensive physical therapy, may be needed.

REFERENCES

Graham, E. M., & Morgan, M. A. (1997). Growth before birth. In M. L. Batshaw (Ed.), *Children with disabilities* (4th ed., pp. 53–69). Baltimore, MD: Paul H. Brookes.

Jones, K. L. (1997). *Smith's recognizable patterns of human malformation* (5th ed.). Philadelphia, PA: Saunders.

Koren, G. (2000). *Varicella virus vaccine before pregnancy*. Motherisk. Retrieved from http://www.motherisk.org/updates/oct00.php3

National Organization for Rare Disorders. (1997). *Congenital varicella syndrome*. Retrieved from http://www.clarian.org/kbase/nord/nord1099.jhtml

ROBERT T. BROWN
University of North Carolina, Wilmington

FETAL WARFARIN SYNDROME

Fetal warfarin syndrome, also known as fetal anticoagulant syndrome, DiSala syndrome, fetal coumarin syndrome, or warfarin embryopathy, is the result of teratogenic effects of the anticoagulant warfarin when taken by women during pregnancy (National Library of Medicine [NLM], 1999). Warfarin is a coumarin derivative that is used to treat clotting disorders such as phlebitis and as an anticoagulant rodenticide (International Programme on Chemical Safety [Inchem], 1997). The most prescribed oral anticoagulant, it is the 11th-most prescribed drug in the United States (Horton & Bushwick, 1999).

The disorder is rare. About one third of pregnancies among women who took warfarin in weeks 6–9 of gestation end in either spontaneous abortion or the birth of infants with congenital abnormalities. Uncertainty exists concerning the effects of ingestion later in pregnancy, but any adverse consequences apparently occur at a very low rate (Jones, 1997).

The disorder has numerous characteristics; some occur more frequently than others (Birth Disorder Information Directory, 2000; NLM, 1999). More common characteristics are listed.

Characteristics

1. Mental retardation and seizures
2. Central nervous system abnormalities (microcephaly hydrocephalus, agenesis of the corpus callosum, spina bifida)
3. Facial anomalies, including nasal hypoplasia
4. Serious visual and auditory impairments
5. Hypoplasia of fingers and toes
6. Abnormalities of cardiovascular and respiratory systems
7. Feeding difficulties and failure to thrive

Because most effects are irreversible, treatment is mainly supportive and directed at the particular complex of symptoms shown. Some skeletal anomalies may be surgically remediable. Special education services will vary with characteristics of the child. Physical therapy, speech therapy, and cognitive therapies will often be needed. Adaptive technology or special schools may be needed in cases involving serious sensory impairments. Owing to the potential number and severity of skeletal, neurological, and muscular impairments, patients may be homebound and require in-home assistance.

Although the disorder is rare, women who are on anticoagulant medication and at risk for becoming pregnant should be aware and advised on the dangers of warfarin.

REFERENCES

Birth Disorder Information Directory. (2000). *Fetal warfarin syndrome*. Retrieved from http://www.orpha.net

Horton, J. D., & Bushwick, B. M. (1999, February 1). Warfarin therapy: Evolving strategies in antcoagulation. *American Family Physician*. Retrieved from http://www.aafp.org/afp/990 201ap/635.html

International Programme on Chemical Safety. (1997). *Warfarin*. Retrieved from http://www.inchem.org/documents/pims/chem ical/pim563.htm

Jones, K. L. (1997). *Smith's recognizable patterns of human malformation* (5th ed.). Philadelphia, PA: Saunders.

National Library of Medicine. (1999). *Fetal anticoagulant syndrome*. Retrieved from http://www.nlm.nih.gov/mesh/jablonski /syndromes/syndrome291.html

PAULA KILPATRICK

ROBERT T. BROWN
University of North Carolina, Wilmington

FEWELL, REBECCA R. (1936–   )

Rebecca R. Fewell received her BA in sociology from Agnes Scott College, Georgia, in 1958. She then went on to receive her MA in 1969 and her doctorate in special education in 1972 from George Peabody College, Tennessee. On graduation she joined the Peabody faculty and remained there until 1979. While at Peabody, Fewell directed projects and a diagnostic training center for children who were deaf-blind and disabled. Additionally, she was chairman of the special education department and was the elected faculty representative to the Peabody College Council on Student Policy.

Fewell's areas of interest have included the following programs: Program for Children with Down's Syndrome and Other Developmental Delays; the Supporting Extended Family Members program, a program for fathers, siblings, and grandparents of handicapped children; the Computer-Assisted Program Project for using resources at the University of Washington to serve children in rural areas throughout the United States; a research program comparing a direct instructional model to a cognitive mediated learning model for preschool intervention; and the Infant Health and Development Program for Premature Infants. Her other research involves the development of affective behavior and play skills in disabled and nondisabled children.

Fewell has served on the editorial boards of five journals and as senior editor of *Topics in Early Childhood Special Education*. Additionally, she has published over 75 articles, several books, and two tests, the Developmental Activities Screening Inventory and the Peabody Developmental Motor Scales and Activity Cards. Her recent work includes publication of a multivolume series dealing with early childhood special education, which included such topics as instructional models, mainstreaming, obtaining family information, and controversies associated with early intervention (Deutscher & Fewell, 2005; Fewell, 1991; Fewell & Neisworth, 1990–1992).

This entry has been informed by the sources listed below.

REFERENCES

Deutscher, B., & Fewell, R. R. (2005). Early predictors of attention-deficit/hyperactivity disorder and school difficulties in low birth weight, premature children. *Topics in Early Childhood Education*, *25*, 445–453.

Fewell, R. R. (1991). Trends in the assessment of infants and toddlers with disabilities. *Exceptional Children*, *58*(2), 166–173.

Fewell, R. R., & Langley, B. (1984). *Developmental activities screening inventory*. Austin, TX: PRO-ED.

Fewell, R. R., & Neisworth, J. T. (1990–1992). *Topics in early childhood special education* (Vols. 10–11). Austin, TX: PRO-ED.

Fewell, R., & Vadasy, P. F. (Eds.). (1986). *Families of handicapped children: Needs and supports across the lifespan*. Austin, TX: PRO-ED

Folio, R., & Fewell, R. R. (1983). *Peabody developmental motor scales and activity cards*. Allen, TX MA: Teaching Resources.

Garwood, S. G., & Fewell, R. R. (1983). *Educating handicapped infants*. Rockville, MD: Aspen.

ROBERTA C. STOKES
Texas A&M University
First edition

TAMARA J. MARTIN
The University of Texas
of the Permian Basin
Second edition

been fatal; however, most children with the disorder have a normal life span.

REFERENCE

Banwell, B. L., Laurence, E. B., Jay, V., Taylor, G. P., & Vajsar, J. (1999). Cardiac manifestations of congenital fiber-type disproportion myopathy. *Journal of Child Neurology, 14*(2), 83–87.

KIMBERLY M. ESTEP
University of Houston–Clear Lake

FIBER-TYPE DISPROPORTION, CONGENITAL

Congenital fiber type disproportion (CFTD) is a rare muscle disease, specifically Type I muscle fibers. It is characterized by scoliosis, loss of muscle tone, short stature, dislocated hips, and foot deformities, all of which are evident at birth. Although CFTD is present at birth, symptoms tend to improve with age. Some cases of CFTD are thought to occur sporadically. Familial transmission also has been evidenced, and in some cases, gene mutations have been identified in genes that encode for muscle proteins. Overall, research presents a rather heterogeneous etiology for CFTD and incidence rates are unknown.

Characteristics

1. Type I muscle fibers are abnormally small, resulting in hypertrophic Type II muscle fibers.
2. At birth, loss of muscle tone, scoliosis, high arched palate, dislocated hips, muscle weakness, and foot deformities are present.
3. Skeletal deformities such as thin face, short stature, congenital hip dislocation, clubfeet, and a hunched back (kyphoscoliosis) are common.

Treatments generally focus on correcting and preventing skeletal abnormalities with surgery; passive stretching and physical therapy to maintain muscle activity are crucial. Orthopedic aids may become necessary as the disease progresses and the child ages. Cardiomyopathy has been documented in a limited number of cases (Banwell, Laurence, Jay, Taylor, & Vajsar, 1999), and intervention will be necessary to prolong life expectancy.

Special education requirements are limited to the progression of the disorder and the degree of impairment. Prognosis is good provided that cardiac or other complications are not present. A few neonatal cases of CFTD have

FIBROSYSPLASIA OSSIFICANS PROGRESSIVA

Fibrodysplasia ossificans progressiva syndrome (FOPS) is a rare hereditary connective tissue disorder. Its salient features include shortening of the big toe and swellings in tendons and other fibrous membranes in muscles of the neck, back, upper arm, and upper leg (fibrodysplasia). The swellings eventually metamorphose into bony deposits within muscle and can therefore cause severe mobility deficits.

The cause of the underlying fibrous tissue defect of FOPS is unknown. The pattern of inheritance is autosomal dominant. A shortened big toe is a constant finding among these patients, but the severity of fibrodysplasia they can have is quite variable. About 90% of cases are new genetic mutations. Advanced paternal age is a factor in this patient subset. Although this condition is considered rare, about 500 cases have appeared in the medical literature since it was first described in 1692 (see Jones, 1997).

Characteristics

1. Short big toe, often with fusion of the joints. Less commonly the thumb is short.
2. Fibrous tissue swellings, sometimes painful and accompanied by fever, leading to bony deposits (ossification) in muscle. The most frequently affected areas are the neck, back, shoulder, upper parts of the extremities, and (less commonly) the jaw. Fibrodysplasia may be evident at birth or may not manifest until the third decade of life. Ossification begins within 2 to 8 months of onset of swelling. By age 7, 80% of patients experience restrictive ossifications. By age 15, 95% have severely limited arm mobility secondary to advanced fibrodysplasia.
3. Progressive fusion of the vertebrae in the neck.
4. Occasional findings include shortened fingers and toes (other than the thumb and big toe),

> inward curving of the little finger (clinodactyly), widely spaced teeth, underdeveloped genitalia, easy bruising, hearing deficits, and abnormalities of heart rhythm.

The efficacy of FOPS therapy is difficult to assess because the natural history of the disorder is characterized by numerous symptomatic exacerbations and remissions. Salicylates (aspirin) and corticosteroids may provide some pain relief. Operative removal of the bony deposits is not an option because surgical sites serve as foci for further fibrodysplasia to develop. In fact, even minor trauma and intramuscular injections can induce bony changes. These patients are also poor surgical risks because of difficulties with anesthesia administration, chronic restrictive lung disease, and cardiac rhythm disturbances.

There is no research to indicate cognitive limitations or the need for remediations academically. However, because of the physical complications, the child with FOPS may require support from physical and occupational therapists who can help with assistive and technological devices to allow the child to continue to progress academically.

No data are available regarding the life expectancy of FOPS patients. Prognosis is largely determined by the degree of fibrodysplasia that the patients develop. This finding is quite variable among affected individuals, may not begin until adulthood, and is relentlessly progressive. Therefore, it is not possible to predict in any reliable way what the future holds for a child with this disease.

For more information and parent support, please contact International Fibrodysplasia Ossificans Progressiva Association, P.O. Box 196217, Winter Springs, FL 32719-6217. Tel.: (407) 365-4194, e-mail: ifopa@vol.com, website: https://www.med.upenn.edu/

REFERENCES

Jones, K. (1997). *Smith's recognizable patterns of human malformations* (5th ed.). Philadelphia, PA: W. B. Saunders.

National Organization for Rare Disorders. (1996). *Fibrodysplasia ossificans progressiva (FOP)*. Retrieved from http://www.stepstn.com/egi-win/nord.exe?proc=GetDocument&rectype=0&recnum=366

BARRY H. DAVISON
Ennis, Texas

FIELD DEPENDENCE–INDEPENDENCE

The concepts field dependence (FD) and independence (FI) were introduced into psychology and education by H.A. Witkin. He identified FD and FI as two distinct cognitive polarities that developed out of the theory of psychological differentiation. They were the terms used to accommodate broad patterns of psychological functioning associated with individual differences.

Witkin's research began with investigations of individual differences in the perception of the "upright" in the rod and frame, body adjustment, rotating room, and embedded figures tests. In each of these tests, subjects differed in the extent to which they used the external visual field or the body itself for locating the upright in space. The rod and frame test was used in early FD–FI research. Seated in darkness, the subject looks at a rod suspended in a frame. The rod and frame are independent of one another. The subject has the examiner adjust the rod to a perceived vertical position. How the subject rotates the rod in relation to the frame indicates field dependence or independence. At one extreme, when perception of the upright is dominated by the previous field (frame), this is designated field dependence. When the person sees the items as distinct from the surrounding field, this is designated field independence. The Embedded Figures Test (Witkin et al., 1977) is used more frequently and especially with younger children because of its simplicity. In this test, subjects are asked to locate a simple figure in a complex background. Witkin used this test to determine FD–FI in children between 3 and 9 years of age. However, there is a scarcity of current research available.

Many of the concepts derived from FD–FI styles may apply to special education. These are applicable to such issues as how children think, perceive, solve problems, and learn to relate to others. Field dependence–independence has been applied to the education of various groups, including the intellectually disabled, gifted, physically disabled, and emotionally disturbed.

REFERENCE

Witkin, H. A., Moore, C. A., Goodenough, D. R., & Cox, P. W. (1977). Field dependent and independent cognitive styles. *Review of Educational Research, 47*, 1–64.

STEVEN GUMERMAN
Temple University

See also **Visual-Motor and Visual-Perceptual Problems;
Visual Perception and Discrimination**

FILIAL THERAPY, SPECIAL EDUCATION AND

Filial therapy was developed in the 1960s by Bernard Gurney and Michael Andronico (Andronico & Gurney, 1967). It is a "psychotherapeutic technique utilizing parents as therapeutic agents for their own children" (Hornsby & Applebaum, 1978). Primarily intended for children with emotional disturbances and their parents in outpatient school settings, filial therapy has been adapted to residential settings with children with intellectual disabilities and children with autism spectrum disorders (Hornsby & Applebaum, 1978; White, Hornsby, & Gordon, 1972). This approach is considered integrative; it empowers the parents as therapists and enlists them as agents of change. Instead of the child being taken away from the family to be helped, the message is clear that the parents are a necessary and integral part of the process. Filial therapy is a method of treatment that can be used as a preventive or remedial approach to help parents become more effective in their parenting skills.

Although filial therapy has been used in the schools (Andronico & Gurney, 1967) to lighten the workloads of school psychologists, current usage is mainly in residential facilities where psychological therapy is the central treatment focus. A typical filial therapy session has a multi-impact format. After the family has undergone initial evaluation, designed to determine the internal dynamics of the family members, the filial sessions begin. The parent who is considered to be the most distant from the child is used as the "primary therapist." It is this parent who will work with the child in the therapy playroom. The psychologist supplies this patient with a "bug" (a hearing device placed in the ear) and retires with the other parent to an observation room. The psychologist gives suggestions and directions to the parent engaging in play with the child, and uses the other parent as a coobserver and resource. After the play session is over, the family and therapist process feelings, observations, and thoughts regarding the relationship and communication patterns between the primary therapist and the child. In addition, there is an emphasis on overall reactions to the filial therapy process. As sessions progress, the bug is removed and therapy focuses on generalizing what has been learned by the parent and child to the home setting. Ultimately, the goals of filial therapy are to enhance and improve family relations, communications, and behavior management and to increase motivation of the parents to succeed and be responsible for changes in the family system.

Filial therapy has not gained widespread recognition in the schools. However, parent training programs such as Parent Effectiveness Training (PET; Gordon, 1970), Systematic Training for Effective Parenting (STEP; Dinkmeyer & McKay, 1976), and Children: The Challenge (Dreikurs & Soltz, 1964), all use essentially the same principles of parents assuming cotherapeutic management of the child with the school. In other words, schools have recognized the importance of offering parental guidance. The resurrection of filial therapy in a residential setting perhaps reflects the reintegration of the emotionally disturbed child back into the public sector and the necessity for change to be supported by the family system.

Special education personnel may use the principles of filial therapy in one of three ways: (1) as a continuation of filial therapy with emotionally disturbed children reentering the public schools from residential or outpatient treatment, (2) where academic and behavioral deficits require support from the home environment, and (3) as a preventive measure in classes with behaviorally disturbed children. Modifications will certainly have to be made in the school setting. For example, the bug could be replaced by the teacher modeling appropriate academic or behavioral instruction in front of the parent or the parent and child engaging in academic or behavioral instruction with the educator observing and making suggestions. The benefits of filial therapy to the special educator include enhanced rapport with the child and parents, emphasizing a cooperative and holistic effort; reinforcement of appropriate learning from home, thereby assisting the child in generalization and transfer of training; and improved communication and interaction among family members.

REFERENCES

Andronico, M. P., & Gurney, B. (1967). The potential application of filial therapy to the school situation. *Journal of School Psychology, 6*, 7–12.

Dinkmeyer, D., & McKay, G. (1976). *Systematic training for effective parenting*. Circle Pines, MN: American Guidance Service.

Dreikurs, R., & Soltz, V. (1964). *Children: The challenge*. New York, NY: Duell, Slone, & Pearce.

Gordon, T. (1970). *Parent effectiveness training*. New York, NY: Wyden.

Hornsby, L. G., & Applebaum, A. S. (1978). Parents as primary therapists: Filial therapy. In N.L.E. Arnold (Ed.), *Helping parents help their children*. New York, NY: Brunner/Mazel.

White, J. H., Hornsby, L. G., & Gordon, R. (1972). Treating infantile autism with parent therapists. *International Journal of Child Psychotherapy, 1*, 83–95.

DAVID FLETCHER-JANZEN
Colorado Springs, Colorado

FINGERSPELLING

The American manual alphabet consists of 26 distinct hand configurations that represent the letters of the alphabet. Fingerspelling is the rapid execution of a series of these configurations to communicate words visually. As such, it is more a representation of written language than of spoken language because it excludes the phonological alterations and prosodic aspects of speech. Fingerspelling skills include the hand configurations, the characteristic positioning of the hand in a fixed central location, and the set of possible transition movements from one configuration to the next (Padden & LeMaster, 1985).

Dactylology (the study or use of the manual alphabet) has attributed the origin of fingerspelling to medieval monks who used it to communicate without breaking their vows of silence. A Spanish Benedictine monk, Pedro Ponce de Leon, is thought to have been the first person to use fingerspelling to instruct the deaf. His work was built on by another Spaniard, Juan Martin Pablo Bonet, who in 1620 published the first book on educating the deaf. This book included a diagram of a manual alphabet that is remarkably similar to the one used in the United States today. It is believed that this alphabet was later brought to France and used to improve the alphabet of Abbé Charles de l'Epée, founder of the first French public school for the deaf in the 18th century. It was de l'Epée's methods and alphabet that were later imported to the United States by Laurent Clerc and Thomas Hopkins Gallaudet. This alphabet, further modified and evolved, has become the American manual alphabet.

There are numerous manual alphabets in use in different countries around the world. The American manual alphabet, however, with only two exceptions (t and d), was adopted by the Fourth Congress of the World Federation of the Deaf in 1963 as the international hand alphabet. This was in part because English and French (which uses a very similar system) are the official languages of the federation, and in part because the American alphabet was already in use in many countries (Carmel, 1975; Schein, 1984).

Fingerspelling is generally used as an adjunct to sign language, especially to render proper nouns, technological terms for which no signs exist, and slang. To the uninitiated, fingerspelling seems an indistinguishable part of sign language. There are, however, several differences between signing and fingerspelling. Signs usually use one or two distinct hand configurations, while in fingerspelling there are as many configurations as there are letters in the word. Fingerspelling is done in a much smaller space than signing, with the hand remaining in a nearly fixed position as only the configuration changes. Palm orientation in fingerspelling is restricted almost exclusively to a palm out position, in contrast to signing, in which there is no such restriction. Another important difference is that while signing evolved as a means of communication in the deaf community, fingerspelling originated as an instructional tool (Padden & LeMaster, 1985).

Although fingerspelling is used primarily as a supplement to sign language, a method of manual communication exists that relies exclusively on the use of fingerspelling. This is known as the Rochester Method, after the Rochester School for the Deaf where the superintendent of the school, Zenas Westervelt, initiated its use in 1878. The method gradually fell into disuse after Westervelt's death in 1912, and though proponents of it still exist, it is seldom used today, not even in the school for which it was named (Schein, 1984).

American deaf people are noted for more frequent use, and more rapid execution, of fingerspelling than other sign communities throughout the world (Padden & LeMaster, 1985). This may in part be responsible for the phenomenon known as loan signs. These are signs that originated as fingerspelled words, but in which the number of hand configurations has been reduced to two. In addition, other features such as palm orientation and movement have been added so that a phonologically well-formed sign is produced (Battison, 1978). Lessons in fingerspelling can be obtained free on the Internet at http://www.asl.ms/

REFERENCES

Battison, R. (1978). *Lexical borrowing in ASL*. Silver Spring, MD: Linstock.

Carmel, S. J. (1975). *International hand alphabet charts*. Rockville, MD: Studio Printing.

Padden, C. A., & LeMaster, B. (1985). An alphabet on hand: The acquisition of fingerspelling in deaf children. *Sign Language Studies, 47*, 161–172.

Schein, J. D. (1984). *Speaking the language of sign*. New York, NY: Doubleday.

Peg Eagney
School for the Deaf, New York, New York

See also **American Sign Language; Deaf Education**

FINLAND, SPECIAL EDUCATION IN

The first Act for public education in Finland dates from the middle of the 19th century. The first schools for children with disabilities started at that time, beginning with special provision for deaf and blind. Compulsory education was enacted in 1921. After that, every community had to organize elementary education and every municipality with more than 10,000 inhabitants had to arrange education for children with intellectual disabilities (Tuunainen, 1994).

Since the first Compulsory Education Act of 1921, the Finnish education system has been based on a philosophy of "Education for All." Following the Nordic social democratic model, Finnish education policy has been based on the idea that everybody needs to have equal access to educate him or herself to the highest possible level without cost. This principle strengthened when the former parallel school system (two graded streams after grade 4) was replaced by united comprehensive schooling by the Comprehensive School Act of 1970. During the gradual shift to comprehensive schooling, the model of "part-time special education" was created to meet the growing diversity of comprehensive school population. Before that the main provision for students with special educational needs was based on special schools and self-contained special classes. The aim of the new part-time provision model was to offer support and prevention to students without administratively transfer them to special education and could be delivered without any diagnosis for students with or without disabilities (Itkonen & Jahnukainen, 2010). This model has expanded during the decades and is in use of every comprehensive school as main part of intensified support of learning and schooling. It is one of those factors explaining recent results of the excellence and equity of Finnish school system in international comparisons like PISA (Kivirauma & Ruoho, 1997).

The Basic Education Act (628/1998) launched Individual Education Plans, which made it possible to serve students requiring significant special support officially in regular classrooms full-time. After that the number of students with significant special education needs in general education classrooms has gradually increased and at the same time both the number of special schools and special school placements has been decreasing over time (Graham & Jahnukainen, 2010) (Figure F.3). The existing special schools are often congregated with the general education schools sharing the same schoolyard and making the social inclusion possible between students.

The Amendment of the Basic Education Act (642/2010) entails again significant changes to the special education regulations. Currently special education is defined under the title of Learning and Schooling Support, which is based on three tiers: (1) general support, (2) intensified support, and (3) special support (National Board of Education, 2010). The first tier consists of every action made by the regular classroom teacher in terms of differentiation as well as in terms of schoolwide efforts to meet the diversity of students. The second tier consists of remedial support by the class teacher, coteaching with the special educator and temporal individual or small group learning with the part-time special educator. The third tier consists of

the whole continuum of special education services from fulltime general education to a special school placement. Every student of the special support tier must have an Individualized Education Plan (Finnish acronym HOJKS).

In school year 2010–2011 there were 46,710 compulsory school students served under the nine categories of special educational needs receiving full-time special education support (Tier 3; special support). This is 8.5 percentages of all compulsory school students (Statistics Finland, 2010). The most typical reason for special support was dysphasia (a learning difficulty caused by impaired linguistic development), following by category of cerebral dysfunction or physical disability (including ADHD) and emotional disturbance or social maladjustment. There has been a significant increase in use of the two first mentioned categories instead of the mild developmental delay, which used to be the largest special education category, but has decreased rapidly since early 2000 (Jahnukainen, 2006). In addition of these students served in full-time special education, 128,657 students (23.3 percentage of compulsory school students), were served under the part-time special support (Tier 2: intensified support) (Statistics Finland, 2010). The most typical reason was reading and writing difficulties, which covers 40 percentage of all intensified support and over 90 percentage of intensified support delivered during elementary school years.

In postcompulsory schools (senior high school or vocational upper secondary school) the most special education services are delivered in vocational schools. In 2009 the special education student percentage in vocational schools was 6.5. Combining statistics from both comprehensive and secondary schooling phases, the percentage of special education students in Finland equivalent to K–12 systems elsewhere was around 6.4% in 2007 (Graham & Jahnukainen, 2011).

The Finnish full-time special education funding used to be based on the idea that the funding follows the child. Students in need of full-time special education did get a higher funding based on the severity of the special

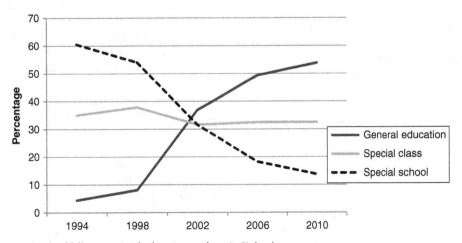

Figure F.3. The placement trends of full-time special education students in Finland.

need. The education funding system was changed recently, and there is currently no extra funding for any students with special educational needs, although the students with severe disabilities will get individually defined extra funding from other than normal education base-funding resources (Jahnukainen, 2011).

The special education teacher education is organized as part of the teacher education in six universities. All teacher education in Finland is based on master-level degrees. Students can either take special education as a major subject of the master studies or, after receiving an elementary or subject teacher degree, apply to a 1-year diploma course in special education. Special teacher education, as well as teacher education in general is highly competitive in Finland, and there are entrance tests with written exam as well as interviews for all applicants.

REFERENCES

Graham, L. J., & Jahnukainen, M. (2011). Wherefore art thou, inclusion? Analysing the development of inclusive education in New South Wales, Alberta and Finland. *Journal of Education Policy, 26*, 261–286.

Itkonen, T., & Jahnukainen, M. (2010). Disability or learning difficulty? Politicians or educators? Constructing special education in Finland and the United States. *Comparative Sociology, 25*, 182–201.

Jahnukainen, M. (2006). Erityisopetuksen tarve ja muutos [The need for and changes in special needs education, in Finnish]. In S. Karvonen (Ed.), *Onko sukupuolella väliä? Hyvinvointi, terveys, pojat ja tytöt.* [Does the gender matter? Well-being, health, boys and girls.] *Nuorten elinolot vuosikirja* [Yearbook of the living conditions of young people] (pp. 119–131). Nuoriso-tutkimusverkosto, Nuorisoasiain neuvottelukunta & Stakes.

Jahnukainen, M. (2011). Different strategies, different outcomes? The history and trends of the inclusive and special education in Alberta (Canada) and in Finland. *Scandinavian Journal of Educational Research, 55*, 489–502.

Kivirauma, J., & Ruoho, K. (2007). Excellence through special education? Lessons from the Finnish school reform. *Review of Education, 58*, 283–302.

National Board of Education (2010). *Perusopetuksen opetussuun-nitelman perusteiden muutokset ja täydennykset.* [The amendments and changes of the national curriculum of compulsory schooling, in Finnish]. Helsinki, Finland: National Board of Education.

Statistics Finland (2010). *Special education* (e-publication). Helsinki: Statistics Finland. Retrieved from http://www.stat.fi/til/erop/tau_en.html

Tuunainen, K. (1994). Country briefing: Special education in Finland. *European Journal of Special Needs Education, 9*, 189–198.

MARKKU JAHNUKAINEN
University of Helsinki
Fourth edition

FITZGERALD KEY, THE

The Fitzgerald key is used to teach deaf children to generate correct language structures. Developed by Elizabeth Fitzgerald, a deaf teacher, the key was originally described in Fitzgerald's book, *Straight Language for the Deaf* (Fitzgerald, 1926). For the next 40 years it was widely used throughout the United States and Canada in schools and programs for the deaf (Moores, 1978; Myers & Hammill, 1976).

The key provides the deaf child with a visual guide for structuring sentences, thus helping to compensate for the lack of hearing. Fitzgerald (1976) recommended that it be used for all subjects and at all age levels. To facilitate its use she suggested that the key be painted in washable yellow paint across the top of the most prominent blackboard in the classroom.

The key consists of ordered (left-to-right) headings (key words) and six symbols that constitute a sentence pattern. Key words are used to classify new vocabulary. Nouns, for example, are classified under the keywords what and who; adjectives under the key words how many, what kind, what color. Symbols are used to classify parts of speech for which there are no associated key words. For example, the symbol for verb is =; for pronoun –. Fitzgerald was careful to point out that each of the six written symbols should always be verbally paired with the name of the part of speech it represents. The teacher may also pair the symbol with its written name. Fitzgerald believed that the use of symbols helps children at beginning levels of instruction to sense the difference between parts of speech more easily than terms such as *verb, participle,* and so forth; however, she recommended that their use be dropped as soon as possible. The following example shows how words are combined into a sentence pattern using key words and symbols:

Who: How many: What color: Whom: Where:
What: What

    =

George brought   a   blue   car   to school

Initially, students are taught to combine words into simple phrases under appropriate key words (Moores, 1978). Instruction emphasizes the use of correct word order. Gradually, the complexity of the phrases is increased until students are able to work with the complete key to formulate sentences.

In 1947 Pugh (1955) published *Steps in Language Development for the Deaf,* a book of carefully sequenced language lessons using the key and based on the principles of instruction set forth by Fitzgerald. Although Pugh slightly modified Fitzgerald's approach, her book complemented Fitzgerald's so well that both books are traditionally used together (Myers & Hammill, 1976).

The Fitzgerald key also has been recommended as an instructional program for learning-disabled students with either severe auditory or visual modality problems

(Myers & Hammill, 1976). The extent of its use with this population and the degree of success achieved in remediating learning disabilities has not been documented.

REFERENCES

Fitzgerald, E. (1926). *Straight language for the deaf*. Washington, DC: Alexander Graham Bell Association for the Deaf.

Moores, D. F. (1978). *Educating the deaf: Psychology, principles, and practices*. Boston, MA: Houghton Mifflin.

Myers, P. I., & Hammill, D. D. (1976). *Methods for learning disorders* (2nd ed.). New York, NY: Wiley.

Pugh, B. L. (1955). *Steps in language development for the deaf*. Washington, DC: Volta Bureau.

MARIANNE PRICE
*Montgomery County Intermediate Unit
Norristown, Pennsylvania*

See also Deaf Education; Language Disorders

FOCUS ON AUTISM AND OTHER DEVELOPMENTAL DISABILITIES (JOURNAL)

Focus on Autism and Other Developmental Disabilities is a practitioner-friendly, empirically based journal published quarterly to support professionals, families, and other advocates committed to improving the lives of children, adolescents, and adults with developmental disabilities, such as autism spectrum disorders, intellectual disability, and cerebral palsy. Researchers, whose work is published in *Focus*, rely on rigorous methodologies to implement studies that reflect a wide range of disciplines, including education, speech–language pathology, physical therapy, occupational therapy, psychology, and social work. The unifying commitment is that all articles contain implications for application in a variety of contexts, including schools, clinics, community agencies, colleges, universities, and homes. Manuscripts are submitted online and undergo masked peer-review by professionals in the field to ensure articles integrate and advance evidence-based practices in assessment, diagnosis, and intervention. The goal is to generate an enhanced understanding of the perspectives and needs of individuals with developmental disabilities, their families, and the professionals who serve them. Toward this end, articles include: (a) original research reports based on single-case designs, group designs, and qualitative investigations; (b) literature reviews and interpretations that offer substantive implications for practice and policy; (c) theoretical and conceptual papers supported by empirical evidence; (d) replication of prior research; and (e) solicited book and product reviews. Biennially,

an entire issue is devoted to one topic selected by the editorial board. Previously published special topic issues have addressed state-of-the-art in "Asperger Syndrome," "Literacy," and "Transition and Adulthood." The journal has evolved, based on demand in the field, from when Dr. Richard Simpson (University of Kansas) created *Focus on Autistic Behavior* in 1986 for disseminating a single article with immediate applicability. In the early 1990s, PRO-ED acquired the journal in 1995 and changed to a multiarticle issue format published under the current name. Sage Publications and the Hammill Institute on Disabilities partnered to begin publishing the journal in 2005. *Focus* was accepted for indexing in *Journal Citation Reports*® (JCR), published by Thomson Reuters (formerly ISI), and impact factors will appear starting in the summer of 2011. *Focus* is provided as a membership benefit to all members of the Division for Autism and Developmental Disabilities of the Council for Exceptional Children. Individual and institutional subscriptions also are available. The current coeditors are Dr. L. Juane Heflin and Dr. Paul A. Alberto, both at Georgia State University in Atlanta, Georgia. The journal's website is: http://mc.manuscriptcentral.com/focus.

L. JUANE HEFLIN
CARINA DEFAZIO, EDITORIAL
ASSISTANT
*Georgia State University
Fourth edition*

FÖLLING DISEASE (*See* Phenylketonuria)

FOLLOW THROUGH

Follow Through was initiated through an amendment to the Economic Opportunity Act. Project Head Start had begun as an early intervention program for children from low-income families under this legislation (Rhine, 1981). Early reports on small groups of Head Start children had shown an average increase in IQ of about 10 points after a year of preschool, but the first major evaluation of Head Start showed initial gains dissipating soon after the children entered elementary school. Follow Through was intended to provide continued support when children were in the elementary grades to help preserve and enhance any gains made in preschool (Haywood, 1982).

Follow Through was plagued by insufficient funds and by conflicting interpretations of data gathered in evaluation studies of planned variations of different educational models. One of the largest studies, by Stebbins and colleagues in 1977 (Hodges & Cooper, 1981), used as primary measures of effectiveness the Metropolitan Achievement Test (MAT), the (Raven) Progressive Matrices, Coopersmith's Self-Esteem Inventory, and the Intellectual Achievement Responsibility Scale. Stebbins reported much variability in scores from site to site, but little significant difference among models. Models emphasizing basic skills facilitated learning of basic skills and yielded higher self-concept scores than other models. If models did not emphasize basic skills, they were not enhanced. No program model was superior to others in increasing cognitive conceptual skills. In general, where there were large effects, they were related to specific program goals (Hodges & Cooper, 1981). Careful consideration of the measures used by Stebbins suggests that high variability of test scores across settings should not have been surprising because of the tests used (only the MAT has unusually well-demonstrated reliability and validity). Other problems in determining the efficacy of Follow Through related to the difficulty of using a true experimental design, confounding variables, and sample loss.

Probably the safest statement to make about the Follow Through planned variation experiment is that with structured approaches such as applied behavior analysis or direct instruction models, scholastic achievement is facilitated, but clearly there is still much to be learned about compensatory programs and their effects.

REFERENCES

Haywood, H. C. (1982). Compensatory education. *Peabody Journal of Education, 59,* 272–300.

Hodges, W., & Cooper, M. (1981). Head Start and Follow Through: Influences on intellectual development. *Journal of Special Education, 15,* 221–238.

Rhine, W. R. (1981). Follow Through: Perspectives and possibilities. In W. R. Rhine (Ed.), *Making schools more effective.* New York, NY: Academic Press.

SUE ALLEN WARREN
Boston University

See also Abecedarian Project; Head Start

FOOD ADDITIVES

In the 1970s and 1980s, one particularly fashionable explanation in the etiology of a number of learning disorders was proposed by Feingold et al. (Feingold, German, Brahm, & Slimmers, 1973). They contended that naturally occurring salicylates in fruits, vegetables, and other foods, artificial food colorings, and preservatives could produce a toxic reaction of cerebral irritability that could result in hyperactivity and other learning disorders in genetically predisposed children. This hypothesis has been subsequently revised by Feingold (1975a, 1976) to mitigate the importance of naturally occurring salicylates and to emphasize the role of two antioxidant preservatives, BHA (butylated hydroxyanisole) and BHT (butylated hydroxytoluene; Feingold & Feingold, 1979). It is important to note that there has been a significant distinction made between food additives' allergic effect, which does occur for a small percentage of hyperactive children (Conners, 1980), and the toxic effect of these additives, which Feingold and Feingold (1979) have more recently hypothesized to explain the origins of learning disorders.

There has been some evidence posited (Brenner, 1979) to suggest that those children who appear to be affected by food additives differ biochemically from children who are not affected. Evidence that low concentrations of food dye (frequently referred to as Red Dye No. 3) used in a number of confections prevent brain cells from ingesting dopamine, a substance having significant effects on motor activity, provide this biochemical hypothesis with further impetus. In fact, in one seminal piece of research, Lafferman and Silbergeld (1979) concluded that the food dyes' blocking of dopamine is consistent with the notion that the dye could induce hyperactivity in some children.

Although some research has tentatively supported the mechanism of the toxic effect of certain food dyes for particular children, Feingold (1975a) has made a plethora of unsupported statements attesting to the efficacy of his additive-free therapeutic diet. In fact, Feingold (1975a) has even suggested that nearly half of his clinical practice evidenced complete remission of symptoms as a function of a diet that was additive-free. Despite the fact that these claims were not based on empirical data and were refuted later by other investigators (National Advisory Committee on Hyperkinesis and Food Additives, 1980), the claims from Feingold (1975b) still continued at high pitch; he contended that eliminating food additives would decrease motor incoordination and increase academic achievement for hyperactive children (Feingold, 1975b).

Feingold's claims resulted in a proliferation of reports by the popular press attesting to the potential link of food additives to hyperactivity (Ross & Ross, 1982). Further, there were also reports of behavioral improvements ascribed to additive-free diets (Ross & Ross, 1982). Understandably, the food industry perceived these claims as a direct threat and thus organized with the Food and Drug Administration committees to review the evidence pertaining to Feingold's claims. The committees concluded that there was no empirical evidence linking food additives to behavioral or learning dysfunctions in children. The committees further recommended (Ross & Ross, 1982) that carefully controlled empirical studies be conducted to test any validity of food additives in causing hyperactivity or other learning disorders in children.

Subsequently, a series of methodologically sophisticated studies were funded by the federal government. In them Feingold's hypotheses regarding food additives were put to careful tests. The results of these studies, which were reviewed by the National Advisory Committee on Hyperkinesis and Food Additives (1980), have generally "refuted the claim that artificial food colorings, artificial flavorings, and salicylates produce hyperactivity and/or learning disability." Based on their findings, the National Advisory Committee also recommended that further funding efforts in this area cease.

REFERENCES

Brenner, A. (1979). Trace mineral levels in hyperactive children responding to the Feingold diet. *Journal of Pediatrics, 94,* 944–945.

Conners, C. K. (1980). *Food additives and hyperactive children.* New York, NY: Plenum Press.

Feingold, B. F. (1975a). *Why your child is hyperactive.* New York, NY: Random House.

Feingold, B. F. (1975b). Hyperkinesis and learning disabilities linked to artificial food flavors and colors. *American Journal of Nursing, 75,* 797–803.

Feingold, B. F. (1976). Hyperkinesis and learning disabilities linked to the ingestion of artificial food colors and flavors. *Journal of Learning Disabilities, 9,* 551–559.

Feingold, H., & Feingold, B. F. (1979). *The Feingold cookbook for hyperactive children and others with problems associated with food additives and salicylates.* New York, NY: Random House.

Feingold, B. F., German, D. F., Brahm, R. M., & Slimmers, E. (1973). *Adverse reaction to food additives.* Paper presented to the annual meeting of the American Medical Association, New York.

Lafferman, J. A., & Silbergeld, E. K. (1979). Erythrosin B inhibits dopamine transport in rat caudate synaptosomes. *Science, 205,* 410–412.

National Advisory Committee on Hyperkinesis and Food Additives. (1980). New York, NY: Nutrition Foundation.

Ross, D. M., & Ross, S. A. (1982). *Hyperactivity: Current issues, research, and theory* (2nd ed.). New York, NY: Wiley-Interscience.

EMILY G. SUTTER
University of Houston, Clear Lake

RONALD T. BROWN
Emory University School of Medicine

See also **Attention-Deficit/Hyperactivity Disorder; Dopamine; Feingold Diet**

FORNESS, STEVEN R. (1939–   )

Steve Forness began his college education at the U.S. Naval Academy but received his BA in English in 1963 and his MA in educational psychology in 1964 from the University of Northern Colorado at Greeley. After 2 years of teaching high school English, he completed his EdD in special education at UCLA in 1968. He has remained at UCLA for his entire career and is currently a professor in the Department of Psychiatry and Biobehavioral Sciences. Forness also holds the position of principal of the UCLA Neuropsychiatric Hospital (NPH) inpatient school and is chief educational psychologist in the child outpatient department. From 1985 to 1992, he was also director of the UAP Interdisciplinary Mental Retardation and Developmental Disabilities Program. His research has been in four main areas: (1) direct classroom observation of children at risk in the primary grades; (2) comorbidity of learning disabilities in children with various psychiatric diagnoses; (3) classroom aspects of psychopharmacologic medications; and (4) special education identification of children in Head Start. In addition to being coauthor of eight textbooks on special education and learning disabilities, he has published more than 200 journal articles and book chapters on school learning and behavior problems.

Winner of CEC's 1992 Wallin Award for outstanding professional and research contributions, Dr. Forness is also a fellow of the American Association on Mental Retardation and of the International Academy for Research on Learning Disabilities. In 1976, he was a Fulbright Scholar assigned to the Ministry of Education in Portugal. He has been national president of the Council for Children with Behavioral Disorders, a member of the *DSM-IV* Committee on Learning Disorders, coauthor of the *Practice Parameters on Learning and Language Disorders* for the American Academy of Child and Adolescent Psychiatry, and author of the education paper for the 1998 NIH Consensus Development Conference on ADHD. Forness also received the Midwest Symposium on Leadership in Behavior Disorders Outstanding Service Award, CCBD Leadership Award, AAMR (Region II) Education Award, and TED/Merrill Teacher Educator of the Year Award.

This entry has been informed by the sources listed below.

REFERENCES

Hewett, F. M., & Forness, S. R. (1984). *Education of exceptional learners* (3rd ed.). Newton, MA: Allyn & Bacon.

Kavale, K. A., & Forness, S. R. (1985). *The science of learning disabilities.* San Diego, CA: Singular.

Kavale, K. A., & Forness, S. R. (1995). *The nature of learning disabilities: Critical elements of diagnosis and classification.* Hillsdale, NJ: Erlbaum.

Kavale, K. A., & Forness, S. R. (1998). *Efficacy of special education and related services*. Washington, DC: American Association on Mental Retardation.

STAFF

FORREST V. AMBACH

Muriel Forrest, a school psychologist with the Edgemont Union Free School District in Winchester, New York, was dismissed with only a five-day notice in May 1979. The district dismissed Forrest ostensibly because her work was unsatisfactory and she had refused to follow orders directing her to change. The dismissal was appealed to the Commissioner of Education for the State of New York (*In re Forrest*, 1980). Forrest based that appeal on three points. First was her contention that she had acquired tenure status. As a four-fifths-time employee, the district argued no, while Forrest argued yes, on the basis of being included in the collective bargaining agreement (tenure status would mandate a formal hearing prior to dismissal). The second point (the crux of system procedure/professional standard interaction) involved the district's order that Forrest shorten reports, delete technical language, and refrain from making recommendations to parents prior to referrals being made to the Committee on the Handicapped. Forrest's position was that these requirements forced her to perform in a manner that violated her professional organization's ethical standards and state and federal law. The third issue was the district's refusal to permit her to present a paper at a professional conference, infringing, therefore, on a constitutionally protected right.

In April 1980, Commissioner Ambach dismissed the appeal on the basis that Forrest had failed to demonstrate that the speech in question is constitutionally protected and that her exercise of her rights was a substantial or motivating factor in the respondent board's decision to terminate her services. Ambach went on to say that

> the Education Law provides that an appeal to the Commissioner of Education may be brought by any party considering himself aggrieved, [and that] the person asserting the claims must demonstrate that he or she is injured in some way by that action. Even if respondents were neglecting their statutory duties regarding handicapped children, an issue I do not here decide, petitioner failed to show how such neglect caused harm to her. Petitioner is not an aggrieved party within the meaning of Section 310 and her claim regarding respondents' performance of statutory duties that do not concern her are dismissed. (p. 5)

With that ruling in hand, Forrest sought judgment in the court to invalidate Ambach's decision (*Forrest v. Ambach*, 1981). Appearing as *amici curiae* were the National Association of School Psychologists, American Psychological Association, New York State Psychological Association, and the Westchester County Psychological Association. Justice Kahn rendered his decision late in 1980. In finding in part for Forrest, the court ordered that Commissioner Ambach review and reconsider the dismissal of Forrest from her position as a school psychologist. The court addressed two issues in the written opinion. First, whether Forrest was a tenured employee and therefore not subject to dismissal without a due process hearing, and second, whether the Commissioner was correct in declining to consider petitioner's specific allegations concerning the reason for her dismissal by holding that she lacked standing to challenge respondents' alleged neglect of their statutory duties regarding handicapped children (p. 920).

With regard to the first question, the court upheld the commissioner's ruling that Forrest had not gained tenured status. However, the court went on to quickly add that the commissioner should have provided a forum for a review of the allegation made by Forrest. Forrest claimed that she was injured (loss of job) by the board's (district's) alleged misconduct. Justice Kahn identifies this as the "hub of her claim" and the commissioner's decision not to review whether the district was neglecting its statutory duties "resulted in a failure to have her grievance aired." Therefore, the opinion identifies the commissioner's determination as "a 'Catch 22' and is arbitrary and capricious in that there is not a rational basis therefore" (p. 920).

While a school board is in the position of an employer, those professionals employed by a school board do have a level of professional competence and standards that must be recognized and respected, not only for the profession itself, but for the purpose of rendering the best service to the school board and ultimately to the students they service. The ethical standards of any professional employed by a school board *cannot be cavalierly dismissed as irrelevant to the employer-employee relationship*, and may indeed become quite relevant in certain circumstances (emphasis added). If, in fact, petitioner was dismissed solely due to her own professional standards as a psychologist, then her dismissal by said school board would be arbitrary, capricious, and unconstitutional (p. 920).

Justice Kahn affirmed the special education legislation and regulation and the explicit requirement of equal educational opportunity with a relevant reminder that "a school board should not be permitted to, in any way, impede the noble goals of such a law" (p. 920). Subsequent to the court's decision and directives, Ambach reheard Forrest's appeal and once again ruled in favor of the school district. Forrest appealed the decision to the state supreme court, and then the appellate division, losing each time. New York's highest court, the Court of Appeals, declined to review the case. The decision of Forrest accentuates the importance of professional standards and serves to underline the real and potential conflict that exists between such standards and system policy and procedure. In that sense, the decision provides an important foundation for establishing legal precedent in similar situations.

REFERENCES

Forrest v. Ambach, 436 N.Y.S. 2d 119, 107 Misc. 2d 920 (Sup. Ct. 1981).

In re Forrest. New York Education Department No. 10237 (April 2, 1980).

DAVID P. PRASSE
University of Wisconsin

See also Ethics; National Association of School Psychologists

FOSTER HOMES FOR CHILDREN WITH DISABILITIES

Foster homes for children and adults with disabilities have been used for many years (Sanderson & Crawley, 1982). With the advent of deinstitutionalization in the 1970s, alternatives to housing had to be considered. Although group homes were predicted to be the primary providers for this population, Roos (1978) affirmed that adoption or foster care would be the preferred residential placement. Willer and Intagliata (1982) compared group home and foster home placements on clients' achievement of self-care skills, adaptive behavior, community living skills, social skills, and community access. Interestingly, few differences were found across the two residential settings. Nevertheless, the authors concluded that family-care homes provided more opportunities to develop age-appropriate personal and interpersonal behaviors, while group homes provided more opportunities to develop community and independent living skills. Two major implications were made from these results. First, placement of persons with disabilities into community residential facilities must be based on the individual needs of the client. Second, "group-home staff members could benefit from training in behavior-management techniques, whereas family-care providers could benefit from training in how to encourage residents to develop and utilize more independent community living skills" (Willer & Intagliata, 1982, p. 594). Although cost-effectiveness data were not examined, the authors concluded that the cost for foster care was significantly lower than for group-home placement.

Despite the issues of best placement, children and adults with disabilities continue to be placed in foster homes. Many questions arise when considering these placements. What kinds of children are being placed in foster homes? What kinds of families take foster children with disabilities? What are the needs of families with foster children with disabilities?

It is estimated that over 513,000 children in the United States live in foster homes (Child Welfare League of America, 2011). Foster homes have served a variety of children with developmental, emotional, physical, and medical problems. Traditionally, abused and neglected children have been in foster care. Many of these children are severely emotionally disturbed. Programs across the country have been developed to place severely mistreated children into safe and secure home environments. For example, the Intensive Treatment Homes (ITH) Project in Sacramento used a complete team approach for placing abused and neglected children into foster care (Harling & Harines, 1980). Less than half of the 43 children served in the first year of the project were able to return to their natural parents. One child was institutionalized, 2 were adopted, 11 were being considered for adoption, and the remaining 10 were referred for long-term foster care placement.

Foster homes for children with intellectual disability and motor delays have been a constructive alternative to residential placement. For example, in a report by Taylor (1980), two case studies were presented from a foster parent's perspective. The achievements made by each of Taylor's foster children were remarkable. To meet the needs of foster parents such as these, Arizona developed a curriculum for foster parents of children with retardation (Drydyk, Mendeville, & Bender, 1980).

Children who are medically fragile also have been placed in foster homes (CASA, 1995). Often it is a nurse who will take a foster child with medical needs such as tracheotomy care, tube feeding, sterile dressing, and physical therapy. In many cases, these children would remain hospitalized indefinitely because of the biological parents' inability to provide care. Additionally, it was estimated that in 1983 the cost of foster care for these children was $1,000 per month, while the average cost of a month's hospitalization was $10,500 (Whitworth, Foster, & Davis, 1983).

What kinds of families take foster children with disabilities into their homes? Demographically, foster parents are often of low to middle socioeconomic status, have little or no education, are married, and have children of their own (Carbino, 1980; CASA, 1995; Enos, 1982; Hampson & Tavormina, 1980). The motives of foster parents vary from love of children, desire to help, and interest in children's well being to wanting a child to nurture or wanting a playmate for another child (Hampson & Tavormina,

1980). Many experience disruptive family patterns when a child is placed within their home; often children with disabilities will be moved from one foster home to another (CASA, 1995).

The specific needs of foster parents vary depending on the child's disability, the family support system, and the coping abilities of the foster parents. Because of the reported emotional strain on families, it is critical that foster parents be provided with intensive orientation, training, and counseling sessions. Enos (1982) reports that foster parents leave foster care programs because of the unexpected demands of foster children, low payments, and interference with their own family's well being. Barsh, Moore, and Hamerlynck (1983) point out that foster parents of children with disabilities have similar problems to those of the biological parents, such as finding babysitters, transporting the child to clinics, and managing disruptive behavior. Furthermore, Edelstein (1981) reports that many foster parents go through a period of grieving when children are returned to their biological parents. It is clear that foster parents need to be aware of the problems inherent in foster parenting and to feel safe in discussing their feelings with professionals or other foster families (Foster, 1984). Training families in first aid, behavior management, therapeutic techniques, and crisis intervention may better prepare families for the care of a child with a disability. Foster homes provide an invaluable service to children with disabilities. Professionals serving children with disabilities need to recognize the needs of foster parents in order to enhance the services provided to them and their foster children.

REFERENCES

Barsh, E. T., Moore, J. A., & Hamerlynck, L. A. (1983). The foster extended family: A support network for handicapped foster children. *Child Welfare, 62*, 349–359.

Carbino, R. (1980). *Foster parenting, an updated review of the literature.* New York, NY: Child Welfare League of America.

CASA. (1995). *Why children are in foster care.* Retrieved from http://www.casanet.org/library/foster-care/why.htm

Child Welfare League of America. (2011). Practice areas: Family foster care: Quick facts about foster care. Retrieved from http://www.cwla.org/programs/fostercare/factsheet.htm

Drydyk, J., Mendeville, B., & Bender, L. (1980). Foster parenting a retarded child. *Children Today, 9*(10), 24–26.

Edelstein, S. (1981). When foster children leave: Helping foster parents grieve. *Child Welfare, 60*, 467–473.

Enos, S. L. (1982). More people to love you: Foster parents look at foster care. *Journal of Human Services Abstracts, 49*, 19.

Foster, P. H. (1984). *Medical foster care: An ethnography.* (Doctoral dissertation, University of Florida).

Hampson, R. B., & Tavormina, J. B. (1980). Feedback from the experts: A study of foster mothers. *Social Work, 25*, 108–112.

Harling, P. R., & Harines, J. K. (1980). Specialized foster homes for severely mistreated children. *Children Today, 9*, 16–18.

Roos, S. (1978). The future residential services for the mentally retarded in the United States: A Delphi study. *Mental Retardation, 16*, 355–356.

Sanderson, H. W., & Crawley, M. (1982). Characteristics of successful family-care parents. *American Journal of Mental Deficiency, 86*, 519–525.

Taylor, S. W. (1980). Foster care: A foster mother's perspective. *Exceptional Parent, 10*, L4–L8.

Whitworth, J. M., Foster, P. H., & Davis, A. B. (1983). *Medical foster care for abused and neglected children of dysfunctional families.* Washington, DC: U.S. Department of Health and Human Services. Federal Grant #90-CA-0932.

Willer, B., & Intagliata, J. (1982). Comparison of family-care and group homes as alternative to institutions. *American Journal of Mental Deficiency, 86*, 588–595.

VIVIAN I. CORREA
University of Florida

See also Adoptees; Family Counseling

FOUNDATION FOR CHILDREN LEARNING DISABILITIES

The Foundation for Children with Learning Disabilities (FCLD) is a charitable foundation incorporated in the state of New York and holding tax-exempt status with the Internal Revenue Service. The FCLD is located at 99 Park Avenue, New York, NY 10016. It was founded in 1977 by Carrie Rozelle, who remains the president of the organization. The FCLD publishes *Their World*, an annual devoted to developing public awareness of learning disabilities. An annual benefit and other activities are carried out each year to raise funds to support the goals of FCLD.

In 1985 FCLD launched two major efforts aimed at service as well as public relations for the learning disabled. The FCLD has a grant program for public libraries to develop live programs for parents, teachers, learning disabled children, and the public about learning differences. A second grant program has been designed and implemented to educate both the public and the judiciary about the potential link between learning disabilities and delinquency. The organization is devoted to developing public awareness of the problems associated with learning disabilities and to providing general educational services to the public on the topic. The FCLD does not provide direct services to children with learning disabilities.

CECIL R. REYNOLDS
Texas A&M University

See also Their World

FOUNTAIN SYNDROME

Fountain syndrome, which is characterized by an association between mental retardation, sensorineural deafness, coarse facies, and skeletal abnormalities, was first described in 1974 (Fountain, 1974). Fountain syndrome is an extremely rare disorder, and the prevalence is unknown (Fryns, 1989). Only seven cases have been documented at this time. The occurrence of this syndrome in siblings of normal parents indicates autosomal recessive inheritance (Fountain, 1974; Fryns, 1987, 1989).

The pathogenesis for Fountain syndrome remains unknown. Chromosomes have been found to be normal (46, XY confirmed with G- and R-banding; Fryns, 1987). Extensive biochemical and metabolic examinations (e.g., calcium, phosphorus, creatine kinase, amino acid chromatography of serum and urine, and mucopolysaccharide excretion), electroencephalography, electromyography, electrocardiography, ophthalmological examinations, and peripheral nerve and rectal biopsies revealed no specific abnormalities (Fountain, 1974; Fryns, 1987, 1989).

Characteristics

1. Mental retardation
2. Sensorineural deafness with cochlear anomalies
3. Round and coarse facies
4. Lip granuloma
5. Plump, stubby hands with broad terminal phalanges
6. Thickened calvaria

All identified individuals have been diagnosed with mental retardation, although the degree varied from mild to severe. All reported cases indicate profound sensorineural deafness that occurred between the ages of 15 and 18 months. Up to that point, hearing development appeared to be normal (Fountain, 1974; Fryns, 1987, 1989). Some rudimentary hearing at the lowest frequencies may be present. Tomography of the inner ear revealed congenital anomalies of the cochlea spirals, ranging from anomalies of the cochlear turns to the presence of a cavity. Vestibular function appears normal.

The face is round and coarse, with swelling of the subcutaneous tissue, particularly of the lips and cheeks (Fountain, 1974; Fryns, 1987, 1989). The swelling of the face has been described as progressive, gross, papular, erythematous, and granulomatous. A biopsy revealed a granulomatous infiltrate marked by large, foamy cells, which contained lipid but not stains for fat (Fountain, 1974). The pathogenesis of the swellings is unknown (Fryns, 1989). The edematous facial characteristics are

similar to those seen in Melkerson-Rosenthal syndrome and Coffin-Lowry syndrome (Fountain, 1974; Fryns, 1989). Skeletal surveys using X-rays show broad and short phalanges and metacarpals with thickened corticalis without ossification anomalies (Fountain, 1974; Fryns, 1987, 1989). Skull X-rays show a gross thickening of the calvarium.

Fountain syndrome may also be linked with other minor and major anomalies (Fryns, 1987, 1989). There may be marked growth retardation, psychomotor impairment, epileptic attacks, infantile seizures, and general hypotonia, which results in secondary scoliotic deformities. These associated disorders must be further delineated in additional patients.

There is no known cure or a specific treatment for Fountain syndrome. A full assessment of the child's mental or developmental age, level of adaptive behavior, and neuropsychological needs is recommended to assist with educational programming. It is important that the educational assessment evaluate the child's special education needs as to not only how they pertain to mental retardation but also how they relate to the child's hearing impairment.

REFERENCES

Fountain, R. B. (1974). Familial bone abnormalities, deaf mutism, mental retardation, and skin granuloma. *Procedures of the Royal Society of Medicine, 67*, 878–879.

Fryns, J. (1987). Mental retardation, deafness, skeletal abnormalities, and coarse face with full lips: Confirmation of the fountain syndrome. *American Journal of Medical Genetics, 26*, 551–555.

Fryns, J. (1989). Fountain's syndrome: Mental retardation, sensorineural deafness, skeletal abnormalities, and coarse face with full lips. *Journal of Medical Genetics, 26*, 722–724.

ALEXANDRA S. KUTZ
MARGARET SEMRUD-CLIKEMAN
University of Texas at Austin

FOURTEENTH AMENDMENT RIGHTS (See Equal Protection)

FOXX, RICHARD M. (1944–)

Richard M. Foxx received his BA from the University of California–Riverside in 1967, his MA from California State University, Fullerton in 1970, and his PhD from Southern Illinois University in 1971. His major fields of interest include mental retardation, autism, and emotionally disturbed adolescents. He is considered a leading authority on the treatment of severe forms of maladaptive behavior.

His current interests include the development of nonintrusive methods of behavioral reduction and the study of the generalization of social skills, staff training, and the interface between environmental design and applied behavior analysis.

Foxx's work includes numerous books, scientific articles, and training films on the use of behavioral principles to treat individuals with mental retardation and autism. Among his most significant publications are *Increasing the Behavior of Retarded and Autistic Persons* (Foxx, 1982b), *Decreasing Behaviors of Persons with Severe Retardation and Autism* (Foxx, 1982a), *Toilet Training for the Retarded* (Foxx, 1980), and *Thinking It Through: Teaching a Problem-Solving Strategy for Community Living* (Foxx, 1989). As a featured speaker at the 1987 annual Conference of the Association for the Severely Handicapped, he presented the paper *Teaching a Generalized Language Strategy*, later published in book form (Foxx, 1990). Foxx is a fellow of the American Psychological Association and American Association on Mental Retardation and is the recipient of numerous awards and honors.

REFERENCES

Foxx, R. M. (1980). *Toilet training for the retarded* [Videocassette]. Champaign, IL: Research.

Foxx, R. M. (1982a). *Decreasing behaviors of persons with severe retardation and autism*. Champaign, IL: Research.

Foxx, R. M. (1982b). *Increasing the behavior of retarded and autistic persons*. Champaign, IL: Research.

Foxx, R. M. (1990). *Teaching a generalized language strategy*. Anna, IL: Anna Mental Health and Development Center.

Foxx, R. M., & Bittle, R. G. (1989). *Thinking it through: Teaching a problem-solving strategy for community living*. Champaign, IL: Research.

TAMARA J. MARTIN
The University of Texas of the Permian Basin

FRAGILE X SYNDROME

Also known as Martin-Bell Syndrome, Fragile X Syndrome (FXS) is a chromosomal abnormality that is now thought to be the most common inherited cause of intellectual disabilities (ID) and the most common single genetic cause of autism (Chonchaiya, Schneider, & Hagerman, 2009). FXS is caused by a premutation (i.e., gene repeats that may become a full mutation in subsequent generations) or full mutation of FMR1 gene, which is located on the X chromosome. FXS mutations cause a family of FXS–associated disorders, being responsible for the

higher prevalence of ID in males than females (Hagerman, Rivera, & Hagerman, 2008).

FXS is unusual genetically in several ways. In typical X-linked disorders, a carrier female, who has no characteristics of the disorder, passes the defective gene, on average, to half of her children. Of those children who inherit the defective gene, males will express any effects, whereas females will be unaffected, but carriers. In FXS, however, the situation is more complicated. Carrier females, who have one normal X chromosome and one with the fragile site, may manifest some FXS characteristics, including intellectual impairments and specific learning disabilities. About 20% of males who inherit the fragile site show no apparent physical or psychological effects and no evidence of fragility. They do, however, pass the X chromosome on to their daughters, who may have affected sons (Brown, 1990; Penagarikano, Mulle, & Warren, 2007).

Research in the 1990s clarified the basis and inheritance patterns of FXS and its precursors. Fragile sites were found to be abnormal expansions or perseveration of the cytosine-guanine-guanine (CGG) triplet repeat, commonly seen in the DNA segment, within the FMR1 gene (Batshaw, 1997; Chonchaiya et al., 2009). Typically, the CGG triplet presents less than 55 repeats. However, individuals with 55–200 CGG repeats are said to have a FMR1 premutation with no or few symptoms, while individuals with more than 200 CGG repeats have a full mutation of FMR1 gene, leading to FXS (Chonchaiya et al., 2009; Wang, Berry-Kravis, & Hagerman, 2010). The increased expansion of CGG repeats over successive generations leads to increased FXS symptomatology over the same generations. Premutations of more than 100 CGG repeats almost always expand into the full mutation range in the next generation. Transmitting males usually have less than 100 CGG repeats, so their daughters will tend also to have premutations and be asymptomatic. Since these daughters will likely have CGG repeats expanded into the 90–200 range, their male and female children who inherit the fragile site are likely to have CGG repeats of over 1,000. That is in the full mutation range, and those children will display FXS symptoms. As Batshaw (1997, p. 379) observed, "Thus, transmitting males tend to have grandchildren manifesting FXS, a very unusual pattern for an X-linked disorder!"

History

From the beginning of the 20th century, researchers noted a considerable excess of males with ID (about 25%). Martin and Bell (1943), and others thereafter, described families in which intellectual disabilities was inherited in an X-linked pattern. Although Lubs (1969) first described the fragile X site, his description drew little interest until

Sutherland (1977) reported that some fragile sites were expressed only if lymphocytes were grown in a culture that lacked folic acid. This discovery led to an exponential growth of interest in X-linked intellectual disabilities (Fryns, 1990). In 1991, the FMR1 gene was identified (Verkerk et al., 1991), confirming the FXS basis for ID initially indicated by Martin and Bell.

Prevalence

Although estimates vary across studies, the prevalence of FXS is about 1 in 1,500 in males and 1 in 2,000 in females. The FMR1 premutation is more common than the full mutation and occurs in 1 in 130 to 260 females and 1 in 250 to 810 males (Wang et al., 2010). Of males with ID serious enough to require extensive support, 6–14% has FXS, as do 3–6% of individuals with autism (Batshaw, 1997). Individuals with ID of unknown cause are now routinely screened for FXS.

Characteristics of Affected Males

Physical Features

About two thirds of affected adult males show a "clinical triad" of characteristics: (1) moderate to severe intellectual impairment; (2) characteristic craniofacial features, including large forehead, protruding chin, and elongated ears; and (3) large testes (macroorchidism; Curfs, Wiegers, & Fryns, 1990; Fryns, 1990). In addition, males with FXS may show a variety of other features, such as hyperextensible joints, high arched palate, mitral valve prolapse (a form of heart murmur), flat feet, and low muscle tone (Chonchaiya et al., 2009). Because affected individuals may show a variety of behavioral and physical characteristics, diagnosis can firmly be based only on cytogenetic analysis. Females and prepubescent males are even more variable. Although most males show an "overgrowth syndrome" from birth, with head size, fontanel, and body measurements exceeding the 97th percentile, macroorchidism and craniofacial features are less distinct in prepubescent boys (Hagerman, 1990).

Cognitive features. Approximately 85% of males with FXS have ID, with intelligent quotient (IQ) below 70 (Loesch, Huggins, & Hagerman, 2004). Affected males present impairment on executive function, visual memory, processing of sequential information, sustained attention and short-term memory, performing poorly on tasks involving series of items or motor movements (Cornish, Turk, & Hagerman, 2008; Roberts, Schaaf, et al., 2005; Zigler & Hodapp, 1991). This deficit in sequential processing differentiates individuals with FXS from those with other forms of ID (Zigler & Hodapp, 1991).

Language

Most affected males have some form of communication disorder (Roberts, Long, et al., 2005). Specifically, individuals with FXS often display characteristics such as verbal perseveration on preferred topics, repetitions, echolalia, disorganized speech, dysfluencies, word-finding problems, and irrelevant associations. Communication deficits are pronounced in individuals with both FXS and autism, particularly in receptive language, including verbal reasoning, recognition of emotions, and labeling of emotions (Lewis et al., 2006).

Behavioral Characteristics

About 75% of affected individuals demonstrate challenging behaviors, including hyperactivity and attention deficits, stereotyped self-stimulatory behaviors, aggression, and anxiety (Wang et al., 2010). About 30% have characteristics of autism (Verkerk et al., 1991) and 10–40% have seizures (Chonchaiya et al., 2009). Many affected individuals are also socially withdrawn, show gaze aversion, and engage in self-injurious behavior, such as self-biting.

Characteristics of Affected Females

About 70% of carrier females show no clear physical, cognitive, or behavioral difficulties. The remaining 30% show a variety of symptoms, which manifest less severely than in males. They may display attention, impulsivity, and executive function deficits even when their IQs are in the normal range (Wang et al., 2010). Learning disabilities involving visual spatial skills and simultaneous processing, communication problems, and emotional and behavioral disorders may also be observed in females (Chonchaiya et al., 2009; Wang et al., 2010). Language problems, similar to males, include disorganized and perseverative speech (Lewis et al., 2006). Some evidence suggests that, unlike males, intelligence quotient of affected carrier females increases with age. Female carriers, particularly those with intellectual impairments, may also have characteristic facial features, including a high broad forehead, long face, and hyperextensibility (Chonchaiya et al., 2009).

Treatment

Although there is no cure for FXS and people remain affected throughout their lives, educational and pharmaceutical treatments can help to minimize the symptoms (Crawford, 2001). Folic acid has often been used in attempts to reduce symptoms associated with FXS (Reiss & Hall, 2007). Double-blind studies (Hagerman, 1990) indicate that such treatment does not affect scores on intelligence tests but may reduce hyperactivity and increase attention span. However, questions exist as to whether folic acid treatment is as effective as traditional treatment for hyperactivity with stimulant medication (Hagerman, 1990, Reiss & Hall, 2007). Several medications are currently available to treat other symptoms of FXS such as aggression, anxiety, distractibility, mood instability, and deviant social behaviors (Chonchaiya et al., 2009; Wang et al., 2010)

Psychological approaches are of importance in treating FXS for two reasons (Curfs et al., 1990): (1) The diffuse and variable physical effects of FXS in children place additional significance on the role of psychological assessment in identifying children for cytogenetic analysis; and (2) cognitive characteristics of those with FXS have important implications for treatment and educational programs. Due to the variety and variation in difficulties exhibited by those with FXS, a team approach is recommended for treatment (Hagerman, 1990). Behavioral and educational interventions can help individuals with FXS be more successful academically. Further studies of neurobiology of FXS will likely lead to other treatments that combined with psychological and educational interventions will likely reduce the deficits caused by the syndrome (Chonchaiya et al., 2009).

REFERENCES

Batshaw, M. L. (1997). Fragile X syndrome. In M. L. Batshaw (Ed.), *Children with disabilities* (4th ed., pp. 377–388). Baltimore, MD: Paul H. Brookes.

Brown, W. T. (1990). Invited editorial: The fragile X: Progress toward solving the puzzle. *American Journal of Human Genetics, 47,* 175–180.

Chonchaiya, W., Schneider, A., & Hagerman, R. J. (2009). Fragile X: A family of disorders. *Advances in Pediatrics, 56,* 165–186.

Cornish, K. K., Turk, J. J., & Hagerman, R. R. (2008). The fragile X continuum: New advances and perspectives. *Journal of Intellectual Disability Research, 52,* 469–482.

Crawford, D. C. (2001). FMR1 and the fragile X syndrome: Human genome epidemiology review. *Genetics in Medicine, 3,* 359–371.

Curfs, L. M. G., Wiegers, A. M., & Fryns, J. P. (1990). Fragile-X syndrome: A review. *Brain Dysfunction, 3,* 1–8.

Fryns, J. P. (1990). X-linked mental retardation and the fragile X syndrome: A clinical approach. In K. E. Davies (Ed.), *The fragile X syndrome* (pp. 1–39). Oxford, England: Oxford University Press.

Hagerman, R. (1990). Behaviour and treatment of the fragile X syndrome. In K. E. Davies (Ed.), *The fragile X syndrome* (pp. 66–75). Oxford, England: Oxford University Press.

Hagerman, R., Rivera, S., & Hagerman, P. (2008). The Fragile X family of disorders: A model for autism and targeted treatments. *Current Pediatric Reviews, 4,* 40–52.

Lewis, P., Abbeduto, L., Murphy, M., Richmond, E., Giles, N., Bruno, L., et al. (2006). Cognitive, language, and social-cognitive skills of individuals with fragile X syndrome with and without autism. *Journal of Intellectual Disability Research, 50,* 532–545.

Loesch, D. Z., Huggins, R. M., & Hagerman, R. J. (2004). Phenotypic variation and FMRP levels in fragile X. *Mental Retardation & Developmental Disabilities Research Reviews, 10,* 31–41.

Lubs, H. A. (1969). A marker X chromosome. *American Journal of Human Genetics, 21,* 231–244.

Martin, J. P., & Bell, J. (1943). A pedigree of mental defect showing sex-linkage. *Journal of Neurology, Neurosurgery, and Psychiatry, 6,* 154–157.

Penagarikano, O., Mulle, J. G., & Warren, S. T. (2007). The pathophysiology of Fragile X Syndrome. *Annual Review of Genomics & Human Genetics, 8,* 109–129.

Reiss, A. L., & Hall, S. S. (2007). Fragile X syndrome: Assessment and treatment implications. *Child and Adolescent Psychiatry Clinics of North America, 16,* 663–675.

Roberts, J. E., Schaaf, J. M, Skinner, M., Wheeler, A., Hooper, S., Hatton, D. D., & Bailey, D. B. (2005a). Academic skills of boys with fragile X syndrome: profiles and predictors. *American Journal of Mental Retardation, 110,* 107–120.

Roberts, J., Long, S. H., Malkin, C., Barnes, E., Skinner, M., Hennon, E. A., & Anderson, K. (2005b). A comparison of phonological skills of boys with Fragile X Syndrome and Down Syndrome. *Journal of Speech, Language & Hearing Research, 48,* 980–995.

Sutherland, G. R. (1977). Fragile sites on human chromosomes: Demonstration of their dependence on the type of tissue culture medium. *Science, 197,* 265–266.

Verkerk, A. J., Pieretti, M., Sutcliffe, J. S., Fu, Y., Kuhl, D. P. A., Pizzuti,...Warren, S. T. (1991). Identification of a gene (*FMR-1*) containing a CGG repeat coincident with a breakpoint cluster region exhibiting length variation in fragile X syndrome. *Cell, 65,* 905–914.

Wang, L. W., Berry-Kravis, E., & Hagerman, R. J. (2010). Fragile X: Leading the way for targeted treatments in autism. *Neurotherapeutics, 7,* 264–274.

Zigler, E., & Hodapp, R. M. (1991). Behavioral functioning in individuals with mental retardation. *Annual Review of Psychology, 42,* 29–50.

ROBERT T. BROWN
ELAINE M. STRINGER
University of North Carolina, at Wilmington

SIGLIA P. H. CAMARGO
MARGOT BOLES
Texas A&M University
Fourth edition

See also Autism; Chromosomes, Human Anomalies, and Cytogenetic Abnormalities; Congenital Disorders; Down Syndrome; Intellectual Disability

FRAIBERG, SELMA HOROWITZ (1918–1981)

Selma Horowitz Fraiberg received her BA in 1940 and MSW in 1945 from Wayne State University. She was a professor of child psychoanalysis at the University of Michigan, Ann Arbor.

As a social worker, Fraiberg advocated using appropriately trained social workers to work with children. Realizing that most caseworkers are trained to help adults, Fraiberg noted that resources are usually not available for a child with problems to be seen by any professional other than a caseworker. Fraiberg saw the difficulty in determining where casework ends and other professions begin when addressing children's problems. She contended that a child with problems affects the lifestyle of an entire family, and that, she believed, is a casework problem that is difficult to resolve without the involvement of a caseworker. She stressed that the effective caseworker must have appropriate training.

Fraiberg's 1977 book, *Every Child's Birthright: In Defense of Mothering*, was written to publicize the practical aspects of research on the rearing of children. Much of the research studied the development of children from the Depression and World Wars I and II who grew up without their parents and frequently without other family as well. Her belief is that the survival of humankind depends at least as much on the nurturing care and love given to a child in infancy and childhood as it does on preventing war and surviving natural disasters. Another of Fraiberg's interests, how blind children develop and form bonding attachments when they cannot see their parents, was the basis of *Insights from the Blind: Comparative Studies of Blind and Sighted Infants* (1977). *The Magic Years* (1969) was another important work by Fraiberg. Among her honors, Fraiberg was elected to *Who's Who of American Women* (1975), and *Who's Who in World Jewry: A Biographical Dictionary of Outstanding Jews* (Karpman, 1972). A native of Detroit, Michigan, Selma Horowitz Fraiberg died on December 19, 1981, in San Francisco, California.

REFERENCES

Fraiberg, S. H. (1969). *The magic years: Understanding and handling the problems of early childhood*. New York, NY: Scribner's Sons.

Fraiberg, S. H. (1977). *Every child's birthright: In defense of mothering*. New York, NY: Basic Books.

Fraiberg, S. H., & Fraiberg, L. (1977). *Insights from the blind: Comparative studies of blind and sighted infants*. New York, NY: Basic Books.

Karpman, I.J. Carmín. (Ed.). (1972). *Who's who in world Jewry: A biographical dictionary of outstanding Jews*. New York, NY: Pitman.

Who's who of American women, ninth edition. (1975). Wilmette, IL: Marquis Who's Who.

E. Valerie Hewitt
Texas A&M University
First edition

Tamara J. Martin
The University of Texas of the Permian Basin
Second edition

FRANCE, SPECIAL EDUCATION IN

During the 18th century, special education in France had various pioneers, including Valentin Haüÿ, who established the first institute for children who were blind, and l'Abbé de l'Epée, who invented a sign language for children who were deaf and mute. Vincent Itard, perhaps the best known, was headmaster of the Institute for Deaf and Mute Children and one of the first French pedagogues to study and educate children with mental retardation. His story was depicted in the movie *The Wild Child* and in the book *Wild Boy of Aveyron*.

In 1909, French law established the first special classes and schools for children with mental retardation. The famous French psychologist Alfred Binet was requested by the Ministry of Public Instruction (now named the Ministry of Education) to develop a test of intelligence, which was later disseminated worldwide.

In 1945, at the end of World War II, 174 special classes in public schools served children with physical, sensory, or mental disabilities. The majority of children with disabilities were serviced in private institutions under the control of the Ministry of Health. During the 1950s and 1960, the Ministry of Education developed special classes and schools and defined various disability categories.

During the 1970s, primary and secondary prevention programs were established using one of two models. In the first, prevention teams consisting of one school psychologist and two specialized teachers worked in psychopedagogic aid groups to help children who were able to follow regular programs in a regular classroom but who might develop future learning or behavior problems if not helped. Younger children (last year of pre-elementary school and first and second grade) were especially targeted. A second model integrated classes for students with moderate learning difficulties.

In 1975, the French Parliament passed the Orientation Law in Favour of Individuals with Disabilities (L. 75-534), which obligated France to work to prevent and, when needed, diagnose handicaps and to provide healing, education, vocational guidance, and professional training for children and adults with disabilities. This law also initiated the school inclusion policy since it recommended their education occur in regular classes and schools without regard for their disabilities. This policy of school inclusion subsequently was promoted and developed through a wide range of regulations issued mainly from the Ministry of Education in partnership with the Ministry of Health and Social Affairs and, for some, the Ministry of Justice. In 1990, the term Groupe d'Aide Psycho-Pédagogique [Psycho Pedagogic Support Group] changed to Réseau d'Aides Spécialisées aux Elèves en Difficulté [Specialized Support Network for Students with Difficulties]. Prevention remained one of its important tasks.

There are 12 million students in public and private schools from ages 2 (pre-elementary school/kindergarten) through 18 (senior high school). Fifty thousand children are enrolled in special classes in both public and private schools. Due to the policy of inclusion promoted since 1990, the number of students in special classes has decreased. Fifty thousand special needs students receive an individual inclusion program in regular classrooms. The "Handiscol" program (handiscol is the general term to qualify a project aiming to facilitate the schooling of handicapped children) recommends children with physical and/or sensory disabilities (blind or deaf) to receive specific material (including computer education). They may be helped by an auxiliaire de vie scolaire [school life assistant], a person paid either by the local education authority and/or the family to provide material support to the child within the classroom. The child also may receive services from Service d'Education Spéciale et de Soins à Domicile [Special Education Service and Remediation at Home].

One hundred fifteen thousand children diagnosed with one or more of the following eight disorders receive their education in special schools: mental retardation, multi-handicaps (usually severe mental retardation together with a motor disability), behavior, emotional and/or personality difficulties, motor disabilities, blind or visually impaired, deaf or hearing impaired, blind and deaf, or psychiatric affections. Twelve thousand children, 50% for less than 1 school year, receive services in classrooms integrated in general hospitals and Health Houses. Seven thousand children are in homes for children with social and family problems (about 50% for a short period before joining their own family or a surrogate family appointed by a judge for children). Four thousand five hundred children are in special classes for students who have been expelled from regular classes for disruptive behavior or who have dropped out before the end of compulsory education (grade 10 or age 16). Usually they stay about four months in these classes before joining a regular school (70%) or a special school. The Ministry of Justice may provide various educational services to children and youths "at risk" or already condemned for criminal offences at Centres d'Action Educative [Educational Action Centres]. In some cases, the youth may stay in his/her family under the control of a specialized educator appointed by the judge for children. Three thousand children are in jail. Closed Educational Centres (Programmatic and Orientation Law on Justice: L.09/10/2002) provide an alternative to jail in which condemned youths receive a special reinforced educational and pedagogical program.

A large number of children with moderate learning and/or behavior-emotional difficulties who receive services from a Specialized Support Network program are not included in the above statistics. These pupils follow a regular school program in a regular class and receive additional educational and psychological services, sometimes within the classroom and most often outside of the classroom. Although they are not eligible for special education (i.e., their case is not studied by the Local Commission for Special Education), the Specialized Support Network staff, including school psychologists and special teachers who help them, are special education personnel.

Professionals who serve students with special needs are employed by the French Ministries of Education, Health and Social Affairs, and Justice. Each is discussed below. The French Ministry of Education employs about 30,000 teachers who work in schools, mainly with primary school students (ages 6 to 10). Another 6,000 general and technical educators are employed by the Ministries of Health and Social Affairs, and Justice and work in special schools and structures depending on these ministries. Teachers hold the Certificat d'Aptitude Professionnelle pour les Aides Spécialisées, les Enseignements Adaptés et la Scolarisation des Elèves en Situation de Handicap [Professional Degree for Specialized Support, Adapted Teaching and Schooling of Students with Disabilities] and work in schools that provide specialized services to students diagnosed with one of the aforementioned eight disabilities, depending on their specialty. Local education authorities employ auxiliaires de vie scolaire [school life-assistants]. They support children with special needs within the classroom and outside and provide a broader level of support when several special needs children are being served.

The Ministry of Education also employs physicians, school nurses, school psychologists and vocational counselors-psychologists to work in a coordinated fashion to contribution to programs designed to prevent disabilities, diagnosis, orientation and decision making, integrate special needs students in regular schools, and develop individual and group programs designed to meet children's needs.

The professional degree of special school principal is prepared at the National Centre for Study and Training in Special Education and delivered by the Ministry of Education. The role of these principals is similar to those in regular schools. Inspectors for special education have administrative responsibilities locally for implementing policies applicable to special needs students and to supervise regular teachers in a given area. Inspectors are given an 8-week program in special education.

The Ministry of Health and Social Affairs employs technical specialized educators (who have a twofold competence in special education and in a professional or technical area and who work with children and adults with special needs in educational and professional settings), specialized educators (who work in various settings in the social or medical-educational fields, at times to support students when they work in Special Education and Remediation at Home or Integrated Pedagogical Units), principals of medical and social cares schools (trained at the National School for Public Health to get a specific professional degree), and inspectors of Health and Social Affairs (who control public and private medicoeducational and socioeducational structures).

The Department for the Judiciary Protection of Children and Youth within the Ministry of Justice employs specialized educators (who play a central role in the support, follow-up, and social inclusions of these children who are either in jail, open structures, or with their families) and technical teachers (who work in various settings to facilitate professional preparation for future social and professional inclusion) to provide services to young delinquents.

Policies from the Ministries of Education and Health and Social Affairs guide the referral, diagnosis, and decision-making practices for children and youth who may be eligible for services provided by special classes or special schools, the Commission Départementale de l'Education Spéciale [Local Commission for Special Education] is responsible for diagnosing and placing children with special needs. The commission is composed of administrators from the Ministries of Education, and Health and Social Affairs, teachers, social workers, and school physicians. One or several technical teams consisting of school psychologists, psychiatrists, social workers and others as needed are attached at the commission. Children proposed for therapy in a Child Guidance Centre need not be referred by the commission. The diagnostic and decision-making process considers information from four reports: a pedagogical evaluation of student's achievement and behavior written by the teacher; a psychological evaluation of cognitive capacities and personality written by the school psychologist who has observed and examined the child; a social evaluation that describes the family's social background, including relationships within the family, educational competencies written by the social worker; and a medical evaluation written by the physician. The child's family is invited to the commission's meeting to present its information and to accept or reject the commission's proposal.

The Local Commission for Special Education decides the financial provisions (e.g., whether special education grants or scholarships will be used to fund needed services), if needed, and may offer other programs that provide social and financial advantages to persons with disabilities. The Local Commission also may recommend ways to transport the student as well as accommodations when taking exams (e.g., use of a calculator, more time).

If the Local Commission decides a child needs specific educational support or to be separated from his/her family temporarily, the work of a Procureur de la République [District Attorney] is needed as well as a social enquiry that includes an evaluation of the child's situation. This issue is referred to a children's court in which a judge decides the case's outcome. During this process, families may solicit help from the Social Help to Children Service in order to resolve the issues before the case reaches the judge.

Local handiscol coordination groups are intended to improve cooperation between regular schools, medical, and social services. These groups are in charge of the observation, follow-up evaluations of special needs students, and those suffering from chronic affecting services for children with special needs. Three important laws recently passed by the French Parliament are summarized below. Their impact on special education is expected to be significant.

The School Orientation Law[1] attempts to combat social inequity and school failure and to offer more opportunities for success. Among the law's 14 tracks, one that is of major concern for school psychologists and special education teachers is the Contrat Individuel pour la Réussite Educative [Individual Contract for Educational Success]. Currently, the Specialized Support Network team and the school psychologist can be required by a school to help children with learning difficulties or other problems that prevent him or her from deriving benefits from schooling. In the new law, the role expected from professionals who currently work to help children with special educational needs has not been clarified.

The Law for Equal Opportunity, Participation, and Citizenship of Handicapped Persons,[2] an implementation of the Orientation Law of 1975, requires all local education authorities, including overseas regions, to create a House of Handicapped Persons with responsibilities to receive, inform, accompany, and advise handicapped persons and their families; to organize multidisciplinary teams to assess competencies and needs of the persons referred and to propose an individual program of schooling and professional development; to create a Commission for the Rights and the Autonomy of Handicapped Persons; and to provide follow-up evaluations and reviews of each handicapped person.

The recently passed Social Cohesion Law[3] focuses on employment and lodging. Chapter II of this law addresses issues of students with difficulties. Programs designed to promote educational success of children and youth (from pre-elementary school through the end of secondary school) are to be implemented by municipalities with financial assistance from the federal government. These programs are to be targeted at children and youth living in culturally and socioeconomically deprived areas. The law recommends the creation of 750 teams to implement these programs. This law is innovative in its cooperative relationships among agencies that do not have a history of working together. Finally, a fiscal law that establishes the national budget for 2006 will clarify which programs within the Ministry of Education are to be directed toward children with special needs both inside and outside of schools.

NOTES

1. L.2005-380.Loi d'orientation pour l'avenir de l'école 2005.04.23.

2. L.2005-102. Loi d'orientation pour l'égalité des droits et des chances, la participation et la citoyenneté des personnes handicapées .2005.02.11.

3. L.2005-32.Loi de programmation pour la cohésion sociale .2005.01.18.

This entry has been informed by the sources listed below.

REFERENCES

Guillemard, J. C., & Guillemard, S. (1997). *Manuel pratique de psychologie en milieu educatif* (Practical Handbook of Psychology in Educational Settings). Paris, France: Masson.

Organisation de l'Adaptation et de l'Intégration Scolaire (Organization of Adaptation and School Inclusion). (2002, May). *Official Bulletin of the French Ministry of Education no. 19.*

Website of the French School Psychologists' Association (AFPS). Retrieved from www.afps.info

Website of the French Ministry of Education. Retrieved from www.education.gouv.fr

Website of the CNEFEI (Centre National d'Etudes et de Formation pour l'Enfance Inadaptée/National Centre for Study and Training in Special Education). Retrieved from http://www.educasources.education.fr/fiche-detaillee-80718.html

Text of laws mentioned in this paper may be found on the website of the Journal Officiel de la Republique francaise [Official Journal of the French Republic]. Retrieved from www.journal-officiel.gouv.fr

J. C. GUILLEMARD
Dourdan, France

See also England, Special Education in; International School Psychology Association

FREE APPROPRIATE PUBLIC EDUCATION

One of the major provisions incorporated in the Education for All Handicapped Children Act (PL 94-142) and reinforced in its reauthorization, the Individuals with Disabilities Education Act, is the requirement that all handicapped children and youths, ages 3 through 21, be afforded a free and appropriate public education (FAPE). Initial federal statutory requirements were that services be provided to all children ages 3 through 5 and youths ages 18 through 21 apply to all states and U.S. territories except where state law or court order expressly prohibits the provision of FAPE to children or youths within these age ranges. The U.S. Congress then passed legislation (PL 99-457) to extend federally supported services to handicapped infants and toddlers from birth through 2 years of age.

The definition of a free and appropriate public education comprises three discrete, yet interrelated, provisions:

1. *Free.* Essentially this component of the FAPE mandate requires that special education and related services be provided at no cost to the parent or guardian.

2. *Appropriate.* This component of the FAPE principle requires that all special education and related services (a) be specifically tailored to the student's unique needs and capabilities (as established during the evaluation process); (b) conform to the content of the student's individualized education program (IEP); and (c) be provided in the least restrictive environment (LRE).

3. *Public Education.* The public education requirement mandates that all local, intermediate, or state agencies that directly or indirectly provide special education or related services must provide for FAPE. In meeting the FAPE requirements, public agencies (e.g., local school districts) may contract with private day or residential facilities to appropriately address the unique educational needs of a handicapped child or youth. Although the provision of FAPE does not fully apply to those handicapped children who, by parental discretion, are enrolled in private or parochial schools, these students must (by federal statute and regulation) be afforded genuine opportunities to participate in special education activities supported under Education for All Handicapped Children Act and IDEA funding.

Turnbull, Leonard, and Turnbull (1982) indicate that the provisions contained in the federal free and appropriate public education requirements have their foundations in several prominent civil rights court cases. These judicial decisions include *PARC v. Commonwealth of Pennsylvania, Mills v. D.C. Board of Education, Wyatt v. Stickney, New York State Association for Retarded Citizens v. Rockefeller, Diana v. State Board of Education,* and *Larry P. v. Riles.*

In establishing the concept of free and appropriate public education, the U.S. Congress (1983) statutorily defined FAPE as:

Special education and related services which (A) have been provided at public expense, under public supervision and direction, and without charge, (B) meet the standards of the State educational agency, (C) include an appropriate preschool, elementary, or secondary school education in the State involved, and (D) are provided in conformity with the individualized education program required under section 614(a)(5).

This definition of FAPE has been maintained unchanged in the most recent reauthorization of the IDEA, the Individuals with Disabilities Education Improvement Act of 2004.

In expanding on the legislative and judicial foundations supporting the provision of FAPE, Turnbull et al. (1982) specify six major principles for the administration of special education: implementation of the zero reject concept, development of nondiscriminatory evaluation models, preparation of IEPs, maintenance of the full continuum of least restrictive placement options, administration of compliant due process systems, and the assurance of full parent participation in all programming decisions.

REFERENCES

Turnbull, A., Leonard, J. L., & Turnbull, H. R. (1982). *Educating handicapped children: Judicial and legislative influences.* Washington, DC: American Association of Colleges for Teacher Education.

U.S. Congress. (1983). The Education of the Handicapped Amendments of 1983 (Public Law 98-199). Washington, DC: U.S. Government Printing Office.

GEORGE JAMES HAGERTY
Stonehill College
Second edition

KIMBERLY F. APPLEQUIST
University of Colorado at Colorado Springs
Third edition

See also Individualized Education Plan; Individuals With Disabilities Education Improvement Act of 2004 (IDEIA); Least Restrictive Environment

FREEDOM FROM DISTRACTIBILITY FACTOR

Numerous factor-analytic studies of the Wechsler Intelligence Scales revealed freedom from distractibility as an additional, smaller factor that underlies test performance, separate from the two larger factors that reflect the Verbal and Performance constructs that underlie all of Wechsler's scales. The first two factors that correspond to Verbal IQ and Performance IQ are typically labeled verbal comprehension and perceptual organization; each is robust in its makeup and generally invariant in its subtest composition. The third, or distractibility factor, usually consisted of the arithmetic, digit span, and coding/digit symbol subtests, although some distractibility factors are composed only of the first two of these subtests (Kaufman & Lichtenberger, 1999). Indeed, the Wechsler Intelligence Scale for Children–Third Edition (WISC-III) included four factor indexes in addition to the IQs, one of which is composed of the arithmetic and digit span subtests and is labeled *freedom from distractibility*. Coding was not aligned with this factor, but instead joined a new speeded subtest (symbol search) to form the fourth factor index, processing speed. Similarly, arithmetic and digit span (plus a new subtest, letter-number sequencing) formed a distractibility-like factor index on the Wechsler Adult Intelligence Scale–Third Edition (WAIS-III). However, in a departure from tradition, the WAIS-III uses the name "working memory" for that factor index.

The freedom from distractibility factor was first reported by Cohen (1952), who used a comparative factor analysis (considered a powerful exploratory technique at that time) to examine the performance of a group of psychiatric patients on the Wechsler-Bellevue. Expressing concern that the rationales for intelligence tests were intuitively developed and lacked needed experimental testing, Cohen found and labeled Factor A (verbal), Factor B (nonverbal organization) and Factor C (freedom from distractibility). The last factor was found to include substantial loadings by the subtests that required alert, undistracted attention for good performance. He followed up this original work with a similar factor analysis of the Wechsler Adult Intelligence Scale (WAIS; Cohen, 1959. In this factor analysis he labeled Factor C as memory. In the Wechsler Intelligence Scale for Children (WISC) factor analysis, Cohen (1959) reverted to his original interpretation of Factor C as freedom from distractibility. Baumeister and Bartlett (1962a, 1962b) identified a third WISC factor that bore a close resemblance to the distractibility factor in their studies of groups of institutionalized and noninstitutionalized retarded individuals; they labeled that factor Stimulus Trace, referring to a hypothetical physiological basis for the construct involving disruption in the amplitude and duration of the stimulus trace.

Although the exact meaning of the so-called freedom from distractibility factor (or memory or stimulus trace factor) remains to be discovered, it has sometimes been identified as the capacity to resist distraction (Wechsler, 1958) and is sometimes referred to as the anxiety triad (Lutey, 1977), although Lutey stressed that the factor may be primarily a measure of number ability. Bannatyne (1974) interpreted the factor as measure of sequential ability. Kaufman (1979, 1990, 1994) suggests that the factor may reflect a variety of cognitive faculties in addition to number facility, such as sequential processing and short-term memory, rather than just the behavioral attributes of distractibility or anxiety. Horn (1989) considers the factor to be primarily a memory dimension, which he labels short-term apprehension and retrieval, one of about eight aspects of intelligence that define his fluid-crystallized (*Gf-Gc*) theory. Wielkiewicz (1990) emphasizes that the distractibility factor may be thought of as a measure of executive processing.

The distractibility factor can play a key role in some individual test interpretations, but caution is advised against using it indiscriminately. For the WISC-R, the composition of the freedom from distractibility factor has been found to vary somewhat from one age group to another; for example, in Kaufman's (1975) study of standardization data, coding did not load meaningfully on the factor at ages 6–7, but did at ages 8–16. Also, a significant WISC-R freedom from distractibility factor has been found in studies of various racial groups (Gutkin & Reynolds, 1981) and socioeconomic groups (Carlson, Reynolds, & Gutkin, 1983), but these findings are not universal. Sandoval (1982), among others, reported that a distractibility factor emerged for Whites but not for groups of African American and Mexican American children. Furthermore, the factor is occasionally not isolated in factor-analysis studies (e.g., Reschly, 1978); the factor is cognitively complex (Stewart & Moely, 1983); and, when compared with the larger factors of verbal comprehension (information, similarities, vocabulary, and comprehension) and perceptual organization (picture completion, picture arrangement, block design, object assembly, and mazes), the third factor clearly accounts for a smaller percentage of variance.

For the WAIS-R, likewise, the distractibility factor varies in composition from age to age (Parker, 1983) and from clinical group to clinical group (Leckliter, Matarazzo, & Silverstein, 1986), sometimes does not emerge in factor-analysis studies (Kaufman, 1990), and accounts for a relatively small amount of variance (Leckliter et al., 1986).

The variability in the subtest composition of the distractibility factor that characterizes the plethora of WISC-R and WAIS-R studies is no longer a pertinent issue for the current editions of Wechsler's scales. The WISC-III, as noted, has a two-subtest distractibility factor that is a formal scale, yields standard scores with mean = 100 and standard deviation = 15, and has been validated (Wechsler, 1991) and cross-validated with large, representative samples in the United States (Roid, Prifitera, & Weiss, 1993) and Canada (Roid & Worrall, 1997); it has also been validated for children with handicapping conditions such as mental retardation and learning disabilities (Konold, Kush, & Canivez, 1997). Its composition is not in question; furthermore, the fact that Symbol Search consistently loads with Coding on a fourth factor (processing speed) virtually eliminates the question of whether or not coding would join arithmetic and digit span or split off. For the

WAIS-III, the addition of letter-number sequencing and the renaming of the factor as a measure of working memory has made the issue of the composition or nature of the adult distractibility factor a moot point; future research will undoubtedly focus on the constructs underlying the working memory index. And, finally, the preschool Wechsler Scale, the WPPSI-R, yields only two interpretable factors, resembling the global verbal and performance IQ scales, and no freedom from distractibility factor at all (Stone, Gridley, & Gyurke, 1991; Wechsler, 1989).

The latter finding for the WPPSI-R is of extreme interest regarding the interpretation of the distractibility factor. Children within the WPPSI-R's age range (3 to 7 years) are by nature distractible. If a third factor does not emerge for the WPPSI-R just as it did not emerge for its predecessor, the WPPSI for ages 4 to 6 years (Hollenbeck & Kaufman, 1973) then how can one justify labeling this dimension in terms of the distractibility behavior? That contention does not mean that poor attention and concentration, or distractible, anxious behavior, will not lower children's scores on oral arithmetic, memory, and highly speeded tasks. Any experienced clinician knows that such behaviors do indeed lower test scores, and those specific types of tasks are the most vulnerable to inattentive and distractible behaviors. However, freedom from distractibility itself cannot lead to high scores on those tasks, and has sometimes been shown not to correlate with objective measures of attention (Riccio, Cohen, Hall, & Ross, 1997). Furthermore, many other reasons, some of them cognitive deficiencies, can also lead to depressed scores on the so-called distractibility factor.

Because the WPPSI-R does not yield a distractibility factor, the WAIS-III yields a working memory index instead of a distractibility score, and the WISC-III includes a simple, well-validated, two-subtest freedom from distractibility index, the composition, or even the existence, of a distractibility factor is of limited current interest. Of greater value are research studies devoted to the score profiles of clinical populations to determine whether they have a strength or weakness on the distractibility factor. It has long been known that low scores on the WISC-R distractibility factor tend to characterize the test performance of groups of reading-disabled and learning-disabled children (Kaufman, 1979; Rugel, 1974). In addition, studies of learning-disabled adolescents, learning-disabled college students, and dyslexic adults also reveal a relative weakness on the distractibility factor (Kaufman, 1990, Table 13.12), although these studies often interpret the dimension as sequential ability from Bannatyne's (1974) perspective.

Kaufman (1994, pp. 212–213), summarizing the results of numerous WISC-R studies, also identified deficits on the distractibility factor for a diversity of populations such as children with attention-deficit/hyperactivity disorder (ADHD), unilateral lesions to either cerebral hemisphere, leukemia (following cranial irradiation treatment), epilepsy, autism, language disorders, schizophrenia, and Duchenne muscular dystrophy. A summary of WISC-III studies, reported in the WISC-III manual (Wechsler, 1991) or a special volume devoted to the WISC-III (Bracken & McCallum, 1993), indicates depressed performance on the distractibility factor for children with learning disabilities, reading disorders, dyslexia, ADHD, hearing impairment, and severe language impairment (Kaufman, 1994, Table 5.1). In contrast, the following samples scored about as well on the distractibility factor as on other WISC-III indexes: gifted, mentally retarded, and severely emotionally disturbed (Kaufman, 1994, Table 5.1).

However, a group weakness on the distractibility factor does not mean that all, or even most, members of that group display a low distractibility profile, a finding that has been shown over and over in research studies (e.g., Joschko & Rourke, 1985). The clinician's goal, therefore, is to interpret the meaning of the distractibility factor for each individual assessed, a goal that is entirely consistent with the notion that the distractibility factor can be interpreted from such a variety of cognitive and behavioral perspectives.

The first question is, When should the freedom from distractibility factor be interpreted? And the second question is, What does the factor mean for the specific individual? For the WISC-R and WAIS-R, Kaufman (1979, 1990) advised adhering to the Wechsler Verbal-Performance dichotomy under ordinary circumstances, and to only interpret the distractibility factor when it seemed to reflect a clear and unitary ability, for example, the person scored about equally well or poorly on its component subtests, and the overall distractibility score differed significantly from at least one of the larger factor scores. For the WISC-III, Kaufman (1994) recommends a more specific set of guidelines for when to interpret the distractibility factor, but the intent is still to determine whether it is a discrete, unitary ability: (a) scaled scores on arithmetic and digit span must not differ by more than 3 points, and (b) the freedom from distractibility index must differ significantly from the verbal comprehension and/or perceptual organization index. Kaufman and Lichtenberger (1999) offer similar guidelines for interpreting the WAIS-III working memory index.

If an examiner determines that an interpretation of the distractibility (or working memory) factor is warranted, the matter of how to interpret the factor still remains. To automatically ascribe an explanation of distractibility to a child who scores low on arithmetic and digit span would be absurd if the child had concentrated on each task and attended closely to each item processed. A hypothesis of distractibility or anxiety should be substantiated by test behavior indicating an attention deficit or failure to concentrate. In addition to behavioral observation, other subtest scores, the nature of wrong responses, and conditions outside the testing situation must also be considered in a comprehensive and individualized interpretation

(Kaufman, 1994; Kaufman & Lichtenberger, 1999). When sequencing ability is believed to be the difficulty (or the strength), the scaled score on the picture arrangement subtest should be examined for corroboration. Also, the examiner should look closely at background and referral information, noting any sequencing deficiency such as failure to follow directions. On the other hand, finger counting or writing and an inability to solve arithmetic problems during the time allowed, along with a low achievement in math, all point to a difficulty with numerical symbols as a probable explanation for a low distractibility index. Individuals who experience more difficulty with reversing digits in digit span (which requires mental number manipulation) than they do repeating the digits forward also may have a number problem. By contrast, a high score on the distractibility index coupled with evidence of very good math achievement suggest an interpretation of strength in number ability.

Lutey (1977) and Kaufman (1979, 1990, 1994) both warn against a simplistic interpretation of the distractibility factor, stressing that the factor can yield valuable information if it is considered in a larger context that features the more global perspective of the entire test performance, the test behavior, and the personal history of the individual. Information yielded by interpreting the distractibility factor provides insight into the cognitive and behavioral functioning of clinical groups, and it offers potentially useful information about an individual's strengths and weaknesses (Kaufman, 1994); differential diagnosis based on the distractibility factor, however, is often not supported by research data (e.g., Anastopolous, Spisto, & Maher, 1994). Nonetheless, the distractibility factor is invariably lower for exceptional than normal samples, impelling Kaufman (1994) to state that the distractibility factor is like a land mine that explodes on a diversity of abnormal populations but leaves most normal populations unscathed (p. 213).

The Freedom from Distractibility factor was retained up to the fourth edition of the WISC for historical continuity. However, during revision the label no longer fit with current neuropsychological research and it was omitted from the fourth edition (Longman, 2005).

REFERENCES

Anastopolous, A. D., Spisto, M. A., & Maher, M. C. (1994). The WISC-III freedom from distractibility factor: Its utility in identifying children with attention deficit hyperactivity disorder. *Psychological Assessment, 6,* 368–371.

Bannatyne, A. (1974). Diagnosis: A note on recategorization of the WISC scaled scores. *Journal of Learning Disabilities, 7,* 212–274.

Baumeister, A. A., & Bartlett, C. J. (1962a). A comparison of the factor-structure of normals and retardates the WISC. *American Journal of Mental Deficiency, 66,* 641–646.

Baumeister, A. A., & Bartlett, C. J. (1962b). Further factorial investigation of WISC performance of mental defectives. *American Journal of Mental Deficiency*, *67*, 257–261.

Bracken, B. A., & McCallum, R. S. (Eds.). (1993). Journal of Psychoeducational Assessment monograph series. *Advances in psychoeducational assessment: Wechsler Intelligence Scale for Children–Third Edition*. Germantown, TN: Psychoeducational Corporation.

Carlson, L., Reynolds, C. R., & Gutkin, T. B. (1983). Consistency of the factorial validity of the WISC-R for upper and lower SES groups. *Journal of School Psychology*, *21*, 319–326.

Cohen, J. (1952). Factors underlying the Wechsler-Bellevue performance of three neuropsychiatric groups. *Journal of Abnormal and Social Psychology*, *47*, 359–365.

Cohen, J. (1959). The factorial structure of the WISC at ages 7–6, 10–6, and 13–6. *Journal of Consulting Psychology*, *23*, 285–299.

Gutkin, T. B., & Reynolds, C. R. (1981). Factorial similarity of the WISC-R for White and Black children from the standardization sample. *Journal of Educational Psychology*, *73*, 227–231.

Hollenbeck, G. P., & Kaufman, A. S. (1973). Factor analysis of the Wechsler Preschool and Primary Scale of Intelligence (WPPSI). *Journal of Clinical Psychology*, *29*, 41–45.

Horn, J. L. (1989). Cognitive diversity: A framework of learning. In P. L. Ackerman, R. J. Sternberg, & R. Glaser (Eds.), *Learning and individual differences* (pp. 61–116). New York, NY: Freeman.

Joschko, M., & Rourke, B. P. (1985). Neuropsychological subtypes of learning-disabled children who exhibit the ACID pattern on the WISC. In B. P. Rourke (Ed.), *Neuropsychology of learning disabilities: Essentials of subtype analysis* (pp. 65–68). New York, NY: Guilford Press.

Kaufman, A. S. (1975). Factor analysis of the WISC-R at 11 age levels between $6^1/_2$ and $16^1/_2$ years. *Journal of Consulting and Clinical Psychology*, *43*, 135–147.

Kaufman, A. S. (1979). *Intelligent testing with the WISC-R*. New York, NY: Wiley.

Kaufman, A. S. (1990). *Assessing adolescent and adult intelligence*. Boston, MA: Allyn & Bacon.

Kaufman, A. S. (1994). *Intelligent testing with the WISC-III*. New York, NY: Wiley.

Kaufman, A. S., & Lichtenberger, E. O. (1999). *Essentials of WAIS-III assessment*. New York, NY: Wiley.

Konold, T. R., Kush, J. C., & Canivez, G. L. (1997). Factor replication of the WISC-III in three independent samples of children receiving special education. *Journal of Psychoeducational Assessment*, *15*, 123–137.

Leckliter, I. N., Matarazzo, J. D., & Silverstein, A. B. (1986). A literature review of factor analytic studies of the WAIS-R. *Journal of Clinical Psychology*, *42*, 332–342.

Longman, R. S. (2005). Tables to compare WISC-IV index scores against overall means. In A. Prifitera, D. H. Sakalofske, & L. Weiss (Eds.), *WISC-IV clinical use and interpretation* (pp. 66–100). Burlington, MA: Elsevier.

Lutey, C. (1977). *Individual intelligence testing: A manual and sourcebook* (2nd ed.). Greeley, CO: Lutey.

Parker, K. (1983). Factor analysis of the WAIS-R at nine age levels between 16 and 74 years. *Journal of Consulting and Clinical Psychology*, *51*, 302–308.

Reschly, D. J. (1978). WISC-R factor structures among Anglos, Blacks, Chicanos, and Native-American Papagos. *Journal of Consulting and Clinical Psychology*, *46*, 417–422.

Riccio, C. A., Cohen, M. J., Hall, J., & Ross, C. M. (1997). The third and fourth factors of the WISC-III: What they don't measure. *Journal of Psychoeducational Assessment*, *15*, 27–39.

Roid, G. H., Prifitera, A., & Weiss, L. G. (1993). Replication of the WISC-III factor structure in an independent sample. In B. A. Bracken & R. S. McCallum (Eds.), *Journal of Psychoeducational Assessment* monograph series. *Advances in psychoeducational assessment: Wechsler Intelligence Scale for Children–Third Edition* (pp. 6–21). Germantown, TN: Psychoeducational Corporation.

Roid, G. H., & Worrall, W. (1997). Replication of the Wechsler Intelligence Scale for Children–Third edition four-factor model in the Canadian normative sample. *Psychological Assessment*, *9*, 512–515.

Rugel, R. P. (1974). WISC subtest scores of disabled readers: A review with respect to Bannatyne's recategorization. *Journal of Learning Disabilities*, *7*, 48–55.

Sandoval, J. (1982). The WISC-R factoral validity for minority groups and Spearman's hypothesis. *Journal of School Psychology*, *20*, 198–204.

Stewart, K. J., & Moely, B. E. (1983). The WISC-R third factor: What does it mean? *Journal of Consulting and Clinical Psychology*, *51*, 940–41.

Stone, B. J., Gridley, B. E., & Gyurke, J. S. (1991). Confirmatory factor analysis of the WPPSI-R at the extreme end of the age range. *Journal of Psychoeducational Assessment*, *8*, 263–270.

Wechsler, D. (1958). *The measurement and appraisal of adult intelligence* (4th ed.). Baltimore, MD: Williams & Wilkins.

Wechsler, D. (1989). *Manual for the Wechsler Preschool and Primary Scale of Intelligence–Revised (WPPSI-R)*. San Antonio, TX: Psychological Corporation.

Wechsler, D. (1991). *Manual for the Wechsler Intelligence Scale for Children–Third Edition (WISC-III)*. San Antonio, TX: Psychological Corporation.

Wielkiewicz, R. M. (1990). Interpreting low scores on the WISC-R third factor: It's more than distractibility. *Psychological Assessment*, *2*, 91–97.

ALAN S. KAUFMAN
Yale University School of Medicine

JAMES C. KAUFMAN
California State University, San Bernardino

***See also* Factor Analysis; Profile Variability; Wechsler Adult Intelligence Scale–Third Edition; Wechsler Intelligence Scale for Children–Fourth Edition**

FREEMAN SHELDON SYNDROME

Freeman Sheldon syndrome, also known as Whistling Face syndrome, is a rare inherited condition that includes a very small mouth, mask-like face, joint contractures, and hypoplasia of the nasal cartilage. Crossed eyes, drooping eyelids, and development of scoliosis may also be encountered. Intelligence is usually normal, although some patients have been mentally retarded. Usually inherited in an autosomal dominant pattern, there are also sporadic cases and others with an autosomal recessive pattern of inheritance. There is no laboratory test to confirm the disorder. There is considerable overlap of symptoms with Schwartz-Janpel syndrome (Fletcher-Janzen, 2003).

The small mouth causes difficulties with speech, oral hygiene, and dental care. Contractures of the fingers complicate fine motor function. Orthopedic and plastic surgery can improve appearance and function but a potentially fatal reaction (malignant hyperthermia) to certain inhaled anesthetic agents necessitates careful preoperative planning with a knowledgeable anesthesiologist. There are several voluntary health agencies focusing on children with craniofacial abnormalities that offer additional information for families and professionals. Two such resources are Children's Craniofacial Association, 13140 Coit Road, Suite 517, Dallas, TX 75240. Tel.: (800) 535-3643, website: http://www.ccakids.com/; and About-Face International, 123 Edward St., Suite 1003, Toronto, ON Canada M5G 1E2. Tel.: (800) 665-3223, website: http://aboutface.ca/index.php

REFERENCES

Fletcher-Janzen, E. (2003). Freeman-Sheldon syndrome. In E. Fletcher-Janzen & C. R. Reynolds (Eds.), *Childhood disorders diagnostic desk reference* (p. 247). Hoboken, NJ: Wiley.

Freeman, E. A., & Sheldon, J. H. (1938). Craniocarpotarsal dystrophy: An undescribed congenital malformation. *Archives of Diseases of Childhood, 13,* 277–280.

Jones, K. L. (1997). Freeman-Sheldon Syndrome. *Smith's recognizable patterns of human malformation* (5th ed., pp. 214–15). New York, NY: W.B. Saunders.

PATRICIA L. HARTLAGE
Medical College of Georgia

FRENCH, EDWARD LIVINGSTON (1916–1969)

Edward Livingston French began his professional career as a teacher at Chestnut Hill Academy in Philadelphia. Following 3 years of military service in World War II, he served as chief psychologist at the Training School at Vineland, New Jersey, where he was associated with Edgar A. Doll. In 1949 both French and Doll joined the Devereux Schools in Pennsylvania, French as director of psychology education. French became a member of the board of trustees of the Devereux Foundation in 1954. Three years later he was made director of the foundation; in 1960 he became president and director.

French received his PhD in clinical psychology from the University of Pennsylvania in 1950. He coauthored *How You Can Help Your Retarded Child*. His chapter on the Devereux Schools in *Special Education Programs within the United States* describes the principles of residential therapy on which the Devereux program is based. He served as president of both the Clinical Biochemistry and Behavioral Institute and the Division of School Psychologists of the American Psychological Association, and he was a trustee of the National Association of Private Psychiatric Hospitals.

REFERENCES

French, E. L. (1968). The Devereux Schools. In M. V. Jones (Ed.), *Special education programs within the United States*. Springfield, IL: Thomas.

French, E. L., & Scott, J. C. (1967). *How you can help your retarded child: A manual for parents*. New York, NY: Lippincott.

PAUL IRVINE
Katonah, New York

FRENCH, JOSEPH L. (1928–   )

Joseph L. French earned his BS (1949) and MS (1950) degrees from Illinois State University at Normal and his EdD (1957) in educational psychology and measurements from the University of Nebraska. He held faculty positions at Illinois State University at Normal, the University of Nebraska at Lincoln, University of Missouri at Columbia, and Penn State University (1964–1997). He is best known for his work with gifted children and those with physical disabilities. His *Pictorial Test of Intelligence* (French, 1964a), designed for use with children with cerebral palsy, has been translated to German, Italian, Korean, and Spanish, and an English variation has been used in Britain. He has authored several chapters on testing exceptional children and on intellectual assessment.

French has also edited books on the gifted that have been widely used in graduate school classes across the United States and abroad. In 1959, he edited *Educating the*

Gifted, a collection of articles on identifying and providing education and services for the gifted and creative (French, 1964b). He has authored five chapters and numerous articles about the education of gifted children, including one article dealing with gifted high school dropouts that was read by Senator Jacob Javits into the *Congressional Record*. In addition, French has had a long-standing interest in intelligence and its assessment (French & Murphy, 1985; Stavrou & French, 1992), and on issues in school psychology (French, 1984, 1985).

French's externally funded research focused on the transition of Head Start alumni through the primary grades, characteristics of high school dropouts of high ability, the effect of test item arrangement on physically measured stress in young children, and the reactions of high school students to televised teachers. He was an active member of the Council for Exceptional Children (CEC) and the American Psychological Association (APA). He served as president of the Association for the Gifted in 1969, was a member of the CEC Research Committee from 1966 to 1969, and was on its Board of Governors from 1969 to 1972. His contributions to APA included serving as president of the Division of School Psychology (1976–1977), on the Council of Representatives (1984–1991), the Committee on Accreditation (1982–1985), and membership on several joint APA-National Association of School Psychologists committees.

French's numerous honors include the Certificate of Merit from The Association for the Gifted (1971), a Certificate of Recognition from the United States Office of Education (1976), a Paul Witty Fellowship (1979), the Distinguished Service Award from the APA Division of School Psychologists (1985), and the Award for Distinguished Contributions to the Science and Profession of Psychology from the Pennsylvania Psychological Association (1996). In 1998 he was named the Distinguished Alumnus of Illinois State University at Normal.

French is currently Professor Emeritus at Pennsylvania State University, and continues to be professionally active.

REFERENCES

French, J. L. (1964a). *The Pictorial Test of Intelligence*. Boston, MA: Houghton Mifflin.

French, L. (Ed.). (1964b). *Educating the gifted* (Rev. ed.). New York, NY: Holt, Rinehart, & Winston.

French, J. L. (1984). On the conception, birth, and early development of school psychology, with special reference to Pennsylvania. *American Psychologist, 39*, 976–987.

French, J. L. (1985). An essay on becoming a school psychologist when school psychology was becoming. *Journal of School Psychology, 23*, 1–12.

French, J. L., & Murphy, J. (1985). Intelligence, its assessment and its role in the comprehensive evaluation. In J. R. Bergan (Ed.), *School psychology in contemporary society*. Columbus, OH: Merrill.

Stavrou, E., & French, J. F. (1992). The K-ABC and cognitive processing styles in autistic children. *Journal of School Psychology, 30*, 259–267.

ANN E. LUPKOWSKI
Texas A&M University
First edition

TAMARA J. MARTIN
The University of Texas of the Permian Basin
Second edition

FREUD, ANNA (1895–1982)

Anna Freud was the youngest of Sigmund Freud's six children. She was educated at the Cottage Lyceum, and although an excellent student, left without a degree in 1912. Her father was her mentor in psychoanalytic theory and practice. Following the Nazi takeover of Austria, the family moved to London in 1938. Anna and her father remained professionally active and influential after their emigration. She was her father's devoted companion and associate until his death in 1939.

Anna Freud's many professional contributions resulted from her interest in applying psychoanalytic theory to the study of child development and in formulating and conducting psychotherapy appropriate to the special needs of young patients. Her work stimulated others, including Erik Erikson, whose study of psychoanalysis she encouraged. Her theoretical contributions included elaborating and extending her father's concept of ego defense mechanisms, particularly displacement and identification. She wrote prolifically, producing more than 100 articles and many important books, including *Introduction to the Technique of Child Analysis* (1927), *Psychoanalysis for Teachers and Parents* (1931), *The Ego and the Mechanisms of Defense* (1936), and *Psychoanalytic Treatment of Children* (1946). She also edited the 24-volume edition of her father's works (1953–1956).

Her interest in promoting child psychoanalysis led her to found in 1947 a clinic and a serial publication, both of which are still active. The Hampstead Child-Therapy Course and Clinic in London treats children and trains psychoanalytic child therapists; *The Psychoanalytic Study of the Child* is a scholarly forum for theoreticians and practitioners.

Anna Freud received the highest professional recognition of her contemporaries in 1970 when she was named the most outstanding living child psychoanalyst. Other distinctions include awards, medals, and honorary degrees from Clark, Yale, Columbia, and Harvard universities, and an honorary MD in 1972 from the University of Vienna.

Because of Anna Freud's modest and private nature, frustratingly little is known about her personal and professional development (Jackson, 1982). However, a memorial section of Volume 39 of *The Psychoanalytic Study of the Child* (1984) includes five papers discussing her contributions to the fields of law, developmental psychology, politics, and training in child analysis.

REFERENCE

Jackson, D. J. (1982). Psychology of the scientist: XLVI. Anna Freud. *Psychological Reports, 50,* 1191–1198.

PAULINE F. APPLEFIELD
University of North Carolina at Wilmington

FREUD, SIGMUND (1856–1939)

Sigmund Freud, the founder of psychoanalysis, entered medical practice as a neurologist in Vienna in 1886. Psychoanalysis, developed out of Freud's clinical practice, revolutionized not only psychiatric treatment but man's view of himself. Freud introduced the concept of the unconscious mind and its influence on behavior. Free association and dream interpretation were developed as techniques for reaching the unconscious. Freud demonstrated the role of mental conflict in human development and identified the motivating forces of sexuality and aggression. He also identified the existence and importance of infantile sexuality, and the influence of childhood development on adult behavior. After the annexation of Austria by Nazi Germany in 1938, Freud moved to London, where he resided until his death the following year.

This entry has been informed by the sources listed below.

REFERENCES

Freud, S. (1933). *New introductory lectures on psycho-analysis.* New York, NY: Norton.

Freud, S. (1970). *An outline of psychoanalysis.* New York, NY: Norton.

Jones, E. (1953–1957). *The life and work of Sigmund Freud* (3 vols.). New York, NY: Basic Books.

PAUL IRVINE
Katonah, New York

FREY'S SYNDROME

Frey's syndrome is a rare neurological disorder resulting from injury or surgery near the parotid glands, damaging the facial nerve and resulting in facial flushing during mastication and possibly profuse sweating, particularly while ingesting hot, spicy, or acidic foods.

Incidence of Frey's syndrome is rare, and treatment is dependent on the severity of symptoms. Most patients have mild symptoms that can be controlled with topical creams, thus making Frey's syndrome a mild nuisance. However, in some cases of Frey's syndrome, the patient may experience excessive discomfort in which surgery on the nerves near the ear may be needed. Recent research has shown injections of botulinum toxin A (BTX) to be effective at relieving symptoms of Frey's syndrome with relatively no side effects.

Special educational needs usually are not required, except counseling to address psychosocial factors, and prognosis is good with full recovery in a majority of patients. Currently, oral medications and better topical ointments to alleviate symptoms of Frey's syndrome are topics of future research.

Characteristics

1. Excessive sweating
2. Flushing of the face
3. Possible temporary lack of sensitivity to heat, pain, or burning in the affected area

---

This entry has been informed by the sources listed below.

REFERENCES

Thoene, J. G., & Coker, N. P. (Eds.). (1995). *Physicians' guide to rare diseases* (2nd ed.). Montvale, NJ: Dowden.

von Lindern, J. J., Niederhagen, B., Berge, S., Hagler, G., & Reich, R. H. (2000). Frey syndrome: Treatment with type A botulinum toxin. *Cancer, 89,* 1659–1663.

KIMBERLY M. ESTEP
University of Houston–Clear Lake

FRIEDREICH'S ATAXIA

Friedreich's ataxia (FA) applies to a varied group of problems whose major symptoms usually appear in the late childhood or early adolescent years. The condition is generally transmitted along family lines through Mendelian inheritance as an autosomal recessive trait, though some cases of dominant mode transmission have been recognized. At the core of the disorder is progressive dysfunction of the spinal cord and cerebellum. Cardiac muscle fiber degeneration may also be present.

The early signs of FA are an increasing disturbance of normal gait followed by progressive loss of muscular coordination in the upper extremities and trunk. Skeletal anomalies such as clubfoot, hammertoes, and highly arched feet, along with scoliosis, may be present. Cardiac failure, enlargement of the heart (or arrhythmias), nystagmus of the eyes, optical nerve atrophy, tremors, dysarthria, and feeding disorders may be noted. Loss of sensation, especially in the feet, is common in this disorder, and the risk of development of seizure disorders is high. The diagnosis of FA is completely reliant on these clinical manifestations. Lab findings are generally of little assistance in diagnosis, except for cases where electrocardiogram changes indicating myocarditis are observed. Most individuals with FA become wheelchair-bound and eventually bedridden. There is no known cure for this disorder, with death from myocardial failure in childhood, adolescence, or early adulthood the usual result.

Friedreich's ataxia has been separated diagnostically from other similar disorders such as ataxia-telangiectasia, Roussy-Levy syndrome, and Bassen-Kornzweig syndrome.

REFERENCES

Batshaw, M. L., & Perret, Y. M. (1981). *Children with handicaps: A medical primer*. Baltimore, MD: Paul H. Brookes.

Bleck, E. E., & Nagel, D. A. (1982). *Physically handicapped children: A medical atlas for teachers*. New York, NY: Grune & Stratton.

Vaughan, V. C., McKay, R. J., & Behrman, R. E. (1979). *Nelson textbook of pediatrics*. Philadelphia, PA: Saunders.

JOHN D. WILSON
Elwyn Institutes

See also Gait Disturbances; Genetic Counseling

FRONTOFACIONASAL DYSPLASIA

Frontofacionasal dysplasia (FFND) is characterized by severe abnormalities of the skull and face. Symptoms include facial asymmetry, coloboma of the iris and retina, malformation of the eyelids, narrowing of the palpebral fissures, ocular hypertelorism, telecanthus, limbic dermoid of the eye, midface hypoplasia, anomalies of the corpus callosum, cleft lip and palate, deformed nostrils, and multiple skin appendages (Al-Gazali, Dawodu, Hamada, Bakir, & Bakalinová, 1996; Temple, Brunner, Jones,

Burn, & Baraitser, 1990). FFND also may be referred to as facio-frontonasal dysplasia, frontofacionasal dysostosis, or nasal-fronto-faciodysplasia; related syndromes include oculoauriculofrontonasal spectrum and frontonasal dysplasia.

FFND is thought to be an extremely rare, low-incidence condition (Temple et al., 1990). Prevalence has not been studied thoroughly, and differences regarding gender and ethnicity in the manifestation of symptoms are unknown. There is evidence for autosomal recessive inheritance of this syndrome (Gollop, Kiota, Martins, Lucchesi, & Alvarenga, 1984).

Characteristics

1. Congenital onset.
2. A variety of deformities of the eyes, nose, mouth, and skull.
3. Child may have poor eyesight due to eyelid malformation and folds of skin obstructing vision.
4. Due to cleft lip and palate, child may experience abnormal dental development and speech difficulties.

The severity of abnormalities associated with FFND is extremely variable, and it is uncertain whether some cases actually are manifesting symptoms of FFND, represent clinical variations of this condition, or represent separate conditions altogether (Al-Gazali et al., 1996). Also variable is the extent to which the eyes are involved (Gollop et al., 1984). The association between intelligence, mental retardation, and FFND is unknown (Temple et al., 1990).

Treatment commonly includes surgery to remove limbal dermoid from the eye(s) if present; this may serve to improve the child's vision. However, poor vision may persist due to coloboma (i.e., partial absence of tissue) of the iris. Cosmetic surgery may be used to remodel the nose and other facial malformations (Temple et al., 1990). Adverse effects of abnormal dental development and speech difficulties may be lessened by extensive dental care and early speech therapy, respectively. Finally, counseling may be sought in order to address self-concept issues and the emotional difficulty of being physically different.

Depending on symptom severity, children with FFND may be eligible to receive special education services under Section 504, IDEA federal regulations, or both. For example, if coloboma of the iris and retina results in partial sight that adversely affects the child's educational performance, the child would qualify for services under the Visual Impairment category of IDEA. Furthermore, if cleft lip and palate result in communication problems, such as impaired articulation or voice impairment, that adversely affect the child's educational performance, then the child would be eligible for services under the Speech or Language Impairment category of IDEA. Visual and speech impairment of children with FFND also would qualify them for services under Section 504.

There is evidence that children with FFND or similar syndromes may develop into intelligent and healthy adults (Guion-Almeida & Lopes, 1997). This likelihood may be enhanced through the surgical, dental, speech, and emotional interventions listed above. However, very little is known regarding the influence of FFND on later development, including intelligence, achievement, and employment status in adulthood. Prognosis, therefore, is difficult to determine. Future research must focus on these issues, in addition to prevalence among different ethnicities, gender differences in prevalence, differential diagnosis between FFND and similar low-incidence syndromes, and the effectiveness of psychosocial interventions in improving the emotional lives of children suffering from this disorder.

REFERENCES

Al-Gazali, L. I., Dawodu, A. H., Hamada, M., Bakir, M., & Bakalinová, D. (1996). Severe facial clefting, limbic dermoid, hypoplasia of the corpus callosum, and multiple skin appendages: Severe frontofacionasal dysplasia or newly recognized syndrome? *American Journal of Medical Genetics, 63*, 346–347.

Gollop, T. R., Kiota, M. M., Martins, R. M. M., Lucchesi, E. A., & Alvarenga, E. (1984). Frontofacionasal dysplasia: Evidence for autosomal recessive inheritance. *American Journal of Medical Genetics, 19*, 301–305.

Guion-Almeida, M. L., & Lopes, V. L. G. S. (1997). Oculoauriculofrontonasal spectrum in an adult Brazilian male. *Clinical Dysmorphology, 6*, 251–255.

Temple, I. K., Brunner, H., Jones, B., Burn, J., & Baraitser, M. (1990). Midline facial defects with ocular colobomata. *American Journal of Medical Genetics, 37*, 23–27.

JEREMY R. SULLIVAN
Texas A&M University

FROSTIG, MARIANNE (1906–1985)

Born in Vienna, Austria, Marianne Frostig received a degree as a children's social worker from the College of Social Welfare, Vienna, Austria, in 1926. Several years later, she and her neuropsychiatrist husband worked in a psychiatric hospital in Poland before he accepted a position in the United States. When the Nazis invaded Poland,

they killed everyone in the hospital. In the United States, Frostig earned the first BA ever issued by the New School for Social Research (1948). She received her MA (1940) from Claremont Graduate School and her PhD (1955) from the University of Southern California. She became ill and died while on a lecture tour in Germany.

Believing that every person is a unique individual who needs to be assessed and treated as such, Frostig was interested in finding the most appropriate education/treatment for each child. She thought that education should be adjusted to meet the needs of all children, especially those who, for various reasons, find learning difficult. To Frostig, a problem child is a child whose needs are not being met. *Education for Dignity* was intended to be a practical guide for the regular classroom teacher to meet those needs.

The Marianne Frostig Developmental Test of Visual Perception was the first test to segregate different visual abilities. Prior to this, all visual problems were grouped together. Frostig retired as director of the Marianne Frostig Center for Educational Therapy in 1972.

Frostig received the *Los Angeles Times* Woman of the Year Award and the Golden Key Award of the International Association for Children with Learning Disabilities. She has been included in *Who's Who of American Women, American Men and Women of Science*, and the *Dictionary of International Biography*.

This entry has been informed by the sources listed below.

REFERENCES

Frostig, M. (1976). *Education for dignity*. New York, NY: Grune & Stratton.

Frostig, M., Lefever, D. W., & Whittlesey, J. R. B. (1964). *The Marianne Frostig Developmental Test of Visual Perception* (3rd ed.). Palo Alto, CA: Consulting Psychologists.

E. VALERIE HEWITT
Texas A&M University

FROSTIG REMEDIAL PROGRAM

The Frostig Program of Visual Perception, developed in 1964, was designed to train children who have visual problems in perceptual and motor skills. Using a series of workbooks and worksheets, the program focuses on five areas. First is eye motor coordination, which involves drawing lines in carefully prescribed boundaries. Second, figure-ground perception is tested, in which the child finds hidden figures in distracting and overlapping backgrounds. Third is perceptual constancy; here the child learns to recognize that an object remains the same even if its shape or color changes. Fourth is position in space; in this part of the program the child discovers that figures and objects remain the same although they may occupy different positions. Often, the child is provided with a model, then given several other models and is asked to select the shape or design that is exactly like the original. The fifth area is spatial relationships; at this point the child develops skills in perceiving positional relationships between objects or points of reference such as the arrangement of material or figures on a printed page (Bannatyne, 1971; Hallahan & Kaufman, 1976).

The assumption underlying the Frostig program is that brain damage in children results in neurological disabilities, giving rise to visual perceptual problems. This assumption, based on the seminal works of Goldstein, Strauss, Werner, and Cruickshank, concludes that manifestations of brain dysfunctions, usually perceptual problems, can occur even if no specific damage to the brain can be found (Hallahan & Kaufman, 1976). The Frostig program is one of several commercially developed training programs to aid learning-disabled children who exhibit perceptual deficiencies (Frostig & Maslow, 1973).

In conjunction with this program, the Frostig Developmental Test of Visual Perception was designed. This test purports to measure the five functions of visual perception and provides a means to compare children's performance with norms for their ages. The assumption on which the test is based, that visual perception is a critical element in school learning, has been questioned. Moreover, the effectiveness of the test and the Frostig training has not been documented. While the test itself provides an adequate measure of global perception of young children, its ability to assess specific areas of perceptual difficulty has not been shown. Mann (1978) cautions that a low score on the test should not be construed as a signal to begin a perceptual training program. In addition, he states that the test and its related training program has "stimulated wide and often injudicious programming for learning-disabled children" (p. 1276). Critics also have claimed that Frostig's names for traits are simply conjecture and the test and program both represent a psychometric era that has passed (Mitchell, 1985).

REFERENCES

Bannatyne, A. (1971). *Language, reading, and learning disabilities*. Springfield, IL: Thomas.

Frostig, M., & Maslow, P. (1973). *Learning problems in the classroom*. New York, NY: Grune & Stratton.

Hallahan, D., & Kaufman, J. (1976). *Introduction to learning disabilities*. Englewood Cliffs, NJ: Prentice Hall.

Mann, L. (1978). Review of the Marianne Frostig developmental test of visual perception. In O. K. Buros (Ed.), *Mental measurements yearbook*. Highland Park, NJ: Gryphon.

Mitchell, J. V. (1985). *Ninth mental measurements yearbook*. Highland Park, NJ: Gryphon.

FORREST E. KEESBURY
Lycoming College

See also Developmental Test of Visual Perception–Second Edition; Movigenics; Visual-Motor and Visual-Perceptual Problems; Visual Perception and Discrimination

FRYNS SYNDROME

Inherited as an autosomal recessive trait, Fryns syndrome is characterized by many abnormalities present at birth. These characteristics include abnormalities of the head and face, protrusion of part of the stomach and the small intestines into the chest cavity, underdeveloped lungs, cleft palate, underdevelopment of the fingers and toes, and some degree of mental retardation.

True incidence of Fryns syndrome is unknown; however, it is estimated to be a very rare disorder affecting 0.7 children per 10,000 births. Fryns syndrome normally results in stillbirths for the children who have inherited this disorder. In the children who live with Fryns syndrome, their existence is meager with severe cognitive and physical deficits, the former the result of brain malformations. Treatment, if viable, could include surgery to correct the internal malformations. In prenatal detection, termination of pregnancy is usually offered.

Characteristics

1. Infants may exhibit a flat, broad nose; a wide mouth; cleft palate; a displaced, abnormally small jaw; underdeveloped ear lobes; and corneal clouding.
2. Many children will have short bones in the tips of their fingers, absent or undersized fingernails, or both.
3. Skeletal abnormalities, congenital cardiac defects, genital anomalies, renal defects, and brain malformation responsible for cognitive sequelae.
4. Infants may also be large for their age.

Special education issues specifically relate to multiple handicaps due to health problems and mental retardation.

Prognosis is poor, and chronic management through assisted living is necessary. Future research is directed toward etiology and treatment through gene mapping.

REFERENCES

Cunniff, C., Jones, K. L., Saal, H. M., & Stern, H. J. (1990). Fryns syndrome: An autosomal recessive disorder associated with craniofacial anomalies, diaphragmatic hernia, and distal digital hypoplasia. *Pediatrics, 85*(4), 499–504.

Jones, K. L. (Ed.). (1997). *Smith's recognizable patterns of human malformation* (5th ed.). Philadelphia, PA: W. B. Saunders.

McKusick, V. A. (1986). Online mendelian inheritance in man [Article 229850]. Retrieved from http://www.ncbi.nlm.nih.gov/Omim

KIMBERLY M. ESTEP
University of Houston–Clear Lake

FUNCTIONAL ANALYSIS

Functional analysis is a term that describes a behavior analytic experimental procedure involving the manipulation of antecedents and consequences that have been hypothesized to predict and/or maintain persistent problem behavior. Considered to be a "hallmark of behavioral assessment" (Hanley, Iwata, & McCord, 2003, p. 147), hypotheses are derived from indirect and/or direct functional assessment data. Indirect methods can include questionnaires or interviews, while direct methods use systematic direct observation techniques (e.g., A-B-C functional assessment). Following the functional analysis, teachers and researchers systematically identify any functional relationships between environmental events and persistent problem behavior to experimentally determine the function or purpose of the problem behavior (Cooper, Heron, & Heward, 2007; Fowler & Schnacker, 1994; O'Neill et al., 1997; Repp & Horner, 1999). For example, a researcher might manipulate a sequence of environmental conditions (e.g., attention, escape, alone, and control conditions) to verify the hypothesis that was derived from a functional assessment. This purpose supports Alberto and Troutman's (2009) assertion that functional analysis is used for hypothesis development, hypothesis refinement, hypothesis verification, or to clarify unclear results from a functional assessment. When the function of the problem behavior has been determined, data-based interventions are identified and incorporated into a comprehensive behavior support plan for the person of concern (Mace, 1994; O'Neill et al., 1997; Wacker, Berg, Asmus, Harding, & Cooper, 1998). In other words, "functional analysis has provided a means to determine in advance which treatments should and should not work" (Hanley, Iwata, & McCord, 2003, p. 149). Functional analysis has been used by researchers to understand and effectively address serious problems such as self-injurious behaviors, aggression, disruption, vocalizations, property destruction, and stereotypy (Hanley, Iwata, & McCord, 2003).

Miltenberger (1998) outlines three methodological features that need to be in place when conducting a functional analysis: (1) objective measurement of the problem behavior under experimental conditions, (2) demonstration of a change in the problem behavior following the systematic manipulation of antecedent and/or consequent events, and (3) systematic replication of the above process. Two different single-case experimental designs are typically used when conducting a functional analysis; these include the ABAB reversal design and the multielement design (Alberto & Troutman, 2009; O'Neill et al., 1997; O'Neill, McDonnell, Billingsley, & Jenson, 2011; Wolery, Bailey, & Sugai, 1988). For example, when using the ABAB reversal design a researcher might try to determine the function of a persistent problem behavior by collecting data on the percent of intervals the student exhibits the problem behavior during "easy tasks" and "hard tasks" phases, whereas the multielement design could be used to measure the effects of "alone," "demand," "tangible," and "attention" conditions on the frequency of the problem behavior (see O'Neill et al., 1997; Repp & Horner, 1999).

Functional analysis can provide special education teachers, school psychologists, behavior specialists, and researchers with an experimental demonstration of the casual factors that occasion or maintain persistent problem behavior. According to Repp and Horner (1999) "functional analysis constitutes the most powerful tool for identifying the purpose of problem behavior. That is so because the sources of variance are controlled experimentally, thereby permitting strong statements about which factors evoke and maintain problem behavior" (p. 21). Cooper, Heron, and Heward (2007) indicate that limitations associated with the use of functional analysis exist, including (a) the possibility that the problem behavior may be temporarily strengthened; (b) misunderstandings about the analytical purposes of functional analysis, including the possibility that the problem behavior may be reinforced as part of the analysis; (c) acknowledgment that functional analysis may not address the full range of problem behaviors encountered in school and community settings; (d) understanding that the use of analog settings (as opposed to naturalistic settings) may produce different results; and (e) awareness that functional analysis requires a level of research expertise related to the systematic implementation and interpretation of results that may prevent the wider adoption or use of this approach in applied settings.

REFERENCES

Alberto, P. A., & Troutman, A. C. (2009). *Applied behavior analysis for teachers* (8th ed.). Upper Saddle River, NJ: Pearson.

Cooper, J. O., Heron, T. E., & Heward, W. L. (2007). *Applied behavior analysis* (2nd ed.). Upper Saddle River, NJ: Pearson Prentice Hall.

Fowler, R. C., & Schnacker, L. E. (1994). The changing character of behavioral assessment and treatment: An historical introduction and review of functional analysis research. *Diagnostique*, *19*, 79–102. doi:10.1177/073724779401900206

Hanley, G. P. Iwata, B. A., & McCord, B. E. (2003). Functional analysis of problem behavior: A review. *Journal of Applied Behavior Analysis, 36*, 147–185.

Mace, F. C. (1994). The significance and future of functional analysis methodologies. *Journal of Applied Behavior Analysis, 27*, 385–392.

Miltenberger, R. G. (1998). Methods for assessing antecedent influences on challenging behaviors. In J. K. Luiselli & M. J. Cameron (Eds.), *Antecedent control: Innovative approaches to behavioral support* (pp. 47–65). Baltimore, MD: Paul H. Brookes.

O'Neill, R. E., Horner, R. H., Albin, R. W., Sprague, J. R., Storey, K., & Newton, J. S. (1997). *Functional assessment and program development for problem behavior: A practical handbook* (2nd ed.). Pacific Grove, CA: Brooks/Cole.

O'Neill, R. E., McDonnell, J. J., Billingsley, F. F., & Jenson, W. R. (2011). *Single case research designs in educational and community settings.* Upper Saddle River, NJ: Pearson Education.

Repp, A. C., & Horner, R. H. (1999). *Functional analysis of problem behavior: From effective assessment to effective support.* Belmont, CA: Wadsworth.

Wacker, D. P., Berg, W. K., Asmus, J. M., Harding, J. K., & Cooper, L. J. (1998). Experimental analysis of antecedent influences on challenging behaviors. In J. K. Luiselli & M. J. Cameron (Eds.), *Antecedent control: Innovative approaches to behavioral support* (pp. 67–86). Baltimore, MD: Paul H. Brookes.

Wolery, M., Bailey, D., Jr., & Sugai, G. (1988). *Effective teaching: Principles and procedures of applied behavior analysis with exceptional students.* Boston, MA: Allyn & Bacon.

RANDALL L. DE PRY
Portland State University

See also **ABAB Design; Behavioral Assessment; Functional Assessment; Multielement Design; Positive Behavior Support**

FUNCTIONAL ASSESSMENT

Functional assessment is a term that describes a process for gathering information about the factors that predict and/or maintain chronic or persistent problem behavior in order to develop and implement an individualized behavior support plan. Data from functional assessments can include information on setting events, immediate antecedents or predictors, and consequent events that are hypothesized to maintain the problem behavior. The behavior support plan delineates the problem behavior(s); diagrams summary statements using a competing behavior model; outlines environmental modifications, curricular adaptations, and instructional strategies that will support the person of concern and the new response; identifies consequent strategies, such as reinforcement contingencies; and outlines typical routines, plans for monitoring and evaluation, and any crisis management plans (O'Neill et al., 1997). Central to the behavior support planning process is the identification of a replacement response that serves the same purpose or function of the problem behavior, but is more acceptable given the individual's home, school, and/or work environments. In other words, the replacement response is "functionally equivalent" to the problem behavior. Functional assessment has a strong evidentiary base (see Chandler & Dahlquist, 2010; Crone & Horner, 2003) and is the preferred method of assessment for persons who exhibit chronic or persistent problem behavior. Function-based support is also a critical component in the design and implementation of Schoolwide Positive Behavior Interventions and Supports at the tertiary (intensive) level (Sugai et al., 2000).

Historically, when students have presented challenging behavior, educators have approached these events by creating reactive interventions that were based on the topography of the problem behavior, that is, how the behavior is performed. For example, students who destroy workbooks, tear up assignments, and carve holes in their desks are all damaging school property. Typically, each student receives a consequence such as a time-out, a response cost procedure, in-school or out-of-school suspension, or exclusion that is designed to reduce the problem behavior and restore teaching and learning. While topographically based interventions may be effective in the short term, it is clear that they do not teach the student positive alternative responses, may fail to generalize to other persons or places, and do not address the function or purpose of the problem behavior (Lewis, Scott, & Sugai, 1994; Scheuermann & Hall, 2012; Wolery, Bailey, & Sugai, 1988). A closer examination of the students' behaviors (from the example above) using a functional assessment process might reveal that the first student typically engages in the problem behavior when she is late for school and misses her breakfast, the second student engages in the problem behavior because he has learned to escape or avoid difficult academic tasks by tearing up his assignments, and the third student engages in the problem behavior because she has learned that damaging school property is an effective way of getting teacher and peer attention. Collecting and using this type of data is critical when designing effective behavioral interventions. In other words, functional assessment helps teachers, psychologist, and other support personnel understand the function or purpose of the problem behavior, which then increases the likelihood that the behavior support team can design behavior support plans that are data-based and ultimately more effective than standard behavior reduction strategies that are topographically based or reactive in nature.

O'Neill et al. (1997) suggest that problem behavior is maintained by getting or obtaining events that are desirable and/or escaping and avoiding events that are undesirable. Examples of desirable conditions include socially mediated conditions such as getting or obtaining attention, access to desired items, access to tangibles, and behaviors that allow a person to get or obtain sensory stimulation (e.g., visual or tactile stimulation). Examples of undesirable conditions include escaping or avoiding social events such as attention, difficult or nonpreferred activities, teacher requests or demands, and behaviors that allow a person to escape or avoid internal stimulation (e.g., pain, voices, hunger). O'Neill et al. (1997) argue that functional assessments should include the following features: (a) an operational definition of the problem behavior; (b) an identification of any events, persons, times, or situations that predict when the problem behavior occurs and when the problem behavior does not occur; (c) documentation of consequences that maintain the problem behavior; (d) summary or hypothesis statements that include any setting events, predictors, and maintaining consequences; and (e) direct observation data that supports or confirms the summary statements that have been created. A comprehensive functional assessment includes both indirect and direct methods for gathering information about the contextual features of the problem behavior. Indirect methods involve gathering information from persons who are familiar with the student (e.g., teacher, parent, caregiver, paraprofessional) and typically incorporate interviews, behavioral rating scales, checklists, and questionnaires. Direct observation methods incorporate the use of systematic direct observation techniques that are conducted in environments where the problem behavior occurs and other environments when feasible. Data from indirect and direct functional assessment procedures are used to develop hypotheses (i.e., summary statements) about the problem behavior and are instrumental in providing a data-based rationale for the development of the behavior support plan.

Indirect functional assessments that are summarized below include the *Functional Assessment Interview* (O'Neill et al., 1997), the *Student-Directed Functional Assessment Interview* (O'Neill et al., 1997), the *Student-Assisted Functional Assessment Interview* (Kern, Dunlap, Clarke, & Childs, 1994), the *Motivation Assessment Scale* (Durand & Crimmins, 1988), *Problem Behavior Questionnaire* (Lewis et al., 1994), and the *Functional Assessment Checklist: Teachers and Staff (FACTS)* (March et al., 2000). Direct functional assessment instruments that are summarized below include *A-B-C Assessment* (Bijou, Peterson, & Ault, 1968), and the *Functional Assessment Observation Form* (O'Neill et al., 1997).

Indirect Functional Assessments

The *Functional Assessment Interview* (O'Neill et al., 1997) is a structured interview that includes the following categories: (a) operational definitions of the behaviors of concern; (b) questions related to setting events that predict or set up the problem behaviors; (c) questions related to antecedents that predict when the behaviors are likely and not likely to occur; (d) questions related to consequences that maintain the problem behavior; (e) a description of the efficiency of the problem behavior; (f) descriptions of alternative behaviors that the person already knows; (g) questions related to the communicative abilities of the person; (h) questions related to known ways of supporting the person; (i) descriptions of what the person finds reinforcing; and (j) descriptions of programs that have been tried in the past and the effect that these interventions have had on the person's behavior. According to the authors, the *Functional Assessment Interview* can take up to 90 minutes to complete. Upon completion of the interview, summary statements are collaboratively created that describe any setting events, antecedents, the problem behavior, and maintaining consequences that were notable from the interview.

Student-Directed Functional Assessment Interview (O'Neill et al., 1997) is an interview that is designed to be given by a person who has a positive relationship with the student. The interview takes up to 40 minutes to complete and includes student-generated responses regarding (a) any behaviors of concern; (b) completion of a schedule analysis where the student indicates the times and places where problem behaviors are least likely and most likely to occur; and (c) the creation of summary statements that diagram what was learned during the interview and possible interventions.

Student-Assisted Functional Assessment Interview (Kern et al., 1994) is comprised of four sections and takes up to 30 minutes to complete. Section I consists of 12 closed-ended questions regarding potential functions of the student's problem behavior. Each question allows the student to respond using one of three options (e.g., "always," "sometimes," and "never"). Section II consists of seven open-ended questions that solicit information about when and where the target behavior is likely to occur. Section III lists academic subject areas and asks the student to rate how much he or she likes each subject using a Likert-type scale. Section IV consists of 22 questions that ask what the student likes and dislikes about selected subjects in school.

Motivation Assessment Scale (Durand & Crimmins, 1988) is a 16-question rating scale that is designed to provide data on four functions (motivations) of problem behavior (e.g., attention, escape, tangibles, and self-stimulation). The instrument has four questions for each of the targeted functions. Upon completion of the *Motivation Assessment Scale*, the educator sums the responses and calculates the mean score and relative ranking for each category.

The *Problem Behavior Questionnaire* (Lewis et al., 1994) is an instrument that includes 15 questions that are correlated with five potential maintaining variables and a series of open-ended questions that allow the respondent to provide data on how often the behavior occurs, where the behavior occurs, relationship of the problem behavior to an academic skills deficit, and the like. The maintaining variables assessed in the *Problem Behavior Questionnaire* include: (1) access to peer attention, (2) access to teacher attention, (3) escape or avoidance of peer attention, (4) escape or avoidance of teacher attention, and (5) setting events.

Functional Assessment Checklist: Teachers and Staff (FACTS) (March et al., 2000) includes a general assessment (Part A) that seeks information on student strengths, problem behaviors, and identification of routines (e.g., activities, settings, times) where the problem behaviors are most likely to occur. The instrument includes a second and more specific assessment (Part B) that examines each of the routines that were highlighted in Part A as being the most problematic and requires the respondent to operationally define the problem behavior, identify antecedents or predictors that occasion the problem behavior, consequences that maintain the behavior, creation of a summary statement (i.e., setting event, antecedent, behavior, and consequence), assessment of the accuracy of the summary statement by the respondent, and strategies that have been used in the past to address the behavior of concern. Scheuermann and Hall (2012) write that "checklists such as the FACTS are quick, easy, and efficient tools to help identify the potential functions of problem behavior" (p. 79).

Direct Functional Assessments

A-B-C Assessment (Bijou et al., 1968) is a direct observation procedure that involves the descriptive analysis of environmental events that are recorded anecdotally over a specified period of time. Direct observation data is collected and recorded on the antecedent-behavior-consequence relations that occur over multiple observation periods (Blakeslee, Sugai, & Gruba, 1994). From this data, educators are able to identify antecedent events that precede problem behavior and consequence events that occur in response to the problem behavior. Data collected over time can provide the behavior support team with important information about possible functional relationships between the environment and the student's problem behavior (Wolery et al., 1988). Guidelines for using *A-B-C Assessment* include: (a) only recording the targeted students' observable behavior (avoid interpretation), (b) recording what happened before the targeted student's behavior (antecedents), (c) recording what happened after the targeted student's behavior (consequences), and (d) conducting multiple observations before developing

summary statements (Alberto & Troutman, 2009; Cooper, Heron, & Heward, 2007).

Functional Assessment Observation Form (FAO; O'Neill et al., 1997) is a direct observation instrument that is used to collect data across settings and over time. O'Neill et al. write that "the FAO documents the predictor events and consequences associated with instances of problem behavior. The form is organized around problem behavior events. An event is different from a single occurrence of a problem behavior. An event includes all the problem behavior in an incident that begins with a problem behavior and ends only after 3 minutes of no problem behavior" (p. 37). The FAO form allows the observer to indicate which problem behaviors (events) were observed, any predictors or immediate antecedents that were observed, and the perceived function the behavior served for the individual. Additional sections are available for indicating the actual consequences the person received and any observer comments that may add to understanding the problem behavior.

The inclusion of functional assessment requirements in the 1997 reauthorization of the Individuals with Disabilities Education Act (IDEA) provides a unique opportunity for all educators to improve current policies, programs, and practices for children and youth with chronic or persistent problem behavior. In particular, IDEA now requires that a functional assessment is used to gather information on the function or purpose of the problem behavior and the development a behavior support plan for students with an IEP who engage in chronic or persistent problem behavior and may need a change of placement due to their behavior. IDEA mandates that the functional assessment is central to the identification and implementation of positive behavioral interventions and supports for the student of concern (Quinn et al., 2000). Tilly et al. (1998) write that this requirement provides the team with useful information, including why the student engages in persistent problem behavior, when the student is least and most likely to engage in the behavior, and summary statements that guide the team as it collaboratively develops strategies that can be used to teach the student more appropriate responses as part of their comprehensive plan of behavior support (Sugai & Horner, 1994). Finally, consideration should be given to having all critical stakeholders involved in the assessment and intervention planning process. This is frequently referred to as "contextual fit" (Albin et al., 1996) and has been implicated as a critical component for improving fidelity of implementation. Including the student in the assessment and intervention planning process may increase self-determination skills, support participatory decision making (Martin, Marshall, & De Pry, 2005) and offer unique and relevant insights that may not be readily apparent to the team without the help and participation of the student (Scheuermann & Hall, 2012).

REFERENCES

Alberto, P. A., & Troutman, A. C. (2009). *Applied behavior analysis for teachers* (8th ed.). Upper Saddle River, NJ: Pearson.

Albin, R. W., Lucyshyn, J. M., Horner, R. H., & Flannery, K. B. (1996). Contextual fit for behavioral support plans: A model for "goodness of fit." In L. K. Koegel, R. L. Koegel, & G. Dunlap (Eds.), *Positive behavioral support: Including people with difficult behavior in the community* (pp. 81–98). Baltimore, MD: Paul H. Brookes.

Bijou, S. W., Peterson, R. F., & Ault, M. H. (1968). A method to integrate descriptive and experimental field studies at the level of data and empirical concepts. *Journal of Applied Behavior Analysis, 1,* 175–191.

Blakeslee, T., Sugai, G., & Gruba, J. (1994). A review of functional assessment use in data-based intervention studies. *Journal of Behavioral Education, 4,* 397–413.

Chandler, L. K., & Dahlquist, C. M. (2010). *Functional assessment: Strategies to prevent and remediate challenging behavior in school settings* (3rd ed.). Upper Saddle River, NJ: Merrill.

Cooper, J. O., Heron, T. E., & Heward, W. L. (2007). *Applied behavior analysis* (2nd ed.). Upper Saddle River, NJ: Pearson Prentice Hall.

Crone, D. A., & Horner, R. H. (2003). *Building positive behavior support systems in schools.* New York, NY: Guilford Press.

Durand, V. M., & Crimmins, D. (1988). Identifying variables maintaining self-injurious behavior. *Journal of Autism and Developmental Disorders, 18,* 99–117.

Lewis, T. J., Scott, T. M., & Sugai, G. (1994). The problem behavior questionnaire: A teacher-based instrument to develop functional hypotheses of problem behavior in general education settings. *Diagnostique, 19,* 103–115.

Kern, L., Dunlap, G., Clarke, S., & Childs, K. E. (1994). Student-assisted functional assessment interview. *Diagnostique, 19,* 29–39.

Martin, J. E., Marshall, L. H., & De Pry, R. L. (2008). Participatory decision-making: Innovative practices that increase student self-determination. In R. W. Flexer, T. J. Simmons, P. Luft, & R. Baer (Eds.), *Transition planning for secondary students with disabilities* (3rd ed., pp. 340–366). Columbus, OH: Merrill.

March, R. E., Horner, R. H., Lewis-Palmer, T., Brown, D., Crone, D. A., Todd, A. W., & Carr, E. G. (2000). *Functional Assessment Checklist for Teachers and Staff (FACTS).* Eugene: University of Oregon.

O'Neill, R. E., Horner, R. H., Albin, R. W., Sprague, J. R., Storey, K., & Newton, J. S. (1997). *Functional assessment and program development for problem behavior: A practical handbook* (2nd ed.). Pacific Grove, CA: Brooks/Cole.

Quinn, M. M., Osher, D., Warger, C. L., Hanley, T. V., Bader, B. D., & Hoffman, C. C. (2000). *Teaching and working with children who have emotional and behavioral challenges.* Longmont, CO: Sopris West Educational Services.

Scheuermann, B. K., & Hall, J. A. (2012). *Positive behavioral support for the classroom* (2nd ed.). Boston, MA: Pearson.

Sugai, G., & Horner, R. (1994). Including students with severe behavior problems in general education settings: Assumptions, challenges, and solutions. In J. Marr, G. Sugai, & G. Tindal (Eds.), *The Oregon Conference Monograph* (pp. 102–120). Eugene: University of Oregon.

Sugai, G., Horner, R. H., Dunlap, G., Hieneman, M., Lewis, T. J., Nelson, C. M., . . . Wilcox, B. (2000). Applying positive behavior support and functional behavioral assessment in schools. *Journal of Positive Behavior Interventions, 2,* 131–143.

Tilly, W. D., III, Kovaleski, J., Dunlap, G., Knoster, T. P., Bambara, L., & Kincaid, D. (1998). *Functional behavioral assessment: Policy development in light of emerging research and practice.* Alexandria, VA: National Association of State Directors of Special Education.

Wolery, M., Bailey, D., Jr., & Sugai, G. (1988). *Effective teaching: Principles and procedures of applied behavior analysis with exceptional students.* Boston, MA: Allyn & Bacon.

RANDALL L. DE PRY
Portland State University

See also Applied Behavior Analysis; Behavioral Assessment; Functional Analysis

FUNCTIONAL CENTERS HYPOTHESIS

The functional centers hypothesis, the Soviet view of learning disorders expounded by and associated primarily with Vygotsky and Luria, was further investigated and supported by other researchers in the Soviet Union (Holowinsky, 1976). It is based on Pavlovian psychology and on the dialectical-materialistic interpretation of human behavior: behavior, that is, on the elementary and higher levels, the product of phylogenetic, ontogenetic, and sociohistorical influences.

Central to the understanding of the hypothesis is the notion that an individual's mental functions (i.e., attention, memory, perception, thinking) are not only adaptive and acquired, but also are localized in and mediated by areas of cerebral cortex centers. Speech problems, language disorders, learning dysfunctions, and other handicaps are related to such centers but have psychoneurological etiologies. However, the functions "as complex functional systems with dynamic levels of localization in the brain" (Luria, 1980) are differentially related to various areas of the brain that are themselves highly differentiated in their structure. Mental functions are not, therefore, totally localized in particular/isolated areas of the brain (e.g., neuron, cortex), but operate as systems of functional combination centers. Localization in the Lurian brain for higher cortical function is dynamic, not static (Reynolds, 1981).

Mental functions appear in the developmental process first in elementary form as a result of natural development (determined by environmental stimulation). They then are changed primarily because of cultural development and self-regulated stimulation by the individual into a higher form (Vygotsky, 1978). Vygotsky considered voluntary control, conscious realization, social origins and nature, and mediation by psychological tools as characteristics of higher mental functioning (Wertsch, 1985). The development of speech is crucial because it provides new tools and signs that on mastery will clarify the operations of mental functioning to the individual.

Society plays a preeminent role in human development and functioning. In fact, higher mental functions (e.g., abstract thought, voluntary action) are formed during everyday activities. In a social context, they enable individuals to use a high level of organization, find new ways of regulating behavior, and establish new functional systems (Luria, 1978). Thus human beings can develop extracerebral connections and have the capacity to form numerous new functional systems and new functional centers in the cerebral cortex.

As a function is "a complex and plastic system performing a particular adaptive task and composed of a highly differentiated group of interchangeable elements" (Luria, 1980, p. 24), damage to any part of the cortical area can lead to a disintegration of the functional system. However, such a disturbance is likely to differ depending on the factors and on the role each part of the brain plays in the organization of the system during different stages of functional development (early or late).

In treating the learning disabled and mentally handicapped, the practitioner operates on the premise that a mental function may be performed by one of several intercenter connections in the functional centers. If one such connection is damaged—the damage or loss is not permanent—another system or cortical function can be trained to compensate for the deficit and take over the lost function. Thus restoring the disturbed or disorganized function is merely reorganizing that function and forming a new functional system.

REFERENCES

Holowinsky, I. Z. (1976). Functional centers hypothesis: The Soviet view of learning dysfunctions. In L. Mann & D. A. Sabatino (Eds.), *The third review of special education* (pp. 53–69). New York, NY: Grune & Stratton.

Luria, A. R. (1978). L. S. Vygotsky and the problem of functional localization. In M. Cole (Ed.), *The selected writings of A. R. Luria* (pp. 273–281). White Plains, NY: Sharpe.

Luria, A. R. (1980). *Higher cortical functions in man* (2nd ed.) (B. Haigh, Trans.). New York, NY: Basic Books. (Original work published 1962)

Reynolds, C. R. (1981). The neuropsychological basis of intelligence. In G. W. Hynd & J. E. Obrzut (Eds.), *Neuropsychological assessment and the school-aged child: Issues and procedures.* New York, NY: Grune & Stratton.

Vygotsky, L. S. (1978). *Mind in society: The development of higher mental processes.* Cambridge, MA: Harvard University Press.

Wertsch, J. V. (1985). *Vygotsky and the social formation of mind.* Cambridge, MA: Harvard University Press.

Hagop S. Pambookian
Elizabeth City, North Carolina

See also **Luria, A. R.; Theory of Activity; Zone of Proximal Development**

FUNCTIONAL COMMUNICATION TRAINING

Functional Communication Training (FCT) is an intervention approach in which individuals with problem behavior are taught specific communicative responses that undermine the necessity for future displays of their problem behavior. In illustration, consider a young girl who throws tantrums to get her mother's attention. The child would be taught specific communicative phrases (e.g., "Look what I drew!") as an alternative way of securing her mother's attention. When Mom responds to these communicative attempts, tantrums decrease. Functional Communication Training highlights an important paradox relevant to effective intervention for problem behavior, namely, that the best time to treat problem behavior is when it is not occurring. Thus, the teaching of communication skills occurs at a time when the child is calm and not displaying problem behavior. FCT is proactive in nature (i.e., focused on prevention), emphasizes an educational (i.e., skill-building) approach to behavior difficulties, and is designed to enhance an individual's quality of life. Since FCT was first introduced into the scientific literature (Carr & Durand, 1985), there have been more than 100 studies published demonstrating its efficacy and effectiveness as a method for reducing or eliminating problem behavior (Durand, 2012).

Background

The conceptual origins of FCT are ancient. Writing in 348 BC, the Greek philosopher, Plato, noted that problem behavior, such as that of a young child crying and screaming, could be viewed as a primitive form of communication. Caregivers attempt to quell the behavior by trying to guess what the child wants: "...if the child is quiet when something is offered it, she (the caregiver) thinks she has found the right thing, but the wrong if it cries and screams" (Plato, 1960, p. 174). The French philosopher, Rousseau, went one step further than Plato and suggested that teaching children to communicate verbally might ameliorate their problem behavior: "When children begin to speak, they cry less...as soon as they can say with words...why would they say it with cries?" (Rousseau, 1979, p. 77).

More recently, psycholinguists have demonstrated that children communicate long before they can speak (Bates, Camaioni, & Volterra, 1975). Protoimperatives, that is, nonverbal prelinguistic communicative forms are an effective means by which young children influence adults. Importantly, some child psychologists (Bell & Ainsworth, 1972; Brownlee & Bakeman, 1981) have suggested that protoimperatives may take the form of crying and aggression and can serve as a primitive form of communication. Taken together, the literature in philosophy, psycholinguistics, and child psychology suggests the usefulness of viewing problem behavior as a primitive form of communication that might be remediated by teaching the child more sophisticated forms of communication.

Variables Influencing the Effectiveness of FCT

Functional Equivalence

What communicative responses should be taught to maximize the likelihood of reducing problem behavior? The answer to this question is the sine qua non of effective use of FCT. Specifically, the communicative response taught should be functionally equivalent to the problem behavior that it is intended to replace (Carr, 1988; Durand, 1990). In lay language, both the communicative act and the problem behavior should serve the same purpose (i.e., have the same function) for the individual. Problem behavior can have many functions and these can be identified through a process known as functional assessment. Functional assessment involves systematically observing and/or manipulating the antecedents and consequences for problem behavior and noting which sets of these variables produce orderly changes in the level of the behavior. From such assessments, many variables (functions) have been identified. These include getting attention from others, escaping/avoiding aversive situations, terminating unwanted social interactions, enhancing access to tangible items (e.g., food, toys) or events (e.g., favorite activities), and generating desired sensory stimulation (Durand, 1990).

Functional assessment information is then used to select appropriate communicative alternatives to problem behavior. In illustration, a young boy might tantrum when his teacher makes requests (e.g., do your math work), but not when he is left alone. The tantrums cause the teacher to withdraw the math demands. This assessment information suggests that tantrums might function to help the boy to escape from an aversive situation (i.e., having to do math). In this case, the boy would be taught to request assistance (i.e., "I can't do these problems. Please

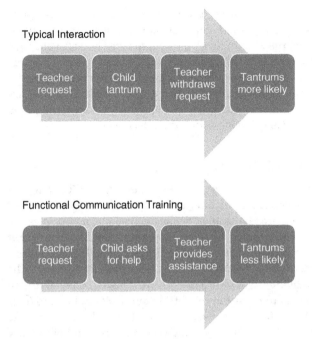

Figure F.4. An illustration of functional equivalence.

help me.") (See Figure F.4). The communicative phrase has the same function as the problem behavior—both help the child to reduce the aversiveness associated with mathematics tasks. In other words, the two responses are functionally equivalent. If a communicative phrase were taught that had a different function, for example, attention seeking (e.g., the boy was taught to say, "Look at all my nice math work"), the two responses would not be equivalent and data suggest that tantrums would likely persist (Durand & Carr, 1991, 1992). Functional equivalence is necessary for FCT to be effective (see Figure F.4).

Efficiency

Functional equivalence is a necessary but insufficient condition for FCT to succeed. It is also necessary for the communicative response to be more efficient than the problem behavior it is intended to replace. The replacement response should require less effort, provide a richer schedule of reinforcement, and pay off (i.e., be reinforced) more rapidly than the problem behavior (Fisher, Thompson, Hagopian, Bowman, & Krug, 2000; Horner & Day, 1991; Reed Schindler & Horner, 2005). Consider the earlier example of the boy who was taught to say, "I can't do these problems" in response to a math assignment. Suppose the boy had severe articulation difficulties due to cerebral palsy. It might require substantial physical effort on his part to utter the sentence. Also, if others could not understand him, then they might respond to his request rarely if at all (i.e., thin schedule of reinforcement). Finally, it might take others some time to ascertain what he was trying to communicate as they repeatedly asked him to clarify what he was trying to say. Therefore, there would be a considerable delay of reinforcement. In this situation, the communicative response is far less efficient than the problem behavior, and the problem behavior would likely persist. On the other hand, if a different, more efficient communicative response were taught (e.g., the use of a communication device to produce the sentence), then problem behavior would likely decrease.

Schedule Thinning

An important issue to address when using FCT is the reinforcement for the alternative communication being used to replace challenging behavior. Initially, a rich schedule of reinforcement is typically recommended to insure that acquisition occurs quickly (Durand, 1990). If reinforcement is delayed too long or is otherwise not sufficient, the individual will return to using challenging behavior to gain access to preferred reinforcers at an acceptable rate (e.g., escape from demands, attention from others) (Horner & Day, 1991). However, continued reinforcement of the new communicative response at high rates (e.g., every time someone makes a request can itself be viewed as problematic. Constant requests for attention, for example, can be difficult for teachers or family members to maintain, regardless of the form they take. Requesting escape from work on a continual basis can seriously interfere with educational and vocational goals.

In order to address this issue, a number of studies examined if and how the schedule of reinforcement for the appropriate communicative behavior can be reduced or "thinned" from a continuous schedule to a more intermittent one that may be more acceptable in typical settings (e.g., Hagopian, Kuhn, Long, & Rush, 2005; Hagopian, Toole, Long, Bowman, & Lieving, 2004; Hanley, Iwata, & Thompson, 2001; Lerman, Kelley, Vorndran, Kuhn, & LaRue, 2002; Shirley, Iwata, Kahng, Mazaleski, & Lerman, 1997; Volkert, Lerman, Call, & Trosclair-Lasserre, 2009; Worsdell, Iwata, Hanley, Thompson, & Kahng, 2000). In one study, for example, researchers gradually increased the time between the appropriate request and the reinforcement (Hagopian, Fisher, Sullivan, Acquisto, & LeBlanc, 1998). They found that although this attempt at schedule thinning was successful in reducing the amount of effort to respond to appropriate requests for some individuals it was not successful for all.

One difficulty with using delayed schedules of reinforcement with the alternative response is that the individual may not be able to discriminate when and if the request will be satisfied, resulting in increased requesting—a pattern typically observed with fixed interval (FI) reinforcement schedules. Some researchers have found more success using signals (e.g., red card signaling no response forthcoming, green card signaling a request will receive a response) to indicate the temporal nature of the responses (e.g., Hanley et al., 2001).

It is unlikely that one approach to schedule thinning will be appropriate for all cases when using FCT. For example, the ability of the individual to discriminate reinforcement schedules and the person's history of reinforcement will likely influence efforts to reduce the level of reinforcement for appropriate requests. At the same time, it is important to consider what the prevailing environment can support. As we discussed in the previous section on "response milieu," some environments can support relatively high rates of requests while others cannot. Research on contextual fit with regard to requests for reinforcement and the environment's ability to maintain responses should be an important next step in researching the nature of responses to appropriate requests for reinforcement in FCT.

Empirical Support

Several published reviews document the depth and breadth of research studies studying the outcomes of FCT across populations, behavior topographies as well as variations in the methods for using this approach (e.g., Bambara, Mitchellkvacky, & Iacobelli, 1994; Durand & Merges, 2008, 2009; Halle, Ostrosky, & Hemmeter, 2006; Mancil, 2006; Matson, Dixon, & Matson, 2005; Mirenda, 1997; Petscher, Rey, & Bailey, 2009). Mirenda (1997), for example, reviewed research that used augmentative and alternative communication strategies (AAC) (e.g., manual signing, communication books, voice output communication aids) as the method for communicating with FCT. Matson and colleagues (Matson et al., 2005) evaluated the literature on a number of techniques used to treat aggression and found that FCT was one of the most heavily researched approaches. Petscher, Rey, and Bailey (2009) broadly review research using differential reinforcement of alternative behavior, which includes variations of FCT. FCT is frequently cited as one of the few behavioral interventions having extensive support from initial efficacy studies (Smith et al., 2007).

Generalization and Maintenance

There is good evidence that the positive effects of FCT can transfer from the original training situation to new situations in which training has not occurred (generalization). There is also good evidence that once FCT effects have been established, they can be quite durable over time (maintenance).

With respect to generalization, Durand and Carr (1991) demonstrated that, after several teachers had successfully implemented FCT across a number of tasks and settings (a strategy known as multiple exemplar training), increases in appropriate communication as well as dramatic reductions in problem behavior were observed across new tasks, environments, and teachers. One explanation for this successful transfer of effects was that the students used their communication skills to recruit relevant reinforcers from new teachers in new situations, thereby undermining the necessity for displaying problem behavior to acquire these reinforcers in the new situations. With respect to maintenance, Durand and Carr (1991, 1992) demonstrated that reductions in problem behavior following FCT were durable and could be maintained for 18 to 24 months after introduction of the procedure.

Generality

Evidence exists that FCT has considerable generality with respect to behavioral topographies, behavioral functions, communicative forms, chronological age, applicable venues, and type of population (Durand, 2012). Clinically significant behavioral topographies that have been successfully treated include aggression, self-injury, elopement, inappropriate sexual behavior, property destruction, tantrums, self-stimulation, and noncompliance/ disruptive behavior. Major functions addressed include attention, task avoidance, social avoidance, and tangible/activity seeking. Further, although the communicative form most commonly taught has been verbal in nature (speech), FCT has also been used successfully when the form taught involved sign language, picture cards, gestures, and microswitches. Importantly, the procedure has been applied to individuals ranging in age from preschool to middle age. In addition, applicable venues have included home, school, community, and the workplace. Finally, many populations have benefited from FCT, namely, individuals exhibiting a variety of types of intellectual disability, Autism Spectrum Disorders (ASD), and Emotional and Behavioral Disorders (EBD).

Limitations

Given that the use of FCT is predicated on the assumption that problem behavior has a social-communicative function, the procedure is likely complicated when it is suspected that the behavior is being influenced by biochemical and/or neurological factors such as those involving genetics, brain dysfunction, or hormonal processes (Schroeder, Oster-Granite, & Thompson, 2002). While it is important to be aware of this potential limitation, it is equally important not to routinely assume that difficult problem behavior that has been unresponsive to prior behavioral/psychoeducational intervention is only biologically based and will therefore not respond to FCT, particularly when FCT is embedded in a multicomponent intervention.

Available Resources

The multifactorial nature of problem behavior and its treatment through FCT pose considerable assessment and intervention challenges. Table F.2 illustrates the key components used to assess behavior and conduct

Table F.2. Step-by-Step Instructions for Functional Communication Training

Steps	Description
1. Determine the function of behavior	Use two or more functional assessment measures to determine maintaining variables.
2. Determine the communication modality	Identify how the individual will communicate with others (e.g., verbally, through alternative communication strategies).
3. Create teaching situations	Determine situations in the environment that are triggers for problem behavior (e.g., difficult tasks) and use these as the settings for teaching the alternative responses.
4. Prompt communication	Prompt the alternative communication in the setting where you want it to occur. Use the least intrusive prompt necessary.
5. Fade prompts	Fade the prompts, insuring that no problem behaviors occur during training.
6. Teach new communicative responses	When possible, teach a variety of alternative communicative responses that can serve the same function (e.g., saying "Help me" or "I don't understand")
7. Environmental modification	When appropriate, changes in the environment—such as improving student-task match in school—should be implemented.

FCT. However, manuals are available to help the teacher, parent, and service provider to implement FCT in an organized, systematic, and effective manner (Carr et al., 1994; Durand, 1990). These resources, as well as the numerous references previously cited, help ensure the continued viability of this widely used strategy for dealing with serious problem behavior.

REFERENCES

Bambara, L. M., Mitchellkvacky, N. A., & Iacobelli, S. (1994). Positive behavioral support for students with severe disabilities: An emerging multicomponent approach for addressing challenging behaviors. *School Psychology Review, 23*(2), 263–278.

Bates, E., Camaioni, L., & Volterra, V. (1975). The acquisition of performatives prior to speech. *Merrill-Palmer Quarterly, 21*(3), 205–226.

Bell, S. M., & Ainsworth, M. D. S. (1972). Infant crying and maternal responsiveness. *Child Development, 43*(4), 1171–1190. doi: 10.2307/1127506

Brownlee, J. R., & Bakeman, R. (1981). Hitting in toddler-peer interaction. *Child Development, 52*(3), 1076–1079. doi: 10.2307/1129115

Carr, E. G. (1988). Functional equivalence as a mechanism of response generalization. In R. H. Horner, G. Dunlap, & R. L. Koegel (Eds.), *Generalization and maintenance: Lifestyle changes in applied settings* (pp. 194–219). Baltimore, MD: Paul H. Brookes.

Carr, E. G., & Durand, V. M. (1985). Reducing behavior problems through functional communication training. *Journal of Applied Behavior Analysis, 18*(2), 111–126. doi: 10.1901/jaba.1985.18-111

Carr, E. G., Levin, L., McConnachie, G., Carlson, J. I., Kemp, D. C., & Smith, C. E. (1994). *Communication-based intervention for problem behavior: A user's guide for producing positive change.* Baltimore, MD: Paul H. Brookes.

Durand, V. M. (1990). *Severe behavior problems: A functional communication training approach.* New York, NY: Guilford Press.

Durand, V. M. (2012). Functional communication training to reduce challenging behavior. In P. Prelock & R. McCauley (Eds.), *Treatment of autism spectrum disorders: Evidence-based intervention strategies for communication & social interaction.* Baltimore, MD: Paul H. Brookes.

Durand, V. M., & Carr, E. G. (1991). Functional communication training to reduce challenging behavior: Maintenance and application in new settings. *Journal of Applied Behavior Analysis, 24*(2), 251–264.

Durand, V. M., & Carr, E. G. (1992). An analysis of maintenance following functional communication training. *Journal of Applied Behavior Analysis, 25*(4), 777–794. doi: 10.1901/jaba.1992.25-777

Durand, V. M., & Merges, E. (2008). Functional communication training to treat challenging behavior. In W. O'Donohue & J. E. Fisher (Eds.), *Cognitive behavior therapy: Applying empirically supported techniques in your practice* (2nd ed., pp. 222–229). Hoboken, NJ: Wiley.

Durand, V. M., & Merges, E. (2009). Functional communication training to treat challenging behavior. In W. O'Donohue & J. E. Fisher (Eds.), *General principles and empirically supported techniques of cognitive behavior therapy* (pp. 320–327). Hoboken, NJ: Wiley.

Fisher, W. W., Thompson, R. H., Hagopian, L. P., Bowman, L. G., & Krug, A. (2000). Facilitating tolerance of delayed reinforcement during functional communication training. *Behavior Modification, 24*(1), 3–29.

Hagopian, L. P., Fisher, W. W., Sullivan, M. T., Acquisto, J., & LeBlanc, L. A. (1998). Effectiveness of functional communication training with and without extinction and punishment: A summary of 21 inpatient cases. *Journal of Applied Behavior Analysis, 31*(2), 211–235.

Hagopian, L. P., Kuhn, S. A. C., Long, E. S., & Rush, K. S. (2005). Schedule thinning following communication training using competing stimuli to enhance tolerance to decrements in reinforcer density. *Journal of Applied Behavior Analysis, 38*(2), 177–193.

Hagopian, L. P., Toole, L. M., Long, E. S., Bowman, L. G., & Lieving, G. A. (2004). A comparison of dense-to-lean and fixed lean schedules of alternative reinforcement and extinction. *Journal of Applied Behavior Analysis, 37*(3), 323–338.

Halle, J. W., Ostrosky, M. M., & Hemmeter, M. L. (2006). Functional communication training: A strategy for ameliorating challenging behavior. In R. J. McCauley & M. E. Fey (Eds.), *Treatment of language disorders in children* (pp. 509–548). Baltimore, MD: Paul H. Brookes.

Hanley, G. P., Iwata, B. A., & Thompson, R. H. (2001). Reinforcement schedule thinning following treatment with functional communication training. *Journal of Applied Behavior Analysis, 34*(1), 17–38.

Horner, R. H., & Day, H. M. (1991). The effects of response efficiency on functionally equivalent competing behaviors. *Journal of Applied Behavior Analysis, 24*(4), 719–732.

Lerman, D. C., Kelley, M. E., Vorndran, C. M., Kuhn, S. A. C., & LaRue, R. H. (2002). Reinforcement magnitude and responding during treatment with differential reinforcement. *Journal of Applied Behavior Analysis, 35*(1), 29–48.

Mancil, G. R. (2006). Functional communication training: A review of the literature related to children with autism. *Education and Training in Developmental Disabilities, 41*(3), 213–224.

Matson, J. L., Dixon, D. R., & Matson, M. L. (2005). Assessing and treating aggression in children and adolescents with developmental disabilities: A 20-year overview. *Educational Psychology, 25*(2), 151–181.

Mirenda, P. (1997). Supporting individuals with challenging behavior through functional communication training and AAC: Research review. *AAC: Augmentative and Alternative Communication, 13*, 207–225.

Petscher, E. S., Rey, C., & Bailey, J. S. (2009). A review of empirical support for differential reinforcement of alternative behavior. *Research in Developmental Disabilities, 30*(3), 409–425.

Plato. (1960). *The laws* (A. E. Taylor, Trans.). London: J.M. Dent. (Original work published circa 348 B.C.)

Reed Schindler, H., & Horner, R. H. (2005). Generalized reduction of problem behavior of young children with autism: Building trans-situational interventions. *American Journal on Mental Retardation, 110*(1), 36–47.

Rousseau, J. J. (1979). *Emile* (A. Bloom, Trans.). New York, NY: Basic Books. (Original work published 1762)

Schroeder, S. R., Oster-Granite, M. L., & Thompson, T. (Eds.). (2002). *Self-injurious behavior: Gene-brain-behavior relationships.* Washington, DC: American Psychological Association.

Shirley, M. J., Iwata, B. A., Kahng, S. W., Mazaleski, J. L., & Lerman, D. C. (1997). Does functional communication training compete with ongoing contingencies of reinforcement? An analysis during response acquisition and maintenance. *Journal of Applied Behavior Analysis, 30*(1), 93–104.

Smith, T., Scahill, L., Dawson, G., Guthrie, D., Lord, C., Odom, S., . . . Wagner, A. (2007). Designing research studies on psychosocial interventions in autism. *Journal of Autism and Developmental Disorders, 37*(2), 354–366.

Volkert, V. M., Lerman, D. C., Call, N. A., & Trosclair-Lasserre, N. (2009). An evaluation of resurgence during treatment with functional communication training. *Journal of Applied Behavior Analysis, 42*(1), 145–160. doi: 10.1901/jaba.2009 .42-145

Worsdell, A. S., Iwata, B. A., Hanley, G. P., Thompson, R. H., & Kahng, S. W. (2000). Effects of continuous and intermittent reinforcement for problem behavior during functional communication training. *Journal of Applied Behavior Analysis, 33*(2), 167–179.

V. Mark Durand
University of South Florida

Jamie Bleiweiss
Hunter College

See also **Behavioral Assessment; Positive Behavioral Support**

FUNCTIONAL DOMAINS

Educators, psychologists, and other health professionals will often assess and describe a child's performance in a number of areas, called functional domains, in addition to describing the child's overall performance and development in a global fashion. Theoretically, an assessment of the child's strengths and weaknesses in the various domains gives a snapshot of the child's functional status or the child's performance and ability to do things most other children do. Functional status is closely related to the concept of health status in the health field (Starfield, 1974; Stein & Jessop, 1984) and to the concept of social competence in the early childhood field (Zigler & Trickett, 1978).

Although typologies for the number and name of the functional domains vary, they generally are divided into four major areas: physical, cognitive, social, and emotional. Sometimes, the social and emotional areas are considered together and called psychological or mental health. The key to assessments in all functional domains is that behavior should be seen in a developmental context or framework so that the dynamic qualities of a child's development are considered (Walker, Richmond, & Buka, 1984).

Examples of behaviors or constructs that might be assessed under each functional domain are the physical (height and weight, activities of daily living); cognitive (intelligence, learning style); social (peer relationships, leadership skills); and emotional (self-concept, depression).

Because the measurements of these domains have been shown to be distinct, it is strongly recommended that researchers and practitioners do not try to combine the individual functional domain measures into an overall index or measure score (Eisen, Donald, Ware, & Brook, 1980). Instead, a profile approach to the child's performance and functioning in terms of his or her strengths and liabilities in the various functional areas is preferred

(Starfield, 1974). Assessments of a child's performance in various functional domain areas are much easier to translate directly into educational and other service programs for the individual child than more generic global index scores. This profile or multidimensional approach is recommended for both individual and group or population descriptions.

REFERENCES

Eisen, M., Donald, C. A., Ware, J. E., & Brook, R. H. (1980). *Conceptualization and measurement of health for children in the health insurance study.* Santa Monica, CA: Rand.

Starfield, B. (1974). Measurement of outcome: A proposed scheme. *Millbank Memorial Fund Quarterly, 52,* 39–50.

Stein, R. E. K., & Jessop, D. J. (1984). Assessing the functional status of children. In D. K. Walker & J. B. Richmond (Eds.), *Monitoring child health in the United States.* Cambridge, MA: Harvard University Press.

Walker, D. K., Richmond, J. B., & Buka, S. L. (1984). Summary and recommendations for next steps. In D. K. Walker & J. B. Richmond (Eds.), *Monitoring child health in the United States.* Cambridge, MA: Harvard University Press.

Zigler, E. F., & Trickett, D. K. (1978). IQ, social competence and evaluation of early childhood intervention programs. *American Psychologist, 33,* 789–798.

Deborah Klein Walker
Harvard University

See also **Adaptive Behavior; Intelligence; Mental Status Exams**

FUNCTIONAL EQUIVALENCE

Functional equivalence has been defined and used in a variety of ways in fields such as psychology and general and special education (Sidman, 1994). This entry discusses the term as it is used in relation to problem behaviors of students with disabilities (Horner & Billingsley, 1988).

The term is typically used in reference to situations in which students are exhibiting problem behaviors, including aggression toward others, self-injurious behavior (e.g., head-hitting), destruction of materials, and other disruptive behaviors (e.g., talking out in the classroom). Over the last several decades, a variety of successful approaches has been developed for intervening in such situations (Scotti & Meyer, 1999). One such approach involves teaching and/or prompting a student to engage in a desired appropriate behavior that is *functionally equivalent* to the problem behavior (Carr, 1988). This means that the appropriate behavior allows the student to access the same outcomes that are reinforcing and maintaining the problem behaviors. Another way to say this is that both the problem and appropriate behaviors can serve the same *function* for the student with regard to accessing the desired outcome (e.g., to get social attention or to escape from an undesired task or activity). From a more technical perspective, one can say that both the problem and appropriate behaviors become part of the same *response class* (Horner & Day, 1990). A response class is a group of behaviors that may differ in how they are performed, but result in the same outcome (e.g., a student can either throw a tantrum or raise their hand to recruit social attention from an adult).

This approach for reducing or eliminating problem behaviors by teaching and/or prompting functionally equivalent behaviors has been referred to by a variety of terms, including functional equivalence training (Horner et al., 1990), differential reinforcement of communication (DRC; Wacker & Steege, 1993), and most frequently, functional communication training (FCT; Carr & Durand, 1985; Durand, 1990). Other terms that have been used in the literature include teaching *alternative* or *replacement* behaviors. The FCT process involves two main steps. First, a functional behavioral assessment (FBA) must be carried out to determine the variables that are (a) triggering and (b) reinforcing and maintaining the problem behaviors (O'Neill et al., 1997). Second, a functionally equivalent appropriate behavior is taught to the student that s/he can use to obtain the same reinforcing outcomes as the problem behavior. (Note: If the desired alternative response is already in the student's repertoire the process becomes more a matter of prompting the student about when and where to exhibit the behavior, versus teaching an entirely new response.) The goal is for the desired alternative response to become functionally equivalent to the problem behavior, and thereby successfully compete with and replace it.

A brief example will illustrate this approach. Horner, Sprague, O'Brien, and Heathfield (1990) reported a study involving David, a 14-year-old student with physical disabilities who had been labeled as having moderate mental retardation. David did not use speech, and his physical limitations made manual signing difficult. He used a Canon Communicator device to type out messages to communicate his wants and needs. However, he often had difficulty manipulating the keys on the device. During difficult task activities he would often become agitated and begin yelling, hitting, or kicking, and tipping over tables and chairs. The teaching staff, working with the researchers, decided to program David's Communicator so that touching a single button would produce the message "Help please." David was taught to use this highly efficient response when he was engaged in difficult tasks for which he required assistance. The data reported demonstrated that he quickly learned to use the desired response to request help, and as a result his aggressive and disruptive behavior very rarely occurred.

Much of the research on and application of FCT has involved teaching social communicative responses as alternatives to problem behaviors, as illustrated in the example described above. This research has demonstrated that appropriate communicative behaviors (e.g., speech, sign language) can successfully compete with and serve as *functionally equivalent* alternatives to problem behaviors (Carr et al., 1994; Halle, Bambara, & Reichle, 2005). This approach to reducing or eliminating problem behaviors has been a main component of an overall approach referred to as *positive behavioral support* (PBS; Bambara, Dunlap, & Schwartz, 2004).

REFERENCES

Bambara, L. M., Dunlap, G., & Schwartz, I. (Eds.). (2004). *Positive behavior support: Critical articles on improving practice for individuals with severe disabilities*. Austin, TX: PRO-ED.

Carr, E. G. (1988). Functional equivalence as a mechanism of response generalization. In R. H. Horner, G. Dunlap, & R. L. Koegel (Eds.), *Generalization and maintenance: Lifestyle changes in applied settings* (pp. 221–241). Baltimore, MD: Paul H. Brookes.

Carr, E. G., & Durand, V. M. (1985). Reducing behavior problems through functional communication training. *Journal of Applied Behavior Analysis, 18*, 111–126.

Carr, E. G., Levin, L., McConnachie, G., Carlson, J. I., Kemp, D. C., & Smith, C. E. (1994). *Communication-based intervention for problem behavior: A user's guide for producing positive change*. Baltimore, MD: Paul H. Brookes.

Durand, V. M. (1990). *Functional communication training: An intervention program for severe behavior problems*. New York, NY: Guilford Press.

Halle, J. W., Bambara, L. M., & Reichle, J. (2005). Teaching alternative skills. In L. M. Bambara & L. Kern (Eds.), *Individualized supports for students with problem behaviors: Designing positive behavior plans* (pp. 237–274). New York, NY: Guilford Press.

Horner, R. H., & Billingsley, F. F. (1988). The effect of competing behavior on the generalization and maintenance of adaptive behavior in applied settings. In R. H. Horner, G. Dunlap, & R. L. Koegel (Eds.), *Generalization and maintenance: Life-style changes in applied settings* (pp. 197–220). Baltimore, MD: Paul H. Brookes.

Horner, R. H., & Day, H. M. (1990). The effects of response efficiency on functionally equivalent competing behaviors. *Journal of Applied Behavior Analysis, 24*, 719–732.

Horner, R. H., Sprague, J. R., O'Brien, M., & Heathfield, L. T. (1990). The role of response efficiency in the reduction of problem behaviors through functional equivalence training: A case study. *Journal of the Association for Persons with Severe Handicaps, 15*, 91–97.

O'Neill, R. E., Horner, R. H., Albin, R. W., Storey, K., Sprague, J. R., & Newton, J. S. (1997). *Functional assessment and program development for problem behavior: A practical handbook* (2nd ed.). Belmont, CA: Wadsworth.

Scotti, J. R., & Meyer, L. (Eds.). (1999). *Behavioral intervention: Principles, models, and practices.* Baltimore, MD: Paul H. Brookes.

Sidman, M. (1994). *Equivalence relations: A research story.* Boston, MA: Author's Cooperative.

Wacker, D. P., & Steege, M. W. (1993). Providing outclinic services: Evaluating treatment and social validity. In R. Van Houten & S. Axelrod (Eds.), *Behavior analysis and treatment* (pp. 297–319). New York, NY: Plenum Press.

ROBERT O'NEILL
University of Utah

See also **Behavioral Assessment; Positive Behavioral Support**

FUNCTIONAL INSTRUCTION

Functional instruction refers to the use of activities and materials that involve skills of immediate usefulness to students as well as the employment of teaching materials that use real rather than simulated materials (Bouck, 2008). For example, a student could be taught to increase fine motor skills by assembling vocational products from local industry rather than by placing pegs in a board or stringing beads. Or a student could be required to place one cup at each place setting as opposed to placing one chip on each colored circle in an effort to teach one-to-one correspondence.

There are several reasons to support the use of functional instruction techniques, especially when considering the needs of students with severe disabilities. First, the use of artificial materials and settings may fail to prepare students for the skills they will need to perform practical tasks in natural settings (Ayres, Douglas, Lowrey, & Sievers, 2011). One cannot make any inferences about the ability of students with severe disabilities to generalize skills taught in simulated settings or with artificial materials to natural environments where these skills will be needed. Second, the actions required to do artificial tasks or use artificial materials may have little or no relation to the actions required in natural settings. For instance, labeling of plastic fruit and placing it in a small plastic shopping cart to be wheeled around the classroom may not prepare students for locating, selecting, bagging, and purchasing fruit in a local supermarket. Third, since the focus of education for students with severe disabilities is on preparing them to function in heterogeneous adult environments, instruction should occur in community-based (natural) settings (Miller & Thompson, 2005). It is only through instruction in such authentic settings that students will learn to attend to and respond to the myriad of activities of individuals without disabilities in such settings. In addition, instruction in community sites will enable students to discriminate among a variety of novel stimuli found in natural environments (Bouck, 2009).

The proliferation of nonfunctional activities in classrooms can be traced to several possible origins. First, the large amount of commercial material that has appeared on the market has significantly influenced the teaching of pupils with severe disabilities. These commercially made materials are not always directly related to materials and activities that will be required by students in natural environments. Second, some educators believe that traditional nonfunctional activities (e.g., pegs in boards, stacking rings on post) are necessary for the student's readiness for more complex activities. Such a philosophy perpetuates the acquisition of isolated skills that have little correlation with skills needed in natural settings in adulthood (Ayres, Douglas, Lowrey, & Sievers, 2011). Unlike individuals without disabilities, individuals with severe disabilities may not generalize skills taught in nonfunctional readiness activities to those needed in natural environments (Tekin-Iftar, 2008). Only with direct instruction of functional skills using authentic materials will students with severe disabilities be able to exhibit competence in nonschool (community) or postschool settings.

The use of functional materials and instruction involves the examination of individual needs in current and future environments. An ecological inventory or ecological assessment can be conducted to determine individual student needs (Baine, Puhan, Puhan, & Puhan, 2000). By looking at aspects of the student's current environments (e.g., home, school, vocational site) and his or her future environments (e.g., group home, community recreation facility, vocational site), one can determine which skills will enable that student to function independently. By further breaking down current and future environments into subenvironments (e.g., group home: bathroom, living room, bedroom) and determining what activities are necessary in those subenvironments, one can determine the types of functional materials to be used during instruction. Careful consultation with parents or guardians as well as staff at future residential sites is also needed to ensure the functionality of skills targeted for instruction during the school years.

REFERENCES

Ayres, K. M., Douglas, K. H., Lowrey, K., & Sievers, C. (2011). I can identify Saturn but I can't brush my teeth: What happens when the curricular focus for students with severe disabilities shifts. *Education and Training in Autism and Developmental Disabilities, 46*(1), 11–21.

Baine, D., Puhan, B., Puhan, G., & Puhan, S. (2000). An ecological inventory approach to developing curricula for rural areas of developing countries. *International Review of Education / Internationale Zeitschrift Fuer Erziehungswissenschaft / Revue Internationale De L'education, 46*(1–2), 49–66.

Bouck, E. C. (2008). Factors impacting the enactment of a functional curriculum in self-contained cross-categorical programs. *Education and Training in Developmental Disabilities, 43*(3), 294–310.

Bouck, E. C. (2009). Functional curriculum models for secondary students with mild mental impairment. *Education and Training in Developmental Disabilities, 44*(4), 435–443.

Miller, J., & Thompson, E. M. (2005). Prevocational services: A resource for enhancing a functional academic curriculum. *RE:View: Rehabilitation Education for Blindness and Visual Impairment, 37*(1), 42.

Tekin-Iftar, E. (2008). Parent-delivered community-based instruction with simultaneous prompting for teaching community skills to children with developmental disabilities. *Education and Training in Developmental Disabilities, 43*(2), 249–265.

CORNELIA L. IZEN
George Mason University

DAVID LOJKOVIC
George Mason University

FUNCTIONAL MRI

Functional MRI (fMRI) is a well-established neuroimaging technique that uses the same equipment as conventional MRI. Functional MRI relies on detecting small changes in the signals used to produce magnetic resonance images that are associated with neuronal activity in the brain. It produces unique and valuable information for applications in both basic and clinical neuroscience. Functional MRI is safe, nonevasive and repeatable in adults and children and thus has widespread potential uses. Functional MRI is a technique for determining which parts of the brain are activated by different types of physical sensation or activity such as sight, sound or tactile response. It is achieved by setting up an advanced MRI scanner in a special way so that increased blood flow to the activated areas of the brain show up on fMRI scans (Gore, 2003).

Functional MRI detects the blood oxygen level–dependent (BOLD) changes in the MRI signal that arises when changes in neuronal activity occur following a change in brain states such as may be produced by a stimulus or task. One of the underlying premises of many current uses of functional imaging is that various behaviors and brain functions rely on the recruitment and coordinated interaction of components of "large scale" brain systems that are spatially distinct, distributed and yet connected in functional networks (Gore, 2003).

Functional MRI has found applications in both clinical and more basic neuroscience. Appropriate experiments may now be designed to address specific hypotheses regarding the nature of distributed systems responsible for various functional responses. For clinical applications, simple mapping of critical sensory and motor functions can be readily performed by subjects lying in the bore of a magnet where they perform simple tasks or experience sensory stimuli in blocks. This is the primary approach for evaluation of the brains of patients prior to neurosurgery or radiation therapy. Standard protocols have been developed at many sites that permit efficient mapping of auditory, visual, motor, and language areas to inform surgeons of the positions of critical functional areas. Functional MRI data can readily be integrated with image guided neurosurgical procedures (Schlosser, Aoyagi, Fulbright, Gore, & McCarthy, 1998).

Functional MRI has several limitations. The use of fast imaging reduces the spatial resolution to a few millimeters, somewhat worse than conventional MRI. The BOLD effect is small and thus the sensitivity is limited so that fMRI experiments require multiple samplings of brain responses. Temporal resolution is poor and the reliability is reduced when there is significant subject motion or physiologically related variations (Gore, 2003).

REFERENCES

Gore, J. C. (2003). Principles and practice of functional MRI of the human brain. *Journal of Clinical Investigation, 112*, 4–9.

Schlosser, M., Aoyagi, N., Fulbright, R. K., Gore, J. C., & McCarthy, G. (1998). Functional MRI studies of auditory comprehension. *Human Brain Mapping, 6*, 1–13.

RICHARD RIDER
University of Utah

See also **Biofeedback; Diffusion Tensor Imaging; Magnetic Resonance Imaging; SPECT**

FUNCTIONAL SKILLS TRAININGS

Functional skills are generally considered to be those skills and competencies that often require problem-solving skills. Functional skills are often relatively simple for many people, such as counting change from a basic purchase, reading the sign for a restroom in an unfamiliar location, or realizing when to walk across an unfamiliar intersection, but can often be complicated and involve the balancing of a checkbook, the completion of an application for employment, or comparative shopping. Many students without disabilities are able to acquire functional skills either within educational environments, through incidental learning or direct instruction. Children with disabilities often acquire functional skill competencies through incidental learning in his or her environment, but acquired skills may not generalize to classroom learning and everyday situations out of the formal learning situation. Teachers recently reported they less frequently teach problem-solving skills often required in functional skill acquirement for students with disabilities than do teachers of typically developing children (Argan, Blanchard, Hughes, & Wehmeyer, 2002).

Techniques for instruction of functional skills within the special education classroom will vary depending on the significance of the disability for each student. With the increase in awareness of students identified with disabilities and the importance of acquiring functional skills for postsecondary employment and education, schools are now required to develop specific IEP goals to address specific functional skills required after graduation, Since all students are required to complete work on their enrolled grade level, accommodations and modifications are developed to help students with disabilities progress through the general education curriculum.

REFERENCE

Agran, M., Blanchard, C., Hughes, C., & Wehmeyer, M. L. (2002). Increasing the problemsolving skills of students with severe disabilities participating in general education. *Remedial Special Education 23*, 279–288.

JAMES H. MILLER
JOHN F. CAWLEY
University of New Orleans

See *also* Functional Domains; Functional Vocabulary

FUNCTIONAL VISION

Functional vision is associated with the name of Natalie Barraga, a pioneer figure in emphasizing the importance of helping children with severe visual limitations to use their residual visual abilities as effectively as possible (Barraga, 1964, 1970, 1976, 1980). Functional vision, as defined by Barraga (1976, p. 15) denotes "how a person uses whatever vision he may have." Vision is functional if a child is able to utilize visual information to plan and carry out a task (Topor, 2006).

The federal regulations for IDEA have defined visual disabilities for school purposes so that the consideration of functional vision is primary. As defined in that law, "Visually handicapped means a visual impairment which, even with correction, adversely affects a child's educational performance." Thus the concept of functional vision is one that emphasizes what the visually impaired child can do, rather than a particular type of physical visual limitation.

A functional vision assessment of children with visual problems attempts to determine how well a visually handicapped student is able to use the visual abilities and skills he or she possesses (Livingston, 1986). It usually involves the use of informal checklists that professionals working with the visually handicapped (e.g., teachers of visually impaired students, low-vision specialists, optometrists, orientation and mobility specialists) are asked to complete as per their particular observations. These assessments can be affected or influenced by the child's visual acuity, visual field, control of eye movements, lighting, color, contrast, the age of onset of the low vision, intelligence, and etiology of the low vision.

The California Ad Hoc Committee on Assessment (Roessing, 1982) developed a comprehensive criterion-referenced checklist for functional vision assessment. This covered the skills required for activities of daily living within a school setting, mobility, and academics. Barraga (1983) developed the Program to Develop Efficiency in Visual Functioning, which provided an observational checklist and a diagnostic assessment procedure (DAP) for the developmental assessment of a wide range of visual skills. She also provided lesson plans to develop visual efficiencies.

The Low Vision Online website (LVO; 2006) cites seven areas of functional vision, based on Barraga's research, that should be assessed: (1) awareness and attention to objects; (2) control of eye movements—tracking; (3) control of eye movements—scanning; (4) discrimination of objects; (5) discrimination of details to identify actions and match objects; (6) discrimination of details in picture; and (7) identification and perception of patterns, numbers, and words.

Children with multiple disabilities require specialized assessment, therefore a number of functional vision assessment devices have been created to meet their needs. Among them is Langley's (1980) Functional Vision Inventory for the Multiply and Severely Handicapped.

REFERENCES

Barraga, N. C. (1964). *Increased visual behavior in low vision children.* New York, NY: American Foundation for the Blind.

Barraga, N. C. (1970). *Teacher's guide for development of visual learning abilities and utilization of low vision.* Louisville, KY: American Printing House for the Blind.

Barraga, N. C. (1976). *Visual handicaps and learning: A developmental approach.* Belmont, CA: Wadsworth.

Barraga, N. C. (1980). *Source book on low vision.* Louisville, KY: American Printing House for the Blind.

Barraga, N. C. (1983). *Visual handicaps and learning.* Austin, TX: Exceptional Resources.

Langley, M. B. (1980). *Functional vision inventory for the multiply and severely handicapped.* Chicago, IL: Stoelting.

Livingston, R. (1986). Visual impairments. In N. G. Haring & L. McCormick (Eds.), *Exceptional children and youth* (4th ed., pp. 398–429). Columbus, OH: Merrill.

Low Vision Online. (2006). Low vision assessment. Retrieved from http://www.lowvisiononline.unimelb.edu.au

Roessing, L. J. (1982). Functional vision: Criterion-referenced checklists. In S. S. Mangold (Ed.), *A teacher's guide to the special educational needs of blind and visually handicapped children*. New York, NY: American Foundation for the Blind.

Topor, I. (2006). Fact sheet functional vision assessment. Retrieved from http://www.cde.state.co.us

JANET S. BRAND
Hunter College, City University of New York

See also Individuals With Disabilities Education Improvement Act of 2004 (IDEIA); Visual Impairment

FUNCTIONAL VOCABULARY

The development of functional reading vocabularies acquired significance as a result of the realization that the acquisition of functional academic skills was the upper limit of academic achievement for persons with moderate to severe retardation (Gearheart & Litton, 1975). Prior to the time of that realization (late 1950s and 1960s) many curricula for retarded individuals, although watered down, were not designed for functionality.

The content of an appropriate functional vocabulary (whether reading or speaking) is determined by analyzing the current and expected environmental demands for the student. Factors that influence the content include the age of the student, the degree of mobility independence the student has, the expected adult environment (e.g., sheltered workshop, competitive employment, custodial care), and the student's likes and dislikes. According to Musselwhite and St. Louis (1982), functional vocabulary content for severely disabled persons should be based on client preferences and should be in the here and now rather than the future or past directed. They should also be words that occur with frequency. Many writers (Baroff, 1974; Holland, 1975; Lichtman, 1974; Schilit & Caldwell, 1980; Snell, 1983) have attempted to develop core functional lexicons or lists of sources for such lexicons. However, most researchers (including the mentioned writers) would agree that for a vocabulary to be truly functional, it must be based on an individual's experience and not on assumed common experience.

Bricker (1983) states that vocabulary instruction for children with moderate and severe retardation must involve the primary caregiver (usually a parent). Instruction must involve association with an object, the client's use of the object, and word recognition in context.

Guess, Sailor, and Baer (1978) provide support and extension for Bricker's statement. Functional words must be used consistently and frequently by all persons in the child's environment if they are to be learned (Musselwhite & St. Louis, 1982). According to Guess et al. (1978) and Bricker (1983), it is important to teach a child words that allow him or her to gain a degree of control over the environment, as these words are likely to lead to reinforcing consequences.

The content of a functional reading vocabulary for an individual is likely to change considerably over time. For elementary-school-aged children, the content is usually aimed at warning signs and survival (e.g., danger, stop, men, women), whereas at the secondary and adult level, the content will include words associated with work, travel, and money management (Baroff, 1974; Drew, Logan, & Hardman, 1984). Sources for functional reading vocabularies include newspapers, street signs, price tags, job applications, recipes, telephone directories, and bank forms. Schilit and Caldwell (1980) produced a list of the 100 most essential career/vocational words, but Brown and Perlmutter (1971) contend that such lists are ineffective since they often do not match the experiences of individual clients.

Although most persons with mental retardation are severely limited with regard to reading, a number of researchers have been able to demonstrate that instruction based on a whole word/task analysis approach is effective (Brown et al., 1974; Sidman & Cresson, 1973). Any functional reading vocabulary should be taught in context. Snell (1983) offers an example of a pedestrian skills program during which students would take walks and read *walk, don't walk,* and *stop* signs. Brown et al. (1974) suggest a similar approach.

REFERENCES

Baroff, G. A. (1974). *Mental retardation: Nature, cause and management*. New York, NY: Holsted.

Bricker, D. (1983). Early communication: Development and training. In M. E. Snell (Ed.), *Systematic instruction of the moderately and severely handicapped* (pp. 269–288). Columbus, OH: Merrill.

Brown, L., Huppler, B., Pierce, F., York, R., & Sontag, E. (1974). Teaching trainable level students to read unconjugated action verbs. *Journal of Special Education, 8,* 51–56.

Brown, L., & Perlmutter, L. (1971). Teaching functional reading to trainable level retarded students. *Education & Training of the Mentally Retarded, 6,* 74–84.

Drew, C. J., Logan, D. R., & Hardman, M. L. (1984). *Mental retardation: A life-cycle approach*. St. Louis, MO: Times Mirror/Mosby.

Guess, D., Sailor, W., & Baer, D. (1978). Children with limited language. In R. L. Schiefelbusch (Ed.), *Language intervention strategies* (pp. 101–143). Baltimore, MD: University Park Press.

Gearheart, B. R., & Litton, F. W. (1975). *Trainable retarded: A foundation approach*. St. Louis, MO: Mosby.

Holland, A. (1975). Language therapy for children: Some thoughts on context and content. *Journal of Hearing Disorders, 40,* 514–523.

Lichtman, M. (1974). The development and validation of R/EAL: An instrument to assess functional literacy. *Journal of Reading Behavior, 6,* 167–182.

Musselwhite, C. R., & St. Louis, K. W. (1982). *Communication programming for the severely handicapped: Vocal and nonvocal strategies.* San Diego, CA: College-Hill.

Schilit, J., & Caldwell, M. L. (1980). A word list of essential career/vocational words for mentally retarded students. *Education & Training of the Mentally Retarded, 15*(2), 113–117.

Sidman, M., & Cresson, O. (1973). Reading and cross modal transfer of stimulus equivalencies in severe retardation. *American Journal of Mental Deficiency, 77,* 515–523.

Snell, M. E. (1983). Functional reading. In M. E. Snell (Ed.), *Systematic instruction of the moderately and severely handicapped* (pp. 445–487). Columbus, OH: Merrill.

JAMES K. MCAFEE
Pennsylvania State University

See also AAMR, American Association on Mental Retardation; Functional Communication Training; Functional Domains; Functional Instruction; Functional Skills Training; Functional Vision; Mental Retardation

FUTURE PROBLEM SOLVING PROGRAM

In an effort to develop an effective model to teach critical and creative thinking, problem solving, and decision-making skills to elementary, middle, and high school students, the Future Problem Solving Program (FPSP) was formulated. According to James Alvino, FPSP is a nonprofit educational program that trains teams of youngsters, grades K–12, in a six-step creative problem-solving process to tackle global and community problems (Alvino, 1993). FPSP seeks to stimulate critical and creative thinking skills in students, while encouraging these students to develop a vision for the future.

The FPSP's six-step problem solving model consists of the following six components: (1) identify challenges; (2) select an underlying problem; (3) produce solution ideas; (4) generate and select criteria; (5) apply criteria to solution ideas; and (6) develop an action plan. Students conduct research on selected topics and are coached in the use of the problem-solving model to address the specified area of need.

The FPSP promotes observance of standards for curriculum and instruction, language arts, social studies, science, the arts, math, geography, civics, technology, life skills, and behavioral studies. The program's use of research and investigation of topics deemed relevant to the student affords opportunities for students to gain skills necessary to achieve and exceed educational standards.

REFERENCE

Alvino, J. (1993). Future problem solving in the year 2000—Challenges and opportunities for business. *Business Horizons, 36*(6), 16–22.

FLOYD HENDERSON
Texas A&M University

See also Creative Problem Solving; Creativity

G

GAIT DISTURBANCES

Walking depends on the integration of sensory-motor-vestibular brain systems, as well as the functional strength and range of motion of the component body parts (Stolov & Clowers, 1981). Normal walking is developmentally linked to the orderly sequential integration of postural reflexes into automated smooth, adaptive responses that permit movement forward, backward, and up and down stairs by approximately 3 years of age. Clinical experience with children with impaired gaits suggests there may be as many gait disturbances as there are muscles and joints within the body (Banus, Kent, Norton, Sudiennick, & Becker, 1979).

Any skeletal or joint injury defect or disease that limits the normal range of joint motion produces a lack of fluidity in walking, or limping gait, because of necessary compensatory movements to maintain balance. Examples may be seen in children with arthritis, arthrogryposis, achondroplastic dwarfism, and fractures. The shortening of one leg produces a characteristic pelvic tilt that can contribute to scoliosis or spinal curvature in a growing child. Pain or foot deformities can also produce a limping gait.

Cerebellar gait or ataxia is a wide-based gait with irregular steps and unsteadiness, with staggering on turning; it is characteristic of children who lack balance. Young children or those with developmental delay often walk with an ataxic-like gait, with arms elevated to assist with balance.

In hemiplegic gait, the child with spastic hemiplegia leans to the afflicted side and swings the affected leg out to the side and in a semicircle (circumduction). The antigravity muscles of upper extremities are often held fixed in flexor patterns.

In scissors gait, the legs are adducted and internally rotated so that with each step the child tends to trip over the opposite foot. Toe walking increases the balance difficulty. Steps are short, jerky, and slow, with many extraneous movements of the upper extremities to facilitate balance. This is the typical pattern for the child with spastic paraplegia or mild quadriplegic cerebral palsy.

Staggering or drunken gait is seen in persons with alcohol intoxication. It may also be observed in children with brain tumor, drug poisoning, or other central nervous system impairment.

Steppage gait is characterized by lifting the knees high to flop the foot down; foot drop is evident. Some children with initial stage muscular atrophy walk in this manner. Children with Duchenne muscular dystrophy show a gait somewhat similar to the steppage gait in initial stages. As their heel cords tighten these children walk more on their toes and often fall. To maintain their tenuous balance they lean back in lordosis. As weakness progresses, these children find it increasingly difficult to come to an erect position after a fall. They use their hands to "walk up their legs" to push themselves into an erect position and achieve balance. This process is the Gower's sign. These children are vulnerable in a regular school setting because a slight touch may disturb their precarious balance and weakness prevents their using their arms to catch themselves when falling; hence, serious head injuries and fractures can result.

The gait patterns of children with involuntary movement disorders are highly variable (Davis, 2003). Some individuals with athetoid and choreiform movements, which are severe and extensive, walk with a fair degree of speed and safety while their windmill involuntary movements occur (Barr, 1979). Others with less involuntary movement may have severe concomitant balance problems that require supportive safety devices.

Specific description, diagnosis, and medical intervention relative to gait disturbances usually occur as a result of consultation among the pediatrician, orthopedist, and neurologist (Chusid, 1978). Assistive devices such as braces, corsets, splints, canes, crutches, and wheelchairs require individualized fitting and training to provide the most effective locomotion compatible with health and safety. Readjustments in the nature and use of these devices must be adapted to changes owed to growth and disease status. Clinical experience suggests that many severely disabled children who learn crutch walking for short distances find the energy required for long distances dictates wheelchair mobility to conserve energy. Mobility evaluation, including transfer and self-care status, has been found to be essential in vocational planning for young adults with gait disturbances to help them achieve more realistic vocational goals. The orthotist (brace maker) and physical and occupational therapists may implement specific exercise and training for cane and crutch walking and assist in the selection and use of wheelchairs.

REFERENCES

Banus, B. S., Kent, C., Norton, Y., Sudiennick, D., & Becker, M. (1979). *The developmental therapist* (2nd ed.). Thorofare, NJ: Slack.

Barr, M. L. (1979). *The human nervous system: An anatomic viewpoint* (3rd ed.). New York, NY: Harper & Row.

Chusid, J. G. (1978). *Correlative neuroanatomy and functional neurology* (16th ed.). Los Angeles, CA: Lang Medical.

Davis, A. (2003). Gait disturbances. In E. Fletcher-Janzen & C. R. Reynolds (Eds.), *Childhood disorders diagnostic desk reference* (pp. 251–252). Hoboken, NJ: Wiley.

Stolov, W. C., & Clowers, M. R. (Eds.). (1981). *Handbook of severe disability* (stock #017-090-00054-2). Washington, DC: U.S. Government Printing Office.

RACHAEL J. STEVENSON
Bedford, Ohio

See also Ataxia; Muscular Dystrophy; Physical Anomalies

GALACTOSEMIA

Galactosemia, first described in 1908, is an inborn error of galactose metabolism resulting in an accumulation of galactose in the blood, tissue, and urine. Three types of galactosemia are known, each due to a specific enzyme deficit. Classic galactosemia (the primary emphasis of this review) is the most prevalent and most severe form. It occurs in approximately 1/70,000 births and is attributed to a marked deficiency of galactose-1-phosphate uridyl transferase. Galactosemia is caused by an autosomal recessive gene, and heterozygotes for the trait exhibit reduced enzyme activity (VHGI, 1999). Galactokinase deficiency, less severe, occurs in 1/155,000 births and leads to the development of cataracts. A rare form, with no clear clinical abnormalities, is attributed to a deficit of EDP-glucose-4-epimerase (Hug, 1979). The overall incidence of variant forms of galactosemia is approximately 1/16,000 (Desposito & Cho, 1996).

Symptoms of classic galactosemia begin within two weeks after birth and may include jaundice, vomiting, hypoglycemia, lethargy, hepatosplenomegaly, cataracts, and failure to thrive (Brown & Sessoms, 2003; Desposito & Cho, 1996; VHGI, 1999). Without treatment, the disorder is usually lethal, and many affected infants die during the first few weeks of life. Failure to thrive, liver failure, and sepsis are associated with additional abnormalities, such as Fanconi syndrome and cerebral edema, and may be fatal if untreated (Desposito & Cho, 1996; Holton & Leonard, 1994). Biochemical changes owing to galactosemia have even been reported in the liver of a second trimester fetus, suggesting the development of the disorder in utero (Allen, Gillett, Holton, King, & Pettit, 1980). The potential prenatal origin may account for the lack of relationship between either the age at which treatment begins or the severity of the neonatal disorder and the long-term outcome (Holton & Leonard, 1994). Other clinical manifestations include cataracts, liver damage, ataxia, seizures, cerebral palsy, proteinuria, and aminoaciduria (Desposito & Cho, 1996). Continued ingestion of galactose may lead to mental retardation, malnourishment, progressive failure, and death (Hug, 1979). Even among treated children, mental retardation and learning disabilities are common (VHGI, 1999).

Diagnosis is determined by severity of the symptoms, previous diagnosis of galactosemia in siblings or parents, amniocentesis, and neonatal screening. The prevalent screening technique is a blood analysis for elevated galactose followed by a test for deficient enzyme activity. Given the disastrous consequences of late diagnosis, nearly all states routinely practice neonatal screening for galactosemia. Although the tests are extremely accurate, especially for classic galactosemia, turnaround time for the results is about 4 to 5 days (Cornell Medical Center, 1962). Some infants may die before the results of the screening test are returned because of susceptibility to E. coli septicemia (Desposito & Cho, 1996).

Treatment consists of elimination of galactose and lactose from the diet as early as possible (Brown & Sessoms, 2003). Since galactose is mainly formed by digestion of disaccharide lactose found in milk (milk sugar), a formula made from cow's milk is replaced with a meat-based or soybean formula. On dietary intervention, most physical symptoms subside. The infant gains weight; vomiting, diarrhea, and liver anomalies disappear; and cataracts regress, although any brain damage is permanent. Since the monosaccharide galactose does not occur in free forms in food, certain carbohydrates, lipids, and proteins that eventually metabolize to galactose must also be eliminated. A balanced galactose-free diet should be maintained throughout life (Desposito & Cho, 1996). The diet does not in any way cure the disorder, but reduces its effects on the developing person. Galactosemic women should adhere to the diet when they become pregnant to reduce levels of circulating toxins and resulting damage to the unborn fetus. Although affected women bear children, the frequency of ovarian failure is high (Desposito & Cho, 1996). Mothers of galactosemic children should also adhere to the diet during subsequent pregnancies to lessen symptoms present at birth (American Liver Foundation, 1995).

Even early dietary intervention may only partially reduce the degree and severity of cognitive damage. IQs cluster in the below normal to low-normal range, although variability is high (Desposito & Cho, 1996; Staff, 1982). Normal IQ has been reported in some cases where treatment was started before 10 days of age (Desposito & Cho, 1996). Other specific difficulties may interfere with the education of treated galactosemic children. About 50% of treated children are developmentally delayed, and learning difficulties increase with age. These effects are apparently due to progressive neurological disease or brain damage sustained at an earlier age that becomes more apparent with age (Holton & Leonard, 1994). Additionally, galactosemic children may show growth retardation; visual-perceptual, speech, motor function, balance, and language difficulties; short attention spans; and difficulty with spatial and mathematical relationships. They generally present no significant behavior problems except for occasional apathy and withdrawal that in some severe cases is shown as a personality disorder characterized by timidity and lack of drive (Holton & Leonard, 1994). According to Roth and Lampe (1995), "[G]alactosemia has humbled us. It has evaded all attempts to categorize and systematize it, consistently becoming more, rather than less, complicated." In other words, "[W]e still have much to learn" (Holton & Leonard, 1994). Those in special education should be aware of the many and varied problems that treated galactosemic children may have.

REFERENCES

Allen, J. T., Gillett, M., Holton, J. B., King, G. S., & Pettit, B. R. (1980). Evidence of galactosemia in utero. *Lancet, 2*, 603.

American Liver Foundation. (1995). *Galactosemia.* Retrieved from http://www.gastro.com/liverpg/galactos.htm

Brown, R. T., & Sessoms, A. (2003). Galactosemia. In E. Fletcher-Janzen & C. R. Reynolds (Eds.), *Childhood disorders diagnostic desk reference* (pp. 252–253). Hoboken, NJ: Wiley.

Desposito, F., & Cho, S. (1996). Newborn screening fact sheets. *Pediatrics, 28*, 473–501.

Holton, J. B., & Leonard, J. V. (1994). Clouds still gathering over galactosemia. *Lancet, 344*, 1242–1243.

Hug, G. (1979). Section 8.15: Defects in metabolism of carbohydrates. Chapter 8: Inborn errors of metabolism. In V. C. Vaughan, R. J. McKay, Jr., & R. E. Behrman (Eds.), *Nelson textbook of pediatrics* (11th ed., p. 546). Philadelphia, PA: W. B. Saunders.

New York Hospital, Cornell Medical Center (1962). Manual of Laboratory, X-ray and Special Procedures. The Hospital. NY.

Roth, K. S., & Lampe, J. B. (1995). Literature reviews: The gene—A multipurpose tool. *Clinical Pediatrics, 34*, 567.

Staff. (1982). Clouds over galactosemia. *Lancet, 2*, 1379–1380.

VHGI. (1999). *Vermont newborn screening program: Galactosemia online.* Retrieved from http://www.vtmednet.org/~m145037/vhgi_mem/nbsman/galacto.htm

Deborah E. Barbour
Robert T. Brown
University of North Carolina at Wilmington

See also Biochemical Irregularities; Congenital Disorders; Inborn Errors of Metabolism

GALLAGHER, JAMES J. (1926–   )

James J. Gallagher earned his BS in psychology from the University of Pittsburgh and went on to obtain the MS and PhD in child and clinical psychology from Pennsylvania State University. During his distinguished career, Gallagher was director of the Frank Porter Graham Child Development Center and Kenan Professor of Education at the University of North Carolina, Chapel Hill. His work has primarily focused on disabled and gifted children, including actively formulating public policies dealing with their special needs (Gallagher, 1984).

In the area of public policy implementation, he served as Associate Commissioner of Education (1967–1970), was the first chief of the Bureau of Education for the Handicapped of the U.S. Office of Education, and chaired the Social Policy Committee for Research in Child Development (1977–1978). As chair of the North Carolina Competency Test Commission, he emphasized the importance of the role of competency testing in remediation (Gallagher, 1979).

Gallagher's (1972a) conception of the Special Education Contract, an agreement between the school and the exceptional child's family detailing the educational plan and its objectives, was instrumental in the development of the individualized education plan (IEP), a tool widely accepted by educators today. His early work in the areas of special and regular education addressed systemic problems such as cost and staffing, frequently emphasizing the need for a "true educational system," one with supporting systems developed using educational technology (Gallagher, 1972b).

As a leader in the field of gifted and talented education, he served as President of the Council for Exceptional Children (1966), the Association for the Gifted (1970), and the World Council for Gifted and Talented Children (1981–1985). Gallagher's prolific body of work includes *Blending Middle School Philosophy and the Education of Gifted Students* (1997), *The Million Dollar Question: Unmet Service Needs for Young Children with Disabilities*

(Gallagher, 1997), *The Study of Federal Policy Implementation* (Gallagher, 1998), and *Educating Exceptional Children* (Kirk, Gallagher, & Anastasiow, 1996).

REFERENCES

Coleman, M. R., Gallagher, J. J., & Howard, J. (1997). *Blending middle school philosophy and the education of gifted students: Five case studies.* Washington, DC: National Association for Gifted Children.

Gallagher, J. (1972a). The special education contract for mildly handicapped children. *Exceptional Children, 38,* 527–535.

Gallagher, J. (1972b). *The search for the educational system that doesn't exist.* Arlington, VA: Council for Exceptional Children.

Gallagher, J. (1979). Minimum competency: The setting of educational standards. *Educational Evaluation & Policy Analysis, 1,* 62–67.

Gallagher, J. (1984). The evolution of special education concepts. In B. Blatt & R. J. Morris (Eds.), *Perspectives in special education.* Glenview, IL: Scott, Foresman.

Gallagher, J. (1985). *Teaching the gifted child* (3rd ed.). Boston, MA: Allyn & Bacon.

Gallagher, J. (1997). *The million dollar question: Unmet service needs for young children with disabilities.* Washington, DC: U.S. Department of Education.

Gallagher, J. (1998). *The study of federal policy implementation: Infants/toddlers with disabilities and their families: A synthesis of results.* Chapel Hill: University of North Carolina.

Kirk, S., Gallagher, J., & Anastasiow, N. J. (1996). *Educating exceptional children* (8th ed.). Boston, MA: Houghton Mifflin.

Ann E. Lupkowski
Texas A&M University
First edition

Tamara J. Martin
The University of Texas of the Permian Basin
Second edition

GALLAUDET, EDWARD M. (1837–1917)

Edward Miner Gallaudet, the originator of higher education for the deaf, was the youngest son of Thomas Hopkins Gallaudet, founder of the first school for the deaf in the United States. While teaching in his father's school, Gallaudet was chosen to organize a new school for the deaf in Washington, DC, the Columbia Institution, which came into existence in 1857 with Gallaudet as superintendent. Believing that deaf students should have the same opportunity as hearing students to receive a higher education, Gallaudet obtained legislation, approved by President Lincoln, giving the Columbia Institution the power to grant college degrees. A higher education department was created, and in 1894 it was named Gallaudet College, in honor of Edward Gallaudet's father.

An early eclectic in the education of the deaf, Gallaudet advocated a system of instruction that combined the language of signs with speech and speech reading. He was primarily responsible for the adoption of oral teaching methods by the state residential schools for the deaf in the United States (Boatner, 1959).

REFERENCE

Boatner, M. T. (1959). *Voice of the deaf: A biography of Edward Miner Gallaudet.* Washington, DC: Public Affairs Press.

Paul Irvine
Katonah, New York

See also Gallaudet College

GALLAUDET, THOMAS HOPKINS (1787–1851)

Thomas Hopkins Gallaudet established the first school for the deaf in the United States in Hartford, Connecticut, in 1817, using methods that he had learned when visiting the *Institution Nationale des Sourds Muets* in Paris, and assisted by a teacher from that school, Laurent Clerc. Gallaudet served as principal of the Hartford school, later named the American School for the Deaf, until 1830, and continued on its board of directors for the rest of his life (DeGerring, 1964).

Gallaudet married one of his first students at the school (Lane, 1984). His oldest son, Thomas, became a minister to the deaf. His youngest son, Edward, established a school for the deaf in Washington, DC, the advanced department of which became Gallaudet College, named in honor of Thomas Hopkins Gallaudet.

REFERENCES

DeGerring, E B. (1964). *Gallaudet, friend of the deaf.* New York, NY: McKay.

Lane, H. (1984). *When the mind hears.* New York, NY: Random House.

Paul Irvine
Katonah, New York

GALLAUDET COLLEGE

Gallaudet College, in Washington, DC, is the only liberal arts college for the deaf in the world. The college was formed in 1864 as a department of the Columbia Institution for the Deaf, now the Kendall School for the Deaf, by Amos Kendall, who had been postmaster general under President Andrew Jackson, and Edward Miner Gallaudet, superintendent of the Columbia Institution. The two men obtained the necessary federal legislation, which was signed by President Lincoln, to establish this national college for the deaf. In 1894 the college department became Gallaudet College, named in honor of Edward Miner Gallaudet's father, Thomas Hopkins Gallaudet, who established the first school for the deaf in the United States.

In addition to a distinguished record of success in the education of its students, Gallaudet College has provided much of the leadership in the education of the deaf in the United States. Its teacher-training program has provided both deaf and hearing teachers of the deaf. Many of the leaders in the field during the past century have been products of the Gallaudet College program.

REFERENCES

Boatner, M. T. (1959). *Voice of the deaf: A biography of Edward Miner Gallaudet*. Washington, DC: Public Affairs.

Gallaudet, E. M. (1983). *History of the College for the Deaf, 1857–1907*. Washington, DC: Gallaudet College Press.

PAUL IRVINE
Katonah, New York

GALTON, FRANCIS (1822–1911)

Sir Francis Galton, born in England in 1822, came from an intellectual family; his mother, Violetta Darwin, was the aunt of Charles Darwin, and his grandfather, Samuel Galton, was a fellow of the Royal Society. The youngest of a family of nine, he was brought up in a large house near Birmingham, where his father ran a bank. Galton was a precocious child. From material in Pearson's biography, Terman (Terman, 1917) estimated Galton's childhood IQ at 200. He was the author of over 300 publications, including 17 books covering a broad range of topics.

Galton pioneered the development of psychological testing and the formulation of the major genetic principle of segregation of inherited characteristics (Galton, 1908). He is perhaps best known for his work on the genetic basis of individual differences in intelligence as discussed in his book, *Hereditary Genius* (Galton, 1869). He was an early proponent of eugenics, a term coined by him.

In his research on the relationship of the characteristics of parents and offspring, Galton discovered the phenomenon of regression toward the mean and developed the concept of correlation, a term first used by him. Galton's measure of correlation was later given mathematical refinement by Karl Pearson, who later wrote a biography of Galton (Pearson, 1914). A more recent biography was prepared by Forrest (1974).

REFERENCES

Forrest, D. W. (1974). *Francis Galton: The life and work of a Victorian genius*. New York, NY: Toplinger.

Galton, F. (1869). *Hereditary genius: An inquiry into its laws and consequences*. London, UK: Macmillan.

Galton, F. (1908). *Memories of my life*. London, UK: Methuen.

Pearson, K. (1914). *The life, letters and labours of Francis Galton*. Cambridge, UK: Cambridge University Press.

Terman, L. M. (1917). The intelligence quotient of Francis Galton in childhood. *American Journal of Psychology, 28*, 209.

ROBERT C. NICHOLS
DIANE JARVIS
State University of New York at Buffalo

GAMMA-AMINOBUTYRIC ACID

Gamma-aminobutyric acid (GABA) is a major inhibitory neurotransmitter in the central nervous system. Specific functions of the brain depend on adequate levels of neurotransmitters in the areas that control such functions. This knowledge has stimulated a search for drugs that can augment or reduce the supply of particular neurotransmitters. A deficiency of GABA has been associated with several diseases, including schizophrenia and epilepsy (Hammond & Wilder, 1985; Swaiman, 1999).

REFERENCES

Hammond, E. J., & Wilder, B. J. (1985). Gamma-vinyl GABA: A new antiepileptic drug. *Clinical Neuropharmacology, 8*(1), 1–12.

Swaiman, K. F. (1999). Movement disorders and disorders of the basal ganglia. In K. F. Swaiman & S. Ashwal (Eds.), *Pediatric neurology* (pp. 801–831). St. Louis, MO: Mosby.

BARBARA S. SPEER
*Shaker Heights City School District,
Shaker Heights, Ohio*

GARGOYLISM (See Hurler Syndrome)

GARRETT, EMMA (1846–1893)

Emma Garrett, seeking a way to demonstrate the effectiveness of the oral method of teaching the deaf, obtained a grant that enabled her, with her sister Mary, to establish the Pennsylvania Home for the Training in Speech of Deaf Children Before They Are of School Age, also known as the Bala Home (Fay, 1893). Located in Philadelphia, the home began operation in 1891. Emma Garrett was superintendent, and both sisters served as teachers. The Bala Home was widely influential as an example of the effectiveness of the oral method of teaching the deaf and of the efficacy of early intervention. Following Emma Garrett's death in 1893, her sister became superintendent of the Bala Home and carried on the work that the two of them had begun.

REFERENCE

Fay, E. A. (1893). *Histories of American schools for the deaf, 1817–1893* (Vol. 3). Washington, DC: Volta Bureau.

PAUL IRVINE
Katonah, New York

GARRETT, MARY SMITH (1839–1925)

Mary Smith Garrett, with her sister Emma, in 1891 founded in Philadelphia the Pennsylvania Home for the Training in Speech of Deaf Children Before They Are of School Age, also known as the Bala Home. Mary Garrett succeeded her sister as superintendent after Emma died in 1893. She continued in this position for the remainder of her life.

Mary Garrett was a leading advocate of the oral method of teaching the deaf and helped to develop a curriculum based on this approach. Her system of teaching oral communication was based on early intervention, with speech training beginning as early as 2 years of age. Through the efforts of Mary and her sister, Pennsylvania became the first state to appropriate funds for preschool speech and language training for deaf children.

Mary Garrett was instrumental in the enactment of legislation establishing a juvenile court and probation system for Pennsylvania. She was also a leader in the National Congress of Mothers, the forerunner of the National Congress of Parents and Teachers, where she promoted such social reforms as child labor laws and juvenile court legislation.

REFERENCE

Fay, E. A. (1893). *Histories of American schools for the deaf, 1817–1893* (Vol. 3). Washington, DC: Volta Bureau.

PAUL IRVINE
Katonah, New York

GARRISON, S. OLIN (1853–1900)

S. Olin Garrison, minister and educator, founded in New Jersey in 1887 the school for "retarded children" that later became the Training School at Vineland. The school featured a cottage system of small, homelike facilities, a strong educational program, and a research department that published some of the nation's most influential works on intellectual disabilities. Garrison served as superintendent of the Training School until his death in 1900. He was also responsible for the establishment by New Jersey of the State Home for Girls and of a school for epileptic children (McCaffrey, 1965).

REFERENCE

McCaffrey, K. R. (1965). *Founders of the Training School at Vineland, New Jersey: S. Olin Garrison, Alexander Johnson, Edward R. Johnstone.* Unpublished doctoral dissertation. Teachers College, Columbia University, New York.

PAUL IRVINE
Katonah, New York

GATES-MACGINITIE READING TEST

The Gates-MacGinitie Reading Test (GMRT), developed by Walter H. MacGinitie, Ruth K. MacGinitie, Katherine Maria, and Lois G. Dreyer, is a formal assessment of balanced reading skills across grade levels. These levels encompass Pre-Reading, Beginning Reading, Level 1, and Level 2. Skills tested include phonemic awareness, decoding skills, phonological awareness, vocabulary, comprehension, word knowledge, and fluency.

Materials required are student test booklets or answer sheets, teacher directions for administering the test, and the manual for scoring and interpretation, which is optional. These tests are also machine scorable.

This instrument is designed to be given to a group of children. The various subtests are timed. The instrument is a multiple-choice test for all grade levels. It is a thorough assessment of reading skills and can be used by the teacher to assess areas of strength or weakness, for both individual students and an entire class. Raw scores are translated into percentile rankings, stanine scores, grade equivalency scores, extended scale scores, and normal curve equivalency scores.

Internal consistency along with means and standard deviations for total scores and subscales for each level of the GMRT are evident for both spring and fall administration. These are quite satisfactory and fall in the upper .80s and .90s for grades 1 to 12 (Swerdlik, 1992). Validity data support the intercorrelations among subtests. Validity data also provide evidence that the GMRT is a powerful test for assessing reading achievement at the lower and upper levels.

The bulk of the validity evidence relates to providing data that support substantial relationships between the GMRT and other instruments that are assumed to measure the same constructs of reading vocabulary and comprehension. These tests include general achievement screening batteries such as the Iowa Test of Basic Skills (ITBS), Tests of Achievement and Proficiency (TAP), the Comprehensive Tests of Basic Skills (CTBS), California Achievement Test (CAT), Metropolitan Achievement Test (MAT), the Survey of Basic Skills (SBS), the Verbal and Mathematics sections of the Preliminary Scholastic Aptitude Test (PSAT) and the Scholastic Aptitude Test (SAT), and the English, Math, Social Science, Natural Science, and Composite sections of the American College Test Program (ACT; Swerdlik, 1992). Reviews of the fourth edition of this test are pending for the *Sixteenth Mental Measurements Yearbook*.

REFERENCES

Dumont, R., & Willis, J. (2006). *A sampling of reading tests.* Retrieved from http://alpha.fdu.edu/psychology/a_sampling_of _reading_tests.htm

Swerdlik, M. (1992). Review of the Gates-MacGinitie Reading Tests, third edition. In J. Kramer & J. Conoley (Eds.), *The mental measurements yearbook* (Vol. 12, pp. 352–353). Lincoln: University of Nebraska.

RON DUMONT
Fairleigh Dickinson University

JOHN O. WILLIS
Rivier College

GAZE AVERSION

Eye contact, the study of facial characteristics during human intercourse, has been a topic that has always captivated inquiry. Why do we maintain eye contact during social interaction? What is there in facial cues that provide others social clues and what do these clues address? Are there normal patterns of gaze aversion?

The answer to the last question is a definite yes. It is neither socially correct nor communicatively enriching to look continuously at another person's face. Researchers (Beattie, 1979) have advanced a hypothesis that gaze aversion is a technique that reduces distractibility and permits thinking and speech planning. Ehrlichman (1981) advanced this hypothesis, which his data supported, as a statement of cognitive interference. Simply, the hypothesis postulates that people look away more often during periods

of speech hesitancy than during periods of fluency. Gaze aversion is used while thinking and planning the next speech pattern.

Coss (1979) believed that the dimensions of gaze in psychotic children were different in several respects. He ran three studies. The first examined 10 nonpsychotic and 10 psychotic children during presentations of five models comprising a blank model and models with one through four concentric discoid elements separated by the same interpupillary distance as human eyes. The second experiment examined 15 psychotic children using models presenting two concentric discoid elements in vertical, diagonal, and horizontal orientations. The third experiment examined 10 nonpsychotic and 10 psychotic children using five models comprising two schematic facing eyes as represented by concentric discoid elements. The psychotic children looked longer at the models than did the nonpsychotic children. However, these groups did not differ for the model with two concentric discoid elements. Both groups, particularly the psychotic children, looked less at the model presenting two concentric discoid elements than at the models presenting other arrangements of concentric discoid elements in the first experiment. Similarly, in the third experiment, both groups looked less at the model with two concentric discoid elements than at models with staring and averted irises. In sum, nonpsychotic children and psychotic children did not differ appreciably in their gaze under varying conditions.

Currently, there is no data to support the long-standing belief that gaze aversion occurs with greater duration or more frequency among emotionally disturbed than among normal children. Scheman and Lockhard (1979) generated data from 573 children suggesting that gaze or stare is developmentally determined. Children under 18 months of age rarely establish eye contact. Children 18 months to 5 years do not avert their gaze. From 5 to 9 years, behavioral patterns specific to the youth are well established. This study took place in a suburban shopping center where the children were unprotected by parents' wishes when confronted by gazes from strange adults. This work lends strong support to the communication theory of gaze aversion. That, in turn, suggests that gaze aversion is not solely a function of development, conditions, difficulty of task (Doherty-Sneddon, Bonner, Longbotham, & Doyle, 2002) or emotional problems, but is a device that provides and protects concentration and is instrumental in speech production. Therefore, children with fluency difficulties (e.g., stutters), may have increased gaze aversion, a contention that is also supported in the research literature.

REFERENCES

Beattie, G. W. (1979). Planning units in spontaneous speech: Some evidence from hesitation in speech and speaker gaze direction in conversation. *Linguistics, 17,* 61–78.

Coss, R. G. (1979). Perceptual determinants of gaze aversion by normal and psychotic children: The role of two facing eyes. *Behavior, 3–4,* 228–253.

Doherty-Sneddon, G., Bonner, B. L., Longbotham, S., & Doyle, C. (2002). Development of gaze aversion as disengagement from visual information. *Developmental Psychology*, 38, 3, 438–445.

Ehrlichman, H. (1981). From gaze aversion to eye movement suppression: An investigation of the cognitive interference explanation of gaze patterns during conversation. *British Journal of Social Psychology*, 20, 233–241.

Scheman, J. D., & Lockhard, J. S. (1979). Development of gaze aversion in children. *Child Development*, 50, 594–596.

DAVID A. SABATINO
West Virginia College of Graduate Studies

See also **Childhood Psychosis; Childhood Schizophrenia**

GEARHEART, BILL R. (1918–2001)

Bill R. Gearheart earned his BA in math and physics from Friends University in Wichita, Kansas, in 1949. He received his MEd in school administration from Wichita State University in 1955 and his PhD in educational psychology and special education from the University of Northern Colorado in 1963. In the early part of his career in public education, Gearheart filled the roles of teacher, elementary principal, director of special services, and assistant superintendent. In 1966 he moved on to the university level and eventually became full professor. During his tenure at the University of Northern Colorado, Gearheart spent 6 years as director of the Navajo Education Project. Gearheart took early retirement and served as professor emeritus of special education at the University of Northern Colorado.

Gearheart's academic interests included preparation of regular classroom teachers to work with mildly disabled students, administration of special education, and professional writing in special education. He was most prolific in this last area, and wrote numerous college texts on special education. One major text, *Learning Disabilities: Educational Strategies* is currently in its fifth edition (Gearheart & Gearheart, 1989), and another text, *The Exceptional Student in the Regular Classroom* (formerly *The Handicapped Child in the Regular Classroom*) is in its sixth edition (Gearheart, Weishahn, & Gearheart, 1996).

Gearheart was a specialist in organizing educational programs for handicapped children and was involved in legislation relating to children with disabilities. He was an active special education advocate at the national level. From 1967 to 1970, he served on the U.S. Office of Education panel involved in awarding federal grants in special education; for two of those years he served as chairperson. He spent 5 years as a field adviser to the Bureau of Education for the Handicapped, evaluating applications for research funds. Gearheart also was a member of different federal site visit teams, visiting numerous major universities that offer the doctorate in special education. At the state level, Gearheart was involved with special education projects for various state departments of education. In addition, he assisted numerous local education agencies in planning and programming various special education services.

Involved in special education for over 25 years, Gearheart's major contributions to the field were twofold. First, he wrote a dozen texts in special education (three in foreign translations). His development of practitioner-oriented texts made his work familiar to many special educators and regular classroom educators. Second, he was involved in the preparation of special educators at the doctoral level. His training contributions are seen in former students who now reside in more than half of the states and several foreign countries. A unique contribution to the field was Gearheart's directorship of the Navajo Education Project, initiating special education programming in Board of Indian Affairs schools of the Navajo reservation. Gearheart taught courses at the University of Northern Colorado and conducted workshops on professional writing. His work in the field of special education continued with the publication of *Exceptional Individuals: An Introduction* (1992).

REFERENCES

Gearheart, B. R., & Gearheart, C. J. (1989). *Learning disabilities: Educational strategies* (5th ed.). Columbus, OH: Merrill.

Gearheart, B. R., Mullen, R. C., & Gearheart, C. J. (1992). *Exceptional individuals: An introduction*. Pacific Grove, CA: Brooks/Cole.

Gearheart, B. R., Weishahn, M. W., & Gearheart, C. J. (1996). *The exceptional student in the regular classroom* (6th ed.). Englewood Cliffs, NJ: Merrill.

KATHRYN A. SULLIVAN
Branson School Online
First edition

TAMARA J. MARTIN
The University of Texas of the Permian Basin
Second edition

GENERAL APTITUDE TEST BATTERY

The General Aptitude Test Battery (GATB) was developed by the U.S. Employment Services as a means of assisting clients (and those at state employment offices) in identifying possible successful occupation areas. The battery is composed of 12 separately timed and scored tests that measure nine aptitudes for individuals age 13 through adulthood. Scores are then used to point out areas of client strengths and weaknesses. There are two forms. The following nine vocational aptitudes are measured:

1. Intelligence—the general learning ability of the client

2. Verbal aptitude—the ability to understand words and their relationships

3. Numerical aptitude—the ability to perform arithmetic quickly and accurately

4. Spatial aptitude—the ability to think visually of geometric forms and to recognize relationships resulting from the movement of objects in space

5. Form perception—the ability to perceive pertinent details and make visual discriminations

6. Clerical perception—the ability to discriminate similarities and differences in verbal material

7. Motor coordination—the ability to coordinate eyes and hands rapidly and accurately

8. Finger dexterity—the ability to move and manipulate small objects with the fingers rapidly and accurately

9. Manual dexterity—the ability to move the hands skillfully in placing and turning motions

In the manual for the GATB (1967), scores on the various subtests are correlated with occupations, and tentative cutoff scores are provided for each occupational area. The test was validated to predict performance in over 400 professional, semi-, and unskilled occupations (USES General Aptitude Test Battery, 1978). A Spanish version of the GATB is available, as is a nonreading measure of the same aptitudes. There is also a special edition for deaf persons. The GATB takes approximately two hours to complete. To administer the GATB, one must obtain certification by attending a workshop that teaches administration and interpretation of the GATB. State employment offices present these workshops.

REFERENCES

United States Employment Services (USES). (1967). *Manual for the USES General Aptitude Test Battery*. Minneapolis, MN: Intran.

USES General Aptitude Test Battery. (1978). In O. K. Buros (Ed.), *The eighth mental measurements yearbook* (Vol. II, pp. 675–680). Highland Park, NJ: Gryphon.

RONALD V. SCHMELZER
Eastern Kentucky University
First edition

ELIZABETH O. LICHTENBERGER
The Salk Institute
Second edition

GENERALIZABILITY THEORY

Generalizability theory was developed by Cronbach and his associates (Cronbach, Gleser, Nanda, & Rajaratnam, 1972) to evaluate the generalizability of results obtained when measurement is carried out for assessing, for example, differences among students. The theory is primarily concerned with identifying and estimating the variances associated with the effects present in the design used to collect the evaluation data. Variances are estimated within an analysis of variance (ANOVA) framework. These estimated variances are then used to describe the relative contribution of each effect to the observed variance and to compute measurement error variance and, if desired, generalizability coefficients for each factor of interest.

Two types of studies are conducted using generalizability theory: G(generalizability)-studies and D(decision)-studies. A G-study is carried out when developing a measurement procedure for use in a D-study later on. Thus, a G-study is designed to encompass the "universe of admissible observations" (Cronbach et al., 1972, p. 20); for instance, a universe including all the variables (factors) under which observations could be collected in subsequent D-studies. A D-study draws observations from the "universe of generalization" (i.e., the universe to which we wish to generalize the results in a specific situation). The universe of generalization is then a subset of, or the same as, the universe of admissible operations. The results of a G-study are used to design D-studies. In many instances, however, a G- and D-study may be conducted using the same data set; for instance, the data are used both for making decisions and for improving the design of future D-studies so that the universe of admissible observations is the same as the universe of generalization.

Suppose a 20-item test is administered for diagnostic purposes to a sample of 30 referred students. To investigate the generalizability of the test for differentiating among the students, a G-study is conducted by first identifying the effects present in the linear ANOVA model associated with the design of the study. These effects are student, item, and student × item interaction, including random error. Next, using the ANOVA technique, the mean squares associated with each effect are obtained, and variances are estimated for each using a procedure such as that proposed by Cornfield and Tukey (1956). For the example above, the variances are estimated as follows: students—.0610 (22.13%), items—.0700 (25.82%), interaction—.1401 (51.68%).

Next, a D-study is carried out using the results of the G-study. First the estimated variances are examined. They show that approximately the same proportion of variation in the design is shown by the students and the items, while twice as much is attributable to the differences between students' responses to items and random error. The measurement error associated with differences among students is .0701/20 = .0025, since differences among students are shown in their differing responses to the same items. Divide by 20, since it is assumed that students are differentiated on the basis of their performance over all 20 items. A generalizability coefficient, p^2, analogous to a reliability coefficient, is estimated as

$$p^2 = \frac{student\ variance}{student\ variance\ and\ error\ variance}$$
$$= .0610$$
$$= .0610 + .0035$$
$$= .8971$$

In summary, from a generalizability analysis we estimate variance associated with each factor in the design, measurement error, and a generalizability coefficient associated with the factor of interest. The practitioner or researcher wishing to conduct generalizability analysis should read Brennan (1983), Fyans (1983), and Shavelson and Webb (1981).

REFERENCES

Brennan, R. L. (1983). *Elements of generalizability theory*. Iowa City, IA: American College Testing Program.

Cornfield, J., & Tukey, J. W. (1956). Average values of mean squares in factorials. *Annals of Mathematical Statistics, 27,* 907–949.

Cronbach, L. J., Gleser, G. C., Nanda, H., & Rajaratnam, N. (1972). *The dependability of behavioral measurements: Theory of generalizability for scores and profiles*. New York, NY: Wiley.

Fyans, L. J. (Ed.). (1983). *Generalizability theory: Inferences and practical applications*. San Francisco, CA: Jossey-Bass.

Shavelson, R. J., & Webb, N. M. (1981). Generalizability theory: 1973–1980. *British Journal of Mathematical & Statistical Psychology, 34,* 133–166.

GWYNETH M. BOODOO
Texas A&M University

See also Research in Special Education

GENERALIZATION

Generalization is the demonstration of a behavior in circumstances other than those in which it was trained. The term is also used to refer to the occurrence of a behavior similar to, but different from, the learned behavior under the same circumstances as during training (Rutherford & Nelson, 1988; Scruggs & Mastropieri, 1984). These two types of generalization are referred to as stimulus generalization and response generalization. Stimulus generalization, the type most commonly studied by special education researchers, may be said to have occurred when a learner demonstrates a skill or behavior in different surroundings, at different times, or with different people. For example, a student who is trained to insert the correct amount of change into a soda machine at school and subsequently performs the same skill at a recreation center is said to have generalized the response. Response generalization refers to the spread of effects to other related behaviors and is exemplified by a student opening a large can after having successfully learned to open a small can.

Generalization is necessary to the development of a wide repertoire of behavior. It was once assumed that generalization occurred automatically with the learning of a behavior, but this principle has not proven true, especially for handicapped learners (Stokes & Baer, 1977). If generalization is to occur, it must be a component of the actual training process (Baer, Wolf, & Risley, 1968).

There is a greater probability of success in training for generalization if several factors are addressed.

- *Initial Training.* The behavior to be generalized should be firmly established in the learner's repertoire. Time between initial acquisition and training for generalization should be short. If conditions during training are tightly controlled, generalization may take more time than if initial training is "loose" (i.e., stimuli and responses are not narrowly defined).

- *Stimulus Variables.* The stimulus variables to be changed (time, number, setting) should be manipulated systematically during training. There is little agreement whether this should be accomplished one variable at a time or all at one time. However, the more similarities between stimuli in the initial learning environment and those in the generalization environment, the easier the process for the learner (Stokes & Baer, 1977).

- *Other Persons.* To the extent possible, significant others in the learner's environment should be included in the training. If they understand the purpose and method, they will be able to reinforce the learner whenever and wherever the behavior occurs.

- *Reinforcers.* Artificial reinforcers should be faded as soon as possible and replaced by those reinforcers found in the environment in which behavior is most likely to occur. Likewise, regardless of the schedule of reinforcement used for training, an intermittent schedule should be in place before generalization is attempted. Intermittent reinforcement will more closely resemble schedules found in the natural environment.

- *Criteria for Completion.* Criteria for successful generalization should be established. The number of exemplars required to assure generalization will vary, but training should continue until some spontaneous generalization is observed in nontraining environments (Stokes & Baer, 1977).

Success in training for generalization has varied and researchers differ in their opinions regarding its efficacy (Scruggs & Mastropieri, 1984). Some propose that failure to train for generalization is due to a lack of educational technology; others contend that inherent deficiencies in the intellectual functioning of persons with disabilities make generalization difficult. The former analysis implies that new and better training techniques are needed and that the problem is a teaching one. The latter implies a learning problem and that attempts to train for generalization should be replaced by more effort spent training desired behaviors in the environments in which they are required (Scruggs & Mastropieri, 1984). The failure of generalization has been a major drawback in the application of strictly behavioral methods to learning (Martens & Witt, 1988).

REFERENCES

Baer, D. M., Wolf, M. M., & Risley, T. R. (1968). Some current dimensions of applied behavior analysis. *Journal of Applied Behavior Analysis, 1*, 91–97.

Martens, B., & Witt, J. (1988). On the ecological validity of behavior modification. In J. Witt, S. Elliott, & F. Graham (Eds.), *Handbook of behavior therapy in education* (pp. 325–339). New York, NY: Plenum Press.

Rutherford, R., & Nelson, C. (1988). Generalization and maintenance of treatment effects. In J. Witt, S. Elliott, & F. Graham (Eds.), *Handbook of behavior therapy in education* (pp. 277–324). New York, NY: Plenum Press.

Scruggs, T. E., & Mastropieri, M. A. (1984). Issues in generalization: Implications for special education. *Psychology in the Schools, 21*, 397–403.

Stokes, T. F., & Baer, D. M. (1977). An implicit technology of generalization. *Journal of Applied Behavior Analysis, 10*, 349–367.

SARA PANKASKIE
PAUL T. SINDELAR
Florida State University

See also **Transfer of Training**

GENERIC SPECIAL EDUCATION

Generic special education is a cross-categorical orientation to training teachers and delivering special education services to children with mild to moderate disabilities. This approach came about as a result of a variety of educational movements in special education. In the 1960s, there was growing dissatisfaction among educators with the use of traditional medical-model categories to identify disabled pupils. This concern was due, in part, to increased recognition of the heterogeneity of learner characteristics within a specific handicap classification and to reports that many pupils have similar educational needs despite differences in their handicapping conditions (Hewett & Forness, 1984).

Legal requirements to educate children with disabilities in the least restrictive educational environment according to an individualized educational plan (IEP) further eroded the historical categorical boundaries to instruction. According to IDEA, selection of instructional services for individuals with disabilities is based on pupils' educational needs as determined by a committee of educators and parents who develop the IEP. After analyzing pupils' levels of performance, the appropriate educational placement is prescribed. A variety of instructional options have been developed to meet pupils' individual needs, including placement in regular classes, the use of consulting and itinerant special education teachers, resource and self-contained special education classes, special day schools, residential centers, hospital schools, and homebound instruction (Deno, 1973; Reynolds & Birch, 1982). The specific nature of instructional services, including decisions concerning curricula and teaching strategies, should be determined by the individual needs and instructional characteristics of the pupil; they should not be arbitrarily prescribed on the basis of the child's handicapping condition.

Concern for individualization is evident throughout the entire continuum of services provided by schools and agencies. From infant stimulation to vocational preparation programs that emphasize the transition from school to work, pupils who require special education services receive them based on their individual needs rather than on their categorical label. Within this context of individualization of instruction, generic special education focuses on identifying and meeting the learning needs and characteristics of specific pupils regardless of disability category. For example, owing to similarities in performance characteristics, many learning-disabled, mildly retarded, and emotionally disturbed youngsters may be effectively served in the same classroom with the same curricula.

As special education instructional services evolved from a rigid categorical approach to a functional orientation, so did teacher training programs change. With the support of federal funds in the early 1970s, several institutions of higher education initiated cross-categorical special education teacher training programs (Brady, Conroy, & Langford, 1984). These programs exhibited a variety of characteristics differentiating them from the traditional categorical orientation to teacher education. For example, each program's name described the role or function of the teacher rather than a particular handicapping condition (e.g., diagnostic-prescriptive teacher, consulting teacher). The programs were primarily developed at the master's degree level for already certified teachers, and although students were trained noncategorically, their certification remained categorical. Later, teacher training programs emphasized greater interaction with regular education, offered programs at both bachelor's and master's levels, and were located in states that began initiating non-categorical certification, primarily by collapsing certain categories into a general one. These training programs tended to collapse categorical course offerings to meet the challenge of noncategorical certification.

Associated with these movements in service delivery and teacher training has been a trend for state education agencies to develop noncategorical teacher certification in special education, growing from only 12 states in 1979 to 34 states and the District of Columbia in 1983 (Idol-Maestas, Lloyd, & Lilly, 1981). Nearly all states now provide some form of generic certification. Names of these new certificates range from descriptions of pupils (e.g., learning disabled, mildly handicapped) to descriptions of programs (e.g., resource room specialist, diagnostic prescriptive teacher) to nonspecific terms such as generic special educator.

REFERENCES

Brady, M. P., Conroy, M., & Langford, C. A. (1984). Current issues and practices affecting the development of noncategorical programs for students and teachers. *Teacher Education & Special Education*, 7(1), 20–26.

Deno, E. N. (Ed.). (1973). *Instructional alternatives for exceptional children*. Arlington, VA: Council for Exceptional Children.

Hewett, F. M., & Forness, S. R. (1984). *Education of exceptional learners* (3rd ed.). Boston, MA: Allyn & Bacon.

Idol-Maestas, L., Lloyd, S., & Lilly, M. (1981). A noncategorical approach to direct service and teacher education. *Exceptional Children*, 48(3), 213–220.

Reynolds, M., & Birch, J. W. (1982). *Teaching exceptional children in all America's schools* (2nd ed.). Reston, VA: Council for Exceptional Children.

CAROL ANDERSON
DOUGLAS J. PALMER
LINDA H. PARRISH
Texas A&M University

See also Holistic Approach and Learning Disabilities; Humanism and Special Education

GENETIC AND RARE DISEASES INFORMATION CENTER

The Genetic and Rare Diseases Information Center (GARD) was created in 2002 by the National Human Genome Research Institute (NHGRI) and the Office of Rare Diseases (ORD)—two agencies at the National Institutes of Health (NIH)—to help people find useful information about genetic and rare diseases. GARD provides immediate, virtually round-the-clock access to experienced information specialists who can furnish current and accurate information, in both English and Spanish, about genetic and rare diseases.

So far, GARD has responded to over 12,000 inquiries on rare and genetic diseases. Requests come not only from patients and their families, but also from physicians, nurses, and other health-care professionals. GARD also has proved useful to genetic counselors, occupational and physical therapists, social workers, and teachers who work with people with a genetic or rare disease. Even scientists who are studying a genetic or rare disease and who need information for their research have contacted GARD, as have people who are taking part in a clinical study.

Community leaders looking to help people find resources for those with genetic or rare diseases and advocacy groups who want up-to-date disease information for their members have contacted GARD. And members of the media who are writing stories about genetic or rare diseases have found the information GARD has on hand useful, accurate, and complete. GARD has information on:

- What is known about a genetic or rare disease
- What research studies are being conducted
- What genetic testing and genetic services are available
- Which advocacy groups to contact for a specific genetic or rare disease
- What has been written recently about a genetic or rare disease in medical journals

STAFF

See also Genetic Mapping; Human Genome Project

GENETIC COUNSELING

What Is Genetic Counseling?

The National Society of Genetic Counselors (NSGC) defines genetic counseling as the process of assisting people with understanding and adapting to the medical, psychological, and familial implications of genetic contributions to disease (National Society of Genetic Counselors, 2012). This process includes the interpretation of family and medical histories to assess the chance of disease occurrence or recurrence. Genetic counseling usually involves providing education about inheritance, testing options, disease management, and prevention. Genetic counseling also promotes informed choices and adaptation to the risk or condition (National Society of Genetic Counselors, 2012). Counseling usually has a specific therapeutic focus such as prenatal, pediatric, psychiatric, or cancer genetic counseling. The aim of genetic counseling is to support individuals in their ability to make an informed decision regarding genetic testing and the implications of such testing (Sequeiros & Guimarães, 2007).

Individuals seek genetic counseling for a variety of reasons. People who have questions about origins of diseases or traits in their family or ethnic group are typical clients of genetic counseling. Those who may find genetic counseling helpful include those who have, or are concerned they might have, an inherited disorder or birth defect. Physicians also refer pregnant women whose ultrasound examinations or blood testing indicate that their pregnancy may be at increased risk for complications or disability, as well as women over 35 who are pregnant. Couples who already have a child with a genetic disability or who give birth to infants diagnosed with a genetic disease by routine newborn screening may also seek genetic counseling (March of Dimes, 2012).

Who Provides Genetic Counseling?

Genetic counselors are health professionals with specific education, training and experience in medical genetics and counseling (National Society of Genetic Counselors, 2006). Genetic counselors usually work as part of a healthcare team, providing information and support to families who have members with birth defects or genetic disorders and to families who may be at risk for a variety of inherited conditions (National Society of Genetic Counselors' Definition Task Force, 2006). Genetic counselors interact with clients and other healthcare professionals in an assortment of clinical and nonclinical settings, such as university-based medical centers, private hospitals, private practice, and industry settings (American Board of Genetic Counseling, 2012). More and more, primary care practitioners are providing facets of genetic counseling and genetic services, resulting in a need to train nurses, social workers, and physicians. Genetic counselors provide a critical role in educating providers and developing standards of practice. Genetic counselors also afford health professionals and patients the opportunity to communicate with others, such as policymakers and the media, about new genetic services and technologies (National Human Genome Research Institute, 2012).

What Does Genetic Counseling Consist Of?

Genetic counselors assess the risk of occurrence or recurrence of a genetic condition or birth defect using a variety of techniques, including knowledge of inheritance patterns, epidemiologic data, and evaluation of clinical data. They obtain and review medical and family histories and explain the nature of genetics evaluation to clients.

They explain medical information regarding the diagnosis or potential occurrence of a genetic condition or birth anomaly (National Society of Genetic Counselors' Definition Task Force, 2006). Also discussed are potential treatment options and possibilities and limitations of tests and assessments in determining the genetic status of the client. Prenatal diagnosis using cytogenetic or biochemical analyses of fetal cells, amniotic fluid, or mother's blood can provide distinct answers to genetic questions (Zych, 2008). In particular, populations where the probability of genetic disorders, such as Tay-Sachs disease or sickle cell anemia, is remarkably high, screening programs have been organized to counsel clients before they start families.

The discovery of disease and susceptibility genes brought forth by the sequencing of the human genome has brought challenges to the field of genetic counseling. The traditional role of genetic counseling has significantly widened to address a diversity of developing needs, ranging from individuals looking for disease susceptibility testing to those looking to find out if a therapeutic treatment option is the right one for them (National Human Genome Research Institute, 2012).

What Common Types of Genetic Disorders Are Discussed and Considered in Genetic Counseling?

Genetic disorders may be detected at any time during the lifespan; however, most disorders are detected during the gestational period or soon after a child is born. Results during the gestational period may reveal Down syndrome or spina bifida, while postnatal testing may reveal phenylketonuria or hypothyroidism. Most disorders occur when one or both of the parents pass on their genes. Couples who are carriers may choose to have their DNA tested before conception to determine if they are carriers for Tay Sachs, cystic fibrosis, or Huntington's disease.

Ethics and Genetic Counseling

Genetic counselors must communicate not only the risks of prenatal testing but also the significance of such testing and the potential for therapeutic intervention (National Human Genome Research, 2012). Most people have limited knowledge about disabilities and prenatal decisionmaking during the screening process occurs within a limited timeline, while requiring families to learn new medical information (Roberts, Stough, & Parrish, 2002). These choices are laden with uncertainty and raise challenging ethical, legal and social issues (National Human Genome Research Institute, 2012). Genetic counselors are trained to facilitate decision-making to promote informed choices. Genetic information can have profound psychological meaning for clients, particularly for members of families affected by a genetic condition (National Human Genome Research Institute, 2012).

REFERENCES

American Board of Genetic Counseling (2012). *Genetic counselors' scope of practice.* Retrieved from http://www.abgc.net/docs/GC_Scope_of_prractice_final.pdf

March of Dimes (2012). *Genetic counseling.* Retrieved from http://www.marchofdimes.com/pregnancy/trying_geneticcounseling.html

National Society of Genetic Counselors' Definition Task Force. (2006). A new definition of genetic counseling: National Society of Genetic Counselors' Task Force report. *Journal of Genetic Counseling, 15*(2), 77–82.

National Society of Genetic Counselors (2012). *Genetic counseling as a profession.* Retrieved from http://www.nsgc.org/Home/ConsumerHomePage/PatientFAQs/tabid/338/Default.aspx

National Human Genome Research Institute. (2012). *The Johns Hopkins University/National Human Genome Research Institute Genetic Counseling Training Program: Introduction.* Retrieved from http://www.genome.gov/10001156

Roberts, C. D., Stough, L. M., & Parrish, L. H. (2002). The role of genetic counseling in the elective termination of pregnancies involving fetuses with disabilities. *Journal of Special Education, 36*(1), 48–55.

Sequeiros, J., & Guimarães, B. (2007). Definitions of genetic testing. *EuroGentest Network of Excellence Project.* Retrieved from http://www.eurogentest.org/web/files/public/unit3/DefinitionsGeneticTesting-3rdDraf18Jan07.pdf

Zych, K. A. (2008). Genetic counseling. In E. Fletcher-Janzen & C. R. Reynolds (Eds.), *Encyclopedia of special education* (3rd ed.). Hoboken, NJ: Wiley.

Laura M. Stough
Marcia L. Montague
Texas A&M University

GENETIC FACTORS IN BEHAVIOR

Behavior genetics is more complex than the study of genetic influences on physical traits because it is hard to define behavioral traits reliably, to assess them validly, and to control situational influences. Nonhuman species offer advantages of convenience and control for genetic research, but the lack of precise analogs between human and animal behavior, especially pathological behavior, limits the value of animal research for human behavior genetics.

However, a number of human pathological genes have more or less specific effects on behavior. The child with phenylketonuria (PKU) is likely to be hyperactive and irritable, have outbursts of temper, abnormal postural attitudes, and agitated behavior; about 10% of those affected show psychotic behavior. Characteristic behavioral changes often precede the choreic movements in Huntington's chorea. Congenital cretinism, which may be recessively inherited, produces effects on personality. Perhaps the most striking example of a gene-induced behavioral defect is the bizarre tendency for self-mutilation in Lesch-Nyhan syndrome.

Chromosomal aberrations also have effects on behavior. Children with Down syndrome are thought to be happier and more responsive to their environment than other children of comparable IQ; they often display musical ability. Girls with Turner syndrome rate high on verbal IQ tests but below average on performance measures; they seem to have a deficit in perceptual organization. The XYY karyotype is alleged to show a predisposition to criminality and aggressive behavior; however, a causal link between an excess or deficiency of chromosomal material and a behavior phenotype is obscure.

There is more information about the genetics of abnormal behavior than about how normal behavior is encoded in the gene loci. Schizophrenia, with incidence in the 1% range, has been studied in families, and 2% to 5% of the parents and 6% to 10% of the siblings are affected. If a propositus and parent are both affected, the risk for the siblings is higher. Concordance is much greater for monozygotic than for dizygotic twin pairs. Children of schizophrenic parents raised by their natural parents and those raised by adoptive parents show the same incidence of schizophrenia. This finding seems to establish a role for heredity in schizophrenia. However, questions of genetic heterogeneity, the role of environmental stress, and the nature of the biochemical abnormalities associated with schizophrenia remain to be answered. At present, it does not seem reasonable to suspect a single gene-determined basic defect.

The affective disorders are somewhat similar to schizophrenia in terms of population incidence and frequency within families. It has been suggested that bipolar disease is an x-linked dominant disease, but so simple a hypothesis seems implausible on the basis of current evidence. Biochemical evidence of a single-gene basis for either the bipolar or the unipolar type is still lacking.

Developmental aphasia appears to be caused by the inability of the aphasic child to process auditory stimuli presented at a normal rate. This ability does develop eventually, but at a later age than average, and it is suspected to be an autosomal dominant trait (Thompson & Thompson, 1980). The evidence favoring the familial nature of dyslexia is compelling, but the factors that account for the aggregation of cases remain unclear. Some types of dyslexia seem to be influenced by the genes and it is speculated that dyslexia is an autosomal dominant condition with some degree of sex limitation (males are affected far more frequently).

A number of disorders that are considered behavioral, such as the pervasive developmental disorders and conduct disorders, have genetic links that are almost certainly polygenetic and cannot be linked to a single gene (Gillberg, 1995; Knopick & Bidwell, 2011). This has made studying the genetic basis of complex human behavior at the single gene level quite complex. It is difficult to predict precise behavioral outcomes or patterns for children, even with extensive data on parents.

By the application of biometrical genetics and twin studies, evidence for heritability has been found for infant behavior and temperament, introversion-extroversion, and neuroticism. Empirical evidence on sibling resemblance in intelligence published since 1915 in the United States and Europe, including more than 27,000 sibling pairs, showed that genetic factors are the major source of individual differences in intelligence (Paul, 1980).

REFERENCES

Gillberg, C. (1995). *Clinical child neuropsychiatry*. Cambridge, UK: Cambridge University Press.

Knopik, V. S., & Bidwell, L. (2011). The landscape of developmental and psychiatric genetics: The example of ADHD. *Brown University Child & Adolescent Behavior Letter, 27*(3), 1–8.

Paul, S. M. (1980). Sibling resemblance in mental ability: A review. *Behavior Genetics, 10*(3), 277–290.

Thompson, J. S., & Thompson, M. W. (1980). *Genetics in medicine* (3rd ed.). Philadelphia, PA: Saunders.

KENNETH A. ZYCH
Walter Reed Army Medical Center

See also Autism; Conduct Disorders; Cretinism; Emotional Disorders; Fragile X; Genetic Counseling; Huntington's Chorea; Lesch-Nyhan Syndrome

GENETIC MAPPING

Developing new and better tools to make gene hunts faster, cheaper, and practical for any scientist was a primary goal of the Human Genome Project (HGP). One of these tools is genetic mapping, the first step in isolating a gene. Genetic mapping—also called linkage mapping—can offer firm evidence that a disease transmitted from parent to child is linked to one or more genes. It also provides clues about which chromosome contains the gene and precisely where it lies on that chromosome.

Genetic maps have been used successfully to find the single gene responsible for relatively rare inherited disorders, like cystic fibrosis and muscular dystrophy. Maps have also become useful in guiding scientists to the many genes that are believed to interact to bring about more common disorders, such as asthma, heart disease, diabetes, cancer, and psychiatric conditions.

To produce a genetic map, researchers collect blood or tissue samples from family members where a certain disease or trait is prevalent. Using various laboratory techniques, the scientists isolate DNA from these samples and examine it for the unique patterns of bases seen only in family members who have the disease or trait. These characteristic molecular patterns are referred to as polymorphisms, or markers.

Before researchers identify the gene responsible for the disease or trait, DNA markers can tell them roughly where the gene is on the chromosome. This is possible because of a genetic process known as recombination. As eggs or sperm develop within a person's body, the 23 pairs of chromosomes within those cells exchange—or recombine—genetic material. If a particular gene is close to a DNA marker, the gene and marker will likely stay together during the recombination process, and be passed on together from parent to child. So, if each family member with a particular disease or trait also inherits a particular DNA marker, chances are high that the gene responsible for the disease lies near that marker.

The more DNA markers there are on a genetic map, the more likely it is that one will be closely linked to a disease gene, and the easier it will be for researchers to zero in on that gene. One of the first major achievements of the HGP was to develop dense maps of markers spaced evenly across the entire collection of human DNA.

Genetic markers themselves usually consist of DNA that does not contain a gene; however, they can tell a researcher the identity of the person a DNA sample came from. This makes markers extremely valuable for tracking inheritance of traits through generations of a family; markers have also proven useful in criminal investigations and other forensic applications.

Although there are several different types of genetic markers, the type most used on genetic maps today is known as a microsatellite map. However, maps of even higher resolution are being constructed using single-nucleotide polymorphisms, or SNPs (pronounced "snips"). Both types of markers are easy to use with automated laboratory equipment, so researchers can rapidly map a disease or trait in a large number of family members.

The development of high-resolution, easy-to-use genetic maps, coupled with the HGP's successful sequencing and physical mapping of the entire human genome, has revolutionized genetics research. The improved quality of genetic data has reduced the time required to identify a gene from a period of years to, in many cases, a matter of months or even weeks. Genetic mapping data generated by the HGP's laboratories is freely accessible to scientists through databases maintained by the National Institutes of Health and the National Library of Medicine's National Center for Biotechnology Information (NCBI; ncbi.nih.gov). The information in this entry was provided by the public domain website for the National Human Genome Research Institute of the National Institute of Health and can be reached online at http://www.genome.gov/.

STAFF

GENETIC TESTING

Genetic tests can be done to confirm a suspected diagnosis, to predict the possibility of future illness, to detect the presence of a carrier state in unaffected individuals (whose children may be at risk), and to predict response to therapy. Genetic tests may be carried out in the prenatal arena, either through preimplantation genetic diagnosis (where the diagnosis is made of an individual embryo before implantation), chorionic villus sampling (CVS), or amniocentesis. Most newborns in industrialized countries are tested at birth for a few genetic disorders that require immediate treatment. Genetic tests may be carried out on children (to confirm a diagnosis, but generally not to predict adult-onset disorders unless an intervention in childhood is essential). Genetic tests may be carried out on adults for all of these indications.

About 900 genetic tests are now offered by diagnostic laboratories (see www.genetests.org for a wealth of information on the specifics). Some genetic tests look at whether the number of chromosomes is correct and whether there is any evidence of a chromosome rearrangement or other abnormality. This kind of test, for instance, would detect Down syndrome (an extra chromosome 21). Most genetic problems are more subtle than this, so tests able to detect them must look at the actual DNA sequence of a particular gene. To detect a carrier of Huntington's disease, for instance, the test must discover a particular expanded repeated sequence of a gene on chromosome 4. If this repeat of CAGCAGCAG is very long, there is a high likelihood of the future onset of illness. For many genes, however, there are multiple different ways that the gene can be misspelled; in that situation, an effective test may need to detect many possible misspellings (usually referred to as mutations). A standard test for cystic fibrosis, for instance, looks for 32 different mutations in the so-called CFTR gene, but will still miss rare ones. Other types of genetic tests do not look at DNA at all, but look at RNA (the messenger that is transcribed from the gene), or at the actual protein product of the gene. Carrier detection for Tay-Sachs disease, for instance, actually measures the enzyme activity of the protein product.

What Kinds of Tests Are Available Now for Predicting Disease Susceptibility?

The number of tests is growing, but most of these are currently applied only in families where there is a strong history of the disorder. For instance, BRCA1 and BRCA2 testing are only offered to individuals with a strong family history of breast and ovarian cancer. Similar situations exist for diseases such as colon cancer or Huntington's disease. But in the next few years, it is expected that a much longer list of susceptibility tests will become available, and may be offered to anyone interested in the information, regardless of family history.

Pharmacogenomics are tests that predict response to therapy. Some such tests are already available, such as a test for estrogen receptors in a breast tumor sample to see whether the drug Herceptin will be effective. A much larger array of tests that predict drug responsiveness for cancer, heart disease, asthma, and other disorders is under development, and some will reach the market soon.

It is likely that the major genetic factors involved in susceptibility to common diseases like diabetes, heart disease, Alzheimer's disease, cancer, and mental illness will be uncovered in the course of the next 5 to 7 years. For many of these conditions, altering diet, lifestyle, or medical surveillance could be beneficial for high-risk individuals. That will open the door to wider availability of genetic tests to identify individual predispositions to future illness, potentially for virtually anyone. If applied properly, this could usher in a new era of individualized preventive medicine that could have considerable health benefits. It will be important to remember, however, that most of these tests will not be "yes or no" but rather will predict relative risk. For this paradigm to succeed, it will also be essential that predictive genetic information is used to benefit individuals, rather than to injure them by discriminatory misuse.

This article was reproduced from public domain resources January 24, 2003, written by Francis S. Collins, MD, PhD, Director of the National Human Genome Research Institute, at http://www.genome.gov/10506784

STAFF

GENETIC TRANSMISSIONS

Genetics, the scientific study of heredity, is the phenomenon wherein biological traits appear to be transmitted from one familial generation to the next. Gregor Mendel, the 19th-century Austrian monk, did the seminal studies leading to the founding of the field of genetics. The history of human genetics since that time has included the development of cytogenetics, biochemical genetics, molecular genetics, immunogenetics, population genetics, applied genetics, and clinical genetics. The science of genetics has shown that inherited traits result from the transmission of the parents' genes to their offspring. Genes interact with one another and with their environment to produce distinctive characteristics or phenotypes. Therefore, offspring tend to exhibit phenotypes similar to those of their parents.

There are two types of cell division that occur within the human body. Mitosis is the process of cell division that occurs in all cells, except for the sex cells or gametes. Gametes are divided during the process of meiosis.

Critical to genetic transmission are chromosomes, which are the small, rod-shaped bodies located in the nuclei of each cell. Each normal human body cell has 23 pairs or 46 chromosomes. During mitosis, cells divide by duplicating themselves, and each daughter cell contains 46 chromosomes that are identical to the 46 chromosomes contained in the original cell. During meiosis, the gametes divide by splitting into two separate distinct cells that each contain 23 chromosomes of the original cell. During reproduction, the male and female gametes join and produce a zygote that contains 46 chromosomes. One pair of the 23 chromosomes is different in size and shape and this atypical pair is related to sex determination. In all mammals, the female has two similarly sized chromosomes, called X, while the male has one X and a smaller Y chromosome. If an ovum is fertilized by a Y-bearing sperm, the zygote will be a male, but if the ovum is fertilized by an X-bearing sperm, the zygote will be female.

The actual units of hereditary transmission are the deoxyribonucleic acid (DNA) molecules or genes residing at specific loci on the chromosome. A recent estimate has indicated there are over 30,000 structural genes per haploid set of 23 chromosomes. The different variants of genes that control a particular trait and occupy corresponding loci on the paired chromosomes are called alleles. For example, one allele, or variant, of the gene for eye color produces blue eyes, while a different allele produces brown eyes. The paternal and maternal alleles for eye color are aligned beside each other in two adjoining chromosomes of the offspring.

According to Mendel's laws, one allele dominates the other in the phenotypic expression of a heterozygous genotype (genetic constitution). Dominant alleles are represented by capital letters and recessive alleles with small letters. Whenever one or both parents are heterozygous for a trait, as often occurs, their children are not all likely to inherit the same genotype as distinguished from its physical appearance (phenotype). For example, a male inherits blue-eyed (b) alleles from both his mother and father. He is therefore homozygous for eye color (bb); both alleles are the same, the zygote is homogeneous for eye color. The boy will have blue eyes and can pass only an allele for blue eyes to his offspring. If the boy mates with a girl who has alleles only for brown eyes, she can pass only a brown-eyed (B) allele to their child. Since this child receives the blue allele (b) from one parent and the brown allele (B) from the other, the child is heterozygous for eye color (Bb). The child will have brown eyes because brown eye color is a dominant trait. Because so many different gene combinations can arise from two parents, two siblings seldom have the same genes, unless they come from the same zygote; these offspring are identical or monozygotic twins.

REFERENCES

King, R. C., & Stansfield, W. D. (1985). *A dictionary of genetics* (3rd ed.). New York, NY: Oxford University Press.

Nora, J. J., & Fraser, F. C. (1981). *Medical genetics: Principles and practice* (2nd ed.). Philadelphia, PA: Lea & Febiger.

Thaddeus, K. E. (1980). *Clinical genetics and genetic counseling.* Chicago, IL: Year Book Medical.

Thompson, J. S., & Thompson, M. W. (1980). *Genetics in medicine* (3rd ed.). Philadelphia, PA: Saunders.

KENNETH A. ZYCH
Walter Reed Army Medical Center

See also **Chromosomes, Human Anomalies, and Cytogenetic Abnormalities; Genetic Counseling; Human Genome Project; Karyotype**

GENETIC VARIATIONS

The independent assortment of chromosomes during meiosis is a major reason for the variation of the genetic constitution in different individuals. Each gamete has 8 million possible combinations of chromosomes from the 23 pairs, and each set of parents has $7 \times 1,013$ possible chromosome combinations to offer their children. Thus, with the incomplete exception of monovular twins, every person is and will be potentially genetically unique.

While genetics is the study of biological variations, medical genetics is the study of those variations that result in, or predispose one to, disease. Genetic diseases make a considerable contribution to the burden of mortality and morbidity in childhood. Mendelian and chromosomal diseases account for about 12% to 15% of childhood mortality, with congenital malformations contributing an additional 25% to 30%. Of all individuals with IQs below 50, at least 40% have a chromosomal disorder (of which Down syndrome accounts for about three-quarters); 15% have a single-gene disease (e.g., Huntington's disease, x-linked mental retardation, Tay-Sachs disease); and 45% have severe developmental malformation (Porter, 1982).

Generally, three major varieties of genetic disease afflict humans: Mendelian disorders caused by a single gene, cytogenetic disorders caused by chromosomal abnormalities, and multifactorial genetic diseases. In Mendelizing or single-gene diseases, the genetic factor is relatively simple. Three distinct patterns are recognized: dominant, recessive, and x-linked, of which there are 800, 550, and 100 known conditions, respectively. The most important of the genetic disorders of early development affect metabolism (e.g., phenylketonuria [PKU], a disorder of amino acid metabolism). Untreated, PKU results in severe mental retardation, decreased attention, and lack of responsiveness to the environment. Well-known autosomal dominant diseases are Huntington's disease, deafness (dominant forms), and neurofibromatosis (Von Recklinghausen disease). Cystic fibrosis is the most prevalent autosomal recessive disorder in White children. Tay-Sachs disease, also an autosomal recessive disorder, has a high prevalence rate among Ashkenazi Jews. Hemophilia is an x-linked recessive disease in which the blood fails to clot normally. Another genetic blood disease characterized by a tendency of the red cells to become grossly abnormal in shape is sickle cell disease, which affects about 0.25% of American Blacks.

The second category of diseases results from failure of chromosomes to develop properly (chromosomal dysgenesis) during the formation of the oocyte or spermatocyte, or during conception and germination, resulting in an irreversibly abnormal chromosome makeup in the embryo. Extra and mismatched chromosomes, as well as structural anomalies, are major forms of dysgenesis. Examples of dysgenesis are trisomy 21, 18, and 13, as well as partial trisomies, mosaicisms, monosomies, deletions, and inversions. Sex chromosomal anomalies include Turner syndrome and Klinefelter's syndrome (XXY). For the most part, the disorders in this category are not inherited, but they involve the genetic material, the chromosomes. Mental retardation and physical abnormalities are the most common consequences of chromosomal disorders.

The more common abnormal genetic conditions are multifactorial in their causation and are characterized by a complex interaction of genetic and environmental factors. The genetic effects are complex and determined by the interaction of many genes, each contributing a small effect. Cleft lip and palate, congenital dislocation of the hip, pyloric stenosis, talipes, and equinovarus are well-known examples; perhaps the best known examples are anencephaly and meningomyelocele, known collectively as neural tube defects. Carcinogens have been found to induce some kind of chromosomal rearrangements that are associated with a variety of human cancers (Radman, Jeggo, & Wagner, 1982).

REFERENCES

Porter, I. H. (1982). Control of hereditary disorders. *Annual Review of Public Health, 3,* 277–319.

Radman, M., Jeggo, P., & Wagner, R. (1982). Chromosomal rearrangement and carcinogenesis. *Mutation Research, 98,* 249–264.

Kenneth A. Zych
Walter Reed Army Medical Center

See also **Genetic Counseling; Genetic Factors in Behavior; Genetic Mapping**

GENIE

The case of Genie involves an adolescent who experienced a degree of social isolation and experiential deprivation so far unparalleled in medical literature. The case came to light in 1970, when Genie was 13½ years of age.

From the age of 20 months to 13 years, 7 months, Genie was confined to a small bedroom at the rear of the family home. There, she was physically harnessed to an infant potty seat. At night, when she was not forgotten, she was removed from the harness and put into a sleeping bag that had been modified to hold Genie's arms stationary. She was then put into a crib with wire mesh sides and a wire mesh cover.

Genie received a minimum of care and stimulation. She was fed only infant food and wore no clothing. There was no TV or radio in the home, and as there were two doors separating her bedroom from the front of the house, where the remainder of the family lived, she could hear little of any family conversations. As her bedroom was set in the back of the house, away from the street, she heard few environmental noises. Her room contained only the potty and crib—no carpet, no pictures on the walls. The room's two windows were covered up except for a few inches at top. Genie's mother, having become blind shortly after Genie's birth, was unable to care for Genie, and so it was Genie's father and brother who were her primary caretakers. Together, they committed many acts of cruelty and abuse, among which was their consistent unwillingness to talk to her and beatings inflicted on Genie for making noise.

When Genie was found, she was extremely malnourished. She weighed only 59 pounds and was only 54 inches tall. Never having been fed solid food, she was unable to chew or bite. She could not stand erect, and could barely walk. She was incontinent for feces and urine. Having been beaten for making noise, she was silent. She knew only a few words. She was essentially unsocialized and untrained.

Genie's case caught the attention of the scientific community because of the unique opportunity it offered for studying the human potential to "catch up" as it were—to develop social, cognitive, and linguistic knowledge after the typical points in development. Particular interest in Genie's potential for linguistic development was fostered by Lenneberg's (1967) critical age hypothesis for language acquisition. Lenneberg proposed that, as is the case with many maturationally timed species-specific behaviors, there is a critical period for first language acquisition—between the ages of 2 and puberty, beyond which a first language could not be learned. Genie faced the task of first language acquisition at 13½. Thus, her ability to learn language directly tested Lenneberg's hypothesis.

In the 9 years she was studied, Genie showed very uneven language learning ability. Most important in this regard is the striking contrast between her acquisition of morphology and syntax on the one hand and her acquisition of semantic knowledge on the other. Genie's acquisition of vocabulary and of how to express meaningful relations through words steadily progressed and increased, whereas her utterances remained largely ungrammatical and hierarchically flat (Curtiss, 1977, 1981, 1982). Genie's case, then, supports a weak form of Lenneberg's hypothesis in that while she developed some language, she did not acquire language fully or normally. Her case also suggests that different components of language are differentially vulnerable to the age at which language acquisition is carried out. In particular, her case points to the separability of a conceptual or referential linguistic component (which involves lexical knowledge and knowledge of semantic roles, and which is resilient in its developmental potential) from a grammatical component, which involves the constraints and rules of grammar, for which the acquisition potential appears to be far more maturationally constrained.

Although most of the scientific investigation carried out with Genie concentrated on her language development, a considerable number of standardized intelligence tests and tests of Piagetian operations were also administered. Remarkably, Genie evidenced 1 year's mental growth every year past her discovery and demonstrated full operational intelligence in spatial knowledge, with less developed ability in some other areas, specifically, those relying on verbal mediation.

The cognitive profile that Genie displayed lends support to a modular view of the mind in which grammar represents a distinct faculty of mind, separate from other components of language and separate from other mental abilities. For details regarding Genie's case history and language acquisition, see Curtiss, 1977. For details regarding her nonlinguistic cognitive abilities, see Curtiss, 1979. For a discussion of Genie's case and the critical age hypothesis, see Fromkin et al., 1974. For a discussion of Genie's case in connection with theories of language learning and cognitive development, see Curtiss, 1981 and 1982. Unfortunately, relations between Genie's mother and the research team studying her soured, and some disputes among those working with her arose. Lawsuits and other disruptions followed, and as a result, not only research on Genie but contact between her and the research team was legally restricted. For an interesting story of this aspect of Genie, see Rymer, 1993.

REFERENCES

Curtiss, S. (1977). *Genie: A psycholinguistic study of a modern-day "wild child."* New York, NY: Academic Press.

Curtiss, S. (1979). *Genie: Language and cognition.* UCLA Working Papers in Cognitive Linguistics, *1*, 16–62.

Curtiss, S. (1981). Dissociation between language and cognition. *Journal of Autism & Developmental Disorders, 11*, 15–30.

Curtiss, S. (1982). Developmental dissociations of language and cognition. In L. Obler & L. Menn (Eds.), *Exceptional language and linguistics*. New York, NY: Academic.

Fromkin et al. (1974). The development of language in Genie: A case of language acquisition beyond the critical period. *Brain & Language, 1*, 81–107.

Lenneberg, E. H. (1967). *Biological foundations of language.* New York, NY: Wiley.

Rymer, R. (1993). *Genie: An abused child's flight from silence.* New York, NY: HarperCollins.

SUSAN CURTISS
University of California, Los Angeles

See also Expressive Language Disorders; Language Disorders; Linguistic Deviance

GENIUS

The original conception of genius was of a deity that would reside within an individual and have a profound influence on the development of his or her mental powers and spiritual growth. Recently the concept of genius has been subsumed within psychology and philosophy. Galton (1869) developed a quantitative concept of genius as an innate or inherited ability, and Lombroso (1891) conceived of genius as a manifestation of abnormal psychology—as akin to madness. Hirsch (1931) even proposed that the genius should be viewed as a separate psychological species.

Historically, the term genius has been used synonymously with the term giftedness as measured by standardized tests of intelligence. In the early stages of Terman's research, Terman equated giftedness with high IQ, and expressed the view on many occasions that from high IQ children "and no where else, our geniuses in every line are recruited" (Terman, 1924). Also, in approaching his monumental longitudinal study of gifted children, Terman (1925) used the term gifted, but he nevertheless titled the entire series of books that resulted *Genetic Studies of Genius*.

Today, researchers note the differences observed between giftedness and genius, and thus make a conceptual distinction between the two constructs (e.g., Jensen, 1996; Simonton, 2000). Also, the term "genius" is used less frequently than it was. When it is used, it often references extremely high levels of adult creativity and accomplishment. Contemporary giftedness researchers incorporate the distinction between childhood giftedness and real world genius into their theories. Renzulli (2005) distinguishes between "schoolhouse giftedness" (which is most important during the grade school years) and "creative-productive giftedness" (which is most important for high levels of adult, real world achievement). Tannenbaum (1986) notes the distinction between those who are consumers of knowledge and those who are the producers of knowledge. Gagné (2005) makes the distinction between giftedness (which can be conceptualized as childhood potential) and talent (which may be conceptualized as adulthood achievement). Contemporary giftedness researchers are interested in determining the factors that link gifted potential to adult eminence.

Research on the origins and nurturance of genius has often taken the form of studies of eminent people or very high achievers, an approach pioneered by Galton (1869). In Volume 2 of *Genetic Studies of Genius* (1926), Catherine Cox and others (including Lewis Terman) studied the early mental traits of 300 geniuses, and estimated their IQs.

The biographical method continues today, with detailed analyses of unambiguously defined geniuses who are no longer living. There has been an increasing recognition among biographical researchers as to the importance of family, schooling, hard work, and other variables in determining giftedness. Howe (1999b) provides case studies suggesting the important influence of a stimulating and intellectual background in the development of genius. Gardner's (1993) analysis of seven eminent creators demonstrates that creators put enormous amounts of time and energy into their work. Taking a more quantitative approach, Simonton (1994) has attempted to identify environmental and personal trends that have affected the quality and quantity of a large number of famous creators. Feist and Barron (2003) examine the impact of intellect, potential, and personality of as predictive factors for the development of genius.

Research by Bloom (1985), however, focused on living subjects who have achieved world recognition. The research by Bloom and his predecessors agree in the finding that genius, giftedness, special talent, and high ability often appear as precocious behavior; for instance, accomplishments in youth that far exceed normal achievements. However, Howe (1999a) notes case studies of individuals who were not particularly precocious while younger, but nonetheless grew up to be highly eminent creators. The reasons why childhood and adulthood are not always linked is an ongoing topic of interest among scholars.

REFERENCES

Bloom, B. S. (Ed.). (1985). *Developing talent in young people.* New York, NY: Ballantine Books.

Cox, C. M. (1926). *Genetic studies of genius: Vol. 2. The early mental traits of three hundred geniuses.* Stanford, CA: Stanford University Press.

Feist, G. J., & Barron, F. X. (2003). Predicting creativity from early to late adulthood: Intellect, potential, and personality. *Journal of Research in Personality, 37*(2), 62–88. doi:10.1016/S0092-6566(02)00536-6

Gagné, F. (2005). From gifts to talents: The DMGT as a developmental model. In R. J. Sternberg & J. E. Davidson (Eds.), *Conceptions of giftedness* (2nd ed., pp. 98–120). New York, NY: Cambridge University Press.

Galton, F. (1869). *Hereditary genius.* London, UK: Macmillan.

Gardner, H. (1993). *Creating minds.* New York, NY: Basic Books.

Hirsch, N. D. M. (1931). *Genius and creative intelligence.* Cambridge, MA: Sci-Art.

Howe, M. J. A. (1999a). Prodigies and creativity. In R. J. Sternberg (Ed.), *Handbook of creativity* (pp. 431–449). New York, NY: Cambridge University Press.

Howe, M. J. A. (1999b). *The psychology of high abilities.* New York, NY: New York University Press.

Jensen, A. R. (1996). Giftedness and genius: Crucial differences. In C. P. Benbow & D. Lubinski (Eds.), *Intellectual talent* (pp. 393–409). Baltimore, MD: Johns Hopkins University Press.

Lombroso, C. (1891). *The man of genius.* London, UK: Scott.

Renzulli, J. S. (2005). The three-ring definition of giftedness: A developmental model for promoting creative productivity. In R. J. Sternberg & J. E. Davidson (Eds.), *Conceptions of giftedness* (2nd ed., pp. 246–280). New York, NY: Cambridge University Press.

Simonton, D. K. (1994). *Greatness.* New York, NY: Guilford Press.

Simonton, D. K. (2000). Genius and giftedness: Same or different? In K. A. Heller, F. J. Monks, R. J. Sternberg, & R. F. Subotnik (Eds.), *International handbook of giftedness and talent* (pp. 111–123). Oxford, UK: Elsevier.

Tannenbaum, A. J. (1986). Giftedness: A psychosocial approach. In R. J. Sternberg & J. E. Davidson (Eds.), *Conceptions of giftedness* (pp. 21–52). New York, NY: Cambridge University Press.

Terman, L. M. (1924). The physical and mental traits of gifted children. In G. M. Whipple (Ed.), *Report of the society's committee on the education of gifted children* (pp. 157–167). The Twenty-Third Yearbook of the National Society for the Study of Education. Bloomington, IL: Public School Publishing.

Terman, L. M. (1925). *Genetic studies of genius: Vol. 1. Mental and physical traits of a thousand gifted children.* Stanford, CA: Stanford University Press.

SCOTT BARRY KAUFMAN
Yale University

See also Gifted Children; Gifted and Talented Children

GEORGE, WILLIAM REUBEN (1866–1936)

William Reuben "Daddy" George was born on June 4, 1866, in the hamlet of West Dryden in central New York. As a young man, he moved to New York City, where he established a small manufacturing business. Through his church, George began working with children in one of the city's most oppressive slums. He had notable success with city gangs, forming his own "law and order" gangs, which transformed young people from lawbreakers to law enforcers. Because children from the slums were often not accepted into the summer fresh air programs for city children, George started a program that provided a camping experience in a rural setting for these needy young people. George's summer program began in 1890 on a farm at Freeville, near West Dryden, and continued until he conceived the idea of a permanent community for young people based on the structure of the U.S. government: "our glorious republic in miniature—a junior republic."

In 1895 George gave up his business to remain at Freeville at the end of the summer with a number of students to begin a year-round program. The community that they developed was based on the principles of self-support—the students worked for their food and lodging—and self-government—the students made and enforced the laws governing the community.

George's ideas attracted the attention of educators and social reformers, and of prominent men and women who provided much of the financial support for the "junior republic." There was great interest in other parts of the country as well, and George supervised the establishment of nine similar communities in other states. None of these institutions consistently followed George's principles, however, and he considered the expansion effort a failure.

At the Freeville junior republic, George developed an elaborate educational and social system based on the principles of self-government and self-support. "Nothing without labor" became the junior republic's motto. The students, or citizens, as they came to be called, attended school, worked in the various jobs that made the junior republic almost entirely self-sufficient, and ran their own government.

George's junior republic, an early demonstration of the progressive education principle of learning by doing, was a major force in the development of programs for deprived, delinquent, and troubled youths in schools and institutions in the first part of the century. George headed the junior republic until his death on April 25, 1936. It is a tribute to the power of his ideas that George's junior republic, which today enrolls 170 adolescents referred by public schools, courts, and parents, still carefully adheres to its founder's precepts of self-support and self-government.

REFERENCES

Holl, J. M. (1971). *Juvenile reform in the progressive era: William R. George and the junior republic movement*. Ithaca, NY: Cornell University Press.

Van Dyck, H. D., & Van Dyck, R. (1983). George junior republic: Fresh start for troubled teens. *Journal of the New York State School Boards Association*, pp. 15–20.

PAUL IRVINE
Katonah, New York

GEORGIA STUDIES OF CREATIVE BEHAVIOR

The Georgia Studies of Creative Behavior was a research program devoted to the study of creativity. Established at the University of Georgia in 1966 by E. P. Torrance, it continued and expanded a similar program of research and development at the University of Minnesota–the Minnesota Studies of Creative Behavior (1958–1966). The Minnesota and Georgia research program has been concerned with the identification of creative potential, developmental patterns in creative thinking abilities, predictions of adult creative achievement, future imaging, instructional models and strategies to enhance creative thinking, the presence of creativity in various population groups, teacher training, creative problem solving, and cross-cultural studies of creative behavior.

The contributions to theory and practice regarding creative behavior from the Minnesota and Georgia studies have been numerous. Significant achievements and events have included the development and refinement of a battery of creative thinking tests, the Torrance Tests of Creative Thinking (TTCT), for use from kindergarten through adulthood; a 22-year longitudinal study to assess the creative achievement of adults whose IQs and creativity had been tested in elementary school; the Incubation Model, an instructional model to enhance creative thinking and incubation; the wide-scale application of this model into the Ginn Reading 360 and 720 series; the Ideal-Pupil Checklist and the Torrance Checklist of Creative Positives; and the founding of the Future Problem Solving Program and the International Network of Gifted Children and their Teachers.

The program of the Georgia studies was supported and directed by Torrance with the assistance of J. Pansy Torrance, numerous graduate research assistants from different countries, postdoctoral students, and visiting scholars. Torrance (1984b) observed that graduate students throughout the world have participated in the studies through their questions, suggestions, and research findings.

Headquarters for the Georgia Studies of Creative Behavior are now located at the University of Georgia. Current activities are concerned with investigating the nature of mentoring relationships; sociodrama as an instructional strategy; developing and revising the streamlined scoring procedures for the TTCT; and verbal and figural work with the Torrance Center for Creative Studies at the University of Georgia in developing the Torrance Creative Scholars Program and the Torrance Creative Scholar-Mentor Network.

The work of the Minnesota and Georgia studies has resulted in the publication of over 1,600 articles, over 40 books, monographs, instructional materials, films, filmstrips, and other creative learning materials. The collection of these materials and other references on creativity, giftedness, and future studies are contained in the library and archives of Torrance, which are housed at the University of Georgia Library and coordinated through the Torrance Center for Creative Studies.

This entry has been informed by the sources listed below.

REFERENCES

Torrance, E. P. (1974). *Georgia studies of creative behavior: A brief summary of activities and results (1966–1974)*. Unpublished paper, Department of Educational Psychology, University of Georgia, Athens.

Torrance, E. P. (1979). *Highlights: Georgia studies of creative behavior (1970–1979)*. Unpublished paper, Department of Educational Psychology, University of Georgia, Athens.

Torrance, J. P. (1984a). *Over the years: Research insights of E. Paul Torrance*. Unpublished paper, Georgia Studies of Creative Behavior, Athens.

Torrance, J. P. (1984b). A retrospective view of the Minnesota and Georgia Studies of Creative Behavior. In *New directions in creativity research* (pp. 65–73). Ventura, CA: National/State Leadership Training Institute on the Gifted and Talented.

MARY M. FRASIER
University of Georgia

See also Creativity; Torrance Center for Creative Studies

GERMANY, SPECIAL EDUCATION IN

Germany provides a well-equipped system of institutions for special education of disabled children and youth. Traditional special education services were developed under the concept of segregation. Not until the 1970s did a movement for integration emerge. It slowly moves forward, against quite a resistance.

Special education in Germany for many children starts in their first years of life. Early intervention for infants who run the risk of becoming handicapped or who are handicapped takes place in the child's home. Young children should not be institutionalized, if possible. In periodical turns—for instance, once a week for one hour—the early educator leaves the responsible resource center to meet the family, provided they agree, in order to give pedagogical and therapeutic help in a playing manner. In practice, this spread method of early intervention can be stonewalled if the family's living circumstances are not suitable or if the adults refuse regular house visits. In these cases, parents can visit the resource center with their handicapped child regularly. Special early intervention can also take place in an institution. In some regions of Germany, this centralized form is still preferred to the

early home intervention. The reasons for this preference are more organizational than pedagogical.

Special early intervention also reaches clinical institutions, especially sociopediatrical clinics, where handicapped children and children at risk can get medical treatment, psychological consultation, and pedagogical support.

Early educational attention often continues during kindergarten time (3 to 6 years old). The early educator can visit the child at home; however, often this educator visits the child in the ordinary kindergarten and gives support in the children's group. The other children may participate in the pedagogical and therapeutic games and exercises. This prevents the handicapped child from being seen by other students as "special" and improves the child's social integration.

In addition, however, there are also many special kindergartens, each of which specializes in one specific kind of handicap. There are working governesses, most of whom have completed an additional course in special education, with groups of, for example, only mentally handicapped infants or only hearing-impaired infants. In some parts of Germany, special kindergartens have begun to open themselves to children without disabilities in order to promote integration. In Germany, for school-aged children and youth with special educational needs, there exist two main options: separate education in special schools, or integrative education with special educational support in ordinary schools. Special educational classes in regular schools exist as well, but are rare. Segregated schooling is built on a 200-year long tradition and still is quite prevalent. In the 1995–1996 school year, 391,100 pupils attended special schools; that equals 3.94% of all 9,931,500 pupils of general schools in Germany (Bundesministerium, 1996). The number of integratively educated children represents only one-tenth of all students; nevertheless, the number is slowly increasing. Exact official statistics showing the number of integrated pupils with special educational needs in Germany do not yet exist.

Since the German reunion in 1990, the Federal Republic of Germany (F.R.G.) consists of 16 Laender. In their territories, the Laender maintain the sovereignty for culture and education. Some Laender with conservative school politics keep special needs students in compulsory special schools; other Laender are promoting integration in regular schools. The Conference of the Ministers for Culture and Education in the F.R.G. (KMK) intends to avoid development in different directions. According to a recommendation given in 1972 by the KMK, 10 types of special schools exist in Germany.

1. *Schools for learning disabilities*: With about 221,000 pupils (95/96), schools for learning disabilities are the most common type of special schools, but at the same time they are especially criticized, because learning disabilities are

only defined in relation to school, and because before education age they cannot actually be diagnosed. Learning deficiencies fundamentally depend on the efficiency of regular schools, which can either support slow learners adequately or not. Through administrative trials, low performance in school is reduced to an intellectual handicap, which is indicated by an IQ of between 55 and 85.

2. *Schools for the mentally handicapped*: Schools for the mentally handicapped were not founded until the 1960s. These schools take pupils who are not able to follow classes in schools for learning disabilities (IQ usually under 60). Nearly 60,000 children attend these schools.

3. *Schools for speech problems*: About 32,000 pupils in Germany attend these special schools. For many of them, it is a school to pass through on their way to another (regular) school or another type of special school.

4. *Schools for behavioral disorders*: In Germany, about 21,000 students with behavioral disorders attend this type of special school, which is in several Laender is called *school for (special) educational support*. This type of special school is meant to be a temporary school, like the schools for speech problems; it should educate the pupils on the learning level of regular schools and send them back to a regular school after a few years' time. However, this happens very rarely.

5. *Schools for physically handicapped students*: Schools have about 20,000 pupils who are all very different from each other in the degree of their physical handicap as well as in their learning abilities. Many children in the schools for physically handicapped students suffer from additional disorders such as speech development, sensory organ impairment, and mental retardation.

6. & 7. *Schools for the hard of hearing and deaf*: Both types of schools together teach about 10,000 pupils, most of them hard of hearing children. In the official statistics, hearing impaired and deaf students are not separated from each other. The Institution for the Deaf and Dumb, founded in 1778 in Leipzig, is considered the oldest special school in Germany. Special schools for hard of hearing children in Germany did not originate until 1900.

8. & 9. *Schools for the visually impaired and blind*: These two types of special schools are attended by only about 4,000 pupils; only about 1,000 of them attend schools for the blind. Quite often, schools for the blind and schools for the visually

impaired are situated next to one another, so single students can easily change from one school to the other according to their educational needs.

10. *Clinic schools*: For most ill young people, this is a transitory school, because they are educated there only during the time of their medical treatment in the hospital. Instruction takes place in the clinic part for children, or if necessary, at the bed or their home.

Besides these 10 special schools, there exist further specialized institutions; for instance, schools for multiple-disordered students, such as deaf-blind students.

The continuously spreading expansion of special schools in Germany was decelerated in 1973 for the first time by the German Education Council, which pled for less segregation and more integration (Deutscher Bildungsrat, 1973). Therefore, since the mid-1970s, educational pilot experiments with integrated schooling ("Integrationsklassen") in primary schools (class 1–4 or 1–6) came into being, first in West Berlin and later in other German cities. Experiments also began later in secondary schools. Integrative classes are classes in regular schools, where three to five children with different disabilities are educated together with other children (without disorders) by two teachers: one teacher for ordinary students and one special education teacher. Since the mid-1980s, integrated schooling can also take place as "single-integration," which means that one single disabled child visits the school appropriate for its residential area, and a special education teacher comes for support only a few hours a week.

Both organizational forms are regarded as successful, and there exists a great deal of literature about the subject of integration (e.g., Eberwein, 1997; Hildeschmidt & Schnell, 1998). Half of the 16 Laender have moved integrated schooling from the experimental into regular status, and have generally opened integrated schooling by law, but always with the restriction that the parents of the disabled child must apply for inclusion and that the necessary conditions for the integration can feasibly be prepared. To establish the required conditions in some cases costs a lot of money and therefore can be refused by local authorities. Then the child with disorders has to visit a special school.

All German Laender still provide a fully developed group of special schools. Even with integrated schooling, only a few special schools have become superfluous. After years of argument and discussion, the KMK passed a recommendation in 1994 that agrees to integrated schooling as well as segregated schooling (KMK, 1994). Each of the Laender can decide on its own how quickly and in which form alternatives for segregated schooling are developed.

Some Laender, so far, only admit inclusion students on *according learning target*. This means that the disabled child has to reach the same curriculum goals as the classmates without a disability do, or else the year has to be repeated. Most of the German educational administrations strictly divide education with according learning target or with a different learning target. If the learning objective differs, an individually adjusted education plan is arranged for the disabled child, with different curriculum goals from the ones that classmates have to approach. Thus a learning disabled, mentally handicapped, or multiple-handicapped child can stay in a regular class without having to fulfill the same standard as the other students. Practice shows that especially learning-disabled students need individual goals only in some of the subjects, and in others are able to share the regular curriculum. Still, some Laender do not allow inclusion with individual learning objectives.

At the moment, all young people have difficulties finding a job, and for young people with special needs it is nearly impossible. Public working administration in Germany certainly provides a complex system of support, but businesses do not use it. In addition to the free market, 600 sheltered workshops offer 160,000 workplaces for disabled people. To continue integrated schooling, for some years now projects of supported employment according to the United States' example are being implemented in many cities.

REFERENCES

Bundesministerium. (1996). *Grund- und Strukturdaten 1996/97*. Bonn, Switzerland: Bundesministerium für Bildung, Wissenschaft, For-schung und Technologie.

Deutscher Bildungsrat. (1973). *Empfehlungen der Bildungskommission: Zur pädagogischen Förderung behinderter und von Behinderung bedrohter Kinder und Jugendlicher*. Stuttgart, Germany: Klett.

Eberwein, H. (Ed.). (1994). *Handbuch Integrationspädagogik. Kinder mit und ohne Behinderung lernen gemeinsam* (4th ed.). Weinheim, Germany: Beltz.

Hildeschmidt, A., & Schnell, I. (Eds.). (1998). *Integrationspädagogik. Auf dem Weg zu einer Schule für alle*. Weinheim, Germany: Juventa.

KMK. (1972). *Empfehlung zur Ordnung des Sonderschulwesens*. Bonn, Switzerland: Sekretariat der Kultusministerkonferenz.

KMK. (1994). *Empfehlungen zur sonderpädagogischen Förderung in den Schulen in der Bundesrepublik Deutschland*. Bonn, Switzerland: Sekretariat der Kultusministerkonferenz.

ALFRED SANDER
Universität des Saarlandes

ANETTE HAUSOTTER
Bis Beratungsstelle Fur Die Integration

See also Denmark, Special Education In; France, Special Education In

GERSTMANN SYNDROME

The Gerstmann syndrome consists of a constellation of problems including finger agnosia, right-left orientation problems, inability to calculate or do math (acalculia), and inability to write (agraphia). When first described by Gerstmann (1940), Gerstmann syndrome was believed to be a discrete, localized neurological problem denoting damage specific to the left parietal lobe of the brain. Considerable disagreement currently exists regarding the specific nature and causes of Gerstmann syndrome. Benton (1961) argued that the syndrome was prematurely described and was based on a serendipitous combination of learning and behavior problems with a variety of causes. Others have argued over its precise nature, some holding that the underlying deficit is aphasic in nature and others arguing that Gerstmann syndrome is related to left-hemisphere neglect. The constellation of behaviors occurring in concert is rare and whether or not they represent a true syndrome is difficult to discern. At present, the syndrome is principally of historical and theoretical interest; there are few treatment implications beyond remediation of the specific symptomatology. Children with this constellation of problems would likely be seen as severely learning disabled and require extensive special education services.

REFERENCES

Benton, A. L. (1961). The fiction of the Gerstmann syndrome. *Journal of Neurology, Neurosurgery, & Psychiatry, 28*, 339–346.

Gerstmann, J. (1940). Syndrome of finger agnosia: Disorientation for right and left, agraphia, and acalculia. *Archives of Neurology & Psychiatry, 44*, 398–408.

CECIL R. REYNOLDS
Texas A&M University

See also Acalculia; Agraphia

GESELL, ARNOLD LUCIUS (1880–1961)

Arnold Lucius Gesell was a high- school teacher and principal before entering graduate school at Clark University, where he received his doctorate in psychology in 1906. In 1911 he became assistant professor of education at Yale University, where he founded the Yale Clinic of Child Development and began the studies of child development that were to occupy him for the rest of his life. To improve his qualifications for this work, Gesell studied medicine at Yale, receiving his MD degree in 1915. Gesell made a detailed, step-by-step analysis of infant behavior, establishing that infant behavior develops in an orderly manner through stages that are alike from child to child (Ames, 1961).

Gesell became a household name in the United States, primarily because of three books that he coauthored: *Infant and Child in the Culture of Today* (1943), *The Child from Five to Ten* (1946), and *Youth: The Years from Ten to Sixteen* (1956).

In addition to his studies of normal development, Gesell made numerous investigations of deviations in development, including mental retardation, Down syndrome, cretinism, and cerebral palsy. Following his retirement from Yale in 1948, Gesell continued his work at the Gesell Institute of Child Development, which was founded in his honor in 1950 (Langfield, Boring, Werner, & Yerkes, 1952).

REFERENCES

Ames, L. B. (1961). Arnold L. Gesell: Behavior has shapes. *Science, 134*, 266–267.

Langfield, H. S., Boring, E. G., Werner, H., & Yerkes, R. M. (1952). *A history of psychology in autobiography* (Vol. 4). Worcester, MA: Clark University Press.

PAUL IRVINE
Katonah, New York

See also **Gesell Developmental Schedules**

GESELL DEVELOPMENTAL SCHEDULES

The Gesell Developmental Schedules were first published by Gesell and his colleagues in 1940, although updated administration and norms are reported by Gesell, Ilg, and Ames (1974) and Ames, Gillespie, Haines, and Ilg (1979). The schedules provide an empirical method of measuring the development of infants and young children from 4 weeks through 5 years of age. Items on the schedules are ordinally arranged, with behaviors typical of successive ages (e.g., 42 months, 48 months, 54 months) listed. The administration of the schedules requires direct observations of children's responses to stimulus objects such as toys and parent interviews.

Four areas of development are included in the schedules: motor, adaptive, language, and personal/social. Items include walking up and down stairs, saying words and sentences, and imitating drawing circles and crosses. Behavioral norms for ages $2\frac{1}{2}$ through 5 years of age are reported in Ames et al. (1979). Interrater reliability coefficients over .95 have been found (Knobloch & Pasamanick, 1974). The scales are quite dated and no longer useful in this form.

REFERENCES

Ames, L. B., Gillespie, B. S., Haines, J., & Ilg, F. L. (1979). *The Gesell Institute's child from one to six: Evaluating the behavior of the preschool child*. New York, NY: Harper & Row.

Gesell, A., Ilg, F., & Ames, L. B. (1974). *Infant and child in the culture of today* (rev. ed.). New York, NY: Harper & Row.

Knobloch, H., & Pasamanick, B. (Eds.). (1974). *Gesell and Amatruda's developmental diagnosis* (3rd ed.). Hagerstown, MD: Harper & Row.

PATTI L. HARRISON
University of Alabama

See also **Bayley Scales for Infant Development–Second Edition**

GESELL SCHOOL READINESS TEST

The Gesell School Readiness Test (Ilg, Ames, Haines, & Gillespie, 1978), a behavior test for children ages 5 through 10 years, determines children's readiness for school and promotions to succeeding grade levels according to developmental level. The administration of the test requires about half an hour. The test consists of an interview with the child (questions about the child's age, birthday, number of siblings, and father's occupation); paper and pencil tests (writing name, address, date, and numbers); copying of forms (e.g., circle, triangle, square); finishing of a drawing of an incomplete man; right and left orientation; the Monroe Visual Tests; and questions about what the child likes to do best at home and at school.

Behavioral norms (i.e., the typical scores for children at each year from 5 through 10 years of age) are provided for each section of the instrument. Ilg et al. (1978) provide detailed descriptions of average children at each year from 5 through 10 years of age. Ilg et al. (1978) also report several psychometric characteristics of the tests. These include a description of the standardization sample and sex and group differences.

REFERENCE

Ilg, F. L., Ames, L. B., Haines, T., & Gillespie, C. (1978). *School readiness: Behavior tests used at the Gesell Institute* (Rev. ed.). New York, NY: Harper & Row.

PATTI L. HARRISON
University of Alabama

See also **Gesell Developmental Schedules**

GETMAN, GERALD N. (1913–1990)

A native of Larchwood, Iowa, Gerald M. Getman earned his doctor of optometry degree from Northern Illinois College of Optometry (NICO) in 1937. He was subsequently awarded an honorary doctor of ocular sciences degree in 1957 from NICO as well as the honorary doctor of sciences degree in 1986 from the State University of New York College of Optometry. Getman conducted most of his work in Minnesota, Pennsylvania, and California, spending 3 years as director of research and child development (1967–1970) at the Pathway School in Norristown, Pennsylvania, and 10 years in education and research in California, first as a member of the faculty at Southern California College of Optometry and subsequently (1978–1985) as part of a group practice in developmental optometry in Newport Beach specializing in children's learning disabilities. He served as a consultant on visually related learning problems to numerous public and private schools and taught special courses and seminars on children's learning problems as a visiting member of the faculties at Ohio State University, Yale University, Temple University, the University of Chicago, and institutions of higher learning in Australia and The Netherlands. Prior to his death in April 1990, Getman had moved to the Washington area where he continued to lecture and consult.

Getman's principal contributions to special education have been equally divided between developmental/behavioral optometry and education. He is widely considered as the father of developmental optometry, with his concept of vision development strongly influenced by his pioneering work with Arnold Gesell on the visual development of infants and children. Their joint research, conducted from 1944 to 1950 at the Yale Clinic of Child Development, contributed to the vision care of children that now enjoys widespread availability from optometrists (Getman, Gesell, Ilg, Bullis, & Ilg, 1949). Getman also had a significant influence on educational procedures used to guide children with learning problems. In order to best prepare children for an increasingly technological and abstract culture, he advocated a parental role in planning their learning programs. In establishing these programs, he viewed clinical labels as ambiguous and useless, creating confusion instead of understanding (Getman, 1976).

Getman authored more than 300 professional papers as well as the book *How to Develop Your Child's Intelligence* (1962), which has become important internationally to both teachers and parents. His numerous publications include *Smart in Everything...Except School* and *Developmental Optometry* (both 1992). He is the recipient of the Pioneer Award of the National Association for Children with Learning Disabilities, the Special Award of Distinction of the International Federation of Learning Disabilities, and the Apollo Award, the highest commendation given by the American Optometric Association. Getman has also been recognized in *Who's Who in the Midwest*.

REFERENCES

Getman, G. N. (1962). *How to develop your child's intelligence.* Luverne, MN: Author.

Getman, G. N. (1976). *Teaching children with learning disabilities: Personal perspectives.* Columbus, OH: Merrill.

Getman, G. N. (1992a). *Developmental optometry: The optometric appraisal of vision development and visual performance.* Santa Ana, CA: Optometric Extension Program.

Getman, G. N. (1992b). *Smart in everything...Except school.* Santa Ana, CA: VisionExtension.

Getman, G. N., Gesell, A., Ilg, F., Bullis, G., & Ilg, V. (1949). *Vision, its development in infant and child.* New York, NY: Hoeber.

E. Valerie Hewitt
Texas A&M University
First edition

Tamara J. Martin
The University of Texas of the Permian Basin
Second edition

G FACTOR THEORY

Charles Spearman (1863–1945) proposed a general intellectual ability, *g*, to account for the fact that all mental abilities are to some degree positively intercorrelated (Spearman, 1904, 1927). Spearman considered *g* to be a hereditary general mental energy that is manifest most strongly in tasks involving "the education of relations and correlates" (i.e., inductive and deductive reasoning) and "abstractness."

Spearman developed the statistical method of factor analysis by which it is possible to determine the *g* loading of a test, or the proportion of variation in the test score that is shared with all other tests in the analysis. This led to Spearman's two-factor theory of mental ability, in which the variation of each measured ability is divided into two parts: a part owed to *g* and a part specific to the particular test. The two-factor theory was later expanded to admit the possibility of group factors, representing groups of tests that share variation in addition to their general and specific variation.

More recent studies confirmed Spearman's observation that nearly all mental abilities are positively correlated. It has proved to be virtually impossible to devise a test that appears to involve mental ability that is not positively correlated with all other such tests when administered to a representative sample of people. Factor analysis of such positively correlating tests can always be made to yield a large general factor representing the variation that the tests share in common as indicated by their positive correlations. In such analyses, the tests with the highest g loadings tend to involve comprehension and abstract reasoning across a broad range of content. The greater the degree of mental manipulation of the input elements of the test items, the higher the general factor loading tends to be.

The observations that led Spearman to develop the theory of g are now well established; however, rival conceptualizations of the same observations have gained wide acceptance among psychologists (Velliotis, 2008). Thurstone (1938) extended Spearman's method of factor analysis to accommodate correlated factors and adopted the criterion of simple structure to determine the best set of multiple factors to represent the abilities contained in the tests being analyzed. The name primary mental abilities, which Thurstone attached to these factors, focused attention on the multiple differential abilities. The general factor, although still present, was hidden in the correlations among the primary factors. Following Thurstone, the number of known ability factors steadily increased. They have been organized into a model of the structure of intellect by Guilford (1967).

There is now general agreement that there are a number of distinct factors of mental ability that are substantially correlated with each other and that the correlation among the distinct factors represents a large general factor. The disagreement centers on which is most important, the multiple distinct factors or the single underlying general factor, g.

Jensen (1979, 1985) interpreted g as the basic biological factor of intelligence and attempted to relate it to general speed of mental processing. He pointed out that g, more than any other factor of ability, corresponds to the commonsense notion of intelligence, that it is most predictive of success in academic and occupational situations demanding mental ability. Today, users of intelligence tests have options as to how they measure g, if at all. The Wechsler Intelligence Scale for Children, Fourth Edition, for example, allows the examiner to calculate purer measures of g, such as the GAI index as opposed to the full scale index that includes processing speed and working memory (Prifitera, Weiss, Saklofske, & Rolfhus, 2005).

On the other hand, Dettermann (1982) suggested that g may simply be an artifact of the difficulty of obtaining independent measures of the specific components of human ability. He pointed out that any complex system will have interrelated parts, which will tend to produce a general factor of functioning. Attending to the general factor, however, will not help in understanding the components of the system, which must be studied if one is to gain insight into the nature of intelligence.

REFERENCES

Dettermann, D. K. (1982). Does "g" exist? *Intelligence, 6*, 99–108.

Guilford, J. P. (1967). *The nature of human intelligence.* New York, NY: McGraw-Hill.

Jensen, A. R. (1979). g: Outmoded theory of unconquered frontier? *Creative Science & Technology, 2*, 16–29.

Jensen, A. R. (1985). The nature of the black-white difference on various psychometric tests: Spearman's hypothesis. *Behavioral & Brain Sciences, 8*, 193–219.

Prifitera, A., Weiss, L., Saklofske, D. H., & Rolfhus, E. (2005). The WISC-IV in the clinical assessment context. In A. Prifitera, D. H. Saklofske, & L. Weiss (Eds.), *WISC-IV clinical use and interpretation* (pp. 3–32). Burlington, MA: Elsevier.

Spearman, C. (1904). General intelligence, objectively determined and measured. *American Journal of Psychology, 27*, 229–239.

Spearman, C. (1927). *The abilities of man.* New York, NY: Macmillan.

Thurstone, L. L. (1938). Primary mental abilities. *Psychometric Monographs, 1*.

Velliotis, E. P. (2008). *Classroom culture and dynamics.* New York, NY: Nova Science.

ROBERT C. NICHOLS
DIANE JARVIS
State University of New York at Buffalo

See also Culture Fair Test; Intelligence Testing; Spearman's Hypothesis

GIFTED AND LEARNING DISABILITIES

The incidence rate of a child to have both giftedness and a learning disability has not yet been adequately determined, although estimates range from less than 1% to as high as 10% (Karnes, Shaunessy, & Bisland, 2004). This discrepancy is due to a lack of common definitions, differences between state policies in program delivery for gifted children with or without learning disabilities, and underidentification of learning disabilities in individuals who are gifted. In a review of state policies for 2001, only 27 states mandated full or partial gifted programs, 9 required an individualized program, and only 4 required identification of gifted children to be conducted in the same manner as identifying children with learning disabilities (Shaunessy, 2003).

Some researchers and parents argue that giftedness is underidentified in children with learning disabilities because these children are able to compensate enough to function in the average range of academic ability. Part of this discrepancy is due to the generic term of "gifted," which may refer to global giftedness, or may refer to areas of giftedness such as cognitive, creative/artistic, leadership, or specific academic fields. Complicating this are the definitions and terms associated with learning disabilities, including the federal definition, state interpretation of federal definition, and ancillary terms (e.g., perceptual disabilities, dyslexia, minimal brain dysfunction). In 1993, Toll developed a conceptual classification of gifted and learning-disabled children that continues to be used. The subtle gifted/learning disabled have been identified as gifted, and also have learning problems that begin to widen the gap between ability and performance. The hidden gifted/learning disabled are those children who may have both giftedness and learning disabilities, but neither is clearly seen. For example, a child with superior cognitive ability and a reading disability may be functioning in the average range, and thus would not be identified as either gifted or having a learning disability. A third group is students who have been identified as learning disabled and are being served as learning disabled; however, giftedness is shunted aside or ignored as the focus is on the learning disability.

Research would suggest that the best practices in assessment for gifted and for learning disabilities are the same. Careful multidimensional assessment of children is essential, whether looking for giftedness or learning disabilities. Identification of strengths and weaknesses is crucial, along with a careful analysis of discrepancies in scores. Information gathering from multiple sources, including teachers and family, is also important. In every situation, the assessment should consider if giftedness or learning disability includes each other.

REFERENCES

Fetzer, E. (2000). The gifted/learning disabled child. *Gifted Child Today Magazine*, 23(4), 44–50.

Karnes, F. A., Shaunessy, E., & Bisland, A. (2004). Gifted students with disabilities: Are we finding them? *Gifted Child Today Magazine*, 27(4), 16–22.

Shaunessy, E. (2003). State policies regarding gifted education. *Gifted Child Today*, 26(3), 16–21.

Toll, M. F. (1993). Learning-disabled and gifted: A kaleidoscope of needs. *Gifted Child Today*, 16(1), 34–35.

CONSTANCE J. FOURNIER
Texas A&M University

See also Acceleration of Gifted Children; Gifted and Talented Children; Gifted and Talented, Counseling the

GIFTED AND TALENTED CHILDREN

Definition of Giftedness

Multiple definitions have been proposed over the years to frame giftedness and different definitions have been given varying weight. Lewis Terman originally proposed that giftedness was simply an individual with an IQ in the top 1% of the school population or an IQ above 140, with giftedness largely a function of genetic inheritance (Terman & Oden, 1925). Leta Hollingworth contributed to the body of knowledge by studying the highly gifted (children with IQs above 180) but subsequently focused on the disparate educational needs of the gifted (Hollingworth, 1942). The Marland Report of 1972 defined giftedness as those who possessed outstanding abilities or potential in the areas of general intellectual capacity, specific academic aptitude, creative or productive thinking, leadership ability, visual or performing arts, and psychomotor ability (Marland, 1972). Tannenbaum (1983) proposed that "giftedness denotes the potential of individuals to become critically acclaimed performers or exemplary producers of ideas in spheres of activity that enhance the moral, physical, emotional, intellectual, social or aesthetic life of humanity." This definition incorporates a number of varying definitions and thus claims a substantial proportion of explanatory power by virtue of its all-inclusive nature. The course of defining giftedness went from one of narrow, specific criteria to one broader and all encompassing. More recently, Renzulli's model of giftedness included the traditional attributes of above-average ability and creativity, while adding a task commitment component (Renzulli, 2002).

Models of Giftedness

Various models have been used to approximate and understand the nature of giftedness. According to the Differentiated Model of Giftedness and Talent, six components interact to produce giftedness and thus make specialized skills or talents (Gagne, 1999). Feldhusen's Purdue Pyramid Model of Talented Development describes talented individuals as human beings with the ultimate goal of realizing commitment to the development of their talent and potential. Howard Gardner proposes that giftedness is not restricted to the intellectual domain, but also manifests itself in multiple arenas such as musical, spatial, or even interpersonal realms (Gardner, 1983). Dabrowski described gifted individuals as having greater overexcitabilities and thus experiencing the world differently (Dabrowski, 1964). Akin to this notion, the Columbus Group advanced a developmental model positing that gifted individuals develop asynchronously where individuals' emotional development rarely keeps pace with their cognitive ones. In the theory, asynchronous development in conjunction with a greater degree of intensity of experiences, leads to a qualitatively different experience (Morelock & Morrison, 1991). The majority of models describe gifted individuals as having both general intellectual capacity and some specialized area of expertise, such as verbal ability, quantitative ability, or spatial ability.

Identification of Giftedness

Gifted identification procedures usually include multiple methods including, but not limited to IQ and achievement test scores, student portfolios, observations, personality measures and even interviews. Though IQ tests are necessary, they are by no means sufficient in identifying giftedness. The complex nature of giftedness and the multiple ways it may manifest, often makes it difficult to rely on any single criterion. However, there is most likely some correlation between higher intelligence and giftedness as some threshold is necessary to produce such achievements. For instance, research has shown that spatial ability is only one of many determinants in gifted and talented identification for some individuals who possess such spatial prowess (Lubinski, 2010). Early identification is advocated though many go unnoticed until later years.

Controversies in Giftedness

Gifted education has suffered from multiple controversies due to claims of elitism, discrimination in selection, and best practice in service provision. Most researchers claim that intelligence plays a role in giftedness but the ongoing polemical debate surrounds to what extent. Arthur Jensen has shown that heritability plays a significant role in intelligence and that it increases over time (Jensen, 1998). Proponents of gifted education have argued against lay beliefs that gifted programs may harm students due to excessive pressure. As an example, Raine, Reynolds, Venables, and Mednick (2002) reported that early stimulation seeking is associated with an increase in cognitive and scholastic test performance in later life. Thus gifted children can be encouraged and motivated to perform to their potential. Tannenbaum (2003) advocated that a strong, special environment enhances the growth of giftedness and that this environment must be in place in order to be gifted.

REFERENCES

Dabrowski, K. (1964). *Positive disintegration*. Boston, MA: Little, Brown.

Feldhusen, J. F. (1986). A conception of giftedness. In R. J. Sternberg & J. E. Davidson (Eds.), *Conceptions of giftedness*. New York, NY: Cambridge University Press.

Gagné, François. (1999). My convictions about the nature of abilities, gifts, and talents. *Journal for the Education of the Gifted, 22*(2), pp. 109–136.

Gardner, H. (1983). *Frames of mind: The theory of multiple intelligences*. New York, NY: Basic Books.

Hollingworth, L. S. (1942). *Children above 180 IQ*. New York, NY: World Book.

Jensen, A. R. (1998). *The g factor*. Westport, CT: Praeger.

Lubinski, D. (2010). Spatial ability and STEM: A sleeping giant for talent identification and development. *Personality and Individual Differences, 49*, 344–351.

Morelock, M. J., & Morrison, K. (1999). Differentiating "developmentally appropriate": The multidimensional curriculum model for young gifted children. *Roeper Review: A Journal on Gifted Education, 21*(3), 195–200. doi:10.1080/02783 199909553961

Marland, S. (1972). *Education of the gifted and talented. Report to the Subcommittee on Education, Committee on Labor and Public Welfare*. Washington, DC: U.S. Senate.

Raine, A., Reynolds, C. Venables, P., & Mednick, S. (2002). Stimulation seeking and intelligence: A prospective longitudinal study. *Journal of Personality and Social Psychology, 82*, 663–674.

Renzulli, J. S. (2002). Emerging conceptions of giftedness: Building a bridge to the new century. *Exceptionality, 10*(2), 67–75.

Tannenbaum, A. J. (1983). *Gifted children, psychological and educational perspectives*. New York, NY: Macmillan.

Tannenbaum, A. J. (2003). Nature and nurture of giftedness. In N. Colangelo & G. Davis (Eds.), *Handbook of gifted education* (3rd ed., pp. 45–59). Boston, MA: Allyn & Bacon.

Terman, L. M., & Oden, M. H. (1925). *Genetic studies of genius: Mental and physical traits of a thousand gifted children*. Stanford, CA: Stanford University Press.

DANNY B. HAJOVSKY
University of Kansas
Fourth edition

GIFTED AND TALENTED, COUNSELING THE

For many years, research related to counseling the gifted populations was relatively scarce, because of prevailing beliefs that those who were gifted were also well adjusted (Keitel, Kopala, & Schroder, 2003; Martin, 2005). Currently, more attention has been seen in this area. Several areas that can be important for counseling children who are gifted have been identified.

One area is self-concept. The child who is labeled gifted may have issues integrating this into a more holistic concept of self. For instance, adults around the child may be focused on the giftedness, at the cost of the child feeling different and alienated from peers. Helping children who are gifted explore all aspects of themselves and feel good about themselves in general is important to overall adjustment.

Social skills development is another area that may require counseling. While many children who are gifted have good social skills, others may need support. For example, children who are gifted may have a difficult time understanding why peers can't see the world the way they do, and may respond with frustration, irritation, or sarcasm. This in turn affects relationships. Helping take another's point of view and having skills in how to deal with social situations that can be uncomfortable can be useful for the gifted child.

Traits often associated with giftedness, such as perfectionism or obsessive thinking, can be a focus of counseling (Lupart, Pyryt, Watson, & Pierce, 2005). The degree to which these conditions interfere with learning and social relationships will dictate the need for counseling.

Additional co-occurrence of mental health problems can occur with children who are gifted. Research suggests that children who are gifted may also have any of the mental health disorders seen in childhood (e.g., Flint, 2001; Little, 2002; Pfeiffer, 2001). Asperger syndrome, a form of autism, has recently come under examination, as some children with this syndrome may also have skills and/or talents that are highly developed and in some cases fall into the gifted range. These children may need counseling and intervention targeted toward symptom clusters, particularly in social interactions, stereotypical behaviors, and interference with social, academic, or occupational areas of functioning (Henderson, 2001).

Family issues can be a focus for counseling, especially in terms of understanding reasonable expectations for the child who is gifted, as well as siblings who may be more typical. For example, how is the family handling the all-"A" report card from the child who is gifted and put forth minimal effort, compared with the "A, B, & C" report card from a sibling who has put forth great effort? In particular, helping families adjust to typical and atypical developmental expectations can be helpful. As another example, the child who is gifted academically may be more typical in emotional development. The child's well-developed vocabulary and reasoning ability may mask emotional needs. Other issues that bring typical families to counseling, such as dealing with loss or behavioral problems, can also be a focus for families with children who are gifted.

Career counseling is important for the adolescent who is gifted. Often, while the child who is gifted can do well academically, there may be issues in deciding on career choices. Some children who are gifted move from interest to interest, making decisions about career choices challenging. Other children who are gifted focus in one area of interest, which may constrict career choices. Having the ability to explore career choices can be helpful, especially in terms of college choices and exploring which interests may be related to career and which interests may lead to important leisure choices.

There is no clear evidence that children who are gifted respond differently to empirically supported interventions for particular mental health support (e.g., career counseling or family psychoeducational counseling) or for specific disorder intervention (e.g., for depression or ADHD) when compared with more typical peers. This suggests that at this time, using empirically supported interventions associated with the presenting (or determined) issue is likely to be a reasonable course of action. There is no one specific theoretical approach or intervention type that appears to be best for counseling with children who are gifted and their families. In general, the counselor needs to be competent in the theoretical approach and interventions used. Further, the counselor must be sensitive to how well family and child expectations meet therapist expectations (Bourdeau & Thomas, 2003). In particular, the counselor may have to assist the family with a gifted child in negotiating the insurance system in order to be able to receive counseling (Anderson, 2001). Finally, the counselor must continue to monitor research to provide the best possible empirically supported interventions to meet the mental health needs of children who are gifted and their families.

REFERENCES

Anderson, C. E. (2001). The role of managed mental health care in counseling gifted children and families. *Roeper Review, 24*(1), 26–32.

Bourdeau, B., & Thomas, V. (2003). Counseling gifted clients and their families: Comparing clients' and counselors' perspectives. *Journal of Secondary Gifted, 12*(2), 114–126.

Flint, L. (2001). Attention-Deficit/Hyperactivity Disorder; gifted children. *Teaching Exceptional Children, 33*(4), 62–70.

Henderson, L. M. (2001). Asperger's syndrome in gifted individuals. *Gifted Child Today Magazine, 24*(3), 28–36.

Jackson, C. M., & Snow, B. M. (2004). *In the eyes of the beholder: Critical issues for diversity in gifted education* (pp. 191–202). Waco, TX: Prufrock.

Keitel, M. A., Kopala, M., & Schroder, M. A. (2003). Counseling gifted and creative students: Issues and interventions. In J. Houtz (Ed.), *The educational psychology of creativity* (pp. 243–270). Cresskill, NJ: Hampton.

Little, C. (2002). Depression and the gifted child. *Understanding Our Gifted, 14*(3), 12–14.

Lupart, J. L., Pyryt, M. C., Watson, S. L., & Pierce, K. (2005). Gifted education and counseling in Canada. *International Journal for the Advancement of Counseling, 27*(2), 173–190.

Martin, L. R. (2005). Counseling the gifted and talented: Editorial and introduction. *International Journal for the Advancement of Counseling, 27*(2), 169–172.

Pfeiffer, S. I. (2001). Professional psychology and the gifted: Emerging practice opportunities. *Professional Psychology: Research and Practice, 32*(2), 175–180.

CONSTANCE J. FOURNIER
Texas A&M University

See also **Gifted and Talented, Underachievement of the; Gifted Children; Gifted Children and Reading; Sidis, William James**

GIFTED AND TALENTED, UNDERACHIEVEMENT OF THE

Underachievement is a discrepancy between ability and demonstrated performance, with performance considerably lower than ability. The child who is gifted may have many causal factors that contribute to underachievement. One set of factors may be in an overall biased attitude toward gifted children. Other children noticing differences or showing envy may influence the gifted child to not show his or her ability in order to fit in with peers. Another bias may be in the school and external support systems, which may act in a belief system that there is no need to provide support and services to help the child reach potential. Both of these biases can contribute to underachievement, where the child does not or cannot develop abilities.

Another key factor in underachievement is motivation. Motivation, which can be described as the inner drive of enthusiasm and direction applied to behavior, can be negatively influenced by frustration and lack of success. The gifted child can be frustrated by curriculum that is unchallenging, a pace that is too slow, repetition of mastered material, too few opportunities to explore areas of interest, and emphasis on lower level thinking skills. In addition, the gifted child can feel support through identification with others who are functioning in a similar range (McCoach & Siegle, 2003). Without support and challenge, gifted children can lose their enthusiasm and drive. Without motivation, the child may not put forth the effort needed to acquire new skills and knowledge.

Underachievement can also occur but not be noticed if the gifted/talented child is not identified, or if the focus on a child with a co-occurring learning disability is solely on the disability. Three key elements in avoiding underachievement in children who have giftedness/talent include identification of ability, challenge and support of ability, and coordinated support of the child at school and at home.

REFERENCES

Ablard, K. E. (2002). Achievement goals and implicit theories of intelligence among academically talented students. *Journal for the Education of the Gifted, 25*(3), 15–32.

Gross, M.U.M. (2000). Exceptionally and profoundly gifted students: An underserved population. *Understanding Our Gifted, 12*(2), 2–9.

McCoach, D. B., & Siegle, D. (2003). Factors that differentiate underachieving gifted students from high-achieving gifted students. *Gifted Child Quarterly, 47*(2), 144–154.

Reis, S. M., & McCoach, D. B. (2002). Underachievement in the gifted and talented students with special needs. *Exceptionality, 10*(2), 113–125.

Smith, D. D. (2004). *Introduction to special education* (pp. 226–246). Boston, MA: Pearson.

Constance J. Fournier
Texas A&M University

See also Gifted and Learning Disabilities; Gifted and Talented Children; Gifted and Talented, Counseling the

GIFTED CHILD QUARTERLY

Gifted Child Quarterly is a major publication in the field of the education of gifted children. It is published by the National Association for Gifted Children, 1707 L St. NW, Ste. 550, Washington, DC 20036-4201. The quarterly was first published in 1958 with an emphasis toward educational researchers, administrators, teachers, and parents of gifted children. The journal publishes manuscripts that offer new or creative insights about giftedness and talent development in the context of the school, the home, and the wider society. The journal also publishes quantitative or qualitative research studies as well as manuscripts that explore policy and policy implications. It is a refereed publication with a panel of 30 reviewers and an editor elected by the association board. All members of the association receive the quarterly as part of their membership privileges.

John F. Feldhusen
Purdue University
First edition

Marie Almond
The University of Texas of the Permian Basin
Second edition

GIFTED CHILDREN

The major pioneer of the scientific study of gifted children in the United States was Lewis Terman, whose research on intellectually gifted students refuted popular myths regarding the physical and social inferiority of highly able children and showed that gifted youths were largely neglected in school (Terman, 1925).

The research of Terman (1925), Hollingworth (1942), Cox (1926), Witty (1930), and others promoted the establishment of prototype programs for the gifted such as

Cleveland's Major Work Program (Barbe, 1957), and special schools for talented students such as the Bronx High School of Science (Galasso & Simon, 1981). Federal support, however, was limited and gifted programming was limited to centers of interest within the major cities.

In 1957 the advent of Sputnik generated national concern regarding the quality of science education in the United States and a concomitant focus on gifted youth. This spurred a second wave of programs for the gifted, this time concentrating on students with specific academic ability, particularly in the sciences and mathematics. The National Education Association commenced its Project on the Academically Talented and issued a series of publications on educating children talented in a range of specific curriculum areas (Bish, 1975).

In 1972 the Marland Report (Marland, 1972) broadened concepts of giftedness still further by defining the gifted as those who possessed outstanding abilities or potential in the areas of general intellectual capacity, specific academic aptitude, creative or productive thinking, leadership ability, visual or performing arts, and psychomotor ability.

The Marland Report also established criteria for differentiated programming for the gifted arising out of the broader definition. Appropriate curriculum for the gifted was defined as (1) based on higher level cognitive concepts and processes; (2) involving instructional strategies that accommodate differentiated learning styles; and (3) accommodating a variety of special grouping arrangements.

The establishment of the Federal Office for the Gifted in 1974 and the appropriation of funding for the establishment of gifted programs led to the strengthening of state support agencies, the establishment of national networks, and increased cross-fertilization of ideas among states and centers of interest in gifted education. The passage of PL 95-561 in 1978 provided for the escalation of funding for gifted education at the federal level. In 1981, however, the Office of Gifted and Talented was eliminated along with many other federal programs.

The early 1980s saw a proliferation of research studies on the effectiveness of gifted programming in the United States. Richert (1982) surveyed methods used to identify gifted and talented youths and found great diversity in procedures. Gallagher, Weiss, Oglesby, and Thomas (1983) surveyed teachers and parents of the gifted to determine which program models were most frequently used and preferred; classrooms serving only gifted students were most common at the elementary level and special classes at the secondary level. More recently, cluster grouping has been promoted as a model of service provision. In the cluster grouping model, gifted students are placed together within the heterogeneous classroom and instructed by a teacher designated and trained in gifted education (Winebrenner & Brulles, 2008).

Definitions of giftedness determine program design and curriculum development. Tannenbaum (1983) stated that "giftedness...denotes their potential for becoming critically acclaimed performers or exemplary producers of ideas in spheres of activity that enhance the moral, physical, emotional, social, intellectual, or aesthetic life of humanity" (p. 86). He goes on to suggest five basic factors related to giftedness. They are (1) general intelligence; (2) special talents, aptitudes, or ability; (3) nonintellective factors such as dedication and ego strength; (4) environmental conditions that are stimulating or supportive; and (5) chance factors. Feldhusen (1986) has added to that definition by suggesting that the gifted need a self-concept that recognizes and accepts their unusual potential for high-level achievement. Feldhusen suggests that giftedness in a child or adolescent consists of psychological and physical predispositions for superior learning and performance in the formative years and high-level achievement or performance in adulthood.

REFERENCES

Barbe, W. B. (1957). What happens to graduates of special classes for the gifted? *Ohio State University Educational Research Bulletin, 36*, 13–16.

Bish, C. E. (1975). The academically talented project, gateway to the present. *Gifted Child Quarterly, 19*(4), 271, 282–289.

Cox, C. M. (1926). *Genetic studies of genius: Vol. 2. The early mental traits of 300 geniuses.* Stanford, CA: Stanford University Press.

Feldhusen, J. F. (1986). A conception of giftedness. In R. J. Sternberg & J. E. Davidson (Eds.), *Conceptions of giftedness.* New York, NY: Cambridge University Press.

Galasso, V. G., & Simon, M. (1981). Model program for developing creativity in science at the Bronx High School of Science. In I. S. Sato (Ed.), *Secondary programs for the gifted/talented* (pp. 55–57). Los Angeles, CA: National/State Leadership Training Institute on the Gifted and Talented.

Gallagher, J. J., Weiss, P., Oglesby, K., & Thomas, T. (1983). *The status of gifted, talented education: United States surveys of needs, practices, and policies.* Los Angeles: National/ State Leadership Training Institute on the Gifted and Talented.

Hollingworth, L. S. (1942). *Children above 180 IQ.* New York, NY: World Book.

Marland, S. (1972). *Education of the gifted and talented.* Report to the Subcommittee on Education, Committee on Labor and Public Welfare. Washington, DC: U.S. Senate.

Richert, E. S. (1982). *National Report on Identification.* Sewell, NJ: Educational Improvement Centre-South.

Tannenbaum, A. J. (1983). *Gifted children, psychological and educational perspectives.* New York, NY: Macmillan.

Terman, L. M. (1925). *Genetic studies of genius: Vol. 1. Mental and physical traits of a thousand gifted children.* Stanford, CA: Stanford University Press.

Winebrenner, S., & Brulles, D. (2008). The schoolwide cluster grouping model (SCGM). *Gifted Education Press Quarterly, 22*(2), 2–6.

Witty, P. A. (1930). *A study of 100 gifted children*. Lawrence, KS: Bureau of School Service and Research.

JOHN F. FELDHUSEN
Purdue University

See also Genius; Gifted and Talented Children

GIFTED CHILDREN AND READING

Four basic reading goals have been offered, in one form or another, for gifted and talented pupils: (1) mechanical skills, (2) appreciation, (3) knowledge of the devices of composition and literature, and (4) evaluation and the application of written material (Barbe, 1961; Cushenbery & Howell, 1974; Endres, Lamb, & Lazarus, 1969; Smutny et al., 2009). Dole and Adams (1983) have suggested that reading programs for the gifted are similar to programs for other students, but in gifted programs there is more stress on evaluation, analysis, research skills, rhetorical techniques, and independence. Housand and Reis (2008) suggested that level of independence varies across gifted students and is improved by the use of self-regulated learning strategies in reading.

Textual analysis, the use of genre examples, and the teaching of social-cultural-historical context are central in teaching rhetoric to students who are gifted and talented (Rindfleisch, 1981). Vida (1979) and Brown (1982) have stressed the instructional importance of well-selected examples of literary genres and nonfiction sources. The appreciation of good writing appears to be based on exposure to good writing and opportunities to react to this writing. McCormick and Swassing (1982) have highlighted access to libraries and resource materials in their consideration of reading programs for the gifted and talented pupil. Further, the modeling of appreciation by significant others, teachers, and parents would seem also to facilitate students' appreciation of good writing.

Critical reading is the evaluation of writing content. Critical reading involves the evaluation of sources: what is known versus what is assumed or stated without support. Critical reading involves the analysis of the cogency of texts. Boothby (1980) has emphasized the differentiation of connotation and denotation. Miller (1982) has recommended that critical reading for the gifted stress propaganda devices, analogy, and the use of euphemism. Criscuolo (1985) offers three suggestions about reading techniques that can teach and reinforce critical reading skills: (1) evaluating the accuracy of written information, (2) discriminating between fact and opinion, and (3) drawing conclusions from unfinished passages. Critical reading includes the evaluation and weighing of evidence, as well as the examination of the structure of written argument or presentation.

Creative reading involves interaction with text, problem solving, and the application of the content of text. In creative reading, a gifted and talented pupil ought to blend what is learned with previous knowledge. A basic goal of creative reading is a pupil's innovative application of knowledge by the creative reader's ability to recognize holes in information, construct new associations, and in turn form new ideas. Torrance and Meyers (1970) have suggested that one instructional step toward creative reading is the setting of reading goals for gifted and talented pupils: (a) the resolution of an ambiguous statement or situation, (b) the presentation of a problem to be solved, or (c) the finding of missing information or a concept that is critical in an argument or explanation.

REFERENCES

Barbe, W. (1961). Reading aspects. In L. Fliegler (Ed.), *Curriculum planning for the gifted*. Englewood Cliffs, NJ: Prentice Hall.

Boothby, P. (1980). Creative and critical reading for the gifted. *Reading Teacher, 33*, 674–676.

Brown, J. E. (1982). Supplementary materials for academically gifted English students. *Journal for the Education of the Gifted, 5*, 67–73.

Criscuolo, N. P. (1985). Helping gifted children become critical readers. *Creative and Adult Quarterly, 9*, 174–176.

Cushenbery, D., & Howell, H. (1974). *Reading and the gifted: A guide for teachers*. Springfield, IL: Thomas.

Dole, J. A., & Adams, P. J. (1983). Reading curriculum for gifted readers: A survey. *Gifted Child Quarterly, 27*, 64–72.

Endres, M., Lamb, P., & Lazarus, A. (1969). Selected objectives in the English language arts. *Elementary English, 46*, 418–430.

Housand, A., & Reis, S. M. (2008). Self-regulated learning in reading: Gifted pedagogy and instructional settings. *Journal of Advanced Academics, 20*(1), 108–136.

McCormick, S., & Swassing, R. H. (1982). Reading instruction for the gifted: A survey of programs. *Journal for the Education of the Gifted, 5*, 34–43.

Miller, M. S. (1982). Using the newspaper with the gifted. *Gifted Child Quarterly, 23*, 47–49.

Rindfleisch, N. (1981). In support of writing. In D. B. Cole & R. H. Cornell (Eds.), *Respecting the pupil: Essays on teaching able students*. Exeter, NH: Phillips Exeter Press.

Smutny, J. F., von Fremd, S. E., Shilhanek, D., Golwitzer, J., Flack, J., Weiner, E., ... Toni, Y. (2009). Literacy strategies: Reading and writing. In J. F. Smutny & S. E. von Fremd (Eds.), *Differentiating for the young child: Teaching strategies across the content areas, preK–3* (pp. 38–76). Thousand Oaks, CA: Corwin Press.

Torrance, E. P., & Meyers, R. E. (1970). *Creative learning and teaching*. New York, NY: Harper & Row.

Vida, L. (1979). Children's literature for the gifted elementary school child. *Roeper Review, 1,* 22–24.

CINDI FLORES
California State University, San Bernardino

See also Gifted and Talented, Underachievement of the

GIFTED EDUCATION RESOURCE INSTITUTE

The Gifted Education Resource Institute (GERI) was founded in 1974 to help develop the gifts of talented people of all ages, through research and through the training of educators and other professionals—working closely with the local school systems, and through services for gifted people and their families. GERI in the Department of Educational Studies at Purdue University provides graduate programs in gifted education and a certification program for K–12 educators. GERI also offers intern opportunities for teaching with their GERI Summer Camps and Super Saturdays, a 9-week program for gifted students based on the three-stage enrichment model of Dr. Feldhusen, the director of GERI. GERI Summer Camps and Super Saturdays have been ongoing for over 25 years. Eight other faculty members besides Dr. Feldhusen and about 15 graduate students also work with GERI.

MICHAEL T. LUCAS
California State University, San Bernardino

See also Creativity, Theories of; Gifted Children and Reading

GIFTED INTERNATIONAL

Gifted International is a journal published by the World Council for Gifted and Talented Children. The founding and current editor is Dr. Dorothy Sisk of the University of South Florida. The journal publishes theory, research on, and discussions of problems and practices in gifted education from around the world. In the first issue Sisk stated the following specific aims of the journal:

1. Provide a forum for the exchange of research, identification procedures, curriculum, and good educational practices for the gifted and talented.

2. Generate cooperative sharing of gifted and talented practices and resources.

3. Stimulate cross-cultural research and provide opportunities for dissemination of findings.

The secretary of the World Council is Sisk; subscription orders for *Gifted International* should be addressed to her at the College of Education, University of South Florida, Tampa, Florida.

JOHN F. FELDHUSEN
Purdue University

GIFTEDNESS, CULTURAL AND LINGUISTIC DIVERSITY (See Culturally/Linguistically Diverse Gifted Students)

GIFTED RATING SCALES

The Gifted Rating Scales (GRS, 2003) provides a standardized method of identifying children for gifted and talented programs based on teacher observations. The scales also allow for identification of relative strengths and specific areas of giftedness. The GRS are based on federal and state guidelines regarding the definition of giftedness.

Preschool and kindergarten teachers complete the GRS-P form for children between the ages of 4:0 and 6:11. The GRS-P contains five domains: intellectual, academic readiness, motivation, creativity, and artistic talent. Convergent validity studies have been conducted with the Wechsler Preschool and Primary Scale of Intelligence–Third Edition (WPPSI-III).

The school-age GRS-S form is used to evaluate children between the ages of 6:0 and 13:11 who are in grades 1–8. The GRS-S includes six domains: intellectual, academic, motivation, creativity, leadership, and artistic talent. Validity studies have been conducted with the Wechsler Intelligence Scale for Children—Third Edition (WISC-III) and the Wechsler Individual Achievement Test—Second Edition (WIAT-II).

This information has been informed by the sources listed below.

REFERENCES

Jarosewich, T., Pfeiffer, S. I. & Morris, J. (2002). Identifying gifted students using teacher rating scales: A review of existing instruments. *Journal of Psychoeducational Assessment, 20,* 322–336.

Li, H., Pfeiffer, S., Petscher, Y., Kumtepe, A., & Mo, G. (2008). Validation of the Gifted Rating Scales—School Form in China. *Gifted Child Quarterly, 52*(2), 160–169.

Li, H., Lee, D., Pfeiffer, S., Kamata, A., Kumtepe, A., & Rosado, J. (2009). Measurement invariance of the Gifted Rating

Scales—School Form across five cultural groups. *School Psychology Quarterly, 24*(3), 186–198.

Margulies, A., & Floyd, R. (2004). Review of "Gifted Rating Scales (GRS)." *Journal of Psychoeducational Assessment, 22*(3), 275–282.

Pfeiffer, S., Petscher, Y., & Jarosewich, T. (2007). The Gifted Rating Scales—Preschool/Kindergarten Form: An analysis of the standardization sample based on age, gender, and race. *Roeper Review, 29*(3), 206–211.

Pfeiffer, S., Petscher, Y., & Kumtepe, A. (2008). The Gifted Rating Scales—School Form: A validation study based on age, gender, and race. *Roeper Review, 30*(2), 140–146.

Pfeiffer, S., & Jaroseiwich, T. (2003). Gifted Rating Scales. Upper Saddle River, NJ: Pearson.

Spies, R. A., & Plake, B. S. (Eds.). (2005). *The sixteenth mental measurements yearbook.* Lincoln, NE: Buros Institute of Mental Measurements.

RON DUMONT
Fairleigh Dickinson University

JOHN O WILLIS
Rivier College

KATHLEEN VIEZEL
Fairleigh Dickinson University

JAMIE ZIBULSKY
Fairleigh Dickinson University
Fourth edition

GILLIAM ASPERGER'S DISORDER SCALE

The Gilliam Asperger's Disorder Scale (GADS) is an individually administered behavior checklist designed to assess for Asperger's Disorder (also called Asperger's Syndrome) in individuals aged 3 to 22 years. After the initial printing in 2001 (Gilliam, 2001), some user concerns, particularly in regards to items asking about early development, led to a second printing in 2003. Therefore, this review refers to the 2003 update (Gilliam, 2003).

The GADS contains 32 items divided across four subscales: Social Interaction, Restricted Patterns of Behavior, Cognitive Patterns, and Pragmatic Skills. Any individual who knows the subject well can complete the form in approximately 5 to 10 minutes, and the manual indicates that it can be appropriate for the examiner to serve as a rater. Items are rated based on frequency of occurrence, ranging from 0 (Never Observed) to 3 (Frequently Observed) The GADS also includes a Parent Interview form that primarily targets early development and can be used to rule out other pervasive developmental disorders. This section can be completed by a parent or caregiver, or administered by the examiner as an interview. Finally, the record form includes a qualitative "Key

Questions" section that can be used to assist an examiner in summarizing findings, as well as an Interpretation and Recommendations section on which the examiner can record relevant notes.

The subject's scores are compared to those obtained by individuals with Asperger's Disorder. After the form is completed, raw scores from each of the four subscales can be converted into standard scores (mean of 10, standard deviation of 3) and percentile ranks. The sum of the standard scores can be converted into the Asperger's Disorder Quotient (mean of 100, standard deviation of 15) and associated percentile rank. The author recommends that only the Asperger's Disorder Quotient be used to assist in the diagnosis of Asperger's Disorder, and the subscale standard scores are only to be used to help identify strengths and weaknesses and to design interventions. As such, the Interpretation Guide on the record form only includes the Quotient score. The probability of the presence of Asperger's Disorder is ranked as Low/Not Probable (standard score $\leq$ 69), Borderline (70–79), or High/Probable ($\geq$80).

The GADS was normed on 371 individuals between the ages of 3 through 22 years who had previously been diagnosed with Asperger's Disorder. There is no information regarding how these diagnoses were confirmed. In the manual, the author acknowledges that this sample size is small, and that individuals with Asperger's Disorder display a wide range of symptoms. The authors present evidence of geographic diversity within the sample. In order to attempt to match the normative sample with a representative sample of those with Asperger's Disorder, there were significantly more males than females (85% of the normative sample were male). With regards to race and ethnicity, the authors attempted to match the normative sample with the U.S. Census. However, due to the low sample size, this presents some difficulty with using the GADS with racial and ethnic minorities. For example, only nine African Americans and two Native Americans were included in the sample, and no information is presented to determine how many of those individuals were male or female or how old they were. The same problems exist regarding the 20 Hispanic Americans included, with the additional difficulty that Hispanic Americans already represent a heterogeneous group from a variety of countries and cultures. Although 79 individuals were listed as having "Other" ethnicity, there is no further indication that any Asian Americans were included in the sample. Overall, examiners should be cautious with using the GADS with non–European American individuals.

The manual presents evidence for reliability by reporting internal consistency, standard error of measurement (SEM), stability, and interrater reliability. Internal consistency coefficients suggested moderate to strong reliability for the GADS subscales and Asperger's Disorder Quotient. Additionally, the SEMs were relatively small. There is initial evidence for test-retest stability; however, the study quoted in the manual used teacher ratings of only 10 students. Similarly, there is initial evidence of parent and teacher interrater reliability, but the sample size presented by the author is small (16 individuals, 10 of whom had Asperger's Disorder).

The author presents initial evidence for content-description, criterion-prediction, and construct-identification validity. Although the manual indicates data analysis guided the process of item selection, the information provided to describe this process is somewhat insufficient (Campbell, 2005). The GADS items were developed to reflect the definitions and symptoms of Asperger's Disorder in the *DSM-IV-TR*, the ICD-10, current literature, and preexisting measures. Item discrimination calculations also provided evidence for content validity. Criterion-prediction validity was presented via correlations with the Gilliam Autism Rating Scale (GARS; Gilliam, 1995) as well as by providing evidence that the GADS could discriminate well between those with Asperger's Disorder and those without—on every GADS subscale the score was significantly higher for those who carried an Asperger's diagnosis. The Asperger's Disorder Quotient scale could correctly classify diagnostic groups with 83% accuracy. Finally, construct validity was argued by proving that scores were not strongly related to age or gender, that the items on each subscale had significant intercorrelation and item discrimination, and that persons with Asperger's Disorder obtain different scores from those with Autism, other disabilities, or who are typically developing.

The GADS is appealing in that it is easy and quick to use, and provides a useful addition to a limited pool of assessment techniques to identify individuals with Asperger's Disorder. The author presents good initial evidence for adequate psychometric properties; however, more research should be conducted given the small sample size for some of these investigations. The main weakness of the GADS appears to be in the small normative sample. Hopefully further revisions of the GADS will address this issue. It should be noted the GADS standardization sample is larger than several other scales designed to measure Asperger's Disorder (Campbell, 2005). Finally, as indicated by the test author, it is not recommended the GADS be used in isolation to diagnose Asperger's Disorder.

REFERENCES

England, C. T. (2005). Review of the Gilliam Asperger's Disorder Scale [2003 Update]. In R. A. Spies & B. S. Plake (Eds.), *The sixteenth mental measurements yearbook*. Lincoln, NE: Buros Institute of Mental Measurements.

Gilliam, J. E. (1995). *Gilliam Autism Rating Scale*. Austin, TX: PRO-ED.

Gilliam, J. E. (2001). *Gilliam's Asperger's Disorder Scale: Examiner's manual*. Austin, TX: PRO-ED.

Gilliam, J. E. (2003). *Gilliam's Asperger's Disorder Scale [2003 Update]*. Austin, TX: PRO-ED.

McGregor, C. M. (2005). Review of the Gilliam Asperger's Disorder Scale [2003 Update]. In R. A. Spies & B. S. Plake, (Eds.), *The sixteenth mental measurements yearbook*. Lincoln, NE: Buros Institute of Mental Measurements.

Campbell, J. M. (2005). Diagnostic assessment of Asperger's Disorder: A review of five third-party rating scales. *Journal of Autism and Developmental Disorders, 35*(1), 25–35.

KATHLEEN VIEZEL
JAMIE ZIBULSKY
Fairleigh Dickinson University

GILLIAM AUTISM RATING SCALE— SECOND EDITION

The Gilliam Autism Rating Scale—Second Edition (GARS-2) is an individually administered measure used to identify individuals ages 3 through 22 who manifest the behavioral problems characteristic of autism. It is a revision of the popular Gilliam Autism Rating Scale (GARS; Gilliam, 1995) and includes revisions to the test, manual, and completely new norms. The scale contains 42 items that are rated on the presence and frequency of certain behaviors. These items form three subscales: Stereotyped Behaviors, Communication, and Social Interaction. Additionally, the record form includes a parent interview to assist examiners with obtaining information about the child's early development. Also present on the record form are "Key Questions" to assist the evaluator in drawing diagnostic conclusions, space for interpretation and recommendation notes, and a brief summary of the GARS-2 psychometric characteristics.

Administration usually takes between 5 and 10 minutes and the measure should be completed by an individual who has had direct, sustained contact with the child or young adult (e.g., parents, teachers). Raw scores for the three subscales can be converted to percentile ranks and derived scores with a mean of 10 and a standard deviation of 3. The sum of these derived scores also produces an overall Autism Index (mean of 100, standard deviation of 15) that indicates the likelihood that an individual has this disorder. The manual includes clear guidelines for interpretations of these scores.

The GARS-2 was normed on a sample of 1,107 individuals between 3 and 22 years of age who had been diagnosed with Autism. Data also was gathered on individuals without Autism; however, their information was not used in developing norms. The sample was representative of the population with autism. For example, there was a larger percentage of males in the sample compared with females, since it has been consistently reported in research that males are significantly more likely to be diagnosed with autism than females.

The internal consistency of the items on the GARS-2 was determined to be .94 for the total test (all 42 items) and .84 to .88 for the subtests. Test-retest reliability of the Stereotyped Behaviors and Social Interaction subscale and Autism Index range from .88 to .90 for a 1-week interval. The Communication subscale demonstrated a test-retest reliability coefficient of .70. No information on interrater reliability was reported. This missing information is concerning due to the wide range of raters who are qualified to complete the form.

The manual provides evidence of content validity by explaining the evidence-based process by which items were selected. Additionally, a concurrent validity study demonstrated the GARS-2 subscales have strong correlations with subscales from the Autism Behavior Checklist (ABC; Krug, Atrick, & Almond, 1993), which theoretically measure similar content. Construct validity studies demonstrated GARS-2 scores were not related to age, subscales were positively correlated, items relate highly with the relevant total subscale score, and the subscales scores are correlated with the Autism Index. An important consideration in the validity of an instrument like the GARS-2 is whether it can accurately identify those with autism. The manual provides evidence that individuals with autism receive significantly higher scores than those with Mental Retardation or multiple disabilities. Nondisabled individuals received significantly lower scores than any of the diagnostic groups. Finally, according to the manual, the GARS-2 appeared to demonstrate good sensitivity, specificity, and positive predictive value for identifying individuals with autism. An independent review (Norris & Lecavalier, 2010) concluded the GARS-2 may not have good sensitivity; however, their data was restricted to the earlier version of the GARS (with the rationale that there was little change between versions). Additionally, the underlying factor structure of the GARS-2 may best be represented by four factors, rather than the three identified by the test author (Pandolfi, Magyar, & Dill, 2010). Overall, although the GARS-2 possesses several strengths and has earned positive remarks (i.e., Fairbank, 2007), more investigation examining its diagnostic utility would be welcome.

REFERENCES

Fairbank, D. W. (2007). Review of the Gilliam Autism Rating Scale, second edition. In K. F. Geisinger, R. A. Spies, J. F. Carlson, & B. S. Plake (Eds.), *The seventeenth mental measurements yearbook*. Lincoln, NE: Buros Institute of Mental Measurements.

Garro, A. (2007). Review of the Gilliam Autism Rating Scale, second edition. In K. F. Geisinger, R. A. Spies, J. F. Carlson, & B. S. Plake (Eds.), *The seventeenth mental measurements yearbook*. Lincoln, NE: Buros Institute of Mental Measurements.

Gilliam, J. E. (1995). *Gilliam Autism Rating Scale*. Austin, TX: PRO-ED.

Montgomery, J., Newton, B., & Smith, C. (2008). Review of "GARS-2: Gilliam Autism Rating Scale-Second Edition." *Journal of Psychoeducational Assessment, 26*(4), 395–401.

Norris, M., & Lecavalier, L. (2010). Screening accuracy of level 2 autism spectrum disorder rating scales: A review of selected instruments. *Autism, 14*(4), 263–284.

Pandolfi, V., Magyar, C., & Dill, C. (2010). Constructs assessed by the GARS-2: Factor analysis of data from the standardization sample. *Journal of Autism and Developmental Disorders, 40*(9), 1118–1130.

JAMIE ZIUBLSKY
KATHLEEN VIEZEL
Fairleigh Dickinson University

GILLINGHAM-STILLMAN: ALPHABETIC APPROACH

Anna Gillingham and Bessie Stillman derived their remedial training for children with specific disabilities in reading, spelling, and penmanship from the work of Dr. Samuel T. Orton (Orton, 1967). Orton was a neurologist who spent his career studying and treating children and adults with specific difficulties in reading, writing, and spelling. Both Gillingham and Stillman were teachers at the Ethical Culture Schools in New York City. Gillingham left the schools to become a research fellow under Orton at the Neurological Institute at Columbia-Presbyterian Medical Center, New York. She worked closely with Orton and later Stillman to devise and refine their teaching approach for children with specific language disabilities.

The Gillingham-Stillman approach was remedial, designed for children from third through sixth grades who had normal intelligence, normal sensory acuity, a tendency for letter or word reversals, and an inability to acquire reading and spelling skills by ordinary methods, for instance, "sight word methods even when these are reinforced by functional, incidental, intrinsic, or analytic phonics, or by tracing procedures" (Gillingham & Stillman, 1960, p. 17).

The technique was based on the close association of visual, auditory, and kinesthetic elements forming what has been called the language triangle. The following is the description of phonogram presentation from the manual by Gillingham and Stillman (1960):

Each new phonogram is taught by the following processes, which are referred to as associations and involve the associations between visual (V), auditory (A), and kinesthetic (K) records on the brain. Association I. This association consists of two parts—association of the visual symbol with the name of the letter, and association of the visual symbol with the sound of the letter: also the association of the feel of the child's speech organs in producing the name or sound of the letter as he hears himself say it. Association I is V–A and A–K. Part b. is the basis for oral reading.

Part a. The card is exposed and the name of the letter is spoken by the teacher and repeated by the pupil.

Part b. As soon as the name has been really mastered, the sound is made by the teacher and repeated by the pupil.

Association II. The teacher makes the sound represented by the letter (or phonogram), the face of the card not being seen by the pupil, and says "Tell me the name of the letter that has this sound." Sound to name is A–A, and is essentially oral spelling.

Association III. The letter is carefully made by the teacher and its form, orientation, etc., explained. It is then traced by the pupil, then copied, written from memory, and finally written again with eyes averted while the teacher watches closely. This association is V–K and K–V.... Now, the teacher makes the sound, saying, "Write the letter that has this sound." This association is A–K, and is the basis of written spelling (p. 40).

Although the initial, primary focus was a direct approach to phonetic decoding via multiple sensory pathways, this was an integrated, total language approach. Each unit is established through hearing, speaking, seeing, and writing it. The visual, auditory, and kinesthetic patterns reinforce each other. It is a systematic, sequential approach, proceeding from the simple to the more complex in the orderly progression of language development. Such a concept originated in the works of Maria Montessori, Grace Fernald, and Samuel Orton. Currently, popular offshoots of the Gillingham-Stillman approach are Enfield and Greene's Project READ, the Slingerland method, Spalding's Writing Road to Reading, the Herman method, and Traub's Recipe for Reading. This method is the basis for most current remediation programs with students with dyslexia.

REFERENCES

Gillingham, A., & Stillman, B. (1960, 1970). *Remedial training for children with specific disability in reading, spelling, and penmanship* (7th ed.). Cambridge, MA: Educators.

Orton, S. T. (1937). *Reading, writing and speech problems in children*. New York, NY: Norton.

SYLVIA O. RICHARDSON
University of South Florida

See also **Reading Disorders; Reading Remediation**

GLAUCOMA (See Visually Impaired)

GLIAL CELLS

In addition to the neuron, there are a variety of brain cells that function in a supportive role. These are the glial or neuroglial cells (Brodal, 1981). The glial cells are 5 to 10 times more numerous than neurons. The name is derived from the Greek derivative *glia*, which means glue. Originally, the glial cells were thought to function only as supportive tissue for the intricate neuronal matrix of the brain. While glial cells do play an important supportive role, it is now known that glial cells may play an even more dynamic, interactive, and regulatory role in brain function. For example, it is now known that many glial cells surround synaptic areas in an apparent network to restrict the escape of and specify the direction of neurotransmitter release between neurons. Glial cells may also play a nutritive role, providing a pathway from the vascular system to individual nerve cells (Rosenzweig & Leiman, 1982). Similarly, glial cells may assist in directing or redirecting blood flow, especially to active cerebral regions (Bloom, Lazerson, & Hofstadter, 1985). Glial cells also participate in regulating neuronal growth and direction of neuronal interaction (Cotman & McGaugh, 1980).

There are several types of glial cells, the most common being the astrocyte (Latin *astra*, meaning star). Another common glial cell is the oligodendrocyte (Greek *oligo*, meaning few), which is considerably smaller than the astrocyte, with fewer processes and appendages. The third major glial cell type is the microglial, which, as its name implies, is very small. The microglial cells function in phagocytosis of neuronal debris.

Abnormal proliferation of glial cells is the basis of many types of cerebral tumors (astrocytomas). Also, the breakdown of glial cells (e.g., the axonal myelin sheath produced by the oligodendroglia) is the basis of certain degenerative brain disorders (e.g., multiple sclerosis).

Some anatomic findings in the brain of dyslexic individuals have demonstrated significant abnormalities in not only neuronal microstructure, but also glial cell development (Duffy & Geschwind, 1985; Galaburda & Kemper, 1979). These and similar findings suggest that glial cell abnormalities may play an important role in the expression of certain neurobehavioral disorders.

REFERENCES

Bloom, F. E., Lazerson, A., & Hofstadter, L. (1985). *Brain, mind, and behavior*. New York, NY: Freeman.

Brodal, A. (1981). *Neurological anatomy* (3rd ed.). New York, NY: Oxford University Press.

Cotman, C. W., & McGaugh, J. L. (1980). *Behavioral neuroscience*. New York, NY: Academic.

Duffy, F. H., & Geschwind, N. (1985). *Dyslexia: A neuroscientific approach to clinical evaluation*. Boston, MA: Little, Brown.

Galaburda, A. M., & Kemper, T. L. (1979). Cytoarchitectonic abnormalities in developmental dyslexia: A case study. *Annals of Neurology, 6*, 94–100.

Rosenzweig, M. R., & Leiman, A. L. (1982). *Physiological psychology*. Lexington, MA: Heath.

ERIN D. BIGLER
Brigham Young University

See *also* Central Nervous System; Dendrites; Multiple Sclerosis

GLIOBLASTOMA

A glioblastoma is a malignant astrocytoma, or brain tumor. A brain tumor is defined as a new growth of tissue in which cells multiple uncontrollably. Like all brain tumors, glioblastomas have no physiological use and are independent of surrounding tissue. One specific type of glioblastoma is a glioblastoma multiforme. These tumors are usually located in the cerebral hemisphere and grow very rapidly. Glioblastomas, regardless of the type, are always malignant and account for approximately 8% to 12% of all pediatric brain tumors (Robertson, 1998). Like other pediatric brain tumors, glioblastomas are usually primary site tumors—that is, they are not metastases.

The 5-year survival rate in children is approximately 35%, or about one in three children (Stewart & Cohen, 1998). Factors that improve survivability, however, are early diagnosis and treatment. If the tumor is totally resected, mortality rates decline. In cases in which the tumor cannot be entirely removed, irradiation, chemotherapy, or both can also improve a child's chance of surviving. Although radiation therapy has some drawbacks—in particular, a negative impact on a child's developing brain and thus cognitive functioning—irradiation is used more often with glioblastomas than with many other brain tumors due to the glioblatoma's highly malignant nature. Chemotherapy, although it is typically more desirable than irradiation, can also cause problems, including kidney and liver damage, cataracts, ulcers, heart and reproductive problems, slowed growth, and future cancers. Some of the short-term side effects include nausea and vomiting, diarrhea, abdominal pain, fever, chills, hair loss, jaw pain, and fluid retention.

Characteristics

1. Malignant tumor that accounts for 8% to 12% of all pediatric brain tumors.
2. Fast-growing tumors that cause rapid onset of symptoms such as headaches, nausea, and vomiting.
3. Other sequelae include vision problems, decreased alertness, disorientation, and personality change.
4. Due to the tumor's typical location in the cerebral hemisphere, seizures and one-sided weakness or paralysis often occurs.

More often than not, children with glioblastoma tumors will qualify for special education services under Other Health Impaired. Services are often needed to address cognitive changes, attentional difficulties, memory problems, and social-emotional concerns, including lack of interest and motivation to achieve and interact with peers. Neuropsychological evaluations may be especially important in identifying deficit areas and designing appropriate interventions. Home-school collaboration will be critical to assess both the child's needs and those of the family. A life-threatening condition such as a glioblastoma affects not only the child but also the child's parents and siblings. Families need information (e.g., what to expect and what resources are available) as well as support; therefore, it is important to put them in touch with local associations where this information can be provided and support can be found with families who are facing a similar situation.

REFERENCES

Robertson, P. L. (1998). Pediatric brain tumors. *Oncology*, *25*, 323–338.

Stewart, E. S., & Cohen, D. G. (1997). Central nervous system tumors in children. *Seminars in Oncology Nursing*, *14*(1), 34–42.

LAURA RICHARDS
ELAINE CLARKE
University of Utah

GLYCOGEN STORAGE DISEASE (VON GIERKE DISEASE)

Von Gierke disease is an inherited disorder caused by an inborn lack of the enzyme glucose-6-phosphatase (G6Pase). G6Pase is critical for its role in the liver's production of glucose, which the body uses for energy. When G6Pase is missing, glycogen accumulates in the liver, kidneys, and intestines. Von Gierke disease is one type of glycogen storage disease (GSD); there are about 11 known types altogether. Von Gierke disease may also be referred to as glycogen storage disease Ia, glycogenosis Type I, and hepatorenal glycogenosis.

In the United States, the lack of newborn screening precludes reliable incidence rate estimates. However, it is suggested that for glycogen storage disorders as a group, the incidence is around 1 case per 20,000–25,000 births. For Von Gierke disease in particular, the incidence is approximately 1 case in 100,000 births. Von Gierke disease can occur in any ethnic group but is more common in Jewish individuals.

Von Gierke disease presents during the first year of life. Symptoms include

Characteristics

1. Low blood sugar levels and liver enlargement (hepatomegaly) that may cause seizures.
2. Slow growth and very short stature.
3. Predispositions to bleeding episodes (e.g., nosebleeds).
4. Delayed onset of puberty.
5. A characteristic "doll-like" facial appearance with full cheeks.
6. Intermittent diarrhea (etiology unknown).

Long-term complications of Von Gierke disease include

1. Gout.
2. Tumors of the liver.
3. Osteoporosis.
4. Kidney stones and other kidney problems (including kidney failure).
5. Symptoms of severe hypoglycemia (low blood sugar) are likely to follow any illness that causes mild anorexia or fasting (e.g., viral gastroenteritis). This may be evidenced by the individual's feeling weak, drowsy, confused, hungry, and dizzy, with paleness, headache, irritability, trembling, sweating, rapid heartbeat, and a cold, clammy feeling. In severe cases, a person can lose consciousness and even lapse into a coma.

Treatment for Von Gierke disease is limited. It primarily consists of giving glucose drinks frequently during the day. For infants glucose drinks are also given continuously overnight through a nasogastric tube. As children get older, a treatment with cornstarch, which releases glucose slowly into the stomach, may be very effective. Any illnesses that may alter glucose intake (e.g., illnesses associated with vomiting or diarrhea) may require IV glucose support until resolution to prevent hypoglycemia. The mainstay therapy for Von Gierke disease is diet; this requires close monitoring and adjustment by specialized personnel. The chief aim is to avoid excessive carbohydrates and calories while supplying adequate nutrition for growth. Close nutritional and biochemical genetic follow-up is critical, especially during initial and pubertal growth periods. Subspecialists should see patients at least every 6 months.

Students diagnosed with Von Gierke disease will probably qualify for special services under the Individuals with Disabilities Education Act (1997) within the physical disability category. This disorder may require students to be absent from school for periods of time for medical reasons. Accommodations and modifications may need to be implemented to help the student keep up with school requirements. School personnel need to be cognizant of the dietary needs and physical limitations of this disorder. These students may not be able to participate in competitive activities because of the propensity for bleeding and potential for liver damage. The student can be encouraged to engage in other physical activities up to individual limits. School personnel should also be able to recognize signs of impending hypoglycemia.

Until recently, most children with this condition died before reaching adulthood. The outlook for those who survived was dismal. Early diagnosis and effective treatment of this condition have undeniably improved the prognosis. Patients receiving proper treatment and education concerning dietary needs should have a reasonable life span. However, it remains unclear whether good control over these children's metabolic problems will reduce the incidence of long-term complications (Weinstein, Somers, & Wolfsdorf, 2001; Restaino, Kaplan, Stanley, & Baker, 1993). Individuals with Von Gierke disease and their families may benefit from contacting support groups such as Association for Glycogen Storage Disease, P.O. Box 896, Durant, IA, 52747, Tel.: (319) 785-6038.

REFERENCES

National Organization for Rare Disorders, Inc. P.O. Box 8923, New Fairfax, CT 06812-8923.

Restaino, I., Kaplan, B. S., Stanley, C., & Baker, L. (1993). Nephrolithiasis, hypocitraturia, and a distal renal tubular acidification defect in type 1 glycogen storage disease. *Journal of Pediatrics, 122*(3), 392–396.

Veiga-da-Cunha, M., Gerin, I., & Van Schaftingen E. (2000). How many forms of glycogen storage disease type I? *European Journal of Pediatrics, 159*, 314–318.

Weinstein, D. A., Somers, M. J., & Wolfsdorf, J. I. (2001). Decreased urinary citrate excretion in type 1a glycogen storage disease. *Journal of Pediatrics, 138*(3), 378–382.

BARRY H. DAVISON
Ennis, Texas

JOAN W. MAYFIELD
Baylor Pediatric Specialty Services, Dallas, Texas

RACHEL TOPLIS
University of Northern Colorado

GLYCOGEN STORAGE DISEASE TYPE II (POMPE DISEASE)

Pompe disease (PD) is a rare, heritable disorder of carbohydrate metabolism. PD is typified by glycogen (a complex carbohydrate polymer) deposition in skeletal and heart muscle, which causes progressive weakness, loss of muscle mass, and failure of the heart's pumping action.

PD is associated with a deficiency of the enzyme lysosomal acid alpha 1, 4 glucosidase (acid maltase). This enzyme is normally present in lysosomes, which are cellular particles containing primarily hydrolyzing enzymes. Acid maltase is essential for the degradation of glycogen into simple sugars.

The gene for acid alpha-glucosidase production is encoded on Chromosome 17. Specific mutations of this site are believed to explain the various clinical forms of PD. The pattern of heredity for PD is autosomal recessive. Its incidence in the general population is 1:50,000 births.

Characteristics

1. PD's most severe form is infantile-onset disease. Infants appear normal at birth but soon develop hypotonia (generalized muscle weakness) and a "floppy baby" appearance, feeding problems, enlargement of the tongue, hepatomegaly (liver enlargement), and progressive cardiomegaly (heart enlargement). Death occurs prior to age 2, secondary to heart failure, respiratory failure, or both.

2. The juvenile form of PD usually manifests itself by delayed motor development and difficulty walking. Swallowing abnormalities, muscle weakness, and respiratory failure (secondary to diaphragm and chest muscle involvement) soon follow. Cardiac abnormalities are not consistently seen. Death from respiratory compromise comes before the end of the second decade.

3. The adult variant of PD is characterized by slowly progressive muscle weakness (myopathy) without associated heart involvement. Symptoms can begin as early as the second decade or as late as age 60. Myopathy is primarily proximal (affecting parts of the limbs closest to the body), with legs more severely involved than arms. Muscles of the pelvic girdle, the spine, and the diaphragm are the most seriously affected. Older children, adolescents, and adults with this disorder may initially complain of sleepiness, morning headache, and exercise-related shortness of breath as symptoms of respiratory insufficiency.

There is no available therapy for the infantile form of PD. A high-protein diet may lessen the severity of juvenile- and adult-onset disease. Nocturnal ventilatory support may be useful in adult patients, particularly during episodes of respiratory illness.

Families affected by PD should receive genetic counseling. Prenatal diagnosis is available and can usually differentiate infantile disease from the less severe types of PD.

There is no research to indicate cognitive dysfunction as a result of PD. Children with juvenile onset may benefit from evaluation and treatment from physical therapy to assist motor development. Swallowing difficulties may be addressed by a speech pathologist.

Prognosis for patients with PD is clearly dependent on the form of the disorder they have. Infantile-onset disease has the worst outlook, with death before or during the second year. Juvenile-onset PD has a somewhat better course, but no patient with this variant has survived to age 20. The adult form of PD actually has a fairly good prognosis and is responsive to dietary management and supportive respiratory care.

For more information, please contact CLIMB (Children Living with Inherited Metabolic Diseases), The Quadrangle, Crewe Hall, Weston Road, Crewe, Cheshire, CW1-6UR, United Kingdom, (127) 02-50221, home page: http://www.CLIMB.org.uk

This entry has been informed by the sources listed below.

REFERENCES

Chen, Y.-T. (2000). Defects in metabolism of carbohydrates. In R. E. Behrman, R. M. Kleigman, & H. B. Jenson (Eds.), *Nelson textbook of pediatrics* (16th ed., pp. 411–412). Philadelphia, PA: W. B. Saunders.

National Organization for Rare Disorders. (1998). *Pompe disease.* Retrieved from http://www.rarediseases.org

BARRY H. DAVISON
Ennis, Texas

JOAN W. MAYFIELD
Baylor Pediatric Specialty Services, Dallas, Texas

GLYCOGEN STORAGE DISEASE TYPE III (FORBES DISEASE)

Forbes disease is a glycogen storage disorder referred to as glycogen storage disease Type III. The disorder usually begins in infancy. Individuals with Forbes disease lack the hepatic debrancher enzyme amylo-1,6-glucosidase, which results in abnormal glycogen accumulation in the liver, muscles, and in some cases the heart. They cannot convert glycogen to glucose, so they must eat frequently or they will suffer from hypoglycemia. Prominent characteristics in children with this disorder include an enlarged liver (hepatomegaly), unusual body fat distribution, hypotonia, and short stature due to retarded physical growth. After puberty, many individuals have a normal growth spurt, they experience few hypoglycemic episodes, and their liver decreases in size (Moses et al., 1986).

The overall incidence of Type III glycogen storage disease in the United States is approximately 1 in 100,000 live births, affecting males and females equally. However, in Israel the disease affects individuals of North African heritage more frequently, with 1 in 5,400 people being affected and 1 in 35 carrying the gene for the disorder (Parvari et al., 1997). The majority of individuals with the disorder have liver and muscle problems (Type IIIa). Approximately 15% of patients have only liver involvement without muscle weakness (Type IIIb), retaining enzymatic activity in muscle (McKusick, 2000). Forbes disease is inherited through autosomal recessive genes. The disorder is caused by a mutation in the glycogen-debranching enzyme gene (amylo-1,6-glucosidase), which is assigned to Chromosome 1p21 (Yang-Feng et al., 1992).

Characteristics

1. Child may have a protruding abdomen, short stature, and frequent bleeding and infections.

2. Infants may have hypotonia with muscle weakness and poor head control, hepatomegaly, failure to thrive, and possibly hypoglycemia and cardiomegaly.

3. During childhood, hepatomegaly may be present but usually disappears after puberty.

4. Hypotonia may be minimal in childhood, but progressive muscle weakness and wasting may be observed during adulthood.

The treatment of Forbes disease primarily focuses on preventing hypoglycemia. Frequent meals of carbohydrates and high-protein diets help combat hypoglycemia. Some children may receive continuous glucose or high-protein tube feedings at night to promote growth and improve muscle function (Slonim, Coleman, & Moses, 1984). The child should also be monitored for liver, heart, and muscle problems. Children with hypotonia may benefit from physical therapy to promote ambulation (Gandy, 1994).

Children with Forbes disease require dietary management during school. Communication between the school dietician, family, and medical professionals is necessary to coordinate dietary plans. Children with this disorder require frequent meals, often with cornstarch, at specific times of the day. School personnel should be able to recognize symptoms of hypoglycemia. The child should also have a health care plan so that the school knows what to do when hypoglycemia occurs. Children with poor muscle tone may benefit from physical therapy services (Plumridge, Bennett, Dinno, & Branson, 1993).

The prognosis of individuals with Forbes disease is good, especially when the disease is confined to the liver. Liver symptoms often disappear after puberty. Adults usually attain normal height and live a normal life span. Individuals with glycogen storage disease Type IIIa may experience progressive muscle weakness and wasting as adults (Gandy, 1994).

REFERENCES

Gandy, A. (1994, June 5). *Forbes disease: Glycogenosis III.* Retrieved from http://www.icondata.com/health/pedbase/.les/Forbesdi.htm

McKusick, V. A. (Ed.). (2000, August 17). *Glycogen storage disease III (Entry no. 232400). Online mendelian inheritance in man (OMIM).* Retrieved from http://www.ncbi.nlm.nih.gov

Moses, W. S., Gadoth, N., Bashan, N., Ben-David, E., Slonim, A. E., & Wanderman, K. L. (1986). Neuromuscular involvement in glycogen storage disease type III. *Acta Paediatrica Scandinavica, 75,* 289–296.

Parvari, R., Moses, S., Shen, J., Hershkovitz, E., Lerner, A., & Chen, Y. T. (1997). A single-base deletion in the 3-prime coding region of glycogen-debranching enzyme is prevalent in glycogen storage disease type IIIA in a population of North African Jewish patients. *European Journal of Human Genetics, 5,* 266–270.

Plumridge, D., Bennett, R., Dinno, N., & Branson, C. (Eds.). (1993). *The student with a genetic disorder.* Springfield, IL: Charles C. Thomas.

Slonim, A. E., Coleman, R. A., & Moses, W. S. (1984). Myopathy and growth failure in debrancher enzyme deficiency: Improvement with high-protein nocturnal enteral therapy. *Journal of Pediatrics, 105,* 906–911.

Yang-Feng, T. L., Zheng, K., Yu, J., Yang, B.-Z., Chen, Y.-T., & Kao, F.-T. (1992). Assignment of the human glycogen debrancher gene to chromosome 1p21. *Genomics, 13,* 931–934.

SUSANNAH MORE
University of Texas at Austin

GLYCOGEN STORAGE DISEASE TYPE IV (ANDERSEN DISEASE)

Andersen disease is one of the glycogen storage diseases and is characterized by cirrhosis and liver failure. Individuals with glycogen storage diseases are unable to break glycogen down to glucose, thus causing abnormal accumulation of glycogen in the liver or muscle (Wynbrant & Ludham, 1999). Storing excess amounts of glycogen results in muscle weakness and an enlarged liver. Individuals with glycogen storage diseases are unable to convert glycogen to glucose, so they must be fed every few hours to ensure constant glucose from ingested food sources. This disease is inherited as an autosomal recessive trait and symptoms are caused by abnormal glycogen levels (Thoene & Coker, 1995).

Andersen disease is one of the rarest of the glycogen storage diseases and affects less than 5% of patients with these diseases. The glycogen storage diseases affect 1 in 40,000 people in the United States.

Characteristics

1. Infants with Andersen disease fail to thrive, develop little weight gain, lack muscle tone, and may have gastrointestinal problems.
2. The liver and spleen progressively enlarge.
3. In addition to hypotonia, neurological abnormalities include muscular atrophy and decreased tendon reflexes.

Treatment for Andersen disease generally targets treating the cirrhosis and other symptoms. Liver transplants are currently an experimental treatment for Andersen disease.

Special education services may be available for students with Andersen disease under the Other Health Impairment category, although most individuals do not survive to school age. In addition to attention to medical problems concerning the liver and spleen, these students may need services targeting motor and neurological deficits. Occupational and physical therapy may be needed to assist with development of gross and fine motor skills. Psychoeducational testing should occur to determine the presence of neurological deficits.

Andersen disease is an extremely rare form of a glycogen storage disease, and cirrhosis of the liver or scarring of muscles and heart can occur. Death usually occurs before the age of 2 years. Current research is investigating liver transplantation as a treatment.

REFERENCES

Thoene, J. G., & Coker, N. P. (Eds.). (1995). *Physicians' guide to rare diseases* (2nd ed.). Montvale, NJ: Dowden.

Wynbrandt, J., & Ludman, M. D. (1999). *The encyclopedia of genetic disorders and birth defects.* New York, NY: Facts on File.

JENNIFER HARGRAVE
University of Texas at Austin

GLYCOGEN STORAGE DISEASE TYPE V (MCARDLE DISEASE)

McArdle disease, or glycogen storage disease Type V, is an autosomal recessive metabolic disorder that results in a defect in glycogen breakdown in skeletal muscle tissue. The breakdown of glycogen is necessary to create the energy that is especially needed during exercise. McArdle disease is characterized by a lack of the enzyme muscle glycogen phosphorylase. The primary store of glucose in the muscle tissue is in glycogen, and muscle glycogen phosphorylase acts as a catalyst in the degradation of glycogen into glucose. Without the capacity to break down glycogen, muscle tissue receives insufficient energy, resulting in fatigue and pain from only minimal activity.

The number of people diagnosed with this rare disease has been steadily growing in the past decades and is conservatively estimated at 1 in 100,000 (Haller, 2000). McArdle disease affects equal numbers of males and females (Gandy, 1994). Age of onset of McArdle disease is during childhood or in adolescence, although due to the nature of the symptoms, diagnosis of McArdle disease is often delayed until persons are in their 20s or 30s. This delay in diagnosis occurs because symptoms present in childhood are less severe and the exercise intolerance usually begins in late childhood or early adolescence (Bartram, Edwards, & Beynon, 1995). Additionally, symptoms of McArdle disease are exercise induced and are often attributed to the patient's being in poor physical condition or lacking in motivation (Haller, 2000).

Characteristics

The following symptoms are brought on by exercise: short duration, intense exercise (e.g., sprinting or lifting and carrying heavy objects) or low exertion, sustained activity (e.g., bike riding).

1. Tenderness or pain in the muscles (myalgia).
2. Severe cramps.
3. Early fatigue and muscle weakness.
4. Myoglobinuria can occur when exercise is continued after muscle pain begins. In severe cases, myoglobinuria can result in renal failure.
5. Patients report that when they rest briefly at the first sign of muscle pain, they then can continue to exercise. This is known as the "second wind" phenomenon.

These characteristics depict the typical picture of McArdle disease; there are variations, including a severe infantile presentation. Diagnosis of McArdle disease can be confirmed by histochemical staining of a muscle biopsy or by an ischemic forearm test (Gandy, 1994). Currently, there is no treatment for McArdle disease, and management focuses on symptom reduction. Symptom reduction aims to increase tolerance to exercise and is achieved by facilitating the use of energy sources other than muscle glycogen. Symptom reduction involves both exercise management and dietary management. Patients with McArdle disease should not avoid exercise. To maximize the function of muscle mitochondrial enzymes, they need to stay as active as is tolerable. Mitochondrial biogenesis reduces the dependence of the muscles on glycogen metabolism for energy. Exercise will increase circulatory capacity, which may increase mitochondrial biogenesis while also increasing delivery of blood-borne fuel to the muscle (Haller, 2000). Dietary management has also been used to reduce symptoms. Although no single diet has been determined to be the most effective for patients with McArdle disease, the diets used aim to provide alternative energy sources to the skeletal muscle. Protein, fatty acid, and carbohydrate supplementation have been used as treatments with some success (Bartram et al., 1995). Vitamin B6 supplements have been successful in some cases, although confirmation of the benefits is needed (Haller, 2000). Patients with McArdle disease must avoid excess weight because it requires more energy during activity.

Special education services may be available to children with McArdle disease under the handicapping condition of Other Health Impaired or Physical Disability, although they may not require special therapy. However, it is important that the exercise encountered in normal play is monitored so as not to cause damage to muscle or to cause episodes of myoglobinuria.

Severity of symptom expression varies for each patient. Exercise intolerance is usually lifelong because there is no cure for McArdle disease. Muscle atrophy and weakness of the muscle may begin in adolescence and become progressively worse later in life (Gandy, 1994). The earlier the diagnosis, the better the overall prognosis because muscle injury and severe episodes of myoglobinuria can be monitored or avoided. In severe cases, myoglobinuria can lead to renal failure. Current research focuses on the nutritional regimen that will best benefit patients with McArdle disease. Creatine therapy is being studied as a dietary management approach for treatment (Vorgerd et al., 2000). Gene therapy using an adenovirus to correct the enzyme deficiency is currently being researched and in the future may be a successful therapy for McArdle disease (Bartam et al., 1995).

REFERENCES

Bartram, C., Edwards, R. H. T., & Beynon, R. J. (1995). McArdle's disease: Muscle glycogen phosphorylase deficiency. *Biochimica et Biophysica Acta, 1272*, 1–13.

Gandy, A. (1994, April 13). McArdle disease: Glycogenosis V. Retrieved from http://www.icondata.com/health/pedbase/.les/MCARDLED.HTM

Haller, R. G. (2000). Treatment of McArdle disease. *Archives of Neurology, 57*, 923–924.

Vorgerd, M., Grehl, T., Jager, M., Muller, K., Freitag, G., Patzold, T., ... Malin, J. P. (2000). Creatine therapy in myophosphorylase deficiency (McArdle disease). *Archives of Neurology, 57*, 56–963.

KELLIE HIGGINS
University of Texas at Austin

GLYCOGEN STORAGE DISEASE TYPE VI

Hers disease, glycogen storage disease VI, is a hereditary glycogen storage disease caused by a deficiency of the enzyme called liver phosphorylase. Typically seen in children between the ages of 1 and 5, Hers disease sometimes goes undiagnosed until adulthood. The most prominent symptom of Hers disease is an enlarged liver. This anomaly occurs as a result of low-level phosphorylase's inability to break down glycogen into glucose, thus causing the glycogen to accumulate in the liver, resulting in the enlargement of the liver.

Prevalence of Hers disease is estimated at 1 in 20,000 persons and is predominantly asymptomatic. Symptoms that are present in childhood often dissipate by puberty. Treatment often involves dietary cognizance, in that meals should be eaten on regular intervals and adjusted as needed to maintain glucose levels. Monitoring by a physician also may be helpful. Often, no special education attention is needed in patients with Hers disease and prognosis is excellent. It should be noted that rare variants of this disease do exist and are associated with fatal cardiomyopathy.

Characteristics

1. Hepatomegaly (enlargement of the liver).
2. Faintness, dizziness, hunger, and nervousness as a result of hypoglycemia.
3. Urine ketones and acetone levels may be high.
4. Growth rate may be slow and mild motor delays are present.

REFERENCES

Burwinkel, B., Bakker, H. D., Herschkovitz, E., Moses, S. W., Shin, Y. S., & Kilimann, M. W. (1998). Mutations in the liver glycogen phosphorylase gene (PYGL) underlying glycogenosis type VI (Hers disease). *American Journal of Human Genetics, 62*, 785–791.

Ierardi-Curto, L. (2001). Glycogen storage disease type IV (Hers Disease). *eMedicine, 2*(3). Retrieved from http://www.emed icine.medscape.com/

KIMBERLY M. ESTEP
University of Houston, Clear Lake

GLYCOGEN STORAGE DISEASE VII (TARUI DISEASE)

Glycogen storage disease Type VII, also called Tarui disease, is characterized by the accumulation of glycogen primarily in skeletal muscle resulting in exercise intolerance, muscle cramps, and fatigue after exercise.

The incidence is rare (about 20 cases worldwide), with equal occurrence in males and females, and it is the rarest of the glycogen storage diseases. The age of onset is late childhood to adolescence. This disorder appeared to be especially prevalent among people of Ashkenazi Jewish descent (McKusick, 2002). The risk factors for this disorder are genetic and are familial from autosomal recessive transmission on Chromosome 1cen-q32 phosphofructokinase (PFK) gene (muscle type). It is diagnosed by observations of decreased PFK activity in erythrocytes (50% of normal) or muscle biopsy biochemistry (<50% of normal).

Characteristics

Musculoskeletal manifestations

1. Symptoms similar to those of McArdle disease
2. Temporary weakness and cramping of muscle after exercise
3. Exercise intolerance and fatigability
4. Normal motor development

Complications (with prolonged vigorous exercise)

1. Gross myoglobinuria due to rhabdomyolysis resulting in acute renal failure (for acute episodes)
2. Chronic renal failure (for prolonged or frequent repetitive episodes of myoglobinuria)
3. Gout
4. Recurrent jaundice
5. Normal mental development

The treatment for glycogen storage disease (GSL) is supportive and needs a multidisciplinary approach with pediatrics monitoring for exercise intolerance, for the avoidance of vigorous exercise, and for complications. Genetic counseling is also advisable.

Special education may be necessary for children with complications that require extensive medical intervention and hospitalization (i.e., renal failure). Adaptive physical education would be necessary as well as helping the child self-monitor exercise and preventing symptoms and complications. Counseling for the family and child may also be necessary to facilitate treatment compliance and home-school collaboration. The prognosis for individuals with this disorder is good with only minimal disability.

REFERENCES

McKusick, V. A. (1998). *Glycogen storage disease Type VII. Online Mendelian inheritance in man.* Retrieved from http://www .ncbi.nlm.nih.gov:80/entrez/dispomim.cgi?id=232800

Pedlynx Online Database. *Tarui disease.* Retrieved May 2002 from http://www.icondata.com/health/pedbase/.les/TARUIDIS .HTM

ELAINE FLETCHER-JANZEN
Chicago School of Professional Psychology

See also Glycogen Storage Disease Type VIII

GLYCOGEN STORAGE DISEASE TYPE VIII

Glycogen storage disease Type VIII is a rare genetic metabolic disorder characterized by an accumulation of glycogen in the central nervous system and can result in substantial abnormalities and dysfunction of the central nervous system (Kornfield & LeBaron, 1984). Glycogen storage disease Type VIII affects the X chromosome and results in a deficiency of a liver enzyme called phosphorylase kinase. This deficiency eventually leads to excessive deposits of glycogen in the liver (National Organization for Rare Disorders [NORD], 2001). Because it is an X-linked, recessive genetic disorder, it is more likely to be masked in females and expressed in males (NORD, 2001).

Glycogen storage disease Type VIII is 1 of 10 identified types of glycogen storage diseases (Kornfield & LeBaron, 1984) that all together affect fewer than 1 in 40,000 persons in the United States (NORD, 2001). Glycogen storage disease Type VIII usually begins in infancy and affects more males than females. Although these symptoms can occur, liver function is usually normal, and glycogen storage disease Type VIII may remain undetected throughout life (NORD, 2001).

Characteristics

1. Child comes into the physician complaining of symptoms of hypoglycemia, including headaches, nausea, dizziness, lightheadedness, and confusion that occur several hours after eating and are relieved by food intake (NORD, 2001). Child could also be identified by blood tests indicating any of the symptoms in the following list.

2. Symptoms of glycogen storage disease may include an enlarged liver, high levels of liver glycogen, mild hypoglycemia, possible liver inflammation (NORD, 2001), possible growth retardation (Vhi Healthcare, 2001), and hypercholesterolemia (elevated levels of choslesterol in the blood; Fernandes et al., 1988).

3. Often the liver function is normal, and the disease may go undetected throughout life (NORD, 2001).

Treatment for this disease in its mild form is often not necessary because the resulting hypoglycemia is mild (Fernandes et al., 1988: NORD, 2001). During a long-term infection, fasting is not recommended, particularly when the infection is accompanied by vomiting or anorexia (Fernandes et al., 1988). Hypercholesterolemia can be also be controlled by dietary changes, such as a diet enriched with polyunsaturated fats (Fernandes et al., 1988). Future treatment research centers on diet and genetic counseling (Fernandes et al., 1988: NORD, 2001). Severe cases of glycogen storage disease that are not responsive to dietary treatment have been treated successfully with liver transplants (Vhi Healthcare, 2001). Patients with glycogen storage disease Type VIII often go undetected, usually do not require treatment, and live normal lives (NORD, 2001).

Academic modifications are usually not necessary for children with glycogen storage disease Type VIII, although cases with severe symptoms of hypoglycemia may need to allow the child to eat small snacks throughout the school day. Special dietary accommodations by the school nutritionists may also be helpful in reducing the symptoms of hypoglycemia.

REFERENCES

Fernandes, J., Leonard, J. V., Moses, S. W., Odievre, M., di Rocco, M., Schaub, J., ... Durand, P. (1988). Glycogen storage disease: Recommendations for treatment. *European Journal of Pediatrics, 147,* 226–228.

Kornfield, M., & LaBaron, M. (1984). Glycogenosis type VIII. *Journal of Neuropathology and Experimental Neurology, 43*(6), 568–579.

National Organization for Rare Disorders. (2001, March 20). *Glycogen storage disease VIII*. Retrieved from http://www .stepstn.com/cgi-win/nord.exe?number=400&proc=ap_fullReport

Vhi Healthcare. (2001, March 18). *Glycogen storage diseases*. Retrieved from https://www.vhi.ie/indexDT.jsp

Moana Kruschwitz
Margaret Semrud-Clikeman
University of Texas at Austin

GOALS, ANNUAL (*See Annual Goals*)

GOALS, USE OF

Educational goals serve three important functions: (1) to structure teaching and curriculum development, (2) to guide learners by helping them recognize errors and discriminate among responses, and (3) to structure the evaluation process (Bloom, Hastings, & Madaus, 1971).

The use of goals in special education was mandated in 1975 by the Education for All Handicapped Children Act (PL 94-142) and has continued under its successor legislation, the Individuals with Disabilities Education Act (IDEIA). Incorporation of educational goals into PL 94-142 and the IDEIA was prompted by congressional concern for accountability, not by a desire to facilitate the educational purposes cited previously (Fuchs & Deno, 1982). In its fact finding for PL 94-142, Congress found that the special education needs of children with disabilities were not being met fully and that the goal specification component of the law would ensure that schools would be accountable for the quality of the programs they provide to such pupils (Turnbull & Turnbull, 1978).

Given this legal mandate, the writing of goals has become standard special education practice; that is, teachers routinely write goals on students' individual educational programs (IEPs). Additionally, as mandated by PL 94-142 and subsequently IDEA, teachers are required to monitor their students' progress toward those goals. This typically translates into informal evaluations of student goal mastery approximately two to three times each year (Fuchs & Fuchs, 1984).

Despite the widespread use of goals and periodic evaluation of goal mastery in special education, research is scant on the effects of goal use among students with disabilities. Moreover, even within the regular education literature, where empirical support for the general effectiveness of goals is provided, only limited information is available concerning specific dimensions of effective goal-writing procedures, and most studies have been conducted with adults (Fuchs, 1986).

Therefore, there is no meaningful database concerning the general effectiveness of goals for students with disabilities or the nature of specific dimensions of effective goals. Not surprisingly, it remains unclear whether special education teachers employ goals for instructional planning (Tymitz, 1981) or systematic progress monitoring (Fuchs & Fuchs, 1984) once they have fulfilled the legal requirement of completing goals on IEPs.

REFERENCES

Bloom, B. S., Hastings, J. T., & Madaus, G. F. (1971). *Handbook on formative and summative evaluation of student learning.* New York, NY: McGraw-Hill.

Fuchs, L. S. (1986). *Use of goals with handicapped learners.* Unpublished paper, Vanderbilt University, Nashville, TN.

Fuchs, L. S., & Deno, S. L. (1982). *Developing goals and objectives for educational programs.* Washington, DC: American Association of Colleges for Teacher Education.

Fuchs, L. S., & Fuchs, D. (1984). Criterion-referenced assessment without measurement: How accurate for special education? *Remedial & Special Education, 5*(4), 29–32.

Turnbull, H. R., & Turnbull, A. P. (1978). *Free appropriate public education: Law and implementation.* Denver, CO: Love.

Tymitz, B. L. (1981). Teacher performance on IEP instructional planning tasks. *Exceptional Children, 48,* 258–260.

LYNN S. FUCHS
DOUGLAS FUCHS
Peabody College, Vanderbilt University
Second edition

KIMBERLY F. APPLEQUIST
University of Colorado at Colorado Springs
Third edition

See also Individual Education Plan; Individuals with Disabilities Education Improvement Act of 2004 (IDEIA); Teacher Effectiveness

GODDARD, HENRY H. (1866–1957)

Henry Herbert Goddard received his PhD in psychology at Clark University. He taught at the Pennsylvania State Teachers College at West Chester before becoming director of research at The Training School at Vineland, New Jersey, in 1906. Specializing in the study of atypical children, his work at the Training School was a major influence on the education of children and adults with mental retardation in the United States. He established the first psychological laboratory devoted to the study of the mentally retarded, and developed and tested educational methods for their instruction. He translated and adapted the Binet-Simon Intelligence Scale and inaugurated its use in the United States. He also participated in the development of the group tests used to classify the men in the U.S. armed forces in World War I. Goddard conducted a classic study of mental retardation as an inherited trait, reported in 1912 in *The Kallikak Family: A Study in the Heredity of Feeblemindedness*.

In 1918 Goddard was appointed director of the State Bureau of Juvenile Research in Ohio. From 1922 until his retirement in 1938, he was professor of abnormal and clinical psychology at Ohio State University.

REFERENCE

Goddard, H. H. (1912). *The Kallikak family: A study in the heredity of feeblemindedness.* New York, NY: Macmillan.

PAUL IRVINE
Katonah, New York

GOLDEN, CHARLES J. (1949–   )

Charles J. Golden received his BA from Pomona College in 1971 and his PhD in clinical psychology from the University of Hawaii in 1975. He completed an internship in clinical psychology at Hawaii State Hospital and established a neuropsychology laboratory at the University of South Dakota (1975–1978) and later at the University of Nebraska Medical Center. He is currently a professor of psychology at Nova Southeastern University in Fort Lauderdale, Florida. His strongest interests are in the areas of psychological assessment, with a major emphasis on clinical neuropsychology.

He is best known for his work in the development of a standardized, American version of Luria's *methode clinique*, a neuropsychological investigation of individual cases known as the Luria-Nebraska Neuropsychological Battery. This battery attempts to integrate the qualitative approach to psychological assessment advocated by Luria with the quantitative, standardized approaches to assessment that have long characterized Western psychology. It also tries to provide a broad evaluation of neuropsychological skill in a general battery applicable to a wide range of patients, administered in diverse settings with a minimum of equipment. The children's version of the battery addresses special education with the assessment of learning deficit suspected of having a neurological base.

Golden is also known for his study of the neurological basis of psychiatric disorders. His work includes an integration of test results from neurological procedures such as computerized tomography and regional cerebral blood flow with psychological and behavioral test results. As a result of this work, a subgroup of psychiatric patients with organic dysfunction that can be hypothesized to be the cause of their disorder has been found.

Golden's major publications include *Clinical Interpretation of Objective Psychological Tests, Interpretation of the Halstead-Reitan Neuropsychological Battery: A Casebook Approach, Diagnosis and Rehabilitation in Clinical Neuropsychology, Item Interpretation of the Luria-Nebraska Neuropsychological Battery*, and *Interpretation of the Luria-Nebraska Neuropsychological Battery.*

REFERENCES

Golden, C. J. (1979). *Clinical interpretation of objective psychological tests*. New York, NY: Grune & Stratton.

Golden, C. J. (1981). *Diagnosis and rehabilitation in clinical neuro-psychology*. Springfield, IL: Thomas.

Golden, C. J., Hammeke, T. A., Purisch, A. D., Berg, R. A., Moses, J. A., Jr., Newlin, D. B.,...Puente, A. E. (1982). *Item interpretation of the Luria-Nebraska Neuropsychological Battery*. Lincoln: University of Nebraska Press.

Golden, C. J., Osmon, D., Moses, J. A., Jr., & Berg, R. A. (1980). *Interpretation of the Halstead-Reitan Neuropsychological Battery: A casebook approach*. New York, NY: Grune & Stratton.

Moses, J. A., Jr., Golden, C. J., Ariel, R., & Gustavson, J. L. (1983, 1984). *Interpretation of the Luria-Nebraska Neuropsychological Battery* (Vols. 1 & 2). New York, NY: Grune & Stratton.

STAFF

GOLDENHAR SYNDROME

Goldenhar syndrome (GS) is a relatively recently enumerated syndrome that is somewhat more common among children with diagnoses of autism than in the general population. The diagnosis of GS is made in the presence of a pattern of 3 physical anomalies: ocular abnormalities that include the epibulbar dermoid; auricular abnormalities including microtia, periauricular tags, and similar abnormalities of the ear; and vertebral abnormalities.

Cases are sporadic and the cause of GS is unknown but anticipated at this time to be due to a teratogen (Gillberg, 1995). Hearing loss of varying degrees is common, and callosal agenesis has also been reported. An increased prevalence of mental retardation, especially in the mild range, occurs, and there is increased incidence of autism and autistic-like behavior, although the latter tends to improve with age, especially after puberty. GS occurs in boys and girls with about equal frequency. There is no cure

and treatment is entirely symptomatic. Special education is typically required but may be associated with one or more of the symptoms noted above. GS has highly variable expressivity and testing is necessary to establish which of the behavioral and mental symptoms are present and to what degree. Outcome is related directly to the degree of hearing loss, the level of intellectual impairment, and the number and severity of any autistic symptoms.

REFERENCE

Gillberg, C. (1995). *Clinical child neuropsychiatry*. Cambridge, UK: Cambridge University Press.

CECIL R. REYNOLDS
Texas A&M University

GOLDMAN-FRISTOE TEST OF ARTICULATION 2

The Goldman-Fristoe Test of Articulation 2 is a systematic measure of articulation of consonant sounds for children and young adults. The second edition of the Goldman-Fristoe Test of Articulation gives updated norms and expanded features, and it remains accurate and easy to administer. The test provides information about a child's articulation ability by sampling both spontaneous and imitative sound production. Examinees respond to picture plates and verbal cues from the examiner with single-word answers that demonstrate common speech sounds. Additional sections provide further measures of speech production. The test is used to measure articulation of consonant sounds, determine types of misarticulation, and compare individual performance to national, gender-differentiated norms.

New items have been added to sample more speech sounds—39 consonant sounds and clusters can now be tested with the Goldman-Fristoe 2. Some objectionable or culturally inappropriate items (e.g., gun, Christmas tree) have been removed. All artwork has been redrawn and reviewed for cultural bias and fairness. The age range for the Goldman-Fristoe 2 has been expanded to include ages 2 through 21. Age-based standard scores include separate normative information for females and males. Normative tables are based on a national sample of 2,350 examinees stratified to match the most recent U.S. Census data on gender, race/ethnicity, region, and SES as determined by mother's education level.

- User-friendly color-coding for recording initial-medial-final sounds
- Multiple testing of speech sounds within a word or plate for efficient test administration

- Broad sampling of the consonant sounds and clusters used in Standard American English
- Opportunity to sample both spontaneous and imitated production of speech sounds

Sounds-in-Words uses colorful, entertaining pictures to prompt responses that sample the major speech sounds in the initial, medial, and final positions. Suggested cues have been added for the examiner to help elicit spontaneous responses by the examinee. Additional sections provide a fuller sampling of the examinee's ability to produce speech sounds and to reproduce sounds when modeled by the examiner.

Three sections sample a wide range of articulation skills:

1. Sounds-in-Words Section uses pictures to elicit articulation of the major speech sounds when the examinee is prompted by a visual and/or verbal cue.

2. Sounds-in-Sentences Section assesses spontaneous sound production used in connected speech. The examinee is asked to retell a short story based on a picture cue. Target speech sounds are sampled within the context of simple sentences.

3. Stimulability Section measures the examinee's ability to correctly produce a previously misarticulated sound when asked to watch and listen to the examiner's production of the sound. The examinee repeats the word or phrase modeled by the examiner.

STAFF

GOLDMAN-FRISTOE-WOODCOCK TEST OF AUDITORY DISCRIMINATION

The Goldman-Fristoe-Woodcock Test of Auditory Discrimination is designed to measure a child's ability to hear speech sounds. It is an individually administered test of the ability to discriminate speech sounds against two different backgrounds—quiet and noise.

The Goldman-Fristoe-Woodcock Test of Auditory Discrimination is specifically designed to assess young children. Geared to children's vocabulary levels and limited attention spans, the test moves rapidly as responses are made by pointing to appealing pictures of familiar objects. Writing and speaking are not required. The test can also be used successfully with adults.

Three parts—Training Procedure, Quiet Subtest, and Noise Subtest—provide practice in word-picture associations and provide two measures of speech-sound discrimination for maximum precision. Separate norms are

provided for each subtest from ages 3 years, 8 months to 70 years and over. In addition, the examiner may use the error analysis matrix in the response form to explore the specific types of errors made on the subtests.

STAFF

See also Goldman-Fristoe Test of Articulation

GOLD, MARC (1931–1982)

Vocational training, job placement, and respect for the moderately, severely, and profoundly mentally disabled was a vision Marc Gold forged into a reality. His interests during his teaching of the intellectually disabled (ID) in Los Angeles led him to pursue a doctoral degree in experimental child psychology and special education. In 1969 he joined the University of Illinois faculty as a research professor and began working at the Institute for Child Behavior and Development.

Gold's strong philosophy of respect for persons ID acted as the foundation for all of his efforts. Gold (1980) believed that (a) the individuals with ID are served best by training them in marketable skills; (b) individuals identified ID respond to learning best in a situation based on respect of their worth and capabilities; (c) given the appropriate training, people with ID have the capability to demonstrate competence; (d) when a lack of learning occurs, it should first be interpreted as a result of inappropriate or insufficient teaching strategies rather than the individual's inability to learn; (e) intellectual testing is limiting to the ID; (6) the labeling of people as ID is unfair and counterproductive; and (f) educators should never assume that they are approaching the maximum potential of their learner.

Extolling this philosophy, Gold developed Try Another Way, a systematic training program for individuals who find it difficult to learn (1980). The strategies employed were physical prompts, modeling, manipulation of the learner's hands, and short specific phrases like, "Try another way." Task completion was met with silence as Gold believed no news is good news. The Try Another Way system is based on task analysis. Components of task analysis include method (the way the task is performed), content (the amount of steps the method is divided into), and process (the way the task is taught). Process is subdivided into format (the presentation of the material), feedback (cues so the learner knows what is wanted), procedure (description of the proposed training plan), criterion (the predetermined point when learning takes place), and data collection (the charting of steps accomplished and still to be mastered).

Gold's research (1972, 1973, 1974, 1976, 1980) consistently supports task analysis as a learning strategy with the autistic, deaf/blind, and multihandicapped for tasks such as self-help, mobility, and vocational and social skills.

In addition to the development of the Try Another Way system, Gold created an organization that disseminated information regarding the program, was the president of the Workshop Division of the Illinois Rehabilitation Association, was a member of the Executive Board of the American Association for the Education of the Severely/Profoundly Handicapped, was vice president of the Vocational Rehabilitation Division of the American Association on Mental Deficiency, and was consulting editor or member of the editorial board of *The American Journal of Mental Deficiency, Mental Retardation,* and *Education and Treatment of Children.*

REFERENCES

Gold, M. W. (1972). Stimulus factors in skill training of retarded adolescents on a complex assembly task: Acquisition, transfer, and retention. *American Journal of Mental Deficiency, 76,* 517–526.

Gold, M. W. (1973). Factors affecting production by the retarded: Base rate. *Mental Retardation, 11*(6), 41–45.

Gold, M. W. (1974). Redundant cue removal in skill training for the mildly and moderately retarded. *Education & Training of the Mentally Retarded, 9,* 5–8.

Gold, M. W. (1976). Task analysis of a complex assembly task by the retarded blind. *Exceptional Children, 4,* 78–84.

Gold, M. W. (1980). *Did I say that?* Champaign, IL: Research.

Gold, M. W., & Barclay, C. R. (1973a). The learning of difficult visual discriminations by the moderately and severely retarded. *Mental Retardation, 11*(2), 9–11.

Gold, M. W., & Barclay, C. R. (1973b). The effects of verbal labels on the acquisition and retention of a complex assembly task. *Training School Bulletin, 70*(1), 38–42.

SHARI A. BEVINS
Texas A&M University

GOLDSTEIN, MAX A. (1870–1941)

Max A. Goldstein, an otolaryngologist, originated the acoustic method of teaching the deaf. The major significance of this method was that it used the student's residual hearing, an avenue largely neglected by educators of the deaf at the time. Goldstein employed amplification to train the student to use any remaining sound perception to understand spoken language and to guide his or her own voice in the production of speech. In 1914 Goldstein founded the Central Institute for the Deaf in St. Louis,

where he demonstrated his methods and where he established the first 2-year training program for teachers of the deaf and began the first nursery school for deaf children.

Goldstein was founder and editor of *The Laryngoscope,* a journal devoted to disorders of the ear, nose, and throat. To promote closer cooperation between teachers of the deaf and physicians, and to standardize teaching methods used in schools for the deaf, Goldstein established the professional society that later became the National Forum on Deafness and Speech Pathology. Goldstein served as president of the American Otological Society, the American Laryngological, Rhinological, and Otological Society, and the organization that was the forerunner of the American Speech and Hearing Association.

This entry has been informed by the sources listed below.

REFERENCES

Goldstein, M. A. (1939). *The acoustic method.* St. Louis, MO: Laryngoscope Press.

In memoriam: Dr. Max A. Goldstein, 1870–1941. (1941). *Laryngoscope, 51,* 726–731.

PAUL IRVINE
Katonah, New York

GOODENOUGH, FLORENCE LAURA (1886–1959)

Florence Laura Goodenough obtained her PhD in psychology under Lewis M. Terman at Stanford University after a number of years of experience as a teacher in the public schools and at the Training School at Vineland, New Jersey. Goodenough is well known for her Draw-A-Man Test (Goodenough, 1926), and the Minnesota Preschool Scale. As a researcher and an authority on research methodology, she was an innovator, applying a variety of research techniques to diverse research questions. Her *Experimental Child Study,* written with John E. Anderson (Goodenough & Anderson, 1982), evaluated the pros and cons of numerous research methodologies. Goodenough served as president of the school psychology division of the American Psychological Association.

REFERENCES

Goodenough, F. L. (1926). *Measurement of intelligence by drawings.* Yonkers, NY: World Book.

Goodenough, F. L., & Anderson, J. E. (1982). *Experimental child study.* Darby, PA: Arden Library.

PAUL IRVINE
Katonah, New York

GOODPASTURE DISEASE

Goodpasture disease is a multisystem, rapidly progressive autoimmune disease that initially presents as a pulmonary-renal syndrome and—if not treated—progresses to respiratory and renal failure. Goodpasture disease in characterized by the presence of autoantibodies in the immune system that attack the lungs and kidneys and cause hemorrhaging in the basement membrane lining of the lungs and kidneys. The disease is a manifestation of human antibasement membrane diseases, but the exact cause is unknown. Smoking and inhaling hydrocarbon fumes as well as viral respiratory infections damage the basement membrane and are implicated in the promotion of Goodpasture disease (Netzer, Merkel, & Weber, 1998). In addition, there does seem to be an inherited predisposition.

The incidence of Goodpasture disease is approximately 0.1 cases per million population. It affects both genders approximately equally.

Characteristics

1. Patients in their 20s usually present with pulmonary and renal manifestations, primarily glomerulonephritis and pulmonary hemorrhage, whereas older patients usually have only nephritis.
2. Time of presentation is often the spring and summer (Savage, Pusey, Bowman, Rees, & Lockwood, 1986).
3. Other signs include coughing up blood, burning sensation while urinating, blood in the urine, flu-like symptoms, fatigue, nausea, pallor, and shortness of breath.
4. Onset is rapid and progresses to death if not treated immediately.

Treatment focuses on slowing the progression of the disease. Since the 1970s, this treatment has consisted of a combined therapy with plasmapheresis and immunosuppression. Corticosteroids are often given intravenously to control bleeding in the lungs. When the autoantibodies have ceased production and are undetectable in the body, renal transplantation is often conducted. After the autoantibodies are not detected and transplantation has occurred, patients are considered cured, although additional transplants are often needed. The recurrence rate is low (Zawada, Santella, Birch, & Jaqua, 1998).

Although presentation of Goodpasture syndrome follows a bimodal distribution with the majority of cases presenting at around ages 30 and 60, young children can also develop Goodpasture syndrome (Savage et al., 1986).

Even if the disorder is detected and cured early, children with Goodpasture syndrome will miss extended amounts of school. They will need special accommodations, including but not limited to additional time on assignments, a home-school liaison to bring them assignments, and an at-home tutor. Emotional support for children with Goodpasture disease and their families is needed for coping with this often fatal disease (Avella & Walker, 1999).

Prognostic factors include percentage of crescents on biopsy and level of creatinine at the time of presentation. If left untreated, Goodpasture disease is usually fatal, but even for patients with the worst prognostic features, Goodpasture is considered curable with early diagnosis and immediate and aggressive treatment. Goodpasture disease can last from a few weeks to as long as 2 years, depending on the extent of damage and whether transplantation is necessary. It does not cause permanent lung damage, but damage to the kidney can be long lasting. Persistent organ failure and additional renal transplantation are often the case, but patients are considered cured after surviving the acute presentation of the disease (Zawada et al., 1998).

REFERENCES

Avella, P., & Walker, M. (1999). Goodpasture's syndrome: A nursing challenge. *Dimensions of Critical Care Nursing, 18,* 2–12.

Netzer, K. O., Merkel, F., & Weber, M. (1998). Goodpasture syndrome and end-stage renal failure: To transplant or not to transplant? *Nephrology, Dialysis, Transplantation, 13,* 1346–1348.

Savage, C. O. S., Pusey, C. D., Bowman, C., Rees, A. J., & Lockwood, C. M. (1986). Antiglomerular basement membrane antibody mediated disease in the British Isles. *British Medical Journal, 292,* 301–304.

Zawada, E. T., Jr., Santella, R. N., Birch, F., & Jaqua, R. A. (1998). Cure of Goodpasture's disease. *South Dakota Journal of Medicine, 51,* 197–201.

ELIZABETH KAUFMANN
University of Texas at Austin

GOTTLIEB, JAY (1942–   )

Jay Gottlieb received his PhD from Yeshiva University in New York in 1972, and is a professor in the Department of Educational Psychology at New York University as well as a researcher in the field of education. His work has included investigations dealing with the social acceptance of children with mental retardation (Goodman, Gottlieb,

& Harrison, 1972), social skills training for handicapped children (Gottlieb, 1984), the impact of instructional group size in resource rooms and speech services (Gottlieb & Alter, 1997), and mainstreaming (Gottlieb, 1981; Kaufman, Gottlieb, Agard, & Kukic, 1975).

In much of his research, Gottlieb has focused on issues that relate to enhancement of the learning experience to provide the maximum benefit for students with learning problems. His studies of children with mental retardation have indicated that these youngsters tend to be easily swayed by their intellectually brighter peers, yet often fail to develop close relationships with them. In some instances, this failure prevents them from learning what is valued by others (Goodman et al., 1972). Also, he has shown that children with disabilities do not progress more rapidly in their schoolwork when taught in segregated classrooms (Kaufman et al., 1975), and that, while they tend to play alone, few differences exist between the play habits of those with learning disabilities and children who do not have learning problems (Levy & Gottlieb, 1984).

More recently, Gottlieb has focused on the area of school placement of children with disabilities, finding an over-representation of students of color referred for special education. He also found that referral is frequently based primarily on academic achievement, misbehavior, and speech and language problems in the absence of standardized educational criteria. Based on his findings, Gottlieb (1994) strongly advocates the development of prereferral instructional activities as a way of maintaining students in general education classes, as well as criteria for determining the success of such activities. He also stresses the necessity of improved teacher training in behavior analysis. Furthermore, he believes that once a child is placed in special education, that individual rarely, if ever, leaves that placement.

REFERENCES

Goodman, H., Gottlieb, J., & Harrison, R. H. (1972). Social acceptance of EMR's integrated into a nongraded elementary school. *American Journal of Mental Deficiency, 76,* 412–417.

Gottlieb, J. (1981). Mainstreaming: Fulfilling the promise? *American Journal of Mental Deficiency, 86,* 115–124.

Gottlieb, J. (1984). *Social skills research integration: Final report.* New York, NY: New York University.

Gottlieb, J. (1994). Special education in urban America: It's not justifiable for many. *Journal of Special Education, 27,* 453–465.

Gottlieb, J., & Alter, M. (1997). *An evaluation study of the impact of modifying instructional group sizes in resource rooms and related service groups in New York City.* New York, NY: New York University.

Kaufman, J. J., Gottlieb, J., Agard, J. A., & Kukic, M. B. (1975). Mainstreaming: Toward an explication of the construct. *Focus On Exceptional Children, 7,* 6–17.

Levy, L., & Gottlieb, J. (1984). Learning disabled and non-learning disabled children at play. *Remedial and Special Education, 5,* 43–50.

E. Valerie Hewitt
Texas A&M University
First edition

Tamara J. Martin
The University of Texas of the Permian Basin
Second edition

GOWAN, JOHN C. (1912–1986)

John C. Gowan earned his BA at Harvard University and his EdM and EdD at the University of California at Los Angeles. During his distinguished career in education, Gowan's interest focused on the areas of psychic science, guidance, and creativity, particularly as related to gifted learners (Gowan, 1980). Prior to his death in 1986, he was a professor at California State University, Northridge, for over 25 years.

Gowan is known for his work in the area of guidance for gifted children (Gowan, Demos, & Kokaska, 1980). He emphasized special problems such as the disparity between social and intellectual development sometimes associated with these children and examined the influence of right-hemisphere imagery on creativity (Gowan, Khatena, & Torrance, 1981). Gowan also noted the importance of using developmental stage theory to enhance creativity in gifted children, and his theories on the subject were explored in his book *Trance, Art, and Creativity* (1987), a psychological analysis of the relationship between the individual ego and the numinous element.

Among his contributions, Gowan served as president of the Association for the Gifted (1971–1972), president of the National Association for Gifted Children (1974–1975), and editor of *Gifted Child Quarterly* (1974–1979). Additionally, he was a Fulbright lecturer at the University of Singapore (1962–1963) and a visiting lecturer at the University of Hawaii (1965, 1967), Southern Connecticut State College (1969), and the University of Canterbury (1970) and Massey University (1975), both in New Zealand. A compilation of his work related to gifted children was published in the 1971 book, *Educating the Ablest.*

REFERENCES

Gowan, J. C. (1971). *Educating the ablest: A book of readings on the education of gifted children.* Itasca, IL: Peacock.

Gowan, J. C. (1980). The use of developmental stage theory in helping gifted children become creative. *Gifted Child Quarterly, 24,* 22–28.

Gowan, J. C. (1987). *Trance, art, and creativity: A psychological analysis of the relationship between the individual ego and the numinous element in three modes—prototaxic, parataxic, and syntaxic.* Buffalo, NY: Creative Education.

Gowan, J. C., Demos, G. D., & Kokaska, C. J. (1980). *The guidance of exceptional children: A book of readings* (2nd ed.). New York, NY: Longman.

Gowan, J. C., Khatena, J., & Torrance, E. P. (Eds.). (1981). *Creativity: Its educational implications* (Rev. ed.). Dubuque, IA: Kendall-Hunt.

ANN E. LUPKOWSKI
Texas A&M University
First edition

TAMARA J. MARTIN
The University of Texas of the Permian Basin
Second edition

GRADE EQUIVALENTS

Grade equivalents (GEs) represent a popular, though much abused and often misinterpreted, score system for achievement tests. A GE is a representation of an average level of performance of all children at a specific grade level. For example, if, on a test of reading, the average number of questions correct (the mean raw score) for children in the third month of fourth grade (typically written as 4.3) is 40, then a raw score of 40 is assigned a GE of 4.3. If the average number correct for children in the second month of fifth grade is 43, then all scores of 43 are henceforth assigned a GE of 5.2, and so forth.

Grade equivalents have numerous problems of interpretation and use, so much so that the 1985 *Standards for Educational and Psychological Testing* asked test publishers to take special care in explaining the calculation, interpretation, and appropriate uses of GEs for any particular test. Many users assume that GEs have the characteristics of standardized or scaled scores when, in fact, they do not. Often GEs are treated as being on an interval scale of measurement when they are only on an ordinal scale; that is, GEs allow the ranking of individuals according to their performance but do not tell us anything about the distance between each pair of individuals. This problem can be illustrated as follows. If the mean score for beginning fourth graders (grade 4.0) on a reading test is 37, then any person earning a score of 37 on the test is assigned a GE score of 4.0. If the mean raw score of a fifth grader (grade 5.0) is 38, then a score of 38 would receive a GE of 5.0. A raw score of 37 could represent a GE of 4.0, 38 could be 5.0, 39 could be 5.1, 40 could be 5.3, and 41, 6.0. Thus, differences of one raw score point can cause dramatic differences in the GE received. The differences will be highly inconsistent across grades with regard to magnitude of the difference in grade equivalents produced by constant changes in raw scores.

Table G.1 illustrates the problems of using GEs to evaluate a child's academic standing relative to his or her peers. Frequently, in both research and clinical practice, children of normal intellectual capacity are diagnosed as learning disabled through the use of grade equivalents such as "two years below grade level for age" on a test of academic attainment. The use of this criterion for diagnosing learning disabilities or other academic disorders is clearly inappropriate (Reynolds, 1981, 1984). As seen in Table G.1, a child with a GE score in reading 2 years below the appropriate grade placement for age may or may

Table G.1. Standard Scores and Percentile Ranks Corresponding to Performance "Two Years Below Grade Level for Age" on Three Major Reading Tests

Grade Placement	Two Years Below Placement	Wide Range Achievement Test		Woodcock Reading Mastery Test[a]		Standard Diagnostic Reading Test[a]	
		SS[b]	%R[c]	SS	%R	S	%R
2.5	K.5	72	1	—		—	
3.5	1.5	69	2	64	1	64	1
4.5	2.5	73	4	77	6	64	1
5.5	3.5	84	14	85	16	77	6
6.5	4.5	88	21	91	27	91	27
7.5	5.5	86	18	94	34	92	30
8.5	6.5	87	19	94	34	93	32
9.5	7.5	90	25	96	39	95	37
10.5	8.5	85	16	95	37	95	37
11.5	9.5	85	16	95	37	92	30

[a] Total test.
[b] All standard scores in this table have been converted for ease of comparison to a common scale having a mean of 100 and an SD of 15.
[c] Percentile rank.
Source: Adapted from Reynolds (1981).

not have a reading problem. At some ages this is within the average range, whereas at others a severe reading problem may be indicated.

Grade equivalents tend to become standards of performance as well, which they clearly are not. Contrary to popular belief, GE scores on a test do not indicate what level of reading text a child should be using. Grade equivalent scores on tests do not have a one-to-one correspondence with reading series placement or the various formulas for determining readability levels.

Grade equivalents are also inappropriate for use in any sort of discrepancy analysis of an individual's test performance and for use in many statistical procedures for the following five reasons (Reynolds, 1981):

1. The growth curve between age and achievement in basic academic subjects flattens out at upper grade levels. This can be seen in the table, where there is very little change in standard score values corresponding to 2 years below grade level for age after about grade 7 or 8. In fact, GEs have almost no meaning at this level since reading instruction typically stops by high school. This difficulty in interpreting GEs beyond about grade 10 or 11 is apparent in an analogy with age equivalents (Thorndike & Hagen, 1977). Height can be expressed in age equivalents just as reading can be expressed as GEs. It might be helpful to describe a tall first grader as having the height of an 8½-year-old, but what happens to the 5'10" 14-year-old female? At no age does the mean height of females equal 5'10". Since the average reading level in the population changes very little after junior high school, GEs at these ages become virtually nonsensical, with large fluctuations resulting from a raw score difference of two or three points on a 100-item test.

2. Grade equivalents assume the rate of learning is constant throughout the school year and that there is no gain or loss during summer vacation.

3. Grade equivalents involve an excess of extrapolation, especially at the upper and lower ends of the scale. However, since tests are not administered during every month of the school year, scores between the testing intervals (often a full year) must be interpolated on the assumption of constant growth rates. Interpolation between sometimes extrapolated values on an assumption of constant growth rates is a somewhat ludicrous activity.

4. Different academic subjects are acquired at different rates and the variation in performance varies across content areas so that "two years below grade level for age" may be a much more serious deficiency in math than in reading comprehension.

5. Grade equivalents exaggerate small differences in performance among individuals and for a single individual across tests. Some test authors even provide a caution on record forms that standard scores only, and not grade equivalents, should be used for comparisons.

Standard scores are a superior alternative to the use of GEs. The principal advantage of standardized or scaled scores with children lies in the comparability of score interpretation across age. By standard scores is meant scores scaled to a constant mean and standard deviation (SD), such as the Wechsler Deviation IQ, and not to ratio IQ types of scales employed by the early Binet and the Slosson Intelligence Test, which give the false appearance of being scaled scores. Ratio IQs or other types of quotients have many of the same problems as grade equivalents and should be avoided for many of the same reasons. Standard scores of the deviation IQ type have the same percentile rank across age since they are based not only on the mean but the variability in scores about the mean at each age level. For example, a score that falls two-thirds of a standard deviation below the mean has a percentile rank of 25 at every age. A score falling two thirds of a grade level below the average grade level has a different percentile rank at every age.

Standard scores are more accurate and precise. When constructing tables for the conversion of raw scores into standard scores, interpolation of scores to arrive at an exact score point is usually not necessary. The opposite is true of GEs. Typically, extrapolation is not necessary for scores within three SDs of the mean, which accounts for more than 99% of all scores encountered. Scaled scores can be set to any desired mean and standard deviation, with the fancy of the test author frequently the sole determining factor. Fortunately, a few scales can account for the vast majority of standardized tests in psychology and education.

Nevertheless, GEs remain popular as a score reporting system in special education. This popularity seems owed to the many misconceptions surrounding their use rather than any true understanding of children's academic attainment or how better to instruct them.

REFERENCES

Reynolds, C. R. (1981). The fallacy of "two years below grade level for age" as a diagnostic criterion for reading disorders. *Journal of School Psychology, 19*, 350–358.

Reynolds, C. R. (1984). Critical measurement issues in learning disabilities. *Journal of Special Education, 18*, 451–476.

Reynolds, C. R., & Mason, B. A. (2009). Measurement and statistical problems in neuropsychological assessment of children. In C. R. Reynolds & E. Fletcher-Janzen (Eds.), *Handbook of clinical child neuropsychology* (pp. 203–230). New York, NY: Springer. doi:10.1007/978-0-387-78 867-8_9

Thorndike, R. L., & Hagen, E. P. (1977). *Measurement and evaluation in psychology and education*. New York, NY: Wiley.

CECIL R. REYNOLDS
Texas A&M University

See also Diagnosis in Special Education; Learning Disabilities, Severe Discrepancy Analysis in

GRADE RETENTION

Retention, the holding back of a child due to poor academic achievement or social immaturity, has been a very controversial topic in the past decade. Schools and researchers are unclear as to whether retention engenders positive effects both academically and socioemotionally in children. The Center for Policy Research in Education (1990) reported that by the ninth grade, approximately 50% of all U.S. school students have been retained. According to the National Association of School Psychologists (NASP; 1991), retention negatively impacts achievement and social-emotional adjustment in children. Though much of the research focuses on the academic effect retention precipitates, a growing number of researchers have begun to examine the effects on the socioemotional development of a child. Academic achievement is crucial for a child's success in school, especially in the primary grades. However, children's socioemotional development is equally important in contributing to a child's overall wellness. Although many children are retained every year, most studies have found it to be ineffective in achievement and adjustment for children. Some studies have agreed that grade retention could be effective if other alternatives have been tried and failed (McCoy & Reynolds, 1999).

Originally, the goal of grade retention was to improve school performance by allowing more time for students to develop adequate academic skills (Reynolds, 1992). By the 1930s, research evidenced the negative effect of retention (Ayer, 1933; Kline, 1933). Goodlad (1954) summarized the research on retention and found that retention did not decrease the variation in student achievement levels and had no positive effect on educational gain.

McCoy and Reynolds (1999) investigated the effects of retention on school achievement, perceived school competence, and delinquency. The sample was composed of low-income, minority children who had been retained at least once by the age of 14. They found that the strongest predictors of grade retention were early achievement, parental involvement, gender (boys were more likely), and number of school moves. Grade retention was found to be associated with lower mathematics and reading achievement, but not perceived school competence and delinquency, by the age of 14.

Jimerson (1997) found similar results when studying the characteristics of children retained in early elementary school and the effects of retention on achievement and adjustment. He found those more likely to be retained were boys with significantly poorer adjustment. He also found higher parental IQ and involvement with the school in nonretained children. The retained children did show a temporary advantage in math, but this quickly disappeared when new material was presented to both groups. Furthermore, the retained group of children showed lower emotional health in the sixth grade.

Research does not support grade retention as an intervention for children with behavior problems. On the contrary, research has shown anxiety, inattentiveness, and disruptive behaviors are not only long lasting, but they also worsen exponentially after retention (Jimerson, 1997; Pagani, Tremblay, Vitaro, Boulerice, & McDuff, 2001). Grade retention has been shown to more greatly affect children's behavior problems when retention occurred in primary school years compared to those retained at a later time (Pagani et al., 2001). If retention has detrimental effects on a child's adjustment, then those children who were retained due to their adjustment will be affected on a greater scale.

While many researchers focus their studies on the negative effects immediately following retention, there have been studies that look at longer-term consequences. Jimerson (1999) found that children who were retained are more likely to drop out of high school by the age of 19 than the low-achieving promoted peers. Those retained students who do graduate from high school are much less likely to go to college or engage in any other type of postsecondary education. Even when socioeconomic status was accounted for, nonretained students were twice as likely to enroll in postsecondary education than those students retained at least once between kindergarten and eighth grades. Those retained during middle school were even less likely to go to college (Fine & Davis, 2003). Children who have been retained also are more likely to be involved in substance abuse, have deviant behaviors, receive public assistance, and end up in prison than those who have not been retained (Jimerson, 1999).

Two main theories explain how children's socioemotional development may be worsened by retention. Gottfredson, Fink, and Graham (1994) suggested that social bonds are created in school formed by relationships with peers. These social bonds prevent children from engaging in self-gratifying, impulsive acts, such as disruptive behavior. As a child is retained, the social bonds formed with peers are broken and the impulsive acts that were being controlled are now being displayed.

Pagani et al. (2001) suggested that retention increases a child's rejection sensitivity, defined as the disposition to misconstrue, expect, and overreact to social rejection. Children experience rejection and feelings of humiliation when they have been retained (Shepard, 1997). Children's feelings of rejection seem to predispose them to situations that trigger similar feelings and, in turn, they misperceive other's interactions with them. This may lead to overreacting to situations with inappropriate, aggressive behavior (Pagani et al., 2001). Other theorists have suggested that problem behaviors are due to poor self-control, and therefore grade retention would have no affect on these behaviors (Gottfredson et al., 1994). Also, self-control may worsen after grade retention due to broken social bonds with peers who had previously kept them socially accountable.

Grade retention has been shown to have many adverse effects on different children. Most research points to the detrimental effects of retention, with few positive outcomes. Keeping a child back so they have an academic advantage or so they can mature may seem like a good idea in theory. However, research has shown that there is no academic or socioemotional advantage after retention. Future research needs to examine more individualized groups. For example, different ethnicities may react differently to grade retention. Most researchers would agree that grade retention is far from the answer to helping children succeed. Others would argue that premature promotion when a child is not academically prepared is also far from perfect. The fact is that retention is detrimental to a child's socioemotional and academic development, and other interventions need to be researched. Extensive research on the effects of retention and promotion will guide future educational interventions to find a way to help children overcome academic disparities.

REFERENCES

Ayer, F. C. (1933). *Progress of pupils in the state of Texas 1932–33.* Austin: Texas State Teachers Association.

Center for Policy Research in Education. (1990). *Repeating grades in school: Current practice and research evidence.* Washington, DC: Author.

Fine, J. G., & Davis, J. M. (2003). Grade retention and enrollment in postsecondary education. *Journal of School Psychology, 41,* 401–411.

Goodlad, J. (1954). Some effects of promotion and non-promotion upon the social and personal adjustment of children. *Journal of Experimental Education, 22,* 301–328.

Gottfredson, D. C., Fink, C. M., & Graham, N. (1994). Grade retention and problem behavior. *American Educational Research Journal, 31,* 761–784.

Jimerson, S. (1997). A prospective, longitudinal study of the correlates and consequences of early grade retention. *Journal of School Psychology, 35,* 3–25.

Jimerson, S. (1999). On the failure of failure: Examining the association between early grade retention and education and employment outcomes during late adolescence. *Journal of School Psychology, 37,* 243–272.

Kline, E. (1933). Significant changes in the curve of elimination since 1900. *Journal of Educational Research, 26,* 608–616.

McCoy, A. R., & Reynolds, A. J. (1999). Grade retention and school performance: An extended investigation. *Journal of School Psychology, 37,* 273–298.

National Association of School Psychologists (NASP). (1991). *Student grade retention: A resource manual for parents and educators.* Silver Spring, MD: Author.

Pagani, L., Tremblay, R. E., Vitaro, F., Boulerice, B., & McDuff, P. (2001). Effects of grade retention on academic performance and behavioral development. *Development and Psychopathology, 13,* 297–315.

Reynolds, A. J. (1992). Grade retention and school adjustment: An explanatory analysis. *Educational Evaluation and Policy Analysis, 14*(2), 101–121.

Shepard, L. A. (1997). Children not ready to learn? The invalidity of school readiness testing. *Psychology in the Schools, 34,* 85–97.

CLARISSA I. GARCIA
Texas A&M University

See also **No Child Left Behind Act; Reading Disorders; Response to Intervention**

GRANDIN, TEMPLE (1947–   )

Dr. Temple Grandin is probably the most recognized person with autism in the United States (Wallis, 2010). She is well known for her influential work in two fields: autism and animal science. Grandin is a Professor of Animal Science at Colorado State University. She also designs livestock handling facilities and runs a private company (Grandin Livestock Handling Systems, Inc.) dedicated to the cause of humane treatment for animals in the food industry. More than one-third of all cattle and hogs in the U.S. food industry are handled using equipment that was designed by Grandin (Grandin, 2006). For many decades she has traveled extensively, given speeches concerning both fields of study, provided insights about what it is like to have autism, and has been a strong advocate for animals and persons with disabilities.

In 1947, Grandin was born in Boston, Massachusetts, to Richard Grandin and Eustacia Cutler. She was the first-born child and had three younger siblings. Within the first 3 years of life, Grandin exhibited some of the classic characteristics of autism including stereotypical and repetitive behaviors (e.g., enjoying excessive spinning, hand flapping), communication difficulties (e.g., delayed speech, odd tone of voice), socialization challenges (e.g., reduced eye contact, difficulties with peer relationships), as well as challenging behaviors such as tantrums (Grandin & Scariano, 1986).

Grandin was diagnosed with autism in 1950, 7 years after the disability was described in the literature for the first time (Future Horizons, 2010). As was common in that period, doctors recommended that Grandin be placed in an institution; her mother refused and instead provided her with care and teaching at home, as well as other treatments (e.g., private speech-language therapy). In 1962, at 14 years of age, her parents sent her to a boarding school in New Hampshire, from which she graduated in 1965 (Future Horizons, 2010; Grandin & Scariano, 1986).

Grandin subsequently earned a BA in Psychology from Franklin Pierce College in 1970 (Grandin, n.d.). She then received two graduate degrees in Animal Science: an MS from Arizona State University in 1975, and a PhD from the University of Illinois in 1989. Grandin has been awarded over 40 distinctions, honors, and awards in both the autism/disability and animal science fields (Grandin, n.d.). Of note, in December 2010, Grandin was included in *Time* magazine's list of the 100 most influential people in the world. Early in 2010, an HBO movie entitled *Temple Grandin* was widely popular and won seven Emmy Awards. This biopic portrayed Grandin's life, the impact of autism on her and her family, and the unique struggles and successes due to her disability. She regularly consults on animal treatment and autism. Grandin has been a guest on dozens of TV shows and radio programs and has been featured in many newspaper and magazine articles (Colorado State University, 2008). She has authored over 400 publications including books, journal articles, book chapters, DVDs, and countless presentations.

In 1986 she authored her first book with Margaret Scariano. *Emergence: Labeled Autistic* was one of the first books to describe what it was like to have autism from the perspective of someone who actually had the disability. Since that time Grandin has written or cowritten a number of other books covering topics important to autism such as relationships, talents, careers, unique experiences of girls, and the specialized thinking of individuals with autism.

Grandin is also the inventor of the Squeeze (or Hug) Machine (Grandin & Scariano, 1986). She developed this device after observing cattle calm down after receiving firm pressure in a restraint system. Carrying this concept over to her own sensitivities to touch, Grandin created the Squeeze Machine and used its deep pressure input for several decades to help her calm down, desensitize to touch, and accept being held. Over time, she reported being able to tolerate touch from others and eventually stopped using the machine (Grandin & Scariano, 1986; Wallis, 2010). Although the efficacy of the Squeeze Machine has not been established, anecdotal reports suggest that the device may help to reduce stress and anxiety. Thus, some individuals with autism or other disabilities use the Squeeze Machine as part of their therapy.

Autism clearly influenced Grandin's career choices and has been critical to her success. Her strong visual thinking skills have allowed her to better understand animal behavior and, thus, impact the care and welfare of these animals (Grandin, & Johnson, 2005). Further, her personal perspective on autism has helped countless individuals with this disability and their families, teachers, and other stakeholders. Critically, Grandin has demonstrated that a person with autism can function well and be successful in a chosen career. Grandin has made an impressive impact on two fields and her contributions have changed the way we look at people with autism, animals, and life in general.

REFERENCES

Colorado State University. (2008). *Animal welfare and autism champion*. Retrieved from http://www.colostate.edu/features/temple-grandin.aspx

Future Horizons. (2010). *Temple Grandin, Ph.D.* Retrieved from http://www.templegrandin.com

Grandin, T. (2006). *Thinking in pictures: And other reports from my life with autism* (2nd ed.). New York, NY: Vintage Books.

Grandin, T. (n.d.). *Temple Grandin, Ph.D.* Retrieved from http://www.grandin.com/professional.resume.html

Grandin, T., & Johnson, C. (2005). *Animals in translation: Using the mysteries of autism to decode animal behavior*. Orlando, FL: Harcourt, Inc.

Grandin, T., & Scariano, M. M. (1986). *Emergence: Labeled autistic*. Novato, CA: Arena Press.

Wallis, C. (2010, February 4). Temple Grandin on *Temple Grandin*. *Time Magazine*. Retrieved from http://www.time.com/time/arts/article/0,8599,1960347,00.html

RESOURCES

Attwood, T., Grandin, T., Bolick, T., Faherty, C., Iland, L., Myers, J. M.,...Wrobel, M. (2006). *Asperger's and girls*. Arlington, TX: Future Horizons.

Grandin, T. (2008). *The way I see it: A personal look at autism and Asperger's*. Arlington, TX: Future Horizons.

Grandin, T. & Barron, S. (2007). *Unwritten rules of social relationships: Decoding social mysteries through the unique perspectives of autism*. Arlington, TX: Future Horizons.

Grandin, T., & Duffy, K. (2004). *Developing talents: Careers for individuals with Asperger Syndrome and high-functioning autism*. Shawnee Mission, KS: Autism Asperger Publishing Company.

PAUL LaCAVA
Rhode Island College

GRAND MAL SEIZURES (*See* Seizure Disorders)

GRANULOMATOUS DISEASE, CHRONIC

An inherited disease of white blood cell bacteria-killing function, chronic granulomatous disease (CGD) results in chronic infections and granuloma formation in skin, lymphatic tissues, respiratory and gastrointestinal tracts, and bones. White blood cells ingest bacteria normally but cannot kill them because of the cell's inability to generate hydrogen peroxide. Some bacteria, like pneumococci and streptococci, produce their own hydrogen peroxide and are normally disposed of by CGC white cells, while many other bacteria, including staphylococci, which do not produce hydrogen peroxide, cannot be killed.

Early in life, eczema-like rashes, enlarged lymph nodes, and perirectal abscesses may be initial signs. Respiratory infections are the most common symptom, and there is gradual enlargement of the liver and spleen. Infections in the central nervous system and the anemia of chronic disease may have cognitive sequelae.

Prophylactic antibiotic treatment, usually with sulfa methoxazole/trimethaprim, has greatly improved life expectancy and steroids are used to shrink granulomas obstructing the airways or gastrointestinal tract. Bone marrow transplant and interferon gamma treatments have been used with success in some patients.

Information for families and professionals is available from the Chronic Granulomatous Disease Association, Inc., 2616 Monterey Rd., San Marino, CA 91108, or at www.cgdassociation.org

REFERENCES

Malech, H. L., & Gallin, J. I. (1987). Neutrophils in human diseases. *New England Journal of Medicine, 317*, 687–694.

Stiehm, E. R. (1989). *Immunological disorders infants and children*. Philadelphia, PA: W. B. Saunders.

PATRICIA L. HARTLAGE
Medical College of Georgia

GRAPHESTHESIA

Graphesthesia is a medical term used to define an individual's ability to identify numbers or figures written on the skin (Hensyl, 1982). For many years, tests of graphesthesia have been a part of the clinical neurological examination to determine the intactness and integration of sensory neural systems related to sensations from within the body, at a distance from the body, and outside the body.

Chusid (1986) reports that sensation may be divided into three types: superficial, concerned with touch, pain, temperature, and two-point discrimination; deep, concerned with muscle and joint position (proprioception), deep muscle pain, and vibration sense (pallesthesia); and combined, concerned with both superficial and deep sensory mechanisms involved in stereognosis (recognition and naming of familiar unseen objects placed in the hand) and topognosis (the ability to localize cutaneous skin stimuli). Stereognosis and topognosis probably depend on the integrity of neural mechanisms within the cortex and are discriminatory in nature. The lower level mechanisms, such as touch, pain, and temperature, seem more protective in nature.

Whether the form identification in graphesthesia is accomplished by identifying numbers traced on the fingertips (Reitan, 1979) or motor form replication (Ayres, 1980), there appears to be a developmental factor in responses favoring greater reliability in 8- to 11-year-olds than in 5- to 6-year-olds. Evaluations of graphesthesia are most useful and reliable when given as part of a battery of sensory, motor vestibular tests of sensory integrative function. These tests usually are given by therapists, psychologists, or neurologists with special training. It has been suggested (Ayres, 1980) that clusters of low scores on somatosensory tests (including graphesthesia) may be associated with a child's having difficulty with motor planning nonhabitual movement (apraxia). Children who have apraxia have severe problems learning fine motor skill tasks such as dressing and writing. A clear definition of the individual child's difficulty can lead to developmentally appropriate classroom responses and therapeutic intervention provided by related services such as occupational and speech therapy.

REFERENCES

Ayres, A. J. (1980). *Southern California Sensory Integration Tests examiner's manual* (rev. ed.). Los Angeles, CA: Western Psychological Services.

Ayres, A. J. (1981). *Sensory integration and the child*. Los Angeles, CA: Western Psychological Services.

Chusid, J. G. (1986). *Correlative neuroanatomy and functional neurology* (16th ed.). Los Angeles, CA: Lange.

Hensyl, W. R. (Ed.). (1982). *Stedman's medical dictionary*. Baltimore, MD: Williams & Wilkins.

Reitan, R. M. (1979). *Manual for administration of neuropsychological test batteries for adults and children*. Tucson, AZ: Reitan Neuropsychology Laboratories.

RACHAEL J. STEVENSON
Bedford, Ohio

See also **Halstead-Reitan Neuropsychological Test Battery; Luria-Nebraska Neuropsychological Battery: Children's Revision; Neuropsychology**

GRAPHIC ORGANIZERS

IDEA requires students be instructed on their enrolled grade level. Students must demonstrate progress in the general education curriculum and be educated with students who do not have a disability (Wehmeyer, Lattin, Lappp-Rincker, & Agran, 2003). One way to ensure that all students are included in general education and make progress towards grade level curriculum is the use of graphic organizers.

Graphic organizers are linked to schema theory, in which new learning is seen as building upon the learner's preexisting knowledge (Dye, 2000). The learner is seen as needing to create a new schema or to utilize an existing schema in order to learn new material. The advance organizer was introduced to help students to learn and retain verbal content containing unfamiliar but significant subject matter (Ausubel, 1960). Because the advance organizer is primarily a written statement, some researchers believed that graphic displays would benefit students to a greater degree than asking a student who was having trouble comprehending a passage to read a statement and relate it to the original passage (Robinson, 1998).

Research points to the efficacy of GOs as aids in learning academic content (Jitendra & DiPipi, 2002; Moore & Readence, 1984). A number of research studies have focused on learning and retaining information from text (Robinson & Kiewra, 1995). Some researchers have focused specifically on using GOs in reading and comprehending mathematics texts (Braselton & Decker, 1994; Monroe, 1997).

While much of the research on the use of graphic organizers points to positive results, Robinson (1998) warns that definitive results regarding the design and use of GOs are difficult to ascertain due to research designs that were flawed and often looked at the wrong dependent variables. Robinson recommends that further research under specific research designs be conducted to determine exactly how GOs should be constructed for use in the classroom setting and how they can most effectively be utilized in teaching students. Dunston (1992) critiqued the research examining the use of GOs in improving reading comprehension and concluded that the research had equivocal results regarding important information that would assist teachers in the classroom. The results did not indicate the type of GO to use or when and with whom they should be used (Dunston). The need for further research is indicated.

A growing body of research in the use of GOs with special needs learners demonstrates the successful use in special education classes and in inclusive classes in general education that serve students with special learning needs. Research regarding the use of GOs has shown promising results in teaching students with learning disabilities to solve mathematics word problems. In one study, the researchers studied a small group of students with learning disabilities who were taught a word problem-solving strategy using graphic representation of the problems. The students' scores on word problem–solving probe sets improved after learning the schema-based strategy

and applying it to their assigned problems (Jitendra & Hoff, 1996).

Weisberg and Balaithy (1990) studied the use of GOs in teaching disabled readers to identify levels of importance of ideas in expository text, to identify main idea statements, and to summarize text. Griffin, Simmons, and Kameenui (1991) found positive results using GOs to improve comprehension and recall of science content by students with learning disabilities, although the results did not reach statistical significance.

Ellis and Lenz (1990), in their discussion of techniques for mediating content-area learning, critiqued a wide variety of research studies that examined the use of GOs as instructional supplements. Students with disorders of learning appeared to perform at a higher level when using GOs.

REFERENCES

Ausubel, D. P. (1960). The use of advance organizers in the learning and retention of meaningful verbal material. *Journal of Educational Psychology, 51,* 267–272.

Braselton, S., & Decker, B. C. (1994). Using graphic organizers to improve the reading of mathematics. *Reading Teacher, 48,* 276–281.

Dunston, P. J. (1992). A critique of graphic organizer research. *Reading Research and Instruction, 31,* 57–65.

Dye, G. A. (2000). Graphic organizers to the rescue: Helping students link—and remember—information. *Teaching Exceptional Children, 32,* 72–76.

Ellis, E. S., & Lenz, B. K. (Eds.). (1990). *Teaching adolescents with learning disabilities: Strategies and methods* (2nd ed.). Denver, CO: Love.

Griffin, C. C., Simmons, D. C., & Kameenui, E. J. (1991). Investigating the effectiveness of graphic organizer instruction on the comprehension and recall of science content by students with learning disabilities. *Reading, Writing, and Learning Disabilities, 7,* 355–376.

Griffin, C. C., & Tulbert, B. L. (1995). The effect of graphic organizers on students' comprehension and recall of expository text: A review of the research and implications for practice. *Reading and Writing Quarterly: Overcoming Learning Difficulties, 11,* 73–79.

Jitendra, A. K., & DiPipi, C. M. (2002). An exploratory study of schema-based word-problem-solving instruction for middle school students with learning disabilities: An emphasis on conceptual and procedural understanding. *Journal of Special Education, 36,* 23–38.

Jitendra, A. K., & Hoff, K. (1996). The effects of schema-based instruction on mathematical word-problem-solving performance of students with learning disabilities. *Journal of Learning Disabilities, 29,* 422–431.

Lerner, J. (2000). *Learning disabilities: Theories, diagnosis, and teaching strategies.* Boston, MA: Houghton-Mifflin.

Monroe, E. E. (1997). *Using graphic organizers to teach vocabulary: How does research inform mathematics instruction?* (ERIC Document Reproduction Service No. 120132)

Moore, D. W., & Readence, J. E. (1984). A quantitative and qualitative review of graphic organizer research. *Journal of Educational Research, 78*(1), 11–17.

Robinson, D. H. (1998). Graphic organizers as aides to text learning. *Reading Research and Instruction, 37,* 85–105.

Robinson, D. H., & Kiewra, K. A. (1995). Visual argument: Graphic organizers are superior to outlines in improving learning from text. *Journal of Educational Psychology, 87,* 455–467.

Wehmeyer, M. L., Lattin, D., Lapp-Rincker, G., & Agran, M. (2003). Access to the general curriculum of middle-school students with mental retardation: An observational study. *Remedial and Special Education, 24,* 262–272.

Weisberg, R., & Balaithy, E. (1990). Development of disabled readers' metacomprehension ability through summarization training using expository text: Results of three studies. *Journal of Reading, Writing, and Learning Disabilities, 6,* 117–136.

JOSEPH R. TAYLOR
Fresno Pacific University

See also **Advanced Organizers**

GRAY DIAGNOSTIC READING TESTS— SECOND EDITION

The *Gray Diagnostic Reading Tests—Second Edition* (GDRT2; Bryant, Widerholt, & Bryant, 2004), a revision of the Gray Oral Reading Tests—Diagnostic (GORT-D), assesses students who have difficulty reading continuous print and who require an evaluation of specific abilities and weaknesses. Two parallel forms are provided to allow the examiner to study a student's reading progress over time.

The GDRT-2 has four core subtests, each of which measures an important reading skill. The four subtests are: Letter/Word Identification, Phonetic Analysis, Reading Vocabulary, and Meaningful Reading. Three supplemental subtests, Listening Vocabulary, Rapid Naming, and Phonological Awareness, measure skills that many researchers and clinicians think have important roles in the diagnosis or teaching of developmental readers or children with dyslexia.

The GDRT-2 was normed in 2001–2002 on a sample of 1,018 students ages 6 through 13. The normative sample was stratified to correspond to key demographic variables (i.e., race, gender, and geographic region). The reliabilities of the test are high; all average internal consistency reliabilities for the composites are .94 or above. Other major improvements include: Studies showing the absence of culture, gender, race, and disability bias have been added, and several new validity studies have been conducted, including a comparison of the Wechsler Intelligence Scale for Children—Third Edition (WISC-III) to the GDRT-2.

The information provided on this test was derived from the following references.

REFERENCES

Bradley-Johnson, S., & Durmusoglu, G. (2005). Evaluation of floors and item gradients for reading and math tests for young children. *Journal of Psychoeducational Assessment, 23*(3), 262–278.

Bryant, B. R., Wiederholt, J. L., & Bryant, D. P. (2004). *Gray Diagnostic Reading Tests, second edition (GDRT-2).* Austin, TX: PRO-ED.

Geisinger, K. F., Spies, R. A., Carlson, J. F., & Plake, B. S. (Eds.). (2007). *The seventeenth mental measurements yearbook.* Lincoln, NE: Buros Institute of Mental Measurements.

RON DUMONT
Fairleigh Dickinson University

JOHN O. WILLIS
Rivier College

KATHLEEN VIEZEL
Fairleigh Dickinson University

JAMIE ZIBULCHSKY
Fairleigh Dickinson University
Fourth edition

GRAY ORAL READING TESTS— FOURTH EDITION

The Gray Oral Reading Tests, Fourth Edition (GORT-4) provides an objective measure of growth in oral reading. Five scores give information on a student's oral reading skills in terms of:

1. *Rate*—the amount of time taken by a student to read a story

2. *Accuracy*—the student's ability to pronounce each word in the story correctly

3. *Fluency*—the student's Rate and Accuracy Scores combined

4. *Comprehension*—the appropriateness of the student's responses to questions about the content of each story read

5. *Overall Reading Ability*—a combination of a student's Fluency (i.e., Rate and Accuracy) and Comprehension Scores

The test consists of two parallel forms, each containing 14 sequenced reading passages with five comprehension questions following each passage. For each reading passage, raw scores are calculated for Accuracy and Rate by calculating the number of words read correctly and the length of time it takes the student to read the passage. Between 0 and 5 points are provided for each Accuracy and Rate score, depending on how quickly and accurately the student reads the passage. Those points are then summed to obtain a Fluency score. A Comprehension score is calculated by summing the number of comprehension items (between 0 and 5) answered correctly for each passage. Raw scores for all four subtests (Accuracy, Rate, Fluency, Comprehension) are then used to compute standard scores, percentile ranks, and age and grade equivalents for the subtests. The sum of the Fluency and Comprehension standard scores are converted to percentile ranks and an Overall Reading Quotient. Error analysis can be completed by recording incorrect words students substitute for words in the passage and categorizing them according to the type of error, including Meaning Similarity, Function Similarity, Graphic/Phonemic Similarity, Multiple Sources, and Self-Correction. A checklist is also provided for an overall analysis of the student's reading behavior, including additions, deletions, prosody, and attitude towards reading. Fluency and Comprehension scores are calculated for each passage read.

GORT-4 was normed on a sample of 1,677 students aged 6 through 18. The normative sample was stratified to correspond to key demographic variables including race, gender, ethnicity, and geographic region. Race in the manual was divided into White (85%), Black (12%), and other (3%). Educational attainment of parents included less than a bachelor's degree (72%), bachelor's degree (21%), and master's, professional, doctoral degrees (7%) categories. Disability status of the sample: included no disability (92%), learning disability (2%), speech-language disorder (<1%), attention-deficit disorder (2%), other handicap (2%) categories.

The reliabilities of GORT-4 are high—average internal consistency reliabilities are .90 or above. The validity is extensive and includes studies that illustrate that GORT-4 may be used with confidence to measure change in oral reading over time. Throughout the validity section of the manual, the authors reference studies correlating earlier versions of the GORT. The authors are assuming that the content of the GORT-4 is similar enough to earlier versions to allow such comparisons. No evidence is provided to support this assumption.

This entry has been informed by the sources listed below.

REFERENCES

Barnhardt, C., Borsting, E., Koo, D., & Vo, B. (2008). Correlations of the grade level equivalent scores among three reading tests. *Journal of Behavioral Optometry, 19*(1), 11–14.

Bryant, B., Shih, M., & Bryant, D. (2009). The Gray Oral Reading Test—fourth edition (GORT-4). *Practitioner's guide to assessing intelligence and achievement* (pp. 417–447). Hoboken, NJ: Wiley.

Champion, T., Rosa-Lugo, L., Rivers, K., & McCabe, A. (2010). A preliminary investigation of second- and fourth-grade African American students' performance on the Gray Oral Reading Test—Fourth Edition. *Topics in Language Disorders, 30*(2), 145–153.

Frasco, R. (2008). Effectiveness of reading first for English language learners: Comparison of two programs. *Dissertation Abstracts International Section A,* 69.

Herman, G. (2009). The value of IQ scores in detecting reading patterns in younger and older elementary aged children referred for learning difficulties. *Dissertation Abstracts International,* 70.

Plake, B. S., Impara, J. C., & Spies, R. A. (Eds.). (2003). *The fifteenth mental measurements yearbook.* Lincoln, NE: Buros Institute of Mental Measurements.

RON DUMONT
Fairleigh Dickinson University

JOHN O. WILLIS
Rivier College

KATHLEEN VIEZEL
Fairleigh Dickinson University

JAMIE ZIBULSKY
Fairleigh Dickinson University
Fourth edition

GREIG CEPHALOPOLYSYNDACTYLY SYNDROME

Greig cephalopolysyndactyly syndrome is characterized by craniofacial anomalies and polydactyly and syndactyly of the hands and feet. This syndrome is inherited as a fully penetrant autosomal dominant disorder. It has four major malformation components: postaxial polydactyly, preaxial polydactyly, syndactyly, and craniofacial anomalies (Duncan, Klein, Wilmot, & Shapiro, 1979). These four manifestations are quite variable, making the diagnosis difficult in mildly affected nonfamilial cases. In other words, they are not uniformly expressed. The origin of this syndrome may be a translocation of one or more chromosomes and may be closely linked to the region of the translocation itself (Gollop & Fontes, 1985). Development tends to be normal, except in the area of motor development, due to deformities of the hands and feet.

As of 1985, 34 patients with varying expression of this syndrome had been described (Gollop & Fontes, 1985). Current incidence rates could not be found.

Characteristics

1. The craniofacial anomalies consist of macro-cephaly with broad forehead, prominent tip of the nose, and broad nasal bridge. The macrocephaly is usually benign (Chudley & Houston, 1982).

2. Postaxial polydactyly is common in the hands, and preaxial polydactyly is common in the feet. This symptom includes having an extra fingerlike appendage, often extending from the pinky finger. The big toes on the feet are often duplicated.

3. The thumbs are frequently broad, with a broad nail and misshapen distal phalanx.

4. Syndactyly is an almost constant finding in affected patients and varies from mild webbing to complete cutaneous fusion, sometimes also with nail fusion.

5. Whorl fingertip patterns on thumbs have also been reported (Duncan et al., 1979).

6. Intelligence is usually normal.

Because most literature on this syndrome consists of case studies, treatment was not often discussed. Several patients had undertaken surgery to remove extra toes and fingers.

Children with this disorder would benefit from extensive physical therapy. With or without surgery to remove the extra digits, such children will need special education assistance in the area of motor development. Other special education issues do not necessarily apply, due to normal intelligence level in children with Greig cephalopolysyndactyly. It may also be necessary to monitor the child's social and emotional well-being. It is possible that the child may encounter difficult peer issues, in which case it may be beneficial to contact a mental health professional.

Children with this disorder have a good prognosis and develop normally, according to the literature.

REFERENCES

Chudley, A. E., & Houston, C. S. (1982). The Greig cephalopolysyndactyly syndrome in a Canadian family. *American Journal of Medical Genetics, 13,* 269–276.

Duncan, P. A., Klein, R. M., Wilmot, P. L., & Shapiro, L. R. (1979). Greig cephalopolysyndactyly syndrome. *American Journal of Disorders of Children, 133,* 818–821.

Gollop, T. R., & Fontes, L. R. (1985). The Greig cephalopolysyndactyly syndrome: Report of a family and review of literature. *American Journal of Medical Genetics, 22,* 59–68.

CATHERINE M. CALDWELL
University of Texas at Austin

GRIEVING PROCESS

It has been recognized for some time that parents of children with disabilities often experience intense traumatic reactions to the diagnosis of their children. Further, these initial feelings are not the only ones that parents experience. It appears that parents go through a continual process of emotional fluctuation in the process of coming to terms with having an exceptional child (Searl, 1978). The intensity or degree of the disabilities does not seem to affect directly the appearance of these feelings. These reactions seem to occur regardless of when the parents become aware of the handicapping condition or how intense the condition is. For example, parents who have been informed that their expected child will be disabled early enough into a pregnancy to make numerous physical and financial preparations still have intense emotional reactions to the child's condition at the time of the child's birth. These reactions continue during the child's maturation (Roos, 1977). These feelings have often been likened to the mourning process experienced at the death of a loved one. Hence the reactions and the subsequent process of coming to terms with a person with disabilities within the family has been labeled the grieving process. Several authors have taken Kübler-Ross's developmental stage model of reaction to dying and have applied it to the loss associated with parenting a child with disabilities (ARCH, 2002).

It has been suggested that parents go through a series of stages. Early work focused on stages of awareness, recognition, search for a cause, and acceptance (Rosen, 1955). Since that time, the literature has focused on psychological concerns, including guilt, denial, ambivalence, depression, anger, and acceptance. Studies of parental reaction often use vastly different terminology. Further, in these studies parents often report differing information concerning the onset, duration, and intensity of a specific feeling. Although the terminology is contradictory, there appear to be common experiences that parents of handicapped children report (Blacher, 1984). These stages are of varied intensity and duration, but seem to appear with predicted regularity. Further, these feelings are experienced throughout the parents' lives. Olshansky (1962) termed this experience "chronic sorrow," referring to the permanent and ongoing grieving that parents of children with disabilities experience. Olshansky holds this is a natural and understandable process. Further, it is in the best interests of parents to work through these feelings at their own pace. Services should be provided to assist parents in managing and living with the disabled child.

Professionals can play a role in helping parents adjust to the added pressures a person with disabilities places on a family (Schleifer, 1971). The thrust of these professional efforts has been to secure appropriate services from the public sector, thus generally ignoring the emotional state of the parents. However, a more complete approach to meeting the needs of parents with exceptional children has received considerable attention for many years. Many professionals have proposed that the grieving process can be an effective tool for understanding parental behavior and a powerful tool for counseling parents to understand and deal with their feelings (Blacher, 1984).

Some have found fault with this approach because of its inability to match all case studies and the misconception that parents resolve the grieving process. Allen and Affleck (1985) have proposed that because of such weaknesses, the grieving process should be disregarded. In place of the grieving process, they have proposed providing coping strategies to parents to help them better deal with the challenges of raising an exceptional individual. The emphasis is placed on problem resolution and emotional regulation. Coping strategies focus the parent on adjustment, which the stage approach to grieving processes often does not do.

Professionals need to be aware that the grieving process may adversely affect their relationship and interactions with parents of children with disabilities. At least three considerations must be understood. First, parents may be experiencing a variety of emotional states at a given time. Single interactions may not be representative of the parents' levels of cooperation or enthusiasm, but rather a stage in grieving (e.g., anger or guilt). Second, interaction with specific agency representatives may cause emotional responses that are not expected by the professionals involved. This may not mean that a parent's total life is focused in that direction, but that current interactions are bringing out certain feelings. Third, parents may spend a prolonged amount of time in one stage or another. A parent may appear to be angry or sad during dealings with a professional. This does not mean that the parent will always remain in this emotional stage; the parent eventually may move on to other feelings in the process. Those who deal with parents must realize that not only do emotions affect interactions, but varied behaviors are normal and to be expected (Searl, 1978).

The implications of the grieving process to those who deal with the parents of children with disabilities may be summarized as follows. First, parents often experience deep and intense feelings that may require counseling. Second, these feelings may continue for long periods of time. Third, feelings change at differing rates and/or varied sequences, necessitating flexibility in interpersonal dealings. Fourth, the grieving process is experienced by parents in an individual manner, necessitating interactions with parents to reflect an individual approach.

REFERENCES

Allen, D. A., & Affleck, G. (1985). Are we stereotyping parents? A postscript to Blacher. *Mental Retardation, 23,* 200–202.

ARCH. (2002). National Resource Center for Respite and Crisis Care Center. *Factsheet Number 21, Families and the grief process.* Retrieved from http://www.archrespite.org/images/docs/Factsheets/fs_21-grief_process.pdf

Blacher, J. (1984). Sequential stages of parental adjustment to the birth of a child with handicaps: Fact or artifact? *Mental Retardation, 22,* 55–58.

Olshansky, S. (1962). Chronic sorrow: A response to having a mentally defective child. *Social Casework, 43,* 190–194.

Roos, P. (1977). Parents of mentally retarded people. *International Journal of Mental Health, 6,* 96–119.

Rosen, L. (1955). Selected aspects in the development of the mother's understanding of her mentally retarded child. *American Journal of Mental Deficiency, 59,* 522.

Schleifer, M. (1971). Let us all stop blaming the parents. *Exceptional Parent, 1,* 3–5.

Searl, S. (1978). Stages of parent reaction. *Exceptional Parent, 8,* 27–29.

ALAN HILTON
Seattle University

See also Family Counseling; Family Response to a Child With Disabilities

GROHT, MILDRED A. (1890–1971)

Mildred A. Groht, a prominent educator of the deaf and developer of one of the major methods of teaching language to deaf children, was a graduate of Swarthmore College, with an honorary doctorate from Gallaudet College. She began her career as a teacher at the New York School for the Deaf and later taught at the Maryland School for the Deaf. In 1926 she joined the faculty of the Lexington School for the Deaf in New York City, where she served as principal until her retirement in 1958.

A talented teacher, she proposed and developed the influential natural language method of teaching language to the deaf. Based on the premise that deaf children can best acquire language through activities that are a natural part of a child's life, Groht's method uses a variety of activities. The teacher consistently creates situations that provide the students with language experiences and continually talks to the children and encourages them to respond with speech. Such practice in real-life situations was seen as more effective than the traditional grammatical or analytical approach, with its emphasis on language analysis and drill. The use of natural methods has increased markedly, and most programs today use a mixture of natural and analytical approaches.

Groht described the natural method in her book *Natural Language for Deaf Children.* In its foreword, Clarence D. O'Connor, then superintendent of the Lexington School for the Deaf, called Groht, "one of America's most distinguished teachers of the deaf, particularly in the field of communication arts." He went on to say:

> She has increasingly expounded the philosophy that deaf children can acquire fluent use of English comparable to that of the hearing through what has come to be known as the "natural" method, and through her own skillful teaching of deaf children and guiding of teachers she has demonstrated that this can be done without question. Through her writings, her demonstrations, and her lecture courses, and now through the chapters of this excellent book, she has very generously passed on to her coworkers the benefits of her rich experience in this specialized field.

Active in the Alexander Graham Bell Association for the Deaf, Groht served on the association's auxiliary board for a number of years and was named to its honorary board in 1965. She died in Ossining, New York, on December 11, 1971.

REFERENCE

Groht, M. A. (1958). *Natural language for deaf children*. Washington, DC: Alexander Graham Bell Association for the Deaf.

PAUL IRVINE
Katonah, New York

GROSENICK, JUDITH K. (1942–)

Judith K. Grosenick obtained her BS in 1964 in elementary education from the University of Wisconsin at Oshkosh (formerly Wisconsin State College), and later earned her MS in 1966 in special education and PhD in 1968 in emotional disturbance from the University of Kansas at Lawrence. She was a professor in the Department of Education and Director of Educational Studies at the University of Oregon, Eugene.

Originally an elementary school teacher, Grosenick encountered more difficulties in the classroom than she had expected or been trained to handle. Attempting to find solutions to these problems subsequently led to her increased involvement in the field of behavior disorders and special education (Grosenick, 1981). She is perhaps best known for her development of in-service training programs for teachers of children with behavior disorders, but is also recognized for her work in teacher and leadership personnel preparation as well as knowledge-building and dissemination.

Grosenick's extensive data-gathering and analysis in the area of district-level programs for behavior-disordered children has influenced issues and practices in the profession nationwide (Grosenick & Huntze, 1983). Her work

with the National Needs Analysis Program in Behavior Disorders has resulted in the development of an evaluation instrument used to assess instructional programs for children with serious emotional disturbance. Nine categories are addressed using this method, including program philosophy, student needs and identification, instructional methods and curriculum, program design and operation, and evaluation. Information regarding the development of instruction is provided as well, outlining several necessary steps ranging from identification of a well-conceptualized program to field testing, revising, and determining the validity of the instrument (Grosenick, 1990, 1991).

Although Grosenick's primary focus is special education, she is also concerned with the integration of special and regular education in public schools as well as teacher education programs. *Educational and Social Issues*, her most recent book, was published in 1996 and coauthored by Daniel W. Close. Dr. Grosenick is currently professor emerita at the University of Oregon.

REFERENCES

Grosenick, J. K. (1981). Public school and mental health services to severely behavior disordered students. *Behavioral Disorders, 6*, 183–190.

Grosenick, J. K. (1990). A conceptual scheme for describing and evaluating programs in behavioral disorders. *Behavioral Disorders, 16*, 66–74.

Grosenick, J. K. (1991). Public school services for behaviorally disordered students: Program practices in the 80s. *Behavioral Disorders, 16*, 87–96.

Grosenick, J. K., & Close, D. W. (1996). *Educational and social issues*. Dubuque, IA: Kendall-Hunt.

Grosenick, J. K., & Huntze, S. L. (1983). *National needs analysis in behavior disorders: More questions than answers: Review and analysis of programs for behaviorally disordered children and youth*. Columbia: University of Missouri.

Grosenick, J. K., & McCarney, S. L. (1984). Preparation of teacher education in behavior disorders. *Teacher Education & Special Education, 7*, 100–106.

E. VALERIE HEWITT
Texas A&M University
First edition

TAMARA J. MARTIN
The University of Texas of the Permian Basin
Second edition

GROSSMAN, HERBERT (1934–)

Herbert Grossman obtained his doctorate in clinical psychology from Columbia University in 1967. Formerly a member of the faculty in the special education department at San Jose State University, Grossman specializes in clinical child psychology and therapy.

His extensive work in the field of education and teacher preparation addresses a variety of topics, including gender inequities in education (Grossman & Grossman, 1994), diversity of students in special education (Grossman, 1995c), behavior management in classrooms (Grossman, 1990), teaching Hispanic-American students (Grossman, 1995b), and discrimination in special education (Grossman, 1998b). Promoting parity of educational opportunity for all students has been the prevailing theme of his writing and research. He has examined gender differences in school experiences and the origins of this disparity, particularly as this factor affects outcomes of education for male and female students. Providing procedures for educators to approach these issues, he focuses primarily on individual emotional reactions, methods of communication and learning, moral development, and interpersonal relationships (Grossman & Grossman, 1994).

Grossman's (1995d) important writing in the area of teacher preparation has promoted recognition of the diversity (i.e., socioeconomic, gender, communication, and so on) of individuals in today's schools, advocating effective, unbiased assessment and instructional methods to reduce these disparities, thus providing all youngsters the same opportunities for learning. His survey of some 500 professionals and parents in various regions of the United States and other countries posed questions related to cultural and contextual factors seen as critical to the formulation of recommendations for improving the academic achievement of Hispanic students (Grossman, 1995b).

During his distinguished career, Grossman has served as coordinator of the Bilingual/Cross Cultural Special Education Program at California State University, and he was the Director of Project Hope in Peru from 1978 to 1980. A prolific writer and researcher, he continues his significant work in the field of education, including *Special Education in a Diverse Society* (1995c), *Ending Discrimination in Special Education* (1998b), *Achieving Educational Equality* (1998a), and *Classroom Behavior Management for Diverse and Inclusive Schools* (2004).

REFERENCES

Grossman, H. (1990). *Instructor's manual to accompany trouble-free teaching: Solutions to behavior problems in the classroom.* Mountain View, CA: Mayfield.

Grossman, H. (1995a). *Classroom behavior management in a diverse society* (2nd ed.). Mountain View, CA: Mayfield.

Grossman, H. (1995b). *Educating Hispanic students: Implications for instruction, classroom management, counseling, and assessment* (2nd ed.). Springfield, IL: Thomas.

Grossman, H. (1995c). *Special education in a diverse society.* Boston, MA: Allyn & Bacon.

Grossman, H. (1995d). *Teaching in a diverse society.* Needham Heights, MA: Allyn & Bacon.

Grossman, H. (1998a). *Achieving educational equality: Assuring all students an equal opportunity in school.* Springfield, IL: Thomas.

Grossman, H. (1998b). *Ending discrimination in special education.* Springfield, IL: Thomas.

Grossman, H. (2004). *Classroom behavior management for diverse and inclusive schools* (3rd ed.). Toronto, Canada: Rowman-Littlefield.

Grossman, H., & Grossman, S. H. (1994). *Gender issues in education.* Boston, MA: Allyn & Bacon.

ROBERTA C. STOKES
Texas A&M University
First edition

TAMARA J. MARTIN
The University of Texas of the Permian Basin
Second edition

JESSI K. WHEATLEY
Falcon School District 49, Colorado Springs, Colorado
Third edition

GROTTOES OF NORTH AMERICA

Grottoes of North America is a humanitarian foundation composed of Master Masons who provide dental care for children with special needs (Humanitarian Foundation, n.d.). In order to qualify for financial assistance for dental treatments from the Grottoes, the child must be under the age of 18 and must meet one of the following conditions: intellectual or developmental disabilities. Developmental disabilities include cerebral palsy, muscular dystrophy and related neuromuscular diseases, or organ transplant recipients. If the child already has dental insurance, Grotto is considered a secondary carrier. They are committed to helping children with special needs to maintain a beautiful healthy smile.

Contact information for a local Dr. of Smiles, located in all 50 states of the United States and Canada, is found on the main website, www.hfgrotto.org. The main office of the Grottoes of North America is located at 430 Beecher Road, Gahanna, Ohio 43230. Tel.: (614) 933-0711.

REFERENCE

Humanitarian Foundation. (n.d.). Retrieved April 1, 2013, from www.hfgrotto.org

DONNA VERNER
Texas A&M University
Fourth edition

GROUP HOMES

The group home design is one model of alternate living environments designed to promote independent living for disabled individuals in our society. As an alternative to large institutions, group homes provide a residential environment within a community that allows disabled individuals to function as independently as possible while protecting their civil rights (Youngblood & Bensberg, 1983). Historically, the developmentally disadvantaged in our society were placed in large institutions housing vast numbers of disabled individuals. In 1969 Kugel and Wolfensberger reported that in the United States, 200,000 persons lived in over 150 public institutions for the retarded. An additional 20,000 resided in private institutions, with tens of thousands awaiting admittance to institutions for the mentally ill. For the most part, these institutions have been shown to be understaffed, overcrowded, and poorly managed. Violation of the rights of individuals with disabilities came into serious question (e.g., *Wyatt v. Stickney*, 1972). As a direct result of this, and in keeping with the civil rights movement that was raging in the late 1960s, a large deinstitutionalization movement began.

The current philosophy is one of normalization, which maintains that developmentally disabled persons have the same legal and civil rights as any other citizen as guaranteed under the Fourteenth Amendment of the U.S. Constitution. Because most alternative living arrangements involve some departure from culturally normative practices, special attention to implementation of normalization and use of the "least restrictive environment" concept must underlie all such arrangements (Accreditation Council for Services for Mentally Retarded and Other Developmentally Disabled Persons, 1984).

To qualify for federal assistance, group homes must be established according to specific guidelines set forth by the Federal Agency of the Administration of Developmental Disabilities (WAC 275.36.010). According to these guidelines, a group home is defined as a residential facility in the form of a single dwelling, series of apartments, or other sound structures that allow for a pleasant and healthful environment for human life and welfare. This structure may be owned, leased, or be part of a larger facility serving other disabled individuals.

A group home is designed to serve a maximum of 20 mentally or physically disabled individuals who participate in various jobs, sheltered workshops, daycare centers, activity centers, educational facilities, or other community-based programs that are designed for their training, rehabilitation, and/or general well-being. These facilities must be located within reasonable proximity to those community resources that are necessary adjuncts to a training, education, or rehabilitation program. The living quarters should provide a homelike atmosphere and the residents should participate in the care of the facility and of themselves.

There are two major types of group home facilities. Both are designed to house 8 to 10 individuals. The first is a transitional group home. As the name implies, this home is designed to house adults (18 or older) with the goal that the disabled person will move on to more independent living quarters (e.g., an apartment) once he or she has mastered important independent living skills. For individuals who exhibit less potential for being capable of independent living, long-term group homes are provided. These more permanent residences offer less restrictive environments than institutions, but not as independent an environment as transitional group homes. There are provisions even with long-term group homes that individuals be allowed to develop to their maximum potential. Thus, there are instances when individuals in long-term group homes have developed independent living skills to the extent that they can enter a transitional group home or can move directly into an independent living setting. Certain other groups of disabled individuals (e.g., deaf-blind) are also afforded chances for group home living. These facilities differ only in that they generally provide additional services to the transitional or long-term group home.

Group home facilities provide a wide range of services from legal assistance to sex education/family planning. The facilities, depending on states' funding patterns, are staffed by individuals ranging from house parents to supervisory professional staff members. Pros and cons of various staffing patterns are discussed by Youngblood and Bensberg (1983).

Establishing alternative living facilities (i.e., group homes) has not been always met with wholesale support, particularly by residents of communities where these residences are to be located. In keeping with the normalization principles and in accordance with state and federal guidelines for their establishment, group homes are to allow disabled individuals to experience community living to the maximum extent possible. Often residents of the community are concerned that their property values will fall because of group homes (Conroy & Bradley, 1985), or that a disabled resident might be dangerous. Researchers in the Pennhurst study found that resident attitudes following actual establishment of a group home were more positive than were attitudes toward the proposal of the same facility. The more negative attitudes were also directed toward group homes for the more severely disabled or mentally ill.

Research regarding the effects of group home living versus institutional living has been overwhelmingly positive. For example, the Pennhurst study (Conroy & Bradley, 1985) investigated whether disabled individuals ordered released from an institution following a court ruling and placed in alternative living environments, including group homes, were better off than a matched group of their peers who remained in the institution. Factors such as adaptive behavior, satisfaction with living arrangements, costs, and family and neighbor attitudes were examined. The study concluded: "the people deinstitutionalized under the Pennhurst court order *are* better off in *every* way measured...the results are not mixed" (pp. 322–323).

Just as residential services for the developmentally disabled today have met Wolfensberger's 1969 predictions, Willer (1981) has proposed that the concept of normalization and alternative living arrangements will again change in the future, out of necessity. He predicts "quality of life" concepts with emphasis on the individual will replace the group homes of today. Group homes as we know them, according to Willer, will be reserved for only the more severely disabled.

REFERENCES

Accreditation Council for Services for Mentally Retarded and Other Developmentally Disabled Persons. (1984). *Standards for services for developmentally disabled individuals.* Washington, DC: Author.

Conroy, J. W., & Bradley, V. J. (1985). *The Pennhurst longitudinal study: A report of five years of research and analysis.* U.S. Department of Health and Human Services. http://aspe.hhs.gov/daltcp/reports/5yrpenn.htm

Kugel, R. B., & Wolfensberger, W. (1969). *Changing patterns in residential services for the mentally retarded.* Washington, DC: President's Committee on Mental Retardation.

Willer, B. (1981). The future of residential services for mentally retarded persons. *Forum, 1*(4), 8–10.

Wyatt v. *Stickney.* 325F. Supp 781 (1972).

Youngblood, G. S., & Bensberg, G. J. (1983). *Planning and operating group homes for the handicapped.* Lubbock, TX: Research and Training Center in Mental Retardation.

JULIA A. HICKMAN
Bastrop Mental Health Association

See also **Adaptive Behavior; Deinstitutionalization; Edgerton, Robert B.; Least Restrictive Environment**

GROUP THERAPY

Group therapy is a general term that refers to any of the various types of therapeutic groups that share the broad purpose of increasing people's knowledge of themselves and others and giving people the skills necessary to enhance their personal competence. According to this general definition, group counseling, encounter groups, human relation groups, and skill-oriented groups are all types of group therapy. There are as many theoretical orientations to group therapy as there are to individual therapy. These include existentialism-humanism, gestalt, psychoanalytic, behavioral, rational-emotive therapy, reality therapy, transactional analysis, and others (Corey & Corey, 1977). The several types of group therapies plus the various theoretical orientations that may characterize group therapy make it difficult to make meaningful statements that generalize to the various types and models.

However, some generalizations do apply to most models of group therapy. First, participants can obtain honest feedback from others about how they appear to others. Thus, participants are provided with an opportunity to explore their style of relating to others and to learn more effective interpersonal skills. This feedback occurs in a group climate characterized by mutual caring and trust. Feedback from several persons, especially persons similar to a group participant, is often more powerful than a therapist's feedback in individual therapy.

Second, the group setting offers support for new behaviors and encourages experimentation. This norm of experimentation combined with the norms of feedback and support create a low-risk setting for participants to practice new behaviors such as showing compassion, intimacy, assertion, or disclosure of weaknesses.

Third, the sharing of experiences allows members to learn about themselves through the experiences of others, to experience emotional closeness, and to empathize with the problems of others. Participants learn that their problems and perceived inadequacies are not unique; they also learn new ways to cope with those problems. Some group therapists select group participants in a way that maximizes the opportunity for learning better ways of dealing with problems. For example, a group designed to help lonely children make friends would include some children who are at least moderately competent in friendship-making skills.

Fourth, group cohesiveness is necessary for a successful group. A cohesive group is characterized by mutual trust and respect and high levels of cooperation, support, encouragement, caring, productive problem solving, and the open expression of conflict. The group therapist directs much of his or her energies and skills to creating cohesive groups in which individuals experience the acceptance that is a necessary precondition for lowering defenses and risking new behaviors.

There are three major types of group therapy used in school settings: skill-oriented groups, personal growth groups, and specific focus therapy groups. The use of all three in schools is justified by the recognition that emotional and behavioral adjustment is important to a child's educational performance. Social-emotional problems like depression, loneliness, or anxiety affect school learning and adjustment.

Skill-oriented group therapy is the most widely accepted type of group therapy in school settings as it focuses on teaching specific adaptive skills such as communication, problem-solving, or social skills. An example of a skill-oriented therapy program is the structured learning therapy model developed and popularized by Goldstein (1981). In this model children with deficient social skills are taught skills through a procedure that employs instruction, modeling, behavior rehearsal, and feedback. Children in the group discuss each skill (e.g., expressing anger, offering help, disagreeing with another), citing their own examples of each skill. The skills are broken into component steps, and members practice the skills in role playing. They receive feedback from the group on their performance. Another example of a skill-oriented group is a communication skill group for adolescents. Members practice such skills as listening and perception-checking in the group setting and discuss how these skills apply outside the group.

In the personal growth group, the group setting provides the emotional support and encouragement necessary for the type of self-exploration that leads to a change in attitudes and behaviors. In schools, members of the group might share a common problem or situation such as having parents who are recently divorced. The group provides members with a place where they can express their feelings regarding their situations and discover that other people experience similar problems and feelings. These groups attempt to help members integrate their thinking and feelings and to experience greater self-acceptance. They are often directed to the normal person who is experiencing unusual stress or who wishes to become more self-actualized.

The specific focus therapy group attempts to correct an emotional or behavioral problem. An example is a group for highly anxious children. Children might share anxiety-producing situations and their reactions to those situations. They learn that different children are afraid of different situations, test the reality of their fears, and learn from other children how to cope with their anxieties. The group therapist might teach children how to use specific anxiety-management techniques such as relaxation, self-talk, or problem solving.

REFERENCES

Corey, G., & Corey, M. S. (1977). *Groups: Process and practice.* Belmont, CA: Wadsworth.

Goldstein, A. P. (1981). *Psychological skill training: The structured learning technique.* New York, NY: Pergamon Press.

JAN N. HUGHES
Texas A&M University

See also **Family Counseling; Psychotherapy**

GROWTH DELAY, CONSTITUTIONAL

Constitutional growth delay is a disorder that is characterized by a temporary delay in skeletal growth (National Organization for Rare Disorders [NORD], 1991). It is often a cause of parental concern about growth. This pattern occurs when a child (usually short) has a slowdown in growth just before puberty and possibly a delay in beginning puberty (Iannelli, 2000). Although children with constitutional growth delay develop slowly, they usually continue growing after other children have stopped, and many times they grow to normal adult height. There are two types of this disorder. Constitutional growth delay (familial) may be found in other individuals in the family. Constitutional growth delay (sporadic) is when the delayed pattern of growth occurs for no apparent reason (NORD, 1991).

Constitutional growth delay is sometimes called constitutional growth delay with delayed adolescence or delayed maturation. This disorder is also known as constitutional short stature, idiopathic growth delay, CDGP, sporadic short stature, or physiological delayed puberty (NORD, 1991).

Children with constitutional growth delay are usually shorter than their peers from early in their development. They grow at a slow but normal rate. The onset of puberty may occur 2 to 4 years later than it does in other children the same age (Rieser, 2001). Many times, after puberty, a growth spurt will occur, and the child will develop to normal height similar that of his or her parents. So-called Bone age is often 1 to 4 years behind the chronological age of the child (eBiocare.com, 2000). Young children with constitutional growth delay are often found to have a deficit in weight for their length (Cheng & Jacobson, 1997).

Many times, a child with constitutional growth delay is normal size at birth (Selig, 1998). In early development, usually between 6 months and 2.5 years, the child's growth slows so that height decreases to below the 5th percentile (Selig, 1998). After this point, growth is normal for the child's chronological age. The delay in skeletal growth will match the delay in height.

Constitutional growth delay is sometimes originally identified as failure to thrive (FTT) in infants and young children. These children should have a thorough evaluation to determine the cause of the growth delay. If a child has constitutional growth delay, he or she is classified as having factitious FTT; this is not considered to be a true form of FTT (Cheng & Jacobson, 1997).

Symptoms of other diseases or conditions that might affect the child's growth should be ruled out by the pediatrician through a thorough examination and family history (Cheng & Jacobson, 1997; eBiocare.com, 2000). It is also recommended that the child be evaluated and possibly treated by a pediatric endocrinologist (Iannelli, 2000).

Characteristics

1. Characterized by a temporary delay in skeletal growth.
2. Slowdown in growth just before puberty and possibly a delay in beginning puberty.
3. Most times, children eventually grow to adult height.
4. May be familial or sporadic.

Most times, this condition resolves itself and treatment is not necessary. However, a patient may undergo elective treatment with monthly hormone injections of either estrogen or testosterone. These hormone treatments can result in closure of growth plates, causing shorter height when the child reaches adulthood (Rieser, 2001). Although it has not been proven that this condition is more prevalent in males, boys are more frequently seen for treatment.

There is no direct link between constitutional growth delay and special education. However, as teenagers, these children may feel uncomfortable because they are less developed and smaller than their peers. It is possible that this condition may cause emotional stress during adolescence. Teenagers with constitutional growth delay should be observed for signs of emotional problems.

Research studies continue to be conducted to determine the physical and psychological impact of hormone treatment for constitutional growth delay.

REFERENCES

Cheng, A., & Jacobson, S. (1997). *Failure to thrive: Approach to diagnosis and management.* Retrieved from http://www.utmj.org/75.1/featurecontents.htm

eBiocare.com. (2000). *Growth hormone deficiency.* Retrieved from http://ebiocare.com/communities/ghd/faqhome.html

Iannelli, V. R. (2000). *Short stature.* Retrieved from http://www.keepkidshealthy.com/welcome/conditions/short_stature.html

National Organization for Rare Disorders. (1991). *Constitutional growth delay.* Retrieved from http://www.rarediseases.org

Rieser, P. A. (2001). *Patterns of growth.* New York, NY: Human Growth Foundation.

Selig, S. (2000). *Constitutional growth delay.* Oak Park, IL: Magic Foundation for Children's Growth.

MICHELE WILSON KAMENS
Rider University

GROWTH HORMONE DEFICIENCY

Growth hormone deficiency is a condition resulting in impaired physical growth, caused by a partial or total absence of the growth hormone produced by the pituitary gland. The affected child will have normal body proportions and yet often look younger than his or her peers (Human Growth Foundation, 2000). If other pituitary hormones are lacking, the condition is called hypopituitarism; in children, the term hypopituitarism may be used interchangeably with growth hormone deficiency. The prevalence of this disorder has been estimated to be between 10,000 and 15,000 children in the United States and to affect 1 of every 4,000 school-aged children. The congenital form of growth hormone deficiency occurs 3 to 4 more times in boys than girls (Vanderbilt University Medical Center, 1998).

Growth hormone deficiency may be congenital (resulting from abnormal formation of the pituitary gland or hypothalamus) or acquired through damage to these glands after birth. There may be either a partial or a total lack of growth hormone production (Human Growth Foundation, 2000). In the case of a total growth hormone deficiency, height and weight are usually normal at birth. However, between 3 and 9 months, growth rate is reduced, and parents may notice additional symptoms such as delayed development of teeth and a diminished ability to gain weight (Netdoctor.co.uk, 2000). Idiopathic hypopituitarism is the most frequent mechanism causing total growth hormone deficiency. Some infants with intrauterine hypopituitarism may at birth have prolonged jaundice, hypoglycemic seizures, and if male, undescended testes and micropenis. In some children, growth hormone deficiency may also be associated with central nervous system and facial defects. These may range from severe abnormalities of brain development to cleft lip and cleft palate.

Characteristics

1. Impaired physical development, usually marked by a growth pattern of less than 2 inches per year.
2. Children often appear younger than their age, with an immature face and chubby body build. (Children may acquire a thick layer of fat under the skin that gives them a chubby body build.)
3. Children have normal body proportions.
4. Many children have heights for bone age that fall below the 3rd percentile.
5. Children may fail to undergo puberty at the appropriate age.

Growth hormone deficiency may be difficult to diagnose because the growth hormone is produced in bursts and in greatest quantities during sleep. Doctors usually first examine a child to rule out other causes (such as thyroid hormone deficiency, malnutrition, or other chronic diseases). Previous growth measurements, an X ray to determine bone age, blood samples, and measurement of growth hormone secretion also play a role in diagnosis (Levy, 1998).

Treatment consists of synthetic growth hormone therapy, usually given by injection daily or several times a week until the child stops growing (Human Growth Foundation, 2000). Although side effects are rare, the correct dosage of growth hormone must be determined exactly and child must be monitored for side effects. After treatment begins, a prompt increase in growth rate can usually be noticed in 3–4 months. Some parents have also reported an increase in appetite and loss of body fat with treatment. During the first year of therapy, children may grow 8–10 cm (Vanderbilt University Medical Center, 1998). Accurate plotting on a growth chart is important. Children who do not respond to treatment should be evaluated for hypothyroidism or the formation of antibodies to human growth hormone (Human Growth Foundation, 2000).

In the educational setting, children who are short for their age may have problems because adults and peers often treat them as younger, not just smaller. Having decreased expectations for a child may result in the child's acting younger than what is appropriate for his or her age (Human Growth Foundation, 2000). Counseling may provide emotional and social support for children. Parents may also wish to communicate with the child's educators about how any side effects of growth hormone treatment may affect learning.

Prognosis is good after a child undergoes treatment. The majority of children treated today reach normal adult height or almost their full growth potential. Early diagnosis and treatment are important for best results. If treatment does not occur before the child's bones fuse, no additional growth can occur. If growth hormone deficiency is not treated, the child's growth will be severely impaired (Levy, 1998).

Research is currently studying alternative methods of treatment, including growth hormone releasing factor (GHRF) and somatomedin. A recent study comparing once-versus twice-daily injections of growth hormone found no significant differences in growth response or bone age after 1 year (Philip et al., 1998). Other researchers have created a prediction model for growth based on the child's size and target height at start of therapy (Südfield, Kiese, Heinecke, & Brämswig, 2000). They conclude that the difference between starting height and target height is an important predictor of first-year growth response. The most current information on research and treatment can be found by contacting the Human Growth Foundation, a national organization of parents with affected children, at the website: http://www.hgfound.org.

REFERENCES

Human Growth Foundation, Inc. (2000, November 26). *Growth hormone deficiency*. Retrieved from http://www .hgfound.org/growth.html

Levy, R. A. (1998). *Growth hormone deficiency*. Retrieved from http://www.magicfoundation.org/ghd.html

NetDoctor.co.uk. (2000, February). *Growth hormone deficiency*. Retrieved from http://www.netdoctor.co.uk/diseases/facts/lack ofgrowthhormone.html

Philip, M., Hershkovitz, E., Belotserkovsky, O., Lieberman, E., Limoni, Y., & Zadik, Z. (1998). Once versus twice daily injections of growth hormone in children with idiopathic short stature. *Acta Paediatrica, 87*, 518–520.

Südfield, H., Kiese, K., Heinecke, A., & Brämswig, J. H. (2000). Prediction of growth response in prepubertal children treated with growth hormone for idiopathic growth hormone deficiency. *Acta Paediatrica, 89*, 34–37.

Vanderbilt University Medical Center. (1998). *Endocrinology: Growth hormone deficiency*. Retrieved from http://www.mc .vanderbilt.edu/peds/pidl/endocr/grohorm.html

LAURA A. GULI
University of Texas at Austin

GUADALUPE V. TEMPE ELEMENTARY SCHOOL (*See Diana v. State Board of Education*)

GUGGENBÜHL, JOHANN J. (1816–1863)

Johann J. Guggenbühl, a Swiss physician, was the originator of institutional care for the mentally retarded. Following an extensive study of cretinism, Guggenbühl established a hospital and school for mentally retarded children, the Abendberg, in the mountains of Switzerland. There he instituted for his students a program that combined healthful living, good diet, and medicine with an educational program that emphasized cognitive, sensory, and physical training. Guggenbühl found that his students, especially those who entered his school at an early age, showed improvement in both physical and mental development. Guggenbühl publicized his results widely, and institutions similar to his were established in many of the countries of Europe and in the United States.

Guggenbühl was much in demand and was often away from the Abendberg for extended periods, during which time the institution was poorly administered. This situation caused problems that, in conjunction with the high expectations that Guggenbühl had fostered, led to the closing of the Abendberg and the departure in disgrace of its founder. Nevertheless, Guggenbühl's contribution was monumental. He originated institutional care for the mentally retarded, demonstrated that young mentally retarded people could be helped to develop both physically and mentally, and developed a system of care and education that served as a model throughout the Western world.

REFERENCE

Kanner, L. (1964). *A history of the care and study of the mentally retarded*. Springfield, IL: Thomas.

PAUL IRVINE
Katonah, New York

GUIDE TO THE ASSESSMENT OF TEST SESSION BEHAVIOR

The Guide to the Assessment of Test Session Behavior for the WISC-III and the WIAT (GATSB; Glutting & Oakland, 1993) is a 29-item behavior rating scale used to evaluate the test behavior of children aged 6 years, 0 months through 16 years, 11 months. Although the scale was conormed with the Wechsler Intelligence Scale for Children–Third Edition (WISC III) and the Wechsler Independent Achievement Test (WIAT), it can be used with all individually administered cognitive tests. The GATSB allows the examiner to evaluate whether a child's behavior during testing differs substantially from behavior displayed by same age and sex peers and whether this behavioral difference affects the quality of the scores. The examiner completes the ratings immediately after the testing session. The instrument is brief, requiring less than 5 minutes to complete and score (Oakland, Glutting, & Watkins, 2005).

The GATSB assesses three broad behaviors known to influence test performance: avoidance, inattentiveness, and uncooperative mood. Children's behaviors are rated on items using a three-point scale (i.e., 0, 1, or 2) in reference to *doesn't apply, somewhat applies*, or *usually applies*. Raw scores are summed and converted to standard T-scores for each of the three scales and for a total score, which is a combination of the three.

The GATSB was standardized on 969 children who were representative of 1988 U.S. Census data according to age, race, ethnicity, gender, and parent education. The children's intellectual abilities and achievement levels matched the general population (Glutting & Oakland, 1993). Internal reliability estimates are high, ranging between .84 and .88 for the three scales and are .92 for the total score. Several studies have supported the construct and criterion-related validity of the GATSB. Coefficients of factorial congruence were sufficiently high to conclude that the three scales were comparable for children who differed in race/ethnicity, gender, and socioeconomic status (Konold, Glutting, Oakland, & O'Donnell, 1995). Children who exhibited higher levels of inattentiveness, avoidance, and uncooperative behaviors when taking tests also tended to exhibit lower WISC-III scores (Glutting, Oakland, & Konold, 1994). Also, children with Attention-Deficit/Hyperactivity Disorder could be distinguished from matched controls on the three test behavior domains (Glutting, Robins, & de Lancey, 1997). Although normed on the WISC-III standardization sample, GATSB scores can accurately assess behavior during testing with the Woodcock-Johnson Psychoeducational Battery–Revised and the Wide Range Assessment of Memory and Learning (Daleiden, Drabman, & Benton, 2002).

The GATSB is a valid and reliable standardized measure of test performance. The GATSB may assist in understanding test session behaviors on measures including the Clinical Evaluation of Language Functions–Third Edition, Differential Abilities Scale, Kaufman Assessment Battery for Children, Stanford-Binet Intelligence Scale: Fifth Edition, and Woodcock-Johnson Tests of Cognitive Abilities (Oakland et al., 2005). Use of the GATSB may be valuable for determining whether a student's test-taking behaviors are atypical and if the quality of his or her scores may be affected.

REFERENCES

Daleiden, E., Drabman, R. S., & Benton, J. (2002). The Guide to the Assessment of Test Session Behavior: Validity in relation to cognitive testing and parent-reported behavior problems in a clinical sample. *Journal of Clinical Child Psychology, 31*, 263–271.

Glutting, J., & Oakland, T. (1993). *Guide to the Assessment of Test Session Behavior for the WISC III and WIAT: Manual*. San Antonio, TX: Psychological Corporation.

Glutting, J., Oakland, T., & Konold, T. R. (1994). Criterion-related bias with the Guide to the Assessment of Test-Session Behavior for the WISC III and WIAT: Possible race/ethnicity, gender, and SES effects. *Journal of School Psychology, 32*, 355–369.

Glutting, J. J., Robins, P. M., & de Lancey, E. (1997). Discriminant validity of test observations for children with attention deficit/hyperactivity. *Journal of School Psychology, 35*, 391–401.

Konold, T. R., Glutting, J. J., Oakland, T., & O'Donnell, L. (1995). Congruence of test-behavior dimensions among child groups that vary in gender, race-ethnicity, and SES. *Journal of Psychoeducational Assessment, 13*, 111–119.

Oakland, T., Glutting, J., & Watkins, M. W. (2005). Assessment of test behaviors with the WISC-IV. In A. Profitera, D. H. Saklofske, & L. G. Weiss (Eds.), *WISC-IV clinical use and interpretation: Scientist practitioner perspectives* (pp. 435–463). San Diego, CA: Elsevier.

JEFFREY DITTERLINE
University of Florida

See also Intelligent Testing

GUILFORD, J. P. (1897–1987)

A native Nebraskan, J. P. Guilford obtained his degree in psychology at the University of Nebraska and later did graduate work at Cornell University. While attending Nebraska, his association with Winifred Hyde led to an interest in psychological testing, with Karl Dallenbach and Kurt Koffka, both of whom he met at Cornell, strongly influencing his later work. Guilford died in 1987.

Guilford spent most of his academic career at the University of Southern California. In addition to writing what some consider classic texts in psychological measurement (e.g., Guilford, 1942, 1967), he is best known for his extensive work in factor analysis, the method used to develop his structure of intellect (SOI) model (Guilford, 1967, 1988). Guilford's model of intelligence postulates some 120 distinct human abilities that contribute to overall intellectual ability and was later revised to contain five content properties, including visual, auditory, symbolic, semantic, and behavioral. In the field of special education, his SOI model, particularly the concepts of convergent and divergent thought, was used to develop programs to foster creativity and improve learning of gifted and creative children.

In 1983, Guilford received the Gold Medal Award of the American Psychological Association. His numerous publications include *The Nature of Human Intelligence* (1967), *Intelligence Education Is Intelligent Education* (1980), and *Fundamental Statistics in Psychology and Education* (1942). A compilation of his work in scholarly journals was published in German (Primmer, 1995).

REFERENCES

Guilford, J. P. (1942). *Fundamental statistics in psychology and education.* New York, NY: McGraw-Hill.

Guilford, J. P. (1967). *The nature of human intelligence.* New York, NY: McGraw-Hill.

Guilford, J. P. (1980). *Intelligence education is intelligent education.* Tokyo, Japan: International Society for Intelligence Education.

Guilford, J. P. (1988). Some changes in the structure-of-intellect model. *Educational & Psychological Measurement, 48,* 1–4.

Guilford, J. P., Anastasi, A., English, H., & Freeman, G. (1948). *Fields of psychology.* New York, NY: Van Nostrand.

Primmer, H. (1995). *Kreativitatsforschung und Joy Paul Guilford.* Munchen, Germany: Akademischer Verlag.

TAMARA J. MARTIN
The University of Texas of the Permian Basin

See also Convergent and Divergent Thinking; Structure of Intellect

GUILLAIN-BARRÉ SYNDROME

Guillian-Barré syndrome (GBS) is one of many autoimmune neuropathies that progress to paralysis and involve inflammation of the peripheral nervous system (Willison, 2005). With the virtual elimination of poliomyelitis, GBS is the leading cause of neuromuscular paralysis following infection or immunization in children (DiMario, 2005). GBS includes acute inflammatory demyelinating polyradiculoneuropathy (AIDP), acute motor axonal neuropathy (AMAN), acute motor and sensory axonal neuropathy (AMSAN), Miller Fisher syndrome (MFS), and acute pandysautonomia (Finsterer, 2005). Across age groups, GBS occurs in 1.5 per 100,000, with a lifetime likelihood that an individual will acquire the disorder of approximately 1 in 1,000 (Hahn, 1998; Willison, 2005). In most cases, GBS is associated with destruction of the myelin sheath of peripheral nerves; however, in some cases there are additional variants (DiMario, 2005).

Onset of GBS is rapid and acute, generally occurring within 2 weeks after some other illness or immunization. Symptoms include weakness of limbs, absent tendon stretch reflexes, limb and back pain, and facial weakness (Bradshaw & Jones, 1992). Onset is rapid and progressive. Diagnostic testing includes evaluation of levels of protein in the cerebral spinal fluid. Following onset, there is symptom manifestation for about 1 month or more. This is followed by varying residual symptoms during what is called the recovery phase (Hartung, Kieseier, & Kiefer, 2001). Secondary deterioration may occur at later times. This pattern of manifestation is particular to GBS. It is believed that the effects in children may be somewhat milder (i.e., better recovery) than with adults (Bradshaw & Jones, 1992).

The optimal treatment window is very short; as a result, in roughly 20 percent of cases, there is total paralysis requiring mechanical ventilation. The current treatment of choice involves whole plasma exchange of intravenous immunoglobulin therapy; this minimizes the severity of syndrome manifestation (e.g., Hughes, Jewitt, & Swan, 2004). Recent studies suggest that introduction of intravenous immunoglobulin therapy decreased the time required to regain motor function (Korinthenberg, Schessl, Kirschner, & Mönting, 2005; see DiMario, 2005, for review). Notably, this intravenous treatment is not without risks (i.e., allergic reactions, headache, infection), and the risks and benefits need to be weighed carefully (DiMario, 2005).

Multiple advances have been made in what is known about GBS (Willison, 2005); however, further advances are needed to improve the outcomes of those affected. Additional information and support can be obtained from the Guillain-Barré Syndrome Foundation, P.O. Box 262, Wynnewood, PA 19096, or on the website: www.guillain-barre.com

REFERENCES

Bradshaw, D. J., & Jones, H. R. (1992). Guillain-Barré syndrome children: Clinical course, electrodiagnosis, and prognosis. *Muscle and Nerve, 15,* 500–506.

DiMario, Jr., F. J. (2005). Intravenous immunoglobulin in the treatment of childhood Guillain-Barré syndrome: A randomized trial. *Pediatrics, 116,* 226–228.

Finsterer, J. (2005). Treatment of immune-mediated, dysimmune neuropathies. *Acta Neurologica Scandinavica, 112,* 115–125.

Hahn, A. F. (1998). Guillain-Barré syndrome. *Lancet, 352,* 635–641.

Hartung, H. P., Kieseier, B. C., & Kiefer, R. (2001). Progress in Guillain-Barré syndrome. *Current Opinion in Neurology, 14,* 597–604.

Hughes, R. A., Jewitt, K. M., & Swan, A. V. (2004). Cochrane systematic reviews of treatments for peripheral nerve disorders. *Journal of Peripheral Nervous System, 9,* 127–129.

Korinthenberg, R., Schessl, J., Kirschner, J., & Mönting, J. S. (2005). Intravenously administered immunoglobulin in the treatment of childhood Guillain-Barré syndrome: A randomized trial. *Pediatrics, 116,* 8–14.

Willison, H. J. (2005). The immunobiology of Guillain-Barré syndromes. *Journal of the Peripheral Nervous System, 10,* 94–112.

Cynthia A. Riccio
Texas A&M University

See also Central Nervous System; Other Health Impaired; Physical Disabilities

H

HABILITATION OF INDIVIDUALS WITH DISABILITIES

Habilitation is the process of using various professional services to help persons with disabilities maximize their vocational, mental, physical, and social abilities (Rosen, Clark, & Kivitz, 1977). Whereas the term *rehabilitation* connotes restoration of abilities, habilitation refers to the *development of abilities* that never existed. The term usually refers to programming for those with developmental disabilities such as cerebral palsy, mental retardation, epilepsy, autism, or sensory impairment.

Present-day habilitation programs have evolved from decades of legislation and litigation addressing the rights and needs of the developmentally disabled (Goldberg, 1984). Three major pieces of legislation promoted early habilitation efforts: the Rehabilitation Act Amendments of 1973 (PL 93-112), the Education for all Handicapped Children Act of 1975 (PL 94-142), and the Education Amendments of 1976 (PL 94-482), efforts that continue to be supported by the Individuals with Disabilities Education Act (IDEA) reauthorizations and the Americans with Disabilities Act (ADA).

Sections 503 and 504 of the Rehabilitation Act mandate affirmative action for all employment openings, prohibit discrimination of individuals with disabilities in hiring, training, advancement, and retention practices, and require that all programs be accessible to persons with disabilities (Trieschmann, 1984). Compliance is necessary to retain federal funding.

Habilitation programs for students with disabilities vary, but are similar in format to those described by Miller and Schloss (1982). Current programs focus not only on vocation, but also on academic, social, leisure, and interpersonal skills. Teaching procedures include identification of the disability, assessment of skills, program design based on needs, interests, and skills of the individual, instruction, and behavior management and evaluation. Career education includes career awareness and exploration, development of vocational prerequisites, and preparation training (Kokaska & Brolin, 1985). Goals of these training programs vary with the individual's skills and abilities.

REFERENCES

Goldberg, R. T. (1984). The human sciences and clinical methods: An historical perspective (Special issue). *Rehabilitation Literature, 45,* 340–344.

Kokaska, C. J., & Brolin, D. E. (1985). *Career education for handicapped individuals* (2nd ed.). Columbus, OH: Merrill.

Miller, S. R., & Schloss, P. J. (1982). *Career-vocational education for handicapped youth.* Rockville, MD: Aspen.

Rosen, M., Clark, G. R., & Kivitz, M. S. (1977). *Habilitation of the handicapped: New dimensions in programs for the developmentally disabled.* Baltimore, MD: University Park Press.

Trieschmann, R. B. (1984). Vocational rehabilitation: A psychological perspective (Special issue). *Rehabilitation Literature, 45,* 345–348.

CHRISTINE A. ESPIN
University of Minnesota

See also Rehabilitation; Vocational Education

HABITUATION

Habituation is a decline in response to a stimulus that is presented repeatedly but that signals the onset of no other stimulus. For example, a loud noise may evoke a startle response at first but little response after its 20th repetition. A new cuckoo clock may awaken people on the hour for the first few nights but not on later nights.

Because habituation is generally perceived as a relatively simple example of learning, it has been a popular focus for study by investigators interested in the physiology of learning. For example, the gill-withdrawal response of the sea slug *Aplysia* habituates after a tactile stimulus is repeated many times. The habituation can be traced to a single, identifiable synapse at which the presynaptic end bulb shrinks and releases less than normal amounts of its synaptic transmitter (Castellucci & Kandel, 1974).

Habituation may be taken as the opposite of distractibility. Someone who fails to habituate to a repeated stimulus will continue to be distracted by it. Biological factors that impair habituation also increase distractibility. Examples include damage to the frontal lobes of the cerebral cortex and a deficit of the synaptic transmitter acetylcholine (Carlton & Markiewicz, 1971). Infant rats fail to habituate before age 25 days (Feigley, Parsons, Hamilton, & Spear, 1972). This failure is attributed to the immaturity of certain areas of the brain, including the frontal cortex, prior to that age (Jansiewicz, Newschaffer, Denckla, & Mostofsky, 2004). High distractibility and slow habituation also characterize many children with an immature nervous system, including most of those who suffer from attention deficit disorder. Slow habituation also is associated with other behaviors that indicate a lack of inhibition such as impulsiveness, unresponsiveness to the threat of punishment, and failure to extinguish an unreinforced response.

Some investigators have used rate of habituation as a diagnostic technique to identify infants or young children who may have been exposed to factors that impair brain maturation. One study examined the rate of habituation by newborns as a function of alcohol use by their mothers during pregnancy (Streissguth, Barr, & Martin, 1983). Habituation was slightly but significantly slower among infants whose mothers drank alcohol during pregnancy, even if they drank a mean of less than one ounce of alcohol per day.

REFERENCES

Carlton, P. L., & Markiewicz, B. (1971). Behavioral effects of atropine and scopolamine. In E. Furchtgott (Ed.), *Pharmacological and biophysical agents and behavior* (pp. 345–373). New York, NY: Academic Press.

Castellucci, V. F., & Kandel, E. R. (1974). A quantal analysis of the synaptic depression underlying habituation of the gill-withdrawal reflex in *Aplysia*. *Proceedings of the National Academy of Sciences, USA, 71*, 5004–5008.

Feigley, D. A., Parsons, P. J., Hamilton, L. W., & Spear, N. E. (1972). Development of habituation to novel environments in the rat. *Journal of Comparative & Physiological Psychology, 79*, 443–452.

Jansiewicz, E. M., Newschaffer, C. J., Denckla, M. B., & Mostofsky, S. H. (2004). Impaired habituation in children with attention deficit hyperactivity disorder. *Cognitive and Behavioral Neurology: Official Journal of the Society for Behavioral and Cognitive Neurology, 17*, 1–8.

Streissguth, A. P., Barr, H. M., & Martin, D. C. (1983). Maternal alcohol use and neonatal habituation assessed with the Brazelton scale. *Child Development, 54*, 1109–1118.

JAMES W. KALAT
North Carolina State University

See also **Attention-Deficit/Hyperactivity Disorder; Behavior Modification; Distractibility**

HALDERMAN VERSUS PENNHURST STATE SCHOOL AND HOSPITAL (1977)

The Halderman case was filed as a class-action suit by a resident, T. L. Halderman, of the Pennhurst State School and Hospital (operated by the Commonwealth of Pennsylvania), the Pennsylvania Association of Retarded Citizens, and the United States of America against the Pennhurst State School and Hospital. The residents made a variety of claims that centered on the lack of rehabilitative and educational efforts at Pennhurst. The plaintiffs argued that custodial care was insufficient for involuntary placement in the Pennhurst institution because the plaintiffs were mentally retarded and not considered dangerous.

In deciding the case, the federal judge for the Eastern District of Pennsylvania, R. J. Broderick, made three rulings that have been of major importance in modifying special education services to the institutionalized retarded. Broderick ruled that mentally retarded residents of state institutions have constitutional rights to minimally adequate habilitation services, to freedom from harm, and to the receipt of habilitation services in a nondiscriminatory manner. Broderick went on to rule in the Halderman case specifically that the resident's rights at Pennhurst had been violated because of failure to provide even minimally adequate habilitative services. In making his rulings, Broderick rejected the argument that improvements at Pennhurst were being made gradually and should be allowed to proceed at an incremental pace, that state law restricted the programs that could be offered, and that funding levels prevented minimally adequate habilitation programs.

Broderick wrote a lengthy decision that reviews assessment practices, programming, and management in institutional settings. All were directed at the provision of habilitative services and special education. For example, Broderick noted that although speech, hearing, and psychological evaluations had been completed on nearly all residents at approximately 3-year intervals, vocational assessments or evaluations of self-care skills were rarely conducted. Broderick saw a need for more extensive evaluations, stating that "Proper habilitation cannot be provided to retarded persons unless those responsible for providing such programs are aware of the individual's needs" (*Halderman v. Pennhurst*, 1977, p. 1305). Broderick required the development of individual educational plans for the institutionalized retarded that would include (1) long- and short-term goals, (2) specification of the conditions under which the individual might achieve these goals, and (3) specification of the criteria to evaluate the individual's mastery of these goals.

Broderick placed many restrictions on the use of punishment, drugs, and physical restraints. He particularly ruled that lack of sufficient staff did not allow the use of otherwise inappropriate methods of control. Physical constraints, for example, could not be used simply because insufficient staff were available to supervise self-injurious residents (Longmore, 1995).

Broderick made strong statements indicating favorable sentiments toward the principles of normalization as applied to the severely and profoundly disabled as well. Since the court found that the environment at Pennhurst was not conducive to normalization, Broderick ruled that the residents were to be moved to community-based living facilities as part of the injunctive relief (Ferleger & Boyd, 1979). He noted that each community facility would be required to provide minimally adequate habilitative services. Broderick's extensive rulings regarding the provisions of habilitative services, including detailed multidisciplinary assessment and movement toward normalization, have had significant impact on the deinstitutionalization of all but the most severely and profoundly mentally retarded. The rulings have greatly impacted the lives of those remaining in institutions such as Pennhurst, and many of these provisions were later incorporated into the Developmental Disabilities Assistance and Bill of Rights Act.

REFERENCES

Ferleger, D., & Boyd, P. A. (1979). Anti-institutionalization: The promise of the Pennhurst case. *Stanford Law Review 31*, 4, 717–752.

Longmore, P. K. (1995). Medical decision making and people with disabilities: A clash of cultures. *Journal of Law, Medicine & Ethics: A Journal of the American Society of Law, Medicine & Ethics, 23*, 1, 82–87.

CECIL R. REYNOLDS
Texas A&M University
Second edition

KIMBERLY F. APPLEQUIST
University of Colorado
at Colorado Springs
Third edition

See also **Developmental Disabilities Assistance and Bill of Rights Act; Normalization; Wolfensberger, Wolf**

HALDOL

Haldol (haloperidol) is considered a major tranquilizer (Physicians Desk Reference, n.d.). Unlike thorazine, which is a phenothiazine, haldol is of the drug class butyrophenone, which tends to have a greater neuroleptic effect than phenothiazine (Bassuk & Schoonover, 1977). Haldol is similar in effect to the piperazine subgroup (e.g., Stelazine) of phenothiazines. Like similar antipsychotic drugs, haldol appears to block dopamine receptors in the brain. In contrast to chlorpromazine, haldol tends to produce less sedation, less decrease in blood pressure, and less change in temperature perception (McEvoy, 1984). Haldol is used primarily for symptomatic management of psychotic conditions. Haldol also appears to have more specific effects on aggression and agitated behavior (Konopasek, 2003). Thus, it tends to be used with psychotic individuals who also show assaultive behavior, with combative adolescents, and with hyperactive brain-impaired children (Bassuk & Schoonover, 1977). Haldol also has been used as an adjunct with manic-depressive patients in the manic phase during the initiation of lithium treatment (Jefferson, Greist, & Ackerman, 1983). Although haldol was once the most popular of the neuroleptic drugs for the treatment of psychotic processes (such as schizophrenia) due to its low side-effect profile, other drugs with even fewer side effects, such as Risperidone, have gained popularity.

As may be expected from its actions, haldol produces anticholinergic side effects (i.e., dry mouth, blurred vision, urinary retention). Side effects (McEvoy, 1984) to haloperidol treatment usually develop during the initial days of treatment; they are similar to the side effects encountered during treatment with phenothiazines (parkinsonian symptoms: drowsiness or lethargy, drooling; neuromuscular reactions: motor restlessness, dystonic reactions, tardive dyskinesia; mental confusion, headache, dizziness, depression, and anxiety may also be seen). Haldol also lowers the seizure threshold, thus otherwise-controlled seizures may recur. Abrupt withdrawal in a pediatric patient, especially after relatively high doses have been used, may produce a syndrome of involuntary movements reminiscent of tardive dyskinesia in adults (Bassuk & Schoonover, 1977; Konopasek, 2003). These problems are often managed with antihistamines or with cogentin.

REFERENCES

Bassuk, E. L., & Schoonover, S. C. (1977). *The practitioner's guide to psychoactive drugs*. New York, NY: Plenum Press.

Jefferson, J. W., Greist, J. H., & Ackerman, D. L. (1983). *Lithium encyclopedia for clinical practice*. Washington, DC: American Psychiatric Press.

Konopasek, D. (2003). *Medication fact sheets*. Longmont, CO: Sopris.

McEvoy, G. K. (1984). *American hospital formulary service: Drug information 84*. Bethesda, MD: American Society of Hospital Pharmacists.

Physicians Desk Reference. (n.d.). *Haloperidol*. Retrieved from http://www.pdr.net/drugpages/concisemonograph.aspx?concise=992

ROBERT F. SAWICKI
Lake Erie Institute of Rehabilitation

See also **Dopamine**

HALLAHAN, DANIEL P. (1944–   )

Daniel P. Hallahan received his BA in psychology from the University of Michigan in 1967 and his PhD in education and psychology from the University of Michigan in 1971. His major fields of interest include learning disabilities, attention problems, cognitive behavior modification, and applied behavior analysis. His earliest work was in information processing. He suggested that many learning-disabled children exhibit strategy deficits when they attempt academic tasks (Hallahan, 1975). His recent research has focused on an educational intervention that will counteract such strategy deficiencies.

Hallahan is currently the Charles S. Robb Professor Education and the director of doctoral studies at the Curry School of Education at the University of Virginia in Charlottesville. He has directed several leadership training projects sponsored by the U.S. Department of Education's Office of Special Education Programs and currently is the co-principal investigator of the federally funded Center of Minority Research in Special Education. This was designed to enhance the capacity of faculty at minority institutions of higher education to conduct research on minority issues in special education. Hallahan has served in various capacities for the Division for Learning Disabilities of the Council for Exceptional Children and was publications chair from 1994 to 1997. He was the 1998 to 1999 president of the organization.

Hallahan is known for having popularized the notion of noncategorical education for the mildly handicapped and also for his research into the use of self-monitoring for children with attention problems. His research is in the area of cognitive interventions, methods of making learning-disabled students independent learners, and policy and ethical issues in special education (Hallahan & Cohen, 2008).

Currently, Hallahan is concerned that the field of special education has lost its instructional momentum. Hallahan is a strong proponent of intensive instruction for students with learning disabilities. He believes that the differences in students with learning disabilities must be recognized not ignored. An effective way to diminish these differences is through intensive instruction (Hallahan, 2007; Hallahan & Ward, 1998).

Hallahan's principal publications include the *Handbook of Special Education* (Hallahan & Kauffman, 1981), *Introduction to Learning Disabilities* (Hallahan, Kauffman, & Lloyd, 1996), and *Exceptional Learners: Introduction to Special Education* (Hallahan & Kauffman, 1997). He has written other books as well as numerous articles concerning special education. He was awarded the Council for Exceptional Children Research Award in 2000 (Employee directory, 2011).

REFERENCES

Employee directory. (2011). *Daniel P. Hallahan*. Curry School of Education. Retrieved from http://curry.virginia.edu/academics /directory/daniel-p.-hallahan

Hallahan, D. P. (1975). Comparative research studies on the psychological characteristics of learning disabled children. In W. M. Cruickshank & D. P. Hallahan (Eds.), *Perceptual and learning disabilities in children, Vol. 1: Psychoeducational practices* (pp. 29–60). Syracuse, NY: Syracuse University Press.

Hallahan, D. P. (2007). Learning disabilities: Whatever happened to intensive instruction? *LDA Newsbriefs, 42*(1), 1, 3–4, 24.

Hallahan, D. P., & Cohen, S. B. (2008). Many students with learning disabilities are not receiving special education. *Learning Disabilities: A Multidisciplinary Journal, 15*, 3–9.

Hallahan, D. P., & Kauffman, J. M. (Eds.). (1981). *Handbook of special education*. Englewood Cliffs, NJ: Prentice Hall.

Hallahan, D. P., & Kaufmann, J. M. (1997). *Exceptional learners: Introduction to special education* (4th ed.). Englewood Cliffs, NJ: Prentice Hall.

Hallahan, D. P., Kaufmann, J. M., & Lloyd, J. W. (1996). *Introduction to learning disabilities* (3rd ed.). Englewood Cliffs, NJ: Prentice Hall.

Hallahan, D. P., & Ward, V. S. (1998, March). *We need more intensive instruction*. Paper presented at the Virginia Council for Learning Disabilities Conference, Charlottesville, VA.

REBECCA BAILEY
Texas A&M University
First edition

MARIE ALMOND
The University of Texas
of the Permian Basin
Second edition

HALL, FRANK H. (1843–1911)

Frank Haven Hall, inventor of the braille typewriter, was a school superintendent prior to becoming superintendent of the Illinois Institution for the Education of the Blind in 1890. In 1892 Hall introduced the braillewriter, a braille typewriter that quickly replaced the laborious writing device then in use—a slate and hand-held stylus—and greatly speeded up the writing of braille. Hall then adapted his machine to print multiple copies. With its speed and efficiency, Hall's machine revolutionized book-making for the blind and made feasible the mass production of braille materials.

Hall's experience at the Illinois institution convinced him that blind students should have the opportunity of participating fully in the activities of sighted individuals. He persuaded the school authorities of Chicago, who were considering the establishment of a boarding school for blind students, to establish day classes instead. As a result, the first public school day class for blind students was initiated in Chicago in 1900, with one of Hall's teachers as supervisor. The last decade of Hall's life was spent as superintendent of the Farmers' Institute of Illinois, where he effectively promoted the cause of agricultural education (Hendrickson, 1956).

REFERENCE

Hendrickson, W. B. (1956). The three lives of Frank H. Hall. *Journal of the Illinois State Historical Society, 44*, 271–293.

PAUL IRVINE
Katonah, New York

HALL, G. STANLEY (1844–1924)

G. Stanley Hall established one of the first psychology laboratories in the United States, at Johns Hopkins University. Later, as the first president of Clark University, he instituted the first child psychology laboratory in the nation. A former student of Wilhelm Wundt in Leipzig, Hall was influential in introducing European theories and methods of psychology into the United States. He carried out pioneering studies of childhood, adolescence, senescence, human genetics, and the psychology of religion. Among Hall's students were many of the next generation of leaders in psychology and education, including John Dewey, James McKeen Cattell, Henry H. Goddard, and Lewis Terman. Hall published nearly 500 articles and books and founded four psychological journals. He was a leading figure in the formation of the American Psychological Association and was its first president (Hall, 1923; Watson, 1968).

REFERENCES

Hall, G. S. (1923). *Life and confessions of a psychologist.* New York, NY: Appleton.

Watson, R. I. (1968). *The great psychologists.* New York, NY: Lippincott.

PAUL IRVINE
Katonah, New York

HALLERMANN-STREIFF SYNDROME

Hallermann-Streiff syndrome is a rare inherited disorder affecting an equal number of males and females. More than 150 cases have been reported in the medical literature, and no known cause has been found other than most likely a new spontaneous genetic mutation. Hallermann-Streiff syndrome is typically diagnosed shortly after birth and usually by the identification of small eyes. Characteristic facial features, premature development of teeth, or deficiency of hair on the face and on the head may also help to confirm the presence of this disorder. Other features become more apparent as the child begins to age (David, Finlon, Genecov, & Argenta, 1999).

Most typically, infants with this disorder are characterized by distinctive craniofacial abnormalities, including an abnormally small head that is usually wide with a prominent forehead; small, underdeveloped lower jaw; small mouth; and a long, narrow nose. In addition, abnormalities of the eyes, malformations of the teeth, and dwarfism (with arms and legs proportional to the body length) also occur. Abnormal widening and delayed hardening of the fibrous joints of the skull and delayed closure of the soft spot may also be evident in infants.

Craniofacial abnormalities may include underdeveloped cheekbones, small nostrils, and underdeveloped cartilage within the nose. Some cases may also include small mouth, an unusually high palate, and an abnormally large or small tongue. The presence of these abnormalities may result in narrow air passages, making it difficult for the infant to swallow, feed, and even breathe. In addition, infants may also experience recurrent respiratory infections, leading to pneumonia, obstruction of the lungs, snoring, and sleep apnea (David et al., 1999).

Ninety percent of infants born with Hallermann-Streiff syndrome experience cataracts and may experience varying degrees of vision loss and even blindness. Some infants may have small eyes, crossed eyes, rapid involuntary eye movements, and bluish discoloration of the whites of the eyes. Frequently, infants with Hallermann-Streiff syndrome experience skin and hair abnormalities, including atrophy of the skin on the scalp and in the middle of the face. The skin is usually thin and taut and may even have patches that lack any coloring. Shortly after birth, the hair commonly becomes very thin, sparse, and brittle (Cohen, 1991).

In approximately 36% of the cases, infants with Hallermann-Streiff syndrome are born prematurely and have low birth weight. Most of these children will continue to experience a deficiency in growth, resulting in a very short stature with arms and legs proportional to the body trunk. Some less common characteristics include hyperactivity, excessive sleepiness during the day, loss of consciousness associated with muscle contractions (generalized tonic-clonic seizures), and jerky movements combined with slow, writhing movements (Cohen, 1991).

Dental abnormalities that may be present include but are not limited to early development of teeth (sometimes prior to birth or shortly thereafter), severe tooth decay, extra teeth, and an underdeveloped hard outer layer.

Other disorders that are similar to Hallermann-Streiff syndrome and useful for differential diagnosis are Hutchinson-Gilford syndrome, Wiedemann Rautenstrauch syndrome, and Seckel syndrome. All of these disorders share but are not limited to symptoms of stunted growth and small facial features.

Characteristics

1. Small head.
2. Small eyes.
3. Wide forehead in comparison to the small head.
4. Small underdeveloped lower jaw.
5. Malformation of teeth.
6. Beak-like nose.
7. Dwarfism (with arms and legs proportional to the body length).
8. Cataract that may result in vision loss in varying degrees.
9. Skin and hair abnormalities.

Due to the complexity of this disorder, a multidisciplinary team is necessary to treat children with this disorder in a comprehensive manner. Pediatricians, surgeons, ophthalmologists, dental specialists, and mental health professionals are some of the professionals necessary for a comprehensive intervention. Other support services that may be beneficial to affected children may include special education services, physical therapy, and social and vocational specialists. Early intervention is crucial.

REFERENCES

Cohen, M. M. (1991). Hallermann-Streiff syndrome: A review. *Journal of Medical Genetics, 41,* 488–489.

David, L. R., Finlon, M., Genecov, M., & Argenta, L. C. (1999). Hallermann-Streiff syndrome: Experience with 15 patients and review of the literature. *Journal of Craniofacial Surgery, 10*(2), 160–168.

LISA FASNACHT-HILL

Children's Hospital, Los Angeles

HALLERVORDEN-SPATZ DISEASE

Hallervorden-Spatz disease (HSD) is a rare, progressive, neurological movement disorder characterized by extrapyramidal and pyramidal motor symptoms, mental deterioration, and abnormally high deposits of iron in the brain (Sheehy, Longhurst, Pool, & Dandekar, 1999). It is an inherited autosomal recessive disorder and has been reported in both males and females (Saito et al., 2000). Incidence data was not available in the literature.

HSD is classified among the primary neuroaxonal dystrophy (NAD) diseases, including infantile, late infantile and juvenile NAD (Angelini, Nardocci, Zorzi, Strada, & Savolardo, 1992). Three subgroups of HSD have been classified, based on age at onset. The classic or postinfantile type of HSD is characterized by progressive clinical symptoms, which start between 7 and 15 years of age. The late infantile type of the disease affects children under the age of 6. The symptoms are slow but progressive and usually lead to death between the ages of 8 and 13 years. The rarest subgroup is the adult form, which starts between 22 and 64 years of age and has a fatal course within 10 years. Symptoms usually become apparent in late childhood, but HSD is often not diagnosed until postmortem inspection. In vivo brain studies using magnetic resonance imaging (MRI) have found varying features during early onset but eventual evidence of iron deposits and neuroaxonal swelling and gliosis, particularly in the globus pallidus of the basal ganglia (Ostergaard, Christensen, & Hansen, 1995).

Characteristics

1. Difficulty walking, unsteady gait, and frequent falls.
2. Abnormal motor movements, such as slow writhing, distorting muscle contractions of the limbs, face, or trunk, and choreoathetosis (involuntary, purposeless, jerky muscle movements).
3. Confusion and disorientation followed by stupor and dementia as disease process progresses.
4. Seizures.
5. Dysphasia and dysarthria.
6. Visual impairment related to retinal deterioration.
7. Brain abnormalities, including MRI evidence of increasing iron deposits in the globus pallidus and substantia nigra, along with neuroaxonal swelling, neuronal loss, and gliosis on microscopy.

There is no cure for HSD and no standard course of treatment. Treatment is symptomatic and supportive. Options include physical and occupational therapy, exercise physiology, and speech therapy (National Institute of Neurological Disorders and Stroke [NINDS], 2000). Sheehy et al. (1999) reported a child with HSD who presented with self-inflicted ulceration of the lip and tongue initiated during periods of intense oral-facial spasms; this behavior was eliminated by placement of upper and lower soft resin bite guards.

Special education considerations include alertness to early symptoms of HSD and referral for neurological and neuropsychological evaluation. In previously healthy young children, the warning signs of HSD include insidious walking difficulties, progressive oromandibular dystonia, and mental deterioration. In 10 cases reported by Angelini et al. (1992), neuropsychological evaluation conducted within 4 years of symptom onset revealed a general loss of intellectual ability from the early stages of the disease in all cases, with full-scale IQ scores ranging from 50 to 72 after 4 years and below 51 after 7 years. In three of these cases, only a nonverbal IQ could be computed due to severe speech impairment. In the remaining cases, verbal abilities exceeded nonverbal abilities. Although the first symptoms were typically of dystonia, in some individuals behavioral disturbance characterized by impulsivity and aggressiveness preceded motor and cognitive decline (Angelini et al., 1992). Diagnosis of HSD will result in special education classification, possibly as Other Health Impaired, Orthopedically Handicapped, or Speech Handicapped. Assistive technology in conjunction with occupational, physical, and speech therapy will be required, with eventual homebound instruction likely. Family education and counseling, with links to appropriate medical and community support, are indicated.

The prognosis for individuals with HSD is poor because of the progressive nature of the disease. Death typically occurs approximately 10 years after onset. However, there have been some reported cases of individuals with HSD surviving for several decades after onset (NINDS, 2000). Future research is needed to address issues of prevention, differential diagnosis, and effective treatment for this debilitating disorder.

REFERENCES

Angelini, L., Nardocci, N., Zorzi, C., Strada, L., & Savolardo, M. (1992). Hallervorden-Spatz disease: Clinical and MRI study of 11 cases diagnosed in life. *Journal of Neurology, 239,* 417–425.

National Institute of Neurological Disorders and Stroke. (2000). *Hallervorden-Spatz disease.* Retrieved from http://www.ninds.nih.gov/disorders/nbia/nbia.htm

Ostergaard, J. R., Christensen, T., & Hansen, K. N. (1995). In vivo diagnosis of Hallervorden-Spatz disease. *Developmental Medicine and Child Neurology, 37*(9), 827–833.

Saito, Y., Kawai, M., Inoue, K., Sasaki, R., Arai, H., Nanba, E.,...Murayama, S. (2000). Widespread expression of alpha-synuclein and tau immunoreactivity in Hallervorden-Spatz syndrome with protracted clinical course. *Journal of Neurological Science, 177*(1), 48–59.

Sheehy, E. C., Longhurst, P., Pool, D., & Dandekar, M. (1999). Self-inflicted injury in a case of Hallervorden-Spatz disease. *International Journal of Pediatric Dentistry, 9*(4), 299–302.

CYNTHIA A. PLOTTS
Texas State University, San Marcos

HALLUCINATIONS

Hallucinations are sensory events that are without any input from the surrounding environment (Barlow & Durand, 2005). Hallucinatory events may occur in any sensory modality, including visual, auditory, olfactory gustatory, and tactile.

Hallucinations are most often associated with the psychotic mental disorder of schizophrenia, but can occur in extreme cases of depression (Comer, 2004), or medical conditions like dementia, brain tumors, Cushing's syndrome, or Substance-Induced Psychotic Disorder (American Psychiatric Association, 1994). Substance abuse disorders can produce episodes of hallucinations when, for example, too much amphetamines are taken by an individual (Mack, Franklin, & Frances, 2003). Amphetamine use stimulates the nervous system by enhancing activity of norepinephrine and dopamine, making them more available throughout the brain, which can lead to hallucinations and even paranoid delusions.

Concerning schizophrenia, hallucinations are regarded as one of four major characteristic symptoms (i.e., criterion A) associated with the disorder. The other characteristic symptoms are delusions, disorganized speech, grossly disorganized or catatonic behavior, and negative symptoms (i.e., affective flattening, alogia, or avolition). Auditory hallucinations are by far the most common type of hallucination in individuals with schizophrenia (American Psychiatric Association, 1994), and are included as one of the top 10 "first-rank" symptoms of schizophrenia (Andersen & Flaum, 1991; Ho, Black, & Andreasen, 2003). Auditory hallucinations usually involve separate/distinct "voices" in the head that are often pejorative, threatening, or can be multiple voices carrying on "conversations" with each other or providing "commentaries" about the individual's thoughts and behaviors. If these types of auditory hallucinations are present, then criterion A of the diagnosis of schizophrenia is satisfied and does not require any more characteristic symptoms in the criteria A list to be present (criteria B, C, D, E, and F still must be considered before making a full diagnosis). The American Psychiatric Association (1994) does not consider hallucinations that occur while falling asleep (hypnogogic) or while waking up (hypnopompic) as indicators of schizophrenia because they are within the range of normal experience. Humming in the head, or isolated occasions where one hears their name called (especially if it lacks the quality of coming from "outside" the head), are also not considered to be associated with schizophrenia. Interestingly, people tend to experience hallucinations more frequently when they are unoccupied or restricted from sensory input, such as in solitary confinement (Margo, Hemsley, & Slade, 1981).

In addition to being considered one of the major characteristic symptoms, hallucinations are also referred to as one of the "positive symptoms," along with delusions, disorganized speech (i.e., frequent derailment or incoherence), and grossly disorganized or catatonic behavior, because of the observed (or reported) excess or distortion of normal functions (Barlow & Durand, 2005). Negative symptoms are regarded as those in which a diminution or loss of normal functions has occurred, such as is the case with symptoms like flattening of affect or loss of personal volition (American Psychiatric Association, 1994). As mentioned, hallucinations are included in the top 10 first rank symptoms list that psychiatry uses for diagnosing schizophrenia, a diagnostic list that is meant to strike an optimal balance between efficient classification and comprehensive description of the disorder (Andreasen & Flaum, 1991).

There has been an increased interest in using brain-imaging techniques to try and localize activity when hallucinations occur. Specifically, single photon emission computed topography (SPECT) is used to study cerebral blood flow in schizophrenic patients when they are having auditory hallucinations and when they are not (cf. Silbersweig et al., 1995). A study by Hoffman, Rapaport, Mazure, and Quinlan, (1999) found that the active part of the brain during hallucinations was Broca's area, which is usually associated with speech production. Researchers expected that Wernicke's area would be most active because it involves language comprehension or understanding the speech of others. This finding supports a growing theory that people who are hallucinating are not hearing the voices of others, but are in fact listening to their own thoughts, but cannot recognize the difference; this also suggests that deficits in language processing are at work as well.

REFERENCES

American Psychiatric Association. (1994). *Diagnostic and statistical manual of mental disorders* (4th ed.). Washington, DC: Author.

Andreasen, N. C., & Flaum, M. (1991). Schizophrenia: The characteristic symptoms. *Schizophrenia Bulletin, 17,* 27–49.

Barlow, D. H., & Durand, V. M. (2005). *Abnormal psychology: An integrative approach* (4th ed.). Belmont, CA: Wadsworth.

Comer, R. J. (2004). *Abnormal psychology* (5th ed.). New York, NY: Worth.

Ho, B-C., Black, D. W., & Andreasen, N. C. (2003). Schizophrenia and other psychotic disorders. In R. E. Hales & S. C. Yudofsky (Eds.), *Textbook of clinical psychiatry* (4th ed., pp. 379–438). Washington, DC: American Psychiatric Association.

Hoffman, R. E., Rapaport, J., Mazure, C. M., & Quinlan, D. M. (1999). Selective speech perception alterations in schizophrenic patients reporting hallucinated "voices." *American Journal of Psychiatry, 156,* 393–399.

Mack, A. H., Franklin, J. E., & Frances, R. J. (2003). Substance use disorders. In R. E. Hales & S. C. Yudofsky (Eds.), *Textbook of clinical psychiatry* (4th ed., pp. 309–377). Washington, DC: American Psychiatric Press.

Margo, A., Hemsley, D. R., & Slade, P. D. (1981). The effects of varying auditory input on schizophrenic hallucinations. *British Journal of Psychiatry, 139,* 122–127.

Silbersweig, D. A., Stern, E., Frith, C., Cahill, C., Holmes, A., Grootoonk, S.,... Frackowiak, R. S. J. (1995). A functional neuroanatomy of hallucinations in schizophrenia. *Nature, 378,* 176–179.

ROLLEN C. FOWLER
Eugene 4J School District, Eugene, Oregon

See also **Childhood Psychosis; Childhood Schizophrenia; Delusions**

HALLUCINOGEN ABUSE

Hallucinogens, also known as psychedelics, cause the distortion of a person's senses, emotions, perceptions, thinking, and self-awareness. These distortions are known as hallucinations. For example, vision can be perceived as sound, and smell can be perceived as vision. Pseudohallucinations are also possible; in these, the user knows that the perceptions are not reality and are due to the use of the drug. In general, the drugs are not considered life threatening. However, because the hallucinations may be very frightening to the user, the user may attempt to escape the perceptions; this has led to very dangerous behavior in some individuals, such as jumping from windows or running in front of moving vehicles (Hallucinogens: Natural and Synthetic).

Hallucinogens are not approved for any kind of medical use. Some hallucinogens are manufactured, such as lysergic acid diethylamide (LSD) and phencyclidine (PCP). Others are produced from natural substances, such as mescaline (peyote), dimethyltryptamine (DMT), and psilocybin (mushrooms). Substances such as LSD are usually ingested in pill, tablet, or liquid form by mouth. LSD is also sometimes produced on a "blotter" paper, which is ingested orally. It can also be injected through a hypodermic needle. Only PCP was initially used as a medication (an anesthetic) but was later discontinued because of its hallucinogenic properties (Meeks, Heit, & Page, 1996). Mescaline (peyote) can be smoked and was used by Native Americans to induce hallucinations. The high that comes from using hallucinogens can last up to 12 hours, and after prolonged use, the user may later experience flashbacks (Hallucinogens, n.d.).

The highest use of hallucinogens occurred in the 1960s. The use has decreased since that time to an all-time low in the 1990s. Currently, there is a concern because of an increase in use among high school students. One survey indicated that 1.1 million persons aged 12 or older in 2007 reported using hallucinogens for the first time within the past 12 months. Also, 9.1% of persons aged 12 or older reported they had used LSD in their lifetime (National Institute on Drug Abuse, 2009). The use of hallucinogens does not appear to be physically addictive (Addictions and Life Page, n.d.).

Characteristics

1. Dilated pupils.
2. Heart and lung failure are possible.
3. Sleeplessness and tremors.
4. Lack of muscular coordination.
5. Decreased awareness of sensation, which can lead to self-injurious behaviors.

6. Mood and personality changes, including depression, anxiety, confusion, paranoia, or psychotic behaviors resembling schizophrenia.
7. Convulsions.
8. Violent behavior.
9. Flashbacks.

The use of hallucinogens does not in itself render a student eligible for special education services. However, a complete evaluation is warranted when a student is chronically unable to make progress in school or drug use is documented. If the etiology is solely due to a drug abuse problem, it is unlikely that the student will be eligible for special education services. However, should the student also appear to have a disability, services should be provided for the appropriate disability. Some students may be eligible for a Section 504 plan based on a drug abuse problem. In the case of hallucinogens, it is possible (but unlikely) that the student may sustain permanent emotional or psychological problems, which may suggest an emotional or behavioral disability. Treatment involves cessation of drug use. Although there are no withdrawal symptoms, it is possible for chronic users to experience unpredictable flashbacks (Strassman, 1995).

Future endeavors with the use of hallucinogens include research with human subjects in several areas (Strassman, 1995). For example, some research is being conducted with hallucinogens to attempt to identify better treatment for schizophrenia. Another study involves use of hallucinogens in the treatment of posttraumatic stress (Strassman, 1995). The use of hallucinogens in research is very controversial and will require stringent regulation. Because of statistics suggesting a recent increase in the use of hallucinogens among adolescents, preventive educational programs in schools and communities should be developed to discourage the use of these dangerous drugs in youth.

REFERENCES

Addictions and Life Page. (n.d.). Retrieved from http://www.addictions.com/lsd.htm

Hallucinogens. (n.d.). Retrieved from http://www.pinehurst.net/~apd/drug/abouthalucin.html

Meeks, L., Heit, P., & Page, P. (1996). Comprehensive School Health Education, (2nd Edition). Blacklick, Ohio: Meeks Heit.

National Institute on Drug Abuse. (2009, June). Hallucinogens: LSD, Peyote, Psilocybin, & PCP. U.S. Department of Health and Human Services, p. 5.

Strassman, R. J. (1995). Hallucinogenic drugs in psychiatric research and treatment: Perspectives and prospects. *The Journal of Nervous and Mental Disease, 183,* 127–138.

DALENE M. MCCLOSKEY
University of Northern Colorado

HALLUCINOGENS

Blum (1984) describes three classes of hallucinogenic drugs: adrenergic compounds (e.g., mescaline, adrenaline); indole types (e.g., lysergic acid diethylamide [LSD]); and anticholinergic hallucinogens (e.g., scopolamine, atropine). An additional hallucinogen, which has been sold as everything from cocaine to LSD, is phencyclidine (PCP), which was originally marketed as an animal anesthetic. For a complete review of hallucinogenic agents, see Blum (1984).

In reviewing the personality characteristics of the users of hallucinogenic drugs, several trends have been noted. LSD users tend to be more introverted and artistic (McGothlin, Cohen, & McGothlin, 1966). Comparisons of personality test findings suggest that persons using hallucinogens are more socially distant, interpersonally suspicious, dominant, anxious, creative, and accident-prone (Kleckner, 1968). These trends have been replicated in additional studies (Pittel et al., 1970, cited in Leavitt, 1995), suggesting a contributory role for childhood chaos and above average stress in substance abuse.

The following are four examples of characteristic hallucinogenic actions (Blum, 1984).

1. *Adrenergic types.* Examples of this class are peyote, mescaline analogs (e.g., DOM/STP 2,5-dimethoxy-4-methyl-amphetamine), epinephrine, and amphetamines. Characteristically, these drugs increase pulse rate, raise blood pressure, and act as a stimulant. Peyote tends to produce colored visual hallucinations as well as hallucinatory experiences. Sensations of depersonalization, ego distortion, and loss of time perception also have been described. The period of intoxication lasts from 4 to 16 hours, with aftereffects (e.g., delusions) occurring, in some cases for several months after intoxication.

2. *Indole types.* LSD-25 is the major example of drugs of this class; however, mushrooms containing psilocybin and the substance DMT (N-dimethyltryptamine) also are included. The major effects of LSD are related to its action on the central nervous system. Responses may be grouped into autonomic symptoms and perceptual symptoms. Autonomic effects include pupillary dilation, rise in blood pressure, and increase in pulse. Perceptual changes include distortions in which objects appear to lose their boundaries, colors are amplified, and new hues are formed. Sensory experiences also seem to merge (synesthesia: e.g., sounds may be perceived as having associated hues). Emotional responsiveness to such experiences and the range of sensory experience appear to be enhanced. LSD intoxication can become frightening since many of the distortions appear related to intrapersonal issues and situational ambience. The degree of perceptual discontinuity itself can produce panic, which is amplified. The

immediate effects of intoxication may last up to 48 hours, with usual periods being between 6 and 18 hours.

Of particular concern is the fact that an LSD experience may recur spontaneously (flashback) even 2 years after the last ingestion. Competing theories for the cause of such flashbacks include intense psychologic reliving and fatty storage of LSD, which creates a flashback on subsequent release of residual LSD. Attempting to calm and reassure an individual who is LSD intoxicated and experiencing a panic reaction is reported to be the most effective intervention. The focus of the technique is to reassure the individual that what is being experienced is a distortion that will stop and that he or she is not alone.

3. *Anticholinergic types.* Examples include plants from which either atropine, or atropine-type alkaloids, or scopolamine may be derived (e.g., belladonna, henbane, mandrake, and datura species). Of particular concern is that the dosage necessary to produce intoxication with these substances is close to dosage that produces toxicity and sometimes poisoning. Along with expected anticholinergic effects, these drugs also may produce a toxic psychosis, lethargy, loss of attention, memory inefficiency for recent events, and delirium. Occasionally these drugs are added to other hallucinogens to increase their effect.

4. *Phencyclidine (PCP).* This substance has become increasingly available and abused owing to the ease of its creation. Besides PCP itself, there are many variations of the PCP formula that also produce hallucinogenic drugs. Effects generated by PCP appear to be related to dose and the chronicity of use. Initially, small doses produce a state similar to alcohol inebriation; larger doses produce analgesia (pain insensitivity) and disorientation; extremely large doses may produce unconsciousness and convulsions. Chronic usage of PCP has been followed by recurrent psychotic episodes, depression, and confusional syndromes. Chronic users, even during periods when the drug is not ingested, are reported to experience memory inefficiency, visual disturbance, disorientation, and communication difficulties. Of particular concern are outbursts of violence and general belligerent, assaultive, and antisocial behavior demonstrated by some intoxicated users. Unlike the visionary experience produced by other hallucinogenic drugs, PCP users experience body image distortions, frank thought disorganization, interpersonal negativism, and aggressiveness. Treatment during the intoxicated episode is symptomatic with a focus on hyperactivity and safety maintenance. Many abusers do not recall much of the intoxicated period, therefore PCP offers nothing in the way of existential experience. For the most part the cost of the inebriation far outweighs its benefit.

REFERENCES

Blum, K. (1984). *The handbook of abusable drugs*. New York, NY: Gardner.

Kleckner, J. (1968). Personality differences between psychedelic drug users and non-users. *Psychology, 5*, 66–71.

Leavitt, F. (1995). *Drugs and behavior* (3rd ed.). New York, NY: Wiley.

McGothlin, W., Cohen, S., & McGothlin, M. (1966). Personality and attitude changes in volunteer subjects following repeated administration of LSD. *Excerpta Medica International Continuing Reports, 129*, 425–434.

ROBERT F. SAWICKI
Lake Erie Institute of Rehabilitation

See also Drug Abuse; Substance Abuse

HALSTEAD-REITAN NEUROPSYCHOLOGICAL TEST BATTERY

The Halstead-Reitan Neuropsychological Battery (Reitan & Halstead, 1993) was developed as a comprehensive neuropsychological test battery and includes three separate test batteries: the Halstead Neuropsychological Test Battery for Adults (ages 15 and older), the Halstead Neuropsychological Test Battery for Children (ages 9 through 14), and Reitan-Indiana Neuropsychological Test Battery for Children. All three tests use the same approach to assess the brain-behavior relationship. The core part of the adult battery is comprised of:

Category Test (CT): Subject is visually presented with seven sets of slides and must press one of four levers in response to each slide. Subject had previously been informed that there was some single principle that underlies each set of slides. Examinees are to figure out what that principle is. This test is related to abstraction and reasoning abilities, particularly concept formation.

Tactual Performance Test (TPT): The TPT employs a version of the Seguin-Goddard Form Board, a flat wooden puzzle board into which differently-shaped blocks can be placed. Without using vision the subject must place the blocks in the board using the dominant, nondominant, and both hands. This test provides a variety of measures, particularly manual dexterity, spatial memory, tactile discrimination.

Seashore Rhythm Test (RT): Derived from a subtest in the Seashore Measures of Musical Talent, the Rhythm Test requires subjects to discriminate between 30 pairs of rhythmic beats as either different or the same. Classified as a measure of nonverbal auditory discrimination, the RT is particularly sensitive to the subject's ability to attend and concentrate, skills frequently impaired in individuals with brain damage.

Speech-Sounds Perception Test (SSPT): A set of 60 nonsense words based on the vowel sound *ee* are played by a tape recorder. The subject must choose which sound is heard from four printed alternatives. The test is a measure of attention, verbal auditory discrimination, and auditory-visual integration.

Finger Tapping Test (FTT): Also called *Finger Oscillation Test* (FOT): Subjects are given multiple 10-second trials on a manual tapping device using the index finger of the dominant and nondominant hand. The test is a measure of motor speed and manual dexterity.

Other recommended tests for this battery are:

Trail Making (TM): The Trail Making test has two forms, Trails A and Trails B. For Trails-A, subjects must connect 25 numbered circles in numeric order. The circles are distributed in a random fashion across a page. The test measures a variety of functions including motor speed, visual scanning, and visual-motor integration. For Trails-B, subjects must perform a task similar to Trails-A, but the circles contain either numbers or letters. The subjects must connect the circles in alternating order between numbers and letters, that is, 1-A-2-B, and so on. In addition to motor speed, visual scanning, and visual-motor integration, this test requires attention and cognitive flexibility.

Reitan-Indiana Aphasia Screening Test: This is a diverse collection of 32 items that require the examinee to demonstrate abilities such as naming, reading, writing, spelling, arithmetic, identifying body parts, identifying and copying shapes.

Reitan-Klove Sensory Perceptual Examination: Similar to many neurological approaches to sensory-perceptual evaluation, this exam employs both unilateral and bilateral simultaneous stimulation across tactile, visual, and auditory channels; finger localization upon tactile stimulation, finger-tip number writing, and the tactile recognition of shapes.

Strength of Grip Test (SOGT): The SOGT employs a standard hand dynamometer to measure the strength of both dominant and nondominant hands.

Lateral Dominance Examination: Right versus left preferences are measured for tasks involving hands, arms, legs, feet, and eyes.

Many of these tests were simplified to create the Halstead Neuropsychological Test Battery for Children. Even more modifications were made to the adult tests in addition to the development of new tests to create the Reitan-Indiana Neuropsychological Test Battery for Children.

The original norms of the Halstead tests were not representative of the patients who undergo testing (Halstead, 1947). However, new norms have been established that take both gender and education into account and allow for conversion to T-scores (Heaton, Grant, & Matthews, 1991). Lezak (1995, p. 493) argues that this test's administration procedures are particularly discomforting and distressing to individuals with brain injuries or among the elderly. She argues that it should only be given under special circumstances.

All three batteries have been shown to be effective in discriminating between those with brain damage and those without (84% to 98% accuracy). Reitan (1986) claimed that the test scores could be used to determine the nature and size of the lesion, although this idea is not supported by everyone.

This entry has been informed by the sources listed below.

REFERENCES

Halstead, W. C. (1947). *Brain and intelligence*. Chicago, IL: University of Chicago Press.

Heaton, R., Grant, I., & Matthews, C. (1991). *Comprehensive norms for an expanded Halstead-Reitan battery*. Odessa, FL: Psychological Assessment Resources.

Horton, A. (2008). The Halstead-Reitan neuropsychological test battery: Past, present, and future. *The neuropsychology handbook* (3rd ed., pp. 251–278). New York, NY: Springer.

Lezak, M. (1995). *Neuropsychological assessment*. New York, NY: Oxford University Press.

Mitchell, J. V. Jr. (Ed.). (1985). *The ninth mental measurements yearbook*. Lincoln, NE: Buros Institute of Mental Measurements.

Nussbaum, N., & Bunner, M. (2009). Halstead–Reitan neuropsychological test batteries for children. *Handbook of clinical child neuropsychology* (3rd ed., pp. 247–266). New York, NY: Springer.

Reitan, R. M. (1986). Theoretical and methodological bases of the Halstead-Reitan neuropsychological test battery. In I. Grant & K. M. Adams (Eds.), *Neuropsychological assessment of neuropsychiatric disorders*. New York, NY: Oxford University Press.

Reitan, R. M., & Wolfson, D. (1993). *The Halstead-Reitan neuropsychological test battery: Theory and clinical interpretation*. Tucson, AZ: Neuropsychology Press.

Reitan, R. M., & Wolfson, D. (2001). The Halstead-Reitan neuropsychological test battery: Research findings and clinical application. In A. S. Kaufman & N. L. Kaufman, *Specific learning disabilities and difficulties in children and adolescents: Psychological assessment and evaluation* (pp. 309–346). New York, NY: Cambridge University Press.

Reitan, R., & Wolfson, D. (2004). Theoretical, methodological, and validational bases of the Halstead-Reitan neuropsychological test

test battery. *Comprehensive handbook of psychological assessment, Vol. 1: Intellectual and neuropsychological assessment* (pp. 105–131). Hoboken, NJ: Wiley.

Sinco, S., D'Amato, R., & Davis, A. (2008). Understanding and using the Halstead-Reitan neuropsychological test batteries with children and adults. *Essentials of neuropsychological assessment: Treatment planning for rehabilitation* (2nd ed., pp. 105–125). New York, NY: Springer.

Vanderslice-Barr, J., Lynch, J., & McCaffrey, R. (2008). Screening for neuropsychological impairment in children using Reitan and Wolfson's preliminary neuropsychological test battery. *Archives of Clinical Neuropsychology, 23*(3), 243–249.

RON DUMONT
Fairleigh Dickinson University

JOHN O. WILLIS
Rivier College

KATHLEEN VIEZEL
Fairleigh Dickinson Unviersity

JAMIE ZIBULSKY
Fairleigh Dickinson University
Fourth edition

HAMMILL, DONALD (1934–   )

Donald Hammill received his BS degree in speech education in 1956, his MA in secondary education in 1961, and an EdD in psychology/special education in 1963. From 1963 to 1965, he was an assistant research professor of logopedics at Wichita State University. He served as a full professor of special education at Temple University in Philadelphia from 1965 to 1972.

Hammill's interests include language development, learning disabilities, remedial education, and assessment methods (Hammill & Bartel, 1995; Hammill & Larsen, 1974). He has authored numerous tests, including the *Tests of Language Development*, the *Detroit Tests of Learning Aptitude*, the *Test of Written Language*, the *Comprehensive Test of Nonverbal Intelligence*, and the *Hammill Mutability Achievement Test* (PRO-ED, 2011).

In the 1970s Hammill demonstrated that disorder processing or ability models for learning disabilities were of questionable value to educators. This evidence was partly responsible for the 1977 guidelines for the implementation of PL 94-142, which minimized the use of ability tests. In addition, it opened the door for the increased use of behavioral or skill models for evaluation and classification (Hammill, 1990, 1993).

Hammill currently is president of PRO-ED Publishing Company in Austin, Texas.

REFERENCES

Hammill, D. D., & Bartel, N. R. (1995). *Teaching students with learning and behavior problems* (6th ed.). Austin, TX: PRO-ED.

Hammill, D. D., & Larsen, S. C. (1974). The effectiveness of psycholinguistic training. *Exceptional Children, 41*, 5–15.

Hammill, D. D. (1990). On defining learning disabilities. *Journal of Learning Disabilities, 23*, 74–84.

Hammill, D. D. (1993). A brief look at the learning disabilities movement in the United States. *Journal of Learning Disabilities, 26*, 295–310.

RO-ED Inc. official website. (2011). Retrieved from http://www.proedinc.com/customer/default.aspx

STAFF

HANDEDNESS AND EXCEPTIONALITY

Handedness, though seemingly a phenomenon in its own right, is actually one component of a more general pattern of lateralization. Lateralization refers to the fact that most people tend to favor one side of their body over the other. A minority of individuals demonstrate inconsistent or weak lateralization, meaning they have a mixed pattern of hand dominance, foot dominance, eye dominance, or cerebral hemisphere dominance.

Research has documented that the left side of the brain controls the right side of the body, and vice versa, for basic sensory and motor activity, and that the left side of the brain is generally more efficient than the right side at processing language. These data, considered along with estimates that right-handers constitute approximately 90% of all humans, indicate that the most common pattern of lateralization includes both right-handedness and left hemisphere cerebral dominance for language. Left-handers, who are more apt to use both hemispheres of the brain for language than right-handers, might then be thought of as having weak or *deviant* lateralization. It is this deviant lateralization, of which handedness is but one component, rather than handedness per se, that has been linked to exceptionalities throughout the literature.

Deviant or weak lateralization may be inherited (Annett, 1964) or it may be caused by injury to the brain (Corballis & Beale, 1983). Whatever the etiology, deviation from the usual pattern of right-handedness and left hemisphere language representation can be manifested in a number of ways. Weakly lateralized left-handers tend to be overrepresented among highly gifted and creative individuals. Leonardo da Vinci, Harpo Marx, and Charlie Chaplin are examples. On the negative side, left-handers may be particularly susceptible to a myriad of pathological conditions. Throughout the ages, left-handers have been overrepresented among schizophrenics, epileptics, and various types of criminals (Corballis & Beale, 1983).

Investigations have revealed a higher incidence of left-handedness in special education populations. Fein, Waterhouse, Lucci, Snyder, and Humes (1984, February) found 18% of a sample of school-age children with autism spectrum disorders were left-handed. This figure is consistent with previous studies of children with autism spectrum disorders, and is comparable to Satz's (1973) estimate of 83% right-handedness in individuals with intellectual disabilities and epileptic populations. Those findings represent an approximate doubling of the left-handedness consistently found in normal populations. Other studies have found markedly greater frequencies of immune disease, migraine, and learning disabilities among left-handers (Geschwind & Behan, 1982).

Two other pathological conditions that have been linked to the deviant lateralization associated with left-handedness are dyslexia, a form of reading disability, and stuttering. The concept of dyslexia, first formulated about 100 years ago, has been surrounded by a great deal of controversy. Disagreement as to whether the disorder actually exists, its nature, and how it should be diagnosed and treated abound. A distinction can be drawn between developmental dyslexia, which implies a developmental or maturational anomaly, and acquired dyslexia, which implies brain damage.

Orton (1928) proposed a unique theory for developmental dyslexia based on his own clinical experience with children suffering from reading and writing problems. Orton believed that reversals of letters and words occurred because the brains of dyslexic children lack cerebral dominance. He argued that the dominant hemisphere recorded events in the correct orientation (e.g., CAT), while the nondominant hemisphere recorded them in the reverse orientation (e.g., TAC). If a child failed to learn to suppress the activity of the nondominant hemisphere, the reversed word would intrude, creating left-right confusion. While Orton's theory generated much research, it soon became apparent that there was no evidence that mirror images of stimuli are projected to the nondominant hemisphere. As such, Orton's theory gradually lost favor.

Within the past 35 years, much progress has been made in understanding the neuropsychological processes involved in developmental dyslexia. Research has shown that dyslexics as a group are deficient in a wide variety of skills necessary for the development of adequate reading ability. Dyslexic children comprise a heterogeneous population that can be subdivided into groups, each with a distinct neurological deficit or cluster of deficits, which are related to dysfunction of left, right, or both cerebral hemispheres; and they may also be related to handedness. One subgroup of developmental dyslexia involves difficulty in integrating written symbols with their sounds, with resulting disability in developing phonic word analysis or decoding, skills often associated with a disordered

function of the left cerebral hemisphere. Another subgroup manifests weaknesses in visual perception and memory for letters and whole-word configurations, resulting in problems with developing a sight vocabulary. The difficulties of this latter group have been associated with the impaired visuospatial functioning of the right side of the brain. A third subgroup demonstrates the difficulties of both of the other subgroups, suggesting dysfunction in both hemispheres (Hynd & Cohen, 1983).

It was also Orton (1937) who originated the dominance theory of stuttering. Stuttering was thought to be caused by a disruption of fine control of articulation resulting from lack of cerebral dominance. The more skilled and meticulous investigators became, however, the more frequently they failed to discover any neurological differences between stutterers and nonstutterers.

Some investigators, however, suggest a return to the dominance theory, as convincing evidence continues to surface suggesting stutterers often exhibit deviant lateralization association with left-handedness. For example, Jones (1966) reported that four left-handers with a family history of left-handedness and bilateral speech representation experienced cessation of stuttering following surgical ablation of a portion of one hemisphere. Other neurosurgical reports have described epileptic stutterers as regaining fluent speech following surgery to either the right or left hemisphere to relieve epilepsy. Studies of stutterers and nonstutterers on dichotic listening tasks have reported a significantly greater number of stutterers than nonstutterers show a left ear advantage, implying right hemisphere language involvement (Corballis & Beale, 1983).

Despite the fact that it is still widely believed that stuttering is related to left-handedness, and in particular that it is caused by forcing a natural left-hander to write with the right hand, there is no evidence to show that changed handedness has any influence on cerebral representation of speech control. Moreover, it is difficult to separate left- or changed-handedness from the more general condition of weak or deviant lateralization (Dean & Reynolds, 1997).

Both dyslexia and stuttering occur more frequently among males than females. Because both of these conditions have been linked to weak or deviant lateralization, it seems contradictory that evidence suggests that generally females have weaker lateralization than males, both with respect to left hemispheric representation of language and right hemispheric representation of spatial functions (Corballis & Beale, 1983). This contradiction may be attributed to several different factors. First, males tend to be more susceptible to pathological influences at birth resulting in injury-induced deviant lateralization (Annett, 1964). Second, weaker female lateralization is specific to adults, as boys tend to lag behind girls in the development of lateralization (Bakker, Teunissen, & Bosch, 1976). The development of lateralization may be complete earlier in girls than in boys because girls generally reach puberty before boys. Dyslexia and stuttering typically develop well before puberty, when lateralization may be more highly developed in girls than in boys. Third, a factor more closely associated with males than females may actually trigger these two conditions. Geschwind and Behan (1982) believe that the male hormone, testosterone, slows development of the brain's left side, allowing the right hemisphere to assume some typically left-brain functions. The end result can be left-handedness or simply weaker or deviant cerebral lateralization.

Overall, there is convincing evidence that weak or deviant lateralization, of which handedness is one important component, is linked to various exceptionalities. While deviant lateralization should not be taken as a sufficient cause of learning disabilities, dyslexia, stuttering, or any of the other pathological conditions herein mentioned, it cannot be overlooked that those who manifest weak cerebral dominance are more apt to develop one of these afflictions than those who manifest strong lateralization. Deviant lateralization is most likely a comorbid symptom, however, and not the fundamental cause of these problems (Dean & Reynolds, 1997).

Some interesting resources about handedness can be found online at the Handedness Research Institute at http://handedness.org/.

REFERENCES

Annett, M. (1964). A model of the inheritance of handedness and cerebral dominance. *Nature, 204,* 59–60.

Bakker, D. J., Teunissen, J., & Bosch, J. (1976). Development of laterality-reading patterns. In R. M. Knights & D. J. Bakker (Eds.), *The neuropsychology of learning disorders* (pp. 207–220). Baltimore, MD: University Park Press.

Corballis, M. C., & Beale, I. L. (1983). *The ambivalent mind.* Chicago, IL: Nelson-Hall.

Dean, R. S., & Reynolds, C. R. (1997). Cognitive processing and self-report of lateral preference. *Neuropsychology Review, 7,* 127–142.

Fein, D., Waterhouse, D., Lucci, D., Snyder, D., & Humes, M. (1984, February). *Cognitive functions in left- and right-handed autistic children.* Presentation at the annual meeting of the International Neuropsychological Society, Houston, TX.

Geschwind, N., & Behan, P. (1982). Left-handedness: Association with immune disease, migraine, and developmental learning disorder. *Proceedings of the National Academy of Science, USA, 79,* 5097–5100.

Hynd, G. W., & Cohen, M. (1983). *Dyslexia: Neuropsychological theory, research, and clinical differentiation.* New York, NY: Grune & Stratton.

Jones, R. K. (1966). Observations on stammering after localized cerebral injury. *Journal of Neurology, Neurosurgery, & Psychiatry, 29,* 192–195.

Orton, S. T. (1928). Specific reading disability-strephosymbolia. *Journal of the American Medical Association, 90,* 105–109.

Orton, S. T. (1937). *Reading, writing, and speech problems in children.* New York, NY: Norton.

Satz, P. (1973). Left-handedness and early brain insult: An explanation. *Neuropsychologia, 11,* 115–117.

GALE A. HARR
Maple Heights City Schools,
Maple Heights, Ohio

See also Dyslexia; Left Brain/Right Brain; Stuttering

HAND-FOOT-MOUTH DISEASE

Hand-foot-mouth disease is a childhood illness caused by various members of the enterovirus family. The most common cause is Coxsackie A16. Other common causes include other strains of Coxsackie A and enterovirus 71 (Ministry of Health, 2000). The virus is commonly recognized by a blister-like rash that appears most commonly on the hands, feet, and mouth. Sometimes the blisters, or vesicles, also appear on the buttocks. It is also possible to have an infection with the Coxsackie virus that causes the ulcers to form only in the mouth; this is called *herpangina*.

Hand-foot-mouth disease usually occurs in children younger than 6 years of age. Because it is often unreported, the number of people infected each year is unknown. It is most commonly seen in the late summer and early fall (Drkoop.com, 1998). The child is contagious when symptoms first appear, and it remains contagious until the blisters disappear. Transmission occurs directly from person to person or indirectly through contaminated articles such as toys or food utensils. The virus can be shed in the stool for several weeks. Diagnosis is usually given by symptoms; however, specific viral tests for diagnosis are available (New York City Department of Health, 2000).

Characteristics

1. A blister-like rash appears most commonly on the hands, feet, and mouth. Several blisters can be found on the palms, on the soles, and in the webs between fingers and toes.

2. The blisters are surrounded by red halos and filled with a clear fluid containing the virus. The blisters have a white or lighter colored area in the center and are approximately 1/16 to 1/8 inch in diameter. These blisters eventually burst, leaving sores.

3. Other symptoms may include low-grade fever, sore throat, headache, runny nose, and loss of appetite.

4. The incubation period is 3 to 6 days. The rash usually develops 1 to 2 days after initial symptoms.

5. The fever generally lasts 2 to 3 days and the blisters usually resolve in 7 to 10 days.

There is no specific treatment other than symptomatic relief of symptoms (Schmitt, 2000). Acetaminophen may be given to the child to treat the fever. Aspirin should not be given for viral illnesses in children. Because the blisters in the mouth are often painful, saltwater mouth rinses may be soothing to the child, as well as a soft diet. An antacid can also be administered to alleviate mouth pain several times a day. Adequate fluids should be given to prevent dehydration and to lower fever. If child shows signs of tachycardia, severe vomiting, dehydration, stiff neck, or a severe headache, parents should contact a doctor immediately (Ministry of Health, 2000).

Because hand-foot-mouth disease is a mild communicable illness with a quick recovery, children do not usually need special education intervention. The child should stay away from school until he or she is not contagious; a good general guideline is usually 1 week after the rash appears or until the blisters resolve (Ministry of Health, 2000). Articles such as toys and eating utensils should be disinfected. If a child has neurological conditions resulting from complications of the disease, he or she may be eligible for special education services.

Hand-foot-mouth disease is generally a mild illness that resolves in 5 to 10 days. The child can gain immunity from a specific strain but catch the disease again from another strain of enterovirus. Prevention through hygienic practice is stressed. Complications of the disease, although they are rare, can be serious and include neurological conditions such as myocardis, meningitis, encephalitis, and acute flaccid paralysis. Research is currently focusing on more serious strains of hand-foot-mouth disease causing neurological complications, such as the serious outbreaks in Taiwan in 1998 caused by enterovirus 71 (Ching-Chuan, Tseng, Wang, Wang, & Su, 2000; Huang et al., 1999). In the United States, however, such complications are rare.

REFERENCES

Ching-Chuan, L., Tseng, H., Wang, S., Wang, J., & Su, I. (2000). An outbreak of enterovirus 71 infection in Taiwan, 1998: Epidemiologic and clinical manifestations. *Journal of Clinical Virology, 17,* 23–30.

Drkoop.com. (1998). Hand-foot-mouth disease. In *Conditions and concerns: Medical encyclopedia. (1998–2000).* Retrieved from http://www.drkoop.com/conditions/ency/article/000965.html

Huang, C. C., Liu, C. C., Chang, Y. C., Chen, C. Y., Wang, S. T., & Yeh, T. F. (1999). Neurologic complications in children with enterovirus 71 infection. *New England Journal of Medicine, 341,* 936–942.

Ministry of Health (2000, September 13). *Hand-foot-mouth disease.* Retrieved from http://app.sgdi.gov.sg/listing.asp?agency_subtype=dept&agency_id=0000000007

New York City Department of Health (2000, October). *Hand, foot, mouth disease (Coxsackie viral infection).* Retrieved from http://www.nyc.gov/html/doh/html/home/home.shtml

Schmitt, B. D. (2000). *Parent care: Hand-foot-mouth disease.* Retrieved from http://www.lebonheur.org/

Laura A. Guli
University of Texas at Austin

HANDICAPISM

Handicapism is a term created by Biklen and Bogdan (1976) to identify both an evolving social movement and a set of behaviors toward individuals with disabilities. It has been defined by its authors as "a theory and set of practices that promote unequal and unjust treatment of people because of apparent or assumed physical or mental disability" (p. 9). Handicapism is evident in our personal lives, social policy, cultural norms, and institutional practices (Biklen & Bogdan, 1976). Like racism and sexism, handicapism is evident in the language often used to describe disabled individuals. Such language tends to be discriminatory and serves to devalue the capabilities of the person (Heward & Orlansky, 1984; Mullins, 1979).

Common words and phrases that devalue rather than enhance a disabled person's characteristics include, "had a fit," "a basket case," and "ree tard." Handicapist phrases such as "he's a moron," handicapist humor such as "what did the twit say," and handicapist behavior, for instance, avoiding contact with a disabled person, are examples of handicapism in our personal lives. People with physical disabilities are often confronted with inaccessible entrances to buildings, bathrooms that do not accommodate wheelchairs, and public transportation systems that are difficult to use. Handicapism is also evident in the limited employment opportunities that prevail for the disabled, in media reporting that often transforms the severely disabled into objects rather than people, and in the attitudes of helping professions that often overlook the disabled person's need for privacy and human dignity.

Handicapism can be corrected. Major steps in eliminating it are (1) learning to identify and correct handicapist statements (Biklen & Bogdan, 1976); (2) providing persons with disabilities opportunities to participate in activities that make them part of the mainstream of society (Mullins, 1979); (3) demanding equal access to all facilities for all people (Biklen & Bogdan, 1976); and (4) recognizing that persons with disabilities deserve the same rights and services as those who are nondisabled. The term is rapidly becoming archaic and has appeared in texts and journals with decreasing frequency since the mid-1980s.

REFERENCES

Biklen, D., & Bogdan, R. (1976, October). Handicapism in America. *WIN, 9–13.*

Heward, W., & Orlansky, M. D. (1984). *Exceptional children* (2nd ed., p. 7). Columbus, OH: Merrill.

Mullins, J. B. (1979). Making language work to eliminate handicapism. *Education Unlimited*, June 20–24.

MARSHA H. LUPI
Hunter College, City University of New York

See also Civil Rights of Individuals With Disabilities; Individuals With Disabilities Education Improvement Act of 2004 (IDEIA)

HANDICAPPED CHILDREN'S EARLY EDUCATION ASSISTANCE ACT (PUBLIC LAW 90-538)

The Handicapped Children's Early Education Program (HCEEP) began in 1968 with the passage of the Handicapped Children's Early Education Assistance Act (PL 90-538). The major goals of the program were to design experimental approaches to meet the special needs of young children with disabilities; to develop programs to facilitate the intellectual, mental, social, physical, and language development of children; to acquaint the community with the problems and potential of young children with disabilities; to coordinate with the local school system in the community being served; and to encourage parental participation in the development of programs. The program originally was composed of one of its five current components—demonstration projects.

Demonstration Projects

To accomplish HCEEP's goals, the Act authorized grants and contracts to public and private agencies and organizations for the establishment of experimental preschool and early education demonstration projects. The chosen projects showed promise of developing comprehensive and innovative approaches for meeting the special needs of children with disabilities from birth to 8 years of age. These projects were expected to serve as models providing highly visible examples of successful practices, and encouraging others to initiate and/or improve services to young children with disabilities. In this respect, HCEEP was viewed not as a direct service mechanism, but as an indirect mechanism for expanding and improving the quality of services.

Geographical dispersion of demonstration projects was extremely important for a program that relied on increasing services by example. Therefore, major efforts were made to establish demonstration projects in as many states as possible. An evaluation of the demonstrations, conducted when the first cohort had reached its third year

of funding, indicated that the demonstrations were only beginning to pay off. To avoid losing the ground gained, and to assist the demonstrations in communicating the results of their efforts, it was decided to make outreach funds available. An additional component was added to HCEEP—the Outreach Component.

Outreach Projects

The Outreach Component, developed in 1972, had two goals: to stimulate and increase high-quality services to preschool children with disabilities, birth through 8 years, and to stimulate replication of innovative models developed in the demonstration projects. Successful demonstration projects were expected to apply for outreach funds at the end of 3 years. To be even eligible for consideration, a demonstration project had to obtain funds from other sources to continue providing direct services to children and their families. Recently, projects not funded previously as early childhood demonstration projects have been allowed to compete for outreach funds.

State Plan Grants

The third component of HCEEP had its roots prior to 1976. Aware of the need for state planning to consider the needs of young children with disabilities, HCEEP had made technical assistance available to states that desired to improve or expand services to the early childhood age range. The expectation was that federal funds would be available in the immediate future to help implement these states' plans. When such funds did become available in 1976 through the State Implementation Grant (SIG) initiative, states applying were awarded grants on a competitive basis. The goal of SIG was to assist state education agencies in building a capacity to plan for the initiation and expansion of early intervention services. To some degree, this planning process was expected to be enhanced simply by creating financial resources for an early childhood planning position within each state.

Public Law 98-199 carried this initiative further with the creation of the current State Plan Grant Component. The state plan grant is intended to enable each state and territory to plan, develop, or implement a comprehensive service delivery system for special education and related services to children with disabilities from birth to 5 years of age. States may apply for a grant to support planning, to support development, or to support implementation activities depending on their assessment of appropriateness and readiness. At least 30% of the HCEEP appropriation must be used for this component in recognition of the need for state commitments to serving these children.

Research Institutes

In 1977, the fourth component of HCEEP was initiated. In cooperation with the Research Projects Branch of the

Office of Special Education Programs, HCEEP funded four research institutes to carry out longitudinal research. Topics of research included social, emotional, physical, cognitive, and behavioral aspects of the child; theories and methods of intervention; parent-child interaction; and assessment techniques.

The institutes were seen as investments in the future, paying off not only in terms of the immediate research results, but in terms of the training of future special education researchers and service providers. A second generation of institutes was funded in 1982 to investigate problems concerning services for autistic-like children, cost and efficacy data for early childhood interventions, and programming for parental involvement. In addition, another institute was funded in 1985 to focus on evaluating the impact of various methods of early intervention for children with disabilities as a whole and in various subgroups.

Technical Assistance

In 1971, the Technical Assistance Development System (TADS) was funded to assist demonstration projects. From 1977 to 1982, two technical assistance systems, TADS and WESTAR, were operating in order to provide geographical coverage for the large number of demonstration projects and SIGs. When the number of demonstrations decreased in 1982, the need for technical assistance also was reduced and TADS again became the sole designated external provider of technical assistance to demonstration projects. A new technical assistance effort, the State Technical Assistance Resource Team (START), was funded in 1985 to provide assistance to the state plan grant projects.

JAMES BUTTON
United States Department of Education
Second edition

KIMBERLY F. APPLEQUIST
University of Colorado at Colorado Springs
Third edition

HANDICAPPED, DEFINITION OF (See Child With a Disability, Definition of)

HANDICAPPING CONDITIONS, HIGH INCIDENCE (See High-Incidence Disabilities)

HAND TEST

The Hand Test (Wagner, 1983) is a brief, performance-based measure of psychopathology and personality used with children and adults. It is a projective measure that is easy to administer; training in the use of projective measures such as the Hand Test is needed in order to understand and interpret the results obtained. The test consists of nine line drawings of hands in ambiguous positions; the child or adult is asked to tell the examiner what the hand might be doing. There is also a blank card; the same direction is given for the blank card. There are 15 quantitative scores and seven summary scores that are generated from the responses of the child or adult for the 10 cards. Adequate reliability and empirical support have been found for the Interpersonal, Environmental, Maladjustive, Withdrawal, Acting Out Score (AOS), and Pathological summary scores as well as the Aggression variable (e.g., Clemence, Hilsenroth, Sivic, & Rasch, 1999; Smith, Blais, Vangala, & Masek, 2005). Of these, the Pathology, AOS, and Aggression scores have proved most useful in discriminating between clinical and typical groups of children. Additional evidence of psychometric properties of the Hand Test has been summarized (e.g., Carter & Moran, 1991; Clemence, Hilsenroth, Sivic, Rasch, & Waehler, 1998; Clemence et al., 1999).

Smith et al. (2005) examined the usefulness of the Hand Test with children who have medical issues as compared to children with psychiatric disorders. They found that the children with psychiatric problems consistently obtained higher scores on the Aggression, Withdrawal, and Pathological scales than the children with medical problems. This supports the use of these scales in the identification of childhood psychopathology and emotional disturbance. Further, they found that the Hand Test added to what was gained from parent and self-report and facilitated (i.e., added to the incremental validity) differentiation of the two groups.

REFERENCES

Carter, D. E., & Moran, J. J. (1991). Interscorer reliability for the Hand Test administered to children. *Perceptual and Motor Skills, 72,* 759–765.

Clemence, A. J., Hilsenroth, M. J., Sivic, H. J., & Rasch, M. (1999). Hand test AGG and AOS variables: Relation with teacher rating of aggressiveness. *Journal of Personality Assessment, 73,* 334–344.

Clemence, A. J., Hilsenroth, M. J., Sivic, H. J., Rasch, M., & Waehler, C. A. (1998). Use of the hand test in the classification of psychiatric inpatient adolescents. *Journal of Personality Assessment, 71,* 228–241.

Smith, S. R., Blais, M. A., Vangala, M., & Masek, B. J. (2005). Exploring the hand test with medically ill children and adolescents. *Journal of Personality Assessment, 85,* 82–91.

Wagner, E. E. (1983). *The hand test manual* (Rev. ed.). Los Angeles, CA: Western Psychological Services.

CYNTHIA A. RICCIO
Texas A&M University

***See also* Personality Assessments; Thematic Apperception Test**

HANDWRITING (See Dysgraphia)

HAPPY PUPPET SYNDROME (See Angelman Syndrome)

HARD OF HEARING

HARING, NORRIS G. (1923–   )

Norris G. Haring obtained a BA from Kearney State Teachers College (Nebraska) in 1948. He went to the University of Nebraska, receiving an MA in 1950 and an EdD from Syracuse University in 1956. He is presently professor of education (special education) and director of the Washington Research Organization in the College of Education at the University of Washington.

Haring's major field of interest lies in dealing with exceptional children in the classroom environment. Haring's philosophy about exceptional children is that they should have the benefit of experiences with their nonexceptional peers whenever possible because they will eventually be required to achieve a satisfactory adjustment within a predominantly normal society (Haring, Stern, & Cruickshank, 1958).

Haring's major research has dealt with the behavior management of children with learning disabilities and behavioral disorders in the classroom. His textbook on this subject, *Educating Emotionally Disturbed Children* (Haring & Phillips, 1962), is now considered a classic.

Subsequent research concentrated on the development and refinement of the learning environment and the ecology that promotes adaptive social behavior. This research resulted from work with the emotionally disturbed and behaviorally disordered and investigations of classroom performance measurement and data-based decisions in terms of instructional procedures, methodology, and curriculum. The application of behavioral principles in special education guided his research for nearly 10 years. His book *Exceptional Teaching* (White & Haring, 1980) concentrates on the application of precision teaching strategies in regular and self-contained classrooms. Haring is known for the research and development of behaviorally validated stages of learning in a learning hierarchy.

Haring was the director of the Experimental Education Unit at the University of Washington for 12 years. During that period he became interested in the application of modern behavior technology to the education of the severely handicapped. Haring worked with national leaders in the field to develop the Association for Persons with Severe Handicaps (TASH), and served as founding president of that organization. He directed the Washington Research Organization in a series of studies designed to investigate ways to promote generalization with severely disabled students and the application of research information to facilitate their transition to vocational success and adult life. Haring remains professionally active and continues to be associated with the University of Washington. A listing of many of his important works are found in the reference list for this entry.

REFERENCES

Haring, K. A., Lovett, D. L., & Haring, N. G. (1992). *Integrated lifecycle services for persons with disabilities: A theoretical and empirical perspective*. New York, NY: Springer-Verlag.

Haring, N. G. (1987). *Assessing and managing behavior disabilities*. Seattle: University of Washington Press.

Haring, N. G. (1994). *Exceptional children and youth: An introduction to special education*. Paramus, NJ: Prentice Hall.

Haring, N. G., & Liberty, K. A. (1990). Matching strategies with performance in facilitating generalization. *Focus on Exceptional Children, 22*, 1–16.

Haring, N. G., & Phillips, E. L. (1962). *Educating emotionally disturbed children*. New York, NY: McGraw-Hill.

Haring, N. G., & Romer, L. T. (1995). *Welcoming students who are deaf-blind into typical classrooms: Facilitating school participation, learning, and friendships*. Baltimore, MD: Paul H. Brookes.

Haring, N. G., Stern, G., & Cruickshank, W. M. (1958). *Attitudes of educators toward exceptional children*. Syracuse, NY: Syracuse University Press.

Haring, N. G., & Whelan, R. J. (1965). Experimental methods in education and management of emotionally disturbed children. In N. J. Long, W. C. Morse, & R. G. Newman (Eds.), *Conflict in the classroom: The education of emotionally disturbed children*. Belmont, CA: Wadsworth.

Romer, L. T., & Haring, N. G. (1994). The social participation of students with deaf-blindness in educational settings. *Education & Training in Intellectual Developmental Disabilities, 29*, 134–144.

Romer, L. T., White, J., & Haring, N. G. (1996). The effect of peer mediated social competency training on the type and frequency of social contacts with students with deaf-blindness. *Education & Training in Intellectual Developmental Disabilities, 31*, 324–338.

White, O. R., & Haring, N. G. (1980). *Exceptional teaching* (2nd ed.). Columbus, OH: Merrill.

ELIZABETH JONES
Texas A&M University
First edition

MARIE ALMOND
The University of Texas of the Permian Basin
Second edition

HARTNUP DISEASE

Hartnup disease is characterized by diminished absorption of monoamino-monocarboxylic amino acids from the intestine and from blood filtered through the kidney. This condition is presumably caused by a defect in the amino acid transporter gene located on Chromosome 2.

Hartnup disease is rare. Its incidence is 1 in 24,000 births. It is inherited in an autosomal recessive manner.

- Most children with Hartnup disease are asymptomatic. Wide variability in the intestinal absorptive defect causes this phenomenon.
- The major finding in symptomatic patients is a rough, red, occasionally itchy rash limited to sun-exposed areas of the skin. This rash may initially appear during the first few weeks of life.
- Neurological manifestations include episodic ataxia (inability to coordinate voluntary muscle movements), irritability, and emotional lability. These symptoms can occur with or without skin abnormalities.
- Diagnosis of Hartnup disease is made in the laboratory. Analysis of amino acid content of the patient's urine shows elevated levels of neutral amino acids but normal excretion of proline, hydroxyproline, and arginine.

In the rare symptomatic patient, treatment includes daily doses of nicotinic acid or nicotinamide and a high-protein diet. Patients with severe absorptive deficits may experience worsening symptoms of the disorder during diarrheic illness and periods of inadequate protein intake.

There is no research to indicate learning difficulties or the need for modifications in the classroom as a result of this disease.

Hartnup disease is considered a benign malady. Most children with this problem have no symptoms. Those who do have symptoms respond well to dietary modifications and daily doses of nicotinic acid. Therefore, the prognosis is excellent.

This entry has been informed by the source listed below.

REFERENCE

Rezvani, I. (2000). Tryptophan. In R. E. Behrman, R. M. Kleigman, & H. B. Jenson (Eds.), *Nelson's textbook of pediatrics* (16th ed., pp. 353–354). Philadelphia, PA: Saunders.

BARRY H. DAVISON
Ennis, Texas

JOAN W. MAYFIELD
*Baylor Pediatric Specialty Services
Dallas, Texas*

HARVARD EDUCATIONAL REVIEW

The *Harvard Educational Review* (*HER*) was first published in 1931 under the name of *Harvard Teachers Record* by the offices of the Harvard Graduate Schools of Education. The present name was taken in 1937. This journal consists of opinions and research related to the field of education. Articles are read blind, then selected, edited, and published by an editorial board of graduate students from various Harvard schools. The selection process of the editorial board involves the distribution of letters to the faculty requesting nominations from the student body and the posting of information on bulletin boards at Harvard schools asking the students to apply for consideration. Students are then selected according to their ability and by their diversity of interests. The board of 20 students is balanced among men and women and minorities, each of whom receives a small stipend. There is one chairperson who receives a slightly larger stipend. This position changes yearly.

For additional information on *HER* visit http://www.hepg.org/page/her-about

TERESA K. RICE
Texas A&M University

HAÜY, VALENTIN (1745–1822)

Valentin Haüy, a French pioneer in the education of the blind, developed a system of raised letters with which he taught blind students to read and write, providing one of the earliest demonstrations that it is possible for a blind person to be educated. It was one of Haüy's students, Louis Braille, who later developed the system in use today, replacing Haüy's raised letters with a system of dots.

In 1784, with support from a philanthropic society, Haüy established in Paris the first school for the blind that admitted both blind and sighted children and educated them together. The great success of Haüy's school led to the rapid development of similar schools throughout Europe (Ross, 1951).

REFERENCE

Ross, I. (1951). *Journey into light.* New York, NY: Appleton-Century-Crofts.

PAUL IRVINE
Katonah, New York

HAVIGHURST, ROBERT J. (1900–1991)

Robert J. Havighurst was born in De Pere, Wisconsin; graduated from Ohio Wesleyan University; and received his doctorate from Ohio State University in 1924. Although trained as a chemist and physicist, he ultimately became interested in the broader aspects of general education. He was a professor of education and psychology at the University of Chicago for more than 40 years: he retired in 1983 but continued to teach and conduct research until 1990. Before joining the University of Chicago faculty in 1941, he had taught at Miami University, the University of Wisconsin, and Ohio State University. Robert Havighurst died in 1991 at the age of 90.

In 1943, Havighurst introduced his theory of developmental tasks, which he continued to develop throughout his career (Havighurst, 1979). Described as skills, knowledge, functions, or attitudes normally acquired by an individual during a specific period of life, he believed in the existence of "teachable moments," meaning those periods when a person is most able and receptive to learning new skills. According to the theory, if a task is not learned at the appropriate time, it is much more difficult to learn later.

Havighurst found that adolescents prefer the approval of the larger community to that of the peer group (Havighurst, 1970). If the larger society does not reward the adolescent meaningfully, the child will usually fail to become socialized. Havighurst believed that the larger society, especially the school system, must learn to provide important reinforcement to adolescents, especially minority or disadvantaged youths.

Havighurst was an early advocate of integrated public schools, believing they were crucial in creating opportunities for poor children. He proposed that children's performance in school depends not upon the socioeconomic status of the child or the child's family, but rather upon the socioeconomic status and character of the school itself. He also focused on the sociological aspects of old age and retirement, identifying and discussing the need for retirees to develop new roles as they aged and new ways of obtaining satisfaction once those previously achieved through work were no longer available.

Havighurst was a student of social and economic conditions in Germany and was Director of the Rockefeller Foundation's European Rehabilitation Program. In the late 1950s, he was co-director of the Brazilian government's effort to prepare a national system of elementary and secondary schools.

REFERENCES

Havighurst, R. J. (1970). Minority subcultures and the law of effect. *American Psychologist, 25,* 313–322.

Havighurst, R. J. (1979). *Developmental tasks and education* (4th ed.). New York, NY: Longman.

E. VALERIE HEWITT
Texas A&M University
First edition

TAMARA J. MARTIN
The University of Texas of the Permian Basin
Second edition

HAWTHORNE EFFECT

The origins of the Hawthorne Effect can be traced to a collection of studies (Roethlisberger & Dickson, 1939) conducted between 1927 and 1932 at the Hawthorne plant of the Western Electric Company. Researchers designed these studies to determine the factors that may lead to more efficient production in the workplace. Variables such as lighting, social interaction, length of the workday, and break time were systematically manipulated. Regardless of how the working conditions were manipulated, researchers noted that productivity steadily increased, suggesting that the special and personal attention given to the workers accounted for improved productivity (Mahoney & Baker, 2002). This unexpected beneficial result has since been labeled the Hawthorne Effect (Raywid, 1979).

The result of these studies substantially affected research practices. Researchers questioned whether positive changes in behavior during controlled studies were the result of the independent variable or the participants' knowledge that they were in an experiment. This concern is especially salient in laboratory experiments in which participants, in novel and artificial settings, are fully aware of their participation. As a result, the use of naturalistic field research methods increased as an alternative to the laboratory research (Adair, 1984). However, unless the participants and experimental observers are unaware of the experimentation, the Hawthorne Effect also may be noticed in naturalistic settings (Mason & Bramble, 1997).

Several critics have challenged the implications of the Hawthorne studies (Chiesa & Hobbs, 2008). For example, Mason and Bramble (1997) noted that if novel treatments result in beneficial outcomes, one would expect new, innovative interventions in education to show greater effects than has been the case thus far. Further, the results of a meta-analysis of 86 studies in educational research employing controls for the Hawthorne Effect failed to support the existence of an overall Hawthorne Effect (Adair, Sharpe, & Huynh, 1989). Considerable disagreement exists as to the description and definition of the Hawthorne Effect (Adair, 1984).

Despite these concerns and the absence of clear evidence supporting the existence of the Hawthorne Effect, it continues to influence research methodologies. Researchers continue to employ techniques to control for the Hawthorne Effect by having a control group receive the same level of attention in a similar unfamiliar setting, yet without receiving the intervention.

REFERENCES

Adair, J. G. (1984). The Hawthorne effect: A reconsideration of the methodological artifact. *Journal of Applied Psychology, 69*(2), 334–345.

Adair, J. G., Sharpe, D., & Huynh, C.-L. (1989). Hawthorne control procedures in educational experiments: A reconsideration of their use and effectiveness. *Review of Educational Research, 59*(2), 215–228.

Chiesa, M., & Hobbs, S. (2008), Making sense of social research: How useful is the Hawthorne Effect? *European Journal of Social Psychology, 38*, 67–74. doi:10.1002/ejsp.401

Mahoney, K. T., & Baker, D. B. (2002). Elton Mayo and Carl Rogers: A tale of two techniques. *Journal of Vocational Behavior, 60*, 437–450.

Mason, E. J., & Bramble, W. J. (1997). *Research in education and the behavioral sciences: Concepts and methods*. Chicago, IL: Brown & Benchmark.

Raywid, M. A. (1979). In praise of the Hawthorne Effect: Perspectives from the profs. *Journal of Teacher Education, 30*(3), 64.

Roethlisberger, F., & Dickson, W. (1939). *Management and the worker*. Cambridge, MA: Harvard University Press.

ERIC ROSSEN
University of Florida

See also Research in Special Education

HAYDEN, ALICE HAZEL (1909–1994)

Alice Hazel Hayden received her MS degree in chemistry from Oregon State University at the age of 19, and later received her PhD from Purdue University. She began teaching at the University of Washington in 1946, and was eventually awarded Professor Emeritus in education from that institution. She stayed at the University of Washington for 33 years, retiring in 1979. Alice Hayden died in 1994, at the age of 85.

Hayden was well known for her research on intellectual developmental disabilities in children, particularly the education of children with Down syndrome. In contrast to the prevailing views of the day, she emphasized the importance of recognizing the disability as early as possible, and strongly advocated that intervention begin in infancy for those identified with Down syndrome. In 1960, she co-directed the experimental Pilot School for children with disabilities, which was the forerunner to the Experimental Education Unit at the Child Development and Intellectual Developmental Disabilities Center at the University of Washington, where she served as associate director following her retirement.

One of her principal publications was *The Improvement of Instruction*, coedited with Norris G. Haring, a book of readings from a workshop designed to provide the classroom teacher with information about various ways of choosing instructional programs to accomplish teaching objectives and to assist teachers in arranging better classroom conditions to improve instruction (Hayden & Haring, 1972). Her book *Systematic Thinking about Education*, co-edited with Gerald M. Torkelson, discusses the technology of education and technology in teaching (Hayden & Torkelson, 1973). It suggests that teachers and the school as an institution must be responsive to the world community and the advancing instruments and processes that people continue to create for a better life, in order to convey the most current techniques and advancements in education to students.

REFERENCES

Hayden, A. H., & Haring, N. G. (Eds.). (1972). *The improvement of instruction*. Seattle, WA: Special Child.

Hayden, A. H., & Torkelson, G. M. (Eds.). (1973). *Systematic thinking about education*. Bloomington, IN: Phi Delta Kappa Educational Foundation.

REBECCA BAILEY
Texas A&M University
First edition

TAMARA J. MARTIN
The University of Texas of the Permian Basin
Second edition

HAY-WELLS SYNDROME OF ECTODERMAL DYSPLASIA

Hay-Wells syndrome (H-WS) is a disorder of ectodermal dysplasia (malformation of skin, hair, nails, and teeth) in association with cleft lip, cleft palate, or both, and string-like, fibrous band between the upper and lower eyelids (ankyloblepharon) (National Organization for Rare Disorders, 1998). H-WS is a congenital, hereditary condition with the previously listed abnormalities present at birth (Jones, 1997).

The mode of transmission of H-WS is autosomal dominant. There is wide variation in the physical abnormalities of individuals with this syndrome. This disorder is rare. Its actual incidence is unknown.

Characteristics

1. Oval face; broad base of the nose; cleft lip, cleft palate, or both; widely spaced, cone-shaped teeth; malformed or missing teeth; ankyloblepharon.

2. Peeling, very reddened skin in the newborn; hyperpigmentation; anhydrosis (lack of sweat glands).

3. Absent or malformed nails.

4. Sparse, wiry hair or complete absence of hair (alopecia).

5. Occasional findings include deafness, malformation of the ear, underdeveloped genitalia, and congenital heart disease.

Ankyloblepharon requires surgical correction during the first month of life. Cleft lip and cleft palate repair is usually done in the first year but may require additional operations as the child ages. Scalp infections are common, and scarring from them may necessitate skin grafting. Ear infections are frequent—probably secondary to palate anomalies—and need appropriate antibiotic treatment. Tympanostomy tube placement is indicated for recurrent middle-ear disease.

There is no research to indicate the need for special education services because the children are of normal intelligence. Because of the cleft lip and palate, the child may require early intervention from a speech pathologist to help with language development.

The prognosis for H-WS patients appears favorable after they are discharged from the surgeons' care. Intelligence is invariably normal. Heat intolerance is common secondary to a sweat gland deficiency, but hyperthermia is rarely seen. These children's eyes are also rather sensitive to bright light. However, there are no other eye anomalies associated with the rather unique and bizarre finding of ankyloblepharon.

For more information and support, contact National Foundation for Ectodermal Dysplasias, 410 East Main Street, P.O. Box 114, Mascoutah, IL 62258–0114. Tel.: (618) 566–2020; home page http://www.nfed.org

REFERENCES

Jones, K. (1997). *Smith's recognizable patterns of human malformations* (5th ed). Philadelphia, PA: Saunders.

National Organization for Rare Disorders. (1998). *Hay Wells syndrome*. Retrieved from http://www.rarediseases.org/rare-disease-information/rare-diseases/byID/880/viewAbstract

BARRY H. DAVISON
Ennis, Texas

JOAN W. MAYFIELD
Baylor Pediatric Specialty Services
Dallas, Texas

HAYWOOD, H. CARL (1931–   )

Carl Haywood holds AB (1956) and MA (1957) degrees from San Diego State College (now San Diego State University) and a PhD from the University of Illinois (1961) in clinical psychology, with minors in experimental psychology and education. He has served on the psychology faculty of Peabody College of Vanderbilt University since 1962 (professor emeritus, 1994). At Peabody he was, successively, director of the Intellectual Developmental Disabilities research training program, director of the Institute on Intellectual Developmental Disabilities and Intellectual Development, director of the John F. Kennedy Center for Research on Education and Human Development, director of the Office of Research Administration, professor of special education, and director of the Cognitive Education Research Group. He served also as professor of neurology in Vanderbilt's School of Medicine until his retirement from Vanderbilt in 1994. In 1993 he established the Graduate School of Education and Psychology at Touro College in New York City, and served as its first dean. This graduate school was the first to be organized entirely around cognitive development and cognitive education principles offering master's degrees in education, special education, school psychology, and school administration/supervision. Haywood retired from Touro College in 2000.

Haywood's program of scholarship and research has centered on intellectual and cognitive development, intellectual developmental disabilities, individual differences in intrinsic motivation, cognitive education, learning efficiency, psychopathology, and public policy relating to the welfare of children. As an advisor to state and federal governments, he served on the National Advisory Child Health and Human Development Council (NIH), the Governor's (Tennessee) special task forces on healthy children and on intellectual developmental disabilities, and as a frequent reviewer of grant applications for the National Institutes of Health and the U.S. Department of Education.

Haywood is principal author (with P. H. Brooks and M. S. Burns) of *Bright Start: Cognitive Curriculum for Young Children*, a cognitive education program that is now used widely in the preschool education of children with special needs. He has published more than 225 research reports, books, chapters, and reviews on intellectual developmental disabilities and cognitive development. He served as president of the American Association on Mental Deficiency (1980–1981; now AAIDD), as editor of the *American Journal of Mental Deficiency* (1969–1979; founder and president, 1988–1992) of the International Association for Cognitive Education and Psychologist, and president (1979–1980) of the American Psychological Association's division on Intellectual Developmental Disabilities. Honors include the leadership and research awards of AAMD/AAMR; the distinguished service award of the International Association for Cognitive Education; the Alexander Heard Distinguished Service Professorship of Vanderbilt University; the Distinguished Alumnus Award of the College of Science, San Diego State University; and the Edgar Doll Award (for research in the field of Intellectual Developmental Disabilities) of Division 33, American Psychological Association. His major works include *Brain Damage in School Age Children* (Haywood, 1968); *Social-Cultural Aspects of Intellectual Developmental Disabilities* (Haywood, 1970); *Bright Start: Cognitive Curriculum for Young Children* (Haywood, Brooks, & Burns, 1992); *Living Environments for Developmentally Retarded Persons* (Haywood & Newbrough, 1981); *Interactive Assessment* (Haywood & Tzuriel, 1992); *Developmental Follow-Up* (Friedman & Haywood, 1994); and *Dynamic Assessment: Clinical and Educational Applications* (Haywood & Lidz, 2007), as well as numerous research and integrative works on task-intrinsic motivation and its relation to learning effectiveness (see, e.g., Haywood, 1997; Haywood & Switzky, 1992).

REFERENCES

Friedman, S., & Haywood, H. C. (Eds.). (1994). *Developmental follow-up: Concepts, domains, and methods.* San Diego, CA: Academic Press.

Haywood, H. C. (Ed.). (1968). *Brain damage in school age children.* Washington, DC: Council for Exceptional Children.

Haywood, H. C. (Ed.). (1970). *Social-cultural aspects of Intellectual Developmental Disabilities.* New York, NY: Appleton-Century-Crofts.

Haywood, H. C. (1997). Interactive assessment. In R. Taylor (Ed.), *Assessment of persons with Intellectual Developmental Disabilities* (pp. 103–129). San Diego, CA: Singular.

Haywood, H. C., Brooks, P. H., & Burns, M. S. (1992). *Bright start: Cognitive curriculum for young children.* Watertown, MA: Charlesbridge.

Haywood, H. C., & Lidz, C. S. (2007). *Dynamic assessment: Clinical and educational applications.* New York, NY: Cambridge University Press.

Haywood, H. C., & Newbrough, J. R. (Eds.). (1981). *Living environments for developmentally retarded persons.* Baltimore, MD: University Park Press.

Haywood, H. C., & Switzky, H. N. (1992). Ability and modifiability: What, how, and how much? In J. S. Carlson (Ed.), *Cognition and educational practice* (Vol. 1, pp. 25–85). Greenwich, CT: JAI Press.

Haywood, H. C., & Tzuriel, D. (Eds.). (1992). *Interactive assessment.* New York, NY: Springer-Verlag.

STAFF

HEAD INJURY (*See Traumatic Brain Injury*)

HEAD START

Head Start began in 1965 as a federally funded 8-week summer program for more than 550,000 children from low-income families. Its initiation reflected the era's optimism for the role of preschool education in fighting the effects of poverty. The program's development also reflected the environmentalist view of intellectual development and a belief in a critical period for human learning. Recommendations put forth in the 1962 report of the President's Panel on Intellectual Developmental Disabilities and the need for a highly visible symbol of President Lyndon Jonson's war on poverty also contributed to the program's development.

The creation of Head Start was fueled by efforts to counteract negative environmental effects heavily influenced by the relationships between low school achievement and factors such as poverty, racial/ethnic membership, and socioeconomic status. Early intervention was envisioned to eliminate the progressive decline in intellectual functioning and academic achievement of many children from disadvantaged communities.

Initial enrollment in Head Start programs delivered services to 561,000 children; as of 2009, the number of children receiving services in Head Start programs included 904,153 children. Since its beginnings, the Head Start program has enrolled more than 27 million children.

During the year of 2008 to 2009, the Head Start program reported:

- 11.5% of the Head Start enrollment consisted of children with disabilities (intellectual developmental disabilities, health impairments, visual handicaps, hearing impairments, emotional disturbance, speech and language impairments, orthopedic handicaps, and learning disabilities).

- 44,109 children participated in home-based Head Start program services.

- 77% of Head Start teachers have at least an AA degree in early childhood education.

- 26% of Head Start program staff members were parents of current or former Head Start children. More than 850,000 parents volunteered in their local Head Start program.

- 94% of Head Start children had health insurance; 82% of those with health insurance were enrolled in the Medicaid/Early and Periodic Screening, Diagnosis and Treatment (EPSDT) program or a state-sponsored child health insurance program.

- The 1994 reauthorization of the Head Start Act established the Early Head Start program for low-income families with infants and toddlers. In the 2009 fiscal year, $709 million was used to support more than 650 programs that provided Early Head Start child development and family support services in all 50 states and in the District of Columbia and Puerto Rico. These programs served more than 66,000 children under the age of 3.

- More than 228,000 Head Start fathers participated in organized regularly scheduled activities designed to involve them in Head Start and Early Head Start programs (U.S. Department of Health and Human Services, 2010).

Mission, Program, and Services

The mission put forth by the Office of Head Start, an advisory to the Assistant Secretary for Children and Families under the United States Department of Health and Human Services. The mission is as follows: "Head Start is a national program that promotes school readiness by enhancing the social and cognitive development of children through the provision of educational, health, nutritional, social, and other services to enrolled children and families" (U.S. Department of Health and Human Services, 2010).

The Head Start program provides public and private non-profit as well as for-profit agencies with grants to facilitate local child development centers. These centers offer services to the economically disadvantaged children and families within the community they operate. Early and heavily documented efforts of Head Start placed strong emphasis on medical, dental, and social services. Millions of children were vaccinated, had vision and hearing tests, and received medical and dental examinations. In order to fulfill the program's mission further, Head Start programs provide early reading and math skills to preschool children. By placing a heavy emphasis on parental engagement in the learning process, the program stimulates social, emotional, and cognitive development of the participants as well as the communities. School readiness services, including those stemming from an educational, nutritional, and social focus promote an increased rate of early scholastic success.

As of 1995, children from birth to 3 years of age became eligible to receive services from Early Head Start programs. Services available for infants and toddlers under these programs include prenatal care, early educational, social, and other services (U.S. Department of Health and Human Services, 2010).

In line with the mission of Head Start, local community involvement has transformed how the delivery of services is presented across the nation; evidenced by the services provided, the central tenants of the mission remain intact.

Research

Early research support for the expectation that preschool education would counteract effects of environmental disadvantages came from early reports of experimental preschool programs for poor, Black children begun in 1958 by Susan Gray in Tennessee, Martin Deutsch in New York City, and David Weikart in Michigan (Lazar & Darlington, 1982). Their experimental work was theoretically anchored, carefully monitored, designed, and implemented by skilled professional educators and psychologists (Cicirelli, 1969).

Since that time, data from dozens of Head Start studies comparing group averages of Head Start program graduates with averages of children without preschool programs reported the following conclusions: Head Start has positive effects on intellectual development (although in most studies average test scores are somewhat below the national average); Head Start children have fewer retentions in grade and fewer special education placements (although they still contribute disproportionally to special education and retention); some Head Start programs produce advantages in reading or arithmetic as measured by standardized tests; different curricula do not appear to produce differential effects (although such differences are found in experimental preschool programs for high-risk children); most parents of Head Start children are highly supportive; and full-year Head Start programs are superior to short summer programs. Other studies report positive effects in the areas of improvement in social behavior, parent-child interactions, skill of parents, and nutrition (Haywood, 1982; Hubbell, 1983).

Edward Zigler, Head Start's first federal administrator, viewed Head Start's goal as the development of social competence. He commented that people should examine the program's true effectiveness. The program cannot be dismissed as a failure but neither should so fragile an effort over 1 year of a child's life be viewed as the ultimate solution to poverty, illiteracy, and failures in life (Zigler, 1979).

Dozens of additional studies have shown that Head Start programs have had a myriad of positive effects on the lives of the children and communities served (Cartwright, Cartwright, & Ward, 1995). More recently, the National Head Start Association, an organization driven by strengthening the quality of Head Start service delivery, reported that long-term studies of the Head Start program continue to reach the following conclusions:

> Head Start results in significant improvements in a wide variety of educational outcomes and life outcomes, such as increased high school graduation rates; fewer grade repetitions; fewer kids going into special education classes; higher vocabulary levels; better emotional development; reduced mortality rates of young kids; families moving out of poverty, and a significant impact on long-term outcomes of adults 19 years or older who attended Head Start. (National Head Start Association, 2011)

Additional Resources

Research. Citations of research studies broken down into the following categories, provided by the National Head Start Association can be found on their website: Cognitive Benefits, Comparison of Head Start to State-Funded Preschool Programs, Economic Benefits, Health Benefits, Social Benefits, Socio-emotional Benefits, Taxpayer, and Early Head Start Research Citations.

- http://www.nhsa.org/research/research_bites.

Legislation. Fact sheets full versions of the most current legislation regarding Head Start programs are provided on the Administration for Children and Families section of the United States Department of Health and Human Services webpage.

- http://www.acf.hhs.gov/programs/ecd/legislation-policies-regulations.

REFERENCES

Cartwright, P., Cartwright, C., & Ward, M. (1995). *Educating special learners.* New York, NY: Wadsworth.

Cicirelli, V. G. (1969). Project Head Start, a national evaluation: Summary of the study. In D. G. Hayes (Ed.), *Britannica review of American education* (Vol. 1). Chicago, IL: Encyclopedia Britannica.

Haywood, H. C. (1982). Compensatory education. *Peabody Journal of Education, 59,* 272–300.

Hubbell, R. (1983). *A review of Head Start research since 1970.* Washington, DC: Administration for Children, Youth, and Families (Superintendent of Documents, U.S. Government Printing Office).

Lazar, I., & Darlington, R. (1982). Lasting effects of early education: A report from the consortium for longitudinal studies. *Monographs of the Society for Research in Child Development, 47* (serial nos. 2–3).

National Head Start Association. (2011). National Head Start association home. Retrieved from http://www.nhsa.org/

U.S. Department of Health and Human Services. (September, 2010). *Administration for Children & Families: Office of Head Start home page.* Retrieved from http://www.acf.hhs.gov/programs/ohs/index.html

Zigler, E. (1979). Project Head Start: Success or failure? In E. Zigler & J. Valentine (Eds.), *Project Head Start: A legacy of the war on poverty.* New York, NY: Free Press.

SUE ALLEN WARREN
JACQUELINE E. DAVIS
Boston University
Third edition

BRITTANY LITTLE
Chicago School of Professional Psychology
Fourth edition

HEALTH IMPAIRMENTS

Public Law 94-142, IDEA, and its reauthorizations divide the classification of physical handicaps into two categories for purposes of special education: orthopedic impairments and health impairments (Bigge & Sirvis, 1986). Health impairments consists of physical conditions that affect a child or youth's educational performance such as "limited strength, vitality or alertness due to chronic or acute health problems such as a heart condition, tuberculosis, rheumatic fever, nephritis, asthma, sickle cell anemia, hemophilia, epilepsy, lead poisoning, leukemia, or diabetes" (U.S. Office of Federal Register, 1977, p. 42478). Children diagnosed with other health impairments require information from a doctor releasing them from school activity as well as medically and socially as chronically ill children. In schools today, the diagnoses of Other Health Impairments (OHI) is given for attention-deficit/hyperactive disorder for children to receive behavioral and academic accommodations. Phelps (1998) provides a review of the educational consequences of more than 95 health impairments of children, and Clay (2004) is an excellent and practical resource for special education personnel. Other health impairments make up 1.3% of the special education population served in United States Schools (National Center for Education Statistics, 2011).

REFERENCES

Bigge, J., & Sirvis, B. (1986). Physical and health impairments. In N. G. Haring & L. McCormick (Eds.), *Exceptional children and youth* (4th ed., pp. 313–354). Columbus, OH: Merrill.

Clay, D. L. (2004). *Helping school children with chronic health conditions.* New York, NY: Guilford Press.

National Center for Education Statistics. (2011). *Digest of Education Statistics, 2010* (NCES 2011–015), Table 45. Washington, DC: U.S. Department of Education.

Phelps, L. (1998). *Health-related disorders in children and adolescents: A guidebook for understanding and educating.* Washington, DC: American Psychological Association.

U.S. Office of Education. (1985). *Seventh annual report to Congress on the implementation of Public Law 94-142: The Education of All Handicapped Children Act.* Washington, DC: U.S. Government Printing Office.

U.S. Office of Federal Register. (1977). National Archives. Washington, DC.

LESTER MANN
Hunter College, City University of New York

See also Chronic Illness in Children; Orthopedic Impairments; Family Educational Rights and Privacy Act (FERPA); Health Maintenance Procedures

HEARING DOGS

Hearing dogs work for the deaf and hard-of-hearing population to notify their owners that a sound needs to be investigated. Commonly, these dogs are taught to recognize phone calls, doorbells, fire alarms, alarm clocks, or a baby's cry—though each individual may teach the dog to respond to the sounds most beneficial to them. Hearing dogs fall under a broader umbrella of "service dogs," which includes seeing-eye dogs, mobility-assistance dogs, wheelchair-assistance dogs, autism-service dogs, diabetic-alert dogs, and seizure-alert dogs.

Service dogs are not "pets" and must serve a physical function for their owners. That is, service animals need to "do" something to provide assistance to their owner, in order to meet the minimum requirements. A hearing dog must be able to recognize a noise, alert its owner and then lead the owner to the sound. In addition, the dog must be housebroken and nonaggressive.

Training, Certification, and Cost

Because there are no current laws dictating the training for service animals, there is still the option of the owner selecting and training a dog, so long as it meets the minimum requirements set by the ADA. While in training the dog may have full access, as a "Service Dog in Training," as the animal will need to sequence his behavior on real world events. Once the owner has deemed the dog trained, their access continues, but now as a fully trained animal. For the person thinking about training their own dog, it is important to investigate legitimate establishments set up to help individuals buy or train a dog that is serviceable in public.

Hearing dogs may be obtained from a center that specializes in the training of service animals. These centers are often comprised of private individuals who train a small number of dogs for service. The dog may also be trained (with or without assistance) by the owner.

Just as the trainer can vary, so can the dog—while most hearing dogs are small to medium-size, there is not a specified size, sex, or breed. All dogs are welcome to be hearing dogs, provided they meet the requirements of the state and the ADA.

There are organizations and individuals that select, raise, and train dogs to be hearing assistance animals. Many dogs are tested and pulled out of shelters, though others select dogs are from breeders who have qualities in their line that are beneficial to the training of the dog. Many assistance dogs require years of training to become safe leaders (seeing eye dogs); others need to pick up on an innate sense (changes in blood sugar levels or oncoming seizures) and their price is reflective of the highly developed specialties. The *New York Times* recently found that "assistance dogs" will cost the owner part or all the cost of raising and training the dog—which can range from $15,000 to $50,000. Hearing assistance dogs, however, can be trained much more easily—many in 6 weeks to 6 months and for a reduced cost of $2,000 to $5,000 per animal. Some states, but not all, require that service dogs pass a certification and carry identification and/or a special harness or leash.

Accessibility

Accessibility is a difficult issue for those with service animals, as the law varies depending on the state. The ADA offers a broad statement of coverage for all service animals, which does not require them to carry any identifiers (ID, harness, cape, or colored leash). The ADA continues to state that assistance dogs must be housebroken and nonaggressive. They otherwise must be given full access to public areas and privately owned areas that serve the public (restaurants, hotels, etc). Additionally, there are national laws that protect the rights of those with hearing dogs: including the "white cane" and "guide dog access" laws, each of which are misdemeanors carrying potential financial penalties and jail time (Konrad, 2009).

In fact, the only two questions that may legally be asked of an individual with a service dog, when it is not obvious, are: Is the dog a service animal required because of a disability? and What work or task has the dog been trained to perform? However, each state may have specific stipulations regarding the access of a hearing dog. Some require that the dog carry an identification card in a backpack or cape, others require the dog to wear an orange harness and leash. To be certain that a hearing dog and owner is in full compliance with the law, it is best to investigate the home state and any states that the owner may be traveling through.

REFERENCE

Konrad, W. (2009, August 8). An aide for the disabled, a companion, and nice and furry. *New York Times*, B5. Retrieved from http://www.nytimes.com/2009/08/22/health/22patient.html

KIRSTEN ARNESEN
*International Center on Deafness and the
Arts through Education
Fourth edition*

HEARING IMPAIRED

HEARING IMPAIRMENT

Hearing impaired is a term used to describe individuals who have a significant hearing loss. Hearing loss can be classified into four types: conductive, sensorineural, mixed, or central. Sensorineural loss, or nerve deafness, is the most common hearing impairment (Better Hearing Institute, 1999). Hearing impairment can also be defined by severity of loss. A decibel (dB) is the unit used to measure the loudness of sound. The higher the dB, the louder the sound. Mild loss refers to sounds less than 40 dB; these individuals are often referred to as hard of hearing and have difficulty with quiet or distant speech. Moderate loss involves sounds between 41 and 70 dB; individuals with this degree of loss typically require a hearing aid but can hear when facing the speaker within 3 to 5 feet. Severe loss includes sounds between 71 and 90 dB; persons suffering this degree of loss require a hearing aid but may hear loud noises one foot from their ear. Profound loss refers to sounds over 90 dB; a hearing aid and specialized training are necessary for individuals with this degree of loss. The term deaf refers to individuals with a loss above 70 dB.

The etiology of hearing impairments is multifaceted, and may include (a) congenital or hereditary factors; (b) obstruction or blockage of the sound pathways; (c) accidental damage to a part of the hearing mechanism; (d) otosclerosis, a spongy bony growth that immobilizes or causes malfunction of the middle-ear bones or cochlea; (e) presbycusis, or age-related hearing impairment; (f) Meniere's disease, which involves the symptoms of vertigo, tinnitus, and hearing loss; and (g) ototoxic drugs or allergies (The Better Hearing Institute, 1999). Exposure to loud noise for extended periods is also a cause of hearing impairment. The U.S. Department of Education (2011) reports that during the 2009 to 2010 school year, 1% of all students with disabilities received special education services under the category of Hearing Impairment. However, the number of children with hearing loss is higher because many of these students may be served under other categories. The Better Hearing Institute (1999) reports that more than 10% of the population have some degree of hearing impairment. Hearing loss is more common with increasing age. Whereas 30% of people over 65 have a hearing loss, only 14% of those 45 to 65 have a loss.

Characteristics

1. Strains or fails to watch speaker.
2. Provides wrong answers to simple questions.
3. Frequently asks for repetition of words or sentences.
4. Often confuses or mispronounces speech sounds.
5. Frequent earaches, colds, respiratory infections, or allergies.
6. Functions below potential in school.
7. Behavioral problems at home or in school.
8. Withdrawn and moody behavior.

Just as the etiology of hearing impairments are varied, multiple forms of treatments are also available. The preferred mode of treatment depends upon several factors, including the degree of impairment, the etiology of the impairment, and the time of onset of hearing loss. Sensorineural, mixed, and central hearing impairments are not as easily aided by amplification devices due to the extent of damage. To gain the most benefit from a hearing aid, the user needs instruction in visual communication, speech reading, and listening skills. The Better Hearing Institute (1999) reports that hearing aids can improve hearing for 95% of those with hearing impairment. Not all individuals who may benefit from a hearing aid actually utilize such a device. Treatment may also involve medical or surgical procedures.

Aural rehabilitation refers to specialized interventions aimed at reducing the degree of hearing impairments, compensating for the loss, and improving expressive and receptive communication skills. Sound and voice awareness training may be implemented to aid in the use of remaining auditory capacity. Early intervention is important to improve the outcome for young children with hearing impairments. Training designed to facilitate parental skills and improve parent-child communications is strongly encouraged (Kranz, 1985). Additionally, multiple types of assistive devices are also available. Modifications of the environment may also be beneficial (Disability Information and Resource Centre, 1999).

As the type and amount of hearing loss vary, so must the degree of educational interventions. The main goal of intervention is to teach the child to communicate. Children with hearing impairment may be eligible for special education services under the category of Hearing Impaired. The extent of special education services will vary greatly depending upon the degree of impairment and the utilization and impact of assistive devices. Training in speech and language is typically a critical component of school-based interventions. There can be profound emotional and social ramifications of hearing impairments that are left untreated.

Although some evidence suggests that hearing loss may be accompanied by additional learning deficits, hearing loss has not been identified as the primary etiology of additional learning problems. Early identification and intervention are important in the determination of prognosis. Outcome is good because multiple interventions are available. Researchers are currently investigating the impact of hearing loss on learning, behavior, and communication.

REFERENCES

Better Hearing Institute. (1999, January 3). *Facts about hearing disorders*. Retrieved from http://www.betterhearing.org/demograp.htm

Disability Information and Resource Centre, Inc. (1999, May 6). *Hearing and hearing loss*. Retrieved from http://www.dircsa.org.au/

Kranz, M. (1985). Parent-infant programs for the hearing impaired. In J. Katz (Ed.), *Handbook of clinical audiology* (3rd ed.), 989–1003. Baltimore, MD: Williams & Wilkins.

U.S. Department of Education. (2011). Office of Special Education Programs, Individuals with Disabilities Education Act (IDEA) database. Retrieved from https://www.ideadata.org/DACAnalyticTool/Intro_2.asp

SHELLEY PELLETIER
JENNIFER NICHOLS
Dysart Unified School District El Mirage, Arizona

HEART BLOCK, CONGENITAL

Congenital heart block occurs when there is an interference with the normal conduction of electrical impulses that control the heart muscle, particularly between the upper and lower heart chambers. Varying degrees of this condition exist: In first-degree heart block, the contractions of the lower chambers (ventricles) lag slightly behind the two upper chambers of the heart (atria). In second-degree heart block, one half of the atrial beats are conducted to the ventricles. In complete heart block (third degree), the ventricles and the atria beat independently.

First-degree heart block occurs primary in young adulthood with an increased prevalence in trained athletes; overall incidence is 1.3 per 1,000. Predominantly asymptomatic, first-degree heart block is generally detected by electrocardiogram (ECG) and monitored on an outpatient basis.

Mobitz I and II heart block are subgroups of second-degree heart block. Sudden occasional blocks or absences of contractions characterize Mobitz II. Mobitz II is likely to progress into complete heart block. Mobitz I type, a progressive prolongation of time between atrial and ventricle beats until one complete beat is skipped, is fairly mild with few to no symptoms. Second-degree heart block occurs in .003% of the population and requires cardiac monitoring, but again on an outpatient basis.

Characteristics

1. In first-degree heart block, the atria beat normally and the ventricles lag slightly behind. Patients may fatigue quickly and have difficulty breathing (dyspnea); however, in most cases the child will be asymptomatic.

2. In second-degree heart block, the child may experience dyspnea, fatigue, bouts of unconsciousness (syncope), or any combination of these.

3. Children presenting with complete heart block may experience lethargy, hypotension, breathlessness, and syncope.

4. Congestive heart failure, chest pains, dizziness, cessation of the heart, and cardiomegaly are commonly seen in individuals with third-degree heart block.

5. In rare cases of complete heart block, an accumulation of fluid in body tissues will be present.

Complete heart block or third-degree heart block occurs in approximately 1 in 20,000 to 25,000 infants. Infants with complete heart block rarely live past 3 years of age, and those who do require the use of a pacemaker.

The cause of congenital heart block is not known; however, research has suggested that it could be inherited as an autosomal recessive trait, that it occurs as a secondary characteristic of underlying myocardium, and most recently that heart block occurs as a result of a maternal autoimmune disease of unknown origin (e.g., systematic lupus erythematosus). Treatment of congenital heart block varies from outpatient monitoring to implantation of a pacemaker to pharmaceuticals. Problems in cognitive realms are usually associated with poor brain perfusion responsible for neurological problems.

Prognosis ranges from poor to good depending on the degree of heart block. Future research is focused on new drug therapies to increase the atrial-ventricular conduction of the heart. Currently, the drug atropine is showing promise in achieving this goal.

This entry has been informed by the sources listed below.

REFERENCES

Brown, F. M. D. (2001a). Heart block, first degree. *eMedicine*, 2(6). Retrieved from http://search.medscape.com/reference-search;jsessionid=B20CC9A675B7ABFE464224D2E6EDB527?newSearch=1&queryText=heart+block

Brown, F. M. D. (2001). Heart block, second degree. *eMedicine*, 2(6). Retrieved from http://search.medscape.com/reference-search;jsessionid=B20CC9A675B7ABFE464224D2E6EDB527?newSearch=1&queryText=heart+block

Brown, F. M. D. (2001). Heart block, third degree. *eMedicine*, 2(6). Retrieved from http://search.medscape.com/reference-search;jsessionid=B20CC9A675B7ABFE464224D2E6EDB527?newSearch=1&queryText=heart+block

Klassen, L. R. (1999). Complete congenital heart block: A review and case study. *Neonatal Network*, 18(3), 33–42.

McKusick, V. A. (1997). Online mendelian inheritance in man, Article 234700. Retrieved from http://www.ncbi.nlm.nih.gov/Omim

KIMBERLY M. ESTEP
University of Houston, Clear Lake

HEBER, RICK F. (1932–1992)

Rick Heber was born January 12, 1932. He received his BA degree from the University of Arkansas in 1953. After a year as principal of the Manitoba School for Mental Deficiency, Heber attended Michigan State University, obtaining his MA degree there in 1955. He then went on to achieve his PhD in 1957 from George Peabody College. Heber joined the faculty of the University of Wisconsin, Madison in 1959 as coordinator of the special education program.

Heber is best known for his work as principal investigator of the Milwaukee Project and the subsequent controversies surrounding the project. A major finding of the project was that the variable of maternal intelligence proved to be by far the best single predictor of the level and character of intellectual development in the offspring (Heber, 1970; Heber & Garber, 1975). Heber believed that the prevalence of intellectual developmental disabilities associated with the slums of U.S. cities is not randomly distributed but is actually strikingly concentrated within individual families who can be identified on the basis of maternal intelligence (Heber, 1988). Heber was a member of the faculty of the University of Wisconsin at Madison when he was indicted on charges stemming from the misuse of federal funds allocated to the project. He was subsequently convicted and served time in the federal prison in Bastrop, Texas. Previously a respected scholar in the field of intellectual developmental disabilities, his academic work on the Milwaukee Project has been called into serious question. It is now questionable whether the project ever actually existed as it had been described by Heber.

REFERENCES

Heber, R. F. (1970). *Epidemiology of Intellectual Developmental Disabilities*. Springfield, IL: Thomas.

Heber, R. F. (1988). Intellectual Developmental Disabilities in the slums. In G. W. Albee & J. M. Joffe (Eds.), *Prevention, powerlessness, and politics: Readings on social change*. Newbury Park, CA: Sage.

Heber, R. F., & Garber, H. (1975). The Milwaukee Project: A study of the use of family intervention to prevent cultural-familial Intellectual Developmental Disabilities. In B. Z. Friedlander, G. Kirk, & G. Sterritt (Eds.), *The exceptional infant* (Vol. 3). New York, NY: Brunner/Mazel.

CECIL R. REYNOLDS
Texas A&M University
First edition

MARIE ALMOND
The University of Texas of the Permian Basin
Second edition

See also Milwaukee Project, The

HECHT SYNDROME

Hecht syndrome (HS) is a rare, hereditary disorder of muscle development and mechanics. The first case report appeared in 1968. Subsequently, several affected individuals in an extended family group were described.

HS is inherited in an autosomal dominant manner. There is a 2:1 female-to-male occurrence, for which there is no clear explanation. No data are available regarding the rate of HS in the general population.

Characteristics

1. Small mouth with inability to open the mouth very widely.
2. Partial flexion (downward curving) of the fingers when the hand is bent upward at the wrist. This finding is secondary to shortened tendons and muscles of the forearm.
3. Occasional findings in the lower extremity are down-turned toes, clubfoot, and inward curving of the fore-foot (metatarsus adductus).

Surgical treatment of clubfoot may be necessary if repeated casting does not correct the deformity. Metatarsus adductus may also require orthopedic intervention (Jones, 1997). Hand and finger deformities tend to improve with age but are not particularly amenable to any type of therapy. Consequently, HS patients have difficulty performing tasks that require more than a moderate degree of manual dexterity.

There is no research to indicate cognitive difficulties; however, because of the physical limitations, children with this syndrome may require assistive devices or technology in the classroom to allow them to achieve their academic potential.

Prognosis for patients with this disorder is favorable. Feeding problems are common in infancy and childhood. Their small mouths make oral surgery, including tonsillectomy, technically difficult. Administering general anesthesia is also a challenge because of problems with intubation.

REFERENCE

Jones, K. (1997). *Smith's recognizable patterns of human malformations* (5th ed.). Philadelphia, PA: Saunders.

BARRY H. DAVISON
Ennis, Texas

JOAN W. MAYFIELD
*Baylor Pediatric Specialty Services
Dallas, Texas*

HEELCORD OPERATION

The heelcord operation is an orthopedic surgical treatment for children with spastic cerebral palsy (Cobeljic, Bumbasirevic, Lesic, & Bajin, 2009). It is performed to compensate for equinus, a condition in which the foot is involuntarily extended owing to contracted tendons in the heel. Children with equinus often have severe gait problems (Batshaw & Perret, 1981). The operation itself involves cutting and lengthening the Achilles tendon and rotating the heel to a normal position. The operation is typically followed by 6 weeks in a cast and roughly 6 months of physical therapy.

Without surgery, treatment of this condition is often painful and unsuccessful. It involves the use of braces, splints worn at night, and regular heelcord stretching exercises. The success rate of the operation is very high. Research has shown an overall recurrence rate for patients receiving surgery of only 9%, although recurrence is related to age; 2-year-olds, for example, have a recurrence rate of 75% (Lee & Bleck, 1980). Improvements

in mobility improve multiple outcomes in cerebral palsy (Nagle & Campbell, 1998).

REFERENCES

Batshaw, M. L., & Perret, Y. M. (1981). *Children with handicaps: A medical primer*. Baltimore, MD: Paul H. Brookes.

Cobeljic, G., Bumbasirevic, M., Lesic, A., & Bajin, Z. (June 1, 2009). The management of spastic equinus in cerebral palsy. *Orthopaedics and Trauma, 23*, 3, 201–209.

Lee, C. L., & Bleck, E. E. (1980). Surgical correction of equinus deformity in cerebral palsy. *Developmental Medicine and Child Neurology, 22*, 287–294.

Nagle, R., & Campbell, L. (1998). Cerebral palsy. In L. Phelps (Ed.), *Health-related disorders in children and adolescents*. Washington, DC: American Psychological Association.

THOMAS E. ALLEN
Gallaudet College

See also Cerebral Palsy

HEGGE, KIRK, KIRK APPROACH

Hegge, Kirk, and Kirk (1936) formulated the phonographo-vocal method of remedial reading while teaching children with mild intellectual developmental disabilities. Emphasizing programmed learning techniques, this method incorporated sound blending and kinesthetic experiences (Kirk & Gallagher, 1983). Basic to this method was a set of remedial reading drills presented in four parts. Part I provided drills in sounding out consonants, short vowels, and vowel combinations such as *ee, ay, ow, ing, all, ight, ur*, and the final *e* marker. Drills in Part I were printed on one line from left to right, reinforcing directional patterns in reading. Early drills were simple, showing that only the initial consonant changes in words such as satmat-rat. More complex drills were successively introduced by changing the first and last consonant of words. After repeated drills on the consonants, the short vowels, a, e, i, o, and u, are emphasized.

In Part II words were presented using the sounds already learned in Part I. Children were taught to read hand as h-an-d instead of h-a-n-d. Through frequent review and drills (the hallmark of this method) children move from vocalizing and recognizing simple sounds to incorporating these sounds into words.

Parts III and IV were for those children who, after having been repeatedly drilled on the sound blends in Parts I and II, were beginning to read by rapidly sounding out words. Part III required children to read new words in syllables or wholes.

In Part IV of this approach children were drilled on sounds that could not be systematically presented in earlier drills. Reinforcement drills were used with children who exhibit problems in specific areas such as confusing b, d, and p or m and n (Kirk, 1940).

Kirk (1940) warned that the Hegge, Kirk, Kirk method, developed in 1936, should not be used as a general teaching method or for children in higher grade levels. Rather it was applicable to first-, second-, and third-grade students whose reading level is at least 2 years below the norm, who are trainable in sound blending, and who demonstrate the desire to learn to read. This program was of little value to those children who were accurate but slow readers because they already possessed the skills inherent in the practice drills.

REFERENCES

Hegge, T., Kirk, S., & Kirk, W. (1936). *Remedial reading drills*. Ann Arbor, MI: Wahr.

Kirk, S. (1940). *Teaching reading to slow-learning children*. Cambridge, MA: Riverside.

Kirk, S., & Gallagher, J. (1983). *Educating exceptional children* (4th ed.). Boston, MA: Houghton Mifflin.

FORREST KEESBURY
Lycoming College

See also Orton-Gillingham Method; Reading Disorders; Reading Remediation

HEINICKE, SAMUEL (1727–1790)

Samuel Heinicke, a German educator, founded the first oral school for the deaf about 1755. He established Germany's first public school for the deaf in 1778 at Leipzig. Using published accounts of the teaching of deaf children by Jacob Pereire and others, Heinicke devised a highly successful method for teaching reading, writing, speech, and speech reading to deaf students, a method that formed the basis for the later development of the oral method in Germany by Moritz Hill (Bender, 1970).

Some of Heinicke's ideas anticipated later educational practice. He taught the reading of whole words before teaching the letters. He advocated classes at the University of Leipzig for preparing teachers of the deaf, and attempted, apparently unsuccessfully, to establish with the university provision for his deaf students to participate in university activities. Heinicke's work was continued after his death by his widow, who took charge of his school, and his son-in-law, who established a school for the deaf near Berlin.

REFERENCE

Bender, R. E. (1970). *The conquest of deafness*. Cleveland, OH: Case Western Reserve University Press.

PAUL IRVINE
Katonah, New York

HELEN KELLER INTERNATIONAL

Founded in 1915, Helen Keller International assists governments and agencies in developing countries in providing services to prevent or cure eye diseases and blindness and to educate or rehabilitate the individuals with blindness and visually impairments. Headquarters are in New York City and there are programs in 22 countries around the world. Subsumed under Helen Keller International are the Association for Chinese; Permanent Blind Relief War Fund; American Braille Press for War and Civilian Blind; and the American Foundation for Overseas Blind (Gruber & Cloyd, 1985).

The organization offers courses for teachers of blind children and adults as well as for field workers dealing with the rural blind. A training focus is prevention and treatment of blindness caused by malnutrition, trachoma, cataracts, and other eye diseases. Additionally, there are programs to prepare volunteers to counsel families of blind babies.

An important function of this international agency is the collection and compilation of statistics on blindness throughout the world. Publications include an annual report, a newsletter, fact sheets, technical reports, educational materials, and training information. There is one annual conference and an annual board meeting. Headquarters are at 352 Park Avenue South, 12th Floor, New York, NY 10010. Additional information and resources can be found at http://www.hki.org/.

REFERENCE

Gruber, K., & Cloyd, I. (1985). *Encyclopedia of associations* (Vol. 1, 20th ed.). Detroit, MI: Gale.

C. MILDRED TASHMAN
College of St. Rose

JESSI K. WHEATLEY
Falcon School District 49, Colorado Springs, Colorado

See also Deaf-Blind

HEMATURIA, BENIGN FAMILIAL (IDIOPATHIC HEMATURIA)

Hematuria is defined as the presence of blood in the urine. It may be further classified as gross hematuria (enough blood to make the urine look abnormal to the naked eye) or microscopic hematuria (blood can be detected only through chemical testing or microscopic examination). Gross hematuria may appear as a brown or cola-colored urine, which suggests a renal (kidney) origin of bleeding. Pink or red urine is associated with lower urinary tract blood loss. Bleeding from the bladder or urethra may also cause tiny blood clots in a urine specimen.

Benign familial hematuria (BFH) is characterized by recurrent episodes of gross hematuria that usually resolve within 1 to 2 weeks. Because the blood is from sites in the kidney, the urine has a brown or smoky color. The onset of hematuria is usually preceded by 1 to 2 days of symptoms of a viral upper respiratory infection (nasal congestion, runny nose, cough, etc.).

No data are available on the prevalence of this disorder. Because multiple individuals in the family group may be affected, the pattern of inheritance seems to be autosomal dominant.

Characteristics

1. Multiple, recurrent episodes of gross hematuria, usually associated with viral respiratory illness.
2. Microscopic hematuria may persist between the gross hematuria events. Occasionally, patients with BFH may just have constant microscopic hematuria and no gross hematuria.
3. A family history of hematuria may be found.
4. Normal blood pressure, no evidence of impaired renal function, and no proteinuria (the presence of abnormal amounts of protein in the urine).
5. Kidney biopsy shows normal findings by the usual microscopic inspections. However, under the electron microscope, many patients will have thinning of the basement membrane. The basement membrane is the supportive structure of the glomerulus, which is the complex network of tiny blood vessels that form the kidney's filtering system.

There is no specific treatment for BFH. However, physicians caring for these children must follow them closely for abnormalities that suggest a more ominous renal disease. Persistent microscopic hematuria in conjunction with other abnormal laboratory data, as well as two or more episodes of gross hematuria, are indications for renal biopsy. This test involves passing a large bore needle into the kidney to obtain tissue for histological examination. The procedure is not without risks.

There is no research to indicate that children with BFH will have cognitive deficits or the need for modifications in the classroom.

As its name implies, BFH has an excellent prognosis. Very rarely these patients will incur progressive renal disease over a period of several decades. They do need close monitoring and may require more than one renal biopsy if hypertension, proteinuria, or deterioration in kidney function develops.

For more information and parent support, contact National Kidney Foundation, 30 East 33rd Street, New York, NY 10016. Tel.: (212) 889-2210, (800) 622–9010; home page http//www.kidney.org.

This entry has been informed by the sources listed below.

REFERENCES

Bergstein, J. M. (2000). Conditions particularly associated with hematuria. In R. E. Behrman, R. M. Kleigman, & H. B. Jenson (Eds.), *Nelson's textbook of pediatrics* (16th ed., pp. 1577–1581). Philadelphia, PA: Saunders.

Gandy, A. (n.d.). *Benign familiar hematuria.* Disease database. Retrieved http://www.pedianet.com/news/illness/disease/.les/benignfa.htm

National Organization for Rare Disorders. (1997). *Hematuria, benign, familial.* Retrieved from http://www.stepstn.com/cgi-win/nord.exe?proc=GetDocument&rectype=&rectype=&recnum=699

Pediatric database (PEDBASE). (1994, January 31). *Hematuria.* Retrieved from http://icondata.com/health/pedbase/.les/HEMATURI.HTM

BARRY H. DAVISON
Ennis, Texas

JOAN W. MAYFIELD
Baylor Pediatric Specialty Services
Dallas, Texas

HEMIBALLISMUS

Hemiballismus is a rare condition that is characterized by violent, flinging, involuntary movements in the extremities on one side of the body. The movements are typically more pronounced in the arm than in the leg and may be severe enough to cause bruising of the soft tissues or exhaustion. Involvement also has been reported in the muscles of the neck. Hemiballistic movements disappear during sleep.

Onset of the condition usually occurs in adulthood and often is associated with a prior cerebral vascular accident (stroke) involving the subthalamic nucleus. Tumors rarely are involved but hemiballism occasionally occurs in multiple sclerosis. In a few instances, the severity of hemiballism spontaneously subsides after several weeks. Death from exhaustion, pneumonia, or congestive heart failure within 4 to 6 weeks of onset also has been reported. Severe movement abnormalities may persist for several months or years without noticeable diminution in many of those who survive these initial weeks. Hemiballistic movements also may subside and be replaced by milder hemichoreatic movements in some instances. Fatalities are rare.

Chlorpromazine and haloperidol have been reported to substantially reduce or eliminate hemiballistic movements over a period of 3 months to more than 1 year. In some individuals, medications have been reduced gradually and ultimately eliminated with no recurrence of the condition (Shannon, 2005). The prognosis has become more optimistic in recent years owing to increased use of these medications. There is also some optimism that other classes of neuroleptics may also be beneficial (e.g., Risperdal).

This entry has been informed by the sources listed below.

Characteristics

1. Involuntary movement of the limbs on one side of the body.
2. In some cases, speech impairments may occur.
3. Stress and anxiety will intensify the movements.
4. Other neurological deficits, including mental deficiencies, muscle tone anomalies, and autonomic and sensory impairments, may be seen. However, these impairments are not necessarily due to hemiballismus but more likely related to the underlying damage of the structures surrounding the STN.

REFERENCES

Berkow, R. (Ed.). (1982). *The Merck manual of diagnosis and therapy* (14th ed.). Rahway, NJ: Merck, Sharp & Dohme.

Fahn, S. (1985). Neurologic and behavioral diseases. In J. Wyngaarden & L. Smith, Jr. (Eds.), *Cecil textbooks of medicine* (17th ed., p. 2075). Philadelphia, PA: Saunders.

Kalawanis, H. L., Moses, H., Nausieda, P. A., Berger, D., & Weiner, W. J. (1976). Treatment and prognosis of hemiballismus. *New England Journal of Medicine, 295,* 1348–1350.

Magalini, S., & Scarascia, E. (1981). *Dictionary of medical syndromes* (2nd ed., pp. 110–111). Philadelphia, PA: Lippincott.

Shannon, K. M. (2005). Hemiballismus. *Current Treatment Options in Neurology, 7,* 3, 203–210.

DANIEL D. LIPKA
Lincoln Way Special Education Regional Resources Center

See also Chorea; Multiple Sclerosis

HEMIPARESIS

Hemiparesis is a condition involving a neurological deficit in which one side of the body has weakness or is partially paralyzed (Hynd & Obrzut, 1981). In hemiparesis, neurological compromise is limited to the hemisphere contralateral to the weakened or partially paralyzed side of the body. The etiology of hemiparesis has been linked to unilateral strokes, transient ischemic attacks, migraines, head injuries, diabetes mellitus, tumors, infections, demyelinating conditions, and hereditary diseases (Family Practice Notebook, 2001; Lezak, 1995). The incomplete paralysis or weakness may present as limb rigidity, spasticity, or both. Weakness and spasticity are usually the main causes of limb deformities associated with hemiparesis. This condition may involve ataxia and gait disorders.

Characteristics

1. Weakness or paralysis on one side of the body.
2. Movement or gait disorders.
3. Poorly coordinated motor skills.
4. Limb deformity.
5. Rigidity or spasticity on the involved side of the body.
6. Excess hip and knee flexion during movement.
7. Decreased weight-bearing capabilities.
8. "Drop-foot" involving limited ankle control.
9. Asymmetrical standing postures and abnormal center of gravity.
10. Decreased walking speed.
11. Becomes fatigued easily.
12. Eyes may track toward the involved hemisphere.

Cognitive deficits in individuals with hemiparesis vary depending on which hemisphere has been compromised. For individuals with left hemiparesis, the right hemisphere is implicated, and for individuals with right hemiparesis, the left hemisphere is involved. The presence of left hemiciated with the right hemisphere (e.g., sensory testing, spatial orientation, and visuospatial construction). Right hemiparesis may involve deficits in functions usually associated with the left hemisphere (e.g., speech, object naming, writing, reading, comprehension, and tactile perception).

The degree of physical and cognitive development varies greatly in children with hemiparesis. Due to the nature of this disability, it is imperative that a transdisciplinary approach to educational and treatment programming be utilized to enhance learning and maximize independent functioning. Most children with hemiparesis would benefit from special services including occupational therapy, physical therapy, speech and language therapy, adapted physical education, and special education. Intervention goals should be designed to assist children with hemiparesis to increase their ability to perform purposeful activities and follow daily routines.

Spasticity in hemiparesis ranges from mild to moderate, which can negatively influence motor control and motor planning. In locomotor movements such as running, a child with hemiparesis may ambulate with a limp and effectively pump with only the noninvolved arm. In hemiparesis, the spastic arm is typically bent and pronated while the spastic leg is noticeably smaller than the normal one. Individuals with hemiparesis generally make two types of movement—either small steps with the paretic limb or larger steps with the nonparetic limb (Jiang, McIlroy, Black, & Maki, 1998). These two motions produce asymmetrical movements that reduce functional stability. Adaptive equipment designed to improve locomotion ability in children with hemiparesis could include therapy balls to reduce spasticity and help with relaxation; rocking on a vestibular board to reduce spasticity and to develop better equilibrium reactions; wearing a shoe lift on the nonparetic limb; and scooter boards, dumbbell kickers, and adaptive tricycles to encourage the use of both hands and both legs (Aruin, Hanke, Chaudhuri, Harvey, & Rao, 2000; Sherrill, 1993).

Coordination skills and motor planning may also be problematic for children with hemiparesis and render them unable to adapt to new settings or to generalize tasks. Due to motor planning deficits, a child with hemiparesis may have difficulty executing coordinated movement patterns or sequences. Activities that may help strengthen a child's motor planning and coordination skills are beanbag activities, obstacle courses, locomotor movements using a ladder on the floor, and motor skills kits to create specific sequential patterns for motor planning skill development (Sherrill, 1993). Due to lack of falling, when developing educational and treatment programs for children with this disorder, caution should be taken to reduce their chance of sustaining physical injury.

Children with hemiparesis often have balance problems, which can affect many areas of the child's performance not only motorically but also academically. The integration of the intersensory skills important to balance is also vital to reading and writing skills (Bailey & Wolery, 1989). In addition to balance problems, hemiparesis may result in visual perception problems. Activities to remediate visual perceptual problems include beeper or jingle balls, auditory guessing games, locomotor movements using a drumbeat, games in which the child must track using his or her eyes to follow a moving object, and exploring different ways to move body parts in a stationary position.

In addition to gross motor delays, children with hemiparesis may experience delays in the development of fine motor skills. The degree of abnormal muscle tone correlates with difficulties in the performance of fine motor tasks. Vision, head, and trunk control, upper extremity function, posture, and volitional movements all need to be carefully assessed to determine their impact on a child's fine motor development (Sherrill, 1993). Treatment programs designed to improve a child's fine motor skills must be conducted in conjunction with activities to improve muscle tone and overall movement patterns.

In the case of hemiparesis, speech and language services may be warranted, depending on which hemisphere of the brain has been damaged and the extent of the impairment. If speech services are provided, it is critical to teach functional communication skills across a variety of settings. Additionally, alternative and augmentative communication modes may need to be taught when a child has highly unintelligible speech or is nonverbal (McCormick & Schiefelbusch, 1984).

The special education teacher's role will depend on the level of cognitive involvement of the child with hemiparesis. As the severity of the cognitive disability increases, the special education teacher's involvement will typically increase. In a transdisciplinary approach, the special education teacher is usually responsible for the coordination and implementation of all services so that an optimal learning environment is provided for the child to learn new skills and to generalize these skills across different environments. In addition to being responsible for assessing and teaching cognitive skills, the special educator may also be responsible for the assessment and daily implementation of sensorimotor, play, social, communication, motor, and self-help skills. Facilitating parent-child interactions and integration issues and strategies may also be a responsibility of the special education teacher.

REFERENCES

Aruin, A. S., Hanke, T., Chaudhuri, G., Harvey, R., & Rao, N. (2000). Compelling weightbearing in persons with hemiparesis following stroke: The effect of a lift insert and goal-directed balance exercise. *Journal of Rehabilitation Research and Development, 37*(1).

Bailey, D. B. Jr., & Wolery, M. (1989). *Assessing infants and preschoolers with handicaps.* New York, NY: Macmillan.

Family Practice Notebook.com. (2001). *Hemiplegia: Hemiparesis.* Retrieved from http://www.fpnotebook.com/Neuro/Exam/Hmplg.htm

Hynd, G. W., & Obrzut, J. E. (1981). *Neuropsychological assessment and the school-age child: Issues and procedures.* Boston, MA: Allyn & Bacon.

Jiang, N., McIlroy, W. E., Black, S. E., & Maki, B. E. (1998, August). *Control of compensatory limb movement in chronic hemiparesis.* Paper presented at the North American Congress on Biomechanics, Waterloo, Ontario, Canada.

Lezak, M. D. (1995). *Neuropsychological assessment* (3rd ed.). New York, NY: Oxford University Press.

McCormick, L., & Schiefelbusch, R. L. (1984). *Early language intervention.* Columbus, OH: Merrill.

Sherrill, C. (1993). *Adapted physical activity, recreation and sport: Crossdisciplinary and lifespan.* Dubuque, IA: WCB Brown & Benchmark.

SHAWN POWELL
United States Air Force Academy

BARBARA CORRIVEAU
SHARINE WEBBER
Laramie County School, District #1, Cheyenne, Wyoming

See also Hemiplegia; Physical Anomalies

HEMIPLEGIA

Hemiplegia, or paralysis of one side of the body, usually is the result of a cerebral vascular insult or injury (Reed, 2001). This condition generally involves rupture or closure of cerebral blood flow in part of the brain (O'Sullivan, 2001). Because some parts of the nerve cells of the brain have been damaged and cannot function, the part of the body controlled by the damaged portion of the brain cannot function (Dzurenko, 1999). For example, when the left side of the brain is involved, the child's right extremities are affected; the results of this may include paralysis, sensory loss, and aphasia that may be temporary or permanent (Young, 2000). In most cases, there will be permanent neurological deficits ranging from slight neurological problems to complete loss of function in motor, sensory, or language ability (Young, 2000). Crossed hemiplegia is characterized by muscular weakness on one side of the body. This condition is extremely rare and generally begins before the child is 18 months old (Misulis, 2000). Monoplegia refers to weakness in one limb on one side of the body (Rowland, 1995).

Pediatric strokes are the most common cause of hemiplegia in children (Gold & Cargan, 2000). The estimated annual incidence of stroke in children under the age of 14 is 2.52 per 100,000 (Gold & Cargan, 2000). Causes of strokes in children have been linked to inherited clotting disorders, congenital heart disease, and sickle cell disease (Gold & Cargan, 2000). Other causes of strokes that may lead to hemiplegia include shaking an infant, sports, and substance abuse by the mother or by a child. Hemiplegia may be caused, in some rare cases, by spinal cord damage or tumors on the spinal cord (Misulis, 2000).

In infants and children, stroke symptoms include seizures, coma, and paralysis of one side of the body (Young, 2000). Additional symptoms may involve the loss of previously acquired speech and seizures (Young, 2000). Hemiplegia is usually diagnosed by a physician using a magnetic resonance imaging (MRI) test (Young, 2000).

Course and outcome of children with hemiplegia are variable and are dependent upon a number of factors. In the case of newborns, most continue to have seizures, motor difficulty, and some cognitive impairment (Young, 2000). In most cases, children will have persistent limb weakness. Children may experience delays in language, processing, memory, attention, and cognition, depending on the side of the brain that is involved (Reed, 2001). For example, if the left hemisphere of the brain was involved, the child may experience difficulty in language and auditory processing as well as motoric impairments. Although the child may always demonstrate residual effects, positive outcomes have been linked to return of adequate blood flow to the brain (Young, 2000).

Special education services will likely be needed to assist the child with hemiplegia. Due to the varying levels of impairment that different children experience, individualized education plans need to be tailored to the child's unique needs. The child may require assistance with many different areas, including learning, academics, self-care, motoric ability, cognitive issues, and psychosocial problems (Reed, 2001). Special education services need to focus on the building of remedial strategies, the teaching of new or lost skills, and compensatory education, the teaching of different skills to accommodate for the skills lost (D'Amato, Rothlisberg, & Work, 1999). The child may benefit from compensatory and remedial strategies in the following areas: physical therapy, occupational therapy, learning interventions, and social skills training. Physical therapy may focus on the reduction of muscle atrophy and an increase in flexion and extension. Occupational therapy could focus on grasping objects and the functional use of both the affected side of the body and compensatory strategies using the unaffected side of the body. Learning interventions may include compensatory and remedial strategies in any affected areas of academics. Social skills training may need to focus on the teaching of prosocial behaviors, increasing self-confidence, and peer relationship development (Reed, 2001). Research needs to progress in the area of intervention studies for children with hemiplegia.

REFERENCES

D'Amato, R. C., Rothlisberg, B. A., & Work, P. H. (1999). Neuropsychological assessment for intervention. In C. R. Reynolds & T. B. Gutkin (Eds.), *The handbook of school psychology*. New York, NY: Wiley.

Dzurenko, J. (1999). Rehabilitation nursing: Educating patients toward independence. In M. G. Eisenberg, R. L. Glueckauf, & H. H. Zaretsky (Eds.), *Medical aspects of disability: A handbook for the rehabilitation professional*. New York, NY: Springer.

Gold, A. P., & Cargan, A. L. (2000). Stroke in children. In L. P. Rowland (Ed.), *Merritt's neurology*. Philadelphia, PA: Lippincott, Williams, & Wilkins.

Misulis, K. E. (2000). Hemiplegia and monoplegia. In W. G. Bradley, R. B. Daroff, G. M. Fenichel, & C. D. Marsden (Eds.), *Neurology in clinical practice: Practice and principles of diagnosis and management*. Woburn, MA: Butterworth-Heinemann.

O'Sullivan, S. B. (2001). Stroke. In S. B. O'Sullivan & T. J. Schmitz (Eds.), *Physical rehabilitation: Assessment and treatment*. Philadelphia, PA: Davis.

Reed, K. L. (2001). *Quick reference to occupational therapy*. Gaithersburg, MD: Aspen.

Young, R. K. (2000). Stroke in childhood. In W. G. Bradley, R. B. Daroff, G. M. Fenichel, & C. D. Marsden (Eds.), *Neurology in clinical practice: The neurological disorders*. Woburn, MA: Butterworth-Heinemann.

NICOLE R. WARNYGORA
University of Northern Colorado

See also Hemiparesis

HEMISPHERECTOMY

Hemispherectomy is a surgical procedure involving the removal of "a cerebral hemisphere, including the frontal, temporal, parietal, and occipital lobes while leaving intact parts of the thalamus and basal ganglia" (Menard, Le Normand, Rigoard, & Cohen, 2000, p. 333). A hemispherectomy may be performed as a treatment for severe seizure disorders, fatal tumors, hemiplegia, and Rasmussen encephalitis (Mathern, 2010). The procedure is usually reserved as a life-saving measure or may be employed to improve the life of a child with intractable seizures resulting from unilateral brain dysfunction (de Bolle & Curtiss, 2000; Estes, 2000).

Characteristics

Note that these symptoms usually result in a hemispherectomy, and some may exist following this surgical procedure.

1. Intractable epileptic seizures of an ongoing severe nature.
2. Hemiplegia or hemiparesis.
3. Progressive declines in cognitive functioning.
4. Visual neglect contralateral to the damaged hemisphere.
5. Impaired expressive and receptive language functioning.
6. Delayed social communication skills.
7. Delayed academic achievement.
8. Increased occurrence of mental illness, specifically those involving thought disorders.

In cases involving a hemispherectomy, cerebral damage from atrophy, sustained seizures, disease processes, tumors, or traumatic insults may be present. The result of such damage usually involves a reduction in cognitive functioning. This reduction in cognition may be widespread or specific, depending on the etiology, course, duration, and age of occurrence when the cerebral damage initially started (Caplan, Curtiss, Chugani, & Vinters, 1996). Additionally, seizure activity may be generalized (i.e., bilateral), or focal (i.e., unilateral). In the case of bilateral seizures, the remaining hemisphere may be damaged, which prompts questions regarding its structural integrity (Boatman et al., 1999).

Depending on the age of disease onset or injury and the age when the hemispherectomy is performed, there is evidence that the remaining cerebral hemisphere may mediate functions normally associated with the removed hemisphere (Caplan et al., 1996; de Bolle & Curtiss, 2000). Thus, the right hemisphere in children with a left hemispherectomy may mediate language functions, and the left hemisphere in children with a right hemispherectomy may mediate visual-spatial functions. The age of injury and age of the hemispherectomy procedure may be more important determinants of future cognitive functions than the severity of the injury or disease process (Bradshaw & Mattingley, 1995). It has been suggested that insults that occur during a critical period of maturation result in less opportunity for the full development of specific abilities. For example, when an insult occurs during a critical period of language development, it reduces the likelihood that a child would acquire full language skills (Menard et al., 2000).

Following a hemispherectomy, a full complement of special education services may be essential to ensure that the child has the best possible opportunity to make educational gains. These services may include speech language therapy, mobility support, occupational therapy, physical therapy, school nursing services, academic support, counseling, and case management. In addition to school-based services, frequent communication with medical care providers is necessary in order to provide the best possible educational services and to better understand the child's recovery. Seizure precautions and protocols should be established and followed because seizure disorders may persist following the hemispherectomy. General guidelines to reduce seizure activity include taking antiseizure medication as prescribed, eating three meals daily, drinking fluids, reducing or eliminating caffeine, following regular sleeping patterns, allowing rest periods, and using stress management techniques (Estes, 2000).

Parental contact should occur on a regular basis with the frequency of these contacts determined by the child's needs. Depending on the age of the child, a daily notebook between home and school may be beneficial in increasing communication. Transitional services and vocational planning with available community resources for children who have had a hemispherectomy will likely increase their ability to adapt and function as independently as possible as they mature.

REFERENCES

Boatman, D., Freeman, J., Vining, E., Pulsifer, M., Miglioretti, D., Minahan, R., . . . McKhann, G. (1999). Language recovery after left hemispherectomy in children with late-onset seizures. *Annals of Neurology, 46*(4).

Bradshaw, J. L., & Mattingley, J. B. (1995). *Clinical neuropsychology: Behavioral and brain science.* San Diego, CA: Academic Press.

Caplan, R., Curtiss, S., Chugani, H. T., & Vinters, H. V. (1996). Pediatric Rasmussen encephalitis: Social communication, language, PET, and pathology before and after hemispherectomy. *Brain and Cognition, 32,* 45–66.

de Bolle, S., & Curtiss, S. (2000). Language after hemispherectomy. *Brain and Cognition, 43,* 135–205.

Estes, R. (2000). A closer look: Seizures. *Premier Outlook, 1*(2).

Mathern, G. W. (November 02, 2010). Cerebral hemispherectomy: When half a brain is good enough. *Neurology, 75,* 18, 1578–1580.

Menard, A., Le Normand, M. T., Rigoard, M. T., & Cohen, H. (2000). Language development in a child with left hemispherectomy. *Brain and Cognition, 43,* 332–340.

SHAWN POWELL
United States Air Force Academy

See also Cerebral Dominance; Left Brain/Right Brain; Neuropsychology

HEMISPHERIC FUNCTIONS

Hemispheric functions refers to the specialization of each cerebral hemisphere of the brain for various processes. The right hemisphere usually has been associated with processing information in a simultaneous, spatial, and holistic fashion (Kinsbourne, 1997; Speery, 1974). In contrast, the left hemisphere of the brain has been shown to best process information in a sequential, temporal, and analytic mode (Kinsbourne, 1997; Speery, Gazzaniga, & Bogen, 1969).

Although hemispheric lateralization usually refers to the processing of specific information by predominantly one hemisphere, undifferentiated hemispheric preference for the processing of certain information also exists. Gordon (1974), for example, found that when melodies recorded from an electric organ were simultaneously presented, one to each ear, no hemispheric superiority was noted. Few reliable hemispheric differences were noted for lower level sensory elements such as brightness, color, pressure, sharpness, pitch, and contour (Gordon, 1970). Symmetrical processing of information does not occur on tasks that require complex cognitive processes such as categorization, integration, and abstraction. As the level of cognitive complexity increases, so does the lateralization for the task in question.

The notion of lateralization of functions within cerebral hemispheres can be dated back to the late 1800s, when Broca and Wernicke demonstrated that aphasia (or the inability to express or comprehend language) resulted from lesions to the left hemisphere. Moreover, the left hemisphere was portrayed as the dominant hemisphere by virtue of its leading role in such activities as speech and calculation, whereas the right hemisphere was seen as the minor hemisphere, serving activities associated with perception and sensation (Geschwind, 1974; Kinsbourne, 1997).

Invasive techniques that have been used to investigate brain functioning consist of electrical stimulation of the brain, hemispheric anesthetization, and split-brain research. Direct electrical stimulation of the brain was pioneered by Penfield (Penfield & Roberts, 1959) as a means of mapping areas of the brain that controlled specific functions prior to other surgical procedures. Given that the brain does not contain pain receptors, electrical stimulation was applied to various parts of the brain while the patient was fully conscious. This technique has been successful in examining areas of the brain associated with vision, hearing, olfaction, and haptic sensations.

Another invasive technique to investigate speech lateralization involved the injection of sodium amytal to the carotid artery, which is located on either the right or left side of the patient's neck. This procedure, which is commonly referred to as the Wada test (Wada & Rasmussen, 1960), quickly anesthetizes or temporarily paralyzes the hemisphere that receives the injection. The hemisphere is anesthetized for approximately 3 to 5 minutes, thereby enabling the examiner to assess which hemisphere is responsible for processing linguistic information. The last invasive technique, split-brain surgery, involves the severing of the corpus callosum, a large band of nerve fibers that permit the left and right hemispheres to communicate with one another. This procedure is primarily performed to prevent the spreading of a seizure from a focal point in one hemisphere to the other hemisphere by way of the corpus callosum. By severing the corpus callosum, communication between the hemispheres is blocked, thereby allowing the examiner to determine the hemispheric lateralization for such functions as language, visual discrimination, touch, olfaction, and motoric control (Hecaen, 1981).

Research that has resulted from the use of the preceding techniques has found that the right hemisphere plays a dominant role in processing certain information. Specifically, the right hemisphere is dominant for processing nonlinguistic information involving nonverbal reasoning, visual-spatial integration, visual-constructive abilities, haptic perception, pattern recognition, and other related tasks (Camfield, 2005; Dean, 1984). Conversely, the left hemisphere has been shown to be responsible for tasks that require speech, general language, calculation, abstract verbal reasoning, and so on (Camfield, 2005; Dean, 1984).

Noninvasive techniques for investigating hemispheric specializations have also been employed. The dichotic listening technique attempts to determine if auditory information for verbal and nonverbal information is lateralized to one hemisphere. Here, the subject is simultaneously presented with different information in each ear and is required to recall or recognize the information presented. Given that greater numbers of nerve connections cross over from ear to hemisphere, the hemisphere opposite the ear that obtains the greatest number of correct responses (ear advantage) is inferred to be the functional hemisphere for the specific information presented. For example, most typical children and adults have a right-ear advantage (left hemisphere) for linguistic information (Dean & Hua, 1982). When nonverbal auditory information such as tones are presented, a left-ear advantage (right hemisphere) is found for most normal right-handed individuals (Kimura, 1967). The dichotic listening paradigm has been successful in suggesting specific functions of each hemisphere.

Similar to the dichotic listening methodology, the split visual-field technique presents visual information to either the left or right visual half fields. It should be noted that each retina is separated into a left and right half visual field. Therefore, information presented to the two left halves of each retina is processed by the right hemisphere and, conversely, information presented to the two right halves is processed by the left hemisphere. To study the lateralization of visual stimuli, different information is simultaneously presented on a tachistoscope. As would be expected, a right visual half advantage (left hemisphere) is found for linguistic information (Marcel & Rajan, 1975) while a left visual half advantage (right hemisphere) has been noted for nonverbal spatial information (Kimura & Durnsford, 1974). One noted difficulty with this technique, however, is the attentional scanning of the stimuli that

occurs once the information has been presented (Dean, 1981).

Differences in hemispheric specializations may be due, in part, to anatomical differences of the cortical hemispheres. In examining anatomical differences, it was found that the left temporal planum structure that serves language functions is larger than the right temporal planum (Geschwind & Levitsky, 1968). Similarly, the Sylvian fissure, a large lateral depression in the brain that contains the major speech area, is found to be larger for the left side of the Sylvian fissure than the right (Geschwind, 1974). In addition, the left hemisphere is noted to be approximately 5 grams heavier than the right hemisphere. Another anatomical difference is the projection of nerve fibers from the left hemisphere that cross over earlier at the base of the brain than do nerve fibers from the right hemisphere. Such structural differences between the hemispheres may partially account for cerebral lateralization of specific functions.

When gender differences are examined, subtle anatomical dissimilarities between males and females are found to exist shortly after birth. Perhaps more striking than anatomical are functional changes that exist between adult male and female brains (Kinsbourne, 1997; Kolata, 1979). As a group, males have been shown to perform better on tasks of spatial ability than females, who present superior verbal facility (Witelson, 1976). The spatial ability of males may be partially due to an earlier right hemisphere lateralization of spatial functions. Males also have been shown to have an earlier hemispheric specialization for language, while females are noted to be less consistent in lateralization for language activities (Levy, 1973). This less established hemispheric specialization for females, however, can be contrasted to their firmer lateralization for peripheral activities such as handedness (Annett, 1976) and visually guided motor activities (Dean & Reynolds, 1997). That is, while females are more bilateral for cognitive activities such as language, they have more established preference than do males for consistently using the same hand, ear, eye, and so on, for related activities.

This paradoxical finding for females seems to be a function of the tenuous relationship between lateral preference patterns for peripheral activities and hemispheric specialization for language. Inferring hemispheric lateralization from lateral preference patterns from simple measures of handedness should be cautioned against. Dean (1982) has shown that lateral preference is a factorially complex variable and a function of the system (e.g., eyes, ears, hands) under study. Lateral preference patterns, then, may be more heuristically represented on a continuum from entirely left to entirely right instead of categorically as either left or right (Dean & Reynolds, 1997).

REFERENCES

Annett, M. (1976). Hand preference and the laterality of cerebral speech. *Cortex, 11*, 305–329.

Camfield, D. (2005). Neurobiology of creativity. In C. Stough (Ed.), *Neurobiology of exceptionality* (pp. 53–72). New York, NY: Kluwer.

Dean, R. S. (1981). Cerebral dominance and childhood learning disorders: Theoretical perspectives. *School Psychology Review*, *10*, 373–380.

Dean, R. S. (1982). Assessing patterns of lateral preference. *Clinical Neuropsychology*, *4*, 124–128.

Dean, R. S. (1984). Functional lateralization of the brain. *Journal of Special Education*, *18*, 239–256.

Dean, R. S., & Hua, M. S. (1982). Laterality effects in cued auditory asymmetries. *Neuropsychologia*, *20*, 685–690.

Dean, R. S., & Reynolds, C. R. (1997). Cognitive processing and self-report of lateral preference. *Neuropsychology Review*, *7*, 127–142.

Geschwind, N. (1974). The anatomical basis of hemispheric differentiation. In S. J. Dimond & J. G. Beaumont (Eds.), *Hemisphere function in the human brain*. New York, NY: Wiley.

Geschwind, N., & Levitsky, W. (1968). Human brain: Left-right asymmetries in temporal speech region. *Science*, *161*, 186–187.

Gordon, H. W. (1970). Hemispheric asymmetries in the perception of musical chords. *Cortex*, *6*, 387–398.

Gordon, H. W. (1974). Auditory specialization of the right and left hemispheres. In M. Kinsbourne & W. L. Smith (Eds.), *Hemispheric disconnection and cerebral function*. Springfield, IL: Thomas.

Hecaen, H. (1981). Apraxias. In S. B. Filskov & T. J. Boll (Eds.), *Handbook of clinical neuropsychology*. New York, NY: Wiley.

Kimura, D. (1967). Functional asymmetry of the brain in dichotic listening. *Cortex*, *3*, 163–178.

Kimura, D., & Durnsford, M. (1974). Normal studies on the function of the right hemisphere in vision. In S. J. Dimond & J. G. Beaumont (Eds.), *Hemisphere function in the human brain*. London. England: Elek Scientific.

Kinsbourne, M. (1997). Mechanisms and development of cerebral lateralization in children. In C. R. Reynolds & E. Fletcher-Janzen (Eds.), *Handbook of clinical child neuropsychology* (pp. 102–119). New York, NY: Kluwer-Plenum.

Kolata, G. B. (1979). Sex hormones and brain development. *Science*, *205*, 985–987.

Levy, J. (1973). Lateral specialization of the human brain: Behavioral manifestations and possible evolutionary basis. In J. A. Kriger (Ed.), *The biology of behavior*. Corvallis: Oregon State University Press.

Marcel, T., & Rajan, P. (1975). Lateral specialization of recognition of words and faces in good and poor readers. *Neuropsychologia*, *13*, 489–497.

Penfield, W., & Roberts, L. (1959). *Speech and brain mechanisms*. Princeton, NJ: Princeton University Press.

Speery, R. W. (1974). Lateral specialization in the surgically separated hemispheres. In F. O. Schmitt & F. G. Worden (Eds.), *The neurosciences: Third study program*. New York, NY: Wiley.

Speery, R. W., Gazzaniga, M. S., & Bogen, J. H. (1969). Interhemispheric relationships: The neocortical commissures: Syndromes of hemisphere disconnection. In P. Vinken & G. W. Bruyn (Eds.), *Handbook of clinical neurology* (Vol. 4). New York, NY: Wiley.

Wada, J. A., & Rasmussen, T. (1960). Intracarotid injection of sodium amytal for lateralization of cerebral speech dominance: Experimental and clinical observation. *Journal of Neurosurgery*, *17*, 266–282.

Witelson, S. F. (1976). Abnormal right hemisphere specialization in developmental dyslexia. In R. M. Knights & D. F. Bakker (Eds.), *Neuropsychology of learning disorders: Theoretical approaches*. Baltimore, MD: University Park Press.

GURMAL RATTAN
Indiana University of Pennsylvania

RAYMOND S. DEAN
Ball State University
Indiana University School of Medicine

See also Cerebral Dominance; Left Brain/Right Brain

HEMOLYTIC UREMIC SYNDROME

Hemolytic uremic syndrome (HUS) is a systemic disease marked by renal failure, hemolytic anemia, thrombocytopenia (platelet deficiency), coagulation defects, and variable neurological signs (MedlinePlus, 2002). This disorder is most common in children. It frequently occurs after a gastrointestinal (enteric) infection, often one caused by a strain of specific E. coli bacteria (*Escherichia coli* O157:H7). It has also been associated with other enteric infections, including shigella and salmonella, and with some nonenteric infections (MedlinePlus, 2002; Rothenberg & Chapman, 1994).

HUS often begins with vomiting and diarrhea (which may be bloody). Within a week the patient develops weakness and irritability. Urine output decreases dramatically and may almost cease. Because red blood cells are being destroyed (a process called hemolysis), the patient rapidly becomes anemic and pale (MedlinePlus, 2002).

The incidence of HUS is 1 to 3 per 100,000, with the highest incidence occurring in the summer and fall. The age of onset is most common under the age of 4 years. HUS is the most common cause of acute renal failure in children (Pedlynx, 2002).

There are two forms of HUS: the typical form (idiopathic) and the atypical or sporadic form. The typical form usually affects children 3 months to 6 years of age (80% < 3 years) and is caused by an E. coli serotype O157:H7 that can produce specific enterocytotoxins. The risk factors for E. coli acquisition are undercooked ground beef and contact with a person with diarrhea within 2 weeks prior to disease onset. One in 10 children who have E. coli 0157:H7 will go on to develop HUS (Pedlynx, 2002).

The atypical or sporadic form may be associated with an inherited autosomal recessive or dominant form and with scleroderma, radiation of kidneys, and essential or malignant hypertension. There is also a pregnancy or oral contraceptive association related to preeclampsia or postpartum renal failure (Pedlynx, 2002).

Characteristics

1. Gastroenteritis
   - Usually precedes illness by 5 to 10 days.
   - Diarrhea, bloody stool, severe colitis.
   - Fever, nausea, and vomiting.
   - Rectal prolapse.
2. Renal manifestations
   - Microscopic or gross hematuria.
   - Proteinuria that can progress to the nephrotic level.
   - Complications such as nephritic syndrome (edema, hypertension, azotemia, oliguria), nephrotic syndrome (edema, hypoalbuminemia, hyperlipidemia), and renal failure that can range from mild renal insufficiency to acute renal failure (ARF).
3. Hematological manifestations
   - Anemia.
   - Sudden onset of pallor, irritability, lethargy, weakness.
   - Hepatomegaly-hepatosplenomegaly.
   - Thrombocytopenia (90%).
4. Complications
   - Irritability, seizures, coma.
   - Colitis with melena and perforation.
   - Acidosis, congestive heart failure, diabetes mellitus, fluid overload, hyperkalemia, rhabdomyolysis.

Treatment usually includes transfusions of packed red cells, and platelets are given as needed. Kidney dialysis may be indicated. Medications prescribed include corticosteroids and aspirin. Plasmapheresis, also called plasma exchange (or passage of the plasma through a Protein A filter) may be performed, although its role is much less well documented than in TTP (thrombotic thrombocytopenic purpura). The blood plasma (the portion that does not contain cells, but does contain antibodies) is removed and replaced with fresh (donated) or filtered plasma to remove antibodies from the circulation (MedlinePlus, 2002). In addition, medical management of the complications such

as nephritic syndrome, nephrotic syndrome, and chronic renal failure may include dialysis, kidney transplant, or both (Pedlynx, 2002).

Special education may or may not be needed for children with HUS. The course and outcome of the disease are highly variable, and individual educational needs will vary as well. Chronic renal problems and medications may well create the need for typical chronic illness counseling and supportive assistance.

Ninety percent of patients survive the acute phase with no renal impairment if aggressive management of acute renal failure (ARF) is instituted. A positive prognosis is associated with the age of the child, typical form, and summer months for diagnosis. A poor prognosis is associated with shock, significant renal involvement, neurological signs and symptoms, and atypical form. The prognosis for children with HUS includes a mortality rate of 7% to 10% and renal dysfunction of 20% (Pedlynx, 2002).

The known cause of HUS, E. coli in hamburger and ground meats, can be prevented by adequate cooking. Other unrecognized causes may not be preventable at this time.

REFERENCES

MedlinePlus. (2002). *HUS*. Retrieved from http://www.nlm.nih.gov/medlineplus/ency/article/000510.htm

Pedlynx Pedbase. (2002). Retrieved from http://icondata.com/

Rothenberg, M. A., & Chapman, C. F. (1994). *Dictionary of medical terms*. New York, NY: Barron's.

ELAINE FLETCHER-JANZEN
Chicago School of Professional Psychology

HEMOPHILIA A, "CLASSIC" HEMOPHILIA

Factor VIII deficiency is one of the most common forms of severe hereditary bleeding disorders. Hemophilia has been known since antiquity, as is evidenced by Talmudic scripts advising against ritual circumcision of male infants whose siblings died from bleeding caused by the procedure.

Hemophilia occurs in about 1 in 5,000 males. Eighty-five percent of these individuals have Factor VIII deficiency. The remainder have Factor IX deficiency (hemophilia B). Both disorders are transmitted in an X-linked recessive manner, with females acting as carriers of the abnormal gene. This carrier state may also cause mild clotting abnormalities.

Multiple mutations of the Factor VIII gene are associated with several clinical classifications of hemophilia. Unimpaired clotting activity requires Factor VIII levels that are 35% to 40% of normal. Severe hemophilia is characterized by less than 1% of normal Factor VIII levels. Moderate cases range from 1% to 5%. Mild hemophilia is over 5%. About 5% to 10% of patients with hemophilia A produce abnormal, nonfunctioning Factor VIII. Forty-five to 50% of those with severe disease have an identical genetic mutation and generate no detectable Factor VIII at all.

Characteristics

1. Bleeding symptoms in the newborn are uncommon. Intracranial hemorrhage is occasionally seen. Only about 30% of affected males have excessive bleeding with circumcision.

2. Easy bruising, bleeding into muscle (intramuscular hematoma), and bleeding into joints (hemarthrosis) usually do not begin until the child starts to crawl and walk. However, 10% of hemophiliacs have no symptoms during their first year.

3. Hemarthrosis is the defining characteristic of this disease. It may be spontaneous or posttraumatic. The ankle is the most commonly affected joint in toddlers. Hemarthroses of the elbow and knee occur more frequently in older children and adolescents. Repeated bleeds into a joint cause scarring, severe pain, erosion of cartilage at the ends of bones forming the joint, and—eventually—complete fusion.

4. Life-threatening hemorrhages are the result of bleeding into the brain, upper airway, or other vital organ. Exsanguination can occur with gastrointestinal bleeds, external blood loss, or massive intramuscular hematomas.

5. Mildly affected patients may not experience spontaneous bleeding. Their most common presenting symptoms is prolonged bleeding following dental work, surgery, or moderate trauma.

Successfully treating hemophilia requires several considerations. Prevention of trauma is important, but many bleeding events are spontaneous. Early family counseling will help parents strike a suitable compromise between overprotecting their child and permitting him reasonable freedom. Hemophiliacs should avoid aspirin and non-steroidal anti-inflammatory drugs (e.g., ibuprofen), because such drugs may aggravate bleeding tendencies. Patients should complete the hepatitis B immunization series during infancy, and they should be screened periodically for hepatitis and abnormal liver function.

Specific therapy with Factor VIII given intravenously is needed to end bleeding events. Serious or life-threatening bleeds require Factor VIII levels to be 100% of normal.

Individuals with mild hemophilia may respond to the drug DDAVP, which causes release of Factor VIII from storage sites in this particular subset of patients.

Previously, Factor VIII infusions were given only when active bleeding was evident or suspected. Prior to the introduction of purification techniques employed for about the past 15 years, repeated Factor VIII administration was associated with a high risk for infection with transmittable viral disease (hepatitis A, B, and C and HIV). The only product available until recently was derived from pooled human plasma and was therefore not totally safe. However, a recombinant Factor VIII produced from genetically altered bacteria is now being marketed. Considerable interest exists for the prophylactic use of this material because it is free from any known viral contaminants. Prophylactic Factor VIII therapy prevents hemarthroses and greatly reduces the incidence of crippling joint pathology in hemophiliacs.

Education of educators and other school personnel is an integral part of keeping the child safe in the school environment. Helping them to provide play and leisure activities that will not result in compromising the health of the child with Factor VIII deficiency will be important. By providing preventive education, the school counselors can work with the other students to understand the need for safety, help the student with Factor VIII adjust to the modifications, and in turn facilitate peer relationships and self-esteem issues. Should the child with Factor VIII experience bleeding in his brain, it will be important to have a comprehensive neuropsychological evaluation completed. Depending on those results, the educators will be able to develop an educational program that focuses on the child's strengths and provides ways to remediate his cognitive weaknesses.

The prognosis for newly diagnosed children with hemophilia A is generally favorable. A referral to large hemophilia comprehensive care centers is imperative for the most satisfactory outcomes. Staffed by professionals in several disciplines, these facilities employ a modern approach to factor replacement therapy (prophylactic treatment), recognize and aggressively treat initial signs of joint debilitation, and manage the complications of prolonged Factor VIII administration (hepatitis and HIV). The most realistic "cure" for this disorder is gene replacement therapy, which should become available during the lifetimes of today's patients.

For more information and parent support, please contact National Hemophilia Foundation, 116 West 32nd Street, 11th Floor, New York, NY 10001. Tel.: (212) 328–3700, (800) 424–2634; e-mail handi@hemophilia.org. Home page http://www.hemophilia.org/NHFWeb/Main Pgs/MainNHF.aspx?menuid=0&contentid=1.

World Federation of Hemophilia, 1425 Rene Levesque Boulevard West, Suite 1010, Montreal, Quebec, H3G-1T7, Canada. Tel.: (514) 87–5–7944; e-mail: wfh@wfh.org; home page: http://www.wfh.org/en/page.aspx?pid=492.

REFERENCES

Montgomery, R. R. (2000). Hemorrhagic and thrombotic disease. In R. E. Behrman, R. M. Kleigman, & H. B. Jenson (Eds.), *Nelson's textbook of pediatrics* (16th ed., pp. 1504–1525). Philadelphia, PA: Saunders.

National Organization for Rare Disorders. (1999). *Factor XIII deficiency*. Retrieved from http://www.rarediseases.org/rare-disease-information/rare-diseases/byID/39/viewAbstract

BARRY H. DAVISON
Ennis, Texas

JOAN W. MAYFIELD
Baylor Pediatric Specialty Service

HEMOPHILIA B

Hemophilia is a sex-linked inherited disorder in which the individual lacks the necessary blood-clotting factors to stop bleeding (Harcourt Health Sciences, 2002). The condition is transmitted via the X chromosome, but it is believed that some individuals are affected by hemophilia due to mutation of the genes on that chromosome. There are two forms of hemophilia: Type A (with the blood-clotting Factor VIII missing) and Type B (with the blood-clotting Factor IV missing; Hemophilia, 2000). Hemophilia A and B are further defined by their severity and range from mild to severe.

The condition exists in all races and ethnicities. The prevalence rate for Hemophilia A is 1 in 10,000 men and for Hemophilia B it is 1 in 40,000 men (Cutler, 2001). Fifty percent of all sons of a female carrier will be affected and 50% of the daughters will be carriers. All daughters of affected men will be carriers, but the disease affects women very rarely (Greene, 2001a). Approximately 17,000 people with hemophilia are currently living in the United States (Mayo Clinic, 2001).

Characteristics

1. The symptoms vary with the degree of the deficiency of the blood-clotting factors.
2. Often diagnosed when infants begin crawling; their injuries cause internal bleeding as in their joints and muscles, which are then visible by bruises, and their injuries bleed profusely.
3. Symptoms associated with the disorder are nosebleeds; bruising; spontaneous bleeding; bleeding into joints and associated pain and swelling; gastrointestinal tract and urinary tract hemorrhage; blood in urine or stool; prolonged bleeding from cuts, tooth extraction, and surgery; and excessive bleeding following circumcision (Greene, 2001a).

Individuals with hemophilia must be under medical care to assist with the replacement of the blood-clotting factors that are administered intravenously. The reduction or prevention of bleeding is essential during treatment because such bleeding can be life-threatening. For example, immunizations should be administered subcutaneously versus intramuscularly to prevent hemorrhages. The importance of dental hygiene must be explained to the individual to prevent tooth decay and possible gum infections. Aspirin and some medications used for arthritis must be avoided because they act as blood thinners. Education of the patient regarding his or her environment and how to interact with it to avoid injury is essential for his or her well being.

Swimming and walking should be preferred over contact or high-impact sports such as boxing or football (Greene, 2001b). MedicAlert tags must be worn by the child, and emergency procedures and emergency numbers must be known by all pertinent individuals in the child's environment (Hemophilia.org, 2001a, 2001b). Serious consideration must be given to any bleeding in the mouth, throat, or neck, because the patient could suffocate as a result of the bleeding. Bleeding in the joints is also a concern and—if untreated—could lead to a loss in mobility (Canadian Hemophilia Society, 2001).

To help the individual cope with the impact of the bleeding disorder, the child is best served if home, school, and medical caregivers form a strong alliance. Joining support groups with other afflicted individuals can help alleviate the stress as well. Genetic counseling for family members and afflicted individuals is also recommended (Cutler, 2001). Depending on the severity of the condition, hospitalizations and longer periods might prevent the child from participating in school on a regular basis (Hemophilia.org, 2001c). Tutoring at home and possibly at school is recommended to help the child compensate for lost school time. As precautionary measures to prevent injuries, some activities might have to be limited or avoided completely. Protective gear such as helmets and padding for elbows and knees should be available. This gear is especially important for smaller children so that the danger from hard toys and sharp edges can be minimized. To prevent the possible trauma to the child of a child abuse investigation, teachers, and care-providers must be educated about the symptoms of hemophilia. These symptoms include visible and recurring bruises and can easily be mistaken for damage resulting from child abuse (Hemophilia.org, 2001).

Due to the advances of modern medicine, individuals with hemophilia can lead happy and successful lives.

Without medical attention, this condition is life threatening. There is no cure for hemophilia at this time.

REFERENCES

Canadian Hemophilia Society. (2001). *The treatment of hemophilia*. Retrieved from http://www.hemophilia.ca/en/bleeding-disorders/hemophilia-a-and-b/

Cutler, T. S. (2001, June 7). Hemophilia. *eMedicine Journal, 2*(6).

Greene, A. R. (2001a). *Disease: Hemophilia A*. Retrieved from http://emedicine.medscape.com/

Greene, A. R. (2001b). *Disease: Hemophilia B*. Retrieved from http://emedicine.medscape.com/

Harcourt Health Sciences. (2002). Hemophilia A & B. In *Mosby's medical, nursing, & allied health dictionary* (6th ed., pp. 800–801). St. Louis, MO: Author.

Hemophilia. (2000). In *Human diseases & conditions* (Vol. 2, pp. 434–438). New York, NY: Scribner.

Hemophilia.org. (2001a). *Child abuse issues*. Retrieved from http://hemophilia.org/NHFWeb/MainPgs/MainNHF.aspx?menuid=0&contentid=1

Hemophilia.org. (2001b). *Information for teachers & childcare providers*. Retrieved from http://hemophilia.org/NHFWeb/MainPgs/MainNHF.aspx?menuid=0&contentid=1

Hemophilia.org. (2001c). *Psychological issues*. Retrieved from http://hemophilia.org/NHFWeb/MainPgs/MainNHF.aspx?menuid=0&contentid=1

Mayo Clinic. (2001, September 14). *Hemophilia*. Retrieved from http://www.mayoclinic.com/

MONIKA HANNON
Colorado Springs, Colorado

HEMOPHILIA C

Hemophilia is a bleeding disorder in which there is a deficiency of selected proteins in the body's blood-clotting system. "Clotting is the process by which your blood changes from a liquid to a solid state in order to stop bleeding" (Mayo Clinic, 2001). There are three main types of hemophilia in which a different clotting factor is missing or deficient. In the most common type, Hemophilia A, clotting Factor VIII is missing or deficient. In Hemophilia B, Factor IX is missing or deficient, and in Hemophilia C, Factor XI is missing or deficient. All three types can cause prolonged bleeding.

Hemophilia is an inherited sex-linked genetic defect in which a defective X chromosome is passed from a mother to her male child. Males cannot pass along the gene that causes hemophilia to their sons because the defect is located on the X chromosome, which is inherited from the mother. In extremely rare cases, a girl may be born with hemophilia, but only if a man with hemophilia has children with a female carrier whose defective X chromosome is passed to the female child. A 1998 study estimated that one of every 5,000 boys of all races born in the United States has some form of hemophilia. The National Hemophilia Foundation estimates that more than 16,000 males in America have hemophilia, whereas in females, the incidence is only 1 in 1 million (Willett, 2001).

Characteristics

1. Abnormal bruising and bleeding.
2. Spontaneous hemorrhages into various joints—knees, elbows, ankles, and hips.
3. Possible limitation of movement and swelling.
4. Internal bleeding.
5. Patient may also suffer from chronic arthritis, anemia, gastritis, and epistaxis (severe and chronic nosebleeds).

There is no cure for hemophilia—it is a lifelong condition (Katz, 1970). Treatment involves injecting the blood clotting factor that is missing into the patient's blood. Clotting factors can be injected on a regular preventive basis in an attempt to keep bleeding from occurring. Prior to the mid-1980s, it was more common for people with hemophilia to become infected with the HIV virus or with hepatitis because of contaminated blood products. The risk of infection through blood products has decreased, however, because of genetically engineered clotting products called recombinant factors, which are free of infection (Mayo Clinic, 2001). With regular injections, even persons with severe cases of hemophilia can lead near-normal lives.

Students with hemophilia could qualify for special education services under the category of Other Health Impairment. The student would most likely require a health plan so that school personnel are adequately prepared in emergencies. It is important that anyone who takes care of the child knows about the condition. The role of the school psychologist is to provide support for the student and his or her family in the form of counseling. The school psychologist could also provide education to the staff and other students about hemophilia to reduce the amount of misinformation that others may have about the disease.

Future research for hemophilia appears to be in the area of genetic therapy. There is also research being conducted into understanding the makeup of the factor VIII protein that is used during treatment.

REFERENCES

Katz, A. (1970). *Hemophilia: A study in hope and reality.* Springfield, IL: Thomas.

Mayo Clinic. (2001). *Hemophilia.* Retrieved from http://www.mayoclinic.com/health/hemophilia/DS00218

Willett, E. (2001). *Hemophilia.* Berkeley Heights, NJ: Enslow.

CHRISTINE D. CDE BACA
University of Northern Colorado

HENOCH-SCHÖNLEIN PURPURA

Henoch-Schönlein (HS) purpura, also called *anaphylactoid purpura*, is a form of hypersensitivity vasculitis. This form of vasculitis is distinguished by erthematouricarial and purpuric rash most prominent in the lower legs and buttocks. The patient may also exhibit signs of arthralgia (pain in one or more joints), gastrointestinal difficulties, and glomerulonephritis (difficulties related to inflammation of the capillaries in or around the kidneys).

The etiology of HS purpura is unknown, although research suggests either an immune system dysfunction or allergic reaction to certain foods, drugs, bacteria, or insect bites (National Organization for Rare Disorders [NORD], 1997). The disorder is more common in children than adults, with an incidence estimated to be as high as 18 cases per 100,000 within the pediatric age group (Henoch-Schonlein Purpura, 1996). Girls and boys appear to be equally affected. Age of onset is variable, although initial symptoms typically begin after age 2 and peak between 4 and 7 years of age. Some literature indicates that HS purpura may be a seasonal disorder because there appears to be a higher incidence in the winter months. A respiratory tract infection has preceded the onset of symptoms in approximately 50% of the cases (Szer, 1996).

Characteristics

1. Child may report sudden onset of headaches.
2. Child may have a marked loss of appetite.
3. Child may have a fever.
4. Red or purple spots (petechiae) may appear on the skin, usually in the area of the legs and buttocks.
5. Child may complain of severe cramping and abdominal pain that becomes worse at night.
6. Child may complain of joint pain, especially in the knees and ankles.
7. Other symptoms may include vomiting and diarrhea or severe constipation and dark stools.
8. Difficulty in kidney function has occurred in 23% to 49% of the reported cases.

The difficulty in treatment is that individual symptoms often mimic other disease processes. Therefore, symptoms are treated individually. If the HS purpura is thought to be the result of an allergic reaction, the offending substance must be avoided. If symptoms include abdominal and joint pain, glucocorticoid (steroid) drugs may be prescribed. The use of steroids in treatment is controversial, however. Although some research indicates that early steroid treatment may reduce the risk of kidney damage, other studies have shown that the steroids neither shorten the length of the illness nor reduce the frequency or recurrence of the symptoms (Causey, Woodall, Wahl, Voelker, & Pollack, 1993; Szer, 1996).

In most cases, this disorder is self-limiting with no long-term complications. The disorder may resolve and recur several times during its course, usually ending in spontaneous resolution. Only in rare cases has the disorder progressed to the point of becoming a chronic disease. Because this disorder usually does not have long-lasting or chronic results, it is unlikely that the child will be eligible for special education services.

Current research is in the area of drug therapy. As stated earlier, the effectiveness of drug therapy remains controversial and requires further research. A procedure for removing unwanted toxins from the blood (plasmapheresis) has also been recommended for severe cases of HS purpura, but this procedure also requires much more investigation and research (NORD, 1997).

REFERENCES

Causey, A., Woodall, B., Wahl, N., Voelker, C., & Pollack, E. (1993). Henoch-Schonlein purpura: Four cases and a review. *Journal of Emergency Medicine, 12*(3), 331–341.

Henoch-Schonlein Purpura. (1996). In *Cecil textbook of medicine* (20th ed., p. 576). Philadelphia, PA: Saunders.

National Organization for Rare Disorders. (1997). *Purpura, Henoch Schonlein.* Retrieved http://rarediseases.org

Szer, I. (1996). Henoch-Schonlein purpura: When and how to treat. *Journal of Rheumatology, 23,* 1661–1665.

CHRISTINE D. CDE BACA
University of Northern Colorado

HEPATITIS

Hepatitis is an inflammation of the liver caused by different viruses, alcoholism, abuse of or side effects of medications, exposure to toxins, or an individual's lowered immune system. Hepatitis viruses are categorized and named according to various attributes, such as hepatitis A, B, C, D, E, F, and G, the first three accounting for the majority of cases and the later four being much less common. This entry focuses on the symptoms and conditions caused by hepatitis viruses A, B, and C.

Each year, 200,000 Americans and 1.4 million people worldwide become infected with hepatitis (Hepatitis Information Network [HIN], 2012). Hepatitis A is transmitted via oral contact with fecal material. People in high-risk areas include military personnel stationed overseas, day-care employees, or individuals working in other less-than-sterile environments such as are found in some institutions and in the waste management industry. Outbreaks have been associated with raw shellfish or fruit that was contaminated with fecal bacteria through the use of unclean water or by infected food handlers (Buggs, 2001). Infections further occur after floods and earthquakes when populations may lack appropriate hygienic conditions.

Hepatitis B is estimated to affect between 1 million to 1.5 million Americans and 400 million people worldwide (HIN, 2012). Hepatitis C is estimated to affect 4 million Americans and 170 million people worldwide. Hepatitis B and C are transmitted through the blood of the carriers. Individuals who are at a higher risk to be infected with hepatitis B and C than the general population are intravenous drug users, health care workers (e.g., nurses, physicians, and dentists), and prisoners ("Hepatitis," 2012). However, since 2005, the number of reported cases has decreased by approximately 56% with .01 to 1.4 cases per 100,000 population (Centers for Disease Control, 2012).

Furthermore, individuals who have sex with many partners, who have organ transplants, or who have contact with shared objects (needles or straws in the drug community), unclean instruments in tattoo and body piercing parlors, unclean hairbrushes and scissors in beauty parlors, shared razors and toothbrushes, or anything that can contain infected blood particles are at risk to contract hepatitis B and C (Buggs, 2001). These viruses can also be transmitted from infected mothers to their infants during labor—a reason why cesarean-section births are recommended to prevent the spread of the disease if the mother is known to be infected.

Characteristics

1. Chronic hepatitis: Loss of appetite, malaise, low-grade fever.
2. Acute hepatitis: Nausea, vomiting, low-grade fever, loss of appetite, rash, tiredness and fatigue, jaundice, darkening of urine, abdominal pain, arthritis.
3. Symptoms for hepatitis A can take between 2 and 7 weeks to develop. These can be mild, last for a limited time, and disappear eventually on their own. In many cases (up to 70%), affected individuals do not notice any symptoms.
4. Symptoms for hepatitis B may not be noticed until 4 to 6 weeks after the infection in both children and adults. Ninety percent of children who become infected with hepatitis B in their first year of life, and 30% to 50% of children from 1 to 4 years of life, become chronically infected. Although this condition may go unnoticed for up to 40 years, the individual could ultimately suffer cirrhosis, which could lead to liver failure and liver cancer.
5. Symptoms for hepatitis C are similar to those for hepatitis B but may not appear until 5 to 12 weeks after the infection, and up to 80% of all infected individuals may never develop any symptoms. However, 50% to 60% of affected individuals may develop a chronic (lasts longer than 6 months) active infection and cirrhosis.

Home care under the supervision of a physician is the treatment of choice for hepatitis A if no severe complications such as dehydration arise. The care should include plenty of rest and a diet that consists of easy-to-digest foods, ample water, and the avoidance of alcohol. The use of over-the-counter medication should be discussed with the physician, as some medications, such as acetaminophen, can be harmful to the liver. Exercise and overexertion of the body should be avoided until the individual's health is regained (Buggs, 2001).

Treatment for hepatitis B is similar to the treatment for hepatitis A. The individual should be placed under the care of a physician as soon as possible to ensure the best possible care according to the latest medical developments. Home care is also recommended, with plenty of rest and fluids to prevent dehydration. Hospitalization may become necessary if symptoms worsen, such as when the patient becomes confused, delirious, or hard to awaken (Buggs, 2001).

The same home-care procedures apply for individuals infected with hepatitis C as discussed earlier for those with hepatitis B. Hospitalization is recommended if the symptoms worsen, such as when the patient vomits foods and fluids, his or her skin turns yellow, the patient experiences increased pain or fever, or the patient becomes disoriented and difficult to awaken. Consultation with a hepatologist is recommended to ensure that the correct medical treatment is chosen to combat the symptoms of hepatitis C because medication and treatment are constantly being researched and improved upon (Buggs, 2001). Interferon is a new medication available for the treatment of hepatitis C. This medication may be recommended by the physician for certain individuals that meet the criterion for its use. The administration of Interferon requires periodic visits (three times weekly) and a proactive approach of the patient. Another new treatment option for some patients with chronic hepatitis C is PEG-INTRON (MayoClinic.com, 2001), which requires the patient to visit the doctor only once each week (Buggs, 2001).

Depending on the physical condition, a child might need hospitalization or home care for a longer period of time. If the physician recommends that the child can return to school and the child is chronically infected with one of the hepatitis viruses, several precautions should be taken. For the safety of others, and to prevent spreading of the viruses, children and teachers should be educated about the possible vaccinations against hepatitis A and B. Sanitary precautions such as hand washing after diaper changes or visits to the bathrooms should be implemented. To prevent the spread of hepatitis B and C, it must be understood that the virus can be spread only through infected blood. Therefore, the children and teachers can interact in a relatively carefree way with a chronically infected child without the worry of becoming infected themselves, yet they should be reminded not to share food, hairbrushes, and other objects that could contain minute blood particles. To help the infected child, teachers must understand that one of the major issues the child has to face in school is the issue of fatigue associated with the chronic condition. This could extensively hinder the child's ability to focus. Tutoring at home and school might be necessary to allow the child to focus on lesson plans or to compensate for lost school time. To help the child with the fatigue during school hours, a rest area should be made available for the child so that he or she can nap if needed. To combat the emotional stress of this disease, self-help groups and support groups should be recommended to the child and family to help alleviate the stress that can accompany a disease of this sort.

With the continued effort of vaccinating children, the spread of hepatitis A and B should eventually be able to be contained. Risks associated with hepatitis A are especially dangerous for the very young or elderly. Death from an infection with hepatitis A is rare. Risks associated with hepatitis B and C are that the diseases can become chronic and lead to liver inflammation, cirrhosis, and liver cancer (Buggs, 2001). Medical advances might be seen in more effective medications to prevent and help with the chronic aspects of the disease.

REFERENCES

Buggs, A. (2001). Hepatitis A. *eMedicine Journal*, 2(6). Retrieved from http://www.eMedicine.com/emerg/topic245.html

Centers for Disease Control and Prevention. (2012). *Viral hepatitis statistics and surveillance*. Retrieved from http://www.cdc.gov/hepatitis/Statistics/index.htm

Hepatitis Information Network. (2000). Hepatitis A. Retrieved from http://www.hepnet.com/hepa/hepafact2000.html

Hepatitis Information Network. (2012). Hepatitis B. Retrieved from http://www.hepfi.org/education/index.htm

Mayo Clinic. (2001). Retrieved from http://www.mayoclinic.com/health/drug-information/DR601737

MONIKA HANNAN
University of Northern Colorado

HEREDITARY SPASTIC PARAPLEGIA

Hereditary spastic paraplegia (HSP; also known as *hereditary spastic paraparesis, Strümpell disease, Strümpell-Lorrain disease, hereditary Charcot disease, hereditary progressive spastic paraplegia*, and *French settlement disease*) is a label used to represent a group of inherited degenerative spinal cord disorders characterized by a slow, gradual, progressive weakness and spasticity (stiffness) of the legs. In the late 1800s, the German neurologist Ernst Adolf von Strümpell first described this disorder. He observed two brothers and their father who had gait disorders and spasticity in their legs. After the death of the brothers, Strümpell was able, through autopsy, to show the degeneration of the motoric nerve fibers leading through the spinal cord (HSPInfo, 2002).

Symptoms may be first noticed in early childhood, or at any age through adulthood. According to some reports in the medical literature, symptom onset may occur as early as infancy or as late as the eighth or ninth decade of life: however, symptoms may most often develop during early to midadulthood. Initial findings typically include stiffness and relatively mild weakness of leg muscles, balance difficulties, unexplained tripping and falls, and an unusually clumsy manner of walking (gait). As the disorder progresses, walking may become increasingly difficult; however, complete loss of the ability to walk is relatively rare (National Organization for Rare Disorders, 2002).

The initial symptoms of HSP may include difficulty with balance, weakness and stiffness in the legs, muscle spasms, and dragging the toes when walking. In some forms of the disorder, bladder symptoms (such as incontinence) may appear, or the weakness and stiffness may spread to other parts of the body. Rate of progression and the severity of symptoms is quite variable even among members of the same family (HSPInfo, 2002).

At the present time, diagnosis of HSP is generally a process of exclusion of other disorders combined with observation of family history. There are some 15 or more gene loci associated with hereditary spastic paraplegia, of which only a few genes have been identified (HSPInfo, 2002).

In Europe the frequency of HSP has been estimated at anywhere from 1 to 9 cases per 100,000 people. HSP is rare, so it is often misdiagnosed, making the frequency rate difficult to determine. However, a reasonable estimate is approximately 3 in 100,000. This would represent less than 10,000 people in the United States. It is further estimated that about 10% of people with HSP have "complicated" HSP, which further complicates diagnosis (HSPInfo, 2002).

Characteristics

1. Uncomplicated HSP: Gradual weakening in the legs, urinary bladder disturbance, and sometimes impaired sensation in the feet.

2. Complicated HSP: Additional symptoms may include peripheral neuropathy, epilepsy, ataxia (lack of muscle control), optic neuropathy, retinopathy (disease of the retina), dementia, ichthyosis (a skin disorder causing dry, rough, scaly skin), intellectual developmental disabilities, deafness, or problems with speech, swallowing, or breathing.

Complicated HSP is rare, and the additional symptoms may be due to a separate disorder in addition to HSP. The patients may actually have uncomplicated HSP plus one or more other disorders. For example, a person with uncom-plicated HSP may have peripheral neuropathy caused by diabetes or may have unrelated epilepsy. Additional symptoms may be present, such as impaired vibration-position sense in the toes, or corticospinal tract signs such as hyperreflexia, extensor toe sign, or ankle clonus.

Currently, there is no specific treatment to prevent, retard, or reverse HSP's progressive disability. Nonetheless, treatment approaches used for chronic paraplegia from other causes are useful. The University of Michigan's HSP laboratory reports that patients in relatively early stages of the illness have obtained symptomatic improvement with oral and intrathecal baclofen and oral dantrolene. Zanaflex has also provided some reduction of spasticity. Bladder spasticity has been improved with oxybutynin (Ditropan; Fink, 2002). Regular physical therapy is important to maintain and improve range of motion and muscle strength. Furthermore, physical therapy is necessary to maintain aerobic conditioning of the cardiovascular system. Although physical therapy does not reduce the degenerative process within the spinal cord, it is considered important that HSP subjects maintain a physical therapy exercise regimen at least several times each week (Fink, 2002).

Children with HSP may well need the support of special education programming due to the chronic nature of this disorder. The obvious physiologic limitations may require extensive medical management that may take away from school attendance and attention to studies. In addition, special education services may provide physical therapy and adaptive physical education for the student. Family and individual counseling may be necessary for adjustment issues related to chronic illness.

REFERENCES

Fink, J. K. (2002). University of Michigan online hereditary spastic paraplegia homepage. Retrieved from http://www.med.umich.edu/hsp/

National Organization for Rare Disorders. (2002). *Hereditary spastic paraplegia*. Retrieved from http://www.rarediseases.org/cgi-bin/nord

ELAINE FLETCHER-JANZEN
Chicago School of Professional Psychology

HERMANSKY-PUDLAK SYNDROME

Hermansky-Pudlak syndrome (HPS), which was first described in 1959 and is named after its discoverers, is characterized by a rare form of albinism that is associated with low visual acuity, bruising and prolonged bleeding, lung fibrosis, and occasionally inflammatory bowel disease and reduced kidney function (National Institute of Child Health and Development [NICHD], 2002).

HPS is seen in many countries but is quite common in northwest Puerto Rico, where 1 in every 1,800 individuals is affected, 1 in 21 is a gene carrier, and more than 400 individuals have the syndrome. Several cases have also been reported in the Puerto Rican community in New York City (NICHD, 2002).

In a study conducted by the NICHD, 27 Puerto Rican patients and 22 non–Puerto Ricans were diagnosed by two symptoms characteristically seen in this syndrome: albinism and defective blood platelets. Twenty-five of the Puerto Rican patients had a specific mutation (a small region of DNA duplication) in the recently cloned gene, HPS, associated with the syndrome. Non–Puerto Ricans did not have this particular mutation. Several different mutations are thought to lead to HPS. Patients with and without the duplication were then compared using clinical and laboratory characteristics (NICHD, 2002).

HPS patients have a biochemical storage disorder; that is, they accumulate a fatty product called ceroid lipofuscin. Researchers believe that this causes inflammation in tissues such as the bowel and lung. Prolonged inflammation leads to fibrosis, which in the case of the lung impairs its ability both to expel air and to exchange carbon dioxide for oxygen (NICHD, 2002).

Characteristics

1. Varying degrees of albinism (lack of skin and eye pigment), which impairs the vision of patients with albinism and often leads to involuntary rhythmic eye movements called nystagmus.

2. Progressive deterioration in lung function, which is particularly prevalent in the Puerto Rican patients carrying the DNA duplication.

3. Tendency to bruise easily and bleed.

4. Females requiring medical intervention during their menstrual cycles or at childbirth.

5. Lung dysfunction beginning with restrictive disease and then progressing inexorably to death usually in the fourth or fifth decade.

In terms of treatment, HPS patients are advised to avoid blood anticoagulants, such as aspirin, and drugs can be used to prevent excessive bleeding during dental extractions and other surgical procedures. The reason HPS patients bleed easily is that their blood platelets are deficient in dense bodies. These subcellular organelles release their contents to make other platelets stick together and form a clot. Without the dense bodies, the clot forms very slowly (NICHD, 2002).

Children with HPS need to be monitored by a multidisciplinary team of professionals for the medical and adaptive monitoring of the disorder. Special education services under the physical and other health impaired handicapping conditions will serve academic and adaptive physical education needs for these children.

The cause of this inherited disease is being investigated by physicians, geneticists, and biochemists at the NICHD; the National Heart, Lung, and Blood Institute (NHLBI); and the National Eye Institute (NEI). From the gene sequence, researchers know what the protein encoded by the HPS gene should look like, but it is not yet known what such a protein actually does. According to William Gahl, many patients with albinism are not aware that they have HPS. They are thus at risk for hemorrhage. Anyone who has albinism and bruises easily should be checked for HPS, which is diagnosed by observing blood platelets under the electron microscope or by performing platelet aggregation studies. The NICHD has started a trial of an investigational drug, that in animal tests has been shown to prevent inflammation. With this drug, the researchers hope that they can prevent the inflammation that leads to the loss of lung function that shortens the lives of individuals with HPS.

REFERENCE

National Institute of Child Health and Development. (2002). *Hermansky-Pudlak syndrome.* Retrieved from http://nichd .nih.gov/Pages/index.aspx

ELAINE FLETCHER-JANZEN
Chicago School of Professional Psychology

HERPES SIMPLEX I AND II

Although clinically and pathologically described as early as 100 BCE, herpesvirus hominus (HVH) was not identified until the 1920s; the existence of two antigenic types was not known until the 1960s; and genital herpes was not recognized as a venereal disease until the late 1960s. In the past, infections above and below the waist have generally been attributed to oral herpes (HVH-1) and genital herpes (HVH-2), respectively. However, the site of the infection does not always point to the particular type of herpes. HVH-1 and 2 now appear in both genital and oral areas, perhaps owing to increased frequency of oral-genital sexual contact (Bahr, 1978). Oral herpes most commonly causes cold sores in infants and children; however, it may cause eye infections and lesions on the fingers as well. Genital herpes has serious effects on both affected individuals and the offspring of affected women; both types of effects are described in this entry.

Genital herpes is a highly contagious and prevalent venereal disease characterized by the appearance of pus-containing sores in the genital region. In 1994, the herpes simplex virus had infected an estimated 45 million Americans. Prevalence has quintupled among White teenagers since 1988, and one out of five Americans 12 years of age or older may be infected with the virus (Fleming et al., 1997). Genital lesions are the most common symptom of herpes in adolescents (Margo & Shaughnessy, 1998). With society's changing mores regarding sexual activity outside of marriage and increasing acceptance of oral sex, as well as increasing numbers of sexual partners, the number of people, including adolescents, with genital manifestations of both genital and oral herpes will probably remain high.

The transfer of genital herpes usually occurs through genital or oral-genital contact. Autoinoculation from infected to uninfected areas of the body commonly occurs through touching the infected area during masturbation, washing, or inspection (Himell, 1981). Inanimate objects such as toilet seats, towels, and medical equipment are generally believed not to contribute to the spread of the herpes virus (Lukas & Corey, 1977), although the virus may survive for up to 72 hours on such objects according to some studies.

Genital Herpes in Adults

Symptoms and Progression of the Infection

Active infection begins, on average, 6 days after exposure (range 2 to 20 days) and lasts approximately 3 weeks, with symptoms most severe between days 10 and 14. Once in the person, the virus can be reactivated with symptoms lasting 10 to 21 days. The first manifestation of the infection is generally the longest and most severe; subsequent infections are shorter and less painful. Patients experience an average of four recurrences a year (Himell, 1981). Local itching and tingling and painful urination are followed by the appearance of painful, blistered red lesions. In females, the lesions may appear on the vulva or vaginal surface, thighs, buttocks, and lower back; in males, the lesions may appear on the penis, thighs, or buttocks. The blisters may open into shallow, open ulcerated areas, which eventually heal without scarring. Other occasional symptoms include enlarged lymph glands, fever, and headaches (Ross, 1997). Genital and oral herpes have been linked with carcinoma of the cervix and lip, respectively. In addition, the occurrence of spontaneous abortion during the first trimester of pregnancy is 3 times greater in women who have genital herpes (Naib, Nahmias, Josey, & Wheeler, 1970).

Herpes increases the risk of acquiring HIV, a virus that causes AIDS, because herpes provides a point of easy entry into the body. In people who have suppressed immune systems, outbreaks can be extremely severe and linger for a much greater amount of time (Schacker et al., 1998).

Friendship and Family Living Concerns

Adolescents with genital herpes are frequently concerned about transmitting the disease to close friends or family members. This may be a genuine concern. However, careful and precise hygienic methods usually prevent the spread of the infection. The herpes victim should thoroughly clean bathroom facilities after using them. During periods when the disease is active or their genital sores are at the weeping stage, victims should not bathe with others in hot tubs or sit on edges of hot tubs and swimming pools.

Because of possible recurrences of infection, genital herpes victims sometimes fear that family members and friends will learn about their disease. If victims understand that direct and intimate sexual contact is the primary mode of transmission, these fears may be reduced.

People with herpes infections of the lips should not kiss anyone, particularly babies, until sores are healed, and should wash their hands well before handling a baby (Ross, 1997).

Pharmacological Treatment

As of yet, no cure for the herpes simplex virus is available. Two types of drug intervention are currently being used for treatment. Acute therapy involves taking a drug to diminish the symptoms of an outbreak, as well as to reduce the duration of the occurrence. This type of therapy requires taking medication for a short length of time, beginning immediately with the first signs of a potential outbreak. The other alternative is suppressive therapy, which requires a daily dose of medication to help prevent reactivation of the virus.

In previous years, the medication acyclovir (Zovirax) was the only option available for treatment. Acyclovir is available by prescription only, and is offered in both oral and topical forms. It works by impeding the spread of

the virus in cells without damaging normal cells (Griffith, 1996).

The U.S. Food and Drug Administration has approved two drugs for treatment of the virus. Famciclovir (Famvir) and Valacyclovir (Valtrex) are being prescribed more frequently than acyclovir. They have been proven to be more effective in absorption by the body, and require fewer daily doses for effectiveness. Famciclovir has proven to be especially useful in suppressive therapy (Diaz-Mitorna et al., 1998). Acyclovir is still regularly prescribed for treatment of herpes infections in newborns (Margo & Shaughnessy, 1998). Treatment with any three of the antiviral medications for 5 days will cost $70 to $80 (Margo & Shaughnessy, 1998).

Sexual Concerns

Having genital herpes does not mean that victims are always infectious; appropriate care can minimize the possibility of transmitting the disease to sexual partners. Prevention should begin with the prodrome, the tingling or itching sensation that many victims have several hours or days before sores are seen. The prodrome state may be infectious itself, and should be thought of as the beginning of the contagious period. Therefore, no oral-genital or genital sexual intercourse should occur from the start of the prodrome to the completion of the healing process as indicated by the disappearance of lesions. Condoms do not prevent the transmission of the disease during an outbreak because the virus can pass through the pores in the condom.

Incidence of cervical herpes has dramatically increased. Females are generally not aware that they have the disease until a gynecological examination has been performed. Since the cervix contains few nerve endings, the victim does not experience the discomfort usually associated with genital herpes. A vaginal discharge may occur, and this usually motivates the woman to seek medical attention. Since these victims do not experience the prodrome or discomfort, they may be unaware that they are having a recurrence. At the first signs of sores on the cervix, restriction of sexual behavior becomes necessary. Health care providers can teach women to perform pelvic self-examinations to enable them to recognize cervical lesions. Also, female victims should be aware that they can spread the virus to the cervix during outbreaks if they use tampons.

Herpes victims also should be aware that having the disease does not immunize against reinfection, as is frequently the case with other diseases. Thus a herpes victim can be reinfected by having sexual relations with a partner who is experiencing a genital herpes attack.

Psychological Consequences

Herpes can have serious psychological consequences, especially for adolescents. Luby (1981) has noted a sequence of responses to genital herpes: (1) shock and emotional numbing; (2) search for an immediate cure; (3) development of feelings of isolation and loneliness and fear that companionship, sexual relations, and children are not in one's future; (4) anger, which can reach homicidal proportions, directed toward the person who is believed to be the transmitter of the disease (at this point fear generalizes and anxiety may result); (5) a "leper" effect, accompanied by depression, which may deepen with time and recurrences. Common feelings at this point include hopelessness, guilt, unworthiness, and self-hatred. Finally, developing herpes can make manifest any latent psychopathology.

Not all victims are emotionally affected, but for many adolescents, it can become a psychologically crippling experience. Individual counseling or membership in a herpes self-help group may be helpful. Herpes self-help groups generally work to achieve several goals, including relief from isolation and loneliness, establishment of a new social network, provision of mentors, and ventilation of rage. If depression with sleep disorder, loss of appetite, psychotic symptoms, or suicidal ideation occur, a psychiatric referral may be required (Luby, 1981). Stress of a variety of kinds appears to increase reactivation of the infection (Keller, Shiflett, Schleifer, & Bartlett, 1994).

Suggestions for Working With Affected Students

Teachers, coaches, and others who work with students who have herpes can help by being sympathetic listeners and having an understanding of the disease that enables them to dispel myths and untruths regarding herpes. Also, they can help students develop a realistic view of their situation by stressing that the disease can be medically managed and is not fatal.

Adolescents' self-esteem can be deeply affected. If this occurs, referral to the school's guidance counselor or family physician should be arranged. Suicide cannot be ruled out. The teacher or coach should not hesitate in making a referral to the guidance counselor or to a mental health professional if emotional disturbances are noted. Remind the victims that they need to isolate active lesions, not themselves.

Effects of Congenital Herpes on Offspring

Transmission from mother to newborn is much more likely if it is the mother's first episode (Margo & Shaughnessy, 1998). Genital herpes may have devastating effects on affected newborns. Although frequently classified with other maternal infections in the STORCH complex (Syphilis, Toxoplasmosis, varicella and other infections, Rubella, Cytomegalovirus, and Herpes; e.g., Graham & Morgan, 1997), herpes generally affects newborns during birth rather than prenatally. Of affected infants, 85% contract the infection during birth as they pass through an infected maternal genital tract or contact the virus through

ruptured fetal-maternal membranes, about 10% contract it later, and 5% earlier in utero. Risk of infection of newborns during birth is about 50% among women who have an active initial infection during labor and delivery, about 5% to 10% among women with recurrent symptoms or lesions present, and less than 1% for women with recurrent infection but asymptomatic at delivery (Graham & Morgan, 1997). Women with herpes lesions in the genital area at the time of delivery are delivered by cesarean section to reduce the likelihood of transmission to the offspring.

Symptoms of perinatal infection, which may include the presence of vesicles, appear a few days after birth. The severity ranges from mild skin infection to death. Common symptoms include irritability, jaundice, and respiratory distress. If untreated, about 75% of affected infants will develop the disseminated infection or encephalitis with a consequent mortality rate of about 70%. Even with antiviral treatment, about 60% of infants with disseminated infections die (Graham & Morgan, 1997). Most survivors show serious sequelae such as intellectual developmental disabilities, epilepsy, and sensory impairments (Douglas, 1985). Infants with congenital herpes infection acquired prenatally show signs common to the STORCH complex, including growth delay, microcephaly, microphthalmia, chorioretinitis, and seizures (Douglas, 1985; Graham & Morgan, 1997).

Assistance can be found at a local chapter of HELP. If there is no local phone number, contact the National Herpes Resource Center, P.O. Box 100, Palo Alto, CA, 94302.

REFERENCES

Bahr, J. (1978). Herpesvirus hominis type 2 in women and newborns. *American Journal of Maternal Child Nursing*, (pp. 16–18).

Diaz-Mitorna, F., Sibbald, R. G., Shafran, S. D., Edmonton, A., Boon, R., & Saltzman, R. L. (1998). Oral Famciclovir for the suppression of recurrent genital herpes. *Journal of the American Medical Association, 280,* 861–944.

Douglas, R. G. Jr. (1985). Herpes simplex virus infections. In J. G. Wyngaarden & L. H. Smith Jr. (Eds.), *Cecil textbook of medicine* (17th ed., pp. 1714–1717). Philadelphia, PA: Saunders.

Fleming, D. T., McQuillan, G. M., Johnson, R. E., Nahmias, A. J., Aral, S. O., Lee, F. K., & St. Louis, M. E. (1997). Herpes simplex virus 2 in the U.S.: 1976–1994. *New England Journal of Medicine, 337,* 1106–1111.

Graham, E. M., & Morgan, M. A. (1997). Growth before birth. In M. L. Batshaw (Ed.), *Children with disabilities* (4th ed., pp. 53–69). Baltimore, MD: Paul H. Brookes.

Griffith, H. W. (1996). *Complete guide to prescription and nonprescription drugs.* New York, NY: Berkley.

Himell, K. (1981). Genital herpes: The need for counseling. *Journal of General Nursing,* 446–447.

Keller, S. E., Shiflett, S. C., Schleifer, S. J., & Bartlett, J. A. (1994). Stress, immunity, and health. In R. Glaser & J. Kiecolt-Glaser

(Eds.), *Handbook of human stress and immunity* (pp. 217–244). San Diego, CA: Academic Press.

Luby, E. (1981). Presentation at the national genital herpes symposium. Philadelphia. *Helper, 3*(4), 2–3.

Lukas, J., & Corey, L. (1977). Genital herpes simplex virus infection: An overview. *Nurse Practitioner, 7*, 7–10.

Margo, K. L., & Shaughnessy, A. F. (1998). Antiviral drugs in healthy children. *American Family Physician, 57*, 1073–1077.

Naib, Z., Nahmias, A., Josey, W., & Wheeler, J. (1970). Association of maternal genital herpetic-infection with spontaneous abortion. *Obstetrics & Gynecology, 35*, 260–263.

Ross, L. M. (1997). *Sexually transmitted diseases sourcebook.* Detroit, MI: Omnigraphics.

Schacker, T., Ryncarz, A. J., Goddard, J., Diem, K., Shaughnessy, M., & Corey, L. (1998). Frequent recovery of HIV-1 from genital herpes simplex virus lesions in HIV-1 infected men. *Journal of the American Medical Association, 280*, 61–66.

C. Sue Lamb
Katherine Falwell
Robert T. Brown
University of North Carolina at Wilmington

See also **Depression, Childhood and Adolescent; Torch Complex**

HESS, ROBERT (1920–1993)

Robert Hess received his BA at the University of California at Berkeley in 1947 and his PhD in developmental psychology at the University of Chicago in 1950. He was the Lee L. Jacks Professor Emeritus of Child Education at Stanford University and codirector of the graduate training program in Interactive Educational Technology. Robert Hess died in 1993 at the age of 73.

Hess's major interests focused on the relationships of teachers who interact with young children's home lives, external realities, and inner lives within the atmosphere of the classroom. He believed that the future of a society rests in its ability to train or socialize the young. He held that the growth of programs in early education and the large-scale involvement of schools and the federal government represented a fundamental shift in the relative roles and potential influence of the two major socializing institutions of society, the family and the school (Hess & Bear, 1968). Thus, he saw the need for social experimentation in order to deal effectively with this shift.

Hess was best known for his work in the late 1950s and early 1960s at the University of Chicago. There he conducted a number of studies on the environmental deprivation of children in poverty, consequently helping to establish the theoretical background for Head Start and other similar government programs. Later research included a 1965 study of communication and instruction methods used by mothers with their children and a longitudinal cross-cultural study, conducted in the 1970s in Japan and the United States, on the interactions of mothers and their children. The latter was one of the first major collaborations between child development researchers in the two countries.

In later years, Hess's interests broadened to include research involving the use of computers in the classroom. Results of this work indicated a distinct gender gap in computer interest and usage among young people.

Some of his major writings include *Early Education: Current Theory, Research, and Action* (Hess & Bear, 1968), *Family Worlds: A Psychosocial Approach to Family Life* (Hess & Handel, 1995), and *Teachers of Young Children* (Hess & Croft, 1972).

REFERENCES

Hess, R. D., & Bear, R. M. (1968). *Early education: Current theory, research, and action.* Chicago, IL: Aldine.

Hess, R. D., & Croft, D. J. (1972). *Teachers of young children.* Boston, MA: Houghton Mifflin.

Hess, R. D., & Handel, G. (1995). *Family worlds: A psychosocial approach to family life.* Lanham, MD: University Press.

Elizabeth Jones
Texas A&M University
First edition

Tamara J. Martin
University of Texas of the Permian Basin
Second edition

HETEROPHORIA (See Strabismus, Effect on Learning)

HEWETT, FRANK M. (1927–   )

Frank M. Hewett received his MA in 1958 and PhD in 1961 in clinical psychology from the University of California in Los Angeles (UCLA). He remained at UCLA as principal of the Neuropsychiatric Institute School until 1964. He then joined the faculty in the Graduate School of Education, gaining his present status of professor of education and psychiatry in 1971.

Hewett's work has mainly dealt with the emotionally disturbed population (Hewett, 1987), and his contribution to the area of learning disabilities has been described as vital (Haring & Bateman, 1977, p. 47). Instead of entering the debate on the definition or etiology of learning disabilities, Hewett has sought educational strategies that allow a wider portion of public school children to learn effectively and efficiently (Hewett, 1988; Hewett & Forness, 1984). From a generalist orientation, he developed a sequence of educational tasks that delineate six levels of learning competence (Hewett & Taylor, 1980). These levels of learning competence are a synthesis of work on developmental stages done by Kephart, Piaget, Maslow, Freud, and others. Hewett's competence levels were operations directly related to classroom learning (Haring & Bateman, 1977). Hewett's principal publications include *Education of Exceptional Learners* and *The Emotionally Disturbed Child in the Classroom: The Orchestration of Success.*

REFERENCES

Haring, N. G., & Bateman, B. (1977). *Teaching the learning disabled child.* Englewood Cliffs, NJ: Prentice Hall.

Hewett, F. M. (1987). The ecological view of disturbed children: Shadow versus substance. *Pointer, 31,* 61–63.

Hewett, F. M. (1988). The engineered classroom re-visited. In R. B. Rutherford & C. M. Nelson (Eds.), *Bases of severe behavioral disorders in children and youth* (pp. 283–289). Boston, MA: College-Hill Press/Little, Brown.

Hewett, F. M., & Forness, S. (1984). *Education of exceptional learners* (3rd ed). Boston, MA: Allyn & Bacon.

Hewett, F. M., & Taylor, F. (1980). *The emotionally disturbed child in the classroom: The orchestration of success* (2nd ed). Boston, MA: Allyn & Bacon.

ELAINE FLETCHER-JANZEN
Chicago School of Professional Psychology
First edition

MARIE ALMOND
The University of Texas of the Permian Basin
Second edition

HIGHER EDUCATION, MINORITY STUDENTS WITH DISABILITIES

It is well known that college campuses are increasingly diverse (Newman, Wagner, Cameto, Knokey, & Shaver, 2010). Included in the diversity are students who are identified as both minority and disabled. In higher education the number of minority students with a disability has grown substantively in part because of legislation mandating the provision of educational services to them. It is now estimated that the percentage of minority students with a disability enrolled in undergraduate programs has doubled in the past three decades (KewalRamani, Gilbertson, Fox,

& Provasnik, 2007) owing to such legislation as Section 504 of the Rehabilitation Act of 1973, the Americans with Disabilities Act Amendments of 2008, and the 2008 Higher Education Opportunity Act.

Data from a national report (Raue, & Lewis, 2011) indicate that the most frequent student reported disabilities in postsecondary institutions include specific learning disabilities, attention-deficit/hyperactivity disorder, orthopedic impairments, and mental illness. Although a full description is beyond the scope of this entry; disabilities have unique characteristics that require varying levels of accommodation. Accommodations services are generally specified by an institution's Department of Disability Services within the Division of Student Affairs after reviewing documentation that establishes a disability and is provided sufficient information on the functional impact of the disability. The documentation provides relevant personnel (e.g., faculty) with an understanding of the student's disability and enough information to anticipate how the current impact of the disability interacts with courses, testing methods, and program requirements. Generally, accommodation services provided to college students with learning disabilities include additional exam time, classroom note-takers, faculty-provided written course notes, learning strategies or study skills, alternative exam formats, and adaptive equipment and technology.

Institutions of higher education have searched for innovative approaches to meet the needs of diverse students with disabilities. One example is the implementation of Universal Design (UD) across campuses nationwide (Raue & Lewis, 2011). UD in education generally refers to an approach that ensures that all learners have complete and equal access to the experience of learning. UD is not an accommodation specific for individuals with disabilities. It, allows, however, for all aspects of the educational experience to become more inclusive not only for students, but also parents, staff, instructors, and administrators regardless of their racial, disability, learning style, and race or ethnicity (Burgstahler, 2011).

UD encompasses a framework of teaching goals, instructional methodology, materials used in class, and assessment methods with the objective of optimizing the educational experience of every student (U.S. Department of Education, 2010). In the classroom, UD targets the improvement of the class climate by incorporating teaching practices that value diversity and inclusiveness. UD integrates various methods of delivery of information that are accessible to all students. Assessment in UD occurs regularly and includes group and cooperative performance, as well as individual achievement. Regular assessment facilitates the monitoring of students' progress and the necessary adjustments in instruction (Burgstahler, 2011). Despite its promise, institutions report obstacles to the full implementation of UD including insufficient staff training and costs associated with purchasing appropriate technology and materials (Raue & Lewis, 2011).

To better serve minority students with disabilities sensitivity and attention to competent multicultural education for all (e.g., administrators, faculty, staff) is important. Multicultural competence among institution professionals can be realized through demonstration of awareness, knowledge, and skills that promote effective and sensitive interactions with students with disabilities (Sue, Arredondo, & McDavis, 1992). At the individual level, professionals need to acknowledge and appreciate diversity as a pre-condition to the provision of services to minority students with special needs (J. Banks & Banks, 2004).

In addition to the focus on multicultural sensitivity and competence among personnel; postsecondary institutes have also turned their attention to academic success and retention of students with disabilities. Specific efforts focus on multifaceted strategies that include administrators, faculty, staff, parents, and students involved in monitoring progress toward meeting the institutional goals of serving the diverse student population with disabilities. These efforts take the form of student-centered evidence-based practices perceived as relevant and consistent with the institutional mission. Evidence-practices are based in theory and result from scientific research, not anecdotal evidence (National Registry of Evidence-Based Programs and Practices, 2011). One example includes having universities offer mentorship programs that facilitate the transition of minority students with disabilities from high school to postsecondary education (Stumbo et al., 2011). In addition to university directed efforts, it is expected that students will also advocate on their own behalves.

Most personnel in higher education who provide services to the diverse student population have the expectation that the students with disabilities will act as their own advocates and openly communicate their needs. As stated earlier, in many institutions, enrollment in the disability office entails bringing secondary school documentation or undergoing a new evaluation as evidence of need for services. Unfortunately, it is not uncommon for minority students with disabilities, especially if they come from another culture, to resist disclosing their need for accommodations or specific services. Often the resistance stems from cultural- or class-bound values or language differences (Valdez, Dvorscek, Budge, & Esmond, 2011). As evidence, a recent national report indicates that only 19% of students identified with a disability in secondary school received accommodations or support services in their higher education institutions (Newman et al., 2011). These students hesitate out of fear of exacerbating the stigma associated with having a disability (Denhart, 2008). For the minority students with disabilities, low disclosure rates stem from their different experiences and dimensions of power, traditions, and social stigma and shame (Harry, 1992).

For the students with disabilities comfortable in disclosing their special needs; the provision of services generally begins by meeting with an Accommodations Counselor who works on a case-by-case basis to identify services that are most suitable to the student (Raue & Lewis, 2011). Although many institutions see this practice as inherently conducive to the academic success of their clientele, this view is not always shared by the minority students with disabilities who access the department specialized in providing them with support. Specifically, when asked about difficulties during college, minority students with disabilities often report not being understood by others, having to work more than nondisabled students, and having to independently seek specific strategies to ensure success in college even though they hesitate to ask for supplemental services.

It is therefore imperative that higher education institutions play a role in the process of facilitating the academic success of their minority students with disabilities through a process of adaptation and commitment to understanding and respecting these students and their specific needs (Bahm & Forchuck, 2009). Some important references and websites include: states' higher education coordinating boards, states' councils for disabilities, the U.S. Department of Education, and the Council for Exceptional Children. These resources include guidelines on the transition from secondary schools to higher education institutions and clear, specific statements about the provision of services to minority students with disabilities. In addition, these references serve as essential tools to be used by the professionals working with minority students with disabilities in their continued search for sensitive and multiculturally competent educational practices so they can best serve their minority students with special needs.

REFERENCES

Bahm, A., & Forchuk, C. (2009). Interlocking oppressions: The effect of a comorbid physical disability on perceived stigma and discrimination among mental health consumers in Canada. *Health & Social Care in the Community, 17*, 63–70. doi:10.1111/j.1365-2524.2008.00799.x

Banks, J. A., & Banks, C. A. M. (2004). *Multicultural education: Issues and perspectives* (5th ed). Hoboken, NJ: Wiley.

Burgstahler, S. (2011). *Universal design of instruction (UDI): Definition, principles, guidelines, and examples.* University of Washington, Seattle. Retrieved from http://www.uw.edu/doit/

Denhart, H. (2008). Deconstructing barriers: Perceptions of students labeled with learning disabilities in higher education. *Journal of Learning Disabilities, 41*(6), 483–497. doi: 10.1177/0022219408321151

Harry, B. (1992). *Cultural diversity, families, and the special education system: Communication and empowerment.* New York, NY: Teachers College Press.

KewalRamani, A., Gilbertson, L., Fox, M., & Provasnik, S. (2007). *Status and trends in the education of racial and ethnic minorities (NCES 2007–039).* National Center for Education Statistics, Institute of Education Sciences, U.S.

Department of Education. Washington, DC. Retrieved from http://nces.ed.gov/pubs2007/2007039.pdf

National Registry of Evidence-Based Programs and Practices. (2011). *Evidence-based practices.* Washington, DC: Substance Abuse and Mental Health Services Administration. Retrieved from http://nrepp.samhsa.gov

Newman, L., Wagner, M., Cameto, R., Knokey, A-M., & Shaver, D. (2010). *Comparisons across time of the outcomes of youth with disabilities up to 4 years after high school.* A report of findings from the National Longitudinal Transition Study (NLTS) and the National Longitudinal Transition Study-2 (NLTS-2) (NCSER 2010–3008). Menlo Park, CA: SRI International. Retrieved from http://policyweb.sri.com/cehs/publications/nlts2_report_2010_09.pdf

Newman, L., Wagner, M., Knokey, A.-M., Marder, C., Nagle, K., Shaver, D.,...Schwarting, M. (2011). *The post-high school outcomes of young adults with disabilities up to 8 years after high school. A report from the national longitudinal transition study-2 (NLTS2)* (NCSER 2011–3005). Menlo Park, CA: SRI International. Retrieved from http://ies.ed.gov/ncser/pubs/20113005/pdf/20113005.pdf

Raue, K., & Lewis, L. (2011). *Students with disabilities at degree-granting postsecondary institutions (NCES 2011–018).* U.S. Department of Education, National Center for Education Statistics. Washington, DC: U.S. Government Printing Office.

Stumbo, N. J., Martin, J. K. Nordstrom, D. Rolfe, T., Burgstahler, S.,...Misquez, (2011). Evidence-based practices in mentoring students with disabilities: Four case studies. *Journal of Science Education for Students with Disabilities, 14,* 1, 33–54.

Sue, D. W., Arredondo, P., & McDavis, R. J. (1992). Multicultural counseling competencies and standards: A call to the profession. *Journal of Counseling & Development, 70,* 477–486.

U.S. Department of education. (2010). Retrieved from www.ed.gov

Valdez, C. R., Dvorscek, M. J., Budge, S. L., & Esmond, S. (2011). Provider perspectives about Latino patients: Determinants of care and implications for treatment. *Counseling Psychologist, 39,* 497–526. doi: 10.1177/0011000010385012

CATHARINA CARVALHO
JORGE E. GONZALEZ
Fourth edition

HIGH-FUNCTIONING AUTISM

The term high-functioning autism (HFA) was first used by DeMyer, Hingtgen and Jackson (1981). HFA is most often used to describe individuals on the autism spectrum without intellectual disabilities (IQ > 70; Gillberg, 1998; Thede & Coolidge, 2007). This classification has generated debate, particularly regarding the distinction between Asperger's Syndrome (AS) and HFA (Ghaziuddin & Mountain-Kimchi, 2004). Although both subgroups are classified as pervasive developmental disorders and are identified by impairments in social interaction and repetitive, stereotypic behaviors, AS, or Asperger's Syndrome is recognized within the American Psychological Association's (APA) *Diagnostic and Statistical Manual of Mental Disorders*, Fourth Edition, Text Revision (*DSM-IV-TR*) and HFA is not (APA, 2000; Noterdaeme, Wriedt, & Hohne, 2010).

Witwer and Lecavalier (2008) reviewed 22 studies examining the subtypes of ASD and concluded that the reports did not support a diagnostic difference between AS and HFA and that any variance among the subgroups might better be accounted for by IQ scores. Other studies have examined differences in anxiety levels, motor skills, and executive functioning and found similarly inconclusive evidence for a clinical distinction (Ghaziuddin & Mountain-Kimchi, 2004; Sciutto & Cantwell, 2005).

REFERENCES

American Psychiatric Association (2000). *Diagnostic and statistical manual of mental disorders* (4th ed., text rev.). Washington, DC: Author.

DeMyer, M., Hingtgen, J., & Jackson, R. (1981). Infantile autism reviewed: A decade of research. *Schizophrenia Bulletin, 7,* 388–451.

Ghaziuddin, M., & Mountain-Kimchi, K. (2004). Defining the intellectual profile of Asperger syndrome: Comparison with high-functioning autism. *Journal of Autism & Developmental Disorders, 34,* 279–284.

Gillberg, C. (1998). Asperger syndrome and high-functioning autism. *British Journal of Psychiatry: The Journal of Mental Science, 172,* 200–209.

Noterdaeme, M., Wriedt, E., & Höhne, C. (2010). Asperger's syndrome and high-functioning autism: Language, motor and cognitive profiles. *European Child & Adolescent Psychiatry, 19,* 475–481.

Sciutto, M., & Cantwell, C. (2005). Factors influencing the differential diagnosis of Asperger's disorder and high-functioning autism. *Journal of Developmental & Physical Disabilities, 17,* 345–359.

Thede, L., & Coolidge, F. (2007). Psychological and neurobehavioral comparisons of children with Asperger's disorder versus high-functioning autism. *Journal of Autism & Developmental Disorders, 37,* 847–854.

Witwer, A., & Lecavalier, L. (2008). Examining the validity of autism spectrum disorder subtypes. *Journal of Autism & Developmental Disorders, 38,* 1611–1624.

BROOKE PFEIFFER
RUSSELL LANG
Texas State University–San Marcos
Fourth edition

HIGH-FUNCTIONING AUTISM/ASPERGER'S IN MATHEMATICS

Few studies have examined mathematics interventions for students with high functioning autism/Asperger's syndrome (HFA/AS), however, these students have been found to respond to interventions that were developed for students with nonverbal learning disabilities (NLD; Donaldson & Zager, 2010; Goldstein, Beers, Siegel, & Minshew; 2001; Joseph, Tager-Flusberg, & Lord, 2002; Mayes & Calhoun, 2003, 2005). Students with NLD typically have difficulties in mathematics. Among the difficulties that students with HFA/AS may have that affect their mathematical performance are remembering steps in a complex algorithm (Goldstein, Minshew, & Siegal, 1994; Griswold, Barnhill, Smith Myles, Hagiwara, & Simpson, 2002; Minshew, Goldstein, Taylor, & Siegel, 1994), organizing information and attention (Mayes & Calhoun, 2003), and understanding instructions or word problems (Minshew et al., 1994; Whitby, Travers, & Harnik, 2009). Self-regulation, direct instruction, goal structure, concrete-representational-abstract (CRA), and Integrated Behavioral Experiential Teaching (IBET) are strategies that have been shown to be effective when used with students with NDL, and can be used effectively with students with HFA/AS (Donaldson & Zager, 2010). In addition, to reviewing these strategies, a strategy instruction curriculum package, *Solve It!* (Montague, 1996, 2003), is discussed.

Self-regulation involves providing the student with a checklist for each step in an algorithm. Self-regulation uses verbal feedback, where the student verbally repeats each step to ensure a stronger relationship between the steps used to arrive at the correct answer and recall of the steps in later independent practice. The final step in the process is teacher feedback following completion of a problem.

Another strategy is direct instruction. This approach is a form of systematic instruction in which the teacher first provides several examples of each step needed to complete a mathematical problem. The teacher works through each step as they model their thinking aloud; the teacher may also model common errors. Next, the students are expected to practice similar problems while the teacher provides prompts and guidance to ensure each student's success. The teacher rewards correct actions/responses and redirects incorrect actions/responses. The goal of direct instruction is to give students enough practice with prompting and guidance so the students can correctly perform each step of the process independently. Direct instruction has been shown to increase success in computation and addition and subtraction word problems.

An additional approach is goal structure, which involves setting a learning goal and rewarding the learner when an appropriate performance level is reached. This method encourages students to collaborate with the teacher in setting goals and rewards; this will lead to greater investment in the process by the student.

Students often set performance levels desired by teachers, which indicates that students understand appropriate levels of performance (Miller, Buller, & Lee, 1998). Goal structure has been used to teach computation.

CRA is another strategy that has been used to teach fractions, computation, and algebra. In CRA, students first work with concrete objects before moving on to a representation of the object, then in the final step, the student works at the abstract level. For example, in studying fractions, a teacher may bring in a cookie, an apple, and a pizza and cut each in half to show a concrete representation of what $\frac{1}{2}$ looks like and what $\frac{1}{2}$ means. In the next stage, the representational stage, the teacher will teach the lesson using photographs of the actual objects that are cut in half. Still at the representational stage, but working toward the abstract stage, the teacher may use black line drawings of things that have been halved, because drawings are more abstract than photographs. At the last stage, the abstract stage, students use numbers to show their understanding.

IBET has been used to instruct students in both basic academic skills as well as social skills. IBET combines parts of direct instruction and CRA to create concrete experiences that students will retain. IBET uses students' personal experiences to make learning meaningful and emphasizes experiential learning or learning by doing. IBET also uses systematic reinforcement and errorless learning, which relies on positive reinforcement.

Finally, *Solve It!* is a curriculum that has been shown to be effective in teaching students with HFA/AS to solve mathematical word problems (Montague, 2003; Whitby, Travers, & Harnik, 2009). The curriculum teaches seven cognitive strategies and three meta-cognitive strategies. The cognitive strategies are read, paraphrase, visualize, hypothesize, estimate, compute, and check. The three meta-cognitive strategies are self-management, self-questioning, and self-evaluation. Instruction is broken into four steps: (1) performance assessment and identification of students to receive *Solve It!* instruction, (2) explicit strategy instruction, (3) modeling, and (4) evaluation of outcomes with emphasis on strategy maintenance and generalization.

In conclusion, it is important for the reader to note the heterogeneous nature of HFA/AS. Due to the heterogeneity, a strategy that leads to success for one student with HFA/AS may not necessarily lead to success with another student with HFA/AS. The mathematical difficulties discussed above are a starting point that should be informed by direct observation of the student with data from curriculum-based assessment (Whitby et al., 2009) used to determine which strategy has the best chance of leading to a positive outcome.

REFERENCES

Donaldson, J. B., & Zager, D. (2010). Mathematics interventions for students with high functioning autism/Asperger's syndrome. *Teaching Exceptional Children, 42,* 40–46.

Goldstein, G., Beers, S. R., Siegel, D. J., & Minshew, N. J. (2001). A comparison of WAIS-R profiles in adults with high-functioning autism or differing subtypes of learning disability. *Applied Neuropsychology*, *8*, 148–154.

Goldstein, G., Minshew, N. J., & Siegal, D. J. (1994). Age differences in academic achievement in high-functioning autistic individuals. *Journal of Clinical and Experimental Neuropsychology*, *16*, 671–680.

Griswold, D. E., Barnhill, G. P., Smith Myles, B., Hagiwara, T., & Simpson, R. (2002). Asperger's syndrome and academic achievement. *Focus on Autism and Other Developmental Disabilities*, *17*, 94–102.

Joseph, R. M., Tager-Flusberg, H., & Lord, C. (2002). Cognitive profiles and social-communicative functioning in children with autism spectrum disorder. *Journal of Child Psychology and Psychiatry*, *43*, 807–821.

Mayes, S. D., & Calhoun, S. L. (2003). Analysis of WISC-III, Stanford-Binet: IV, and academic achievement test scores in children with autism. *Journal of Autism and Developmental Disorders*, *33*, 329–341.

Mayes. S. D., & Calhoun, S. L. (2005). Frequency of reading, math, and writing disabilities in children with clinical disorders. *Learning and Individual Differences*, *16*, 145–157.

Miller, S. P, Buller, F. M., & Lee. K. (1998). Validated practices for teaching mathematics to students with learning disabilities: A review of the literature. *Focus on Exceptional Children*, *31*, 1–24.

Minshew, N. J., Goldstein. G., Taylor, H. G., & Siegel, D. J. (1994). Academic achievement in high functioning autistic individuals. *Journal of Clinical and Experimental Neuropsychology*. *16*, 261–270.

Montague, M. (1996). Assessing mathematical word problem solving. *Learning Disabilities Practice*, *11*, 238–248.

Montague, M. (2003). *Solve It! A Practical Approach to Teaching Mathematical Problem Solving Skills*. Reston, VA: Exceptional Innovations.

Whitby, P. J. S., Travers, J. C., & Harnik, J. (2009). Academic achievement and strategy instruction to support the learning of children with high-functioning autism. *Beyond Behavior*, *19*, 3–9.

JAMIE DURAN
Texas A&M University
Fourth edition

HIGH-INCIDENCE DISABILITIES

Although often used synonymously, the terms incidence and prevalence are not equivalent and therefore interchangeable use is erroneous. Marozas, May, and Lehman (1980) note that incidence represents new cases during some specified period of time (frequently 1 year), while prevalence denotes the total number of individuals affected at any particular point in time. Hypothetically, a school system might find 75 previously unidentified cases of learning disabilities during a specific academic year. If 150 previously identified cases are then added, prevalence is 225. This total may then be used to specify a prevalence rate; if the school system contains 10,000 students the prevalence rate is 225/10,000, or about 2%.

Prevalence and incidence need not reflect the same proportions of the population. For example, if an effective preventive technique could be found to prevent the occurrence of a disabling condition (but not remediate it), the incidence rate (new cases) approaches zero. However, the prevalence rate would fall off more gradually since existing cases would continue. The terms are related but distinct. Blurring the distinction can result in the development of inaccurate statistics or the erroneous interpretation of statistics.

The expression high-incidence disability refers to an exceptionally large proportion of a particular type of exceptionality during some particular period of time relative to the incidence of other conditions. The expression high incidence is arbitrarily defined, however, as no specific numerical proportion is required. Unfortunately, the special education literature provides mention of both high-incidence and high-prevalence disability; therefore, the reader must keep this distinction in mind.

REFERENCE

Marozas, P. S., May, D. C., & Lehman, L. C. (1980). Incidence and prevalence: Confusion in need of clarification. *Intellectual Developmental Disabilities*, *18*, 229–230.

TED L. MILLER
University of Tennessee at Chattanooga

See also Categorical Education

HIGH INTEREST–LOW VOCABULARY

High interest–low vocabulary refers to reading materials that have been designed to interest older students who have low vocabularies and low reading levels. Often, adolescents who have reading levels in the lower elementary grade levels become even more frustrated if given the reading books that have been designed for their reading levels. Such reading books can insult adolescents because they are geared for the interest level of a third grader, not a ninth grader.

Many publishers have designed materials to deal with this problem. For example, the *Corrective Reading* series (Engelmann et al., 1978) was designed for students from

4th to 12th grade who have not developed adequate reading, decoding, and comprehension skills. The vocabulary introduced in these stories was very controlled. Only word patterns that have been taught and practiced were included in the lessons (low vocabulary). More important, however, the interest level of the stories was geared to the older reader; the topics covered did not insult the older reader by assuming his or her interests were similar to those of a third grader.

Other published materials were also designed to be used as supplements for the older, lower reader's instructional program. C. Mercer and Mercer (1985) present a listing of 35 such materials, with corresponding reading grade levels and approximate interest grade levels. The *Pal Paperback Kits* (Xerox Education Publications) and the *Mystery Adventure Series* (Benefic Press) are two examples. These series, however, do not present as carefully sequenced phonetic skills as a linguistic basal reader series or *Corrective Reading* series previously mentioned.

Online resources for individuals interested in these types of books and related products abound. The Resource Room, an online resource for special educators and parents, supplies a broad analysis of high-interest–low vocabulary books and rationale for their design. The Resource Room website can be found at http://resourceroom.net/.

REFERENCES

S., Johnson, G., Hanner, S., Carnine, L., Meyers, L., Osborn, S., ... Becker, J. (1978). *Corrective reading program*. Chicago, IL: Science Research.

Mercer, C. D., & Mercer, A. R. (1985). *Teaching students with learning problems* (2nd ed). Columbus, OH: Merrill.

Thomas E. Scruggs
Margo A. Mastropieri
Purdue University

HIGHLY QUALIFIED TEACHERS

The passage of the No Child Left Behind Act (NCLB) of 2001 marked a growing, bipartisan recognition to address the challenge of raising the academic achievement for all students. At the core of NCLB are measures designed to close achievement gaps between different groups of students, offering more flexibility to states, giving parents more options, and teaching students based on what works (Office of Elementary and Secondary Education, 2005). The NCLB, signed into law on January 8, 2002 (Tuerk, 2005), has expanded the federal role in education and set requirements in place that affect every public school in the United States. To meet the standard of high academic achievement for all students, NCLB issued the mandate that every child be instructed by a teacher who meets the rigorous standards for earning a "highly qualified" classification.

NCLB is the latest revision of the 1965 Elementary and Secondary Education Act (ESEA) and is regarded as the most significant federal education policy initiative in a generation (deBettencourt, 2004). Under the law's strong accountability provisions, states must describe how they will close the achievement gap and make sure all students, including those with disabilities, achieve academically. The specific goals of the law, as spelled out in the *Federal Register* issued on March 6, 2002, are:

- All students will reach high standards, at a minimum attaining proficiency or better in reading and mathematics by 2013 to 2014.
- By 2013 to 2014, all students will be proficient in reading by the end of the third grade.
- All limited English proficient students will become proficient in English.
- All students will be educated in learning environments that are safe, drug free, and conducive to learning.
- All students will graduate from high school.

To help schools and districts meet these goals, the law provides a blend of requirements, incentives, and resources. The requirements include (Paige, 2004):

- Annual testing of all students against state standards in reading and mathematics in grades 3 to 8 and in science at three times in a student's school career (including once in high school).
- "Verification" of each state's assessment system via required participation (every other year) by selected districts in the NAEP test.
- Aggregate and disaggregate analysis and reporting of student achievement results.
- A state definition and timeline for determining whether a school, district, and the state are making "adequate yearly progress" (AYP) toward the goal of 100% of students meeting state standards by the 2013 to 2014 school year.
- Support for students not meeting standards and/or for those who have special needs (e.g., homeless, limited English proficiency).
- The use of "scientifically based" programs and strategies.
- Technical assistance, and then sanctions, for schools, districts, and the state for failure to make AYP.
- Highly qualified teachers in core academic subjects by 2005 to 2006.
- Highly qualified aides or paraprofessionals.

Highly Qualified Teachers

A major objective of NCLB is to ensure high-quality teachers for all students, regardless of race, ethnicity or income, because a well-prepared teacher is vitally important to a child's education (Rosenberg, Sindelar, & Hardman, 2004). In fact, research demonstrates the clear correlation between student academic achievement and teacher quality (Sanders & Rivers, 1996). Subsequent to the full implementation of the highly qualified mandate, all school principals are required by law to send a notification to each child's parent/guardian informing them if their child's teacher does not meet the mandate. According to Sanders and Rivers, parents should never hesitate to inquire within their school and district about the qualifications of teachers instructing their children.

The purpose of NCLB is to help states and school districts ensure that all students have highly qualified teachers; that is, teachers with the subject matter knowledge and teaching skills necessary to help all children achieve high academic standards, regardless of individual learning styles or needs. The NCLB Act requires local school districts to ensure that all teachers hired to teach core academic subjects after the first day of the 2002 to 2003 school year are highly qualified (Paige, 2004). The requirements to be considered "highly qualified" are threefold (Office of Elementary and Secondary Education, 2005): (1) teachers should hold at least a bachelor's degree; (2) teachers should be fully licensed by the State; and (3) teachers should demonstrate competency in each core subject area in which they teach. According to NCLB, core subjects include English, reading or language arts, mathematics, science, foreign languages, civics and government, economics, arts, history and geography. NCLB also calls for all teachers of the core academic subjects (teaching in Title I programs or elsewhere) to be highly qualified by the end of school year 2005 to 2006 (Paige, 2004).

Current teachers do not have to return to school or take a test in every subject to demonstrate that they meet highly qualified requirements. NCLB allows states to create an alternative method (High, Objective, Uniform State Standard of Evaluation or HOUSSE) for teachers not new to the field—as determined by each state—to certify that they know the subject they teach by demonstrating content-related competencies that recognize, among other things, the experience, expertise, and professional training garnered over time in the profession (Paige, 2004).

Highly Qualified Provisions for Special Education Teachers

NCLB does not differentiate between special educators and general educators. This is most evident within the recent reauthorization of the Individuals with Disabilities Act, known as the Individuals with Disabilities Education Improvement Act (IDEIA). IDEIA specifies the requirements for a highly qualified special education teacher in that only special education teachers who teach core academic subjects must meet highly qualified teacher requirements (Mooney, Denny, & Gunter, 2004). The professionals who do *not* need to meet highly qualified requirements include the following (Paige, 2004): (1) special education teachers who provide consultation to teachers of core academic subjects by adapting curricula or selecting appropriate teaching strategies/accommodations; (2) resource room teachers who do not teach core academic subjects for a grade or credit; and (3) special education teachers who team teach in a general education classroom (this also holds true whether the special education teacher gives the grade for the team-taught class). If a special education teacher is providing direct instruction in multiple subject areas at the secondary level, he or she *must* satisfy the highly qualified definition at the secondary level for each of those content areas (Office of Elementary and Secondary Education, 2005). Teachers at the secondary level can demonstrate their qualifications if they meet one or more of the following requirements (deBettencourt, 2004): (1) a major in the subject they teach; (2) a minimum of 24 credit hours of professional development courses that are equivalent to a major in the subject; (3) passage of a state-developed test; (4) a graduate degree; (5) an advanced certification from the state; or (6) HOUSSE. HOUSSE allows current teachers to demonstrate subject matter competency and meet highly qualified teacher requirements. Proof may consist of a combination of teaching experience, professional development, and knowledge in the subject garnered over time in the profession (deBettencourt, 2004).

Conclusion

An integral component within NCLB is that it will provide substantial funding to help states and districts recruit, train, reward, and retain effective teachers, toward ensuring that teachers of core academic subjects meet certain minimum requirements they need to become effective educators. To further the goal of having a highly qualified teacher in every classroom, traditional approaches for preparing teachers must be expanded to include preparation programs that are innovative and nontraditional and can be made available to "*anyone, anytime, and anywhere*" (Paige, 2004, p. 39). States should be provided with financial assistance in the form of personnel preparation grants, which can prompt this innovation and reform. Through these efforts, the goal of providing all students with highly qualified teachers will be achieved.

REFERENCES

deBettencourt, L. (2004). Critical issues in training special education teachers. *Exceptionality, 12*, 193–194.

Mooney, P., Denny, R., & Gunter, P. (2004). The impact of NCLB and the reauthorization of IDEA on academic instruction of students with emotional or behavioral disorders. *Behavioral Disorders, 29,* 237–246.

Office of Elementary and Secondary Education. (2005). *Improving teacher quality state grants: Non-regulatory guidance.* U.S. Department of Education. Retrieved from www.ed.gov/programs/teacherqual/

Paige, R. (2004). *The secretary's third annual report on teacher quality.* U.S. Department of Education, Office of Postsecondary Education. Retrieved from http://www.ed.gov/

Rosenberg, M., Sindelar, P., & Hardman, M. (2004). Preparing highly qualified teachers for students with emotional or behavioral disorders: The impact of NCLB and IDEA. *Behavioral Disorders, 29,* 266–278.

Sanders, W., & Rivers, J. (1996). *Cumulative and residual effects of teachers on future academic achievement.* Knoxville: University of Tennessee Value-Added Research and Assessment Center.

Tuerk, P. (2005). Research in the high-stakes era: Achievement, resources, and no child left behind. *Psychological Science, 16,* 419–425.

JULIE A. ARMENTROUT
University of Colorado at Colorado Springs

See also Individuals With Disabilities Education Improvement; Act of 2004 (Ideia); Response to Intervention

HIGH RISK

The phrase high risk refers to a baby at risk for the development of a disability owing to factors present prior to conception, during pregnancy, delivery, or the first three years of life. Presently, couples contemplating having a baby take a 3% to 5% chance of producing a high-risk child (Deppe, Sherman, & Engel, 1981). This percentage can be reduced by developing awareness of factors that can place a child at risk and taking steps to minimize their impact.

The first set of factors that place a child at risk occurs prior to conception and is hereditary in nature. Hereditary factors include the genetic history of both parents. Specifically, parents may produce a high-risk child if either has a mentally or physically disabled child in the extended family; is a known or suspected carrier of a chromosome abnormality; is Black or of Jewish or Mediterranean descent. In addition, hereditary factors include previous miscarriages during the first trimester of pregnancy and a maternal age greater than 35 at the time of anticipated birth. Couples falling into any of these categories may seek genetic counseling to estimate the risk of occurrence of a genetic disorder, understand options available for dealing with the risk, decide on a course of action, and increase their knowledge of diagnosis, prognosis, and management techniques available.

The second set of factors increasing the probability of producing a high-risk child occurs during pregnancy. Specific factors include maternal malnutrition, use of alcohol or drugs, smoking, and exposure to diseases. Maternal malnutrition has been related to intellectual developmental disabilities, cerebral palsy, and learning disabilities. Use of alcohol during pregnancy has been linked to intellectual developmental disabilities, joint distortions, facial abnormalities, and congenital heart disease (Furey, 1982; Merck, 2003). Medicine purchased over the counter or by prescription may adversely influence the health of a baby. For example, disabled babies were born to women using thalidomide. Similarly, there is an increased incidence of vaginal cancer in young women whose mothers used diethylstilbestrol to prevent miscarriages. Other drugs, such as heroin, have been linked to an increased incidence of low birth weight, intrauterine growth, retardation, and prematurity (Crain, 1984; Merck, 2003). Smoking has been associated with smaller birth weight and may be a factor in sudden infant death syndrome. Exposure to diseases such as German measles is associated with visual impairments, hearing impairments, and heart disease. Couples anticipating the birth of a child can take precautionary steps to reduce the chance of producing a high-risk baby. These steps include proper diet, use of medicines only under the supervision of a physician, limited consumption of alcohol, and no cigarette or drug use.

The third set of factors associated with the birth of high-risk babies occurs during the perinatal period. These factors include the use of an anesthesia, hemorrhage, knotting of the umbilical cord, and shock owing to loss of blood in the mother (Cartwright, Cartwright, & Ward, 1995; Merck, 2003). All of these factors may cause fetal anoxia (lack of oxygen), resulting in intellectual developmental disabilities, cerebral palsy, or convulsive disorders.

Finally, factors placing a child at high risk may occur from birth to 3 years of age and include physical trauma, deprivation, and severe infection. Physical traumas such as accidents may result in brain damage or a physical disability. Similarly, children who suffer nonaccidental injuries such as child abuse may be brain damaged, physically disabled, or emotionally disturbed. Deprivation includes physical neglect (e.g., inadequate levels of medical attention, food, clothing, supervision, and housing) and emotional neglect (an environment nonconducive to a child's learning and development). Severe infections such as meningitis, rheumatic fever, or encephalitis frequently result in hearing impairments, heart damage, or convulsive disorders. Many of the factors placing a child at risk from birth to 3 years of age can be controlled by parents or professionals. Careful supervision of young children, adequate physical and emotional care, and prompt medical attention can minimize the impact of high-risk factors during the first three years of life.

The U.S. National Library of Medicine and the National Institutes of Health provide prodigious resources concerning high-risk situations on MedlinePlus at http://www.nlm.nih.gov/.

REFERENCES

Cartwright, G. P., Cartwright, C. A., & Ward, M. E. (1995). *Educating special learners*. Belmont, CA: Wadsworth.

Crain, L. S. (1984). Prenatal causes of atypical development. In M. J. Hanson (Ed.), *Atypical infant development* (pp. 27–55). Baltimore, MD: University Park Press.

Deppe, P. R., Sherman, J. L., & Engel, S. (1981). *The high risk child: A guide for concerned parents*. New York, NY: Macmillan.

Furey, E. M. (1982). The effects of alcohol on the fetus. *Exceptional Children, 49*, 30–34.

Merck. (2003). *Risk factors that develop during pregnancy*. Retrieved from http://www.merck.com/index.html

Maureen A. Smith
Pennsylvania State University

See also **Genetic Counseling; High-Risk Registry; Prematurity**

HIGH-RISK REGISTRY

A high-risk registry is based on the premise that early identification of infants and young children with disabilities is critical to the success of an early intervention treatment program. The registry contains factors associated with an increased risk for the development of a handicapping condition (Feinmesser & Tell, 1974). These factors typically include birth weight of less than 1,500 gram; bilirubin level of less than 20 mg/100 ml of serums; exposure to or the presence of bacterial infections such as meningitis; exposure to or the presence of nonbacterial infections such as rubella or herpes; multiple apneic spells; and 5-minute Apgar scores less than 5.

The Apgar score (Apgar, 1953) is a simple measure of neonatal risk routinely obtained during the medical assessment of a newborn infant 1 and 5 minutes after delivery. The infant's heart rate, respiration, reflex irritability, muscle tone, and skin color are rated on the basis of 0, 1, or 2. For example, a heart rate between 100 and 140 beats per minute is rated a 2, while a heart rate less than 100 beats per minute is rated 1; no heartbeat is rated 0. A composite score reflects the infant's ability to adapt to the postnatal environment (Gorski, 1984). Scores under 3 at the 5-minute Apgar assessment predict quite certainly that neurodevelopmental impairments and

learning difficulties will be present later on in life (Moster, Lie, & Markestad, 2002).

The staff at a hospital participating in a high-risk registry typically completes a card after each live birth. Information regarding birth weight, billirubin levels, the presence of bacterial or nonbacterial infections, apneic spells, and Apgar scores is provided by the obstetric staff or the attending physician. Maternal interviews provide additional information regarding exposure to bacterial or nonbacterial infections and any parental concern for the health of the baby. The presence of any one of these factors tentatively identifies an infant as at risk and warrants referral for additional evaluation at 6, 9, and 12 months of age. If during subsequent evaluation, the baby no longer displays any abnormal characteristics, and if parents express no concern, the baby's name is removed from the files. If subsequent evaluation does indicate the presence of a disability, the parents are encouraged to pursue additional assessment, a medical evaluation, and a treatment program.

REFERENCES

Apgar, V. (1953). A proposal for a new method of resolution of the newborn infant. *Current Researchers in Anesthesia & Analgesia, 32*, 260–267.

Feinmesser, M., & Tell, L. (1974). Evaluation of methods for detecting hearing impairment in infancy and early childhood. In G. T. Mencher (Ed.), *Early identification of hearing loss* (pp. 102–113). Pratteln, Switzerland: Thur AG Offsetdruck.

Gorski, P. A. (1984). Infants at risk. In M. J. Hanson (Ed.), *Atypical infant development* (pp. 59–75). Baltimore, MD: University Park Press.

Moster, D., Lie, R. T., & Markestad, T. (2002). Joint association of Apgar scores and early neonatal symptoms with minor disabilities at school age. *Archives of Disease in Childhood Fetal and Neonatal Edition, 86*, 16–21.

Maureen A. Smith
Pennsylvania State University

See also **Early Experience and Critical Periods; Early Identification of Children With Disabilities; High Risk; Infant Stimulation; Prematurity**

HIGH SCHOOLS, POSITIVE BEHAVIOR SUPPORTS

High School School-wide Positive Behavior Support (SWPBS) is a multitiered framework used in high schools to build a school-wide culture that supports both academic and social success. The SWPBS framework was developed in the early 1990s and has primarily been implemented in elementary and middle schools. Though SWPBS was not implemented in high schools until 1998, the number of high schools implementing SWPBS is growing at a steady rate. Of the more than 11,000 schools now adopting SWPBS, more than 1,000 are high schools.

Similar to any initiative, the adoption of SWPBS in high schools requires attention to two things: (1) the key features (SWPBS) and (2) the context (high school). Since SWPBS is a framework, the same key features are applicable across all grade levels. The key features within SWPBS are: (a) investment in prevention, (b) selection and definition of valued outcomes by stakeholders, (c) academic and behavioral practices at multiple levels of intensity, (d) use of data for decision making, and (e) use of organizational systems (Colvin, Kameenui, & Sugai, 1993; Sugai & Horner, 2002; Sugai, Sprague, Horner, & Walker, 2000).

What makes SWPBS in high schools unique is the context in which it is implemented. High schools that are successful have attended to five contextual variables in the implementation of SWPBS: size, infrastructure, student age, teacher philosophies, and expected school outcomes. High schools by and large have average student bodies of 1,000 to 2,000 and faculty/staff of about 110 to 150. They have larger buildings with more open space, more resources (e.g., counseling, career centers, security), and multiple levels of courses and clubs/activities for students. This impacts the number of people who must buy in to the initiative, the needed communication systems between administrators, teachers, and students, and the number of both settings and students that need to be considered when implementing practices.

Most high school principals have an administrative team from assistant principals to department chairs to whom they delegate management, instructional and decision-making responsibilities. To reduce fragmentation, it is critical for the principal to work with the administrative team to ensure philosophical alignment, consistency and integration of SWPBS into the team's responsibilities (Flannery, Guest, & Horner, 2010). Due to the focus of high schools on student achievement toward graduation and postsecondary life, they often utilize departmental or curricular organization that allows for maximized content expertise. A drawback, however, is that this structure provides few opportunities for interdisciplinary collaboration among content instructors and specialists. The faculty are used to working within their department structure and pedagogical approach rather than across departments for a more school-wide approach. High schools often need additional assistance to establish a team focused on school-wide systems and practices. The school-wide team needs to use the infrastructure of departments or divisions to obtain representation and input from the diverse faculty and staff.

The students in high school are at the adolescent stage of development and, thus, the students place greater value on being actively involved in decision making and are influenced greatly by their peer groups. Implementation in high schools, unlike in the lower grade levels, must involve students in the development and evaluation of SWPBS. Put simply, if students do not value the system, it will not likely be successful. Schools need to seek input from the students through mechanisms such as membership on the School-Wide Leadership Team, establishment of an advisory group, survey input, or systematically soliciting input from existing student groups (e.g., Link Crew, student government). Schools also have given students a role in the implementation efforts such as developing videos to teach expectations, students teaching the expectations to small groups of students, students developing and implementing student surveys, or math classes taking the responsibility of analyzing and graphing school-wide data.

High school teachers are hired because of their expertise in a specific content area. They often place the emphasis of their role on the teaching of the content itself and less on the impact of the learning for individual students. Additionally, high school teachers' expectations of their students are different from those in the lower grades (Lane, Pierson, Stang, & Carter, 2010). The expectation is that students take increased responsibility for their behavioral and academic performances (Isakson & Jarvis, 1999) and are often removed to other classes or alternative environments when there is a discrepancy with the expected level of performance. When teachers understand the linkage between academic and behavioral performance as well as the relationship to discipline issues and available instructional time, they see the need to expand their role as a teacher to not only their content area but the social behaviors necessary for learning it. The high school SWPBS Leadership Teams need to work with teachers to see the link between teaching of academics and teaching of social behaviors and include the teaching of social behaviors relevant to academic performance (e.g., note taking, group participation, managing books and materials).

High schools implementing SWPBS work to build a school culture where teachers and staff are responsible for, not only what happens in their classroom, but for all school locations (for example, cafeteria, hallways, locker room, restroom, athletic events). High schools, different from elementary schools and most middle schools, have more open and common areas in the school, schedules in which students change classrooms each period, and schedules that allow students to have periods when they are not in a supervised class. The results of the student interactions during any of these unsupervised times often impacts how the student acts in the classroom—they don't leave it at the classroom door. As teachers are impacted by what happens outside of their classroom, they and administrators need to attend to what happens in other locations of the school as well.

Last, high school completion rates (graduation, credit accrual), engagement rates (attendance, skip/truancy, drop out), and achievement scores (state assessments) are used as measures of accountability for high schools. Current data systems are developed for district and state accountability rather than for school-level decision making. High schools are working to be able to examine these categories of data on a regular basis (Kennedy et al., 2009) and publicly disseminate their outcomes.

REFERENCES

Colvin, G., Kameenui, E., & Sugai, G. (1993). Reconceptualizing behavior management and school-wide discipline in general education. *Education and Treatment of Children, 16*, 361–381.

Flannery, K. B., Guest, E. M., Horner, R. H. (2010). The principal's role in establishing school-wide positive behavior support in high schools. *Principal Leadership, 11*(1), 38–43.

Isakson, K., & Jarvis, P. (1999). The adjustment of adolescents during the transition into high school: A short-term longitudinal study. *Journal of Youth and Adolescence, 28*(1), 1–26.

Kennedy, M. J., Horner, R. H., McNelly, D., Mimmack, J., Sobel, D., Tillman, D. R. (2009). Data-based decision making in high schools: Informed implementation of school-wide positive behavior support. In B. Flannery & G. Sugai (Eds.), *SWPBS implementation in high schools: Current practice and future directions* (pp. 81–114). Retrieved from www.pbis.org

Lane, K. L., Pierson, M. R., Stang, K. K. & Carter, E. W. (2010). Teacher expectations of students' classroom behavior: Do expectations vary as a function of school risk? *Remedial and Special Education, 31*(3), 163–174. doi: 10.1177/0741932508327464

Sugai, G., & Horner, R. (2002). The evolution of discipline practices: School-wide positive behavior supports. *Child & Family Behavior Therapy, 24*(1–2), 1–50.

Sugai, G., Sprague, J., Horner, R., & Walker, H. (2000). Preventing school violence: The use of office discipline referrals to assess and monitor school-wide discipline interventions. *Journal of Emotional and Behavioral Disorders, 8*(2), 94–101.

K. Brigid Flannery
University of Oregon
Fourth edition

HIRSCHSPRUNG DISEASE

Hirschsprung disease is a congenital genetic disorder characterized by a lack of nerve cells in a segment of the bowel resulting in constipation, diarrhea, and abdominal distention. This condition was originally named for Harold Hirschsprung, a Danish physician in Copenhagen who first described the disease in 1886 (Passarge, 1993). It is also referred to as *aganglionic megacolon.*

Hirschsprung disease is caused by the absence of nerve cells, called ganglia, in the wall of the intestines (McKusick, 1993). From the 5th to the 12th week of pregnancy, nerve cells form in a downward manner through the alimentary tract from the mouth to the anus. These nerve cells control the squeezing and relaxation of the intestinal wall, which moves the stool through the bowel. In the baby with Hirschsprung disease, the downward migration of nerve cells is not completed, and a portion of the intestine remains aganglionic, or lacking nerve cells. The portion of intestine that is aganglionic is unable to relax and the stool is unable to pass through. This condition causes a buildup of bowel contents behind the obstruction. Most often the disease begins in the last foot or two of the bowel, called the *sigmoid colon* and the *rectum,* and always ends at the anus. The length of the aganglionic portion of the bowel varies, but rarely involves the entire bowel.

Hirschsprung disease occurs in about one out of every 5,000 live births (Kessmann, 2006). More males than females are affected with the disease, with a ratio as high as 4:1. When more than half of the large intestine is aganglionic, the ratio of boys to girls is lower. Parents of Hirschsprung children have an increased risk for having additional children with the disease. Diagnosis may be considered when an infant does not pass meconium, the dark sticky substance that is a newborn's first bowel movement, within 24 hours of birth. The newborn may also exhibit abdominal distention and vomiting after the first feedings. Other symptoms may include constipation or diarrhea, anemia, and growth delay. Other children may develop chronic constipation and abdominal distention, but do not become acutely ill. Enterocolitis, a severe inflammatory condition of the bowel wall, is the most life-threatening emergency in Hirschsprung disease. Diagnosis is usually made by a barium enema X-ray to identify the affected intestinal area. A biopsy, or tissue sample, may be necessary to confirm the absence of nerve cells. An anorectal manometry test may also be conducted.

Treatment may include a temporary colostomy (surgically opening the large intestine) or ileostomy (opening the lower part of the small intestine), which will later be surgically closed. Surgical removal of the diseased section of the intestine may also be necessary. For most children with Hirschsprung disease, there are no long-term complications after successful surgery. A small but significant minority of children, however, do experience persistent constipation, encopresis, or persistent enterocolitis.

REFERENCES

Kessmann, J. (2006). Hirschsprung's disease: Diagnosis and management. *American Family Physician, 74*, 8, 1319–1322.

McKusick, V. (1993). *Hirschsprung disease.* Online Mendelian Inheritance in Man OMIM, developed by the National Center for Biotechnology Information (NCBI). Retrieved from http://www.ncbi.nlm.nih.gov/

Passarge, E. (1993). Wither polygenic inheritance: Mapping Hirschsprung disease. *Nature Genet, 4*, 325–326. PubMed ID: 8401573.

STAFF

HISKEY-NEBRASKA TEST OF LEARNING

The Hiskey-Nebraska Test of Learning Aptitude (HNTLA) is individually administered to assess the learning aptitude of persons age 3 through 17. The test is appropriate for use with individuals with auditory impairments as well as those without sensory defects. The HNTLA is composed of 12 subtests; 3 of the 12 are administered to subjects of all ages; 5 are administered only to children under age 12; and 4 are administered only to students over age 11. Items are uniformly administered either in pantomime fashion or by verbal directions. Examinees respond to items motorically, by pointing to one of several response alternatives, drawing picture parts, or manipulating objects such as beads, colored sticks, picture cards, or wooden blocks. The type of tasks on the HNTLA range from memory for color sequences to puzzle completion, picture analogy, and spatial reasoning. The tasks administered to children ages 3 to 11 primarily involve short-term visual memory, perceptual organization, visual discrimination abilities, and freedom from distractibility. The tasks administered to older examinees primarily involve perceptual organization, visual discrimination abilities, and analogical reasoning.

An examinee's raw score is based on the median subtest performance and converted to a learning age (LA) if pantomimed directions were used or a mental age (MA) if verbal directions were used. Learning ages are based on norms for children with deafness; MAs are based on norms for children with typical hearing. By using norms tables, LAs and MAs can be converted to learning quotients and IQs respectively. The current edition of the HNTLA was normed in 1966 for children with deafness and typical hearing. Reviewers have consistently noted the lack of more current reliability or validity for the test, but frequently acknowledge it as the best, and only appropriate, device available for the assessment of deaf children. It is a useful instrument for evaluating the intellectual functioning of children with language disorders.

This entry has been informed by the sources listed below.

REFERENCES

Bolton, B. F. (1978). Review of the Hiskey-Nebraska test of learning aptitude. In O. K. Buros (Ed.), *The eighth mental measurements yearbook* (pp. 307–308). Highland Park, NJ: Gryphon.

Mira, M., & Larson, A. D. (1986). Review of the Hiskey-Nebraska test of learning aptitude. In D. J. Keyser & R. C. Sweetland (Eds.), *Test critiques* (Vol. 3, pp. 331–339). Kansas City, MO: Test Corporation of America.

Newland, T. E. (1972). Review of the Hiskey-Nebraska test of learning aptitude. In O. K. Buros (Ed.), *The seventh mental measurements yearbook* (pp. 738–740). Highland Park, NJ: Gryphon.

Salvia, J., & Ysseldyke, J. E. (1985). *Assessment in special and remedial education* (3rd ed.). Boston, MA: Houghton Mifflin.

GEORGE MCCLOSKEY
Philadelphia College of Osteopathic Medicine

See also Intelligence Testing

HISTORY OF SPECIAL EDUCATION

Prehistoric societies, whose survival could depend on the fitness of each member, did not protect children who were born with defects, generally allowing them to die at birth or in infancy. Some ancient peoples, believing that physical deformities and mental disorders were the result of possession by demons, rejected, punished, or killed those who were afflicted. However, there is some evidence of persons with disabilities being treated with kindness, or even revered as being possessed of supernatural powers.

The ancient Greek and Roman societies gave us the first recorded attempts at the scientific understanding and treatment of disability in children. Some physicians and scholars in these cultures began to look on such conditions as treatable, and although infanticide was common, some efforts were made to preserve the lives of children with disabilities.

In the Middle Ages, persons with disabilities were often objects of amusement, and sometimes were used for entertainment. More often, however, they were derided, imprisoned, or executed. During this period, the church began to foster humane care for people with disabilities and to provide asylums for them. The Renaissance brought a greater belief in the value of human life, and laid the groundwork for the popular revolutions that later overthrew the domination of royalty in much of Europe and in the United States. Interest in educating children with disabilities, then, grew out of the new humanism of the Renaissance, the belief in the worth of every individual, and the associated struggles for freedom for the common man.

Education of Individuals With Hearing Impairments

Special education, as the scientific study and education of exceptional children, started about 1555 when a Spanish monk, Pedro Ponce de Leon (1520–1584), taught a small number of children who were deaf to read, write, speak, and to master academic subjects. Another Spaniard, Juan Pablo Bonet (1579–1629?), wrote the first book on the education of individuals who were deaf in 1620. He described his methods, probably derived from those of Ponce de Leon, and set forth a one-handed manual alphabet that provided the basis for the one used today.

In 1644 in England, John Bulwer (1614–1684) published the first book in English on the education of the deaf. This was followed in 1680 by the most significant of the early books in English, *Didasopholus; or, The Deaf and Dumb Man's Tutor*, by George Dalgarno (1628?–1687). The author made the startling assertion that people who are deaf have as much capacity for learning as those who can hear, and outlined instructional methods that came to be widely used by subsequent educators.

The first permanent school for the deaf in Great Britain was established in 1767 in Edinburgh by Thomas Braidwood (1715–1806). Braidwood's school was successful from the beginning, and in 1783 he moved it to Hackney, near London, to draw students from the larger population of the London area. Braidwood's nephew and assistant, Joseph Watson (1765–1829), later established the first school in Great Britain for children who were poor and deaf, in the London area. Braidwood's method combined manual and oral elements, teaching his students a manual alphabet and signs as well as articulation.

In Germany, at about the same time, Samuel Heinicke (1729–1784) developed a purely oral method of instruction, emphasizing the development of lip reading and speaking skills. Heinicke's method, as further developed by Friedrich Moritz Hill (1805–1874), was the basis for the oral method that became accepted practice throughout the world.

In France, Abbé Charles Michel de L'Epée (1712–1789) and Abbé Roch Ambroise Sicard (1742–1822) were developing the modern language of signs. Based on earlier work by Jacob Pereire (1715–1790), the instructional system was characterized by use of signs and a manual alphabet for communication. The French system also emphasized training of the senses of sight and touch, a forerunner of the sensory training that became an integral part of special education in the next century.

Organized education for children who were deaf in the United States began with the training of Thomas Hopkins Gallaudet (1787–1851) by Sicard in the French method of teaching persons who were deaf. Gallaudet, who had been chosen to start America's first school for the deaf, returned to Hartford, Connecticut, well trained in Sicard's methods and accompanied by a recruit from France, Laurent Clerc (1785–1869), a teacher of the deaf who was deaf himself. In 1817, they established the first school for children who were deaf in the United States, now the American School for the Deaf. This was the first educational program for

exceptional children established in the United States. The New York Institution for the Deaf opened the next year, and by 1863, 22 schools for the deaf existed in the nation. In 1867, the first oral schools for the deaf were established in the United States, the Clarke School for the Deaf in Massachusetts and the Lexington School for the Deaf in New York. Gallaudet College, the only liberal arts college for students who are deaf in the world, was established in 1864. The first day school classes for any exceptionality in the United States were established for children who were deaf in Boston in 1869. Adult education for persons who were deaf began in New York City in 1874.

The subsequent development of services for persons who were deaf in the United States was aided immeasurably by a number of prominent advocates, most notably Alexander Graham Bell (1847–1922), inventor of the telephone and tireless worker for education for the deaf, and Helen Keller (1880–1957), who, deaf and blind from early childhood, was a living example of the effectiveness of special educational methods in overcoming even the most severe disabilities.

The development of services for persons who were deaf was hindered in the United States and elsewhere by bitter disagreements between advocates of oral and manual methods of instruction, with a resulting lack of cohesive effort toward common goals. These disagreements continue to this day, with some educators advocating oral speech-language and others promoting gestural language or a combination of methods. Most educators agree that the goal is to provide an adequate means of communication for the individual, and the predominant teaching method today is total communication, which incorporates various modes of communication.

Education of Children With Visual Impairments

Education for children who were blind began in France with the work of Valentin Haüy (1745–1822), a French philanthropist who, in 1784, founded the National Institution for the Young Blind in Paris. The school admitted students who were both blind and sighted so as not to isolate students who were blind from their peers with sight. Its success led to the formation of seven similar schools in Europe during the next 15 years. The first school for children who were blind in the United States, now the Perkins School for the Blind in Watertown, Massachusetts, was begun in 1829 with Samuel Gridley Howe (1801–1876) as its first director. There followed a rapid development of residential schools, which soon began also to enroll students who were partially sighted. These residential schools provided the nation's only education services to children with visual impairments until the development of special classes in the public schools, a movement that began with the formation of a special class for children who were blind in Chicago in 1900. The first special class for children with partial sight was opened 13 years later in Boston.

Crucial to the education of students who are blind was the development of a system of reading and writing. Haüy developed a system of embossed letters to be read with the fingers and, using this system, he printed the first books for the blind. Raised letters proved to be extremely difficult to read, however, and Louis Braille (1809–1852), blind from childhood and one of Haüy's students, developed the system of reading that has become universal. Known as *braille*, the system uses raised dots to represent the letters of the alphabet. For many years all braille materials had to be prepared individually by hand. Two inventions by Frank H. Hall (1843–1911) greatly expanded the amount of materials in braille: a braille typewriter (1892) and a braille printing system (1893). English language braille, which developed in many variations, was standardized in 1932 with an international agreement on the code that is now called Standard English Grade Two.

Education for Children With Intellectual Developmental Delays

Education for children with Intellectual Developmental Disabilities began with the attempt by a French physician, Jean Marc Gaspard Itard (1775–1838), to educate an 11-year-old boy who had been found living as a savage in the woods. Itard's efforts to educate and civilize the boy were only partially successful, apparently because the boy was mentally retarded. Itard documented his methods in a book, *The Wild Boy of Aveyron* (1801). His instructional materials and procedures formed the basis for more than a century of development in the education of those with Intellectual Developmental Disabilities, most notably by Edouard Seguin (1812–1880) in France and the United States and by Maria Montessori (1870–1952) in Italy. Seguin, in his influential book, *Idiocy and Its Treatment by the Physiological Method*, published in 1866, enunciated many ideas that have persisted to the present time: education of the whole child, individualization of instruction, beginning instruction at the child's current level of functioning, and the importance of rapport between teacher and pupil. These concepts and Seguin's emphasis on sensory training were incorporated in the 20th century into the famous Montessori method, used worldwide in the education of children both with and without disabilities. Ovide Decroly (1871–1932) in Belgium developed an effective curriculum for children with intellectual developmental disabilities early in the 20th century and established schools that served as models throughout Europe. Alfred Binet (1857–1911), working in the public schools of Paris, made an immense contribution with the invention of intelligence testing, providing in 1905 the first objective instrument for selecting children for placement in special education programs.

The first instance of schooling for children with intellectual developmental disabilities in the United States took place in 1839 with the admission of a student who was blind and mentally retarded to the Perkins Institute for the Blind in Massachusetts. The first school designed specifically for children with intellectual developmental disabilities, a residential facility, was opened in 1848 in Barre, Massachusetts, by Hervey Backus Wilbur (1820–1883). Public residential facilities for children and adults with intellectual developmental disabilities were opened in all parts of the country during the next half century, and by 1917 all but four states were providing institutional care for individuals with intellectual developmental disabilities.

The first public school special class for children with intellectual developmental disabilities was formed in Germany in 1859, and a small number of such classes were formed in other European nations during the next several decades. In the United States the first public school special class for children with intellectual developmental disabilities was opened in 1896 in Providence, Rhode Island. Several cities followed suit between 1896 and 1900. During this same period "streamer classes" were set up for non-English speaking children. These special education facilities soon were a "hodgepodge bin" for nearly every sort of variant child that could not be handled with regular classrooms.

In the 1930s special education was incorporated into the secondary schools primarily in the large cities. Up until that time special education programs serving adolescents were primarily residential or housed in elementary schools. Martens (1947) cited the inclusion of exceptional students in secondary schools as a significant and gratifying indication that secondary schools were being modified to meet the needs of disabled adolescents. Special divisions in city high schools were set up for the "mentally subnormal" coming from elementary schools, and some city junior high schools offered modified programs of instruction.

In the years that followed, children with milder forms of intellectual developmental disabilities were educated primarily in separate classes in public schools or in residential facilities. Children with more severe intellectual developmental disabilities were kept at home, provided for in private programs, or were institutionalized. The normalization and deinstitutionalization movements, which began in the 1940s and continue to the present, led to an increasing number of children classified as mentally retarded being educated in the public schools. The passage of PL 94-142 in 1975 began a major shift in special educational services received by children classified as mentally retarded. More and more children classified as "educable" by the school systems were "mainstreamed" into general education and fewer were placed in separate classes and schools. Children classified as "trainable" and "severe" were educated in the public schools and no longer expected to be educated in segregated facilities.

Education of Children With Orthopedic Disabilities and Other Health Problems

Few special educational provisions for children with orthopedic and health impairments existed prior to the 20th century. In the United States, the first special class for orthopedically disabled children was established in the Chicago public schools in 1899 or 1900. A class for students with lowered vitality was initiated in Providence, Rhode Island in 1908, and one for children with epilepsy was formed in Baltimore, Maryland in 1909. Special educational and related services, such as occupational and physical therapy for children with a wide variety of orthopedic and health-related problems, expanded with the passage of PL 94-142 and IDEA.

Education of Emotionally/Behaviorally Disordered Children

References to emotionally disturbed children do not appear in the scientific literature until the 19th century; there is a puzzling absence of references to the subject in any literature prior to that time. The first description of childhood psychosis was published in 1838 by Jean Etienne Esquirol (1772–1840) in *Des Maladies Mentales*, a work that constituted the first scientific treatment of mental illness.

The development of school services for children with emotional disabilities is not easy to trace because of imprecision in the classification of disabilities, difficulty in diagnosis, and a tendency to place children with these types of problems in classes designed for children with other disabilities. Late in the 19th century, a few schools in the United States began to make formal provision for students with emotional disabilities. The New Haven, Connecticut public schools established a class in 1871 to provide for children exhibiting unmanageable behavior and the New York City public schools formed classes for unruly boys in 1874. It is noteworthy that these were the first public school special classes for exceptional students to be established in the United States.

Children with severe emotional problems began to be studied in a systematic way only in the 1930s, and even then public schools were slow to accept responsibility for educating them. But with psychiatry developing as a discipline, with individual differences a central topic in psychology, and with psychological testing increasingly useful as a diagnostic tool, schools began to assume responsibility for educating these students and for developing programs based on psychiatric diagnosis and treatment recommendations.

In 1975, 10 categories of handicapped children were recognized as eligible for special education, and in 1990 PL 101-476 defined the categories of disabilities which qualify children for special education. These disabilities are intellectual developmental disabilities, hearing impairments (including deafness), speech or language impairments, visual impairments (including blindness), serious emotional disturbance, orthopedic impairments, autism, traumatic brain injury, other health impairments, or specific learning disabilities.

Parent Involvement

The years since World War II have been characterized by the rapid development of services for children with disabilities in the United States, with greatly increased involvement of parents and governmental entities. Parents of children with disabilities, who had long been in the background of special education, began in the 1940s and 1950s to organize themselves to represent the needs of their children and, where necessary, to provide educational services for those children not being served by the public schools. Organizations such as the National Association of Retarded Citizens (now known as the *Arc*), the United Cerebral Palsy Association, and the Association for Children with Learning Disabilities (now known as the *Learning Disabilities Association*) have been major forces in the development of public school services for all disabled children. They have had great influence in establishing the educational rights of all children and their families, obtaining legislation relating to the rights of persons with disabilities, changing attitudes toward those with disabilities, and establishing the right of parents to participate in public school decisions about their child.

Legislative and Governmental Action

The federal government conducted a variety of programs designed to improve educational services for children with disabilities in the years following World War II. These governmental activities included grants to the states to assist in the development of new programs for children with disabilities, funding of research and demonstration projects, funding of training of special education personnel, establishment of regional resource centers for teachers, and establishment of a network of centers for children who are deaf-blind. In 1967, the Bureau of Education for the Handicapped was established in the U.S. Office of Education to administer the training, research, and educational programs supported by the federal government throughout the nation.

The landmark legislation for children with disabilities in the United States is PL 94-142, the Education for All Handicapped Children Act, enacted by Congress in 1975. Its stated purpose is ensuring that all disabled children have available a free appropriate public education that provides special education and related services as needed to meet the student's unique needs. Public Law 94-142 required that state and local education agencies ensure that all children who are disabled be identified and evaluated; that a comprehensive, nondiscriminatory, multidisciplinary educational assessment be made; that a reassessment be made at least every 3 years; that a written individualized educational plan (IEP) be developed and maintained for each child who has been determined to be disabled; and that each child be educated in the least restrictive environment that is consistent with his or her disability. The law also granted certain rights to parents to review their child's school record, to obtain an independent evaluation of the child, to receive written notice prior to placement in special education services, and to have an impartial hearing if they wish to challenge the proposed classification or placement of their child. Compliance with the requirements of PL 94-142 has brought modest amounts of federal financial aid to the states, to be used with state and local funds to support the cost of educating disabled children. A far-reaching effect of PL 94-142 has been the virtual elimination of the exclusion of disabled children from school. As the title of the act states, the legislation provides for the education of all disabled children.

PL 94-142 was amended a number of times to increase the age of children covered under the provisions of the law and to emphasize transition services and assistive technology. A major reauthorization of PL 94-142 in 1990 changed the name of the law from Education of All Handicapped Children Act to Individuals with Disabilities Education Act, or IDEA (PL 101-476). This act increased the number of categories of disabilities to include autism and traumatic brain injury and attempted to address what were perceived to be injustices in the previous act. Amendments to IDEA in 1997 significantly changed the requirements for the IEP (Individualized Education Plan) and combined the "categorical" approach with the "functional" approach. A "child with a disability" between the ages of 3 through 9 may include a child experiencing developmental delays in one or more of the following areas: physical development, cognitive development, communication development, social or emotional development, or adaptive development. This provision allows states to serve "at-risk" children.

A number of court decisions laid the groundwork for the enactment of PL 94-142. The decision in *Pennsylvania Association for Retarded Children* v. *Commonwealth of Pennsylvania* in 1972 established that the public schools have the responsibility to provide appropriate programs for disabled children and that a child may not be excluded from school without due process. *Mills* v. *Board of Education* in the same year established that a disabled child may not be denied an appropriate, publicly supported education, and that the school system may not use lack of funds as a reason for failing to provide the services to which a disabled child is entitled.

Section 504 of the Vocational Rehabilitation Act of 1973 (PL 93-112) serves as a statement of civil rights for the disabled, providing that no otherwise qualified disabled individual will, because of his or her disability, be denied participation in any activity or program that receives federal financial assistance. This provision established public education as a right for all disabled children, regardless of how serious the disability might be, and is also the basis for a nationwide effort to make school buildings accessible to the disabled.

The Americans with Disabilities Act (ADA) of 1990 extended the nondiscriminatory provisions of Section 504 of the Rehabilitation Act amendment in 1975 to the private sector and with its emphasis on accessibility impacts on the provision of special education. IDEA and the Rehabilitation Act deal with education and training for employment and Section 504 and ADA make sure that students with disabilities can put their education and training to use.

Growth in Services

Special education services expanded rapidly after World War II, both in number and types of children served. New special classes and special schools dramatically increased, as did college and university preparation programs for special education personnel. Additional types of children included in the population served were children classified as trainable mentally retarded, previously served primarily in institutions or in special schools operated by parent groups, and, beginning in the 1960s, children with learning disabilities, a group that had mostly been achieving poorly in regular classes or misplaced in special classes for students with other kinds of disabilities. In addition, interest increased in providing special programs for a group of students who are not disabled but who are generally included in the definition of exceptional children: gifted and talented children. Programs for these students appeared only slowly, as they lacked strong support from most educators. Consequently, programs for the gifted and talented have not shown the rapid growth that took place in programs for students with disabilities.

Early or preschool education for children with disabilities, long provided for children who had hearing impairments or cerebral palsy and other physical disabilities, became generally available for other categories of children with disabilities in the 1970s. This development was based on research findings corroborating commonly held beliefs that the development of young children can be changed through early educational intervention. Often initiated with federal funding, these programs provided several new emphases in special education, including organized "child-find" procedures to locate young children in need of special programming, improved multidisciplinary approaches, and parent education.

Under the provisions of PL 94-142 and Section 504 of the Vocational Rehabilitation Act, public schools are required to make appropriate educational services available to students with severe, profound, and multiple disabilities, a category that includes various degrees and combinations of intellectual developmental disabilities, behavior disorders, physical disabilities, and sensory disabilities. Programs for such children with severe disabilities, many of whom were previously unserved by the public schools, have become a major element of special education, and have brought with them services (such as physical therapy and occupational therapy) that had not previously been considered within the province of the schools. These programs also have necessitated the downward extension of the curriculum to include instruction in infant-level self-help skills.

Increased enrollment of students with disabilities in vocational education programs was fostered by the Vocational Education Amendments of 1976 (PL 94-482), which require each state to allocate 10% of its vocational funds for the education of students with disabilities. Increasingly since the enactment of these amendments, high school students with disabilities have had a variety of occupational preparation options available to them, in both regular and special vocational education programs.

The explosion of technology that characterizes our time has directly benefited students with disabilities in some significant ways. The use of computers by children with disabilities is becoming commonplace, as it is for all students. Adaptive technology, including improved prostheses, motorized wheelchairs, and other transportation devices, has greatly increased the mobility of children with physical disabilities. Persons who are hearing impaired have benefited from vastly improved hearing aid technology, advances in surgical techniques, and increased captioning of films and television programs. Of special significance are telecommunication devices for persons who are deaf or hearing impaired, the best known being the teletypewriter and teleprinter (TTY), a device that enables the deaf to communicate by telephone, typing into the system messages that are then printed at the receiving end. Reading for persons with visual impairments is being made more effective by a number of devices. The recorded "talking book" can now be enhanced by a technique known as *compressed speech*, which can double the speed at which the recording is played without producing distortion in pitch or quality. The Optacon converts print into a vibrating image that can be read with the fingers. The Kurzweil Reading Machine converts print into spoken English. In the important area of mobility, the Sonicguide aids those with visual impairments by producing a sound that indicates the presence and distance of an object that lies in their path. Other technologies include translation of printed language into spoken language and braille, synthetic speech, speech-producing handheld calculators, closed-circuit television with enlargers, optical-to-tactile and print-to-braille converters, and various portable devices. Although the cost of such devices remains high in some instances, they are enhancing the quality of services to children with disabilities in a variety of educational and community settings.

The 1970s saw the emergence of mainstreaming and least restrictive environment as dominant concepts in special education. The requirement in PL 94-142 that disabled students be educated in the least restrictive environment was a reaction to doubts about the educational and social efficacy of the existing special class model and about the willingness of the schools to give disabled students access to the regular school program. The least restrictive environment requirement has led to a significant shift in special education placements in the last decade. The shift is toward a reduction in placements in residential schools and special day schools, and increased enrollment of disabled students in special classes in regular school buildings and in regular classes, usually with assistance in the form of some type of supplementary special instruction. Placement in less restrictive environments and the provision of appropriate educational services in this context, while not without its difficulties, is serving to eliminate needless segregation of disabled students.

The debate still continues regarding the best environments in which to educate children with disabilities. IDEA creates a presumption in favor of educating students with disabilities with those who do not have disabilities to the maximum extent possible and of the school providing supplementary aids and support services. The presumption in favor of inclusion can only be set aside if the student cannot benefit from regular education. In this case the student may be placed in a less typical, more specialized, less inclusive program. IDEA also set forth the provision that schools must offer a continuum of services from more to less typical and inclusive. On the other hand, organizations such as the Learning Disabilities Association (LDA) believe that the regular classroom is not the appropriate place for many students with learning disabilities. They advocate for alternative instructional environments or teaching strategies that cannot be provided with the regular classroom. Other organizations and professionals support the LDA position, but do not advocate a return to the previous total segregation models of special education.

The history of special education reveals evolution from initial education of specific groups in segregated settings to a movement toward total inclusion within the public schools. The restructuring of general education taking place in the 1990s (Goals, 2000, etc.) and the accompanying reforms have impacted special education. These reforms are cooperative learning, cooperative/collaborative teaching, site-based management, outcomes-based education and assessment, academic standards, effective assessment tools, accountability, and state and federal legislation.

More recent legislative developments that will continue to impact special education services in this country well into the future include the 2001 passage of the No Child Left Behind Act (NCLB), which significantly alters programs instituted under the Elementary and Secondary Education Act (ESEA), and the recent reauthorization of the IDEA in 2004. While the ESEA provided a program of federal grants to school districts based on the number of children in the district from families living in poverty, NCLB provides grants to all qualifying public schools, regardless of the socioeconomic status of the children attending the schools, but imposes numerous burdens on state and local education agencies as a condition of receiving those funds, including extensive testing requirements, stringent teacher qualification standards, and a requirement that schools demonstrate adequate yearly progress toward the ultimate goal of having 100% of their students achieve academic proficiency goals established by each state. NCLB remains controversial among parents and educators, with many decrying what is described as the punitive nature of the statute, and with special educators expressing concerns about the statute's requirement that all but those students with the most severe learning disabilities be included in each district's testing program. The 2004 reauthorization of the IDEA, while retaining many of the requirements of earlier iterations of the statute, also includes a number of changes to bring the provisions of the IDEA into compliance with NCLB, particularly in the area of establishing goals and monitoring individual student progress under individualized education programs (IEPs) as those requirements relate to district testing requirements. These changes have generated significant controversy, and it is anticipated that the future should hold much research to evaluate the impact of these changes on children in special education.

This entry has been informed by the sources listed below.

REFERENCES

Bender, R. (1970). *The conquest of deafness.* Cleveland, OH: Case Western Reserve University Press.

Blatt, B., & Morris, R. J. (1984). *Perspectives in special education: Personal orientations.* Glenview, IL: Scott, Foresman.

Despert, J. L. (1965). *The emotionally disturbed child: Then and now.* New York, NY: Brunner.

Fancher, R. E. (1979). *Pioneers of psychology.* New York, NY: Norton.

Fancher, R. E. (1985). *The intelligence men: Makers of the I. Q. controversy.* New York, NY: Norton.

Gannon, J. R. (1981). *Deaf heritage: A narrative history of deaf America.* Silver Spring, MD: National Association of the Deaf.

Hatlen, P. H., Hall, A. P., & Tuttle, D. (1980). Education of the visually handicapped: An overview and update. In L. Mann & D. A. Sabatino (Eds.), *The fourth review of special education* (pp. 1–33). New York, NY: Grune & Stratton.

Irwin, R. B. (1955). *As I saw it.* New York, NY: American Foundation for the Blind.

Jan, J. E., Freeman, R. D., & Scott, E. P. (1977). *Visual impairment in children and adults.* New York, NY: Grune & Stratton.

Kanner, L. (1964). *A history of the care and study of the mentally retarded.* Springfield, IL: Thomas.

Kanner, L. (1970). Emotionally disturbed children: A historical review. In L. A. Faas (Ed.), *The emotionally disturbed child: A book of readings.* Springfield, IL: Thomas.

Kirk, S. A., & Gallagher, J. J. (1983). *Educating exceptional children* (4th ed.). Boston, MA: Houghton Mifflin.

Kirk, S. A., Gallagher, J. J., & Anastasiow, N. J. (1997). *Educating exceptional children* (8th ed.). Boston, MA: Houghton Mifflin.

Koestler, F. A. (1976). *The unseen minority: A social history of blindness in the United States.* New York, NY: McKay.

Lane, H. (1984). *When the mind hears.* New York, NY: Random House.

Lerner, J. (1985). *Learning disabilities: Theories, diagnosis, and teaching strategies* (4th ed.). Boston, MA: Houghton Mifflin.

Lowenfeld, B. (1976). *The changing status of the blind: From separation to integration.* Springfield, IL: Thomas.

Martens, E. H. (1947). *Statistics of special schools and classes for exceptional children 1947–48.* Washington, DC: Federal Security Agency.

Meyen, E. L., & Skrtic, T. M. (Eds.). (1995). *Special education and student disability: Traditional, emerging, and alternative perspectives.* Denver, CO: Love.

Moores, D. F. (1982). *Educating the deaf—Psychology, principles, and practices* (2nd ed.). Boston, MA: Houghton Mifflin.

Reynolds, M. C., & Birch, J. W. (1977). *Teaching exceptional children in all America's schools.* Reston, VA: Council for Exceptional Children.

Rhodes, W. C., & Head, S. (1974). *A study of child variance.* Ann Arbor: University of Michigan.

Rosen, M., Clark, G. R., & Kivitz, M. S. (Eds.). (1976). *The history of Mental Retardation: Collected papers.* Baltimore, MD: University Park Press.

Ross, I. (1951). *Journey into light: The story of the education of the blind.* New York, NY: Appleton-Century-Crofts.

Scheerenberger, R. C. (1983). *A history of Mental Retardation.* Baltimore, MD: Paul H. Brookes.

Smith, S. (1983). *Ideas of the great psychologists.* New York, NY: Harper & Row.

Swanson, B. M., & Willis, D. J. (1979). *Understanding exceptional children and youth.* Chicago, IL: Rand McNally.

Turnbull, A., Turnbull, R., Shank, M., & Leal, D. (1999). *Exceptional lives: Special education in today's schools* (2nd ed.). Upper Saddle River, NJ: Merrill.

Turnbull, R., & Cilley, M. (1999). *Explanations and implications of the 1997 Amendment to IDEA.* Upper Saddle River, NJ: Merrill.

Wallin, J. E. W. (1955). *Education of mentally handicapped children.* New York, NY: Harper & Row.

Watson, R. I. (1968). *The great psychologists: From Aristotle to Freud* (2nd ed.). Philadelphia, PA: Lippincott.

Wiederholt, J. L. (1974). Historical perspectives on the education of the learning disabled. In L. Mann & D. A. Sabatino (Eds.), *The second review of special education* (pp. 103–152). Philadelphia, PA: JSE.

Wright, E. B. (1980). *Noncategorical special education programs for the mildly handicapped in secondary schools: A review of the literature.* Unpublished manuscript.

PAUL IRVINE
Katonah, New York
First edition

ELEANOR BOYD WRIGHT
University of North Carolina at Wilmington
Second edition

KIMBERLY APPLEQUIST
University of Colorado at Colorado Springs
Third edition

See also Americans With Disabilities Act; Inclusion; Individuals with Disabilities Education Improvement Act of 2004 (IDEIA); No Child Left Behind Act; Politics and Special Education

HISTRIONIC PERSONALITY DISORDER

Hysterical personality is an obsolete term that evolved from the 18th and 19th century diagnostic label *hysteria*, whose Greek root meant "wandering uterus." Used prior to 1980 to describe a personality disorder characterized by pervasive, excessive, and exaggerated emotionality, attention-seeking behavior, a focus on physical appearance as an attention-getting device, seductiveness, suggestibility, and the propensity to assume that relationships are more intimate than they really are (American Psychiatric Association, 1994), it was applied almost exclusively by male clinicians to female clients. In 1980, the third edition of the *Diagnostic and Statistical Manual of Mental Disorders* (American Psychiatric Association, 1980) replaced "hysterical" personality with the designation *histrionic personality disorder*, which was retained in the most recent revision of the manual (*DSM-IV*). Although the *DSM-IV* notes that some research studies have found similar prevalence rates among men and women when structured assessments are employed, actual clinical practitioners rarely use such structured assessments, and thus the diagnosis continues to be much more frequently diagnosed in women. Histrionic personality disorder is commonly diagnosed in conjunction with other personality disorders, most frequently borderline personality disorder, dependent personality disorder, or narcissistic personality disorder. Other frequent co-occurring conditions include alcohol/drug abuse, various physical complaints, depression, and anxiety.

Rather than a primary mental disorder, personality disorders are considered to be long-lasting, chronic patterns of maladaptive behaviors that represent a person's typical, customary way of responding to the everyday conditions and demands of their environment. The representative behavioral patterns of those people designated as personality-disordered cause considerable impairment in the person's interpersonal relationships, and endure over time in spite of the negative consequences such patterns characteristically provoke.

The diagnostic manual does not attempt to identify the causes of any of the diagnoses it describes. Traditionally, most attempts to specify the causes of histrionic personality disorder have committed the logical fallacy of circular reasoning, which involves using description as explanation. For example, Millon (1981) saw the histrionic personality disorder as a result of an extreme longing for attention and approval from others mixed with a fear of independence. Such a statement, however, is no more than a description of the symptoms by which the disorder is identified. It essentially says that the disorder is both characterized by, as well as caused by, craving for attention and other symptoms. Such a statement is only superficially explanatory as it offers no further clarification of the disorder.

More useful attempts to explain the etiology of this disorder have focused on problems/deficits in identity development of the young child. Mahler's (1972) views on the separation-individuation process, and Mahler, Pine, and Bergman's (1975) perspectives on the "psychological birth" of the human child describe a process wherein the child develops a strong, coherent sense of self, capable of psychological independence only in the context of a reliable, dependable relationship with a primary caretaker. Serious deficits in that primary relationship would logically result in a strong "neediness" for others' attention and approval. Kohut (1971), addressing histrionic personality disorder as a subset of narcissistic personality disorder, considers it as a disorder of the self and self/identity development.

The histrionic's typical interpersonal shallowness and extreme sensitivity to perceived criticism are almost always serious obstacles to treatment for people with this disorder. Clinicians typically find these people to be self-centered, demanding, and manipulative clients, and the therapeutic relationship is frequently difficult to establish and maintain at a level sufficient for successful psychological treatment. Masterson (1993) employs a combination of developmental and self-psychological tenets, along with object relations theory, in his approach to the treatment of disorders of the self, and provides additional information for those interested in treatment strategies for this condition.

REFERENCES

American Psychiatric Association. (1980). *Diagnostic and statistical manual of mental disorders* (3rd ed.). Washington, DC: Author.

American Psychiatric Association. (1994). *Diagnostic and statistical manual of mental disorders* (4th ed.). Washington, DC: Author.

Kohut, H. (1971). *The analysis of the self: A systematic approach to the treatment of narcissistic personality disorders.* New York, NY: International Universities Press.

Mahler, M. (1972). On the first three subphases of the separation-individuation process. *International Journal of Psycho-Analysis, 53,* 333–338.

Mahler, M., Pine, F., & Bergman, A. (1975). *The psychological birth of the human infant.* New York, NY: Basic Books.

Masterson, J. F. (1993). *The emerging self: A developmental, self, and object relations approach to the treatment of the closet narcissistic disorder of the self.* New York, NY: Brunner/Mazel.

Millon, T. (1981). *Disorders of personality DSM-III: Axis II.* New York, NY: Wiley.

KAY E. KETZENBERGER
University of Texas of the Permian Basin

HOBBS, NICHOLAS (1915–1983)

Nicholas Hobbs began his professional career as a high school teacher, earned his PhD degree in clinical psychology from Ohio State University in 1946, and served on the faculties of Teachers College, Columbia University, Louisiana State University, and George Peabody College of Vanderbilt University. From the time of his arrival at George Peabody College in 1951 until his retirement in 1980, he held a number of positions, including chairman of the division of human development, director of the Center for the Study of Families and Children, which he created, and provost of Vanderbilt University.

Hobbs was widely known for his pioneering Project Re-ED, dedicated to "the reeducation of emotionally disturbed children." An educational approach to the treatment of emotionally disturbed children, Project Re-ED, which grew into a nationwide program, is described in Hobbs's *The Troubled and Troubling Child* (Hobbs, 1982).

Hobbs was appointed to a number of presidential panels and commissions and participated in the creation of the Peace Corps. He served as president of the American Psychological Association.

REFERENCE

Hobbs, N. (1982). *The troubled and troubling child.* San Francisco, CA: Jossey-Bass.

PAUL IRVINE
Katonah, New York

HOLLAND, SPECIAL EDUCATION IN
(See Netherlands, Special Education in)

HOLLINGWORTH, LETA A. S. (1886–1939)

Leta A. S. Hollingworth, psychologist, received her PhD from Teachers College, Columbia University, in 1916, after serving as a high school teacher in Nebraska and as a clinical psychologist in New York City. She was a member of the faculty of Teachers College from 1916 until her death in 1939.

Hollingworth made pioneering studies of the psychology of women, correcting prior misconceptions regarding differences in abilities between the sexes and providing the basis for her strong advocacy of professional equality between men and women (Gates, 1940). She was a leader in the establishment of standards for clinical psychologists and carried out significant investigations of both mentally retarded and gifted children (Hollingworth, 1926, 1943).

REFERENCES

Gates, A. I. (Ed.). (1940). Education and the individual. *Teachers College Record, 42,* 183–264.

Hollingworth, H. L. (1943). *Leta Stetter Hollingworth.* Lincoln: University of Nebraska Press.

Hollingworth, L. (1926). *Gifted children: Their nature and nurture.* New York, NY: Macmillan.

PAUL IRVINE
Katonah, New York

HOLT-ORAM SYNDROME

Holt-Oram syndrome, also known as heart-hand syndrome or cardiac-limb syndrome, refers to a rare genetic condition involving abnormalities of the heart and upper limbs. Those affected have malformations or abnormalities of the bones in the thumbs, wrists, and arms, but lower extremities are not affected. Bones may be missing, extra, underdeveloped, or malformed. There may also be problems with the shoulder blades and collarbones. In some children the thumb is absent (National Organization for Rare Disorders [NORD], 2000). The severity varies greatly with the individual and may be as slight as limited range of motion or as great as complete absence of upper limbs (Jeanty & Silva, 1999).

Holt-Oram syndrome is also characterized by cardiac abnormalities. There may be structural defects such as holes in the heart or electrical impulse problems that cause the heart to beat improperly. As in the limb malformations, these may also range from mild (asymptomatic) to severe (life-threatening).

A very rare disorder, only about 100 or so cases of Holt-Oram syndrome have been documented since it was first described in 1960. A parent with Holt-Oram syndrome has about a 50% chance of passing the disorder on to each child. The condition is the result of heredity about 60% of the time; the other 40% of cases are apparently the result of a spontaneous mutation. The severity of the child's condition is unrelated to the severity of the parent's condition; a parent who is only slightly affected may produce a severely affected child.

Characteristics

1. Malformed or abnormal bones in upper body.
2. May be missing bones entirely.
3. Impaired range of motion.
4. Normal lower body.

For the children without thumbs, surgery to allow the index finger to act as a thumb has been cautiously explored, with positive results (Weber, Wenz, van Riel, Kaufmann, & Graf, 1997). In the school setting, children with orthopedic impairments that impact their learning may receive special services under the Orthopedically Impaired umbrella; such services may well include occupational therapy for fine motor skills and physical therapy for gross motor. An assistive technology system, such as a special keyboard and mouse or voice-activated software, may be appropriate for those having difficulty with handwriting. Children with serious heart complications affecting alertness, stamina, or concentration may be eligible for services under Other Health Impairment, allowing them to have adapted physical education and other modifications as needed.

REFERENCES

Jeanty, P., & Silva, S. (1999). *Holt-Oram syndrome. The fetus.* Retrieved from http://thefetus.net/

National Organization for Rare Disorders. (2000). *Holt-Oram syndrome.* Retrieved from http://www.rarediseases.org

Weber, M., Wenz, W., van Riel, A., Kaufmann, A., & Graf, J. (1997). The Holt-Oram syndrome: Review of the literature and current orthopedic treatment concepts. *Zeitschrift für Orthopädie und thre Grenzgebiete, 135*(4), 368–375.

SHARLA FASKO
Rowan County Schools Morehead, Kentucky

HOLT, WINIFRED (1870–1945)

Winifred Holt founded the New York Association for the Blind in 1905. She was responsible for the creation of the committee that eventually became the National Society for the Prevention of Blindness. With a special interest in training and employment for the blind, she developed the New York Lighthouse, a workshop devoted to education, employment, and recreation for the blind (Bloodgood, 1952). Dedicated by President William Howard Taft in 1913, the Lighthouse was so successful that Lighthouses were established in many cities in the United States, and eventually in 34 other countries.

A leader in the campaign to get blind children into the public schools, Holt helped the New York City Board of Education to establish its program for the education of blind students in classes with sighted children. She wrote two influential books, a biography of Henry Faucett, the blind English postmaster general (Hold, 1914), and *The Light Which Cannot Fail*, (Holt, 1922) which contained stories about blind men and women and a useful "handbook for the blind and their friends." In 1922 Holt married Rufus Graves Mather, a research and lecturer on art who joined her in her work for the blind.

REFERENCES

Bloodgood, E. H. (1952). *First lady of the Lighthouse.* New York, NY: The Lighthouse, New York Association for the Blind.

Holt, W. (1914). *A beacon for the blind: Being a life of Henry Faucett, the blind postmaster-general.* Boston, MA: Houghton Mifflin.

Holt, W. (1922). *The light which cannot fail.* New York, NY: Dutton.

PAUL IRVINE
Katonah, New York

HOLTZMAN, WAYNE H. SR. (1923–   )

Wayne H. Holtzman received his BS and MS degrees from Northwestern University. In 1950, he was awarded his PhD degree in psychology and statistics from Stanford University. Since 1949, he has been a faculty member in psychology at The University of Texas at Austin. Associated with the Hogg Foundation since 1954, he is currently Professor Emeritus, Hogg Professor Emeritus in Psychology and Education, Department of Psychology. Holtzman served as Foundation President from 1970 to 1993 and as dean of the College of Education at the University from 1964 to 1970.

From 1953 to 1954, Holtzman received a faculty research fellowship from the Social Science Research Council, and in 1962 his research in the field of inkblot perception and personality was recognized by the Helen D. Sargent Memorial Award from the Menninger Foundation. The inkblot technique, devised by Holtzman and designed to stir the imagination, focuses on the analysis of inkblots as a means of studying personality by determining individual modes of perception. This technique was ultimately revised by Holtzman, utilizing more inkblots and simplifying procedures for administration.

His numerous honorary awards and doctorates include a fellowship at the Center for Advanced Study in the Behavioral Sciences, Stanford, California (1962–1963); the title of *Professor Honorario* at the Universidad San Martin de Porres in Lima, Peru in 1979; the Doctor of Humanities degree from Southwestern University in Georgetown, Texas in 1980; the Bruno Klopfer Award for Distinguished Contributions to Personality Assessment of the Society for Personality Assessment in 1988; the Centennial Citation for International Advancement of Psychology in Education from the American Psychological Association (APA) in 1992; and a 1996 award from the APA for Distinguished International Contributions to Psychology.

Holtzman has authored more than 150 articles in scientific journals, and served as editor of the *Journal of Educational Psychology* from 1966 to 1972. His books include *Holtzman Inkblot Technique* (Holtzman, 1961); *Tomorrow's Parents* (Holtzman, 1965); *Computer-Assisted Instruction, Testing, and Guidance* (Holtzman, 1970); *Placing Children in Special Education: A Strategy for Equity; Mental Health of Immigrants and Refugees;* and *School of the Future.*

REFERENCES

Holtzman, W. H. (1961). *Holtzman inkblot technique.* New York, NY: Psychological Corporation.

Holtzman, W. H. (1965). *Tomorrow's parents.* Austin: University of Texas Press.

Holtzman, W. H. (1970). *Computer-assisted instruction, testing, and guidance.* New York, NY: Harper & Row.

TAMARA J. MARTIN
University of Texas of the Permian Basin

HOMEBOUND INSTRUCTION

Homebound instruction is defined as education for the child confined to home owing to illness, physical injury, or emotional condition, provided by an itinerant or visiting teacher. A child is eligible for a home instruction program if school attendance is made impossible by such physical or emotional conditions. The Education for All Handicapped Children Act of 1975 (PL 94-142) and the Individuals with Disabilities Education Act (IDEA) have categorized home instruction as one of the most restrictive in the available cascade of services; as a result, such placement is to be considered temporary whenever possible (Berdine & Blackhurst, 1985).

The homebound teacher is used as the provider of this instruction in those areas or school districts where such services are available. The homebound instructional component must consist of direct service to the child and regular consultation with in-school personnel, as the nature of the service will vary from helping students at home for short periods of time to maintain the pace and assignments of their classes, to providing a complete instructional program for those confined for longer periods. Authorities agree that regular liaison with school and peers to maintain contacts and social skills is vital to the student on homebound instruction, who must be brought back to school as quickly as the handicapping condition allows (Polloway, Payne, Patton, & Payne, 1985).

Some instances of the abuse of homebound instruction have been noted in urban areas with a relatively high-frequency use of such services, primarily with students who are disruptive, delinquent, or emotionally disturbed prohibited from school for behavioral reasons. Homebound services for the individuals with emotional disturbances have also been overemployed with disadvantaged, black, and male students (Safer, 1982). Additional criticisms of home instruction include the danger of segregating children for prolonged periods of time, the expense to school systems, and the use of inadequately trained teachers as service providers (Haring, 1982).

New directions in special education are extending traditional homebound instruction to include home-based services for children with severe disabilities, infants who are deaf and blind and preschool children, individuals with intellectual disabilities, and other high-risk infants (Cartwright, Cartwright, & Ward, 1995). These services include the use of teacher-trainers to teach parents and children, with emphasis on self-help skills, communications, and language arts, using the natural surroundings of the home environment to promote development (Kiernan, Jordan, & Saunders, 1984).

Technological advances in telecommunications and computer-linked instruction increasingly assist the homebound child and teacher until a return to a less restrictive environment is accomplished (Kirk & Gallagher, 1986).

REFERENCES

Berdine, W. H., & Blackhurst, A. E. (1985). *An introduction to special education* (2nd ed). Boston, MA: Little, Brown.

Cartwright, G. P., Cartwright, C. A., & Ward, M. J. (1995). *Educating special learners* (2nd ed). Belmont, CA: Wadsworth.

Haring, N. R. (Ed.). (1982). *Exceptional children and youth.* Columbus, OH: Merrill.

Kiernan, C., Jordan, R., & Saunders, C. (1984). *Stimulating the exceptional child: Strategies for teaching communication and behavior change to the mentally disabled.* Englewood Cliffs, NJ: Prentice Hall.

Kirk, S. A., & Gallagher, J. J. (1986). *Educating exceptional children* (5th ed). Boston, MA: Houghton Mifflin.

Polloway, E. A., Payne, J. S., Patton, J. R., & Payne, R. A. (1985). *Strategies for teaching retarded and special needs learners.* Columbus, OH: Merrill.

Safer, D. J. (1982). *School programs for disruptive adolescents.* Baltimore, MD: University Park Press.

RONALD S. LENKOWSKY
Hunter College, City University of New York
Second edition

KIMBERLY APPLEQUIST
University of Colorado at Colorado Springs
Third edition

See also Cascade Model of Special Education Services; Least Restrictive Environment

HONG KONG, SPECIAL EDUCATION IN

Hong Kong, located on the southeastern coast of the mainland China, is a Special Administrative Region (SAR) of the People's Republic of China. The SAR, with a total land area of 1,054 km, comprises Hong Kong Island, Kowloon, the New Territories and the Outlying Islands. The population of Hong Kong was just over 7.1 million in July 2011. The two official languages used in the SAR are Chinese (the spoken dialect being Cantonese) and English. Hong Kong was a British colony from 1843 until 1997, so it is not surprising that education in Hong Kong during that period was modeled largely on the British system. However, important changes in education policies, school organization and curricula have occurred since 1997. The principal changes are highlighted later in this brief overview.

In the school year 2010 to 2011, approximately 970,000 students were enrolled in Hong Kong's 951 kindergartens, 572 primary schools, 533 secondary schools, and 61 special schools (Education Bureau, 2011a). The number of children attending primary and secondary schools has declined in recent years because the fertility rate in Hong Kong has remained at a low level (1.04 in 2009) (Information Services Department, 2011a).

The needs of students with disabilities or learning difficulties are met through either support in mainstream schools or by placement in special schools. In the school year 2010 to 2011, 7,803 students were enrolled in the 61 special schools, which cater for students under several categories of special need or disability, namely, visual impairment, hearing impairment, physical disability, social adjustment, and intellectual disability (Education Bureau, 2011b). Residential facilities are available in more than one-third of these special schools. The Education Bureau provides funding for special schools under the *Code of Aid for Special Schools*, and also subsidizes any allied health, social work, nursing, and residential care services that are required.

Currently, the Education Bureau (formerly the Education Department) promotes a policy of inclusive education, which began with a small-scale integration project in 1997. The Education Bureau states that the main objective of special education in Hong Kong is to enable children with special educational needs to develop to their full potential; and as far as possible they will receive their education in ordinary schools. Special schools will continue to exist to meet the needs of students with severe forms of disability.

Development of Special Education

Prior to 1960, the Hong Kong government (through its Education Department) had little involvement in the provision of special education services. Care for children with special educational needs was mainly provided by religious bodies and by voluntary organizations. Some of the earliest endeavors involved the establishment of a school for blind students in 1863, and for hearing impaired students in 1935. Religious and charitable bodies also made provision for students with intellectual or physical disabilities. In 1960, a Special Education Section was established within the Education Department. At first, this section was responsible only for the monitoring and support of special education services provided by voluntary organizations. But gradually it took a stronger lead. Many new special schools were established, and the provision of remedial and resource-room teaching in mainstream schools was strengthened. At this time and for the next three decades special education remained largely segregated from mainstream schooling (Board of Education, 1996).

In 1977, the government published the first White Paper on Rehabilitation, *Integrating the Disabled into the Community: A United Effort.* This document advocated, inter alia, the inclusion of children with less severe disabilities such as the children with partial hearing and children with adjustment problems in ordinary schools and classes. It also recommended a significant increase in the number of places to be offered in special schools, as well as an increase in special classes and resource classes in ordinary schools. In 1978, the government's introduction of "9-year free and compulsory education for all" impacted on the area of special education, resulting in rapid expansion of special education services. This was particularly evident in the areas of psychological and educational assessment and in remedial teaching. Despite the good intentions during this period, the resulting easy availability of special placement for students with special needs tended to maintain a system of segregation rather than integration. This situation continued into the early 1990s. It was only then that integrating students with special educational needs *fully* into ordinary schools became central in the planning of special education in Hong Kong. A key impetus for this was the UNESCO World Conference on Special Needs Education, held in Salamanca in 1994, which called on all governments to endorse the approach of "inclusive schooling."

In 1995, the government issued a second White Paper on Rehabilitation, *Equal Opportunities and Full Participation: A Better Tomorrow for All*, reaffirming the policy of integration. In addition, a Disability Discrimination Ordinance now safeguards equal opportunities for disabled persons in various domains, including education.

Since 2000, all secondary schools, previously "banded" into five levels, have been reorganized into only three bands, increasing the range of ability in each band. To some extent this removed the significant stigma felt by students of low ability or with learning difficulties who had found themselves in a "Band 5" school.

Toward Inclusive Education

The first "pilot project on integration" in 1997 involved only seven primary schools and two secondary schools. Selected students with mild disabilities were placed into ordinary classrooms with support, and their progress was monitored. Although there were some positive results (according to the students' and parents' perceptions), the general response from schools was not enthusiastic. Teachers felt ill-equipped professionally to teach these students effectively in regular classes. In an attempt to improve this situation, a "Whole school approach to integrated education" (WSA) became a major initiative of the Education Bureau. The WSA seeks to involve all staff in devising and implementing effective strategies for teaching and supporting students with special needs (Education Bureau, 2010).

To further the inclusive policy, the government improved funding arrangements in 2003 to 2004 for primary schools adopting a WSA to inclusion. This was extended to secondary schools in 2008 to 2009. The new funding arrangement facilitates more flexible deployment of resources for implementing and supporting inclusion. A grant of HK$10,000 or HK$20,000 per student per annum (with a maximum of HK$1 million per school) is provided depending on the degree of support the students require. By 2008 to 2009, the number of schools opting to provide inclusive education had risen to 344 (Forlin, 2010).

The Education Bureau also developed a more comprehensive framework for facilitating the implementation of inclusive education. Starting from 2006, a "3-Tier Intervention Model" was introduced to provide appropriate levels of support according to students' learning needs. A five-year framework for teachers' professional development was established in 2007 to 2008 to provide courses to enhance teachers' professional capacity in supporting children with special educational needs. To empower ordinary schools in supporting students with special educational needs, 18 special schools and 10 ordinary schools have been designated to act as "resource schools" in 2011 to 2012. They support other ordinary schools through workshops, on-site support, case conferences, and district-based sharing sessions.

Special Schools

Special schools in Hong Kong will continue to exist to meet the special needs of students with severe or multiple disabilities who cannot cope with even a modified and adapted curriculum in the mainstream. Many of these students require various forms of therapy or treatment on a daily basis.

The class size in special schools ranges from 8 to 20 students per class; and the staffing ratio ranges from 1.7 to 1.9 teachers per class depending on the age and disability of children served. In the school year 2009 to 2010, the academic structure for secondary schools was revised. Under the new system, students attend junior secondary (3 years), then senior secondary (3 years) before commencing tertiary studies (4 years). In line with these structural changes in secondary grades, special schools now offer 6 years of free secondary education for their students (Education Bureau, 2011c).

Early Identification and Assessment

A pilot implementation of the "Comprehensive Child Development Service" was first launched in 2005, to facilitate earlier identification of children's difficulties. The service aims to identify the varied needs of children aged 0 to 5 years and their families at an early stage. Preprimary children who are suspected of having health, developmental or behavior problems are initially assessed by the Maternal and Child Health Centres of the Department of Health. Children who required further assessment are served by the Child Assessment Services. Screening tools for pre-primary educators include *Pre-Primary Children Development and Behaviour Management—Teacher Resource Kit* (Cheung, 2008) and the *Hong Kong Reading Ability Screening Test for Preschool Children* (Ho et al., 2011). The Education Bureau also operates an Early Identification and Intervention for Learning Difficulties Programme for pupils in their first school year, and an Early Identification and Intervention Programme for Speech and Language Problems (Information Services Department, 2011b).

Instruments commonly used to evaluate children with special needs include: the *Wechsler Intelligence Scale for Children, Fourth Edition (Hong Kong)* with updated local norms (2010); and an assessment tool titled the *Hong Kong Cantonese Oral Language Assessment Scale* (Tsou, Lee, Cheung, & Tung, 2006) for diagnosing language impairment among Cantonese speaking preprimary and primary school children.

Two areas in which Hong Kong has made significant advances in recent years are the identification of students with specific learning difficulties (e.g., dyslexia), and the recognition of students with various forms of giftedness or talent. The most commonly assessment tools for the former are the *Hong Kong Test of Specific Learning Difficulties in Reading and Writing for Primary School Students, Second Edition* (Ho et al., 2007) and the *Hong Kong Test of Specific Learning Difficulties in Reading and Writing for Junior Secondary School Students* (Chung, Ho, Chan, Tsang, & Lee, 2007). Observation checklists for teachers are also available. Children with gifts and talents are usually identified by using multiple methods, such as performance in local and international competitions, achievements in schools, standardized achievement tests, intelligence tests, behavioral checklists, and principal/teacher/parent/peer/self nominations (Yuen, 2010).

Challenges and Future Directions

Hong Kong still faces significant challenges in its movement toward inclusion. At the moment, only 10% of teachers are provided with basic training necessary for effectively implementing inclusive education. Many teachers are still not attuned to ways of differentiating instruction and addressing diversity in mainstream classrooms.

Large class size remains an obstacle to implementing a more student-centered and individualized approach particularly in secondary schools, where classes of 40-plus are not unusual. The government has proved to be extremely resistant to the notion of reducing class sizes in mainstream schools. Key personnel in the Education Bureau remain unconvinced that lowering the student/teacher ratio is cost effective.

The education system in Hong Kong remains highly competitive and examination oriented. Many schools are reluctant to include students with special educational needs who may lower the overall school performance in public examinations. Major reforms in academic structure and curriculum have been introduced quite rapidly over the past few years. These placed pressures on teachers resulting in them having less time and inclination to cater for students' special needs.

Future directions must include an expansion of the preservice and in-service teacher professional training to equip them with a wider repertoire of strategies and skills for addressing students' learning and adjustment problems. In particular, more attention needs to be given to effective and feasible methods for differentiating curriculum content according to students' ability level, adapting teaching activities, selecting alternative curriculum resources, structuring group-work, modifying assessment procedures, and using peer and classroom support.

To make better use of the expertise of teachers in special schools (who have more experience, knowledge and skills in catering for students with special needs), more professional collaboration and exchanges between special schools and mainstream schools should be encouraged. Mainstream schools where inclusive practices are working well can be tapped as a source of practical advice for other schools.

To help advance inclusive education, significantly reducing class sizes is a priority for the future. Meanwhile, special schools should continue to receive sufficient funding to meet their requirements and to enable them to use resources in flexible ways. Funding must continue to support the buying-in of outside services where necessary, and to facilitate the purchasing of various form of assistive technology required by students with severe sensory, physical and intellectual impairments.

REFERENCES

Board of Education (1996). *Sub report of the sub-committee on special education*. Retrieved from http://edb.gov.hk/

Chung, K., Ho, C. S.-H., Chan, D., Tsang, S.-M., & Lee, S.-H. (2007). *The Hong Kong test of specific learning difficulties in reading and writing for junior secondary school students (HKT-JS)*. Hong Kong, China: Hong Kong Specific Learning Difficulties Research Team.

Cheung, M. (Ed.) (2008). *Pre-primary children development and behaviour management—Teacher resource kit*. Hong Kong, China: Department of Health, Hong Kong Special Administrative Region Government.

Education Bureau, Hong Kong Special Administrative Region Government. (2010). *Operation guide on the whole school approach to integrated education*. Retrieved from http://edb.gov.hk/

Education Bureau, Hong Kong Special Administrative Region Government. (2011a). *Figures and statistics*. Retrieved from http://www.edb.gov.hk/en/about-edb/publications-stat/figures/enrol-by-level.html

Education Bureau, Hong Kong Special Administrative Region Government. (2011b). *Figures and statistics*. Retrieved from http://www.edb.gov.hk/en/about-edb/publications-stat/figures/special.html

Education Bureau, Hong Kong Special Administrative Region Government. (2011c). *Figures and statistics*. Retrieved from http://edb.gov.hk/

Forlin, C. (2010). Developing and implementing quality inclusive education in Hong Kong: Implications for teacher education. *Journal of Research in Special Educational Needs, 10*, 177–184.

Ho, C. S.-H., Chan, D., Chung, K., Tsang, S.-M., Lee, S.-H., & Cheng, R. W.-Y. (2007). *The Hong Kong test of specific learning difficulties in reading and writing for primary school students, 2nd ed. (HKT-PII).* Hong Kong, China: Hong Kong Specific Learning Difficulties Research Team.

Ho, C.S.H., Leung, K.N.K., Yeung, P.S., Chan, D. W., Chung, K. K. H., Tsang, S. M., & Lee, S. H. (2011). *The Hong Kong reading ability screening test for preschool children.* Hong Kong, China: Hong Kong Specific Learning Difficulties Research Team.

Information Services Department, Hong Kong Special Administrative Region Government. (2011a). *Hong Kong: The facts.* Retrieved from http://www.gov.hk/en/about/abouthk/facts heets/docs/population.pdf

Information Services Department, Hong Kong Special Administrative Region Government. (2011b). *Hong Kong: The facts.* Retrieved from http://www.gov.hk/en/about/abouthk/facts heets/docs/rehabilitation.pdf

Tsou, B., Lee, T., Cheung H., & Tung, P. (2006). *HKCOLAS: Hong Kong Cantonese oral language assessment scale 《香港兒童口語（粵語）能力量表》.* Hong Kong, China: Language Information Sciences Research Center, City University of Hong Kong/Department of Health, HKSAR.

Yuen, M. (2010). Giftedness and talent development. In L.-F. Zhang, J. Biggs, & D. Watkins, (Eds.), *Understanding the learning and development of Asian students: What the 21st century teacher needs to know* (pp.167–192). Singapore: Pearson.

RESOURCES

General information on special education in Hong Kong can be found on the Education Bureau website at http://edb.gov.hk/

A list of all special schools in Hong Kong (as of September 2011) can be located online at http://edb.gov.hk/

PUI-SZE
MANTAK YUEN
University of Hong Kong
Fourth edition

HORNER, ROBERT H. (1949–   )

Rob Horner has used behavioral science to address challenges in education and developmental disabilities. He is the son of a school superintendent, and received his BS from Stanford University in psychology in 1971. After 2 years working as a teacher for children with emotional disorders, and another year as a teacher for children with severe disabilities, he entered graduate school. His master's degree in experimental psychology was received from Washington State University in 1975, and his PhD in special education was earned from the University of Oregon in 1978.

Horner worked closely with Dr. G. Thomas Bellamy from 1978 to 1988 when the strategies for supported employment were being developed and applied to adults with severe developmental disabilities. Central to this work was the application of task analysis, and systematic instruction to build employment skills. In collaboration with Dr. Dean Inman, Bellamy and Horner defined strategies not only for building effective employment skills, but for implementing supported employment across state developmental disabilities services. Many of the strategies developed during this period are still part of supported employment efforts across the United States.

A central challenge in both employment and education is the generalization of skills to the full array of settings where they are needed. Social skills should be used in home, school, and community contexts. Employment skills need to generalize across tasks and materials. Educational skills need to generalize across texts, settings, teachers, and ideas. For children and adults with intellectual and developmental disabilities, the problems of generalization are extreme. Rob Horner collaborated with Tom Bellamy, Bob Koegel, and Glen Dunlap to apply General Case Programming to this challenge. Together they completed a series of research studies documenting that with careful selection and sequencing of teaching examples, children and adults with significant learning disabilities could not only acquire useful skills, but apply those skills throughout the natural settings in their life. General Case Programming was based on early work by Siegfried Engelmann and stimulus control research championed by H. S. Terrace. Horner and his colleagues brought this conceptual knowledge to the practical tasks faced by children and adults who have difficulty learning. The result has been an approach to teaching that is now part of nearly every special education training program across the United States.

In 1987 Horner led a group of researchers and teachers in the creation of a national center focused on positive behavior support. This center originally emphasized "nonaversive behavior support" and included Edward Carr, Glen Dunlap, Robert and Lynn Koegel, Wayne Sailor, Richard Albin, and Jacki Anderson. Over the next 15 years, the guiding principles of positive behavior support that were initially asserted by Drs. Luanna Meyer, Ian Evans, Gary LaVigna, Anne Donnellan, and Mark Durand were validated through systematic research studies. This research emphasized (a) the importance of conducting functional behavioral assessment of problem behavior to understand the events that maintain a behavior before launching an intervention, (b) changing the context in which a person behaves (e.g., those events that happen before a problem behavior) to "prevent" problem situations, (c) careful use of data to assess both the impact of support, and whether support was delivered as planned. Following the clear guidance of Ted Carr, positive behavior support laid out the central importance of letting the values of the learners and their family guide not only the goals of a support plan, but the active practices within the plan.

In 1994 Rob Horner and George Sugai began collaboration on what has become known as "School-Wide Positive Behavioral Interventions and Supports" (SWPBIS). This approach to behavior support emphasizes the whole school as the unit of analysis, and argues that effective behavior support for an individual student cannot be divorced from the classroom and whole-school systems. Led by standards that Sugai developed with Edward Kame'enui and Geoffrey Colvin SWPBIS emerged as a practical approach for organizing schools where a wider array of students could be successful. Horner and Sugai emphasized the importance of functional behavioral assessment at the individual student level, but they also argued that if schools were going to be effective learning environments for all children (for children with autism, learning disabilities, emotional disorders, and intellectual disabilities) then we need whole school systems of support that will work for all these students. Essentially, the message was that the teaching and behavior support strategies that have been so valuable for children with disabilities are also exceptionally effective for children without disabilities. By making schools more efficient and effective learning settings all students benefit.

Horner and Sugai have co-directed a national technical assistance center since 2000 that is funded by the U.S. Department of Education's Office of Special Education Programs. This center has combined systematic research on how best to provide effective instruction and behavior support in schools, and launched a nationwide effort to better understand how practices that have been proven through systematic research can be implemented at scales of social importance. This center now supports more than 14,000 schools across the United States in implementation of SWPBIS, and current work is underway with Drs. Dean Fixsen and Karen Blase to better define the implementation technology needed to scale-up sustainable use of SWPBIS practices.

A recent research direction for Rob Horner has focused on better understanding and assisting school teams to use data in problem solving. A large literature indicates that the technology age is making information available to teachers, administrators, families, and related services personnel. These data are too often unused for active decision making in schools. Horner is collaborating with J. Stephen Newton, Robert and Kate Algozzine, and Anne Todd in the development of (a) Team Initiative Problem Solving (TIPS), and (b) a direct observation measure of team meeting decision making. Results from this research indicate that teams can run meetings more efficiently, and use data more effectively if they follow meeting protocols, and make data instantly available to the team during the meeting.

In addition to his research program, Rob Horner is an endowed professor of special education at the University of Oregon, where he has remained since he took his PhD and launched his research efforts. He has been the editor (or co-editor) of the *Journal for the Association of Persons with Severe Handicaps* (JASH), and the *Journal for Positive Behavioral Intervention* (JPBI). He also has served as associate editor for the *Journal of Applied Behavior Analysis, JASH, JPBI*, and the *American Journal on Intellectual Developmental Disabilities* (AJMR). He currently serves on nine journal research boards, and regularly serves as a reviewer on federal grant review panels. His publications include more than 263 research articles and chapters. He has authored or co-authored or co-edited 27 texts. Horner's leadership and contributions in educational science and systems change at state, regional, district, school, and individual students contexts has been instrumental in developing effective practices that embed data-based decision making to monitor fidelity of implementation and the effects of the intervention on student outcomes.

ANNE W. TODD
University of Oregon
Fourth edition

HORSEBACK RIDING FOR STUDENTS WITH DISABILITIES (*See Equine Therapy*)

HORTICULTURAL THERAPY

Horticultural therapy is also known as *hortitherapy, agritherapy, therapeutic horticulture, plant therapy*, and *hort-therapy*. Horticultural therapy for individuals with disabilities has its roots in the 19th century, during the rise of the large state institutions. Many of these institutions were located in rural areas and included areas for propagation of crops. Residents were trained to plant, care for plants, and harvest. The purpose of this farming was primarily economic rather than therapeutic. However, as a secondary benefit many residents were able to obtain work in agriculture and, in fact, before World War II, agriculture was one of the strongest occupational areas for the disabled.

Contemporary hortitherapy has several underpinnings. It may be a branch of occupational therapy (Burton & Watkins, 1978) used to enhance motor development. It has also been employed as a form of psychotherapy (Watson & Burlingame, 1960) to develop motivation and provide clients with a sense of responsibility for living things (Saever, 1985). Horticultural therapy has also been used as a vocational activity (Downey, 1985; Good-Hamilton, 1985; Schrader, 1979). Such training may be in a sheltered work setting or in a vocational school program for competitive employment.

There are a number of unique hortitherapy programs. Burton and Watkins (1978) described a public school program for students with physical disabilities in which academic concepts were taught while students were involved in plant care. The program was designed from a Piagetian point of view and was transdisciplinary, incorporating physical, occupational, and speech therapy, and classroom instruction. Saever (1985) employed agritherapy with students with learning disabilities (8 to 12 years old) as a means of promoting responsibility, order, and structure, following through on plans, respect for nature, cooperative effort, and positive relationships with adults. Good-Hamilton (1985) described another public school program in which students with intellectual disabilities and learning-disabilities worked in greenhouse production to develop vocational skills (primarily work habits). More than 50% of the students were able to obtain employment at the conclusion of training. The American Horticultural Therapy Association provides many resources for individuals who wish to be trained in horticultural therapy, a journal for the presentation of research, and professional support. The association can be reached online at http://ahta.org/.

REFERENCES

Burton, S. B., & Watkins, M. (1978). *The green scene: Horticultural experiences for the physically impaired student*. Paper presented at the 56th annual International Conference, Council for Exceptional Children, Kansas City, MO.

Downey, R. S. (1985). Teaching the disadvantaged and handicapped. *Agricultural Education Magazine, 57*(8), 5–7.

Good-Hamilton, R. (1985). Plants breed success. *Agricultural Education Magazine, 57*(8), 8–10.

Saever, M. D. (1985). Agritherapy, plants as learning partners. *Academic Therapy, 20*(4), 389–397.

Schrader, B. (1979). *Working hands and 3,000 chrysanthemums. Special report: Fresh views on employment of mentally handicapped people*. Washington, DC: President's Committee on Employment of the Handicapped.

Watson, D. P., & Burlingame, A. W. (1960). *Therapy through horticulture*. New York, NY: Macmillan.

JAMES K. MCAFEE
Pennsylvania State University

See *also* Occupational Therapy; Vocational Education

HOUSE, BETTY J. (1923–   )

Betty J. House earned her BA from Oklahoma University in 1948 and her MA from Brown University in 1949. She received her PhD in 1952 from the University of Connecticut. Beginning as a research assistant at the University of Connecticut in 1954, she has remained there throughout her career and has been a professor in residence in the department of psychology since 1972. Her research interests include learning, memory, cognitive processes, intelligence, and intellectual developmental disabilities.

In collaboration with her husband, Dr. David Zeaman, House has conducted research in intellectual developmental disabilities for more than 30 years. A permanent laboratory was established for their research at the Mansfield State Training School in Connecticut; the National Institute of Mental Health provided funding for their projects for more than 20 years. The major accomplishment of their research has been the development and elaboration of an attention theory of retardation discrimination learning. Their model was first published in 1963. A history of their research and theory development from 1963 to 1979 can be found in Ellis' *Handbook of Mental Deficiency, Psychological Theory and Research* (Zeaman & House, 1970).

House has been associate editor of the *American Journal on Mental Deficiency*. She was a consulting editor for *Child Development* from 1968 to 1981 and has been a consulting editor for the *Journal of Experimental Child Psychology*. She served as associate editor for *Psychology Bulletin* from 1982 to 1984 and became editor in 1985.

REFERENCE

Zeaman, D., & House, B. J. (1970). A review of attention theory. In N. R. Ellis (Ed.), *Handbook of mental deficiency, psychological theory and research* (2nd ed). Hillsdale, NJ: Erlbaum.

KATHRYN A. SULLIVAN
Texas A&M University

See *also* Zeaman, David; Zeaman-House Research

HOUSE-TREE-PERSON

The House-Tree-Person (HTP), developed by J. N. Buck (1948), is a projective drawing technique used to assess personality and psychological adjustment in children and adults; the individual is asked to make freehand drawings of a house, a tree, and a person. It is considered one of the most frequently used projective instruments (Piotrowski & Zalewski, 1993; Watkins, Campbell, Nieberding, & Hallmark, 1995), most likely due to its ease of administration and students' enthusiasm for drawing. In addition, it is often viewed as a nonthreatening way to obtain clinical information and establish rapport early in the assessment process. Drawings such as the HTP are frequently used in the assessment of children who have been abused or maltreated (see Veltman & Browne, 2002), as the child is less likely to exhibit the same restraints of expression as in other formats (Groth-Marnat, 1997).

There are various administration procedures; however, the examinee is typically provided with a pencil with an eraser and three 8½ × 11-inch blank sheets of paper and then asked to draw a picture of a house, tree, and person on each sheet. The examinee is then asked to describe and elaborate on their illustrations. For example, questions such as, "Who is the person you drew?" or "What can you tell me about this house?" can be used to investigate the child's drawings. Each drawing can then be interpreted using a qualitative scoring system such as one devised by Buck (1992); Wenck (1977) also provided an illustrated handbook, with 183 sample illustrations, to facilitate the interpretation of HTP drawings. With the qualitative scoring, the clinician looks for certain characteristics in the drawings that can provide meaningful information about the psychological adjustment of the examinee (i.e., broken windows, heavily drawn tree, or person with no eyes).

Some cautions relative to HTP interpretation are needed. Any interpretation of children's drawings must take into consideration any motor production problems and motor developmental issues that could impact on their representational abilities (e.g., Thomas & Jolley, 1998). Reliability issues have been raised with regard to drawing techniques as well (e.g., Thomas & Jolley, 1998; Veltman & Browne, 2002). Although often used as a nonbiased measure that assumes cross-cultural consistency, there are some indications that, in fact, children's drawings reflect cultural differences as well as individual differences that need to be accounted for (e.g., LaVoy et al., 2001).

REFERENCES

Buck, J. N. (1948). The H-T-P technique. *Journal of Clinical Psychology, 4*, 319–327.

Buck, J. N. (1992). *House-tree-person projective drawing technique: Manual and interpretive guide* (Rev. ed). Los Angeles, CA: Western Psychological Services.

Groth-Marnat, G. (1997). *Handbook of psychological assessment* (3rd ed). New York, NY: Wiley.

LaVoy, S. K., Pedersen, W. C., Reitz, J. M., Brauch, A. A., Luxenberg, T. M., & Nofsinger, C. C. (2001). Children's drawings: A cross-cultural analysis from Japan and the United States. *School Psychology International, 22*, 53–63.

Piotrowski, C., & Zalewski, C. (1993). Training in psychodiagnostic testing in APA-approved PsyD and PhD clinical training programs. *Journal of Personality Assessment, 61*, 394–405.

Thomas, G. V., & Jolley, R. P. (1998). Drawing conclusions: A re-examination of empirical and conceptual bases for psychological evaluation of children from their drawings. *Journal of Clinical Psychology, 37*, 127–139.

Veltman, M. W. M., & Browne, K. D. (2002). The assessment of drawings from children who have been maltreated: A systematic review. *Child Abuse Review, 11*, 19–37.

Watkins, C. E. Jr., Campbell, V. L., Nieberding, R., & Hallmark, R. (1995). Contemporary practice of psychological assessment by clinical psychologists. *Professional Psychology: Research and Practice, 26*(1), 54–60.

Wenck, L. S. (1977). *House-tree-person drawings: An illustrated diagnostic handbook*. Los Angeles, CA: Western Psychological Services.

OLGA L. RODRIGUEZ-ESCOBAR
CYNTHIA A. RICCIO
Texas A&M University

See also Draw-a-Person Test; Kinetic-Family-Drawing; Kinetic School Drawing

HOWE, SAMUEL GRIDLEY (1801–1876)

Samuel Gridley Howe, pioneer educator of the blind and the mentally retarded, was a Massachusetts physician who became superintendent of that state's first school for the blind, which opened in Howe's home in 1832 (Kanner, 1964). Later named the Perkins Institution and Massachusetts School for the Blind, Howe's school led in the development of programs to enable blind students to become academically competent, self-reliant, and competitively employable. Howe's most famous student was a deaf-blind child, Laura Bridgeman, and the school's success in educating her led Helen Keller's father (50 years later) to appeal to the Perkins Institution for help, with the result that Anne Sullivan became young Helen's teacher.

Howe published books for the blind, and through appeals to Congress was instrumental in the establishment of the American Printing House for the Blind in 1879 (Schwartz, 1956). Howe accepted a student with blindness and intellectual disability in 1839, demonstrated that such a child could be successfully educated, and, in 1848, established an experimental program at Perkins for same. With encouraging results in this program, Howe convinced the legislature that education of the intellectual disabilities should be a public responsibility, and a state school for the "mentally retarded" was authorized (Scheerenberger, 1983). That school, established in 1855, became the Walter E. Fernald State School.

REFERENCES

Kanner, L. (1964). *A history of the care and study of the mentally retarded*. Springfield, IL: Thomas.

Scheerenberger, R. C. (1983). *A history of Intellectual Developmental Disabilities*. Baltimore, MD: Paul H. Brookes.

Schwartz, H. (1956). *Samuel Gridley Howe, social reformer*. Cambridge, MA: Harvard University Press.

PAUL IRVINE
Katonah, New York

HUMAN GENOME PROJECT

The Human Genome Project (HGP) was the international, collaborative research program whose goal was the complete mapping and understanding of all the genes of human beings. All our genes are together known as our *genome*. The HGP was the natural culmination of the history of genetics research. In 1911, Alfred Sturtevant, then an undergraduate researcher in the laboratory of Thomas Hunt Morgan, realized that he could—and had to, in order to manage his data—map the locations of the fruit fly (Drosophila melanogaster) genes whose mutations the Morgan laboratory was tracking over generations. Sturtevant's very first gene map can be likened to the Wright brothers' first flight at Kitty Hawk. In turn, the Human Genome Project can be compared to the Apollo program's bringing humans to the moon.

The hereditary material of all multicellular organisms is the famous double helix of deoxyribonucleic acid (DNA), which contains all of our genes. DNA, in turn, is made up of four chemical bases, pairs of which form the rungs of the twisted, ladder-shaped DNA molecules. All genes are made up of stretches of these four bases, arranged in different ways and in different lengths. HGP researchers have deciphered the human genome in three major ways: determining the order, or sequence, of all the bases in our genome's DNA; making maps that show the locations of genes for major sections of all our chromosomes; and producing what are called linkage maps, complex versions of the type originated in early Drosophila research, through which inherited traits (such as those for genetic disease) can be tracked over generations.

The HGP has revealed that there are probably somewhere between 30,000 and 40,000 human genes. The completed human sequence can now identify their locations. This ultimate product of the HGP has given the world a resource of detailed information about the structure, organization, and function of the complete set of human genes. This information can be thought of as the basic set of inheritable instructions for the development and function of a human being.

The International Human Genome Sequencing Consortium published the first draft of the human genome in the journal *Nature* in February 2001, with the sequence of the entire genome's 3 billion base pairs some 90% complete. A startling finding of this first draft was that the number of human genes appeared to be significantly fewer than previous estimates, which ranged from 50,000 genes to as many as 140,000. The full sequence was completed and published in April 2003.

On publication of the majority of the genome in February 2001, Francis Collins, the director of the National Human Genome Research Institute (NHGRI), noted that the genome could be thought of in terms of a book with multiple uses: "It's a history book—a narrative of the journey of our species through time. It's a shop manual, with an incredibly detailed blueprint for building every human cell. And it's a transformative textbook of medicine, with insights that will give health care providers immense new powers to treat, prevent and cure disease" (NHGRI, 2006).

The tools created through the HGP also continue to inform efforts to characterize the entire genomes of several other organisms used extensively in biological research, such as mice, fruit flies, and flatworms. These efforts support each other, because most organisms have many similar, or homologous, genes with similar functions. Therefore, the identification of the sequence or function of a gene in a model organism, for example, the roundworm *C. elegans*, has the potential to explain a homologous gene in human beings, or in one of the other model organisms. These ambitious goals required and will continue to demand a variety of new technologies that have made it possible to relatively rapidly construct a first draft of the human genome and to continue to refine that draft. These techniques include:

- DNA Sequencing
- The Employment of Restriction Fragment-Length Polymorphisms (RFLP)
- Yeast Artificial Chromosomes (YAC)
- Bacterial Artificial Chromosomes (BAC)
- The Polymerase Chain Reaction (PCR)
- Electrophoresis

Information is only as good as the ability to use it, however, and therefore, advanced methods for widely disseminating the information generated by the HGP to scientists, physicians, and others is necessary in order to ensure the most rapid application of research results for the benefit of humanity. Biomedical technology and research are particular beneficiaries of the HGP.

However, the momentous implications for individuals and society for possessing the detailed genetic information made possible by the HGP were recognized from the outset. Another major component of the HGP—and an ongoing component of NHGRI—is therefore devoted to the analysis of the ethical, legal, and social implications (ELSI) of our newfound genetic knowledge, and the subsequent development of policy options for public consideration. The information in this entry was provided by the public domain web site for the National Human Genome Research Institute of the National Institute of Health and can be reached online at http://www.genome.gov.

REFERENCE

National Human Genome Research Institute (NHGRI). (2006). *All about the Human Genome project*. Retrieved from http://www.genome.gov/10001772

STAFF

See also Genetic Counseling; Genetic Mapping

HUMANISM AND SPECIAL EDUCATION

Humanistic approaches to education draw heavily from humanistic philosophy and humanistic psychology. Examples may be found in the alternative or free schools, the most prominent of these being Summerhill, founded by A. S. Neill (1960). It was Neill's belief that children do not need teaching as much as they need love, understanding, approval, and responsible freedom. Self-direction, self-evaluation, and self-fulfillment were emphasized at his school. Another humanistic approach to education was Brown's (1971) confluent education. Believing that education of the whole person is important, he described confluent education as a philosophy and a process of teaching and learning that focuses on both the affective and the cognitive domains. Other humanistic strategies included Simon's values clarification exercises, Kohlberg's moral development activities, Ojemann's causal orientation, Glasser's classroom meetings, Palomares' magic circle, Dinkmeyer's Developing Understanding of Self and Others, Alschuler's organizational approach, Redl's life space interviewing, and Weinstein's trumpet technique. Whatever the approach or strategy, all seemed to be directed toward the goal of the fullest use of capacities by all human beings (Simpson & Gray, 1976).

Prior to 1800 little or no attention was given to the development of the capacities of individuals with disabilities. Among the earliest to provide humane treatment was Pinel. His methods, which became known as moral treatment, were elaborated on and extended by his students and admirers, the best known of whom was perhaps Itard. Not only did Itard attempt to socialize a boy found in the forests of Aveyron, France, but he also attempted to understand the mind and emotions of the child and to feel with and care for him.

The first children with disabilities to receive the attention of organized groups were probably individuals with visual and auditory impairments. Noteworthy here is the work of Howe, who was able to make a significant breakthrough in the education of these children owing, in part, to his unique ability to understand their inner world. Also influential was Rush, whose emphasis on love-oriented methods of control foreshadowed current appeals for more caring relationships with children (Kauffman, 1981; Suran & Rizzo, 1979).

The positivism and humane care associated with moral treatment in the first half of the 1800s gave way to pessimism and dehumanizing institutionalization that continued into the 1900s. In works such as *Christmas in Purgatory, Exodus from Pandemonium*, and *Souls in Extremis*, Blatt (1981) revealed how society treated individuals with intellectual disabilities. *In and Out of Intellectual Developmental Disabilities* is his plea for more humane treatment. "This book took 30 years to write," he said, "and I hope it will teach someone that what we can learn from the life of Helen Keller isn't only that she was educable but that all people are educable" (p. xv). Echoing Blatt were persons such as Baum (1982), Hobbs (1974), and Long, Morse, and Newman (1980). Others calling for freedom, openness, and humanism in special education included Dennison, Grossman, Knoblock, Schultz, Heuchert, and Stampf (Kauffman, 1981).

As attitudes began to change, the rights of children were reinforced at three distinct levels: policy statements of national and international organizations such as the Bill of Rights for Children; court decisions such as *Brown* v. *Board of Education*, providing equal access to educational opportunities; and legislation enacted by Congress, the most important being the Education for All Handicapped Children Act (PL 94-142) passed in 1975 to ensure a free and appropriate public education for all children with special needs (Suran & Rizzo, 1979). However, with regard to the legislation, Morse (1979) noted that the child too often got lost. He called for the humanization of special education with the individual student as the focus. Fischer and Rizzo (1974), Newberger (1978), Shelton (1977), and Zeff (1977) were among those suggesting ways to humanize special education. Fischer and Rizzo offered the following suggestions in their paradigm for humanizing special education. Recognize that children with special needs are experiencing, purposive beings; deemphasize testing and give priority to assessing how the child does what in specific circumstances; replace diagnosis with concrete recommendations; allow the child to be a co-assessor/planner (Rayder, 1978, March); provide students with access to their files, allowing them to have input; and shift focus from limitation to possibility, with the child participating in the direction of his or her life as much as possible.

Newberger presented a mainstreaming reintegration process, situational socialization, through which individuals with disabilities could be helped to acquire the knowledge, behaviors, and attitudes needed to interact successfully with others. Shelton focused on considerations necessary when planning a successful affective program for the learning disabled. Zeff described the implementation and outcome of a group tutorial program designed to help students who underachieve.

An illustrative humanistic approach to special education was in operation at the P. K. Yonge School in Florida. There all pupils were in regular heterogeneous classroom groups. Goals were that each student develop increasingly positive perceptions of himself or herself; accept increasing responsibility for his or her behavior and learning; develop those skills and attitudes necessary for effective group living and interaction; learn to adapt to change and effect change constructively; become an effective lifelong learner; and find real meaning in life. Underlying values included sensitivity, authenticity, self-realization, involvement, creativity, pursuit of excellence, and responsibility (Brown, 1973).

Humanistic approaches to teacher education have been proposed in order to prepare humanistic teachers of children with special needs (Bruininks, 1977; Simpson & Gray, 1976). In these programs teacher education was not centered on learning how to teach but rather on learning how to use one's self and surroundings to help students learn (Wass, Blume, Combs, & Hedges, 1974).

A teacher who devises an education for children with special needs based on a humanistic model will be more of a resource and catalyst for children's learning than a director of activities (Bernard & Huckins, 1974). The classroom atmosphere will be nontraditional, affectively charged, and personal (Kauffman, 1981). Interactions between the teacher and students will be characterized by respect and acceptance, and students' needs for identity, achievement, and individual treatment will be recognized.

REFERENCES

Baum, D. D. (Ed.). (1982). *The human side of exceptionality*. Baltimore, MD: University Park Press.

Bernard, H. W., & Huckins, W. C. (1974). *Humanism in the classroom*. Boston, MA: Allyn & Bacon.

Blatt, B. (1981). *In and out of intellectual developmental disabilities*. Baltimore, MD: University Park Press.

Brown, G. I. (1971). *Human teaching for human learning*. New York, NY: Viking.

Brown, J. W. (1973). *A humanistic approach to special education*. (Resource Monograph No. 8). Gainesville, FL: P. K. Yonge Laboratory School.

Bruininks, V. L. (1977). A humanistic competency-based training for teachers of learning disabled students. *Journal of Learning Disabilities, 10*, 518–526.

Fischer, C. T., & Rizzo, A. A. (1974). A paradigm for humanizing special education. *Journal of Special Education, 8*, 321–329.

Hobbs, N. (1974). *The future of children*. San Francisco, CA: Jossey-Bass.

Kauffman, J. M. (1981). *Characteristics of children's behavior disorders* (2nd ed.). Columbus, OH: Merrill.

Long, N. J., Morse, W. C., & Newman, R. G. (1980). *Conflict in the classroom* (4th ed.). Belmont, CA: Wadsworth.

Morse, W. C. (Ed.). (1979). *Humanistic teaching for exceptional children*. Syracuse, NY: Syracuse University Press.

Neill, A. S. (1960). *Summerhill*. New York, NY: Hart.

Newberger, D. A. (1978). Situational socialization: An affective interaction component of the mainstreaming reintegration construct. *Journal of Special Education, 12*, 113–121.

Rayder, N. F. (1978, March). *Public outcry for humane evaluation and isomorphic validity*. Paper presented at the meeting of the American Educational Research Association, Toronto, Canada.

Shelton, M. N. (1977). Affective education and the learning disabled student. *Journal of Learning Disabilities, 10*, 618–624.

Simpson, E. L., & Gray, M. A. (1976). *Humanistic education: An interpretation*. Cambridge, MA: Ballinger.

Suran, B. G., & Rizzo, J. V. (1979). *Special children: An integrative approach*. Glenview, IL: Scott, Foresman.

Wass, H., Blume, R. A., Combs, A. W., & Hedges, W. D. (1974). *Humanistic teacher education: An experiment in systematic curriculum innovation*. Fort Collins, CO: Shields.

Zeff, S. B. (1977). A humanistic approach to helping underachieving students. *Social Casework, 58*, 359–365.

GLENNELLE HALPIN
Auburn University

See *also* Ecological Education for Children With Disabilities; History of Special Education

HUMAN RESOURCE DEVELOPMENT

Human resource development (HRD) in special education involves the implementation of approaches and interventions designed to improve the functioning of professionals and paraprofessionals in their delivery of special education services. The need for HRD in special education has been exacerbated by four historical trends and events: (1) the changing nature of special education, (2) burnout of special services providers, (3) new professional and legal requirements, and (4) the increasing demand for special education services. The changing nature of special education is evident in many ways, including the introduction of new technologies such as computers. For special services providers to keep abreast of advances, it is important that they participate in skill and knowledge development activities. Burnout and stress have been recognized as important problems for many types of employees, and a review of the literature suggests that special services providers are not exempt from burnout and high levels of job-related stress (Cherniss, 1985).

The HRD approaches and interventions may have the potential for reducing burnout and stress in special education by enriching the work experience of special services providers. The significance of HRD for special education is further underscored by changing professional and legal requirements. The advent of PL 94-142, for example, placed new demands on many special services providers such as multidisciplinary team decision making. It has been argued (Yoshida, 1980) that special services providers and others may have been ill prepared to participate in team decision making. The need for HRD in special education is evident from the increasing demand for special education services. As Sarason (1982) has noted, it is unlikely that traditional approaches to training will be able to generate the number of individuals needed to provide the requested services. Therefore, it is also important to engage various nonprofessional groups (e.g., classroom instructional aides, parents, and even students) in special education HRD.

In contrast to traditional staff development efforts, which have almost exclusively focused on technical competencies, HRD interventions can focus on a broad spectrum of areas that might be functionally related to job performance. These areas include: (1) technical competencies, (2) interpersonal competencies, (3) professional responsibilities, and (4) job satisfaction. Technical competencies refer to job-related knowledge and skills. Interpersonal competencies concern conflict resolution and assertiveness skills that are important to maintaining productive work relationships. Professional responsibilities encompass fulfilling job-related duties in a reliable and timely manner. Job satisfaction is a multidimensional concept referring to both task satisfaction and satisfaction with the organizational climate of the work setting.

Interventions intended to develop these HRD areas can be implemented within the context of several general approaches to HRD, such as in-service training, supervision, consultation, team building, job design, and professional self-management. In-service training has typically involved performance evaluations, participation in conventions and workshops, reading of professional literature, and courses at local colleges (Maher, Cook, & Kruger, 1990). Supervision that is intended to facilitate HRD might involve participatory decision making, goal setting, performance review, and feedback activities. Consultation for the purpose of HRD is voluntarily engaged in by the consultee and might involve the consultee in activities similar to those described with respect to supervision. Team-building approaches to HRD can focus on either improving the functioning of existing work teams or the development of new work teams (Woodman & Sherwood, 1980). Job design as an HRD approach focuses on changing elements of work tasks and setting work conditions so that tasks can be performed in an exemplary manner (Gilbert, 1978). A sixth approach to HRD is professional self-management (Maher, 1985). Professional self-management is characterized by self-initiated and self-sustained efforts to improve one's management of time, stress, intervention cases, interpersonal conflicts, and continuing education.

REFERENCES

Cherniss, C. (1985). Stress, burnout, and the special services providers. *Special Services in the Schools, 2,* 45–61.

Gilbert, T. (1978). *Human competence: Engineering worthy performance.* New York, NY: McGraw-Hill.

Maher, C. A. (1985). *Professional self-management: Techniques for special services providers.* Baltimore, MD: Paul H. Brookes.

Maher, C. A., Cook, S. A., & Kruger, L. J. (1990). A behavioral approach to human resources development in schools. In C. A. Maher & S. G. Forman (Eds.), *Providing effective educational services: Behavioral approaches.* Hillsdale, NJ: Erlbaum.

Sarason, S. B. (1982). *The culture of the school and the problem of change* (2nd ed.). Boston, MA: Allyn & Bacon.

Woodman, R. W., & Sherwood, J. J. (1980). The role of team development in organizational effectiveness. *Psychological Bulletin, 88,* 166–186.

Yoshida, R. K. (1980). Multidisciplinary decision making in special education: Review of the issues. *School Psychology Review, 9,* 221–227.

CHARLES A. MAHER
Rutgers University

LOUIS J. KRUGER
Tufts University

See also Multidisciplinary Teams

HUMPHREY, ELLIOTT S. (1888–1981)

Elliott S. (Jack) Humphrey, after early experiences as a jockey and a cowboy, made a career of the breeding and training of animals. He trained lions and tigers for circuses, and bred some of the dogs used by Admiral Richard E. Byrd in his Antarctic expedition. Dorothy Eustis, who later founded the Seeing Eye, the first American organization to train dogs as guides for the blind, hired Humphrey to breed and train guide dogs for the blind. His teaching methods are credited with the immediate success of the Seeing Eye when it was established in 1928. His methods are used today by more than half a dozen other programs that train guide dogs. Faced with difficulty in finding competent instructors for the Seeing Eye, Humphrey designed and operated a school for instructors that provided not only teachers needed at the Seeing Eye but staff for other guide-dog programs as well (Humphrey & Warner, 1934). Humphrey published a book on the breeding of working dogs, and lectured on his specialty at Columbia University (Putnam, 1979). During World War II he served as a commander in the Coast Guard, with responsibility for organizing and directing a school for dog trainers for the armed forces.

REFERENCES

Humphrey, E. S., & Warner, L. H. (1934). *Working dogs.* Baltimore, MD: Johns Hopkins University Press.

Putnam, P. B. (1979). *Love in the lead.* New York, NY: Dutton.

PAUL IRVINE
Katonah, New York

HUNGERFORD, RICHARD H. (1903–1974)

Richard H. Hungerford, a leader in the field of intellectual developmental disabilities, served from 1942 to 1953 as director of the Bureau for Children with Retarded Mental Development in the New York City public schools. Subsequently he was superintendent of the Laconia, New Hampshire, State School; executive director of the Gulf Bend Center for Children and Youth in Victoria, Texas; executive director of Mental Health and Intellectual Developmental Disabilities Services for the diocese of Galveston-Houston; and professor of special education at Boston University.

During the 1940s, Hungerford developed for New York City's schools a comprehensive curriculum for students with intellectual disabilities that emphasized specific occupational preparation, training in home living skills, and activities aimed at the development of social competence (Blatt, 1975). In 1943 he co-founded, with Chris J. DeProspo, *Occupational Education*, a journal for teachers of mentally retarded pupils. Hungerford's thoughtful writings, especially his beautifully written essays, such as "On Locusts," (Hungerford, 1950) inspired both laypeople and colleagues in the field of intellectual developmental disabilities. Hungerford served as president of the American Association on Mental Deficiency and was editor of its *American Journal of Mental Deficiency* from 1948 to 1959.

REFERENCES

Blatt, B. (1975). Toward an understanding of people with special needs: Three teachers. In J. M. Kauffman & J. S. Payne (Eds.), *Intellectual developmental disabilities: Introduction and personal perspectives*. Columbus, OH: Merrill.

Hungerford, R. H. (1950). On locusts. *American Journal of Mental Deficiency, 54*, 415–418.

Paul Irvine
Katonah, New York

HUNTER, MADELINE CHEEK (1916–1994)

Madeline Cheek Hunter developed a model for teaching and learning that has been widely disseminated in schools throughout the United States and abroad since the 1960s (Hunter, 1969, 1971). Her principles of instruction, based on the premise that the teacher is a decision maker, translated psychological theory into practical language that teachers can understand and apply in the classroom (Goldberg, 1990).

Hunter viewed her model as one that increased the probability of learning by identifying decisions teachers must make, using research evidence to support those decisions, and using student data to augment or correct those decisions (Hunter, 1985). According to Hunter, every decision a teacher makes falls into one of three categories: (1) what you are going to teach, (2) what the students will do to learn it and to let you know they've learned it, and (3) what the teacher will do to facilitate and escalate that learning (Goldberg, 1990). Applied correctly, Hunter asserted that her principles of instruction are appropriate for a variety of teaching circumstances, audiences, and disciplines (Brandt, 1985).

Born in Canada, Hunter emigrated to California with her family at an early age, receiving her education (BA, MA, and PhD) at the University of California at Los Angeles. Working as a psychologist in the inner city of Los Angeles, first at Children's Hospital and later at Juvenile Hall, she found the interventions, which focused on remediation, not prevention, to be "too little, too late" (Goldberg, 1990, p. 42). Convinced that real progress could only be made through prevention, she became a school psychologist in the urban, multicultural schools of Los Angeles. In that capacity, she observed that even very dedicated and capable teachers often failed to see the connection between research and practice (Goldberg, 1990).

After 13 years in Los Angeles area public schools, in 1962 she became associated with the University of California at Los Angeles (UCLA) as principal of the University Elementary School (aka UCLA Lab School) and professor in the College of Education (Goldberg, 1990). During those years, she worked closely with John Goodlad, renowned educator and dean of the UCLA Graduate School of Education. Because Hunter was both a trained psychologist and an experienced educator, she considered herself well-versed in both theory and practice (Brandt, 1985).

During her tenure at UCLA, Hunter developed her model of instruction, which she regarded as professional decision making (Hunter, 1979). In 1967, Hunter published a series of booklets to help teachers translate theory into practice—*Motivation Theory for Teachers, Reinforcement Theory for Teachers,* and *Retention Theory for Teachers*. These programmed, or self-instructional, booklets led the educator through a series of decisions, providing both instruction and application of her model in the process. In addition to her publications, she provided professional development training for teachers and administrators throughout the United States, Asia, Russia, and Europe (Brandt, 1985).

Hunter regarded teaching as a kind of "performance behavior like music, like dancing, like athletics, like surgery. You have to automate many behaviors so you can perform them artistically at high speed" (Goldberg, 1990, p. 42). She emphasized that the basic principles of sound teaching must underlie every lesson. Although these principles form the basis of the lesson, no lesson should look the same; the teacher should decide which elements to include in a particular lesson (Hunter, 1986). "There is absolutely nothing you should expect to see in every lesson and nothing you have to do in education—except *think*" (Goldberg, 1990, p. 43).

Over the years, she developed an entourage of educators who were practicing her model and training others to use them (Coulombe, 1994). Reflecting her belief that effective teachers are active decision makers, Hunter chose to not certify instructors nor standardize her training (Hunter, 1986). Although her principles of instruction were designed to help teachers plan and deliver instruction, in its dissemination this model was oversimplified (Hunter, 1986). This lack of standardization led to various interpretations of the "Hunter model," some of which may have been less than accurate representations of her work, sometimes becoming rigid formulas. Hunter's work is known by several different names, including a clinical theory of instruction, mastery teaching, clinical teaching, the UCLA model, and the Hunter Model (Ryan, Jackson, & Levinson, 1986).

The Hunter Model has not been without critics; debate about its pros and cons has flourished for decades, continuing into the 21st century (Gibboney, 1987; Johnson, 2000; Wolfe, 1998). To many, "doing the Madeline Hunter Model" meant strictly including seven elements in every lesson plan, much to Hunter's dismay (Goldberg, 1990). The oft-cited elements are (1) objectives, (2) standards, (3) anticipatory set, (4) teaching (which also includes input, modeling, and checking for understanding), (5) guided practice, (6) closure, and (7) independent practice. Hunter vehemently disavowed such practices, and was openly critical of principals who evaluated teacher performance using a checklist of these elements (Hunter, 1985).

The oversimplification of the Hunter model may lie, not in the fundamental principles of her model, but in the traditional implementation of inservice teacher education, frequently limited to a few hours (Goldberg, 1990). To successfully internalize her model of instruction, Hunter recommended about 2 years of dedicated study, with coaching as an essential component. She believed that the lack of coaching during and after inservice training of any kind is a grievous error, with the result that teachers rarely translate theory into "artistic procedures" (Hunter, 1985). Her greatest hope was that her work will help teaching become a profession, where its practitioners are decision makers who never stop learning (Goldberg, 1990).

REFERENCES

Brandt, R. (1985). On teaching and supervising: A conversation with Madeline Hunter. *Educational Leadership*, *42*(5), 61–66.

Coulombe, G. (1994). Remembering Madeline Hunter. *Educational Leadership*, 67, 337–338.

Gibboney, R. A. (1987). A critique of Madeline Hunter's teaching model from Dewey's perspective. *Educational Leadership*, *44*(5), 46–50.

Goldberg, M. F. (1990). Portrait of Madeline Hunter. *Educational Leadership*, *47*(5), 141–143.

Hunter, M. (1967). *Motivation theory for teachers*. El Segundo, CA: TIP.

Hunter, M. (1967). *Reinforcement theory for teachers*. El Segundo, CA: TIP.

Hunter, M. (1967). *Retention theory for teachers*. El Segundo, CA: TIP.

Hunter, M. (1969). *Teach more—faster!* El Segundo, CA: TIP.

Hunter, M. (1971). *Teach for transfer*. El Segundo, CA: TIP.

Hunter, M. (1979). Teaching is decision making. *Educational Leadership*, *37*(1), 62–64, 67.

Hunter, M. (1985). What's wrong with Madeline Hunter? *Educational Leadership*, *42*(5), 57–60.

Hunter, M. (1986). Madeline Hunter replies: Develop collaboration; build trust. *Educational Leadership*, *43*(6), 68.

Johnson, A. P. (2000). It's time for Madeline Hunter to go: A new look at lesson plan design. *Action in Teacher Education*, *22*(1), 72–78.

Ryan, C. W., Jackson, B. L., & Levinson, E. M. (1986). Human relations skills training in teacher education: The link to effective practice. *Journal of Counseling & Development*, 65(2), 114–116.

Wolfe, P. (1998). Revisiting effective teaching. *Educational Leadership*, *56*(3), 61–64.

ELAINE A. CHEESMAN
University of Colorado at Colorado Springs

HUNTER SYNDROME

Hunter syndrome (mucopolysacchridosis II, or MPS II), a progressive disorder arising from a deficiency in the enzyme iduronate sulfatase, is a sex-linked inborn error of metabolism (IEM) affecting only males. The enzyme's absence or deficiency prevents complete breakdown of the mucopolysacchrides heparen sulphate and dermatan sulfate, which then accumulate in bodily cells (National MPS Society, 2001). One of a group of lycosomal storage disorders that arise from altered mucopolysaccharide metabolism, Hunter syndrome is of two types, MPS IIA, having severe effects commonly leading to death by age 10 to 15 years, and MPS IIB, having milder effects and a life span of about 50 years (Flagler, 2000; Jones, 1997). Collapse of the trachea, cardiac failure, and neurological problems are usual causes of death (Jones, 1997; Pediatric Database, 1994). In both types, development is apparently normal for about the first 2 years of life followed by progressive deterioration. Major features of both types are presented here; Pediatric Database (1994) contains a more complete list.

Hunter syndrome is a rare disorder affecting an estimated 1 in 100,000 to 150,000 males worldwide (National MPS Society, 2001). Because females are carriers, those with family histories of Hunter syndrome may want to have genetic counseling before having children (National MPS Society, 2001).

No treatment or cure is currently available. Bone marrow transplantation has had limited effects (Meyer, 1997). The best that can be done is to provide support to these children and their families. As children with severe Hunter syndrome may have recurrent ear infections, hydrocephalus, congestive heart failure, respiratory problems, hernias, and gastrointestinal problems (Knoell, 2000; Naggs, 1999), a variety of medical interventions may be frequently needed.

Characteristics

Type MPS IIA

1. Growth retardation and short terminal height.
2. Progressive intellectual developmental disabilities and hearing and vision loss, often to severe levels.
3. Hyperactivity and aggressive behavior.
4. Coarse facial features, full lips, macrocephaly.
5. Enlarged internal organs, leading to large abdomen.
6. Progressive stiffening of joints, especially fingers.
7. Severe neurologic, cardiac, and airway complications in advanced stages.

Type MPS IIB

1. Normal to mild intellectual developmental disabilities.
2. Somatic abnormalities, including respiratory and cardiovascular, of the same type and ultimate severity as in MPS IIA but developing much more slowly.
3. Carpal tunnel syndrome.
4. Visual impairment owing to corneal opacities and hearing impairment.

Boys with Hunter syndrome need extensive special education interventions. Having recurrent problems and a progressive disease, they need teachers who are skilled in basic medical care. These boys can have problems chewing and swallowing their food, so caretakers must ensure that they have easily managed food such as soft puddings or pureed food (Naggs, 1999). Their progressive stiffening of joints will call for physical therapy. Boys with severe

Hunter syndrome may never speak or have a very small vocabulary and be prone to repetition of words or short phrases (Naggs, 1999) and will benefit from speech therapy to improve basic communication. Because their hyperactive and aggressive behavior may be disruptive (Pediatric Database, 1994), their instructors should be skilled in working with profoundly impaired students. Boys with the milder form of Hunter syndrome may be placed in a more normal school setting, although they may still need services for mild retardation and disruptive behavior disorders.

The prognosis for boys with the severe form is poor. Their progressive deterioration leads to increasing dependency, physical problems, and early death. Boys with the less severe form can be expected to live a more normal life but will still need considerable medical and educational intervention. Current research focuses on gene therapy and enzyme replacement therapy as ways of controlling Hunter syndrome (Meyer, 1997).

REFERENCES

Flagler, S. F. (2000). Hunter's syndrome (mucopoly sacchridosis II). In C. R. Reynolds & E. Fletcher-Janzen (Eds.), *Encyclopedia of special education* (2nd ed., Vol. *2*, pp. 909–910). New York, NY: Wiley.

Jones, K. L. (1997). *Smith's recognizable patterns of human malformation* (5th ed.). Philadelphia, PA: Saunders.

Knoell, K. (2000). Denoument and discussion: Hunter syndrome (mucopolysacchardosis IIA). *Pediatrics and Adolescent Medicine*, *154*, 86–89.

Meyer, G. (1997). Syndromes and inborn errors of metabolism. In M. L. Batshaw (Ed.), *Children with disabilities* (4th ed., pp. 813–834). Baltimore, MD: Paul H. Brookes.

Naggs, T. (1999). *Hunter's syndrome: Description and educational considerations.* (ERIC Document Reproduction Service No. EC 307 023)

National MPS Society. (2001). *MPS II Hunter syndrome.* Retrieved from http://www.mpssociety.org/mps2.htm

Pediatric Database. (1994). *Hunter syndrome.* Retrieved from http://www.icondata.com/health/pedbase/.les/HUNTERSY.HTM

AMY MORROW
ROBERT T. BROWN
University of North Carolina, Wilmington

HUNTER SYNDROME (MUCOPOLY SACCHARIDOSIS II)

Hunter syndrome (mucopoly saccharidosis II), which belongs to a general family of mucopolysaccharide disorders (including Hurler, Scheie, Hurler-Scheie, Marquio, and Sanfillipo syndromes; Brown & Trivette, 1998), is transmitted as an X-linked recessive trait that occurs primarily in males. Growth during the first 2 years is normal, with malformations occurring during years 2 to 4. There are two types of Hunter syndrome, A (severe) and B (mild). In type A, there is no clouding of corneas and death usually occurs before year 15. Concomitant intellectual developmental disabilities and learning levels are higher than for children with Hurler syndrome (Carter, 1978). However, behavior disorders and hyperactive and destructive behavior are often seen as a result, and the children tend to become difficult to manage as they mature. With type B, survival rates may extend to age 50, with fair intelligence possible (Wortis, 1981).

Children having Hunter syndrome will appear short in stature with stiff joints and a large abdomen (associated with enlarged organs like the spleen and liver). Children have a large head, prominent forehead, long skull, and coarse eyebrows. Thick lips, broad flat nose, and misaligned teeth are seen as the child develops. Hairiness, especially in brows and lashes, is characteristic and usually apparent by 2 to 4 years of age. Hands are clawlike, with short and stubby fingers; stiff hands and feet may present mobility and coordination problems (Lemeshaw, 1982).

Intellectual developmental disabilities occurs in varying degrees but because development is normal to age 2 or beyond, cognitive and verbal capabilities may be higher than in other syndromes having similar physical characteristics. Motor retardation may be more likely as the child matures. Seizures also have been noted in older children. Progressive nerve deafness and occasional vision problems are present in some Hunter syndrome children (Illingworth, 1983). Many learning-disabled like symptoms (low attention span, hyperkinesis, negative behavior) may also be displayed.

Health and behavior problems, coupled with the motoric and mental disabilities that occur later in development, may require placement in a more restricted setting than the regular classroom. Visual, speech, and hearing impairments that may occur will need to be assessed and remediated by a special education specialist. Physical and occupational therapy may also be necessary. Hunter syndrome is quite rare, occurring in about 1 per 140,000 male births (Brown & Trivette, 1998).

REFERENCES

Brown, M. B., & Trivette, P. S. (1998). Mucopolysaccharide disorders. In L. Phelps (Eds.), *Health-related disorders in children and adolescents*. Washington, DC: American Psychological Association.

Carter, C. (Ed.). (1978). *Medical aspects of Intellectual Developmental Disabilities* (2nd ed.). Springfield, IL: Thomas.

Illingworth, R. (1983). *Development of the infant and young child: Abnormal and normal* (7th ed.). New York, NY: Churchill, Livingstone.

Lemeshaw, S. (1982). *The handbook of clinical types in Intellectual Developmental Disabilities*. Boston, MA: Houghton Mifflin.

Wortis, J. (Ed.). (1981). *Intellectual Developmental Disabilities and developmental disabilities: An annual review*. New York, NY: Brunner/Mazel.

SALLY F. FLAGLER
University of Oklahoma

See also Hurler Syndrome; Physical Anomalies

HUNTINGTON'S CHOREA

Huntington's chorea, or Huntington's disease, is a degenerative condition, the progression of which is insidious. Its onset generally occurs between 25 and 50 years of age and is characterized by involuntary, irregular, jerking movements (i.e., chorea). Although the condition is often not correctly diagnosed until the onset of the chorea, Bellamy (1961) found that 29% of his patients manifested emotional disturbance prior to the abnormal motor movements. As the disease progresses, mental deterioration occurs and, after 10 to 20 years, ends with the death of the afflicted individual.

Huntington's chorea is rare; most prevalence studies agree that it occurs in from 4 to 7 individuals per 100,000 in the population. Although it was long thought not to occur among certain ethnic groups (e.g., Jewish families), such is not the case. However, it is apparently true that, among Japanese, the disease occurs at a much lower rate (about .4 per 100,000).

The major symptoms of the disease had been reported in earlier literature by several individuals: Charles O. Waters in 1841, Charles L. Gorman in 1848, George B. Wood in 1855, and Irving W. Lyon in 1863. Nevertheless, George S. Huntington is widely considered to deserve the use of his name in the medical nomenclature because his 1872 description of the symptoms of the disease was so accurate (DeJong, 1973).

Huntington's chorea is transmitted by a dominant autosome. That is, half of the children of a parent who carries the gene will become afflicted (Coleman, 1964). The prevalence could be reduced to zero in one generation if affected individuals would forego bearing children. Nevertheless, this solution is difficult to implement because the carrier is often unaware of the problem until after the prime reproductive years. In addition, since the disease originates as a defective gene mutation, abstinence on the part of the gene carrier from parenthood remains only a partial solution.

Unfortunately, there is no cure for Huntington's chorea. Though both drug therapy and neurosurgery have been applied successfully to alleviate the symptoms of the disease, the ultimate problem is most likely to be resolved through prevention. The precisely affected genetic structure has been mapped to 4p16.3 (Nation, Turk, & Reynolds, 1998).

Compared to adult-onset HC, juvenile Huntington's chorea (JHC) has a greater paternal inheritance pattern, less prominent choreiform movements, greater rigidity, facial grimacing, and dysfluent speech. Unlike the adult who exhibits hyperkinetic movement patterns, children present more like Parkinson's patients, that is, with rigid musculature and slowed movements. With JHC there is also a propensity to develop epilepsy, often in the form of generalized myoclonic seizures. Although the disease progresses more slowly than when it begins in adulthood, the disease is often more severe in children and adolescents. Psychological problems, especially depression and paranoid ideations, are fairly common among individuals with JHC, and the disease eventually causes dementia and death.

Characteristics

1. Rigidity, epilepsy, and paternal inheritance pattern are more common in JHC.

2. Children with JHC have ataxic gait, speech dysfluency, and facial grimacing.

3. Chorea is less pronounced in children with JHC, but involuntary jerking does show.

4. There is an eventual decline in cognitive functioning and academic performance.

5. Significant psychological problems, including depression, are present.

6. The disease is more severe in JHC, and lifespan may be shorter than in adult HC.

Diagnosis is typically based on symptom presentation and family history of the disease (i.e., at least one affected parent). Magnetic resonance imaging and computerized tomography scans do, however, show a characteristic pattern of atrophy in areas of the caudate nucleus, corpus striatum, and cerebral cortex. Genetic studies can also provide information as to the likelihood that a person will develop the disease because having the HC gene predicts having the disease. Genetic testing can be done, however, when an individual is asymptomatic; testing protocols often include a minimum age of 18 and consent for follow-up counseling. Prenatal testing can also be done when parents have HC or are at 50% risk.

Children and adolescents with JHC often require special education services (e.g., as Other Health Impairment). Psychological services are also likely to be needed given the degenerative nature and severity of the disease. Supportive therapy for both the child and family should be offered, as well as help making contact with community agencies.

Treatment for the disease itself consists of symptom relief, that is, drugs that improve movements by reducing the impact on the dopaminergic and cholinergic systems and drugs that treated associated problems (e.g., valproic acid, baclofen, haloperidol, and phenothiazine). Neuroleptics have the advantage of treating both abnormal movements and psychiatric symptoms.

Prognosis for HC is poor. Not only is quality of life compromised, but life span is also shortened. On average individuals with HC live 8 years from the time of onset (Fenichel, 1993). In males who have JHC with early onset of rigidity and a pattern of paternal inheritance, the duration of the disease is even shorter. Although research has made great strides in identifying the gene responsible for HC, little has been done to change the outcome. Prevention methods currently consist of genetics testing and counseling regarding pregnancy.

REFERENCES

Bellamy, W. E., Jr. (1961). Huntington's chorea. *North Carolina Medical Journal, 22,* 409–412.

Coleman, J. C. (1964). *Abnormal psychology and modern life* (3rd ed.). Chicago, IL: Scott, Foresman.

DeJong, R. N. (1973). The history of Huntington's chorea in the United States of America. In A. Barbeau, T. Chase, & G. W. Paulson (Eds.), *Advances in neurology—Huntington's chorea* (Vol. *1*). New York, NY: Raven.

Fenichel, G. (1993). *Clinical pediatric neurology.* Philadelphia, PA: Saunders.

Nation, P., Turk, K., & Reynolds, C. R. (1998). Huntington's disease. In L. Phelps (Ed.), *Health-selected disorders in children and adolescents* (pp. 337–342). Washington, DC: American Psychological Association.

RONALD C. EAVES
Auburn University
First edition

CECIL R. REYNOLDS
Texas A&M University
Second edition

ELAINE CLARK
University of Utah

See also Chorea; Genetic Counseling

HUNT, JOSEPH MCVICKER (1906–1991)

Joseph McVicker Hunt was born in Scottsbluff, Nebraska, on March 19, 1906. He attended the University of Nebraska, receiving his BA there in 1929 and his MA in 1930. He then received his PhD in 1933 from Cornell University. On graduating, he became a National

Research Council fellow in psychology, spending the year 1933 to 1934 at New York Psychiatric Institute and Columbia University and 1934 to 1935 at Worcester State Hospital and Clark University. After a year as visiting assistant professor of psychology at the University of Nebraska in 1935, Hunt went to Brown University as an instructor in psychology in 1936, advancing to assistant professor in 1938 and associate professor in 1944. While at Brown, Hunt became associated with Butler Hospital in Providence, Rhode Island, acting as research associate (1944–1946) and as director (1946–1951). In 1951, Hunt joined the department of psychology at the University of Illinois as professor of psychology, a position he held until gaining Professor Emeritus status in 1974. Hunt died in 1991.

Hunt is well-known for his many studies in child psychology. Aside from being professor of psychology, he was also professor of early education at the University of Illinois (1967–1974). He was chair of the White House Task Force on Early Childhood Education and was instrumental in the preparation of the report "A Bill of Rights for Children." That report recommended extending Head Start programs to very young children and promoted a follow-through program that would extend the age limits of Head Start children.

Hunt's long list of publications (Hunt, 1950, 1965, 1986, 1987, 1988) have dealt with problems of clinical psychology, child psychology, social casework, personality and behavior disorders, and intelligence.

REFERENCES

Hunt, J. McV. (1950). *Measuring results in social casework: A comparison of diagnostic and functional casework concepts.* New York, NY: Family Service Association of America.

Hunt, J. McV. (1965). *Intrinsic motivation and its role in psychological development.* Proceedings of the Nebraska Symposium on Motivation. Lincoln: University of Nebraska Press.

Hunt, J. McV. (1986). Effect of variations in quality and type of early child care on development. *New Directions for Child Development, No. 32,* 31–48.

Hunt, J. McV. (1987). Effects of differing kinds of experience in early rearing conditions. In I. C. Uzgiris & J. McV. Hunt (Eds.), *Infant performance and experience: New findings with the ordinal scales.* Urbana: University of Illinois Press.

Hunt, J. McV. (1988). Relevance to educability: Heritability or range of reaction. In S. G. Cole & R. G. Demaree (Eds.), *Applications of interactionist psychology: Essays in honor of Saul B. Sells.* Hillsdale, NJ: Erlbaum.

RAND B. EVANS
Texas A&M University
First edition

MARIE ALMOND
The University of Texas of the Permian Basin
Second edition

HURLER SYNDROME

Hurler syndrome (gargoylism; lipochondrodstrophy), a mucopolysaccharide disorder of the same family as Hunter syndrome, is an inherited metabolic disorder that can affect an individual's physical or mental development. There are two distinct forms of this disease (Stanbury, Wyngaarden, & Fredrickson, 1966). The milder form of this disorder results from an inherited sex-linked recessive gene commonly carried by the X chromosome of the 23rd pair of chromosomes. It is more likely to be expressed in the male population. The more severe form is inherited by way of an autosomal recessive gene that may affect any one of the 22 genes inherited from either parent (H. Robinson & Robinson, 1965).

In its milder form, clinical indicators of Hurler syndrome may not be evident at birth, although symptoms generally begin to appear by 6 months of age. By 2 years of age, affected children may reflect retarded physical or mental growth. In its more severe form, individuals may manifest a variety of physical characteristics. Owing to a build-up of mucopolysaccharides throughout the body, abnormal growths will result. Tissues in the liver, heart, lungs, and spleen are most often the areas affected. Abnormal lipid deposits may result in lesions in the gray matter of the brain. Even in its severe form, this genetic defect accounts for less than 1% of the severe intellectual developmental disabilities in children.

Physical characteristics of this disorder typically include an underdeveloped body with significant disproportion between the head and body. Limbs are short and mobility may be limited as fingers and toes are often fixed in a partial flexed position. Bone abnormalities may affect the vertebrae and result in a shortened neck and protruding belly, with possible umbilical hernia.

Individuals severely affected by Hurler disease often have an enlarged head and protruding forehead. Facial characteristics may include bushy eyebrows, a saddle-shaped nose, double chin, and enlarged tongue. The more common form of this disorder is characterized by dwarfism and corneal clouding. In this more severe form of the disorder, individuals may live only into their teens, with death resulting from heart failure or respiratory disease. In milder cases, there is an absence of corneal clouding and dwarfism, but there is a high frequency of deafness from nerve damage.

Diagnostic advances in detecting fetal abnormalities have accurately confirmed the presence of Hurler syndrome as early as 14 to 16 weeks into gestation. This diagnosis is made on the basis of finding elevated levels of the compound mucopolysaccharide in amniotic fluid (Henderson & Whiteman, 1976). A positive in vitro diagnosis of Hurler syndrome is questionable owing to the variety of related diseases. As advances are made in microtechnology, the efficacy of in vitro diagnosis will increase.

Characteristics

1. The syndrome may be detected before birth through amniocentesis.
2. Symptoms become apparent after the first few months.
3. Subsequent to birth, the syndrome is diagnosed through urine samples, skeletal changes observed in X-rays, and family history.
4. Symptoms include enlarged spleen and liver, coarse features (low forehead and enlargement of head), dwarfism, chest deformity, stiff joints, clouding of the cornea, deafness, heart murmurs, and mental deterioration.
5. The progressive syndrome leads to physical and mental retardation and severely decreased life expectancy.

REFERENCES

Henderson, H., & Whiteman, P. (1976). Antenatal diagnoses of Hurler's disease. *Lancet, 2*, 1024–1025.

Robinson, H. B., & Robinson, N. M. (1965). *The mentally retarded child*. New York, NY: McGraw-Hill.

Stanbury, J. B., Wyngaarden, J. B., & Fredrickson, D. S. (Eds.). (1966). *The metabolic bases of inherited diseases* (2nd ed). New York, NY: McGraw-Hill.

Francine Tompkins
University of Cincinnati

See also Amniocentesis; Chromosomes, Human Anomalies, and Cytogenetic Abnormalities; Hunter Syndrome

HUTCHINSON-GILFORD PROGERIA SYNDROME

Hutchinson-Gilford progeria syndrome is a very rare progressive disorder characterized by an appearance of accelerated aging in children (National Organization for Rare Disorders [NORD], 2012). Progeria is a Greek term meaning "prematurely old." The classic type is Hutchinson-Gilford progeria syndrome, first described in England in 1886 by Jonathan Hutchinson and again in 1886 and 1904 by Hastings Gilford (Brown, 2000). Signs of progeria become visible from age 6 months to 1 year, after an apparently normal early infancy. Affected individuals seldom exceed the size of a healthy 5-year-old, although they have the appearance of 60-year-old adults by the time they are 10 years of age (NORD, 2012).

Hutchinson-Gilford progeria syndrome has a reported incidence of about 1 in 8 million newborns. The number of published cases since 1886 is just over 100. The disease appears to affect sexes and races equally, and cases have been reported around the world. Although the cause of progeria remains a mystery, this disorder is believed to be the result of an autosomal dominant mutation. Because neither parent carries the mutation, each case is believed to represent a sporadic new mutation that probably occurs at the time of conception (Brown, 2000; NORD, 2012).

Characteristics

Primary (Almost Always Present When Condition Is Apparent)

1. Growth failure during first year of life with diminished subcutaneous fat.
2. Generalized alopecia (baldness).
3. Small face relative to head size.
4. Micrognathia (small jaw).
5. Delayed tooth formation.
6. Stiffness of joints and limited range of motion.
7. Wide-based, shuffling gait.
8. Atherosclerosis and cardiovascular problems.
9. Infantile sex organs.

Frequently Present Characteristics

1. Dry, scaly, aged-looking skin.
2. Prominent superficial veins.
3. Loss of eyebrows and eyelashes.
4. Open anterior fontanelle.
5. Beaked nose.
6. Brittle bones, with repeated nonhealing fractures.

No specific tests exist for this disorder; diagnosis is based on symptoms and features found on physical examination. Diagnosis typically occurs between 1 and 2 years of age, when symptoms that resemble the regular aging process become apparent. The skin becomes wrinkled and dry; hair becomes lighter and begins to fall out; and circulatory and respiratory complications occur. Motor and cognitive development appears to be normal, although muscles may begin to atrophy (NORD, 2012).

Treatments may include injections of growth hormone and coronary bypass surgery (Dyck et al., 1987) although no effective treatment for progeria has been discovered. Special education considerations include possible heart disease, insulin-resistant diabetes, and other physical abnormalities that may require medical treatment and interfere with regular school attendance or progress. Because of quickly progressing atherosclerosis, stroke is a possible complication. A few individuals are mentally retarded; however, most have normal intelligence and may even be academically advanced. Emotional support for affected individuals and their families, including support groups, counseling, and education, is certainly warranted. School-age children with Hutchinson-Gilford progeria syndrome will likely be eligible for special education services under Other Health Impairment, and the categories of Mentally Retarded or Orthopedically Handicapped may be appropriate depending on specific symptoms and their severity. Information regarding neuropsychological or educational functioning in individuals affected with progeria is not available in the literature.

Life expectancy for patients with progeria is minimal. By age 10, extensive arteriosclerosis and heart disease have typically developed, and most patients die during adolescence. According to reviews of the literature, the age at death ranges from 7 to 27 years, with a median age of death at 13.4 (NORD, 2012). Rodriguez, Perez-Alonso, Funes, and Perez-Rodriguez (1999) reported a case of a 35-week-old fetus with a severe prenatal form of progeria. Although the precise diagnosis for this fetus, who died shortly after birth, has been debated (Faivre et al., 1999), future research efforts should be directed toward prenatal identification, both for study of the development of the pathology and for possible prevention and early intervention. Treatment options should increase as a result of greater understanding of the pathology that characterizes this disorder. More information is needed about the psychosocial and educational functioning of affected individuals so that appropriate school programs and parent support can be provided.

REFERENCES

Brown, T. (2000). *The progeria syndrome fact sheet*. Progeria Research Foundation. Retrieved from http://www.progeria research.org

Dyck, J. D., David, T. E., Burke, B., Webb, G. D., Henderson, M. A., & Fowler, R. S. (1987). Management of coronary artery disease in Hutchinson-Gilford syndrome. *Journal of Pediatrics, 111,* 407–410.

Faivre, L., Van Kien, P. K., Madinier-Chappat, N., Nivelon-Chevallier, A., Beer, F., & LeMerrer, M. (1999). Can Hutchinson-Gilford progeria syndrome be a neonatal condition? *American Journal of Medical Genetics, 87,* 450–452.

National Organization for Rare Disorders. (2012). *Hutchinson Gilford progeria syndrome*. Retrieved from http://www .rarediseases.org

Rodriguez, J. I., Perez-Alonso, P., Funes, R. & Perez-Rodriguez, J. (1999). Lethal neonatal Hutchinson-Gilford progeria syndrome. *American Journal of Medical Genetics, 82,* 242–248.

CYNTHIA A. PLOTTS
Texas State University, San Marcos

HYDROCEPHALUS

Hydrocephalus is a condition caused by an accumulation of cerebrospinal fluid (CSF) inside the skull. Most often this condition occurs when the pathways of CSF are somehow blocked, not allowing the fluid to drain as it normally would, but it may also occur with overproduction or lack of reabsorption of CSF (Mathie & Clark, 2003). Hydrocephalus is usually a secondary outcome of another disorder. These underlying etiologies include: neural tube defects (e.g., spina bifida), aqueductal stenosis, Dandy-Walker syndrome (DWS), intraventricular hemorrhage (IVH), and complications from hypoxic-ischemic encephalopathy in premature infants (Fletcher, Dennis, & Northrup, 2000).

Congenital or early-onset hydrocephalus is diagnosed before infants reach 12 months of age. Most cases of congenital hydrocephalus are detected very early—either before, at, or shortly after birth (Fletcher et al., 2000). Babies with this condition often appear lethargic and irritable, with pupils that are sluggish. Also, because the skull sutures of infants have not completely closed, hydrocephalus at this age typically results in an abnormally large head and prominent forehead. Atrophy of the brain, mental deterioration, and convulsions are often common results of early-onset or congenital hydrocephalus. Less commonly, hydrocephalus can occur later in childhood or adulthood, usually as a result of head trauma, infections, or with dementia in adults (Fletcher et al., 2000).

The most common and effective method of treatment for hydrocephalus involves the surgical insertion of a shunt. The shunt acts as an artificial pipeline, directing the CSF around any obstructions so that it can drain away into another area, such as the abdominal cavity (Fletcher et al., 2000).

The extra intracranial pressure caused by the overaccumulation of CSF in hydrocephalus often causes other problems, damaging or impairing brain structures. Additionally, children born with the condition many times also exhibit other malformations of the brain. The corpus callosum may be deformed, the cerebellum may be displaced or partially missing, and there may be reduced brain mass overall or thinning in certain areas (Fletcher et al., 2000).

Children with hydrocephalus commonly experience a wide range of developmental and other difficulties. Specific deficiencies vary depending on the etiology and severity of each child's condition, but many trends have been noted. For example, children afflicted with hydrocephalus commonly exhibit poorly developed motor skills, below-average visual-motor abilities, and difficulty with other areas of nonverbal ability (Mathie & Clark, 2003). Once these children reach school age, a host of learning and behavior problems may arise. While not all children with hydrocephalus require special education placement, many receive services for Specific Learning Disabilities, Emotional Disturbance, Other Health Impairment, or Traumatic Brain Injury.

In addition to special education placement, children with hydrocephalus may need tutoring or extra instruction to help them catch up, if they have missed school for hospital stays and medical procedures (Mathie & Clark, 2003). They also may have problems with attention, though these difficulties may be related to nonverbal skills deficiencies (Fletcher et al., 2000).

REFERENCES

Fletcher, J. M., Dennis, M., & Northrup, H. (2000). Hydrocephalus. In K. O. Yeates, M. D. Ris, & H. G. Taylor (Eds.), *Pediatric neuropsychology* (pp. 25–46). New York, NY: Guilford Press.

Mathie, H., & Clark, E. (2003). Hydrocephalus, X-linked. In E. Fletcher-Janzen & C. R. Reynolds (Eds.), *Childhood disorders diagnostic desk reference* (pp. 301–302). Hoboken, NJ: Wiley.

LISA A. LOCKWOOD
Texas A&M University

See *also* Dandy-Walker Syndrome; Other Health Impaired; Spina Bifida

HYDROCEPHALUS, X-LINKED

Hydrocephalus is a condition that is caused by abnormal buildup or accumulation of cerebrospinal fluid (CSF) in the ventricles or subarachnoid space of the brain. As a result, intracranial pressure is increased by overproduction of CSF, obstruction of the flow of CSF, or failure to reabsorb the fluid. Hydrocephalus can be either congenital with an early onset or acquired. The principal etiologies of congenital hydrocephalus include Dandy-Walker syndrome (DWS), neural tube defects, aqueductal stenosis, intraventricular hemorrhage (IVH), and complications from hypoxicischemic encephalopathy affecting premature infants (Fletcher, Dennis, & Northrup, 2000).

The prevalence rate for hydrocephalus is dependent on the specific etiology. Neural tube defects are estimated to occur in 1% to 2% of 1,000 births in North America, with spina bifida occurring at a rate of 0.5% to 1.0% in 1,000. Hydrocephalus occurs in 80% to 90% of children diagnosed with spina bifida and affects 70% to 80% of children with DWS, which has a rate of 1 in 30,000 live births. Hydrocephalus is present in 100% of cases of aqueductal stenosis, a condition that affects 0.5 in 1,000 live births. Hydrocephalus is also associated with IVH, a condition that occurs in 20% of premature infants (Fletcher et al., 2000). Acquired hydrocephalus can be caused by a number of conditions, including brain tumor, arachnoid cyst, traumatic brain injury (TBI), central nervous system infections such as meningitis, and intracranial and intraventricular hemorrhaging.

Congenital, or early-onset, hydrocephalus is identified and treated before 12 months of age. More often, however, it is diagnosed within the first few days of life. Early signs include abnormal increase in the circumference of the head in the first 8 weeks, head circumference exceeding the infant's chest, prominent veins in the scalp, and widely spaced eyes (Eaves, 2000). The pupils are often sluggish and respond unequally to light, and these infants present as lethargic and irritable. In cases of acquired hydrocephalus, the older child often complains of severe headache pain (especially on awakening) and has problems with ataxic gait.

Characteristics

1. Abnormal growth of the skull and/or ventricles as a result of accumulated CSF.
2. Headaches, irritability, and lethargy.
3. Poor gross and fine motor skills, including motor slowing.
4. Poor visual-motor and spatial abilities.

The most common treatment of hydrocephalus is the surgical placement of a shunt to divert CSF to other areas of the body (e.g., abdominal cavity). This treatment usually allows the child to have a normal life span; however, repeated shunting and complications caused by surgical interventions (e.g., shunt obstructions and infections) often reduce the quality of life. Frequent hospitalizations can also make an impact due to lengthy absences from school and interruption in academic and social activities. Nonetheless, appropriately treated hydrocephalus (i.e., surgical and medical management) gives patients the best chance to lead a normal life and have a good prognosis.

Although the cognitive abilities of a child with hydrocephalus are largely dependent on the etiology of the condition, deficits are commonly seen in nonverbal skill areas. Children with early-onset hydrocephalus have poorly developed gross and fine motor skills and have problems with visual-motor and spatial ability. Children with hydrocephalus also have high rates of behavior disorders compared to the general population (Fletcher et al., 2000). Not all children with hydrocephalus warrant special education placements. However, when serious learning and psychological problems occur, the child should be evaluated by the school psychologist and considered at an Individual Educational Plan meeting. Which category of service, if any, will depend on the severity and nature of the child's difficulty; however, possible considerations include Specific Learning Disabilities, Emotional Disturbance, Other Health Impairment, and Traumatic Brain Injury. Regardless of the need for special education, children with this condition are likely to benefit from accommodations in the regular classroom. As a result of motor slowing and poor fine motor skills, children with hydrocephalus may need extra time to take down notes from the board and complete written assignments. Tutoring may also be needed to catch the child up after lengthy absences for treatment or associated illness. Given the likelihood that the child will struggle with nonverbal skills, including math, regular monitoring and the provision of math tutoring services may be critical. Children with hydrocephalus may also need counseling to assist them with issues of self-esteem and finding better ways to cope with their problems. Collaboration with parents is also critical to ensure that children with hydrocephalus receive adequate services in the school, as well as help outside (e.g., special camp experiences and recreational activities).

Ongoing research is needed in the medical field to find ways that reduce the number of shunt revisions a child has to undergo. Further research is needed to find more effective ways to identify children who are in need of treatment before complications arise and functioning is diminished.

REFERENCES

Eaves, R. C. (2000). Hydrocephalus. In C. R. Reynolds & E. Fletcher-Janzen (Eds.), *Encyclopedia of special education* (Vol. 2, pp. 911–912). New York, NY: Wiley.

Fletcher, J. M., Dennis, M., & Northrup, H. (2000). Hydrocephalus. In K. O. Yeates, M. D. Ris, & H. G. Taylor (Eds.), *Pediatric neuropsychology* (pp. 25–46). New York, NY: Guilford Press.

HEIDI MATHIE
ELAINE CLARK
University of Utah

HYDROLETHALUS SYNDROME

Hydrolethalus syndrome is a recessively inherited lethal malformation syndrome involving the central nervous system. Prenatal diagnosis is most common, and the fetuses commonly present with hydrocephaly (with significant functional deficits), micrognathia (underdevelopment of the jaw), polydactyly (more than the normal number of fingers and toes), and a key-shaped defect of the occipital bone.

Incidence rates are estimated at 1 in 20,000, and hydrolethalus belongs to the Finnish disease heritage (Norio, Nevanlinna, & Perheentupa, 1973); many of the reported cases originate in Finland. There is no treatment for this

lethal disorder; however, survival upwards of 5 to 8 months of age in a limited number of hydrolethalus cases has been documented (Aughton & Cassidy, 1987).

Characteristics

1. Hydrocephaly, micrognathia, polydactyly, and an absence of midline structures of the brain are present.

2. Abnormal eyes and nose, cleft lip or palate, low-set ears, defective lung lobes, clubfeet, cardiac myopathy, and abnormal genitalia have been frequently observed in hydrolethalus syndrome.

3. Most cases result in stillbirths, and those children born alive survive only minutes to a few hours at most.

REFERENCES

Aughton, D. J., & Cassidy, S. B. (1987). Hydrolethalus syndrome: Report of an apparent mild case, literature review, and differential diagnosis. *American Journal of Medical Genetics, 27,* 935–942.

Norio, R., Nevanlinna, H. R., & Perheentupa, J. (1973). Hereditary diseases in Finland: Rare flora in rare soil. *Annuals of Clinical Research, 5*(3), 109–141.

KIMBERLY M. ESTEP
University of Houston, Clear Lake

HYPERACTIVITY (See Attention-Deficit/ Hyperactivity Disorder)

HYPERCALCEMIA

Resulting from excessive amounts of calcium in the blood, hypercalcemia most often occurs in conjunction with or as a result of other underlying endocrine conditions (Nelson, Behrman, Kliegmen, & Arvin, 1996). Hypercalcemia commonly results from malignancy or hyper-parathyroidism. In the body, calcium levels are maintained by the interplay of three major hormones: parathyroid hormone (PTH), calcitriol, and calcitonin. For hypercalcemia to develop, the normal calcium regulation system must be overwhelmed with an excess of PTH, calcitriol, or other hormones mimicking these hormones. Hyperthyroidism-related hypercalcemia is caused by increased calcium absorption in the intestines. Hypercalcemia is most commonly seen in patients with breast and lung cancer. An autosomal dominant trait has also been associated with hypercalcemia in children, and it is characterized by persistent hypercalcemia.

Hypercalcemia is a fairly common metabolic disorder affecting 10% to 20% of cancer patients. Hyperthyroidism is the most common cause of hypercalcemia, and 50,000 new cases occur in the United States each year (Dent, Miller, Klaff, & Barron, 1987). Hyperthyroidism incidence in females is much higher than in males; thus, hypercalcemia associated with this disorder is more often seen in women. Hypercalcemia associated with cancer affects males and females alike.

Characteristics

1. Calcium levels are elevated.
2. Patients with mild elevations are asymptomatic; cognitive sequelae observed in more severe cases include changes in mental status.
3. Nausea, vomiting, lethargy, constipation, depression, headache, polyuria, muscle weakness, and altered mental status are common.
4. In individuals with increased calcium, abdominal examinations may suggest pancreatitis or ulcers; however, severe hypercalcemia is associated with enlargement of the pancreas and spleen.

Hypercalcemia also may be caused by antacids, an abundance of vitamins D or A, AIDS, advanced liver disease, milk alkali, lithium, and other syndromes (e.g., Williams syndrome). Dialysis will be necessary in patients with renal failure (Bilezikian, 1993). Cognitive sequelae are sometimes observed leading to alterations in mental status and cognition. Mental deficiency may be observed in select cases.

Due to the medical condition of the child, special education services may be needed under Other Health Impairment. However, in cases of mild hypercalcemia, children normally do not present with any special needs. Prognosis is dependent on the underlying causes. In people with cancer, morbidity rates are high when hypercalcemia is also present. A majority of incidences of hypercalcemia occurring in conjunction with other disorders are manageable. Research is ongoing in the disorders often associated with hypercalcemia, and although hypercalcemia is manageable, often the underlying disorder results in complications for the patient.

REFERENCES

Bilezikian, J. P. (1993). Management of hypercalcemia. *Journal of Endocrinology Metabolism, 77*, 1445–1449.

Dent, D. M., Miller, J. L., Klaff, L., & Barron, J. (1987). The incidence and causes of hypercalcemia. *Postgraduate Medical Journal, 63*, 745–750.

Nelson, W. E., Behrman, R. E., Kliegmen, R. M., & Arvin, A. M. (1996). *Nelson textbook of pediatrics* (15th ed). Bangalore, India: Prism Books.

KIMBERLY M. ESTEP
University of Houston, Clear Lake

HYPERCHOLESTEROLEMIA

Hypercholesterolemia (high cholesterol), a metabolic disorder, is characterized by high accumulations of fats in the blood. High cholesterol is the leading cause of death in the United States. In a majority of cases, symptomatology culminates as one gets older; however, rare instances of childhood onset have been documented. Particularly deadly to children is familial hypercholesterolemia (FH), which is a rare form of hypercalcemia that is believed to be an autosomal dominant trait characterized by absent or malfunctioning low-density lipoprotein (LDL) receptors. If the trait is homozygous, complications arise, and most children will not survive into young adulthood. Heterozygous FM will likely present itself in middle adulthood, and if treatment is swift, the patient can survive. Affected FM patients normally develop premature coronary artery disease (CAD) in which early detection is of the utmost importance.

As noted, hypercholesterolemia is common, occurring in about 1 in 500 persons worldwide. Men normally have earlier onset than women; however, childhood onset is rare.

Characteristics

1. Individuals have unusually high blood serum cholesterol.
2. Patients with high levels of cholesterol eventually develop coronary disease.
3. Children with the homozygous familial type will have symptoms that mimic ischemic heart disease, peripheral vascular disease, or aortic stenosis (constriction or narrowing of an opening).
4. Children with the heterozygous familial type may remain asymptomatic until adulthood.
5. Patients may have cutaneous xanthomas at birth, and planar xanthomas are most commonly seen.

Treatment includes dietary modifications and exercise. Cholesterol-lowering medications may also be needed. However, homozygous FH does not respond well to medication and requires a more aggressive approach. For instance, a liver transplant dramatically reduces low-density lipoprotein levels; however, complications then arise as a result of the transplant.

Symptomatic children qualify for special education services under Other Health Impairment, and such services vary depending on the particular child's needs. Prognosis is dependent on presentation, and if CAD is present, premature death is almost imminent. However, age of morbidity is highly varied, and early detection is the key to longevity.

This entry has been informed by the sources listed below.

REFERENCES

Citkowitz, E. (2001). Hypercholesterolemia. *eMedicine*, *2*(5). Retrieved from http://emedicine.medscape.com/

Granot, E., & Deckelbaum, R. J. (1989). Hypocholesterolemia in childhood. *Journal of Pediatrics*, *115*, 171.

Illingworth, D. R., Duell, P. B., & Connor, W. E. (1995). Disorders of lipid metabolism. In P. Felig, J. D. Baxter, & L. A. Frohmin (Eds.), *Endocrinology and metabolism* (3rd ed, pp. 1315–1403). New York, NY: McGraw-Hill.

Nelson, W. E., Behrman, R. E., Kliegmen, R. M., & Arvin, A. M. (1996). *Nelson textbook of pediatrics* (15th ed.). Bangalore, India: Prism Books.

KIMBERLY M. ESTEP
University of Houston–Clear Lake

Characteristics

1. In infancy, failure to thrive, low muscle tone (hypotonia), seizures, respiratory distress, and lethargy are common.
2. Most patients die within the first year of life. Those who survive manifest severe psychomotor retardation and seizures.
3. Glycine amounts in the blood, urine, and cerebrospinal fluid are high.
4. Severe adaptive and intellectual impediments are present.

Treatment focuses on the reduction of glycine concentrations by administration of sodium benzoate; however, treatment outcomes vary greatly in the literature. Even with early diagnosis and treatment, infants who survive present with profound intellectual developmental disabilities and physical disabilities. Other treatment issues surround neurotransmitter activity involved in NKH. Elevated glycine levels influence two receptors in the body. The inhibitory glycine receptor, mainly in the brain stem and spinal cord, is responsible for the respiratory difficulties and the lethargy associated with NKH, and the inhibitory glycine activates the N-methyl-D-aspartate (NMDA) receptor, an excitatory receptor of glutamate. Research suggests that the latter plays the more important role in the difficulties associated with NKH; therefore, treatments aimed at protecting the NMDA receptor are advantageous (Von Wendt, Hirvasniemi, & Simila, 1979). Unfortunately, this NMDA treatment is still in a preliminary phase.

Special education placement is necessary for children living with NKH. These children present with multiple health problems, developmental delays, and mental deficiencies. Most are unable to communicate with their environment.

Prognosis is not favorable, and future research is focusing on protecting the NMDA receptors and finding an antagonist to offset the effects of overstimulation (Boneh, Degani, & Harari, 1996). Antagonists such as dextromethorphan, ketamine, and tryptophan are currently under study.

REFERENCES

Boneh, A., Degani, Y., & Harari, M. (1996). Prognosis clues and outcome of early treatment of nonketotic hyperglycinemia. *Pediatric Neurology*, *15*, 137–141.

Lu, F. L., Wang, P., Hwu, W., Yau, K., & Wang, T. (1999). Neonatal type of nonketotic hyperglycinemia. *Pediatric Neurology*, *20*, 295–300.

HYPERGLYCINEMIA, NONKETOTIC

Nonketotic hyperglycinemia (NKH) is a rare autosomal-recessive trait involving an error of glycine metabolism (Nissenkorn, Michelson, Ben-Zeev, & Lerman-Sagie, 2001). Large amounts of the amino acid glycine accumulate in the body fluids, particularly in the cerebrospinal fluid. Two subtypes of this disorder exist: nonclassic NKH and neonatal NKH. The former appears later in life and presents with milder neurological deficits and varying degrees of intellectual developmental disabilities (Lu, Wang, Hwu, Yau, & Wang, 1999).

NKH is rare and the prevalence unknown; however, high occurrences of NKH have been found in Finland (von Wendt, Hirvasniemi, & Simila, 1979).

Nissenkorn, A., Michelson, M., Ben-Zeev, B., & Lerman-Sagie, T. (2001). Inborn errors of metabolism: A cause of abnormal brain development. *Neurology, 56*, 1265–1272.

Von Wendt, L., Hirvasniemi, A., & Simila, S. (1979). Nonketotic hyperglycinemia: A genetic study of 13 Finnish families. *Clinical Genetics, 15*, 411–417.

KIMBERLY M. ESTEP
University of Houston, Clear Lake

HYPERHIDROSIS, PRIMARY

Primary hyperhidrosis is a genetic disorder of hyperactivity of the sweat glands. Sweating may occur in the hands and feet, face, underarms, groin area, and under the breasts. Patients with more severe hyperhidrosis may experience excessive sweating all over the body. More common than primary hyperhidrosis, secondary hyperhidrosis develops because of an underlying disorder.

Primary hyperhidrosis is rare, equally affecting men and women. Often, the symptoms of overactive sweat glands dissipate with age without medical intervention. However, treatment is available and consists of surgery or topical medications that have proven effective at alleviating symptomatology (Glasnapp & Schroeder, 2001). Botulinum toxin A injections have also been successful in the treatment of primary hyperhidrosis (Heckman, Ceballos-Baumann, & Plewig, 2001).

Patients with primary hyperhidrosis do not present with any special education issues; however, due to the possible embarrassment that excessive sweating causes, psychosocial issues may arise, especially for adolescents (O'Donoghue, Finn, & Brady, 1980). Prognosis is good, and future research lies in the development of effective management tools that lessen the symptoms associated with primary hyperhidrosis.

Characteristics

1. Excessive sweating is either generalized over the whole body or localized to areas such as the hands and feet, the most common areas affected.
2. Some children experience facial flushing.
3. Individuals suffering from primary hyperhidrosis may experience heightened reactions to anxiety or nervousness, exercise, and caffeine.
4. The skin may become unusually soft and smooth, scaly, or cracked, and the palms and soles of the affected individual may appear abnormally pink or bluish-white in appearance.

REFERENCES

Glasnapp, A., & Schroeder, B. J. (2001). Topical therapy for localized hyperhidrosis. *International Journal of Pharmaceutical Compounding, 5*, 28–29.

Heckman, M., Ceballos-Baumann, A. O., & Plewig, G. (2001). Botulinum toxin A for axillary hyperhidrosis (excessive sweating). *New England Journal of Medicine, 344*, 488–493.

O'Donoghue, G., Finn, D., & Brady, M. P. (1980). Palmar primary hyperhidrosis in children. *Journal of Pediatric Surgery, 15*, 172–174.

KIMBERLY M. ESTEP
University of Houston, Clear Lake

HYPERKINESIS

Hyperkinesis involves excessive involuntary movements that interfere with motor control. Both hyperkinetic and hypokinetic movement disorders are attributed to chemical and electrical imbalances that result in the malfunction of the body's motor circuit (Bogdanov, Pinchuk, Pisar'kova, Shelyakin, & Sirbiladze, 1994). Hyperkinesis is characterized by repetitive movements that may involve the face, limbs, or the entire body. Hyperkinesis was formerly the diagnosis now referred to in the *Diagnostic and Statistical Manual of Mental Disorders, Fourth Edition* (DSM-IV) as attention-deficit/hyperactivity disorder. Presently, the European Diagnostic Manual ICD-10 still emphasizes the presence of abnormal levels of inattention and overactivity across multiple settings in its identification of hyperkinetic disorders (Tripp, Luk, Schaughency, & Singh, 1999).

The prevalence and severity of hyperkinesis varies according to the disorder. Hyperkinesis may manifest a variety of symptoms including tremors, dystonia, tics, chorea, athetosis, ballism, and myoclonus. Some hyperkinetic movement disorders include Huntington's disease, Tourette syndrome, and an infantile cerebral palsy classified as hyperkinetic (Bogdanov et al., 1994; Kishore & Calne, 1997). There can be instances of drug-induced hyperkinesia as well (Vitek & Giroux, 2000).

Although there is still uncertainty as to the exact neurological role played by the basal ganglia, the portion of the brain most responsible for the body's motor control, it has been implicated in the development of these movement disorders (Litvan, Paulsen, Mega, & Cummings, 1998). Decreased output from the basal ganglia reduces the level of inhibition to the thalamus and subsequently results in excessive movements. Moreover, certain drugs that stimulate dopamine neurotransmitters have also been found to induce hyperkinetic movements (Vitek & Giroux, 2000).

Characteristics

1. Involuntary movements occur at rest, while standing still, or during voluntary movement.

2. The rate of movements can range from very fast to slow.

3. The pattern of movements can be rhythmic or irregular.

4. Generally, voluntary movements of affected body parts are slow.

5. Movement is intensified in uncontrolled or stressful situations.

6. There may be a greater frequency of hyperactive behaviors such as agitation, irritation, euphoria, or anxiety.

When a child's presenting symptoms include hyperkinetic movements, physicians should first consider whether the hyperkinesis is a side effect of any medication. However, certain medical procedures have been used successfully to alleviate the hyperkinetic movements. In particular, transcranial micropolarization has been found to alleviate hyperkinesis and improve functional movements of the joints (Bogdanov et al., 1994). Biochemical therapy and motor rehabilitation therapy also have been used to treat and alleviate symptoms.

Many children with movement disorders have intelligence within the normal range. However, some may have developmental delays in several domain areas, such as motor, cognitive, socioemotional, and adaptive skills. Children with movement disorders may need adaptive physical education, alternatives to writing, and extra time to transition between locations. Physical and occupational therapists can assist children in strengthening their fine and gross motor skills as well as in learning to control their movements (Paulson & Reider, 1997).

Moreover, children may experience increased frustration at their inability to control their movements. Thus, children with movement disorders may be socially isolated due to embarrassment. As increased stress exacerbates the hyperkinetic movements, and may even limit the efficacy of physical therapy, children may benefit from counseling to address the emotional consequences of having a movement disorder (Paulson & Reider, 1997).

REFERENCES

Bogdanov, O. V., Pinchuk, D. Y., Pisar'kova, E. V., Shelyakin, A. M., & Sirbiladze, K. T. (1994). The use of the method of transcranial micropolarization to decrease the severity of hyperkinesis in patients with infantile cerebral palsy. *Neuroscience and Behavioral Physiology, 24*(5), 442–445.

Kishore, A., & Calne, D. B. (1997). Approach to the patient with a movement disorder and overview of movement disorders.

In R. L. Watt & W. C. Koller (Eds.), *Movement disorders: Neurological principles and practice* (pp. 3–14). New York, NY: McGraw-Hill.

Litvan, I., Paulsen, J. S., Mega, M. S., & Cummings, J. L. (1998). Neuropsychiatric assessment of patients with hyperkinetic and hypokinetic movement disorders. *Archives of Neurology, 55*, 1313–1319.

Paulson, G. W., & Reider, C. R. (1997). Movement disorders in childhood. In R. L. Watt & W. C. Koller (Eds.), *Movement disorders: Neurological principles and practice* (pp. 661–672). New York, NY: McGraw-Hill.

Tripp, G., Luk, S. L., Schaughency, E. A., & Singh, R. (1999). DSM-IV and ICD-10: A comparison of the correlates of ADHD and hyperkinetic disorder. *American Academy of Child and Adolescent Psychiatry, 38*(2), 156–159.

Vitek, J. L., & Giroux, M. (2000). Physiology of hypokinetic and hyperkinetic movement disorders: Model for dyskinesia. *Annals of Neurology, 47*(1), S131–S138.

MICHELLE PERFECT
University of Texas at Austin

HYPERLEXIA

While some inconsistency in the use of the term *hyperlexia* has occurred, the predominant view is that hyperlexia refers to a developmental disorder characterized by a spontaneous and intense early interest in letters and words. According to Oberschneider, two variants of childhood hyperlexia have been proposed and supported: (1) those who demonstrate hyperlexic characteristics, while also meeting the criteria for pervasive developmental delay spectrum disorder; and (2) those who demonstrate milder impairments of cognitive, speech/language, and social/emotional functioning while meeting the criteria for communication disorder. At present, hyperlexia is not diagnosed by itself, and, depending on the severity, occurs with other disorders such as Asperger's disorder, autistic disorders, pervasive developmental disorder, or one of the communication disorders: mixed receptive-expressive disorder or expressive language disorder (Oberschneider, 2003).

Healy (1982, as cited in Sparks, 1995) noted three major symptoms in children with hyperlexia: (1) spontaneous reading of words before the age of 5; (2) impaired comprehension on both reading and listening tasks; and (3) word recognition (decoding) skills above expectations, based on other measured cognitive and linguistic abilities. Even though these children, as a group, evidence a wide range of intelligence, the majority of them present at least some degree of general intellectual limitation and many have been classified as borderline or mildly retarded

(Sparks, 1995). In addition, there are social and behavioral problems that can manifest in hyperlexia. Examples of some problematic behaviors that are associated with childhood hyperlexia include infrequent initiation of social conversation, an intense need to develop or keep to routines in daily life, difficulty with transitions and ritualistic behaviors, age-appropriate development until 18 to 24 months and then regression, selective listening, or the appearance of being deaf, and specific yet unusual fears (Oberschneider, 2003).

It has been suggested that hyperlexia is associated with abnormal neurobiologic functioning and/or genetic basis because it sometimes accompanies conditions such as Prader-Willi syndrome, Tourette syndrome, Turner syndrome, and intellectual developmental disabilities; however, no consistent pattern of clinical neurobiological findings, laboratory findings, or prenatal, perinatal, or postnatal events have been identified so far (Oberschneider, 2003). Hyperlexia occurs more common in males, with an overall gender ratio of greater than 7:1 males:females (Aram, 1997).

Children with hyperlexia usually receive professional attention because they do not develop speech and language as expected. They rarely produce single words by age 1 and they demonstrate marked delays in the use of word combinations. However, a defining characteristic of children with hyperlexia is early reading, especially when compared to the emergence of oral language. The majority demonstrate word recognition between the ages of 2½ and 3½ years of age (Aram, 1997). Soon, they become preoccupied with reading at the expense of other age-appropriate activities. Children with hyperlexia learn to read more rapidly than controls, and scrambling word order in text disrupts their reading speed far less relative to normal readers (Nation, 1999). Most children with hyperlexia recognize words by utilizing grapheme-phoneme correspondence rules, which demonstrates good use of phonologic rules for word decoding. However, these children demonstrate the dissociation between word decoding and meaningful comprehension. This suggests that hyperlexia is a disorder of language comprehension and that decoding is a splinter skill dissociated from meaning. Therefore, the clinician should begin with an assessment of language comprehension abilities in order to determine abilities in both meaning (semantic) and structural (syntax) domains. The assessment of comprehension abilities should be ongoing throughout treatment, and the goals of therapy should be continually modified as new behaviors and/or information is presented (Aram, 1997).

REFERENCES

Aram, D. M. (1997). Hyperlexia: Reading without meaning in young children. *Topics in Language Disorders*, *17*(3), 1–13.

Nation, K. (1999). Reading skills in hyperlexia: A developmental perspective. *Psychological Bulletin*, *125*, 338–355.

Oberschneider, M. S. (2003). A case of a four-year-old boy with hyperlexia: Some considerations for diagnosis and treatment from a psychodynamic perspective. *Clinical Child Psychology and Psychiatry*, *8*, 205–214.

Sparks, R. L. (1995). Phonemic awareness in hyperlexic children. *Reading & Writing: An Interdisciplinary Journal*, *7*, 217–235.

ESMERELDA LÓPEZ
Texas A&M University

See also **Reading Disorders; Reading Remediation**

HYPEROPIA

Hyperopia, better known as *farsightedness*, is defined as a condition in which refracting optics of the eye are too weak given the length of the eye such that images of distant objects are focused behind the retina. This occurs in a normal sized eye when the cornea and lens power are insufficient, or in an eye that is too short when the cornea and lens power are adequate (Bullimore & Gilmartin, 1997). In other words, hyperopia is caused by an imbalance between the refractive action and the size and shape of the eye.

Bullimore and Gilmartin (1997) have described hyperopia as a regular part of the developmental process in that hyperopia is present in most newborns. Over time the natural growth cycle of the eye reduces the magnitude of the disorder. However, in cases where eye growth is halted or delayed, hyperopia becomes an ailment instead of a developmental milestone. Bullimore and Gilmartin suggested that hyperopia waxes and wanes throughout the human life span and that prevalence is a function of age. Most everyone is born hyperopic, outgrows it by adolescence, and most likely relapses in old age. Unfortunately, there is little agreement regarding prevalence rates among children and adolescents, but at the extremes of the age range there seems to be more consensus. In fact, the American Optometric Association (AOA, 1997) stated that most infants delivered full term are mildly hyperopic, whereas premature and low-birthweight infants tend to be less hyperopic. In the 6- to 8-month age range, Ingram, Arnold, Dally, and Lucas (1990) reported that approximately 6% to 9% of infants have hyperopia to some degree. Further, Wang, Klein, Klein, and Moss (1994) studied almost 5,000 adults and discovered that hyperopia existed in 67% of participants aged 65 to 74 years and in only 22% of participants aged 43 to 54 years.

The AOA (1997) pointed out that there are no known gender differences in the prevalence of hyperopia. However, Crawford and Haamar (1949) and Post (1962) discovered ethnic differences in prevalence rates. They reported that Native Americans, African Americans, and Pacific Islanders are among the groups with the highest reported rates of hyperopia.

Hyperopia is most commonly measured and diagnosed by retinoscopy. Static retinoscopy (measurement of the accommodation of the eye when viewing a distant object) may also be accompanied by subjective refraction and autorefraction as diagnostic techniques (AOA, 1997).

Characteristics

1. Constant to intermittent blurred vision
2. Asthenopia
3. Red, teary eyes
4. Frequent blinking
5. Decreased binocularity
6. Difficulty reading
7. Amblyopia
8. Strabismus

The most common and least invasive treatment for hyperopia is the prescription of spectacles or contact lenses. Vision therapy may also be required in some cases because lens correction alone will not be sufficient. Several other treatment options such as the use of pharmaceuticals, habit and environment modification, and refractive surgery are available. Refractive surgery has recently gained much support among professionals and popularity among the public, but as Fundingsland and Sher (1997) pointed out there are many forms of refractive surgery with no one form recognized as superior. According to Fundlingsland and Sher, corneal reshaping can be achieved through incisions (hexagonal keratotomy), burns (thermokeratoplasty), laser ablations (hyperopic photorefractive keratectomy or the Excimer laser technique), lamellar cuts (keratophakia and keratomileusis), and replacement of the posterior lens.

In an educational setting, children with hyperopia may require glasses or contact lenses. While in the past such aids have been a source of teasing, hyperopia is now so common that most children find glasses or contacts to be perfectly acceptable.

REFERENCES

American Optometric Association. (1997). *Optometric clinical practice guideline: Care of the patient with hyperopia—Reference guide for clinicians*. St. Louis, MO: Author.

Bullimore, M. A., & Gilmartin, B. (1997). Hyperopia and presbyopia: Etiology and epidemiology. In N. A. Sher (Ed.), *Surgery for hyperopia and presbyopia* (pp. 3–10). Baltimore, MD: Williams & Wilkins.

Crawford, H. E., & Haamar, G. E. (1949). Racial analysis of ocular deformities in schools of Hawaii. *Hawaii Medical Journal, 9,* 90–93.

Fundlingsland, B., & Sher, N. A. (1997). Hyperopia and presbyopia: Etiology and epidemiology. In N. A. Sher (Ed.), *Surgery for hyperopia and presbyopia* (pp. 11–20). Baltimore, MD: Williams & Wilkins.

Ingram, R., Arnold, P., Dally, S., & Lucas, J. (1990). The results of a randomized trial of treating abnormal hypermetropia from the age of 6 months. *British Journal of Ophthalmology, 74,* 158–159.

Post, R. H. (1962). Population differences in visual acuity: Review with speculative notes on selection relaxation. *Eugenics Quarterly, 9,* 189–192.

Wang, Q., Klein, B. E. K., Klein, R., & Moss, S. E. (1994). Refractive status in the Beaver Dam eye study. *Investigative Ophthalmology and Visual Science, 35,* 4344–4337.

TRACY A. MUENZ
Alliant University

See also **Visual Acuity; Visual Efficiency**

HYPERSOMNIA, PRIMARY

Primary hypersomnia is a disorder characterized by excessive daytime sleepiness or extremely long periods of nighttime sleep (greater than 10 hours) on a regular basis. In the recurrent form of this disorder known as Kleine-Levin syndrome, symptoms occur for at least 3 days at a time and reoccur several times per year for 2 or more years (American Psychiatric Association [APA], 1994).

The true prevalence of hypersomnia is unknown, as many who suffer from this disorder perceive their sleepiness as normal and never seek treatment. Five to 10% of patients who seek help at sleep disorder clinics are diagnosed with primary hypersomnia, whereas in the general adult population .5% to 5.0% report daytime sleepiness (APA, 1994). Kleine-Levin syndrome is exceedingly rare but affects males more often than females and generally begins in adolescence (National Organization for Rare Disorders [NORD], 1997).

Characteristics

1. Excessive sleepiness for a period of 1 month or more (if recurrent, sleepiness may last only 3 days but returns several times per year).
2. Long periods of sleep (10 to 20 hours).

3. Inability to remain awake during the day, especially in situations where stimulation is lacking (in class, when driving, while watching television).

In individuals with Kleine-Levin syndrome, the sleep episodes are associated with a lack of inhibition, hypersexuality, excessive eating, irritability, depression, and confusion (NORD, 1997). In diagnosing primary hypersomnia, it is important to determine whether the symptoms are caused by another disorder, such as depression or bipolar disorder, by another medical condition, by substance abuse, or by the side effects of prescribed medication (APA, 1994). Consultation with a sleep disorders specialist for assessment is often necessary (Talk About Sleep, 2000).

Treatment for the symptoms of primary hypersomnia may involve the use of stimulant medications such as methylphenidate, modafinil, or pemoline (Talk About Sleep, 2000) during periods when excessive sleepiness occurs. In some cases individuals with Kleine-Levin syndrome have responded to treatment with the anticonvulsant drug phenytoin, with lithium, or with antidepressant medication (NORD, 1997). During episodes of hypersomnia, affected individuals should not be permitted to drive or operate machinery.

Adolescents and children with primary hypersomnia are likely to need special education services under the Other Health Impairment handicapping condition. During symptomatic periods, waking in time for school and remaining awake in class is difficult. In students suffering from Kleine-Levin syndrome, school attendance may not be possible while symptoms persist. Modifications to students' class schedules and at-home study arrangements may be necessary to help those with hypersomnia maintain their academic progress.

The cause of hypersomnia is not known, but research is ongoing to discover the cause and to improve treatment. Some researchers believe that Kleine-Levin syndrome has a genetic basis and may be related to a malfunction in the hypothalamus (NORD, 1997). In most cases, symptoms of Kleine-Levin syndrome eventually dissipate by middle age (APA, 1994).

REFERENCES

American Psychiatric Association. (1994). *Diagnostic and statistical manual of mental disorders* (4th ed.). Washington, DC: Author.

National Organization for Rare Disorders. (1997). *Kleine-Levin syndrome.* Retrieved from http://www.rarediseases.org

Talk About Sleep. (2000). *An introduction to hypersomnia.* Retrieved from http://www.talkaboutsleep.com/

NANCY K. SCAMMACCA
University of Texas at Austin

HYPERTELORISM

Hypertelorism is a descriptive term designating wide orbital separation characterized by separation of the eyes. This represents a retention of the wide, primitive interorbital angle. While early studies suggested a single cause, subsequent evaluations show great variety in the clinical and radiologic appearances of the skull. The condition is distinguished from telecanthus (lateral displacement of the medical canthal tissue), where the interocular (between the eyes) distance is normal (Duke-Elder, 1963).

The retention of a wide interorbital angle is attributed to early ossification of the lesser wings of the sphenoid bone, fixing the orbits in lateral positions (Jones, 1997). An alternative hypothesis suggests the anomaly results from failure of maxillary process development with compensatory overgrowth of the frontonasal process. Further, it is important to differentiate this anomaly from physiologic variance often associated with racial groups and patients with secondary hypertelorism. Secondary forms follow disturbances in development resulting from various disorders such as frontal encephalocele and trauma. The primary, dysgenetic type may accompany a variety of congenital disorders, including craniofacial abnormalities and many chromosomal aberrations (Jones & Jakobiec, 1979).

Hypertelorism is a frequent feature of nearly 50 syndromes and genetic disorders. It is occasionally seen in about 20 more. It can be a minor morphologic variation, such as a familiar trait. Finally, hypertelorism may be a developmental abnormality secondary to an underlying brain anomaly or the persistence of a midline cleft, which separates rapidly growing blocks of tissue that form an embryo's face and head. Physicians caring for children affected with hypertelorism should search for related findings because their presence (or absence) certainly has prognostic significance.

Divergent strabismus is the most common associated ocular disorder (Olitsk & Nelson, 2000), although other abnormalities such as microphthalmos, microcornea, and optic atrophy may occur. Mentation is generally good and most patients are described as even-tempered and gentle.

The significance of this anomaly is minimal to the educator except as a clue to other developmental defects. In general, the eye, face, and brain develop concurrently; defects in one area suggest the possibility of defects in another. Only if associated with ocular or central nervous system defects would this anomaly be of particular significance.

REFERENCES

Duke-Elder, S. (1963). *System of ophthalmology: Vol. III, Part 2, Congenital deformities.* St. Louis, MO: Mosby.

Jones, I. S., & Jakobiec, F. A. (1979). *Diseases of the orbit.* Hagerstown, MD: Harper & Row.

Jones, K. (1997). *Smith's recognizable patterns of human malformations* (5th ed.). Philadelphia, PA: Saunders.

Olitsk, S. E., & Nelson, L. B. (2000). Orbital abnormalities. In R. E. Behrman, R. M. Kleigman, & H. B. Jenson (Eds.), *Nelson's textbook of pediatrics* (16th ed., p. 1934). Philadelphia, PA: Saunders.

GEORGE R. BEAUCHAMP
Cleveland Clinic Foundation

BARRY H. DAVISON
Ennis, Texas

JOAN W. MAYFIELD
Baylor Pediatric Specialty Services, Dallas, Texas, CDDR

HYPERTHYROIDISM

Hyperthyroidism, also known as thyrotoxicosis, is a metabolic imbalance caused by an overproduction of thyroid hormone. The overproduction of thyroid hormone causes an overall increase in the organism's metabolic rate, which is responsible for a host of medical problems (St. Germain, 2000). Hyperthyroidism is classified as a syndrome, and diagnosis is made based on the presence of symptoms. Two medical conditions lead to the development of hyperthyroidism. In one condition, the thyroid produces too much thyroid hormone. This can occur as a result of tumors of the thyroid gland, pituitary gland, ovaries, or testes; inflammation of the thyroid; ingestion of too much iodine; and Grave's disease (in which the immune system attacks the thyroid). In the second cause, the thyroid gland becomes damaged and leaks thyroid hormone (St. Germain, 2000).

Hyperthyroidism occurs in 1:1,000 people or about 2.5 million Americans each year. Several causative conditions are more prevalent in women, including postpartum thyroiditis and Grave's disease, leading to a greater female than male incidence rate. Grave's disease accounts for about 85% of the cases of hyperthyroidism and is much more prevalent among women, especially age 20 to 50 years. There also appears to be an increased incidence among individuals with Down syndrome.

Characteristics

1. Increased appetite with concurrent weight loss. Children and adolescents may be unusually tall and thin (Vaughan, McKay, & Behrman, 1979).

2. Changes in mood and thinking skills, including increased nervousness, restlessness, depression, fatigue, memory, and concentration problems that may impact school or job performance (Vaughan et al., 1979).

3. Heat intolerance and increased sweating.

4. Increased metabolism leading to muscle cramping, irregular heartbeat, chest pains, and perhaps heart attack (St. Germain, 2000).

5. Frequent bowel movements related to overactivity of the intestines (St. Germain, 2000).

6. Menstrual irregularities.

7. The development of goiters or enlargements of the thyroid gland (St. Germain, 2000).

The treatment of hyperthyroidism includes the use of medicine called beta-blockers, such as Inderol, to block the effect of too much thyroid hormone. This treatment is used to deter the effects of overproduction of thyroid on the heart and nervous system (St. Germain, 2000). Beta-blockers are usually the only intervention needed when there is a leakage and the condition tends to be temporary. In cases of overproduction, three types of treatments are available, including antithyroid drug therapy (Porpylthiouracil or Methimazole) to decrease the production of thyroid hormone; use of radioiodine, which often results in hypothyroidism that persists; and surgical removal of the thyroid gland (St. Germain, 2000). Treatment of Grave's disease tends to result in short-term remediation of the symptoms, and reoccurrence is common. In children, drug therapy lasting up to 36 months is effective for permanent remediation of symptoms in 75% of the children (Vaughan et al., 1979).

Hyperthyroidism occurs in children but is more prevalent among adults. If the symptoms are significant enough to interfere with a child's academic or social functioning, it will likely be labeled under Other Health Impairment according to criteria from the Individuals with Disabilities Education Act. Down syndrome children with hyperthyroidism may receive services under the Mental Disability category or Multiple Disability category. However, hyperthyroidism is a treatable disorder that should not by itself make a child eligible for special education services.

The symptoms of hyperthyroidism tend to develop slowly and are generally not painful. As a result, there may be a lag in diagnosis. The medical field may improve diagnosis so that treatment can be initiated earlier in the course of the syndrome. It is a treatable condition, but treatments may be improved in the future. For example, radioactive iodine therapy is effective, but when using this treatment, the individual must avoid being around others, especially children. In addition, radioactive iodine therapy may induce hypothyroidism, which must then be corrected by introducing natural thyroid hormone. Surgical removal of the thyroid gland also causes hypothyroidism, which must be treated.

REFERENCES

St. Germain, D. (2000). *All about hyperthyroidism*. Retrieved from http://www.healthcentral.com/

Vaughan, V. C., McKay, R. J., & Behrman, R. E. (1979). In W. E. Nelson (Ed.), *Nelson textbook of pediatrics* (11th ed., pp. 1164–1167). Philadelphia, PA: Saunders.

DALENE M. MCCLOSKEY
University of Northern Colorado

HYPERTONIA-RD

Hypertonia is increased tension of the muscles that can make movement difficult. It can also be defined as resistance to passive movement that is not velocity dependent (Pediatric Services, n.d.). Hypertonia usually occurs in definite patterns of flexion or extension (Pedretti & Zoltan, 1990). Difficulties are most predominant in the flexor patterns for the upper extremities and in the extensor patterns of the lower extremities.

There are two main types of hypertonia—rigidity and spasticity—but both can be present in the same individual. Specifically, spasticity is an increase in resistance to sudden passive movement that is velocity dependent. It involves an imbalance between the agonist and antagonist muscle groups. The severity of spasticity is directly related to the speed of the stretch placed on the muscle. In contrast, rigidity is increased muscle tone in both agonist and antagonist muscles simultaneously (Pedretti & Zoltan, 1990). Hypertonia is the opposite of hypotonia.

Hypertonia is commonly associated with other medical disorders such as cerebral palsy (CP), multiple sclerosis (MS), amyotrophic lateral sclerosis (ALS), spina bifida, Parkinson's disease, and head injury. Although identification of the presence of hypertonia is not difficult, determination of the actual cause is significantly more problematic. Children with hypertonia may have difficulty with both fine and gross motor movements and with motor coordination depending on the severity of the condition. Prolonged hypertonicity with spasticity can lead to shortening of the muscles and subsequent contracture and deformity, resulting in severely decreased mobility.

It is not possible to estimate the prevalence of hypertonia because it is not a specific disease, and records do not necessarily specify the frequency of particular symptoms.

Characteristics of hypertonia include: (1) resistance to passive movement that is not dependent on the velocity of the movement; and (2) spasticity or rigidity of muscles.

Following the identification of the presence of hypertonia, a treatment program can be developed. Although treatment will not cure the symptoms, it will aid in the prevention of future complications due to the condition. Treatment may also serve to facilitate the child's most appropriate development and teach compensatory skills. Treatment programs incorporate instruction to the child and caregivers in positioning and movement strategies. Medical and surgical interventions and drug treatments that may serve to decrease muscle tone are available.

Collaboration among parents, educators, and medical professionals is crucial to enable the most positive outcome for the child with hypertonia. Children with hypertonia are often identified at an early age through primary care medical settings. It is important for parents to be placed in contact with the local school district or state agencies that provide early intervention services for children ages 0 to 3 years.

Infants with hypertonia may be eligible for special education services under the provisions of Public Law 99-457 and its reauthorization in 1991 as Public Law 102-119, which mandates services for children from birth to age 3. Eligibility is dependent on associated disabilities rather than on the presence of hypertonia in and of itself. If eligible, an Individual Family Service Plan (IFSP) would be developed to identify goals and services as mandated by Part C of the Individuals with Disabilities Education Act. Preschool and elementary school children may remain eligible to receive services provided that the child falls into one of the specific eligibility classifications and meets the specific state requirements for service provision. Although a child may not be directly eligible to receive services due to the presence of hypertonia, per se, eligibility may be based on associated conditions or disorders. Specific services will be determined on an individualized basis. If educationally necessary, students with hypertonia may receive the related services of occupational, physical, and speech therapies.

The prognosis for children with hypertonia varies depending on several factors, including the root cause of the condition, the severity of the symptoms, and the provision of appropriate early interventions.

REFERENCES

Pediatric Services. (n.d.). *Understanding the lingo*. Retrieved from http://www.pediatricservices.com/

Pedretti, L. W., & Zoltan, B. (1990). *Occupational therapy: Practice skills for physical dysfunction* (3rd ed.). St. Louis, MO: Mosby.

SHELLEY L. F. PELLETIER
SUSAN SAGE
Dysart Unified School District, El Mirage, Arizona

See also **Congenital Disorders**

HYPNOSIS

While no generally accepted definition exists, hypnosis is usually considered to be an altered state of consciousness characterized by a heightened susceptibility to suggestion. As an altered state of consciousness, hypnosis is seen as a condition distinct from sleep or wakefulness, perhaps similar to deep meditation, yoga, or some other trancelike state. The heightened susceptibility characteristic relates to the observation that the hypnotized person accepts ideas more uncritically and wholeheartedly than ordinarily (American Society of Clinical Hypnosis, 1973).

Research suggests that the practice of hypnosis extends far back into the history of man. Support for such claims is found in ancient writings from many cultures, including India, Persia, China, and Egypt (Gravitz & Gerton, 1984). The modern history of hypnosis began with Franz Anton Mesmer, a Viennese physician of the late 18th and early 19th centuries. Mesmer is most famous for his theory of hypnotism as animal magnetism, a force that he believed came from within living bodies and was passed to other living bodies and objects. Mesmer's animal magnetism supposedly could be used to cure serious illnesses. His work gave rise to the term mesmerism, a synonym for hypnosis.

Mesmer's work came to the attention of James Braid, a Scottish physician of the early 19th century. Braid, who coined the term *hypnotism*, rejected Mesmer's animal magnetism theory but emphasized the importance of suggestion and concentration in hypnosis. Braid's experience led him and others to use hypnosis in the treatment of disease; during the 1800s this technique was used successfully as an anesthetic for many surgical procedures (E. Hilgard & Hilgard, 1975).

Since Braid's time, the use of hypnosis has gone through several periods of public and professional interest and disinterest, and has been studied by such famous scientists as Charles Darwin and Sigmund Freud. Presently, the interest in hypnosis as a medical and psychological aid is high and research into its effective use is expanding. Hypnosis is now viewed by the majority of the professional community as a respectable and useful technique for helping with medical and psychological problems.

Little agreement about the nature of hypnosis exists among the authorities in the field. Numerous competing theories have been proposed, but none seem to explain adequately the phenomenon and no theory has gained wide acceptance. Many theories fit into one of two categories, physiological and psychological. Physiological theories of hypnosis emphasize physical changes that are reported to occur during or as a result of hypnosis: alteration in metabolism, changes in the nervous system, and unusual electrical activity in the brain. Psychological theories stress the importance of psychological factors: learning, suggestion, role-playing, and modeling.

Ernest R. Hilgard, a leader in the scientific study of hypnosis, has proposed a neodissociation theory, which holds that hypnotic procedures rearrange control systems in the brain (Hilgard, 1977). Research by Hilgard and others supports this model. However, at the present time, the scientific understanding of hypnosis is at an early stage of development.

Regardless of the true nature of hypnosis, it can be used to produce some conditions in a subject that are helpful and therapeutic: relaxation, concentration, the ability to put oneself in imaginary situations, and the capacity to accept suggestions more fully. These conditions provide a basis for the application of hypnosis to the treatment of a number of medical and psychological problems.

Hypnosis has been used successfully alone or in combination with other treatment methods in dealing with the following: emotional problems, including anxiety; control of pain; surgery; psychosomatic problems; obesity and dietary problems; smoking; pediatric problems; neurological problems; rehabilitation; conditions related to obstetrics and gynecology; skin problems; sexual dysfunction; and dental procedures. Practical application of hypnosis is extensive. The American Society of Clinical Hypnosis offers extensive resources on the subject at http://www.asch.net/

REFERENCES

American Society of Clinical Hypnosis–Education and Research Foundation. (1973). *A syllabus on hypnosis and a handbook of therapeutic suggestions*. Des Plains, IL: Author.

Gravitz, M. A., & Gerton, M. I. (1984). Hypnosis in the historical development of psychoanalytic psychotherapy. In W. C. Wester & A. H. Smith (Eds.), *Clinical hypnosis: A multidisciplinary approach*. Philadelphia, PA: Lippincott.

Hilgard, E. R. (1977). *Divided consciousness*. New York, NY: Wiley.

Hilgard, E. R., & Hilgard, J. R. (1975). *Hypnosis in the relief of pain*. Los Altos, CA: Kaufman.

ROBERT R. REILLEY
Texas A&M University

See also Psychosocial Adjustment; Psychotherapy With Individuals With Disabilities

HYPOACTIVITY

Hypoactivity is a condition characterized by insufficient or inadequate motor activity and the inability to focus and sustain attention on external stimuli. Myers and Hammill

(1969) describe the hypoactive child as one who is lethargic and quiet, and who causes little disturbance in the classroom. These children are more difficult to recognize and identify than are their hyperactive counterparts, and their problems may escape detection.

Although hyperactive and hypoactive children are at opposite ends of an activity level continuum, both show attentional deficits that may interfere with learning. Dykman, Ackerman, Clements, and Peters (1971) discuss the child who is unable to focus attention on the written or spoken word, and who, therefore, cannot easily learn to read or spell. Most frequently, such attention deficits take the form of impulsivity and overreaction to stimuli. However, in the case of hypoactive children, inhibition, passivity, and underreaction to stimuli are symptomatic of the deficit.

The Russian psychologist A. R. Luria (1959, 1961) has written extensively on attention deficits, and has addressed the problem of hypoactivity specifically. He refers to the syndrome of cerebral asthenia, characterized by an inability to concentrate, distractibility, and short attention span. Luria points out that this syndrome often can be expressed in two externally different but essentially similar forms. He states that nervous processes are reducible to the two basic components of excitation and inhibition, present in all individuals. The strength, concentration, equilibrium, and mobility of excitation and inhibition may be affected by brain pathology. If the pathological state of the cortical cells primarily affects the inhibitory processes, the child displays excessive impulsivity and the loss of control associated with hyperactivity. However, if the pathology is expressed in a decline of the excitatory processes, the child experiences a sharp fall of the tone of the nervous processes and enters into a state of passivity. Luria refers to such children as *inhibitory types* and describes them as sluggish, torpid, and slow to form new positive reactions to stimuli, much like the hypoactive, learning-disabled child.

Although the literature reflects considerable research focused on hyperactivity, there have been relatively few studies dealing with the hypoactive child. Luria (1961) investigated the role of speech as an influence on the disequilibrium between the basic nervous processes. In experiments that required sustained, focused attention, he found inhibited children failed to make correct motoric responses to stimuli. However, when these children were asked to respond verbally as well as motorically, the accuracy and frequency of their responses increased significantly. Luria concluded that the combination of verbal and motoric responses tones up the activity level of the child, and that the compensatory influence of speech serves to heighten the level of the excitatory processes.

Research by Ozolins and Anderson (1980) showed that behavioral approaches could be used successfully to influence the performance of hypoactive children. In experiments requiring sustained attention, the authors found that such children performed better when given feedback reinforcing correct answers. Knowledge of errors served only to increase already excessive levels of inhibition and reduced correct answers. Positive reinforcement made this group feel more secure and less inhibited in their responses.

REFERENCES

Dykman, R. A., Ackerman, P. T., Clements, S. D., & Peters, J. E. (1971). Specific learning disabilities: An attentional deficit syndrome. In H. R. Myklebust (Ed.), *Progress in learning disabilities* (Vol. 2, pp. 56–94). New York, NY: Grune & Stratton.

Luria, A. R. (1959). Experimental study of the higher nervous activity of the abnormal child. *Journal of Mental Deficiency Research, 3,* 1–22.

Luria, A. R. (1961). *The role of speech in the regulation of normal and abnormal behavior.* New York, NY: Liveright.

Myers, P. I., & Hammill, D. D. (1969). *Methods for learning disorders.* New York, NY: Wiley.

Ozolins, D. A., & Anderson, R. P. (1980). Effects of feedback on the vigilance task performance of hyperactive and hypoactive children. *Perceptual and Motor Skills, 50*(2), 415–424.

Barbara S. Speer
Shaker Heights City School District, Shaker Heights, Ohio

See also Attention-Deficit/Hyperactivity Disorder; Attention Span

HYPOCHONDROPLASIA

Hypochondroplasia is a rare, hereditary type of short-limbed dwarfism (Jones, 1997). Originally described in 1913, this disorder has many similarities to achondroplasia, with which it is, and has been, often confused. Physical findings in hypochondroplasia include short stature, mildly shortened extremities, malformed vertebrae of the lower spine, and nearly normal appearance of the face and head. This last characteristic helps to distinguish hypochondroplasia from achondroplasia.

Hypochondroplasia is about one twelfth as common as achondroplasia, making its incidence 1 in 180,000 births (Horton & Hecht, 2000). Like achondroplasia, it has an autosomal dominant mode of inheritance. Advanced paternal age is associated with "new" cases that appear to be fresh mutations. The abnormal gene is located on Chromosome 4, at the same site as the gene for achondroplasia. Therefore, hypochondroplasia may just represent a slightly different and clinically milder form of the mutated achondroplasia gene.

Characteristics

1. Mean birth length and weight within the low normal range.
2. Growth deficiency usually apparent by age 3; adult height ranging from 46.5 to 60 inches.
3. Mild, symmetric shortening of the extremities.
4. Stubby hands, feet, fingers, and toes.
5. Outward bowing of the legs with genu varum (bowleg deformity of the knee) that becomes more pronounced when the child starts to walk.
6. Nine percent to 25% incidence of intellectual developmental disabilities (IQ 50–80); mental deficiency rare in achondroplasia.
7. Normal-looking head and face, although macrocephaly (abnormally large head) possible in infancy.

Treatment for this disorder addresses the orthopedic problems. Although genu varum can improve during childhood, it may need surgical straightening. Exercise causes mild aching in the knees, ankles, and elbows in children. These pains usually intensify in adults, who also experience low-back discomfort. Oral analgesics (acetaminophen and ibuprofen) can provide symptomatic relief for suffering patients.

Like children with achondroplasia, children with hypochondroplasia may benefit from modifications in the classroom environment, such as providing appropriate-sized desks and chairs. Evaluation and treatment by occupational and physical therapists also may be beneficial. These children should be treated in an age-appropriate manner and not according to their short statures. Because of the incidence of intellectual developmental disabilities in children with hypochondroplasia, educational modifications under the umbrella of special education are needed to facilitate learning. The extent of modifications is contingent on the individual child's intellectual functioning and is based on educational need.

Because of the relatively high occurrence of mental retardation in hypochondroplasia, physicians caring for affected children should be cautious when discussing their prognoses (Gandy, n.d.). Until formal psychological testing can be done, optimism about their outlook appears ill advised. On the other hand, early delays in psychomotor development suggest that cognitive impairment is likely.

For more information and parent support, please contact Little People of America, Inc., P.O, Box 745, Lubbock, TX 79408. Tel.: (888) 572-2001.

REFERENCES

Gandy, A. (n.d.). *Hypochondroplasia*. Disease database. Retrieved from http://www.pedianet.com/news/illness/disease/.les/hypochon.htm

Horton, W. A., & Hecht, J. T. (2000). Disorders involving transmembrane receptors. In R. E. Behrman, R. M. Kleigman, & H. B. Jenson (Eds.), *Nelson's textbook of pediatrics* (16th ed., p. 2123). Philadelphia, PA: Saunders.

Jones, K. (1997). Smith's recognizable patterns of human malformations (5th ed) Philadelphia, PA: Saunders.

BARRY H. DAVISON
Ennis, Texas

JOAN W. MAYFIELD
Baylor Pediatric Specialty Services, Dallas, Texas

HYPOGLYCEMIA

Hypoglycemia is a clinical syndrome that results from an imbalance between glucose production and glucose utilization such that glucose levels in the bloodstream are depleted faster than they are replaced. Hypoglycemia is defined by a blood glucose concentration less than 2.2 mmol/L (Gandy, 1994). Hypoglycemia deprives the brain and nervous tissue of their primary source of energy and, as a result, may cause central nervous system dysfunction. Causes of hypoglycemia are highly varied and include numerous metabolic and endocrine disorders. Recent reviews have identified as many as 12 distinct hypoglycemic disorders (see Lteif & Shwenk, 1999) and more than 30 causes of hypoglycemia (see Schwartz, 1997).

Incidence of hypoglycemia in infants is estimated at 4.4 per 1,000 live births and is more common among infants of low birth weight (15.6:1,000; Gandy, 1994). Incidence in older children is 2 to 3 per 1,000 (Gandy, 1994). Onset can occur at any age.

Characteristics

1. In newborn infants, symptoms of hypoglycemia are nonspecific and can include the following: hypotonia, irritability, feeding difficulties, cyanosis, tachypnea, apnea, hypothermia, seizures, lethargy, and coma.
2. Older infants and children exhibit nonspecific signs consistent with autonomic nervous system arousal including sweating, hunger, tingling, heart pounding, nervousness or anxiety, and being shaky or tremulous.
3. If hypoglycemia is not treated, neuroglycopenic symptoms will emerge signaling brain glucose

deprivation. These symptoms include weakness, headache, confusion, fatigue, blurred vision, dizziness, slurred speech, abnormal behavior, amnesia, seizures, and coma.

4. In addition to symptoms consistent with hypoglycemia, a low plasma-glucose concentration is present (less than 2.2 mmol/L).

5. Symptoms resolve when plasma glucose level is restored to normal levels.

Treatment of hypoglycemia is a two-step process. First, acute symptoms are treated by normalizing blood glucose concentrations through food intake, intravenous glucose infusion, or subcutaneous injection of glucagon. The next phase of treatment involves diagnosing and correcting the underlying disorder that caused the hypoglycemia. Depending on the cause, treatment may involve medication, hormone replacement therapy, or surgery (Schwartz, 1997).

The long-term effects of hypoglycemia are highly varied and depend on timing, duration, and severity of the hypoglycemic episodes. Hypoglycemia can result in structural damage or death to nerve cells. In infants who experience hypoglycemia, neurological impairment can range from none to severe. Intellectual developmental disabilities can occur when hypoglycemia is severe, recurrent, and prolonged. Because outcomes may include a broad range of dysfunction, special education requirements will correspondingly vary.

Infants with asymptomatic hypoglycemia without convulsions have been shown to have a better prognosis than infants who experience symptomatic hypoglycemia with convulsions (Schwartz, 1997). Frequency of hypoglycemic episodes also appears to be an important factor in determining outcomes. In a sample of preterm neonates, those experiencing frequent moderate hypoglycemia were found to have poorer neuropsychological outcomes than were those experiencing more severe but less frequent episodes (Lteif & Schwenk, 1999).

REFERENCES

Gandy, A. (1994). *Hypoglycemia*. Pediatric database. Retrieved from http://www.icondata.com/health/pedbase/.les/hypoglyc.htm

Lteif, A. N., & Schwenk, W. F. (1999). Hypoglycemia in infants and children. *Endocrinology and Metabolism Clinics of North America, 28,* 619–646.

Schwartz, R. P. (1997). Hypoglycemia in infancy and childhood. *Indian Journal of Pediatrics, 64,* 43–55.

HEIDI A. MCCALLISTER
University of Texas at Austin

HYPOHIDROTIC ECTODERMAL DYSPLASIA

Hypohidrotic ectodermal dysplasia (HED) is one of a diverse group of disorders that affect the skin and skin derivatives (teeth, hair, nails, sweat glands, and sebaceous glands). Disturbances in other organ systems are common in these diseases. The hallmarks of HED are a deficiency or complete absence of sweat glands, malformed or missing teeth, and a generalized decrease in body hair.

HED is hereditary. The most common form, which is found exclusively in males, is transmitted in an X-linked recessive manner. Subtle abnormalities are usually present in carrier females. There is another clinically indistinguishable variant of HED, in which both parents are normal and their male and female offsprings are equally affected. The mode of inheritance for this subset appears to be autosomal recessive. Both types of the disorder are rare. Fewer than 150 cases of HED have been reported since its original description in 1848.

Characteristics

1. Thin skin with decreased pigmentation; considerable wrinkling around the eyes with hyperpigmentation; eczema.

2. Fine, dry, light-color hair that is sparse; complete baldness possible.

3. Absent or markedly diminished number of sweat glands, which makes affected children prone to hyperthermia when they are exposed to warm environmental temperatures.

4. Deficiency of mucous glands in the mouth, nose, trachea, and bronchi; chronic, foul nasal discharge, ear infections, and pneumonia possible.

5. Underdeveloped and missing teeth; cone-shaped front teeth.

6. Small nose; flat nasal bridge; prominent forehead; prominent bony ridge above the eyes; thick, protruding lips; large, low-set ears.

7. Occasionally hoarse voice; absence of tears; obstruction of the tear duct; absence of a breast or nipple; cataracts; conductive hearing loss; varying degrees of nail malformation; and asthma.

Treatment of HED requires protecting patients from heat exposure. Hyperthermia secondary to high ambient temperature not only is life-threatening but also can cause brain injury resulting in intellectual developmental disabilities. Dental referral is indicated early. Prostheses are provided for cosmetic reasons and to ensure that the child is able to chew food adequately. If tear glands are absent, artificial tears may be needed to prevent corneal damage. Upper and lower respiratory infections are managed with appropriate antibiotic therapy. Finally, a wig can be helpful in cases of marked hair loss.

There is no research to indicate the need for special education support services in the classroom. However, providing the child's teacher with information about HED is important to the safety of the child in the prevention of heat exposure.

The prognosis for HED is guarded. Approximately 30% of males with this disorder die before their second birthday, either from hyperthermic events or overwhelming respiratory infections.

In families where there is a concern about having a baby with HED, 90% of women carrying the defective gene can be identified by dental examination and a simple test measuring sweat gland activity. Prenatal testing is also available for detecting affected fetuses during the first trimester of pregnancy.

For more information, please contact National Foundation for Ectodermal Dysplasias, 410 East Main Street, P.O. Box 114, Mascoutah, IL 62258–0114. Tel.: (618) 566–2020: e-mail: nfedddd1@aol.com; http://www.nfed.org

This entry has been informed by the sources listed below.

REFERENCES

Darmstadt, G. L. (2000). Ectodermal dysplasias. In R. E. Behrman, R. M. Kleigman, & H. B. Jenson (Eds.), *Nelson's textbook of pediatrics* (16th ed, pp. 1974–1975). Philadelphia, PA: Saunders.

Gandy, A. (n.d.). *Hypohidrotic (anhidrotic) ectodermal dysplasis*. Disease database. Retrieved from http://www.pedianet.com/news/illness/disease/.les/hypohidr/htm

Pediatric database (PEDBASE). (1998, July 8). *Hypohidrotic (anhidrotic) ectodermal dysplasia*. Retrieved from http://www.icondata.com/pedbase/.les/HYPOHIDR.HTM

National Organization for Rare Disorders (NORD). (1998). *Hypohidrotic ectodermal dysplasia*. (Retrieved from http://www.rarediseases.org)

Jones, K. (1997). *Smith's recognizable patterns of human malformations* (5th ed). Philadelphia, PA: Saunders.

BARRY H. DAVISON
Ennis, Texas

JOAN W. MAYFIELD
Baylor Pediatric Specialty Services, Dallas, Texas

HYPOPHOSPHATASIA

Hypophosphatasia is an uncommon disorder of bone and cartilage formation. Its salient features include poor mineralization of the skull, short ribs resulting in an underdeveloped thorax and respiratory insufficiency, and poorly formed, fragile bones. A severe deficiency of the enzyme alkaline phosphatase is present in tissue and bone.

Hypophosphatasia is hereditary and conforms to an autosomal recessive mode of transmission. There are four clinically distinct forms of the disease. Mutations of the abnormal gene are considered to be responsible for these variations. The defect has been traced to Chromosome 1. The incidence of hypophosphatasia is unknown, but since the disorder was first recognized in 1948, many cases of the uniformly lethal perinatal subset have been reported.

Characteristics

1. Short-limbed dwarfism.
2. Generalized poor mineralization of bone.
3. Poorly formed, globular skull.
4. Bowed lower extremities.
5. Short ribs with multiple fractures.
6. Small thoracic cage.
7. Occasionally polyhydramnios (excessive amount of amniotic fluid) and blue sclerae (the normally white part of the eyeball).

No available references for this abnormality contain therapeutic recommendations. This lack of information regarding treatment could be explained by the dismal outlook for the perinatal and infantile variants of hypophosphatasia.

There is no research to indicate cognitive dysfunction or the need for special education services.

Prognosis for hypophosphatasia depends on the clinical form affecting the child. In the perinatal group, death usually occurs in early infancy, secondary to respiratory insufficiency. In those patients who survive, poor growth, diminished muscle tone, seizures, irritability, anemia, derangements of calcium metabolism, and calcification of kidney tissue are common findings. Children with the infantile type usually develop growth failure, rickets-like skeletal changes, and increased intracranial pressure by 6 months of age. Fifty percent die during the first year. There is a milder form in children that usually presents after 6 months of age. It is characterized by premature loss of the baby teeth, ricket-like skeletal pathology, and premature fusion of the cranial sutures. Finally, the adult variant occurs later in life and therefore carries the most favorable outlook. It manifests as premature loss of teeth and recurring bone fractures.

Prenatal diagnosis of hypophosphatasia is currently available from analysis of the alkaline phosphatase content in membranes surrounding the fetus. Findings can be obtained as early as the 10th to 12th week of pregnancy.

However, results require interpretation based on the history and clinical course of the disorder in each individual family.

For more information, please contact CLIMB (Children Living with Inherited Metabolic Diseases), The Quadrangle, Crewe Hall, Weston Road, Crewe, Cheshire, CW1–6UR, United Kingdom. Tel.: (127) 0 2-50221; http://www.CLIMB.org.uk

REFERENCES

Jones, K. (1997). *Smith's recognizable patterns of human malformations* (5th ed). Philadelphia, PA: Saunders.

National Organization for Rare Disorders. (1966). *Hypophosphatasia*. Retrieved from http://www.rarediseases.org

Barry H. Davison
Ennis, Texas

Joan W. Mayfield
Baylor Pediatric Specialty Services, Dallas, Texas

HYPOPLASTIC LEFT HEART SYNDROME

Hypoplastic left heart syndrome (HLHS) describes a group of complex congenital heart defects that occur in newborns (Barber, 1998). HLHS is characterized by the underdevelopment of the left atrium and ventricle of the heart. Additionally, the valve that connects these two chambers (the mitral orifice) and the aortic valve are narrowed or closed. The defects on the left side put unusual strain on the right side of the heart, causing enlargement of the chambers and the vessels on this side. When the baby is born, she or he may appear normal, but within a few days the baby will develop a bluish color to the skin (cyanosis and hypoperfusion). The infant will soon go into shock, and emergency surgery is usually required. Problems in cognition are usually the result of neurological complications associated with hypoperfusion of the brain and other structures of the central nervous system (CNS) (Freedom & Benson, 1995).

The cause of HLHS is unknown, and the prevalence rate is estimated to be somewhere between 0.16 and 0.36 in 1,000 live births.

Characteristics

1. Underdevelopment of the left side of the heart resulting in impaired oxygenated blood flow to the rest of the body, including the brain.

2. Difficulty breathing, rales (high-pitched noise while inhaling), and a grayish blue color to the skin occurring within the first 48 hours of life.

3. Hepatomegaly (an enlarged liver) in some infants.

4. Symptoms such as poor feeding habits, vomiting, lethargy, and shock.

5. CNS abnormalities and cognitive sequelae.

Before surgical therapies were made available, mortality rates reached 100% in most cases. However, with the advent of heart transplants and multistage operations, survival rates have reached 90% or better. Staged palliation involves three operations, the first of which is the Norwood operation. The second is the bidirectional Glenn operation, and the Fontan operation is the final procedure. The Norwood is performed shortly after birth and converts the right ventricle into the main or systemic ventricle. The second procedure, performed around 6 months of age, diverts one half of the blood returning from the body to the lungs. In the Fontan procedure, all of the blood returning from the body is diverted into the lungs. This final procedure is performed around 2 years of age.

Special education issues will be nonexistent in some children because once the corrective surgeries are performed, development proceeds normally with few residual effects. In a few cases, neurological impairment may be seen, and special education and labeling (e.g., Other Health Impairment) should be commensurate with degree of impairment.

Medical intervention has transformed a once fatal disorder into a syndrome with a positive prognosis. Instances will occur in which undiagnosed children will not survive and other children will succumb to complications associated with the surgical interventions. As etiology is unknown, future research has much of its focus on designing a method of detection. Currently, this deformity of the heart is not detectable in utero, and only after life-threatening manifestations is the disorder diagnosable.

REFERENCES

Barber, G. (1998). Hypoplastic left heart syndrome. In A. Garson, Jr., J. T. Bricker, D. J. Fisher, & S. R. Neish (Eds.), *Science and practice of pediatric cardiology* (pp. 1625–1645). Baltimore, MD: Williams & Wilkins.

Freedom, R. M., & Benson, L. N. (1995). Hypoplastic left heart syndrome. In H. D. Allen, H. D. Gutgesell, E. B. Clark, & D. J. Driscoll (Eds.), *Moss and Adams heart disease in infants, children, and adolescents* (pp. 1133–1153). Philadelphia, PA: Lippincott Williams & Wilkins.

Kimberly M. Estep
University of Houston, Clear Lake

HYPOTHYROIDISM

Hypothyroidism results from depletion in the concentration of thyroid hormone in the body. Thyroid hormone is released by the thyroid gland situated at the base of the neck. This important hormone is fundamental for normal metabolic rates in adults and is essential for growth and maturation in children. Depletion of thyroid hormone may occur as a result of treatment for *hyperthyroidism*, damage to the thyroid gland (i.e., primary hypothyroidism), a deficiency of iodine in the diet, or by a disorder of the pituitary gland (i.e., secondary hypothyroidism). There are three major types of hypothyroidism, and these include congenital, juvenile, and adult (Noble, Leyland, & Clark, 2000; Price & Wilson, 1997).

Congenital hypothyroidism (cretinism) is noticeable at birth and is often the result of a developmental defect (Price & Wilson, 1997). Most infants with this disorder have a defective thyroid gland or no gland at all. The infant usually has prolonged jaundice and a hoarse cry. Other noteworthy physical abnormalities include a large tongue that protrudes from the mouth and an umbilical hernia. Difficulty with feeding, excessive sleep, lethargy, and intellectual developmental disabilities are common (Kunz & Finkel, 1987; Price & Wilson, 1997). These infants fail to meet normal developmental milestones, and their teeth are often underdeveloped. Congenital hypothyroidism is incurable. However, immediate medical treatment at birth can circumvent intellectual developmental disabilities and growth failure (Beckwith & Tucker, 1988; Clayman, 1989; Dallas, 2000; Price & Wilson, 1997). Permanent intellectual deficits are typical if the condition is left untreated during the first 30 months of life (Beckwith & Tucker, 1988).

Although the age of onset differentiates juvenile from adult hypothyroidism, both types share common characteristics. Juvenile hypothyroidism becomes evident around 1 or 2 years of age, whereas adult hypothyroidism (myxedema) develops during adulthood. Juveniles and adults with hypothyroidism typically present with slowing of intellectual and motor activity, cold intolerance, decreased sweating, facial puffiness, weight gain, and fatigue (Price & Wilson, 1997). Frequently, symptoms of clinical depression are also reported (Beckwith & Tucker, 1988).

About 13 million Americans have a thyroid disorder, and more than half go undiagnosed because onset is typically gradual. Women suffer from the disorder 7 times more than men, and the frequency of occurrence increases with age. Indeed, adult onset is usually seen among elderly women. The disorder remains undetected in many middle-aged women because several symptoms, including fatigue, mood swings, sleep disturbances, and depression, resemble signs of menopause (Portyansky, 1999). Hypothyroidism rarely occurs in newborns (Kunz & Finkel, 1987), affecting only about 1 in every 4,000 infants (Dallas, 2000).

The disorder occurs more frequently in children with Down syndrome than in the general population. However, these children often go untreated because the two disorders share common characteristics (e.g., weight gain, poor growth, and dull affect). For this reason, physicians recommend that persons with Down syndrome be routinely screened for hypothyroidism (Noble et al., 2000).

Characteristics

Congenital

1. Persistent jaundice and hoarse cry.
2. Constipation, somnolence, and feeding problems.
3. Short stature and coarse features.
4. Protruding tongue; broad, flat nose; widely spaced eyes; and sparse hair.
5. Dry skin, protuberant abdomen, and umbilical hernia.
6. Hearing impairment.

Juvenile and Adult

1. Fatigue and hoarseness.
2. Cold intolerance and decreased sweating.
3. Cool, dry skin and facial puffiness. Slow movements.
4. Slowing of intellectual and motor activity.
5. Slow relaxation of deep tendon reflexes.
6. Impaired recent memory and difficulty in concentrating.
7. Weight gain.
8. Major depressive symptomology.

Treatment for all types of hypothyroidism involves replacement therapy with the artificial thyroid hormone thyroxine (Clayman, 1989). Infants and children with hypothyroidism should take thyroid hormone as soon as possible in order to avoid irreversible damage to their nervous systems including retarded growth, delayed sexual maturity, and inhibited normal brain development (Clayman, 1989; Kunz & Finkel, 1987). Adults should feel better a few days after beginning treatment, and they should be back to normal within a few days. Biochemical tests showing either elevated (primary hypothyroidism) or lowered (secondary hypothyroidism) thyroid-stimulating hormone levels and reduced thyroxine (T4) levels make diagnosis easy (Portyansky, 1999; Price & Wilson, 1997).

The prognosis for infants who do not receive treatment is poor. Left untreated, infants will suffer irreversible brain damage and growth failure. Prognosis is good for infants who are diagnosed early, with most of the effects of hypothyroidism being reversible. Indeed, infants who are treated for hypothyroidism within the first months after birth are usually of average intelligence and grow at a normal rate.

Researchers recommend screening for congenital hypothyroidism by measuring the thyroid hormone (T4) with a blood spot test. Since the implementation of screening procedures and early childhood medical intervention, intellectual developmental disabilities and growth failure rarely occur (Dallas, 2000). Without early intervention, however, these children will require special education services in school and will need constant care and supervision into adulthood.

REFERENCES

Beckwith, B. E., & Tucker, D. M. (1988). Thyroid disorders. In R. E. Tarter, D. H. Van Thiel, & K. L. Edwards (Eds.), *Medical neuropsychology: The impact of disease on behavior* (pp. 197–221). New York, NY: Plenum Press.

Clayman, C. B. (1989). *The American Medical Association home medical encyclopedia*. New York, NY: Random House.

Dallas, J. S. (2000). *Congenital hypothyroidism*. The Thyroid Society. Retrieved from www.thyroid.org

Kunz, J. R. M., & Finkel, A. J. (1987). *The American Medical Association family medical guide*. New York, NY: Random House.

Noble, S. E., Leyland, C. A., & Clark, C. E. (2000). School based screening for hypothyroidism in Down's syndrome by dried blood spot TSH measurement. *Archives of Disease in Childhood, 82,* 27–32.

Portyansky, E. (1999). Hard-to-diagnose subclinical hypothyroidism often undertreated. *Drug Topics, 143,* 29–31.

Price, S. A., & Wilson, L. M. (1997). *Pathophysiology clinical concepts of disease processes*. St. Louis, MO: Library of Congress.

MELLISA BECKHAM
KERRY S. LASSITER
The Citadel

HYPOTONIA

Hypotonia involves decreased tension of the fine muscles, making upright postures difficult to hold and independent movement difficult to produce (Pediatric Services, n.d.). It is also referred to as *decreased muscle tone, flaccidity,* or *floppiness.* Hypotonia is the opposite of hypertonia. Hypotonia is commonly associated with multiple genetic, metabolic, cerebral, spinal, or muscular disorders including muscular dystrophy, myasthenic gravis, Down syndrome, meningitis, and encephalitis. Hypotonia can also be caused by injury or trauma. Although identification of the presence of hypotonia is not difficult, determination of the actual cause of the symptom is more problematic.

Obviously, children with hypotonia are at risk for developmental delays in motor skills, poor reflexes, and limited sense of balance. Moreover, children with hypotonia are more likely to suffer from dislocations of joints, such as the hip, jaw, shoulders, and neck due to the inadequate support from the muscles to hold the joints together. Additionally, skeletal deformities are more common in children with hypotonia due to their tendency to assume abnormal positions (i.e., "W" sitting and sleeping prone in a frog-like position). Finally, other domains of functioning may be affected by hypotonia, including overall development and cognitive skill development, as the child may not be able to benefit from exploration of the environment or the child may have delayed development of language skills due to decreased muscle tone in the face and mouth.

It is difficult to estimate the actual prevalence of hypotonia, as it is not a specific disease, and records do not specify the frequency of particular symptoms.

Characteristics

1. Low tone, floppy, rag-doll appearance.
2. Extreme flexibility, range of motion beyond normal.
3. Delayed motor skills.
4. Shallow breathing.
5. Limited gag reflex, open mouth, protruding tongue.
6. Abnormal posture (may cause skeletal deformities).
7. Unable to sustain movements (sucking, chewing, holding head up, sitting position, weight bearing).
8. Poor reflexes and balance reactions.

Following identification of the presence of hypotonia, a treatment program can be developed. Although treatment will not cure the symptoms, it will aid in the prevention of future complications due to the condition. Treatment may also serve to facilitate the child's most appropriate development and teach compensatory skills. Treatment programs incorporate instruction to the child and caregivers in positioning and movement strategies. Hypotonic children may need extra stimulation through treatment programs that incorporate the use of sensory stimuli (i.e., touch, sound, sight, taste, smell, movement). Provision of general stimulation through swinging, rolling, and spinning activities may be beneficial (Trombly, 1989). Physical therapy, occupational therapy, and speech services are often provided to facilitate skill development. Ankle-foot orthoses are sometimes used for weak ankle muscles.

Collaboration between parents, educators, and medical professionals is important to enable the most positive outcome for the child with hypotonia. Children with hypotonia will often be identified at an early age through primary care medical settings. It is important for parents to be placed in contact with the local school district or state agencies that provide early intervention services for children ages 0 to 3. Infants with hypotonia may be eligible for special education services. If eligible, an Individual Family Service Plan (IFSP) would be developed to identify goals and services. Preschool and elementary school students may continue to be eligible for special education services under provisions of the Individuals with Disabilities Education Act. Although a child may not be directly eligible to receive services due to the presence of hypotonia, per se, eligibility may be based on associated conditions or disorders. Specific services will be determined on an individualized basis. If educationally necessary, children may receive the related services of occupational, physical, and speech therapies.

The prognosis for children with hypotonia varies dependent on several factors, including the root cause of the condition, the severity of the symptoms, and the provision of appropriate early interventions.

REFERENCES

Pediatric Services (n.d.). *Understanding the lingo.* Retrieved from www.pediatricservices.com

Trombly, C. A. (1989). Neurophysiological and developmental treatment approaches. In C. Trombly (Ed.), *Occupational therapy for physical dysfunction* (3rd ed.). Baltimore, MD: Williams & Wilkins.

SHELLEY PELLETIER
SUSAN SAGE
Dysart Unified School District, El Mirage, Arizona

Characteristics

Perinatal Hypoxia (Gross, 1990; Hill & Volpe, 1994)

1. Widespread damage to white matter, particularly in the periventricular regions and brain stem.
2. Damage to the watershed regions of the cerebral cortex parasagitally.
3. Focal areas of neuronal necrosis in the cerebral and cerebellar cortices, thalamus, basal ganglia, brain stem, and anterior horn cells due to concomitant ischemia or hemorrhage.
4. Status marmoratus of the basal ganglia and thalamus characterized by neuronal loss, gliosis, and hypermyelination, causing a marbled appearance of these structures.
5. In the preterm infant a similar pattern of white matter and brain stem damage but parasagital cortical areas less vulnerable due to anastomoses with meningeal arteries.
6. The encephalopathy that ensues from perinatal hypoxia often immediately apparent and associated with loss of consciousness, hypotonia, seizures, and brain stem findings including impairments of extraocular movements, sucking response, and respiration.

Hypoxia in Older Children (Brierley & Graham, 1976; Taylor, Quencer, Holzman, & Naidich, 1985)

1. Brain stem and white matter become more resistant to hypoxia with age.
2. Cerebral cortex remains vulnerable, as do the hippocampus, thalamus, cerebellum, and basal ganglia.
3. Problems with attention and memory are common.
4. Less impairment with muscle tone occurs.

HYPOXIA

Cerebral hypoxia refers to reduced oxygenation of brain tissue and is a leading cause of perinatal neurologic morbidity and encephalopathy in children (Hill & Volpe, 1994; Schwartz, Ahmann, Dykes, & Brann, 1993). In the absence of oxygen, cells switch to anaerobic glycolysis, which can sustain the brain for only a short time before cell death occurs (Brierley & Graham, 1976). In addition, hypoxia can initiate a cascade of toxic biochemical events that evolve over the course of hours to days, including glutamatergic excito-toxicity (Johnston, 1997).

Perinatal hypoxia is estimated to occur in 2 to 4 per 1,000 live-term births. The incidence is much higher in premature births at approximately 60% due to immaturity of the lungs (Schwartz et al., 1993). Hypoxia can occur at the antepartum, intrapartum, and postpartum periods. Antepartum, the fetus is vulnerable to diseases or disorders affecting oxygen content of the mother's blood, such as cardiac arrest or hemorrhage. During the intrapartum period hypoxia may occur from abruptio placentae, uterine rupture, or traumatic delivery (Rivkin, 1997). Postpartum hypoxia can result from aspiration of meconium as well as respiratory or cardiac distress. The risk of perinatal hypoxia increases with maternal diabetes, toxemia or hypertension, delivery by cesarean section not preceded by labor, and in second twins (Gross, 1990).

In older children hypoxia can occur due to a variety of causes, including processes affecting the passage of oxygen at the alveolar level (e.g., pneumonia, asthma), inhibition of the bellows function of the chest wall (e.g., polio, spinal cord lesion), obstruction of the tracheobronchial tree (e.g., choking, hanging), and situations in which insufficient oxygen is available (e.g., drowning, high altitudes, smoke inhalation). Hypoxia can also occur secondary to ischemia, hypoglycemia, anemia, shock, cardiac disease, and histotoxic effects interfering with the cells ability to utilize oxygen (Brierley & Graham, 1976).

The newborn tends to be more resistant to the effects of hypoxia than the older child or adult. Mild perinatal hypoxia often does not result in detectable encephalopathy. The longer-term effects of moderate to severe perinatal hypoxia include Intellectual Developmental Disabilities, dystonia, cerebral palsy, seizures, and death. Perinatal hypoxia has long been suspected as a causal factor in learning disabilities and ADHD. Up to 40% of infants with moderate hypoxia have been reported to have problems with school readiness at age 5 years (Hill & Volpe, 1994). In older children, dystonia and cerebral palsy are not as frequent, but cerebellar dysfunction may occur. Problems with attention, memory, and executive functions predominate. Impairment of visuospatial functions is also common.

Given the frequent motor involvement, physical and occupational therapy may be indicated. In addition, early evaluation and intervention to facilitate school readiness should be routinely considered. Special education services and specific cognitive rehabilitation therapy may be necessary with children of school age.

REFERENCES

Brierley, J. B., & Graham, D. I. (1976). Hypoxia and vascular disorders of the central nervous system. In W. Blackwood & J. A. N. Corsellis (Eds.), Greenfield's neuropathology. Chicago, IL: Year Book Medical.

Gross, I. (1990). Respiratory distress syndrome. In F. Oski (Ed.), Principles and practice of pediatrics. Philadelphia, PA: Lippincott.

Hill, A., & Volpe, J. J. (1994). Hypoxic-ischemic cerebral injury in the newborn. In K. F. Swaiman (Ed.), Pediatric neurology. St. Louis, MO: Mosby.

Johnston, M. V. (1997). Hypoxic and ischemic disorders of infants and children: Lecture for the 38th meeting of Japanese Society of Child Neurology, Tokyo, Japan, July, 1996. Brain and Development, 19, 235–239.

Rivkin, M. J. (1997). Hypoxic-ischemic brain injury in the term newborn: Neuropathology, clinical aspects, and neuroimaging. Clinics in Perinatology, 24(3), 607–625.

Schwartz, J. F., Ahmann, P. A., Dykes, F. D., & Brann, A. W. (1993). Neonatal intracranial hemorrhage and hypoxia. In J. M. Pellock & E. C. Myer (Eds.), Neurologic emergencies in infancy and childhood. Boston, MA: Butterworth-Heinemann.

Taylor, S. B., Quencer, R. M., Holzman, B. H., & Naidich, T. P. (1985). Central nervous system anoxic-ischemic insult in children due to near drowning. Radiology, 156(3), 641–646.

DAVID M. TUCKER
REBECCA VAURIO
Austin, Texas

See also Anoxia

HYSTERICAL PERSONALITY (See Histrionic Personality Disorder)

I

ICHTHYOSIS, CHANARIN DORFMAN SYNDROME

Chanarin Dorfman syndrome is a hereditary disorder of lipid metabolism almost always accompanied by dry, scaly skin (ichthyosis). Myopathy (degeneration of the muscles) and fat deposits appearing in the white blood cells also are commonly seen in patients with Chanarin Dorfman syndrome.

Chanarin Dorfman syndrome is believed to be a rare disorder inherited as an autosomal recessive trait. Treatment is symptomatic and generally includes skin-softening ointments and medical interventions directed toward fatty liver, ocular abnormalities, disorders of the central nervous system, and liver enlargement, which comprise part of the long list of other abnormalities occasionally seen in these patients.

Characteristics

1. Chanarin Dorfman syndrome can be detected by the presence of fat droplets in certain white blood cell in a blood smear taken from a finger, toe, heel, or ear.
2. In addition to the fat deposits, ichthyosis is present.
3. Additional symptoms include deafness, short stature, fatty liver (the liver being the most commonly affected organ), central nervous system disorders with cognitive sequelae, ocular abnormalities, myopathy, and developmental lags.

Some children will not need special education services, whereas others may require assistance. Special education issues can vary greatly from minimal intervention such as tutoring to keep a child on track to qualification of a child as handicapped due to health problems.

Prognosis is highly dependent on the affected individual. This disorder is fatal and merely a nuisance in others. Future research on this disorder includes gene mapping in the hopes of attainment of a cure and more definitive information regarding etiology.

This entry has been informed by the sources listed below.

REFERENCES

Pena-Penabad, C., Almagro, M., Martinez, W., Garcia-Silva, J., Del Pozo, J., Yebra, M. T.,...Fonseca, E. (2001). Dorfman-Chanarin syndrome (neutral lipid storage disease): New clinical features. *British Journal of Dermatology, 144*, 430432.

Tullu, M. S., Muranjan, M. N., Save, S. U., Deshmukh, C. T., Khubchandani, S. R., & Bharucha, B. A. (2000) Dorfman Chanarin syndrome: A rare neutral lipid storage disease. *Indian Pediatrics, 37*, 8893.

KIMBERLY M. ESTEP
University of Houston–Clear Lake

ICHTHYOSIS, CHILD SYNDROME

CHILD (congenital hemidysplasia with ichthyosis erythroderma and limb defects) syndrome is an inherited disorder that is usually present at birth. It is characterized by skin anomalies and limb defects on one side of the body.

CHILD syndrome is a rare disorder transmitted through an X-linked dominant gene and thus occurs more frequently in females. Males affected by CHILD syndrome, an extremely rare occurrence, present with an XXY genetic code (Klinefelter syndrome).

Characteristics

1. The syndrome predominantly affects females at birth or in early childhood.
2. Dry, scaly, itchy, and red skin (ichthyosis erythrodermia) appears on one side of the body, although minor skin abnormalities may be seen on the opposite side of the body.

---

3. Children may have clawlike nails and be bald on one side of the head.

4. Pulmonary, cardiovascular, renal, and endocrine abnormalities may be present.

5. Anomalies of the central nervous system and the thyroid and adrenal glands may also occur.

6. Limb defects may be present on the same side of the body as the skin symptoms, and they may include an absence of fingers and toes or an underdevelopment of the fingers and toes, as well as deformities of the long bones.

7. A majority of the aberrations seen in affected children are a result of underdevelopment of the affected side of the body.

Treatment of the skin disease involves the use of emollients. Surgery may become necessary to correct musculoskeletal abnormalities. Keratolytics, a category of drugs, may be administered to alleviate dry, scaly skin and help exfoliate the skin. Special education issues revolve around handicapping issues associated with health problems.

Prognosis is fatal in affected males, and in females morbidity is more often caused by anomalies not associated with the skin condition. Congenital cardiac defects are the primary cause of death among individuals with CHILD syndrome, whereas abnormalities in the lungs, skeleton, kidneys, and central nervous system pose other potential complications. Future research is focused on gene mapping to understand better the etiology and to find more effective treatments for this disorder.

This entry has been informed by the sources listed below.

REFERENCES

Fenske, N. A., & Roshdieh, B. (2001). CHILD syndrome. *eMedicine, 2*. Retrieved from http://emedicine.medscape.com/

Hebert, A. A., Esterly, N. B., Holbrook, K. A., & Hall, J. C. (1987). The CHILD syndrome. *Archives of Dermatology, 123*, 503–509.

KIMBERLY M. ESTEP
University of Houston–Clear Lake

ICHTHYOSIS, CONGENITA

Ichthyosis congenita is an inherited skin disorder characterized by generalized dry and rough skin. All babies who suffer from an autosomal recessive congenita ichthyosis are collodion babies at birth. Collodion babies are born with a translucent or opaque membrane that covers the entire body and lasts for days to weeks. Congenita ichthyosis presents on a spectrum in which lamellar ichthyosis is the most severe and nonbullous congenital ichthyosis is a mild form of congenita ichthyosis. In lamellar ichthyosis the collodion membrane is replaced by dark brown plate-like scales without erythroderma (abnormal redness of the skin). The nonbullous type presents with erythroderma with fine white scales.

Prevalence is estimated at 1 in 200,000 individuals in the United States. The disease affects all racial and ethnic groups and males and females alike.

Characteristics

1. Most newborns with congenita ichthyosis are collodion babies with a transparent membrane covering their body that will eventually be shed.

2. On the congenita ichthyosis spectrum is lamellar ichthyosis, which is a more severe form presenting with large dark brown and shedding scales that cover almost the entire body.

3. Children affected with the more severe form may also suffer sepsis (infection) and protein and electrolyte loss, which can lead to complications associated with death.

4. In the nonbullous cases, erythroderma and white scales are present.

Treatment involves keeping the child moist with petroleum-based ointments, and hygienic handling should be carefully followed to avoid infection. As the child ages, alphahydroxy acid preparations can aid in peeling and thinning of the skin. Keeping the infant hydrated is also of importance.

Given that most congenita ichthyosis resolve themselves, no long-term effects are seen except the outward signs of the ichthyosis. Therefore, no special education issues arise. However, psychological needs might surface in regard to the child's or adolescent's outward appearance. Overall, prognosis is good, and research is ongoing to find a cure for this disorder.

This entry has been informed by the sources listed below.

REFERENCES

Masashi, A. (1998). Severe congenital ichthyosis of the neonate. *International Journal of Dermatology, 37*, 722–728.

Williams, M. L., & Elias, P. M. (1987). Genetically transmitted, generalized disorders of cornification: The ichthyoses. *Clinical Dermatology, 5,* 155–178.

KIMBERLY M. ESTEP
University of Houston–Clear Lake

Williams, M. L., & Elias, P. M. (1987). Genetically transmitted, generalized disorders of cornification: The ichthyoses. *Dermatology Clinics, 5,* 155–178.

KIMBERLY M. ESTEP
University of Houston–Clear Lake

ICHTHYOSIS, ERYTHROKERATODERMIA PROGRESSIVA SYMMETRICA

A form of ichthyosis, erythrokeratodermia progressiva symmetrica (EPS) is a very rare hereditary skin disorder characterized by keratotic (hardened red) plaques distributed over the body and the extremities. However, the chest and abdomen area are normally void of any plaques. Cornification normally appears during the first year of life; some cases involving EPS have been documented to disappear spontaneously later in life.

Incidence rates are equal for males and females, and EPS is transmitted through autosomal dominant genes. Other than the outward manifestation of EPS, children show no other physical symptoms, and no mental deficiencies have been noted.

Characteristics

1. Keratotic plaques cover a majority of the body, including the buttocks, head, and extremities.
2. In most cases, the chest and abdomen are spared cornification.
3. EPS appears during the first year of life and stabilizes after 1 or 2 years and in some cases even dissipates during puberty.
4. Lesions may also appear on the palms of the hands and the soles of the feet.

Treatment is limited to topical medications, and relief is sometimes not achieved. Prognosis is good, and future research focuses on alleviation of symptomology.

This entry has been informed by the sources listed below.

REFERENCES

Khoo, B. P., Tay, Y. K., & Tan, S. H. (2000). Generalized erythematous plaques: Progressive symmetric erythrokeratodermia (PSEK) (erythrokeratodermia progressiva symmetric). *Archives of Dermatology, 136,* 665–668.

ICHTHYOSIS, ERYTHROKERATODERMIA VARIABILIS

Ichthyosis erythrokeratodermia variabilis (IEV) is one of a diverse group of disorders of skin keratinization (the process in which skin cells form and are eventually shed). It is distinguished from the other members of the ichthyosis group by its unique clinical features and pattern of inheritance.

IEV is transmitted in an autosomal dominant manner. No data are available regarding its frequency in the general population. Evidence points to a genetic linkage between IEV and Rh blood type.

Characteristics

1. Skin abnormalities usually appear early in life, progress throughout childhood, and cease during adolescence.
2. Distinct, thickened plaques (hyperkeratosis) with irregular borders occur in normal skin. Their appearance may be preceded by discrete patches of redness (erythema).
3. Patches of erythema may vary in size, shape, and location. They may migrate or remain in the same place and eventually become hyperkeratotic.
4. Hyperkeratosis tends to be generalized, but the face, buttocks, armpits, and outer surfaces of the extremities are most commonly involved.
5. Thickened skin of the palms and soles is common.
6. The teeth, hair, and nails are not involved.

No therapeutic recommendations for IEV can be found in the literature about this disorder. Presumably, the ichthyotic changes respond to the same treatment modalities that are effective for other diseases in this general classification of skin maladies.

There is no research to indicate that children with IEV have any specific cognitive deficits or require special education resources. The prognosis for IEV should be considered favorable. Although skin changes progress during childhood, they stabilize during adolescence. Therefore, adults with this problem can anticipate that their cutaneous abnormalities will, at least, not get any worse.

For more information, please contact the Foundation for Ichthyosis and Related Skin Types, 650 North Cannon Ave., Suite 17, Lansdale, PA 19446. Tel.: (215) 631–1411 or (800) 545–3286, e-mail: ichthyosis@aol.com; http://www.firstskinfoundation.org/.

This entry has been informed by the sources listed below.

REFERENCES

Darmstadt, G. L. (2000). Disorders of keratinization. In R. E. Behrman, R. M. Kleigman, & H. B. Jenson (Eds.), *Nelson's textbook of pediatrics* (16th ed., p. 2009). Philadelphia, PA: Saunders.

National Organization for Rare Diseases. (1997). *Ichthyosis, erythrokeratodermia variabilis.* Retrieved from http://www.rarediseases.org

BARRY H. DAVISON
Ennis, Texas

JOAN W. MAYFIELD
*Baylor Pediatric Specialty Services,
Dallas, Texas*

ICHTHYOSIS, ERYTHROKERATOLYSIS HIEMALIS

Erythrokeratolysis hiemalis (EH) or keratolytic winter erythema (KWE) is an autosomal dominant skin disorder characterized by circles of erythema (redness or inflammation of the skin) and hyperkeratosis (excessive skin lesions in which there is overgrowth and thickening of the skin). With age, the symptoms grow milder, eventually disappearing all together. This disorder is mostly seen in South Africa, where the incidence is 1 in 7,000 people.

Characteristics

1. Redness and inflammation of the skin.
2. Overgrowth and thickening of the skin leading to recurrent and intermittent peeling of the palms and soles.
3. Symptoms that generally subside during the summer months.

The peeling and redness cause no physical discomfort, and moisturizing the affected areas or submerging them in water only exacerbates the condition. Peeling of the affected areas causes no discomfort and is done with

ease. No special education issues arise as a result of EH. Future research is interested in finding the etiology of this disorder, and prognosis is good for those who are affected.

This entry has been informed by the sources listed below.

REFERENCES

Botha, M. C., & Beighton, P. (1983). Inherited disorders in the Afrikaner populations of southern Africa: Part II. Skeletal, dermal, and haematological conditions; the Afrikaners of Gamkaskloof; demographic considerations. *South African Medical Journal, 64,* 664–667.

Findaly, G. H., & Morrison, J. G. L. (1978). Erythrokeratolysis hiemalis—keratolytic winter skin or "oudtshoorn skin" *British Journal of Dermatology, 98,* 491–495.

Starfield, M., Hennies, H. C., Jung, M., Jenkins, T., Wienker, T., Hull, P.,...Reis, A. (1997). Localization of the gene causing keratolytic winter erythema to chromosome 8p22p23, and evidence for a founder effect in South African Afrikaansspeakers. *American Journal of Human Genetics, 61,* 370–378.

KIMBERLY M. ESTEP
University of Houston–Clear Lake

ICHTHYOSIS, HARLEQUIN TYPE (HARLEQUIN FETUS)

Harlequin fetus (HF) is a rare disorder of keratinization, the process by which skin tissue forms and eventually sloughs off the body. It most likely represents several genetic mutations that have common clinical findings.

No data are available on the incidence of HF in the general population. HF is transmitted in an autosomal recessive manner. One subtype of HF has been traced to an enzyme deficiency that is encoded on chromosome 11.

Characteristics

1. Newborns covered with extremely thick, fissured skin that obscures facial features and causes severe constriction of the digits.
2. Flat nose and ears.
3. Marked eversion of the eyelids with inflammation of the eyeball.
4. Absent nails and hair (occasionally).
5. Eversion of the lips, gaping mouth.
6. Restricted joint mobility; hands and feet are fixed, and their blood flow is impaired.
7. Respiratory distress, poor suck.
8. Skin infections common and potentially life-threatening.

Initial therapy for affected newborns requires attention to fluid intake to replace water losses that occur through denuded skin. A warm, humid environment and application of lubricating ointments help to reduce cutaneous evaporation. Oral retinoids, drugs that correct some of the defects in the keratinization process, are also useful.

Because of the poor prognosis, there is no research available concerning cognitive deficits associated with HF.

The prognosis for HF is poor. The majority of these babies die in the first few weeks after birth. Those infants who survive the neonatal period suffer from severe ichthyosis (inflamed, scaling skin) and varying degrees of neurological damage.

Prenatal diagnosis of HF is available for individuals with a family history of this disorder. Direct visualization of the fetus (fetoscopy), biopsy of fetal skin, and culture of fetal cells found in amniotic fluid all provide valuable data for clinicians caring for concerned parents-to-be.

For more information, contact the Foundation for Ichthyosis and Related Skin Types, 650 North Cannon Ave., Suite 17, Lansdale, PA 19446. Tel.: (215) 631–1411 or (800) 545–3286, e-mail: ichthyosis@aol.com; http://www .firstskinfoundation.org/.

This entry was informed by the following references.

REFERENCES

Darmstadt, G. L. (2000). Disorders of keratinization. In R. E. Behrman, R. M. Kleigman, & H. B. Jenson (Eds.), *Nelson's textbook of pediatrics* (16th ed., p. 2007). Philadelphia, PA: Saunders.

National Organization for Rare Disorders. (1997). *Ichthyosis, harlequin type*. Retrieved from http://www.rarediseases.org

BARRY H. DAVISON
Ennis, Texas

JOAN W. MAYFIELD
*Baylor Pediatric Specialty Services,
Dallas, Texas*

ICHTHYOSIS, HYSTRIX, CURTH-MACKLIN TYPE

Ichthyosis is the name for a group of rare genetic disorders that causes the skin to build up and scale (Ichthyosis Information, 2001). The forms of ichthyosis vary and range in severity. The ichthyosis disorders all involve the normal growth and shedding cycle of skin; the filament network is critical to this process. In ichthyosis hystrix, Curth-Macklin type (IHCM), the filaments are rudimentary with a greater production of mucus than typically occurs (Anton-Lamprecht, 1978). IHCM is a very rare type of ichthyosis. It is believed to result from an abnormality in the genes that encode proteins with resulting disruption of the keratin filament network (Curth & Macklin, 1954), possibly due to a mutation in a keratin gene (KRT1). The altered appearance of the skin in IHCM tends to be localized and may have the appearance of multiple birthmarks or nevi.

As a result of the various forms of ichthyoses, the incidence rate for IHCM is very hard to establish. Two families with IHCM have been discussed extensively in the research literature (Curth & Macklin, 1954; Niemi, Virtanen, Kanerva, & Muttilainen, 1990). ICHM is genetic with autosomal dominant transmission; it also can occur through spontaneous mutation, but this is even rarer. Reliable data on the incidence of the ichthyoses in general are minimal. There is no evidence of greater likelihood of occurrence of IHCM in any specific ethnic group or gender.

The disruption of the shedding process has multiple effects. The scaling that results can be painful and can restrict movement. If untreated, in the more severe forms and depending on the localization, the scaling can interfere with hearing or vision. Additionally, because skin normally is involved in the regulation of body temperature, individuals with ICHM can be very sensitive to temperature changes. Individuals with ICHM can have significant problems with overheating because the scaling may interfere with the usual cooling process of perspiration. Finally, depending on the localization and severity of the disorder, appearance can be affected negatively, and individuals with ICHM may be subjected to teasing or recurrent questions (Ichthyosis Information, 2001).

Characteristics

1. Extremely dry skin.
2. Buildup and scaling of skin.
3. Thick, furrowed overgrowth of skin or hyperkeratosis over the joints.
4. Sensitivity to temperature fluctuations.
5. Problems with heat exhaustion or overheating.

Treatment of ichthyosis is a lifelong endeavor (Ichthyosis Information, 2001) that involves frequent exfoliation and moisturizing of the affected areas of skin. Additional treatment may be needed to address itching that is associated with the scaling as well as the potential for infection. The extent of time required may vary, but skin care is needed not only to improve the appearance of the skin but also to avoid pain or restricted movement, vision, or hearing that may be associated with the scaling. Scaling can restrict range of movement, and at that level of severity, accommodations may be appropriate to compensate for the restricted motion. For children and adolescents, inservice programs on skin disorders, as well as behavior management of any teasing, may be appropriate. There is a national registry for individuals with all forms of ichthyosis supported by the National Institutes for Health, as well as support groups (Ichthyosis Information, 2001).

REFERENCES

Anton-Lamprecht, I. (1978). Electron microscopy in the early diagnosis of genetic disorders of the skin. *Dermatologica, 157*, 65–85.

Curth, H. O., & Macklin, M. T. (1954). The genetic basis of various types of ichthyosis in a family group. *American Journal of Human Genetics, 6*, 371–381.

Ichthyosis Information. (2001). *Ichthyosis information: Providing a Web-based resource for ichthyosis.* Retrieved from www.ichthyosis.com

Niemi, K. M., Virtanen, I., Kanerva, L., & Muttilainen, M. (1990). Altered keratin expression in ichthyosis hystrix Curth-Macklin. *Archives of Dermatology Research, 282*, 227–233.

CYNTHIA A. RICCIO
Texas A&M University

ICHTHYOSIS, KERATOSIS FOLLICULARIS SPINULOSA DECALVANS

Keratosis follicularis spinulosa decalvans (KFSD) is a form of ichthyosis characterized by hardening of the skin around the hair follicles eventually leading to baldness (alopecia) and scarring. During infancy, keratosis begins on the face and moves to the extremities and trunk by childhood. Around puberty, alopecia of the scalp and eyebrows develops. KFSD is a rare X-linked disease that affects more males than females.

Characteristics

1. The skin around the hair follicles hardens, leading to scarring and alopecia.
2. Patients develop sensitivity to bright light, and corneal abnormalities may be present.
3. Eyebrows and eyelashes may be absent or thinned.

Treatment involves topical ointments to alleviate some of the discomfort associated with the dry, scaly skin.

Pharmacological advances have been made with regard to alopecia, but effectiveness varies by individual. Ophthalmologists should be consulted regarding any emerging ocular abnormalities. Special education issues revolve around any ocular anomalies that arise, and many children

will suffer no deficits that require intervention other than those associated with the keratosis and hair loss. Research is ongoing in the hopes of attaining a cure for this disorder.

This entry has been informed by the sources listed below.

REFERENCES

Rand, R., & Baden, H. P. (1983). Keratosis follicularis spinulosa decalvans: Reports of two cases and literature review. *Archives of Dermatology, 119*(1), 22–26.

van Osch, L. D., Oranje, A. P., Keukens, F. M., van Voorst Vader, P. C., & Veldman, E. (1992). Keratosis follicularis spinulosa decalvans: A family study of seven male cases and six female carriers. *Journal of Medical Genetics, 29*(1), 36–40.

KIMBERLY M. ESTEP
University of Houston–Clear Lake

ICHTHYOSIS, LAMELLAR RECESSIVE (LAMELLAR ICHTHYOSIS)

Lamellar ichthyosis (LI) is one of the two major forms of hereditary, autosomal recessive, congenital disorders of keratinization, the process by which skin tissues form and are eventually shed from the body's surface. Abnormalities are present at birth or shortly thereafter. The incidence of LI has not been determined. The mode of inheritance is autosomal recessive.

Characteristics

1. Newborns with LI present either as collodion babies (these infants are covered with a thick, parchment-like membrane that sloughs off within a few days) or with generalized redness of the skin (erythroderma) and scaling.
2. Initial cutaneous findings give way to the development of generalized ichthyosis in which the body is completely covered by large, dark, quadrangular scales.
3. Marked facial involvement is common. Eversion of the eyelids (ectropion) and small, crumpled ears may be present.
4. The palms and soles have thick skin.
5. Hair is sparse and fine.
6. The teeth or mucous glands are not involved.
7. Erythroderma is not seen beyond the newborn period.
8. Blistering is not a feature of this disorder.

Treatment goals for children with LI are to relieve their intense itching, improve their appearance, and provide support and counseling for the serious psychological problems that their disease imposes. Unfortunately, the itching responds only minimally to antihistamine therapy. Prolonged bathing with moisturizing oils helps to remove scales, reduce skin dryness, and prevent bacterial colonization of dead skin. This last phenomenon causes LI patients to have a very foul body odor. High humidity environments provide the most comfortable settings for these patients during the winter, and air conditioning during the summer is imperative. Moisturizing creams may help the scaling to some degree, but they can cause intense burning if they are applied to cracked, fissured skin. A group of medications called retinoids are given orally to reduce the severity of ichthyosis. However, they must be administered indefinitely for maximum effectiveness and are not without significant side effects (bone toxicity and severe damage to fetal tissue). Ectropion may necessitate referral to an eye specialist. Plastic surgery consultation is occasionally needed. Genetic counseling should be offered to families.

There is no current research to indicate the need for special education services due to cognitive deficits as result of the LI. Children with LI, however, will require additional psychological support to help with self-esteem as a result of the physical abnormalities. Providing educational resources to the teacher and peers in the classroom will facilitate understanding of the disease and help foster peer relationships.

Prognosis for children with LI is guarded. Their disease requires constant treatment. There is no evidence that their problems remit at all with age. In addition, their disturbing physical appearance gives rise to multiple psychological difficulties that challenge the abilities of even the most gifted and skilled therapists.

For more information and parent support, contact Foundation for Ichthyosis and Related Skin Types, 650 North Cannon Avenue, Suite 17, Lansdale, PA 19446. Tel.: (215) 631–1411 or (800) 545–3286, e-mail: ichthyosis@aol.com; http://www.firstskinfoundation.org/.

This entry has been informed by the sources listed below.

REFERENCES

Darmstadt, G. L. (2000). Disorders of keratinization. In R. E. Behrman, R. M. Kleigman, & H. B. Jenson (Eds.), *Nelson's textbook of pediatrics* (16th ed., p. 2008). Philadelphia, PA: Saunders.

National Organization for Rare Disorders. (1997). *Ichthyosis, lamellar recessive.* Retrieved from http://www.rarediseases.org

BARRY H. DAVISON
Ennis, Texas

JOAN W. MAYFIELD
*Baylor Pediatric Specialty Services,
Dallas, Texas*

ICHTHYOSIS, NETHERTON SYNDROME

Netherton syndrome (NS) is a rare, congenital, hereditary disorder characterized by ichthyosis (an abnormality of skin development that manifests as scaling and redness), several distinct anomalies of hair, and a tendency toward a variety of allergic illnesses. Skin findings are usually evident within 2 weeks after birth.

NS is reportedly rare. No data are available on its incidence. The mode of inheritance is autosomal recessive. The vast majority of cases have occurred in females.

Characteristics

1. Ichthyosis is present shortly after birth. Skin around the eyes, mouth, and anus are most commonly affected. The pattern of ichthyosis has a distinctive circular shape (ichthyosis linearis circumflexa).
2. There is sparse, short scalp hair that breaks easily with minimal pressure. Eyebrow, eyelash, and body hair are also abnormal.
3. Allergic disease includes hives (urticaria), angioedema (swelling of the tissues beneath the skin or inside the respiratory or gastrointestinal tract), atopic dermatitis (skin inflammation caused by an allergic reaction), and asthma.
4. There is growth failure (failure to thrive).
5. Recurrent bacterial and yeast infections occur.
6. Mental retardation is found in some patients.

No recommendations regarding therapy can be found in the literature. Presumably, the ichthyotic skin abnormalities respond to treatments used in other disorders of this type. Infectious diseases should be managed with appropriate antibiotic or antifungal (for yeast) agents. Patients with significant allergic illness or asthma may need referral to a specialist for the best outcome.

Because some patients with NS have cognitive deficiencies, it is important to provide a comprehensive neuropsychological evaluation to determine the child's cognitive strengths and weaknesses. Based on those results, specific school recommendations, including classroom modifications, can be made to help the child reach his or her academic potential.

No data are available concerning the prognosis for NS. The rarity of this syndrome may make an understanding of its usual course impossible. Although the physical abnormalities of NS appear remedial, the possibility of mental retardation should make clinicians cautious about predicting what the future holds for an NS patient.

For more information, contact Foundation for Ichthyosis and Related Skin Types, 650 North Cannon

Avenue, Suite 17, Lansdale, PA 19446. Tel.: (215) 631–1411 or (800) 545-3286, e-mail: ichthyosis@aol.com; http://www.firstskinfoundation.org/.

This entry has been informed by the sources listed below

REFERENCES

Darmstadt, G. L. (2000). Diseases of keratinization. In R. E. Behrman, R. M. Kleigman, & H. B. Jenson (Eds.), *Nelson's textbook of pediatrics* (16th ed., pp. 1577–1581). Philadelphia, PA: Saunders.

National Organization for Rare Disorders. (1999). *Ichthyosis, Netherton syndrome*. Retrieved from http://www.raredis eases.org

BARRY H. DAVISON
Ennis, Texas

JOAN W. MAYFIELD
Baylor Pediatric Specialty Services, Dallas, Texas

ICHTHYOSIS, SJOGREN-LARSSON SYNDROME

Sjogren-Larsson syndrome (SLS) is a hereditary disorder of the skin and central nervous system. It is characterized by ichthyosis (red, scaly patches of skin), mental retardation, and spasticity (increased muscle tone). A deficiency of the enzyme fatty aldehyde dehydrogenase is the primary defect in SLS.

SLS is transmitted in an autosomal recessive manner. It is rare, and no data are available regarding its actual incidence.

Characteristics

1. Lamellar ichthyosis (large, thick, dark scales) or ichthyosiform erythroderma (red skin with fine white scales); ichthyosis is distributed all over the body but is more pronounced on the arms, legs, and lower abdomen.
2. Delayed motor and speech development apparent during the first year.
3. Seizures.
4. Mental retardation obvious by age 3.
5. Spasticity of the legs or both the arms and the legs.

Therapy for SLS patients is limited. The skin changes respond to measures used for ichthyosis associated with other disorders. Anticonvulsants may be needed for seizure control. Some patients may eventually become ambulatory with the use of leg braces or other orthopedic appliances. Most, however, will require a wheelchair.

Children diagnosed with SLS require occupational, physical, and speech therapy through early childhood intervention (ECI) programs to help them attain appropriate developmental milestones. As they reach school age, children with SLS continue to require additional educational support under the umbrella of special education because of their cognitive deficits. Assistive technology and devices may also be required.

The prognosis for SLS is poor. Mental retardation and other significant neurologic deficits are common. Prenatal diagnosis and detection of the carrier state of SLS are available. Families who are concerned about having a child with SLS should be counseled about the accessibility of these diagnostic procedures.

For more information and support, contact Foundation for Ichthyosis and Related Skin Types, 650 North Cannon Avenue, Suite 17, Lansdale, PA 19446. Tel.: (215) 631–1411 or (800) 545–3286, e-mail: ichthyosis@aol.com; http://www.firstskinfoundation.org/

This entry has been informed by the sources listed below.

REFERENCES

Darmstadt, G. L. (2000). Disorders of keratinization. In R. E. Behrman, R. M. Kleigman, & H. B. Jenson (Eds.), *Nelson's textbook of pediatrics* (16th ed., p. 2009). *Philadelphia*, PA: Saunders.

National Organization for Rare Disorders. (1999). *Ichthyosis, Sjogren Larsson syndrome*. Retrieved from http://www.rare diseases.org

BARRY H. DAVISON
Ennis, Texas

JOAN W. MAYFIELD
Baylor Pediatric Specialty Services, Dallas, Texas

ICHTHYOSIS, TAY SYNDROME

Tay syndrome is a hereditary disorder characterized by trichothiodystrophy (brittle, sulfur deficient hair) and dry, scaly skin (ichthyosis). Males and females are equally affected, and Tay syndrome is believed to be an autosomal recessive trait.

Characteristics

1. Children present with ichthyosis consisting mainly of fine, dark scales covering most of the body, trichothiodystrophy, abnormal finger and toe nails, and loss of subcutaneous (beneath the skin) fat resulting in aged facial features. Reproductive

organs are usually underdeveloped, and cataracts often develop in the eyes.

2. Mental retardation is evident at an early age, and physical development is slow. Some children may also be short in stature.

3. Central nervous system abnormalities include seizures, ataxia (lack of muscle control), tremors, and neurosensory deafness. Hypomyelination has also been associated with children affected with Tay syndrome.

4. Susceptibility to infection is increased, and abnormalities of the teeth and bones may be present.

Treatment is symptomatic, and medical intervention is necessary in a majority of cases. Cognitive involvement usually results in mental deficiency. Ichthyosis is treated with skin emollients. Special education qualification is handicapped due to health problems, and remediation commonly associated with mental retardation is necessary. Prognosis is poor, and future research is focusing on genetic characteristics that delineate Tay syndrome from other disorders of ichthyosis to enable researchers and health care professionals better to help the patients affected with these disorders.

This entry has been informed by the sources listed below.

REFERENCES

Happle, R. H., Taube, H., Grobe, H., & Bonsmann, G. (1984). The Tay syndrome (congenital ichthyosis with trichothiodystrophy). *European Journal of Pediatrics, 141,* 147–152.

Ostergaard, J. R., & Christensen, T. (1996). The central nervous system in Tay syndrome. *Neuropediatrics, 27,* 326–330.

KIMBERLY M. ESTEP
University of Houston–Clear Lake

ICHTHYOSIS VULGARIS

Ichthyosis vulgaris (IV) is one of a heterogeneous group of disorders of skin cornification or keratinization (the process in which skin cells are produced and eventually shed). It is typified by a specific pattern of scaling of the skin and a unique form of inheritance.

IV is the most common of abnormalities of skin keratinization. Its incidence is about 1 in 300 live births. It is transmitted in an autosomal dominant manner.

Characteristics

1. The onset of symptoms is during the first year of life. Rarely, newborns are affected with a thick, membranous covering of the skin that eventually sloughs off in large sheets during the first few days after birth (so-called collodion baby).

2. Slightly rough, scaling skin is most noticeable on the outer surfaces of the extremities (particularly the legs) and back.

3. Skin of the abdomen, neck, and face are usually normal.

4. The palms and soles are thick skinned.

5. Scaling is more severe during the winter and typically abates during the summer months.

6. Skin findings improve as patients age.

7. Disorders of the teeth, hair, mucosal surfaces, and other organs are absent.

Treatment of IV is directed toward amelioration of the scaling tendency of the skin. The use of bath oil, skin lubricants, and soaps (e.g., Dove, Caress, and Tone) that are less likely to leach out the skin's protective oils is beneficial. Patients with IV may experience considerable itching and skin irritation, particularly in low-humidity environments. Topical corticosteroids and, occasionally, oral antihistamines will improve these symptoms. Humidifiers also are helpful.

There is no research to indicate any cognitive deficiencies associated with IV.

The prognosis for IV is excellent. Usually only minimal therapeutic intervention is required to provide these patients symptomatic relief. In most cases, the problem is considered more of a nuisance than a significant illness.

For more information, contact the Foundation for Ichthyosis and Related Skin Types, 650 North Cannon Avenue, Suite 17, Lansdale, PA 19446. Tel.: (215) 631–1411 or (800) 545–3286. Also contact the National Registry of Ichthyosis and Related Disorders, University of Washington, Dermatology Department, Box 356524, 1959 N.E. Pacific, Seattle, WA 98195–6524. Tel.: (206) 616–3179 or (800) 595–1265, e-mail: eck@u.washington .edu or geogg@u.washington.edu

This entry has been informed by the sources listed below.

REFERENCES

Darmstadt, G. L. (2000). Disorders of keratinization. In R. E. Behrman, R. M. Kleigman, & H. B. Jenson (Eds.), *Nelson's textbook of pediatrics* (16th ed., pp. 2008). Philadelphia, PA: Saunders.

National Organization for Rare Disorders. (1998). *Ichthyosis vulgaris*. Retrieved from http://www.rarediseases.org

BARRY H. DAVISON
Ennis, Texas

JOAN W. MAYFIELD
*Baylor Pediatric Specialty Services,
Dallas, Texas*

ICHTHYOSIS, X-LINKED

X-linked ichthyosis (XLI) is a hereditary disorder of the skin that affects males almost exclusively. Female carriers of the abnormal gene may occasionally demonstrate clinical findings. Corneal opacities (clouding of the clear part of the eyeball that overlies the iris) and cryptorchism (undescended testicles) are also commonly seen in patients with XLI. Ichthyosis (reddened, scaling skin) is caused by a deficiency of the enzyme steroid sulfatase. Individuals with XLI do not possess the gene for steroid sulfatase production.

XLI is rare. Its occurrence in the general population is unclear. It is inherited in an X-linked recessive manner, in much the same way as classic hemophilia (Factor VIII deficiency).

Characteristics

1. Dry, scaly skin is occasionally present at birth. This finding usually resolves quickly but returns between 3 and 6 months of age.
2. Scaling is most severe on the neck, lower face, in front of the ears, on the front of chest and abdomen, and, particularly, on the legs.
3. Skin of the palms and soles is mildly thickened.
4. Ichthyosis worsens as patients age.
5. Corneal opacities develop in late childhood or adolescence. There is no visual impairment. Carrier females may also have this abnormality.
6. Cryptorchism occurs in 25% of patients. Testicular cancer is an occasional finding.

Treatment of the ichthyosis in patients with XLI is similar to strategies employed for the skin problems of related disorders. Liberal use of bath oils as well as skin lubricants is helpful. Cryptorchism may need surgical repair unless spontaneous descent of the testicles occurs during the first year. Because of the increased incidence of testicular malignancy, particularly in a cryptorchic organ,

patients with XLI should be taught how to detect signs of a tumor through self-examination. Periodic visits to the primary care physician for screening checks for testicular cancer should be strongly encouraged.

There is no research to indicate cognitive deficits or the need for special education services for children with XLI, and the prognosis for XLI is generally favorable. Ichthyosis responds well to treatment. The ophthalmologic findings do not inhibit visual acuity and are not associated with any other eye anomalies. Testicular cancer is a worrisome problem, but it generally responds well to treatment, as long as the diagnosis is not delayed.

Families concerned about the occurrence of XLI in their children should be advised of the availability of prenatal diagnosis, as well as testing for detection of the carrier state. Gene replacement therapy may not be that far off and will result in a cure for this disorder.

For more information and support, contact the Foundation for Ichthyosis and Related Skin Types, 650 North Cannon Avenue, Suite 17, Lansdale, PA 19446. Tel.: (215) 631–1411 or (800) 545–3286, e-mail: ichthyosis@aol.com; http://www.firstskinfoundation.org/.

This entry has been informed by the sources listed below.

REFERENCES

Darmstadt, G. L. (2000). Disorders of keratinization. In R. E. Behrman, R. M. Kleigman, & H. B. Jenson (Eds.), *Nelson's textbook of pediatrics* (16th ed., pp. 2008–2009). Philadelphia, PA: Saunders.

National Organization for Rare Disorders. (1997). *Ichthyosis, x linked*. Retrieved from http://www.rarediseases.org

BARRY H. DAVISON
Ennis, Texas

JOAN W. MAYFIELD
*Baylor Pediatric Specialty Services,
Dallas, Texas*

IDIOT

Idiot is an archaic technical and legal term used from the turn of the century through the 1950s to denote an individual with an intellectual disability whose measured IQ fell below 25 or 30. It represented the most severe level of cognitive impairment and was used comparatively with lesser degrees of impairment (i.e., imbecile and moron). The term acquired a pernicious quality among lay people over the years of its use and, during the 1950s, led to several revised systems of nomenclature. In the United States the classification system that was to become most widely adopted was published by the American Association on Mental Deficiency (which became the American Association on Mental Retardation; Heber, 1959). This classification system replaced the term *idiot* with the current levels of Severe and Profound Retardation. In 2010, the American Association on Intellectual and Developmental Disabilities published a revised definition manual (AAIDD, 2010).

Originally, the terms *idiocy*, *imbecility*, and *moronity* represented the three levels of mental deficiency (otherwise known as amentia or feeblemindedness). These terms were considered separate from dementia, which denoted those who had acquired mental illnesses. Amentia, on the other hand, denoted "persons whose minds (had) never developed very far" (Peterson, 1925, p. 20).

The exact level of functioning of individuals designated as idiots has never been clear. However, attempts to characterize the level often focused on the use of language. In general such individuals could learn only a few simple words, but were not capable of substituting words for objects in their behavior. In addition, they were not expected to learn to wash or dress themselves and were generally cared for in institutions. Finally, the mental age of those classified as idiots did not exceed 3 years.

REFERENCES

American Association on Intellectual and Developmental Disabilities. (2010). *Intellectual disability: Definition, classification, and systems of supports*. Washington, DC: Author.

Heber, R. F. (1959). A manual on terminology and classification in mental retardation. *Monograph Supplement American Journal of Mental Deficiency*, 64.

Peterson, J. (1925). *Early conceptions and tests of intelligence*. Chicago, IL: World Book.

RONALD C. EAVES
Auburn University

IDIOT SAVANT (*See Savant Syndrome*)

IEP (*See Individualized Educational Plan*)

IGA NEPHROPATHY

IGA nephropathy (IGAN) is an endochrine (renal) disorder or unknown cause. IGAN occurs when deposits of the protein immunoglobulin A (IGA) enter the kidneys. The IGA protein interrupts the filtering process of the kidneys, causing blood and protein to build in the urine and resulting in swelling of the feet and hands.

As this condition progresses, the filtering units of the kidneys (glomeruli) are permanently damaged, and renal failure will eventually ensue. Researchers have come to no definitive conclusions about the etiology of IGAN. Select studies claim that IGAN occurs following a flu-like viral infection of the upper respiratory tract or the gastrointestinal tract. This condition could also be the result of an autoimmune disease in which the IGA antibodies interfere with normal kidney functioning. Another possibility is that the disorder is familial. In fact, recent, research has shown more definitively that IGAN may be of genetic origin and that these genetic factors may influence severity and course of IGAN.

IGAN normally occurs in adolescence or young adulthood and affects males two to three times more often than females. It is one of the leading causes of acute nephritis (inflammation and abnormal function of the kidney) in young people in the United States. Cognitive and neuropsychological sequelae may be observed as a result of chronic renal disease.

Characteristics

1. The disorder is marked by hematuria (blood in the urine) and a mild loss of protein in the urine (proteinuria) caused by acute nephritis.
2. Groin pain is common.
   a. High blood pressure is seen in most patients.
3. A predominant number of cases are seen in the Native American population.
4. The course can range from benign to acute renal failure.
5. Cognitive and neuropsychological sequelae (alterations in attention, memory, etc.) may be observed as a result of prolonged renal malfunction.

Treatment is on a case-by-case basis and much of the focus is on maintaining kidney health and longevity. When high blood pressure is present, medication and diet regulation are treatments of choice. Affected persons developing kidney failure require dialysis or possibly a kidney transplant.

Special education requirements may involve health-related difficulties, but many children presenting with IGAN lead normal lives with minimal symptomology. In that regard, prognosis is good, and serious complications develop only in rare instances.

Etiology is the focus of future research in the hopes of developing better treatment and avoidance therapies.

This entry has been informed by the sources listed below.

REFERENCES

Fennell, R. S., Fennell, E. B., & Carter, R. L. (1990). Association between renal function and cognition in childhood chronic renal failure. *Pediatric Nephrology, 4*, 16–20.

Floege, J. & Feehally, J. (2000). IGA nephropathy: Recent developments. *Journal of the American Society of Nephrology, 11*, 2395–2403.

Julian, B. A., Quiggins, P. A., Thompson, J. S., Woodford, S. Y., Gleason, K., & Wyatt, R. J. (1985). Familial IGA nephropathy: Evidence of an inherited mechanism of disease. *New England Journal of Medicine, 312*, 202–208.

Yoshikawa, N., Tanaka, R., & Iijima, K. (2001). Pathophysiology and treatment of IGA nephropathy in children. *Pediatric Nephrology, 16*, 446–457.

KIMBERLY M. ESTEP
University of Houston–Clear Lake

ILLINOIS TEST OF PSYCHOLINGUISTIC ABILITIES, THIRD EDITION

The Illinois Test of Psycholinguistic Abilities, Third Edition (ITPA-3, 2001) measures spoken and written language. All of the subtests measure some aspect of language, including semantics, grammar, phonology, reading comprehension, word identification, and spelling. The ITPA3 uses the following subtests to assess a children's specific linguistic ability:

Spoken Analogies: Examiner says a four-part analogy, with the last part missing. The child gives the missing part (e.g., "Dogs bark, cats ____").

Spoken Vocabulary: Examiner says a sentence or phrase that describes a noun and the child must provide the correct word (e.g., "I am thinking of something with wheels").

Morphological Closure: Examiner gives an oral prompt with the last part missing and the child completes the phrase by saying the missing part (e.g., "big, bigger, ___").

Syntactic Sentences: Examiner says a sentence that is syntactically correct but semantically nonsensical and the child repeats the sentence (e.g., "Purple hammers are smart").

Sound Deletion: Examiner asks the child to delete words, syllables, and phonemes from spoken words. (e.g., say "weekend" without the "end").

Rhyming Sequences: Examiner says strings of rhyming words that increase in length, and the child repeats them (e.g., "noon," "soon," "moon").

Sentence Sequencing: Child reads sentences silently and then puts them in orders to form a plausible sequence (e.g., rearrange: I go to school, I get up, I get dressed).

Written Vocabulary: After reading an adjective the child writes a noun that is closely associated with the stimulus word (e.g., complete this: "A broken ____").

Sight Decoding: The child pronounces a list of printed words that contain irregular parts (e.g., "would," "laugh," "height").

Sound Decoding: The child reads aloud phonically regular names of make-believe animal creatures (e.g., Flant, Yang).

Sight Spelling: Examiner reads aloud irregular words from a list. The child is given a printed list in which the irregular part of the words and one or more phonemes are missing. The child writes in the omitted part of the words (e.g., Examiner reads "said," and the child sees s___d, and fills in the missing letters).

Sound Spelling: The examiner reads aloud phonically regular nonsense words, and the child writes the word or the missing part.

These ITPA3 subtests can be combined to form the following composites: General Language, Spoken Language, Written Language, Semantics, Grammar, Phonology, Comprehension, Spelling, Sight Symbol Processing, Sound Symbol Processing.

Subtest raw scores are transformed into standard scores, percentile ranks, and age equivalents.

Normative data for a sample of 1,522 children was collected in 27 states during the years 1999 and 2000 and reflected the population characteristics of the United States for 1999. Data was stratified according to ethnicity, race, gender, disability status, geographic region, parental education, rural/urban residence, and family income, and the results were a close match to projected percentages. In each of the 1-year age groups, the number in the samples exceeded 100 (range 138 to age 12 to 239 to age 10).

Internal consistency, stability, and interscorer reliability for all subtests and composites are high (greater than .90).

This entry has been informed by the source listed below.

REVIEWED IN:

Plake, B. S., Impara, J. C., & Spies, R. A. (Eds.). (2003). *The fifteenth mental measurements yearbook*. Lincoln, NE: Buros Institute of Mental Measurements.

IMAGERY

Imagery is the mental representation of objects, events, or concepts in some nonverbal form, a process thought to be basic to human functioning. Although this representation is often assumed to be visual, such as a picture according to Klinger (1981), mental imagery includes any of the almost unceasing sensation-like experiences that are a part of our stream of consciousness and that are representative of any of our sense modalities. Although the study of mental imagery was a central part of psychology until 1920, interest by psychologists in the United States in this phenomenon did not become active until the 1960s, with the work of psychologists such as Eleanor and James Gibson, Piaget, Neisser and others. These psychologists were concerned with determining how the brain constructs and stores models through which sense can be made of the sensations that occur as the individual interacts with the environment. This latter process, labeled perception, guides the individual's actions or response to the environment. Thus the imagery constructed by an individual is central to psychological functioning and whoever can shape that imagery holds a powerful tool for controlling and altering human functioning, whether the shaper be the individual or another person (Klinger, 1981).

The facilitative effect of imagery on comprehension and recall or memory was described by early Greek scholars and experienced by Roman orators as they delivered lengthy speeches using imagery as a mnemonic tool. Pioneering work of Canadian psychologist Allan Paivio has provided theoretical explanations and firm empirical support for this aspect of imagery. Paivio (1971) effectively developed the case for dual coding of information by individuals. In dual coding retrieval of information is enhanced by the fact that many concrete words or concepts can be represented in both verbal and imagery systems, thus providing dual cues for recalling the information. Present investigations on imagery as an important concept in cognitive psychology are focusing on individual differences in imagery, its usefulness in problem solving and other complex human behaviors including creativity, imagery through sensory modalities other than the visual, and the possibility of affective coding of experiences.

Mental imagery appears to play a critical role in the creative processes in diverse fields, from architecture and sports (Hall, Mack, Paivio, & Housenblas, 1998), to molecular science (Shepard, 1978). The ability to process information through imagery has been used to predict and enhance creative imagination in children and adults (Khatena, 1979). In addition, directed focusing of imagery has been found to be a powerful enhancer, eliciting from the individual a holistic and directly felt bodily sense of a situation or issue (Gendlin, 1980). Perfection of various athletic or performance skills, as well as a wide variety of classroom applications, have evolved, and scripts have been developed for using such guided imagery (Roberts, 1983). Rose (1980) describes his technique for using guided fantasies in the elementary classroom to acquire new concepts, build confidence for oral reports, or handle conflicts. In special education, imagery can be used to help individuals identify negative or positive attitudes regarding a physical disability (Morgan, 1980); or as a component of cognitive-restructuring interventions (Vannest, Reynolds, & Kamphaus, 2008).

Imagery has been a particularly useful tool for the psychotherapist: the patient expresses in drawings or paintings, to be interpreted clinically, information unlikely to have been offered verbally. The advantage of this type of communication is that it is given in less threatening situations, avoiding times when the patient may be withdrawn, overly aroused, or frightened (Barrios & O'Dell, 1998). In addition, imagery can be used to establish empathetic understanding, manage anxiety and stress, and even reduce pain, giving symptomatic relief to patients. Through imagery, then, humans can alter mental and physical functioning in positive ways for themselves and others.

REFERENCES

Barrios, B. A., & O'Dell, S. L. (1998). Fears & anxieties. In E. J. Mash & R. A. Barkley (Eds.), *Treatment of childhood disorders* (pp. 249–337). New York, NY: Guilford Press.

Gendlin, E. T. (1980). Imagery is more powerful with focusing: Theory and practice. In J. E. Schorr, G. E. Sobel, P. Robin, & J. A. Connella (Eds.), *Imagery. Its many dimensions and applications* (pp. 65–73). New York, NY: Plenum Press.

Hall, C. R., Mack, D. E., Paivio, A., & Housenblas, H. A. (1998). Imagery use by athletes: Development of the Sport Imagery Questionnaire. *International Journal of Sport Psychology*, *29*(1), 73–89.

Khatena, J. (1979). *Teaching gifted children to use creative imagination imagery*. Starkville, MI: Allan.

Klinger, E. (Ed.). (1981). *Imagery. Concepts, results and applications*. New York, NY: Plenum Press.

Morgan, C. (1980). Imagery experiences of disabled persons. In J. E. Schorr, G. E. Sobel, P. Robin, & J. A. Connella (Eds.), *Imagery. Its many dimensions and applications* (pp. 232–244). New York, NY: Plenum Press.

Paivio, A. (1971). *Imagery and verbal processes*. New York, NY: Holt, Rinehart & Winston.

Roberts, N. M. (1983). Imagery: A second look: Expanding its use in the classroom. *Reading Improvement*, *20*(1), 22–27.

Rose, R. (1980). Guided fantasies in elementary classrooms. In J. E. Schorr, G. E. Sobel, P. Robin, & J. A. Connella (Eds.), *Imagery. Its many dimensions and applications* (pp. 605–622). New York, NY: Plenum Press.

Shepard, R. N. (1978). Externalization of mental images and the act of creation. In B. S. Randhawa & W. E. Coffman (Eds.), *Visual learning, thinking, and communication*. New York, NY: Academic Press.

Vannest, K. J., Reynolds, C. R., & Kamphaus, R. W. (2008). *BASC-2: Intervention guide.* Minneapolis, MN: Pearson.

PATRICIA A. HAENSLY
Texas A&M University

See also Creativity; Hypnosis

IMPERSISTENCE (*See Perseveration*)

IMPULSE CONTROL

An impulse is a psychological term given to a feeling that results in an action. Research about impulse control can be found as it relates to many psychiatric disorders such as attention-deficit/hyperactivity disorder (Barkley, 2003; Pulkkinen, 1996), manic depression (McElroy, Pope, Keck, & Hudson, 1996), and so on. As used here, it refers to a trait normally measured by a test such as the Matching Familiar Figures Test. The resulting outcome of the test is an indication of whether the learner is reflective or impulsive. A reflective learner examines a stimulus slowly and takes more time to make a decision than an impulsive learner. Generally, there is some relationship between impulsive responders and high error rates. Thus, there is a need to control the response rate of the learner to cut down on errors (Kagan, Pearson, & Welch, 1966; Kendall & Wilcox, 1979).

A variety of interventions exist (Vannest, Reynolds & Kamphaus, 2008). The predominant method for the control of impulsive behavior is cognitive training (Barkley, 2003; Kendall & Finch, 1978; Kendall & Wilcox, 1979, 1980). Investigators have combined cognitive and behavioral methods. Two of the most successful strategies for the control of impulsive behavior are modeling and self-instructional training. Modeling is based on social learning theory. A learner observes a high-status adult or peer engaging in acts that are reflective and purposeful. If the tasks performed by the model are similar to the types of tasks to be performed by the learner, there is a likelihood that the reflective behavior will be modeled by the learner. As the tasks become dissimilar, the degree of transfer decreases.

Self-instructional training is based on a theory that states that voluntary control over motor behavior requires the internalization of verbal commands (Barkley, 2003; Meichenbaum & Goodman, 1971). To improve impulsive behavior by self-instruction, the learner verbalizes either aloud, in a whisper or subvocally. The practice becomes a thinking outloud intervention that reminds a learner to slow down, to be careful, and to follow the steps in a process.

Cognitive modeling plus self-instructional training is generally superior to cognitive modeling alone. The following five-step procedure has been used successfully to control impulsive behavior: (1) the leader models a reflective problem solving style using overt self-instructions; (2) the learner is guided by the teacher through the same problem with verbal instructions; (3) the learner solves the problem while providing overt self-instruction; (4) the learner solves the problem while whispering; and (5) the learner solves the problem with subvocal self-instruction. This procedure appears to work well for modifying impulsive behavior on specific tasks but general classroom behavior on unrelated tasks remains unchanged.

Adding a response cost procedure to the cognitive modeling and self-instructional training enhances the training program for the control of impulsive behavior (Meichenbaum & Anarnow, 1979). In response cost, a punishment procedure is imposed for errors. The procedure is designed to discourage the child from making quick responses. Positive reinforcement is not a highly effective strategy to add to cognitive modeling and self-instructional training. The problem with using positive reinforcement in this process is that lucky guesses may be reinforced and thus maladaptive problem-solving strategies may be maintained.

Another approach to cognitive training involves the following six-step problem-solving sequence (Meichenbaum & Goodman, 1971): (1) problem definition; (2) problem approach; (3) focusing attention; (4) problem solution; (5) self-reinforcement; and (6) coping with errors. In studies following this sequence, there is a greater generalization of reflective behavior if the training deals with self-statements that are global rather than problem specific. If training focuses only on a specific problem situation, the generalization of reflective behavior is restricted. If the problem situations are broad and the strategies applicable to a wide range of behavior, generalization will be enhanced.

A final procedure for the control of impulsive behavior is the imposed delay. Students are prevented from responding for a specified number of seconds after a problem is presented. Used in isolation, learners will slow down in their responding time but errors will not change. To be effective, the strategy must be coupled with other strategies discussed previously.

REFERENCES

Barkley, R. A. (2003). Attention-deficit hyperactivity disorder. In E. J. Mash & R. A. Barkley (Eds.), *Childhood psychopathology* (pp. 75–143). New York, NY: Guilford Press.

Kagan, J., Pearson, L., & Welch, L. (1966). Modifiability of an impulsive tempo. *Journal of Educational Psychology, 57,* 359–365.

Kendall, P. C., & Finch, A. J. (1978). A cognitive behavioral treatment for impulsivity: A group comparison study. *Journal of Consulting & Clinical Psychology, 46,* 110–118.

Kendall, P. C., & Wilcox, L. E. (1979). Self control in children: Development of a rating scale. *Journal of Consulting & Clinical Psychology, 47,* 1020–1029.

Kendall, P. C., & Wilcox, L. E. (1980). Cognitive behavioral treatment for impulsivity: Concrete versus conceptual training in non-self-controlled problem children. *Journal of Consulting & Clinical Psychology, 48,* 80–91.

McElroy, S. L., Pope, H. G., Keck, P. E., & Hudson, J. I. (1996). Are impulse control disorders relaxed to bipolar disorder? *Comprehensive Psychiatry, 37*(4), 229–240.

Meichenbaum, D. H., & Anarnow, J. (1979). Cognitive behavioral modification and meta-cognitive development: Implications for the classroom. In P. C. Kendall & S. D. Hollon (Eds.), *Cognitive-behavioral interventions: Theory, research, and procedures.* New York, NY: Academic Press.

Meichenbaum, D. H., & Goodman, J. (1971). Training impulsive children to talk to themselves: A means of developing self control. *Journal of Abnormal Psychology, 77,* 115–126.

Pulkkinen, L. (1996). Impulse control in children. *Journal of Forensic Psychiatry, 7*(2), 228–233.

Vannest, K. J., Reynolds, C. R., & Kamphaus, R. W. (2008). *BASC-2: Intervention guide.* Minneapolis, MN: Pearson.

ROBERT A. SEDLAK
University of Wisconsin at Stout

See also Behavior Modeling; Behavior Modification; Self-Monitoring

IMPULSIVITY-REFLECTIVITY

Impulsivity-reflectivity is a cognitive dimension defined by Kagan (1965) that describes the way children resolve uncertainty. Impulsivity-reflectivity describes the tendency to reflect on the validity of problem solving when several choices are presented. The instrument most often used to measure reflectivity and impulsivity in children is the Matching Familiar Figures Test (MFFT), which also comes in a computerized version (Hummel-Schulgar & Baer, 1996). Based on test performance, reflective children will make fewer errors and have longer response latencies than impulsive children (Kagan, 1965). The test format involves presentation of a figure such as a boat, animal, or pair of scissors with as many as eight facsimiles differing in one or more details. The subject is asked to select from the alternatives the one that exactly matches the figure. Time and response are computed. Children who score above the median on the MFFT response time and below the median on errors are called *reflective*. Children who score below the median on response time and above the median on errors are called *impulsive* (Messer, 1976). Impulsive children tend to respond quickly and make many mistakes; reflective children tend to respond more slowly and carefully and make fewer errors (Finch, 1982).

Educators and psychologists have used impulsivity and reflectivity as a way to implement programs for childhood education (Borkowski, Peck, Reid, & Kurtz, 1983). This has been useful with emotionally disturbed children who display problem behavior (Finch, Saylor, & Spirito, 1982; Finch, Spirito, & Brophy, 1982). Finch also examined reflectivity and impulsivity in Wechsler Intelligence Scale for Children Revised performance in children with behavior problems. Reflective children scored significantly higher than impulsive children on verbal, performance, and full-scale IQ. Although there is no evidence that consistently links impulsivity and reflectivity to IQ scores, this does suggest that cognitive style may be related to performance on standard intelligence tests.

Sergeant, Van Velthoven, and Virginia (1979) explored hyperactivity, impulsivity, and reflectivity and their relationship to clinical child psychology. The MFFT was used to measure hyperactivity. Although impulsivity is thought to be related to hyperactivity, their research showed that measuring hyperactivity by determining the level of impulsivity could be misleading. Impulsivity-reflectivity has been found to be related to other clinical syndromes including brain damage, epilepsy, and mental retardation (Messer, 1976). This work also indicates that impulsivity and reflectivity may be related to school performance as shown by the greater impulsivity in children with learning disabilities, reading problems, and general school failure. Messer found that reflective children will gather information more carefully and systematically than impulsive children. This same study indicated that reflectivity and impulsivity cannot accurately be measured in preschool children, since they have not yet learned to examine alternatives.

Social reasoning has also been measured in reflective and impulsive children (Peters & Bernfeld, 1983) by using the Peabody Picture Vocabulary and the MFFT. Reflective children made decisions more slowly; impulsive children made decisions more rapidly. Reflective children favored a more direct approach; impulsive children favored a more passive approach.

Kagan (1983) studied children who were given visual matching problems. The subjects with fast response times and higher error scores made more errors in reading words than subjects with long decision-making times and lower error scores. This supported the notion that primary-grade children who reflected over alternative hypotheses would be more accurate in word recognition than children who reported hypotheses impulsivity.

Reflectivity and impulsivity seem to develop with age as children typically become more reflective as they grow older (Messer, 1976). Messer reported that response times increased with age, while the amount of errors decreased. Siegelman (1969) examined the ways in which reflective and impulsive children of different ages actually deploy alternatives and scan the objects presented to them. The hypothesis was that impulsive children devote a greater amount of time to a chosen stimulus and ignore the alternatives, in contrast to the reflectives, who spent more time weighing alternatives. Results suggested that impulsive and reflective children may be using different search strategies. This indicates that the impulsive dimension may be modifiable. Kagan (1983) and Messer (1976) found that impulsivity may be modified by teaching impulsives to improve their scanning strategies. The researchers accomplished this by having children who were impulsive verbalize what they were doing.

Impulsivity and reflectivity have also been examined from a teaching perspective that has implications for classroom learning. Teachers need to be aware of individual differences among children to cope with each individual learner. Readance and Bean (1978) reported that the impulsive child has a tendency to act on his or her initial response with little reflection when solving problems. A reflective child usually delays, weighing all choices available. Reflective children are not necessarily brighter or better learners; however, the research did suggest that teachers may perceive impulsive children less favorably. Reflective students were seen as highly attentive. Impulsive boys were seen as less able to concentrate in class. This supported the notion that this particular individual difference of impulsivity and reflectivity is important for classroom learning. Evidence supports the contention that the cognitive and meta-cognitive (Palladino, Poli, Masi, & Marcheschi, 1997) dimensions of impulsivity and reflectivity are important individual differences. These dimensions will play a role in helping assess a child's ability, ultimately improving the learning process within the field of special education.

REFERENCES

Borkowski, J. G., Peck, V. A., Reid, M. K., & Kurtz, B. E. (1983). Impulsivity and strategy transfer: Metamemory as mediator. *Child Development, 54,* 469–473.

Finch, A. J., Saylor, C. F., & Spirito, A. (1982). Impulsive cognitive style and impulsive behavior in emotionally disturbed children. *Journal of Genetic Psychology, 141,* 293–294.

Finch, A. J., Spirito, A., & Brophy, C. J. (1982). Reflection-impulsivity and WISC-R performance in behavior-problem children. *Journal of Genetic Psychology, 111,* 217–221.

Hummel-Schulgar, A. O., & Baer, J. S. (1996). A computer-controlled administration of the matching familiar figures test. *Behavior Research Methods, 28*(1), 93–95.

Kagan, J. (1965). *Conceptual development in children.* New York, NY: International University Press.

Kagan, J. (1983). Reflection-impulsivity and reading ability in primary grade children. *Child Development, 54,* 609–628.

Messer, S. B. (1976). Reflection-impulsivity: A review. *Psychological Bulletin, 83,* 1026–1052.

Palladino, P., Poli, P., Masi, G., & Marcheschi, M. (1997). Impulsive-reflective cognitive style, metacognition and emotion in adolescence. *Perceptual and Motor Skills, 84*(1), 47–57.

Peters, R. D., & Bernfeld, G. A. (1983). Reflection-impulsivity and social reasoning. *Developmental Psychology, 19,* 78–81.

Readance, J. E., & Bean, T. W. (1978). Impulsivity-reflectivity and learning: An individual difference that matters. *College Student Journal, 11,* 367–371.

Sergeant, J. A., Van Velthoven, R., & Virginia, A. (1979). Hyperactivity, impulsivity and reflectivity. *Journal of Child Psychology & Psychiatry, 20,* 47–60.

Siegelman, E. (1969). Reflective and impulsive observing behavior. *Child Development, 40,* 1213–1222.

STEVEN GUMERMAN
Temple University

See also Creative Problem Solving; Impulse Control

INBORN ERRORS OF METABOLISM

Inborn errors of metabolism are classified as a group of genetic diseases and involve single-gene defects that interfere with the process of metabolism. Metabolism refers to the process in which the body breaks down food into fats, proteins, and carbohydrates. The conversion of the food into energy to maintain the life cycle of body cells is carried out by enzymes. The enzymes assist in the maintenance of homeostasis and the control of functions of blood pressure, blood sugar levels, and rate of growth. A single-gene defect may lead to a missing or malfunctioning enzyme, which if left untreated, may result in severe mental retardation or impaired bodily functions such as poor digestion. Such disorders occur in approximately 1 in 5,000 births (Batshaw & Perret, 1981).

Robinson and Robinson (1965) divided metabolic disorders into three areas: (1) ongoing faulty digestive processes identified by biochemical substances in the urine or the bloodstream; (2) storage diseases in which materials are stored because of decreased rate of metabolism or overproduction; and (3) disorders in endocrine secretions that result in anomalies in the structure of the brain and cranium or other difficulties.

Koch and Koch (1974) reported that 40 to 50 such serious diseases often are passed on by consanguineous parents. The body is constantly producing, maintaining, and recycling cells. In the metabolic process of mitosis, the cell dies and is recycled and changed into chemicals and proteins. These components are then absorbed and reused by the body. Any genetic disease that interferes with the process is called an inborn error of metabolism. For many metabolic disorders, there is no effective therapy. For some, therapy is successful only if begun immediately. When untreated, profound mental retardation, seizures, aberrant behavior, and stunted growth may accompany the metabolic abnormality. Some inborn errors of metabolism (e.g., Gaucher's) are asymptomatic and may pose little threat to a reasonably normal existence (Holland, 2003; Stanbury, Wyngaarden, & Fredrickson, 1978). However, many of these disorders have serious consequences and may be fatal if untreated. Age of onset affects severity. In several of the lipid storage diseases such as Gaucher's and Niemann-Pick disease, if the disorder is manifested during the infantile period when the brain is being myelinated, the result is a much more serious disability. Conversely, many of the hereditary metabolic disorders such as gout, hemochromatosis, or familial periodic paralysis do not become fully manifest until adulthood.

In galactosemia, a carbohydrate disorder, the infant appears normal at birth. However, because of a missing enzyme, the sugar or galactose is not used properly. It accumulates in the blood, body tissue, and urine. The injurious waste products can cause brain damage if proper dietary controls are not exercised immediately. The affected individual is unable to metabolize the galactose in milk. If milk and dairy products are withheld, the development will proceed normally (Brown & Sessoms, 2003).

Phenylketonuria (PKU) is the most well-known and successfully treated metabolic disorder. Two similar recessive genes, one from each parent, combine and produce a deficiency of the liver enzyme that normally breaks down the amino acid phenylalanine (Telford & Sawrey, 1977). The parents are carriers of the defective genes but are not themselves affected. Brain damage results from an accumulation of phenylalanine, one of the nine amino acids essential for growth. Prenatal diagnosis does not detect PKU and a child has no symptoms in infancy, hence early screening is critical. More than 90% of all newborns in the United States are tested for PKU (Bearn, 1979). Although it is not a general test for mental retardation, it does successfully detect PKU and a few other rare inborn errors. The currently used heel-stick test was developed by Dr. Robert Guthrie in 1959 (Guthrie, 1972). Phenylketonuria occurs at a rate of 1/14,000 births. Parents who have one affected child have a 25% chance of having another (Batshaw & Perret, 1981). In the past, this disorder led to death or severe mental retardation. Diet therapy has greatly improved prognosis. However, early treatment is not perfect. Individuals with PKU are still found to score significantly lower on IQ tests than their parents. Longitudinal studies of PKU children have found a high incidence of perceptual difficulties that interfere with academic achievement (Koch & Koch, 1974). Diet therapy can lead to malnutrition because of reduced food intake. It also is problematic to gain the full cooperation of the affected individual.

Robinson and Robinson (1965) detailed several of the storage diseases. Hurler's disease, gargoylism, results in a deformed and stunted body as well as mental retardation. Affected individuals also may exhibit visual and hearing impairments. Gaucher's, when severe, is manifested by enlarged liver, spleen, and lymph nodes. Most do not live beyond adolescence.

Some of the inherited metabolic disorders are sex linked. Hemochromatosis is more common in males because the menstrual cycle in females decreases the iron stored in the system. Hemophilia, Fabray's disease, childhood muscular dystrophy, and hyperuricemia all occur predominantly in males.

Some metabolic disorders appear to improve as the affected individual ages (Stanbury et al., 1978). Some galactosemics gradually develop the ability to metabolize galactose (Brown & Sessoms, 2003). Individuals with adrynamia epidocis hereditaria and periodic paralysis may also cease to have attacks as they grow older.

Inborn errors of metabolism are the subject of continued intensive research. Reports of newly discovered syndromes frequently are announced. Screening still offers the best hope. The most direct method detects qualitative changes in the structure of the protein (Bearn, 1979). Mass screening for all possible single gene defects is still prohibitive financially. Therefore, with the exception of PKU, the focus is on families and at-risk populations. Amniocentesis, the use of cultured fibroblasts, and the applications stemming from the Human Genome Project will increase in the years ahead as a means of making screening programs more comprehensive. Currently, scientists apply a sophisticated battery of laboratory procedures to identify and elucidate suspected metabolic disorders.

REFERENCES

Batshaw, M. L., & Perret, Y. M. (1981). *Children with handicaps: A medical primer*. Baltimore, MD: Paul H. Brookes.

Bearn, A. G. (1979). Inborn errors of metabolism and molecular disease. In P. Beeson, W. McDermott, & J. Wyngaarden (Eds.), *Cecil textbook of medicine* (15th ed., pp. 40–48). Philadelphia, PA: Saunders.

Brown, R. T., & Sessoms, A. (2003). Galactosemia. In E. Fletcher-Janzen & C. R. Reynolds (Eds.), *Childhood disorders diagnostic desk reference* (pp. 252–253). Hoboken, NJ: Wiley.

Guthrie, R. (1972). Mass screening for genetic disease. *Hospital Practice, 7*, 93.

Holland, A. (2003). Gaucher's disease. In E. Fletcher-Janzen & C. R. Reynolds (Eds.), *Childhood disorders diagnostic desk reference* (pp. 256–258). Hoboken, NJ: Wiley.

Koch, R., & Koch, K. (1974). *Understanding the mentally retarded child: A new approach*. New York, NY: Random House.

Robinson, H. B., & Robinson, N. M. (1965). *The mentally retarded child: A psychological approach*. New York, NY: McGraw-Hill.

Stanbury, J., Wyngaarden, J., & Fredrickson. D. (1978). *The metabolic basis of inherited disease* (4th ed.). New York, NY: McGraw-Hill.

Telford, C., & Sawrey, J. (1977). *The exceptional individual.* Englewood Cliffs, NJ: Prentice Hall.

SALLY E. PISARCHICK
Cuyahoga Special Education Service Center

Schifani, J. W., Anderson, R. M., & Odle, S. J. (Eds.). (1980). *Implementing learning in the least restrictive environment.* Baltimore, MD: University Press.

PHILIP R. JONES
Virginia Polytechnic Institute and State University

See *also* **Demography of Special Education**

INCIDENCE

The term *incidence* refers to the estimated number of people in a given population who possess or exhibit a given characteristic at some point during their lives (Blackhurst & Berdine, 1981). Dunn (1973) believes that incidence gives the rate of occurrence of a condition while Schifani, Anderson, and Odle (1980) define incidence as the number of new cases of disabled children identified in a given period of time—usually a year. Incidence most often relates to the occurrence of some characteristic.

Incidence is often confused with prevalence but the two terms have different meanings. Prevalence refers to currently existing disabled children as opposed to those who might be considered exceptional at some point in their lives. Incidence results in a higher figure since it estimates future occurrence, where prevalence deals with a point in time figure.

Because incidence is usually an estimate, it is more difficult to validate or substantiate. Meyen (1978) states that state education agencies and school districts generally establish prevalence rates when conducting needs assessment surveys. He suggests that surveys and studies would be better able to establish incidence rates given the data becoming available from referral requests for service under IDEA. For general education planning purposes prevalence estimates continue to be used.

Educational planning requires an estimate of the number of children with disabilities requiring service. If program planners, for example, assume the incidence of mental retardation is 3% and project needed programs and services based on that figure, the result could be an overestimate of 100% if the actual prevalence was $1\frac{1}{2}\%$.

REFERENCES

Blackhurst, A. E., & Berdine, W. H. (1981). (Eds.). *An introduction to special education.* Boston, MA: Little, Brown.

Dunn, L. M. (Ed.). (1973). *Exceptional children in the schools.* New York, NY: Holt, Rinehart, & Winston.

Meyen, E. L. (1978). *Exceptional children and youth: An introduction.* Denver, CO: Love.

INCIDENTAL LEARNING AND VISUAL IMPAIRMENTS

Incidental learning is a term used to refer to information and concepts that are learned automatically or informally through observation or experimentation. For most children, incidental learning is the beginning of concept development and is a critical part of the learning process. For example, a young child watches his parents cook dinner, wash dishes, and put things away. Later, he is able to spontaneously imitate these actions in his own play or partially participate in these activities as they occur within the home. Through play and partial participation, he is practicing sequencing and hand movements, developing motor skills, and involving himself in activities as an active manager of life skills. As he grows older, he is able to fully or independently participate in these activities without extensive, if any, direct instruction. Instead, they were learned incidentally, through observation, imitation, and practice.

Potential breakdowns in learning incidentally may occur for students with limited vision or who are blind, as they cannot visually glance around the environment to make observations, leading to challenges with imitation, knowledge of detail, spontaneous feedback, and practice in natural environments (Fazzi & Petersmeyer, 2001; Ferrell, 2011). They may not be able to see their parents cooking and therefore do not imitate those actions in play, missing important opportunities to spontaneously develop these living skills altogether or until years after peers have acquired them. Limited opportunities for incidental learning, and the resultant deficits in conceptual understanding, also have the potential to reduce the engagement of children in the activities around them, leading to passivity and learned helplessness.

In order for students with visual impairments to learn what most students learn incidentally, they need extra verbal descriptions of events occurring around them, explicit instruction of how tasks are performed, and repeated experiences using all their senses, especially touch (Ferrell, 2011). For these students, the more they are actively engaged through touch and manual involvement in the tasks around them, the more they learn.

Related to incidental learning is the limited ability of students with visual impairments to understand the gestalt of a situation, object, or concept. Typical vision allows individuals to see the whole at one time, then to focus on the details that make up that whole. Children with visual impairments are often limited in what they can touch or see at one time, and therefore, first learn the details without seeing and understanding how those details combine to form the whole concept. Repeated experiences and explanations that relate current experiences to past experiences help the student form the whole concept (Ferrell, 2011).

When aware that incidental learning may not spontaneously occur, parents and teachers can purposefully create these learning and practice opportunities (Fazzi & Petersmeyer, 2001). By creating these opportunities in a way that is meaningful to the student (i.e., through opportunities to engage in activities occurring around them, involvement of multiple sensory modalities, and use of concrete objects, meaningful routines, and consistent language), the student will be given the best opportunity for learning.

REFERENCES

Fazzi, D. L., & Petersmeyer, B. A. (2001). *Imagining the possibilities: Creative approaches to orientation and mobility instruction for persons who are visually impaired.* New York, NY: AFB Press.

Ferrell, K. A. (2011). *Reach out and teach: Helping your child who is visually impaired learn and grow.* New York, NY: AFB Press.

Kitty Greeley
Florida State University
Fourth edition

INCLUSION

Special education services can be offered in various settings, ranging from regular education classes to hospitals. Regular education classes and others that resemble them constitute the least restrictive settings. Hospitals and others that resemble them (e.g., residential programs, juvenile detention settings) constitute the most restrictive settings.

Inclusion refers to the placement of students who display one or more disabilities in age-appropriate general education classrooms together with needed accommodations and supports. Inclusion is based on the belief that all children are capable of learning, children with disabilities benefit from being educated with students who do not display disabilities, and inclusion promotes equal educational opportunities. Inclusion directly affects students with disabilities, their teachers, and support staff. Additionally, the impact of inclusion can be school-wide, affecting many aspects of schooling (McLeskey & Waldron, 2000).

The 1975 Education for All Handicapped Children Act (Public Law 94-142) advocated an appropriate education for all students with disabilities. The 1990 Individuals with Disabilities Education Act (IDEA) established standards for eligibility, types of services, and procedural safeguards (Murphy, 1996). Advocacy for mainstreaming, or educating students to the maximum extent appropriate with peers without disabilities (Kavale & Forness, 2000) is consistent with this legislation. Both laws promulgate placement in the least restrictive environment. The provision reflects the belief that a student should be removed from general education only when the severity of their disability requires their need for services unattainable in general education classrooms. The 2004 amendments to IDEA continued to emphasize the importance of the least restrictive environment by noting the provision of a free, appropriate public education in the least restrictive environment as a priority area for monitoring.

Arguments in Favor of Inclusion

Those who advocate for inclusion typically emphasize one or more of the following beliefs. Some adopt philosophical value-based attitudes that parallel the ideological underpinnings of the Civil Rights movement. For them, inclusion is seen as an issue of social justice in which all forms of segregation are unacceptable, including those in education (Stainback & Stainback, 1990). The belief that "the burden of proof should fall upon the shoulders of those who wish to segregate students with disabilities" (Cole, Waldron, & Majd, 2004, p. 42) is consistent with this viewpoint.

Others believe the educational and social needs of students with disabilities are not being met in self-contained classrooms. Thus, their placement in alternative settings should be explored (Kavale & Forness, 2000). Students with disabilities are thought to benefit from inclusion because the curriculum to which they are exposed is more age-appropriate, and they learn from peers who serve as suitable role models. Inclusion is thought to lead to fewer behavior problems and higher levels of self-esteem.

Still others suggest that inclusion promotes desired change in attitudes, leading to more positive views toward persons with disabilities (Burstein, Sears, Wilcoxen, Cabello, & Spagna, 2004). Students learn to appreciate differences and take pride in assisting their classmates. Over time, inclusion programs promote positive attitudes toward children with disabilities among both general and special educators.

Some research supports inclusion. For example, preschool children with disabilities who are educated with typically developing peers display more improvement than those who are educated with peers with disabilities (Odom, 2000). Students with learning disabilities in reading and math who received their instruction in inclusive school programs, compared to those who received their education in resource rooms, made comparable progress in math and more progress in reading (Waldron & McLeskey, 1998).

Advocates of inclusion indicate that principals and administrators as well as general education and special education teachers must support inclusion programs for them to be effective. Teachers and administrators must feel as if they own the change that is occurring in their school and it is not being imposed on them (Waldron & McLeskey, 2000).

Arguments Against Inclusion

Those who oppose inclusion typically emphasize one or more of the following beliefs. Some dissenters believe that advocates of inclusion who base their support on philosophical and moral grounds are wishful in their thinking and instead should base their judgments on empirical evidence. Attempts to link noninclusion practices with apartheid and slavery lack evidence, are emotional in nature, and do not benefit the educational process (Mock & Kaufman, 2002). Some research confirms the belief that many students need more intense instruction and support than is provided in mainstream classrooms (Kauffman, Bantz, & McCullough, 2002).

The belief that all children can learn has been described as naive liberalism (Raines, 1996). Raines believes the broad scale use of inclusion is fallacious and contends that efforts by courts to support inclusion arise from a desire to emphasize the promotion of social goals consistent with the least restrictive environment rather than promoting suitable academic environments. He believes the fundamental purpose of the education system is to foster learning, not socialization (Raines, 1996).

Dissenters of inclusion point to difficulties encountered by teachers attempting to meet the needs of diverse students, especially those with moderate to severe disabilities (Chelsey & Calaluce, 1997). Many are not prepared for these responsibilities. Some teachers utilize classroom peers to provide needed instruction even though they are untrained and ill prepared (Zigmond & Baker, 1996). In some locations, teacher contracts allow them to decide which types of disabilities and the number of students with disabilities they will accept in their classrooms.

Regular education teachers often feel unprepared and thus lack confidence in their abilities to teach students with disabilities. Some dissenters of inclusion argue against the idea that good teachers can teach all students and that general education classrooms can be successful in managing all students without some form of administrative differentiation (Kavale & Forness, 2000).

Those who advocate for full inclusion may not place much importance on research evidence and instead focus on issues of compassion and caring (Kavale & Forness, 2000).

Inclusion: National and State Trends

Students with learning disabilities constitute the majority of those receiving special education services. During the 1980s, students with learning disabilities generally were being educated in the more restrictive settings (McLeskey & Pacchiano, 1994). Later studies found an increase in placement of students with learning disabilities in general education classrooms and a 31% decrease in placement in separate school settings (McLeskey, Henry, & Axelrod, 1999). This increase in the number of students with learning disabilities being educated in general education classrooms may be attributed to an increase in the number of students being identified with learning disabilities (McLeskey, Hoppey, Williamson, & Rentz, 2004). During the 1990s, only 15 states educated more students in less restrictive settings while many states ended the decade educating more students in more restrictive settings.

Studies of the placement of students with intellectual developmental disabilities generally suggest a movement toward inclusive education. For example, one study conducted with 1990 data (McLeskey et al., 2004) found an increase of 27% to 43% being educated in general education classrooms and a decrease from 73% to 56% being educated in segregated settings. Furthermore, the number of students with mental retardation being educated in separate facilities decreased by more than half. Identification rates for this disability remained fairly stable during this period.

Conclusions

The United States and other countries continue to struggle in their efforts to develop more effective methods to prevent disabilities and to educate those with disabilities. This theme is echoed in various entries from various countries described within this Encyclopedia. Some view inclusion as an opportunity and others view it as pathway that provides few benefits, except to those with the more mild handicapping conditions. Individualized decisions regarding inclusion should be determined by a multidisciplinary team to determine the best educational placement for a student with disabilities. Teacher training and support levels are a consideration when considering inclusion for children with more significant disabilities. An increase in academic rigor requires all students make progress in their enrolled grade level curriculum.

This discussion is brief and is not intended to provide a full discussion of inclusion. Various models of inclusion have been advanced. No one model of inclusion is necessarily best for every school district. Research and other forms of scholarship are needed to evaluate the impact of inclusion models on students with various levels and types of disabilities and disorders, their teachers, and nondisabled peers.

REFERENCES

Burstein, N., Sears, S., Wilcoxen, A., Cabello, B., & Spagna, M. (2004). Moving toward inclusive practices. *Remedial and Special Education, 25,* 104–116.

Chelsey, G. M., & Calaluce, P. D., Jr. (1997). The deception of inclusion. *Mental Retardation, 35,* 488–490.

Cole, C. M., Waldron, N., & Majd, M. (2004). Academic progress of students across inclusive and traditional settings. *Mental Retardation, 42*(2), 136–144.

Kauffman, J. M., Bantz, J. B., & McCullough, J. M. (2002). Separate and better: A special public school class for students with emotional and behavioral disorders. *Exceptionality, 10*(3), 149–170.

Kavale, K., & Forness, S. (2000). History, rhetoric, and reality: Analysis of the inclusion debate. *Remedial and Special Education, 21*(5), 279–296.

McLeskey, J., Henry, D., & Axelrod, M. I. (1999). Inclusion of students with learning disabilities: An examination of data from reports to congress. *Exceptional Children, 66,* 55–66.

McLeskey, J., Hoppey, D., Williamson, P., & Rentz, T. (2004). Is inclusion an illusion? An examination of national and state trends toward the education of students with learning disabilities in general education classrooms. *Learning Disabilities Research & Practice, 19*(2), 109–115.

McLeskey, J., & Pacchiano, D. (1994). Mainstreaming students with learning disabilities: Are we making progress? *Exceptional Children, 60*(6), 508–517.

McLeskey, J., & Waldron, N. (2000). *Inclusive schools in action: Making differences ordinary.* Alexandria, VA: Association for Supervision and Curriculum Development.

Mock, D. R., & Kauffman, J. M. (2002). Preparing teachers for full inclusion: is it possible? *Teacher Educator, 37*(3), 202–215.

Murphy, D. (1996). Implications of inclusion for general and special education. *Elementary School Journal, 96*(5), 470–493.

Odom, S. L. (2000). Preschool inclusion: What we know and where we go from here. *Topics in Early Childhood Special Education, 20*(1), 20–27.

Raines, J. C. (1996). Appropriate versus least restrictive educational policies and students with disabilities. *Social Work in Education, 18*(2), 113–127.

Stainback, W., & Stainback, S. (1990). *Support networks for inclusive schooling: Interdependent integrated education.* Baltimore, MD: Paul H. Brookes.

Waldron, N., & McLeskey, J. (1998). The effects of an inclusive school program on students with mild and severe learning disabilities. *Exceptional Children, 64,* 395–405.

Waldron, N., & McLeskey, J. (2000). *Inclusive education in action: Making differences ordinary.* Alexandria, VA: Association for Supervision and Curriculum Development.

Zigmond, N., & Baker, J. M. (1996). Full inclusion for students with learning disabilities: Too much of a good thing? *Theory Into Practice, 35*(1), 26–34.

MARIA ARZOLA
University of Florida

See also Teaching: Inclusion and Co-Teaching; Teaching and Consultation

INCONTINENTIA PIGMENTI (BLOCH-SULZBERGER SYNDROME)

Incontinentia pigmenti (IP) is a rare, hereditary disorder with abnormalities in the skin, skin derivatives (hair, nails, and teeth), eyes, skeleton, and nervous system. The original cases were described in 1925 and occurred in twin sisters. Since then, several hundred affected individuals have been reported.

IP is transmitted in an X-linked dominant manner. The gene is felt to be almost uniformly lethal in males, which accounts for the observations that more than 97% of patients with IP are females. IP is reportedly rare, but its incidence has not been clearly delineated.

Characteristics

1. Skin. Skin findings are the most common manifestation of IP. In the newborn, groups of blisters develop in straight lines, preceded by red streaks. These lesions occur on the limbs and trunk. By about 4 months of age, these abnormalities clear, except on the legs, where the blisters evolve into scaly, wart-like plaques. Likewise, these plaques usually resolve by the end of the first year of life. Finally, the pigmentary stage, which gives this syndrome its name, may be present at birth or develop over several months. The characteristic lesion of this phase is extensive areas of increased pigmentation, more common on the trunk than on the limbs. The pattern can be whorl-like, linear, or in scattered flecks. These areas persist throughout childhood but usually fade completely by mid-adolescence.

2. Teeth. Missing teeth, delayed tooth eruption, cone-shaped teeth.

3. Hair. Patchy hair loss, especially on the back of the scalp. Hair may also be coarse, wiry, and thin.

4. Nails. Minor anomalies (pitting) to severe malformation.

5. Nervous system. One third have mental retardation, seizures, and spasticity (increased muscle tone).

6. Eyes. About one third of patients have poor vision, strabismus (uncoordinated eye movement), cataracts, underdevelopment of the optic nerve, and detached retina.

7. Skeletal. Scoliosis, vertebral anomalies, extra ribs, hemiatrophy (deficient development of one side of the body).

Treatment for patients with IP addresses problems that are unrelated to the skin pathology, which tends to resolve over time. Seizures require control with anticonvulsant medication. Eye abnormalities, particularly retinal detachment, are best handled by pediatric ophthalmologists. Significant skeletal defects should be promptly referred to pediatric orthopedic specialists.

The need for special education services for a child with IP will be variable based on the involvement of the nervous system. Because mental retardation is reported in approximately one third of the known cases, special cognitive support services are required. A comprehensive neuropsychological evaluation is helpful to determine a child's strengths and weaknesses and provide valuable recommendations to the school personnel. Vision support and physical therapy may also be required. The school counselor can provide emotional support to help the child with IP develop good self-esteem and peer relationships. Providing education to the child's teacher and classmates will facilitate understanding of this syndrome.

The prognosis for children with IP is dependent on what nonskin-related manifestations of the disorder they have. Seizures during the first month of life usually indicate a very poor outlook and significant defects in the central nervous system. However, unless this problem occurs, the vast majority of patients with IP should do well.

For more information and support, contact National Incontinentia Pigmenti Foundation, 30 East 72nd Street #16, New York, NY 10021. Tel.: (212) 452-1231, e-mail: nipf@pipeline.com http://www.medhelp.org/.

This entry has been informed by the sources listed below.

REFERENCES

Darmstadt, G. L. (2000). *Hyperpigmented lesions*. In R. E. Behrman, R. K. Kleigman, & H. B. Jenson (Eds.), *Nelson's textbook of pediatrics* (16th ed., pp. 1984–1985). Philadelphia, PA: Saunders.

Gandy, A. *Incontinentia pigmenti*. Disease database. Retrieved from http://www.pedianet.com/news/illness/disease/files/incontin.htm

Pediatric database (PEDBASE). (n.d.). *Incontinentia pigmenti*. Retrieved from http://www.icondata.com/health/pedbase/files/incontin.htm

Jones, K. (1997). *Smith's recognizable patterns of human malformations* (5th ed.). Philadelphia, PA: Saunders.

National Organization for Rare Disorders. (1999). *Incontinentia pigmenti*. Retrieved from http://www.rarediseases.org/

BARRY H. DAVISON
Ennis, Texas

JOAN W. MAYFIELD
Baylor Pediatric Specialty Services, Dallas, Texas

INCORRIGIBILITY (*See Conduct Disorder*)

INDEPENDENCE LIVING CENTERS

In discussing this select topic that addresses independent living for individuals who live with disabilities the author of this article would like to state to the reader that for more than four decades he has personally been involved as a classroom teacher with students who experience disabilities as well as the preparation of special and general education credential students who themselves are preparing to be classroom teachers. Experience gained from working with and knowing numerous individuals over the years has left a significant mark not only in terms of one being an educator but, also, in terms of how significant it is that individuals are viewed by others in terms of ability, prominence, stature, and self-worth. Indeed the Independent Living Movement is a Civil Rights Movement for individuals with disabilities. In its infancy, during the 1960s and 1970s, it was a time of protests, sit-ins, and media coverage. Newspapers, magazines, and the evening news told of these activities by college students living with disabilities and those who supported their efforts. These activities took place at the University of California, Berkeley on the West and the University of Illinois in the East and were considered revolutionary in their nature. The movement represented human rights of persons with disabilities; however, more than this is how as a nation, all persons would be treated and respected by other individuals simply because they are human beings. If we trivialize the notion that some in society simply deserve to live more freely or openly and enjoy individual rights more so than others then perhaps we have played a trick on ourselves. In this case, we have lost our way. Instead we should be members of a society in which we search for unity within a nation.

The three cornerstones of the independent living philosophy are consumer sovereignty, self-reliance, and political and economic rights. The philosophy rejects the supremacy of professionals as decision makers and views disability as an interaction with the society and the environment rather than as a medical condition or physical or mental impairment (DeJong, 1978). Models of service delivery that help foster independent living for persons with disabilities vary by region and locale. Although centers hold commonalities in services offered to individuals there is ample variance in how these services may be made available based on the type of disabilities encountered by individuals in a given locale. Also a good deal of variation in services available may depend on location such as an urban environment as compared to a rural environment. Such locations play significantly in what and how services are delivered or made available. Ward (1998) produced an internationally acclaimed film titled: *A Little History Worth Knowing* (1998) that is a primer on disability and the vast stereotypes that individuals living with disabilities have endured over many centuries in society. Clearly indicated within the film is the necessary sweeping away of harmful stereotypes illustrated in print and other media while replacing such negativity with positive imagery of individuals with disabilities being active contributors within our communities.

There are a number of essential features of the independent living service model discussed in the literature. These include consumer control, a cross-disability emphasis (inclusion of people with all types of disabilities, mental, physical, sensory), a community-based and community-responsive approach, peer role modeling, provision of a wide range of services, a community advocacy orientation and open and ongoing access to services (Counts, 1978; Goodall, 1988; Lachat, 1988).

Centers for Independent Living (CILs) are designed to assist individuals with disabilities to achieve their maximum potential. Typically, CILs are nonresidential, private, nonprofit, community-based organizations providing services and advocacy by and for persons with disabilities. In discussing living options for those living with disabilities Goodall (1988), suggests that independent living philosophy calls for options and individual control. That is, when social and environmental options are available, persons with disabilities can live independently like other people in the community. To become fully independent, disabled persons must select their options, specify their goals, and take responsibility for achieving those goals. In this way, persons with disabilities can gain control of their lives and minimize reliance on others (Frieden, 1978). Moreover, Garboden (2011), suggests for people with disabilities the world of rents and benefits is a harsh one that may see them forced to live away from social networks. Local rents or housing availability may be prohibitive because of expense but, also, availability for suitable housing may cause hardship due to distance

from support networks such as family and friends as well as transportation hampered by availability and cost. In their work dealing with models for independent living Nosek, Zhu, and Howard (1992), suggest that inequalities that existed could be remedied if consideration was given based on the uniqueness and individuality of people with disabilities along with provision of reasonable accommodations and appropriate services. Individuals living with severe disabilities were the real pioneers in the CIL movement because it afforded them options for living a more integrated life in their communities. Ironically it was individuals with some of the most serious as well as limiting disabilities that opened the door for other individuals with less serious disabilities to experience and enjoy models of living independence.

The term *severe disabilities* has been defined somewhat differently by various individuals and agencies. Generally, however, it implies a condition in which the development of typical abilities is in some way adversely affected (Sailor & Guess 1983; Snell & Brown, 2011; Westling & Fox, 2009). Persons with severe disabilities are often challenged by significant weaknesses in general learning abilities, personal and social skills, and frequently in areas of sensory and physical development.

According to Westling and Fox (2009), individuals who experience severe disabilities commonly do not demonstrate general ability in skills necessary to maintain themselves independently. Most often these individuals require assistance and ongoing support from persons who do not experience disabilities, such as family members, friends, professionals, and care providers.

The traditional categories of persons usually referred to as having a severe disability, as suggested by Westling and Fox (2009), include those who have been classified as having moderate, severe, or profound intellectual disabilities; some who have autism spectrum disorders (ASD); and those who have multiple physical or sensory disabilities as well as intellectual disabilities. Recent developments in defining the condition of severe disabilities and their impact on the lives of individuals as reported by Westling and Fox (2009) have focused on quality of life issues with regard to necessary support. TASH, an organization supporting equity, opportunity and inclusion for people with disabilities and the American Association on Intellectual and Developmental Disabilities (AAIDD) in its most recent characterization of intellectual disabilities considered it as a human manifestation in which different levels of support are required. Since 1992, AAIDD ceased making distinctions using the traditional subclasses of intellectual disabilities, but instead proposed that an individual must be described within a multidimensional context that provides a comprehensive description of the person and the necessary supports (see Figure I.1).

The theoretical model of intellectual disabilities presented in Figure I.1 has five dimensions: (1) intellectual abilities, (2) adaptive behavior, (3) participation,

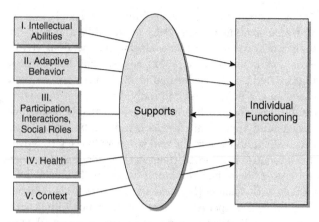

Figure I.1. Theoretical model of mental retardation.
Source: Westling and Fox (2009, p. 4).

interactions, and social roles, (4) health, and (5) context. These are mediated by a support system to affect an individual's functioning. Using this model the impact of all dimensions on the individual is influenced by the support that buffers the person's life. The model implies that a person's functioning is not due solely to characteristics of the individual, but also to the supportive context in which the person must operate. Intellectual disabilities experienced by an individual as illustrated (see Figure I.1) is seen not as deficiency, but in terms of needed supports.

As suggested by Westling and Fox (2009) the AAIDD states five assumptions "essential" to the application of its definition:

1. Limitations in present functioning must be considered within the context of community environments typical of the individual's age peers and culture.

2. Valid assessment considers cultural and linguistic diversity, as well as differences in communication, sensory, motor, and behavioral factors.

3. Within an individual, limitations often coexist with strengths.

4. An important purpose of describing limitations is to develop a profile of needed supports.

5. With appropriate personalized supports over a sustained period, the life functioning of the person with intellectual disabilities generally will improve (p. 34).

Although the AAIDD eliminated categories of intellectual disabilities based on levels of measured intelligence, these categories are still maintained in the American Psychiatric Association's *Diagnostic and Statistical Manual of Mental Disorders, Fourth Edition, Text Revision* (*DSM-IV-TR*; American Psychiatric Association, 2000). Stated levels and their corresponding approximate IQ ranges include mild (50 to 70), moderate (35 to 50), severe (20 to 35), and profound (below 20 to 25) intellectual disabilities.

DeJong (1978) and Wilson (1998) state that the independent living movement is characterized as the civil rights movement of people with disabilities. It was initiated by individuals, and quickly became a national, informal network of community organizations and individuals, including not only people with disabilities but also human rights advocates, political lobbyists, and the like. As stated previously in this article the author saw and experienced firsthand the effects of this movement both in terms of educational implications for students with special needs receiving an education in public and private schools as well as adults with disabilities (and their advocates) demanding full accessibility for employment and living independently within their communities. Consumers (those living with disabilities) sought to live a more fulfilling life in the able-bodied world and the efforts of the rehabilitation professionals to reach disabled persons for whom a vocational goal was, until recently, unthinkable (Switzer, 2003). It was not until the early 1970s that the CIL movement gained greater visibility and recognition with the creation of the Center for Independent Living (CIL) in Berkeley, California.

Professionals in the field of rehabilitation have held common beliefs that rehabilitation programs are built on the "medical model" of service delivery, while the disability rights and CIL movement promotes a completely different approach to service delivery. The approach is based on the principles of self-determination, choice, and consumer control (Nosek et al., 1992).

Self-determination refers to an individual's ability to express preferences and desires, make decisions, and initiate actions based on these decisions. Simply, self-determination refers to choice. Control focuses on the extent to which individuals are independent, self-sufficient, and capable of gaining access to the resources necessary to freely act on their choices and decisions (Wilson, 1998).

The medical model labeled people with disabilities as helpless, passive, dependent, unable, and perhaps disinterested in gaining or maintaining employment. The independent living model completely turned the medical model (and those who adhere to it) on its head. A comparison of these two divergent models of disability is illustrated vividly (Table I.1).

In addition to established independent living models in communities Garboden (2011) and Wilson (1998) both assert the requirement of every community needing the rehabilitation paradigm for the provision of adequate medical-based services. Equally important, however, is that each community needs an equal amount of service and advocacy stemming from the independent living paradigm. At this time approximately 99% of all public dollars go into the rehabilitation paradigm while less than 1% goes into independent living.

The passage of P.L. 101-336: Americans with Disabilities Act of 1990 (ADA) creates a vision for equal

Table I.1. Comparison of a "Medical Model" and "Independent Living Model" of Disability

Issue	Medical Model	Independent Living Model
What is the problem?	Clinical condition resulting in dependence and apathy	Discrimination and lack of supports
What is the solution?	Diagnose, prescribe, and support	Reasonable, appropriate accommodations, support services, and programs facilitating independence
Who is in control?	Physicians and allied health care professionals	Consumers

Source: Wilson, 1998. Contrasting the two models of disability illustrates the desired outcomes for CILs to assist individuals in decision making for taking control over one's daily life as paramount. The term *control* does not necessarily mean having the physical or mental capacity to do everyday tasks for one's self. Individuals who have worked or are in the process of initiating careers that bring them into contact with persons who live with disabilities understand firsthand the harsh realities of these individuals gaining full independence in their lives. What they ask for or request of us is the opportunity to experience as much independence and decision making in their lives as is feasible given the limitations they may live with. For some persons, complete control may not be possible but the CIL movement continues to work toward complete consumer control wherever and whenever possible.

opportunity and access for all persons. This vision according to Wilson (1998) is shared by people involved in both the traditional rehabilitation system and the newer disability rights and CIL movement. CILs enhance not only the lives of persons with disabilities, but also the individual communities where these centers are located. Additionally, CILs provide an advocacy voice on a wide range of national, state, and local issues. The more than 700 CILs in the United States are working to establish physical and programmatic access to housing, employment, communities, transportation, recreational facilities, as well as health and social services. The movement for independent living has been evolving for more than four decades. The CIL movement will continue to grow because committed individuals will seek ways to assist all persons to feel that they are valued members of their community, whether they happen to live with or without disabilities.

REFERENCES

American Psychiatric Association (2000). *Diagnostic and statistical manual of mental disorders* (4th ed., text rev.). Washington, DC: Author.

Counts, R. (1978). *Independent living rehabilitation for severely handicapped people: A preliminary appraisal*. Washington, DC: Urban Institute.

DeJong, G. (1978, November 17). *The movement for independent living: Origins, idealogy, and implications for disability research*. Boston, MA: Medical Rehabilitation Institute, Tuffs New England Medical Center. A paper presented at the annual meetings of the American Congress of Rehabilitation Medicine, New Orleans, Louisiana.

Frieden, L. (1978). Independent living: Movement and programs. *American Rehabilitation*, 3(6), 69.

Garboden, M. (2011, November 24). Independence—at a price. *Community Care*. Retrieved from http://go.galegroup.com.ezproxylocal.Library.nova.edu/ps/

Goodall, J. (1988). Living options for physically disabled adults: A review. *Disability, Handicap & Society*, 3(2), 173–193.

Lachat, M. (1988). *The independent living service model: Historical roots, core elements and current practices*. Hampton, NH: Center for Resource Management.

Nosek, A., Zhu, Y., & Howard, C. (1992). The evolution of independent living programs. *Rehabilitation Counseling Bulletin*, 35(3), 175–189.

Sailor, W., & Guess, D. (1983). *Severely handicapped students: An instructional design*. Boston, MA: Houghton Mifflin.

Snell, M., & Brown, F. (2011). *Instruction of students with severe disabilities* (7th ed). Upper Saddle River, NJ: Pearson.

Switzer, J. (2003). *Disabled rights: American disability policy and the fight for equality*. Washington, DC: Georgetown University Press.

Ward, I. (Director). (1998). *A little history worth knowing*. (Film). Cicero, NY: Program Development.

Westling, D., & Fox, L. (2009). *Teaching students with severe disabilities* (4th ed). Upper Saddle River, NJ: Pearson.

Wilson, K. (1998). Centers for independent living in support of transition. *Focus on Autism and Other Developmental Disabilities*, 13(3), 246–252.

PETER KOPRIVA
Fresno Pacific University
Fourth edition

INDEPENDENT AND FUNCTIONAL LIVING SKILLS

The purpose of a functional life skills curriculum for students with disabilities is to maximize their independent functioning in everyday settings where people without disabilities live, work, and spend time. Early instructional programs in Madison, Wisconsin schools that addressed naturally occurring, functional activities in everyday contexts, including general education and the community, resulted in improved postschool outcomes for students, including increased employment in integrated settings with co-workers without disabilities (Van Deventer et al., 1981). Similarly, Benz, Lindstrom, and Yovanoff (2000) demonstrated that a functional skills curriculum (Youth

Transition Program) was associated with improved postschool outcomes for participating students, including higher rates of graduation, employment, and participation in postsecondary education.

More than 30 years after the first of these early demonstrations of the effectiveness of a functional curriculum for students with disabilities, the field of special education appears to be in a quandary about what comprises an appropriate curriculum for these students (Alper, Ryndak, Hughes, & McDonnell, 2011; Hughes, in press). On the one hand, federal legislation (e.g., No Child Left Behind Act [NCLB] of 2002) calls for an increased access to general education curricula and focus on academic outcomes and standardized testing. On the other hand, special education is not producing the positive postschool outcomes nationwide demonstrated in the early studies. Having a disability is persistently associated with poor postschool outcomes, such as low graduation and postsecondary enrollment rates and increased unengagement, unemployment, and underemployment (Newman, Wagner, Cameto, & Knokey, 2009). For example, Newman et al. (2009) reported that, after leaving high school, only 33% of youth with intellectual disabilities are employed (primarily part time), only 7% attend postsecondary school as a sole postschool activity, only 14% live independently or semi-independently, only 26% have a checking account, and only 11% participate in a community group, such as a sports team or church club. One factor related to such poor postschool outcomes may be the inappropriateness of the prevailing special education curriculum, instructional strategies, and service delivery model, which have increasingly deemphasized a functional skills curriculum.

Balancing Academic and Functional Skills

Increasing numbers of special educators are beginning to question the relevance of a curriculum strictly focused on achieving grade-level general education standards versus functional skills (e.g., Bouck, 2009; Patton, Polloway, & Smith, 2000; Wehman, 2009). For example, Storey and Miner (in press) remind us that "although specific curriculum content decisions must be based on standards and benchmarks as well as more individualized preferences and interests, the general goal of all instruction must be to enhance a person's capacity to function successfully in the community" (p. 4). Therefore, the curriculum should comprise skills that teach a person to function in employment, residential, community living, and recreational/leisure domains and that are personally meaningful and valuable to the individual (Hughes, in press). Similarly, the curriculum should consist of skills that are useful in an immediate (e.g., learning to operate a microwave in order to cook and eat breakfast) or future environment (e.g., learning to ride the bus to get to work). When we consider the poor adult outcomes generally experienced by individuals with disabilities (e.g., Newman et al., 2009),

a renewed emphasis in the curriculum on the "criterion of ultimate functioning"—the skills a person must possess "to function as productively and independently as possible in socially, vocationally, and domestically integrated adult community environments" (Brown, Nietupski, & Hamre-Nietupski, 1976, p. 8)—is invaluable as we enter an era of "curriculum wars" in special education.

Critical Skills Areas

Test, Walker, and Richter (2008) referred to functional skills as "skills that help a person to live in, and get around in, the community" (p. 132). The breadth of such skills is extensive, given the range of community and home environments and subenvironments that individuals frequent. Test et al. (2008) suggest five general skills areas: travel and community safety (e.g., transportation, pedestrian safety), grocery and general shopping (e.g., preparing a shopping list, finding items, purchasing), eating out (e.g., ordering and paying for meals), community services (e.g., using medical and recreational services, post office), and money and budgeting (e.g., banking, using credit cards). The extent to which individuals achieve mastery in these skills areas will clearly enhance their independence and competence and both increase and broaden their participation in their respective communities.

Additional skills areas include those skills needed to function independently at home. Steere and Burcroff (2004) suggest competence in nine general activity areas is necessary. These areas include: planning and preparing meals; self-care, bathing, and hygiene; cleaning and care of the home; cleaning and care of clothing; telephone use; leisure activities; safety procedures; time management and scheduling; and negotiating with others (roommates) and self-advocacy.

Successful performance of these and the community functional skills mentioned earlier require that individuals know when to perform these skills, how their actions may impact others (e.g., waiting to use the shower), and what support they may need to complete tasks. Also, one issue that warrants serious attention is that participants need to be aware of the numerous risks that exist in home and community environments (e.g., crosswalks, appliances) (Agran, 2004). Learning how to recognize such risks (e.g., spilled water on kitchen floor) and appropriately responding to risk stimuli (e.g., extinguishing a fire) must be included in instruction.

Teaching in Community and Home Settings

As discussed in the entry "Community-Based Instruction," there is considerable controversy regarding where the instruction of independent living skills should be conducted. Numerous researchers have suggested that instruction should be delivered in natural settings in which the tasks are typically performed (e.g., using a public Laundromat). That said, this focus precludes or limits student participation in inclusive, general education setting (Fisher & Sax, 1999) and may limit instruction in academics. Conversely, proponents of community-based instruction maintain that failure to teach independent living skills in community environments will only compromise generalization and skill transfer. When planning instructional programs, it is critical that the planning team consider the relative benefits of both approaches when determining the instructional site. As a reasonable compromise, several researchers suggest that both general education and community settings be used (e.g., teach skill in school but probe in community).

Systematic Instruction and Promoting Generalization

Direct instruction in the actual settings in which students are expected to perform valued behavior has been shown to be effective in teaching critical functional and independent living skills to students, especially those with severe disabilities (e.g., Downing, 2010; McDonnell & Hardman, 2010). The first step is to analyze the performance demands in a setting or across different settings and then observe the student performing these skills. Areas in which the student is not performing required skills should then be taught by direct instructional methods, such as modeling, prompting, reinforcing, and providing corrective feedback (Downing, 2010). As the student acquires targeted skills, the teacher, job coach, or other instructor should begin fading assistance to promote the student's independent performance. For example, if a teacher has been accompanying a student on a bus route from school to a job site, the teacher can begin fading assistance by sitting in a different section of the bus, checking to see that the student gets off at the correct bus stop. When the student is performing all steps of the bus riding routine independently (e.g., boarding the correct bus, paying for the ride, finding and sitting in an unoccupied seat, signaling for and disembarking at the correct bus stop), the teacher can replace accompanying the student on each ride with occasional spot checks.

To promote generalization of acquired skills across people, settings, tasks, and time, instructional personnel should introduce into training multiple exemplars of stimuli that occur across environmental settings (Horner, Sprague, & Wilcox, 1982; Stokes & Baer, 1977). For example, if a student is learning to use a bank card at an ATM machine, the teacher should expose the student to ATM machines that have different stimulus features, such as where to insert the bank card and information provided on the keypad. If students learn to perform a task across a variety of relevant stimuli, they are more likely to generalize tasks to new situations and environmental demands. For example, Hughes et al. (2000) taught four high school students with intellectual disabilities and autism to initiate conversation across a variety

of peers and settings (multiple exemplars). All four students generalized their initiations to novel peers in both trained and untrained settings after instruction had been terminated.

Summary

Grigal, Test, Beattie, and Wood (1997) examined a sample of IEPs of students with disabilities to examine the transition components in their IEPs. Independent living skills were included in just over one half of the IEPS; home making skills were in about 40%; and transportation, financial, and medical-related skills were in less than 25%. Additionally, IEP goals were evaluated to determine if they were: Detailed, Adequate, or Minimal. The majority of goals in the area of living skills were determined to be at best minimal, with many goals being "vague and illegible." Last, in a study by Lynch and Beare (1990) on IEP objectives for students with intellectual disabilities or behavioral disorders, their education was exclusively on academic skills. From the available data, it appears that a large number of students with disabilities are not receiving satisfactory, if any, instruction in living skills. This is regrettable given the many challenges individuals with disabilities will face as they transition into the myriad of employment, residential, commercial, public, and medical environments and services available to them as adults. Instruction in independent living skills is a curriculum domain that cannot be neglected for many students with disabilities.

REFERENCES

Agran, M. (2004). Health and safety. In P. Wehman & J. Kregel (Eds.), *Functional curriculum* (pp. 357–383). Austin, TX: PRO-ED.

Alper, S., Ryndak, D. L., Hughes, C., & McDonnell, J. (2011). *Documenting long-term outcomes of inclusive education for students with significant disabilities: Methodological issues.* Manuscript submitted for publication.

Benz, M. R., Lindstrom, L. E., & Yanvanoff, P. (2000). Improving graduation and employment outcomes of students with disabilities: Predictive factors and student perspectives. *Exceptional Children, 66*, 509–529.

Bouck, E. C. (2009). No Child Left Behind, the Individuals with Disabilities Education Act, and functional curricula: A conflict of interest? *Education and Training in Developmental Disabilities, 44*, 313.

Brown, L., Nietupski, J., & Hamre-Nietupski, S. (1976). Criterion of ultimate functioning. In M. A. Thomas (Ed.), *Hey, don't forget about me!* (p. 215). Reston, VA: Council for Exceptional Children.

Downing, J. E. (2010). *Academic instruction for students with moderate and severe intellectual disabilities in inclusive classrooms.* Thousand Oaks, CA: Corwin.

Fisher, D., & Sax, C. (1999). Noticing differences between and postsecondary education: Extending Agran, Snow, and

Swaner's discussion. *Journal of the Association for Persons with Severe Handicaps, 24*, 303–305.

Grigal, M., Test, D., Beattie, J., & Wood, W. M. (1997). An evaluation of transition components of Individualized Education Programs. *Exceptional Children, 63*(3), 357–372.

Horner, R. H., Sprague, J., & Wilcox, B. (1982). Constructing general case programs for community activities. In B. Wilcox & G. T. Bellamy (Eds.), *Design of high school programs for severely handicapped students* (p. 6198). Baltimore, MD: Paul H. Brookes.

Hughes, C. (in press). Foreword. In K. Storey & C. Miner, *Systematic instruction of functional skills for students and adults with disabilities*. Springfield, IL: Thomas.

Hughes, C., Rung. L. L., Wehmeyer, M. L., Agran, M., Copeland, S. R., & Hwang, B. (2000). Selfprompted communication book use to increase social interaction among high school students. *The Journal of the Association for Persons with Severe Handicaps, 25*, 153–166.

Lynch, E. C., & Beare, P. L. (1990). The quality of IEP objectives and their relevance to instruction for students with mental retardation and behavior disorders. *Remedial and Special Instruction, 11*, 44–55.

McDonnell, J., & Hardman, M. L. (2010). *Successful transition programs: Pathways for students with intellectual disabilities and developmental disabilities*. Thousand Oaks, CA: Sage.

Newman, L., Wagner, M., Cameto, R., & Knokey, A. M. (2009). *The post-high school outcomes of youth with disabilities up to 4 years after high school. A report of findings from the National Longitudinal Transition Study2 (NLTS2)*. Menlo Park, CA: SRI.

No Child Left Behind Act of 2001, Pub. L. No. 107110, 115 Stat. 1425 (2002).

Patton, J. R., Polloway, E. A., & Smith, T. E. C. (2000). Educating students with mild mental retardation. *Focus on Autism and Other Developmental Disabilities, 15*, 80–89.

Steere, D. E., & Burcroff, T. L. Living at home. In P. Wehman & J. Kregel (Eds.), *Functional curriculum* (pp. 293–316). Austin, TX: PRO-ED.

Stokes, T., & Baer, D. (1977). An implicit technology of generalization. *Journal of Applied Behavior Analysis, 10*, 349–367.

Storey, K., & Miner, C. (2010). *Systematic instruction of functional skills for students and adults with disabilities*. Springfield, IL: Thomas.

Test, D., Walker, A., & Richter, S. (2008). Community functioning skills. In K. Storey, P. Bates, & D. Hunter (Eds.), *The road ahead: Transition to adult life for persons with disabilities* (pp. 131–150). St. Augustine, FL: Training Resource Network.

Van Deventer, P., Yelinek, N., Brown, L., Schroeder, J., Loomis, R., & Gruenewald, L. (1981). A followup examination of severely handicapped graduates of the Madison Metropolitan School District from 1971–1978. In L. Brown, K. Baumgart, I. Pumpian, J. Nisbet, A. Ford, A. Donnellan, M....J. Schroeder (Eds.), *Educational programs for severely handicapped students* (Vol. XI). Madison, WI: Madison Metropolitan School District.

Wehman, P. (2009, October). *Transition from school to adulthood for youth with disabilities: Where are we in 2009?* Paper presented to the U.S. Department of Education, Office of Special Education and Rehabilitative Services. Washington, DC.

CAROLYN HUGHES
Vanderbilt University

MARTIN ARGRAN
University of Wyoming
Fourth edition

INDEPENDENT VARIABLE

Independent variable is a term used to describe the intervention or treatment that will be implemented as part of an experimental manipulation (Alberto & Troutman, 2012). Independent variables can include antecedent-oriented strategies (e.g., teacher directives), consequent strategies (e.g., schedules of reinforcement), environmental modification (e.g., moving a student's desk), setting event strategies (e.g., touching base with the student following a difficult interaction), and biological strategies (e.g., methods for decreasing physical symptoms of agitation; Bailey & Burch, 2002).

The independent variable is usually implemented following a period of baseline data collection. As a rule, the independent variable is only initiated when the baseline data shows stability, such as minimal variability and/or a flat or contratherapeutic trend (Tawney & Gast, 1984). Bailey and Burch (2002) offer several considerations for selecting and implementing an independent variable, including (a) knowing your consumer, that is, being sure to select procedures with the understanding that the teacher or student is willing to use the procedure and/or considers the procedure feasible given his or her learners or context; (b) considering potential side effects, that is, determining if there are any detrimental effects associated with the proposed procedure prior to implementation (e.g., use of aversives, loss of privileges, health or safety concerns); and (c) operationally defining your intervention, that is, providing an observable and measurable statement that exactly defines what you plan to do as part of your intervention (see Gresham, 1996).

In conclusion, the independent variable represents the treatment or intervention that the experimenter implements to determine if he or she can demonstrate a functional relationship between the intervention and changes in the dependent variable. Gresham (1996) argues that researchers should always be mindful of treatment integrity, which is verifying that the intervention was delivered as intended. Treatment integrity can be evaluated using direct, indirect, and statistical methodologies.

REFERENCES

Alberto, P., & Troutman, A. C. (2012). *Applied behavior analysis for teachers*. Upper Saddle River, NJ: Merrill.

Bailey, J. S., & Burch, M. R. (2002). *Research methods in applied behavior analysis*. Thousand Oaks, CA: Sage.

Gresham, F. M. (1996). Treatment integrity in single-subject research. In R. D. Franklin, D. B. Allison, & B. S. Gorman (Eds.), *Design and analysis of single-case research* (pp. 93–117). Mahwah, NJ: Erlbaum.

Tawney, J. W., & Gast, D. L. (1984). *Single subject research in special education*. New York, NY: Merrill.

RANDALL L. DE PRY
Portland State University

See also Research in Special Education

INDIA, SPECIAL EDUCATION IN

Fifty million of India's 1 billion people are disabled or have special needs. Information as to the number of special needs children currently receiving educational services is unavailable. In 1992, 12,590,000 children reportedly received special education services (Ministry of Human Resource Development, 1998; National Policy on Education, 1992).

All children in India who attend school have the right to education. The term *special education* denotes the education of children who deviate socially, mentally, or physically from the average to such an extent that they require major modifications of usual school practices. Students who warrant special education services include the gifted; the mentally challenged; those with communication or emotion disorders; attention deficit disorders; autism; vision, hearing, or speech impairments; or those with orthopedic and neurological problems. An understanding of the status of special education in India requires some understanding of its history.

The first special school was established around 1869 when Jane Leupot started one for the blind in Benares with the support of the Church Missionary Society and Raja Kali Shankar Ghosal (Miles, 1997). Another special school was established in Amritsar in 1887 by Anne Sharpe, a missionary manager (Mani, 1988; Pandey & Advani, 1997). The first school for mentally and physically disabled children was established at Kurseong in 1918 (Pandey & Advani, 1997).

The following initiatives were taken recently at the national level. The Indian Education Commission (1964 to 1966) observed that, although the Indian constitution had issued specific directives on compulsory education for all, including children with disabilities, little had been done in this regard. At the time the commission made its recommendations, there were fewer than 250 special schools. The commission recognized that services for children with disabilities were extremely inadequate and recommended the adoption of two approaches, special schools and classes as well as integrated education. The commission set the following targets to be achieved by 1986: education for about 15% of the country's blind, deaf, and orthopedically disabled and 5% of its mentally retarded persons. The commission emphasized the importance of integrated education in meeting this target as it considered integrated education to be cost effective and useful in developing mutual understanding between children with and without disabilities.

In 1974, the Ministry of Welfare initiated the Integrated Education for Disabled Children program to promote the integration of students with mild to moderate disabilities into regular schools. Children were to be provided financial support for books, stationery, school uniforms, transport, special equipment, and aides. State governments were provided 50% financial assistance to implement this program in regular schools. However, the program met with little success. Major contributory factors for its failure were the nonavailability of trained and experienced teachers, lack of orientation among school staff on the problems of disabled children and their educational needs, and nonavailability of equipment and educational materials. By 1979 to 1980, only 1,881 children from 81 schools had benefited from this program (Mani, 1988). Due to the program's failure, it was revised in 1992, incorporating various recommendations of Project Integrated Education for the Disabled. Various nongovernment organizations were entitled to implement this program. Until 1990, it was implemented in only 14 states.

The Indian government's 1986 National Policy on Education (1986 to 1992), one that applied to all government schools, articulated a need to integrate students with disabilities and attempted to promote the following goals. Children with mild disabilities were to be educated in regular schools. Children with severe disabilities were to be in special residential schools located near their homes. Vocational education was to be initiated along with teacher training programs redesigned to prepare educators to teach disabled children. All voluntary efforts were encouraged.

Again in 1986, the National Policy on Education devoted a specific section to the education of students with disabilities. It emphasized that, whenever feasible, the education of children with motor and other mild disabilities should be provided in regular schools. This policy also stressed that children whose needs could not be met in regular schools were to be enrolled in special schools. Children in special schools were to be integrated into regular schools as soon as they acquired reasonable levels of daily living, communication, and basic academic skills. The need to restructure primary teacher training programs to prepare teachers to deal with the special difficulties of children with disabilities was emphasized (National Policy on Education, 1992).

In 1987, the Ministry of Human Resource Development, in association with UNICEF and the National Council for Educational Research and Training, undertook Project Integrated Education for the Disabled. Its goal was to strengthen the implementation of the Integrated Education for the Disabled program. Instead of confining this program to a particular institution or school, this program adopted a composite area approach to address the needs of students with special needs. Schools in a particular area were requested to share resources such as specialized equipment, instructional materials, and special education teachers. The key aspect of the project was the teacher training program. Selected teachers undertook 6 weeks' intensive training in special education and were provided practical experiences in integrated and special school settings.

The project produced several positive results, including improved program planning and better management skills, thus increasing the capacity of various states to implement integration (Jangira, 1990). About 13,000 children with disabilities in eight states and two urban slums were enrolled in the program.

The 1994 District Primary Education Program emphasized in-service training of primary school teachers in such areas as early detection of disabilities, functional assessment, use of aids and appliances, and implementation of individualized education plans. This program utilized resource rooms to implement integrated education in primary schools.

The 1995 Persons with Disabilities Act marked a turning point in special education services. Although the government had made several attempts to implement integrated education programs, it lacked a firm commitment to promote integration. This largely was due to considering the provision of special education services to be a welfare issue rather than an educational issue that should be addressed by the Ministry of Education. With the passage of the 1995 Persons with Disabilities Act, the integration of students with disabilities became the legal responsibility of the Ministry of Education. The Act proposed the provision of improved educational services, medical care, vocational training and employment, and social security for all persons with disabilities. The Act further stated that, whenever possible, students with disabilities should be educated in regular school settings. The federal government's recent Five Year Plan earmarked Rs. 1,000 million (1US dollar = Rs. 43.70) for integrated education programs (Miles, 1997).

The federal government has established four national institutes of disability. These are the National Institute for the Orthopaedically Handicapped located in Calcutta and established in 1978, the National Institute for the Visually Handicapped located in Dehradun and established in 1979, the Ali Yavar Jung National Institute for the Hearing Handicapped located in Bombay and established in 1983, and the National Institute for the Mentally Handicapped located in Secunderabad and established in 1984. These institutes have played a major role in research, manpower development, documentation and information services, providing consultative services to nongovernmental organizations, and in developing service delivery models for the care and rehabilitation appropriate for local situations.

However, their manpower training efforts tended to emphasize teaching students with special needs in segregated settings. Although the educational services provided by special schools and the national institutes have contributed to some extent in meeting the needs of a large number of individuals with disabilities, current educational provisions for children with disabilities remain largely inadequate. The latest estimates indicate that more than 16 million children do not have access to any form of education (Ministry of Human Resource Development, 1998).

Various conditions are needed to contribute to the success of special education in India. Specialized teachers are needed to serve as resource persons, supported by appropriate educational texts and selected aids and appliances, to prepare special materials, and to provide special instruction according to individual needs. Consultation for regular classroom teachers, school administrators, families, local health authorities, and the general public is needed on matters dealing with education of disabled children, specialized training techniques, and selection of appropriate materials. Parent education, appropriate technology, and awareness of parent attitudes toward disabilities are needed (Jayachandran, 2000). Individual educational plans should be prepared while integrating children in regular classrooms.

Evaluation also is crucial to the development and maintenance of effective special education programs and services. The aim of the evaluation process is to encourage the best possible learning conditions for exceptional children. An important step toward the achievement of this aim is the promotion of professional classroom practices. A special educator has to be specially assigned to conduct follow-up evaluations for special children.

Sensitivity to the needs of communities in rural areas, where educational facilities are poor and one teacher schools are common, is needed. Special education is a major component of community-based rehabilitation programs and requires trained personnel for effective delivery of services. However, most services are concentrated in urban areas. Sevainaction, a voluntary organization, has attempted to understand the needs of people in rural areas and has developed a cost effective, socioculturally appropriate, comprehensive, sustainable, and holistic community–based rehabilitation program with the goal to rehabilitate all persons with disabilities in rural areas of Karnataka, South India (Nanjurdaiah, 2000).

REFERENCES

Jangira, N. K. (1990). Desirability and feasibility of integrated education for mentally retarded children. In P. Usha Rani & P. P. Reddy (Eds.), *Mental retardation in India*. Hyderabad, India: Institute of Genetics.

Jayachandran, K. R. (2000, July). *Possibility of inclusive education in India based on success of integrated education in Kerala State, India*. Paper presented in the International Special Education Congress held in Manchester, England.

Mani, C. (1988). *The physically handicapped in India*. New Delhi, India: Ashish.

Miles, M. (1997). *Disability care and education in the 19th century India: Some dates, places and documentation*. (ERIC Document No. 408747)

Ministry of Human Resource Development. (1998). *Selected educational statistics: 1998–99*. New Delhi, India: Department of Education, Planning, Monitoring & Statistics Division.

Nanjundaiah, Manjula. (2000). *Shift from rehabilitation to inclusion: Implementation of Inclusive Education (IE) through rural community based rehabilitation program of Sevainaction, India*. Paper presented in the International Special Education Congress held in Manchester, England.

National Policy on Education. (1992). Ministry of Human Resource Development, Government of India.

Pandey, R. S., & Advani, L. (1997). *Perspectives in disability and rehabilitation*. New Delhi, India: Vikas.

RUMKI GUPTA
*Indian Statistical Institute,
Kolkata, India*

INDIVIDUALIZATION OF INSTRUCTION

Individualization of instruction is a method of teaching in which instruction is tailored to the unique needs of students, enabling them to advance at their own rates and to achieve their potential. Individualized instruction requires that students be placed individually within a curriculum or sequence of objectives, and that teaching methods be prescribed so as to maximize individual growth and accomplishment. Both elements—placement and prescription—are essential to the process. Schwartz and Oseroff (1975) traced the roots of individualized instruction to Harris, who in 1868, "vigorously [sic] challenged the validity of requiring all pupils to do the same amount of work and to advance at the same time" (p. 26). Nonetheless, formal recognition of its critical role in special education awaited the enactment of the Education for All Handicapped Children Act of 1975 (PL 94-142).

Public Law 94-142 and subsequent legislation, including in particular the Individuals with Disabilities Education Act (IDEA), assigned to state and local education agencies the responsibility to provide free, appropriate education to meet the unique needs of exceptional children. The act delineated guidelines for individualized placement and prescription by requiring an individual educational program (IEP) for every student with a disability. The IEP includes, among other things, statements of present levels of educational performance, annual goals, short-term objectives, and specific educational services to be provided. Ideally, then, an IEP must embody the elements of individualized instruction and in so doing "represents a formalization of the diagnostic/prescriptive approach to education" (Safer, Morrissey, Kaufman, & Lewis, 1978, p. 1).

Individualized placement within a curriculum or sequence of objectives may be accomplished through a variety of means. Many curricula include placement tests that can be used to identify the material that students have and have not mastered. However, these instruments are apparently not developed with the same rigor as standardized tests because their technical properties (reliability and validity) often fall short of established standards. Criterion referenced tests, those that sample performance within a specified instructional domain, have stronger technical properties but may not necessarily correspond to particular curricula. Recent efforts to link performance on criterion referenced tests to placement levels within curricula bode well for their continued use in the future. Precision teaching (PT) and databased program modification (DBPM) define instructional levels in terms of performance within the curriculum itself and represent another useful alternative for making individualized placements.

The prescription of individualized instructional methodologies represents a more difficult problem because efforts to predict how teaching methods interact with learner characteristics have not yet proved fruitful. At the present, post hoc validation represents the most well established approach to determining the effectiveness of instructional programs (Salvia & Sindelar, 1982). Frequent and repeated assessments of performance are evaluated against predetermined criteria to establish the adequacy of an instructional program. Here again, PT and DBPM provide methodologies for conducting such post hoc analyses.

Individualization of instruction is not synonymous and should not be confused with one-to-one instruction. The latter may or may not be individualized; the former may be accomplished with groups. Similarly, individualized instruction does not necessarily require that students work independently on seatwork tasks. Effective individualized instruction can occur in teacher led groups (Stevens & Rosenshine, 1980).

REFERENCES

Safer, D., Morrissey, A., Kaufman, J., & Lewis, L. (1978). Implementation of IEPs: New teacher roles and requisite support systems. *Focus on Exceptional Children, 10,* 1–20.

Salvia, J., & Sindelar, P. T. (1982). Aptitude testing and alternative approaches to maximizing the effects of instruction. In T. L. Miller & E. E. Davis (Eds.), *The mildly handicapped student* (pp. 221–240). New York, NY: Grune & Stratton.

Schwartz, L., & Oseroff, A. (1975). *The clinical teacher for special education: Vol. 1. Establishing the model.* Final Report, USOE, HEW/BEH Grant No. OEG0711688 (603). Tallahassee: Florida State University.

Stevens, R., & Rosenshine, B. (1980). Advances in research on teaching. *Exceptional Education Quarterly, 2,* 1–9.

PAUL T. SINDELAR
RHONDA COLLINS
Florida State University
Second edition

KIMBERLY F. APPLEQUIST
University of Colorado at Colorado Springs
Third edition

See also Data-Based Instruction; Individualized Educational Plan; Precision Teaching

INDIVIDUALIZED EDUCATIONAL PLAN

IEP is the acronym for the individualized educational plan that must now be written for each identified child with a disability prior to his or her placement in a special education program. The Education of All Handicapped Children Act of 1975 (PL 94-142) and subsequent legislation such as the Individuals with Disabilities Education Act (IDEA) required that states receiving federal funds for special education services develop and implement a written statement regarding the specific special educational services and related services each child with a disability is to receive. At a minimum, it is mandatory that each written plan include five points:

1. A statement of the child's present levels of educational performance, including:

    (i) How the child's disability affects the child's involvement and progress in the general curriculum (i.e., the same curriculum as for nondisabled children); or

    (ii) For preschool children, as appropriate, how the disability affects the child's participation in appropriate activities.

2. A statement of measurable annual goals, including benchmarks or short-term institutional objectives related to:

    (i) Meeting the child's needs that result from the child's disability to enable the child to be involved in and progress in the general curriculum (i.e., the same curriculum as for nondisabled children), or for preschool children, as appropriate, to participate in appropriate activities; and

    (ii) Meeting each of the child's other educational needs that result from the child's disability.

3. A statement of special education and related services and supplementary aids and services to be provided to the child, or on behalf of the child, and a statement of the program modifications or supports for school personnel that will be provided for the child:

    (i) To advance appropriately toward attaining the annual goals.

    (ii) To be involved and progress in the general curriculum in accordance with paragraph 1, and to participate in extracurricular and other nonacademic activities; and

    (iii) To be educated with other children with disabilities and nondisabled children in the activities described in this section.

4. An explanation of the extent, if any, to which the child will not participate with nondisabled children in the regular class and in the activities described in paragraph 3.

5. (i) A statement of any individual modifications in the administration of state or district-wide assessments of student achievement that are needed in order for the child to participate in the assessment; and

    (ii) If the IEP team determines that the child will not participate in a particular state or district-wide assessment of student achievement (or part of an assessment) a statement of:

    a. Why that assessment is not appropriate for the child; and

    b. How the child will be assessed.

6. The projected date for the beginning of services and modifications, and the anticipated frequency, location, and duration of those services and modifications.

7. A statement of:

    (i) How the child's progress toward the annual goals described in paragraph 2 will be measured; and

    (ii) How the child's parents will be regularly informed (through such means as periodic report cards), at least as often as parents are informed of their nondisabled child's progress, of:

a. Their child's progress toward the annual goals; and

b. The extent to which that progress is sufficient to enable to achieve the goals by the end of the year. (34 CFR § 300.347[a])

In addition, beginning at age 14 (or earlier if deemed appropriate by the IEP team), the IEP must include a statement of the transition service needs of the student, focusing on the student's course of study. Beginning at the age of 16 (or earlier, again, as deemed appropriate by the IEP team), the IEP must also include "a statement of needed transitions services for the student, including, if appropriate, a statement of the interagency responsibilities or any needed linkages" (34 CFR § 300.347[b]). There are additional requirements regarding notice to the student in states where rights are transferred when the student reaches his or her majority. There are also special requirements for students with disabilities convicted of criminal offenses as adults and imprisoned in adult correctional facilities (34 CFR § 300.311[b] and [c]). Proposed regulations implementing the most recent reauthorization of the IDEA, issued June 21, 2005, would make minor, primarily non-substantive changes to the requirements of 34 CFR § 300.347 (70 Fed. Reg. 35865).

Under these guidelines, the IEP team must meet at least once a year to review and, if necessary, revise the educational program as originally outlined. It is obvious that the goals—long or short range—specified in the initial IEP would periodically be in need of revision for a number of reasons: The original goals may be inappropriate for the individual child, or the child may meet or make progress on many of the goals, thus requiring revision and development of new goals.

According to some authorities (e.g., Reynolds, Gutkin, Elliot, & Witt, 1984), once a year reviewing is not enough to ensure the best educational programming for a handicapped child. They do, however, acknowledge that this mandated requirement is far better than prior practices that seldom ensured the review of educational plans for handicapped students.

Although the intent of the law is commendable, the actual implementation is often less than satisfactory. One example involves the extent to which the IEP is in fact individualized for the child. It is not uncommon for educational programs to be designed specific to the child's classification (e.g., learning disabled) rather than the unique abilities of the child involved. Often individualized educational plans will simply be a reflection of the specific district or school the child attends. For example, states will frequently mandate that all children meet certain objectives within a given subject (e.g., reading). Therefore, it is not uncommon to find the short-range objectives specified for the learning disabled child in reading to be simply a list of the reading objectives common to the district. This practice would seem in direct contradiction to the intent of the law and certainly not always in the best interests of the child with disabilities involved. Indeed, special educators have questioned the general value of these types of IEPs (Ryan & Rucher, 1991).

The law also stipulates who should be present at each IEP meeting, whether it be for the purposes of developing, reviewing, or revising a child's IEP. The educational agency is charged with ensuring that those individuals are present. According to the IDEA implementing regulations, the IEP team must include:

1. The parents of the child.
2. At least one regular education teacher of the child (if the child is, or may be, participating in the regular education environment).
3. At least one special education teacher of the child, or if appropriate, at least one special education provider of the child.
4. A representative of the public agency who:
   a. Is qualified to provide, or supervise the provision of, specially designed instruction to meet the unique needs of children with disabilities.
   b. Is knowledgeable about the general curriculum.
   c. Is knowledgeable about the availability of resources of the public agency.
5. An individual who can interpret the instructional implications of evaluation results, who may be a member of the team described in paragraphs (2) through (6) of this section.
6. At the discussion of the parent or the agency, other individuals who have knowledge or special expertise regarding the child, including related services personnel as appropriate.
7. If appropriate, the child. (34 CFR §300.344)

The proposed regulations issued in June of 2005 make only nonsubstantive changes to these requirements (70 Fed. Reg. 35866).

In keeping with another major intent of IDEA to protect the rights of parents of children with disabilities to fully participate in their child's education, each public agency is charged with the responsibility of exerting maximum effort in ensuring that one or both parents are present and participating (Van Reusen & Bos, 1994) at meetings where the IEP is developed, reviewed, and revised. To be in compliance with the law, the public agency serving the child with disabilities must have proof that they not only gave parents notice of the meeting, including all details, but that the meeting was arranged at a time that is mutually convenient to all involved. If the parents cannot attend the meeting, the agency must show that parent participation was elicited via other means (e.g., telephone conversations). Whether or not the parents are able to attend, they are to be given a copy of the IEP.

Various studies have been conducted investigating parental participation in IEP development and planning (e.g., Lusthaus, Lusthaus, & Gibbs, 1981; Polifka, 1981; Roit & Pfohl, 1984; Scanlon, Arick, & Phelps, 1981; Yoshida, Fenton, Kaufman, & Maxwell, 1978). Yoshida et al. (1978) found that educational personnel involved in the planning meeting expected parents to simply provide information as opposed to actively participating in the decisions as to what would constitute the plan. Interestingly, results of a parental survey conducted by Lusthaus et al. (1981) found that parents agreed that their role should be that of information giver and receiver instead of equal decision maker. This has slowly changed (Van Reusen & Bos, 1994). Roit and Pfohl (1984) indicated that printed information provided to parents regarding PL 94-142 and their rights (including their right to participate in the IEP process) was often not comprehensible to a large number of parents. More recent legislation and rulemaking has imposed stricter requirements about the notice to be provided to parents to make such notice more comprehensible to parents of children with disabilities.

Polifka (1981) reported on the results of a survey conducted as part of the Iowa Department of Public Instruction evaluation of special education services by a specific area agency. He found that parent satisfaction with the services their child received was significantly related to, among other variables, whether they were asked to help develop the IEP and whether they were invited to a meeting to review the IEP. It is impossible to determine the actual involvement these parents were allowed or whether the involvement was responsible for their satisfaction, but it does seem that active involvement should be fostered not only to ensure compliance but to promote active decision making roles for the parents of children with disabilities.

REFERENCES

Lusthaus, C. S., Lusthaus, E. W., & Gibbs, H. (1981). Parents' role in the decision process. *Exceptional Children, 48*(3), 256–257.

Polifka, J. C. (1981). Compliance with Public Law 94-142 and consumer satisfaction. *Exceptional Children, 48*(3), 250–253.

Reynolds, C. R., Gutkin, T. B., Elliot, S. N., & Witt, J. C. (1984). *School psychology: Essentials of theory and practice*. New York, NY: Wiley.

Roit, M. L., & Pfohl, W. (1984). The readability of PL 94-142 parent materials: Are parents truly informed? *Exceptional Children, 50*(6), 496–506.

Ryan, L. G., & Rucher, C. N. (1991). The development and validation of a measure of special education teachers' attitudes toward the IEP. *Educational and Psychological Measurement, 51*(4), 877–882.

Scanlon, C. A., Arick, J. R., & Phelps, N. (1981). Participation in development of the IEP: Parents' perspective. *Exceptional Children, 47*(5), 373–376.

Van Reusen, A. K., & Bos, C. S. (1994). Facilitating student participation in individualized education programs through motivational strategy instruction. *Exceptional Children, 60*(5), 466–475.

Yoshida, R., Fenton, K., Kaufman, M. J., & Maxwell, J. P. (1978). Parental involvement in the special education pupil planning process: The school's perspective. *Exceptional Children, 44*, 531–533.

Julia A. Hickman
Bastrop Mental Health Association
Second edition

Kimberly F. Applequist
University of Colorado at Colorado Springs
Third edition

INDIVIDUALIZED TRANSITION PLAN

The Individuals with Disabilities Education Improvement Act (IDEIA) mandates public schools to develop Individualized Transition Plans (ITP) for students, no later than 16 years of age, who need to prepare for adult life after leaving high school. Transition services are defined as a set of coordinated activities that assist the students' movement from school into self-determined, independent, satisfying, adult lives. The 2004 reauthorization of the IDEA includes more effective transition planning requirements to benefit students with Individualized Education Programs (IEPs). The ITP should be the focal point of the IEP meeting and is the section of the IEP that outlines transition goals and services for the student and is the template for mapping out long-term adult outcomes from which annual goals and objectives are defined. The ITP is a written plan identifying the progressive steps a student will take to meet postgraduation goals. Required elements of transition planning begin with the transition assessment process (transition assessments should be an ongoing process and not a onetime event) including multiple relevant assessments such as student interviews, interest inventories, and self-determination skills assessments. The ITP is made up of five core components: (1) postsecondary goals, (2) annual goals/objectives, (3) course of study, (4) transition activities, and (5) linkages with adult agencies.

1. *Postsecondary goals.* The IEP for a student of transition age must include measurable postsecondary goals that articulate what the student would like to achieve after high school. These goals must be based on the student's strengths, preferences, interests and age-appropriate transition assessment information.

Postsecondary goals should be discussed, developed, and written into the IEP transition plan before developing the rest of the IEP for a transition-age student. Postsecondary goals and outcomes must be written for the following two areas: (1) education and/or training (e.g., community college, university, trade, technical or vocational school, career field training, apprenticeship, on-the-job training) and (2) employment (e.g., competitive, supported, or military). If appropriate for individual students, postsecondary goals and outcomes should be written for independent living skills.

2. *Annual goals/objectives.* Measureable annual goals must be included so that adequate progress toward postsecondary goals are being met. Some states require the inclusion of short-term objectives in the ITP.

3. *Course of study.* The course of study is the series of courses and/or settings in which students will receive instruction. A course of study (i.e., classes and after-school clubs/organizations) should be determined mostly by the student's desired postschool outcomes. The purpose is to create a long-range educational plan or multiyear description of the educational program that directly relates to the student's anticipated postschool goals.

4. *Transition activities.* Transition services and activities should be clearly articulated in the ITP and should support the student's course of study. Activities and services may address areas such as academic instruction, related services as defined by IDEIA, community participation, career development; adult living; daily living skills, and functional vocation evaluation (McPartland, 2005). This section of the IEP may be thought of as the "action plan" and it should be easily understood by the student, parents, and professionals.

5. *Linkages with adult agencies.* IEP team members must identify adult agencies that are likely to work with the transitioning student post high school. This section must delineate responsible individuals and/or agencies and request that they are a member of the transition planning team. Each transition activity must have a designated person (i.e., adult service provider or secondary education provider) that is aligned with each activity.

REFERENCES

McPartland, P. (2005). *Implementing ongoing transition plans for the IEP: A student-driven approach to IDEA mandates.* Verona, WI: IEP Attainment.

ANTHONY J. PLOTNER
University of South Carolina
Fourth edition

INDIVIDUALS WITH DISABILITIES EDUCATION ACT, HISTORY OF

In the early 1970s only 20% of children with disabilities were educated in America's public schools. These students were denied educational opportunities in two major ways. First, many students were completely excluded from public schools. Congressional findings in 1974 indicated that more 1.75 million students with disabilities did not receive educational services. In fact, some states had laws that actually excluded certain categories of students with disabilities. Second, more than 3 million students with disabilities who were admitted to school did not receive an education that was appropriate to their needs. Because of limited educational opportunities offered by public schools, families were often forced to look elsewhere for appropriate services, often at great distance from their homes and at their own expense. The lack of educational programs and the haphazard nature of services for students with disabilities often led to parents and advocates to seek solutions through court actions.

Litigation and the Education of Students With Disabilities

The civil rights movement of the 1950s and 1960s encouraged the use of courts in forcing states to provide appropriate public education for disabled children's unique educational needs. Advocates for students with disabilities argued that if racial segregation was a denial of equal educational opportunity, then the exclusion of students with disabilities from schools was a denial as well.

Beginning in the early 1970s, advocates for students with disabilities began to sue states, claiming that exclusion and inappropriate educational services violated students' rights to equal educational opportunity under the U.S. Constitution. In 1972, two landmark court cases, *PARC v. Commonwealth of Pennsylvania* and *Mills v. Board of Education of the District of Columbia* helped establish the right of students with disabilities to receive public education. Both cases resulted in schools being required to provide access to students with disabilities.

Within the next two years, 46 similar right-to-education cases were heard in 28 states. These cases clearly established the rights of students with disabilities to participate in publicly supported educational programs. Despite these rulings and the enactment of laws in states establishing these educational rights, however, many students with disabilities were still denied services. Additionally, a great variability of level and quality of services existed across the states. Because of this unevenness in the special education services, many parents, educators, and legislators believed a federal standard was needed.

Federal Legislation and the Education of Students With Disabilities

Given the challenges faced by students with disabilities in their efforts to access educational services, the uneven attempts to provide education to these students, and the activism by concerned parents, the U.S. Congress began enacting legislation to assure the educational rights of students with disabilities. In this legislation, Congress sought to establish a federal mandatory base to create a floor of educational responsibility that cut across state and local boundaries.

On November 29, 1975, President Gerald Ford signed into law the most significant increase in the role of the federal government in special education to date—the Education for All Handicapped Children Act of 1975 (hereafter EAHCA), often called *PL 94-142*, the EAHCA combined an educational bill of rights with the promise of federal financial incentives to states that chose to accept EAHCA funds. The law offered grants to states that provided direct services to students with disabilities covered by the law.

Through this law, the federal government offered grants to states that provided appropriate educational programs for students with disabilities who were covered by the EAHCA. To receive funding under the EAHCA, states had to pass laws and prove they were educating students with disabilities in accordance with the law's principles. With the passage of the EAHCA, therefore, the federal government partnered with states in educating students with disabilities. In 1990 the EAHCA was amended in the Individuals with Disabilities Education Act (IDEA). The name of the law, EAHCA, was changed to the IDEA.

The Structure of the Individuals With Disabilities Education Act

The IDEA is divided into four provisions. Part A contains definitions of terms, the general provision of the Act. Part B contains the explanation of the provisions of providing assistance for education of all children with disabilities. Part C covers infants and toddlers from birth through age 2. Part D of the IDEA contains provisions for national activities to improve education of children with disabilities. The activities funded by Part D include research and innovation activities to improve services and results for children with disabilities, through technical assistance activities of parents and personnel preparation to improve such services.

States that meet the IDEA requirements receive federal funding for the education of children with disabilities. The IDEA funds are received by the state educational agency (SEA) for distribution to the local educational agencies (LEA). The federal funds do not cover the entire cost of special education, but rather are intended to provide financial assistance to the states. Congress originally intended to fund 40% of states' costs in providing special education and related services through the IDEA. The actual levels of funding to the states, however, usually amounted to approximately 8% to 10% of states' total special education expenditures. Thus, the IDEA has never been fully funded in accordance with the original Congressional intentions in 1975.

The Major Principles of the Individuals With Disabilities Education Act

Some scholars have divided Part B into six major principles for discussion purposes. Although this is a useful structure for purposes of discussion, neither the IDEA's statutory language nor the U.S. Department of Education recognizes the division of the law into these six principles.

Zero Reject

The zero reject principle requires that all students with disabilities who are eligible for services under the IDEA receive a special education services designed to meet their unique needs. This principle applies regardless of the severity of the child's disability.

States must ensure that all students with disabilities, from age 3 to 21, residing in the state who are in need of special education and related services, or are suspected of having disabilities and in need of special education, are identified, located, and evaluated. A student is eligible for the IDEA if he or she has at least one of 13 types of disability specifically listed under the IDEA and who needs special education and related services.[1]

Protection in Evaluation

Before a student can receive special education and related services for the first time, he or she must receive a full and individual evaluation. Prior to conducting an evaluation for special education eligibility, however, a school district must obtain parental consent. When consent is received, the team must conduct the individualized evaluation. The IDEA contains extensive procedural requirements that must be followed when conducting the evaluation. A fair and accurate evaluation is extremely important to ensure proper programming and placement.

On completing the administration of tests and other evaluation materials, a group of qualified professionals and the parents of the child must determine whether the child has a disability under the IDEA. Additionally, the team must determine whether the disability adversely

---

[1]The disability categories are: autism, deaf-blind, deafness, emotional disturbance, hearing impairment, mental retardation, multiple disabilities, orthopedic impairments, other health impairment, specific learning disability, speech and language impairment, traumatic brain injury, and visual impairment including blindness.

affects a child's educational performance, and therefore requires that he or she receive special education services. When an evaluation team has decided that a student qualifies for special education under the IDEA, a team is appointed to develop the student's individualized education program (IEP).

Free Appropriate Public Education

Students who are eligible for special education under the IDEA have the right to receive a FAPE, consisting of special education and related services that (a) are provided at public expense; (b) are under public supervision and direction, and without charge; (c) meet the standards of the SEA; (d) include preschool, elementary school, or secondary school education in the child's state; and (e) are provided in conformity with an IEP that meets the requirements of the IDEA.

The key to providing a FAPE is individualized programming. To ensure that each student covered by the IDEA receives a FAPE, Congress required that school-based teams develop IEPs for all students with disabilities receiving special education services. The IEP is both a collaborative process between the parents and the school, and a written document, developed by a team of educators and a student's parents. The IEP describes a student's educational needs and details the special education and related services that will be provided to the student. The document also contains a student's goals and how his or her educational progress will be measured. Students' IEPs must address involvement and participation in the general education curriculum. The IDEA mandates the process and procedures for developing the IEP.

Least Restrictive Environment

The IDEA mandates that students with disabilities are educated with their peers without disabilities to the maximum extent appropriate. This requirement ensures that students with disabilities are educated in the least restrictive environment (LRE) that is suitable for their individual needs.

Moreover, students in special education can only be removed from the regular classroom when the nature or severity of the child's disability means that the child cannot receive an appropriate education in a general education classroom with supplementary aids and services. The exact nature of the placement that is the LRE for a particular student can only be determined, therefore, after the team has decided what educational services are necessary for the student to receive a FAPE. This requirement allows school districts to move students to more restrictive settings when a general education setting is not appropriate for the student and a more restrictive setting is need to provide a FAPE. Thus, program appropriateness is the primary IDEA mandate, and LRE is secondary.

To ensure that students are educated in the appropriate LRE, school districts must provide a complete continuum of alternative placements ranging from less restrictive settings to more restrictive and specialized settings. The purpose of the continuum of placements is to allow school personnel to choose from a number of options when determining the most appropriate and least restrictive placement for a student. The most typical and least restrictive setting on the continuum of placements is the regular education classroom. Additional settings that must be available include special classes, special schools, home instruction, and instruction in hospitals and institutions.

When determining the educational placement of a child with a disability each public agency shall ensure that the placement decision is made by a group of persons, including the parents and other persons knowledgeable about the child, the meaning of the evaluation data, and the placement options are made in conformity with the LRE provisions of the IDEA. The child's placement is determined at least annually and must be based on the child's IEP and be as close as possible to the child's home. Unless IEPs require some other arrangement, students should be educated in the school that they would attend if they did not have a disability.

Procedural Safeguards

The IDEA contains an extensive system of procedural safeguards to ensure that all eligible students with disabilities receive a FAPE. Schools must follow these safeguards when developing special education programs for students with disabilities. The purpose of the these procedures is to safeguard a student's right to a FAPE by ensuring that parents are meaningfully involved in the education of their children. These safeguards include (a) prior notice, (b) informed parental consent, (c) an opportunity to examine records, (d) the right to an independent educational evaluation at public expense, and (e) the right to request an impartial due process hearing.

Additionally, when there is disagreement between the school and the parents on any proposals to initiate or change the identification, evaluation, educational placement, or the provision of FAPE to the child, or if the school refuses to initiate or change any of these areas, parents, school districts, or the SEA may initiate an impartial due process hearing. States offer parents the option of resolving their disputes through mediation prior to a due process hearing. The mediation process is voluntary, however, and must not be used to deny or delay a parent's right to a due process hearing. Additionally, prior to going to a due process hearing, a school must enter into a resolution session to try to solve the problem before it goes to hearing.

Any party in a due process hearing has the right to be accompanied and advised by counsel and individuals with special knowledge or training regarding the problems of children with disabilities. While this decision is binding on both parties, either party may appeal the decision to state or federal court.

Parent Participation

Since the early days of special education litigation, parents of children with disabilities have played important roles in helping schools meet the educational needs of their children. In fact, parents are coequal partners in the IEP process.

Summary

Few parents, educators, advocates, and researchers would dispute the tremendous benefits children and youth with disabilities and their families have received as a result of the IDEA. In 25 years, the IDEA has clearly met its original goal: To open the doors of public education to students with disabilities. Today, this right is assured for virtually all eligible students with disabilities, including children with severe and profound disabilities.

This entry has been informed by the sources listed below.

REFERENCES

U.S. Department of Education. (2002). *No child left behind: A desktop reference*. Washington, DC: Education Publications Center. Available at http://www.ed.gov/

Yell, M. L. (2012). *The law and special education* (3rd ed). Upper Saddle River, NJ: Pearson.

MITCHELL YELL
South Carolina State University
Fourth edition

INDIVIDUALS WITH DISABILITIES EDUCATION IMPROVEMENT ACT OF 2004 (IDEIA)

The Individuals with Disabilities Education Act (IDEA), formerly known as the Education for All Handicapped Children Act of 1975 (EHA; PL 94-142), and most recently amended in 2004 by the Individuals with Disabilities Education Improvement Act (IDEIA; PL 108-446), represents a more than 30-year national commitment, beginning with EHA, to children with disabilities. IDEA, a federal statute, is the main special education law in the United States, and when initially enacted in 1975, it represented the most sweeping statement this nation has ever made regarding the rights of children with disabilities (Haring, McCormick, & Haring, 1994). The purpose of the law, as most recently articulated by the IDEA, is:

(1)(A) to ensure that all children with disabilities have available to them a free appropriate public education that emphasizes special education and related services designed to meet their unique needs and prepare them for further education, employment, and independent living; (B) to ensure that the rights of children with disabilities and parents of such children are protected; and (C) to assist States, localities, educational service agencies and Federal agencies to provide for the education of all children with disabilities; (2) to assist States in the implementation of a statewide, comprehensive, coordinated, multidisciplinary, interagency system of early intervention services for infants and toddlers with disabilities and their families; (3) to ensure that educators and parents have the necessary tools to improve educational results for children with disabilities by supporting system improvement activities; coordinated research and personnel preparation; coordinated technical assistance, dissemination, and support; and technology development and media services; and, (4) to assess, and ensure the effectiveness of, efforts to educate children with disabilities. (20 U.S.C. § 1400[d]; Sec. 601[d])

Historical Background

Early legislation and case law, spanning over a 20-year period, foreshadowed the enactment of the initial version of the law, EHA, in 1975 (Jacob-Timm & Hartshorne, 1995). Three landmark court cases, *Brown* v. *Board of Education of Topeka* (1954), *Pennsylvania Association for Retarded Children* v. *Commonwealth of Pennsylvania* (PARC; 1971, 1972), and *Mills* v. *Board of Education* (1972), marked a turning point in the education of children with disabilities and provided the impetus for the development and enactment of federal legislation assuring a free appropriate public education for children with disabilities. Prior to the *Brown* case, many school districts throughout the nation were operated under the "separate but equal" policy (i.e., segregated classrooms based on race) that were in actuality not equal. Many minorities (African Americans, in the case of *Brown*) were excluded from an equal educational opportunity in public schools. This practice, according to the *Brown* ruling, was in violation of the "equal protection clause" of the 14th Amendment to the U.S. Constitution. Education, which is considered to be a property right, is protected under the equal protection clause, and in the *Brown* ruling, the property right of African Americans to an education at the public expense was violated by the school district's racially discriminatory policies (Jacob-Timm & Hartshorne, 1995).

Following the *Brown* ruling and other successful court challenges to racial discrimination in the public schools, parents of children with disabilities began to file lawsuits on behalf of their children, alleging that the children's right to an education at the public expense was being violated under the equal protection clause. Prior to the 1970s, many schools denied children with disabilities access to a public education based on school district policies, which required a child to meet certain admission standards (e.g., possession of a certain level of adaptive living and cognitive skills). In *PARC*, parents of children with Mental Retardation brought suit against Pennsylvania because their children were denied access to a public education. In a consent decree, the parents of the children with Mental Retardation won access to the public schools for their children. Similarly, in *Mills*, the parents of children with behavioral, emotional, and learning problems brought suit on behalf of their children against the District of Columbia for denial of access to a public education. In a consent decree followed by a court order, the court ruled that the schools were required to provide each child with a disability a free and public-supported education, regardless of the degree of severity or nature of the child's disability (Jacob-Timm & Hartshorne, 1995).

In response to the successful resolution of the *PARC* and *Mills* cases, 36 additional "right-to-education" cases were filed in 27 different jurisdictions by parents on behalf of their children with disabilities (Martin, 1979). These cases served as a signal to the U.S. Congress that federal legislation was needed to ensure a full educational opportunity to all children with disabilities (Jacob-Timm & Hartshorne, 1995).

In addition to case law, early attempts were made by the U.S. Congress to address the needs of children with disabilities. Funds were made available through various education laws and amendments to develop or improve special education resources, programs, services, and personnel. Beginning as early as the 1960s with the passage of PL 87-276, Congress authorized support for the training of teachers to work with the deaf and for speech pathologists and audiologists to work with individuals with speech and hearing impairments (Abramson, 1987; Reynolds & Fletcher-Janzen, 1990). In 1965, the Elementary and Secondary Education Act (ESEA; PL 8910), one of the first major federal programs to aid education, was enacted. One year later, Congress amended the ESEA (PL 89-750) and, with these amendments, grants were provided to states to assist in the development and improvement of programs to educate children with disabilities (Jacob-Timm & Hartshorne, 1995). Students with disabilities were also assisted when the 1968 Amendments to the Vocational Education Act (PL 90-576) were passed. With these amendments, funds were made available for students with disabilities in vocational education programs (Abramson, 1987; Reynolds & Fletcher-Janzen, 1990). The needs of young children with disabilities were addressed with the establishment of model programs under the Handicapped Children's Early Education Assistance Act (PL 90-538) in 1968 (Abramson, 1987; Reynolds & Fletcher-Janzen, 1990). In 1970, Congress repealed and replaced the 1966 amendments to the ESEA (PL 89-750; Jacob-Timm & Hartshorne, 1995). Public Law 99-230, which replaced PL 89-750, established a grant program similar to PL 89-750 to encourage states to develop special education resources and personnel (Turnbull, 1990). Federal

government assistance to states for special education increased with the passage of the Education Amendments of 1974 (PL 93-380). This act also put schools on notice that federal funding for special education purposes would be contingent on the development of a state plan with the goal of providing children with disabilities a full educational opportunity (Jacob-Timm & Hartshorne, 1995).

Congress also attempted to address the needs of children with disabilities through antidiscrimination legislation (Martin, 1979). An amendment to Title VI of the Civil Rights Act of 1964 was one of the first pieces of legislation that attempted to ensure equal educational opportunities for children with disabilities. Nine years later, this amendment became part of Section 504 of the Rehabilitation Act of 1973. Section 504 is a civil rights act that prohibits discrimination against children with disabilities in schools receiving federal funds. Federal funds are not available to schools not in compliance with the act (Jacob-Timm & Hartshorne, 1995).

Through enactment of antidiscrimination legislation and education laws, passage of amendments to existing education laws, and litigation, the stage was set for the introduction of a comprehensive federal statute that would reaffirm and strengthen the educational rights of children with disabilities and increase the federal government's financial commitment to children with disabilities (Abramson, 1987; Reynolds & Fletcher-Janzen, 1990). The Education for All Handicapped Children Act was originally introduced as a Senate bill in 1972. After 3 years of extensive hearings, the U.S. Congress passed the bill in 1975 and President Gerald Ford signed the bill into law on November 29, 1975. EHA was amended in 1978 (PL 98-733), 1983 (PL 98-199), twice in 1986 (PL 99-457 and PL 99-372), in 1988 (PL 100-630), and 1990 (PL 101-476; Jacob-Timm & Hartshorne, 1995).

In 1990, President George H. W. Bush signed PL 104-476 into law. The 1990 Amendments changed the EHA's name to the Individuals with Disabilities Education Act. The law was significantly amended and reauthorized in 1997 (PL 105-17) and signed into law by President Bill Clinton. The 1997 act restructured the IDEA into four parts: Part A, General Provisions; Part B, Assistance for Education of All Children with Disabilities; Part C, Infants and Toddlers with Disabilities; and Part D, National Activities to Improve Education of Children with Disabilities (PL 105-17).

In 2002, Congress passed the cornerstone of President George W. Bush's education reform package, the controversial No Child Left Behind Act (NCLB; PL 107-110), which made significant changes to the ESEA. The intent behind the NCLB is to improve education by increasing teacher and school accountability, primarily through increased testing of all students' reading and math skills and requirements that schools demonstrate "adequate yearly progress" in their students' proficiency. Students in special education programs are not exempt from the

NCLB's requirement that schools demonstrate adequate yearly progress. States and school districts are allowed to use alternate assessment standards in determining whether certain students meet proficiency requirements, but only for a maximum of 1% of their students, regardless of the number of students who might have serious learning disabilities or otherwise be considered children with disabilities under the IDEA. The NCLB also imposes teacher education requirements, promotes the use of evidence-based educational interventions, and provides parents with some ability to choose alternate schools if their child's local school fails to demonstrate adequate yearly progress for a specified period of time (Applequist, 2005). The law continues to generate controversy due to what one organization describes as the law's focus on "punishments rather than assistance, mandates rather than support for effective programs, [and] privatization rather than teacher-led, family oriented solutions" (National Education Association, n.d.).

When the IDEA next came before Congress for reauthorization, numerous changes were made in the statute to bring it into compliance with NCLB. The reauthorizing bill, IDEIA (PL 108-446), was enacted on December 3, 2004, by President George W. Bush. The majority of the IDEA's provisions went into effect on July 1, 2005, though most of the regulations regarding implementing IDEA were not published until 2006 (Jacob, Decker, & Hartshorne, 2011).

The Department of Education published regulations to implement the 2004 legislation for IDEA Part B in the Federal Register on August 14, 2006 (71 Fed. Reg. 46,540), with supplemental regulations published on December 1, 2008 (73 Fed. Reg. 73,006). Proposed regulations for IDEA Part C were published in 2007 but were withdrawn. As of August 2011, revised proposed new rules for Part C had not been published (Jacob et al., 2011).

The IDEA consists of three titles. Title I, which is the primary focus of this article, amends and restates the IDEA, retaining the four-part structure established by the 1997 amendments. It is in Title I that the majority of changes relating to NCLB appear. Title II amends the Education Sciences Reform Act of 2002 (20 U.S.C. § 9501 et seq.), establishing a National Center for Special Education Research to sponsor research into the needs of infants, toddlers, and children with disabilities to improve their developmental, educational, and transitional results and research to improve services provided under the IDEA and support its implementation (20 U.S.C. § 9567). Title III makes miscellaneous changes to other statutory provisions, primarily in order to make them consistent with the changes to the law made by Titles I and II.

IDEA Overview

The key provisions of IDEA include the requirement that states provide a free appropriate public education (FAPE) for all children qualified under the statute, nondiscriminatory assessment, the individualized education program (IEP), procedural safeguards, confidentiality of records, provision of education services in the least restrictive environment (LRE), and related services. State educational agencies (SEAs) are responsible for ensuring that local educational agencies (LEAs) provide FAPE to all children with disabilities. A free appropriate public education must be made available to all children with disabilities, regardless of the nature or severity of their disability, and consists of special education and related services. *Related services* are support services required to assist children with disabilities to benefit from special education. Examples of related services include psychological services, physical and occupational therapy, speech pathology, audiology, and orientation and mobility services. Related services cannot stand alone under Part B of the IDEA. Instead, such services must be attached to a special education program. In other words, a child must be eligible for special education under IDEA Part B in order to receive related services (34 C.F.R. § 300.8). Special education and related services must be provided to children with disabilities at no cost to the children's parents or the children (34 C.F.R. § 300.34[c]).

Another key requirement of the IDEA is nondiscriminatory assessment. Testing and evaluation materials must be selected and administered so as not to be culturally or racially discriminatory. In addition, tests must be administered in the child's native language or other mode of communication, unless it is unfeasible to do so. LEAs must also ensure that standardized tests given to a child are validated for the purpose for which they are used and are administered by trained personnel in accordance with the test producer's instructions. The child must be assessed in all areas of suspected disability. The child must also be assessed with a variety of technically sound assessment tools and strategies, the instruments must be technically sound, and no single procedure must be used as the sole criterion for determining eligibility (34 C.F.R. § 300.306[a][2]).

Prior to the 2004 amendments, IDEA regulations stated that a team could only determine that a child has a specific learning disability if the child had a severe discrepancy between an area of academic achievement and intellectual ability. Under IDEA 2004, schools no longer are required to take into consideration whether a severe discrepancy exists between achievement and intellectual ability; states "must permit the use of a process based on the child's response to scientific, research based interventions" 34 C.F.R. § 300.307[a][2]). In practice, this means that standardized tests of intellectual ability and academic achievement are no longer requirements for the diagnosis of a learning disability.

An IEP is required for each child with a disability who is receiving special education. The initial IEP meeting must be held within 30 days after the determination that the child needs special education and related services (34.

C.F.R. § 300.323 [c][1]). Each LEA must have an IEP in place for each such child at the beginning of each school year. The child's IEP is reviewed and revised on at least an annual basis by the IEP team, and a reevaluation is conducted at least once every 3 years. The IEP team consists of the parent of the child, at least one special education teacher and one regular education teacher if the child is or may be participating in the regular education program, a representative of the LEA who is qualified to provide or supervise the provision of specially designed instruction and who is knowledgeable about the general curriculum and resources available, an individual who can interpret the instructional implications of evaluation results, other individuals at the discretion of the parent or LEA, and the child when appropriate (34. C.F.R. § 300.321 [b][3]). The IEP serves as the mechanism by which goals and objectives are established, programs are planned, and progress of the child is monitored (Abramson, 1987; Reynolds & Fletcher-Janzen, 1990).

Procedural safeguards are also included in the IDEA. Such safeguards are discussed at length later in this article. These safeguards are intended to ensure that children with disabilities and their parents have certain rights and that these rights are protected under the law. Parents are given the opportunity to present their complaints regarding possible violations of their rights through mediation, due process hearings, and/or civil action with respect to any matter relating to the identification, evaluation, or placement of a child (34 C.F.R. 300.300).

Parents' rights also extend to the educational records of their child. Educational and psychological records pertaining to the child must remain confidential except to those individuals who are directly involved in a child's education and who have a specific reason for reviewing the records (34 C.F.R. § 99.3). Parents have the right to examine all records, not just relevant records, with respect to the identification, evaluation, and placement of their child, and the provision of FAPE (34 C.F.R. § 99.10). Additional limitations and requirements regarding the confidentiality of students' records can be found in the entry for the Family Educational Rights and Privacy Act (FERPA).

Special education and related services must be provided in the Least Restrictive Environment (LRE) for children with disabilities in public or private institutions. In selecting the LRE, consideration is given to any potential harmful effect on the child or on the quality of services he or she needs, and a child with a disability is not removed from education in a general education classroom if modifications can be reasonably made to accommodate these needs (300 C.F.R. § 300.116[d–e]).

Part A: General Provisions

Part A, General Provisions, includes the congressional findings that constitute the underpinnings of the IDEA, definitions of key terms used in the statute (e.g., "child

with a disability"), and provisions establishing an Office of Special Education and Rehabilitative Services to administer the terms of the IDEA, revoking state immunity under the 11th Amendment to the U.S. Constitution for violation of the IDEA, and various other administrative provisions (relating to, e.g., promulgation of federal regulations under the IDEA; requirements that State rules, regulations, and policies be in compliance with the IDEA; and questionably named "paperwork reduction" provisions; 20 U.S.C. § 1400–1409; Sec. 601-610).

The new legislation made some changes to the congressional findings, including some adjustment to the language used to describe certain demographic changes over time and the addition of a specific reference to "improvement efforts under the Elementary and Secondary Education Act of 1965" (20 U.S.C. § 1400[c][5][C]), a reference to the changes promulgated under NCLB. It also made minor changes to the statement of the IDEA's purposes (e.g., replacing "systemic change activities" with "system improvement activities" and adding "further education" to subsection [1][A] of the statement of purposes; see introductory portion of this article for the full text of the statement of purposes; 20 U.S.C. § 1400[d]; Sec. 601[d]).

The 2004 legislation also adds a number of new defined terms, including *core academic subjects, highly qualified* (as in, "highly qualified special education teachers"), *homeless children*, and *limited English proficiency*, that relate to provisions of ESEA/NCLB and are part of the new statute's push to make IDEA consistent with, or possibly subordinate to, NCLB (20 U.S.C. § 1401; Sec. 602). Furthermore, the new statute expands the definition of *parent* to include natural, adoptive, and foster parents, as well as guardians, and individuals acting in place of a natural or adoptive parents (e.g., grandparent, stepparent, other relative) of children who may be eligible to receive special education services under the IDEA, thus allowing for greater participation by those filling parenting roles in the processes outlined by the statute (20 U.S.C. § 1401; Sec. 602). The new statute also adds school nurse services to the list of services that make up the defined term *related services*, and makes other minor changes and additions to the defined terms list.

Part B: Assistance for Education of All Children With Disabilities

Part B, Assistance for Education of All Children with Disabilities, contains what many would argue are the key components of the IDEA, including the formulas for calculating the maximum amounts states are eligible to receive under the act; provisions governing state and LEA eligibility for assistance under the IDEA; provisions governing evaluations, individual eligibility, IEPs, and educational placements; procedural safeguards for children and their parents; monitoring and enforcement provisions; and preschool grants. This section will look at the regulations for each section in Part B separately for ease of reference.

Authorization, Allotment, and Use of Funds

IDEA includes information on the authorization of federal funds to the states and state requirements to receive federal funds. The federal government provides funds to the states to financially assist the states in the education of children with disabilities. The IDEA regulations increased funding for this act on an annual basis going from just over $12 billion in FY 2005 to more than $26 billion in FY 2011 [20 U.S.C. 1411(i)]. These funds are used to serve over 6 million students between the ages of 3 and 21 who have been identified (NECTAC, 2011), and are divided among states based on a formula that looks at the number of students identified with disabilities and the number of students who are living in poverty [34 CFR 300.700(b)(2) [20 U.S.C. 1411(a)(2)(B)].

It is required that portions of these funds be used to carry out monitoring, enforcement and complaint investigation; and to establish and implement the mediation process required by IDEA, including providing for the cost of mediators and support personnel [34 CFR 300.704(b)(3)] [20 U.S.C. 1411(e)(2)(B)]. States have the discretion to use funds for several other activities such as including support and direct services; expanding technology to reduce paperwork; assisting local educational agencies (LEAs) in providing positive behavioral interventions and supports and mental health services for children with disabilities; improving the use of technology in the classroom by children with disabilities to enhance learning; and providing technical assistance to schools and LEAs including professional development for regular and special education teachers in order to help improve academic achievement of students with disabilities [34 CFR 300.704(b)(4)] [20 U.S.C. 1411(e)(2)(C)(x),(xi)]. States are also allowed to use some of these funds to provide early intervention services to children with disabilities to promote school readiness [34 CFR 300.704(f)] [20 U.S.C. 1411(e)(7)].

State Eligibility

In order for states to receive federal funding, they have to document that they provide an education for students with disabilities that complies with IDEA provisions that include:

- *Free appropriate public education (FAPE).* The state must ensure that a free appropriate public education is available to all children with disabilities. However, under the 2004 legislation, a state that provides early intervention services in accordance with Part C of the IDEA (which covers infants and toddlers with disabilities) to a child who is eligible for services under Section 619 (which relates to preschool

grants) is not required to provide such child with a free appropriate public education (20 U.S.C. § 1412[a][1]; Sec. 612[a][1]).

- *Child find.* The state must actively seek to locate all children with disabilities within a state. The state must implement policies and procedures to assure that all children with disabilities, including those who are homeless, wards of the state, or attending private schools, are evaluated (34 CFR. § 300.111[a]. The state must identify students who are suspected of being disabled and in need of special education even if they are advancing from grade to grade, highly mobile, or migrant children (34 CFRCFR § 300.11[c]. An accurate report of children receiving services under IDEA must be made to the federal government each year (34 CFR § 300.640).

- *Individualized education program (IEP).* An individualized education program or individualized family service plan (IFSP) must be developed, reviewed, and revised for each child with a disability (CFR § 300.321).

- *Least restrictive environment (LRE).* The state must establish procedural safeguards to ensure that children with and without disabilities are educated together to the maximum extent appropriate, and students with disabilities are only removed from the regular classroom environment "when the nature or severity of the disability is such that education in regular classes with the use of supplemental aids and services cannot be achieved satisfactorily" (34 CFR § 300.114 [a][2]).

- *Procedural safeguards.* Parents are afforded the right to confidentiality of identifiable information, the right to examine records, and the right to consent or decline any intervention service without jeopardizing the right to other services (34 CFR § 300.300). Greater detail on procedural safeguards is provided in a later section of this article.

- *Evaluation.* Evaluations must be completed within 60 days of receiving parental consent for evaluation, and must establish procedures to assure that a full and individual evaluation is provided for every child who may qualify as having a disability (34 CFR § 300.301 [a-c]).

- *Children in private schools.* The child must retain all IDEA rights in the private school setting, and the state must monitor the services provided to ensure compliance with IDEA requirements (34 CFR § 300.146). If the placement is made by the state or local educational agency, the cost of placement must be paid by that agency (34 CFR § 300.146[a][2]).

- *Ensuring services.* The SEA must establish interagency agreements with public agencies responsible for providing and paying for special education or related services used by children with disabilities. The State Education Agency is now responsible for making an appropriate education available for all students in the state, including those who are homeless, residing in mental health facilities or hospitals, and are in homes for individuals with disabilities (34 CFR § 300.149).

- *Personnel qualifications.* The state must ensure that personnel who work with children with disabilities have the highest qualified standards. In particular, under the new legislation, individuals who are employed as special education teachers must be *highly qualified* as that term is defined in Part A (which in turn is designed to conform to requirements under NCLB) in accordance with the deadlines established by NCLB. Trained and supervised paraprofessionals may assist in providing services to children with disabilities (20 U.S.C. § 1412[a][14]; Sec. 612[a][14]).

- *Performance goals and indicators.* Under the new legislation, the state must establish goals for the performance of children with disabilities that are the same as the state's definition of *adequate yearly progress* under NCLB, address graduation and dropout rates, and are consistent (to the extent appropriate) with any other goals and standards for children adopted by the state. The state must also develop indicators to judge children's progress, including measurable annual objectives for progress under ESEA/NCLB for children with disabilities, and must report to the secretary of the Department of Education (DOE) and to the public on the state's progress, and the progress of children with disabilities in the state, toward meeting the goals established (20 U.S.C. § 1412[a][15]; Sec. 612[a][15]).

- *Participation in assessments.* According to the new legislation, all children with disabilities must be included in all general state and district-wide assessment programs, including NCLB-required assessments, "with appropriate accommodations and alternate assessments where necessary and as indicated in their respective IEPs" (20 U.S.C. § 1412[a][16][A]; Sec. 612[a][16][A]). States are required to develop guidelines for the provision of appropriate accommodations, and such guidelines must be aligned with the state's academic achievement standards under NCLB (20 U.S.C. § 1412[a][16]; Sec. 612[a][16]).

- *Prohibition on mandatory medication.* The 2004 legislation added a new provision prohibiting SEA and LEA personnel from requiring any child to obtain a prescription for a substance covered by the Controlled Substances Act as a condition of attending school, receiving an evaluation under Section 614, or receiving services under this statute, generally (20 U.S.C. § 1412[a][25]; Sec. 612[a][25]).

The Office of Special Education Programs (OSEP) within the DOE monitors compliance with IDEA by reviewing each state's plan. OSEP does not monitor individual school districts, rather it reviews state plans for ensuring compliance with IDEA. These reviews are all available on the U.S. Department of Education public web site (U.S. Department of Education, n.d). IDEA Part B now requires the State Education Agency be responsible for making available an appropriate education for all children with disabilities in the state including those who are homeless, residing in mental health facilities or hospitals, or in homes for individuals with developmental disabilities (Jacob et al., 2011).

Local Educational Agency Eligibility

IDEA Part B requires the State Educational Agency to ensure that all children with disabilities aged 3 to 21 meet key IDEA standards (34 CFR § 300.101, 300.149). The law also allows the SEA to delegate the responsibility of providing special education and remedial services to local education agencies (LEAs). The LEA is usually the board of education of a public school district, the educational administrative unit of a public institution, or a charter school that is established by the state (Jacob et al., 2011). Section 613 of the IDEA outlines the conditions LEAs must meet to be eligible for funding. To be eligible for funding, each LEA's plan must be consistent with the state plan. Once funding is received, LEAs are not allowed to reduce financial support for education of children with disabilities to schools by more than 50% of the amount of the current grant that is in excess of the amount of the grant in the previous fiscal year under the IDEA, and to the extent that the LEA reduces any such financial support it must use an amount equal to the amount of the reduction to carry out activities authorized under the ESEA/NCLB. LEAs must provide funding and serve children with disabilities who attend public charter schools in the same manner as children with disabilities who attend public schools. The new legislation also allows LEAs to allocate as much as 15% of the money they receive under the IDEA to develop and implement coordinated early intervening services. These services are targeted to students who "need additional academic and behavior support to succeed in the general education environment" but who have not been identified as having a disability (34 CFR § 300.226[a]).

The state may require LEAs to meet other conditions as well. The state may require LEAs to include disciplinary information in the records of children with disabilities and to transmit the record with the disciplinary information included in the same manner that disciplinary information is included in, and transmitted with, the student records of nondisabled children. The information transmitted may include a description of the behavior and disciplinary action taken, and any other additional information that is relevant to the safety of the child or others. When the child with a disability transfers to another school (e.g., to another elementary school), the child's most current IEP and all disciplinary action would be included in and transferred with the child's records (20 U.S.C. § 1413; Sec. 613).

Evaluations, Eligibility Determinations, IEPs, and Educational Placements

Under IDEA Part B, a child with a disability is defined as a child having:

> [M]ental retardation, a hearing impairment (including deafness), a speech or language impairment, a visual impairment (including blindness), a serious emotional disturbance (referred to in this part as "emotional disorder"), an orthopedic impairment, autism, traumatic brain injury, an other health impairment, a specific learning disability, deafblindness, or multiple disabilities. (34 CFR § 300.8[a])

For a child to be eligible for services under IDEA Part B, the student must have one of the disabilities categorized above, and a need for special education services must be established. Also, a child is not eligible for special education and related services if the determinant factor for that determination is a lack of appropriate instruction in reading, including the essential components of reading instruction; lack of appropriate instruction in math; or limited English proficiency (CFR § 300.306 [b]). If a state requires a medical evaluation to determine whether a child has a disability, this evaluation must be provided at no cost to the parent (Jacob et al., 2011).

A significant change from previous versions of this legislation is found in the requirements for determining whether a child has a specific learning disability. Previous IDEA regulations stated that a team could only determine that a child has a specific learning disability only if the child had a severe discrepancy between an area of academic achievement and intellectual ability. Under IDEA 2004, schools no longer are required to take into consideration whether a severe discrepancy exists between achievement and intellectual ability; states "must permit the use of a process based on the child's response to scientific, research based interventions" 34 CFR § 300.307[a][2]). In practice, this means that standardized tests of intellectual ability and academic achievement are no longer requirements for the diagnosis of a learning disability.

An initial evaluation of a child may be requested by a parent, and SEA, another state agency, or an LEA. The law generally requires a full and individual initial evaluation of the child to be conducted within 60 days (a change from the previous law of 60 *school* days) of receipt of parental consent to the evaluation in order to determine the educational needs of such child, before the initial provision for special education and related services is provided. The initial evaluation must be conducted with a variety of assessment tools and strategies and must use technically sound instruments. The child must be initially assessed in all areas of suspected disability. Assessments and evaluation materials used must meet certain statutory requirements, including nonbiased protections as well as the need to address the child's educational experiences and primary language. IDEA also indicates that each state or local agency must ensure that parents of a child with a disability are members of any group that makes decisions on the identification, evaluation, and educational placement of a child (34 CFR § 300.501).

The IEP team must include, as appropriate, (a) the parent(s) of the child; (b) one (or more) of the child's regular education teachers; (c) one (or more) of the child's special education teachers or, where appropriate, special education providers; (d) a representative of the LEA who is qualified to provide or supervise the provision of specially designed instruction to meet the needs of children with disabilities, knowledgeable about the general education curriculum, and knowledgeable about the availability of resources of the LEA; (e) an individual who can interpret the instructional implications of the evaluation results (e.g., a school psychologist), (f) at the discretion of the LEA or parent, other individuals who have knowledge or special expertise regarding the child; and (g) when appropriate, the child with the disability. The new legislation provides that a member of the IEP team may be excused from a meeting of the IEP team if the parent and LEA agree that the attendance of the team member is not necessary for the purposes of the scheduled meeting (e.g., the member's area of the child's curriculum or related services is not being modified or discussed in the meeting), or if the parents and LEA consent to the member's excusal from the meeting and the member submits written input into the development or modification of the IEP prior to the meeting (34 CFR § 300.321).

Upon completion of the evaluation process, a determination is made as to whether a child qualifies as a child with a disability or not. A team of qualified professionals and a parent of the child make the determination about the child's eligibility and the educational needs of the child. The parent must be given a copy of the evaluation report and documentation of the determination of eligibility at no cost (CFR § 300.322).

After eligibility for special education and related services has been determined, an IEP must be developed. The 2004 legislation expands upon prior requirements about what must be included in the IEP. An IEP is a written statement developed, reviewed, and revised by the IEP team for a child with a disability. It includes information regarding (a) the child's present level of academic achievement and functional performance, (b) measurable annual goals (including academic and functional goals), (c) a description of how the child's progress toward meeting the annual goals will be measured and how the parent will be informed of such progress, (d) an explanation of the extent to which the child will not participate with nondisabled children in academic or nonacademic settings, (e) program modifications or supports for school personnel that will be provided to the child, (f) projected date for the beginning of services and anticipated frequency, location, and duration of services, (g) if the child is 16, the IEP must include appropriate postsecondary goals related to training, education, employment, independent living skills, and or transition services, and (g) a statement of rights that will be transferred to the student if he/she will reach the age of majority within the year (34 CFR § 300.320[a]).

Each child's IEP must be reviewed and revised at least annually, and each child must be seen for reevaluation at least once every 3 years, or more often if warranted (34 CFR § 300.323 [c][2]). If the IEP team determines that no additional assessment data are required for a reevaluation, they are not required to conduct further assessment unless requested by the child's parents or teacher. During the annual review of the IEP, the team must determine whether the annual goals for the child are being achieved and revise the IEP as appropriate to address: (a) any lack of progress toward goals, (b) the results of any reevaluations, (c) information about the child provided by parents, or (d) child's anticipated needs (34 CFR § 300.324[b][1]).

In addition, the 2004 legislation establishes a pilot program permitting states to allow parents and LEAs to conduct long-term planning by offering the option of a comprehensive, multiyear IEP, not to exceed 3 years, that is designed to coincide with natural transition points for the child (e.g., from elementary school to middle school). The program must be optional for parents, and the IEP must include annual review of the child's IEP to determine the child's levels of progress and whether the child's annual goals are being met (20 U.S.C. § 1414[d][5]; Sec. 614[d][5]).

Procedural Safeguards

IDEA requires procedural safeguards to be put into place to assure the rights of children with disabilities and their parents. The procedural safeguards include:

- *Consent*: Parental written consent must be obtained before conducting an evaluation or placing a child in special education (34 CFR § 300.300[a][1]). If the parent refuses consent to the initial evaluation, the school agency may request mediation or a hearing to override a parent's refusal to give consent (34 CFR § 300.300 [a][3]). Parent consent is also required for subsequent reevaluations of a child, or for any changes in placement for the child (34 CFR § 300.300[c][2]; 34 CFR § 300.300[b][23]).
- *Notice*: IDEA divides information sent to parents into two different types of notice: prior written notice and procedural safeguards notice. Prior notice is required

a reasonable time before the proposed school action whenever the SEA or LEA proposes to initiate or change the identification, evaluation, education placement, or program (Jacob & Hartshorne, 2011). IDEA requires that notice be provided in a way understandable to the parent and must include a description of the proposed action; a description of each evaluation procedure, record, or report; a statement that parents have protection under procedural safeguards; sources for parents to contact to obtain assistance in understanding the provisions; a description of other options considered and why they were rejected (CFR § 300.503 [b]).

- The procedural safeguards notice must include a full explanation of the procedural safeguards in an understandable manner (34 CFR § 300.504[d]). The notice must include information pertaining to independent educational evaluations, prior written notice, parental consent, access to education records, opportunity to present and resolve complaints, the availability of mediation, procedures for students who are subject to placement in an interim alternative educational setting, requirements for unilateral placements by parents of children in private schools at public expense, hearings on due process complaints, statelevel appeals, civil actions and attorney's fees (34 CFR § 300.504[c]).
- *Complaints*: The IDEA requires the school to have procedures that require a school or parent to provide the other party with a written due process complaint, which must remain confidential (34 CFR § 300.508[a]). The complaint must include the description of the nature of the problem and a proposed resolution to the problem (34 CFR § 300.508[b]). The party receiving the complaint has 10 days to send the other party a response that specifically addresses the issues raised in the due process complaint (34 CFR § 300.508[f]).
- *Resolution meetings*: Within 15 days of receiving notice of the parents due process complaint, and prior to the initiation of a hearing, the school must convene a resolution meeting with the parents and members of the IEP team who have knowledge of the facts identified in the complaint (CFR § 300.510[a]), unless the school and parent agree in writing to waive the meeting or use the mediation process (34 CFR § 300.510 [a][3]). If the dispute is resolved in the meeting the parties sign a legally binding agreement, but if the complaint is not resolved, a due process hearing is held within 30 days of the receipt of the due process complaint (34 CFR § 300.510).
- *Mediation*. Procedures for resolving disputes through a mediation process must be established by an educational agency and must ensure that the process is voluntary, does not deny or delay a due process hearing, and is conducted by a qualified and impartial mediator

(34 CFR § 300.506[b]). The educational agency bears the cost of the process, and must maintain a list of qualified mediators that are selected on an impartial basis. (34 CFR § 300.506[b]). Discussions that occur during mediation are confidential and may not be used as evidence in any subsequent due process hearing or civil proceeding that arises from the dispute (34 CFR § 300.506[b][8]).

- *Due process hearing*: Parents and the school have a right to an impartial due process hearing on any matter regarding the identification, evaluation, or educational placement of a child. The educational agency maintains the list of hearing officers and qualifications. Each party has the right to be accompanied by legal counsel and other experts and the meeting must occur at a time and place convenient to the parents (34 CFR § 300.512). The hearing can be open to the public if the parents choose, and a final decision must be made by the officer within 45 days. The decision is final unless a party initiates an appeal to the SEA or begins a court action (34 CFR § 300.514[b]).

Discipline of Students With Disabilities

School personnel may order a change in placement for not more than 10 school days to an interim AES, another setting, or suspension for a child with a disability who violates the school's code of student conduct, to the same extent such alternatives are applied to children without disabilities (20 U.S.C. § 1415[k][1]; Sec. 615[k][1]). Within 10 school days of any decision to change the placement of the child under this section, the LEA, the parent, and relevant members of the IEP team are required to review all relevant information in the student's file, including his or her IEP, to determine if the conduct in question was caused by, or had a direct and substantial relationship to, the child's disability, or if the conduct was a direct result of the LEA's failure to implement the IEP. If either of these is found to be the case, then the IEP is required to determine that the conduct at issue was a manifestation of the child's disability (20 U.S.C. § 1415[k][1][E]; Sec. 615[k][1][E]). If the behavior that prompted an LEA is not the result of either the child's disability or inadequate services, the child may be disciplined under the general code of conduct in the same manner and severity as a nondisabled peer, but the child must continue to receive FAPE. However, upon any determination that the conduct was a manifestation of the child's disability, the IEP team is required to conduct a functional behavioral assessment and implement a behavioral intervention plan for the child, or, if a behavioral intervention plan was already in existence, the IEP team must review such behavioral intervention plan and modify it as necessary, and, except as described in the following, return the child to the placement from which he

or she was removed, unless the parent and the LEA agree to change the placement as part of the modification of the behavioral intervention plan (20 U.S.C. § 1415[k][1][F]; Sec. 615[k][1][F]). Parents have the right to appeal any step of this process (20 U.S.C. § 1415; Sec. 615).

Notwithstanding the foregoing, school personnel are permitted to move a student to an interim AES for not more than 45 school days, even if the conduct was determined to be a manifestation of the child's disability, in cases where the child (a) carries a weapon to school or to a school function, (b) possesses, uses, or sells illegal drugs at school or a school function, or (c) inflicts serious bodily injury upon another person while at school or a school function. Under these circumstances, the child must continue to receive educational services to enable the child to continue to participate in the general education curriculum and to progress toward meeting the goals set out in the child's IEP, and should receive, as appropriate, a functional behavioral assessment and behavioral intervention services and modifications that are designed to address the behavior violation so that it does not recur (20 U.S.C. § 1415[k][1][D]; Sec. 615[k][1][D]).

A hearing officer may also order a change in placement for a child with a disability. The hearing officer may order a change in placement to an interim AES for not more than 45 school days if the hearing officer finds that keeping the child in his or her current placement is substantially likely to result in injury to the child or to others (20 U.S.C. § 1415[k][3]; Sec. 615[k][3]).

Monitoring, Technical Assistance, and Enforcement

The 2004 legislation has resulted in significant changes to this section of the IDEA. Each state must have in place a performance plan that evaluates the state's efforts to implement the provisions of the IDEA and describes how the state will improve such implementation. The performance plan must establish measurable and rigorous targets for improvement in certain priority areas (20 U.S.C. § 1416[b]; Sec. 616[b]). The performance plan is reviewed and approved by the secretary of the DOE (20 U.S.C. § 1416[c]; Sec. 616[c]). Based on the information provided by the state in its annual performance report, the secretary determines if the state (a) meets the requirements of the IDEA, (b) needs assistance in implementing its requirements, (c) needs intervention in implementing its requirements, or (d) needs substantial intervention in implementing its requirements (20 U.S.C. § 1416[d]; Sec. 616[d]). If the secretary determines that a state needs assistance or intervention for 2 or 3 consecutive years, respectively, the new legislation provides certain options for the secretary to help (or force) the state to improve its performance. If the secretary determines that a state needs substantial intervention, the secretary is permitted to take stronger actions, including certain enforcement actions and the withholding of further payments to the state under the IDEA until identified problems are corrected (20 U.S.C. § 1416[e]; Sec. 616[e]). If any state does not agree with the secretary's decision with respect to the state plan, then the state may file a petition with the U.S. Court of Appeals for judicial review of the secretary's action. The judgment of the court shall be subject to review by the U.S. Supreme Court (20 U.S.C. § 1416[e][8]; Sec. 616[e][8]).

In the most recent (20092010) report, OSEP rated 28 states as "meets the requirements of IDEA," 20 states as "needs assistance," and 2 states (Illinois and Utah) as "needs intervention." As of this time, the federal government has not withheld funding from any state for failing to meet the requirements of IDEA (Education Week, 2011).

Preschool Grants

Preschool grants are available to states to assist the states in providing special education and related services to children with disabilities aged 3 to 5, though states at their own discretion may also include 2-year-old children with disabilities who will turn 3 during the school year (20 U.S.C. § 1419[a]; Sec. 619[a]). Under the new legislation, the funding formula has changed to conform to the formula change in Part B (20 U.S.C. § 1419[c]; Sec. 619[c]). Section 619 also establishes limitations on the percentage of funds allocated under Section 619 that a state may retain for state administrative and other state-level activities (20 U.S.C. § 1419[d]; Sec. 619[d]).

Part C: Infants and Toddlers With Disabilities

Part C of the Act, Infants and Toddlers with Disabilities, contains information about children under the age of 3. Similar to part B, it establishes regulations of how children with disabilities are identified, assessed, and served. It is designed to encourage states to develop and implement a statewide, comprehensive, coordinated, multidisciplinary, interagency program of early intervention services for infants and toddlers with disabilities and their families (34 CFR § 303.1). Each state must develop a public awareness program and a comprehensive directory of early intervention services that is available to the general public, and a lead agency in charge of assisting the needs of infants and toddlers with disabilities (34 CFR § 303.1). IDEA Part C defines an infant or toddler with (a) a disability as one who is experiencing developmental delays in one or more areas of cognitive, physical, communication, social or emotional, or adaptive development; or (b) has a diagnosed physical or mental condition that has a high probability of resulting in developmental delay. These factors may be biological or environmental (34 CFR § 303.16). Evaluations must be made available to assess the unique needs of the child to assess cognitive, physical, communication, social/emotional, or adaptive needs of the child, and of the family if the family consents (34 CFR § 303.322). This evaluation must be completed within 45 days of a referral. At the conclusion of the evaluation, a written individualized family service plan (IFSP) is developed rather than an IEP. Services rendered as a result of the IFSP are (a) designed to meet the developmental needs of the child and the needs of the family related to enhancing the child's development, (b) selected in collaboration with the parents, (c) provided under public supervision by qualified personnel in conformity with an individualized family service plan, and (d) provided at no cost, unless federal or state law provides for a system of payments by families. Services include family training, counseling, home visits; speech-language pathology and audiology services; occupational therapy; physical therapy; psychological services; service coordination services; medical diagnostic services; early screening services; nursing services; social work services; vision services; assistive technology; and transportation to such services (34CFR §§ 303.1213).

Part D: National Activities to Improve Education of Children With Disabilities

Part D, National Activities to Improve Education of Children with Disabilities, includes all other discretionary programs (i.e., state improvement grants, personnel preparation, research, technical assistance, parent training, dissemination). State improvement grants are made available to assist SEAs and their partners in reforming and improving systems for providing educational, early intervention, and transitional services to improve results for students. Grants are also made available for research and innovation and personnel preparation to improve services and results for children with disabilities (20 U.S.C. §§ 1451–1482; Sec. 651–682).

Controversies in IDEA

As mentioned earlier, this legislation is the main special education law in the United States, and has had a great impact on how children with disabilities are educated in the country. Each version of IDEA has produced controversies, and this article will discuss two controversies that exist in the current version. One area of concern is the fact that the law serves as a federal mandate to states, but does not fully fund the requirements; the other area of concern is the way in which schools have implemented the new Response to Intervention (RTI) system of evaluating children suspected of having a learning disability.

The IDEA is a piece of federal legislation that imposes significant costs on school and local education agencies to provide services for children with disabilities. The law requires schools to provide a wide range of services, including speech therapy, audiology, physical therapy, nursing, counseling, and educational interventions that can be quite expensive. The cost of special education in the United States has been estimated to be estimated at close to $80 billion, with federal funding for the program usually falling below 15% (New America Foundation, 2011). In 2009, the American Recovery and Reinvestment Act (PL 111-5) was passed; nearly doubling funds provided for IDEA by adding $12.5 billion, but this was a 1-year addition of funds. This means that state and local educational agencies are often tasked with the challenge of raising funds for these very expensive requirements when states have many other competing needs.

An area of controversy that is specific to the most recent amendment is the way in which students with a specific learning disability are evaluated. As mentioned earlier, previous versions of the legislation required students to demonstrate a significant discrepancy between measured intelligence and achievement in a given academic area. Under IDEA 2004, schools no longer are required to take into consideration whether a severe discrepancy exists between achievement and intellectual ability; states "must permit the use of a process based on the child's response to scientific, research based interventions" (34 CFR § 300.307[a][2]). In implementing this new Response to Intervention (RTI) system of evaluating students, some parents have complained that school districts have used this system as a way to delay providing a full evaluation. For example, an Office of Civil Rights (OCR) investigation was triggered by a parent's complaint that a school district had a policy of requiring an 8-week RTI intervention before a student could be considered for an evaluation (Acalanes Union High School District Office for Civil Rights, Western Division, San Francisco [California], 2009). Investigation such as these led to a memo from the U.S. Department of Education's Office of Special Education Programs (OSEP), clarifying that "States and LEAs have an obligation to ensure that evaluations of children suspected of having a disability are not delayed or denied because of implementation of an RTI strategy."

REFERENCES

Abramson, M. (1987). Education for All Handicapped Children Act of 1975 (PL 94-142). In C. R. Reynolds & L. Mann (Eds.), *Encyclopedia of special education* (pp. 583–585). New York, NY: Wiley.

Applequist, K. F. (2005). Special education legislation. In E. Fletcher-Janzen & C. R. Reynolds (Eds.), *Special educators' almanac*. Hoboken, NJ: Wiley.

Focus on IDEA. (1997, July). *Span update*. Bethesda, MD: National Association of School Psychologists.

Education Week. (2011). *State Ratings in Special Education*. Retrieved from http://www.edweek.org/ew/section/infographics/36idea_map.html

Haring, N. G., McCormick, L., & Haring, T. (1994). *Exceptional children and youth: An introduction to special education* (6th ed). New York, NY: Prentice Hall.

Individuals with Disabilities Act of 1997, 20 U.S.C. §§1400 et seq. (West, 1997).

Jacob, S., Decker, D. M., & Hartshorne, T. S. (2011). *Ethics and law for school psychologists* (6th ed). Hoboken, NJ: Wiley.

Jacob-Timm, S., & Hartshorne, T. (1995). *Ethics and law for school psychologists*. Brandon, VT: Clinical Psychology Publishing.

Martin, R. (1979). *Educating handicapped children: The legal mandate*. Champaign, IL: Research Press.

Moore v. District of Columbia, 907 F.2d 165 (D.C. Cir. 1990).

National Association of State Directors of Special Education. (1997). *Comparison of key issues: Current law & 1997 IDEA Amendments*. Washington, DC: Author.

National Education Association. (n.d.). *No Child Left Behind Act (NCLB)/ESEA*. Retrieved from http://www.nea.org/home/NoChildLeftBehindAct.html

New America Foundation (2011). *Federal Education Budget Project*. Retrieved from http://febp.newamerica.net/

Reynolds, C. R., & Fletcher-Janzen, E. (1990). Education For All Handicapped Children Act of 1975 (PL 94-142). In C. R. Reynolds & L. Mann (Eds.), *Concise encyclopedia of special education* (pp. 386–88). New York, NY: Wiley.

Turnbull, H. R. (1990). *Free appropriate public education* (3rd ed). Denver, CO: Love.

U.S. Department of Education (n.d.). *Special education and rehabilitative services: IDEA 2004 resources*. Retrieved from http://www.ed.gov/

U.S. Department of Education (2011) *Part B State Performance Plans (SPP) Letters and Annual Performance Report (APR) Letters*. Retrieved from http://www2.ed.gov/fund/data/report/idea/partbspap/allyears.html

CECIL R. REYNOLDS
Texas A&M University
Second edition

PATRICIA A. LOWE
University of Kansas
Third edition

JAMES E. WALSH
Chicago School of Professional Psychology
Fourth edition

INFANT ASSESSMENT

The term *infant assessment* has come to represent a variety of formal and informal screening and diagnostic procedures used for the systematic collection of data. The initial purpose of assessment is to determine whether development of the infant is progressing normally.

Advances in genetics and biochemistry have made it possible to begin this assessment process prior to the birth of the infant. Information about the health of the mother and her fetus, including the identification of genetic and chromosomal disorders, can be obtained through prenatal diagnostic techniques.

The common areas of focus for the assessment of infants from birth through 2 years of age include physical and sensory attributes, cognitive and general communication abilities, and social/emotional responses and interactions.

Infant assessment begins with procedures that can be carried out quickly and inexpensively. These screening measures constitute the initial stage of the assessment process and allow for the identification of at risk infants (i.e., individuals with known or suspected disorders or developmental delays).

For those infants considered to be at risk, the focus of assessment is expanded to include more in-depth or diagnostic procedures. The purpose for using diagnostic measures is to collect information that will help to identify and understand the nature of an impairment as it affects the development of the infant.

Screening and diagnostic information can be gathered through the combined use of direct testing (using standardized norm, criterion, or curriculum reference measures), naturalistic observations, and parent interviews. The resulting information is analyzed and used to make strategic diagnostic, placement, and intervention decisions.

Historically, the assessment of infants can be traced back to the intelligence testing movement of the 19th and 20th centuries (Brooks & Weintraub, 1976). Among the first tests designed specifically for the purpose of gathering normative data on infant behavior were Gesell's Developmental Schedules and Bayley's California First Year Mental Scale.

Although many advances have been made in the development of diagnostic instruments, a lack of predictive validity for these standardized measures has continued to be the major issue in infant assessment. Research has consistently shown that it is not possible to predict the future cognitive performance of a child on the bases of infant test results (McCall, 1979).

According to Lewis and Fox (1980), the major reason for this lack of predictive validity is the nature of the tests themselves, in that the resulting scores are inaccurate indicators of a child's functioning. Lewis and Fox (1980) point out that it is not possible to validly predict future infant performance without considering the nature of parent infant interactions and the influence these interactions can have on the future development of the child. Kagan and Moss (1962) have concluded that the predictive validity of infant assessment tests could be improved if the socioeconomic status of the parents was combined with the child's test scores.

Although there is little long-range predictive validity in the assessment of normal infants, research with infants with disabilities (DuBose, 1977; Kamphaus, 2001; Meir, 1975) has provided evidence that predictive validity is greater with severely handicapped individuals. This increase appears to be related to the overall rate of development in the infant. Unlike normally developing infants, who are in a constant state of change (Honzik, 1976), infants with severe delays or deficits often exhibit very low-functioning behaviors that remain relatively stable, and thus more predictable over time (Brooks-Gunn & Lewis, 1981; Kamphaus, 2001).

It is clear that the most pervasive issue with respect to the validity of assessing infant behavior is that it may not be possible to accurately predict long-range performance based on early test results. As Sheehan and Gallagher (1984) suggest, it may be more productive for infant assessment to be used to address immediate needs of diagnoses, placement, and intervention rather than long-range predictions of a child's developmental outcome.

The assessment process should begin with the identification of the specific behaviors to be measured. Following this identification, selection of appropriate screening and diagnostic measures can be made. In-depth, diagnostic procedures must include the use of reliable and valid standardized tests (with appropriate use of adaptive equipment); multiple, systematic observations of the infant in various settings and situations; and parent interviews.

The collection and subsequent analysis of assessment data should be conducted by a multidisciplinary team, which might include a pediatrician, a psychologist, a communications specialist, and a physical therapist as well as the parents of the infant. The resulting information is used for the purpose of establishing appropriate objectives for intervention. This process of assessment also must include an evaluation of the intervention program.

REFERENCES

Brooks, J., & Weintraub, M. (1976). A history of infant intelligence testing. In M. Lewis (Ed.), *Origins of intelligence* (pp. 19–58). New York, NY: Plenum Press.

Brooks-Gunn, J., & Lewis, M. (1981). Assessing young handicapped children: Issues and solutions. *Journal of the Division for Early Childhood, 2*, 84–95.

DuBose, R. F. (1977). Predictive value of infant intelligence scales with multiply handicapped children. *American Journal of Mental Deficiency, 81*(4), 388–390.

Honzik, M. (1976). Value and limitations of infant tests: An overview. In M. Lewis (Ed.), *Origins of intelligence*. New York, NY: Plenum Press.

Kagan, J., & Moss, H. A. (1962). *Birth and maturity: A study in psychological development*. New York, NY: Wiley.

Kamphaus, R. (2001). *Clinical assessment of child and adolescent intelligence* (2nd ed). Needham Heights, MA: Pearson.

Lewis, M., & Fox, N. (1980). Predicting cognitive development from assessment in infancy. *Advances in Behavioral Pediatrics, 1,* 53–67.

McCall, R. B. (1979). The development of intellectual functioning in infancy and the prediction of later I.Q. In J. Osofsky (Ed.), *Handbook of infant development.* New York, NY: Wiley.

Meir, J. H. (1975). Screening, assessment and intervention for young children at developmental risk. In N. Hobbs (Ed.), *Issues in the classification of children* (Vol. 2). San Francisco, CA: Jossey-Bass.

Sheehan, R., & Gallagher, R. J. (1984). Assessment of infants. In M. J. Hanson (Ed.), *A typical infant development.* Baltimore, MD: University Park Press.

FRANCINE TOMPKINS
University of Cincinnati

See also **Apgar Rating Scale; Developmental Milestones; Infant Stimulation; Measurement**

INFANTILE HYPERCALCEMIA

Infantile hypercalcemia (also called *hypercalcemia,* or *William's syndrome*) is a rare syndrome caused by deletion of genetic material from a specific region of chromosome 7 (Genetics Home Reference, 2008). It is characterized by abnormal calcium chemistry and is associated with circulatory and cardiac (particularly supravalvular aortic stenosis) defects. Many children with this syndrome have low birth weights. They may have heart murmurs, kidney problems, and gastrointestinal problems early in life. There may be reduced muscle tone and general motor difficulties (listlessness, lethargy), also noted in infants. Most children will have mild to moderate intellectual disability, although some children may have normal intelligence. Some mild neurologic dysfunction has been noted (Bergsma, 1979).

Children are short in stature (and skeletal defects are often seen), with pointed chins and ears, and are often described as having elfin-like features (full cheeks, small, broad foreheads). Widespread and squinted eyes with epicanthal folds are typical. Teeth tend to be underdeveloped but the mouth is wide with a "cupid bow" upper lip. No significant characteristics in upper or lower extremities are usually noted (Lemeshaw, 1982).

Affected individuals show a severe deficit of spatial cognition but have a modicum of language and face recognition (Atkinson et al., 1997). Because of the varying degree of mental retardation and concomitant health and skeletal problems that may exist, a comprehensive assessment is necessary for proper placement of these children. Support medical services are usually required, and in some instances children will respond to medical treatment and surgery. Motoric problems may cause extensive immobility and may result in more restricted education placement than in a regular classroom. This decision can be made only by a complete evaluation of all the factors of this syndrome. Related services are often necessary as well.

REFERENCES

Atkinson, J., King, J., Braddick, O., Nores, L., Anker, S., & Braddick, F. (1997). A specific deficit of dorsal stream junction in William's Syndrome. *Neuroreport, 8*(8), 1919–1922.

Bergsma, D. (1979). *Birth defects compendium* (2nd ed.). New York, NY: National Foundation, March of Dimes.

Genetics home reference. (2008). http://ghr.nlm.nih.gov/condition/williamssyndrome

Lemeshaw, S. (1982). *The handbook of clinical types in mental retardation.* Boston, MA: Allyn & Bacon.

SALLY L. FLAGLER
University of Oklahoma

See also **Hunter Syndrome; Hurler Syndrome; Low Birth Weight/Prematurity; Mental Retardation; Physical Anomalies**

INFANT STIMULATION

The term infant stimulation is used to represent a variety of early intervention activities (i.e., perceptual, sensorimotor, cognitive, language, and/or social/emotional) that are designed to facilitate development. The value of early intervention is based on a body of research that has demonstrated that infants, including those with disabilities, are capable of learning as a result of sustained, meaningful interactions with people and events within their environment (Osofsky, 1979).

It is believed that early experiences of the infant serve as the foundation for future growth of the individual. According to developmental theory, an infant's early sensorimotor experiences such as visually tracking and reaching for objects are precursors for later cognitive attainments such as object permanence, mean sends, and spatial relationships (Gallagher & Reid, 1981).

Since many at-risk infants (i.e., infants with known or suspected handicapping conditions) manifest deficits in perceptual or sensorimotor areas, early intervention is particularly important. Deficits that limit an infant's interaction with his or her physical and social environment often will result in delayed or deficient development (Bobath & Bobath, 1972).

There is no clear agreement about how much or what type of stimulation is most effective for facilitating development. This issue is unresolved because it is not known how to validly evaluate the effects of stimulation activities. There is general agreement, however, that the stimulation of infants does have a positive effect on immediate and future development (Alberto, Briggs, & Goldstein, 1983; Hanson & Hanline, 1984; Sheehan & Gallagher, 1983).

Over the years many programs have been developed for the purpose of stimulating the development of handicapped and at-risk infants. Detailed reviews of these programs (Bailey, Jens, & Johnson, 1983; Sheehan & Gallagher, 1983) reveal that they vary greatly in their content and effectiveness. Infant stimulation programs can be center based (i.e., carried out by professionals in hospitals, clinics, or schools) or home-based (i.e., conducted by parents and professionals within the infant's home). There are also programs that combine center-based instruction with a home-based component.

Infant stimulation programs have been shown to be successful with low-vision infants (Leguire, Fellows, Rogers, & Bremer, 1992), with premature infants (Dieter & Emory, 1997), infants with gastric problems (de Roiste & Bushnell, 1995), and many other conditions.

Fortunately, there are general guidelines suggested for the purpose of guiding the development of programs, including the selection of intervention methods and materials, as well as program evaluation. According to these guidelines, there is a clear need for programs to use a sound theoretical framework to direct instructional content and intervention strategies. Professionals need to be clear about the purpose of instruction and to identify the population(s) most appropriate for their programs.

Activities must be meaningful and instruction should emphasize natural learning opportunities and interactions within a variety of domains (i.e., perceptual, cognitive, psychomotor, and social/emotional). Staff must be properly trained and a program evaluation plan developed. Most important, any stimulation or early intervention program must involve the parents and family of the infant.

REFERENCES

Alberto, P. A., Briggs, T., & Goldstein, D. (1983). Managing learning in handicapped infants. In S. G. Garwood & R. R. Fewell (Eds.), *Educating handicapped infants* (pp. 417–454). Rockville, MD: Aspen.

Bailey, D. B. Jr., Jens, K. G., & Johnson, N. (1983). Curricula for handicapped infants. In S. G. Garwood & R. R. Fewell (Eds.), *Educating handicapped infants* (pp. 387–416). Rockville, MD: Aspen.

Bobath, K., & Bobath, B. (1972). Cerebral palsy. In P. H. Pearson & C. Williams (Eds.), *Physical therapy services in the developmental disabilities*. Springfield, IL: Thomas.

Dieter, J. N. I., & Emory, K. (1997). Supplemental of stimulation of premature infants: A treatment model. *Journal of Pediatric Psychology, 22*(3), 281–295.

de Roiste, A., & Bushnell, I. W. R. (1995). The immediate gastric effects of a tactile stimulation programme on premature infants. *Journal of Reproductive & Infant Psychology, 13*(1), 57–62.

Gallagher, J., & Reid, D. K. (1981). *The learning theory of Piaget and Inhelder*. Monterey, CA: Brooks/Cole.

Hanson, M. J., & Hanline, M. F. (1984). Behavioral competencies and outcomes: The effects of disorder. In M. J. Hanson (Ed.), *A typical infant development* (pp. 109–178). Baltimore, MD: University Park Press.

Leguire, L. E., Fellows, R. R., Rogers, G. L., & Bremer, D. L. (1992). The CCH vision stimulation program for infants with low vision: Preliminary results. *Journal of Visual Impairment & Blindness, 86*(1), 33–37.

Osofsky, J. D. (Ed.). (1979). *Handbook of infant development*. New York, NY: Wiley.

Sheehan, R., & Gallagher, R. J. (1983). Conducting evaluations of infant intervention programs. In S. Garwood & R. R. Fewell (Eds.), *Educating handicapped infants*. Rockville, MD: Aspen.

FRANCINE TOMPKINS
University of Cincinnati

See also **Deprivation; Enrichment; Infant Assessments; Low Birth Weight/Prematurity**

INFANTS & YOUNG CHILDREN

Infants & Young Children (IYC) is an interdisciplinary journal of early childhood intervention, published quarterly. The journal's clinical focus is on children ages birth to 5 years and their families who have, or are at risk of acquiring developmental problems. The purpose of the journal is to link the extensive knowledge emerging from the developmental science of normative development, the developmental science of risk and disability and intervention science relevant to the field of early childhood development to practice and policy.

Articles consist of summaries of research developments in the field and implications in application into practices such as therapeutic, diagnostic, educational, and family support concepts. While doing so, the journal incorporates theory, consensus, and debate. As well, articles address policy and law, professional development, and other high priority topics. Current topics in IYC include, screening for sleep problems in early childhood special education populations, early intervention services for children with physical disabilities, and experiences of parents of toddlers with autism spectrum disorder.

Current editor Mary Beth Bruder, PhD, works to publish four issues per year and encourages an open submission format. The journal is available through paper copies as well as electronically through its dedicated web site, and as part of Ovid collections to universities. The online link below provides access to subscription and gives information about how potential authors can submit manuscripts.

Written communication should be submitted to the publisher, Lippincott Williams and Wilkins at: LWW Business Offices, Two Commerce Square, 2001 Market Street, Philadelphia, PA 19103; http://journals.lww.com/iycjournal/pages/default.aspx

NICOLE M. CASSIDY
Chicago School of Professional Psychology
Fourth edition

INFORMAL READING INVENTORY

Informal reading inventory (IRI) is a generic term that refers to some type of nonstandardized technique used to assess aspects of reading performance. According to Smith and Johnson (1980), the most informal application of the diagnostic method involves having the child read selections of material silently and orally, asking comprehension questions about what has been read, and making note of the quality of reading, particularly word identification errors. Typically, the reading selections cover a range of grade or difficulty levels, from the pre-primer through the eighth or ninth reader levels, as found in basal reading series. The comprehension questions based on the reading passages are usually of three types: factual or literal recall, inferential thinking, and vocabulary knowledge.

Johnson and Kress (1965) identified four purposes for administering an informal reading inventory. The IRI can be used to determine the level at which a reader can function independently, the level at which he or she can profit from instruction, the level at which the reader is frustrated by the material (Pehrsson, 1994), and the level of listening comprehension. Results of an IRI aid in determining specific strengths and weaknesses in reading, thus leading to a program of instruction or remediation. Also, the results of an IRI enable the reader to become aware of his or her own abilities and can be used as a measure of reading progress.

Betts (1946) established the earliest criteria for determining the four pedagogical levels. He determined that a child should read words in context with 99% accuracy and answer 90% of the comprehension questions correctly to be able to handle material independently. To profit from instruction in certain materials, the reader should recognize 95% of the words in context and respond correctly to comprehension questions with 75% accuracy. When the reader can recognize words with only 90% accuracy, or

respond correctly to only half of the comprehension questions, then the material is too difficult and is frustrating. Finally, listening comprehension is determined by reading selections to the child with the expectation that he or she will answer 75% of the related questions correctly.

REFERENCES

Betts, E. A. (1946). *Foundation of reading instruction*. New York, NY: American Book.

Johnson, M. S., & Kress, R. A. (1965). *Informal reading inventories*. Newark, DE: International Reading Association.

Pehrsson, R. S. (1994). Challenging frustration level. *Reading and Writing Quarterly*, *10*(3), 201–208.

Smith, R. J., & Johnson, D. D. (1980). *Teaching children to read* (2nd ed.). Reading, MA: Addison-Wesley.

JOHN M. EELLS
Souderton Area School District,
Souderton, Pennsylvania

See also Basal Readers; Cloze Technique; Johnston Informal Reading Inventory; Reading

INFORMATION PROCESSING

Webster's Third World International Dictionary defines a process as:

> The action of moving forward progressively from one point to another on the way to completion; the action of passing through continuing development from a beginning to a contemplated end; the action of continuously going along through each of a succession of acts, events, to developmental stages.

Succinctly, process may be considered a manipulation. Information processing, then, in the context of psychological study, is the manipulation of incoming stimuli, and existing or stored information, and the creation of new information by the human brain. This would include such common activities as perception, encoding, decoding, retrieval from memory, rehearsal, general reasoning ability, and a growing multitude of "new" cognitive processes. As new theories of cognitive processes occur, new names and new constructs are devised and added to the list. Implicit in theories of information processing is the assumption that each individual's behavior is determined by the information processing that occurs internally. In combination, the form, depth, and breadth of information processing is what controls behavior, overt and covert, though in all likelihood in a reciprocal relationship with the outside world.

Information processing is in the midst of a revival of study in psychology and related fields, generally under the rubric of cognitive science. During the age of behaviorism, when only clearly observable behaviors were appropriate for study, research on the internal processes of the mind continued but at a much slower pace. There were clear biases present in many journals against the publication of such work. During the 1960s a resurgence began that came to full force only in the 1980s. This resurgence was in some ways related to advances in computer technology, as analogies to computer terminology are common and provide a paradigm for how humans might analyze information. In special education, information processing has always been a major interest because of its relationship to learning and the remediation of learning disorders (Mann, 1979). Disturbances of normal information processing are believed to be at the core of the etiology of learning disabilities. The terminology of information processing has fluctuated over the years, with *central processing* being the most frequently used alternative term.

Since at least the early 1900s, special educators have been interested in training children in various information-processing methods as a technique for the remediation of learning disorders. Past efforts to improve academic skills through the training of processing have been notable in their failures (Glass, 1983; Mann, 1979; Myers & Hammill, 1969; Reynolds, 1981). With the revival of cognitivism has come a new wave of cognitive processes and higher order information-processing strategies to train. The effectiveness of training cognitive processes for the purpose of improving academic skills has yet to be demonstrated, and the potential of such efforts has been hotly debated (Gresham, 1986; Haywood & Switzky, 1986a, 1986b; Reynolds, 1986).

The information-processing skills of exceptional children will always be of interest to special educators. Most mentally handicapped children have some form of information-processing disorder, whether it is a mild deviation from the average skill level of other same-age children or a massive disruption of higher order skills. Treating these children requires extensive knowledge of their information-processing skills.

Theories of information processing abound. The best theory on which to base generalizations about a child may vary from child to child. New theories are being formulated and old theories revised almost daily in this rapidly expanding area of research. However, we must be particularly careful in evaluating work in information processing for its application to special education. As Mann (1979) reminds us, many fads in information processing have come and gone and too many of the "new" information processing approaches are simply yesterday's failures shrouded in new jargon and repackaged for today's thinking.

Contemporary information processing models attempt to duplicate or prepare a representation of the internal flow of information in the brain. The various information-processing theories create numerous variations in number and arrangement of subsystems of processing. Information-processing models of human thinking can be represented mathematically, though most often researchers prefer to display the theory as a series of boxes connected by various arrows, much as in a flowchart with feedback loops and various checks and balances.

There are basically only three kinds of models. The first treats information processing as a linear activity, a form of processing that is serial, wherein stages of processing are linked in a straight line and the output of one stage is the input for the next stage; processing proceeds very much in a sequential step-by-step manner. Each stage must await the outcome of the preceding stage. The second primary model of processing does not need to wait for each link in the chain to be completed, but rather carries on parallel processing, doing many tasks simultaneously without awaiting output from a prior step. In parallel processing, several stages can access output from any other stage at the same time. An information processing theory with both components interlinked (serial stages and parallel stages) is a hybrid model (Kantowitz, 1984). These models tend to be more complex but may not always be more useful. They continue to be challenged by organizations such as Neural Information Processing Systems (NIPS) that study broad-based and inclusive approaches (Tesauro, Touretzky, & Leen, 1995).

Information processing has progressed to the point of now being a major force in experimental psychology. It is likely to continue to occupy a significant amount of space in the leading scientific journals of psychology for some years to come. Discussions, reviews, and research related to information processing and its related theories will grow in importance in journals related to the education of exceptional children.

REFERENCES

Glass, G. V. (1983). Effectiveness of special education. *Policy Studies Review, 2,* 65–78.

Gresham, F. (1986). On the malleability of intelligence: Unnecessary assumptions, reifications, and occlusion. *School Psychology Review, 15,* 261–263.

Haywood, H. C., & Switzky, H. N. (1986a). The malleability of intelligence: Cognitive processes as a function of polygenic-experiential interaction. *School Psychology Review, 15,* 245–255.

Haywood, H. C., & Switzky, H. N. (1986b). Transactionalism and cognitive processes: Reply to Reynolds and Gresham. *School Psychology Review, 15,* 264–267.

Kantowitz, B. H. (1984). Information processing. In R. Corsini (Ed.), *Encyclopedia of psychology* (Vol. 2). New York, NY: Wiley.

Mann, L. (1979). *On the trail of process.* New York, NY: Grune & Stratton.

Myers, P., & Hamill, D. (1969). *Methods for learning disorders.* New York, NY: Wiley.

Reynolds, C. R. (1981). Neuropsychological assessment and the habilitation of learning: Considerations in the search for the aptitude × treatment interaction. *School Psychology Review, 10,* 343–349.

Reynolds, C. R. (1986). Transactional models of intellectual development, yes. Deficit models of process remediation, no. *School Psychology Review, 15,* 256–260.

Tesauro, G., Touretzky, D., & Leen, T. (Eds.). (1995). *Advances in neural information processing systems.* Cambridge, MA: MIT Press.

CECIL R. REYNOLDS
Texas A&M University

See also Perceptual Development (Lag in); Perceptual Training; Reciprocal Determinism; Remediation, Deficit-Centered Models; Sequential and Simultaneous Cognitive Processing

INFORMED CONSENT (*See* Consent, Informed)

INHALANT ABUSE

Inhalant abuse involves the voluntary inhalation of gases or fumes in an effort to achieve an intoxicated state. These substances include many household products that are legal to buy and possess, including such things as airplane glue, nail polish remover, and propellants used in certain commercial products, such as whipped cream dispensers. Generally, the vapors are inhaled through the nose or mouth, a practice referred to as huffing, but they can also be ingested or absorbed through the skin. Adolescent abusers usually choose inhalants based on availability, the desired physiological effect, and the degree of social and legal risk associated with possessing the substance (Fullwood & Ginther, 1994).

Unlike nearly all other classes of drugs, the use of inhalants is most common among younger adolescents and tends to decline as youth grow older. A recent study indicated that 19.7% of eighth graders admitted to inhalant use (Johnston, O'Malley, & Bachman, 1999), with a wide range of reported use based on gender and ethnicity. Use by African American students appears to be least prevalent, with 4.2% reporting inhalant use in the past year, compared with 13.3% of White and 11.5% of Hispanic eighth graders. Among eighth graders, females consistently have a slightly higher annual prevalence rate (11.6% in 1998 versus 10.6% for males); however, this trend does not hold for the older grades, in which there

were 7.6% of 10th-grade females using inhalants compared with 8.4% of 10th-grade males. Native American females show very high rates for lifetime use (23.9%), exceeded only by White males (28.8%; Bates, Plemons, Jumper-Thurman, & Beauvais, 1997).

Characteristics

1. Short-term memory loss or other cognitive impairments.
2. Emotional instability such as irritability or anxiety.
3. Slow, slurred, or incoherent speech.
4. Uncoordinated movements.
5. Loss of smell and taste, sometimes accompanied by loss of appetite.
6. Chemical smell in clothing, hair, or breath.
7. Possible sores or spots around the mouth.

Most inhalant use is either one time or for a brief period of time; only 2% to 5% of youth report chronic use (Beauvais, 2000). Unfortunately, the consequences of even a single use can be deadly as a result of asphyxia, suffocation, or sudden sniffing death syndrome, most often from cardiac arrest. Studies have suggested that inhalant abusers respond poorly to traditional drug treatment programs (Dinwiddie, Zorumski, & Rubin, 1987), and the long-term outcomes tend to be poor for these youth: high rates of school dropout, poor social and emotional adjustment, and increased involvement in illegal activities (Beauvais, 2000; Simpson & Barrett, 1991). Programs that have focused on positively impacting the adolescents' social environment by increasing family involvement and social support for the adolescents, fostering healthy peer relationships, and maximizing client interest in and commitment to treatment have had some success (Simpson & Barrett, 1991). Additionally, treatment programs should focus on increasing users' self-efficacy and teaching adaptive coping strategies so that users are better able to deal with difficult situations in the future (Gunning & D'Amato, 1999).

Because of the associated academic and emotional difficulties reported among abusers, it is likely that many of these youth will be involved in special education programming. Although students may be enrolled in any special education program, those with learning disabilities and emotional/behavioral disturbances are especially at risk (Gunning & D'Amato, 1999). This is also the case with students that are socially maladjusted or involved with the law and the legal system. Therefore, it is especially important that special education teachers and school psychologists be aware of the signs of inhalant abuse as well as the long-term neurological damage that can occur from inhalant abuse, including poor attention and concentration and memory difficulties (Filley, Heaton, & Rosenberg, 1990). Educational professionals should be familiar with the treatment resources available in their communities to provide immediate referral as needed. If a student presents with a history of chronic inhalant abuse, classroom instruction should be modified to accommodate the student's concentration and memory difficulties. Schools can also help prevent inhalant use by incorporating curriculum materials that contain straightforward information on the effects of inhalant abuse on learning and its physical and emotional effects.

Specific treatment and prevention strategies for inhalant abuse must be developed and tested before successful intervention can be achieved. Future research should be directed toward longitudinal studies that help identify the predictors of solvent abuse and the outcomes of such abuse. Although research has demonstrated the relationship between poor academic performance, dropping out, and volatile solvent abuse, the direct and causal nature of those relationships remains unclear.

REFERENCES

Bates, S. C., Plemons, B. W., Jumper-Thurman, P., & Beauvais, F. (1997). Volatile solvent use: Patterns by gender and ethnicity among school attenders and dropouts. *Drugs and Society*, *10*(1/2), 61–78.

Beauvais, F. (2000). Inhalant abuse: Causes, consequences, and prevention. *Prevention Researcher*, *7*(3), 3–6.

Dinwiddie, S. H., Zorumski, C. F., & Rubin, E. H. (1987). Psychiatric correlates of chronic solvent abuse. *Journal of Clinical Psychiatry*, *48*, 334–337.

Filley, C. M., Heaton, R. K., & Rosenberg, N. L. (1990). White matter dementia in chronic toluene abuse. *Neurology*, *40*, 532–534.

Fullwood, H., & Ginther, D. W. (1994). Inhalant abuse: The silent epidemic. *Principal*, *74*, 52–53.

Gunning, M. P., & D'Amato, R. C. (1999). Understanding and preventing inhalant abuse among children and adolescents in schools. *Communiqué*, *25*, 31–32.

Johnston, L. D., O'Malley, P. M., & Bachman, J. G. (1999). *National survey results on drug use from the Monitoring the Future study, 1975–1998: Vol. 1*. Secondary school students (NIH Publication No. 994660). Bethesda, MD: National Institute on Drug Abuse.

Simpson, D. D., & Barrett, M. E. (1991). A longitudinal study of inhalant use: Overview and discussion of findings. *Hispanic Journal of Behavioral Sciences*, *13*, 341–355.

ROBYN S. HESS
University of Colorado at Denver

RIK CARL D'AMATO
University of Northern Colorado

INITIAL TEACHING ALPHABET

The Initial Teaching Alphabet, popularly known as i.t.a., was devised by Sir James Pitman of England. His work was the amalgamation of earlier work done by British advocates of the simplification of English spelling. Pitman promoted the concept of a simplified spelling of the English language requiring the addition of new symbols that augmented the alphabet from 26 characters to 44 characters. These early efforts at changing the orthography of English were known as the *Augmented Roman Alphabet* (Aukerman, 1971).

The 44-character Augmented Roman Alphabet was developed and publicized by the Pitman organization in 1960 under the original title *Initial Teaching Medium* (Aukerman, 1971). The purpose behind the development of the new orthographic system was to permit a one-letter character to represent only one English sound or phoneme. Twenty characters were added for speech sounds not represented by a single letter of the English alphabet, and no characters were provided for q and x. No distinction was made between lowercase and capital letters; capital letters were a larger type size of the lowercase form. Use of the augmented alphabet was proposed for teaching beginning reading only.

The i.t.a. was used in British and American schools in the 1960s and the early 1970s. The i.t.a. a provided beginning readers with a true symbol approach to encoding and decoding the sounds of the English language. It made phoneme-grapheme correspondence more regular and simplified spelling for beginning readers. Downing (1964) stated that i.t.a. was not a method of instruction; rather, it was a teaching tool that could be used with any type of reading instruction.

Research comparing i.t.a. instruction and traditional orthographic (TO) instruction was conducted in England by John Downing (1964). Longitudinal studies showed that even though various instructional methods were used, i.t.a.–trained students showed significant differences in the speed with which they learned to read, their levels of comprehension, their spelling levels, and their creative writing abilities.

The i.t.a. program in the United States, Early to Read, was developed by Albert Mazurkiewicz and Harold Tanyzer (1966). This program, like the British i.t.a., was divided into three phases. In Phase I, students were introduced to the i.t.a. characters through the use of the language-experience approach. Phase II reinforced and extended writing, spelling, and reading skills. Phase III, which usually began during the second year of instruction, emphasized the transfer to TO. Early to Read differed from the British program in that a new reading series was written. British publishers transliterated the *Janet and John* basal series into i.t.a.

Mazurkiewicz (1967) conducted the first i.t.a. research in the United States in Bethlehem, Pennsylvania.

This initial study and later studies showed that pupils instructed in i.t.a. continuously showed better abilities in word discrimination, word knowledge, spelling, and creative writing.

The Initial Teaching Alphabet Foundation at Hofstra University was founded to collect and disseminate information on the i.t.a. In reviewing 70 control group studies that compared i.t.a. programs to TO, Block (1971) found that two thirds of the studies indicated that i.t.a. was more successful in teaching beginning reading and writing skills, that one third showed i.t.a. equally as successful as TO, and that no studies showed adverse effects of using the i.t.a. approach.

Block (1971) cites the following as four frequent criticisms of i.t.a.: (1) children who learn i.t.a. have difficulty transferring to TO; (2) i.t.a. materials and training are expensive; (3) the majority of the children's environment uses TO; and (4) children in i.t.a. programs experience the Hawthorne effect.

Downing (1979) reviewed the use of i.t.a. with exceptional children. He reported that even though i.t.a. had been successful in teaching diverse students including those with learning disabilities, students from poverty, and English language learners, further research is needed. Longitudinal studies in Britain showed that the gifted benefited most from the i.t.a. method (Downing, 1979).

REFERENCES

Aukerman, R. C. (1971). *Approaches to beginning reading.* New York, NY: Wiley.

Block, J. R. (1971). *i.t.a.—A status report—1971: The beginnings of a second decade.* Hempstead, NY: Initial Teaching Alphabet Foundation.

Downing, J. (1964). The i.t.a. (Initial Teaching Alphabet) reading experiment. *Reading Teacher, 18,* 105–109.

Downing, J. (1979). "i.t.a." in special education. *Special Education in Canada, 53,* 25–27.

Mazurkiewicz, A. J. (1967). *The initial teaching alphabet in reading instruction, evaluation-demonstration project on the use of i.t.a.* Bethlehem, PA: Lehigh University.

Mazurkiewicz, A. J., & Tanyzer, H. J. (1966). *The i.t.a. handbook for writing and spelling: Early-to-read i.t.a. program.* New York, NY: Initial Teaching Alphabet.

Joyce E. Ness
Montgomery County Intermediate Unit, Norristown, Pennsylvania

INSATIABLE CHILD SYNDROME

Insatiable child syndrome is characterized by a chronic inability to be satisfied (Levine, Brooks, & Schonkoff, 1980). Usually the child craves specific foods, certain activities, attention from others, or material goods. The child's insatiability may be organic or could be learned, such as when humiliating experiences leave the child feeling useless and craving for the attention of others.

The prevalence of the disorder is not well documented, and it usually appears secondary to an attention deficit disorder (Templeton, 1995). Correct diagnosis depends on ruling out the genetic disorder Prader-Willi syndrome due to similar characteristics including food insatiability. Current societal pressures and mores may increase the prevalence rates of this disorder.

Characteristics

1. Onset beginning in early infancy if the disorder is organic.
2. Onset later in life if the disorder is related to environmental influences.
3. An uncontrollable desire for food, activities, attention, or material goods.
4. Children presenting as whiney, irritable, and unpleasant.
5. Parents reporting that children are demanding and difficult to live with.
6. Usually associated with a diagnosed attention deficit disorder.
7. Insatiability not better accounted for by Prader-Willi syndrome, a genetic disorder characterized by overeating and gross obesity.

Due to the low incidence of the disorder, treatment of insatiable child syndrome depends mostly on correct diagnosis (Reynolds, 1999). To increase the probability of an appropriate diagnosis and offer proper treatment, a functional behavior assessment should be conducted to assess the setting events, antecedents, and consequences linked to the child's insatiability.

After the data are analyzed, home and school treatment should be developed to change the behavior of the child, such as by building the child's ability to delay receiving gratification, helping the child understand that parents or other adults cannot be available all the time, and encouraging sharing with other children (Levine et al., 1980). In addition, relationship development between the child and the parents and between the child and his or her teacher should be a target of intervention. One-on-one time or special playtime with significant individuals to reinforce appropriate attention behaviors should be encouraged. The goal of special playtime is to help the child feel more secure and to decrease feelings of helplessness and deprivation (Levine et al., 1980). Another objective may be to set up specific collaborative activities with other children, such as turn-taking games, to promote sharing. Traditional family therapy may also be warranted.

School teachers should also develop special activities with the child to promote positive reinforcement (Levine et al., 1980). Teachers may use praise for completed tasks and delayed gratification to help the child feel more competent and self-sufficient. This in turn may decrease the child's insatiability.

Because insatiability is a behavior problem, prognosis is good if there is sufficient home-school collaboration on interventions. This entails school personnel and parents working together toward common goals to decrease insatiability in the home and school settings. Such collaboration increases the probability of generalization within all environments. Future research should focus on prevalence rates, etiology, and intervention strategies.

REFERENCES

Levine, M. D., Brooks, R., & Shonkoff, J. P. (1980). *A pediatric approach to learning disorders.* New York, NY: Wiley.

Reynolds, C. R. (1999). Insatiable child syndrome. In C. R. Reynolds & E. Fletcher-Jansen (Eds.), *The encyclopedia of special education* (Vol. 2). New York, NY: Wiley.

Templeton, R. (1995, February). *ADHD: A teacher's guide.* Oregon Conference Monograph, 7.

SHERRI LYNN GALLAGHER
RIK CARL D'AMATO
University of Northern Colorado

IN-SERVICE TRAINING FOR SPECIAL EDUCATION TEACHERS (*See* Highly Qualified Teachers)

INSIGHT (IN THE GIFTED)

Advocates of the Gestalt school typically believe that learning takes the form of an insight, a sudden occurrence of a reorganization of the field of experience, as when one has a new idea or discovers a solution to a problem. Two authors (Koffka, 1929; Kohler, 1929) used a variety of problem situations to study the role of insight in the learning of animals. For example, Kohler studied chimpanzee behaviors associated with retrieving a banana that had been placed out of reach by the investigator. As opposed to trial-and-error behavior, the chimpanzee successfully reached the banana as if by plan. Thus, Kohler interpreted the insight involved as a seeing of relations or a putting together of events that were internally represented.

Insight has also been described in human beings by researchers such as Wertheimer (1945) and Sternberg and Davidson (1983). Wertheimer studied children's insightful solutions to geometric problems. Some children used a rote fashion to solve problems; others, however, could see the essential structure of a problem situation, and consequently used insight as their approach to learning. Sternberg and Davidson (1983), on the other hand, developed a subtheory of intellectual giftedness based on the centrality of insight skills.

In a later work, Davidson and Sternberg (1984) proposed that insight involves not one, but three separate but related psychological processes. They referred to the products of the three operations as insights, understood in terms of three types of insight skills: (1) selective encoding, by which relevant information in a given context is sifted from irrelevant information; (2) selective combination, by which relevant information is combined in a novel and productive way; and (3) selective comparison, by which new information is related in a novel way to old information.

The authors' three-process view of insight constitutes what they believe to be a subtheory of intellectual giftedness. Whereas selective encoding involves knowing which pieces of information are relevant, selective combination involves knowing how to blend together the pieces of relevant information. Selective comparison involves relating the newly acquired information to information acquired in the past (as when one solves a problem by using an analogy). In addition, the authors reason that the three processes are not executed in simple serial order, but rather, continually interact with each other in the formation of new ideas. Thus, it is the products of these operations that they refer to as insights.

To test their subtheory, Davidson and Sternberg (1984) completed three experiments with gifted and nongifted children in grades 4, 5, and 6. Results of all three experiments support the subtheory of intellectual giftedness. It was learned that insight plays a statistically significant role in the learning of the gifted as compared with that of the nongifted.

Davidson and Sternberg (1984) suggest several benefits of their approach to understanding and assessing intellectual giftedness over alternative psychometric and information processing approaches. First, they propose that their theoretically based approach deals with what it is that makes the gifted special. For example, they believe that what primarily distinguishes the intellectually gifted in their performance is not that they are faster, but that they are better in their insightful problem solving skills. Second, because their measurement of insight skills has no demands on prior knowledge, their approach is appropriate for individuals with nonstandard backgrounds. Researchers are using EEG technology to investigate insight in problem solving (Jansovec, 1997).

REFERENCES

Davidson, J. E., & Sternberg, R. J. (1984). The role of insight in intellectual giftedness. *Gifted Child Quarterly, 28*(2), 58–64.

Jansovec, N. (1997). Differences in EEG activity between gifted and nonidentified individuals: Insights into problem solving. *Gifted Child Quarterly, 41*(1), 26–32.

Koffka, K. (1929). *The growth of the mind* (2nd ed.). New York, NY: Harcourt.

Kohler, W. (1929). *Gestalt psychology*. New York, NY: Liveright.

Sternberg, R. J., & Davidson, J. E. (1983). Insight in the gifted. *Educational Psychologist, 18*(1), 51–57.

Wertheimer, M. (1945). *Productive thinking*. New York, NY: Harper & Row.

JUNE SCOBEE
University of Houston,
Clear Lake

See also **Culturally/Linguistically Diverse Gifted Students; Gifted Children**

INSTITUTES FOR RESEARCH ON LEARNING DISABILITIES

The Institutes for Research on Learning Disabilities were created to encourage basic and applied research in order to develop and validate successful practices with learning disabled (LD) pupils. Originally sponsored by the Bureau of Education for the Handicapped and later funded through Special Education Programs within the Department of Education, the five 6-year institutes were awarded on a contractual basis to the University of Illinois–Chicago Circle, Teachers College at Columbia University, the University of Kansas, the University of Minnesota, and the University of Virginia.

The Chicago Institute for the Study of Learning Disabilities focused on the social competence of LD children. Studies addressed LD pupils' communicative competence and reading abilities, causal attributions of success and failure, and the immediate impression the pupils make on naive observers (Bryan, Pearl, Donahue, Bryan, & Pflaum, 1983).

The Teachers College Institute at Columbia University was organized as five task forces, each of which conducted research in a specific academic skill area (Connor, 1983). One task force studied memory and study skills of LD students (Gelzheiser, 1982; Shepherd, Frank, Solar, & Gelzheiser, 1982). Two task forces investigated learning problems in the basic skills of arithmetic, reading, and spelling (Fleischner & Garnett, 1979; Fleischner, Garnett, & Preddy, 1982). The final two task forces studied reading comprehension, one from the perspective of interaction of text and reader and one from the perspective of semantics and application of schemata (Williams, 1986).

At the University of Kansas institute, research concentrated on the problems of LD adolescents. Epidemiological studies revealed the unique characteristics of LD students of high school age, and a curriculum comprised of strategy training, social skills, modified materials, and instructional procedures was investigated and developed (Schumaker, Deshler, Alley, & Warner, 1983).

The major purpose of the University of Minnesota's Institute for Research on Learning Disabilities was to study the assessment of LD children. This research incorporated two major lines of investigation. The first explored the characteristics of students referred for psycho-educational evaluation and of those found eligible for placement in school-based LD programs (Ysseldyke et al., 1983). The second line of research developed and validated repeated and direct assessment procedures for assessing students' academic progress and for formatively developing effective instructional programs (Deno, 1985).

The University of Virginia Learning Disabilities Research Institute focused its efforts on LD students with attention problems. It emphasized developing cognitive behavior modification techniques that improve children's on task behavior and that provide children with strategies for approaching academic tasks. Studies included investigations of metacognition, information processing, self-recording of task related behavior, and strategy training (Hallahan et al., 1983).

The work of the five Institutes for Research on Learning Disabilities began amidst considerable controversy about the nature of learning disabilities (McKinney, 1983). Nevertheless, it is generally accepted that the institutes, through the collective resources of many investigators pursuing a complex set of problems in programmatic fashion, contributed significantly to what we now know about the nature and treatment of learning disabilities (Keogh, 1983; McKinney, 1983).

REFERENCES

Bryan, T., Pearl, R., Donahue, M., Bryan, J., & Pflaum, S. (1983). The Chicago institute for study of learning disabilities. *Exceptional Education Quarterly, 4*(1), 1–22.

Connor, F. P. (1983). Improving school instruction for learning disabled: The teachers college institute. *Exceptional Education Quarterly, 4*(1), 23–44.

Deno, S. L. (1985). Curriculum-based measurement: The emerging alternative. *Exceptional Children, 52,* 219–232.

Fleischner, J. E., & Garnett, K. (1979). *Arithmetic learning disabilities: A literature review* (Research Review Series 1979–1980, Vol. 4). New York, NY: Teachers College, Columbia University, Research Institute for the Study of Learning Disabilities.

Fleischner, J. E., Garnett, K., & Preddy, D. (1982). *Mastery of basic number facts by learning disabled students: An intervention study* (Technical Report No. 17). New York, NY: Teachers College, Columbia University, Research Institute for the Study of Learning Disabilities.

Gelzheiser, L. M. (1982). *The effects of direct instruction on learning disabled children's ability to generalize study behaviors for deliberate memory tasks*. Unpublished doctoral dissertation, Teachers College, Columbia University.

Hallahan, D. P., Hall, R. J., Ianna, S. O., Kneedler, R. D., Lloyd, J. W., Loper, A. B., & Reeve, R. E. (1983). Summary of research findings at the University of Virginia Learning Disabilities Research Institute. *Exceptional Education Quarterly*, 4(1), 95–114.

Keogh, B. K. (1983). A lesson from Gestalt psychology. *Exceptional Education Quarterly*, 4(1), 115–128.

McKinney, J. D. (1983). Contributions of the Institutes for Research on Learning Disabilities. *Exceptional Education Quarterly*, 4(1), 129–144.

Schumaker, J. B., Deshler, D. D., Alley, G. R., & Warner, M. M. (1983). Toward the development of an intervention model for the learning disabled adolescents: The University of Kansas Institute. *Exceptional Education Quarterly*, 4(1), 45–74.

Shepherd, J. J., Frank, B., Solar, R. A., & Gelzheiser, L. M. (1982). *Progress report*. New York, NY: Teachers College, Columbia University, Research Institute for the Study of Learning Disabilities.

Williams, J. P. (1986). The role of phonemic analysis in reading. In J. K. Torgeson, & B. Y. L. Wong (Eds.), *Psychological and educational perspectives on learning disabilities*. Orlando, FL: Academic.

Ysseldyke, J., Thurlow, M., Graden, J., Wesson, C., Algozzine, B., & Deno, S. (1983). Generalizations from five years of research on assessment and decision making: The University of Minnesota Institute. *Exceptional Education Quarterly*, 4(1), 75–94.

DOUGLAS FUCHS
LYNN S. FUCHS
*Peabody College,
Vanderbilt University*

INSTITUTIONALIZATION

In the past, persons with disabilities (notably persons with intellectual disabilities or mental illness) were left to fend for themselves, were shut away in rooms or houses, or worse, were placed in prisons (Wolfensberger, 1972). This often resulted in illness or death, a situation that led to the establishment of institutional residences in the 19th century. These facilities, called *hospitals, asylums*, or *colonies*, were constructed in rural areas with residents having little contact with community members. The original intent of such facilities was to provide a higher level of care for handicapped persons needing such care. Anywhere from 500 to 5,000 residents were maintained in each facility. The facilities often had large staffs and became communities unto themselves.

Disabled residents of institutions typically were not prepared to live and work in the community. Emphasis was placed on physical care in contrast to vocational preparation. In addition, the standard of care often was poor. Residents lived in barracks style arrangements that were dehumanizing. Crowding was commonplace, with waking hours spent in idle activity.

Placement in a residential facility was often for life. Through the 1950s, the number of disabled persons residing in institutions increased. Then, with the advent of the deinstitutionalization movement, promoted by those who thought the physical and social environment of institutions to be detrimental, the resident institutional population declined. From 1955 to 1973, the resident population declined from 500,000 to 250,000 in spite of a 40% increase in the U.S. population (Telford & Sawrey, 1977). Currently, the emptying of residential institutions has slowed, with most states controlling new admissions instead of removing residents.

Although many formerly institutionalized persons with disabilities can be accommodated in the community, care and treatment facilities have not kept pace with the deinstitutionalization movement. Consequently, a number of those who returned to the community have been unable to obtain needed services and have become part of the homeless contingent found in many cities. Institutions will always be required for at least some small segment of the disabled population. However, with early intervention, education, and community-based alternatives, few individuals will require intensive and lifelong care.

REFERENCES

Telford, C. W., & Sawrey, J. M. (1977). *The exceptional individual* (2nd ed.). Englewood Cliffs, NJ: Prentice Hall.

Wolfensberger, W. (1972). *The principle of normalization in human services*. Downsview, CT: National Institute of Mental Retardation.

PATRICIA ANN ABRAMSON
*Hudson Public Schools,
Hudson, Wisconsin*

See also Community Residential Programs; Deinstitutionalization

INSTITUTION NATIONALE DES SOURDS-MUETS

The Institution Nationale des Sourds-Muets, the first public nonpaying school for the deaf in the world, was founded in Paris in 1755 by the Abbot Charles Michel de l'Epée (1712–1789). Its name was changed in 1960 to Institut National de Jeunes Sourds (INJS; National Institute for Young Deaf). Despite its location in the heart of Paris, it has retained spacious grounds (19,300 square meters) comprising playgrounds, gardens, orchards, and vegetable gardens.

De l'Epée started to teach the deaf when he was asked to give religious instruction to two deaf twin sisters who communicated by signs. He understood that signs could express human thought as much as oral language and decided to use them for his teaching. However, probably unaware that a more elaborate sign system existed among the Paris deaf community (Moody, 1983), de l'Epée felt compelled to create additional signs. These, the methodical signs, were intended to expand the vocabulary and to adapt the existing signs so as to follow French syntax and morphology. The successor of de l'Epée was the abbot Sicard (1808), who continued to expand the methodical signs. However, their excessive development resulted in a cumbersome system unsuitable for communication. During his tenure, a trend towards greater use of natural signs gained momentum and was established as a principle by the following director, Bébian (Moores, 1978).

As early as 1805, the institute's physician, J. M. Itard (1821), introduced auditory and speech training for some pupils, and tried to teach speech to Victor, the wild child of the Aveyron (Lane, 1981). Bébian, who took charge in 1817, is probably the first protagonist of a bilingual education. He considered that the acquisition of French was facilitated when concepts were first established through signs. This official use of natural sign language allowed more and more former pupils to become teachers. Already under Sicard, however, some deaf teachers had been trained; in 1816 one of them, Laurent Clerc, accompanied Thomas Hopkins Gallaudet back to the United States to establish a school along the same model as the Paris institution.

During most of the 19th century, sign language for teaching flourished, although its use was criticized by Itard and his followers. The latter were unsuccessful in defending oralism until the 1880 Milano Congress of Educators of the Deaf, which decided that signs were inappropriate for teaching and had an adverse effect on the acquisition of spoken language. Signs were henceforth suppressed, and deaf teachers discharged.

For the rest of the 19th century and for more than two thirds of the 20th, oral education prevailed as the only official method. Signs were tolerated among pupils as a low-grade communication medium, although they were still covertly used by some teachers. Following the congresses of the World Federation of the Deaf in Paris (1971) and Washington (1975), a renewal of interest in sign language took place in France. This movement shook the strictly oralist position of the INJS and other European schools for the deaf and led several of its teachers to adopt a total communication philosophy. Today the INJS is a place where energies are expended in several directions in an attempt to revitalize deaf education. The school, which formerly was entirely residential, presently has a larger population of day pupils. Efforts are being made towards mainstreaming and some teachers have become itinerant in order to support pupils integrated into ordinary schools. Sign language teaching is organized within the institution and several teachers use it in their classrooms. Training of interpreters for the deaf has been organized. Other teachers have adopted cued speech, while some have remained exclusively oral. The venerable library contains many publications by former deaf teachers and pupils, including detailed accounts of the life of the deaf community in 18th- and 19th-century France.

The INJS deserves the title of cradle of sign language for deaf education. In its front courtyard, visitors are greeted by the statue of the Abbot de l'Epée, to whose robe clings a grateful deaf child. Many deaf people throughout the world consider de l'Epée as their spiritual father, and the INJS as the living historical landmark of his action.

REFERENCES

Itard, J. M. (1821). *Traité des maladies de l'oreille et de l'audition.* Mequignon Marvis. Paris, France.

Lane, H. (1981). *L'enfant sauvage de l'Aveyron.* Paris, France: Payot.

Moody, B. (1983). *La langue des signes.* Vincennes, France: International Visual Theatre.

Moores, D. F. (1978). *Educating the deaf: Psychology, principles and practices.* Boston, MA: Houghton Mifflin.

Sicard, A. (1808). *Théorie des signes.* Paris, France: Dentu, Delalain.

OLIVIER PÉRIER
Université Libre de Bruxelles,
Centre Comprendre et Parler,
Belgium

See also Deaf Education; Inservice Training for Special Education Teachers; Total Communication

INSTRUCTIONAL TECHNOLOGY FOR INDIVIDUALS WITH DISABILITIES

The federal definition of assistive technology involves two components: Assistive Technology Devices (*see also* Assistive Technology Devices) and Assistive Technology Services. The wisdom in this approach recognizes that positive outcomes associated with assistive technology use are not solely dependent on having access to a device but also several types of supports. These six support factors are outlined in the following federal definition of assistive technology services:

Assistive technology service.
. . . Assistive technology service means any service that directly assists a child with a disability in the selection, acquisition, or use of an assistive technology device. The term includes:

a. The evaluation of the needs of a child with a disability, including a functional evaluation of the child in the child's customary environment.

b. Purchasing, leasing, or otherwise providing for the acquisition of assistive technology devices by children with disabilities.

c. Selecting, designing, fitting, customizing, adapting, applying, maintaining, repairing, or replacing assistive technology devices.

d. Coordinating and using other therapies, interventions, or services with assistive technology devices, such as those associated with existing education and rehabilitation plans and programs.

e. Training or technical assistance for a child with a disability or, if appropriate, that child's family.

f. Training or technical assistance for professionals (including individuals providing education or rehabilitation services), employers, or other individuals who provide services to, employ, or are otherwise substantially involved in the major life functions of that child. (20 U.S.C. 1401(2))

The assistive technology services definition was far ahead of its time in that it recognized that successful assistive technology outcomes are dependent on more than simply acquiring new devices. Indeed, the comprehensive nature of "wraparound services" are essential to success in the adoption, use, and benefit of assistive technologies that augment human performance. Unfortunately, many disputes between school districts and parents concerning assistive technology focus on the interpretation of the assistive technology services requirements associated with evaluation (section a), determination of need/benefit (sections b and c), funding (section b), training (sections e and f), and home use (sections b, d, e, and f) (Day & Huefner, 2003; Edyburn, 2009).

A considerable literature has emerged supporting the preparation of professionals who work with assistive technology (Cook, Polgar, & Hussey, 2008; Dell, Newton, Petroff, 2011; Newton, 2004) thereby ensuring that they are acquainted with the federal requirements associated with assistive technology devices and services. Significant attention has also been placed on the collaborative decision making required to provide interdisciplinary assistive technology services (Bodine & Melonis, 2005; Downing, 2004; Newton, 2004). However, research on assistive technology services is relatively rare and reveals that there are significant disparities in the way services are provided (Bausch, Ault, Evmenova, & Behrmann, 2008; McLaren, Bausch, & Ault, 2007).

The definitions of assistive technology devices and assistive technology services provide a comprehensive perspective on processes that enable individuals with disabilities to acquire and use assistive technologies in ways that enhance functional capabilities. Unfortunately, the federal definitions overlook one necessary component of a three-legged stool: outcomes. Since federal law is silent concerning the need to measure the outcomes of assistive technology use, or quantify the benefits derived from assistive technology, the field has focused on procedural compliance with federal law rather than engage in

systemic research that would inform the development of evidence-based practices.

REFERENCES

Bausch, M. E., Ault, M. J., Evmenova, A. S., & Behrmann, M. M. (2008). Going beyond AT devices: Are AT services being considered? *Journal of Special Education Technology, 23*(2), 116.

Bodine, C., & Melonis, M. (2005). Teaming and assistive technology in educational settings. In D. Edyburn, K. Higgins, & R. Boone (Eds.), *Handbook of special education technology research and practice* (pp. 209–227). Whitefish Bay, WI: Knowledge by Design.

Cook, A. M., Polgar, J. M., & Hussey, S. M. (2008). *Assistive technologies: Principles and practices* (3rd ed.). St. Louis, MO: Mosby Elsevier.

Day, J. D., & Huefner, D. S. (2003). Assistive technology: Legal issues for students with disabilities and their schools. *Journal of Special Education Technology, 18*(2), 2334.

Dell, A. G., Newton, D. A., Petroff, J. G. (2011). *Assistive technology in the classroom: Enhancing the school experiences of students with disabilities* (2nd ed.). Upper Saddle River, NJ: Pearson.

Downing, J. A. (2004). Related services for students with disabilities: Introduction to the special issue. *Intervention in School and Clinic, 39*(4), 195–208.

Edyburn, D. (2009). Assistive technology advocacy. *Special Education Technology Practice, 11*(2), 15–17.

McLaren, E. M., Bausch, M. E., & Ault, M. J. (2007). Collaboration strategies reported by teachers providing assistive technology services. *Journal of Special Education Technology, 22*(4), 16–29.

Newton, D. A., (2004). Assistive technology teams: A model for developing school district teams. *Journal of Special Education Technology, 19*(3), 47–49.

DAVE EDYBURN
University of Wisconsin–Milwaukee
Fourth edition

INTEGRATED THERAPY

The provision of specialized therapy services in the classroom and in other natural environments has been termed integrated therapy (Nietupski, Schutz, & Ockwood, 1980; Sternat et al., 1977). Integrated therapy has a number of advantages over the isolated therapy model, in which students are removed from their classroom for therapy in a segregated environment, usually a clinic or therapy room. One advantage is the potential for continuous as opposed to episodic training sessions. Therapists and classroom teaching staff are able to coordinate both training goals and procedures. Moreover, in an integrated therapy model, there are more opportunities for sharing of professional skills and information concerning students' programs.

Another important advantage of integrated therapy conditions is the potential to enhance generalization. This is particularly critical for very young students with severe disabilities who often fail to perform new skills in other than the training environment.

There are many other theoretical and practical considerations (e.g., the importance of longitudinal intervention in natural environments, the reality of limited resources and personnel) that suggest the superiority of integrated therapy conditions in most school situations, but these considerations are less important than professional commitment. The effectiveness of integrated therapy depends on the willingness of teachers and therapists to alter traditional beliefs and practices and negotiate new role functions. They must discard the notion that only a therapist can provide therapy and agree to share intervention responsibilities in natural settings.

REFERENCES

Nietupski, J., Scheutz, G., & Ockwood, L. (1980). The delivery of communication therapy services to severely handicapped students: A plan for change. *Journal of the Association for the Severely Handicapped*, 5(1), 13–23.

Sternat, J., Messina, R., Nietupski, J., Lyon, S., & Brown, L. (1977). Occupational and physical therapy services for severely handicapped students: Toward a naturalized public school service delivery model. In E. Sontag, J. J. Smith, & N. Certo (Eds.), *Educational programming for the severely and profoundly handicapped*. Reston, VA: Council for Exceptional Children.

LINDA MCCORMICK
*University of Hawai,
Manoa*

See also Inclusion; Least Restrictive Environment; Mainstreaming

INTELLECTUAL DEFICIENCY (*See* Intelligence; Mental Retardation)

INTELLIGENCE

Intelligence has proven to be a difficult construct to define. From as early as 1921 (Intelligence and Its Measurement: A symposium, 1921) to the present (e.g., Detterman, 1994; Neisser et al., 1996; Sternberg & Detterman, 1986), psychologists have consistently failed to agree on a common conceptual definition, general theoretical approach,

or assessment device. Boring's (1923, p. 35) response to the inconsistencies was his famous pronouncement that "intelligence as a measurable capacity must at the start be defined as the capacity to do well in an intelligence test. Intelligence is what the tests test." Psychologists were not thrilled, perhaps not only because of the circularity of the definition but because it appeared in the *New Republic*, bringing our confusion to the attention of a wide audience. But if we consider Boring's qualifying phrase, "as a measurable capacity," the definition makes some sense, particularly given the great influence of the psychometric approach to research on intelligence.

The confusion over definition has not diminished. Indeed, a larger number and greater variety of approaches may exist now than at any other time since the outset of interest in the topic. Whether the number of theories of intelligence exceeds the combined memberships of the American Psychological Association and American Psychological Society is undetermined at this time. Further, as Neisser (1979, p. 185) has convincingly argued, intelligence cannot be defined in the absolute, but only in so far as an individual can be seen as resembling a prototypical imaginary "intelligent person": "There are no definitive criteria of intelligence...it is a fuzzy edged concept to which many features are relevant. Two people may both be quite intelligent and yet have very few traits in common—they resemble the prototype along different dimensions. Thus, there is no such quality as *intelligence*...resemblance is an external fact and not an internal essence. There can be no process-based definition of intelligence because it is not a unitary quality. It is a resemblance between two individuals, one real and the other prototypical." Neisser suggests, however, that intelligence tests are good measures of the academic intelligence subset of the larger prototype of intelligent person.

Some commonality of agreement at a fairly global level holds both among psychologists and the public at large. Consider the well-known study of implicit theories of intelligence by Sternberg, Conway, Ketron, and Bernstein (1981), who asked laypeople at a supermarket, train station, and university library to describe behaviors that they would consider intelligent, academically intelligent, or everyday intelligent. Sternberg et al. (1981) then sent the entire list of behaviors to academic psychologists whose research interest was psychology and asked them to indicate how important each behavior was in characterizing intelligent, academically intelligent, or everyday intelligent people. The authors also asked a group of laypeople to do essentially the same task in a laboratory setting. Factor analysis of the psychologists' ratings of intelligence revealed three factors: Verbal Intelligence ("is verbally fluent"), Problem-Solving Ability ("is able to apply knowledge to problems at hand"), and Practical Intelligence ("sizes up situations well"). Factor analysis of the laypeople's ratings also revealed three factors: Practical Problem Solving Ability ("reasons logically and well"), Verbal Ability ("speaks clearly and articulately"), and Social Competence ("accepts others for what they are"). Clearly, these factors are similar for the two groups and indicate that professionals and laypeople have well-developed and similar implicit theories of intelligence. Sternberg et al. (1981) suggest that problem solving, which they equated to fluid intelligence, and verbal ability, which they equated to crystallized intelligence (see the following discussion) are "integral aspects of intellectual functioning" (p. 54). Further, two elements are common to many experts' definitions of intelligence: (1) the ability to learn from experience, and (2) the capacity to adapt to one's environment.

Theories of Intelligence

As implied previously, psychologists and educators have proposed far more theories of intelligence than can be reviewed in this entry. Summarized below are some of the more influential past and current theories. Broader and more in-depth presentations are in Detterman (1994) and Sternberg and Detterman (1986).

Psychometric Approaches

Psychometric theories of intelligence derive from statistical analyses, particularly factor analysis, of scores on intelligence tests. Such theories could be seen as following the Boring prototype of the intelligent person, someone who does well on intelligence tests. Several strong arguments can be made in support of a single general intelligence factor, called g. As early as 1904, Spearman reported that scores on a variety of then available tests all intercorrelated; that is, high scores on one test tended to be associated with high scores on others, and vice versa. The intercorrelations suggested that one intellectual factor predicted performance on the tests. He later (e.g., Spearman, 1927) conducted factor analyses, a technique he invented, on large numbers of intelligence test scores and found that scores intercorrelated, reflecting a general factor of intelligence (g), but that each group of tests also tapped a more specific factor (s).

Support for a single general intelligence has been offered in studies of reaction time. Reaction time is measured by the time it takes an individual to complete an uncomplicated task. Eysenck (1994) has provided evidence for a biological basis of the g factor, and Jensen (1993) claims that the essence of g relies on the speed of neural transmission. The faster an individual's neural processes, the faster their reaction time. Reaction time has been related to intelligence through its positive correlation with IQ. Others have argued against this position by claiming it does not make sense that reaction time speed and intelligence should correlate. They counter that intelligence is an engaging process that involves problem solving. Reaction time is different; it is an automatic response over which one has little control. The importance and basis of g

remain contentious as seen in the pro and con arguments in Modgil and Modgil (1987).

Opposed to g theory, Thurstone (1938) proposed that intelligence was comprised of seven independent factors, which he called primary mental abilities: verbal comprehension, verbal fluency, inductive reasoning, spatial visualization, number, memory, and perceptual speed. However, he found that scores on his tests of these factors, the Primary Mental Abilities Test, actually intercorrelated moderately, supporting the existence of a second order common factor. However, Thurstone chose to emphasize the factors' separate identities.

Cattell (1971) proposed a hierarchical model of intelligence in which g was divided into two components, fluid intelligence and crystallized intelligence. Fluid intelligence, now referred to as Gf, is the ability to apply cognitions to novel problems, to acquire new information, and to induce new relationships among known information. This type of intelligence is considered abstract and culture free. Crystallized intelligence, now referred to as Gc, includes skills and knowledge acquired across the lifespan that enable individuals to apply proven problem solving skills to familiar challenges. This form of intelligence is acquired, and relies heavily on culture and experience. Under each of these two major subfactors are other more specific ones. Horn (1985) has presented new evidence for Gf and Gc, and has suggested that they are highly correlated in young children but tend to become less and less correlated as children grow and have various experiences. Eysenck's (1985) intelligence A, which includes all biological and genetically determined intelligence and is the type he and Jensen have proposed is measured through reaction time, is very similar to Gf, whereas intelligence B, which is any type of intelligence that is formed through the environment and experience, is similar to Gc.

The ultimate factor analytic model of intelligence is Guilford's three-dimensional structure of the intellect (SOI), represented as a cube comprised of all combinations of five operations, four contents, and six products for a total of 120 factors. Guilford attempted to develop tests for these individual factors that would be independent of g. Little evidence supports Guilford's theory, and it has been much criticized. For example, Kline (1991) suggests that the model relies on human intuition more than scientific evidence. The SOI now appears largely of historic interest for the role it played in Guilford's resurrection of interest in the topic of creativity.

Carroll (e.g., 1994) has developed a hierarchical theory of intelligence based on factor analysis of a large sample of data sets. His model proposes more than 40 primary factors in various domains (language competence, reasoning and thinking, memory and learning, visual perception, auditory reception, idea production, and cognitive speed). Analysis of the primary factors revealed seven secondary factors, many of them similar to aspects of the theories of

Horn, Cattell, Eysenck, and Jensen: *Gf*, fluid intelligence; *Gc*, crystallized intelligence; *Gv*, visualization capacity; *Gs*, general cognitive speed; *Gm*, general memory; *Gr*, general retrieval capacity; and *Ga*, general auditory perception capacity. Analyses of these factors revealed, not surprisingly, Spearman's *g*. Carroll (1994, p. 62) suggests that *g* mainly loads on tasks involving "the *level of complexity* at which individuals are able to handle basic processes of induction, deduction, and comprehension."

Beyond Psychometrics: Intelligence Broadly Conceptualized

Concerned among other things about limitations of *g*, Gardner (1983, 1993) proposed seven "multiple intelligences" (MI) as individual components that perform separately at differing levels. He (Gardner, 1983, p. 9) claims support for MI through "studies of prodigies, gifted individuals, idiots savants, normal children, normal adults, experts in different lines of work, and individuals from diverse cultures." His seven MI are: (1) linguistic intelligence, reflected in tasks such as reading or language comprehension; (2) logical mathematical intelligence, involving calculations and logic; (3) spatial intelligence, involving transformations of objects and perception of forms; (4) musical intelligence, which supposedly develops earliest, involving such capabilities as composing or playing an instrument; (5) bodily kinesthetic intelligence, reflected in control over the motions of one's body as well as ability to manipulate objects; (6) interpersonal intelligence, the ability to understand other individuals; and (7) intrapersonal intelligence, which relates to the ability to view oneself objectively in terms of strengths and weaknesses. Although the seven intelligences are viewed as functioning separately, they often interact to produce particular kinds of intelligent behavior.

Although generating much interest in both psychology and education, Gardner's proposal is questionable from a scientific standpoint. In the first place, he has offered no tests of his intelligences, leaving their presumed independence as well as their very existence in question. The evidence he offers is interesting, but hardly systematic or compelling, particularly since comparable evidence could be found for other presumed "intelligences." As others (e.g., Neisser et al., 1996) have pointed out, separate categories of intelligence are not all that independent; individuals who have talent in one area tend to be talented in other areas as well, relating again to the *g* factor premise. Further, also pointed out by Neisser et al. (1996), Gardner's intelligences are others' talents. Indeed, Gardner's approach conceptually resembles Taylor's (e.g., Taylor & Ellison, 1975) earlier multiple talent model. Finally, as Hunt (1994, p. 233) has observed, Gardner attempts to incorporate far too much under the concept of intelligence: "If we make 'intelligence' coterminous with 'all the nice little abilities a human might have,' the topic will be so incoherent that it will never be understood." To be fair, Gardner (1983, p. 11) specifically stated, "I want to underscore that the notion of multiple intelligences is hardly a proven scientific fact: it is, at most, an idea that has recently regained the right to be discussed seriously." That cautionary note still appears appropriate.

Also concerned about limitations of *g* as well as believing that all good things come in threes, Sternberg (1985) has proposed a triarchic componential theory of intelligence. Intelligence is viewed as involving three types of abilities that operate on three different levels and that draw on three components of information processing. The triarchy of abilities are the analytic, creative, and practical abilities. Analytic abilities are used to evaluate and judge information to deal with problems that have only one right answer. Creative abilities are used to deal with novel problems that require thinking in a different way and that may have no one solution. Practical abilities deal with real-world problems that may have various solutions. The three levels on which the abilities operate are the internal world, the external world, and individual experience. The three information-processing components are: (1) metacomponents are executive processes that plan, monitor, and evaluate; (2) performance components implement metacomponents; and (3) knowledge acquisition components are used for initial learning of problem solving strategies. These three components operate interdependently. Sternberg's argument against the emphasis on *g* is that general reasoning, such as previously noted in crystallized intelligence, may be a highly regarded aspect in some cultures, but other cultures have no use for it at all. This should not mean that they have a mental deficiency—it is simply a skill that they have never acquired.

Proponents of *g* contend that Sternberg's theory lacks any biological basis and that his concepts are not empirically supported. Some (e.g., Eysenck, 1994) have provided evidence that originality and creativity are not aspects of cognitive ability, but traits of personality. On the other hand, a variety of evidence (Neisser et al., 1996) supports Sternberg's contention that practical intelligence is both largely independent of scores on standard intelligence tests and an important correlate of real-world problem solving.

Aspects of Measured Intelligence

Intelligence as measured by standardized tests can be used as predictors of various criterion variables, correlated with presumptive underlying processes such as processing time, used to describe individual and group differences, and analyzed for genetic and environmental bases. The following is a brief summary of some of these findings, based on reviews by Gottfredson (1997), Humphreys (1992), and Neisser et al. (1996).

Prediction of Scholastic Achievement

Since the time of Binet, the major purpose of intelligence tests has been to predict academic performance. As would be expected, scores on such tests do correlate with scholastic achievement as measured both by grades and standardized achievement tests. Correlations between IQs and measures of school achievement for children average about .50. At a higher educational level, SAT and scores also predict college grades, although the correlations vary considerably from one study to another. These correlations only account for about 25% of the total variance, indicating that a host of other factors, including personality, social, and cultural factors are also important in school performance.

Other Correlates

Intelligence test scores correlate with years of education, occupational status, and job performance. They also correlate with socioeconomic status, but interpretation is difficult owing to the number of other correlates. The speed with which people perform a number of cognitive tasks also correlates positively with measured intelligence, and the magnitude of the correlations appears to increase with task complexity.

Genetic and Environmental Bases

Although a topic of much research and controversy, the degree to which genetic and environmental factors contribute to intelligence remains uncertain. Many reasons are responsible for this uncertainty, including the statistical techniques and subject samples used. Further, by necessity, the more environmental factors are similar for subjects in the samples, the larger must be the contribution of genetic ones. That is, if environment differences are negligible, then any variability must owe to genetic differences. Estimates of the proportion of differences in intelligence that may be attributed to differences in genetic background range from .40 to .80, with a mean of about .50. These estimates are, however, based on studies in which subjects from very low socioeconomic levels were underrepresented. Since environmental differences are correlated with socioeconomic status, artifactually small environmental differences would necessarily exaggerate the effect of genetic differences. The proportion tends to increase with age, perhaps because as individuals develop, they increasingly select their own environments, partly to be compatible with other genetically based traits. Particular genetic conditions, such as Down syndrome, may be responsible for individual cases of mental retardation.

Although even the highest estimates of the role of differences in genetics indicate a considerable role of environmental differences in determining differences in intelligence, determining the nature of the responsible environmental factors has been difficult. Researchers have identified numerous environmental factors as being potentially important in influencing normal variations in intelligence, including cultural, familial, social, and academic ones, but firm identification remains elusive. Doubtless, environmental factors, such as lead exposure, prenatal alcohol, prolonged malnutrition, perinatal factors (prematurity, very low birth weight) are responsible for individual cases of lowered intelligence and mental retardation, but their role in normal individual differences is small.

Group Differences

Consistent differences exist among cultural/ethnic subgroups in measured intelligence, although the degree of difference is not as consistent. Mean IQ of Whites is the same as the standardized mean, 100, whereas that of Asian Americans is somewhat higher, about 105, and that of African Americans considerably lower, about 85. Means for Latinos and Native Americans fall in between. Many explanations, both environmental and genetic, have been offered for these differences, but all are subject to criticism. One consistent finding, however, is that group differences cannot be attributed to bias in the tests, for which no scientific evidence exists. Absence of test bias should not, however, be taken as support of a genetic interpretation. Flynn (1999), for example, has recently offered a cogent criticism of genetic interpretations of group differences. Virtually no direct evidence supports a genetic explanation, but reliable evidence of environmental factors also remains elusive. What can be said at this time is that firm claims to either position likely rest more on belief than on scientifically supported evidence.

The Rising IQ

"Perhaps the most striking of all environmental effects is the steady worldwide rise in intelligence test performance" (Neisser et al., 1996, p. 89). The "Flynn Effect," named after the person who first systematically reported it (e.g., Flynn, 1984, 1999), refers to the consistent and sizable increases in measured intelligence that have occurred in the United States and other Western countries since at least the 1930s. The gain is approximately 0.3 IQ points each year (Flynn, 1999). Of particular interest, gains on the Ravens Progressive Matrices test, a culture-reduced and thus more g loaded test, are even higher and occur in 20 different countries (Flynn, 1999). The increases must be environmental, since positing genetic change over that period of time is simply untenable. Furthermore, the increases occur in the absence of any increases in achievement test scores. The reasons for the increase are unclear. Neisser et al. (1996) argue that increased test sophistication is an unlikely basis and suggest that increased cultural complexity and/or improved nutrition may play a role. But possible also is Flynn's (1987) position that the improved scores cannot reflect a comparable increase in real intelligence, or several countries would be experiencing a true cultural renaissance owing to a dramatic increase in the number of their geniuses. Flynn suggests that what has increased actually may be only a relatively narrow, for practical purposes, type of abstract problem solving.

Some Implications

The validity of intelligence tests as predictors of school performance supports their continued use to identify children in need of special education services. The relatively low correlations between IQ and academic performance indicate that many other factors are involved. Although a hierarchical theory of intelligence with *g* as the highest factor is supported by much research, additional aspects of intelligence, particularly practical intelligence, appear to be important determinants of a wide range of behavior. The Flynn Effect is a clear reflection of environmental influences on measured intelligence for which theories will need to account. Formal adequate schooling, including preschools and appropriate intervention, is an important influence on intellectual development. Finally, a separation of the scientific aspects of the study of intelligence from its political implications is needed.

REFERENCES

Boring, E. (1923). Intelligence as the tests test it. *New Republic*, *36*, 35–37.

Carroll, J. B. (1994). Cognitive abilities: Constructing a theory from data. In D. K. Detterman (Ed.), *Current topics in human intelligence, volume 4: Theories of intelligence* (pp. 43–63). Norwood, NJ: Ablex.

Cattell, R. B. (1971). *Abilities: Their structure, growth, and action*. Boston, MA: Houghton Mifflin.

Detterman, D. K. (1994). A system theory of intelligence. In D. K. Detterman (Ed.), *Current topics in human intelligence*: Vol. 4. *Theories of Intelligence* (pp. 85–115). Norwood, NJ: Ablex.

Eysenck, H. J. (1994). A biological theory of intelligence. In D. K. Detterman (Ed.), *Current topics in human intelligence*: Volume 4. *Theories of intelligence* (pp. 117–149). Norwood, NJ: Ablex.

Eysenck, H. J., & Eysenck, M. W. (1985). *Personality and individual differences: A nature science approach*. New York, NY: Plenum Press.

Flynn, J. R. (1984). The mean IQ of Americans: Massive gains 1932 to 1978. *Psychological Bulletin*, *95*, 29–51.

Flynn, J. R. (1987). Massive IQ gains in 14 nations: What IQ tests really measure. *Psychological Bulletin*, *101*, 171–191.

Flynn, J. R. (1999). Searching for justice: The discovery of IQ gains over time. *American Psychologist*, *54*(1), 5–20.

Gardner, H. (1983). *Frames of mind: The theory of multiple intelligences*. New York, NY: Basic Books.

Gardner, H. (Ed.). (1993). *Multiple intelligences: The theory in practice*. New York, NY: Basic Books.

Gottfredson, L. S. (1997). Mainstream science on intelligence: An editorial with 52 signatories, history, and bibliography. *Intelligence*, *24*, 13–23.

Horn, J. L. (1985). Remodeling old models of intelligence: *GfGc* theory. In B. B. Wolman (Ed.), *Handbook of intelligence* (pp. 267–300). New York, NY: Wiley.

Humphreys, L. G. (1992). Ability testing. *Psychological Science*, *3*, 271–274.

Hunt, E. (1994). Theoretical models for the study of intelligence. In D. K. Detterman (Ed.), *Current topics in human intelligence volume 4: Theories of intelligence* (pp. 233–256). Norwood, NJ: Ablex.

Intelligence and its measurement: A symposium. (1921). *Journal of Educational Psychology*, *12*, 123–147, 195–216, 271–275.

Jensen, A. R. (1993). Why is reaction time correlated with psychometric *g*? *Current Directions in Psychological Science*, *2*, 53–56.

Kline, P. (1991). *Intelligence*. New York, NY: Routledge.

Modgil, S., & Modgil, C. (Eds.). (1987). *Arthur Jensen: Consensus and controversy*. Falmer, England: Falmer Press.

Neisser, U. (1979). The concept of intelligence. *Intelligence*, *3*, 217–227.

Neisser, U., Boodoo, G., Bouchard, T. J. Jr., Boykin, A. W., Brody, N., Ceci, S. J.,... Urbina, S. (1996). Intelligence: Knowns and unknowns. *American Psychologist*, *51*, 77–101.

Spearman, C. (1904). "General intelligence" objectively determined and measured. *American Journal of Psychology*, *15*, 201–293.

Spearman, C. (1927). *The abilities of man: Their nature and measurement*. New York, NY: Macmillan.

Sternberg, R. J. (1985). *Beyond IQ: A triarchic theory of human intelligence*. New York, NY: Cambridge University Press.

Sternberg, R. J., Conway, B. E., Ketron, J. L., & Bernstein, M. (1981). People's conception of intelligence. *Journal of Personality and Social Psychology*, *41*, 37–55.

Sternberg, R. J., & Detterman, D. K. (Eds.). (1986). *What is intelligence?* Norwood, NJ: Ablex.

Taylor, C. W., & Ellison, R. L. (1975). Moving toward working models in creativity: Utah creativity experiences and insights. In I. A. Taylor & J. W. Getzels (Eds.), *Perspectives in creativity* (pp. 191–223). Chicago, IL: Aldine.

Thurstone, L. L. (1938). Primary mental abilities. *Psychometric monographs*, No. 1.

ROBERT C. NICHOLS
DIANE JARVIS
State University of New York at Buffalo
First edition

ROBERT T. BROWN
KATHERINE D. FALWELL
University of North Carolina at Wilmington
Second edition

INTELLIGENCE: A MULTIDISCIPLINARY JOURNAL

Intelligence, first appearing in January 1977, has been edited since its inception by Douglas K. Detterman. David Zeaman and Robert J. Sternberg served as associate editors until 1984; no associate editors are currently listed. Joseph Hogan, III, served as book review editor until 1980, when James Pellegrino took the position. Presently, Ian Deary is listed as book review editor. *Intelligence* has a large editorial board comprised of notable scholars from different disciplines within the behavioral sciences.

When *Intelligence* was established in 1977, there were no other journals devoted exclusively to basic research in human intelligence, even though many prestigious journals were available in the field of learning. By establishing a new journal, the founder sought to "formalize the importance of the study of human intelligence and the major role it has played in the development of the behavioral sciences" (p. 2). In past years, the journal published issues quarterly but has now increased publication to six issues per year.

Intelligence is a scientifically oriented journal, publishing papers that strive to substantially contribute to research regarding the nature and function of intelligence. The journal is devoted to the publication of original research, but also accepts theoretical and review articles. Studies concerned with application are considered only if the work also contributes to basic knowledge. *Intelligence* publishes on a variety of topics ranging from IQ's correlation with crime to cultural test bias. Though a multidisciplinary journal, recent publications on mental retardation and early childhood development may be of note to special educators.

This entry has been informed by the source listed below.

REFERENCE

Detterman, D. K. (1977). Is intelligence necessary? *Intelligence: A Multidisciplinary Journal, 1*(1), 13.

ADAM C. PULLARO
JAMES C. KAUFMAN
*California State University,
San Bernardino
Fourth edition*

INTELLIGENCE, EMOTIONAL

Although all humans experience emotions, individuals markedly differ in the extent to which they experience, attend to, identify, understand, regulate, and use their emotions and those of others. The term *emotional intelligence* (EI) first appeared in a book by Van Ghent (1961),

soon followed by an article by Leuner (1966). Because the former was unrelated to psychology and the latter was published in German, the concept remained largely unnoticed. The first English occurrence in Psychology was in a doctoral dissertation by Payne (1985). Peter Salovey and John Mayer (1989–1990) opened a modern line of research, started a hot topic in psychology, and coined a catchphrase that has made its way into the common vernacular. The subsequent fame and widespread use of the term *emotional intelligence* is due mostly to the popular best seller of the same name by Daniel Goleman (1995). This enormous popularity, however, has come at the unfortunate cost of obscuring Salovey and Mayer's original conception of emotional intelligence and overshadowing subsequent empirical research. This resulted in the formation of three distinct concepts of EI, each containing its own definition and approach. Caruso, Mayer, and Salovey (2002) dubbed two of these approaches the mixed model and the ability model. The mixed model, the more popular of the two, merges EI with characteristics of personality and certain skills. The ability model characterizes emotional intelligence as a class of intelligence where emotions and thinking are integrated (Caruso et al., 2002). Other authors held that EI was conceptually (inversely) related to the personality dimensions of neuroticism and alexithymia (among others) and should therefore be conceived as a set of affect-related traits (Petrides & Furnham, 2003).

The idea that emotion is a significant part of our intellectual being has roots in Darwin and Freud and, more recently, in the work of Howard Gardner (1983). In Gardner's theory of multiple intelligences, two of his proposed seven intelligences involve emotions: interpersonal intelligence (understanding other people) and intrapersonal intelligence (understanding one's self). Robert Sternberg's theory of successful intelligence (also known as *practical intelligence*) is another major theory of intellect that takes into consideration the importance of emotional well-being (see Sternberg & Kaufman, 1998). The common historical view, however, is that emotions are secondary—indeed, inferior to intellect (Mayer, Salovey, & Caruso, 2004).

In 1990, Salovey and Mayer proposed a model of emotional intelligence that had three factors: appraisal and expression of emotion, regulation of emotion, and utilization of emotion. Appraisal and expression of emotion is comprised of emotion in the self (which can be both verbal and nonverbal), and emotion in others. Emotion in others consists of nonverbal perception of emotion and empathy. The second factor, regulation of emotion, is the ability to regulate emotion in the self, and the ability to regulate and alter emotions in other people. The final factor, utilizing emotional intelligence, has four aspects: flexible planning, creative thinking, redirected attention, and motivation. Flexible planning refers to the ability to produce a large number of different plans for the future, enabling the planner to better respond to opportunities. This production of many plans can result from using emotion and mood changes to one's advantage and from looking at a wide variety of possibilities. Creative thinking, the second aspect, may be more likely to occur if a person is happy and in a good mood. Redirected attention involves the idea that when strong emotions are experienced, a person's resources and attentions may be tuned to new problems. People who can use this phenomenon to their own benefit will be able to use a potentially stressful situation to focus on the most important or pressing issues involved. Motivation emotions, the final principle of emotional intelligence, refers to the art of making one's self continue to perform difficult tasks by focusing one's anxiety or tension toward the performance of that task.

Mayer and Salovey compressed their theory into four branches of ability: (1) perceiving, appraising, and expressing emotions; (2) accessing and producing feelings in aid of cognition; (3) comprehending information on affect and using emotional knowledge; and (4) regulating emotions for growth and contentment (Mayer & Salovey, 1997). These branches are categorized in a certain order to show how much ability is incorporated into personality (Mayer et al., 2004). The branches create a hierarchy where the ability to regulate emotions is positioned at the top and the capacity to perceive emotion is placed at its bottom. The first branch, perception of emotion, is the degree to which one is able to distinguish emotion in other individuals, by utilizing cues from facial expression and body language. The second branch, facilitation, comes into play once emotion is recognized, which involves the integration of emotion with cognitive processes. The third branch, the understanding of emotions, is the ability to analyze emotions, to recognize the most likely path they will take over time, and to become aware of their aftereffects. The fourth branch, the management of emotion, is the ability to control emotions in order to meet an individual's set goals, having an understanding of one's self, and having societal awareness (Mayer et al., 2004).

Contrary to the ability perspective that was theory-driven and then empirically tested, the trait EI perspective was empirically driven and then theorized. To facilitate EI testing in research, educational, and business settings, several authors translated ability models into self-report instruments (e.g. Schutte et al., 1998). The high correlations found between self-reported EI scores and personality traits led Petrides and Furnham (2001) to coin the term *trait emotional intelligence*. From the trait EI perspective, EI is a constellation of emotion-related dispositions capturing the extent to which people attend to, identify, understand, regulate, and utilize their emotions and those of others. Greater trait EI corresponds to a profile of dispositions that leads to greater adaptation.

The trait EI perspective views EI as a cluster of lower-order personality traits (Petrides, Pita, & Kokkinaki, 2007). EI therefore encompasses two kinds of variance: one portion of variance already covered by established personality taxonomies (e.g., the Giant Three or the Big Five) and one portion of variance that lies outside these dimensions (Petrides et al., 2007). In accordance with this view, trait EI has been evaluated using personality-like questionnaires.

The trait EI perspective uses self-reports, which barely reflect self-perceptions and therefore constitute unreliable assessments of objective competencies. Although this premise appears acceptable in the first instance, this argument proved to be incorrect as trait EI does relate to objective criteria. First, trait EI has neurobiological correlates, such as the level of asymmetry in the resting activation of frontal cortical areas (i.e., Kemp et al., 2005) or the hypothalamic-pituitary-adrenal axis reactivity in stressful situations (Mikolajczak, Roy, Luminet, Fillée, & de Timary, 2007; Salovey, Woolery, Stroud, & Epel, 2002). Studies on individuals with lesions in key emotion brain areas also revealed that these people have lower levels of trait EI than normal controls (Bar-On, Tranel, Denburg, & Bechara, 2003). It is noteworthy that the effect sizes in these studies were not only statistically significant, but that most of them were large according to Cohen's norms (1988). Second, trait EI correlates with the speed of emotional information processing (Austin, 2004, 2005). Third, trait EI predicts objective life-outcomes such as work performance (e.g., Bradberry & Su, 2006; Law, Wong, & Song, 2004; Van Rooy, & Viswesvaran, 2004), income (Petrides & Furnham, 2006), number of school exclusions or unauthorized absences (e.g., Mavroveli, Petrides, Shove, & Whitehead, 2008), cooperation (Schutte et al., 2001) or peer-rated sociability and popularity (Petrides, Sangareau, Furnham, & Frederickson, 2006).

The second critique addressed to the trait EI perspective is that it correlates too much with existing personality traits to be useful. According to Gignac, Jang, and Bates (2009), the common practice of comparing EI to the NEO PIR is flawed logic, as the NEO is such a big construct that it encompasses almost everything and is so general that there is redundancy within the NEO itself. The trait EI construct is useful because it organizes under a single framework the main individual differences in affectivity, which have been up to now scattered across the basic Big Five dimensions (neuroticism, extraversion, openness, agreeableness, and conscientiousness) and other models (Gignac, 2009). This critique is also refuted by the numerous studies showing that trait EI explains additional variance over and above related traits such as alexithymia or the Big Five, to predict criteria as diverse as cortisol secretion amid stress (e.g., Mikolajczak et al., 2007), academic success (e.g., Van der Zee, Thijs, & Schakel, 2002), and work performance (e.g., Van Rooy, & Viswesvaran, 2004), to name but a few.

The trait EI perspective is criticized for measuring abilities that may not have been put into practice. However, it is not because abilities are not always used that they ought not to be measured. On the contrary, it is extremely useful to know whether the individuals who behave in a nonemotionally intelligent manner lack the underlying abilities or just do not use their abilities. Remediation perspectives (therapies in clinical settings, trainings in organizational settings) would indeed drastically differ depending on the source of the problem. The second critique addressed to the ability perspective concerns the psychometrical properties of its measures (i.e., scoring method at odds with the theory, low reliabilities), which would prove that abilities cannot be measured. However, the fact that the tests are not yet optimal does not undermine the quality of the underlying idea. Moreover, abilities have long been successfully measured in assessment centers (e.g., through role plays) or in laboratories (e.g., by asking people to regulate their emotions and measuring their physiological parameters; Mikolajczak, 2009).

Mikolajczak (2009) suggests a unifying three-level model of EI. According to the three-level model, EI aims to capture individual differences in emotion-related knowledge, abilities, and dispositions. Knowledge refers to the complexity of emotion-related knowledge. Abilities refer to emotion-related abilities to implement a given strategy in an emotional situation and dispositions refer to the propensity to behave in a certain way in emotional situations.

Can emotional intelligence be measured? There are some tests of emotional intelligence that exist: The Bar-On Emotional Quotient Inventory (EQI; Bar-On, 1997), the Self Report Emotional Intelligence Test (SREIT; see Brackett & Mayer, 2003), the Mayer-Salovey-Caruso Emotional Intelligence Test (MSCEIT; Brackett & Mayer, 2003), the Trait Meta-Mood Scale (TMMS; Salovey, Mayer, Goldman, Turvey, & Palfai, 1995), the Schutte Self Report Emotional Intelligence (SSREI: Schutte, Malouff, & Bhullar, 2009), the adolescent Swinburne University Emotional Intelligence Test (Adolescent SUEIT; Luebbers, Downey, & Stough, 2003). The validity of such tests has been called into question as most of these measures are self reports and have psychometric properties that are largely unknown. However, the MSCEIT uses a consensus to score participants in place of self reports (Mayer et al., 2004) and measures emotional intelligence based on cognitive ability (Brackett & Mayer, 2003), making it a more reliable measure than tests solely using methods of self-report.

Mayer et al. (2004) argue that emotional intelligence meets many of the current standards used to measure intelligence. Indeed, they make the assertion that emotional intelligence works through cognitions that deal directly with matters of personal, or emotional, importance. In their study, they showed that measures of emotional intelligences meet three standard criteria of a new intelligence by using the MSCEIT. The first criterion is that the test questions could be confirmed as either correct or incorrect. The second condition is that there are connections in emotional intelligence that directly relate to the ones of a standard intelligence. The third decisive

factor is that when time passes, emotional intelligence continues to develop within that individual.

Emotional intelligence is still a young discipline, and much of the research and scholarship to date has been in defining exactly what are the parameters and boundaries of "emotional intelligence." While Salovey, Mayer, and colleagues define emotional intelligence in terms of how well people can understand and control their own emotions and those of others, there are several other extensions of the terms. Motivation, cognition, and morality have also been dubbed aspects of emotional intelligence (Salovey et al., 1999). Goleman (1995), in his popular book on the topic, extended the definition even further. His conception of emotional intelligence encompasses impulse control, enthusiasm, social acumen, and persistence, as well as the other variables already mentioned. In 1998, Goleman revised his model of emotional intelligence (Mayer, 2001), extending its fields to include self-awareness, self-regulation, motivation, empathy, and social skills.

Future directions in emotional intelligence research, according to Mayer et al. (2004), will likely be concentrated in the following areas: finding the correlations between emotional intelligence and more traditional types of intelligence and personality traits; assessing cultural differences and similarities in emotional intelligence (both abilities and definitions); developing more empirical measures of the construct, and determining if these measures predict an advantageous effect on academic, personal, and professional success; and using a larger range of age groups to determine how emotional intelligence develops over time.

REFERENCES

Austin, E. J. (2004). An investigation of the relationship between trait emotional intelligence and emotional task performance. *Personality and Individual Differences, 36*, 1855–1864.

Austin, E. J. (2005). Emotional intelligence and emotional information processing. *Personality and Individual Differences, 39*, 403–414.

Bar-On, R. (1997). *EQI: Bar-On emotional quotient inventory*. Toronto, Canada: Multihealth Systems.

Bar-On, R., Tranel, D., Denburg, N. L., & Bechara, A. (2003). Exploring the neurological substrate of emotional and social intelligence. *Brain, 126*, 1790–1800.

Brackett, M. A., & Mayer, J. D. (2003). Convergent, discriminant, and incremental validity of competing measures of emotional intelligence. *Personality and Social Psychology Bulletin, 29*, 1147–1158.

Bradberry, T., & Su, L. D. (2006). Ability versus skill-based assessment of emotional intelligence. *Psicothema, 18*, 59–66.

Caruso, D. R., Mayer, J. D., & Salovey, P. (2002). Relation of an ability measure of emotional intelligence to personality. *Journal of Personality Assessment, 79*(2), 306–320.

Cohen, J. (1988). *Statistical power analysis for the behavioral sciences*. Hillsdale, NJ: Erlbaum.

Gardner, H. (1983). *Frames of mind: The theory of multiple intelligences*. New York, NY: Basic Books.

Gignac, G. E. (2009). Psychometric and the measurement of emotional intelligence. In C. Stough, D. H. Saklofske, & J. D. A. Parker (Eds.), *Assessing emotional intelligence: Theory, research, and applications* (pp. 9–40). New York, NY: Springer.

Gignac, G. E., Jang, K. L., & Bates, T. C. (2009). Construct redundancy within the five-factor model as measured by the NEO PIR: Implications for emotional intelligence and incremental coherence. *Psychology Science, 51*(1), 7686.

Goleman, D. (1995). *Emotional intelligence.* New York, NY: Bantam.

Kemp, A. H., Cooper, N. J., Hermens, G., Goron, E., Bryant, R. & Williams, L. M. (2005). Toward an integrated profile of emotional intelligence: Introducing a brief measure. *Journal of Integrative Neuroscience, 4*, 41–61.

Law, K. S., Wong, C., & Song, L. J. (2004). The construct and criterion validity of emotional intelligence and its potential utility for management studies. *Journal of Applied Psychology, 89*(3), 483–496.

Luebbers, S. S., Downey, L. A., & Stough, C. C. (2007). The development of an adolescent measure of EI. *Personality and Individual Differences, 42*(6), 999–1009.

Leuner, B. (1966). Emotional intelligence and emancipation. A psychodynamic study on women. *Praxis der Kinderpsychologie und Kinderpsychiatrie, 15*(August–September), 193–203.

Mavroveli, S., Petrides, K., Shove, C., & Whitehead, A. (2008). Investigation of the construct of trait emotional intelligence in children. *European Child & Adolescent Psychiatry, 17*(8), 516–526.

Mayer, J. D. (2001). A field guide to emotional intelligence. In J. Ciarrochi, J. P. Forgas, J. D. Mayer, J. Ciarrochi, J. P. Forgas, & J. D. Mayer (Eds.), *Emotional intelligence in everyday life: A scientific inquiry* (pp. 324). New York, NY: Psychology Press.

Mayer, J. D., Salovey, P., & Caruso, D. R. (2004). Emotional intelligence: Theory, findings, and implications. *Psychological Inquiry, 17*(3), 197–215.

Mayer, J. D., & Salovey, P. (1997). What is emotional intelligence? In P. Salovey & D. Sluyter (Eds.), *Emotional development and emotional intelligence: Implications for educators* (pp. 3–31). New York, NY: Basic Books.

Mikolajczak, M. (2009). Going beyond the ability-trait debate: The three-level model of emotional intelligence. *E-Journal of Applied Psychology, 5*(2), 25–31.

Mikolajczak, M., Roy, E., Luminet, O., Fillee, C., & de Timary, P. (2007). The moderating impact of emotional intelligence on free cortisol responses to stress. *Psychoneuroendocrinology, 32*(810), 1000–1012.

Payne, W. L. (1985). *A study of emotion: Developing emotional intelligence; self-integration; relating to fear, pain and desire.* Unpublished dissertation, the Union for Experimenting Colleges and Universities, United States, Ohio.

Petrides, K. V., & Furnham, A. (2001). Trait emotional intelligence: Psychometric investigation with reference to established trait taxonomies. *European Journal of Personality, 15*(6), 425–448.

Petrides, K. V., & Furnham, A. (2003). Trait emotional Intelligence: Behavioral validation in two studies of emotion recognition and reactivity to mood induction. *European Journal of Personality, 17*, 39–57.

Petrides, K. V., & Furnham, A. (2006). The role of trait emotional intelligence in a gender-specific model of organizational variables. *Journal of Applied Social Psychology, 36*(2), 552–569.

Petrides, K. V., Sangareau, Y., Furnham, A., & Frederickson, N. (2006). Trait emotional intelligence and children's peer relations at school. *Social Development, 15*(3), 537–547.

Petrides, K. V., Pita, R., & Kokkinaki, F. (2007). The location of trait emotional intelligence in personality factor space. *British Journal of Psychology, 98*(2), 273–289.

Salovey, P., & Mayer, J. D. (1989–1990). Emotional intelligence. *Imagination, Cognition, and Personality, 9*(3), 185–211.

Salovey, P., Mayer, J. D., Goldman, S., Turvey, C., & Palfai, T. P. (1995). Emotional attention, clarity, and repair: Exploring emotional intelligence using the trait meta-mood scale. In J. W. Pennebaker (Ed.), *Emotion, disclosure, & health* (pp. 125–154). Washington, DC: American Psychological Association.

Salovey, P., Stroud, L. R., Woolery, A., & Epel, E. S. (2002). Perceived emotional intelligence, stress reactivity, and symptom reports: Further explorations using the trait meta-mood scale. *Psychology and Health, 17*, 611–627.

Schutte, N. S., Malouff, J. M., & Bhullar, N. (2009). The assessing emotions scale. In C. Stough, D. H. Saklofske, & J. A. Parker (Eds.), *Assessing emotional intelligence: Theory, research, and applications* (pp. 119–134). New York, NY: Springer Science + Business Media.

Schutte. N. S., Malouff, J. M., Hall, L. E., Haggerty, D. J., Cooper, J. T., Golden, C. J., & Dornheim, L. (1998). Development and validation of a measure of emotional intelligence. *Personality and Individual Differences, 25*, 167–177.

Sternberg, R. J., & Kaufman, J. C. (1998). Human abilities. *Annual Review of Psychology, 49*, 479–502.

Van Ghent, D. (1961). *The English novel: Form and function.* New York, NY: Harper & Row.

Van der Zee, K., Thijs, M., & Schakel, L. (2002). The relationship of emotional intelligence with academic intelligence and the big five. *European Journal of Personality, 16*(2), 103–125.

Van Rooy, D. L., & Viswesvaran, C. (2004). Emotional Intelligence: A metaanalytic investigation of predictive validity and nomological net. *Journal of Vocational Behavior, 65*(1), 71–95.

RAUL SALCEDO
JAMES C. KAUFMAN
*California State University,
San Bernardino*

INTELLIGENCE, PRACTICAL

Although most people in society are aware of the existence of both "street smarts" and "book smarts," psychology, in general, has chosen to focus on the latter when it examines intelligence. Intelligence tests sometimes measure topics that have real-world implications (e.g., auditory comprehension on the Kaufman Adolescent and Adult Intelligence Test assesses understanding of a mock news broadcast; Kaufman & Kaufman, 1993), but psychometric testing of intelligence has been more focused on academic intelligence (Sternberg & Kaufman, 1998).

The history of scientific research on practical intelligence is a short one (Sternberg, 1996; Torff & Sternberg, 1998). Neisser (1976) provided a theoretical distinction between academic and everyday intelligence, and Sternberg, Conway, Ketron, and Bernstein (1981) demonstrated that both laypeople and intelligence researchers had implicit beliefs that academic and practical intelligence were separate things. Ceci and Liker (1986) and Scribner (1984) did early research on how adult subjects performed much better on tasks of mathematical reasoning when these tasks were presented in the context of a more familiar domain (e.g., filling orders in a factory), showing subjects who may not do well on traditional intelligence tests may be able to solve similar problems if they are presented in the guise of their day-to-day work. Connecting such a result with other findings that suggest practical intelligence is linked to expertise (Cianciolo, Grigorenko, Jarvin, Gil, Drebot, & Sternberg, 2009; Sternberg, 1999), may indicate that previous forms of psychometric testing are less informative than previously thought.

Robert Sternberg (1984; Sternberg, Kaufman, & Grigorenko, 2008), in his triarchic theory of intelligence, proposed that there are three kinds of intelligences: analytical intelligence, practical intelligence, and creative intelligence (see entry for Intelligence, Triarchic Theory). He defines practical intelligence, being similar to "street smarts," as the ability to apply one's knowledge in a hands-on, real-world manner. One key element required for practical intelligence is tacit knowledge (Sternberg, Wagner, Williams, & Horvath, 1995; Wagner & Sternberg, 1985, 1986), that is, knowledge that is acquired without being explicitly taught. There are three features of tacit knowledge that are considered characteristic: (1) it is procedural; (2) it is related to the pursuit and achievement of valued outcomes; and (3) it is learned without assistance from other people. The third condition is one of the key distinctions between tacit and academic knowledge.

Several tacit knowledge tests have been developed and researched, including the Tacit Knowledge Inventory for Managers (TKIM; Wagner & Sternberg, 1991), the Academic Tacit Knowledge Scale (Insch, McIntyre, & Dawley, 2008), and measures included on the Sternberg Triarchic Abilities Test (STAT; Sternberg, 1993) and used in studies with the College Board (Sternberg & the Rainbow Project Collaborators, 2005, 2009). These tests examine a subject's tacit knowledge by presenting scenarios specific to a particular job (e.g., business manager, military officer) and then asking questions about what actions should be taken in each situation. One typical question might be to ask subjects what they would do if a colleague asked for their advice on a project that looked terrible. Would the correct response be to give an honest assessment of the project's worth, or to give complimentary but inaccurate feedback? The subject rates each potential answer on a 1 to 7 scale, with 1 meaning that the solution is "extremely bad" and 7 meaning the solution is "extremely good."

Empirical research by Sternberg, Wagner, and others (Sternberg, 1997; Sternberg, Okagaki, & Jackson, 1990; Sternberg, Wagner, & Okagaki, 1993; Wagner & Sternberg, 1986) has found several consistent results. Tacit knowledge increases with hands-on experience; measures of tacit knowledge have repeatedly correlated at significant levels with job performance and innovation (Seidler-de Alwis & Hartmann, 2008), yet show only small correlations with traditional measures of intelligence; and early results show that if one wants to teach tacit knowledge, such training should improve results on tests of practical intelligence and tacit knowledge. The behaviors obtained can differ from one culture to another (Sternberg & Kaufman, 1998; Yang & Sternberg, 1997). Practical intelligence has many important implications for education. Sternberg, Gardner, and other colleagues have combined to form a collaborative project called "Practical Intelligence for Schools" (PIFS; see Gardner, Krechevsky, Sternberg, & Okagaki, 1994). The authors defined the practically intelligent student as one who is aware of his or her individual learning styles; knows how to draw on individual strengths; understands the requirements for the variety of problems encountered across many different school subjects; and can function well interpersonally as well as academically. The authors propose a curriculum for enhancing PIFS that has three units: one that focuses on self-awareness and self-management, another that focuses on task management, and a final unit that shows students how to interact beneficially with others (Gardner et al., 1994; Sternberg et al., 1990). This curriculum resulted in improvement on a variety of measures of practical intelligence. The PIFS project went on to inspire further work by Sternberg and colleagues (Grigorenko, Jarvis, & Sternberg, 2002; Sternberg, Grigorenko, Ferrari, & Clinkenbeard, 1999; Sternberg, Torff, & Grigorenko, 1998) as well as work by the Cornell Institute's Research on Children's (CIRC) in their program Thinking Like a Scientist (Williams, Papierno, Makel, & Ceci, 2004)

REFERENCES

Alwis, R.S.D., & Hartmann, E. (2008). The use of tacit knowledge within innovative companies: Knowledge management in innovative enterprises. *Journal of Knowledge Management*, *12*(1), 133–147.

Ceci, S., & Liker, J. (1986). Academic and nonacademic intelligence: An experimental separation. In R. J. Sternberg & R. K. Wagner (Eds.), *Practical intelligence: Nature and origins of competence in the everyday world* (pp. 119–142). New York, NY: Cambridge University Press.

Cianciolo, A. T., Grigorenko, E. L., Jarvin, L., Gil, G., Drebot, M. E., & Sternberg, R. J. (2009). Practical intelligence and tacit knowledge: Advancements in the measurement of developing expertise. In J. C. Kaufman, E. L. Grigorenko, & R. J. Sternberg, (Eds.), *The essential Sternberg: Essays on intelligence, psychology, and education* (pp. 119–144). New York, NY: Springer.

Gardner, H., Krechevsky, M., Sternberg, R. J., & Okagaki, L. (1994). Intelligence in context: Enhancing students' practical intelligence for school. In K. McGilly (Ed.), *Classroom lessons: Integrating cognitive theory and classroom practice* (pp. 105–127). Cambridge, MA: Bradford Books.

Grigorenko, E. L., Jarvis, L., & Sternberg, R. J. (2002). School-based tests of the triarchic theory of intelligence: Three settings, three samples, three syllabi. *Contemporary Educational Psychology, 27*, 167–208.

Insch, G. S., McIntyre, N., & Dawley, D. (2008). Tacit knowledge: A refinement and empirical test of the academic tacit knowledge scale. *Journal of Psychology: Interdisciplinary and Applied, 142*(6), 561–579.

Kaufman, A. S., & Kaufman, N. L. (1993). *Manual for the Kaufman adolescent and adult intelligence test (KAIT)*. Circle Pines, MN: American Guidance Service.

Neisser, U. (1976). General academic and artificial intelligence. In L. Resnick (Ed.), *Human intelligence: Perspectives on its theory and measurement* (pp. 135–146). Norwood, NJ: Ablex.

Scribner, S. (1984). Studying working intelligence. In B. Rogoff & J. Lave (Eds.), *Everyday cognition* (pp. 9–40). Cambridge, MA: Harvard University Press.

Seidler-de Alwis, R., & Hartmann, E. (2008). The use of tacit knowledge within innovative companies: Knowledge management in innovative enterprises. *Journal of Knowledge Management, 12*(1), 133–147.

Sternberg, R. (1999). The theory of successful intelligence. *Review of General Psychology, 3*(4), 299–316.

Sternberg, R. J. (1984). A triarchic theory of human intelligence. *Behavioral and Brain Sciences, 7*, 269–287.

Sternberg, R. J. (1993). *Sternberg triarchic abilities test*. Unpublished test.

Sternberg, R. J. (1996). What should we ask about intelligence? *American Scholar, 65*(2), 205–217.

Sternberg, R. J. (1997). Tacit knowledge and job success. In N. Anderson & P. Herriot (Eds.), *International handbook of selection and assessment* (pp. 201–213). New York, NY: Wiley.

Sternberg, R., & Kaufman J. (1998). Human abilities. *Annual Review of Psychology, 49*, 479–502.

Sternberg, R. J., Conway, B. E., Ketron, J. L., & Bernstein, M. (1981). Aegnie's conception of intelligence. *Journal of Personality and Social Psychology, 41*, 37–55.

Sternberg, R. J., Grigorenko, E. L., Ferrari, M., & Clinkenbeard, P. (1999). A triarchic analysis of an aptitude-treatment interaction. *European Journal of Psychological Assessment, 15*, 313.

Sternberg, R. J., Kaufman, J. C., & Grigorenko, E. L. (2008). *Applied intelligence*. New York, NY: Cambridge University Press.

Sternberg, R. J., Okagaki, L., & Jackson, A. (1990). Practical intelligence for success in school. *Educational Leadership, 48*, 35–39.

Sternberg, R. J., & the Rainbow Project Collaborators. (2005). Augmenting the SAT through assessments of analytical, practical, and creative skills. In W. J. Camara & E. W. Kimmel (Eds.), *Choosing students* (pp. 159–176). Mahwah, NJ: Erlbaum.

Sternberg, R. J., & the Rainbow Project Collaborators. (2009). The rainbow project: Enhancing the SAT through assessments of analytical, practical, and creative skills. In J. C. Kaufman & E. L. Grigorenko (Eds.) *The essential Sternberg: Essays on intelligence, psychology, and education* (pp. 273–319). New York, NY: Springer.

Sternberg, R. J., Torff, B., & Grigorenko, E. L. (1998). Teaching triarchically improves school achievement. *Journal of Educational Psychology, 90*, 374–384.

Sternberg, R. J., Wagner, R. K., & Okagaki, L. (1993). Practical intelligence: The nature and role of tacit knowledge in work and at school. In H. Reese & J. Puckett (Eds.), *Advances in lifespan development* (pp. 205–227). Hillsdale, NJ: Erlbaum.

Sternberg, R. J., Wagner, R. K., Williams, W. M., & Horvath, J. A. (1995). Testing common sense. *American Psychologist, 50*(11), 912–927.

Torff, B., & Sternberg, R. J. (1998). Changing mind, changing world: Practical intelligence and tacit knowledge in adult learning. In R. Sternberg, C. M. Smith, & T. Pourchot (Eds.), *Adult learning and development: Perspectives from educational psychology* (pp. 109–126). Mahwah, NJ: Erlbaum.

Wagner, R. K., & Sternberg, R. J. (1985). Practical intelligence in realworld pursuits: Theory of tacit knowledge. *Journal of Personality and Social Psychology, 49*, 436–458.

Wagner, R. K., & Sternberg, R. J. (1986). Tacit knowledge and intelligence in the everyday world. In R. J. Sternberg & R. K. Wagner (Eds.), *Practical intelligence: Nature and origins of competence in the everyday world* (pp. 51–83). New York, NY: Cambridge University Press.

Wagner, R. K., & Sternberg, R. J. (1991). *Tacit knowledge inventory for managers (TKIM)*. New York, NY: Psychological Corporation.

Williams, W. M., Papierno, P. B., Makel, M. C., & Ceci, S. J. (2004). Thinking Like A Scientist About RealWorld Problems: The Cornell Institute for Research on Children Science Education Program. *Journal of Applied Developmental Psychology, 25*, 107–126.

Yang, S. Y., & Sternberg, R. J. (1997). Taiwanese Chinese people's conceptions of intelligence. *Intelligence, 25*, 21–36.

KYLE J. JAQUESS
*California State University,
San Bernardino*

LAN LAN
Shanghai University of Finance and Economics

JAMES C. KAUFMAN
California State University, San Bernardino

INTELLIGENCE QUOTIENT

The intelligence quotient represents a measurement concept that was used extensively in the early days of intelligence testing but is less commonly used today. After Alfred Binet's death in 1911, Stern (1914) introduced the notion of a mental quotient, suggesting that the index of intellectual functioning derived from the Binet-Simon Scale could be expressed as the ratio of a test taker's mental age to his or her chronological age multiplied by 100 to eliminate decimals ($MQ = 100 \times MA/CA$). This MQ represented something about a person's rate of mental growth up to the time of the test. If examinees earned a mental age (MA) equivalent to chronological age (CA), their mental quotient (MQ) would be 100. An MQ of 100 represented average performance.

Working at Stanford University in California, Lewis M. Terman developed what was to become the most widely used American version of the Binet test, the Stanford-Binet. Terman (1916) incorporated Stern's notion of a mental quotient but renamed it, calling it a ratio intelligence quotient, or IQ.

The concept of the ratio intelligence quotient became increasingly popular, but it was used in a number of inappropriate ways. Its decline over the past quarter century can be attributed to a number of inherent characteristics that have been highly criticized by measurement specialists and practitioners.

Because the ratio intelligence quotient has minor differences in the magnitude of its standard deviation at various ages, a constant intelligence quotient from one age to another does not represent the same relative status. Similarly, even if the test taker's relative status remained the same from one year to another, the intelligence quotient would have to change. This suggests that intelligence quotients at different age levels are not comparable statistically (Tyler & Walsh, 1979). For example, a very bright child could obtain a higher IQ at age 12 than at age 6, even if the child's growth rate was unchanged. This difference would simply be due to the differences in the variability or standard deviations, with the variability of the IQ distribution being greater for 12-year-olds than for 6-year-olds.

Critics also point to the conceptual difficulty of the ratio intelligence quotient. For example, a 5-year-old with a mental age of 6 and a 10-year-old with a mental age of 12 would both have identical intelligence quotients of 120. However, the 6-year-old is a year advanced in mental age while the 10-year-old is 2 years advanced.

Another criticism of the intelligence quotient relates to its inability to describe adult intelligence (Tyler & Walsh, 1979). Critics suggest that like physical growth, adult mental growth lacks the predictable regularity characteristic of the mental development of children. Age standards lack meaning after the mid-teens, rendering mental age and therefore the intelligence quotient concept meaningless.

Owing to these criticisms of the ratio intelligence quotient, major intelligence tests in use today yield IQs but not ratio intelligence quotients. Because of the inherent limitations of the ratio intelligence quotient, they should be interpreted cautiously.

REFERENCES

Stern, W. (1914). *The psychological methods of testing intelligence.* Baltimore, MD: Warwick & York.

Terman, L. M. (1916). *The measurement of intelligence.* Boston, MA: Houghton Mifflin.

Tyler, L. E., & Walsh, W. B. (1979). *Tests and measurements.* Englewood Cliffs, NJ: Prentice Hall.

MARK E. SWERDLIK
Illinois State University

See also Deviation IQ; IQ; Ratio IQ

INTELLIGENCE TESTING

The practice of formally testing skills and abilities dates back nearly 3,000 years (Wang, 1993). Moreover, individual differences in human performance have been discussed among history's greatest thinkers, including Socrates, Plato, and Darwin. Despite a history of interest in exploring human abilities, standardized and validated intelligence tests first were developed in 1905 by Binet and Simon to help predict how well children would achieve in school (French & Hale, 1990). Since then, the intelligence testing movement has gained considerable momentum as a result of the need to differentiate among individuals when providing educational services (French & Hale, 1990).

Intelligence testing is a means to observe the actual performance of individuals under standardized conditions. Its purpose is to accurately assess cognitive strengths and weaknesses. However, individual scores are samples of behavior. In addition, many other nonintellective factors influence everyday functioning and behavior. As a result, intelligence testing is used to make inferences and predictions about an individual's ability rather than serve as a direct indicator of the traits and capacities of an individual (Sattler, 1992).

Standardized measures of intelligence are used by psychologists on a daily basis. Data from intelligence tests often are used to predict school performance, especially achievement. Intelligence tests do this fairly well (Neisser et al., 1996). Approximately 25% of the variance associated with achievement can be attributed to intelligence. Although 75% of the variance in school performance can be attributed to other factors, intelligence testing remains the best single predictor of academic performance (Sattler, 1993). Further, although intelligence test scores may fluctuate due to changes in environment and quality of schooling, they are quite stable over time (Kamphaus, 2001; Neisser et al., 1996).

In addition to their predictive validity, intelligence tests provide several other benefits to students, adults, educators, and researchers. They may reveal unsuspected or unnoticed talents in children and adults that may positively impact their educational and vocational success. Similarly, tests may provide information about areas of weakness that may guide early intervention efforts. By providing a profile of strengths and weaknesses, intelligence tests may help teachers and parents develop individualized interventions to promote a child's development (Sattler, 1993).

Classroom assessments and observations provide educators and parents with information about a student's ability. However, this information is collected in relation to students in the same classroom or district. Standardized tests provide educators with an accurate method of comparing one child's performance to his or her peers nationally. In this sense, intelligence tests may be considered as a measure of an individual's ability to compete and achieve economically and socially in society. Finally, intelligence tests provide useful insight into cultural and biological differences among individuals (Sattler, 1993).

Despite the apparent benefits of intelligence testing, their use has been criticized. Some racial/ethnic groups differ in mean IQs. For example, compared to mean IQs for White/non-Hispanics, those for Blacks and Hispanics are lower and those for Asian Americans are higher (Neisser et al., 1996). Consequently, some conclude intelligence tests are culturally biased and promote racism. However, mean differences do not necessarily indicate bias. When considering intelligence tests as predictors of performance, most researchers agree that intelligence tests are not biased in that they predict behaviors similarly for all groups (Neisser et al., 1996; Valdes & Figueroa, 1994). Nonetheless, critics argue that mean IQ differences lead to overrepresentation of some minority children in special education classes and the overrepresentation of White, middle- to upper-class children in gifted and talented programs.

In response to such criticisms, test developers have attempted to preserve the utility of intelligence tests through revisions that better reflect the abilities of individuals from diverse backgrounds. As a result, some nonverbal and newly revised intelligence tests claim to have smaller racial differences and therefore may be perceived as less biased.

Additional criticisms include the importance placed on scores obtained from a single test administration, the negative stigma associated with a low score, and that they assess a narrow range of intellectual abilities (Sattler, 1993). Moreover, some disagreement exists as to the nature of the construct of intelligence. For these and other reasons, intelligence testing may be disregarded among some psychologists and educators (Papanastasiou, 1999).

Although these criticisms should not be ignored, substantial empirical data support intelligence testing. Intelligence tests have considerable value in assessing processing abilities and guiding intervention design (e.g., memory deficits, processing speed deficits). The use of intelligence tests also continues to be of considerable value when assessing developmental delays, brain injury, gifted, and mental disabilities.

REFERENCES

French, J. L., & Hale, R. L. (1990). A history of the development of psychological and educational testing. In C. R. Reynolds & R. W. Kamphaus (Eds.), *Handbook of psychological and educational assessment of children* (pp. 3–28). New York, NY: Guilford Press.

Kamphaus, R. W. (2001). *Clinical assessment of children's intelligence* (2nd ed.). Needham Heights, MA: Allyn & Bacon.

Neisser, U., Boodoo, G., Bouchard, T. J., Boykin, A. W., Brody, N., Ceci, S. J., ... Urbina, S. (1996). Intelligence: Knowns and unknowns. *American Psychologist, 51*(2), 77–101.

Papanastasiou, E. C. (1999). *Intelligence: Theories and testing.* (ERIC Document Reproduction Service No. ED441859)

Sattler, J. M. (1992). *Assessment of children: Revised and updated* (3rd ed.). San Diego, CA: Author.

Valdes, G., & Figueroa, R. A. (1994). *Bilingualism and testing: A special case of bias.* Norwood, NJ: Ablex.

Wang, Z. M. (1993). Psychology in China: A review dedicated to Li Chen. *Annual Review of Psychology, 44*, 87–116.

Eric Rossen
University of Florida

See also Intelligence; Intelligence Testing

INTELLIGENCE TESTING, HISTORY OF

Intelligence testing, although called by many different names and used in many different forms, has been around for many centuries (Kaufman, 2009; Urbina, 2004). The Chinese have been using mental tests for 3,000 years, and in the seventh and eighth centuries the Imperial Court established tests of speaking and writing and verbal and nonverbal reasoning that are similar to tasks on today's tests. The ancient Greeks, followers of Socrates, and universities in the Middle Ages, all developed methods of assessing intellectual skills.

As summarized by Kaufman (2009), the 1800s saw the beginning of the development of ideas about mental abilities and methods of measuring intelligence; these ideas formed the foundation for contemporary assessment. Not surprisingly, the scholars involved in the roots of intelligence testing were concerned with the two extremes of ability. Jean Esquirol in the early 1800s and Edouard Seguin in the mid-1800s, two French physicians, studied intelligence of mentally retarded individuals. Francis Galton, in the mid- to late 1800s, focused on the ability of men of genius. In the 1890s, James McKeen Cattell brought intelligence testing to the United States.

Esquirol's contributions included distinguishing between those people with very low intelligence, or those with mental retardation, and those people with emotional disturbances. He indicated that there is a hierarchy of mental retardation along a continuum, and coined terms like imbecile and idiot to describe different levels of mental deficiency. Although Esquirol studied several procedures, he concluded that a person's use of language is the most dependable criterion for determining intelligence, a philosophy that is apparent on many intelligence tests today.

Seguin rejected the notion that mental retardation is incurable and served as a pioneer in education for people with mental retardation. Unlike Esquirol, Seguin stressed the importance of sensory discrimination and motor control as aspects of intelligence. He developed procedures that were adopted by later developers of performance and nonverbal intelligence tests. An example is the Seguin Form board, which requires rapid placement of variously shaped blocks into their correct holes.

The English biologist Galton was primarily responsible for developing the first comprehensive individual intelligence test. As part of his research of men of genius and the heredity of intelligence, he administered tasks of sensory discrimination and sensory motor coordination in his Anthropometric Laboratory. His belief that intelligence comes to us through the senses led to the development of tasks such as weight discrimination, reaction time, strength of squeeze, and visual discrimination.

In the early 1890s, Cattell, an assistant in Galton's laboratory, established similar laboratories in the United States. During this time, Cattell used the term *mental test* for the first time in the psychological literature. Cattell shared Galton's view that intelligence is best measured through sensory tasks, but expanded his mentor's ideas by emphasizing that test administration must be standardized so that results are comparable from person to person and time to time.

In the early 1900s, significant advances were made in both individual and group intelligence testing (Sattler, 2008; Vane & Motta, 1984). In France, Alfred Binet, assisted by Theophile Simon and Victor Henri, rejected Galton's notions about the sensory and motor aspects of intelligence and claimed that tests of higher mental processes more effectively distinguish among the individual differences in people's intellectual abilities. This group developed numerous tests of complex intellectual functions such as memory, comprehension, imagination, and moral sentiments. The specific appointment by the French minister of public instruction to study the education of children with mental retardation led to the development of the individually administered Binet-Simon Scale in 1905, constructed to separate children with typical abilities and those with mental retardation in the Paris public schools. Two of the key aspects of Binet's approach to intelligence testing were that he "discarded the specific test for the specific ability and took a group of tests, which seemed to cover in general the chief psychological characteristics that go to make up intelligence. And, further, as the norm or standard of intelligence he took what the average child at each age could do" (Pintner & Patterson, 1925, p. 7).

The Binet-Simon Scale, including the 1911 revision that extended through adulthood, was almost immediately adapted and translated in the United States. The most successful revision was Terman's Stanford-Binet Scale in 1916. Terman carefully standardized his scale and introduced the application of the term intelligence quotient (mental age divided by chronological age multiplied by 100). The Stanford-Binet was widely adopted by individual examiners in the United States, and it is still popular today. The Binet was revised and restandardized in 1937, revised in 1960, and again restandardized in 1972. The ratio IQ, although retained in the 1937 Binet, was replaced by the deviation IQ (a standard score with a mean of 100 and standard deviation of 16) for the 1960 and 1972 Stanford-Binets. Thoroughly new versions of the Binet were published in 1986 (4th edition) and by Roid in 2003.

David Wechsler, in 1939, was the first to challenge the Stanford-Binet monopoly on individual intelligence tests by publishing the Wechsler-Bellevue Scale. Wechsler, like Binet, included the concept of global intelligence in his scale, but instead of having one score, as did the Stanford-Binet, he included three scores: a verbal IQ, a performance IQ, and a full-scale IQ. Wechsler did not employ the methodology of the Stanford-Binet, which used a large number of brief and primarily verbal tasks. His scale was limited to a small number of longer tasks, half of them verbal and half nonverbal. Several versions of the Wechsler scales have been published since his Wechsler-Bellevue, and the types of tasks on later versions are virtually identical to the first scale. The main sources of Wechsler's verbal tasks were the Binet and the Army Group Examination Alpha; his performance tests came primarily from the Army Group Examination Beta and the Army Individual Performance Scale Examination (Kaufman, 2009; Wasserman, in press).

Wechsler, chief psychologist at Bellevue Psychiatric Hospital in New York City from 1932 to 1967, changed the field of intellectual assessment from primarily a *psychometric* endeavor—emphasis on reliability, norms, individual differences among groups—to a *clinical* procedure. That is to say, the master clinician David Wechsler implemented his basic tenets, that intelligence is an aspect of personality and that a clinician learns as much about the individual by observing behaviors and evaluating the person's responses as by examining test scores. Individual IQ tests have been used for generations as the staple for neuropsychological, psychoeducational, and clinical evaluations. Wechsler's (2003, 2008) current scales, the Wechsler Intelligence Scale for Children, Fourth Edition (WISCIV) and Wechsler Adult Intelligence Scale, Fourth Edition (WAISIV), remain the most popular IQ tests in the United States and, indeed, in the world. There has, however, been a key transformation in IQ test development over the past quarter century, namely the reliance on Luria's neuropsychological theory (Kaufman & Kaufman, 1983, 2004; Naglieri & Das, 1997) and, especially, on the Cattell-Horn-Carroll (CHC) model of intelligence (Elliott, 2007; Roid, 2003; Woodcock & Johnson, 1989; Woodcock, McGrew & Mather, 2001) as the foundations of most contemporary measures of intelligence.

The emerging fields of learning disabilities and neuropsychology in the 1960s gave an advantage to Wechsler's multiscore tests over the one score (general intelligence) Stanford-Binet. The passage of the Education of All Handicapped Children Act of 1975 (PL 94-142) and subsequent revisions resulted in the common use of individual intelligence tests as part of larger assessment batteries for determination of special education eligibility of children with mental retardation, specific learning disabilities, and emotional disturbance and for the development of individual educational programs for these children. However, the latest revision of the law, commonly referred to as IDEA 2004, signaled less reliance on testing and more reliance on children's response to instruction and interventions in general education and the use of alternate forms of assessment, such as curriculum-based assessment, to measure their progress. This new emphasis on Response-To-Intervention (RTI) has dramatically changed the way individuals are diagnosed as having a specific learning disability (SLD), with a number of leaders in the field advocating the use RTI (without IQ testing, usually referred to as *cognitive assessment*) as the best way to diagnose SLD (e.g., VanDerHayden & Burns, 2010). However, many leaders in the field stress that both cognitive assessment and RTI need to work hand in hand for the most appropriate identification of students with SLD (Flanagan & Alfonso, 2011). Assessment of intellectual functioning, as well as adaptive behavior, continues to be emphasized in IDEA 2004 for the disability category of mental retardation (now termed "intellectual disability" by the American Association on Intellectual and Developmental Disabilities).

The widespread use of group intelligence tests began, like the first Binet Scale, to meet a practical need (Anastasi & Urbina, 1997). The entry of the United States into World War I in 1917 required a rapid means of classifying 1.5 million recruits for assignment into different types of training, discharge from service, and officer ability. A committee of the American Psychological Association, headed by Robert M. Yerkes, was directed to develop two group intelligence tests; these came to be known as the Army Alpha and Army Beta. The former, a verbal test modeled after the Binet, was designed for general use with literate recruits; the latter employed nonverbal items and was designed for illiterate recruits, or those recent immigrants who did not speak English well. (The Army Individual Performance Scale, mentioned previously, was given to those recruits who could not be tested validly on either the Army Alpha or Army Beta.)

The tests were released for civilian use soon after the war ended. Because of the belief that intelligence tests were better than teacher evaluations for identifying abilities, these tests became widely accepted in education (Vane & Motta, 1984). A short time after, revisions of the Army tests, as well as new group intelligence tests that used the Army tests as models, were being administered to thousands of preschool through graduate students all over the country, and to special adult groups such as employees or prisoners. The group format was attractive because it allowed the testing of many individuals simultaneously and it incorporated simple administration procedures that required little examiner training. The rapid growth of group intelligence testing resulted in the development of 37 group tests in only 5 years! (Pintner, 1923).

A new surge in group intelligence testing occurred in 1958, after the launching of Sputnik. The passage of the National Defense Education Act provided funds for states to test the abilities of schoolchildren and identify outstanding students. This testing was facilitated by the development of optical scanning for test scoring by Lindquist in 1955. Also in 1958, the National Merit Scholarship program was established to select exceptional high school students. According to Vane and Motta (1984), another significant upturn in testing happened in the late 1970s, and this interest continues to this day.

Intelligence tests, both group and individual, are used in many different ways today. The largest users of intelligence tests are schools. Group intelligence tests are used at the preschool and kindergarten levels to distinguish children who are ready to participate in educational activities from those who need remedial preparation. At the elementary, middle, and high school levels, group tests are used to identify students with exceptional abilities. Group intelligence tests are commonly used as one criterion for admission into colleges and universities. Individual intelligence tests have been administered for about three quarters of a century by well-trained clinicians for psychological, psychoeducational, and neuropsychological diagnosis. For adults, group and individual intelligence tests are used in a variety of settings, including business and industry, prisons, mental health centers, hospitals, and private clinical practice.

Group intelligence tests find their principal application in education, business, government, and military, in circumstances where it is feasible to obtain valid test data from many individuals at once; they are useful as well with individuals who are able to take a test by themselves without need of an examiner. In contrast, individual intelligence tests are used in clinics and special education centers, where an intensive study of individual clients is needed and a trained examiner is necessary to secure valid test results. The reasons for using group and individual tests are many and provide a basis for understanding the type of information provided by the two testing formats. A summary of these reasons, as reported by Anastasi and Urbina (1997), follows.

Group tests can be administered to a large number of individuals at the same time by using booklets of printed items and forms for the examinee to indicate his or her answer. The training and experience required by the examiner is minimal, as most group tests only require the examiner to read simple instructions and accurately keep time. The minimal role of the examiner in group testing provides more uniform testing conditions than in individual testing.

Objective scoring is a key aspect of group tests. Test items are usually multiple choice, true-false, or some other type that produces responses that can be scored as correct or incorrect with no deliberation. Items on group tests can usually be scored by a clerk or a computer. In addition, group tests typically include answer sheets, separate from the test booklets that contain the items, allowing economical reuse of test booklets.

Because group tests can be administered to large groups of individuals at the same time, larger numbers of individuals can be used in the standardization programs for group tests than for individual tests. Group test norms are generally better established because they are based on standardization samples of 100,000 to 200,000 instead of the 1,000 to 4,000 used for individual tests.

On the other hand, individual intelligence tests have several characteristics that make them suitable for a variety of clinical purposes. In individual testing, the examiner has the opportunity to obtain cooperation, establish rapport, and enhance motivation of the examinee. The trained examiner in individual testing detects, reports, and uses in the interpretation of test scores the many characteristics of the examinee that may affect test performance such as anxiety, fatigue, and problem-solving style. In addition, some individuals such as children and adults with learning, behavior, or cognitive difficulties may perform better on individual tests than on group tests. Since most group tests require the examinee to read instructions and test items, individually administered tests, which demand little or no reading, are especially useful for individuals with disabilities, and others who may have reading problems.

Individual intelligence tests, because they typically include short questions that require oral and open-ended responses, allow examinees to give creative and original responses to items. In individual testing, examinees are not limited to selecting one of four multiple-choice answers or indicating if an item is true or false. The contents of an examinee's response on an individual intelligence test can therefore be analyzed in order to generate hypotheses about, for example, the examinee's creativity, style of thinking, cognitive development, or defense mechanisms.

Another aspect of individual intelligence testing concerns the flexibility of administration. On a group test, an examinee is required to respond to all items, or as many items as he or she can in a certain time limit. On an individual test, testing time is more effectively used because the examinee is administered only those items in the range appropriate to his or her ability level. This characteristic of individual tests helps avoid the boredom an examinee may have when working on items that are too easy or the frustration of working on items that are too difficult.

Intelligence testing has been a controversial topic since the 1960s (A. S. Kaufman, 1979). The most pressing issues that are debated within both professional and public forums concern test bias, the influence of heredity versus environment on IQ, race differences in test scores, and disproportionate placement of minority children into classes such as those for students with gifted abilities or with disabilities. These issues have been the subject of research, debate, federal guidelines, laws, and lawsuits. Just as major law cases differ on whether intelligence tests are unfair to minority children (*Larry P. v. Riles;* PASE decision in Chicago), so do professionals in the field of intelligence testing continue to disagree on these issues. It is likely that the future will be filled with arguments on the appropriate use of intelligence tests (Flanagan & Harrison, in press; Fletcher-Janzen & Reynolds, 2008; Geisinger, in press; Kaufman, 2009; Sternberg & Kaufman, 2011) and claims that they should be banned; at the same time, it is equally certain that there will continue to be a proliferation of new and revised instruments of both the individual and group variety.

REFERENCES

Anastasi, A., & Urbina, S. (1997). *Psychological testing* (7th ed.). Upper Saddle River, NJ: Prentice Hall.

Elliott, C. D. (2007). *Differential Ability Scales—Second Edition (DASII) administration and scoring manual.* San Antonio, TX: Psychological Corporation.

Flanagan, D. P., & Alfonso, V. C. (Eds.). (2010). *Essentials of specific learning disability identification.* Hoboken, NJ: Wiley.

Flanagan, D. P., & Harrison, P. L. (in press). (Eds.). *Contemporary intellectual assessment: Theories, tests, and issues* (3rd ed.). New York, NY: Guilford Press.

Fletcher-Janzen, E., & Reynolds, C. R. (Eds.). (2008). *Neuropsychological perspectives on learning disabilities in the era of RTI: Recommendations for diagnosis and intervention.* Hoboken, NJ: Wiley.

Geisinger, K. F. (Ed.). (in press). *APA handbook of testing and assessment in psychology*. Washington, DC: American Psychological Association.

Kaufman, A. S. (1979). *Intelligent testing with the WISC-R*. New York, NY: Wiley.

Kaufman, A. S. (2009). *IQ testing 101*. New York, NY: Springer.

Kaufman, A. S., & Kaufman, N. L. (1983). *Kaufman Assessment Battery for Children (KABC) interpretive manual*.

Kaufman, A. S., & Kaufman, N. L. (2004). *Kaufman Assessment Battery for Children—Second Edition (KABC-II)*. Circle Pines, MN: American Guidance Service.

Naglieri, J. A., & Das, J. P. (1997). *Das-Naglieri Cognitive Assessment System*. Itasca, IL: Riverside.

Pintner, R. (1923). *Intelligence testing*. New York, NY: Holt, Rinehart, & Winston.

Pintner, R., & Patterson, D. G. (1925). *A scale of performance*. New York, NY: Appleton.

Roid, G. H. (2003). *Stanford-Binet Intelligence Scales—5th Edition*. Itasca, IL: Riverside.

Sattler, J. M. (2008). *Assessment of children: Cognitive foundations* (5th ed.). San Diego, CA: Author.

Sternberg, R. J., & Kaufman, S. B. (Eds.). (2011). *Cambridge handbook of intelligence*. New York, NY: Cambridge University Press.

Urbina, S. (2004). *Essentials of psychological testing*. Hoboken, NJ: Wiley.

VanDerHayden, A. M., & Burns, M. K. (2010). *Essentials of response to intervention*. Hoboken, NJ: Wiley.

Vane, T. R., & Motta, R. W. (1984). Group intelligence tests. In G. Goldstein & M. Hersen (Eds.), *Handbook of psychological assessment* (pp. 100–116). New York, NY: Pergamon Press.

Wasserman, J. D. (in press). A history of intelligence assessment: The unfinished tapestry. In D. P. Flanagan & P. L. Harrison (Eds.), *Contemporary intellectual assessment: Theories, tests, and issues* (3rd ed.). New York, NY: Guilford Press.

Wechsler, D. (2003). *Wechsler Intelligence Scale for Children (4th ed.). (WISC-IV) administration and scoring manual*. San Antonio, TX: Psychological Corporation.

Wechsler, D. (2008). *Wechsler Adult Intelligence Scale (4th ed.) (WAIS-IV)*. San Antonio, TX: Pearson.

Woodcock, R. W., & Johnson, M. B. (1989). *Woodcock-Johnson Psycho-Educational Battery Revised*. Itasca, IL: Riverside.

Woodcock, R. W., McGrew, K. S., & Mather, N. (2001). *Woodcock-Johnson Psycho-Educational Battery, Third Edition (WJ III)*. Itasca, IL: Riverside.

ALAN S. KAUFMAN
*Yale University Child Study Center,
School of Medicine*

PATTI L. HARRISON
University of Alabama

See also Intelligence; Intelligence Quotient; Intelligent Testing; *see specific tests*

INTELLIGENCE, TRIARCHIC THEORY OF

The triarchic theory of intelligence, also referred to as the *theory of successful intelligence*, has expanded the understanding of human intelligence. In contrast to traditional intelligence theories, particularly the general or *g* theory of intelligence (Spearman, 1946), the triarchic theory has provided a superior notion of intelligence. Although similar to other efforts to broaden explanations of human abilities, such as Gardner's (1983) multiple intelligence theory, the triarchic theory of intelligence has focused on three specific components of intellectual functioning. These three components are: (1) analytical intelligence (the ability to critique, judge, evaluate, and assess), (2) creative intelligence (the ability to invent, imagine, and predict), and (3) practical intelligence (the ability to apply, use, and implement one's knowledge into the real world; Sternberg, 1997).

The triarchic theory of intelligence is composed of four main elements (Sternberg, 1997). The first element states that success is accomplished from using analytical, creative, and practical intelligence abilities. Schools more often place a higher priority on teaching that focuses on analytical intelligence than practical and creative intelligence. Sternberg, Torff, and Grigorenko (1998) have found that students who receive education that balances teaching all three abilities will outperform students who receive more traditional instruction on assessments of memory and performance. Emphasis on a range of all three intellectual abilities would address concerns that have been raised by creativity scholars (e.g., Csikszentmihalyi, 2003) who have criticized schools for not providing education that involves creativity into their curriculum as well, but by mainly focusing on teaching analytical abilities.

The second element states that intelligence is defined based on the ability to achieve success from one's own personal standards they hold as well as their cultures (Sternberg, 2010). For instance, teaching that is targeted on emphasizing each component has resulted in increased scores on traditional measures of student performance, such as the SAT (Sternberg, 2006). The third element proposes that for one to achieve, they must take advantage of their strengths and use them to compensate for their weaknesses (Sternberg, 1997, 2009). The fourth element is that one can balance their abilities and use them to adapt to, shape, and select environments where once can achieve more effectively. In other words, intelligence does not involve simply modifying oneself to the environment; it also involves the ability to modify the environment itself to suit one's abilities and to find new settings that are better for one's skills, values, or desires.

The Sternberg Triarchic Abilities Test (STAT) was developed to measure the three components of intellectual functioning. Researchers have demonstrated that the STAT test is a reliable way for assessing learning outcomes of teaching in the classroom aimed at the three components of the triarchic theory (Sternberg & the Rainbow Project

Collaborators, 2006). Sternberg and colleagues have suggested this type of triarchically based measure yields stronger predictive validity for first-year college GPA than high school GPA or the SAT.

Research has shown that an analytic-ability teaching style in public schools and standardized tests tends to favor learning styles of Caucasian students (for a review see Kaufman, 2010). The STAT may be a useful tool for reducing ethnic bias in college admissions. Sternberg (& Rainbow Collaborators, 2006, 2009), through programs such as the Rainbow Project and Kaleidoscope Project, has shown that by utilizing tests such as the STAT, students of different ethnicities perform as well as students who were accepted based on standardized admissions tests. Furthermore, in the Kaleidoscope Project at Tufts University, Sternberg (2009) found that by giving students tests measuring other aspects of intelligence, such as creative and practical intelligence, students of all ethnicities who were accepted performed as well as students admitted based on regular admissions tests. These could hold the future for college admission tests in the future (Sternberg, 2010).

REFERENCES

Csikszentmihayli, M. (2003). Key issues in creativity and development. In R. K. Sawyer, V. John-Steiner, S. Moran, R. J. Sternberg, O. H. Feldman, H. Gardner, J. Nakamura, & M. Csikszentmihayli (Eds.), *Creativity and development* (pp. 149–162). New York, NY: Oxford University Press.

Gardner, H. (1983). *Frames of mind: The theory of multiple intelligences*. New York, NY: Basic Books.

Kaufman, J. C. (2010). Using creativity to reduce ethnic bias in college admissions. *Review of General Psychology, 14*(3), 189–203.

Spearman, C. (1946). Theory of general factor. *British Journal of Psychology, 36*, 117–131.

Sternberg, R. J. (1997). *Successful intelligence: How practical and creative intelligence determine success in life*. New York, NY: Plume.

Sternberg, R. J. (2009). The rainbow and kaleidoscope projects: A new psychological approach to undergraduate admissions. *European Psychologist, 14*(4), 279–287.

Sternberg, R. J. (2010). *College admissions for the 21st century*. Cambridge, MA: Harvard University Press.

Sternberg, R. J., & the Rainbow Project Collaborators (2006). The rainbow project: Enhancing the SAT through assessments of analytical, practical, and creative skills. *Intelligence, 34*, 321–350.

Sternberg, R. J., Torff, B., & Grigorenko, E. L. (1998). Teaching triarchically improves school achievement. *Journal of Educational Psychology, 90*(3), 374–384.

ALEXANDER S. MCKAY
JAMES C. KAUFMAN
California State University, San Bernardino

INTELLIGENT TESTING

Intelligent testing is a philosophy or model of assessment widely espoused and best represented in the writings of Kaufman et al. (Kaufman, 1979, 1994; Kaufman & Kaufman, 1977; Kaufman & Lichtenberger, 1999; Reynolds & Clark, 1982; Reynolds & Kaufman, 1986). The intent of the intelligent testing model is to bring together empirical data, psychometrics, clinical acumen, psychological theory, and careful reasoning to build an assessment of an individual leading to the derivation of an intervention to improve the life circumstances of the subject. The promulgation of this philosophy was prompted by many factors, but particularly extremist approaches to the use of tests.

Conventional intelligence tests and even the entire concept of intelligence testing have been the focus of considerable controversy for several decades. Always the subject of scrutiny, the past two decades have witnessed intelligence tests placed on trial in the federal courts (*Larry P.*, 1979; *PASE*, 1980), state legislatures (New York's "trust in testing" legislation), the lay press, and open scholarly forums (Reynolds & Brown, 1984). At one extreme are issues such as those brought up by Hilliard (1984), who contends that IQ tests are inherently unacceptable measurement devices with no real utility. At the other extreme are such well-known figures as Herrnstein (1973) and Jensen (1980), who believe the immense value of intelligence tests is self-evident. While critics of testing demand a moratorium on their use with children, psychologists often are forced to adhere to rigid administrative rules that require the use of precisely obtained IQs when making placements or diagnostic decisions. No consideration is given to basic psychometric principles including measurement error (Reynolds, 1999), the influence of behavioral variables on performance, or appropriate sensitivity to the child's cultural or linguistic heritage.

A middle ground is sorely needed. Tests must be preserved, along with their rich clinical heritage and their prominent place in the neurological, psychological, and educational literature. At the same time, the proponents of tests need to be less defensive and more open to rational criticism of the current popular instruments. Knowledge of the weaknesses as well as the strengths of individually administered intelligence tests can serve the dual functions of improving examiners' ability to interpret profiles of any given instrument and enabling examiners to select pertinent supplementary tests and subtests to secure a thorough assessment of the intellectual abilities of any child, adolescent, or adult referred for evaluation. The quality of individual mental assessment is no longer simply a question answered in terms of an instrument's empirical or psychometric characteristics. High reliability and validity coefficients, a meaningful factor structure, and normative data obtained by stratified random sampling techniques do not ensure that an intelligence test is valuable for all or even most assessment purposes. The skills and training of the psychologist engaged in using intelligence tests will certainly interact with the utility of intelligence testing beyond the level of simple actuarial prediction of academic performance. Intelligent testing provides an appropriate model.

For children with low IQ, the primary role of the intelligent tester is to use the test results to develop a means of intervention that will "beat" the prediction made by global IQs. A plethora of research during the twentieth century has amply demonstrated that very low IQ children show concomitantly low levels of academic attainment. The clinical purpose of administering an intelligence test to a child with low IQ, then, is at least twofold: (1) to determine that the child is indeed at high risk for academic failure, and (2) to articulate a set of learning circumstances that defeat the prediction. For individuals with average or high IQs, the specific tasks of the intelligence tester may change, but the philosophy remains the same. When evaluating a child with a learning disability (LD), for example, the task is primarily one of fulfilling the prediction made by the global IQs. Most children with LD exhibit average or better general intelligence, but have a history of academic performance significantly below what would be predicted from their intelligence test performance. The intelligent tester takes on the responsibility of preventing the child from becoming an "outlier" in the prediction (i.e., he or she must design a set of environmental conditions that will cause the child to achieve and learn at the level predicted by the intelligence test).

When psychologists engage in intelligent testing, the child or adult becomes the primary focus of the evaluation and the tests fade into the background as only vehicles to understanding. The test setting becomes completely examinee oriented. Interpretation and communication of test results in the context of the individual's particular background, referral behaviors, and approach to performance on diverse tasks constitute the crux of competent evaluation. Global test scores are deemphasized; flexibility, a broad base of knowledge in psychology, and insight on the part of the psychologist are demanded. The intelligence test becomes a dynamic helping agent, not an instrument for labeling, placement in dead end programs, or disillusionment on the part of eager, caring teachers and parents.

Intelligent testing through individualization becomes the key to accomplishment; it is antithetical to the development of computerized or depersonalized form reporting for individually administered cognitive tests such as espoused by Alcorn and Nicholson (1975) and Vitelli and Goldblatt (1979) (Reynolds, 1980a, 1980b). For intelligent testers, it is imperative to be sensitive and socially aware, and to be aware that intelligence and cognition do not constitute the total human being. The intelligence testing model is inconsistent with "checklist" approaches to the development of individual education plans (IEPs). It is a mode of true individualization and does not lend itself to mimeographed IEPs that are checked off, or to special education programs where all children are taught with the same methodology. Computer generated reports with "individualized" recommendations are anathema to the intelligent testing philosophy.

Intelligent testing urges the use of contemporary measures of intelligence as necessary to achieve a true understanding of the individual's intellectual functioning. The approach to test interpretation under this philosophy has been likened to the approach of a psychological detective (Kaufman, 1979, 1994). It requires melding of clinical skill, mastery of psychometrics and measurement, and extensive knowledge of cognitive development and intelligence. A far more extensive treatment of this approach to test interpretation appears in the book *Intelligent Testing with the WISC-R* (Kaufman, 1979), a volume updated in 1994 by Kaufman to apply directly to the WISC-III. The philosophy is not, however, test-specific. Discussion of applications of this philosophy to preschool children may be found in Kaufman and Kaufman (1977) and Reynolds and Clark (1982).

Clinical skills with children are obviously important to the intelligent tester in building rapport and maintaining the proper ambience during the actual testing. Although adhering to standardized procedures and obtaining valid scores are important, the child must remain the lodestar of the evaluation. Critical to the dynamic understanding of the child's performance is close, insightful observation and recordings of behavior during the testing period. Fully half of the important information gathered during the administration of an intelligence test comes from observing behavior under a set of standard conditions. Behavior at various points in the course of the assessment often will dictate the proper interpretation of test scores. Many individuals earn IQs of 100, but each in a different manner, with infinite nuances of behavior interacting directly with a person's test performance.

Knowledge and skill in psychometrics and measurement are requisite to intelligent testing (Reynolds, 1999). The clinical evaluation of test performance must be directed by careful analyses of the statistical properties of the test scores, the internal psychometric characteristics of the test, and the data regarding their relationship to external factors. As one example, difference scores have long been of inherent interest for psychologists, especially between subparts of an intelligence scale. Difference scores are unreliable, and small discrepancies between levels of performance may be best attributed to measurement error. If large enough, however, difference scores can provide valuable information regarding the choice of an appropriate remedial or therapeutic program. The psychometric characteristics of the tests in question dictate the size of the differences needed for statistical confidence in their reflecting real rather than chance fluctuations. Interpretation of subscale differences often requires integrating clinical observations of the child's behavior with data on the relationship of the test scores to other factors, and with theories of intelligence, but only after first establishing that the differences are real and not based on error.

One major limitation of most contemporary intelligence tests is their lack of foundation in theories of intelligence, whether these theories are based on research in neuropsychology, cognitive information processing, factor analysis, learning theory, or other domains. Nevertheless, many profiles obtained by children and adults on intelligence tests are interpretable from diverse theoretical perspectives, and can frequently be shown to display a close fit to one or another theoretical approach to intelligence. Theories then become useful in developing a full understanding of the individual. Competing theories of intelligence abound (Kaufman, 1994; Reynolds, 1981; Vernon, 1979; White, 1979).

Well-grounded, empirically evaluated models of intellectual functioning enable one to reach a broader understanding of the examinee and to make specific predictions regarding behavior outside of the testing situation. Predictions will not always be correct; however, the intelligent tester has an excellent chance of making sense out of the predictable individual variations in behavior, cognitive skills, and academic performance by involving the nomothetic framework provided by theory. The alternative often is to be stymied or forced to rely on trial and error or anecdotal, illusionary relationships when each new set of profile fluctuations is encountered. Theories, even speculative ones, are more efficient guides to developing hypotheses for understanding and treating problems than are purely clinical impressions, armchair speculations, or clinical anecdotes.

Through the elements of clinical skill, psychometric sophistication, and a broad base of knowledge of theories of individual differences emerges intelligent testing. None is sufficient, yet, when properly implemented, these elements engage in a synergistic interaction to produce the greatest possible understanding. The intelligent testing model places a series of requirements on the test but also on the tester; not every test can be used intelligently nor can everyone be an intelligent tester. The examiner's breadth of knowledge of psychometrics, differential psychology, child development, and other areas is crucial. Equally, the test must have multiple scales that are reliable, with good validity evidence, and be standardized on a sufficiently large, nationally stratified random sample. The test must offer the opportunity for good clinical observations. Without all of these characteristics, intelligent testing is unlikely to take place; when it does, however, the child is certain to benefit.

REFERENCES

Alcorn, C., & Nicholson, C. (1975). A vocational assessment battery for the educable mentally retarded and low literate. *Educating and Training the Mentally Retarded*, *10*(2), 78–83

Herrnstein, R. (1973). *IQ in the meritocracy*. Boston, MA: Little, Brown.

Hilliard, A. G. (1984). IQ testing as the emperor's new clothes: A critique of Jensen's bias in mental testing. In C. R. Reynolds & R. T. Brown (Eds.), *Perspectives on bias in mental testing*. New York, NY: Plenum Press.

Jensen, A. R. (1980). *Bias in mental testing*. New York, NY: Free Press.

Kaufman, A. S. (1979). *Intelligent testing with the WISC-R*. New York, NY: Wiley.

Kaufman, A. S. (1994). *Intelligent testing with the WISC-III*. New York, NY: Wiley.

Kaufman, A. S., & Kaufman, N. L. (1977). *Clinical evaluation of young children with the McCarthy scales*. New York, NY: Grune & Stratton.

Kaufman, A. S., & Lichtenberger, L. (1999). Intellectual assessment. In C. R. Reynolds (Ed.), *Assessment*, Vol. 4 of M. Hersen & A. Bellack (Eds.), *Comprehensive clinical psychology*. Oxford, England: Elsevier.

Reynolds, C. R. (1980a). Two commercial interpretive systems for the WISC-R. *School Psychology Review*, *9*, 385–386.

Reynolds, C. R. (1980b). Review of the TARDOR interpretive scoring system for the WISC-R. *Measurement & Evaluation in Guidance*, *14*, 46–48.

Reynolds, C. R. (1981). The neuropsychological basis of intelligence. In G. W. Hynd & J. E. Obrzut (Eds.), *Psychoeducational assessment of the school aged child: Issues and procedures*. New York, NY: Grune & Stratton.

Reynolds, C. R. (1999). Fundamentals of measurement and assessment in psychology. In C. R. Reynolds (Ed.), *Assessment*, Vol. 4 of M. Hersen & A. Bellack (Eds.), *Comprehensive clinical psychology*. Oxford, England: Elsevier.

Reynolds, C. R., & Brown, R. T. (Eds.). (1984). *Perspectives on bias in mental testing*. New York, NY: Plenum Press.

Reynolds, C. R., & Clark, J. H. (1982). Cognitive assessment of the preschool child. In K. Paget & B. Bracken (Eds.), *Psychoeducational assessment of preschool and primary aged children*. New York, NY: Grune & Stratton.

Reynolds, C. R., & Kaufman, A. S. (1986). Assessment of children's intelligence with the Wechsler scales. In B. Wolman (Ed.), *Handbook of intelligence*. New York: Wiley.

Vernon, P. A. (1979). *Intelligence: Heredity and environment*. San Francisco, CA: Freeman.

Vitelli, R., & Goldblatt, R. (1979). *The TARDOR interpretive scoring system for the WISC-R*. Manchester, CT: TARDOR.

White, W. (Ed.). (1979). Intelligence [Special issue]. *Journal of Research & Development in Education*, *12*(1).

CECIL R. REYNOLDS
Texas A&M University

See *also* Cultural Bias in Testing; Intelligence Testing; Kaufman, Alan S.; Remediation, Deficit-Centered Models of; Sequential and Simultaneous Cognitive Processing

INTERACTIVE LANGUAGE DEVELOPMENT

The notion of interactive language development has its roots in the philosophy of pragmatism and in child language pragmatics research. Pragmatics refers to the study of the social uses of language and research in the area of pragmatic language development in children. It is concerned primarily with three major focuses: (1) understanding how children learn to adapt their language to various linguistic and nonlinguistic contexts; (2) tracking development relative to the increasing repertoire of language functions; and (3) determining the role of social context in facilitating various aspects of language development (Bates, 1976; Prutting, 1982).

Interactive language development approaches rely heavily on social psychological research involving the study of adult child interaction. Rees (1982) found a recurring theme in this literature: that pragmatic considerations have a prominent role in language acquisition "not only as a set of skills to be acquired but as motivating and explanatory factors for the acquisition of the language itself" (p. 8). Rees argues that pragmatic interactional factors assume an important role in the child's mastery of native language. Interactional factors may be seen as the source or origin of language in the child. Bruner (1975) cites the interaction between mother and infant during the first year of life, particularly in shared attention objects, people, and events of interest, as the basis of the child's capacity for reference and more broadly for meaning that eventually characterizes the human use of symbols.

Second, pragmatic interactional factors may be seen as the motivation for language learning as exemplified in the research of Halliday (1975) and Bates (1976). These researchers demonstrate how communicative functions emerge prior to the acquisition of linguistic skills. In addition to forming the basis for the development of particular linguistic structures, pragmatic interactional factors explain the development of linguistic style and code switching ability. As Rees (1982) notes, "language users typically control a range of style and code variants that are appropriate to particular listeners and particular settings, and they use these variants in establishing and maintaining social role relationships" (p. 10). Children as young as 3 or 4 years have been found to use different styles or "registers" for speaking to their parents, siblings, friends, strangers, younger and older children (Gleason, 1973; Snow & Ferguson, 1977).

As descriptions of the acquisition of pragmatic interactional abilities increased in the normal child language literature, language and communication practitioners began to develop pragmatically based assessment and intervention programs for children with language disorders (Prinz, 1982). Professionals involved in the treatment of children with language disorders stressed the importance of viewing communication as an interpersonal behavior that occurs in interaction with the environment. The interactional component, in which language is used to establish and maintain contact with other persons, is an integral part of many current intervention programs for language-disabled children. Specific procedures have been developed to facilitate the child's communication with the environment, including initiating and sustaining communicative interactions with others, consideration of a listener's perspective when encoding messages, and appropriate responses to listener feedback indicating a lack of understanding. Procedures for pragmatic interactional language treatment are discussed in Wilcox (1982).

REFERENCES

Bates, E. (1976). Pragmatics and sociolinguistics in child language. In D. Morehead & A. Morehead (Eds.), *Normal and deficient child language* (pp. 247–307). Baltimore, MD: University Park Press.

Bruner, J. (1975). The ontogenesis of speech acts. *Journal of Child Language, 2*, 1–20.

Gleason, J. (1973). Codeswitching in children's language. In T. Moore (Ed.), *Cognitive development and the acquisition of language* (pp. 167–169). New York, NY: Academic Press.

Halliday, M. (1975). *Learning how to mean*. London, England: Arnold.

Prinz, P. M. (1982). Development of pragmatics: Multiword level. In J. V. Irwin (Ed.), *Pragmatics: The role in language development*. La Verne, CA: Fox Point and University of La Verne Press.

Prutting, C. (1982). Pragmatics as social competence. *Journal of Speech & Hearing Disorders, 47*, 123–134.

Rees, N. (1982). An overview of pragmatics or what is in the box? In J. V. Irwin (Ed.), *Pragmatics: The role in language development* (pp. 15–27). La Verne, CA: Fox Point and University of La Verne Press.

Snow, C., & Ferguson, C. (1977). *Talking to children: Language input and acquisition*. Cambridge, England: Cambridge University Press.

Wilcox, M. (1982). The integration of pragmatics into language therapy. In J. V. Irwin (Ed.), *Pragmatics: The role in language development* (pp. 29–48). La Verne, CA: Fox Point and University of La Verne Press.

PHILIP M. PRINZ
Pennsylvania State University

See also Communication Disorders; Language Therapy; Pragmatics and Pragmatic Communication Disorders; Social Learning Theory; Theory of Activity

INTERDISCIPLINARY TEAMS

Before any child receives special education services, he or she must receive an individual assessment to identify areas of educational need, determine the child's aptitude for achievement, and identify other factors that might be interfering with school performance. This individual assessment is the basis for all instructional planning. With the advent of the Education for All Handicapped Children Act of 1975 (PL 94-142) came the requirement that an interdisciplinary team (IDT), also known as a multidisciplinary team (MDT), be used to determine pupil eligibility for special education services. Public agencies assessing children suspected of having a disability must include the individuals identified by regulations as necessary for an individualized education program (IEP) team, specifically:

1. The parents of the child.
2. At least one regular education teacher of the child (if the child is, or may be, participating in the regular education environment).
3. At least one special education teacher of the child, or if appropriate, at least one special education provider of the child.
4. A representative of the public agency who:
   a. Is qualified to provide, or supervise the provision of, specially designed instruction to meet the unique needs of children with disabilities.
   b. Is knowledgeable about the general curriculum.
   c. Is knowledgeable about the availability of resources of the public agency.
5. An individual who can interpret the instructional implications of evaluation results, who may be a member of the team described in paragraphs (2) through (6) of this section.
6. At the discretion of the parent or the agency, other individuals who have knowledge or special expertise regarding the child, including related services personnel as appropriate.
7. If appropriate, the child.

(34 CFR §300.344), plus "other qualified professionals, as appropriate" (34 CFR §300.533). The proposed regulations issued in June of 2005 make only nonsubstantive changes to these requirements (70 Fed. Reg. 35866).

The IDT is required by the regulations to review all relevant evaluation data on the child, including:

- Evaluations and information provided by the parents of the child.
- Current classroom based assessments and observations.
- Observations by teachers and related services providers. (34 CFR §300.533)

On the basis of this information and input from the child's parents, the team identifies any additional data that may be needed to determine the child's present level of performance and needs; arranges for the administration of any tests needed; and determines whether the child is indeed eligible for special education and related services.

Since PL 94-142 and subsequently the IDEA, IDTs have become incorporated into the organizational routine of most school systems in the United States. Nevertheless, school professionals, parents, and the general public have expressed differing views regarding their value (Masters & Mori, 1986).

The IDT model is often cited as the organizational unit best suited to making evaluation and programming decisions because the different perspectives made possible by it prevent biased eligibility and placement decisions (Abelson & Woodman, 1983). However, there is no empirical evidence to support the use of teams. Ballard-Campbell and Semmel (1981) suggest forces such as litigation, parental and educator opinions, and state level administrative practices, rather than research evidence, have been responsible for the spread of interdisciplinary practices.

Indeed, recent research findings concerning the effectiveness of the IDT model are discouraging. According to Ysseldyke (1983), the IDT model uses conceptual definitions that have not been translated into scientific or practical assessment procedures.

While IDT functioning has been widely researched, the results have been mixed; some inquiries into whether IDTs make better decisions than individuals have revealed few differences between decisions made by IDTs and those made by individual decision makers (Pfeiffer, 1982). Some researchers (Pfeiffer & Naglieri, 1983) have demonstrated that teams make more consistent and less variable decisions than do individuals. Interpretive and methodological differences between positive and negative studies make it difficult to arrive at definitive answers.

REFERENCES

Abelson, M. A., & Woodman, R. W. (1983). Review of research on team effectiveness: Implications for teams in schools. *School Psychology Review, 12*(2), 125–138.

Ballard-Campbell, M., & Semmel, M. I. (1981). Policy research and special education issues affecting policy research and implementation. *Exceptional Education Quarterly, 2*, 59–68.

Masters, L. F., & Mori, A. A. (1986). *Teaching secondary students with mild learning and behavior problems*. Rockville, MD: Aspen.

Pfeiffer, S. I. (1982). Special education placement decisions made by teams and individuals. *Psychology in the Schools, 19*, 335–340.

Pfeiffer, S. I., & Naglieri, J. A. (1983). An investigation of multidisciplinary team decision making. *Journal of Learning Disabilities, 15*(10), 586–590.

Ysseldyke, J. E. (1983). Current practices in making psychoeducational decisions about learning disabled students. *Journal of Learning Disabilities, 16*(4), 226–233.

JOSEPH M. RUSSO
Hunter College,
City University of New York
Second edition

KIMBERLY F. APPLEQUIST
University of Colorado at Colorado Springs
Third edition

See also Individuals with Disabilities Education Improvement Act of 2004 (IDEIA); Multidisciplinary Teams

INTERMITTENT REINFORCEMENT

Reinforcement is a rule of human behavior. To increase in the frequency of a response it is followed by the presentation of a reinforcer, generally something considered pleasant (e.g., increase in homework completion following verbal praise from a parent) or the removal of something aversive (e.g., increase in screaming following the removal of difficult math work). A reinforcement schedule refers the ratio of reinforcer delivery to the behavior. There are two basic schedules of reinforcement: continuous and intermittent. Continuous reinforcement involves reinforcing the student's behavior or response each time it occurs whereas intermittent reinforcement involves reinforcing the behavior or response on some occasions but not others (Chance, 1999). In schools, the majority of student behavior is reinforced under intermittent schedules as it is typically impossible to reinforce each appropriate academic or social behavior that a student exhibits. More specifically, continuous schedules of reinforcement are best used when students are learning new behaviors or responses. In contrast, intermittent schedules are more appropriate to use when maintaining behavior over time (Kazdin, 2000).

There are four different types of intermittent schedules of reinforcement: fixed interval, variable interval, fixed ratio, and variable ratio. Interval schedules involve reinforcing behavior related to time whereas ratio schedules involve reinforcing behavior related to the frequency of responses (Alberto & Troutman, 2003). In the research literature, the name of a reinforcement schedule is often shortened (i.e., fixed interval = *FI*, variable interval = *VI*, fixed ratio = *FR*, and variable ratio = *VR*). In addition, the type of schedule is paired with a number that indicates the actual schedule of reinforcement (e.g., *FR* 3 = behavior will be reinforced after three responses).

A fixed interval (FI) schedule refers to the delivery of a reinforcer after a set amount of time has passed and a student has engaged in an appropriate behavior or response. For example, a student can receive a sticker each hour for engaging in no talk outs or after every 10 minutes of being on task. A problem with FI schedules is that students can begin to predict when a reinforcer is about to be delivered based on time and thus may only engage in the appropriate behavior close to time period that he or she will be reinforced (Kazdin, 2000). In addition, there is often a drop in student performance right after the reinforcer is delivered if the student learns that a certain amount of time must pass before he or she will be able to receive a reinforcer for appropriate responding (Pryor, 1999).

In contrast to the FI schedule of reinforcement, variable interval (VI) schedules involve the delivery of a reinforcer after an average length of time rather than a set amount of time. For example, a VI schedule in a school setting is when teachers use computer signaling programs to cue themselves to provide verbal praise to students. These computer programs can be set to beep at random intervals and the average length of time can be determined by the teacher. For a VI 7-minute schedule, students will be reinforced on average every 7 minutes. Sometimes students will be reinforced after 4 or 5 minutes have passed and they are engaging in the appropriate behavior and sometimes students will receive a reinforcer after 8, 9, or 10 minutes. In general, VI schedules produce higher rates of responding compared to FI schedules (Kazdin, 2000).

A fixed ratio (FR) schedule involves the delivery of a reinforcer after a set number of correct responses or occurrences of appropriate behavior. For example, a teacher implementing an FR 5 schedule to increase completion of math problems would provide reinforcement (e.g., praise, points on a chart) after every five problems completed correctly. Similar to FI schedules of reinforcement, FR schedules may also produce a delay in responding following the delivery of the reinforcer, particularly if the ratios are large—such as requiring students to complete 40 math problems before delivering a reinforcer (Alberto & Troutman, 2003). Another characteristic of FR schedules is that students may work quickly in order to complete the number of problems or responses required to receive the reinforcer and the quality of work may suffer (Kazdin, 2000). Individuals interested in implementing this type of reinforcement schedule should focus on both quality and quantity as criteria for delivery of the reinforcer.

A variable ratio (VR) schedule of reinforcement involves delivering a reinforcer after an average number of correct responses rather than a set number of responses. That is, a different number of responses are required each time in order to receive a reinforcer. The most common example of a VR schedule is gambling: sometimes a slot machine will pay off after 10 pulls and sometimes it will pay off after one pull. Typically, variable ratio schedules lead to high, stable rates of responding and are quite frequently used in educational and clinical settings (Kazdin, 2000; Lerman, Iwata, Shore, & Kahng, 1996). Another reason for the frequent use of VI schedules is that behavior is more likely to maintain once reinforcement is discontinued compared to FR or continuous schedules (Pryor, 1999).

Overall, it is important to consider which schedule of reinforcement to implement as it will greatly affect both rates of responding and the extent to which the behavior will maintain once it is no longer being reinforced. Continuous schedules of reinforcement are more appropriate during the acquisition stages of learning. In contrast, intermittent schedules of reinforcement are more appropriate after the student has learned the skill and understands the relationship between engaging in a particular behavior and receiving a reinforcer.

REFERENCES

Alberto, P. A., & Troutman, A. C. (2003). *Applied behavior analysis for teachers* (6th ed.). Upper Saddle River, NJ: Pearson.

Chance, P. (1999). *Learning and behavior*. Pacific Grove, CA: Brooks/Cole.

Kazdin, A. E. (2000). *Behavior modification in applied settings*. Belmont, MA: Wadsworth.

Lerman, D. C., Iwata, B. A., Shore, B. A., & Kahng, S. (1996). Responding maintained by intermittent reinforcement: Implications for the use of extinction with problem behavior in clinical settings. *Journal of Applied Behavior Analysis, 29*, 153–171.

Pryor, K. (1999). *Don't shoot the dog*. New York, NY: Bantam Books.

LEANNE S. HAWKEN
JASON BURROW-SANCHEZ
University of Utah

See also Negative Reinforcement; Positive Reinforcement

INTERNATIONAL CENTER FOR DISABILITY RESOURCES ON THE INTERNET

The International Center for Disability Resources on the Internet (ICDRI) was founded in 1998 and is a nonprofit center based in the United States. It is an internationally recognized public policy center "organized by and for people with disabilities"; and "ICDRI seeks to increase opportunities for people with disabilities by identifying barriers to participation in society and promoting best practices and universal design for the global community." ICDRI provides disability rights education and customized programs for the public and is an active participant in public policy strategic planning and implementation for governments in the United States and abroad.

ICDRI describes the organization strengths as follows.

- ICDRI is operated by people with disabilities and benefits from the expertise of an International Advisory Board.
- ICDRI embraces a cross disability perspective, rather than a singular focus on one type of disability, in order to include the entire community of people with disabilities.
- ICDRI is a neutral research institute that maintains independence and control over its strategic planning, business work plan, and budget.
- ICDRI is committed to be on the cutting edge of global disability law, policy, and electronic and information technology.
- ICDRI seeks to enable replication of best practices and to enable other organizations to address disability issues.
- ICDRI operates within a framework of collaboration with local, national, and international organizations in the exchange of information and cultural perspectives.

ICDRI's website establishes a formal knowledge base of quality disability resources and best practices and provides education, outreach, and training. ICDRI makes this information available in an accessible format through its website at http://icdri.org/

STAFF

See also Web Accessibility

INTERNATIONAL CHILD NEUROLOGY ASSOCIATION

The International Child Neurology Association (ICNA) was founded in 1973, with Articles of Association approved by Royal Decree by Baudouin, King of Belgium, the following year. ICNA is a nonprofit organization composed of child neurologists and related professionals dedicated to the promotion of research in the field of child neurology and encouraging recognition of the ability and scope of those who practice within the profession. In the interest of advancing and benefiting child and infant neurological science, the association provides a forum for the exchange of scientific and professional opinions by organizing international meetings, international cooperative studies, publications, and translations as well as supporting international exchange of teachers and students in the field. The 9th International Child Neurology Congress and the Asian and Oceanian Congress of Child Neurology are two other conferences.

This entry has been informed by the source below.

REFERENCE

International Child Neurology Association. (2012). *8th International Child Neurology Congress.* Retrieved from www.icna pedia.org

MARILYN P. DORNBUSH
Atlanta, Georgia
First edition

TAMARA J. MARTIN
The University of Texas of the Permian Basin
Second edition

INTERNATIONAL CLASSIFICATION OF DISEASES

The International Classification of Diseases (ICD) is used to classify morbidity and mortality data for statistical purposes and to index hospital records on diseases and operations for information storage and retrieval. Classifying operations for this purpose has traditionally involved structuring according to type of operative procedure, anatomic site, or a combination of these two methods. Surgical specialty serves as the primary axis for classification in the present ICD as well as in most hospitals. The way in which a classification system of diseases is applied depends on the particular data to be classified and on the final product desired. As of yet, there exists no internationally agreed on method for classifying multiple causes of death.

Although the statistical study of diseases began as early as the 1700s, the roots of the ICD are found in the work of William Farr (1807–1883), a medical statistician who produced the best classification of diseases for his time—the International List of Causes of Death. Although this classification was never universally accepted, it did lay the basis for classifying by anatomical site. In the early 1900s, Dr. Jacque Bertillon prepared the Bertillon Classification of Causes of Death. Several revisions were put forth and, in 1923, M. Michel Huber (Bertillon's successor) managed to involve other international organizations, such as the Health Organization of the League of Nations, in drafting revisions, stating that the system should be reviewed every 10 years. The Sixth Decennial Revision Conference was marked by the adoption of a system calling for international cooperation in establishing national committees on vital and health statistics to coordinate statistical activity in the United States as well as through the World Health Organization. The present ICD is in its 10th revision.

The 10th revision of the ICD is an extension of the system of causes of morbidity and mortality. Furthermore, it provides a means for developing an efficient basis for indexing diagnostic information on hospital charts so that this data may later be reviewed and studied. The ICD is divided into 17 main sections, among them: diseases caused by well-defined infective agents; endocrine, neoplasmic, metabolic, and nutritional diseases; mental diseases; complications of pregnancy and childbirth; diseases of the perinatal period; ill-defined conditions; and a classification of injuries (puncture, burn, or open wound). The last category involves a dual classification system: external cause and nature of injury. This section is designed to bear the numbers 800 to 999; external cause is distinguished by the prefix "E," while nature of injury is distinguished by the prefix "N."

Although the broad section headings aid organization, much significance should not be placed on their inherent value, since they have never represented a consistent collection of disease conditions to serve as statistically stable and usable areas. The detailed list is comprised of 671 categories, in addition to 187 categories characterizing injuries according to the nature of the wound, and 182 categories classifying external causes of injuries. A decimal numbering system is used; thus the categories are designated by three-digit numbers. The initial two digits pinpoint important or summary groups, while the third digit sections each group into categories representing classifications of diseases according to a specific axis of specific disease entities. The three-digit categories are not numbered consecutively. Four-digit subcategories provide additional specificity regarding etiology or manifestations of the condition. While the list of categories in the ICD provides a structure for classification, it is essential to be familiar with the diagnostic terms included within each category before the ICD can be of practical use.

MARY LEON PEERY
Texas A&M University

INTERNATIONAL CLASSIFICATION OF FUNCTIONING, DISABILITY, AND HEALTH

As a new member of the World Health Organization Family of International Classifications, the International Classification of Functioning, Disability, and Health (ICF) describes how people live with their health conditions. ICF is a classification of health and health related domains that describe body functions and structures, activities, and participation. The domains are classified from body, individual, and societal perspectives. Since an individual's functioning and disability occurs in a context, ICF also includes a list of environmental factors.

The ICF is useful to understand and measure health outcomes. It can be used in clinical settings, health services, or surveys at the individual or population level. Thus ICF complements the ICD10, The International Statistical Classification of Diseases and Related Health Problems, and therefore is looking beyond mortality and disease.

The ICF is a multipurpose classification designed to serve various disciplines and different sectors. Its specific aims can be summarized as:

• To provide a scientific basis for understanding and studying health and health related states, outcomes, and determinants.

• To establish a common language for describing health and health-related states in order to improve communication between different users, such as health care workers, researchers, policy makers, and the public, including people with disabilities.

• To permit comparison of data across countries, health care disciplines, services, and time.

• To provide a systematic coding scheme for health information systems.

These aims are interrelated because the need for and uses of ICF require the construction of a meaningful and practical system that can be used by various consumers for health policy, quality assurance, and outcome evaluation in different cultures.

Since its publication as a trial version in 1980, ICF's predecessor, the International Classification of Impairment, Disability, and Handicap (ICIDH), has been used for various purposes, for example:

• As a statistical tool—in the collection and recording of data (e.g., in population studies and surveys, in management information systems).

• As a research tool—to measure outcomes, quality of life, or environmental factors.

• As a clinical tool—in needs assessment, matching treatments with specific conditions, vocational assessment, rehabilitation, and outcome evaluation.

• As a social policy tool—in social security planning, compensation systems, and policy design and implementation.

• As an educational tool—in curriculum design and to raise awareness and undertake social action.

ICF is inherently a health and health-related classification; therefore it is also used by sectors such as insurance, social security, labor, education, economics, social policy and general legislation development, and environmental modification. It has been accepted as one of the United Nations social classifications and is referred to in and incorporates The Standard Rules on the Equalization of Opportunities for Persons with Disabilities. Thus ICF provides an appropriate instrument for the implementation of stated international human rights mandates as well as national legislation.

ICF is useful for a broad spectrum of different applications, for example, social security, evaluation in managed health care, and population surveys at local, national, and international levels. It offers a conceptual framework for information that is applicable to personal health care, including prevention, health promotion, and the improvement of participation by removing or mitigating societal hindrances and encouraging the provision of social supports and facilitators. It is also useful for the study of health care systems, in terms of both evaluation and policy formulation. Information for this entry was taken directly from the ICF webpage and this and other excellent resources can be found online at http://www.who.int/en/.

STAFF

See also **International Classification of Diseases; World Health Organizations**

INTERNATIONAL DYSLEXIA ASSOCIATION

The International Dyslexia Association (IDA) is an international, nonprofit organization dedicated to the study and treatment of dyslexia. The IDA was established to continue the pioneering work of Dr. Samuel T. Orton, a neurologist who was one of the first to identify dyslexia and develop effective teaching approaches. Since then, the association has been a strong force in educational and scientific communities. For nearly 65 years, the IDA has been helping individuals with dyslexia, their families, teachers, physicians, and researchers to better understand dyslexia. The IDA believes that all individuals have the right to achieve their potential; that individual learning abilities can be strengthened; and that social, educational, and cultural barriers to language acquisition and use must be removed. The IDA actively promotes effective teaching approaches and related clinical educational intervention strategies for people with dyslexia. The IDA supports and encourages interdisciplinary research. They facilitate the exploration of the causes and early identification of dyslexia and are committed to the responsible and wide dissemination of research based knowledge.

IDA defines their purpose as:

The Purpose of the International Dyslexia Association is to pursue and provide the most comprehensive range of information and services that address the full scope of dyslexia and related difficulties in learning to read and write.... In a way that creates hope, possibility and partnership.... So that every individual has the opportunity to lead a productive and fulfilling life, and society benefits from the resource that is liberated.

According to their website, IDA has approximately 8,500 members, 60% of which come from the field of education. IDA provides information to approximately 30,000 people annually through international offices and/or one of the 40-plus local branches. According to the IDA website, more than 1.5 million visitors access their website annually. IDA conducts conferences, seminars and hosts support groups. Their international conference brings together 200 to 300 experts in learning disabilities and 2,500 individuals interested in learning disabilities and dyslexia. IDA publishes the *Annals of Dyslexia* annually, a print newsletter, *Perspectives on Language and Literacy*, quarterly and an e-newsletter, the *eXaminer*, is electronically distributed to nearly 20,000 subscribers monthly. IDA also provides fact sheets through their website that are free to the public. IDA has an online store that sells other related publications. IDA is funded by private donations, membership dues, foundation grants, sales of publications, our annual national conference, and other development efforts. IDA receives no government funding. IDA funds research on neurological, educational and developmental issues as they relate to dyslexia.

Information for this entry was provided directly from the International Dyslexia Association's webpage. This Internet website is an excellent source of information for individuals interested in dyslexia and the association. The website address is http://interdys.org/. The association can be contacted at: The International Dyslexia Association, 40 York Rd., 4th floor, Baltimore, MD 21204. Tel.: (410) 296-0232.

RACHEL TOPLIS
Falcon School District 49,
Colorado Springs, Colorado

ELIZABETH M. ZORN
Chicago School of Professional Psychology
Fourth edition

INTERNATIONAL ETHICS AND SPECIAL EDUCATION (See Ethics, International and Special Education)

INTERNATIONAL READING ASSOCIATION

The International Reading Association (IRA) is a nonprofit, global network of individuals and institutions committed to worldwide literacy. The mission of the IRA is to promote reading by continuously advancing the quality of literacy instruction and research worldwide. Membership in IRA is open to individuals who are interested in the field of reading, including teachers, administrators, reading specialists, special educators, college-level instructors and researchers, psychologists, librarians, and parents. According to their website, the Association currently has more than 70,000 members. Membership is also available to institutions and agencies that are involved with the teaching of reading or the preparation of reading teachers. The IRA is comprised of more than 1,150 councils and national affiliates in various countries around the world.

The IRA endorses the study of reading as a process, promotes research into improvement of reading programs, and advocates better teacher education. The organization is also closely involved with the worldwide literacy movement and the role of reading in the general welfare of society and individuals, as promulgated in the IRA Code of Ethics (1985).

Local, national, and international meetings and conventions provide an opportunity for members to come together. The four major professional journals and numerous individual volumes on reading-related topics published annually by the IRA provide other means through which members are kept informed of current practices in reading education, these tools are available to members through the Association's website.

Information for this entry was provided through the International Reading Association's webpage. Their website address is http://reading.org/. The IRA may also be contacted at: International Reading Association, 800 Barksdale Rd., P.O. Box 8139, Newark, DE 19714-8139. Tel.: (800) 336-7323 (U.S. and Canada), (302) 731-1600 (elsewhere).

ELIZABETH M. ZORN
Chicago School of Professional Psychology

INTERNATIONAL SCHOOL PSYCHOLOGY ASSOCIATION

The International School Psychology Association (ISPA) emerged from efforts by Calvin Catterall and Francis Mullins to broaden the views of school psychologists within the United States to include international perspectives. They initiated the International School Psychology Committee, first within the American Psychological Association's Division of School Psychology and later within the National Association of School Psychologists.

This committee served as a vehicle through which Dr. Catterall established contacts with various school psychologists outside of the United States. This committee sponsored its first international conference in 1975.

In 1979, the U.N.-sponsored International Year of the Child attracted the interests of many school psychologists internationally. Participants recognized the need for an international association that would serve ongoing interests of school psychologists internationally and in 1982 ISPA was founded. ISPA's constitution and bylaws were adopted that same year and Anders Poulsen was named the organization's first president.

ISPA has five major objectives: to promote the use of sound psychological principles within the context of education all over the world, to promote communication between professionals who are committed to the improvements of the mental health of children in the world's schools, to encourage the use of school psychologists in countries where they are not currently being used, to promote the psychological rights of all children all over the world, and to initiate and promote cooperation with other organizations working for purposes similar to those of ISPA in order to help children and families.

Membership approximates 400 and comes from approximately 45 countries. Twenty-five professional associations are affiliated with ISPA, across five continents. Each year, ISPA hosts colloquia in a different country. The purpose of these colloquia is to bring together diverse perspectives and research from around the world to improve the quality of school psychology internationally. During the 5-day annual colloquium, participants discuss practices that help parents raise healthy, resilient children, and that help teachers meet the needs of all students, including those with challenging learning and emotional problems. In addition, ISPA publishes a quarterly newsletter, *World Go Round*, and sponsors a scholarly journal, *School Psychology International*. ISPA has approved three policy statements: an ethics code, a definition of professional practice, and a model professional preparation program. ISPA's Central Office is located in the Netherlands. See Oakland (2000) as well as ISPA's website (www.ispaweb.org) for more details.

This entry has been informed by the sources listed below.

REFERENCES

Oakland, T. (2000). International school psychology. In T. Fagan & P. S. Wise (Eds.), *School psychology: Past, present, and future* (pp. 412–419). Washington, DC: National Association of School Psychologists.

International School Psychology Association. (2009). Retrieved from http://ispaweb.org/

THOMAS OAKLAND
University of Florida

ELIZABETH ZORN
*Chicago School of Professional Psychology
Fourth edition*

INTERNATIONAL TEST USE IN SPECIAL EDUCATION

Although the origins of testing occurred at least 3,000 years ago in China (Wang, 1993), current methods of test development and use can be traced directly to attempts to meet four sets of needs which grew in importance during the past 150 years: to utilize reliable and valid measures in research, to educate more students at more advanced levels, to help ensure that people with special needs were cared for properly, and to provide special services to those with more severe disorders. This section reviews the international availability and uses of tests with children and youth typically served in special education.

An international survey of test use in 44 countries, not including the United States, identified 455 tests used frequently with children and youth (Hu & Oakland, 1991; Oakland & Hu, 1991, 1992, 1994). Among these tests, 46% were imported for use as they were developed outside of the countries in which they were being used. Tests commonly imported for use originally were developed in the United States (22%), the United Kingdom (7%), West Germany (7%), France (5%), and Sweden (5%). Foreign-developed tests are used more frequently than locally developed tests in 68% of the countries surveyed. Locally developed tests are used more frequently than foreign developed tests in only 27% of the reporting countries. Seven countries report no nationally developed tests.

Test use is not uniform throughout the world. Highest test use was reported by three pre-1990 socialist nations: Yugoslavia (principally Slovenia), East Germany, and Czechoslovakia. Lowest test use was reported by the least developed nations. Reliance on foreign developed tests is most common in the Middle Eastern and least developed nations.

Types of Tests Used

Measures of intelligence (39%), personality (24%), and achievement (10%) appear most frequently. Tests assessing perceptual motor abilities, vocational interests and aptitudes, school readiness, and social development are not found commonly. The 10 most frequently used tests, in rank order of frequency of use, are the Wechsler Intelligence Scales for Children, the Raven's Progressive Matrices, Bender Gestalt, Rorschach, Stanford-Binet, Wechsler Adult Intelligence Scales, Thematic Apperception Test, Differential Aptitude Test, Minnesota Multiphasic Personality Inventory, and Frostig Developmental Test of Visual Perception.

Two thirds of the countries surveyed report a critical need for additional group and individual tests of achievement, intelligence, vocational interest and aptitudes, social development, and personality. The need for tests that assess qualities important to persons who are mentally retarded, blind, deaf, slow learners, emotionally and socially disturbed, physically impaired, and gifted were identified by almost 85% of the countries. Tests to assess students with learning disabilities are needed most, given an estimated 150 million worldwide.

Psychometric Studies

Standardized tests are expected to be suitably normed and to have reliability and validity estimates (American Educational Research Association, 1985). As noted below, these important qualities often do not exist. Local norms are available on 80% of achievement tests, 65% of intelligence tests, and 58% of personality tests. Among measures of achievement, studies of concurrent validity are available on 71%, predictive validity on 43%, and construct validity on 48%. Among measures of intelligence, studies of concurrent validity are available on 63%, predictive validity on 56%, and construct validity on 54%. Among measures of personality, concurrent validity studies are available on 53% and predictive and construct validity studies on approximately 39%.

Reliability studies have been conducted on 50% to 60% of measures of intelligence, personality, achievement, vocational interests and aptitudes, and school readiness. Studies examining the reliability of other types of measures appear less frequently. Thus, information often is unavailable to determine the adequacy of measures commonly used with children and youth (Oakland & Hu, 1994).

Professionals Who Use Tests

At least 16 professional groups commonly use tests with children and youth. School or educational psychologists often assume leadership for testing. Other frequently cited specialists include regular and special education teachers, clinical psychologists, and counselors (Oakland & Hu, 1991).

The educational levels of these professionals differ considerably, ranging from 2.5 years of postsecondary education for nurses to 6.5 years for physicians. The correlation between the number of years of postsecondary education and the perceived competence of the professional groups is substantial ($r = .50$, $p = .001$). Thus, professions with more education are thought to be more competent in the use of tests. In addition, professionals who use individually administered tests often are educated more highly than those who use only group tests.

Levels of professional preparation differ considerably between countries. The levels are lowest among professionals working in developing third world nations, Middle Eastern, and least developed nations. These countries also tend to have fewer tests developed nationally and with national norms. The combination of these qualities (i.e., less adequately prepared professionals together with fewer and less adequate tests) severely limits efforts to deliver adequate assessment services to children and youth in these countries and to conduct needed research.

Implication Concerning Test Use in Special Education

The availability and quality of tests used with children and youth internationally varies greatly by region and country. Resources are strongest in Western Europe and some Eastern European countries, in English speaking countries affiliated with the United Kingdom, and Israel. Fewest resources are found in the Middle East, and Central and South America. The number of studies examining test reliability and validity clearly is deficient. Professionals commonly are required to make decisions about children and youth using measures whose psychometric qualities are unknown and whose norms were developed on children from technologically advanced countries. As a result, professional standards and professional respect are jeopardized along with the quality of services delivered to children, youth, and their families.

Efforts to promote proper test development and use internationally should address three major needs: for additional studies that examine test reliability and validity, for additional measures that have nationally representative norms, and for greater reliance on nationally developed tests.

REFERENCES

American Educational Research Association. (1985). *Standards for educational and psychological testing*. Washington, DC: Author.

Hu, S., & Oakland, T. (1991). Global and regional perspectives on testing children and youth: An empirical study. *International Journal of Psychology, 26*, 329–344.

Oakland, T., & Hu, S. (1991). Professionals who administer tests with children and youth: An international survey. *Journal of Psychoeducational Assessment, 9*(2), 108–120.

Oakland, T., & Hu, S. (1992). The top 10 tests used with children and youth worldwide. *Bulletin of the International Test Commission, 19*, 99–120.

Oakland, T., & Hu, S. (1994). International perspectives on tests used with children and youth. *Journal of School Psychology, 31*, 501–517.

Wang, Z. M. (1993). Psychology on China: A review. *Annual Review of Psychology, 44*, 87–116.

THOMAS OAKLAND
HARRISON KANE
University of Florida

INTERNATIONAL YEAR OF DISABLED PERSONS, 1981

The General Assembly of the United Nations proclaimed 1981 the International Year of Disabled Persons (Resolution 31/123, December 16, 1976). Previous initiatives had set the stage. These included the Declaration on the Rights of Mentally Retarded Persons (Resolution 2856 [xxvi], adopted on December 20, 1971) and the Declaration on the Rights of Disabled Persons (Resolution 3447, adopted December 9, 1975).

The resolution on the International Year of Disabled Persons stressed the theme of full participation by persons with disabilities in the social, political, and economic life and development of the societies in which they live. It also promoted national and international efforts to provide disabled persons with proper assistance, training, care, and guidance, and encouraged study and research projects designed to facilitate the practical participation of disabled persons in daily life by improving such things as transport and access. One hundred and thirty-one countries took an active part in the International Year of Disabled Persons. They formed national commissions and carried out national programs, many of them focusing formally on the problem of disability for the first time.

Perhaps the greatest contribution of the International Year of Disabled Persons at the world level was the development by the United Nations of a World Plan of Action. The plan was adopted by the General Assembly at its 34th session, which concluded in December 1979. The plan set forth (on a global scale) the steps nations, nongovernment organizations, the United Nations, and individuals must take to continue the commitment and momentum of the International Year of Disabled Persons (Resolution A/RES/34/158, adopted January 30, 1980). Activities included measures at the national, regional, and international levels, including the organization of meetings and symposiums, the development of statistical data on disability, a review of existing legislation relating to disabled persons, the development of mass media campaigns relating to disability, and the identification of prophylaxis for disease and the prevention of disability.

On December 3, 1982, at the conclusion of its 37th session and the end of the International Year of Disabled Persons, the United Nations' General Assembly proclaimed the United Nations Decade of Disabled Persons, 1983–1992. It also formally adopted the World Program of Action, with its stress on the prevention of disability and its effort to identify major problems facing people with disabilities throughout the world, and made recommendations of actions to be taken to respond to these problems. The majority of recommendations address strategies for prevention, rehabilitation, and equalization of opportunity. The last category includes such issues as legislation, the physical environment, income maintenance, social security, education and training, employment, recreation, culture, religion, and sports.

REFERENCES

Rehabilitation International. (1981). *International statements on disability policy*. New York, NY: Author.

United Nations. (1983). *For the benefit of the disabled, activities undertaken during the international year of disabled persons*. New York, NY: Author.

United Nations. (1983). *U.N. decade of disabled persons, 1983–1992: World programme of action concerning disabled persons*. New York, NY: Author.

United Nations General Assembly adopts IYPD action plan. (1980). *International Rehabilitation Review*, 1, 1.

United Nations proclaims 1983–1992 decade of disabled persons. (1982). *International Rehabilitation Review*, 4th quarter, 1.

CATHERINE HALL RIKHYE
Hunter College,
City University of New York

INTERNET ACCESSIBILITY (See Web Accessibility)

INTEROBSERVER AGREEMENT

Systematic direct observation of behavior has become a widely used assessment approach within school systems (Kratochwill, Sheridan, Carlson, & Lasecki, 1999). When conducted with fidelity, systematic direct observation provides a snapshot of the environment of interest. This data allows one to consider the effects of environmental contingencies, thus placing behavior within a contextual framework. Understanding a behavior in relation to the environment is one of the key components to intervention. However, the utility of systematic direct observation depends on the trustworthiness of the observation data. Assessing the reliability of observation data is a necessary prerequisite to interpreting that data and developing interventions.

Determining the Credibility of Observation Data

One method to examine the reliability of observation data is to train two or more observers to use the same observation coding system so that the agreement between these two observers' findings can be determined. This method, called *interobserver agreement* or *interrater reliability*, evaluates the degree of consistency in findings from different observers who rate the same behaviors. Disagreement between observers could occur for a variety of reasons and it typically is a function of training. For example, if observers are not adequately trained to use the coding scheme or if the target behaviors of interest are not clearly defined, interobserver agreement may be compromised. Even when the coding system is clear and followed with integrity, there may be variability in observers' interpretations of certain behaviors. This is the error source we hope to capture. Whether observers are conscious of it or not, their personal biases or expectations may influence behavior recording.

The possibility for the miscoding of behavior highlights the need to consider interobserver agreement. Methods used to measure behavioral change are dependent upon accurate measurement of target behaviors. Consequently, researchers and practitioners must consider interobserver agreement to determine the reliability and validity of their behavioral assessments. In addition, we are in an age of accountability in our school systems, which dictates that we employ the most methodologically sound procedures we have available to ensure the credibility of our assessment data, and thus, the effectiveness of our resulting interventions. As a result, it is clear that the measurement of interobserver agreement also plays a role in day-to-day school procedures.

Measures of Interobserver Agreement

Although this is by no means an exhaustive review of the various methods for calculating interobserver agreement, three popular procedures will be presented. In addition to describing each method, potential uses and limitations of each will be discussed. There are a few important similarities among these various procedures. They all share the same core concept in that each measures consistency between two or more observations of the same behavior sample. Second, all but the first method (percentage of agreement) share the same resulting coefficients in that scores of interobserver agreement range from 0 to 1, and a value as close to 1 as possible indicates greater agreement. While percentage of agreement does not result in a coefficient, it is similar in that scores range from 0% to 100% agreement, with scores as close to 100% being desirable on the part of the researcher.

Percentage of Agreement

This is a popular procedure that compares two observers' observation data on a point to point basis (Salvia & Ysseldyke, 2001; Steege, Davin, & Hathaway, 2001). Percentage of interobserver agreement is calculated by dividing the number of agreements by the total number of agreements plus disagreements, and then multiplying this by 100. If there is not at least 80% agreement between

evaluators, it is advisable to discuss differences, clarify the behavioral coding system, and repeat the training process until satisfactory agreement can be achieved. Steege and colleagues (2001) used the percentage of agreement procedure to examine the reliability of two observers' ratings after a 15-minute observation interval. Observers coded the duration of target behaviors, such as opposition, based on a 5-point Likert scale. For example, a rating of 2 indicated that the oppositional behavior occurred for 3 to 6 minutes during the 15-minute interval. If both observers coded identical ratings, it was counted as an agreement. The resulting percentage of agreement was then calculated. In this example, the ratings of two observers showed 98% agreement in the coding of the duration of a child's oppositional behavior.

The use of percentage of agreement persists as a popular method for reporting interobserver agreement perhaps, in part, due to its ease of calculation. However, this approach to interobserver agreement has been criticized for psychometric reasons. The primary concern is that this method is unable to take chance into account, and chance is likely to inflate agreement percentages in all cases, but especially with two coders. Or, as in the example above, near miss ratings are not counted the same as dramatic differences. This "closeness of approximation" discussion can be addressed with a different calculation method. Thus, other approaches have been proposed to correct for the possibility that two observers' ratings may agree at times simply by chance alone.

Cohen's Kappa

Cohen's kappa statistic (Cohen, 1960) has long been proposed as a more psychometrically sound statistic for assessing interobserver agreement. Like the simple percentage of agreement method, kappa considers the proportion of actual agreement (P_o), but it also accounts for the proportion of agreement that would be expected by chance alone (P_c). Specifically, kappa is calculated as the difference between chance agreement and actual agreement, divided by one minus chance agreement ($[P_o—P_c]/[1—P_c]$).

Kappa is appropriate for examining interobserver agreement when the observed data is frequency or categorical data. For example, Theodore and colleagues (Theodore, Bray, & Kehle, 2004) used a partial interval time sampling method to code the presence or absence of disruptive behavior during 15-second intervals. Interobserver agreement calculated with kappa revealed an average of .83. A value as close to 1 as possible is desirable; perfect agreement would equate to a kappa of 1, and chance agreement would equate to 0. Generally a kappa greater than .70 is considered satisfactory.

Intraclass Coefficients (ICC)

When observation data includes continuous scores as opposed to ranks or categorical classifications, interclass coefficients are the most appropriate measure. As with kappa, high agreement is reflected by an ICC close to 1. If there is significant disagreement between two observers' data, the resulting ICC will be a low or negative correlation. It is important to note that several ICC procedures exist, and each can result in quite different results when applied to the same data. Differentiation among the various types of ICC procedures is beyond the scope of this article (see Shrout & Fleiss, 1979, for a complete review of these procedures). Instead, be aware that researchers using ICC should report which procedure was used and the reason behind the choice made.

A study by Walcott and Landau (2004) used ICC to check the reliability of a coding scheme in which observers coded 3-minute behavior samples for the presence or absence of specific expressive behaviors during consecutive 10-second intervals. The resulting scores were a frequency count of the number of behaviors exhibited by a child in each behavioral category. Intraclass correlation coefficients, using the ICC (3, 1) procedure, were calculated to measure the consistency of the two ratings while treating the observers as fixed effects (Shrout & Fleiss, 1979). Coefficients revealed satisfactory levels of consistency between observers' measurements on most categories. As with kappa, intraclass coefficients greater than .70 are generally considered satisfactory.

Several methods for determining interobserver agreement were discussed, and researchers or practitioners should consider the type of observation data being collected when choosing an appropriate method. Above all, it is crucial that we assess the credibility of direct observation data with a viable method of interobserver agreement before using it to design school-based interventions or make important educational decisions.

REFERENCES

Cohen, J. (1960). A coefficient of agreement for nominal scales. *Educational and Psychological Measurement, 20,* 37–46.

Kratochwill, T. R., Sheridan, S. M., Carlson, J., & Lasecki, K. L. (1999). Advances in behavioral assessment. In C. R. Reynolds & T. B. Gutkin (Eds.), *The handbook of school psychology* (3rd ed, pp. 350–382). New York, NY: Wiley.

Salvia, J., & Ysseldyke, J. E. (2001). *Assessment* (8th ed). New York, NY: Houghton Mifflin.

Shrout, P. E., & Fleiss, J. L. (1979). Intraclass correlations: Uses in assessing rater reliability. *Psychological Bulletin, 86,* 420–428.

Steege, M. W., Davin, T., & Hathaway, M. (2001). Reliability and accuracy of a performance-based behavioral recording procedure. *School Psychology Review, 30,* 252–261.

Theodore, L. A., Bray, M. A., & Kehle, T. J. (2004). A comparative study of group contingencies and randomized reinforcers to reduce disruptive classroom behavior. *School Psychology Quarterly, 19,* 253–271.

Walcott, C. M., & Landau, S. (2004). The relation between disinhibition and emotion regulation in boys with attention deficit hyperactivity disorder. *Journal of Clinical Child and Adolescent Psychology, 33,* 772–782.

CHRISTY M. WALCOTT
T. CHRIS RILEY-TILLMAN
East Carolina University

KIMBERLY VANNEST
Texas A&M University
Fourth edition

See also **Behavioral Assessment; Positive Behavioral Support**

INTERPRETERS FOR THE DEAF

Interpreters for the deaf are hearing individuals who listen to a spoken message and communicate it in some way to hearing impaired people. Departing from the exact words of the speaker to paraphrase is permissible in interpreting. Interpreting is differentiated from translating, which is a verbatim presentation of another person's remarks (Quigley & Paul, 1984).

Until 1964 interpreters were mainly family friends or relatives who knew sign language (Levine, 1981). In 1964 the National Registry of Interpreters for the Deaf was established to promote the recruitment and training of interpreters, to clarify their functions, to specify the competencies required for interpreting, and to maintain a list of certified interpreters.

There are various types of interpreters for the deaf: sign language interpreters, who communicate what has been said in some form of sign language or finger spelling; oral interpreters, who inaudibly repeat the speaker's message, (clearly enunciated and somewhat more slowly) to facilitate its speech reading by deaf persons (Northcott, 1984); and reverse interpreters, who convert a deaf person's sign language or difficult to understand speech into normally spoken English (Bishop, 1979). Specialized interpreters, familiar with the pertinent technical language, serve in legal, medical, psychiatric, and rehabilitative settings. Educational interpreters facilitate the mainstreaming of deaf students in schools and universities. Theatrical interpreters sign operatic performances and Broadway shows (Kanter, 1985).

The first case involving PL 94-142, the Education for all Handicapped Children Act—the precursor to IDEA—decided by the U.S. Supreme Court, was a demand for a sign language interpreter by the parents of a mainstream deaf child, Amy Rowley. The Court decided that this particular deaf child did not need an interpreter. However, in other cases, sign language interpreters have been ordered, even for elementary school students when teachers state that interpreters are needed for pupils to benefit from their classes and actively participate in them (DuBow & Geer, 1983). In 1982 the U.S. Court of Appeals mandated state vocational rehabilitation agencies to provide interpreters for deaf clients attending college.

The Vocational Rehabilitation Act of 1965 provided that interpreter services must be included as part of vocational rehabilitation services. Since then, most states have mandated that deaf individuals must be offered sign language interpreters whenever their civil rights are involved. Interpreter training programs are available throughout the United States. Many colleges offer an AA or BA degree in interpreting.

REFERENCES

Bishop, M. (1979). *Mainstreaming*. Washington, DC: Alexander Graham Bell Association for the Deaf.

DuBow, S., & Geer, S. (1983, July). Education decisions after Rowley. *National Center for Law and the Deaf Newsletter, 1–3*.

Kanter, A. (1985, Summer). A night at the opera. N.T.I.D. *Focus*, 3–4.

Levine, E. (1981). *The ecology of early deafness*. New York, NY: Columbia University Press.

Northcott, W. (1984). *Oral interpreting: Principles and practices*. Baltimore, MD: University Park Press.

Quigley, S., & Paul, P. (1984). *Language and deafness*. San Diego, CA: College Hill Press.

ROSEMARY GAFFNEY
Hunter College,
City University of New York

See also Deaf Education; Lipreading/Speechreading

INTERVAL RECORDING

Interval recording is a data collection method used to measure behavior that could occur continuously or consistently across time. This method is a time-based measurement system where the passage of a predetermined amount of time, not each occurrence of a behavior, is the signal for the teacher or researcher to record data (Wolery, Bailey, & Sugai, 1988). Like all time-based systems, interval recording provides a close approximation of the targeted behavior, not an exact count of each occurrence. Interval recording is suitable for behaviors such as academic engagement, playing, engaging in off-task behaviors, such as being out of an assigned seat and/or walking around the classroom, cooperative learning, and self-stimulatory behaviors, such as rocking. The two types of interval

recording that are used by teachers and researchers are partial interval recording and whole interval recording.

Interval recording first requires an operational definition of the behavior of concern. An operational definition (which originated in 1914) is a written statement that precisely defines the behavior you wish to measure in terms that are observable, measurable, and replicable (Bridgeman, 1954; Fletcher-Janzen & De Pry, 2003). Next, the observer determines the length of time for each interval. Intervals are predetermined periods of time that are equivalent in length. Interval length is determined by (a) the frequency of the target behavior, (b) the context that elicits the behavior (e.g., times, place, conditions), and (c) the time demands or schedule of the teacher (Wolery et al., 1988). Interval lengths for this method usually range from 5 to 30 seconds. As a general rule, the shorter the interval length the more accurate the data that is collected (Alberto & Troutman, 2006).

When the interval length has been determined, a data collection form should be created. The form should have the student's name, the date, the observer's name, the classroom teacher's name, information about the setting or context of the observation (to be completed at each observation session), the start and stop times, and the interval grid. Teachers who use interval recording need a signal that lets them know when to observe and record data. The signal can be visual (e.g., classroom clock, watch) or auditory (e.g., kitchen timer, countdown timer).

The rules for using partial interval recording and whole interval recording are different. Partial interval recording follows the rule that you record the behavior if it occurs at any time during the interval being observed. For example, an observer is measuring "time in seat" using a 30-second partial interval recording method. The student is observed to be in her seat for 20 of the 30 seconds, but gets up to get a drink of water for the remaining 10 seconds. Because she met the operational definition for time in seat and was observed being in her seat for part of the interval, the observer would put a plus mark in the appropriate interval box (this method allows only one plus or minus mark per interval). The only time that the observer would put a minus mark in an interval box would be if the student did not meet the operational definition at all for the designated interval.

Whole interval recording follows the rule that the student needs to meet the operational definition for the entire 30-second interval for that interval to be counted as met. Using our example, the student is observed to be in her seat the entire 30-second interval, therefore a plus mark is put in the appropriate interval box. If, however, the student met the definition for 25 seconds, but stood up to stretch for 5 seconds, the observer would put a minus sign in the appropriate interval box because our rule for whole interval recording requires that the student meets the operational definition for the entire 30-second interval. End of interval recording or time-sampling procedure would record only if the behavior were occurring at the point of the recording time.

Maag (1999) suggests that interval recording has two advantages. This method provides a good estimate of the frequency or duration of the targeted behavior and it can be used to detect temporal patterns of occurrence, such as when the behavior is more likely to occur (beginning, middle, or end of the observation session). Disadvantages include the possibility of underestimating or overestimating the behavior of concern and the time demands made on the teacher or researcher for conducting the observation. This last point is especially a concern for whole interval recording (Wolery et al., 1988) given the intensity of this observation method. As with all direct observation systems, collecting interobserver reliability data is critical, particularly in a response to intervention framework where decisions will be made based on this type of data. See inter-rater reliability for details on calculations.

REFERENCES

Alberto, P. A., & Troutman, A. C. (2006). *Applied behavior analysis for teachers* (7th ed). Upper Saddle River, NJ: Prentice Hall.

Bridgeman, P. W. (1954). *The way things are*. Cambridge, MA: Harvard University Press.

Fletcher-Janzen, E., & De Pry, R. L. (2003). *Teaching social competence and character: An IEP planner with goals, objectives, and interventions*. Longmont, CO: Sopris West.

Maag, J. W. (1999). *Behavior management: From theoretical implications to practical applications*. San Diego, CA: Singular.

Wolery, M., Bailey, D. B., Jr., & Sugai, G. M. (1988). *Effective teaching: Principles and procedures of applied behavior analysis for exceptional students*. Boston, MA: Allyn & Bacon.

RANDALL L. DE PRY
University of Colorado at Colorado Springs

KIMBERLY VANNEST
Texas A&M University
Fourth edition

See also **Behavioral Assessment; Behavior Charting**

INTERVAL SCHEDULES

At home, school, and in the workplace, the quality of our interactions and performance is often judged by our sensitivity to the contingencies of reinforcement. Sometimes, for example, rapid, precise movements are required, such as when engaging in factory piecework or completing a timed math quiz in the classroom. At other times, a steady, moderate work pace is desirable, such as during individual activities in the classroom while the teacher circulates from one student to the next. It is useful for parents, teachers, and employers to take careful note of what kinds of work patterns are desirable and to set schedules of reinforcement that are likely to influence the rate and consistency of behavior in a manner congruent with the expectations of the environment.

A schedule of reinforcement describes the conditions that must be in effect for reinforcers to be delivered (Ferster & Skinner, 1957). Interval schedules involve delivery of a reinforcer following the first response that occurs after a specified time period. During a fixed interval (FI) schedule, the time specified after which a response is reinforced is held constant. For example, every 3 minutes, when a vibrating timer alerts a teacher, he writes the names of all students who are engaged in a reading activity on the whiteboard. At the end of 12 minutes, students whose names were written on the board may select from a bin the activities for which they have indicated a preference. Fixed interval schedules should not be confused with fixed time (FT) schedules, in which reinforcement is available after a specified amount of time independent of behavioral responses. In an FT schedule, it is left to chance whether desired behaviors that are being taught are occurring when the reinforcement is provided, and unless behaviors that have been taught are occurring at a very high rate, it is probable that unwanted behaviors will be reinforced.

Variable interval (VI) schedules are similar to FI schedules, except responses are reinforced after an average amount of time. A teacher circulating throughout the classroom is unlikely to be able to reinforce all on task behaviors every minute, but may on average get to each student who is working diligently once every 3 to 4 minutes.

Behavior is emitted in characteristic patterns depending on the schedule of reinforcement (Ferster & Skinner, 1957). Many schedules produce consistent patterns of responding across species. Human behavior under FI schedules is consistent among infants and adults with less well-developed verbal skills (Lowe, Beasty, & Bentall, 1983). People with limited verbal repertoires respond and then pause briefly, engage in other behaviors, then gradually increase the rate of responses until there is a payoff, after which the pattern repeats. Although such postreinforcement pauses are not always evident or pronounced in adults, they are common enough to merit analysis. When quizzes are given each week on Friday, students may play and work on other assignments throughout the week, study briefly on Tuesday and Wednesday, and then cram Thursday night. Unscheduled quizzes given on a VI schedule would likely produce more consistent study habits because the specific timing of the quizzes, though on average still once a week, would be unpredictable. This central difference between behavior on FI and VI schedules is prescriptive: When steady, moderate rates of behavior are desired, VI schedules are preferable.

Behavior reinforced continuously may decrease in frequency, while behavior reinforced intermittently becomes more resilient, or resistant to extinction. When praised every 3 minutes for staying in his seat, John begins testing his teacher and standing up when she is not looking. Soon other children notice and laugh, maintaining John's behavior with their attention. After recognizing this pattern, his teacher switches to a VI schedule and praises John intermittently. She offers praise on average once every 3 minutes when John is seated properly. The unpredictability of this praise schedule brings John's behavior under control.

John's teacher may do more at this point with the schedule of reinforcement to maintain the desired response. She may enlist other students' cooperation in ignoring John's behavior should he jump out of his seat. Then, to capitalize on the effect of others ignoring his behavior, she may offer praise of increased magnitude when John is seated appropriately. By adding an extinction schedule of reinforcement, John's teacher makes use of the contrast phenomenon, which is seen when two schedules are concurrently in effect and a change in one schedule produces contrasting changes in behavior under both schedules (McSweeney, 1982). Making use of contrast between behavior in the extinction schedule for being out of his seat and the intermittent reinforcement schedule for appropriate behavior fosters an increase in the desired behavior. Thus VI schedules can be used both for teaching new behaviors and for maintaining previously taught behaviors.

Investigations into the way verbal stimuli influence behavior on VI schedules have demonstrated that rules, both those provided by others and those that are self-generated, may assist or hinder learning. In one study, participants who were asked to generate their own rules describing the schedule contingency that determined reinforcement were more likely to show schedule-typical behavior than participants who were told the rules in advance (Rosenfarb, Newland, Brannon, & Howey, 1992). Horne and Lowe (1993), on the other hand, found nearly equal numbers of participants given a task to perform created rules for themselves that did not correspond to the schedule of reinforcement as participants who created functional rules. Those whose rules did not match the contingencies for earning money continued to follow the rules they had generated, in spite of failure.

Recent investigations have focused on functional combinations of instructions and modeling to promote schedule sensitivity. A preschooler who was taught to ask for preferred items but whose requests persisted when no longer reinforced developed schedule sensitivity when taught specific signals for when teacher attention was and was not available (Tiger & Hanley, 2004). Neef et al. (2004) found that children with attention-deficit/hyperactivity disorder developed greater schedule sensitivity when a teacher modeled choice-making than when rules for making decisions were taught in advance of an activity. The implication for those who provide care to children with special needs is that discriminative stimuli can be used to aid a child to learn behaviors that are consistent with environmental contingencies. Clearly explaining rules, asking children to hypothesize or to generate their own statements of the rules, and modeling decision making that follows the schedule in effect can aid children to acquire sensitivities necessary for success at home, school, and in the workplace.

During interval schedules of reinforcement, behavior occurs at a lower rate than in other schedules. One way to increase the rate of performance under an interval schedule is to require that responses occur within a specific time frame. When under a limited hold schedule (Reynolds, 1968), a person must hurry to avoid losing the opportunity to be reinforced for producing a desired behavior. Arriving at the bus stop after the bus has left means that you have to wait for the next one. Handing in her homework on time means that Jean gets full credit for the assignment. Using limited holds can augment rates of responding sufficiently to maintain behavior on an interval schedule.

In summary, interval schedules are easy to implement and are valuable because they promote moderate rates of performance and do not require constant monitoring by teachers or staff. FI schedules reinforce following the first response after a specified amount of time but maintain desired behavior less efficiently than VI schedules, in which a behavior is reinforced when it occurs after an average amount of specified time. Using behavioral contrast helps to maintain behaviors that have been taught on a VI schedule. Teaching individuals the rules that apply in a given schedule, asking learners to form their own rules and then reviewing these with them, and modeling choice making in difficult situations are strategies that foster the development of behaviors that are consistent with environmental contingencies. Though interval schedules produce characteristically lower rates of responding, limited holds can be placed on behavior to help pick up the pace when this is desirable.

REFERENCES

Ferster, C. B., & Skinner, B. F. (1957). *Schedules of reinforcement.* New York, NY: Appleton.

Horne, P. J., & Lowe, C. F. (1993). Determinants of human performance on concurrent schedules. *Journal of the Experimental Analysis of Behavior, 59,* 29–60.

Lowe, C. F., Beasty, A., & Bentall, R. P. (1983). The role of verbal behavior in human learning: Infant performance on fixed interval schedules. *Journal of the Experimental Analysis of Behavior, 39,* 157–164.

McSweeney, F. K. (1982). Positive and negative contrast as a function of component duration for key pecking and treadle pressing. *Journal of the Experimental Analysis of Behavior,* 37, 281–293.

Neef, N. A., Marckel, J., Ferreri, S., Jung, S., Nist, L., & Armstrong, N. (2004). Effects of modeling versus instructions on sensitivity to reinforcement schedules. *Journal of Applied Behavior Analysis,* 37, 267–281.

Reynolds, G. S. (1968). *A primer of operant conditioning.* Glenview, IL: Scott, Foresman.

Rosenfarb, I. S., Newland, M. C., Brannon, S. E., & Howey, D. S. (1992). Effects of self-generated rules on the development of schedule-controlled behavior. *Journal of the Experimental Analysis of Behavior,* 58, 107–121.

Tiger, J. H., & Hanley, H. P. (2004). Developing stimulus control of preschooler demands: An analysis of schedule-correlated and contingency-specifying stimuli. *Journal of Applied Behavior Analysis,* 37, 517–521.

THOMAS G. SZABO
Western Michigan University

Behavioral Assessment; Negative Reinforcement; Positive Reinforcement

INTERVENTION

Intervention consists of all planned attempts to promote the general welfare of exceptional individuals. There are three broad types of interventions: preventive, remedial, and compensatory. School may provide intervention services as part of a multitier model using terms like Tier 1, 2, and 3 or primary, secondary, tertiary, or universal, targeted, individual to refer to their types of interventions.

Efforts to thwart the appearance of disabilities are considered preventive. For example, phenylketonuria is an inherited condition that ultimately results in brain damage and arrested mental development. Early diagnosis and intervention via a special diet effectively prevent the otherwise predictable neurological damage and intellectual disability. Though it is not invariably so, preventive interventions are most often introduced by the medical profession for medical conditions, although preschool efforts are a prevention. Universal teaching of social expectations is preventative for social, emotional, and behavioral disorders.

Remedial intervention is the process of overcoming a deficit by correcting or otherwise improving it directly. When a struggling reader is brought up to read at a level that is comparable to that of his or her peer group, it is called *remedial intervention*. When targeted programs such as mentoring or practices like a daily behavior report card are used to improve behavior or emotional problems it is a remedial practice. Remedial interventions introduced

in school, by parent, or physicians after risk or early stages of problems are identified.

In compensatory intervention, the usual approach is to provide a child with the means to circumvent, substitute, or otherwise offset an irremediable deficit. The best-known and most widely used compensatory interventions consist of teaching a child to use technological advances that at least partially obviate the need for remediation. For example, the development of closed-captioned television programs effectively compensates for the inability of people who are deaf to hear the program.

Several theoretical models exist by which interventions may be classified. They include biophysical, psychological, behavioral, ecological, and sociological models. In the following sections, each model is discussed and at least one example is provided to illustrate an application of the model. The illustrations are often not pure applications but may borrow from other theoretical models.

Biophysical theorists believe that abnormalities result from physical anomalies within the organism. The causes of affective, cognitive, and motoric difficulties may be either endogenous (i.e., originating within the body) or exogenous (originating outside of the body), and generally are considered to be genetic, nutritional, neurological, or biochemical in nature.

Genetic counseling is an intervention intended to prevent hereditary disorders from occurring. Prime candidates for genetic counseling are adults who have known hereditary disorders or who find themselves in circumstances that increase the probability of bearing a child with a genetic disorder. Sickle cell anemia, hemophilia, and osteogenesis imperfecta (*tarda*) are just three conditions that are genetically caused and, therefore, can be prevented through genetic counseling. On the other hand, genetic counselors provide a service to older couples by informing them of the probabilities of bearing a child with a genetic abnormality such as Down syndrome.

Nutritional deficiencies can result in severe, irreversible intellectual and physical disorders. Although nutritional problems are not particularly extensive in the United States, they do exist; in many third-world nations (e.g., Ethiopia) the extent of such disorders is nothing short of catastrophic. The introduction of a balanced, nutritional diet is the obvious biophysical intervention of choice.

Neurological damage incurred following accidents, low levels of oxygen in the blood, and so on, also result in behavioral abnormalities. When instruction in sign language is used with victims of electrical shock or stroke in order to circumvent the resulting neurological impairment, a compensatory intervention is implemented.

Remedial interventions are also employed to overcome assumed neurological dysfunctions. For instance, cognitive interventions are those that deal with teaching the individual how to think or think about thinking and learning. This label is somewhat misleading as it refers to both process or verbal mediation strategies such as problem solving. Also included here are approaches once referred to as *process* or *ability* training (Mann & Sabatino, 1985; Ysseldyke & Algozzine, 1984). Such interventions primarily intend to improve perception, memory, and problem solving and have a long history of research, regardless of terminology. In some types of cognitive intervention, the tasks involved are neuropsychologically specific. That is, they are characterized by modality specificity (e.g., auditory, visual, or haptic) or hemisphere specificity (i.e., they are analytical, sequential, and highly language-based or global, simultaneous, and nonlanguage-based). Cognitive intervention strategies overall, however, cover a wide range of topics (Hallahan, 1980). Although "brain remediation" remains among the most controversial approaches to intervention, verbal mediation, cognitive restructuring, problem solving and the like are considered evidence-based practice.

In another theoretical area of "intervention" the core belief in the psychological intervention model is that abnormality is the result of internalized conflicts that prevent the individual from fully participating in the social and academic environment. According to the earliest view, that of Freud's psychoanalysis, these conflicts interfere with the individual's normal progression through several stages of personality development presumed to take place during childhood and adolescence.

An outgrowth of Freudian psychology, the psychodynamic model seeks to reduce the individual's conflicts by helping him or her to better understand both behavior and the reasons for exhibiting it. Fritz Redl was one of the primary contributors to this approach, introducing such classroom techniques as the life space interview (LSI). The LSI is actually a set of interventions designed to take place immediately following crisis situations. The interventions have a temporal advantage over traditional therapy in that life events are not allowed to grow distant before the child and the teacher or therapist deal with them. Psychoeducational approaches are an outgrowth of the work of Fritz Redl and have been proposed by his students and co-workers. These interventions are deliberate attempts to adapt psychodynamic concepts to the classroom environment and to date demonstrate little empirical evidence for their use.

Although the behavioral intervention tradition in special education is often tied most closely to B. F. Skinner's work in instrumental (or operant) conditioning, its roots are much broader. It is true that most of the interventions known today as *behavior modification* do stem from Skinner's groundbreaking research in reinforcement, punishment, and extinction. However, many of the more powerful interventions being introduced to the field lately (e.g., in the writings of Kathryn Blake, Siegfried Engelman, and Douglas Carnine) come from the traditional psychological research on concept learning, verbal learning, discrimination learning, and problem solving. So there are cognitive, behavioral and cognitive behavioral approaches to intervention.

Both approaches share the common characteristic that the specific techniques they employ have been well validated through a rich research history. However, they are somewhat particular in their effects. Generally, conditioning approaches powerfully affect the motivation of the individual. That is, they provide the individual with the need or desire (the motive) to act in a specific manner. They probably influence the acquisition of skills as well, but their primary effect is motivational. On the other hand, conditions that influence the various types of learning primarily affect the speed with which the individual acquires, retains, and transfers new skills. Both behavioral interventions are powerful, well documented approaches that enjoy considerable support in the research literature.

In contrast to proponents of the biophysical and psychological models, ecological theorists consider disturbance to be the result of the dynamic interaction between the child and the environment (Rhodes & Tracy, 1974). According to the ecological intervention approach, such events as physical abuse by the parents, slothful behavior by the child, or the death of a sibling are not isolated phenomena, but are interactive in nature. That is, the individual's behavior and other environmental conditions both affect and are affected by the people and conditions within the ecosphere. Consequently, advocates of this model discuss disturbed environments, not disturbed people.

Given their views on disturbance, it follows that ecological practitioners attempt to intervene on entire ecologies or at least those aspects of the environment considered to be disturbed. In practice, this means that virtually any existing intervention may be used within the ecological model if it is considered to be of potential benefit. For instance, the biophysical intervention of drug therapy, the psychodynamic LSI, and such behavioral techniques as positive reinforcement and extinction would not be unusual within an ecological intervention system.

Without question, the best-known implementation of an ecological intervention system is that of Project ReEd (Hobbs, 1966). In this project, children are temporarily removed from their homes to a residential setting that focuses on education. Two teacher counselors are responsible for eight children during the day and at night. During their relatively brief stay in the residential facility, the teacher counselors, aided by a host of supportive personnel, "reeducate" their charges regarding the virtues of trust, competence, cognitive control, the healthy expression of feelings, and so on. Prior to the reintegration of the child into the community, additional staff members prepare the home and the community for his or her return. It is the liaison teacher's task to ensure that the faculty and staff of the child's school are sufficiently aware of the child's needs so as to provide effectively for them. The psychiatric social worker engages community services (e.g., family counseling) that are expected to be needed to enhance the probability that the child's return will be successful.

Three distinct views characterize the sociological intervention model: (1) labeling theory, (2) societal rule breaking and rule following, and (3) anomie. Specific interventions that are the result of these views are difficult to identify. Rather, in labeling theory and societal rule breaking and rule following, the opposite seems true; that is, it may be the interventions themselves that lead to *deviance* (as it is termed by sociologists).

Labeling theorists suggest that deviance itself is sometimes the result of the painfully focused attention that the individual's behavior may receive. They contend that labels such as *troublemaker* and *dunce* are pejorative and can actually be powerful stimuli for deviant behavior. Some individuals (e.g., Lemert, 1962) further contend that the most debilitating form of deviance is that which results from a falsely applied label (i.e., instances in which significant deviance did not exist until after the application of the label). Since the label was falsely applied, there is little hope that the child will work to overcome the deviance; instead, it is likely that the label itself will produce rebellion and other forms of deviance where none existed before.

Unlike other perspectives, sociological theorists generally view abnormality as behavior that is significantly contrary to the rules established by society. Because normal people break rules some of the time and abnormal individuals follow established rules much or even most of the time, it is important to note the agents who enforce societal rules (e.g., police, teachers) are in the unhappy position of deciding which rule breakers to label as *abnormal*. Clearly, only a few rule breakers are labeled by society. Because deviance is only a vaguely defined concept, it seems certain that many injustices in the form of false positives and false negatives are committed. In particular, many believe that individuals from poor or culturally different backgrounds are especially susceptible to the application of false labels. Such logic would seem to support the notion of labeling theory.

Anomie refers to deviance that results from social changes that occur at rates too fast for society to effectively establish norms for behavior. One example might be the United States' rapid shift from an agrarian society (in which large families were an advantage) to modern U.S. society, in which the role of children remains marked by ambiguity. The frustrations one feels in attempting to deal with an inoperable vending machine or a billing error committed by a computer are minor examples of anomie.

Interventions based on sociological models are difficult to implement. Nevertheless, society has implemented a number of them in an attempt to prevent or remediate deviance. Local, state, and federal police forces are intended to both prevent and enforce societal rules that have been codified into laws. Our judicial system is intended to mete out justice to those accused of offenses.

Public school programs clearly play a similar role, particularly with regard to values and mores that have not been codified as laws. Prison systems and youth detention centers assume both a punitive and a remedial intervention role where lawbreakers are concerned. Some attempts by society to intervene more effectively include an increase in mental health centers, better organized community services, crisis intervention centers, suicide help lines, normalization projects, and not least, public school inclusion programming with children who have disabilities.

REFERENCES

Hallahan, D. (Ed.). (1980). *Teaching exceptional children to use cognitive strategies*. Rockville, MD: Aspen.

Hobbs, N. (1966). Helping disturbed children: Psychological and ecological strategies. *American Psychologist, 21*, 1105–1115.

Lemert, E. (1962). Paranoia and the dynamics of exclusion. *Sociometry, 25*, 2–20.

Mann, L., & Sabatino, D. A. (1985). *Foundations of cognitive processes in special and remedial education*. Rockville, MD: Aspen.

Rhodes, W. C., & Tracy, M. I. (Eds.). (1974). *A study of child variance: Conceptual models* (Vol. 1). Ann Arbor: University of Michigan.

Ysseldyke, J. E., & Algozzine, B. (1984). *Introduction to special education*. Boston, MA: Houghton Mifflin.

RONALD C. EAVES
Auburn University
First edition

JAMES A. POTEET
Ball State University
First edition

KIMBERLY J. VANNEST
Texas A&M University
Fourth edition

See also **Behavior Modification; Child Psychology; Ecological Assessment**

INTERVENTION IN SCHOOL AND CLINIC

In 1988, PRO-ED, Inc. purchased the journal *Academic Therapy* from Academic Therapy Publications. In 1990, PRO-ED changed the title of the journal to *Intervention in School and Clinic;* however, the emphasis remained the same as when John Arena began *Academic Therapy* in 1965. *Intervention* is a practitioner-oriented journal designed to provide practical, research-based ideas to those who work with students with severe learning disabilities or emotional and behavioral problems for whom typical classroom instruction is not effective. The articles are easy to read, and the interventions and strategies provided can be implemented in school or special clinical settings. *Intervention* is published five times during a volume year: September, November, January, March, and May.

JUDITH K. VORESS
PRO-ED Inc,

INTERVENTION PROGRAMS, EARLY

The 25-year period between 1970 and 1995 was a most remarkable time for the field of early intervention. Evolving from a collection of disparate activities and therapeutic approaches, far more coherent, highly visible, and well-established programs of early intervention supports and services for children and families have emerged (Guralnick, 1997, p. 3).

Indeed, Guralnick and others suggest that the first generation of intervention programs has ended with the demonstration of overall effectiveness, and that now the second generation of programs must attempt the more difficult task of determining "what interventions work best, for whom, under what conditions, and toward what ends" (Guralnick, 1997, p. xvi). In general, across programs and handicapping or potentially handicapping conditions, intervention is effective, producing average effects of about half or greater standard deviations (Guralnick, 1997). However, conclusions about effectiveness in many cases are qualified by many evaluation studies that have serious methodological problems. Further, as would be expected, intervention is far more effective for some conditions than for others and for some domains within conditions than others. Some programs have had effects much smaller than initially anticipated, and some conditions (neuromotor and sensory ones, for example) are likely to be relatively resistant to modification. In addition, children with the same condition may benefit to quite different degrees from intervention, depending not only on the severity of their condition, but on a variety of factors, including the presence of other risk factors, the adequacy of family and environmental support, and where appropriate, availability of follow-up services. Although some conditions may themselves be resistant to modification, adaptive technological developments are increasing dramatically the extent to which affected children may be able to function in normal settings and develop in domains other than the one in which they are disabled.

Federal legislation mandates intervention services for children with disabilities. 1986 Amendments to PL 94-142, the Education of All Handicapped Children Act of 1974, extended services to children 3 to 5 years of age, and 1997 Amendments to what had become the Individuals with Disabilities Education Act (IDEA 97, PL 105-17) further mandate services to infants and toddlers who either manifest a developmental delay or have a diagnosed condition likely to lead to a developmental delay. Although some (e.g., S. Ramey & D. Ramey, 1998) use the term *intervention program* to describe services for children at risk for developmental delay and *treatment program* to describe services for children who have a specific diagnosed condition, many (e.g., Bryant & Graham, 1993; Guralnick, 1997) use intervention program inclusively, as will be the case with this section.

Intervention programs now exist for children with 11 potentially handicapping and handicapping conditions: (1) disadvantaged at-risk children; (2) premature and low birth weight infants; (3) infants exposed to prenatal alcohol or other substances; (4) infants with various neuromotor disorders, including cerebral palsy; (5) infants whose parents are mentally retarded; (6) infants with Down syndrome; (7) infants with autism; (8) young children with communication (speech and language) disorders; (9) young children with conduct problems; (10) children with vision or hearing impairments; and (11) maltreating parents and their children, among others. Summaries and evaluations of these programs are described in individual chapters in Guralnick (1997b). Development of programs has progressed to the point that Bryant and Graham (1993) have collected recommendations for implementing such programs.

Several sets of guiding principles have been proposed to guide intervention programs. The following 8-point list was compiled largely from those (a) developed by the Division for Early Childhood Task Force on Recommended Practices as presented in Bryant and Graham (1993b) and (b) presented in Guralnick (1997a).

1. Whatever the service delivery model, it should be the least restrictive and most natural environment for the child and family.

2. Programs should center on the needs of individual families and children, and be responsive to families' priorities.

3. Programs should not only be interdisciplinary, but should fully integrate components from each discipline.

4. Empirical results and professional and family values should guide service delivery practices.

5. Each child's and each family's services should be individualized and developmentally appropriate.

6. Intervention programs should be based in local communities.

7. Intervention programs should integrate services from a variety of agencies using a systems model.

8. Intervention programs should begin as early and be as intense as realistically possible and appropriate

for the child and family. However, for some conditions, timing and intensity of treatment must be based carefully on each child's level of development since manipulations that occur too early or are too intense may have iatrogenic effects, being actually harmful.

REFERENCES

Bryant, D. M., & Graham, M. A. (1993a). *Implementing early intervention: From research to effective practice.* New York, NY: Guilford Press.

Bryant, D. M., & Graham, M. A. (1993b). Models of service delivery. In D. M. Bryant & M. A. Graham (Eds.), *Implementing early intervention: From research to effective practice* (pp. 183–215). New York, NY: Guilford Press.

Guralnick, M. J. (1997a). Second-generation research in the field of intervention. In M. J. Guralnick (Ed.), *The effectiveness of early intervention* (pp. 3–20). Baltimore, MD: Paul H. Brookes.

Guralnick, M. J. (1997b). *The effectiveness of early intervention.* Baltimore, MD: Paul H. Brookes.

ROBERT T. BROWN
University of North Carolina at Wilmington

See also Asperger Syndrome; Autism

INTERVENTION PROGRAMS FOR CHILDREN WHO ARE AT RISK

Children raised in impoverished conditions are at greater risk for a host of adverse outcomes including developmental delay, school failure, and behavioral difficulties (Crosnoe & Huston, 2007; McCoy & Reynolds, 1999; Meisels & Liaw, 1993). These children generally score below average on standardized intelligence and achievement tests, are overrepresented in special education classes, and are more likely to drop out of school (Finn & Rock, 1997). In Birch and Gussow's (1970) representation of the poverty cycle, school failure contributed directly to unemployment and underemployment, which in turn were the major perpetuators of the cycle. Such failure and resulting poverty are costly to the affected individuals, their children, and society at large.

Intervention programs beginning in infancy or early childhood have been implemented in an attempt to promote healthy development for children at risk of these outcomes. Each focuses on prevention instead of rehabilitation, integrated provision of a variety of services through a variety of agencies, and a holistic approach that includes family participation (Belsky & MacKinnon, 1994; Sameroff, McDonough, & Rosenblum, 2004). Each also has a primary goal of preventing developmental delays and school failure. Thus, they are sometimes (e.g., Ramey & Ramey, 1998) described as *preventive interventions*.

The effectiveness of these programs has been long and regularly questioned (Herrnstein & Murray, 1994; Jensen, 1969; Spitz, 1986), particularly in terms of attempts to raise intelligence (e.g., Brown & Campione, 1986), and indeed, the large IQ increases of children in most programs generally fade after program cessation, with IQ gains of Head Start disappearing by third grade (Barnett & Hustedt, 2005). However, evidence indicates that the programs are successful in a number of other ways, including reducing school failure (Schweinhart & Weikart, 1993). Unfortunately, programs differ in intensity, scope, and duration, rendering outcome comparison difficult (Ramey & Ramey, 1998).

Historical Background

Most developers of intelligence tests in the United States, including Goddard and Terman, were firm believers in the concept of fixed, innate intelligence. A major opponent of this view was not a psychologist or educator, but a journalist, Walter Lippmann, who debated Terman in a series of articles and letters in the *New Republic* in the 1920s. But by the 1930s, the Iowa Group began to present evidence of considerable increases in intelligence of adopted children and others whose environments had changed. Although justifiably criticized for methodological problems, their research nonetheless supported the view that IQs are modifiable. Further, data on military inductees indicated that Whites overall had higher IQs than Blacks, and northern Blacks had higher IQs than southern Blacks, suggesting that environmental factors influenced intelligence. More detail on the early nature-nurture debate, including reprints of the Terman-Lippmann papers, is in Block and Dworkin (1976).

Beginning in the 1930s and 1940s and expanding greatly in the 1950s and 1960s, experimental research demonstrated dramatic effects of early experience and environment on animals' learning and problem solving. Hebb (1949) used that research as the basis for his theory that varied early experience is necessary for adequate "primary learning" that in turn was a necessary precursor to adequate later learning. Hebb proposed that primary learning was perceptual and led to the development of particular structures in the brain. In an influential book, Hunt (1961) integrated Hebb's theory with Piaget's theory of child development and suggested that human intelligence could be modified through enrichment of early experiences. Research indicating enhanced brain development in animals exposed to environments providing greater stimulation (e.g., Bennett, Diamond, Krech, & Rosenzweig, 1964) supported the views of Hebb and Hunt. In addition, a variety of research suggested that environmental factors related to socioeconomic status (SES) might have positive or negative influences on children's cognitive development. For example, Hess and Shipman (1965) reported that relatively mothers of higher SES backgrounds used more complex and child-oriented language styles with their children than did mothers from poverty-level backgrounds and that these differences correlated with differences in the children's performance on problem-solving tasks (Hart & Risley, 1995). Thus, research in a variety of areas supported the possibility that early intervention might raise IQs and school performance of at-risk children. Out of this convergence came Head Start in 1964, now including Early Head Start, and other intervention programs.

Specific Intervention Programs

This section reviews the content and evaluations of two intervention programs for disadvantaged at-risk children for which long-term follow-up evaluation is available. Many other programs, including the Chicago Child and Parent Centers, Syracuse University Family Development Research Program. Houston Parent Child Development Center, and Project CARE have had positive effects, although the results across projects differ by program components and measured outcomes. Summaries and evaluations of these programs were reviewed by Bryant and Maxwell (1997).

The Carolina Abecedarian Project

The Abecedarian Project may be the most intense and longest-lasting early intervention program. Some participants received intervention services from early infancy to 8 years of age. As summarized in Campbell and Ramey (1995), the participant sample was almost entirely African American and raised in poverty-level households headed by a single female who had not graduated from high school. They were predicted to be at risk for impaired cognitive development on the basis of a 13-point high-risk index that emphasized parental education and income. The project used a true 2 × 2 factorial experimental design, initially matching children at birth on the basis of scores on the high-risk index and then randomly assigning them to an experimental or control group. Each of those two groups

was then randomly divided into two subgroups based on 48-month IQs. The two factors were: (1) preschool intervention (experimental) versus no preschool intervention (control); and (2) school-age intervention (E) versus no school-age intervention (C). Thus, the study had two conditions initially (E and C) and four beginning at kindergarten (EE, EC, CE, and CC). Control children received no special services, but were assessed with the experimental children.

The preschool intervention was implemented for 5 full days a week for 50 weeks a year. The program was comprehensive and dealt with four domains: language development, cognitive development, gross and fine motor skills, and social skills, with a particular emphasis on language development and interaction. Teacher:child ratios ranged from 1:3 for infants to 1:6 for 4-year-olds. In the summer before participating students entered kindergarten, E children participated in a 6-week program to assist in the transition to public school classrooms. Parents served on the preschool's advisory board, had the opportunity to attend social events and information meetings, and were provided with information on child health and development.

The school-age intervention program supported the children's academic performance in school by involving parents in the educational process. A home/school resource teacher (HST) worked with each EE and CE child and his or her parent(s) for the first 3 years of school. The HST, developed individualized home curricula for each child, consulted with each child's regular teacher, served as an advocate for the parents and children, and taught parents to work with their children on a home curriculum that emphasized basic math and reading skills. The HST visited each home approximately 15 times a year for about 30- to 45 minutes and made additional visits if necessary to help families deal with various crises.

A follow-up evaluation of the participants at age 15 showed significant effects of preschool program on several measures. Major results are shown in Table I.2. Participants in the EE and EC groups had higher scores on reading and mathematics achievement tests, fewer assignments to special education programs, and roughly half as many grade retentions than did children in the CC and CE groups. Differences in measured intelligence, although

Table I.2. Summary of Results from the Carolina Abecedarian Project

Measure	Treatment Condition			
	EE	EC	CE	CC
Intelligence at age 15 years	95.0	94.5	87.3	92.0
Woodcock-Johnson reading scores	95.3	92.0	88.8	87.5
Woodcock-Johnson mathematics scores	92.3	92.3	87.0	86.0
Percentage ever retained in grade to age 15	31	30	52	56
Percentage assigned to special education, K–9	36	12	48	48

Note: Data derived from figures in Campbell and Ramey (1995).

small, favored the EE and EC participants. The preschool program had notably large and durable positive effects on participant's academic achievement.

The Perry Preschool

Owing to its long-term effects and cost-effectiveness, the Perry Preschool program was well-known to policy makers (Bryant & Maxwell, 1997). The program, which ran from 1962 through 1965, served disadvantaged preschool children with initial IQs 90 or less. Children were randomly assigned to a preschool that used a specially designed High/Scope Curriculum or an untreated control group. The High/Scope Curriculum, based on Piaget's constructivist developmental theory, treated participants as active learners and focused on child-initiated learning. Participants planned and carried out their own activities, supervised and encouraged by teachers. Experiences related to broad aspects of development, including initiative, creativity, language, logic and mathematical relations, and social relations. Participants attended preschool for 2.5 hours a day, 5 days a week, for 2 years before entering school.

Follow-up evaluation indicated that the High/Scope Curriculum was successful on not only academic but also socioemotional levels. During their school years, children who attended the High/Scope preschool spent fewer than half as many years as control children (1.1 versus 2.8) in special education programs for those with *educable mental retardation* (a term of the day reflecting children with an IQ between 50 and 75; Murphy, 1986) and scored higher on educational achievement tests on every evaluation. Although by the age of 27, no differences in cognitive scores between the two groups remained, preschool participants had higher rates of completion of grade 12 or more, lower rates of arrest, higher income, higher rate of home ownership, and lower participation in welfare programs (Schweinhart & Weikart, 1993). These differences are shown in Table I.3. Of particular importance are cost-effectiveness analyses that indicate that return on investment for the public was $7.16 for each dollar spent on the program. The program developers (Schweinhart & Weikart, 1993) attributed the success of the intervention to the program's empowerment of children, parents, and teachers.

Table I.3. Summary of Results of the Perry Project

Measure	Treatment Condition	
	Preschool	Control
Completed grade 12	71%	54%
Had five or more arrests	7%	35%
Earned at least $2,000 month	29%	7%
Owned home	36%	13%
Received welfare as an adult	59%	80%

Note: Data from Schweinhart and Weikart (1993).

Possible Adverse Long-Term Effects of Some Forms of Early Intervention

A strong caution about necessary effectiveness of early intervention comes from a comparison among three different types of early intervention. The same group (Schweinhart & Weikart, 1997) that conducted the Perry Preschool project also compared the effects of three different early intervention programs. Their High/Scope Preschool Curriculum Comparison study compared the High/Scope project, described earlier, with a traditional nursery school, and what they termed a *Direct Instruction* program. Direct Instruction was a highly structured and teacher-initiated Bereiter and Englemann (1966) program in which teachers led groups of children in 20-minute planned question and answer sessions dealing with language, mathematics, and reading. Duration of the intervention was similar to that of the Perry Preschool project.

Evaluation of the effects of the different preschools when the participants were about 23 years old revealed an interesting pattern of results. Virtually no differences in educational attainment occurred across the three programs, although participants in the High/Scope program required more compensatory education. However, adults who had participated in the Direct Instruction program showed significantly more years of identified emotional disturbance in school and were identified as having more felony and property crime arrests compared to the High/Scope program. Results interpretation must be qualified for the small number of subjects (total $n = 68$) and the large number of variables studied, which increases the likelihood of chance significant differences.

Principles for Intervention Programs for At-Risk Children

Based on an extensive review of intervention programs for both at-risk children and children with diagnosed disabilities, Ramey and Ramey (1998) developed a set of six general principles that apply to the development, implementation, and effects of intervention programs.

1. *Principle of developmental timing.* Generally speaking, the earlier in development intervention begins and the longer it lasts, the more effective it is. For intervention with specific conditions the infant/child must have developed to the point where intervention will have functional impact. In many cases, however, intervention most effectively should begin in early infancy as is the case with premature, low birth weight, or at-risk children.

2. *Principle of program intensity.* Programs increase in effectiveness with increases in number of intervention hours per day and days per week, number of intervention settings, and number of intervention activities. In addition, Ramey and Ramey (1998) suggest that the greatest benefits are in children who,

along with their parents, participate most regularly and actively.

3. *Principle of direct provision of learning experiences.* Whether conducted in centers or at children's homes, programs whose staff members directly provide learning experiences to participants are more effective than those that train parents to provide the experiences. A number of studies have demonstrated the relative ineffectiveness of parent-oriented home visits only in comparison with programs that combine home visits with direct provision of services. These findings are particularly important, given the fact that the most widely implemented intervention programs in the United States involve only infrequent home visits (Ramey & Ramey, 1998).

4. *Principle of program breadth and flexibility.* As would be expected, programs increase in effectiveness with increases in the range of services provided and the routes through which intervention is implemented. Thus, programs that provide transportation, health, and nutritional assistance as necessary; specific therapies; parent training; and educational programs are more effective than those providing a more restricted range of services.

5. *Principle of individual differences in program benefits.* Children respond differently to the same programs, related at least in part to their initial degree risk. Who benefits more from a given program, those initially more or less impaired, may depend on the type of initial impairment. Thus, programs for low birth weight infants are effective overall, but very low birth weight infants benefit less than do those whose birth weights are higher. On the other hand, results from the Abecedarian Project indicate that children of the lowest IQ mothers showed the greatest relative increase in performance (Ramey & Ramey, 1998). Further, different programs may be needed for children with different risk factors.

6. *Principle of ecological dominion and environmental maintenance of development.* Effects of early intervention will likely decrease or even disappear in the absence of follow-up programming and a supportive environment. The original notion, based partly on theorizing of Hebb (1949) that early intervention would have some permanent "inoculation effect," protecting the child from the effects of an adverse environment, has proved incorrect. Learning and adaptation to current environments are continuous processes, so a child returned to a maladaptive environment is likely to adapt to it. Further, as Ramey and Ramey indicate, for a child to maintain long-term benefit from intervention, its development must continue at a normal or near normal rate throughout the developmental period. Supplemental services may well be necessary to support this development.

Summary and Conclusions

Intervention, if early, intense, and of long duration, can benefit at-risk children and thereby society in a number of ways. Several programs have had considerable impact scholastically, improving children's school performance, reducing retention in grade, and reducing referrals for special services or assignment to special education classes. This effect may, although the participants are as yet too young to evaluate, increase future employability and therefore help interrupt the poverty cycle (Birch & Gussow, 1970).

REFERENCES

Barnett, W. S., & Hustedt, J. T. (2005). Head Start's lasting benefits. *Infants and Young Children, 18,* 16–24.

Belsky, J., & MacKinnon, C. (1994). Transition to school: Developmental trajectories and school experiences. *Early Education and Development, 5*(2), 106–119.

Bennett, E. L., Diamond, M. C., Krech, D., & Rosenzweig, M. R. (1964). Chemical and anatomical plasticity of the brain. *Science, 146,* 610–619.

Bereiter, C., & Engelmann, S. (1966). *Teaching the disadvantaged child in the preschool.* Englewood Cliffs, NJ: Prentice-Hall.

Birch, H. G., & Gussow, J. D. (1970). *Disadvantaged children: Health, nutrition, and school failure.* New York, NY: Gruen & Stratton.

Block, N. J., & Dworkin, G. (Eds.). (1976). *The IQ controversy.* New York, NY: Pantheon Press.

Brown, A. & Campione, J. (1986). Psychological theory and the study of learning disabilities. *American Psychologist 41*(10), 1059–1068.

Bryant, D. M., & Maxwell, K. (1997). The effectiveness of early intervention for disadvantaged children. In M. J. Guralnick (Ed.), *The effectiveness of early intervention* (pp. 23–46). Baltimore, MD: Paul H. Brookes.

Campbell, F. A., & Ramey, C. T. (1995). Cognitive and school outcomes for high-risk African-American students at middle adolescence: Positive effects of early intervention. *American Educational Research Journal, 32,* 743–772.

Crosnoe, R., & Huston, A. (2007). Socioeconomic status, schooling, and the developmental trajectories of adolescents. *Developmental Psychology, 43,* 1097–1110.

Finn, J. D., & Rock, D. A. (1997). Academic success among students at-risk. *Journal of Applied Psychology, 82,* 221–234.

Hart, B., & Risley, T. R. (1995). *Meaningful differences in the everyday experience of young American children.* Baltimore, MD: Paul H. Brookes.

Hebb, D. O. (1949). *Organization of behavior.* New York, NY: Wiley.

Herrnstein, R. J., & Murray, C. (1994). *The bell curve: Intelligence and class structure in American life*. New York, NY: Free Press.

Hess, R. D., & Shipman, V. C. (1965). Early experience and the socialization of cognitive modes. *Child Development, 36*, 869–886.

Hunt, J. M. (1961). *Intelligence and experience*. New York, NY: Ronald.

Jensen, A. R. (1969). How much can we boost IQ and scholastic achievement? *Harvard Educational Review, 39*, 1–123.

McCoy, A. R., & Reynolds, A. J. (1999). Grade retention and school performance: An extended investigation. *Journal of School Psychology, 37*, 273–298.

Meisels, S. J., & Liaw, F. R. (1993). Failure in grade: Do retained students catch up? *Journal of Educational Research, 87*(2), 69–77.

Murphy, D. M. (1986). The prevalence of handicapping conditions among juvenile delinquents. *Remedial and Special Education, 7*(3), 7–17.

Ramey, C. T., & Ramey, S. L. (1998). Early intervention and early experience. *American Psychologist, 53*, 109–120.

Sameroff, A. J., McDonough, S. C., & Rosenblum, K. L. (Eds.). (2004). Treating early relationship problems: Infant, parent, and interaction therapies. New York, NY: Guilford Press.

Schweinhart, L. J., & Weikart, D. P. (1993). Success by empowerment: The High/Scope Perry preschool study through age 27. *Young Children, 49*(1), 54–58.

Schweinhart, L. J., & Weikart, D. P. (1997). The High/Scope preschool curriculum comparison study through age 23. *Early Childhood Research Quarterly, 12*, 117–143.

Spitz, H. H. (1986). *The raising of intelligence: A selected history of attempts to raise retarded intelligence*. Hillsdale, NJ: Erlbaum.

ROBERT T. BROWN
ALISON SHANER
University of North Carolina at Wilmington

See also Abecedarian Project, the; Head Start

INTERVENTIONS FOR AUTISM SPECTRUM DISORDERS

Interventions for individuals with autism spectrum disorders (ASD) have been the subject of much controversy and inaccurate information is widespread (Simpson, Myles, & Ganz, 2008; Simpson et al., 2005). Thus, recently, autism experts and panels have attempted to summarize the evidence base for ASD interventions to provide some guidance for families and service providers in choosing evidence-based strategies. The most recent entity to do so is the National Standards Project from the National Autism Center. This report may be downloaded via: http://www.nationalautismcenter.org/affiliates/ Those deemed to be highly evidence-based, based on a large amount of high quality research support, by the National Autism Center (2009) and by Simpson and colleagues (2005) include antecedent based intervention packages, applied behavior analysis, behavioral intervention packages, comprehensive behavioral intervention for young children with ASD, discrete trial training, joint attention instruction, LEAP preschool, modeling, naturalistic instruction, peer-mediated interventions, pivotal response treatment, schedules, self-management, and story-based interventions.

The literature support for interventions for individuals with ASD continues to expand. Although most of the research in this area has been small scale, single-case research, several recent meta-analyses have provided syntheses of this data, which is more generalizable. Results of these studies indicate that (a) video modeling and video self-modeling are effective in improving social communication, behavior, and functional skills in children and adolescents (Bellini & Akullian, 2007; P. Wang & Spillane, 2009; S. Wang, Cui, & Parrila, 2011); (b) behavioral interventions effectively reduce challenging behaviors in individuals with ASD (Campbell, 2003); (c) early intensive behavioral interventions improve cognitive and adaptive behavioral functioning (Eldevik et al., 2009; Makrygianni & Reed, 2010; Peters-Scheffer, Didden, Korzilius, & Sturmey, 2011; Reichow & Wolery, 2009); (d) the Picture Exchange Communication System is a promising practice for improving functional communication skills in young children with ASD (Flippin, Reszka, & Watson, 2010); and (e) self-management is effective in improving behavioral skills in school aged students with ASD (Lee, Simpson, & Shogren, 2007). A recent meta-analysis on Social Stories contradicted the National Autism Center's (2009) ranking of the intervention as strongly evidence based (Kokina & Kern, 2010).

The following encyclopedia entries provide detailed information on several evidence based interventions and promising practices for individuals with ASD, as well as an overview of controversial interventions:

Applied Behavior Analysis

Applied Verbal Behavior

Augmentative and Alternative Communication

Controversial and Nonconventional Autism Interventions

Peer-Mediated Instruction

Picture Exchange Communication System

Pivotal Response Treatment

TEACCH

REFERENCES

Bellini, S., & Akullian, J. (2007). A meta-analysis of video modeling and video self modeling interventions for children and adolescents with autism spectrum disorders. *Exceptional Children*, *73*, 264–287.

Campbell, J. M. (2003). Efficacy of behavioral interventions for reducing problem behavior in persons with autism: A quantitative synthesis of single-subject research. *Research in Developmental Disabilities*, *24*, 120–138.

Eldevik, S., Hastings, R. P., Hughes, J. C., Jahr, E., Eikeseth, S., & Cross, S. (2009). Meta analysis of early intensive behavioral intervention for children with autism. *Journal of Clinical Child and Adolescent Psychology*, *38*, 439–450.

Flippin, M., Reszka, S., & Watson, L. R. (2010). Effectiveness of the picture exchange communication system (PECS) on communication and speech for children with autism spectrum disorders: A meta analysis. *American Journal of Speech-Language Pathology*, *19*, 178–195.

Kokina, A., & Kern, L. (2010). Social story[TM] interventions for students with autism spectrum disorders: A meta-analysis. *Journal of Autism and Developmental Disorders*, *40*, 812–826.

Lee, S., Simpson, R. L., & Shogren, K. A. (2007). Effects and implications of self management for students with autism: A meta-analysis. *Focus on Autism and Other Developmental Disabilities*, *22*, 213.

Makrygianni, M. K., & Reed, P. (2010). A meta-analytic review of the effectiveness of behavioural early intervention programs for children with autistic spectrum disorders. *Research in Autism Spectrum Disorders*, *4*, 577–593.

National Autism Center. (2009). *National Standards Project: Findings and Conclusions*. Randolph, MA: Author.

Peters-Scheffer, N., Didden, R., Korzilius, H., & Sturmey, P. (2011). A meta-analytic study on the effectiveness of comprehensive ABA-based early intervention programs for children with autism spectrum disorders. *Research in Autism Spectrum Disorders*, *5*, 60–69.

Reichow, B., & Wolery, M. (2009). Comprehensive synthesis of early intensive behavioral interventions for young children with autism based on the UCLA young autism project model. *Journal of Autism & Developmental Disorders*, *39*, 2341.

Simpson, R. L., deBoer-Ott, S., Griswold, D., Myles, B. S., Byrd, S., Ganz, J. B.,...Adams, L. (2005). *Autism spectrum disorders: Interventions and treatments for children and youth*. Thousand Oaks, CA: Corwin Press.

Simpson, R. L., Myles, B. S., & Ganz, J. B. (2008). Efficacious interventions and treatments for learners with autism spectrum disorders. (pp. 477–512). In R. L. Simpson & B. S. Myles (Eds.), *Educating children and youth with autism: Strategies for effective practice* (2nd ed). Austin, TX: PRO-ED.

Wang, P., & Spillane, A. (2009). Evidence based social skills interventions for children with autism: A metaanalysis. *Education and Training in Developmental Disabilities*, *44*, 318–342.

Wang, S., Cui, Y., & Parrila, R. (2011). Examining the effectiveness of peer-mediated and video modeling social skills interventions for children with autism spectrum disorders: A meta-analysis in single case research using HLM. *Research in Autism Spectrum Disorders*, *5*, 562–569.

JENNIFER B. GANZ
Texas A&M University

INVESTMENT THEORY OF CREATIVITY

Creativity operates just like investment banking, argue Robert J. Sternberg and Todd I. Lubart, with the difference being that the currency of creativity is ideas. A creative person will "buy low" and "sell high," just like a Wall Street trader. The key is knowing when to "invest" in ideas, and when to move on and pursue other projects (Sternberg & Lubart, 1995, 1996). According to the Sternberg-Lubart theory, there are six personal resources that are required for the production of creative work: Intelligence, Knowledge, Thinking Styles, Personality, Motivation, and Environmental Context. Intelligence, Personality, Motivation, and Environmental Context are commonly viewed as necessary (but not sufficient) variables in other theories of creativity (e.g., Amabile, 1996; Simonton, 2009).

Intelligence, Sternberg and Lubart argue, plays a part in creativity according to the theory of successful intelligence (Sternberg, 1999; Sternberg, Kaufman & Grigorenko, 2008), which has evolved from Sternberg's (1984) triarchic theory. The three subtheories are a *componential subtheory*, which relates intelligence to the internal world of the individual; an *experiential subtheory*, which relates intelligence to both the external and the internal worlds of the individual; and a *contextual subtheory*, which relates intelligence to the external world of the individual. The experiential subtheory, which focuses on those behaviors that involve either adjustment to relative novelty, automatization of information processing, or both, is the most connected to creativity. Personality is another factor in the Sternberg-Lubart model. Creative individuals must be risk-taking and persistent, they believe, especially as the most brilliant ideas are also the ones that encounter the most resistance.

Motivation is an area that is the subject of an active debate in the field of creativity, with one side (Amabile, 1996) arguing for the importance of intrinsic motivation (e.g., enjoyment) over extrinsic motivation (e.g., rewards), and others (e.g., Eisenberger & Shanock, 2003) arguing that extrinsic motivation is not damaging and may be helpful The investment theory does not take a strong stance on this debate, impressing the importance of both intrinsic and extrinsic motivators. The final factor found in several other theories, Environmental Context, is clearly important, as some environments foster creativity, while others crush it. An individual growing up in an environment that values creativity will have an easier time producing creative works than one who does not. However, there is actually a debate over whether a "bull-market" (accepting, reinforcing) or "bear-market" (cold, traumatic) environment most leads to a creative individual. Sternberg and Lubart (1995) believe that a synthesis of the two environments is likely the answer, with creativity being encouraged and highly regarded—and yet with some obstacles to overcome.

In addition to these four factors that are common to several other theories, the authors also make a strong case for two other variables, Knowledge and Thinking Styles. Knowledge refers to both formal knowledge (i.e., if you don't know the basic laws of mathematics, you aren't going to make a creative mathematical contribution) and informal knowledge. Informal knowledge, also called *tacit* knowledge, refers to knowledge, usually procedural, that is practical, yet not taught (Cianciolo et al., 2006). The contribution of Thinking Styles is rooted in the theory of Mental Self-Government (Zhang & Sternberg, 2006), which has three primary components: Legislative, Executive, and Judicial. According to this theory, legislative thinkers prefer to create things individually, with little inherent structure. Executive thinkers prefer to follow directions and carry out orders with a great deal of structure. Judicial thinkers like to judge and evaluate things. Sternberg and Lubart argue that at least some degree of legislative thinking is required for creativity.

These six variables are all needed for buying low and selling high. "Buying low," Sternberg and Lubart (1995, 1996) say, can be defined as choosing to pursue ideas that are either unknown or unfashionable. "Selling high" is having the insight to know when to move on and pursue other ideas. This strategy does mean, however, that an element of risk is involved. The authors define two types of risk: market risk and specific risk. Market risk refers to the larger area involved, while specific risk involves the more distinct types of creative production. One reason why everyone does not "buy low" is that there are these risks, and many people are risk-averse. A strong tendency in psychology, according to Sternberg (1997), is for "fads" to dominate the field. Someone who "buys low" has to resist this temptation to research fads, which would nearly guarantee journal publications and grants, and instead attack less popular topics, risking rejection and loss of funding.

In addition to affecting psychological research, however, risk aversion affects education as well. Sternberg and Lubart (1995, 1996) point to students who select the easiest courses to take instead of challenging courses because of concern over grades. This process results, the authors argue, in the students never learning to take "sensible risks." However, this skill is needed for creative production. The Investment Theory offers a number of possible strategies (also using the investment banker analogy) for creative production. One is technical analysis, which (as it applies to creativity) is studying past trends in your chosen field. This information can then be used to anticipate coming trends—and whether to challenge them or utilize them. Fundamental analysis is deciding which areas are not overexposed or overrepresented (i.e., a student assigned to write about a state in America may pick a less visible state, such as Montana, rather than New York or California). Finally, Sternberg and Lubart (1995) cover the random-walk theory, which holds that the odds of predicting future trends and topics of interest is practically chance.

One variable that Sternberg and Lubart (1995) discuss is school climate and its relationship to creativity. They report that personal experience has led them to believe that students "often become less able to produce creative work as they progress through school" (p. 267). One reason for this phenomenon may be that teaching usually has an end goal, which is measured through standardized testing. These tests traditionally are more knowledge-based and do not usually give credit for creativity.

REFERENCES

Amabile, T. M. (1996). *Creativity in context*. Boulder, CO: Westview.

Cianciolo, A. T., Grigorenko, E. L., Jarvin, L., Gil, G., Drebot, Kaufman J. C, & Sternberg, R. J. (2006). Practical intelligence and tacit knowledge: Advancements in the measurement of developing expertise. *Learning and Individual Differences, 16*, 235–253.

Eisenberger, R., & Shanock, L. (2003). Rewards, intrinsic motivation, and creativity: A case study of conceptual and methodological isolation. *Creativity Research Journal, 15*, 121–130.

Simonton, D. K. (2009). *Genius 101*. New York, NY: Springer.

Sternberg, R. J. (1984). Toward a triarchic theory of human intelligence. *Behavioral and Brain Sciences, 7*, 269–287.

Sternberg, R. J. (1997). Fads in psychology: What we can do. *APA Monitor, 28*, 19.

Sternberg, R. J. (1999). The theory of successful intelligence. *Review of General Psychology, 3*, 292–316.

Sternberg, R. J., Kaufman, J. C., & Grigorenko, E. L. (2008). *Applied intelligence*. New York, NY: Cambridge University Press.

Sternberg, R. J., & Lubart, T. I. (1995). *Defying the crowd*. New York, NY: Free Press.

Sternberg, R. J., & Lubart, T. I. (1996). Investing in creativity. *American Psychologist, 51*, 677–688.

Zhang, L. F., & Sternberg, R. J. (2006). *The nature of intellectual styles*. Mahwah, NJ: Erlbaum.

JAMES C. KAUFMAN
MARIA J. AVITIA
Learning Research Institute
California State University,
San Bernardino

IQ

In psychoeducational assessment, a difference exists between an IQ and an intelligence quotient or ratio IQ. Since the ratio IQ or intelligence quotient has decreased in use, the IQ has taken on more of a generic meaning as an index of a test taker's current level of intellectual functioning or general cognitive ability. The IQ has been found useful in understanding and predicting a number of important behaviors such as academic achievement (Sattler, 1982). In addition, diagnoses of a variety of learning disorders such as mental retardation and learning disabilities are dependent in part on determining the IQ of the student.

A test taker's composite performance on a test consisting of cognitive or intellectual tasks is represented by the IQ score. Intelligence tests can be very different from each other in item composition and consequently may yield divergent IQ estimates for the same individual. The magnitude of the IQ score and the interpretation of its meaning is dependent on the test author's theory or definition of intelligence. For example, the Wechsler Intelligence Scales yield verbal and performance IQs and a full-scale IQ. The meaning of these IQ estimates relate to Wechsler's theory of intelligence, which includes verbal and nonverbal reasoning and a heavy emphasis on language and acquired knowledge such as is tapped on the information, vocabulary, and arithmetic subtests. This theory is in contrast to Kaufman and Kaufman's (1983) definition of intelligence, which minimizes the role of language and acquired knowledge. Interpretations of IQ estimates based on Wechsler's and Kaufman and Kaufman's definitions of intelligence will certainly be different; the tests would likely yield different IQ estimates for the same individual.

Although most tests of intelligence currently in use yield IQs, they do not yield intelligence quotients representing the ratio of the test taker's mental age to his or her chronological age multiplied by 100. Rather, these intelligence tests provide tables for converting raw scores into age-corrected deviation standard scores or IQs.

David Wechsler, author of the Wechsler Intelligence Scales, proposed what he called a deviation IQ. The deviation IQ is a measure that describes how much a test taker's intellectual ability deviates from the average performance of others of the same chronological age within the standardization sample. Initially, developing a test to measure adult intelligence, Wechsler (1939) culled the standardization sample's data and constructed tables so that the person who scored at the average level for his or her age group would receive an IQ of 100. The standard deviation for all age groups was set at 15 by Wechsler. For the Wechsler Intelligence Scale for children, IQs were obtained by comparing a child's performance with the average performance of those in his or her age group. This deviation IQ is a standard score that represents how many standard deviations above or below the average the test taker's intellectual ability falls. To further aid in communicating the meaning of the IQ to nonprofessionals, IQ standard scores are often translated into a descriptive classification such as mentally deficient, a percentile rank, or an age equivalent.

The deviation IQ now represents the most common composite standard score yielded by intelligence tests, including the Wechsler scales and the Stanford-Binet. This popularity can be attributed primarily to the deviation IQ's overcoming many of the criticisms leveled at the ratio intelligence quotient. The means and standard deviations are equal across all age levels for the deviation IQ, allowing comparability for similar IQs across different ages. However, it is important for the test user to remember that deviation IQs yielded by different intelligence tests can only be compared if they have the same or similar standard deviations.

Finally, the generic terms IQ and IQ tests have often been misinterpreted by nonprofessionals and they possess a number of unfortunate negative connotations. The IQ test and the IQ have also been the subject of litigation in state and federal courts (Jensen, 1980). As a result of these negative connotations and litigation, some contemporary test developers have avoided the term *IQ* in labeling their composite standard scores yielded from their intelligence tests. For example, McCarthy's (1972) General Cognitive Index (GCI), Kaufman and Kaufman's (1983) Mental Processing Composite (MPC), and Reynolds and Kamphaus's (2003) Composite Intelligence Index (CIX) can be used interchangeably with the IQ.

REFERENCES

Jensen, A. R. (1980). *Bias in mental testing.* New York, NY: Free Press.

Kaufman, A. S., & Kaufman, N. S. (1983). *Kaufman Assessment Battery for Children.* Circle Pines, MN: American Guidance Service.

McCarthy, D. (1972). *Manual for the McCarthy scales of children's abilities.* New York, NY: Psychological Corporation.

Reynolds, C. R., & Kamphaus, R. W. (2003). *Reynolds Intellectual Assessment Scales.* Odessa, FL: PAR.

Sattler, J. M. (1982). *Assessment of children's intelligence and special abilities.* Boston, MA: Allyn & Bacon.

Wechsler, D. (1939). *The measurement of adult intelligence.* Baltimore, MD: Williams & Wilkins.

MARK E. SWERDLIK
Illinois State University

See also Deviation IQ; Intelligence; Intelligence Testing

IRAN, SPECIAL EDUCATION IN

In old Iran (Persia), in particular in Zarathostrian teachings, special care for individuals with disabilities is emphasized. Persian literature and Iranian Islamic educational philosophy also are rich in sagely counsel for people with special needs. However, before the 20th century, there was no systematic and organizational attempt to provide special education services for exceptional children.

In 1925, a German minister, E. Kristofel, founded the Institute for the Blind Students in Tabriz. At about the same time, a group of German Protestant missioners founded the Efta junior school in Tehran for students with hearing impairment. In 1929, Jabbar Baghchehbaan, an Iranian teacher, started a school for hearing impaired students in Tabriz. Subsequently, several unofficial institutions were established to serve exceptional children, including NooreAeen in Esfahan in 1929 for blind girls by English missionary Geven Gester, Esfahan Blind Boys' School in 1950 by Kristofel, Roudaki, Work and Education Association for the Blind in 1928 by the Social Services Organization in Tehran, Golbidi Hearing Impaired School in Esfahan in 1935 by Hossein Golbidi, Tabriz Exceptional Institute in 1937 by Hassan Osouli, Khazaeli Institute for Blind Adults by Mohammad Khazaeli in 1943 in Tehran, Reza Pahlavi Blind Boarding School in Tehran by the Pahlavi Foundation, Nezam Mafi Institute in 1943 by the 13th Educational District in Tehran for hearing impaired students, Nimrouz Deaf Students Institute in 1943 in Tehran by Mahmood Pakzad, Mash'had Deaf and Mute Junior School in 1947 by Parichehre Ghafforian, and Baghchehban Institute No. 2 in 1847 by Samineh Baghcheban in Tehran.

The official beginning of special education in Iran was in 1987. Laws helped open the doors of public schools to students with disabilities and mandated their absorption to the greatest degree possible into normal life. The 1990 Rehabilitation Act outlawed discrimination against exceptional children in education and mandated the elimination of all barriers that may prevent them from attending school. In 1991 the Education Department and the National Welfare Organization began to work jointly to improve special education in regular school. Colleges began training regular classroom teachers and specialists in ways to assist special needs students.

Preschool education is mandatory for all children between ages 5 and 6. This period is considered to be important and marks the beginning of the Department of Education's efforts to focus on assessing, identifying, and providing special education services for special needs students in both private and the public schools. Special education programs include those for students with learning disabilities; mental retardation; hearing, speech, or visual impairments; emotional disturbance; orthopedic or other physical disabilities; those with multiple handicaps; and gifted students.

All children, including those with special needs, are examined physically and mentally each year and receive psychological assessment provided by joint personnel from the departments of Health and Education.

Special education is provided for students with special needs from primary school through high school. Depending on the severity of their disability, students are placed in one of eight settings: special day schools; specialized residential facilities, including homes and hospitals; full-time residential schools; full-time special classrooms exclusive to special education students in regular schools; regular classrooms attendance with part-time special education services in a special classroom; regular classroom attendance with part-time special education services in a regular classroom with part-time help or tutoring in a resource room; full-time attendance in regular classrooms with occasional help from itinerant specialists; and full-time attendance in regular classrooms with occasional help from the regular teacher. Children with special needs receive services in 2,029 ordinary schools, 815 special schools, and 219 special classes in regular schools.

The majority of special education students able to attend public schools are assigned to regular classrooms for all or part of the day and receive instruction from regular teachers. Depending on the particular student and the degree of disability, a special resource teacher may be assigned to a classroom to provide special help, especially with students who disrupt the classroom. Resource teachers may work with special education students individually or in small groups for part of the day in resource rooms for the learning disabled. The main objectives of special education emphasize training students with skills that will facilitate their achieving independence socially and economically.

Among Iran's 18 million children, special education services are provided to 99,972. They include 60,114 who have mental retardation, 17,633 who have a hearing impairment, 3,615 who have a visual impairment, 7,281 who have language impairment, 6,868 who have severe learning disabilities, 3,021 preschoolers with multiple disabilities, 1,190 who have physical disability, and 250 who have serious emotional disturbance. Not all children with special needs are enrolled in school. Some students in remote areas are ignored, some families are too shy to admit they have a child with special needs, and some receive special education at home. Thus, exact numbers of those with disabilities are unobtainable.

In 1967, gifted student education began unofficially in the Hoshdar educational complex in Tehran. In 1988, responsibility for gifted education was assumed by the Education Department, was separated from special education, and was expanded nationally. Each year students are informed of the entry competition date and conditions for gifted classes. The brightest students are selected through an extensive nationwide competitive entry examination process in two preliminary and one advanced stages that includes achievement, academic aptitude, creativity tests, and grade point averages. These students receive highly advanced scientific and technological education in 44 cities. In 2005, 5,000 boys and 5,000 girls were in classes for gifted students.

Additional opportunities for students with special needs, including the gifted, are needed, especially in rural areas. Discussions center on the best approaches to implement effective educational intervention, budgetary allocations, the training of personnel, and entry criteria.

This entry has been informed by the sources listed below.

REFERENCES

Department of Education. (2005). *National Organization for Development of Educational Talents*. Retrieved from http://en.wikipedia.org/wiki/National_Organization_for_Development_of_Exceptional_Talents

Hajibabaei, M., & Dehghani, H. Y. (2004). *Characteristics and problems of special education in Iran*. Department of Education Publishing.

MONIR SALEH
*Beheshti University,
Tehran, Iran*

See also International School Psychology Association

IRELAND, REPUBLIC OF, SPECIAL EDUCATION IN

Policy Developments

In the past decade the Irish educational system has made a significant investment in the development of special education services and has demonstrated a trend toward inclusion of students with special educational needs in mainstream schools. National policies in special education have been influenced by international policy documents such as the Salamanca Statement on Special Needs Education UNESCO (1994), the UN Convention on the Rights of the Child (UN) (1990) and the UN International Convention on the Rights of Persons with Disabilities (2006). Irish policy documents relating to special education have adopted the philosophy of the Special Education Review Committee (SERC), favoring "as much integration as is appropriate and feasible with as little segregation as is necessary" (SERC, 1993). The Education Act of 1998 gave practical effect to the constitutional rights of children to education, including children with disabilities, and influenced a large body of legislation including the Employment Equality Acts 1998 and 2004, the Equal Status Acts 2000 to 2004, the Education (Welfare) Act 2000, the Education for Persons with Special Educational Needs Act (EPSEN) 2004 and the Disability Act 2005.

While the Education Act of 1998 asserted the role of the Minister of Education and Skills in the provision of educational access, the Education for Persons with Special Educational Needs Act of 2004 (EPSEN) detailed specific practices regarding individual assessment and proper levels of service provision in schools for students with disabilities. The EPSEN Act established the National Council for Special Education (NCSE) to coordinate resources to support schools and students. According to EPSEN (Government of Ireland, 2004), special educational needs are defined as a "restriction in the capacity of the person to participate in and benefit from education on account of an enduring physical, sensory, mental health or learning disability, or any other condition that results in a person learning differently from a person without that condition." Each policy document has been complemented by a full complement of departmental circulars, research and task force reports, curricular planning, policy, and practice guidelines. Children and families have also seen an increase in the resources provided to the system in terms of statutory bodies, learning support, resource, language support teachers, Special Educational Needs Organizers (SENO) and Special Needs Assistants (SNA).

The National Council for Special Education (NCSE) is a statutory body established to handle the planning and coordination of education and support services for children with special educational needs in conjunction with schools and the Health Service Executive (Department of Education and Science, DES, 2005). In addition to coordination of services, the NCSE also disseminates information on best practices, advises the Minister of Education and Skills, conducts research, provides information to parents regarding eligibility/entitlement, and coordinates the assessment, review, and monitoring of educational resources (NCSE, 2010).

Legal Rights and Safeguards

In relation to education, the Constitution of Ireland outlines that the family is the main source of education for the child (Article 42). Parents are entitled to provide education outside the school system if they wish. The state may require that children receive a certain minimum education, but this has not yet been defined in legislation or official policy. The state is obliged to provide for free primary education, but not to provide it directly. In practice, there are some private schools but the majority are state funded, originally established by Catholic religious orders, and currently administered by local boards of management.

The Education Act 1998 does not define inclusive education but states that a child with special educational needs shall be educated in an inclusive environment with children who do not have such needs unless the nature or degree of those needs of the child preclude it (Government of Ireland, 2004). The phrase *"as far as is practicable"* acknowledges that there should not be a statutory obligation in all cases to educate a child in an integrated setting

(McGrath, 2002). Special education services in Ireland can include supports from state and voluntary/nonprofit sectors such as:

- Consultation and casework about individual children, including psychological assessment (NEPS).
- Guidance and counseling services are often provided by schools.
- Technical aids and equipment, including means of access to schools, adaptations to buildings to facilitate access and with special needs and their families, provided by ENABLE IRELAND (nonprofit organization providing free services to individuals and families with disabilities: http://www.enableireland.ie/).
- Transportation for students (Department of Education and Skills DES).
- Provision for students learning through Irish sign language or other sign language, including interpreting services (DES).
- Therapy services (speech therapy, occupational therapy and social work support are usually provided by HSE or voluntary sector).
- Provision for early childhood, primary, post primary, adult or continuing education to students with special needs otherwise than in schools or centers for education.
- DES also provides a visiting teacher service for pupils with hearing or visual impairments.
- Support to schools through the Special Education Support Service (SESS).

Provision of Services

Public schools or school agencies were not always the providers of special education in Ireland. Although a few special schools were established by the State, parent groups, advocates, and voluntary organizations have been allowed to establish special schools independently since the 1960s. The service provided by schools was limited, and the services of voluntary organizations linked to the Health Boards (Department of Health) were heavily relied upon. Until the legislative changes in the past 10 years, the Department of Health provided a good deal of the educational services for students with moderate and severe disabilities. A new cross sector team comprised of representatives from the Departments of Health and Children, Education and Skills (DES), the Health Service Executive (HSE), and the National Council for Special Education (NCSE) has been established to plan implementation of Part 2 of the Disability Act of 2005 (DES, 2007d).

More than half of children with special educational needs are now educated in ordinary classes in mainstream primary schools or in special classes within these schools, and there is a strong emphasis on inclusion (NCSE, 2009). In Ireland and the United Kingdom, the term *learning*

disability is typically used instead of *intellectual disability* and there are generally two categories of teachers working within this special education area in Irish schools. Teachers categorized as learning support teachers generally provide support to pupils with literacy, numeracy and mild learning difficulties in mainstream schools, while resource teachers support pupils with more severe and less common learning difficulties (although overlap in caseloads can occur due to staffing issues). Both categories of teachers engage in regular planning with mainstream teachers and parents, and target the individual pupil's needs through the Individual Education Plan process as articulated by the NCSE, and the DES provides special needs assistants (SNAs) in classrooms to pupils with care or safety needs (NCSE, 2009).

Assessment

The needs of pupils with special educational needs are considered and provided for in terms of a continuum. In a three-stage model developed through the agency of DES, classroom-based assessment and intervention are provided to pupils with mild and/or transient needs (Stage 1: Classroom Support Stage) by classroom teachers and learning support teachers. More complex and/or enduring needs are supported at Stage 2 (School Support Stage) and Stage 3 (School Support Plus Stage) by learning support and resource teachers with the classroom teacher still maintaining a primary role (DES, 2007d). Generally, formal psychological assessment takes place at Stage 3, and is for students with more complex needs. This school-based formal referral process for psychological assessment is provided by the National Educational Psychological Service (NEPS).

Assessment of children for special needs does not occur until the learning support teacher and the class teacher have made efforts to address the child's problems. Children who continue to have difficulty coping with the curriculum are referred by the school principal to the National Educational Psychological Service (NEPS). As an executive agency of the Department of Education and Skills, NEPS provides psychological services to primary and post primary schools, both state and private; NEPS also processes applications for reasonable accommodations on State examinations for children with disabilities (NEPS, n.d.).

General Allocation Model

Students with special educational needs are accommodated in both mainstream and special schools. A revised system, the General Allocation Model (GAM), for the allocation of teaching resources to mainstream primary schools to cater for pupils who need additional support, involves a general allocation for primary schools to cater for pupils who are eligible for learning support (for high incidence needs) and pupils with borderline mild and mild general learning disability and specific learning disability (DES, 2005). Requests are assessed by regional Special Educational Needs Organizers (SENOs). The school must make an individual application for resource teaching hours for children with low incidence special needs or disabilities, such as hearing impairment, visual impairment, and autism spectrum disorders. Each school determines how its resources for high incidence support are to be used. Specific guidelines for practice and pupil/teacher ratios have been established by the DES for each disability (DES, 2005). For example, special classes for pupils diagnosed with moderate speech and language disorders are attached to mainstream primary schools. Schools must have at least five eligible pupils in order to retain a class and the pupil/teacher ratio is 7:1. An enhanced capitation grant is paid in respect of each pupil enrolled in these classes. The Health Service Executive (HSE) funds the provision of speech and language therapy services for these children. If a special class is not available, resource teacher support for individual children will be provided (DES, 2005).

There are approximately 5,500 teachers working directly with children with special educational needs in the primary school system (DES, 2011a). The National Council for Special Education (NCSE) administers and processes applications for support resources using its network of Special Educational Needs Organizers (SENOs). Schools may also apply for funding from the NCSE to buy special equipment to help children with special needs. Specific provisions have been made for children on the autistic spectrum, including special classes attached to special and mainstream schools; preschool classes to facilitate the demand for early intervention provision for children on the autistic spectrum; standalone facilities providing an applied behavioral analysis (ABA) specific methodology on a pilot basis (DES, 2006b).

Special needs assistants (SNAs) are provided by the DES to work with children needing instructional support due to a physical disability, medical need, mobility need, or behavioral difficulties, and may work with more than one child, on a full or part-time basis (NCSE, 2009). A recent review by the DES Inspectorate have found an overallocation of SNAs in the schools, which may have led to an overidentification of students with special educational needs (DES, 2011a). The report indicates that the DES is currently working to bring staffing levels and pupil/teacher ratios in line with the need that exists within individual schools, as opposed to the special school's designation or diagnostic label.

Postprimary Education

Postprimary or secondary level students with special educational needs are integrated into mainstream schools and classes with the assistance of a learning support/resource teacher and/or SNA. More than 2,300 whole-time equivalent teachers support students with special educational needs in post primary schools, a quarter of whom are learning support teachers (NCSE, 2009). Special classes at postprimary schools typically cater for the learning needs of students with a moderate level of learning disability. The NCSE may request a school to make specific provision for students in a category of special educational need (for example, visual impairment, moderate general learning disability, or autism) within a particular geographical area. In such circumstances, additional staffing is usually allocated to enable the school to establish a special class/unit for students within the category of special educational needs involved.

The DES promotes a model of assessment and intervention at both primary and postprimary levels that recognizes that special educational needs occur along a continuum, from mild to severe and from transient to long term following the recommendations of the SERC report (SERC, 1993). The response to the needs of students is also offered along a continuum, from whole school, universal and preventative approaches to individual and specialist approaches. The Continuum of Support encompasses a graduated solution-orientated model of assessment and intervention in schools and comprises three distinct school-based processes, which are summarized as: *Support for All* is a process of prevention, effective mainstream teaching and early identification. These systems are available to all students and effectively meet the needs of most students; *Support for Some*, including classroom and subject support, is an assessment and intervention process directed to some students, or groups of students who require some additional input. *Support for a Few* is generally characterized by more intensive and individualized supports (DES, 2007d). This level of intervention is for students with complex and/or enduring needs and relatively few students will need this level of support.

Special Schools

Students with disabilities are also accommodated in a variety of special schools and in special classes attached to mainstream primary and postprimary schools. The special schools cater to students with mild general learning disability, moderate general learning disability, and severe/profound general learning disability; for emotionally disturbed students; for students with autistic spectrum disorders; for students with physical and multiple disabilities; for students with visual and hearing impairment; and students with specific learning disability. Special classes for students in most of these categories are attached to mainstream schools, mainly at primary level.

Recent statistics from the Department of Education and Skills report that there are 140 special schools in Ireland catering for mild, moderate, and severe/profound special needs, serving more than 7,000 students, while over

9,500 students are served in mainstream schools (DES, 2011a). Special schools are staffed primarily on the basis of their official school designations (type of disability served), pupil numbers in the school, and teacher staffing ratios.

Preschool Education

Ireland operates a split system of governance with the Department of Education and Skills having responsibility for early childhood education provision in targeted initiatives for "at risk of educational disadvantage" children age 3 to 4 (e.g., Early Start and Traveller Preschools) and the Infant Classes in primary schools catering for children age 4 to 6 years. Infant classes cater to 95% of all 56-year-olds and 59% of 45-year-olds and include more than 1,000 children with identified special educational needs in mainstream primary schools. The Early Years Education Policy Unit, an executive office of the Department of Education and Skills, was established to improve the quality of educational provision in early childhood care and education settings and is collocated in the Office of the Minister for Children and Youth Affairs to ensure that policy developments in the early childhood sector are developed within an overall strategic policy framework for children (Centre for Early Childhood Development and Education [CECDE], 2006).

Training

Special education training is now available through a variety of master's degree and certificate programs in all teacher training colleges, many universities, and educational centers. The current provision is a large improvement on limited supports available between the 1960s and 1990s. Developments spearheaded by the Vocational Education Committees (VEC) may have foreshadowed a number of changes instituted by the Department of Education. Prior services were largely dependent on the enthusiasm and creativity of individual teachers. Without doubt, international trends have had a large impact on public awareness and the direction of policy. Currently, there is a strong focus on Applied Behavioral Analysis, autism, social emotional skill development, and inclusion in continuing education opportunities.

The Irish Association of Teachers in Special Education is an important resource for teachers of pupils with special needs and for other professionals, through the publication of articles reflecting research findings, best practices, and international perspectives. Through the association journal *REACH*, the Irish Association of Teachers of Special Education (IATSE) promotes cooperation and understanding between teachers across the spectrum of educational settings, including primary, post primary schools and special schools (Irish Association of Teachers of Special Education [IATSE], 2011). The association aims to engage parents, service providers, policy makers and people with disabilities themselves in fruitful dialogue. For further information on the association and the REACH journal, the reader is directed to the IATSE website (www.iatse.ie) or the association office: Irish Association of Teachers in Special Education, Drumcondra Education Centre, Dublin 9, Ireland.

The Special Education Support Service (SESS) is an initiative of Teacher Education Section of the Department of Education and Skills, funded by the Irish Government under the National Development Plan 2007–2013, "Transforming Ireland A Better Quality of Life for All" (Government of Ireland, 2007). Under the remit of the Department of Education and Science, the role of SESS is to enhance the quality of learning and teaching in relation to special educational provision, through the coordination, development and delivery of a range of professional development initiatives and support structures for school personnel working with students across all school levels (SESS, n.d.). The organization facilitates a partnership involving support teams of practicing teachers, Education Centers, the education Inspectorate, the National Psychological Service (NEPS), the National Council for Curriculum and Assessment (NCCA), the National Council for Special Education (NCSE), Third Level Colleges, Health Board Personnel, Teacher Unions and other relevant bodies and services (SESS, n.d.).

Challenges for the Future

DES audits of the special education support provision in mainstream schools have found an increase in the number of students with special needs and an increase in support and teaching staff, but a need for more detailed guidelines about entitlement to resources (Ware et al., 2009). The current climate of economic austerity adds to the challenge of ensuring that resources reach those most in need. Awareness of the benefits of early identification and the responsibility of all sectors to work together in that effort are heightened. The DES is challenged with embedding the principles of current legislation throughout the educational system, and accountability for the consistency of implementation and outcomes. In this regard, continued preservice and inservice support is still needed to develop more clearly defined roles and responsibilities for teachers providing special education services (Ware et al., 2009). With centralized budgetary control, this is a constant challenge for local schools.

Under the Education for Persons with Special Educational Needs Act 2004, each child assessed with a special educational need should have a personal education plan (Government of Ireland, 2004). This system is not yet in place but implementation is being coordinated by the National Council for Special Education (NCSE), which has published Guidelines for the Individual Education Plan process (NCSE, 2006). A cross-sector team representative of officials from the Departments of Health and Children, Education and Science, the Health Service Executive and the National Council for Special Education has been established to ensure that the arrangements for the implementation of Part 2 of the Disability Act 2005, and the EPSEN Act 2004 are progressed in tandem.

At a policy level, the Irish Government appears committed to the development of a national system of early education placement for children with intellectual disabilities and is currently engaging with the Health Service Executive (HSE) in this context. Due to the demand regarding specific issues (e.g., autism), the DES has established preschool classes to facilitate the demand for early intervention provision for children with Autistic Spectrum Disorders. The white paper on early childhood education "Ready to Learn" set out a comprehensive strategy for the development of early childhood education up to 6 years with a particular focus on disadvantage and special needs (Government of Ireland, 1999).

Development might seem to suggest that the concept of inclusion has become embedded in legislation and in schools but confusion still exists as to what constitutes government policy in relation to children with special needs. Special education continues to be provided on a continuum that ranges from separate special schools for children with severe, moderate, or mild intellectual disability, to special classes within mainstream schools, to inclusion within mainstream classes with appropriate support. DES policy and the charge of the NCSE is currently to ensure that a continuum of special education provision is available as required in relation to each type of disability, necessitating an individualized approach for each child. Making room for the voices of children and their families is an important step towards inclusive practice and most recent legislation.

REFERENCES

Centre for Early Childhood Development and Education (CECDE). (2006). *Synergy: An exploration of high quality early intervention for children with special needs in diverse early childhood care and education settings*. Dublin, Ireland: CECDE.

Department of Education and Science (DES). (2005). Special education circular letter SP ED 01/05: The National Council for Special Education (NCSE). Dublin, Ireland: DES

Department of Education and Science (DES). (2006b). The evaluation of educational provisions for children with autistic spectrum disorders. Dublin, Ireland: Stationery Office.

Department of Education and Science (DES). (2007b). *Circular letter 051/2007: Education for Persons with Special Educational Needs (EPSEN) Act 2004 and Disability Act 2005*. Dublin, Ireland: DES.

Department of Education and Science (DES). (2007d). Special education needs: A continuum of support. *Guidelines for teachers*. Dublin, Ireland: Stationery Office.

Department of Education and Skills. (2011a). *Education and statistics database*. Retrieved from http://www.cso.ie/px/des/database/des/des.asp

Government of Ireland. (1998). *Education Act 1998*. Dublin, Ireland: Stationery Office.

Government of Ireland. (1999). *Ready to learn: White paper on early childhood education*. Dublin, Ireland: Stationery Office.

Government of Ireland. (2000). *Education (Welfare) Act 2000*. Dublin, Ireland: Stationery Office.

Government of Ireland. (2004). *Education for Persons with Special Educational Needs Act 2004* (EPSEN). Dublin, Ireland: Stationery Office.

Government of Ireland. (2005). *Disability Act 2005*. Dublin, Ireland: Stationery Office.

Government of Ireland. (2007). *National Development Plan 2007–2013. Transforming Ireland: A better quality of life for all*. Dublin, Ireland: Stationery Office.

Irish Association of Teachers of Special Education (IATSE). (2011). *REACH*. Retrieved from http://www.iatse.ie/Reach.aspx

McGrath, B. (2002). *The social context of inclusion: A three-country study*. Unpublished dissertation. Loyola University Chicago.

National Council on Special Education (NCSE). (2006). *Guidelines on individual education plan process*. Dublin, Ireland: Stationery Office.

National Council on Special Education (NCSE). (2010). *Customer charter*. Dublin, Ireland: Stationery Office.

National Disability Authority. (2005). *Special education provision for children with disabilities in Irish primary schools–the views of stakeholders*. Retrieved from http://www.nda.ie/cntmgmtnew.nsf/0/5B4CE56E1452B0E18025717E00525CDE/$File/primary_ed_report_04.htm

National Educational Psychological Service (NEPS). (n.d.). *State examinations commission*. NEPS submission to the advisory group on reasonable accommodations at the certificate examinations (RACE). Retrieved from http://examinations.ie/

Special Education Review Committee. (1993). *Report of the Special Education Review Committee* (SERC). Dublin, Ireland: Stationery Office.

Special Education Support Services (SESS) (n.d.). *Information for and about special schools*. Retrieved from http://sess.ie/sess/Main/Special_Schools.htm

Ware, J., Balfe, T., Butler, C., Day, T., DuPont, M., Harten, C.,... Travers, J. (2009). *Research report on the role of special schools and classes in Ireland. Trim, Co. Meath, Ireland: National Council of Special Education (NCSE).

BREEDA MCGRATH
Chicago School of Professional Psychology

IRWIN, ROBERT BENJAMIN (1883–1951)

Robert Benjamin Irwin, blind from the age of 5, in 1909 became superintendent of classes for the blind in the

Cleveland, Ohio, public schools, one of the first school systems in the United States to educate blind children. He organized braille reading classes and, most significantly, established the first "sightsaving" classes for partially seeing students rather than group them with blind children.

Irwin became director of research and education for the newly formed American Foundation for the Blind in 1923, and served as its executive director from 1929 until his retirement in 1950. He promoted federal legislation relating to the blind, including laws authorizing the Library of Congress to manufacture and distribute "talking books" and books in braille, providing Social Security for the blind, providing income tax exemptions for the blind, and giving priority to the blind in the operation of vending stands in federal buildings. Believing that the blind should not be segregated, he opposed a movement to establish a national college for the blind.

This entry has been informed by the sources listed below.

REFERENCES

Allen, A. (1952). Robert B. Irwin—A lifetime of service. *New Outlook for the Blind, 46,* 1–3.

Irwin, R. B. (1955). *As I saw it.* New York, NY: American Foundation for the Blind.

PAUL IRVINE
Katonah, New York

ISOVALERIC ACIDEMIA

Isovaleric acidemia is characterized by a deficiency of the enzyme isovaleryl CoA dehydrogenase. This enzyme is essential to normal metabolism of the amino acid lysine. Clinical manifestations of this disorder are caused by accumulations of large amounts of isovaleric acid and its metabolites in tissue and body fluids.

Isovaleric acidemic is rare. Its frequency in the general population is unknown. The abnormal gene is located on the long arm of Chromosome 15. Like most hereditary enzyme deficiencies, isovaleric acidemia is an autosomal recessive disorder.

Characteristics

1. The acute form causes symptoms in the first few days of life, once protein intake is established. Milder clinical forms may remain asymptomatic for a few months or even 2 to 3 years. The acute form accounts for 50% of cases.

2. Symptoms of the acute form include vomiting, lethargy, seizures, and a peculiar odor of sweaty feet about the baby.

3. Babies with the acute form become comatose and eventually die within a few days from the onset of illness unless prompt diagnosis is made and appropriate therapy is started.

4. Laboratory findings include severe acidosis, low white blood cell and platelet counts, low calcium, elevated ammonia, and occasionally elevated blood glucose.

5. Diagnosis is confirmed by finding elevated levels of isovaleric acid and its metabolites in body fluids, especially urine. This assay is not generally available in hospitals other than tertiary pediatric centers that specialize in the care of critically ill infants and children.

Treatment of acute attacks requires rehydration with intravenous fluids, correction of acidosis, and removal of excess isovaleric acid. Some patients may need exchange transfusions or dialysis to ensure rapid clinical and biochemical improvement. Chronic treatment of isovaleric acidemia includes a low protein diet and glycine and carnatine supplements.

The prognosis for this disorder is generally good, provided that it is promptly diagnosed and treated. Normal development can occur if these requirements are met. However, the initial symptoms of an acute attack are nonspecific and suggest many other clinical entities, such as sepsis, that are far more common than isovaleric acidemia. The astute clinician must always consider an abnormality of amino acid metabolism when confronted with an extremely ill newborn, even though it may be the only case he or she will ever encounter.

This entry has been informed by the source listed below.

REFERENCES

Rezvani, I., & Rosenblatt, D. S. (2000). Defects in metabolism of amino acids. In R. E. Behrman, R. M. Kleigman, & H. B. Jenson (Eds.), *Nelson's textbook of pediatrics* (16th ed., pp. 344–377). Philadelphia, PA: Saunders.

BARRY H. DAVISON
Ennis, Texas

JOAN W. MAYFIELD
Baylor Pediatric Specialty Services, Dallas, Texas

ISRAEL, SPECIAL EDUCATION IN

Special education services for children with special needs have been provided in Israel since the establishment of the state in 1948. However, in 1988, the first special education law was enacted. According to this law, the purpose of special education is to advance and develop the abilities and potential of disabled children, to correct and improve their physical, mental, psychological, and behavioral performance, to convey knowledge, skills, and habits, and to adapt them to behavior acceptable to society, for the purpose of becoming part of that society and being integrated in the world of work (Meadan & Gumpel, 2002).

The law provides for special education services for individuals between the ages of 3 and 21, including teaching and systematic learning and treatment, including physiotherapy, speech therapy, occupational therapy, and other interventions as they may be defined (Israel Ministry of Education, 1988). The disabilities covered include deafness, blindness, children in hospital, mild to severe retardations, behavior disorders, cerebral palsy, learning disabilities, autism, retarded developmental and language development, and mental illness. All children with special needs in these categories are provided with all the professional and educational services required, and all costs are covered by the ministry of education and the local municipalities.

A child experiencing difficulty in school is diagnosed by a professional in the relevant area (e.g., school psychologist, child neurologist, psychiatrist, speech pathologist) and, if deemed eligible for special education services, is referred to a local committee that makes formal decisions on eligibility and placement. The committee includes a representative of the local education authority, two ministry of education superintendents, a school psychologist, a pediatrician, a social worker, and a representative of the National Special Education Parents' Organization. The committee decides where the child will be educated and gives *priority to placing the child in a recognized school that is not a special education school*. The child's parents are allowed to attend and be represented, and are entitled to read all the documents concerning their child. The psychological tests most widely used to evaluate intellectual ability are the Wechsler-III and the Kaufman KABC, both of which have been standardized for the Israeli population (norms for these tests are currently being developed for the Arab population). Recently, the WAIS was standardized for high school students, and Israeli norms have been developed for several specific tests for learning disabilities.

The child with special needs, a parent, or a representative of a public organization can, within 21 days, submit an appeal concerning a decision of the placement committee to a seven-member board appointed by the ministry of education. Parents are usually granted wide latitude concerning placement, and a child will seldom be placed in a special education framework against parental wishes (usually if the child presents a clear danger to self or others).

Nearly all severe problems are detected at an early age, often soon after birth, thanks to a highly developed pre- and postnatal care system in the country and to child development centers functioning in most hospitals where children diagnosed with serious developmental and physical disorders can be observed and treated. These children are later placed in special kindergartens and schools.

The special education law has undergone major revisions since 2000, partly in response to the advocacy of parents who demanded that their children with special needs receive services within regular classrooms. In 2002, the ministry of education began implementing a policy striving to include every child with special needs in regular schools whenever possible. A multilevel hearing system has been established, and a school based statutory committee convened by the principal of the school makes decisions about children with special needs at the school level, that determines their eligibility for assistance. This committee includes the child's teacher, the school psychologist, a special education specialist, and medical and paramedical professionals relevant to the area of disability being discussed, with parents and other teachers also invited. Similar procedures are in place for kindergartens.

Local Support and Resource Centers are the organizational and operational arm of the inclusion program. These centers currently serve only mild disability categories, function in a semiautonomous manner, and are able to allocate resources according to specific local needs. These centers are changing the very nature of service provision in Israel: special education teachers are no longer associated with specific schools, but rather with their centers. In this way, teachers and paramedical services are provided from within an itinerant consultative/collaborative framework. A major criticism against this new structure is that it has become very bureaucratic and too large a proportion of the funds allocated to children with special needs is being used to administer the new system.

In special schools, a multidisciplinary team develops an individualized education program for each special needs child at the beginning of every school year. The individualized education program includes a plan that describes the child's current performance level, the learning aims and objectives, a timetable for achieving them, the required resources, and the measuring standards.

During the 2004 to 2005 academic year, 17,000 students received special education services in special education settings, and about 25,000 students received special education services through Local Support and Resource Centers in preschool and general education schools. Special education does not relate to a place but rather to a range of educational, didactic, and therapeutic procedures carried out in different settings. The percentage of pupils diagnosed with special needs in separate schools in 2005 is 2.3%. This is a dramatic drop from a figure of about 8% over the past 20 years, reflecting the inclusion policy of the ministry of education.

REFERENCES

Israel Ministry of Education: Special Education Law, 1988.

Meadan, H., & Gumpel, T. P. (2002). Special education in Israel. *Council for Exceptional Children, 30*(5), 16–20.

BERNIE STEIN
Tel Aviv, Israel

ITA (*See Initial Teaching Alphabet*)

ITALY, SPECIAL EDUCATION IN

Italian educational regulations did not include official provisions for students with disabilities until 1932, though religious and institutional leaders were aware of their special learning needs since the late 1800s.

The field of *special pedagogy* (pedagogia speciale) developed with the early work of researchers such as De Santis, Montesano, Provolo, and Montessori, who focused on determining the learning needs of children with physical, sensory, and cognitive impairments. Such children were largely institutionalized, which afforded consistent and long-term access to a wide range of disabilities. The earliest studies in special pedagogy shed light on how learning can be influenced by environmental impact, cognitive function, reading theory, and socioeconomic status (Cornoldi, 1990).

In the mid-19th century, Italy's unification movement used the education system as a vehicle for creating Italian citizenry by galvanizing a national identity through schooling. During this time, religious, municipal, and state institutions had to abandon individualized philosophical approaches to students to participate in forming the new republic by educating children of the elite to become leaders in the new sociopolitical identity (White, 1991). Despite these directives, De Santis, Montesano, Montessori, and other researchers continued their work in private institutions, furthering the development of pedagogia speciale. They developed individual educational plans for children with disabilities, established teacher training initiatives, opened the country's first orthophrenic schools (residential schools specialized in innovative instructional techniques for children with disabilities while providing specialized training for teachers), and brought considerable attention to the needs of students with disabilities and otherwise marginalized children in a society eager to assert its identity as a unified country. In 1907, Montessori opened the first school specifically designed for teaching children with disabilities (Cornoldi, 1991).

In 1923, the Gentile Education Reform outlined provisions for children who were deaf or blind, and included the first education regulations that recognized the civil rights of students with disabilities. By 1926, Montessori's methods were the most widely recognized examples of differentiated instruction and student centered instruction and learning (Cornoldi, 1991). Soon thereafter, compulsory public education was extended to students who were deaf or blind provided they had no other disabilities. Students with psychological disabilities were put in special classes or in institutes for juvenile offenders (European Commission, 1995).

The First Constitution of the Italian Republic in 1948 proclaimed that all citizens had equal social dignity and were therefore equal before the law. All children between ages 6 and 14 were granted the right to a free public education. Article 34 of the Constitution specifically provides persons with disabilities the right to an education and work (Einaudi, 1948). This provision paved the way for the eventual development of inclusionary education models where students with disabilities are educated alongside their peers with support of specialized teachers in the classroom.

In the late 1960s, throughout Europe and the United States, efforts were made to challenge established social order and dismantle power structures, which had become immobile. Italy was one of the countries caught in this social upheaval. The demands of trade unions helped modify social policies by calling on social services to prevent and contain marginalization. These sociopolitical changes significantly impacted the three subcultures of Italian life (Catholic, Marxist, and secular progressive) which, in turn, had a particular impact on special education by calling for the closing of institutions whereby psychoeducational issues could be dealt with in the social realm (White, 1991). This sentiment gained sociopolitical momentum and became known as the *antiinstitutional movement*, spearheaded by psychiatrist Franco Basaglia. By 1977, Law #517 provided all Italians the constitutional right to be educated, free from discrimination. This antiinstitutional mandate became known as Basaglia's Law. In a similar spirit, Article 28 of Law 118 of 1971 mandated that students with disabilities were to be instructed equally alongside their nondisabled peers in public schools, unless their disabilities were of such gravity that they learning or successful inclusion was impeded (European Commission, 1995).

Law 104 of 1992, known as the *Framework Law* (Legge Quaddro), is the principal legislative mandate for school inclusion. It extends inclusionary practice to nursery, primary, and secondary schools, universities, rehabilitation centers, and hospitals. It outlines procedures for identifying students for entitlement to special education services. It was reinforced in 1994 with a presidential decree that called for cooperation among schools, local health units, and families to address the special needs of students with disabilities in inclusionary settings (Organization for Economic Cooperation and Development, 2003).

New legislation was put into effect through Law 170/2010, which makes provisions for children with specific learning disabilities at school (Gazzetta Ufficiale, 2010). This mandate, with language pertaining specifically to dyslexia, was added to Ministerial Decree No. 5669 of July 12, 2011. It outlines State-recognized rights for children with learning disabilities adequate safeguards be exposed to the same educational objectives as nondisabled peers. Law 170 provides teacher training initiatives and individualized instruction. In addition, it establishes provisions for assessment and learning interventions through an individualized Custom Learning Plan (*Piano Didattico Personalizzato*), which is drawn up within the first school term of eligibility determination and amended as needed during the school year. The diagnosis of learning disabilities (*disturbi specifici di apprendimento*) is designated privately or by accredited specialists through the National Health Service (Ministry of Instruction, University and Research, 2011). A disability certificate is registered which parents must then provide the school either by hand or by registered mail if they wish their child to receive support.

In order to streamline the process of assessment and service delivery in terms of special education, Law 170/2010 calls for a "functional diagnosis" which is more implicit than a clinical label certifying that a child has a disability (Gazzetta Ufficiale, 2010). A functional diagnosis describes the disorder in practical terms and provides a clear account for how the child is impacted in the school setting and provides guidance for compensatory tools and strategies needed to design an adequate Custom Learning Plan. Law 17/2010 also provides guidelines for frequent contact between teachers and parents, and calls for monthly or bimonthly meetings with families to monitor the student's school performance, verify the actual use of accommodations and modifications. Textbooks are available for free in digital format online. Law 170/2010 also addresses learning foreign languages. In cases of severe disorder, a student with disabilities may be exempt from the written portion of the test and participate by taking an oral equivalent in its stead (Ministry of Instruction, University and Research, 2011).

Special Education in Italy is subject to legislative developments that continue to move it forward, with the latest law specifically outlining provisions for students with learning disabilities. Inclusionary practices with support from specialized staff in the classroom with diagnostic assessment mainly conducted off-site endure as distinguishing characteristics of Italian special education.

REFERENCES

Cornoldi, C. (1990). *I Disturbi dell'Apprendimento. Aspetti Psicologici Neuropsicologici* [*Learning Disabilities: Psychologicaland Neuropsychological Aspects*]. Bologna, Italy: Il Mulino.

Cornoldi, C. (1991). I disturbi di apprendimento [learning disorders]. Bologna, Italy: Il Mulino.

Einaudi, M. (1948). The Constitution of the Italian Republic. *American Political Science Review, 42*, 661–676.

European Commission. (1995). *Structures of the education and initial training systems of the European Union (2nd ed.), prepared by EURYDICE and CEDEFOP*. Luxembourg, Luxembourg: Office for Official Publications of the European Community.

Gazzetta Ufficiale. (2010). http://www.gazzettaufficiale.it/archivio Completo

Ministero dell'Istruzione, dell'Universita' e della Ricerca, Departimento per l'Istruzione, Direzione Generale per lo Studente, l'Integrazione, la Partecipazione e la Comunicazione, allegate al Decreto Ministriale luglio 2011. (Ministry of Instruction, University and Research, Department for Instruction, General Management for the Student, Integration, Participation and Communication, attachment to Ministerial Decree of July 12, 2011), Italy.

Organisation for Economic Co-operation and Development. (2003). *Education at a glance*. Paris, France: Author.

White, S. (1991). *Progressive renaissance: America and the reconstruction of Italian education 1943–62*. New York, NY: Garland.

JULIA H. COYNE
Chicago School of Professional Psychology

ITARD, JEAN M. G. (1775–1838)

Jean Itard, a French physician who served on the medical staff of the famous National Institution for Deaf Mutes in Paris, is best known for his work with the wild boy of Aveyron. This child of 11 or 12 was found naked in the woods, where he had been living as a savage. He was brought to Itard for training, and Itard set out to civilize the boy, to teach him to speak and to learn. Five years of work with the boy, whom Itard named Victor, led to the conclusion that his pupil was mentally retarded. Victor learned to read and write many words and could even exchange simple written communications with others, but he never learned to speak. He became socialized to some degree; he could, for example, dine in a restaurant with his tutor. The experiment ended unhappily when, with the onset of puberty, Victor changed from a gentle boy into a rebellious youth. Itard abandoned his work with the boy, and Victor lived in custodial care until his death at the age of about 40.

Itard's work was not in vain, however. He demonstrated that mentally retarded individuals could be trained in both cognitive and social skills and he provided essential groundwork for the development of the first educational programs for mentally retarded children by Edouard Seguin and others.

This entry was informed by the following references.

REFERENCES

Itard, J. M. G. (1932). *The wild boy of Aveyron.* New York, NY: Appleton-Century-Crofts.

Kanner, L. (1960). Itard, Seguin, Howe—Three pioneers in the education of retarded children. *American Journal of Mental Deficiency, 65,* 2–10.

Lane, H. (1976). *The wild boy of Aveyron.* Cambridge, MA: Harvard Press.

PAUL IRVINE
Katonah, New York

ITINERANT SERVICES

Itinerant services are shared, mobile, or traveling resource programs. This program model is most practical in areas that have limited funds for full-time services in each school or that do not have enough eligible children to warrant a full-time teacher. In addition to serving schools, itinerant services can provide instruction in the hospital or home to recuperating and chronically ill children by establishing a curriculum and offering teaching services.

Visual impairment was one of the first areas to demonstrate that itinerant instruction on a resource basis could be used in conjunction with a regular school program. Only a few decades ago, according to Reynolds and Birch (1977), it was common in many states to have blind and partially sighted students automatically referred and placed in residential schools. It has now become the prevailing practice in a great many school districts to start visually impaired children in regular school programs and to maintain them there by delivering the special instruction they need in that environment or nearby resource rooms. In many states, there are more legally blind children being educated in regular classes as a result of itinerant service programs than are being educated in special schools or classes for the blind (Deighton, 1971). Although itinerant services as a derivative of the resource room have been used primarily with visually impaired children, this program model is being employed with hearing impaired, emotionally disturbed, learning-disabled, and gifted children.

A comparative study, designed by Pepe (1973), concerned the effectiveness of itinerant services and resource room programs serving children with learning disabilities. Each group consisted of 20 students identified as learning disabled, of average ability, and 9 to 12 years of age. There was no significant difference in the treatment effect gains of students, indicating that the itinerant and resource room programs were equally effective in providing services for mildly learning-disabled children. Since there was no significant difference in gains made by students of comparable ability who were afforded less time by the special education teachers, the itinerant programs appeared to be more efficient. Similar results were obtained by Sabatino (1971).

Difficulties in operating itinerant services are described by Wiederholt, Hammill, and Brown (1978). First, teachers must carry their materials from school to school. Second, they frequently must work in the furnace room, in the lunchroom, or in the principal's or counselor's office, and may even share a room with other staff. Third, they are rarely able to provide instruction on a daily basis. Fourth, they may serve several schools, which makes it difficult for them to develop social and professional bonds.

An advantage of itinerant services is flexible scheduling, allowing the student's instructional program to be altered to meet changing needs. Because large numbers of young children with developing problems can be accommodated less expensively, later severe disorders may be prevented, making room for the disabled students for whom self-contained classes were originally developed. Through itinerant services, most students can receive help in their neighborhood schools; thus, the necessity of busing disabled children is reduced. Finally, in contrast to the self-contained special class program, children start the day in an integrated program with their age mates and become special for specific services. The itinerant service setting helps avoid the stigma of the special class.

REFERENCES

Deighton, L. C. (1971). *The encyclopedia of education* (Vol. 4). New York, NY: Macmillan.

Pepe, H. J. (1973). A comparison of the effectiveness of itinerant and resource room model programs designed to serve children with learning disabilities (Doctoral dissertation, University of Kansas, 1973). *Dissertation Abstracts, 34,* 7612A.

Reynolds, M. C., & Birch, J. W. (1977). *Teaching exceptional children in all America's schools.* Reston, VA: Council for Exceptional Children.

Sabatino, D. A. (1971). An evaluation of resource rooms for children with learning disabilities. *Journal of Learning Disabilities, 4,* 341.

Wiederholt, J. L., Hammill, D. D., & Brown, V. (1978). *The resource teacher.* Boston, MA: Allyn & Bacon.

WARNER H. BRITTON
Auburn University

See also Homebound Instruction; Itinerant Teacher; Resource Room

ITINERANT TEACHER

An itinerant teacher has received specialized training in a particular category and provides services to homebound students, or students in hospital programs. The itinerant teacher may also travel between schools within a district, or between districts. The service rendered supplements the instruction provided by the student's classroom teacher. Although teaching is the major responsibility of itinerant teachers, they are involved in related activities such as procuring special materials, conferring with parents, assessing students, or participating in case conferences (Dejnozka & Kapel, 1982). According to Wiederholt, Hammill, and Brown (1978), itinerant teachers must also be able to manage daily details, such as scheduling and grading. In addition, they must possess considerable knowledge of many specific school-related abilities, including reading, spelling, writing, arithmetic, spoken language, and classroom behavior.

The use of itinerant teachers has developed particularly in the field of speech and hearing impairments, where only small group or individual instruction will work. In the past few years, itinerant teachers have been employed to serve learning-disabled, emotionally disturbed, and gifted students.

Disadvantages, reported by Ellis and Mathews (1982), indicate that itinerant teachers have larger caseloads than special education teachers with a self-contained classroom, which usually has an established teacher pupil ratio prescribed by state law. The larger caseload often prevents the itinerant teacher from becoming completely familiar with the child. According to Cohen (1982), the role of the itinerant teacher has several drawbacks. For example, itinerant teachers rarely become accepted as a part of a school faculty because they are divided between schools. They are available only on a limited basis, creating problems in scheduling. Because of their itinerant schedules, these teachers are sometimes perceived to be inaccessible both by classroom teachers and parents. Itinerant teachers confess that at times their instructional roles seem dictated by schedule rather than by choice. In addition, the physical burden of transporting materials between resource rooms, the sharing of locations with other staff, and the general feeling of isolation can make itinerant teachers question their contribution to a school's program.

Advantages to employing an itinerant teacher occur when the teacher serves as an in-school consultant based on broad experience with many children exhibiting different educational and behavioral problems. More children can be served by itinerant teachers working extensively with classroom teachers through indirect services to students with mild problems. Another important advantage, according to Deighton (1971), is the effect of changing the attitude of the classroom teacher in dealing with the special student. As the classroom teacher becomes more skillful in meeting the needs of the special child, the itinerant teacher can become involved in the more severe cases that require direct services.

REFERENCES

Cohen, J. H. (1982). *Handbook of resource room teaching*. New York, NY: Aspen.

Deighton, L. C. (1971). *The encyclopedia of education* (Vol. 4). New York, NY: Macmillan.

Dejnozka, E. L., & Kapel, D. E. (1982). *American educators' encyclopedia*. Westport, CT: Greenwood.

Ellis, J. R., & Mathews, G. J. (1982). *Professional role performance difficulties of first-year itinerant specialists*. Northern Illinois University, Educational Resources Information Center.

Wiederholt, J. L., & Hammill, D. D., & Brown, V. (1978). *The resource teacher*. Boston, MA: Allyn & Bacon.

WARNER H. BRITTON
Auburn University

See also **Homebound Instruction; Itinerant Services; Resource Teacher**

ITO'S HYPOMELANOSIS

Hypomelanosis of Ito (HMI) is a rare skin condition characterized by hypopigmentation (unusual lack of skin color) caused by lack of melanin. Hypopigmentation may appear on any area of the body except the palms of the hands, the soles of the feet, and the scalp. Numerous other congenital defects may be present including neurological, skeletal, hair, and dental abnormalities. Causes of HMI elude researchers, but theories point to a chromosomal mosaicism (an occurrence in an individual of two or more cell populations of different chromosomal constitutions derived from a single zygote). Sporadic mutations also may occur. Intellectual and adaptive deficits are usually present.

HMI is usually diagnosed in childhood, and genetic links have been noted with no consensus on an exact locus. HMI occurs 1.5 to 2.5 times more often in females than in males.

Characteristics

1. Hypopigmentation of the skin occurs in patches, whirls, or streaks.
2. Often the child presents with seizures, dental abnormalities such as extra cuspids or incisors, deafness, and megaloencephaly (enlargement of the brain).
3. Visual problems including cataracts, a cleft along the edge of the iris of the eye, nearsightedness, and crossed eyes may be present.

4. Varying degrees of mental retardation are evident in children, as are developmental delays.

5. Affected individuals do not have the ability to sweat in the areas of hypopigmentation.

A team of specialized health care professionals is usually required to work with these children. For example, dentists are required to address dental anomalies. Orthopedists and ophthalmologists are required to assist patients with orthopedic and visual abnormalities. Psychologist are usually necessary to address cognitive limitations.

No treatment exists for the hypopigmentation, and some patients may wish to use makeup to conceal the affected areas. Medications to control seizures are usually necessary.

Affected children need special education services, and these services vary by degree of impairment, thereby making appropriate assessment vital. Children affected by HMI likely qualify for special education services as Other Health Impairment with behavior problems and speech and language delays associated with mental retardation. Occupational therapy may also be needed.

Prognosis is highly dependent on the severity of the disorders associated with HMI and is excellent for patients presenting with only cutaneous manifestations of HMI. Morbidity rates increase with the number of associated defects and complications. Anticonvulsant drugs are an area of research interest as well as research on birth defect causality and etiology.

This entry has been informed by the sources listed below.

REFERENCES

Donnai, D., Read, A. P., & Mckeown, C. (1988). Hypomelanosis of Ito: Manifestation of mosaicism or chimerism. *Journal of Medical Genetics, 25*, 809–818.

Glover, M. T., Brett, E. M., & Atherton, D. J. (1989). Hypomelanosis of Ito: Spectrum of the disease. *Journal of Pediatrics, 115*, 75–80.

Gross, N., & Ratz, J. (2000). Hypomelanosis of Ito. *eMedicine, 1*(5). Retrieved from http://emedicine.medscape.com/

Pascual-Castroviejo, I., Roche, C., & Martinez-Bermejo, A. (1998). Hypomelanosis of Ito: A study of 76 infantile cases. *Brain Development, 20*(1), 36–43.

KIMBERLY M. ESTEP
University of Houston–Clear Lake

J

JACTATIO CAPITIS

Prior to puberty, it is common for children, especially during the preschool years, to engage in rhythmic body movements and rhythmic vocalizations. Some is inconsequential beyond being annoying to adults (e.g., body rocking or incessant humming). Some will engage in more serious forms of rhythmic behavior that may include head banging. Zappert was the first to use the term "jactatio capitis nocturna," in 1905 (Gourineni, 1995), a synonymous term for head banging. All of such behaviors are subsumed under the term Jactatio Capitis (JC), with the additional modifier of "nocturna" in those cases where the behavior occurs only at night (Gillberg, 1995).

About 10% of otherwise normal children will display behavior that is consistent with JC; however, a disproportionate percentage of these children go on to develop diagnoses of disorders of attention and motor control (Gillberg, 1995). The male-to-female ratio of JC is estimated to be 3:1. It is suspected to be an inheritable disorder, but its true etiology and pathogenesis are not known. In most cases no intervention beyond reassurance of the parents and the child will be required, as the disorder is most commonly benign. There is no special treatment beyond behavioral interventions when the symptoms may be injurious to the child. Outcome is excellent in those cases that do not progress to motoric and attentional deficiencies, with most cases being entirely asymptomatic by adulthood with no intervention.

REFERENCE

Gillberg, C. (1995). *Clinical child neuropsychiatry*. Cambridge, England: Cambridge University Press.

Gourineni, R. (1995, August 16.) *Sleep-related rhythmic movement disorders. Clinical summary*. MedLink Neurology. Retrieved from www.medlink.com/medlinkcontent.asp

Zappert, J. (1905). Uber nactliche Kopfbewegungen bei kindern (jactatio capitis nocturna). *Jahrbuch fuer Kinderheilkunde, 62*, 70–83.

CECIL R. REYNOLDS
Texas A&M University

JAPAN, SPECIAL EDUCATION IN

Special Education Within the Formal Education System

In Japan, the compulsory education system consists of 6 years of primary school education followed by 3 years of junior high school education. Children start their compulsory education at the age of 6 and finish it at 15.

School education that is provided for mentally and physically challenged children, in accordance with the type and extent of their disability and their aptitude, is called *tokushu kyoiku*, or special education. This aims to help develop children's potentials and to broaden their abilities.

Unlike the United States and some countries in Europe, Japan does not include vocational training, professional education, or the education of gifted children under the label of special education. Subsequently, in recent years, *tokushu kyoiku* has been more often referred to as *shogaiji kyoiku*, or the education of children with physical and/or intellectual disabilities. For the purpose of this paper, the author uses the English term "special education" to describe Japan's formal school education for children with physical and/or intellectual disabilities.

System of Special Education

The special education provided for disabled children of school age is given according to the type and extent of their disability. The definition of disability includes visual and hearing impairment, intellectual development disability, physical disability, infirmity/invalidism, and emotional disturbance. Within the school education system, there are special schools, special classes offered by ordinary primary schools and junior high schools, and *tsukyu*, or resource rooms.

The special schools include schools for the visually impaired, schools for the hearing impaired, and schools for mentally and physically disabled children (including children with mental deficiency and children with a weak constitution). These schools cater to relatively seriously disabled children. Some special schools have a kindergarten and a senior high school. For those children who have difficulty commuting to school because of the severity of their impediments, teachers visit the children at their home, hospital, or other institution.

The special classes cater to children with relatively mild disabilities. The children are given special education suitable to their individual needs, considering the type and extent of their disability—mental deficiency, physical disability, weak constitution, weak sight, difficulty in hearing, speech impediment, or emotional disturbance. The law provides for ordinary senior high schools to open special classes, but in reality, none offer them.

Tsu-kyu literally means attending class. In the current special education system, it is a form of guidance offered in special classrooms (resource rooms) to school children with weak eyes, difficulty in hearing, a speech impediment, or emotional disturbances. These children attend classes in ordinary schools; however, in addition, they may receive a specialist's guidance appropriate to their individual needs.

Incidentally, the use of the Japanese term *seishin haku-jaku* (mental deficiency) was banned on April 1, 1999. It was replaced by *chiteki shogai* (intellectual disability). Therefore, the school or class for children with mental deficiency will be called the school or class for children with intellectual disability.

History of Special Education

The first provisions regarding special education were made in 1872, when the modern system of formal education in Japan was inaugurated. In 1878, a school for the visually impaired and the hearing impaired came into being in Kyoto. In 1923, a legal obligation was laid on each prefecture to establish schools for the visually impaired and schools for the hearing impaired.

For children with intellectual developmental disabilities, a private school known as Takinogawa Gakuen was opened in Tokyo in 1891. During the 1920s, special classes for those with intellectual development disabilities were introduced in Tokyo and in many other parts of Japan. Classes for children who stuttered, were weak-sighted, or were hard-of-hearing were also opened one after another. In 1941, immediately before the outbreak of the Pacific War, the National Elementary School decree was instituted. Education for disabled children, in addition to the establishment of schools for the visually impaired and hearing impaired, was incorporated into the nation's school education system. However, because of the war, no progress was made in the area of special education.

After World War II

In the aftermath of World War II, drastic educational reform was introduced. In 1947, the School Education Law was enacted based on the spirit of the new Constitution and the Fundamental Law of Education. Chapter VI, "Special Education" (Articles 77–76), presented the outline of special education. At this time, various forms of education for physically and/or mentally disabled children of school age were put together and termed special education. Thus, special education took its place legally as part of the compulsory education system for the first time in the educational history of Japan.

The law provided for the establishment of special schools, which were classified into three divisions—schools for the visually impaired (*mo gakko*), schools for the hearing impaired (*ro gakko*), and schools for physically and/or mentally disabled children (*yogo gakko*). The extent of children's handicaps was also defined by law, providing a standard teachers could use regarding special education.

Compulsory education at schools for the visually impaired and schools for the hearing impaired was introduced in 1948. However, plans for building schools for physically and/or mentally disabled children across the nation made little progress. It was not until 1979 that compulsory education was instituted at these schools. All special schools introduced compulsory education into their syllabus. The home visit system, which had already been put into practice, formally took its place as one method of instruction offered by the schools for physically and/or mentally disabled children.

Children who were expected to attend special classes were divided according to the type of disability—intellectual disability, physical disability, physical weakness, amblyopia (weak sight), impaired hearing, speech impediment, and emotional disturbance. In 1993, the system of *tsu kyu* was inaugurated, under which disabled children enrolled in ordinary schools could receive lessons in special classrooms (resource rooms).

Numbers of Schools and Children Receiving Special Education

As of May 1996, children receiving special education accounted for 1.067% of all children of school age from 6 to 15 years. This percentage is low when compared with figures in the United States and other developed nations in Europe. The rate of attendance at special schools was 0.39% of all school-aged children.

Schools for intellectually disabled children numbered 511 with a total enrollment of 52,102. Special classes for intellectually disabled children numbered 15,511 at primary schools and 7,260 at junior high schools. These special classes were attended by 44,061 primary school pupils and 22,101 junior high school students.

There were 19,424 primary school children and 582 junior high school students who received special lessons at resource rooms under the *tsu-kyu* system. Their cases were broken down by the type of impediment: speech impediment, 83%; emotional disturbance, 10%; and impaired hearing, 6%.

Curriculum

The law stipulates that special schools must offer, in principle, the same education as ordinary schools. To help improve and overcome physical and mental disabilities, special courses in such subjects as therapeutic training and exercises are provided. The objective of each lesson and the curriculum at schools for mentally disabled children are not bound by the government guidelines for teaching. The curriculum can be organized in a flexible manner in accordance with the needs of the children.

The curriculum for special classes is organized on the basis of teaching guidelines set by the Ministry of Education. However, special curriculums can be drawn up to suit any child's individual needs.

The course of study for disabled children who receive lessons in resource rooms under the *tsu-kyu* system includes therapeutic training classes, in addition to ordinary subjects, aimed at encouraging them to improve and to overcome their disabilities.

Standard for Class Organization

Classes at special schools for disabled children and special classes at ordinary schools are small. This is to meet the educational needs of all of the children. The maximum number of children per class is six for special schools and eight for special classes. However, a check of the 1996 statistics reveals that the average number of children per class is three at both special schools and special classes.

Textbooks

In addition to the textbooks compiled by the Ministry of Education for the purpose of special education, the textbooks used in ordinary primary and junior high schools are also used in special schools. The textbooks made by the Ministry of Education include braille books for the visually impaired, speech and music texts for the hearing impaired, and Japanese, math, and music texts for the intellectually disabled.

In case the textbooks authorized by the Ministry of Education are unsuitable for use in special classes, books placed on the market can be used as textbooks if approved by the Board of Education.

Home Visit System and Interaction With Other People

A survey of 970 special schools in 1998 showed that the system of home visits was practiced by 403 schools—one school for the visually impaired, 115 schools for physically disabled children, 239 schools for mentally disabled children, and 48 schools for sickly children.

Special school children sometimes have the opportunity to get together with their peers at ordinary primary and junior high schools. Children in special classes also sometimes mix with children in ordinary classes to do schoolwork or engage in other activities together. Disabled children also have opportunities to participate in events organized by neighborhood associations.

These opportunities are helpful not only in enriching the experience and social life of the disabled and building their characters, but also by increasing society's understanding of disabled children as well as special education.

Counseling on Education and Schooling

Counseling to parents on education prior to enrollment at school is given by the Board of Education. This counseling before school age is helpful to the parents who have physically and mentally disabled children. Counselors are able to give pertinent advice on the care of disabled children in their infancy, alleviating anxiety experienced by the parents about their children's upbringings, in addition to advice on the right course of education. The Board of Education decides whether special education should be taken, with the parents' opinions always held in high regard.

Advice About What to Do After Graduation

Most of the special school and special class children who completed their compulsory education in March 1996 went on to tertiary education—96.9% of the graduates from the schools for the visually impaired, 98.5% of those from the schools for the hearing impaired, 84.9% of those for mentally and physically handicapped, and 73.8% of those at special classes in junior high schools. Although recently the number of graduates from special schools for the intellectually disabled has been decreasing, the percentage of those who go on to the next stage of education has been increasing. The ratio was 56% in 1984 and it rose to 83% in 1996. After graduation from special schools, 43.7% of graduates from the schools for the visually impaired and 43.4% of those from the schools for the hearing impaired went on to special training courses attached to the school or university. Meanwhile, the rate of employment was 21.9% for graduates from the schools for the visually impaired and 35.9% for those from the schools for the hearing impaired.

Most graduates from the senior classes of special schools for the physically and mentally disabled entered social welfare facilities: 63% for the schools for the intellectually disabled, 78.9% for the schools for the physically disabled, and 55.5% for the schools for the physically weak children. The employment rates were 34.4%, 12.1%, and 16.8%, respectively. It has become increasingly difficult for the intellectually disabled to find employment since 1990 because of the long-term business depression in Japan.

Teachers and Teacher Training Program

In addition to the standard teaching certification, teachers at special schools for the visually impaired, hearing impaired, and physically and/or mentally disabled are required to obtain extra certification. Instructors of acupuncture at the schools for the visually impaired have to possess an acupuncturist's license and instructors of haircutting must have a barber's license. Because of the nature of the profession, it is compulsory for teachers at special schools to undergo special vocational training on a regular basis. In special classes and resource rooms, teachers can work only if they have the standard teaching certification.

National Expenditure for Special Education and Subsidies

The fiscal 1997 national budget showed that a total of ¥30,480 million was appropriated for special education, of which the largest ¥15.7 billion was allocated for compulsory education at schools for the visually impaired, hearing impaired, and physically and/or mentally disabled. The next largest expenditure was ¥6.07 billion for financial assistance for encouragement of special school attendance.

Problems to Be Addressed and the Future of Special Education in Japan

Japan's special education system has long kept physically and/or mentally disabled children separated from their peers in ordinary schools. However, the trend in society today is toward the creation of equal opportunities for children, disabled or otherwise, to participate in social activities. In view of this steps are being taken in Japan to promote an educational system in which children with physical and/or mental disabilities receive the same education as children without such disabilities.

A real problem is that uniform education still prevails in some schools where the needs of the individual and the characteristics of disabilities are disregarded. Few plans, if any, of individual guidance have been implemented. Most plans scarcely reflect parental wishes, because of inadequate teacher-parent relationships. Another problem is that there are few teachers who are able to devise plans for individual guidance and carry them out.

After compulsory education is complete, most students now, instead of getting jobs, go on to a higher stage of education. This means that it will be at least three additional years before they go out into the world and become productive members of society. Consequently, the urgent need has arisen to examine educational programs during this transient period.

Furthermore, for the disabled to lead productive lives, it would be necessary to establish a regional system to support them and invite them to the open school for youth and to special classes for adult education.

This entry has been informed by the sources listed below.

REFERENCES

Ministry of Education, Science, Sports and Culture. (1997). *To encourage zest for living: Special education in Japan*. Tokyo, Japan: Author.

Ministry of Education, Science, Sports and Culture. (1994). *Japanese government policies in education, science and culture*. Tokyo, Japan: Author.

The Japan League for the Mentally Retarded. (1996). *Rehabilitation services for people with mentally retardation in Japan*. Tokyo, Japan: Author

CATHERINE HALL RIHKYE
Hunter College,
City University of New York
First edition

MASATAKA OHTA
NAOJI SHIMIZU
Tokyo Gakujei University
Second edition

See also China, Special Education In; Hong Kong, Special Education In

JARGON APHASIA

Jargon aphasia refers to an expressive language deficit in which a dysphasic individual produces a profusion of unintelligible utterances. Language structure may be retained, but meaning is unclear. Intonation, rhythm, and stress patterns are normal. Speech is fluent with few if any of the hesitations or pauses characteristic of some other dysphasic speech patterns. Bizarre responses, often consisting of clichés, stock phrases, neologisms, and unusual word combination patterns are produced. Speakers seem unaware that their utterances are not meaningful, and receptive language is impaired.

Although meaningless to the listener, Eisenson (1973) feels that jargon may not be so to the speaker. Analysis of a patient's jargon speech revealed some regular sound and morpheme substitutions, confirming Eisenson's impression that some underlying meaning may exist. Eisenson considers jargon aphasia to be a transitory condition rather than a true aphasic condition.

REFERENCE

Eisenson, J. (1973). *Adult aphasia: Assessment and treatment.* New York, NY: Appleton-Century-Crofts.

K. Sandra Vanta
Cleveland Public Schools
Cleveland, Ohio,

See also Aphasia; Communication Disorders; Developmental Aphasia;
Dysphasia; Language Disorders

ARTHUR R. JENSEN (1923–   )

Arthur Jensen has been on the faculty of the University of California at Berkeley since 1958, and in 1994 he became professor emeritus of educational psychology. A graduate of Berkeley and Columbia University, he served his internship in clinical psychology at the University of Maryland Psychiatric Institute and was a postdoctoral research fellow at the Institute of Psychiatry at the University of London, where he studied with and was strongly influenced by Hans J. Eysenck.

Jensen turned to the study of differential psychology after a decade of research on classical problems in verbal learning. In 1969 he argued that genetic, as well as environmental and cultural, factors should be considered for understanding not only individual differences, but also social class and racial differences in intelligence and scholastic performance (Jensen, 1969). This hypothesis, that both individual and racial differences in abilities are in part a product of the evolutionary process and have a genetic basis, created a storm of protest from scientists and educators. The subject is still a sensitive one and has been explicated by Jensen in several books such as *Educability and Group Differences* (1973), *Bias in Mental Testing* (1980), and *Straight Talk about Mental Tests* (1981). The controversy has also led him to two other areas of research: the study of culture bias in psychometric tests and the investigation of the nature of *g* (the general intelligence factor).

Jensen presently views the *g* factor as (a) reflecting some property or processes of the human brain manifest in many forms of adaptive behavior in which individuals (and probably populations) differ; (b) increasing from birth to maturity and declining in old age; (c) showing physiological as well as behavioral correlates; (d) having a hereditary component; (e) being subject to natural selection in the course of human evolution; and (f) having important educational, occupational, economic, and social correlates in all industrialized societies. Jensen's theories and prolific empirical research on the nature of human mental ability are comprehensively explicated in his latest major works, *The g Factor* (Jensen, 1998), and "Thirty Years of Research on Black-White Differences in Cognitive Ability" (Rushton & Jensen, 2005).

Author of over 400 publications, Jensen has been a Guggenheim fellow (1964–1965), a fellow of the Center for Advanced Study in the Behavioral Sciences (1966–1967), and a research fellow at the National Institute of Mental Health (1957–1958).

REFERENCES

Jensen, A. R. (1969). How much can we boost IQ and scholastic achievement? *Harvard Educational Review, 39,* 1–123.

Jensen, A. R. (1973). *Educability and group differences.* New York, NY: Harper & Row.

Jensen, A. R. (1980). *Bias in mental testing.* New York, NY: Free Press.

Jensen, A. R. (1981). *Straight talk about mental tests.* New York, NY: Free Press.

Jensen, A. R. (1998). *The g factor.* Westport, CT: Praeger.

Rushton, J. P., & Jensen, A. R. (2005). Thirty years of research on black-white differences in cognitive ability. *Psychology, Public Policy, and Law, 11,* 235–294.

Elaine Fletcher-Janzen
Chicago School of Professional Psychology
First edition

Tamara J. Martin
The University of Texas of the Permian Basin
Second edition

See also Cultural Bias in Tests; *g* Factor Theory

J.E.V.S. HUMAN SERVICES

The J.E.V.S. evaluation was developed by the Jewish Employment Vocational Service in Philadelphia (Vocational Research Institute, 1973), Pennsylvania, during the 1960s. An evaluation of the capabilities of a client is completed through a comprehensive evaluation of a person's employability skills. Initial stages of the evaluation begin with simple work samples, which gradually advance to more complex skills.

The J.E.V.S. Human Services work to improve the chance of employability through increasing independence and the quality of life provided through a spectrum of services. With over 1,000 employees and more than 20 programs, J.E.V.S. Human Services provide programs to improve job readiness skills of individuals with disabilities, those facing hardships from unemployment, and at-risk adolescents. Providing direct service along with policy development for persons struggling to find employment is a perspective of JEVS founded on the Jewish principles of social justice and repairing the world. For more information on services provided by JEVS, please visit: http://www.jevshumanservices.org/index.html

This entry has been informed by the sources listed below.

REFERENCES

Vocational Research Institute. (1973). *Work sample evaluator's handbook*. Philadelphia, PA: Jewish Employment and Vocational Services.

Jewish Employment Vocational Service. (2012). *About JEVS Human Services*. Retrieved from http://www.jevshuman services.org/learnmore/learnmore.html

PAUL C. RICHARDSON
Elwyn Institutes

See also Vocational Evaluation

JOB ACCOMMODATION NETWORK

The U.S. Department of Labor, Office of Disability Employment Policy, provides assistance to individuals with disabilities via the Job Accommodation Network (JAN). JAN is a collaboration of resources, information, and referral service on job accommodations for people with disabilities, on the employment provisions of the Americans with Disabilities Act, and on resources for technical assistance, funding, education, and services related to the employment of people with disabilities. In addition, JAN analyzes trends and statistical data related to the technical assistance it provides. JAN can be accessed by phone or TTY at 1-800-526-7234 or 1-800-ADA-WORK (1-800-232-9675) or via its website at http://askjan.org/

STAFF

JOB SYNDROME

The National Organization for Rare Disorders (NORD, 1999) states that Job syndrome (JS) is a congenital immunodeficiency disorder that is characterized by recurrent bacterial (staphylococcal) infections that focus primarily on the skin. JS is a very rare disorder that affects an equal number of males and females. Symptoms of JS are present at birth or early childhood. JS causes extremely elevated immunoglobulin E (IgE) levels. Job syndrome is also known as HIE syndrome, hyper-IgE syndrome, hyperimmunoglobulin E syndrome, hyperimmunoglobulin E staphylococcal, and Job-Buckley syndrome (NORD, 1999). Eppinger, Greenberger, White, Brown, and Cunningham-Rundles (1999) report that patients with JS have increased susceptibility of catching bacterial and fungal infections. The staphylococcal infection is the most common infection to attack patients with JS and may involve the skin, lungs, joints, and other sites. More rarely, a patient with JS will develop a potentially deadly Aspergillus species infection (Eppinger et al., 1999). NORD (1999) reported that JS, like other immune disorders, may impair the white blood cells (neutrophils) that destroy bacteria, cell debris, and solid particles in the blood. Job syndrome can be inherited through an autosomal dominant trait. This means that in order for a child to inherit JS, both parents must be carriers and have one normal gene and one recessive gene for JS. There is a 25% chance that a child of two carriers will receive a JS gene from both parents. A child of this couple would have a 50% chance of being a genetic carrier of JS and a 25% chance of receiving both normal genes (NORD, 1999). The minimum criteria for a diagnosis of JS can be made on the basis of the presence of elevated IgE levels, a history of staphylococcal pulmonary infections, and the presence of an eczematous skin rash (Eppinger et al., 1999).

Characteristics

1. Cold staphylococcal abscesses, which are pus-filled holes caused by bacterial infection. These abscesses are usually found on the skin but may also present on the mastoid bone behind the ear, joints, gums, bronchi (air passages in the lungs), and in the lungs.

2. Granulocyte chemotactic defect, a problem experienced by patients with JS, in which the leukocytes (the living substance of white blood cells) are unable to protectively destroy bacteria, fungi, and viruses, thereby allowing bacteria to thrive.

3. Chronic eczema, a swelling of the outer skin surface with the presence of itchy, small red blisters that become thick, scaly, and crusted.

4. Hyperimmunoglobulinemia E, a condition in which there is an excess of immunoglobulin E, one of the five fluid antibodies the human body produces, which reacts with foreign substances by releasing

chemicals that redden the skin. This antibody is concentrated in the lungs, skin, and mucous membrane cells.

5. Mild eosinophilia, a mild increase in the number of leukocyte white blood cells (eosinophils), which increase when infection or allergies are present in the body.

Symptoms of JS are most effectively treated with continuous oral antibiotic prophylaxis, which serves to reduce infections from chronically recurring (Eppinger et al., 1999). Although antibiotic treatment (usually trimethoprim or sulfamethoxazole) is usually effective, patients generally experience repeated infections (NORD, 1999). NORD (1999) suggested that patients with JS and their families may be referred to genetic counseling, and other treatments may include providing relief from symptoms and a possible mental health referral for supportive therapy if needed.

In the classroom, teachers need to be aware that students with JS experience repeated health problems and may need to miss school at times. Teachers should also be aware that the student may have difficulty with peer teasing and may have self-esteem issues. In order to work with these issues, teachers can be helpful to JS students by providing make-up work or extra homework assignments as well as tutoring sessions in order to prevent a student with JS from falling behind their classmates. In addition, a teacher may want to contact the parent or refer the student to the school counselor in order to help the student deal with emotional conflicts that may result from his or her condition.

JS is a chronic disorder that usually can be managed successfully by prophylactic medication (Eppinger et al., 1999).

However, an individual with JS may be susceptible to uncommon diseases, such as aspergillus fumigatus infections, which may become deadly. Future research could focus on understanding the link between JS and granulocyte dysfunction, which leads to a possible diagnosis of aspergillus fumigatus, which has a high morbidity rate (Eppinger et al., 1999). NORD (1999) stated that the long-term safety and effectiveness of the treatment of interferon gamma for JS patients, which is designed to ameliorate excessive immunoglobulin E production, is currently being explored.

REFERENCES

Eppinger, T. M., Greenberger, P. A., White, D. A., Brown, A. E., & Cunningham-Rundles, C. (1999). Sensitization to Aspergillus species in the congenital neutrophil disorders chronic granulomatous disease and hyper-Ige syndrome. *Journal of Allergy and Clinical Immunology, 104,* 1265–1272.

National Organization for Rare Disorders. (1999). *Job syndrome.* Retrieved from http://www.rarediseases.org

JENNIE KAUFMAN SINGER
California Department of Corrections,
Region 1 Parole Outpatient Clinic
Sacramento, California

JOHANSON-BLIZZARD SYNDROME

Johanson-Blizzard syndrome is a disorder characterized by a thin, beaklike nose due to abnormalities in nostril development; coarse, thin scalp hair that grows in a distinctive upsweeping pattern; and abnormal development and functioning of the pancreas that results in a failure to grow and gain weight as expected. Approximately 60% of individuals with the disorder have a moderate developmental delay. Others may have a mild delay or normal intelligence (Moeschler & Lubinsky, 1985; National Organization for Rare Disorders [NORD], 1998). The range and severity of symptoms varies widely from case to case (Hurst & Baraitser, 1989; NORD, 1998).

Johanson-Blizzard syndrome is extremely rare, with only 22 (Hurst & Baraitser, 1989) to 26 (Gershoni-Baruch et al., 1990) reported cases. It is a genetic disorder with an autosomal recessive inheritance that is present at birth (NORD, 1998).

Characteristics

1. Thin, beak-shaped nose with absent or underdeveloped nostrils; other facial anomalies (NORD, 1998)
2. Dry, patchy scalp hair with an upsweep at the forehead (Hurst & Baraitser, 1989)
3. Pancreatic defect; malabsorption of fats and nutrients caused by enzyme deficiencies
4. Microcephaly
5. Failure to thrive; short stature
6. Developmental delay
7. Dental abnormalities including malformed primary teeth and absent permanent teeth
8. Anorectal, genitourinary, and cardiac malformations

Treatment of individuals with Johanson-Blizzard syndrome has focused on treating the pancreatic defect. Success rates have varied (Hurst & Baraister, 1989).

Children with Johanson-Blizzard syndrome may require special education services for physical weakness and psychomotor retardation, speech and hearing impairments, and medical needs. Speech and language therapy and physical and occupational therapy may be necessary. Additionally, many require placement in an educational environment that is appropriate for individuals with developmental delays. Students with the disorder may also need home-based schooling or home visits from a teacher because medical difficulties often require them to be absent from the classroom.

The prognosis for individuals with this disorder is poor. Infections and complications from malabsorption and failure to thrive often develop and lead to death in childhood (Hurst & Baraister, 1989). The focus of current and future research is on continued symptom identification and treatment.

REFERENCES

Gershoni-Baruch, R., Lerner, A., Braun, J., Katzir, Y., Iancu, T. C., & Benderly, A. (1990). Johanson-Blizzard syndrome: Clinical spectrum and further delineation of the syndrome. *American Journal of Medical Genetics, 35,* 546–551.

Hurst, J. A., & Baraitser, M. (1989). Johanson-Blizzard syndrome. *Journal of Medical Genetics, 26,* 45–48.

Moeschler, J. B., & Lubinsky, M. S. (1985). Brief clinical report: Johanson-Blizzard syndrome with normal intelligence. *American Journal of Medical Genetics, 22,* 69–73.

National Organization for Rare Disorders. (1998). *Johanson-Blizzard syndrome.* Retrieved from http://www.rarediseases .org

STACEY L. BATES
University of Texas at Austin

JOHNSON, DORIS (1932–)

Doris Johnson obtained her BA (1953) in speech pathology from Augustana College and went on to earn her MA (1955) in speech and language pathology and PhD (1971) in counselor education from Northwestern University. She is currently the Jo Ann and Peter Dolle Professor of Learning Disabilities at Northwestern University. Her work at Northwestern has included training learning disability specialists and extensive research at the Center for Learning Disabilities.

Johnson's primary area of interest has focused on relationships among oral language, written language, reading,

and mathematics. Her work with Helmer Myklebust called attention to the significance of language disorders in learning disabilities, describing a specific disabilities model that showed that certain abilities are required for normal language development and noting that such abilities can be measured and deficits remediated (Johnson & Myklebust, 1967).

Johnson's current work includes the study of early writing development of normal and learning disabled children and the identification of co-occurring problems of adults with learning disabilities, including problems of comprehension, verbal disorders, and nonverbal learning. Her research has indicated that nonverbal disorders, including problems associated with social perception, problem solving, spatial orientation, and nonverbal communication, are often the most debilitating (Johnson, 1987, 1993, 1995; Johnson & Blalock, 1987).

Among her numerous awards, Johnson has received the Outstanding Service Award of the Association of Children with Learning Disabilities. Additionally, she has been an active member of many professional organizations, chairing the Professional Advisory Board of the Learning Disabilities Association and serving as executive director of the International Association for Research in Learning Disabilities for several years Johnson's (1967) publication with Myklebust, *Learning Disabilities: Educational Principles and Practices*, has been translated into four languages.

REFERENCES

Johnson, D. (1987, February). Nonverbal learning disabilities. *Pediatric Annals, 16,* 133–141.

Johnson, D. (1993). Relationships between oral and written language. *School Psychology Review, 22*(4), 595–609.

Johnson, D. (1995). An overview of learning disabilities: Psycho-educational perspectives. *Journal of Child Neurology, 10*(1), 2–5.

Johnson, D. J., & Blalock, J. (Eds.). (1987). *Adults with learning disabilities: Clinical studies.* Orlando, FL: Grune & Stratton.

Johnson, D. J., & Myklebust, H. R. (1967). *Learning disabilities: Educational principles and practices.* New York, NY: Grune & Stratton.

TAMARA J. MARTIN
*The University of Texas
of the Permian Basin*

JOHNSON, G. ORVILLE (1915–)

G. Orville Johnson was born in Cameron, Wisconsin, and attended the University of Wisconsin, Milwaukee (formerly Milwaukee State Teachers College), obtaining his BS degree in 1938. He later earned his EdM (1949) and EdD (1950) at the University of Illinois. In the years between his undergraduate and graduate studies, Johnson worked as a public school teacher in Sheboygan and Wawatosa, Wisconsin, and from 1946 to 1947 he was principal of the South Wisconsin Colony and Training School. During his distinguished career, he was associate professor of education and director of special education at the University of Denver, and also taught at the University of Syracuse, Ohio State University, and the University of South Florida at Tampa.

Johnson's research focused on the psychological characteristics of individuals with mental retardation and the effects of labeling. He proposed that the two basic classifications, behavioral and medical, are not mutually exclusive, with adequate descriptions of persons with mental retardation requiring the use of both categories.

He also advocated a behaviorally oriented, cognitive approach for teachers, counselors, and other professionals to use for management of individuals with behavior disorders. Using what he termed the coping style model, Johnson concluded that analysis of coping style was an essential element in the development of programs for these children, emphasizing removal of opportunities in the classroom to use coping styles common to children with emotional disorders and teaching more appropriate, adaptive styles (Boyd & Johnson, 1984). Johnson and Boyd (1984) also developed an assessment tool utilizing drawings of persons interacting in various settings for identification of individual coping styles.

Among his many contributions, Johnson served as associate editor of the professional publication *Exceptional Children*, and was a featured speaker at the 62nd Annual Convention of the Council for Exceptional Children (1984). His major works include *Education for the Slow Learner* (1963), *Education of Exceptional Children and Youth* (1975), and *Analysis of Coping Style: A Cognitive-Behavioral Approach to Behavior Management* (1981).

REFERENCES

Boyd, H. F., & Johnson, G. O. (1981). *Analysis of coping style: A cognitive-behavioral approach to behavior management.* Columbus, OH: Merrill.

Boyd, H. F., & Johnson, G. O. (1984, April). *The coping style approach to understanding and dealing with behavior disorders. I. Theory and definitions.* Paper presented at the meeting of the Council for Exceptional Children, Washington, DC.

Johnson, G. O. (1963). *Education for the slow learner.* Englewood Cliffs, NJ: Prentice Hall.

Johnson, G. O., & Boyd, H. F. (1984, April). *The coping style approach to understanding and dealing with behavior disorders. II. Assessment and intervention strategies.* Paper presented at the meeting of the Council for Exceptional Children, Washington, DC.

Johnson, G. O., & Cruickshank, W. A. (1975). *Education of exceptional children and youth.* Englewood Cliffs, NJ: Prentice Hall.

ELIZABETH JONES
Texas A&M University
First edition

TAMARA J. MARTIN
The University of Texas
    of the Permian Basin
Second edition

JOHNSTONE, EDWARD RANSOM (1870–1946)

Edward Ransom Johnstone began his career as a teacher and principal in the public schools of Cincinnati. He then served as a teacher in the Indiana School for Feeble Minded Youth, subsequently becoming principal there. In 1898 he moved to the Training School at Vineland, New Jersey, where he was employed as vice principal under the Reverend Stephen Olin Garrison, who had founded the school 10 years before. After Garrison's death in 1900, Johnstone was made superintendent. He became executive director in 1922, and director emeritus in 1944.

During Johnstone's years there, the Training School exerted tremendous influence on the education and training of mentally retarded children and adults, on the preparation of teachers of disabled children, and on educational testing. Johnstone founded a research laboratory with Henry H. Goddard as director. There numerous studies were conducted using data from the school's mentally retarded population. A summer school was conducted for teachers.

Johnstone inaugurated *The Training School Bulletin*, an influential journal in special education from its inception in 1904. Johnstone served on numerous boards and commissions and was elected to two terms as president of the American Association on Mental Deficiency.

REFERENCES

McCaffrey, K. R. (1965). Founders of the Training School at Vineland, New Jersey: S. Olin Garrison, Alexander Johnson, Edward R. Johnstone. Unpublished doctoral dissertation. Teachers College, Columbia University, New York.

The *Training School Bulletin* (1947, May), p. 44.

PAUL IRVINE
Katonah, New York

JOHNSTON INFORMAL READING INVENTORY

The Johnston Informal Reading Inventory (JIRI; Johnston, 1982) is an informal reading scale that assesses understanding of antonyms and synonyms, and silent reading comprehension skills. The test is designed for use for students in the seventh grade through adulthood. The test can be group administered or individually administered. Results of the JIRI may be used for diagnostic as well as placement purposes, according to the author.

Three types of tasks are used in the JIRI: word opposites, word synonyms, and graded narrative passages. The Word Opposites test results determine the level of the passages at which the examinee is to begin. The passages contain nine levels that progress from simple stories to more complex narratives. The examinees are asked a series of short-answer questions about the passages, which require written responses, assessing the main idea, detail, vocabulary, cause-effect, and inference. The role of the third test, Word Synonyms, is not clearly articulated by the author (Rogers, 1995).

Several problems have been noted on the JIRI. The scoring procedures lack clarity and sound empirical foundation (Rogers, 1995). The content of the JIRI is of questionable relevance to the contemporary audience, and the reliability and validity evidence is lacking altogether (Rogers, 1995; Wright, 1995). Wright (1995) notes that the JIRI is a time-efficient instrument for estimating a student's reading level; however, Rogers (1995) states that, in his opinion, other informal reading inventories made by teachers to go with their curricula may be a better choice than the JIRI.

REFERENCES

Johnston, M. C. (1982). *Johnston Informal Reading Inventory.* Tucson, AZ: Educational Publications.

Rogers, M. R. (1995). Review of the Johnston Informal Reading Inventory. In J. C. Conoley & J. C. Impara (Eds.), *The twelfth mental measurements yearbook* (pp. 523–524). Lincoln, NE: Buros Institute of Mental Measurements.

Wright, C. R. (1995). Review of the Johnston Informal Reading Inventory. In J. C. Conoley & J. C. Impara (Eds.), *The twelfth mental measurements yearbook* (pp. 524–525). Lincoln, NE: Buros Institute of Mental Measurements.

ELIZABETH O. LICHTENBERGER
The Salk Institute

See also **Reading Disorders**

JOINT TECHNICAL STANDARDS FOR EDUCATIONAL AND PSYCHOLOGICAL TESTS (*See* Standards for Educational and Psychological Testing)

JONES, REGINALD L. (1931–2005)

Reginald L. Jones received his AB in psychology, cum laude, from Morehouse College in 1952 and his MA in clinical psychology from Wayne State University. He later earned his PhD in psychology, with a minor in special education, from the Ohio State University. He served as the department chair for psychology and form director of the Center for Minority Special Education at Hampton University (HU), was a Distinguished Professor of psychology and special education at that school.

Prior to his HU appointments in August 1991, he was professor of African American studies and education for 17 years at the University of California at Berkeley, and he also served as the university's faculty assistant to the Vice Chancellor. In addition, for several years he was director of Berkeley's doctoral program in special education. Other positions held by Jones include professor of psychology and special education and vice-chair of the department of psychology at Ohio State University; professor and chair of the department of education at University of California, Riverside; and professor and director of the University Testing Center, Haile Sellassie I University in Addis Abada, Ethiopia. He also taught at Miami, Fisk, and Indiana Universities, and at UCLA. For more than 25 years, Jones was a fellow of the American Psychological Association (APA).

He produced 28 instructional videotapes in psychology, written and/or presented more than 200 papers, articles, chapters, reviews, and technical reports, and edited 17 books, including *Black Psychology* (3rd ed., 1991); *Attitudes and Attitude Change in Special Education* (1984); *Psychoeducational Assessment of Minority Group Children* (1988); *Black Adolescents* (1989a), *Black Adult Development and Aging* (1989b), and *The Handbook of Tests and Measurements for Black Populations* (1996). From 1979 to 1983, he was the editor of *Mental Retardation*, an official journal of the American Association on Mental Retardation, and he served as an associate, advisory, or guest editor of more than a dozen other professional journals in psychology and education.

He is especially noted for his work on special education labeling, attitudes toward individuals with disabilities, and the special ducation of minority children. Jones was a recipient of the J. E. Wallace Wallin Award, the Council for Exceptional Children's highest honor.

Among his numerous appointments to governmental task forces and advisory committees, Jones served on President Clinton's Council of Advisors to the Education Transition Team and received various appointments by the National Academy of Sciences, Congress, and the Secretary of Health, Education, and Welfare. His service in this area led to recommendations of new and/or modified policies, programs, and practices in mental health, mental retardation, special education, and the education of African American children and youth.

Jones' many honors and awards include the Citation for Distinguished Achievement from the Ohio State University, the Distinguished Alumni Award from Wayne State University, the Education Award from the American Association on Mental Retardation, the Distinguished Psychologist and Scholarship Awards from the Association of Black Psychologists, and the Outstanding Faculty Award from the Class of 1991 African American Students of the University of California at Berkeley. He also received special recognition from the APA "... for unusual and outstanding contributions in the field of psychology," and the Berkeley Citation "for distinguished achievement and for notable service to the University," one of the highest honors bestowed by the university.

REFERENCES

Jones, R. L. (1984). *Attitudes and attitude change in special education: Theory and practice*. Reston, VA: Council for Exceptional Children.

Jones, R. L. (1988). *Psychoeducational Assessment of Minority Group Children: A Casebook*. Berkeley, CA: Cobb & Henry.

Jones, R. L. (1989a). *Black adolescents*. Berkeley, CA: Cobb & Henry.

Jones, R. L. (1989b). *Black adult development and aging*. Berkeley, CA: Cobb & Henry.

Jones, R. L. (1991). *Black psychology* (3rd ed.). Berkeley, CA: Cobb & Henry.

Jones, R. L. (1996). *Handbook of tests and measurements for Black populations*. Berkeley, CA: Cobb & Henry.

TAMARA J. MARTIN
*The University of Texas
of the Permian Basin*

in Dandy-Walker syndrome (Greenspan, 1998). Joubert syndrome results in mental retardation that is typically severe or profound coupled with pronounced autistic-like behaviors, ataxia, hypotonia, tongue protrusion, and abnormal patterns of eye movements. Exceptional cases exist with IQs reported as high as 85, but diagnoses of autism are common in the higher-IQ JS patient. Diagnosis may occur prenatally via ultrasound in some cases, but traditionally the diagnosis has been made on the basis of the clinical exam and MRI findings. Academic and psychosocial outcomes are typically quite limited due to the level of retardation and the social deficits noted. Special education services and continuous psychoeducational workups are required in all cases.

Characteristics

1. Absence or underdevelopment of cerebellar vermis, resulting in ataxia and hypotonia
2. Malformation of brain stem and possibly the cerebral hemispheres resulting in abnormal breathing that initially presents as panting in infancy and may be followed by apnea
3. Abnormal eye and tongue movement
4. Hypotonia
5. Symptoms contributing to global developmental delay
6. Commonly mild or moderate mental retardation
7. Molar tooth sign in the mesencephalon

REFERENCES

Gillberg, C. (1995). *Clinical child neuropsychiatry*. Cambridge, England: Cambridge University Press.

Greenspan, S. (1998). Dandy-Walker syndrome. In L. Phelps (Ed.), *Health-related disorders of children and adolescents* (pp. 219–223). Washington, DC: American Psychological Association.

CECIL R. REYNOLDS
Texas A&M University

JOUBERT SYNDROME

Joubert syndrome (JS) is a rare genetic disorder that is autosomal recessive, characterized by partial or complete agenesis of the cerebellar vermis (Gillberg, 1995), but without the formation of cysts and hydrocephalus common

JOURNAL FOR THE EDUCATION OF THE GIFTED

The *Journal for the Education of the Gifted (JEG)* is the official journal of The Association for the Gifted (TAG), a division of the Council for Exceptional Children (CEC). Members of CEC-TAG receive the quarterly issues published by *JEG* and online access to current and past issues as a benefit of membership. The journal was first published in 1978 and currently is distributed internationally.

JEG provides a forum for the analysis and communication of knowledge about the gifted and talented, as well as the exchange of information regarding the educational and psychological needs of children within this unique population. The journal address topics such as, school evaluation, gifted children with learning disabilities, program development, and prominent themes and diverse ideas related to the gifted and talented. *JEG* specifically solicits (a) original research relevant to the education of the gifted and talented; (b) theoretical and position papers; (c) descriptions of innovative programming and instructional practices based on existing or novel models of gifted education; (d) review of literature related to gifted education, and (e) historical perspectives. Submitted writings are evaluated by referees and undergo a blind reviewing process. The current editor is Tracy L. Cross, Teachers College, Ball State University, Muncie, Indiana.

CECIL R. REYNOLDS
Texas A&M University
First edition

TAMARA J. MARTIN
The University of Texas of the Permian Basin
Second edition

ERIN E. K. SHINNERS
The Chicago School of Professional Psychology
Fourth edition

JOURNAL OF ABNORMAL CHILD PSYCHOLOGY

The *Journal of Abnormal Child Psychology* was established in 1973 by Herbert Quay, PhD. In 1995 the journal became the official publication of the International Society for Research in Child and Adolescent Psychopathology. The journal is published bimonthly by Springer Netherlands. The editor-in-chief is John E. Lochman, who is also the president of the American Board of Clinical Child and Adolescent Psychology. The journal focuses on child and adolescent psychopathology with an emphasis on empirical studies of the major childhood disorders (the disruptive behavior disorders, depression, anxiety, and pervasive developmental disorders). Research addresses the epidemiology, assessment, diagnosis, etiology, developmental course and outcome, and treatment of childhood disorders. Studies on risk and protective factors, and on the correlates of children's psychiatric disturbances, especially family and peer processes, are of interest. Treatment outcome research is also published, with an emphasis on studies that include randomized clinical trials with appropriate controls. Occasional special issues highlight a particular topic of importance in the field and conceptual articles are included from time to time.

STAFF
Third edition

ASHLEY T. GREENAN
The Chicago School of Professional Psychology
Fourth edition

JOURNAL OF APPLIED BEHAVIOR ANALYSIS

The *Journal of Applied Behavior Analysis (JABA)* was founded in 1968 by Montrose M. Wolf, Donald Baer, Sidney W. Bijou, and Todd Risley. Since then, the journal has published over 2,600 articles devoted to research that applies the experimental analysis of behavior to problems of social importance. *JABA's* current editor is Dorothea C. Lerman of the University of Houston-Clear Lake. She is responsible for issues published in 2011, 2012, and 2013.

JABA is published quarterly by the Society for the Experimental Analysis of Behavior, Inc. (SEAB). All articles are available free of charge online through PubMed Central of the National Library of Medicine. Articles are presented in PDF and full-text HTML format. These articles are made available 6 months after publication. However, *JABA* subscribers receive the journal immediately upon publication. One can subscribe to *JABA* online through the *JABA* or SEAB websites. One can also register online to receive the latest *JABA* table of contents via e-mail. Additionally, for Facebook users, by becoming a fan of *JABA* on Facebook, one can receive notifications via Facebook wall of new *JABA* publications.

Manuscripts can be submitted online for review. Inquiries regarding manuscript submissions and subscription information should be directed to Kathy Hill, *JABA*, Department of Applied Behavioral Science, University of Kansas, 1000 Sunnyside Ave. Lawrence, Kansas 66045-2133. Email: behavior@mail.ku.edu. Phone: (916) 482-2426.

This entry has been informed by the source below.

REFERENCE

Journal of Applied Behavior Analysis. (2011). Retrieved from http://seab.envmed.rochester.edu/

RAND B. EVANS
Texas A&M University
First edition

TAMARA J. MARTIN
The University of Texas of the Permian Basin
Second edition

LAUREN K. EBY
The Chicago School of Professional Psychology
Fourth edition

JOURNAL OF AUTISM AND DEVELOPMENTAL DISORDERS (JADD)

The *Journal of Autism and Developmental Disorders (JADD)*, was first published under the title of the *Journal of Autism and Childhood Schizophrenia*. It was born from the collaboration of Leo Kanner, regarded as the founding father of child psychiatry in the English-speaking world, and publisher V.H. Winston, the father of an autistic child. The journal was dedicated to stimulating and disseminating from diverse sources "ways to understand and alleviate the miseries of sick children." As founding editor and the discoverer of autism, Kanner convened a task force of outstanding researchers and clinicians to contribute from multidisciplinary sources. Fields such as ethology, genetics, psychotherapy, chemotherapy, behavior modification, special education, speech pathology, and neurobiology contributed. Research was conducted by investigators from the professions of medicine, psychology, neuroscience, biochemistry, physiology, and education. The unifying basis for the publication of such diverse material was the direct relevance to the understanding and remediation of autism, childhood psychoses, and related developmental disorders.

In 1974 Eric Schopler took over as editor of the journal, with Michael Rutter collaborating as European editor. Editorial policies remained the same, but there was increasing emphasis on studies demonstrating the connection between research and clinical application. Toward that end, a "Parents Speak" column was added. It was intended to raise issues of practical concern not always accessible to current research methodologies and research issues not always clear as to their practical implications. The purpose of the column was to provide a forum for parents and researchers.

By 1979 the title of the journal was changed from the *Journal of Autism and Childhood Schizophrenia* to its current title. This change reflected primarily the growth of empirical knowledge. Initially, autism was regarded as the earliest form of childhood schizophrenia. However, increasing data suggested that autism and childhood schizophrenia were different both in onset and symptoms. Autism was usually related to early onset, before age 3, whereas childhood schizophrenia came with later onset and somewhat different symptoms. Moreover, the effects of development were recognized for a wide range of disorders, as was the coexistence of autism with other developmental disorders such as mental retardation. An unusual convergence of scientific knowledge and political action occurred when autism was included in the Developmental Disabilities Act of 1975. The journal's change of title and scope was intended to proclaim this infrequent marriage of science and policy.

Currently, the *Journal of Autism and Developmental Disorders* is the "leading peer-reviewed, scholarly periodical focusing on all aspects of autism spectrum disorders and related developmental disabilities. Published monthly, *JADD* is committed to advancing the understanding of autism, including potential causes and prevalence (e.g., genetic, immunological, environmental); diagnosis advancements; and effective clinical care, education, and treatment for all individuals. Studies of diagnostic reliability and validity, psychotherapeutic and psychopharmacological treatment efficacy, and mental health services effectiveness are encouraged. *JADD* also seeks to promote the well-being of children and families by publishing scholarly papers on such subjects as health policy, legislation, advocacy, culture and society, and service provision as they pertain to the mental health of children and families" (www.springer.com/psychology). The current editor is Fred R. Volkmar, Yale University School of Medicine, New Haven, Connecticut.

ERIC SCHOPLER
University of North Carolina at Chapel Hill

RACHEL TOPLIS
*Falcon School District 49,
    Colorado Springs, Colorado*
First Edition

ANITA M. ROGINSKI
The Chicago School of Professional Psychology
Second Edition

JOURNAL OF CLINICAL CHILD AND ADOLESCENT PSYCHOLOGY

The *Journal of Clinical Child and Adolescent Psychology* (*JCCAP*) is the official journal of the Section on Clinical Child Psychology (Section 1), Division of Clinical Psychology (Division 12) of the American Psychological Association. *JCCAP* publishes original research, reviews, and articles on the development and evaluation of assessment and intervention, development and maintenance of problems, cross-cultural and social factors, and training and practice within the discipline of clinical child psychology. Authors need not be members of the section in which publications are submitted. Colleagues in other disciplines, students, and consumers are also encouraged to contribute. *JCCAP* is published six times a year. Publications may be sent to: Taylor & Francis, Inc., 325 Chestnut Street, Suite 800, Philadelphia, PA 19106. The current editor for JCCAP is Mitchell J. Prinstein, University of North Carolina at Chapel Hill. For additional information on *JCCAP* please visit: http://www.tandf.co.uk/journals/titles/15374416.asp

All information retrieved from http://www.tandf.co.uk /journals/ on January 15, 2012.

RACHEL TOPLIS
Falcon School District 49,
Colorado Springs, Colorado

JOURNAL OF COMMUNICATION DISORDERS

The *Journal of Communication Disorders* publishes articles related to speech, language, and hearing disorders. Special topics issues entitled Clinics in Communication Disorders offer information for speech-language pathologists, audiologists, psychotherapists, otolaryngologists, and other professionals on the assessment, diagnosis, and treatment of these disorders. This bimonthly journal encourages articles of experimental or descriptive investigations, theoretical or tutorial papers, case reports, or letters to the editor.

Originally founded by its first editor, R. W. Riever of John Jay College and Columbia University, the aim of the journal has remained the same since its inception: to publish articles on "problems related to the various disorders of communication, broadly defined." Its interests include the biological foundations of communications as well as psychopathological, psychodynamic, diagnostic, and therapeutic aspects of communication disorders.

The current editor is Luc de Nil, University of Toronto, Toronto, Ontario. Elsevier Science, Inc. publishes the journal. Readers can purchase articles on the journals website. Elsevier B.V. publishes the *Journal of Communication Disorders* and is located at 3251 Riverport Lane, Maryland Heights, MO 63043.

This entry has been informed by the source below.

REFERENCE

Elsevier B.V. (2011). *Guide for authors*. Retrieved from http://www.elsevier.com/wps/find/journaldescription.cws_home /505768/authorinstructions

ERESA K. Rice
Texas A&M University
First edition

TAMARA J. MARTIN
The University of Texas of
the Permian Basin
Second edition

KRISTIN T. HOLSKER
The Chicago School of
Professional Psychology
Fourth edition

JOURNAL OF CONSULTING AND CLINICAL PSYCHOLOGY

The *Journal of Consulting and Clinical Psychology* was first published in 1937 by the American Psychological Association (APA) under the name *Journal of Consulting Psychology*. Its original managing editor was J. P. Symonds. The editor, appointed by the APA, is currently Aurthur M. Nezu, a Distinguished Professor of Psychology at Drexel University. There are nine associate editors and approximately 50 consulting editors appointed by the managing editor.

The journal publishes original contributions on such topics as the development and use of diagnostic techniques in the treatment of disordered behaviors; studies of populations of clinical interest; studies of personality and of its assessment and development related to consulting and clinical psychology; and cross-cultural and demographic studies of interest for behavioral disorders.

The journal considers manuscripts dealing with diagnosis or treatment of abnormal behavior. Manuscripts are submitted and blind-reviewed by a board of consulting editors. The journal receives approximately 400 manuscripts a year; about 25% of these are published. For additional information please visit: http://www.apa.org/pubs/journals/ccp/index.aspx.

TERESA K. RICE
Texas A&M University
First edition

DONNA WALLACE
The University of Texas
of the Permian Basin
Second edition

JOURNAL OF EMOTIONAL AND BEHAVIORAL DISORDERS

The *Journal of Emotional and Behavioral Disorders (JEBD)* is a refereed quarterly journal publishing articles on research, practice, and commentary related to children and adolescents with emotional and behavioral disorders. Established in 1993 by PRO-ED, the journal contains articles with implications for a range of disciplines, including counseling, education, early childhood care, juvenile corrections, mental health, psychiatry, psychology, public health, rehabilitation, social work, and special education. *JEBD* provides an impartial forum and draws on a wide variety of fields to further services for children and adolescents at-risk or diagnosed with emotional and behavioral problems. For additional information on JEBD, please visit: http://www.hammill-institute.org/journals/JEBD.html.

JUDITH K. VORESS
PRO-ED, Inc.

JOURNAL OF FLUENCY DISORDERS

The *Journal of Fluency Disorders* is currently the only publication devoted specifically to fluency. The official journal of the International Fluency Association, the *Journal of Fluency Disorders* was begun in 1974. It provides extensive coverage of current clinical, experimental, and theoretical aspects of stuttering. The journal also provides the latest research on remediation techniques. The journal, which is published yearly by Elsevier Incorporated, features research and clinical reports, theoretical and philosophical articles, reviews, and various other communications.

The *Journal of Fluency Disorders* is a valuable resource for speech-language pathologists and audiologists. It is approved by the Continuing Education Board of the American Speech-Language-Hearing Association as a means of obtaining continuing education units (CEUs). The journal offers professionals a way of acquiring new knowledge, obtaining up-to-date professional information, and ideas for improving service delivery. Members of the International Fluency Association have the option of accessing the *Journal of Fluency Disorders* online at www.theifa.org Ashley Craig, who practices and teaches in Sydney, Australia, edits the *Journal of Fluency Disorders*. He is associated with The Northern Clinical Medical School and University of Sydney.

CECIL R. REYNOLDS
Texas A&M University
First edition

MARIE ALMOND
The University of Texas of
the Permian Basin
Second edition

JEFFRY FINLAYSON
The Chicago School of
Professional Psychology
Fourth edition

JOURNAL OF FORENSIC NEUROPSYCHOLOGY

The *Journal of Forensic Neuropsychology (JFN)* was founded in 1998 by Jim Hom of the Neuropsychology Center of Dallas. The current editor is Bruce A. Arrigo of the University of North Carolina–Charlotte. The journal publishes articles involving legal aspects of the practice of clinical neuropsychology. It is published quarterly by the Haworth Press.

Its interest to special educators lies in its focus on head injury and litigation of head injury cases, many of which involve children and the schooling and education of brain-injured children. The journal includes original research, reviews of research, opinions, and topical presentations on matters of timely interest. For additional information on *JFN*, please visit: http://web.me.com/gregdeclue/Site/Home.html.

CECIL R. REYNOLDS
Texas A&M University

JOURNAL OF INTELLECTUAL DISABILITY RESEARCH

The *Journal of Intellectual Disability Research* is the official journal of the International Association for the Scientific Study of Intellectual Disability and the European

Association for Mental Health and Mental Retardation. It began publication as the *Journal of Mental Deficiency Research* in 1956 and was renamed in 1992. This international journal is devoted exclusively to the scientific study of intellectual disability. The journal publishes papers reporting original observations, including clinical case reports; pathological reports; biochemical investigations; genetics; and psychological, educational, and sociological studies. The results of animal experiments or studies in any discipline that may increase knowledge of the causes, prevention, or treatment of intellectual disability are also discussed. Reviews are submitted from experts from time to time on themes in which recent research has produced notable advances. All papers are reviewed by expert referees. The journal also reports the activities of special interest groups and the meetings and conferences of the International Association for the Scientific Study of Intellectual Disability.

The journal is published six times per year by Wiley-Blackwell Publishing. The current editor-in-chief is A. J. Holland, Developmental Psychology Section, Cambridge, England. For additional information on *JIDR*, please visit: http://www.blackwellpublishing.com/journal.asp?ref= 0964-2633.

STAFF

JOURNAL OF LEARNING DISABILITIES

The *Journal of Learning Disabilities (JLD)* is the oldest and most prestigious journal in the area of learning disabilities. The journal continues to publish reports of empirical research, opinion papers, and discussions of issues concerning learning disabilities. The journal has been published consecutively since 1968. *JLD* is currently edited by Lee Swanson, University of California at Riverside, and covers topics concerning successful interventions, empirical research, literature reviews, and theoretical positions or perspectives in the areas of mathematics and the sciences pertaining to learning disabilities. For additional information on *JLD*, please visit: http://intl-ldx.sagepub.com.

JUDITH K. VORESS
PRO-ED, Inc.

JOURNAL OF POSITIVE BEHAVIOR INTERVENTIONS

The *Journal of Positive Behavior Interventions (JPBI)* deals exclusively with principles of positive behavioral

support in school, home, and community settings for people who exhibit challenges in behavioral domains across settings. Established in 1999, *JPBI* publishes empirical research reports, commentaries, program descriptions, discussion of family supports, and coverage of timely issues. Contributors and editorial board members are leading authorities representing different disciplines involved with intervention for individuals with challenging behaviors. Robert Koegel and V. Mark Durand serve as the Journal's Editors. For additional information on JPBI, please visit: http://intl-pbi.sagepub.com.

JUDITH K. VORESS
PRO-ED, Inc.

JOURNAL OF PSYCHOEDUCATIONAL ASSESSMENT

The *Journal of Psychoeducational Assessment (JPA)* was founded in 1983, and for the past 23 years has continuously published quarterly issues as well as special topic monographs on topics of interest to all assessment specialists, including psychologists, educational diagnosticians, special educators, and academic trainers. The internationally known journal originated as an outlet for the publication of research on assessment practices and procedures common to the fields of psychology and education. It provides school psychologists with current information regarding psychological and educational assessment practices, legal mandates, and instrumentation; and includes topics such as cross-cultural assessment practices, differential diagnoses, and dynamic assessment neuropsychology.

JPA publishes brief reports, position papers, and book and test reviews routinely addressing issues related to achievement, adaptive behavior, classroom behaviors, creativity, motor skills, intelligence, language skills, memory, and other constructs. An editorial board of some 50 members representing a wide range of expertise in assessment-related issue employs a double-blind peer review process for manuscripts submitted for publication. *JPA* is published by Sage Publications. Donald H. Saklofske of the University of Calgary, Canada, is the current editor. For additional information about *JPA*, please visit: http://intl-jpa.sagepub.com.

MARY LEON PEERY
Texas A&M University
First edition

TAMARA J. MARTIN
The University of Texas
of the Permian Basin
Second edition

JOURNAL OF SCHOOL PSYCHOLOGY

The *Journal of School Psychology (JSP)* is the journal of the Society for the Study of School Psychology (SSSP). It commenced publication in 1963. *JSP* publishes full-length quantitative and qualitative research articles and critical reviews of literature on research and practices relevant to psychology and behavior in schools. *JSP* strives to publish methodologically and statistically sophisticated research in order to contribute to the science of school psychology. Article topics include assessment, consultation, intervention mechanisms and approaches, and schooling effects on social, cognitive, mental health, and achievement-related outcomes. The vast majority of *JSP*'s articles focus on issues directly relevant to children, adolescents, or families in school and related settings. The current editor of *JSP* is Randy G. Floyd.

JSP is published bimonthly for the intended audience of psychologists, educators, social workers, and sociologists. One can subscribe online to receive the print journal, and there are discounted rates for students, American Psychological Association Division 16 members, and National Association of School Psychologists members. Individual articles can also be purchased online and received in a PDF format via ScienceDirect.

Manuscripts for JSP can be submitted online. Any questions regarding submission should be directed to the editor: Randy G. Floyd, University of Memphis, 202 Psychology Building, 400 Innovation Drive, Memphis, Tennessee 38152. E-mail: rgfloyd@memphis.edu.

REFERENCE

Journal of School Psychology. (2011). Retrieved from www.elsevier.com/wps/find/journaldescription.cws_home/699/description

THOMAS OAKLAND
University of Florida
First edition

TAMARA J. MARTIN
The University of Texas
of the Permian Basin
Second edition

LAUREN K. EBY
The Chicago School of
Professional Psychology
Fourth edition

JOURNAL OF SPECIAL EDUCATION

First published in 1966, the *Journal of Special Education (JSE)* is internationally known as the prime research journal in the field of special education. This quarterly, multidisciplinary publication presents primary research and scholarly reviews by experts in all subspecialties of special education for individuals with disabilities ranging from mild to severe. *JSE* includes critical commentaries; intervention studies; integrative reviews of timely problems; traditional, ethnographic, and single-subject research; and articles on families, transition, technology, general/special education interface, and legislation and litigation. Robert F Algozzine, University of North Carolina at Charlotte and Fred Spooner, University of North Carolina at Charlotte, currently serve as Co-Editors of *JSE*. All published articles have undergone a rigorous peer review process. For additional information on the *JSE*, please visit: http://intl-sed.sagepub.com.

JUDITH K. VORESS
PRO-ED, Inc.

JOURNAL OF SPECIAL EDUCATION TECHNOLOGY

The *Journal of Special Education Technology (JSET)* is a peer-reviewed journal first published in 1985 that focuses on research and policies in the field of assistive technology. According to their website, the journal focuses on "up-to-date information and opinions about issues, research, policy, and practice related to the use of technology in the field of special education. *JSET* supports the publication of research and development activities, provides technological information and resources, and presents important information and discussion concerning important issues in the field of special education technology to scholars, teacher educators, and practitioners" (*JSET*, 2005). The journal is geared more toward K–12 assistive technology rather than higher education, but a fair number of articles in recent years have focused on issues interesting to both constituencies, such as web accessibility and universal design.

The journal is a publication of the Technology and Media (TAM) division (CEC, 2005) of the Council for Exceptional Children (CEC). The journal is published four times per year and annual subscription rates are currently $55 per year for individuals and $109 per year for institutions. Members of the TAM division of the CEC receive the publication as a member benefit. Web-based archives of the journal are located on their website.

For more information, call 800-877-2693 or visit their website at: http://www.tamcec.org/.

REFERENCE

Journal of Special Education Technology. (2012). About the journal. Retrieved from http://www.tamcec.org/about-2/

DAVID SWEENEY
Texas A&M University

JOURNAL OF SPEECH AND HEARING DISORDERS

The *Journal of Speech and Hearing Disorders (JSHD)* was discontinued in November of 1990, but it merged with the *Journal of Speech and Hearing Research* in 1991. The archives of *Journal of Speech and Hearing Disorders* from March 1936 to November 1990 are available, with a subscription, online at http://jshd.asha.org/archive The merged journals then began publishing under the title *Journal of Speech, Language, and Hearing Research (JSLHR)* in 1997. The American Speech-Language-Hearing Association currently publishes the *JSLHR*, and can be located online at http://jslhr.asha.org The website provides general information about the journal, archives and current issues, the process of submission, and lists editors. The *JSLHR* can be contacted at American Speech-Language Hearing Association, 2200 Research Boulevard, #427 Rockville, MD 20850-3289. The phone number is 1-888-498-6699.

The *JSLHR* is an online-only journal that circulates four issues a year, which are divided into three major categories: language, speech, and hearing. The mission of the *JSLHR* is to provide information pertaining to peer-reviewed, empirical research, theoretical approaches, and clinical management related to areas of normal and disordered speech, language, and hearing. Understanding both normal and disordered processes involved in speech, language, and hearing expands knowledge of screening, diagnosis, habilitation, or rehabilitation of communication disorders. Topics covered are screening, assessment, treatment techniques, prevention, professional issues, supervision, and administration. The *JSLHR* also encourages evidenced-based practice by disseminating the results of new experiments as well as critical reviews and meta-analyses of existing experimental work.

TERESA K. RICE
Texas A & M University
First edition

MARIE ALMOND
The University of Texas
of the Permian Basin
Second edition

MARIE GALAN
The Chicago School of
Professional Psychology
Fourth edition

JOURNAL OF THE AMERICAN ASSOCIATION FOR THE SEVERELY HANDICAPPED (See *TASH.*)

JOURNAL OF VISUAL IMPAIRMENT AND BLINDNESS

The *Journal of Visual Impairment and Blindness (JVIB)* is an international journal of record on blindness and visual impairments. When first published this journal was known as *Outlook for the Blind*, and later *New Outlook for the Blind*. For a century, *JVIB* has kept professionals up to date on all the major developments and trends of the field of visual impairment and blindness, serving as the cornerstone of the field's literature. *JVIB* is a monthly publication of research articles and discussion articles on topics of interest related to the field of visual impairment. *JVIB* provides its interdisciplinary, international subscribers with a forum for the exchange of ideas and information as well as a means of discussing controversies and issues relevant to practitioners and researchers concerned with visually impaired and blind individuals (*JVIB*, 1998).

A publication of the American Foundation for the Blind, *JVIB* contains features pertinent to all ages, which cover various aspects of visual impairment, including international news, short reports, research, innovative practice techniques, worldwide events, employment updates, and evaluation of new products and publications. A sampling of past articles finds that topics include parental concerns and involvement, educational issues of the visually impaired and blind, assessment, language development, residential schools, rehabilitation, employment, orientation, mobility, and physical fitness.

Information pertaining to the impact of technology on individuals with visual impairment is continually updated in the segment "Random Access." Another feature, entitled "Research Note," contains brief reports on cutting-edge research and relevant work from other fields. Additionally, *JVIB* presents important statistical information about blindness, and reviews fiction and nonfiction books as well as videos related to blindness. Duane R. Geruschat, Johns Hopkins Wilmer Eye Institute, is the current Editor in Chief. For additional information on *JVIB*, please visit: jvib@afb.net.

E. CAMPBELL
Purdue University
First edition

TAMARA J. MARTIN
The University of Texas
of the Permian Basin
Second edition

RACHEL TOPLIS
Falcon School District 49 Colorado
Springs, Colorado
Third edition

JUBERG-MARSIDI SYNDROME

Juberg-Marsidi syndrome (JMS) is a rare, multisystem, congenital condition characterized by pronounced mental retardation, stunted growth, sensory deficiencies, and microgenitalism (Juberg & Marsidi, 1980). JMS is X-linked recessive; all affected cases have been males born to phenotypically normal mothers.

Although born of full-term pregnancies, infants with JMS show low birth weight, height, and head circumference (in the 5th or lower percentile), with small penis, scrotum, and impalpable testes. There are also dysmorphic facial features, such as flattened nasal bridge, dysplastic and sometimes asymmetrical ears, and high forehead. JMS children eventually show marked delays in bone maturation, hypotonia, and gross motor function (e.g., late in sitting and walking), as well as delays in speech production. In addition, JMS children show sensory deficits; most are hearing-impaired or completely deaf with some visual problems, such as retinal pigmentation and crossed eyes (Mattei, Collignon, Ayme, & Giraud, 1983). Children with JMS show severe mental retardation, manifested as disinterested gaze, poor visual tracking, and absent or limited speech production. Although the details of psychometric evaluation of JMS patients have not been reported, patients with other X-linked mental retardation syndromes typically show IQ scores well below 70.

Characteristics

1. X-linked recessive syndrome
2. Mental retardation, growth retardation, facial dysmorphisms, microgenitalism, and sensory deficiencies
3. Poor prognosis: death occurring by late childhood

Prognosis for children with JMS is poor. There is no cure, and JMS patients die by late childhood. Older JMS patients (over 5 years of age) can be incapacitated by illness or severe hypotonia.

JMS is an X-linked recessive mental retardation syndrome. There are numerous other forms of X-linked mental retardation, such as Borjeson and Lowe syndromes, that have some but not all of the characteristics of JMS (Glass, 1991). However, a recent study in which the genetic locus of JMS was isolated and a key genetic mutation in JMS-carrying families was identified that further distinguishes JMS from other X-linked syndromes (Villard et al., 1996). Such advances in understanding the genetic basis of JMS

will help provide reliable genetic counseling for at-risk women. In addition, identified gene mutations will lead to an understanding of the mechanisms underlying JMS symptoms and yield new treatments.

REFERENCES

Glass, I. A. (1991). X-linked mental retardation. *Journal of Medical Genetics, 28*, 361–371.

Juberg, R. C., & Marsidi, I. (1980). A new form of X-linked mental retardation with growth retardation, deafness, and microgenitalism. *American Journal of Human Genetics, 32*, 714–722.

Mattei, J. F., Collignon, P., Ayme, S., & Giraud, F. (1983). X-linked mental retardation, growth retardation, deafness and microgenitalism: A second familial report. *Clinical Genetics, 23*, 70–74.

Villard, L., Gecz, J., Mattei, J. F., Fontes, M., Saugier-Veber P., Munnich, A., & Lyonnet, S. (1996). XNP mutation in a large family with Juberg-Marsidi syndrome. *Nature Genetics, 12*, 359–360.

ADAM S. BRISTOL
Yale University

THE JUKES AND THE KALLIKAKS

In the late 19th and early-20th centuries, Americans became increasingly concerned with overpopulation and unrestricted immigration. It was believed that the high birth rate of intellectual disabilities would have an adverse impact on the economy and social order. The eugenics movement promoted compulsory sterilization of people with undesirable traits as well as restricted immigration of unwanted races (Bajema, 1976). Research on human pedigrees provided scientific support for these efforts by showing intellectual disabilities could be genetically linked. Many studies of family degeneracy were published, but the two most influential were based on the pedigrees of the Juke and the Kallikak families.

One of the most influential studies of family degeneration, *The Jukes*, written by Richard L. Dugdale as a report for the Prison Association of New York (Dugdale, 1895), was the first comprehensive study of the history of an entire family over a number of generations. By examining prison records, Dugdale discovered a family with a long history of arrest and dependence on charity. Dugdale traced 709 members of the Juke family, spanning seven generations, who were related by blood, marriage, and cohabitation.

Dugdale found that the Juke family had a high incidence of feeblemindedness, pauperism, prostitution, illegitimacy, and crime among its members. The family tended to marry its own members and produce large numbers of offspring. Dugdale calculated the cost of the Juke family in confinement and charity to be over $1 million (over $12 million in 1985).

The study concluded that crime and poverty are mainly the result of heredity, but that the environment does have some influence. Dugdale argued that crime and poverty are avoidable if the proper environmental conditions are met. He advocated a program of industrial education and personal hygiene, with imprisonment only as a last resort for the habitual criminal. Heredity was viewed as an innate force that impinged on individuals throughout their lives. In spite of Dugdale's emphasis on environmental interventions, his report of the Juke family was widely used in support of the argument that only heredity determines human behavior and consequently poverty and crime.

Although Dugdale claimed that his data-gathering methods were sound, the study has been severely criticized on methodological grounds (Gould, 1981). One problem is that individuals with intellectual developmental disabilities were identified mainly on the basis of hearsay, rather than by testing or other standardized methods. In addition, it has been charged that the self-fulfilling prophecy may have biased the results, in that the researcher's strong expectations may have influenced his judgment of the cases.

A follow-up of the Juke family (Estrabrook, 1915) reported that the incidence of intellectual developmental disabilities, prostitution, pauperism, illegitimacy, and crime had continued at about the same rate as reported by Dugdale. This report argued against imprisoning people with intellectual developmental disabilities, proposing instead that they receive permanent custodial care and sterilization. Sterilization was particularly advocated because persons diagnosed with intellectual developmental disabilities produced large numbers of offspring and put high demands on welfare systems. It was claimed that the Juke family history demonstrated that criminal fathers would produce criminal offspring, making sterilization the only remedy.

The second most influential study of family degeneracy was Henry Goddard's 1912 book *The Kallikak Family: A Study of the Heredity of Feeble-Mindedness* (Goddard, 1912). Goddard's work was based on the family background of a young girl with the pseudonym of Deborah Kallikak; she was a resident at the Vineland Training School for Feeble-Minded Girls and Boys in New Jersey. Deborah's family was traced back through six generations to Martin Kallikak. Martin first married a woman of good repute and founded a line of offspring that were upstanding citizens of normal intelligence. Martin Kallikak also had an illegitimate child with a barmaid, and this branch of the family produced large numbers of criminals, intellectual developmental disabilities, and charity cases. Goddard summarized the findings as follows:

The Kallikak family presents a natural experiment in heredity. A young man of good family becomes through two different women the ancestor of two lines of descendants,—the one characterized by thoroughly good, respectable, normal citizenship, with almost no exceptions; the other being equally characterized by mental defect in every generation.... In later generations, more defect was brought in from other families through marriage....

We find on the good side of the family prominent people in all walks of life and nearly all of the 496 descendants owners of land or proprietors. On the bad side we find paupers, criminals, prostitutes, drunkards, and examples of all forms of social pest with which modern society is burdened. (Goddard, 1912, p. 116)

It is interesting to note that Goddard interpreted the striking difference between the two lines of the Kallikak family as evidence for the strong influence of heredity, an interpretation uncritically accepted at the time. Later writers have pointed out, however, that this difference is actually stronger evidence for the importance of the environment, since the two lines of the family have a common ancestor, yet differed greatly in social standing (Smith, 1985).

Goddard's methodology has been subject to the same criticism as was Dugdale's study of the Jukes. He relied on untrained field workers to make diagnostic decisions about the mental abilities and personalities of family members, both living and dead. For example, the following report of a home visit was submitted by a research associate.

The girl of twelve should have been at school, according to the law, but when one saw her face, one realized it made no difference. She was pretty, with olive complexion and dark languid eyes, but there was no mind there.... Benumbed by this display of human degeneracy, the field worker went out into the icy street. (Goddard, 1912, p. 73)

There is also uncertainty over whether Goddard's original diagnosis of Deborah's intellectual disability was correct (Smith, 1985). Smith reviewed Goddard's diagnostic evidence and concluded that using modern standards, Deborah would not be classified as intellectually developmentally disabled.

Although the studies of the Jukes and the Kallikaks are seriously flawed by present-day standards, they provided all the evidence needed to convince the eugenicists of the time that something must be done to stem the proliferation of intellectual developmental delays. Armed with these inflammatory studies, they successfully lobbied for compulsory sterilization laws in 30 states, and helped pass the Immigration Restriction Act of 1924.

REFERENCES

Bajema, C. J. (1976). *Eugenics then and now*. Stroudsburg, PA: Hutchinson Ross.

Dugdale, R. L. (1895). *The Jukes: A study in crime, pauperism, disease, and heredity* (5th ed.). New York, NY: AMS.

Estrabrook, A. H. (1915). *The Jukes in 1915.* New York, NY: Macmillan.

Goddard, H. H. (1912). *The Kallikak family: A study in the heredity of feeble-mindedness.* New York, NY: Macmillan.

Gould, S. J. (1981). *The mismeasure of man.* New York, NY: Norton.

Smith, J. D. (1985). *Minds made feeble: The myth and legacy of the Kallikaks.* Rockville, MD: Aspen.

ROBERT C. NICHOLS
DIANE JARVIS
*State University of New York
at Buffalo*

See also Eugenics; Socioeconomic Status

JUVENILE ARTHRITIS (See Arthritis, Juvenile)

JUVENILE CEREBROMACULAR DEGENERATION

Juvenile cerebromacular degeneration (also known as juvenile neuronal ceroid lipofuscinosis) is a progressive disorder transmitted on an autosomal recessive basis. If the onset occurs between the ages of 1 and 3 years, it may be known as infantile cerebromacular degeneration or Bielschowsky syndrome. The juvenile variety occurs at 5 to 7 years of age and may also be known as Spielmeyer-Vogt disease. Both types involve a degenerative process of the gray matter of the brain and are generally classified with the lipid storage diseases, the most common of which is Tay-Sachs or amaurotic familial idiocy (Behrman & Vaughan, 1983).

Onset usually begins with visual disturbances (eventually leading to blindness; Gillberg, 1995) because of degenerative changes in the retina. These range from retinitis pigmentosa to generalized retinal atrophy, resulting in blindness, despite the fact that the pupils may remain reactive to light. The visual disturbances are followed by a progressive degeneration of cortical gray matter, which may be detected by EEG exam long before observable behavioral changes are seen. The child may develop seizures, become hyperactive, and show a severe pattern of cognitive and motor degeneration. Speech is lost, as are most other motor functions. The later the onset of the disease, the slower it progresses. Some have survived into adolescence but there remains no cure for the disorder

(Behrman & Vaughan, 1983). Treatment consists only of symptom alleviation and supportive care. Many eventually require feeding through gastrostomy tube (Kolodny, 1979). Death, with current methods of intervention, occurs between 16 and 35 years of age (Gillberg, 1995).

A blood test can detect carriers of the disease: It is strongly recommended for all those of Ashkenazic Jewish background where heterogenous carriers have been identified at the rate of about 1:30 (Bennett, 1981).

Characteristics

1. Infants with TSD appear to develop normally for the first few months of life.
2. Infants' physical and mental abilities start to deteriorate relentlessly: a loss of peripheral vision, abnormal startle response to noises, decreased eye contact, listlessness, and recurrent seizures (uncontrolled electrical disturbances in the brain).
3. Infants and children with this disorder may develop cherry-red spots within the middle layer of the eyes, gradual loss of vision, deafness, uncontrolled electrical disturbances in the brain (seizures), and deterioration of cognitive processes (dementia).
4. The infant gradually increases muscle stiffness and restricted movement (spasticity). The infant loses skills and is eventually unable to crawl, turn over, sit, or reach out.
5. The infant may experience loss of coordination, inability to swallow, and breathing difficulties.
6. The child may become mentally retarded, blind, or paralyzed.

REFERENCES

Behrman, R., & Vaughan, V. (1983). *Nelson textbook of pediatrics* (12th ed.). Philadelphia, PA: Saunders.

Bennett, J. (1981). *Diseases, the nurse's reference library series.* Horsham, PA: Informed Communications Book Division.

Gillberg, C. (1995). *Clinical child neuropsychiatry.* Cambridge, England: Cambridge University Press.

Goodman, A., & Motulsky, R. (Eds.). (1979). *Genetic disorders of Ashkenazi Jews.* New York, NY: Raven.

Kolodny, E. H. (1979). Tay-Sachs disease. In A. Goodman & R. Motulsky (Eds.), *Genetic disorders of Ashkenazi Jews.* New York, NY: Raven.

JOHN E. PORCELLA
Rhinebeck Country School

See also Tay-Sachs Syndrome

JUVENILE COURT SYSTEM AND INDIVIDUALS WITH DISABILITIES

The number of delinquents with disabilities being disposed of by the juvenile courts is not known, since this datum currently is not recorded by any U.S. governmental office. In a recent study, Nelson, Rutherford, and Wolford (1985) reported that the prevalence of disabilities among incarcerated youth is approximately two times that expected in a hypothetical average school. The implication of this study is that a higher number of juveniles with disabilities are being disposed of by the courts.

The juvenile courts are organized in various manners within the different states. Whatever their organizational structure, they process juvenile cases under a separate system that is based on concepts of nonculpability and rehabilitation (U.S. Department of Justice, 1983). In 1989, Illinois established the first juvenile court based on the concept that a juvenile is worth saving and is in need of treatment rather than punishment, and that the juvenile court had a mission to protect the juvenile from the stigma of criminal proceedings.

Juvenile courts differ from criminal courts in that the language used in juvenile courts is less harsh. A juvenile court accepts "petitions of delinquency" rather than criminal complaints; conducts "hearings," not trials; adjudicates "juveniles to be delinquent" rather than guilty of a crime; and orders one of a number of available dispositions rather than sentences (U.S. Department of Justice, 1983).

The number of juveniles under the age of 21 who were processed through the juvenile courts during 1980 was 1,345,200. There were approximately three times more male than female cases being disposed of by the courts (U.S. Department of Justice, 1983). In 1977, 83% of the under-18-year-old population was held in detention facilities prior to court disposition (including 122,503 in jails and 507,951 in other juvenile detention facilities) as suspected delinquent or status offenders (U.S. Department of Justice, 1980).

Once referred to a juvenile court, a juvenile may be located at an intake facility or a detention facility that is either secured (similar to a jail facility) or nonsecured. During the judicial process, a juvenile may experience several of the following hearings: the detention hearing; the preliminary hearing; the fitness hearing (to certify as an adult or juvenile); the hearing of motions filed; the adjudication hearing (a hearing of fact); or the disposition hearing (placement, release, and probation; U.S. Department of Justice, 1980).

A study by the U.S. Department of Justice (1980) to determine the relationship between juvenile delinquency and learning disabilities found that learning-disabled youths are disproportionately referred to the juvenile justice system and that the juvenile courts need to use procedures for identifying and referring learning-disabled youths for remediation. These findings suggest that the juvenile court could expand its available range of dispositional alternatives by incorporating the use of special education program options.

Few studies have attempted to determine the current relationship between the juvenile court and special education. Karcz (1984) found that youths in a juvenile court secure detention facility in Lake County, Illinois, who were suspected of having disabilities, or who had disabilities, were provided with screening for disabilities, referral for diagnosis, an interim special education program at the detention facility, guarantees of due process procedures, and transition services through a new special education-related service position known as the Youth Advocate Liaison (YAL). As a result of these efforts, the YAL program increased the likelihood that the average detainee with disabilities would attend school in the home school district.

REFERENCES

Karcz, S. A. (1984). *The impact of a special education related service on selected behaviors of detained handicapped youth.* Unpublished doctoral dissertation, University of Syracuse, New York.

Nelson, C. M., Rutherford, R. B., & Wolford, B. J. (1985). *Juvenile and adult correctional special education data.* (Corrections 1/Special Education Training [C/SET] Project). Washington, DC: U.S. Department of Education.

U.S. Department of Justice. (1980). *Juvenile justice: Before and after the onset of delinquency.* Washington, DC: U.S. Government Printing Office.

U.S. Department of Justice. (1983). *Report to the nation on crime and justice: The data.* National Criminal Justice Reference Series, NCJ-87060. Rockville, MD: Bureau of Justice Statistics.

STAN A. KARCZ
University of Wisconsin at Stout

See also Conduct Disorder; Juvenile Delinquency

JUVENILE DELINQUENCY

Prior to the enactment of the federal Juvenile Delinquency Act in 1938, juvenile offenders violating the laws of the United States were subject to prosecution in the same manner as adults. Since the act, juvenile delinquents have been treated procedurally as juveniles (not adults) by our justice system. Juvenile delinquency is defined as the violation of the law of the United States committed by a person prior to his or her 18th birthday that would have been a crime if committed by an adult (Karcz, 1984). Delinquency refers to those encounters with the law in which the juvenile custody (called an "arrest" for adults) is entered into the record books. Any act that could place the juvenile who committed it in jeopardy of adjudication if it were to be detected is referred to as delinquent behavior (Hopkins, 1983).

Broadly speaking, there are two categories of children and/or youth who commit a delinquent offense: status offenders and juvenile offenders. Status offenses are those subject to legal action only if committed by a juvenile. Examples of status offenses are truancy, incorrigibility, smoking, drinking, and being beyond the control of the parent or guardian (Hopkins, 1983). This category includes minors in need of supervision (MINS), dependent minors, and neglected and abused minors. Juvenile offenders are those children and/or youth who commit index crimes. Index crimes are criminal acts that are illegal regardless of the person's age or status (e.g., shoplifting, robbery, homicide; Kauffman, 2005). A major difference between juvenile offenders and adult offenders is the importance that the juvenile places on gang membership and the tendency of the juvenile to engage in group criminal activity. Violent juvenile offenders, however, have similar characteristics to those of adult felons. Juvenile offenders and adult felons are predominately male, disproportionately Black and/or Hispanic, typically disadvantaged, likely to exhibit interpersonal difficulties and behavioral problems in school, and likely to come from one-parent families with a high degree of conflict, instability, and inadequate supervision (U.S. Department of Justice, 1983).

The Office of Juvenile Justice and Delinquency Prevention (OJJDP) data indicate that juveniles had 8.6% of all arrests for murder (1 out of every 12 arrests), 1 out of every 9 arrests for drug abuse, and 1 out of every 4 arrests for both weapons violations and robbery. Walker, Ramsey, and Gresham (2004) write that research shows "that youths who are chronic offenders (i.e., having three or more arrests by age 12) are much more likely to be early starters in their pattern of antisocial behavior." They found that 100% of boys arrested before age 10 had at least three arrests before reaching age 17. They also identified 17 boys in their longitudinal sample who had committed violent acts; each of these 17 boys was found to be a chronic offender. "Thus a severe pattern of antisocial behavior that is clearly in evidence early in the schooling process, coupled with an early start in committing delinquent acts, may identify the future chronic offender" (p. 29, emphasis added).

Prevention programs that address youth violence and juvenile delinquency fall under two broad categories: prevention at the societal and community levels and prevention at the individual and school levels (Walker, Colvin, & Ramsey, 1995). Kauffman (2005) notes that intervention efforts are typically multifaceted and focus on the reduction of risk factors, as well as proactive and preventative measures that involve the family, juvenile justice agencies, and schools and other educational agencies as part of a comprehensive system of supervision, support, and care.

REFERENCES

Hopkins, J. R. (1983). *Adolescence: The transitional years.* New York, NY: Academic Press.

Karcz, S. A. (1984). *The impact of a special education related service on selected behaviors of detained handicapped youth.* Unpublished doctoral dissertation, University of Syracuse, New York.

Kauffman, J. M. (2005). *Characteristics of emotional and behavioral disorders of children and youth.* Upper Saddle River, NJ: Prentice Hall-Merrill.

Office of Juvenile Justice and Delinquency Prevention (OJJDP). (2005). *FAQs on law enforcement and juvenile crime.* Retrieved from http://www.ojjdp.gov/

Walker, H. M., Colvin, G., & Ramsey, E. (1995). *Antisocial behavior in school: Strategies and best practices.* Pacific Grove, CA: Brooks/Cole.

Walker, H. M., Ramsey, E., & Gresham, F. M. (2005). *Antisocial behavior in school: Evidence-based practices* (2nd ed.). Belmont, CA: Wadsworth/Thomson Learning.

STAN A. KARCZ
University of Wisconsin at Stout
Second edition

RANDALL L. DE PRY
University of Colorado at Colorado Springs
Third edition

See also Crime and Individuals With Disabilities

DATE DUE

PRINTED IN U.S.A.